The Gigantic Book
of
Hunting Stories

Edited by
Jay Cassell

Skyhorse Publishing

Skyhorse Publishing books may be purchased in bulk at special discounts for sales promotion, corporate gifts, fund-raising, or educational purposes. Special editions can also be created to specifications. For details, contact the Special Sales Department, Skyhorse Publishing, 555 Eighth Avenue, Suite 903, New York, NY 10018 or info@skyhorsepublishing.com.

www.skyhorsepublishing.com

10 9 8 7 6 5 4 3 2 1

Illustrations © John Rice: Pages 13; 25; 45; 101; 146; 177; 187; 211; 215; 231; 237; 249; 259; 273; 279; 287; 315; 321; 327; 333; 341; 345; 349; 365; 377; 431; 439; 457; 473; 479; 491; 649; 659; 665; 685; 687; 709; 721; 739; 769
Photo © Greg Rodriguez: Page 485
Photo courtesy of the Theodore Roosevelt Collection, Harvard College Library: Page 3

All stories are reprinted by permission of the author unless otherwise indicated.

The authors and texts included in this book represent more than a century of literature. The integrity of their individual styles, including spelling, punctuation, and grammar, has been respected. The stories reflect the attitudes of their times, and do not necessarily represent the views or opinions of Skyhorse Publishing, Inc.

Library of Congress Cataloging-in-Publication Data

The gigantic book of hunting stories / edited by Jay Cassell.
    p. cm.
  Includes bibliographical references.
  ISBN 978-1-60239-301-1
1. Hunting—Anecdotes. 2. Hunting stories. I. Cassell, Jay.
  SK33.G47 2008
799.2—dc22
                                                2008024256

Printed in the United States of America

This book is dedicated to combat medic Keith Gibson, 25, with the 3-142nd aviation unit out of Latham, New York; and specialist Alan 'Ham' Hamilton, 25, also with the 3-142nd aviation unit out of Latham, New York.

As I write this, they are in Iraq, defending our freedom and way of life.

May they fight well, with honor, dignity, and intelligence; and may they come home safely, to be with their families again. I look forward to next November, when they can come back to our Catskill Mountain deer camp and hunt with the Over the Hill Gang.

Jay Cassell
Katonah, New York
9/3/2008

Contents

Part III

Big Game

Part IV

Small Game

Part V
Upland Birds

Part VI
Waterfowl

Part IX

Africa and Asia

Part X

Reflections on Our Sport

Preface

JAMES D. RANGE

As Chairman of the Theodore Roosevelt Conservation Partnership, it is my pleasure and honor to introduce *The Gigantic Book of Hunting Stories*. Between its covers, you will find some of the best sporting yarns ever woven together. Sit down, open it up, and enjoy a cornucopia of adventurous tales. You'll find everything from Teddy Roosevelt's wanderings in the wilds of Africa and the Wild West a century ago to stories about big- and small-game hunts across North America and the globe, by the best of contemporary writers. Whether you're a hunter of dangerous game, whitetail deer, elk, upland birds, or waterfowl, there's something for you in this wonderful collection that celebrates the hunt and the animals and the places that drew TR, which continue to draw American sportsmen and -women to life in the open.

Our hunting and sporting community, led by non-profit groups like Ducks Unlimited, National Wildlife Federation, Pheasants Forever, Whitetails Unlimited and dozens of other great organizations, has voluntarily raised and donated billions of dollars in support of wildlife and wildlife habitat over the last three quarters of a century. But until recently, they have not spoken with a single and unified voice, one that can truly and effectively influence and redirect the course of fish- and wildlife-management policy in this country. We have done a great job at restoring fish and wildlife in America, but the truth is that we can and must do an even better job if hunting is to survive and continue to be available to the average man and woman.

Today, as human population growth and expanding development threaten the basic essentials and underpinnings of our nation's wildlife conservation model and the hunting traditions enjoyed by millions of our citizens, we must reawaken to the spirit of Teddy Roosevelt and other giants of conservation who bequeathed to us a legacy that is the envy of the world.

That is why a group of concerned leaders representing dozens of sportsmen-conservation groups, along with representatives from some of America's leading labor unions—nearly 70 percent of whose rank-and-file members hunt and fish—have joined forces to create and support the Theodore Roosevelt Conservation Partnership, named in honor of the 26th president and America's greatest hunter-conservationist. The organization's purpose is to speak with one unified voice for the hunting and angling community so as to influence major conservation legislation and policy in a manner rarely seen or experienced in more than half a century. At the time of this writing, we're working to strengthen our nation's Farm Bill, which is the single largest source of funding for conservation in the country, and are concurrently promoting important advancements on a number of fronts including energy development, fisheries management, and wetlands protection.

Guaranteeing every American a place to hunt and fish is one of TRCP's biggest goals, because no matter how many whitetails, turkeys, and pheasants we have, and no matter how many guns we own, if there is no place to hunt, especially for the average citizen—whom Teddy recognized was the foundation upon which our democracy is built—our hunting traditions might die. The time to work together to guarantee a bright future for today's hunters and the hunters of tomorrow is now!

I hope and trust you will enjoy this fine book and that it inspires you to join the TRCP as America's hunters and anglers move forward to guarantee us all places to hunt and fish, while ensuring a bright future for, in the words of T.R., "the generations yet unborn."

Please join the TRCP today. Membership is free, all you need to do is visit www.trcp.org. Working together, we can save and ensure our hunting and fishing legacy; it's what Teddy would do and it's what we must do.

James D. Range
Chairman

Foreword

JAY CASSELL

The idea to assemble *The Gigantic Book of Hunting Stories* came to me in 2006, when I bought a copy of *The Gigantic Book of Fishing Stories*, edited by Nick Lyons. Nick had assembled more than 100 selections on fishing, from the days of Izaak Walton right up to present times. What fun it would be to put together a similar tome on hunting, an activity that has always been such an important part of my very being. What better excuse to read as many hunting stories as I possibly could, by a variety of authors—some from the 1800s, some from 2007, most in between? What better way to discover those obscure gems or to re-read masterpieces that I hadn't seen in years?

As I soon discovered, what better way, also, to tie up all of my weekends and weeknights, practically all of my spare time. But now that this daunting project is done, it was clearly worth the time and effort, for I feel I've assembled as good a collection of hunting stories as you can find anywhere. I hope you'll agree.

I'm also honored to say that the Theodore Roosevelt Conservation Partnership gladly and enthusiastically got on board with this book from the start. The TRCP is a worthwhile and important organization, dedicated to preserving hunting grounds across the country—to preserving our sport—and it just keeps getting stronger and stronger, as more organizations and individuals recognize how critical its work is to our future. A portion of every book sale will be donated to the TRCP.

You'll naturally find many of the writings of Theodore Roosevelt, our 26th president, in here. He was our best-known conservationist president, responsible for creating many new national parks during his tenure. It's fun to read his take on hunting mountain goats in the Canadian Rockies, elk in the American West, and elephants in Africa.

He is just one of many famous names and respected authors whom you'll find in these pages. I did not attempt to gather every 'name' author who has ever written on our sport, as that would have been impossible. I also did not attempt to include the likes of Hemingway or Faulkner. You can read them in so many other anthologies, as well as in their own works, so why repeat their splendid words yet again?

On the other hand, in here you will find authors who aren't particularly well known for their words on hunting. Trollope is here, for example, as are Ivan Turgenev, Charles Dickens, and even Grover Cleveland. Hunting writers from days gone by are also here, including the likes of Nash Buckingham, Zane Grey, Lt. Townsend Whelen, Corey Ford, and Aldo Leopold. Then, of course, there are contemporary writers such as Philip Caputo, Jim Harrison, Rick Bass, Nelson Bryant, and David E. Petzal.

One of my favorite stories in the book is by Thomas McGuane. Written in 1990, "The Heart of the Game" really gives insight into this sport of hunting, why we take it so deeply to heart, and why we all must take it so seriously.

As Nick Lyons did in his fishing book, I've also included a few of my own stories, some of my personal favorites. I hope you enjoy them as much as I do.

Trying to organize all of these fine pieces was another matter. One problem was that while I found vast bodies of literature on waterfowl and upland bird hunting, and hunting in Africa, there was relatively little on the pursuit of small game. It seems that most folks who write about rabbits and squirrels stick strictly to the how-to aspects of those sports, and I tried to avoid how-to in this book. Maybe rabbit and squirrel hunters pursue their sports so often that they find it hard to rhapsodize on them. Maybe the sports just don't lend themselves to that kind of treatment. I don't know the answer, although I do know that my respect for "The Bear," by William Faulkner, has increased tenfold after searching high and low for solid squirrel narratives. I was unable to obtain permission to run that selection in this book, but I did find a few goodies, such as those written by Jim Casada and T. Edward Nickens.

As you'll see, I have divided the book into ten distinct sections; they all contain strong pieces, from "The Forest and The Steppe," by Ivan Turgenev in *The Olden Days*, to "Trail's End," by Sigurd Olson in 'Deer,' to "The Ledge," by Lawrence Hall and "Just A Dog," by Corey Ford, in *Reflections*. Those last two will rip your heart right out.

Lastly, I know you'll think of selections I should have included, but didn't. Some were just impossibly expensive to procure from the copyright holders; others, as noted, have simply appeared in too many other places to merit publication yet again.

Now that I've completed this, I know I'm going to come across pieces that I will regret not having included. Might I consider a second volume someday? Time will tell. In the meantime, I hope you enjoy this one.

Jay Cassell
Katonah, New York
February 24, 2008

Introduction

THOMAS MCINTYRE

"Why should I not be serious? I am speaking of hunting."
—General Zaroff, *The Most Dangerous Game*, Richard Connell

This will be a brief introduction to a gigantic book because I don't want to delay you from making your way into the storytelling—storytelling being, of course, the earliest form of art and the one emerging directly from the hunt. The tales in this exceptional compendium reflect the wide diversity of the hunting experience. Yet while each is unique, they all follow a similar set of tracks, deriving from the identical coil of racing heart and illuminating soul, the spark of which is traced to the first of our ancient hunting fathers. Not only the original storyteller, this hunter was also, perforce, the original reader—of spoor, light, wind, and more. He was the earth's initial interpreter of abstract signs, precursors to the black letters and words marked, like hoof- and pawprints, across the pages you now hold in your hands. So the reading of this book is also, like the hunt, being on the trail, giving chase to an object of pursuit.

It would seem right, then, to wish the reader "good hunting." The old *cacciatori* of Italy's Piedmont, though, accounted it the very worst of luck to express such a sentiment. Instead they made another petition, to camouflage their true intentions: *In bocca al lupo*, "Fall into the jaws of the wolf!" May you, as well, and with great pleasure.

PART I

Theodore Roosevelt

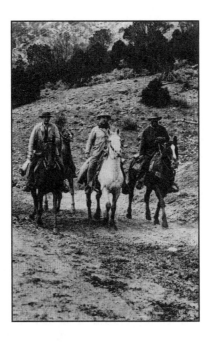

Theodore Roosevelt: America's Greatest Hunter/Conservationist

JIM CASADA

Throughout his years, Theodore Roosevelt strove to live what he called "the strenuous life." Following that credo, he was, at various times in his career, a soldier, diplomat, politician, author, reformer, and visionary—a true Renaissance man. Yet if one sought for bright, shining threads that ran through the fabric of his entire life, none would stand out more vividly than his love of hunting and his staunch commitment to conservation. The more one learns of his activities in these areas, the greater becomes one's appreciation of his zest for life and incredible accomplishments.

Born on October 27, 1858, in New York City, young Theodore Roosevelt, Jr., enjoyed many of the privileges associated with being the child of affluent parents, but from a tender age he also had firsthand acquaintance with adversity. A sickly, asthmatic lad, he faced health problems throughout his adolescent years. At an early age though, TR demonstrated the dogged perseverance that would characterize him as a hunter and in so many other arenas, saying simply: "I'll make my body." Through boxing, wrestling, horseback riding, climbing, rowing, swimming, hiking, camping, and most of all, hunting, he did just that.

His father, although the owner of some lovely guns (such as a set of W. W. Greener percussion pistols and a Lefaucheux pinfire 12-gauge shotgun), had little interest in the outdoors. Instead, young Theodore found inspiration in the novels of Mayne Reid, books on exploration by the likes of Dr. David Livingstone, and in the accounts of African hunting by Roualeyn Gordon-Cumming and Sir Samuel Baker. His mentor for outdoor pursuits, at least at the outset, was his uncle, Robert Barnwell Roosevelt. A respected authority on fishing and ichthyology, he also wrote two hunting-related books, *Game Birds of the Coasts* and *Florida and the Game Water Birds.* As a long-time member of the New York Fish and Game Commission and some one who was quite active in politics, Uncle Robert probably had much more to do in shaping TR's philosophical outlook than did his father.

Another influential figure in shaping his perspectives and nurturing the budding outdoorsman was a Maine guide, outfitter, and lumberman, Bill Sewall. Even as Roosevelt was proving himself, as a collegian, an individual of great intellect possessing an exceptional work ethic (he earned a Phi Beta Kappa key at Harvard), he spent summers in the Maine wilderness. The first of these adventures came in 1878, following his father's death late in the previous year. Its original intent was, likely, simple escape from the sorrow that threatened to consume the young man, but TR's linkage with Sewall proved to be a real watershed in his life.

Sewall initially saw him as "a thin, pale youngster with bad eyes and a weak heart," and he fully expected three weeks of nursemaiding lay before him. Furthermore, by his own admission Roosevelt shot so poorly that he was moved to comment "I am disgusted with myself." Yet the tenacity and sheer determination to succeed, no matter what the odds, which would become hallmarks of his career, served him well, and he insisted on arduous dawn-to-dusk activity every day. His confidence blossomed, as did his hardiness, and two subsequent Maine outings, both in 1879, added immensely to his education in the school of the outdoors.

Meanwhile, TR completed his undergraduate studies. With graduation a time for momentous decisions was at hand. Before considering these—graduate study, a career path, possibly marriage, and other matters—Roosevelt took an extended hunting trip in company with his brother, Elliott. This type of escape to the wilderness and engagement in what he described as "manly pursuits" would become a prominent feature of his entire life. On this occasion and many subsequent ones, when faced by pressures in his personal or political life, TR would find that the solitude of the wild world, often shared with a close companion, was the ideal way to clear his mind and strengthen his resolve when critical decisions lay before him. During this particular trip, the brothers hunted upland birds and small game. TR treated himself to a new shotgun, and he got his first taste of the West, a region that would exert magnetic influence on him the rest of his life.

In his heart of hearts, he found that nothing held as much appeal for him as sport. Indeed, when writing of an 1883 trip on the Little Missouri River, he commented: "I am fond of politics, but fonder still of a little big-game hunting." This was quite introspective as well as being a statement of simple reality. As Paul Cutright would note in the preface to his book, *Theodore Roosevelt: The Naturalist* (1956), "Roosevelt began his life as a naturalist, and he ended it as a naturalist. Throughout a half century of strenuous activity his interest in wildlife, though subject to ebb and flow, was never abandoned at any time."

In the fall of 1883, bothered by a return of the asthma that had periodically plagued him throughout his youth and tired of the grind of politics (he had, after a brief stint as a graduate student at Columbia University, been elected to the State Assembly in New York), TR went on a hunting trip in the Dakota Badlands. He shot a buffalo and encountered various misadventures including miserable weather, proving along the way that he almost welcomed obstacles as a challenge. As TR suggested to his guide on the trip, Joe Ferris, "It's dogged as does it." Ferris for his part, while initially harboring serious doubts about the hardihood of his client, in the end evaluated him as "a plumb good sort."

Roosevelt's exposure to the Badlands made a deep impression, and for the next decade he would find himself torn between a life lived close to nature in that rugged area and one devoted to national affairs back East. Before boarding a train to return home, he set in motion plans to buy a ranch, Chimney Butte, in the Badlands. He would be back in the Badlands less than a year later, and in the intervening months his life and outlook changed dramatically. His wife and mother died within hours of one another on February 14, 1884, the former succumbing to kidney disease in the aftermath of childbirth while his mother, Mittie, fell victim to typhoid fever. His diary for the day shows a black *X* followed by a single sentence: "The light has gone out of my life."

It was in the Badlands that TR found a refuge and renewed purpose in life. He persuaded his old Maine guide and mentor, Bill Sewell, to join him as ranch manager, and in short order was, by his own calculations, "well hardened." He discovered the surcease of solitude first in daily outings then in a longer trip by himself, and soon Roosevelt was planning a more ambitious adventure in Wyoming. Until his great African safari late in life, this would be TR's longest hunt. It lasted seven weeks and he and members of his party took six elk, seven deer, three grizzlies, and 109 head of various "small game," with Roosevelt meticulously recording the daily bag in his diary. This trip to the Bighorns also soothed his troubled soul, and with its conclusion he was once more ready to look back to the East, the responsibilities of public service that were a family tradition, and his destiny. Henceforth, while his mind and most of his time belonged to public affairs in the East, the West would have a firm hold on his heart.

Out of his experiences would come two of his most enduring books, *Hunting Trips of a Ranchman* and *Ranch Life and the Hunting-Trail,* while the best-known of all his outdoor books, *The Wilderness Hunter,* drew in part on these years. He left this period of his life determined to preserve the West that had firmly seized a corner of his soul. It is a measure of both his determination and ability that Roosevelt would, to a greater degree than any other American, be responsible for protecting this western wonderland.

After a devastating winter in the Badlands in 1886–87, one that saw TR lose most of his cattle, he reluctantly gave up the ranching life. Meanwhile, he married again, and ever a busy, boisterous individual, late in December, 1887, he hosted a dinner that led directly to the founding of the Boone and Crockett Club. He wrote its constitution, with the concept of fair chase being at the heart of its philosophy, and over the years Roosevelt would both edit and contribute to a number of the organization's publications.

During the late 1880s and early 1890s he watched his boys grow (all would eventually become keen sportsmen) and managed to take at least one extended hunt every year. He made outings to British Columbia, the Rockies, his old haunts in the Badlands, and the Yellowstone River region. In them he was living out the plea he posited, in *The Wilderness Hunter,* "for manliness and simplicity and delight in a vigorous outdoor life."

From the time he became the reformist police commissioner of New York City in 1895, on through his exploits with the Rough Riders in the Spanish-American War, election as governor of New York, and then as William McKinley's successful vice presidential running mate, TR experienced the busiest time of an incredibly busy life. McKinley's death at the hands of an anarchist put him at the head of the nation, but even so, he would find a surprising amount of time to hunt.

His first hunt as president took him to Mississippi, where to his lasting chagrin he found that his guide, a highly experienced bear hunter named Holt Collier, had captured a bear and had it bound in ropes awaiting a presidential shot. TR bluntly refused to have in part in such a charade, and from this the "Teddy" bear fad was born. Disgusted with the whole affair, which would be a source of embarrassment for the remainder of his life (and a major factor in the widespread use of the nickname he detested), Roosevelt took the ethically appropriate path.

Other aspects of his two terms as president (he was elected in his own right after completing McKinley's term) associated with sport and conservation were far more satisfying. He traveled to Yosemite with the great naturalist, John Muir, and made a similar trip to Yellowstone with another noted conservationist/writer, John Burroughs. More significant, however, were his concrete accomplishments in promoting conservation. He founded the Forest Service and persuaded Gifford Pinchot to serve as its first director. Both men fully understood that their mission involved conserving, with practical use by hunters and others, not mindless preservation with no provision whatsoever for sensible utilization of natural resources. TR also signed bills creating five new national parks, established game reserves and the National Bison Range, and in general instilled in the American populace awareness of the importance of protecting wildlife and habitat. Unquestionably his work as a conservationist looms large among his many legacies to posterity.

While president, TR hunted regularly—taking a wild turkey in Virginia and a bear in Louisiana; coursing after wolves, coyotes, and foxes in several states; killing rattlesnakes and wolves in Oklahoma; and chasing bears and bobcats in Colorado. He also regularly entertained noted sportsmen, ranging from fellow members of the Boone and Crockett Club to renowned foreign hunters such as Fred Selous, at the White House.

As his second term drew toward an end, he began thinking about and then planning a grand African safari. His papers contain correspondence with a number of individuals—Selous, J. H. Patterson, Carl Akeley, Edward North Buxton, and R. J. Cuninghame—who knew the continent well. Andrew Carnegie helped subsidize the safari, and TR contracted with *Scribner's Magazine* to write a series of articles about it.

The undertaking was a striking success from start to finish. Accompanied by his son, Kermit, Roosevelt bagged Africa's Big Five along with an incredible variety of lesser game. His experiences are fully detailed in *African Game Trails* (1910) and the two-volume *Life-Histories of African Game Animals* (with Edmund Heller, 1914). Altogether the hunters and scientists involved in the expedition collected 4,897 mammals, some 2,000 reptiles, 500 fish, and 4,000 birds, not to mention numerous invertebrates. The holding, one of the most important of its kind, went to the Smithsonian.

The end of the African safari was a bittersweet one, but in 1913 TR, despite having lost all vestiges of sight in his left eye, nonetheless planned a final expedition to Brazil's storied River of Doubt. It was, as he put it, "a last chance to be a boy." The journey, described in *Through the Brazilian Wilderness* (1914), was what TR reckoned "a thorough success." Nonetheless, it took its toll on the aging giant. He was injured in a canoe accident, and when the party emerged from the jungle he was lame, utterly exhausted, and had lost 35 pounds. Still he was at peace with himself as only a bone-weary, inwardly happy sportsman can be.

The Great War brought great tragedy to the Roosevelt family. His son, Quentin, died in aerial combat late in the war, and James Amos, TR's beloved butler and bodyguard, said the death of "Quinikins" left his father a changed man "eating his heart out." To make matters worse, TR suffered a severe attack of jungle fever, a holdover from his earlier adventures in the tropics. It left him with limited mobility and some deafness, but characteristically, even when warned he might spend the remainder of his life in a wheelchair, he shrugged it off and said, "All right, I can work that way."

Late in 1918, TR was once more quite ill. He rallied briefly with the New Year, and on January 5 worked a full eleven hours. At bedtime though, he told his wife, Edith, that he had "such a strange feeling." He died that night in his sleep, and his son, Archibald, at home recuperating from wounds suffered on the Western Front, cabled family members and friends: "The old Lion is dead."

Thus ended what TR had often called "the great adventure." For him, all of life was an ongoing adventure, and he characterized those who dared to be adventurous as "torch-bearers." He was in the forefront of those carrying the flame, and nowhere was that more obvious than in his efforts as a hunter, naturalist, and advocate of protecting the nation's natural resources for enjoyment and use by future generations.

Roosevelt remains the only American president to have had a true sense and a sure feel for balancing human and environmental needs. He left a lasting, romantic legacy, one that places today's lovers of nature, whether their outlook is that of Thoreau or of hunters like Davy Crockett and Daniel Boone, deeply in his debt. He lived, with incredibly fullness, the strenuous life in which he so staunchly believed. Even today, a full four score years and more later, TR's legacy inspires us and his *joie de vivre* invigorates us. To join him vicariously, in the pages of his many books on the outdoors, is to savor his inspiration and share the invigoration that moved a masterful writer and a genuinely great American.

Reprinted with permission of the author. Jim Casada has written or edited more than forty books. Readers can order his books by going to his website, www.jimcasadaoutdoors.com. His website offers a free monthly e-newsletter.

A Man-Killing Bear

THEODORE ROOSEVELT

Almost every trapper past middle age who has spent his life in the wilderness has stories to tell about exceptionally savage bears. One of these stories was told in my ranch house one winter evening by an old mountain hunter, clad in fur cap, buckskin hunting shirt and leather trousers, who had come to my ranch at nightfall, when the cowboys were returning from their day's labor.

The old fellow, who was known by the nickname of "Buckskin," had camped for several months in the Bad Lands but a score of miles away from my ranch. Most of his previous life had been spent among the main chains of the Rockies. After supper the conversation drifted to bears, always a favorite subject of talk in frontier cabins, and some of my men began to recount their own adventures with these great, clumsy-looking beasts.

This at once aroused the trapper's interest. He soon had the conversation to himself, telling us story after story of the bears he had killed and the escapes he had met with in battling against them. In particular he told us of one bear which, many years before, had killed the partner with whom at the time he was trapping.

The two men were camped in a high mountain valley in northwestern Wyoming, their camp being pitched at the edge of a "park country"—that is, a region where large glades and groves of tall evergreen trees alternate.

They had been trapping beaver, the animal which, on account of its abundance and the value of the fur, was more eagerly followed than any other by the old-time plains and mountain trappers. They had with them four shaggy pack ponies, such as most of these hunters use, and as these ponies were not needed at the moment, they had been turned loose to shift for themselves in the open glade country.

Late one evening three of the ponies surprised the trappers by galloping up to the campfire and there halting. The fourth did not make his appearance. The trappers knew that some wild beast must have assailed the animals and had probably caught one and caused the others to flee toward the place which they had learned to associate with safety.

Before dawn the next morning the two men started off to look for the lost horse. They skirted several great glades, following the tracks of the ponies that had come to the fire the previous evening. Two miles away, at the edge of a tall pine wood, they found the body of the lost horse, already partially eaten.

The tracks round about showed that the assailant was a grizzly of uncommon size, which had evidently jumped at the horses just after dusk, as they fed up to the edge of the woods. The owner of the horse decided to wait by the carcass for the bear's return, while old Buckskin went off to do the day's work in looking after traps, and the like.

Buckskin was absent all day, and reached camp after nightfall. His friend had come in ahead of him, having waited in vain for the bear. As there was no moon he had not thought it worthwhile to stay by the bait during the night.

The next morning they returned to the carcass and found that the bear had returned and eaten his full, after which he had lumbered off up the hillside. They took up his tracks and followed him for some three hours; but the wary old brute was not to be surprised. When they at last reached the spot where he had made his bed, it was only to find that he must have heard them as they approached, for he had evidently left in a great hurry.

After following the roused animal for some distance they found they could not overtake him. He was in an ugly mood, and kept halting every mile or so to walk to and fro, bite and break down the saplings, and paw the earth and dead logs; but in spite of this bullying he would not absolutely await their approach, but always shambled off before they came in sight.

At last they decided to abandon the pursuit. They then separated, each to make an afternoon's hunt and return to camp by his own way.

Our friend reached camp at dusk, but his partner did not turn up that evening at all. However, it was nothing unusual for either one of the two to be off for a night, and Buckskin thought little of it.

Next morning he again hunted all day, and returned to camp fully expecting to see his friend there, but found no sign of him. The second night passed, still without his coming in.

The morning after, the old fellow became uneasy and started to hunt him up. All that day he searched in vain, and when, on coming back to camp, there was still no trace of him, he was sure that some accident had happened.

The next morning he went back to the pine grove in which they had separated on leaving the trail of the bear. His friend had worn hobnail boots instead of moccasins, and this made it much easier to follow his tracks. With some difficulty the old hunter traced him for some four miles, until he came to a rocky stretch of country, where all sign of the footprints disappeared.

However, he was a little startled to observe footprints of a different sort. A great bear, without doubt the same one that had killed the horse, had been travelling in a course parallel to that of the man. Apparently the beast had been lurking just in front of his two pursuers the day they followed him from the carcass; and from the character of the "sign" Buckskin judged that as soon as he separated from his friend, the bear had likewise turned and had begun to follow the trapper.

The bear had not followed the man into the rocky piece of ground, and when the old hunter failed in his efforts to trace up his friend, he took the trail of the bear instead.

Three-quarters of a mile on, the bear, which had so far been walking, broke into a gallop, the claws making deep scratches here and there in the patches of soft earth. The trail then led into a very thick and dark wood, and here the footprints of the man suddenly reappeared.

For some little time the old hunter was unable to make up his mind with certainty as to which one was following the other; but finally, in the decayed mold by a rotten log, he found unmistakable sign where the print of the bear's foot overlaid that of the man. This put the matter beyond doubt. The bear was following the man.

For a couple of hours more the hunter slowly and with difficulty followed the dim trail.

The bear had apparently not cared to close in, but had slouched along some distance behind the man. Then in a marshy thicket where a mountain stream came down, the end had come.

Evidently at this place the man, still unconscious that he was followed, had turned and gone upward, and the bear, altering his course to an oblique angle, had intercepted him, making his rush just as he came through a patch of low willows. The body of the man lay under the willow branches beside the brook, terribly torn and disfigured.

Evidently the bear had rushed at him so quickly that he could not fire his gun, and had killed him with its powerful jaws. The unfortunate man's body was almost torn to pieces. The killing had evidently been done purely for malice, for the remains were uneaten, nor had the bear returned to them.

Angry and horrified at his friend's fate, old Buckskin spent the next two days in looking carefully through the neighboring groves for fresh tracks of the cunning and savage monster. At last he found an open spot of ground where the brute was evidently fond of sunning himself in the early morning, and to this spot the hunter returned before dawn the following day.

He did not have long to wait. By sunrise a slight crackling of the thick undergrowth told him that the bear was approaching. A few minutes afterward the brute appeared. It was a large beast with a poor coat, its head scarred by teeth and claw marks gained in many a combat with others of its own kind.

It came boldly into the opening and lay down, but for some time kept turning its head from side to side so that no shot could be obtained.

At last, growing impatient, the hunter broke a stick. Instantly the bear swung his head around side-wise, and in another moment a bullet crashed into its skull at the base of the ear, and the huge body fell limply over on its side, lifeless.

Old Ephraim

THEODORE ROOSEVELT

Few bears are found in the immediate neighborhood of my ranch; and though I have once or twice seen their tracks in the Bad Lands, I have never had any experience with the animals themselves except during the elk-hunting trip on the Bighorn Mountains.

The grizzly bear undoubtedly comes in the category of dangerous game, and is, perhaps, the only animal in the United States that can be fairly so placed, unless we count the few jaguars found north of the Rio Grande. But the danger of hunting the grizzly has been greatly exaggerated, and the sport is certainly very much safer than it was at the beginning of this century. The first hunters who came into contact with this great bear were men belonging to that hardy and adventurous class of backwoodsmen which had filled the wild country between the Appalachian Mountains and the Mississippi. These men carried but one weapon: the long-barrelled, small-bored pea-rifle, whose bullets ran seventy to the pound, the amount of powder and lead being a little less than that contained in the cartridge of a thirty-two-calibre Winchester. In the eastern states almost all the hunting was done in the woodland; the shots were mostly obtained at short distance, and deer and black bear were the largest game; moreover, the pea-rifles were marvellously accurate for close range, and their owners were famed the world over for their skill as marksmen. Thus these rifles had so far proved plenty good enough for the work they had to do, and indeed had done excellent service as military weapons in the ferocious wars that the men of the border carried on with their Indian neighbors, and even in conflict with more civilized foes, as at the battles of Kings' Mountain and New Orleans. But when the restless frontiersmen pressed out over the Western plains, they encountered in the grizzly a beast of far greater bulk and more savage temper than any of those found in the Eastern woods, and their small-bore rifles were utterly inadequate weapons with which to cope with him. It is small wonder that he was considered by them to be almost invulnerable, and extraordinarily tenacious of life. He would be a most unpleasant antagonist now to a man armed only with a thirty-two-calibre rifle that carried but a single shot and was loaded at the muzzle. A rifle, to be of use in this sport, should carry a ball weighing from half an ounce to an ounce. With the old pea-rifles the shot had to be in the eye or heart; and accidents to the hunter were very common. But the introduction of heavy breech-loading repeaters has greatly lessened the danger, even in the very few and far-off places where the grizzlies are as ferocious as formerly. For nowadays these great bears are undoubtedly much better aware of the death-dealing power of men, and, as a consequence, much less fierce, than was the case with their forefathers, who so unhesitatingly attacked the early Western travellers and explorers. Constant contact with rifle-carrying hunters, for a period extending over many generations of bear life, has taught the grizzly by bitter experience that man is his undoubted overlord, as far as fighting goes; and this knowledge has become an hereditary characteristic. No grizzly will assail a man now unprovoked, and one will almost always rather run than fight; though if he is wounded or thinks himself cornered he will attack his foes with a headlong, reckless fury that renders him one of the most dangerous of wild beasts. The ferocity of all wild animals depends largely upon the amount of resistance they are accustomed to meet with, and the quantity of molestation to which they are subjected.

The change in the grizzly's character during the last half-century has been precisely paralleled by the change in the characters of its Northern cousin, the polar bear, and of the South African lion. When the Dutch and Scandinavian sailors first penetrated the Arctic seas, they were kept in constant dread of the white bear, who regarded a man as simply an erect variety of seal, quite as good eating as the common kind. The records of these early explorers are filled with examples of the ferocious and man-eating propensities of the polar bears; but in the accounts of most of the later Arctic expeditions, they are portrayed as having learned wisdom, and being now most anxious to keep out of the way of the hunters. A number of my sporting friends have killed white bears, and none of them were ever even charged. And in South Africa the English sportsmen and Dutch Boers have taught the lion to be a very different creature from what it was when the first white man reached that continent. If the Indian tiger had been a native of the United States, it would now be one of the most shy of beasts. Of late years our estimate of the grizzly's ferocity has been lowered; and we no longer accept the tales of uneducated hunters as being proper authority by which to judge it. But we should make a parallel reduction in the cases of many foreign animals and their describers. Take, for example, that purely melodramatic beast, the North African lion, as portrayed by Jules Gérard, who bombastically describes himself as *"le tueur des lions."* Gérard's accounts are self-evidently in large part fictitious, while, if true, they would prove less for the bravery of the lion than for the phenomenal cowardice, incapacity, and bad marksmanship of the Algerian Arabs. Doubtless Gérard was a great hunter; but so is many a Western plainsman, whose account of the grizzlies he has killed would be wholly untrustworthy. Take, for instance, the following from page 223 of *La Chasse au Lion:* "The inhabitants had assembled one day to the number of two or three hundred, with the object of killing (the lion) or driving it out of the country. The attack took place at sunrise; at midday five hundred cartridges had been expended; the Arabs carried off one of their number dead and six wounded, and the lion remained master of the field of battle." Now, if three hundred men could fire five hundred shots at a lion without hurting him, it merely shows that they were wholly incapable of hurting anything, or else that M. Gérard was more expert with the long-bow than with the rifle. Gérard's whole book is filled with equally preposterous nonsense; yet a great many people seriously accept this same book as trustworthy authority for the manners and ferocity of the North African lion. It would be quite as sensible to accept M. Jules Verne's stories as being valuable contributions to science. A good deal of the lion's reputation is built upon just such stuff.

How the prowess of the grizzly compares with that of the lion or tiger would be hard to say; I have never shot either of the latter myself, and my brother, who has killed tigers in India, has never had a chance at a grizzly. Any one of the big bears we killed on the mountains would, I should think, have been able to make short work of either a lion or a tiger; for the grizzly is greatly superior in bulk and muscular power to either of the great cats, and its teeth are as large as theirs, while its claws, though blunter, are much longer; nevertheless, I believe that a lion or a tiger would be fully as dangerous to a hunter or other human being, on account of the superior speed of its charge, the lightning-like rapidity of its movements, and its apparently sharper senses. Still, after all is said, the man should have a thoroughly trustworthy weapon and a fairly cool head, who would follow into its own haunts and slay grim Old Ephraim.

A grizzly will only fight if wounded or cornered, or, at least, if he thinks himself cornered. If a man by accident stumbles on to one close up, he's almost certain to be attacked really more from fear than from any other motive; exactly the same reason that makes a rattlesnake strike at a passer-by. I have personally known of but one instance of a grizzly turning on a hunter before being wounded. This happened to a friend of mine, a Californian ranchman, who, with two or three of his men, was following a bear that had carried off one of his sheep. They got the bear into a cleft in the mountain from which there was no escape, and he suddenly charged back through the line of his pursuers, struck down one of the horsemen, seized the arm of the man in his jaws and broke it as if it had been a pipe-stem, and was only killed after a most lively fight, in which, by repeated charges, he at one time drove every one of his assailants off the field.

But two instances have come to my personal knowledge where a man has been killed by a grizzly. One was that of a hunter at the foot of the Bighorn Mountains who had chased a large bear and finally wounded him. The animal turned at once and came straight at the man, whose second shot missed. The bear then closed and passed on, after striking only a single blow; yet that one blow, given with all the power of its thick, immensely muscular forearm, armed with nails as strong as so many hooked steel spikes, tore out the man's collar-bone and snapped through three or four ribs. He never recovered from the shock, and died that night.

The other instance occurred to a neighbor of mine—who has a small ranch on the Little Missouri—two or three years ago. He was out on a mining trip, and was prospecting with two other men near the headwater of the Little Missouri, in the Black Hills country. They were walking down along the river, and came to a point of land thrust out into it, which was densely covered with brush and fallen timber. Two of the party walked round by the edge of the stream; but the third, a German, and a very powerful fellow, followed a well-beaten game trail, leading through the bushy point. When they were some forty yards apart the two men heard an agonized shout from the German, and at the same time the loud coughing growl, or roar, of a bear. They turned just in time to see their companion struck a terrible blow on the head by a grizzly, which must have been roused from its lair by his almost stepping on it; so close was it that he had no time to fire his rifle, but merely held it up over his head as a guard. Of course, it was struck down, the claws of the great brute at the same time shattering his skull like an eggshell. Yet the man staggered on some ten feet before he fell; but when he did he never spoke or moved again. The two others killed the bear after a short brisk struggle as he was in the midst of a most determined charge.

In 1872, near Fort Wingate, New Mexico, two soldiers of a cavalry regiment came to their death at the claws of a grizzly bear. The army surgeon who attended them told me the particulars, as far as they were known. The men were mail-carriers, and one day did not come in at the appointed time. Next day a relief party was sent out to look for them, and after some search found the bodies of both, as well as that of one of the horses. One of the men still showed signs of life; he came to his senses before dying, and told the story. They had seen a grizzly, and pursued it on horseback with their Spencer rifles. On coming close, one had fired into its side, when it turned with marvellous quickness for so large and unwieldy an animal, and struck down the horse, at the same time inflicting a ghastly wound on the rider. The other man dismounted and came up to the rescue of his companion. The bear then left the latter and attacked the other. Although hit by the bullet, it charged home and threw the man down, and then lay on him and deliberately bit him to death, while his groans and cries were frightful to hear. Afterward it walked off into the bushes without again offering to molest the already mortally wounded victim of its first assault.

At certain times the grizzly works a good deal of havoc among the herds of the stockmen. A friend of mine, a ranchman in Montana, told me that one fall bears became very plenty around his ranches, and caused him severe loss, killing with ease even full-grown beef-steers. But one of them once found his intended quarry too much for him. My friend had a stocky, rather vicious range stallion, which had been grazing one day near a small thicket of bushes, and, towards evening, came galloping in with three or four gashes in his haunch, that looked as if they had been cut with a dull axe. The cowboys knew at once that he had been assailed by a bear, and rode off to the thicket near which he had been feeding. Sure enough, a bear, evidently in a very bad temper, sallied out as soon as the thicket was surrounded, and, after a spirited fight and a succession of charges, was killed. On examination, it was found that his under jaw was broken, and part of his face smashed in, evidently by the stallion's hoofs. The horse had been feeding when the bear leaped out at him, but failed to kill at the first stroke; then the horse lashed out behind, and not only freed himself, but also severely damaged his opponent.

Doubtless the grizzly could be hunted to advantage with dogs, which would not, of course, be expected to seize him, but simply to find and bay him, and distract his attention by barking and nipping.

Occasionally, a bear can be caught in the open and killed with the aid of horses. But nine times out of ten the only way to get one is to put on moccasins and still-hunt it in its own haunts, shooting it at close quarters. Either its tracks should be followed until the bed wherein it lies during the day is found, or a given locality in which it is known to exist should be carefully beaten through, or else a bait should be left out, and a watch kept on it to catch the bear when he has come to visit it.

For some days after our arrival on the Bighorn range we did not come across any grizzly.

Although it was still early in September, the weather was cool and pleasant, the nights being frosty; and every two or three days there was a flurry of light snow, which rendered the labor of tracking much more easy. Indeed, throughout our stay on the mountains, the peaks were snowcapped almost all the time. Our fare was excellent, consisting of elk venison, mountain grouse, and small trout—the last caught in one of the beautiful little lakes that lay almost up by timber line. To us, who had for weeks been accustomed to make small fires from dried brush, or from sage-brush roots, which we dug out of the ground, it was a treat to sit at night before the roaring and crackling pine logs; as the old teamster quaintly put it, we had at last come to a land "where the wood grew on trees." There were plenty of black-tail deer in the woods, and we came across a number of bands of cow and calf elk, or of young bulls; but after several days' hunting we were still without any head worth taking home, and had seen no sign of grizzly, which was the game we were especially anxious to kill; for neither Merrifield nor I had ever seen a wild bear alive.

Sometimes we hunted in company; sometimes each of us went out alone; the teamster, of course, remaining in to guard camp and cook. One day we had separated; I reached camp early in the afternoon, and waited a couple of hours before Merrifield put in an appearance.

At last I heard a shout—the familiar long-drawn *Eikoh-h-h* of the cattlemen—and he came in sight galloping at speed down an open glade, and waving his hat, evidently having had good luck; and when he reined in his small, wiry, cow-pony, we saw that he had packed behind his saddle the fine, glossy pelt of a black bear. Better still, he announced that he had been off about ten miles to a perfect tangle of ravines and valleys where bear sign was very thick; and not of black bear either, but of grizzly. The black bear (the only one we got on the mountains) he had run across by accident, while riding up a valley in which there was a patch of dead timber grown up with berry bushes. He noticed a black object which he first took to be a stump; for during the past few days we had each of us made one or two clever stalks up to charred logs, which our imagination converted into bears. On coming near, however, the object suddenly took to its heels; he followed over frightful ground at the pony's best pace, until it stumbled and fell down. By this time he was close on the bear, which had just reached the edge of the wood. Picking himself up, he rushed after it, hearing it growling ahead of him; after running some fifty yards the sound stopped, and he stood still listening. He saw and heard nothing, until he happened to cast his eyes upwards, and there was the bear, almost overhead, and about twenty-five feet up a tree; and in as many seconds afterwards it came down to the ground with a bounce, stone dead. It was a young bear, in its second year, and had probably never before seen a man, which accounted for the ease with which it was treed and taken. One minor result of the encounter was to convince Merrifield—the list of whose faults did not include lack of self-confidence—that he could run down any bear; in consequence of which idea we on more than one subsequent occasion went through a good deal of violent exertion.

Merrifield's tale made me decide to shift camp at once, and go over to the spot where the bear tracks were so plenty. Next morning we were off, and by noon pitched camp by a clear brook, in a valley with steep, wooded sides, but with good feed for the horses in the open bottom. We rigged the canvas wagon-sheet into a small tent, sheltered by the trees from the wind, and piled great pine logs near by where we wished to place the fire; for a night camp in the sharp fall weather is cold and dreary unless there is a roaring blaze of flame in front of the tent.

That afternoon we again went out, and I shot a fine bull elk. I came home alone toward nightfall, walking through a reach of burnt forest, where there was nothing but charred tree-trunks and black mould. When nearly through it I came across the huge, half-human footprints of a great grizzly, which must have passed by within a few minutes. It gave me rather an eerie feeling in the silent, lonely woods, to see for the first time the unmistakable proofs that I was in the home of the mighty lord of the wilderness. I followed the tracks in the fading twilight until it became too dark to see them any longer, and then shouldered my rifle and walked back to camp.

That evening we almost had a visit from one of the animals we were after. Several times we had heard at night the musical calling of the bull elk—a sound to which no writer has yet done justice. This particular night, when we were in bed and the fire was smouldering, we were roused by a ruder noise—a kind of grunting or roaring whine, answered by the frightened snorts of the ponies. It was a bear which had evidently not seen the fire, as it came from behind the bank, and had probably been attracted by the smell of the horses. After it made out what we were, it stayed round a short while, again uttered its peculiar roaring grunt, and went off; we had seized our rifles and had run out into the woods, but in the darkness could see nothing; indeed, it was rather lucky we did not stumble across the bear, as he could have made short work of us when we were at such a disadvantage.

Next day we went off on a long tramp through the woods and along the sides of the canyons. There were plenty of berry bushes growing in clusters; and all around these there were fresh tracks of bear. But the grizzly is also a flesh-eater, and has a great liking for carrion. On visiting the place where Merrifield had killed the black bear, we found that the grizzlies had been there before us, and had utterly devoured the carcass, with cannibal relish. Hardly a scrap was left, and we turned our steps toward where lay the bull elk I had killed. It was quite late in the afternoon when we reached the place. A grizzly had evidently been at the carcass during the preceding night, for his great footprints were in the ground all around it, and the carcass itself was gnawed and torn, and partially covered with earth and leaves—for the grizzly has a curious habit of burying all of his prey that he does not at the moment need. A great many ravens had been feeding on the body, and they wheeled about over the tree-tops above us, uttering their barking croaks.

The forest was composed mainly of what are called ridge-pole pines, which grow close together, and do not branch out until the stems are thirty or forty feet from the ground. Beneath these trees we walked over a carpet of pine needles, upon which our moccasined feet made no sound. The woods seemed vast and lonely, and their silence was broken now and then by the strange noises always to be heard in the great forests, and which seem to mark the sad and everlasting unrest of the wilderness. We climbed up along the trunk of a dead tree which had toppled over until its upper branches struck in the limb crotch of another, that thus supported it at an angle half way in its fall. When above the ground far enough to prevent the bear's smelling us, we sat still to wait for his approach; until, in the gathering gloom, we could no longer see the sights of our rifles, and could but dimly make out the carcass of the great elk. It was useless to wait longer; and we clambered down and stole out to the edge of the woods. The forest here covered one side of a steep, almost canyon-like ravine, whose other side was bare except of rock and sagebrush. Once out from under the trees there was still plenty of light, although the sun had set, and we crossed over some fifty yards to the opposite hillside, and crouched down under a bush to see if, per-chance, some animal might not also leave the cover. To our right the ravine sloped downward toward the valley of the Bighorn River, and far on its other side we could catch a glimpse of the great main chain of the Rockies, their snow-peaks glinting crimson in the light of the set sun. Again we waited quietly in the growing dusk until the pine trees in our front blended into one dark, frowning mass. We saw nothing; but the wild creatures of the forest had begun to stir abroad. The owls hooted dismally from the tops of the tall trees, and two or three times a harsh wailing cry, probably the voice of some lynx or wolverine, arose from the depths of the woods. At last, as we were rising to leave, we heard the sound of the breaking of a dead stick from the spot where we knew the carcass lay. It was a sharp, sudden noise, perfectly distinct from the natural creaking and snapping of the branches; just such a sound as would be made by the tread of some heavy creature. "Old Ephraim" had come back to the carcass. A minute afterward, listening with strained ears, we heard him brush by some dry twigs. It was entirely too dark to go in after him; but we made up our minds that on the morrow he should be ours.

Early next morning we were over at the elk carcass, and, as we expected, found that the bear had eaten his full at it during the night. His tracks showed him to be an immense fellow, and were so fresh that we doubted if he had left long before we arrived; and we made up our minds to follow him up and try to find his lair. The bears that lived on these mountains had evidently been little disturbed; indeed, the Indians and most of the white hunters are rather chary of meddling with "Old Ephraim," as the mountain men style the grizzly, unless they get him at a disadvantage; for the sport is fraught with some danger and but small profit. The bears thus seemed to have very little fear of harm, and we thought it likely that the bed of the one who had fed on the elk would not be far away.

My companion was a skilful tracker, and we took up the trail at once. For some distance it led over the soft, yielding carpet of moss and pine needles, and the footprints were quite easily made out, although we could follow them but slowly; for we had, of course, to keep a sharp lookout ahead and around us as we walked noiselessly on in the sombre half-light always prevailing under the great pine trees, through whose thickly interlacing branches stray but few beams of light, no matter how bright the sun may be outside. We made no sound ourselves, and every little sudden noise sent a thrill through me as I peered about with each sense on the alert. Two or three of the ravens that we had scared from the carcass flew overhead, croaking hoarsely; and the pine-tops moaned and sighed in the slight breeze—for pine trees seem to be ever in motion, no matter how light the wind.

After going a few hundred yards the tracks turned off on a well-beaten path made by the elk; the woods were in many places cut up by these game trails, which had often become as distinct as ordinary footpaths. The beast's footprints were perfectly plain in the dust, and he had lumbered along up the path until near the middle of the hillside, where the ground broke away, and there were hollows and boulders. Here there had been a windfall, and the dead trees lay among the living, piled across one another in all directions; while between and around them sprouted up a thick growth of young spruces and other evergreens. The trail turned off into the tangled thicket, within which it was almost certain we would find our quarry. We could still follow the tracks, by the slight scrapes of the claws on the bark, or by the bent and broken twigs; and we advanced with noiseless caution, slowly climbing over the dead tree trunks and upturned stumps, and not letting a branch rustle or catch on our clothes. When in the middle of the thicket we crossed what was almost a breastwork of fallen logs, and Merrifield, who was leading, passed by the upright stem of a great pine. As soon as he was by it, he sank suddenly on one knee, turning half round, his face fairly aflame with excitement; and as I strode past him, with my rifle at the ready, there, not ten steps off, was the great bear, slowly rising from his bed among the young spruces. He had heard us, but apparently hardly knew exactly where or what we were, for he reared up on his haunches sideways to us. Then he saw us, and dropped down again on all fours, the shaggy hair on his neck and shoulders seeming to bristle as he turned towards us. As he sank down on his forefeet I had raised the rifle; his head was bent slightly down, and when I saw the top of the white bead fairly between his small, glittering, evil eyes, I pulled trigger. Half rising up, the huge beast fell over on his side in the death throes, the ball having gone into his brain, striking as fairly between the eyes as if the distance had been measured by a carpenter's rule.

The whole thing was over in twenty seconds from the time I caught sight of the game; indeed, it was over so quickly that the grizzly did not have time to show fight at all or come a step toward us. It was the first I had ever seen, and I felt not a little proud, as I stood over the great brindled bulk, which lay stretched out at length in the cool shade of the evergreens. He was a monstrous fellow, much larger than any I have seen since, whether alive or brought in dead by the hunters. As near as we could estimate (for of course we had nothing with which to weigh more than very small portions) he must have weighed about twelve hundred pounds, and though this is not as large as some of his kind are said to grow in California, it is yet a very unusual size for a bear. He was a good deal heavier than any of our horses; and it was with the greatest difficulty that we were able to skin him. He must have been very old, his teeth and claws being all worn down and blunted; but nevertheless he had been living in plenty, for he was as fat as a prize hog, the layers on his back being a finger's length in thickness. He was still in the summer coat, his hair being short, and in color a curious brindled brown, somewhat like that of certain bulldogs; while all the bears we shot afterward had the long thick winter fur, cinnamon or yellowish brown. By the way, the name of this bear has reference to its character and not to its color, and should, I suppose, be properly spelt grisly—in the sense of horrible, exactly as we speak of a "grisly spectre"—and not grizzly; but perhaps the latter way of spelling it is too well established to be now changed.

In killing dangerous game, steadiness is more needed than good shooting. No game is dangerous unless a man is close up, for nowadays hardly any wild beast will charge from a distance of a hundred yards, but will rather try to run off; and if a man is close it is easy enough for him to shoot straight if he does not lose his head. A bear's brain is about the size of a pint bottle; and any one can hit a pint bottle offhand at thirty or forty feet. I have had two shots at bears at close quarters, and each time I fired into the brain, the bullet in one case striking fairly between the eyes, as told above, and in the other going in between the eye and ear. A novice at this kind of sport will find it best and safest to keep in mind the old Norse viking's advice in reference to a long sword: "If you go in close enough your sword will be long enough." If a poor shot goes in close enough he will find that he shoots straight enough.

I was very proud over my first bear; but Merrifield's chief feeling seemed to be disappointment that the animal had not had time to show fight. He was rather a reckless fellow, and very confident in his own skill with the rifle; and he really did not seem to have any more fear of the grizzlies than if they had been so many jack-rabbits. I did not at all share his feelings, having a hearty respect for my foes' prowess, and in following and attacking them always took all possible care to get the chances on my side. Merrifield was sincerely sorry that we never had to stand a regular charge; while on this trip we killed five grizzlies with seven bullets, and, except in the case of the she and cub spoken of farther on, each was shot about as quickly as it got sight of us. The last one we got was an old male, which was feeding on an elk carcass. We crept up to within about sixty feet, and as Merrifield had not yet killed a grizzly purely to his own gun, and I had killed three, I told him to take the shot. He at once whispered gleefully: "I'll break his leg, and we'll see what he'll do!" Having no ambition to be a participator in the antics of a three-legged bear, I hastily interposed a most emphatic veto; and with a rather injured air he fired, the bullet going through the neck just back of the head. The bear fell to the shot, and could not get up from the ground, dying in a few minutes; but first he seized his left wrist in his teeth and bit clean through it, completely separating the bones of the paw and arm. Although a smaller bear than the big one I first shot, he would probably have proved a much more ugly foe, for he was less unwieldy, and had much longer and sharper teeth and claws. I think that if my companion had merely broken the beast's leg, he would have had his curiosity as to its probable conduct more than gratified.

We tried eating the grizzly's flesh, but it was not good, being coarse and not well flavored; and besides, we could not get over the feeling that it had belonged to a carrion feeder. The flesh of the little black bear, on the other hand, was excellent; it tasted like that of a young pig. Doubtless, if a young grizzly, which had fed merely upon fruits, berries, and acorns, was killed, its flesh would prove good eating; but even then it would probably not be equal to a black bear.

A day or two after the death of the big bear, we went out one afternoon on horseback, intending merely to ride down to see a great canyon lying some six miles west of our camp; indeed, we went more to look at the scenery than for any other reason, though, of course, neither of us ever stirred out of camp without his rifle. We rode down the valley in which we had camped, through alternate pine groves and open glades, until we reached the canyon, and then skirted its brink for a mile or so. It was a great chasm, many miles in length, as if the table-land had been rent asunder by some terrible and unknown force; its sides were sheer walls of rock, rising three or four hundred feet straight up in the air, and worn by the weather till they looked like towers and battlements of some vast fortress. Between them, at the bottom, was a space, in some places nearly a quarter of a mile wide, in others very narrow, through whose middle foamed a deep, rapid torrent, of which the sources lay far back among the snow-topped mountains around Cloud Peak. In this valley, dark green sombre pines stood in groups, stiff and erect; and here and there among them were groves of poplar and cottonwood, with slender branches and trembling leaves, their bright green already changing to yellow in the sharp fall weather. We went down to where the mouth of the canyon opened out, and rode our horses to the end of a great jutting promontory of rock, thrust out into the plain; and in the cold, clear air we looked far over the broad valley of the Bighorn as it lay at our very feet, walled in on the other side by the distant chain of the Rocky Mountains.

Turning our horses, we rode back along the edge of another canyon-like valley, with a brook flowing down its center, and its rocky sides covered with an uninterrupted pine forest—the place of all others in whose inaccessible wildness and ruggedness a bear would find a safe retreat. After some time we came to where other valleys, with steep, grass-grown sides, covered with sage-brush, branched out from it, and we followed one of these out. There was plenty of elk sign about, and we saw several black-tail deer. These last were very common on the mountains, but we had not hunted them at all, as we were in no need of meat. But this afternoon we came across a buck with remarkably fine antlers, and accordingly I shot it, and we stopped to cut off and skin out the horns, throwing the reins over the heads of the horses, and leaving them to graze by themselves. The body lay near the crest of one side of a deep valley, or ravine, which headed up on the plateau a mile to our left. Except for scattered trees and bushes the valley was bare; but there was heavy timber along the crests of the hills on its opposite side. It took some time to fix the head properly, and we were just ending when Merrifield sprang to his feet and exclaimed: "Look at the bears!" pointing down into the valley below us. Sure enough, there were two bears (which afterwards proved to be an old she and a nearly full-grown cub) travelling up the bottom of the valley, much too far off for us to shoot. Grasping our rifles and throwing off our hats, we started off as hard as we could run, diagonally down the hillside, so as to cut them off. It was some little time before they saw us, when they made off at a lumbering gallop up the valley. It would seem impossible to run into two grizzlies in the open, but they were going up hill and we down, and, moreover, the old one kept stopping. The cub would forge ahead and could probably have escaped us, but the mother now and then stopped to sit up on her haunches and look round at us, when the cub would run back to her. The upshot was that we got ahead of them, when they turned and went straight up one hillside as we ran straight down the other behind them. By this time I was pretty nearly done out, for running along the steep ground through the sage-brush was most exhausting work; and Merrifield kept gaining on me and was well in front. Just as he disappeared over a bank, almost at the bottom of the valley, I tripped over a bush and fell full-length. When I got up I knew I could never make up the ground I had lost, and, besides, could hardly run any longer; Merrifield was out of sight below, and the bears were laboring up the steep hillside directly opposite and about three hundred yards off, so I sat down and began to shoot over Merrifield's head, aiming at the big bear. She was going very steadily and in a straight line, and each bullet sent up a puff of dust where it struck the dry soil, so that I could keep correcting my aim; and the fourth ball crashed into the old bear's flank. She lurched heavily forward, but recovered herself and reached the timber, while Merrifield, who had put on a spurt, was not far behind.

I toiled up the hill at a sort of trot, fairly gasping and sobbing for breath; but before I got to the top I heard a couple of shots and a shout. The old bear had turned as soon as she was in the timber, and came towards Merrifield, but he gave her the death wound by firing into her chest, and then shot at the young one, knocking it over. When I came up he was just walking toward the latter to finish it with the revolver, but it suddenly jumped up as lively as ever and made off at a great pace—for it was nearly full-grown. It was impossible to fire where the tree trunks were so thick, but there was a small opening across which it would have to pass, and, collecting all my energies, I made a last run, got into position, and covered the opening with my rifle. The instant the bear appeared I fired, and it turned a dozen somersaults down hill, rolling over and over; the ball had struck it near the tail, and had ranged forward through the hollow of the body. Each of us had thus given the fatal wound to the bear into which the other had fired the first bullet. The run, though short, had been very sharp, and over such awful country that we were completely fagged out, and could hardly speak for lack of breath. The sun had already set, and it was too late to skin the animals; so we merely dressed them, caught the ponies—with some trouble, for they were frightened at the smell of the bear's blood on our hands—and rode home through the darkening woods. Next day we brought the teamster and two of the steadiest pack-horses to the carcasses, and took the skins into camp.

The feed for the horses was excellent in the valley in which we were camped, and the rest after their long journey across the plains did them good. They had picked up wonderfully in condition during our stay on the mountains; but they were apt to wander very far during the night, for there were so many bears and other wild beasts around, that they kept getting frightened and running off. We were very loath to leave our hunting-grounds, but time was pressing, and we had already many more trophies than we could carry; so one cool morning, when the branches of the evergreens were laden with the feathery snow that had fallen overnight, we struck camp and started out of the mountains, each of us taking his own bedding behind his saddle, while the pack-horses were loaded down with bearskins, elk and deer antlers, and the hides and furs of other game. In single file we moved through the woods, and across the canyons to the edge of the great table-land, and then slowly down the steep slope to its foot, where we found our canvas-topped wagon; and next day saw us setting out on our long journey homewards, across the three hundred weary miles of treeless and barren-looking plains country.

Last spring, since the above was written, a bear killed a man not very far from my ranch. It was at the time of the floods. Two hunters came down the river, by our ranch, on a raft, stopping to take dinner. A score or so of miles below, as we afterwards heard from the survivor, they landed, and found a bear in a small patch of brushwood. After waiting in vain for it to come out, one of the men rashly attempted to enter the thicket, and was instantly struck down by the beast, before he could so much as fire his rifle. It broke in his skull with a blow of its great paw, and then seized his arm in its jaws, biting it through and through in three places, but leaving the body and retreating into the bushes as soon as the unfortunate man's companion approached. We did not hear of the accident until too late to go after the bear, as we were just about starting to join the spring round-up.

The Game of the High Peaks:
The White Goat

THEODORE ROOSEVELT

In the fall of 1886 I went far west to the Rockies and took a fortnight's hunting trip among the northern spurs of the Cœur d'Alêne, between the towns of Heron and Horseplains in Montana. There are many kinds of game to be found in the least known or still untrodden parts of this wooded mountain wilderness—caribou, elk, ungainly moose with great shovel horns, cougars, and bears. But I did not have time to go deeply into the heart of the forest-clad ranges, and devoted my entire energies to the chase of but one animal, the white antelope-goat, then the least known and rarest of all American game.

We started from one of those most dismal and forlorn of all places, a dead mining town, on the line of the Northern Pacific Railroad. My foreman, Merrifield, was with me, and for guide I took a tall, lithe, happy-go-lucky mountaineer, who, like so many of the restless frontier race, was born in Missouri. Our outfit was simple, as we carried only blankets, a light wagon sheet, the ever-present camera, flour, bacon, salt, sugar, and coffee: canned goods are very unhandy to pack about on horseback. Our rifles and ammunition, with the few cooking-utensils and a book or two, completed the list. Four solemn ponies and a ridiculous little mule named Walla Walla bore us and our belongings. The Missourian was an expert packer, versed in the mysteries of the "diamond hitch," the only arrangement of the ropes that will insure a load staying in its place. Driving a pack train through the wooded paths and up the mountain passes that we had to traverse is hard work anyhow, as there are sure to be accidents happening to the animals all the time, while their packs receive rough treatment from jutting rocks and overhanging branches, or from the half-fallen tree-trunks under which the animals wriggle; and if the loads are continually coming loose, or slipping so as to gall the horses' backs and make them sore, the labor and anxiety are increased tenfold.

In a day or two we were in the heart of the vast wooded wilderness. A broad, lonely river ran through its midst, cleaving asunder the mountain chains. Range after range, peak upon peak, the mountains towered on every side, the lower timbered to the top, the higher with bare crests of gray crags, or else hooded with fields of shining snow. The deep valleys lay half in darkness, hemmed in by steep, timbered slopes and straight rock walls. The torrents, broken into glittering foam masses, sprang down through the chasms that they had rent in the sides of the high hills, lingered in black pools under the shadows of the scarred cliffs, and reaching the rank, tree-choked valleys, gathered into rapid streams of clear brown water, that drenched the drooping limbs of the tangled alders. Over the whole land lay like a shroud the mighty growth of the unbroken evergreen forest—spruce and hemlock, fir, balsam, tamarack, and lofty pine.

Yet even these vast wastes of shadowy woodland were once penetrated by members of that adventurous and now fast-vanishing folk, the American frontiersmen. Once or twice, while walking silently over the spongy moss beneath the somber archways of the pines, we saw on a tree-trunk a dim, faint ax-scar, the bark almost grown over it, showing where, many years before, some fur-trapper had chopped a deeper blaze than usual in making out a "spotted line"—man's first highway in the primeval forest; or on some hill-side we would come to the more recent, but already half-obliterated, traces of a miner's handiwork. The trapper and the miner were the pioneers of the mountains, as the hunter and the cowboy have been the pioneers of the plains: they are all of the same type, these sinewy men of the border, fearless and self-reliant, who are ever driven restlessly onward through the wilderness by the half-formed desires that make their eyes haggard and eager. There is no plain so lonely that their feet have not trodden it; no mountain so far off that their eyes have not scanned its grandeur.

We took nearly a week in going to our hunting-grounds and out from them again. This was tedious work, for the pace was slow, and it was accompanied with some real labor. In places the mountain paths were very steep and the ponies could with difficulty scramble along them; and once or twice they got falls that no animals less tough could have survived. Walla Walla being the unfortunate that suffered most. Often, moreover, we would come to a windfall, where the fallen trees lay heaped crosswise on one another in the wildest confusion, and a road had to be cleared by ax work. It was marvelous to see the philosophy with which the wise little beasts behaved, picking their way gingerly through these rough spots, hopping over fallen tree-trunks, or stepping between them in places where an Eastern horse would have snapped a leg short off, and walking composedly along narrow ledges with steep precipices below. They were tame and friendly, being turned loose at night, and not only staying near by, but also allowing themselves to be caught with out difficulty in the morning; industriously gleaning the scant food to be found in the burnt places or along the edges of the brooks, and often in the evening standing in a patient, solemn semicircle round the camp fire, just beyond where we were seated. Walla Walla, the little mule, was always in scrapes. Once we spent a morning of awkward industry in washing our clothes; having finished, we spread the half-cleansed array upon the bushes and departed on a hunt. On returning, to our horror we spied the miserable Walla Walla shamefacedly shambling off from the neighborhood of the wash, having partly chewed up every individual garment and completely undone all out morning's labor.

At first we did not have good weather. The Indians, of whom we met small band—said to be Flat-heads or their kin, on a visit from the coast region—had set fire to the woods not far away, and the smoke became so dense as to hurt our eyes, to hide the sun at midday, and to veil all objects from our sight as completely as if there had been a heavy fog. Then we had two days of incessant rain, which rendered our camp none too comfortable; but when the cleared we found that it had put out the fire and settled all the smoke, leaving a brilliant sky overhead.

We first camped in a narrow valley, surrounded by mountains so tall that except at noonday it lay in the shadow; and it was only when we were out late on the higher foot-hills that we saw the sun sink in a flame behind the distant ranges. The trees grew tall and thick, the underbrush choking the ground between their trunks, and their branches interlacing so that the sun's rays hardly came through them. There were very few open glades, and these were not more than a dozen rods or so across. Even on the mountains it was only when we got up very high indeed, or when we struck an occasional bare spur, or shoulder, that we could get a glimpse into the open. Elsewhere we could never see a hundred yards ahead of us, and like all plainsmen or mountaineers we at times felt smothered under the trees, and longed to be where we could look out far and wide on every side; we felt as if our heads were in hoods. A broad brook whirled and eddied past our camp, and a little below us was caught in a deep, narrow gorge, where the strangling rocks churned its swift current into spray and foam, and changed its murmurous humming and splashing into an angry roar. Strange little water wrens—the water-ousel of the books—made this brook their home. They were shaped like thrushes, and sometimes warbled sweetly, yet they lived right in the torrent, not only flitting along the banks and wading in the edges, but plunging boldly into midstream, and half walking, half flying along the bottom, deep under water, and perching on the slippery, spray-covered rocks of the waterfall or skimming over and through the rapids even more often than they ran along the margins of the deep, black pools.

White-tail deer were plentiful, and we kept our camp abundantly supplied with venison, varying it with all the grouse that we wanted, and with quantities of fresh trout. But I myself spent most of my time after the quarry I had come to get—the white goat. White goats have been known to hunters ever since Lewis and Clarke crossed the continent, but they have always ranked as the very rarest and most difficult to get of all American game. This reputation they owe to the nature of their haunts, rather than to their own wariness, for they have been so little disturbed that they are less shy than either deer or sheep. They are found here and there on the highest, most inaccessible mountain peaks down even to Arizona and New Mexico; but being fitted for cold climates, they are extremely scarce everywhere south of Montana and northern Idaho, and the great majority even of the most experienced hunters have hardly so much as heard of their existence. In Washington Territory, northern Idaho, and north-western Montana they are not uncommon, and are plentiful in parts of the mountain ranges of British America and Alaska. Their preference for the highest peaks is due mainly to their dislike of warmth, and in the north—even south of the Canadian line—they are found much lower down the mountains than is the case farther south. They are very conspicuous animals, with their snow-white coats and polished black horns, but their pursuit necessitates so much toil and hardship that not one in ten of the professional hunters has ever killed one; and I know of but one or two Eastern sportsmen who can boast a goats head as a trophy. But this will soon cease to be the case: for the Canadian Pacific Railway has opened the haunts where the goats are most plentiful, and any moderately adventurous and hardy rifleman can be sure of getting one by taking a little time, and that, too, whether he is a skilled hunter or not, since at present the game is not difficult to approach. The white goat will be common long after the elk has vanished, and it has already outlasted the buffalo. Few sportsmen henceforth—indeed, hardly any—will ever boast a buffalo head of their own killing: but the number of riflemen who can place to their credit the prized white fleeces and jet-black horns will steadily increase.

The Missourian, during his career as a Rocky Mountain hunter, had killed five white goats. The first he had shot near Canyon City. Colorado, and never having heard of any such animal before had concluded afterward that it was one of a flock of recently imported Angora goats, and accordingly, to avoid trouble, buried it where it lay: and it was not until fourteen years later, when he came up to the Cœur d'Alêne and shot another, that he became aware of what he had killed. He described them as being bold, pugnacious animals, not easily startled, and extremely tenacious of life. Once he had set a large hound at one which he came across while descending an ice-swollen river in early spring. The goat made no attempt to flee or to avoid the hound, but coolly awaited its approach and killed it with one wicked thrust of the horns; for the latter are as sharp as needles, and are used for stabbing, not butting. Another time he caught a goat in a bear trap set on a game trail. Its leg was broken, and he had to pack it out on pony-back, a two-days journey, to the settlement; yet in spite of such rough treatment it lived a week after it got there, when, unfortunately, the wounded leg mortified. It fought most determinedly, but soon became reconciled to captivity, eating with avidity all the grass it was given, recognizing its keeper, and grunting whenever be brought it food or started to walk away before it had had all it wished. The goats he had shot lived in ground where the walking was tiresome to the last degree, and where it was almost impossible not to make a good deal of noise: and nothing but their boldness and curiosity enabled him ever to kill any. One he shot while waiting at a pass for deer. The goat, an old male, came up, and fairly refused to leave the spot, walking round in the underbrush and finally mounting a great fallen log, where he staid snorting and stamping angrily until the Missourian lost patience and killed him.

For three or four days I hunted steadily and without success, and it was as hard work as any that I had ever undertaken. Both Merrifield and I were accustomed to a life in the saddle, and although we had varied it with an occasional long walk after deer or sheep, yet we were utterly unable to cope with the Missourian when it came to mountaineering. When we had previously hunted, in the Big Horn Mountains, we had found stout moccasins most comfortable, and extremely useful for still-hunting through the great woods and among the open glades; but the multitudinous sharp rocks and sheer, cliff-like slopes of the Cœur d'Alêne rendered our moccasins absolutely useless, for the first day's tramp bruised our feet till they were sore and slit our foot-gear into ribbons, besides tearing our clothes. Merrifield was then crippled, having nothing else but his cowboy boots; fortunately, I had taken in addition a pair of shoes with soles thickly studded with nails.

We would start immediately after breakfast each morning, carrying a light lunch in our pockets, and go straight up the mountain sides for hours at a time, varying it by skirting the broad, terrace-like ledges, or by clambering along the cliff crests. The climbing was very hard. The slope was so steep that it was like going upstairs; now through loose earth, then through a shingle of pebbles or sand, then over rough rocks, and again over a layer of pine needles as smooth and slippery as glass, while brittle, dry sticks that snapped at a touch, and loose stones that rattled down if so much as brushed, strewed the ground everywhere, the climber stumbling and falling over them and finding it almost absolutely impossible to proceed without noise, unless at a rate of progress too slow to admit of getting anywhere. Often, too, we would encounter dense underbrush, perhaps a thicket of little burnt balsams, as prickly and brittle as so much coral; or else a heavy growth of laurel, all the branches pointing downward, and to be gotten through only by main force. Over all grew the vast evergreen forest, except where an occasional cliff jutted out, or where there were great land-slides, each perhaps half a mile long and a couple of hundred yards across, covered with loose slates or granite bowlders.

We always went above the domain of the deer, and indeed saw few evidences of life. Once or twice we came to the round foot-prints of cougars, which are said to he great enemies of the goats, but we never caught a glimpse of the sly beasts themselves. Another time I shot a sable from a spruce, up which the little fox-headed animal had rushed with the agility of a squirrel. There were plenty of old tracks of bear and elk, but no new ones; and occasionally we saw the foot-marks of the great timber wolf.

But the trails at which we looked with the most absorbed interest were those that showed the large, round hoof-marks of the white goats. They had worn deep paths to certain clay licks in the slides, which they must have visited often in the early spring, for the trails were little traveled when we were in the mountains during September. These clay licks were mere holes in the banks, and were in spring-time visited by other animals besides goats; there were old deer trails to them. The clay seemed to contain something that both birds and beasts were fond of, for I frequently saw flocks of cross-bills light in the licks and stay there for many minutes at a time, scratching the smooth surface with their little claws and bills. The goat trails led away in every direction from the licks, but usually went up-hill, zigzagging or in a straight line, and continually growing fainter as they went farther off, where the animals scattered to their feeding-grounds. In the spring-time the goats are clad with a dense coat of long white wool, and there were shreds and tufts of this on all the twigs of the bushes under which the paths passed; in the early fall the coat is shorter and less handsome.

Although these game paths were so deeply worn, they yet showed very little fresh goat sign; in fact, we came across the recent trails of but two of the animals we were after. One of these we came quite close to, but never saw it, for we must have frightened it by the noise we made; it certainly, to judge by its tracks, which we followed for a long time, took itself straight out of the country. The other I finally got, after some heart-breaking work and a complicated series of faults committed and misfortunes endured.

I had been, as usual, walking and clambering over the mountains all day long, and in mid-afternoon reached a great slide, with half-way across it a tree. Under this I sat down to rest, my back to the trunk, and had been there but a few minutes when my companion, the Missourian, suddenly whispered to me that a goat was coming down the slide at its edge, near the woods. I was in a most uncomfortable position for a shot. Twisting my head round, I could see the goat waddling down-hill, looking just like a handsome tame billy, especially when at times he stood upon a stone to glance around, with all four feet close together. I cautiously tried to shift my position, and at once dislodged some pebbles, at the sound of which the goat sprang promptly up on the bank, his whole mien changing into one of alert, alarmed curiosity. He was less than a hundred yards off, so I risked a shot, all cramped and twisted though I was. But my bullet went low; I only broke his left fore-leg, and he disappeared over the bank like a flash. We raced and scrambled after him, and the Missourian, an excellent tracker, took up the bloody trail. It went along the hill-side for nearly a mile, and then turned straight up the mountain, the Missourian leading with his long, free gait, while I toiled after him at a dogged trot. The trail went up the sharpest and steepest places, skirting the cliffs and precipices. At one spot I nearly came to grief for good and all, for in running along a shelving ledge, covered with loose slates, one of these slipped as I stepped on it, throwing me clear over the brink. However, I caught in a pine top, bounced down through it, and brought up in a balsam with my rifle all right, and myself unhurt except for the shaking. I scrambled up at once and raced on after my companion, whose limbs and wind seemed alike incapable of giving out. This work lasted for a couple of hours.

The trail came into a regular game path and grew fresher, the goat having stopped to roll and wallow in the dust now and then. Suddenly, on the top of the mountain, we came upon him close up to us. He had just risen from rolling and stood behind a huge fallen log, his back barely showing above it as he turned his head to look at us. I was completely winded, and had lost my strength as well as my breath, while great bead-like drops of sweat stood in my eyes; but I steadied myself as well as I could and aimed to break the backbone, the only shot open to me, and not a difficult one at such a short distance. However, my bullet went just too high, cutting the skin above the long spinal bones over the shoulders; and the speed with which that three-legged goat went down the precipitous side of the mountain would have done credit to an antelope on the level.

Weary and disgusted, we again took up the trail. It led straight downhill, and we followed it at a smart pace. Down and down it went, into the valley and straight to the edge of the stream, but half a mile above camp. The goat had crossed the water on a fallen tree-trunk, and we took the same path. Once across, it had again gone right up the mountain. We followed it as fast as we could, although pretty nearly done out, until it was too dark to see the blood stains any longer, and then returned to camp, dispirited and so tired that we could hardly drag ourselves along, for we had been going to speed for five hours, up and down the roughest and steepest ground.

But we were confident that the goat would not travel far with such a wound after he had been chased as we had chased him. Next morning at daybreak we again climbed the mountain and took up the trail. Soon it led into others and we lost it, but we kept up the hunt nevertheless for hour after hour, making continually wider and wider circles. At last, about midday, our perseverance was rewarded, for coming silently out on a great bare cliff shoulder, I spied the goat lying on a ledge below me and some seventy yards off. This time I shot true, and he rose only to fall back dead; and a minute afterward we were standing over him, handling the glossy black horns and admiring the snow-white coat.

After this we struck our tent and shifted camp some thirty miles to a wide valley through whose pine-clad bottom flowed a river, hurrying on to the Pacific between unending forests. On one hand the valley was hemmed in by an unbroken line of frowning cliffs, and on the other by chains of lofty mountains in whose sides the ravines cut deep gashes.

The clear weather had grown colder. At night the frost skimmed with thin ice the edges of the ponds and small lakes that at long intervals dotted the vast reaches of woodland. But we were very comfortable, and hardly needed our furs, for as evening fell we kindled huge fires, to give us both light and warmth; and even in very cold weather a man can sleep out comfortably enough with no bedding if he lights two fires and gets in between them, or finds a sheltered nook or corner across the front of which a single great blaze can be made. The long walks and our work as cragsmen hardened our thews, and made us eat and sleep as even our life on the ranch could hardly do: the mountaineer must always be more sinewy than the horseman. The clear, cold water of the swift streams too was a welcome change from the tepid and muddy currents of the rivers of the plains; and we heartily enjoyed the baths, a plunge into one of the icy pools making us gasp for breath and causing the blood to tingle in our veins with the shock.

Our tent was pitched in a little glade, which was but a few yards across, and carpeted thickly with the red kinnikinic berries, in their season beloved of bears, and from the leaves of which bush the Indians make a substitute for tobacco. Little three-toed woodpeckers with yellow crests scrambled about over the trees near by, while the great log-cocks hammered and rattled on the tall dead trunks. Jays that were dark blue all over came familiarly round camp in company with the ever-present moose-birds or whisky jacks. There were many grouse in the woods, of three kinds—blue, spruce, and ruffed—and these varied our diet and also furnished us with some sport with our rifles, as we always shot them in rivalry. That is, each would take a shot in turn, aiming at the head of the bird, as it perched motionless on the limb of a tree or stopped for a second while running along the ground; then if he missed or hit the bird anywhere but in the head, the other scored one and took the shot. The resulting tally was a good test of comparative skill; and rivalry always tends to keep a man's shooting up to the mark.

Once or twice, when we had slain deer, we watched by the carcasses, hoping that they would attract a bear, or perhaps one of the huge timber wolves whose mournful, sinister howling we heard each night. But there were no bears in the valley; and the wolves, those cruel, crafty beasts, were far too cunning to come to the bait while we were there. We saw nothing but crowds of ravens, whose hoarse barking and croaking filled the air as they circled around overhead, lighted in the trees, or quarreled over the carcass. Yet although we saw no game it was very pleasant to sit out, on the still evenings, among the tall pines or on the edge of a great gorge, until the afterglow of the sunset was dispelled by the beams of the frosty moon. Now and again the hush would be suddenly broken by the long howling of a wolf, that echoed and rang under the hollow woods and through the deep chasms until they resounded again, while it made our hearts bound and the blood leap in our veins. Then there would be silence once more, broken only by the rush of the river and the low moaning and creaking of the pines; or the strange calling of the owls might be answered by the far-off, unearthly laughter of a loon, its voice carried through the stillness a marvelous distance from the little lake on which it was swimming.

One day, after much toilsome and in places almost dangerous work, we climbed to the very top of the nearest mountain chain, and from it looked out over a limitless, billowy field of snow-capped ranges. Up above the timber line were snow-grouse and huge, hoary-white woodchucks, but no trace of the game we were after; for, rather to our surprise, the few goat signs that we saw were in the timber. I did not catch another glimpse of the animals themselves until my holiday was almost over and we were preparing to break camp. Then I saw two. I had spent a most laborious day on the mountain as usual, following the goat paths, which were well-trodden trails leading up the most inaccessible places; certainly the white goats are marvelous climbers, doing it all by main strength and perfect command over their muscles, for they are heavy, clumsy seeming animals, the reverse of graceful, and utterly without any look of light agility. As usual, towards evening I was pretty well tired out, for it would be difficult to imagine harder work than to clamber unendingly up and down the huge cliffs. I came down along a great jutting spur, broken by a series of precipices, with flat terraces at their feet, the terraces being covered with trees and bushes, and running, with many breaks and interruptions, parallel to each other across the face of the mountains. On one of these terraces was a space of hard clay ground beaten perfectly bare of vegetation by the hoofs of the goats, and, in the middle, a hole, two or three feet in width, that was evidently in the spring used as a lick. Most of the tracks were old, but there was one trail coming diagonally down the side of the mountain on which there were two or three that were very fresh. It was getting late, so I did not stay long, but continued the descent. The terrace on which the lick was situated lay but a few hundred yards above the valley, and then came a level, marshy plain a quarter of a mile broad, between the base of the mountain and the woods. Leading down to this plain was another old goat-trail, which went to a small, boggy pool, which the goats must certainly have often visited in the spring; but it was then unused.

When I reached the farther side of the plain and was about entering the woods, I turned to look over the mountain once more, and my eye was immediately caught by two white objects which were moving along the terrace, about half a mile to one side of the lick. That they were goats was evident at a glance, their white bodies contrasting sharply with the green vegetation. They came along very rapidly, giving me no time to get back over the plain, and stopped for a short time at the lick, right in sight from where I was, although too far off for me to tell anything about their size. I think they smelt my footprints in the soil; at any rate they were very watchful, one of them always jumping up on a rock or fallen log to mount guard when the other halted to browse. The sun had just set; it was impossible to advance across the open plain, which they scanned at every glance; and to skirt it and climb up any other place than the pass down which I had come—itself a goat-trail—would have taken till long after nightfall. All that I could do was to stay where I was and watch them, until in the dark I slipped off unobserved and made the best of my way to camp, resolved to hunt them up on the morrow.

Shortly after noon next day we were at the terrace, having approached with the greatest caution, and only after a minute examination, with the field-glasses, of all the neighboring mountain. I wore moccasins, so as to make no noise. We soon found that one of the trails was evidently regularly traveled, probably every evening, and we determined to lie in wait by it, so as either to catch the animals as they came down to feed, or else to mark them if they got out on some open spot on the terraces where they could be stalked. As an ambush we chose a ledge in the cliff below a terrace, with, in front, a breastwork of the natural rock some five feet high. It was perhaps fifty yards from the trail. I hid myself on this ledge, having arranged on the rock breast-work a few pine branches through which to fire, and waited, hour after hour, continually scanning the mountain carefully with the glasses. There was very little life. Occasionally a chickaree or chipmunk scurried out from among the trunks of the great pines to pick up the cones which he had previously bitten off from the upper branches; a noisy Clarke's crow clung for some time in the top of a hemlock; and occasionally flocks of cross-bill went by, with swift undulating flight and low calls. From time to time I peeped cautiously over the pine branches on the breastwork; and the last time I did this I suddenly saw two goats, that had come noiselessly down, standing motionless directly opposite to me, their suspicions evidently aroused by something. I gently shoved the rifle over one of the boughs; the largest goat turned its head sharply round to look, as it stood quartering to me, and the bullet went fairly through the lungs. Both animals promptly ran off along the terrace, and I raced after them in my moccasins, skirting the edge of the cliff, where there were no trees or bushes. As I made no noise and could run very swiftly on the bare cliff edge, I succeeded in coming out into the first little glade, or break, in the terrace at the same time that the goats did. The first to come out of the bushes was the big one I had shot at, an old she, as it turned out; while the other, a yearling ram, followed. The big one turned to look at me as she mounted a fallen tree that lay across a chasm-like rent in the terrace; the light red frothy blood covered her muzzle, and I paid no further heed to her as she slowly walked along the log, but bent my attention towards the yearling, which was galloping and scrambling up an almost perpendicular path that led across the face of the cliff above. Holding my rifle just over it, I fired, breaking the neck of the goat, and it rolled down some fifty or sixty yards, almost to where I stood. I then went after the old goat, which had lain down; as I approached she feebly tried to rise and show fight, but her strength was spent, her blood had ebbed away, and she fell back lifeless in the effort. They were both good specimens, the old one being unusually large, with fine horns. White goats are squat, heavy beasts; not so tall as black-tail deer, but weighing more.

Early next morning I came back with my two men to where the goats were lying, taking along the camera. Having taken their photographs and skinned them we went back to camp, hunted up the ponies and mules, who had been shifting for themselves during the past few days, packed up our tent, trophies, and other belongings, and set off for the settlements, well pleased with our trip.

All mountain game yields noble sport, because of the nerve, daring, and physical hardihood implied in its successful pursuit. The chase of the white goat involves extraordinary toil and some slight danger on account of the extreme roughness and inaccessibility of its haunts; but the beast itself is less shy than the mountain sheep. How the chase of either compares in difficulty with that of the various Old World mountain game it would be hard to say. Men who have tried both say that, though there is not in Europe the chance to try the adventurous, wandering life of the wilderness so beloved by the American hunter, yet when it comes to comparing the actual chase of the game of the two worlds, it needs greater skill, both as cragsman and still-hunter, to kill ibex and chamois in the Alps or Pyrenees—by fair stalking I mean; for if they are driven to the guns, as is sometimes done, the sport is of a very inferior kind, not rising above the methods of killing white-tail in the Eastern States, or of driving deer in Scotland. I myself have had no experience of Old World mountaineering, beyond two perfectly conventional trips up the Matterhorn and Jungfrau—on the latter, by the way, I saw three chamois a long way off.

My brother has done a good deal of ibex, mountain sheep, and mark hoor shooting in Cashmere and Thibet, and I suppose the sport to be had among the tremendous mountain masses of the Himalayas must stand above all other kinds of hill shooting; yet, after all, it is hard to believe that it can yield much more pleasure than that felt by the American hunter when he follows the lordly elk and the grizzly among the timbered slopes of the Rockies, or the big-horn and the white-fleeced, jet-horned antelope-goat over their towering and barren peaks.

The Ranchman's Rifle
on Crag and Prairie

THEODORE ROOSEVELT

The ranchman owes to his rifle not only the keen pleasure and strong excitement of the chase, but also much of his bodily comfort; for, save for his prowess as a hunter and his skill as a marksman with this, his favorite weapon, he would almost always be sadly stinted for fresh meat. Now that the buffalo have gone, and the Sharps rifle by which they were destroyed is also gone, almost all ranchmen use some form of repeater. Personally I prefer the Winchester, using the new model, with a 45-caliber bullet of 300 grains, backed by 90 grains of powder, or else falling back on my faithful old stand-by, the 45–75. But the truth is that all good modern rifles are efficient weapons; it is the man behind the gun that makes the difference. An inch or two in trajectory or a second or two in rapidity of fire is as nothing compared to sureness of eye and steadiness of hand.

From April to August antelope are the game we chiefly follow, killing only the bucks; after that season, black-tail and white-tail deer. Now and then we get a chance at mountain sheep, and more rarely at larger game still. As a rule, I never shoot anything but bucks. But in the rutting season, when the bucks' flesh is poor, or when we need to lay in a good stock of meat for the winter, this rule of course must be broken.

The smoked venison stored away in the fall lasts us through the bitter weather, as well as through the even less attractive period covering the first weeks of spring. At that time we go out as little as possible. The roads are mere morasses, crusted after nightfall with a shell of thin ice, through which the shaggy horses break heavily. Walking is exceedingly tiresome, the boots becoming caked with masses of adhesive clay. The deer stay with us all the time; but they are now in poor condition, the does heavy with fawn and the bucks with ungrown antlers.

Antelope gather together in great bands in the fall, and either travel south, leaving the country altogether, or else go to some out-of-the-way place where they are not likely to be disturbed. Antelope are queer, freaky beasts, and it is hard to explain why, when most of these great bands go off south, one or two always stay in the Bad Lands. Such a band having chosen its wintering ground, which is usually in a valley or on a range of wide plateaus, will leave it only with great reluctance, and if it is discovered by hunters most of its members will surely be butchered before the survivors are willing to abandon the place and seek new quarters.

In April the prong-horned herds come back, but now all broken up into straggling parties. They have regular passes, through which they go every year: there is one such not far from my ranch, where they are certain to cross the Little Missouri in great numbers each spring on their return march. In the fall, when they are traveling in dense crowds, hunters posted in these passes sometimes butcher enormous numbers.

Soon after they come back in the spring they scatter out all over the plains, and for four months after their return—that is, until August—they are the game we chiefly follow. This is because at that time we only hunt enough to keep the ranch in fresh meat, and kill nothing but the bucks; and as antelope, though they shed their horns, are without them for but a very short time, and as, moreover, they are always seen at a distance, it is easy to tell the sexes apart.

Antelope shooting is the kind in which a man most needs skill in the use of the rifle at long ranges; for they are harder to get near than any other game—partly from their wariness, and still more from the nature of the ground they inhabit. Many more cartridges are spent, in proportion to the amount of game killed, in hunting antelope than is the case while after deer, elk, or sheep. Even good hunters reckon on using six or seven cartridges for every prong-horn that they kill; for antelope are continually offering standing shots at very long distances, which, nevertheless, it is a great temptation to try, on the chance of luck favoring the marksman. Moreover, alone among plains' game, they must generally be shot at over a hundred and fifty yards, and often at between two and three hundred. Over this distance a man will kill occasionally—I have done so myself—but at such long range it is mainly a matter of accident. The best field-shot alive lacks a good deal of always killing, if the distance is much over two hundred yards; and with every increase beyond that amount, the chances of failure augment in geometrical proportion. Exceptional individuals perform marvelous feats with the rifle, exactly as still more exceptional individuals perform marvelous feats with the revolver; but even these men, when they have to guess their distances, miss very often when firing at game three hundred yards, or thereabouts, distant.

As in all other kinds of big-game shooting, success in hunting antelope often depends upon sheer, downright luck. A man may make a week's trip over good ground and get nothing; and then again he may go to the same place and in two days kill a wagon-load of venison.

In the fall the prairie fires ravage the land, for at the close of summer the matted, sun-dried grass burns like tinder, and the fires are sometimes so numerous as to cover whole counties beneath a pall of smoke, while at night they look very grand, burning in curved lines of wavering flame, now advancing fastest at one point, now at another, as if great red snakes were writhing sideways across the prairie. The land across which they have run remains a blackened, charred waste until the young grass begins to sprout in the spring. The short, tender blades at once change the cinder-colored desert into a bright emerald plain, and are so much more toothsome than the dry, withered winter grass that both stock and game forsake the latter and travel out to the tracts of burned land. The feed on these places is too sparse to support, of itself, horses or cattle, who accordingly do not penetrate far beyond the edges; but antelope are like sheep, and prefer scanty, short herbage, and in consequence at this time fairly swarm in the burned districts. Indeed, they are sometimes so numerous that they can hardly be stalked, as it is impossible to approach any animal without being seen by some of its countless comrades, which at once run off and give the alarm.

While on these early spring trips we sometimes vary the sport, and our fare as well, by trying our rifles on the mallards in the reedy sloughs, or on the jack rabbits as they sit up on their haunches to look at us, eighty or a hundred yards off. Now and then we creep up to and kill the cock prairie fowl, when they have gathered into their dancing rings to posture with outstretched neck and outspread wings as they shuffle round each other, keeping up a curious clucking and booming that accord well with their grotesque attitudes.

Late in the season any one of us can usually get antelope in a day's hunt from the ranch by merely riding off alone, with a good hunting horse, to a great tract of broken, mound-dotted prairie some fifteen miles off, where the prong-horns are generally abundant.

On such a trip I leave the ranch house by dawn, the rifle across my saddle-bow, and some strips of smoked venison in the saddle-pockets. In the cool air the horse lopes smartly through the wooded bottoms. The meadow-larks, with black crescents on their yellow breasts, sing all day long, but the thrushes only in the morning and evening; and their melody is heard at its best on such a ride as this. By the time I get out of the last ravines and canter along the divide, the dark bluff-tops in the east have begun to redden in the sunrise, while in the flushed west the hills stand out against a rosy sky. The sun has been up some little time before the hunting-grounds are fairly reached; for the antelope stands alone in being a diurnal game animal that from this peculiarity, as well as from the nature of its haunts, can be hunted as well at midday as at any other hour. Arrived at the hunting-grounds I generally, but not always, dismount and hunt on foot, leaving the horse tethered out to graze.

Lunch is taken at some spring, which may be only a trickle of water at the base of a butte, where a hole must be dug out with knife and hands before the horse can drink. Once or twice I have enjoyed unusual delicacies at such a lunch, in the shape of the eggs of curlew or prairie fowl baked in the hot ashes.

The day is spent in still-hunting, a much easier task among the ridges and low hills than out on the gently rolling prairies. Antelope see much better than deer, their great bulging eyes, placed at the roots of the horns, being as strong as twin telescopes. Extreme care must be taken not to let them catch a glimpse of the intruder, for it is then hopeless to attempt approaching them. On the other hand, there is never the least difficulty about seeing them; for they are conspicuous beasts, and, unlike deer, they never hide, being careless whether they are seen or not, so long as they can keep a good lookout. They trust only to their own alert watchfulness and quick senses for safety. The game is carried home behind the saddle; and the bottom on which the ranch house stands is not often reached until the moon, showing crimson through the haze, has risen above the bluffs that skirt the river.

Antelope are very tough, and will carry off a great deal of lead unless struck in exactly the right place; and even when mortally hit they sometimes receive the blow without flinching, and gallop off as if unharmed. They always should be followed up a little distance after being fired at, as if unhurt. Sometimes they show the rather curious trait of walking backwards a number of steps just before falling in death.

Although ordinarily harder to get at than deer, they are far more frequently killed in what may be called accidental ways. At times they seem to be heedless of danger, and they suffer from occasional panic fits of fear or curiosity, when it is no feat at all to slay them. Hunters can thus occasionally rake very large bags of antelope, but a true sportsman who only shoots for peculiarly fine trophies, or to supply the ranch table, will not commit such needless butcheries. Often accidents have thrown it into my power to make a big killing; but the largest number I have ever shot was on one day when I bagged four, all bucks, and then we were sorely in need of fresh meat, and it was an object to get as much as possible. This day's shooting was peculiar because it took place during a heavy rain storm, which, taken in connection with my own remarkable costume, apparently made the animals act with less than their usual shyness. I wore a great flapping yellow slicker, or oilskin overcoat, about as unlikely a garb as a hunter could possibly don; but it seemed to fascinate the game, for more than once a band huddled up and stood gazing at me, while I clambered awkwardly off the horse. The cold rain numbed my fingers and beat into my eyes, and I was hampered by the coat; so I wasted a good many cartridges to get my four head.

Bringing Home the Game

In some places they now seem to have learned wisdom, for the slaughter among them has been so prodigious that the survivors have radically changed their character. Their senses are as keen as ever, and their wits much keener. They no longer give way to bursts of panic curiosity; they cannot be attracted by any amount of flagging, or by the appearance of unknown objects, as formerly. Where they are still common, as with us, they refuse, under any stress of danger, to enter woodland or thickets, but keep to the flat or broken plains and the open prairies, which they have from time immemorial inhabited. But elsewhere their very nature seems to have altered. They have not only learned to climb and take to the hills, but, what is even more singular, have intruded on the domain of the elk and the deer, frequently making their abode in the thick timber, and there proving the most difficult of all animals to stalk.

In May and June the little antelope kids appear: funny little fellows, odd and ungainly, but at an astonishingly early age able to run nearly as fast as their parents. They will lie very close if they think that they are unobserved. Once several of us were driving in a herd of cattle while on the round-up. The cattle, traveling in loose order, were a few paces ahead, when, happening to cast down my eyes, I saw, right among their hoofs, a little antelope kid. It was lying flat down with outstretched neck, and did not move, although some of the cattle almost stepped on it. I reined up, got off my horse, and lifted it in my arms. At first it gave two or three convulsive struggles, bleating sharply, then became perfectly passive, standing quietly by me for a minute or two when I put it down, after which it suddenly darted off like a flash. These little antelope kids are very easily tamed, being then very familiar, amusing, and inquisitive—much more so than deer fawns, though they are not so pretty. Within a few days of their birth they stop seeking protection in hiding and adopt the habits of their parents, following them everywhere, or going off on their own account, being almost as swift, although, of course, not nearly so enduring.

Three of us witnessed a rather curious incident last spring, showing how little the bringing forth of a fawn affects the does of either deer or antelope. We were walking through a patch of low brushwood, when up got a black-tail doe and went off at full speed. At the second jump she gave birth to a fawn; but this did not alter her speed in the least, and she ran off quite as well and as fast as ever. We walked up to where she had been lying and found in her bed another fawn, evidently but a few seconds old. We left the two sprawling, unlicked little creatures where they were, knowing that the mother would soon be back to care for them.

Although sometimes we go out to the antelope ground and back in one day, yet it is always more convenient to take the buckboard with us and spend the night, camping by a water hole in one of the creeks. The last time we took such a trip I got lost, and nearly spent the night in the open. I had been riding with one of my cowboys, while another acted as teamster and drove the buckboard and pair. We killed two antelope and went into camp rather early. After taking dinner and picketing out the four horses we found it still lacked an hour or two of sunset, and accordingly my companions and I started out on foot, leaving our teamster in camp, and paying no particular heed to our surroundings. We saw a herd of prong-horn and wounded one, which we followed in vain until dusk, and then started to go back to camp. Very soon we found that we had quite a task before us, for in the dim starlight all the hollows looked exactly alike, and the buttes seemed either to have changed form entirely or else loomed up so vaguely through the darkness that we could not place them in the least. We walked on and on until we knew that we must be far past the creek, or coulée, where our camp lay, and then turned towards the divide. The night had grown steadily darker, and we could hear the far-off mutter and roll that told of an approaching thunder-storm. Hour after hour we trudged wearily on, as fast as we could go without stumbling, the gloom and the roughness of the unknown ground proving serious drawbacks to our progress. When on the top of a hillock, the blackness of the hollow beneath was so intense that we could not tell whether we were going to walk down a slope or over a cliff, and in consequence we met with one or two tumbles. At last we reached the top of a tall butte that we knew must be on the divide. The night was now as dark as pitch, and we were so entirely unable to tell where we were that we decided to give up the quest in despair and try to find some washout that would yield us at least partial shelter from the approaching rain storm. We had fired off our rifles several times without getting any response; but now, as we took one last look around, we suddenly saw a flash of light, evidently from a gun, flare up through the darkness so far off that no sound came to our ears. We trotted towards it as fast as we could through the inky gloom, and when no longer sure of our direction climbed a little hill, fired off our rifles, and after a minute or two again saw the guiding flash. The next time we had occasion to signal, the answering blaze was accompanied by a faint report; and in a few minutes more, when it was close on midnight, we were warming our hands at the great camp-fire, and hungrily watching the venison steaks as they sizzled in the frying-pan.

The morning after this adventure I shot an antelope before breakfast. We had just risen, and while sitting round the smoldering coals, listening to the simmering of the camp-kettle and the coffee-pot, we suddenly caught sight of a large prong-horn buck that was walking towards us over the hill-crest nearly half a mile away. He stopped and stared fixedly at us for a few minutes, and then resumed his course at a leisurely trot, occasionally stopping to crop a mouthful of grass, and paying no further heed to us. His course was one that would lead him within a quarter of a mile of camp, and, grasping my rifle, I slipped off as soon as he was out of sight and ran up over the bluff to intercept him. Just as I reached the last crest I saw the buck crossing in front of me at a walk, and almost two hundred yards off. I knelt, and, as he halted and turned his head sharply towards me, pulled trigger. It was a lucky shot, and he fell over, with his back broken. He had very unusually good horns; as fine as those of any of his kind that I ever killed.

A Prong-Horn Buck Visits Camp

Antelope often suffer from such freaks of apathetic indifference to danger, which are doubly curious as existing in an animal normally as wary as that wildest of game, the mountain sheep. They are fond of wandering too, and appear at times in very unlikely places. Thus once, while we were building the cow corral, in an open bottom, five antelope came down. After much snorting and stamping, they finally approached to within fifty yards of the men who were at work, and, as the latter had no weapons with them, retired unmolested.

In winter the great herds consist of the two sexes; and this is true also of the straggling parties that come back to us in spring, soon to split up into smaller ones. During early summer the males may be found singly, or else three or four together, with possibly a barren doe or two; while two or three does, with their kids, and perhaps the last year's young, will form the nucleus of a little flock by themselves. With the coming of the rutting season they divide into regular bands, for they are polygamous. Every large, powerful buck gathers his little group of does, driving out all his rivals, though perhaps a yearling buck or two will hang round the outskirts at a respectful distance, every now and then rousing the older one to a fit of jealous impatience. More often the young bucks go in small parties by themselves, while those older ones that have been driven out by their successful rivals wander round singly. The old bucks are truculent and courageous, and do fierce battle with each other until it is evident which is master, when the defeated combatant makes off at top speed. One of these beaten bucks will occasionally get hold of a single doe, whom he promptly appropriates and guards with extreme watchfulness; and, not being overconfident in his own prowess, drives her off very rapidly if any other antelope show signs of coming near. A successful buck may have from four or five to ten or fifteen does in his harem. In such a band there is always an old doe that acts as leader, precisely as with deer and elk. This doe is ever on the alert, is most likely to take the alarm at the approach of danger, and always leads the flight. The buck, however, is prompt to take command, if he sees fit, or deems that the doe's fears have overpowered her judgment; and frequently, when a band is in full flight, the buck may be seen deliberately to round it up and stop it, so that he may gaze on the cause of the alarm—a trait the exercise of which often costs him his life. The bucks occasionally bully the does unmercifully, if they show symptoms of insubordination. Individual antelope vary very widely in speed. Once I fairly rode one down, but this is generally an almost impossible feat. Among deer, the fat, heavy antlered bucks are usually slower than the does and the young males; but there seems to be little difference of this sort among prong-horns.

With the first touch of sharp fall weather we abandon the chase of the antelope for that of the deer. Then our favorite quarry is the noble black-tail, whose haunts are in the mountains and the high, craggy hills. We kill him by fair still-hunting, and to follow him successfully through the deep ravines and across the steep ridges of his upland home a man should be sound in wind and limbs, and a good shot with the rifle as well. Many a glorious fall morning I have passed in his pursuit; often, moreover, I have slain him in the fading evening as I walked homeward through the still dim twilight—for all wild game dearly love the gloaming.

Once on a frosty evening I thus killed one when it was so dark that my aim was little but guess-work. I was walking back to camp through a winding valley, hemmed in by steep cedar-crowned walls of clay and rock. All the landscape glimmered white with the new-fallen snow, and in the west the sky was still red with the wintry sunset. Suddenly a great buck came out of a grove of snow-laden cedars, and walked with swift strides up to the point of a crag that overlooked the valley. There he stood motionless while I crouched unseen in the shadow beneath. As I fired he reared upright and then plunged over the cliff. He fell a hundred feet before landing in the bushes, yet he did not gash or mar his finely molded head and shapely, massive antlers.

On one of the last days I hunted, in November, 1887, I killed two black-tail, a doe and a buck, with one bullet. They were feeding in a glen high up the side of some steep hills, and by a careful stalk over rough ground I got within fifty yards. Peering over the brink of the cliff-like slope up which I had clambered, I saw them standing in such a position that the neck of the doe covered the buck's shoulder. The chance was too tempting to be lost. My bullet broke the doe's neck, and of course she fell where she was; but the buck went off, my next two or three shots missing him. However, we followed his bloody trail, through the high pass he had crossed, down a steep slope, and roused him from the brushwood in a valley bottom. He soon halted and lay down again, making off at a faltering gallop when approached, and the third time we came up to him he was too weak to rise. He had splendid antlers.

Sometimes we kill the deer by the aid of hounds. Of these we have two at the ranch. One is a rough-coated, pure-blood Scotch stag-hound, named Rob. The other, Brandy, is a track-hound, bell-mouthed, lop-eared, keen-nosed, and not particularly fast, but stanch as Death himself. He comes of the old Southern strain; and, indeed, all the best blooded packs of American deer-hounds or fox-hounds come from what was called the Southern Hound in early seventeenth century England. Thus he is kin to the hounds of Bellemeade, wherewith General Jackson follows the buck and the gray fox over the beautiful fertile hills of middle Tennessee; and some of the same blood runs in the veins of Mr. Wadsworth's Geneseo hounds, behind which I have ridden as they chased the red fox through the wooded glens and across the open fields of the farms, with their high rail fences.

I often take Rob out when still-hunting black-tail, leading him along in a leash. He is perfectly quiet, not even whimpering; and he is certain to overhaul any wounded deer. A doe or a flying buck is borne to the ground with a single wrench, and killed out of hand; but a buck at bay is a formidable opponent, and no dog can rush in full on the sharp prong points. If the two dogs are together, Rob does most of the killing; Brandy's only function is to distract the attention of an angry buck and then allow Rob to pin him. Once a slightly wounded and very large black-tail buck, started just at nightfall, ran down to the river and made a running bay of nearly two hours, Rob steadily at him the whole time; it was too dark for us to shoot, but finally, by a lucky throw, one of the men roped the quarry.

The Buck Overtaken

Not only will a big black-tail buck beat off a dog or a wolf coming at him in front, but he is an awkward foe for a man. One of them nearly killed a cowboy in my employ. The buck, mortally wounded, had fallen to the shot, and the man rushed up to stick him; then the buck revived for a moment, struck down the man, and endeavored to gore him, but could not, because of the despairing grip with which the man held on to his horns. Nevertheless the man, bruised and cut by the sharp hoofs, was fast becoming too weak to keep his hold, when in the struggle they came to the edge of a washout, and fell into it some twelve or fifteen feet. This separated them. The dying buck was too weak to renew the attack, and the man crawled off; but it was months before he got over the effects of the encounter.

Sometimes we kill the white-tail also by fair still-hunting, but more often we shoot them on the dense river bottoms by the help of the track-hound. We put the dogs into the woods with perhaps a single horseman to guide them and help them rout out the deer, while the rest of us, rifle in hand, ride from point to point outside, or else watch the passes through which the hunted animals are likely to run. It is not a sport of which I am very fond, but it is sometimes pleasant as a variety. The last time that we tried it I killed a buck in the bottom right below our ranch house, not half a mile off. The river was low, and my post was at its edge, with in front of me the broad sandy flat sparsely covered with willow-brush. Deer are not much afraid of an ordinary noisy hound; they will play round in front of him, head and flag in air; but with Rob it was different. The gray, wolfish beast, swift and silent, threw them into a panic of terror, and in headlong flight they would seek safety from him in the densest thicket.

On the evening in question one of my cowboys went into the brush with the hounds. I had hardly ridden to my place and dismounted when I heard old Brandy give tongue, the bluffs echoing back his long-drawn baying. Immediately afterwards a young buck appeared, coming along the sandy river-bed, trotting or cantering; and very handsome he looked, stepping with a light, high action, his glossy coat glistening, his head thrown back, his white flag flaunting. My bullet struck him too far back, and he went on, turning into the woods. Then the dogs appeared, old Brandy running the scent, while the eager gaze-hound made wide half-circles round him as he ran; while the cowboy, riding a vicious yellow mustang, galloped behind, cheering them on. As they struck the bloody trail they broke into clamorous yelling, and tore at full speed into the woods. A minute or two later the sound ceased, and I knew that they had run into the quarry.

Sometimes we use the hounds for other game besides deer. A neighboring ranchman had a half-breed fox-and-greyhound, who, single-handed, ran into and throttled a coyote. I have been very anxious to try my dogs on a big wolf, intending to take along a collie and a half-breed mastiff we have to assist at the bay. The mastiff is a good fighter, and can kill a wildcat, taking the necessary punishment well, as we found out when we once trapped one of these small lynxes. Shep, the collie, is an adept at killing badgers, grabbing them from behind and whirling them round, whereas Brandy always gets his great lop-ears bitten. But how they would do with a wolf I cannot say; for one of these long-toothed wanderers is usually able to outrun and outfight any reasonable number of common hounds, and will kill even a big dog very quickly.

A friend of mine, Mr. Heber Bishop, once coursed and killed a wolf with two Scotch deer-hounds. After a brisk run the dogs overtook and held the quarry, but could not kill it, and were being very roughly handled when Mr. Bishop came to their assistance. But a ranchman in the Indian Territory has a large pack of these same Scotch dogs trained especially to hunt the wolf; and four or five of the fleet, high-couraged animals can not only soon overhaul a wolf, but can collar and throttle even the largest. Accidents to the pack are, of course, frequent. They say that the worry is enough to make one's hair stand on end.

Before leaving the subject, it is worth noting that we have with us the Canada lynx as well as his smaller brother; and, more singular still, that a wolverine, usually found only in the northern forests, was killed two winters ago in a big woody bottom on the Little Missouri, about forty miles north of Medora. The skin and skull were unmistakable; so there could be no doubt as to the beast's identity.

I have had good sport on the rolling plains, near Mandan, in following a scratch pack of four fleet, long-legged dogs. One was a wire-haired Scotch deer-hound; his mate was a superb greyhound, the speediest of the set. Both were possessed of the dauntless courage peculiar to high-bred hunting dogs. The other two were mongrels, but, nevertheless, game fighters and swift runners: one was a lurcher, and the other a cross between a greyhound and a fox-hound—the only one of the four that ever gave tongue. The two former had been used together often, and had slain five coyotes, two deer (white-tails), and an antelope. Both the antelope and the deer they had fairly run down, having come up close on them, so that they had good send-offs; but there is a wide individual variation among game animals as regards speed, and those that they caught—at any rate the antelope—may not have been as fleet as most of their kind. They were especially fond of chasing coyotes, and these they easily overtook. When at bay the coyotes fought desperately but unavailingly, the two hounds killing their quarry very quickly, one seizing it by the throat and the other by the flanks, and then stretching it out in a trice. They occasionally received trifling injuries in these contests. The animal that gave them most trouble was a badger which they once found and only killed after prolonged efforts, its squat, muscular form and tough skin making it very difficult for them to get a good hold.

We did not have time to go far from Mandan, and so confined our coursing to jack rabbits, swifts, and foxes. Of the latter, the great red prairie fox, we saw but one, which got up so close to the dogs that it had no chance at all, and after a fine burst of a few hundred yards was overtaken and torn to pieces. The swifts are properly called swift foxes, being rather smaller than the southern gray fox. Ever since the days of the early explorers they have been reputed to possess marvelous speed, and their common name of "swift," by which they are universally known, perpetuates the delusion; for a delusion it emphatically is, since they are, if anything, rather slow than otherwise. Once, in a snow storm, I started one up under my horse's feet while riding across the prairie, overtook him in a few strides, and killed him by a lucky shot with the revolver. The speed of the coyote also has been laughably exaggerated. Judging by the records of the hounds, the antelope is the fastest plains' animal, the white-tail deer and the jack rabbit coming next; then follow, in order, the coyote, the fox, and the swift, which is the slowest of all. Individuals vary greatly, however; thus a fast jack rabbit might well outrun a slow deer, and of course both coyote and fox will outlast the swifter jack rabbits. Several dogs should run together, as otherwise a jack or a swift, although overtaken, may yet escape by its dexterity in dodging. The cactus beds often befriend the hunted animals, as the dogs rush heedlessly into them and are promptly disabled, while a rabbit or a fox will slip through without injury.

Two or three of us usually went out together. Our method of procedure was simple. We scattered out, dogs and men, and rode in an irregular line across the country, beating with care the most likely looking places, and following at top speed any game that got up. Sometimes a jack rabbit, starting well ahead, would run for two miles or over, nearly in a straight line, before being turned by the leading hound; and occasionally one would even get away altogether. At other times it would be overhauled at once and killed instantly, or only prolong its life a few seconds by its abrupt turns and twists. One swift gave us several minutes' chase, although never getting thirty rods from the place where it started. The little fellow went off as merrily as possible, his handsome brush streaming behind him, and, though overtaken at once, dodged so cleverly that dog after dog shot by him. I do not think that a single dog could have killed him.

Coursing is the sport of all sports for ranchmen, now that big animals are growing scarce; and certainly there can be no healthier or more exciting pastime than that of following game with horse and hound over the great Western plains.

The Wapiti, or Round-Horned Elk

THEODORE ROOSEVELT

This stately and splendid deer, the lordliest of its kind throughout the world, is now fast vanishing. In our own neighborhood it is already almost a thing of the past. But a small band yet lingers round a great tract of prairie and Bad Lands some thirty-five miles from the ranch house.

One fall I killed a good bull out of the lot. I was hunting on horseback, and roused the elk out of a deep, narrow coulée, heavily timbered, where he was lying by himself. He went straight up the steep side directly opposite to where I stood, for I had leaped off my horse when I heard the crash of the underbrush. When on a level with me, he halted and turned half round to gaze at me across the ravine, and then I shot him.

The next season, when we were sorely in need of meat for smoking and drying, we went after these elk again. At the time most of the ponies were off on one of the round-ups, which indeed I had myself just left. However, my two hunting-horses, Manitou and Sorrel Joe, were at home. The former I rode myself, and on the latter I mounted one of my men who was a particularly good hand at finding and following game. With much difficulty we got together a scrub wagon team of four as unkempt, dejected, and vicious-looking broncos as ever stuck fast in a quicksand or balked in pulling up a steep pitch. Their driver was a crack whip, and their load light, consisting of little but the tent and the bedding; so we got out to the hunting-ground and back in safety; but as the river was high and the horses were weak, we came within an ace of being swamped at one crossing, and the country was so very rough that we were only able to get the wagon up the worst pitch by hauling from the saddle with the riding-animals.

We camped by an excellent spring of cold, clear water—not a common luxury in the Bad Lands. We pitched the tent beside it, getting enough timber from a grove of ash to make a large fire, which again is an appreciated blessing on the plains of the West, where we often need to carry along with us the wood for cooking our supper and breakfast, and sometimes actually have to dig up our fuel, making the fire of sage-brush roots, eked out with buffalo chips. Though the days were still warm, the nights were frosty. Our camp was in a deep valley, bounded by steep hills with sloping, grassy sides, one of them marked by a peculiar shelf of rock. The country for miles was of this same character, much broken, but everywhere passable for horsemen, and with the hills rounded and grassy, except now and then for a chain of red scoria buttes or an isolated sugar-loaf cone of gray and brown clay. The first day we spent in trying to find the probable locality of our game; and after beating pretty thoroughly over the smoother country, towards nightfall we found quite fresh elk tracks leading into a stretch of very rough and broken land about ten miles from camp.

We started next morning before the gray was relieved by the first faint flush of pink, and reached the broken country soon after sunrise. Here we dismounted and picketed our horses, as the ground we were to hunt through was very rough. Two or three hours passed before we came upon fresh signs of elk. Then we found the trails that two, from the size presumably cows, had made the preceding night, and started to follow them, carefully and noiselessly, my companion taking one side of the valley in which we were and I the other. The tracks led into one of the wildest and most desolate parts of the Bad Lands. It was now the heat of the day, the brazen sun shining out of a cloudless sky, and not the least breeze stirring. At the bottom of the valley, in the deep, narrow bed of the winding water-course, lay a few tepid little pools, almost dried up. Thick groves of stunted cedars stood here and there in the glen-like pockets of the high buttes, the peaks and sides of which were bare, and only their lower, terrace-like ledges thinly clad with coarse, withered grass and sprawling sage-brush; the parched hill-sides were riven by deep, twisted gorges, with brushwood in the bottoms; and the cliffs of coarse clay were cleft and seamed by sheer-sided, cañon-like gullies. In the narrow ravines, closed in by barren, sun-baked walls, the hot air stood still and sultry; the only living beings were the rattlesnakes, and of these I have never elsewhere seen so many. Some basked in the sun, stretched out at their ugly length of mottled brown and yellow; others lay half under stones or twined in the roots of the sage-brush, and looked straight at me with that strange, sullen, evil gaze, never shifting or moving, that is the property only of serpents and of certain men; while one or two coiled and rattled menacingly as I stepped near.

Yet, though we walked as quietly as we could, the game must have heard or smelt us; for after a mile's painstaking search we came to a dense thicket in which were two beds, evidently but just left, for the twigs and bent grass-blades were still slowly rising from the ground to which the bodies of the elk had pressed them. The long, clean hoof-prints told us that the quarry had started off at a swinging trot. We followed at once, and it was wonderful to see how such large, heavy beasts had gone up the steepest hill-sides without altering their swift and easy gait, and had plunged unhesitatingly over nearly sheer cliffs down which we had to clamber with careful slowness.

They left the strip of rugged Bad Lands and went on into the smoother country beyond, luckily passing quite close to where our horses were picketed. We thought it likely that they would halt in some heavily timbered coulées six or seven miles off; and as there was no need of hurry, we took lunch and then began following them up—an easy feat, as their hoofs had sunk deep into the soft soil, the prints of the dew-claws showing now and then. At first we rode, but soon dismounted, and led our horses.

We found the elk almost as soon as we struck the border of the ground we had marked as their probable halting-place. Our horses were unshod, and made but little noise; and coming to a wide, long coulée filled with tall trees and brushwood, we as usual separated, I going down one side and my companion the other. When nearly half-way down he suddenly whistled sharply, and I of course at once stood still, with my rifle at the ready. Nothing moved, and I glanced at him. He had squatted down and was gazing earnestly over into the dense laurel on my side of the coulée. In a minute he shouted that he saw a red patch in the brush which he thought must be the elk, and that it was right between him and myself. Elk will sometimes lie as closely as rabbits, even when not in very good cover; still I was a little surprised at these not breaking out when they heard human voices. However, there they staid; and I waited several minutes in vain for them to move. From where I stood it was impossible to see them, and I was fearful that they might go off down the valley and so offer me a very poor shot. Meanwhile, Manitou, who is not an emotional horse, and is moreover blessed with a large appetite, was feeding greedily, rattling his bridle-chains at every mouthful; and I thought that he would act as a guard to keep the elk where they were until I shifted my position. So I slipped back, and ran swiftly round the head of the coulée to where my companion was still sitting. He pointed me out the patch of red in the bushes, not sixty yards distant, and I fired into it without delay, by good luck breaking the neck of a cow elk, when immediately another one rose up from beside it and made off. I had five shots at her as she ascended the hill-side and the gentle slope beyond; and two of my bullets struck her close together in the flank, ranging forward—a very fatal shot. She was evidently mortally hit, and just as she reached the top of the divide she stopped, reeled, and fell over, dead.

We were much pleased with our luck, as it secured us an ample stock of needed fresh meat; and the two elk lay very handily, so that on the following day we were able to stop for them with the wagon on our way homeward, putting them in bodily, and leaving only the entrails for the vultures that were already soaring in great circles over the carcasses.*

Much the finest elk antlers I ever got, as a trophy of my own rifle, were from a mighty bull that I killed far to the west of my ranch, in the eastern chains of the Rockies. I shot him early one morning, while still-hunting through the open glades of a great pine forest, where the frosty dew was still heavy on the grass. We had listened to him and his fellows challenging each other all night long. Near by the call of the bulls in the rutting season—their "whistling," as the frontiersmen term it—sounds harsh and

---

*No naturalist ever described the way vultures gather with more scientific accuracy than Longfellow:

"Never stoops the soaring vulture   Sees the downward plunge, and follows;
On his quarry in the desert,   And a third pursues the second,
On the sick or wounded bison,   Coming from the invisible ether,
But another vulture, watching   First a speck, and then a vulture,
From his high aërial lookout,   Till the air is dark with pinions."

grating; but heard in the depths of their own mountain fastnesses, ringing through the frosty night, and echoing across the ravines and under the silent archways of the pines, it has a grand, musical beauty of its own that makes it, to me, one of the most attractive sounds in nature.

At this season the bulls fight most desperately, and their combats are far more often attended with fatal results than is the case with deer. In the grove back of my ranch house, when we first took possession, we found the skulls of two elk with interlocked antlers; one was a royal, the other had fourteen points. Theirs had been a duel to the death.

In hunting, whether on the prairie or in the deep woods, a man ought to pay great heed to his surroundings, so as not to get lost. To an old hand, getting lost is not so very serious; because, if he has his rifle and some matches, and does not lose his head, the worst that can happen to him is having to suffer some temporary discomfort. But a novice is in imminent danger of losing his wits, and therefore his life. To a man totally unaccustomed to it the sense of utter loneliness is absolutely appalling: the feeling of being lost in the wilderness seems to drive him into a state of panic terror that is frightful to behold, and that in the end renders him bereft of reason. When he realizes that he is lost he often will begin to travel very fast, and finally run until he falls exhausted—only to rise again and repeat the process when he has recovered his strength. If not found in three or four days, he is very apt to become crazy; he will then flee from the rescuers, and must be pursued and captured as if he were a wild animal.

Since 1884, when I went to the Big Horn Mountains, I have killed no grizzlies. There are some still left in our neighborhood, but they are very shy, and live in such inaccessible places, that, though I have twice devoted several days solely to hunting them, I was unsuccessful each time. A year ago, however, two cowboys found a bear in the open, and after the expenditure of a great number of cartridges killed it with their revolvers, the bear charging gamely to the last.

But this feat sinks into insignificance when compared with the deed of General W. H. Jackson, of Bellemeade, Tennessee, who is probably the only man living who ever, single-handed, killed a grizzly bear with a cavalry saber. It was many years ago, when he was a young officer in the United States service. He was with a column of eight companies of mounted infantry under the command of Colonel Andrew Porter, when by accident a bear was roused and lumbered off in front of them. Putting spurs to his thoroughbred, he followed the bear, and killed it with the saber, in sight of the whole command.

Elephant Hunting on Mount Kenia

THEODORE ROOSEVELT

On July 24th, in order to ship our fresh accumulations of specimens and trophies, we once more went into Nairobi. It was a pleasure again to see its tree-bordered streets and charming houses bowered in vines and bushes, and to meet once more the men and women who dwelt in the houses. I wish it were in my power to thank individually the members of the many East African households of which I shall always cherish warm memories of friendship and regard.

At Nairobi I saw Selous, who had just returned from a two months' safari with McMillan, Williams, and Judd. Their experience shows how large the element of luck is in lion hunting. Selous was particularly anxious to kill a good lion; there is nowhere to be found a more skilful or more hardworking hunter; yet he never even got a shot. Williams, on the other hand, came across three. Two he killed easily. The third charged him. He was carrying a double-barrelled .450, but failed to stop the beast; it seized him by the leg, and his life was saved by his Swahili gun-bearer, who gave the lion a fatal shot as it stood over him. He came within an ace of dying; but when I saw him, at the hospital, he was well on the road to recovery. One day Selous while on horseback saw a couple of lionesses, and galloped after them, followed by Judd, seventy or eighty yards behind. One lioness stopped and crouched under a bush, let Selous pass, and then charged Judd. She was right alongside him, and he fired from the hip; the bullet went into her eye; his horse jumped and swerved at the shot, throwing him off, and he found himself sitting on the ground, not three yards from the dead lioness. Nothing more was seen of the other.

Continually I met men with experiences in their past lives which showed how close the country was to those primitive conditions in which warfare with wild beasts was one of the main features of man's existence. At one dinner my host and two of my fellow-guests had been within a year or eighteen months severely mauled by lions. All three, by the way, informed me that the actual biting caused them at the moment no pain whatever; the pain came later. On meeting Harold Hill, my companion on one of my Kapiti Plains lion hunts, I found that since I had seen him he had been roughly handled by a dying leopard. The government had just been obliged to close one of the trade routes to native caravans because of the ravages of a man-eating lion, which carried men away from the camps. A safari which had come in from the north had been charged by a rhino, and one of the porters tossed and killed, the horn being driven clear through his loins. At Heatley's farm three buffalo (belonging to the same herd from which we had shot five) rushed out of the papyrus one afternoon at a passing buggy, which just managed to escape by a breakneck run across the level plain, the beasts chasing it for a mile. One afternoon, at Government House, I met a government official who had once succeeded in driving into a corral seventy zebras, including more stallions than mares; their misfortune in no way abated their savagery toward one another, and as the limited space forbade the escape of the weaker, the stallions fought to the death with teeth and hoofs during the first night, and no less then twenty were killed outright or died of their wounds.

Most of the time in Nairobi we were the guests of ever-hospitable McMillan, in his low, cool house, with its broad, vine-shaded veranda, running around all four sides, and its garden, fragrant and brilliant with innumerable flowers. Birds abounded, singing beautifully; the bulbuls were the most noticeable singers, but there were many others. The dark ant-eating chats haunted the dusky roads on the outskirts of the town, and were interesting birds; they were usually found in parties, flirted their tails up and down as they sat on bushes or roofs or wire, sang freely in chorus until after dusk, and then retired to holes in the ground for the night. A tiny owl with a queer little voice called continually not only after nightfall, but in the bright afternoons. Shrikes spitted insects on the spines of the imported cactus in the gardens.

It was race week, and the races, in some of which Kermit rode, were capital fun. The white people—army officers, government officials, farmers from the country roundabout, and their wives—rode to the races on ponies or even on camels, or drove up in rickshaws, in gharries, in bullock tongas, occasionally in automobiles, most often in two-wheel carts or rickety hacks drawn by mules and driven by a turbaned Indian or a native in a cotton shirt. There were Parsees, and Goanese dressed just like the Europeans. There were many other Indians, their picturesque womenkind gaudy in crimson, blue, and saffron. The constabulary, Indian and native, were in neat uniforms and well set up, though often barefooted. Straight, slender Somalis with clear-cut features were in attendance on the horses. Native negroes, of many different tribes, flocked to the race-course and its neighborhood. The Swahilis, and those among the others who aspired toward civilization, were well clad, the men in half-European costume, the women in flowing, parti-colored robes. But most of them were clad, or unclad, just as they always had been. Wakamba, with filed teeth, crouched in circles on the ground. Kikuyu passed, the men each with a blanket hung round the shoulders, and girdles of chains, and armlets and anklets of solid metal; the older women bent under burdens they carried on the back, half of them in addition with babies slung somewhere round them, while now and then an unmarried girl would have her face painted with ochre and vermilion. A small party of Masai warriors kept close together, each clutching his shining, long-bladed war spear, their hair daubed red and twisted into strings. A large band of Kavirondo, stark naked, with shield and spear and head-dress of nodding plumes, held a dance near the race-track. As for the races themselves, they were carried on in the most sporting spirit, and only the Australian poet Patterson could adequately write of them.

On August 4th I returned to Lake Naivasha, stopping on the way at Kijabe to lay the corner-stone of the new mission building. Mearns and Loring had stayed at Naivasha and had collected many birds and small mammals. That night they took me out on a springhaas hunt. Thanks to Kermit we had discovered that the way to get this curious and purely nocturnal animal was by "shining" it with a lantern at night, just as in our own country deer, coons, owls, and other creatures can be killed. Springhaas live in big burrows, a number of them dwelling together in one community, the holes close to one another, and making what in the West we would call a "town" in speaking of prairie dogs. At night they come out to feed on the grass. They are as heavy as a big jack-rabbit, with short forelegs, and long hind legs and tail, so that they look and on occasion move like miniature kangaroos, although in addition to making long hops or jumps, they often run almost like an ordinary rat or rabbit. They are pretty creatures, fawn-colored above, and white beneath, with the terminal half of the tail very dark. In hunting them we simply walked over the flats for a couple of hours, flashing the bull's eye lantern on all sides, until we saw the light reflected back by a springhaas's eyes. Then I would approach to within range, and hold the lantern in my left hand so as to shine both on the sight and on the eyes in front, resting my gun on my left wrist. The number 3 shot, in the Fox double-barrel, would always do the business, if I held straight enough. There was nothing but the gleam of the eyes to shoot at; and this might suddenly be raised or lowered as the intently watching animal crouched on all-fours or raised itself on its hind legs. I shot half a dozen, all that the naturalists wanted. Then I tried to shoot a fox; but the moon had risen from behind a cloud bank; I had to take a long shot and missed; but my companions killed several, and found that they were a new species of the peculiar African long-eared fox.

While waiting for the safari to get ready, Kermit went off on a camping trip and shot two bushbuck, while I spent a couple of days trying for singsing waterbuck on the edge of the papyrus. I missed a bull, and wounded another which I did not get. This was all the more exasperating because interspersed with the misses were some good shots: I killed a fine waterbuck cow at a hundred yards, and a buck tommy for the table at two hundred and fifty; and, after missing a handsome black and white, red-billed and red-legged jabiru, or saddle-billed stork, at a hundred and fifty yards, as he stalked through the meadow after frogs, I cut him down on the wing at a hundred and eighty, with the little Springfield rifle. The water-buck spent the daytime outside, but near the edge of, the papyrus; I found them grazing or resting, in the open, at all times between early morning and late afternoon. Some of them spent most of the day in the papyrus, keeping to the watery trails made by the hippos and by themselves; but this was not the general habit, unless they had been persecuted. When frightened they often ran into the papyrus, smashing the dead reeds and splashing the water in their rush. They are noble-looking antelope, with long, shaggy hair, and their chosen haunts beside the lake were very attractive. Clumps of thorn-trees and flowering bushes grew at the edge of the tall papyrus here and there, and often formed a matted jungle, the trees laced together by creepers, many of them brilliant in their bloom. The climbing morning-glories sometimes completely covered a tree with their pale-purple flowers; and other blossoming vines spangled the green over which their sprays were flung with masses of bright yellow.

Four days' march from Naivasha, where we again left Mearns and Loring, took us to Neri. Our line of march lay across the high plateaus and mountain chains of the Aberdare range. The steep, twisting trail was slippery with mud. Our last camp, at an altitude of about ten thousand feet, was so cold that the water froze in the basins and the shivering porters slept in numbed discomfort. There was constant fog and rain, and on the highest plateau the bleak landscape, shrouded in driving mist, was northern to all the senses. The ground was rolling, and through the deep valleys ran brawling brooks of clear water; one little foaming stream, suddenly tearing down a hill-side, might have been that which Childe Roland crossed before he came to the dark tower.

There was not much game, and it generally moved abroad by night. One frosty evening we killed a duiker by shining its eyes. We saw old elephant tracks. The high, wet levels swarmed with mice and shrews, just as our arctic and alpine meadows swarm with them. The species were really widely different from ours, but many of them showed curious analogies in form and habits; there was a short-tailed shrew much like our mole shrew, and a longhaired, short-tailed rat like a very big meadow mouse. They were so plentiful that we frequently saw them, and the grass was cut up by their runways. They were abroad during the day, probably finding the nights too cold, and in an hour Heller trapped a dozen or two individuals belonging to seven species and five different genera. There were not many birds so high up. There were deer ferns; and Spanish moss hung from the trees and even from the bamboos. The flowers included utterly strange forms, as for instance giant lobelias ten feet high. Others we know in our gardens; geraniums and red-hot-pokers, which in places turned the glades to a fire color. Yet others either were like, or looked like, our own wild flowers: orange lady-slippers, red gladiolas on stalks six feet high, pansy-like violets, and blackberries and yellow raspberries. There were stretches of bushes bearing masses of small red or large white flowers shaped somewhat like columbines, or like the garden balsam; the red flower bushes were under the bamboos, the white at lower level. The crests and upper slopes of the mountains were clothed in the green uniformity of the bamboo forest, the trail winding dim under its dark archway of tall, close-growing stems. Lower down were junipers and yews, and then many other trees, with among them tree ferns and strange dragon trees with lily-like frondage. Zone succeeded zone from top to bottom, each marked by a different plant life.

In this part of Africa, where flowers bloom and birds sing all the year round, there is no such burst of bloom and song as in the northern spring and early summer. There is nothing like the mass of blossoms which carpet the meadows of the high mountain valleys and far northern meadows, during their brief high tide of life, when one short joyous burst of teeming and vital beauty atones for the long death of the iron fall and winter. So it is with the bird songs. Many of them are beautiful, though to my ears none quite as beautiful as the best of our own bird songs. At any rate there is nothing that quite corresponds to the chorus that during May and June moves northward from the Gulf States and southern California to Maine, Minnesota, and Oregon, to Ontario and Saskatchewan; when there comes the great vernal burst of bloom and song; when the mayflower, bloodroot, wake-robin, anemone, adder's tongue, liverwort, shadblow, dogwood, redbud, gladden the woods; when mocking-birds and cardinals sing in the magnolia groves of the South, and hermit thrushes, winter wrens and sweetheart sparrows in the spruce and hemlock forests of the North; when bobolinks in the East and meadowlarks East and West sing in the fields; and water ousels by the cold streams of the Rockies, and canyon wrens in their sheer gorges; when from the Atlantic seaboard to the Pacific wood thrushes, veeries, rufous-backed thrushes, robins, bluebirds, orioles, thrashers, cat-birds, house finches, song sparrows—some in the East, some in the West, some both East and West—and many, many other singers thrill the gardens at sunrise; until the long days begin to shorten, and tawny lilies burn by the roadside, and the indigo buntings trill from the tops of little trees throughout the hot afternoons.

We were in the Kikuyu country. On our march we met several parties of natives. I had been much inclined to pity the porters, who had but one blanket apiece; but when I saw the Kikuyus, each with nothing but a smaller blanket, and without the other clothing and the tents of the porters, I realized how much better off the latter were simply because they were on a white man's safari. At Neri boma we were greeted with the warmest hospitality by the District Commissioner, Mr. Browne. Among other things, he arranged a great Kikuyu dance in our honor. Two thousand warriors, and many women, came in; as well as a small party of Masai moran. The warriors were naked, or half-naked; some carried gaudy blankets, others girdles of leopard skin; their ox-hide shields were colored in bold patterns, their long-bladed spears quivered and gleamed. Their faces and legs were painted red and yellow; the faces of the young men who were about to undergo the rite of circumcision were stained a ghastly white, and their bodies fantastically painted. The warriors wore bead necklaces and waist belts and armlets of brass and steel, and spurred anklets of monkey skin. Some wore head-dresses made out of a lion's mane or from the long black and white fur of the Colobus monkey; others had plumes stuck in their red-daubed hair. They chanted in unison a deep-toned chorus, and danced rhythmically in rings, while the drums throbbed and the horns blared; and they danced by us in column, springing and chanting. The women shrilled applause, and danced in groups by themselves. The Masai circled and swung in a panther-like dance of their own, and the measure, and their own fierce singing and calling, maddened them until two of their number, their eyes staring, their faces working, went into fits of berserker frenzy, and were disarmed at once to prevent mischief. Some of the tribesmen held wilder dances still in the evening, by the light of fires that blazed in a grove where their thatched huts stood.

The second day after reaching Neri the clouds lifted and we dried our damp clothes and blankets. Through the bright sunlight we saw in front of us the high rock peaks of Kenia, and shining among them the fields of everlasting snow which feed her glaciers; for beautiful, lofty Kenia is one of the glacier-bearing mountains of the equator. Here Kermit and Tarlton went northward on a safari of their own, while Cuninghame, Heller, and I headed for Kenia itself. For two days we travelled through a well-peopled country. The fields of corn—always called mealies in Africa—of beans, and sweet potatoes, with occasional plantations of bananas, touched one another in almost uninterrupted succession. In most of them we saw the Kikuyu women at work with their native hoes; for among the Kikuyus, as among other savages, the woman is the drudge and beast of burden. Our trail led by clear, rushing streams, which formed the head-waters of the Tana; among the trees fringing their banks were graceful palms, and there were groves of tree ferns here and there on the sides of the gorges.

On the afternoon of the second day we struck upward among the steep foot-hills of the mountain, riven by deep ravines. We pitched camp in an open glade, surrounded by the green wall of tangled forest, the forest of the tropical mountain sides.

The trees, strange of kind and endless in variety, grew tall and close, laced together by vine and creeper, while underbrush crowded the space between their mossy trunks, and covered the leafy mould beneath. Toward dusk crested ibis flew overhead with harsh clamor, to seek their night roosts; parrots chattered, and a curiously home-like touch was given by the presence of a thrush in color and shape almost exactly like our robin. Monkeys called in the depths of the forest, and after dark tree-frogs piped and croaked, and the tree hyraxes uttered their wailing cries.

Elephants dwelt permanently in this mountainous region of heavy woodland. On our march thither we had already seen their traces in the "shambas," as the cultivated fields of the natives are termed; for the great beasts are fond of raiding the crops at night, and their inroads often do serious damage. In this neighborhood their habit is to live high up in the mountains, in the bamboos, while the weather is dry; the cow and calves keeping closer to the bamboos than the bulls. A spell of wet weather, such as we had fortunately been having, drives them down in the dense forest which covers the lower slopes. Here they may either pass all their time, or at night they may go still further down, into the open valley where the shambas lie; or the may occasionally still do what they habitually did in the days before the white hunter came, and wander far away, making migrations that are sometimes seasonal, and sometimes irregular and unaccountable.

No other animal, not the lion himself, is so constant a theme of talk, and a subject of such unflagging interest round the camp-fires of African hunters and in the native villages of the African wilderness, as the elephant. Indeed the elephant has always profoundly impressed the imagination of mankind. It is, not only to hunters, but to naturalists, and to all people who possess any curiosity about wild creatures and the wild life of nature, the most interesting of all animals. Its huge bulk, its singular form, the value of its ivory, its great intelligence—in which it is only matched, if at all, by the highest apes, and possibly by one or two of the highest carnivores—and its varied habits, all combine to give it an interest such as attaches to no other living creature below the rank of man. In line of descent and in physical formation it stands by itself, wholly apart from all the other great land beasts, and differing from them even more widely than they differ from one another. The two existing species—the African, which is the larger and finer animal, and the Asiatic—differ from one another as much as they do from the mammoth and similar extinct forms which were the contemporaries of early man in Europe and North America. The carvings of our palaeolithic forefathers, etched on bone by cavern dwellers, from whom we are sundered by ages which stretch into an immemorial past, show that in their lives the hairy elephant of the north played the same part that his remote collateral descendant now plays in the lives of the savages who dwell under a vertical sun beside the tepid waters of the Nile and the Congo.

In the first dawn of history, the sculptured records of the kings of Egypt, Babylon, and Nineveh show the immense importance which attached in the eyes of the mightiest monarchs of the then world to the chase and the trophies of this great strange beast. The ancient civilization of India boasts as one of its achievements the taming of the elephant, and in the ancient lore of that civilization the elephant plays a distinguished part.

The elephant is unique among the beasts of great bulk in the fact that his growth in size has been accompanied by growth in brain power. With other beasts growth in bulk of body has not been accompanied by similar growth of mind. Indeed sometimes there seems to have been mental retrogression.

The rhinoceros, in several different forms, is found in the same regions as the elephant, and in one of its forms it is in point of size second only to the elephant among terrestrial animals. Seemingly the ancestors of the two creatures, in that period, separated from us by uncounted hundreds of thousands of years, which we may conveniently designate as late miocene or early pliocene, were substantially equal in brain development. But in one case increase in bulk seems to have induced lethargy and atrophy of brain power, while in the other case brain and body have both grown. At any rate the elephant is now one of the wisest and the rhinoceros one of the stupidest of big mammals. In consequence the elephant outlasts the rhino, although he is the largest, carries infinitely more valuable spoils, and is far more eagerly and persistently hunted. Both animals wandered freely over the open country of East Africa thirty years ago. But the elephant learns by experience infinitely more readily than the rhinoceros. As a rule, the former no longer lives in the open plains, and in many places now crosses them if possible only at night. But those rhinoceros which formerly dwelt in the plains for the most part continued to dwell there until killed out. So it is at the present day. Not the most foolish elephant would under similar conditions behave as the rhinos that we studied and hunted by Kilimakiu and in the Sotik behaved. No elephant, in regions where they have been much persecuted by hunters, would habitually spend its days lying or standing in the open plain; nor would it, in such places, repeatedly, and in fact, uniformly, permit men to walk boldly up to it without heeding them until in its immediate neighborhood. The elephant's sight is bad, as is that of the rhinoceros; but a comparatively brief experience with rifle-bearing man usually makes the former take refuge in regions where scent and hearing count for more than sight; while no experience has any such effect on the rhino. The rhinos that now live in the bush are the descendants of those which always lived in the bush; and it is in the bush that the species will linger long after it has vanished from the open; and it is in the bush that it is most formidable.

Elephant and rhino differ as much in their habits as in their intelligence. The former is very gregarious, herds of several hundred being sometimes found, and is of a restless, wandering temper, often shifting his abode and sometimes making long migrations. The rhinoceros is a lover of solitude; it is usually found alone, or a bull and cow, or cow and calf may be in company; very rarely are as many as half a dozen found together. Moreover, it is comparatively stationary in its habits, and as a general thing stays permanently in one neighborhood, not shifting its position for very many miles unless for grave reasons.

The African elephant has recently been divided into a number of sub-species; but as within a century its range was continuous over nearly the whole continent south of the Sahara, and as it was given to such extensive occasional wanderings, it is probable that the examination of a sufficient series of specimens would show that on their confines these races grade into one another. In its essentials the beast is almost everywhere the same, although, of course, there must be variation of habit with any animal which exists throughout so wide and diversified a range of territory; for in one place it is found in high mountains, in another in a dry desert, in another in low-lying marshes or wet and dense forests.

In East Africa the old bulls are usually found singly or in small parties by themselves. These have the biggest tusks; the bulls in the prime of life, the herd bulls or breeding bulls, which keep in herds with the cows and calves, usually have smaller ivory. Sometimes, however, very old but vigorous bulls are found with the cows; and I am inclined to think that the ordinary herd bulls at times also keep by themselves, or at least in company with only a few cows, for at certain seasons, generally immediately after the rains, cows, most of them with calves, appear in great numbers at certain places, where only a few bulls are ever found. Where undisturbed elephant rest, and wander about at all times of the day and night, and feed without much regard to fixed hours. Morning or evening, noon or midnight, the herd may be on the move, or its members may be resting; yet, during the hottest hours of noon they seldom feed, and ordinarily stand almost still, resting—for elephant very rarely lie down unless sick. Where they are afraid of man, their only enemy, they come out to feed in thinly forested plains, or cultivated fields, when they do so at all, only at night, and before daybreak move back into the forest to rest. Elsewhere they sometimes spend the day in the open, in grass or low bush. Where we were, at this time, on Kenia, the elephants sometimes moved down at night to feed in the shambas, at the expense of the crops of the natives, and sometimes stayed in the forest, feeding by day or night on the branches they tore off the trees, or, occasionally, on the roots they grubbed up with their tusks. They work vast havoc among the young or small growth of a forest, and the readiness with which they uproot, overturn, or break off medium-sized trees coveys a striking impression of their enormous strength. I have seen a tree a foot in diameter thus uprooted and overturned.

The African elephant has never, like his Indian kinsman, been trained to man's use. There is still hope that the feat may be performed; but hitherto its probable economic usefulness has for various reasons seemed so questionable that there has been scant encouragement to undergo the necessary expense and labor. Up to the present time the African elephant has yielded only his ivory as an asset of value. This, however, has been of such great value as wellnigh to bring about the mighty beast's utter extermination. Ivory hunters and ivory traders have penetrated Africa to the haunts of the elephant since centuries before our era, and the elephant boundaries have been slowly receding throughout historic time; but during the century just passed its process has been immensely accelerated, until now there are but one or two out-of-the-way nooks of the Dark Continent to the neighborhood of which hunter and trader have not penetrated. Fortunately the civilized powers which now divide dominion over Africa have waked up in time, and there is at present no danger of the extermination of the lord of all four-footed creatures. Large reserves have been established on which various herds of elephants now live what is, at least for the time being, an entirely safe life. Furthermore, over great tracts of territory outside the reserves regulations have been promulgated which, if enforced as they are now enforced, will present any excessive diminution of the herds. In British East Africa, for instance, no cows are allowed to be shot save for special purposes, as for preservation in a museum, or to safeguard life and property; and no bulls with tusks weighing less than thirty pounds apiece. This renders safe almost all the females and an ample supply of breeding males. Too much praise cannot be given the governments and the individuals who have brought about this happy result; the credit belongs especially to England and to various Englishmen. It would be a veritable and most tragic calamity if the lordly elephant, the giant among existing four-footed creatures, should be permitted to vanish from the face of the earth.

But of course protection is not permanently possible over the greater part of that country which is well fitted for settlement; nor anywhere, if the herds grow too numerous. It would be not merely silly, but worse than silly, to try to stop all killing of elephants. The unchecked increase of any big and formidable wild beast, even though not a flesh eater, is incompatible with the existence of man when he has emerged from the state of lowest savagery. This is not a matter of theory, but of proved fact. In place after place in Africa where protection has been extended to hippopotamus or buffalo, rhinoceros or elephant, it has been found necessary to withdraw it because the protected animals did such damage to property, or became such menaces to human life. Among all four species cows with calves often attack men without provocation, and old bulls are at any time likely to become infected by a spirit of wanton and ferocious mischief and apt to become mankillers. I know settlers who tried to preserve the rhinoceros which they found living on their big farms, and who were obliged to abandon the attempt, and themselves to kill the rhinos because of repeated and wanton attacks on human beings by the latter. Where we were by Neri, a year or two before our visit, the rhinos had become so dangerous, killing one white man and several natives, that the District Commissioner who preceded Mr. Browne was forced to undertake a crusade against them, killing fifteen. Both in South Africa and on the Nile protection extended to hippopotamus has in places been wholly withdrawn because of the damage done by the beast to the crops of the natives, or because of their unprovoked assaults on canoes and boats. In one instance a last surviving hippo was protected for years, but finally grew bold because of immunity, killed a boy in sheer wantonness, and had to be himself slain. In Uganda the buffalo were for years protected, and grew so bold, killed so many natives, and ruined so many villages that they are now classed as vermin and their destruction in every way encouraged. In the very neighborhood where I was hunting at Kenia but six weeks before my coming, a cow buffalo had wandered down into the plains and run amuck, had attacked two villages, had killed a man and a boy, and had then been mobbed to death by the spearmen. Elephant, when in numbers, and when not possessed of the fear of man, are more impossible neighbors than hippo, rhino, or buffalo; but they are so eagerly sought after by ivory hunters that it is only rarely that they get the chance to become really dangerous to life, although in many places their ravages among the crops are severely felt by the unfortunate natives who live near them.

The chase of the elephant, if persistently followed, entails more fatigue and hardship than any other kind of African hunting. As regards risk, it is hard to say whether it is more or less dangerous than the chase of the lion and the buffalo. Both Cuninghame and Tarlton, men of wide experience, ranked elephant hunting, in point of danger, as nearly on the level with lion hunting, and as more dangerous than buffalo hunting; and all three kinds as far more dangerous than the chase of the rhino. Personally, I believe the actual conflict with a lion, where the conditions are the same, to be normally the more dangerous sport; though far greater demands are made by elephant hunting on the qualities of personal endurance and hardihood and resolute perseverance in the face of disappointment and difficulty. Buffalo, seemingly, do not charge as freely as elephant, but are more dangerous when they do charge. Rhino when hunted, though at times ugly customers, seem to me certainly less dangerous than the other three; but from sheer stupid truculence they are themselves apt to take the offensive in unexpected fashion, being far more prone to such aggression than are any of the others—man-eating lions always excepted.

Very few of the native tribes in Africa hunt the elephant systematically. But the 'Ndorobo, the wild bush people of East Africa, sometimes catch young elephants in the pits they dig with slow labor, and very rarely they kill one with a kind of harpoon. The 'Ndorobo are doubtless in part descended from some primitive bush people, but in part also derive their blood from the more advanced tribes near which their wandering families happen to live; and they grade into the latter, by speech and through individuals who seem to stand half-way between. Thus we had with us two Masai 'Ndorobo, true wild people, who spoke a bastard Masai; who had formerly hunted with Cuninghame, and who came to us because of their ancient friendship with him. These shy wood creatures were afraid to come to Neri by daylight, when we were camped there, but after dark crept to Cuninghame's tent. Cuninghame gave them two fine red blankets, and put them to sleep in a little tent, keeping their spears in his own tent, as a matter of precaution to prevent their running away. The elder of the two, he informed me, would certainly have a fit of hysterics when we killed our elephant! Cuninghame was also joined by other old friends of former hunts, Kikuyu 'Ndorobo these, who spoke Kikuyu like the people who cultivated the fields that covered the river-bottoms and hill-sides of the adjoining open country, and who were, indeed, merely outlying, forest-dwelling members of the lowland tribes. In the deep woods we met one old Dorobo, who had no connection with any more advanced tribe, whose sole belongings were his spear, skin cloak, and fire stick, and who lived purely on honey and game; unlike the bastard 'Ndorobo, he was ornamented with neither paint nor grease. But the 'Ndorobo who were our guides stood farther up in the social scale. The men passed most of their time in the forest, but up the mountain sides they had squalid huts on little clearings, with shambas, where their wives raised scanty crops. To the 'Ndorobo, and to them alone, the vast, thick forest was an open book; without their aid as guides both Cuninghame and our own gun-bearers were at fault, and found their way around with great difficulty and slowness. The bush people had nothing in the way of clothing save a blanket over the shoulders, but wore the usual paint and grease and ornaments; each carried a spear which might have a long and narrow, or short and broad blade; two of them wore head-dresses *of tripe*—skull-caps made from the inside of a sheep's stomach.

For two days after reaching our camp in the open glade on the mountain side it rained. We were glad of this, because it meant that the elephants would not be in the bamboos, and Cuninghame and the 'Ndorobo went off to hunt for fresh signs. Cuninghame is as skilful an elephant hunter as can be found in Africa, and is one of the very few white men able to help even the wild bushmen at their work. By the afternoon of the second day they were fairly well satisfied as to the whereabouts of the quarry.

The following morning a fine rain was still falling when Cuninghame, Heller, and I started on our hunt but by noon it had stopped. Of course we went in single file and on foot; not even a bear hunter from the cane-brakes of the lower Mississippi could ride through that forest. We left our home camp standing, taking blankets and a coat and a change of underclothing for each of us, and two small Whymper tents, with enough food for three days; I also took my wash kit and a book from the Pigskin Library. First marched the 'Ndorobo guides, each with his spear, his blanket round his shoulders, and a little bundle of corn and sweet potato. Then came Cuninghame, followed by his gun-bearer. Then I came, clad in khaki-colored flannel shirt and khaki trousers buttoning down the legs, with hob-nailed shoes and a thick slouch hat; I had intended to wear rubber-soled shoes, but the soaked ground was too slippery. My two gun-bearers followed, carrying the Holland and the Springfield. Then came Heller, at the head of a dozen porters and skinners; he and they were to fall behind when we actually struck fresh elephant spoor, but to follow our trail by the help of a Dorobo who was left with them.

For three hours our route lay along the edge of the woods. We climbed into and out of deep ravines in which groves of tree ferns clustered. We waded through streams of swift water, whose course was broken by cataract and rapid. We passed through shambas, and by the doors of little hamlets of thatched beehive huts. We met flocks of goats and hairy, fat-tailed sheep guarded by boys, strings of burden-bearing women stood meekly to one side to let us pass; parties of young men sauntered by, spear in hand.

Then we struck into the great forest, and in an instant the sun was shut from sight by the thick screen of wet foliage. It was a riot of twisted vines, interlacing the trees and bushes. Only the elephant paths, which, of every age, crossed and recrossed it hither and thither, made it passable. One of the chief difficulties in hunting elephants in the forest is that it is impossible to travel, except very slowly and with much noise, off these trails, so that it is sometimes very difficult to take advantage of the wind; and although the sight of the elephant is dull, both its sense of hearing and its sense of smell are exceedingly acute.

Hour after hour we worked our way onward through tangled forest and matted jungle. There was little sign of bird or animal life. A troop of long-haired black and white monkeys bounded away among the tree tops. Here and there brilliant flowers lightened the gloom. We ducked under vines and climbed over fallen timber. Poisonous nettles stung our hands. We were drenched by the wet boughs which we brushed aside. Mosses and ferns grew rank and close. The trees were of strange kinds. There were huge trees with little leaves, and small trees with big leaves. There were trees with bare, fleshy limbs, that writhed out through the neighboring branches, bearing sparse clusters of large frondage. In places the forest was low, the trees thirty or forty feet high, the bushes, that choked the ground between, fifteen or twenty feet high. In other places mighty monarchs of the wood, straight and tall, towered aloft to an immense height; among them were trees whose smooth, round boles were spotted like sycamores, while far above our heads their gracefully spreading branches were hung with vines like mistletoe and draped with Spanish moss; trees whose surfaces were corrugated and knotted as if they were made of bundles of great creepers; and giants whose buttressed trunks were four times a man's length across.

Twice we got on elephant spoor, once of a single bull, once of a party of three. Then Cuninghame and the 'Ndorobo redoubled their caution. They would minutely examine the fresh dung; and above all they continually tested the wind, scanning the tree tops, and lighting matches to see from the smoke what the eddies were near the ground. Each time after an hour's stealthy stepping and crawling along the twisted trail a slight shift of the wind in the almost still air gave our scent to the game, and away it went before we could catch a glimpse of it; and we resumed our walk. The elephant paths led up hill and down—for the beasts are wonderful climbers—and wound in and out in every direction. They were marked by broken branches and the splintered and shattered trunks of smaller trees, especially where the elephant had stood and fed, trampling down the bushes for many yards around. Where they had crossed the marshy valleys they had punched big round holes, three feet deep, in the sticky mud.

As evening fell we pitched camp by the side of a little brook at the bottom of a ravine, and dined ravenously on bread, mutton, and tea. The air was keen, and under our blankets we slept in comfort until dawn. Breakfast was soon over and camp struck; and once more we began our cautious progress through the dim, cool archways of the mountain forest.

Two hours after leaving camp we came across the fresh trail of a small herd of perhaps ten or fifteen elephant cows and calves, but including two big herd bulls. At once we took up the trail. Cuninghame and his bush people consulted again and again, scanning every track and mark with minute attention. The signs showed that the elephants had fed in the shambas early in the night, had then returned to the mountain, and stood in one place resting for several hours, and had left this sleeping ground some time before we reached it. After we had followed the trail a short while we made the experiment of trying to force our own way through the jungle, so as to get the wind more favorable but our progress was too slow and noisy, and we returned to the path the elephants had beaten. Then the 'Ndorobo went ahead, travelling noiselessly and at speed. One of them was clad in a white blanket, and another in a red one, which were conspicuous; but they were too silent and cautious to let the beasts see them, and could tell exactly where they were and what they were doing by the sounds. When these trackers waited for us they would appear before us like ghosts; once one of them dropped down from the branches above, having climbed a tree with monkey-like ability to get a glimpse of the great game.

At last we could hear the elephants, and under Cuninghame's lead we walked more cautiously than ever. The wind was right, and the trail of one elephant led close alongside that of the rest of the herd, and parallel thereto. It was about noon. The elephants moved slowly, and we listened to the boughs crack, and now and then to the curious internal rumblings of the great beasts. Carefully, every sense on the alert, we kept pace with them. My double-barrel was in my hands, and, wherever possible, as I followed the trail, I stepped in the huge footprints of the elephant, for where such a weight had pressed there were no sticks left to crack under my feet. It made our veins thrill thus for half an hour to creep stealthily along, but a few rods from the herd, never able to see it, because of the extreme denseness of the cover, but always hearing first one and then another of its members, and always trying to guess what each one might do, and keeping ceaselessly ready for whatever might befall. A flock of hornbills flew up with noisy clamor, but the elephants did not heed them.

At last we came in sight of the mighty game. The trail took a twist to one side, and there, thirty yards in front of us, we made out part of the gray and massive head of an elephant resting his tusks on the branches of a young tree. A couple of minutes passed before, by cautious scrutiny, we were able to tell whether the animal was a cow or a bull, and whether, if a bull, it carried heavy enough tusks. Then we saw that it was a big bull with good ivory. It turned its head in my direction and I saw its eye; and I fired a little to one side of the eye, at a spot which I thought would lead to the brain. I struck exactly where I aimed, but the head of an elephant is enormous and the brain small, and the bullet missed it. However, the shock momentarily stunned the beast. He stumbled forward, half falling, and as he recovered I fired with the second barrel, again aiming for the brain. This time the bullet sped true, and as I lowered the rifle from my shoulder, I saw the great lord of the forest come crashing to the ground.

But at that very instant, before there was a moment's time in which to reload, the thick bushes parted immediately on my left front, and through them surged the vast bulk of a charging bull elephant, the matted mass of tough creepers snapping like packthread before his rush. He was so close that he could have touched me with his trunk. I leaped to one side and dodged behind a tree trunk, opening the rifle, throwing out the empty shells, and slipping in two cartridges. Meanwhile Cuninghame fired right and left, at the same time throwing himself into the bushes on the other side. Both his bullets went home, and the bull stopped short in his charge, wheeled, and immediately disappeared in the thick cover. We ran forward, but the forest had closed over his wake. We heard him trumpet shrilly, and then all sound ceased.

The 'Ndorobo, who had quite properly disappeared when this second bull charged, now went forward, and soon returned with the report that he had fled at speed, but was evidently hard hit, as there was much blood on the spoor. If we had been only after ivory we should have followed him at once; but there was no telling how long a chase he might lead us; and as we desired to save the skin of the dead elephant entire, there was no time whatever to spare. It is a formidable task, occupying many days, to preserve an elephant for mounting in a museum, and if the skin is to be properly saved, it must be taken off without an hour's unnecessary delay.

So back we turned to where the dead tusker lay, and I felt proud indeed as I stood by the immense bulk of the slain monster and put my hand on the ivory. The tusks weighed a hundred and thirty pounds the pair. There was the usual scene of joyful excitement among the gun-bearers—who had behaved excellently—and among the wild bush people who had done the tracking for us; and, as Cuninghame had predicted, the old Masai Dorobo, from pure delight, proceeded to have hysterics on the body of the dead elephant. The scene was repeated when Heller and the porters appeared half an hour later. Then, chattering like monkeys, and as happy as possible, all, porters, gun-bearers, and 'Ndorobo alike, began the work of skinning and cutting up the quarry, under the leadership and supervision of Heller and Cuninghame, and soon they were all splashed with blood from head to foot. One of the trackers took off his blanket and squatted stark naked inside the carcass the better to use his knife. Each laborer rewarded himself by cutting off strips of meat for his private store, and hung them in red festoons from the branches round about. There was no let up in the work until it was stopped by darkness.

Our tents were pitched in a small open glade a hundred yards from the dead elephant. The night was clear, the stars shone brightly, and in the west the young moon hung just above the line of tall tree tops. Fires were speedily kindled and the men sat around them, feasting and singing in a strange minor tone until late in the night. The flickering light left them at one moment in black obscurity, and the next brought into bold relief their sinewy crouching figures, their dark faces, gleaming eyes, and flashing teeth. When they did sleep, two of the 'Ndorobo slept so close to the fire as to burn themselves; an accident to which they are prone, judging from the many scars of old burns on their legs. I toasted slices of elephant's heart on a pronged stick before the fire, and found it delicious; for I was hungry, and the night was cold. We talked of our success and exulted over it, and made our plans for the morrow; and then we turned in under our blankets for another night's sleep.

Next morning some of the 'Ndorobo went off on the trail of Cuninghame's elephant to see if it had fallen, but found that it had travelled steadily, though its wounds were probably mortal. There was no object in my staying, for Heller and Cuninghame would be busy for the next ten days, and would ultimately have to use all the porters in taking off and curing the skin, and transporting it to Neri; so I made up my mind to go down to the plains for a hunt by myself. Taking one porter to carry my bedding, and with my gun-bearers, and a Dorobo as guide, I struck off through the forest for the main camp, reaching it early in the afternoon. Thence I bundled off a safari to Cuninghame and Heller, with food for a week, and tents and clothing; and then enjoyed the luxury of a shave and a warm bath. Next day was spent in writing and in making preparations for my own trip. A Kikuyu chief, clad in a cloak of hyrax skins, and carrying his war spear, came to congratulate me on killing the elephant and to present me with a sheep. Early the following morning everything was in readiness; the bullnecked porters lifted their loads, I stepped out in front, followed by my led horse, and in ten hours' march we reached Neri boma with its neat building, its trees, and its well-kept flower beds.

My hunting and travelling during the following fortnight will be told in the next chapter. On the evening of September 6th we were all together again at Meru boma, on the north-eastern slopes of Kenia—Kermit, Tarlton, Cuninghame, Heller, and I. Thanks to the unfailing kindness of the Commissioner, Mr. Horne, we were given full information of the elephant in the neighborhood. He had no 'Ndorobo, but among the Wa-Meru, a wild martial tribe, who lived close around him, there were a number of hunters, or at least of men who knew the forest and the game, and these had been instructed to bring in any news.

We had, of course, no idea that elephant would be found close at hand. But next morning, about eleven, Horne came to our camp with four of his black scouts, who reported that three elephants were in a patch of thick jungle beside the shambas, not three miles away. Horne said that the elephants were cows, that they had been in the neighborhood some days, devastating the shambas, and were bold and fierce, having charged some men who sought to drive them away from the cultivated fields; it is curious to see how little heed these elephants pay to the natives. I wished a cow for the museum, and also another bull. So off we started at once, Kermit carrying his camera. I slipped on my rubber-soled shoes, and had my gun-bearers accompany me bare-footed, with the Holland and the Springfield rifles. We followed footpaths among the fields until we reached the edge of the jungle in which the elephants stood.

This jungle lay beside the forest, and at this point separated it from the fields. It consisted of a mass of rank-growing bushes, allied to the cotton-plant, ten or twelve feet high, with only here and there a tree. It was not good ground in which to hunt elephant, for the tangle was practically impenetrable to a hunter save along the elephant trails, whereas the elephants themselves could move in any direction at will, with no more difficulty than a man would have in a hay-field. The bushes in most places rose just above their backs, so that they were completely hid from the hunter even a few feet away. Yet the cover afforded no shade to the mighty beasts, and it seemed strange that elephants should stand in it at mid-day with the sun out. There they were, however, for, looking cautiously into the cover from behind the bushes on a slight hill crest a quarter of a mile off, we could just make out a huge ear now and then as it lazily flapped.

On account of the wind we had to go well to one side before entering the jungle. Then in we went in single file, Cuninghame and Tarlton leading, with a couple of our naked guides. The latter showed no great desire to get too close, explaining that the elephants were "very fierce." Once in the jungle, we trod as quietly as possible, threading our way along the elephant trails, which crossed and re-crossed one another. Evidently it was a favorite haunt, for the sign was abundant, both old and new. In the impenetrable cover it was quite impossible to tell just where the elephants were, and twice we sent one of the savages up a tree to locate the game. The last time the watcher, who stayed in the tree, indicated by signs that the elephant were not far off; and his companions wished to lead us round to where the cover was a little lower and thinner. But to do so would have given them our wind, and Cuninghame refused, taking into his own hands the management of the stalk. I kept my heavy rifle at the ready, and on we went, in watchful silence, prepared at any moment for a charge. We could not tell at what second we might catch our first glimpse at very close quarters of "the beast that hath between his eyes the serpent for a hand," and when thus surprised the temper of "the huge earth-shaking beast" is sometimes of the shortest.

Cuninghame and Tarlton stopped for a moment to consult; Cuninghame stooped, and Tarlton mounted his shoulders and stood upright, steadying himself by my hand. Down he came and told us that he had seen a small tree shake seventy yards distant; although upright on Cuninghame's shoulder he could not see the elephant itself. Forward we stole for a few yards, and then a piece of good luck befell us, for we came on the trunk of a great fallen tree, and scrambling up, we found ourselves perched in a row six feet above the ground. The highest part of the trunk was near the root, farthest from where the elephants were; and though it offered precarious footing, it also offered the best lookout. Thither I balanced, and looking over the heads of my companions I at once made out the elephant. At first I could see nothing but the shaking branches, and one huge ear occasionally flapping. Then I made out the ear of another beast, and then the trunk of a third was uncurled, lifted, and curled again; it showered its back with earth. The watcher we had left behind in the tree top coughed, the elephants stood motionless, and up went the biggest elephant's trunk, feeling for the wind; the watcher coughed again, and then the bushes and saplings swayed and parted as three black bulks came toward us. The cover was so high that we could not see their tusks, only the tops of their heads and their backs being visible. The leader was the biggest, and at it I fired when it was sixty yards away, and nearly broadside on, but heading slightly toward me. I had previously warned every one to kneel. The recoil of the heavy rifle made me rock, as I stood unsteadily on my perch, and I failed to hit the brain. But the bullet, only missing the brain by an inch or two, brought the elephant to its knees; as it rose I floored it with the second barrel. The blast of the big rifle, by the way, was none too pleasant for the other men on the log and made Cuninghame's nose bleed. Reloading, I fired twice at the next animal, which was now turning. It stumbled and nearly fell, but at the same moment the first one rose again, and I fired both barrels into its head, bringing it once more to the ground. Once again it rose—an elephant's brain is not an easy mark to hit under such conditions—but as it moved slowly off, half stunned, I snatched the little Springfield rifle, and this time shot true, sending the bullet into its brain. As it fell I took another shot at the wounded elephant, now disappearing in the forest, but without effect.

On walking up to our prize it proved to be not a cow, but a good-sized adult (but not old) herd bull, with thick, short tusks weighing about forty pounds apiece. Ordinarily, of course, a bull, and not a cow, is what one desires, although on this occasion I needed a cow to complete the group for the National Museum. However, Heller and Cuninghame spent the next few days in preserving the skin, which I after gave to the University of California; and I was too much pleased with our luck to feel inclined to grumble. We were back in camp five hours after leaving it. Our gun-bearers usually felt it incumbent on them to keep a dignified bearing while in our company. But, the death of an elephant is always a great event; and one of the gun-bearers, as they walked ahead of us campward, soon began to improvise a song, reciting the success of the hunt, the death of the elephant, and the power of the rifles; and gradually, as they got farther ahead, the more lighthearted among them began to give way to their spirits and they came into camp frolicking, gambolling, and dancing as if they were still the naked savages that they had been before they became the white man's followers.

Two days later Kermit got his bull. He and Tarlton had camped about ten miles off in a magnificent forest, and late the first afternoon received news that a herd of elephants was in the neighborhood. They were off by dawn, and in a few hours came on the herd. It consisted chiefly of cows and calves, but there was one big master bull, with fair tusks. It was open forest with long grass. By careful stalking they got within thirty yards of the bull, behind whom was a line of cows. Kermit put both barrels of his heavy double .450 into the tusker's head, but without even staggering him; and as he walked off Tarlton also fired both barrels into him, with no more effect; then, as he slowly turned, Kermit killed him with a shot in the brain from the .405 Winchester. Immediately the cows lifted their ears, and began trumpeting and threatening; if they had come on in a body at that distance, there was not much chance of turning them or of escaping from them: and after standing stock still for a minute or two, Kermit and Tarlton stole quietly off for a hundred yards, and waited until the anger of the cows cooled and they had moved away, before going up to the dead bull. Then they followed the herd again, and Kermit got some photos which, as far as I know, are better than any that have ever been taken of wild elephant. He took them close up; at imminent risk of a charge.

The following day the two hunters rode back to Meru, making a long circle. The elephants they saw were not worth shooting, but they killed the finest rhinoceros we had yet seen. They saw it in an open space of tall grass, surrounded by lantana brush, a flowering shrub with close-growing stems, per-haps twenty feet high and no thicker than a man's thumb; it forms a favorite cover for elephants and rhinoceros, and is well nigh impenetrable to hunters. Fortunately this particular rhino was outside it, and Kermit and Tarlton got up to about twenty-five yards from him. Kermit then put one bullet behind his shoulder, and as he whipped round to charge, another bullet on the point of his shoulder; although mor-tally wounded, he showed no signs whatever of being hurt, and came at the hunters with great speed and savage desire to do harm. Then an extraordinary thing happened. Tarlton fired, inflicting merely a flesh wound in one shoulder, and the big, fearsome brute, which had utterly disregarded the two fatal shots, on receiving this flesh wound, wheeled and ran. Both firing, they killed him before he had gone many yards. He was a bull, with a thirty-inch horn.

By this time Cuninghame and Heller had finished the skin and skeleton of the bull they were pre-serving. Near the carcass Heller trapped an old male leopard, a savage beast; its skin was in fine shape, but it was not fat, and weighed just one hundred pounds. Now we all joined, and shifted camp to a point eight or nine miles distant from Meru boma, and fifteen hundred feet lower among the foot-hills. It was much hotter at this lower level; palms were among the trees that bordered the streams. On the day we shifted camp Tarlton and I rode in advance to look for elephants, followed by our gun-bearers and half a dozen wild Meru hunters, each carrying a spear or a bow and arrows. When we reached the hunting grounds, open country with groves of trees and patches of jungle, the Meru went off in every direction to find elephant. We waited their return under a tree, by a big stretch of cultivated ground. The region was well peopled, and all the way down the path had led between fields, which the Meru women were tilling with their adze-like hoes, and banana plantations, where among the bananas other trees had been planted, and the yam vines trained up their trunks. These cool, shady banana plantations, fenced in with tall hedges and bordered by rapid brooks, were really very attractive. Among them were scattered villages of conical thatched huts, and level places plastered with cow dung on which the grain was threshed; it was then stored in huts raised on posts. There were herds of cattle, and flocks of sheep and goats; and among the burdens the women bore we often saw huge bottles of milk. In the shambas there were platforms, and sometimes regular thatched huts, placed in the trees; these were for the watchers, who were to keep the elephants out of the shambas at night. Some of the natives wore girdles of banana leaves, looking, as Kermit said, much like the pictures of savages in Sunday-school books.

Early in the afternoon some of the scouts returned with news that three bull elephants were in a piece of forest a couple of miles distant, and thither we went. It was an open grove of heavy thorn timber beside a strip of swamp; among the trees the grass grew tall, and there were many thickets of abutilon, a flowering shrub a dozen feet high. On this the elephant were feeding. Tarlton's favorite sport was lion hunting, but he was also a first-class elephant hunter, and he brought me up to these bulls in fine style. Although only three hundred yards away, it took us two hours to get close to them. Tarlton and the "shenzis"—wild natives, called in Swahili (a kind of African chinook) "washenzi"—who were with us, climbed tree after tree, first to place the elephants, and then to see if they carried ivory heavy enough to warrant my shooting them. At last Tarlton brought me to within fifty yards of them. Two were feeding in bush which hid them from view, and the third stood between, facing us. We could only see the top of his head and back, and not his tusks, and could not tell whether he was worth shooting. Much puzzled, we stood where we were, peering anxiously at the huge, half-hidden game. Suddenly there was a slight eddy in the wind, up went the elephant's trunk, twisting to and fro in the air; evidently he could not catch a clear scent; but in another moment we saw the three great dark forms moving gently off through the bush. As rapidly as possible, following the trails already trampled by the elephants, we walked forward, and after a hundred yards Tarlton pointed to a big bull with good tusks standing motionless behind some small trees seventy yards distant. As I aimed at his head he started to move off; the first bullet from the heavy Holland brought him to his knees, and as he rose I knocked him flat with the second. He struggled to rise; but, both firing, we kept him down; and I finished him with a bullet in the brain from the little Springfield. Although rather younger than either of the bulls I had already shot, it was even larger. In its stomach were beans from the shambas, abutilon tips, and bark, and especially the twigs, leaves, and white blossoms of the smaller shrub. The tusks weighed a little over a hundred pounds the pair.

We still needed a cow for the museum; and a couple of days later, at noon, a party of natives brought in word that they had seen two cows in a spot five miles away. Piloted by a naked spearman, whose hair was done into a cue, we rode toward the place. For most of the distance we followed old elephant trails, in some places mere tracks beaten down through stiff grass which stood above the head of a man on horseback, in other places paths rutted deep into the earth. We crossed a river, where monkeys chattered among the tree tops. On an open plain we saw a rhinoceros cow trotting off with her calf. At last we came to a hill-top with, on the summit, a noble fig-tree, whose giant limbs were stretched over the palms that clustered beneath. Here we left our horses and went forward on foot, crossing a palm-fringed stream in a little valley. From the next rise we saw the backs of the elephants as they stood in a slight valley, where the rank grass grew ten or twelve feet high. It was some time before we could see the ivory so as to be sure of exactly what we were shooting. Then the biggest cow began to move slowly forward, and we walked nearly parallel to her, along an elephant trail, until from a slight knoll I got a clear view of her at a distance of eighty yards. As she walked leisurely along, almost broadside to me, I fired the right barrel of the Holland into her head, knocking her flat down with the shock; and when she rose I put a bullet from the left barrel through her heart, again knocking her completely off her feet; and this time she fell permanently. She was a very old cow, and her ivory was rather better than in the average of her sex in this neighborhood, the tusks weighing about eighteen pounds apiece. She had been ravaging the shambas over night—which accounted in part for the natives being so eager to show her to me—and in addition to leaves and grass, her stomach contained quantities of beans. There was a young one—just out of calfhood, and quite able to take care of itself—with her; it ran off as soon as the mother fell.

Early next morning Cuninghame and Heller shifted part of the safari to the stream near where the dead elephant lay, intending to spend the following three days in taking off and preparing the skin. Meanwhile Tarlton, Kermit, and I were to try our luck in a short hunt on the other side of Meru boma, at a little crater lake called Lake Ingouga. We could not get an early start, and reached Meru too late to push on to the lake the same day.

The following morning we marched to the lake in two hours and a half. We spent an hour in crossing a broad tongue of woodland that stretched down from the wonderful mountain forest lying higher on the slopes. The trail was blind in many places because elephant paths of every age continually led along and across it, some of them being much better marked than the trail itself, as it twisted through the sun-flecked shadows underneath the great trees. Then we came out on high downs, covered with tall grass and littered with volcanic stones; and broken by ravines which were choked with dense underbrush. There were high hills, and to the left of the downs, toward Kenia, these were clad in forest. We pitched our tents on a steep cliff overlooking the crater lake—or pond, as it might more properly be called. It was bordered with sedge, and through the water-lilies on its surface we saw the reflection of the new moon after nightfall. Here and there thick forest came down to the brink, and through this, on opposite sides of the pond, deeply worn elephant paths, evidently travelled for ages, wound down to the water.

That evening we hunted for bushbuck, but saw none. While sitting on a hillock at dusk, watching for game, a rhino trotted up to inspect us, with ears cocked forward and tail erect. A rhino always has something comic about it, like a pig, formidable though it at times is. This one carried a poor horn, and therefore we were pleased when at last it trotted off without obliging us to shoot it. We saw new kinds of whydah birds, one with a yellow breast, one with white in its tail; at this altitude the cocks were still in full plumage, although it was just past the middle of September; whereas at Naivasha they had begun to lose their long tail feathers nearly two months previously.

On returning to camp we received a note from Cuninghame saying that Heller had been taken seriously sick, and Tarlton had to go to them. This left Kermit and me to take our two days' hunt together.

One day we got nothing. We saw game on the open downs, but it was too wary, and though we got within twenty-five yards of eland in thick cover, we could only make out a cow, and she took fright and ran without our ever getting a glimpse of the bull that was with her. Late in the afternoon we saw an elephant a mile and a half away, crossing a corner of the open downs. We followed its trail until the light grew too dim for shooting, but never overtook it, although at the last we could hear it ahead of us breaking the branches; and we made our way back to camp through the darkness.

The other day made amends. It was Kermit's turn to shoot an elephant, and mine to shoot a rhinoceros; and each of us was to act as the backing gun for the other. In the forenoon, we saw a bull rhino with a good horn walking over the open downs. A convenient hill enabled us to cut him off without difficulty, and from its summit we killed him at the base, fifty or sixty yards off. His front horn was nearly twenty-nine inches long; but though he was an old bull, his total length, from tip of nose to tip of tail, was only twelve feet, and he was, I should guess, not more than two-thirds the bulk of the big bull I killed in the Sotik.

We rested for an hour or two at noon, under the shade of a very old tree with glossy leaves, and orchids growing on its gnarled, hoary limbs, while the unsaddled horses grazed, and the gun-bearers slept near by, the cool mountain air, though this was midday under the equator, making them prefer the sunlight to the shade. When we moved on it was through a sea of bush ten or fifteen feet high, dotted here and there with trees; and riddled in every direction by the trails of elephant, rhinoceros, and buffalo. Each of these animals frequents certain kinds of country to which the other two rarely or never penetrate; but here they all three found ground to their liking. Except along their winding trails, which were tunnels where the jungle was tall, it would have been practically impossible to traverse the thick and matted cover in which they had made their abode.

We could not tell what moment we might find ourselves face to face with some big beast at such close quarters as to insure a charge, and we moved in cautious silence, our rifles in our hands. Rhinoceros were especially plentiful, and we continually came across not only their tracks, but the dusty wallows in which they rolled, and where they came to deposit their dung. The fresh sign of elephant, however, distracted our attention from the lesser game, and we followed the big footprints eagerly, now losing the trail, now finding it again. At last near a clump of big trees we caught sight of three huge, dark bodies ahead of us. The wind was right, and we stole toward them, Kermit leading, and I immediately behind. Through the tangled branches their shapes loomed in vague outline; but we saw that one had a pair of long tusks, and our gun-bearers unanimously pronounced it a big bull, with good ivory. A few more steps gave Kermit a chance at its head, at about sixty yards, and with a bullet from his .405 Winchester he floored the mighty beast. I rose, and we both fired in unison, bringing it down again; but as we came up it struggled to get on its feet, roaring savagely, and once more we both fired together. This finished it. We were disappointed at finding that it was not a bull; but it was a large cow, with tusks over five feet long—a very unusual length for a cow—one weighing twenty-five, and the other twenty-two pounds.

Our experience had convinced us that both the Winchester .405, and the Springfield .300 would do good work with elephants; although I kept to my belief that, for such very heavy game, my Holland .500–.450 was an even better weapon.

Not far from where this elephant fell Tarlton had, the year before, witnessed an interesting incident. He was watching a small herd of elephants, cows and calves, which were in the open, when he saw them begin to grow uneasy. Then, with a shrill trumpet, a cow approached a bush, out of which bounded a big lion. Instantly all the cows charged him, and he fled as fast as his legs could carry him for the forest, two hundred yards distant. He just managed to reach the cover in safety; and then the infuriated cows, in their anger at his escape, demolished the forest for several rods in every direction.

PART II

The Olden Days

The Forest and the Steppe

IVAN TURGENEV

And slowly something began to draw him
Back to the country, to the garden dark,
Where lime-trees are so huge, so full of shade,
And lilies of the valley, sweet as maids,
Where rounded willows o'er the water's edge
Lean from the dyke in rows, and where the oak
Sturdily grows above the sturdy field,
Amid the smell of hemp and nettles rank. . . .
There, there, in meadows stretching wide,
Where rich and black as velvet is the earth,
Where the sweet rye, far as the eye can see,
Moves noiselessly in tender, billowing waves,
And where the heavy golden light is shed
From out of rounded, white, transparent clouds:
There it is good. . . .

(From a poem consigned to the flames)

The reader is, very likely, already weary of my sketches: I hasten to reassure him by promising to confine myself to the fragments already printed; but I cannot refrain from saying a few words at parting about a hunter's life.

Hunting with a dog and a gun is delightful in itself, *für sich*, as they used to say in old days; but let us suppose you were not born a hunter, but are fond of nature and freedom all the same; you cannot then help envying us hunters. . . . Listen.

Do you know, for instance, the delight of settling off before daybreak in spring? You come out on to the steps. . . . In the dark-grey sky stars are twinkling here and there; a damp breeze in faint gusts flies to meet you now and then; there is heard the secret, vague whispering of the night; the trees faintly rustle, wrapt in darkness. And now they put a rug in the cart, and lay a box with the samovar at your feet. The trace-horses move restlessly, snort, and daintily paw the ground; a couple of white geese, only just awake, waddle slowly and silently across the road. On the other side of the hedge, in the garden, the watchman is snoring peacefully; every sound seems to stand still in the frozen air—suspended, not moving. You take your seat; the horses start at once; the cart rolls off with a loud rumble. You ride—ride past the church, downhill to the right, across the dyke. . . . The pond is just beginning to be covered with mist. You are rather chilly; you cover your face with the collar of your fur cloak; you doze. The horses' hoofs splash sonorously through the puddles; the coachman begins to whistle. But by now you have driven over four versts . . . the rim of the sky flushes crimson; the jackdaws are heard, fluttering clumsily in the birch-trees; sparrows are twittering about the dark hayricks. The air is clearer, the road more distinct, the sky brightens, the clouds look whiter, and the fields look greener. In the huts there is the red light of flaming chips; from behind gates comes the sound of sleepy voices. And meanwhile the glow of dawn is beginning; already streaks of gold are stretching across the sky; mists are gathering in clouds over the ravines; the larks are singing musically; the breeze that ushers in the dawn is blowing; and slowly the purple sun floats upward. There is a perfect flood of light; your heart is fluttering like a bird. Everything is fresh, gay, delightful! One can see a long way all round. That way, beyond the copse, a village; there, further, another, with a white church, and there a birch-wood on the hill; behind it the marsh, for which you are bound . . . Quicker, horses, quicker! Forward at a good trot! . . . There are three versts to go—not more. The sun mounts swiftly higher; the sky is clear. It will be a glorious day. A herd of cattle comes straggling from the village to meet you. You go up the hill. . . . What a view! the river winds for ten versts, dimly blue through the mist; beyond it meadows of watery green; beyond the meadows sloping hills; in the distance the plovers are wheeling with loud cries above the marsh; through the moist brilliance suffused in the air the distance stands out clearly . . . not as in the summer. How freely one drinks in the air, how quickly the limbs move, how strong is the whole man, clasped in the fresh breath of spring! . . .

And a summer morning—a morning in July! Who but the hunter knows how soothing it is to wander at daybreak among the underwoods? The print of your feet lies in a green line on the grass, white with dew. You part the drenched bushes; you are met by a rush of the warm fragrance stored up in the night; the air is saturated with the fresh bitterness of wormwood, the honey sweetness of buckwheat and clover; in the distance an oak wood stands like a wall, and glows and glistens in the sun; it is still fresh, but already the approach of heat is felt. The head is faint and dizzy from the excess of sweet scents. The copse stretches on endlessly. Only in places there are yellow glimpses in the distance of ripening rye, and narrow streaks of red buckwheat. Then there is the creak of cart wheels; a peasant makes his way among the bushes at a walking pace, and sets his horse in the shade before the heat of the day. You greet him, and turn away; the musical swish of the scythe is heard behind you. The sun rises higher and higher. The grass is speedily dry. And now it is quite sultry. One hour passes, another. . . . The sky grows dark over the horizon; the still air is baked with prickly heat. "Where can one get a drink here, brother?" you inquire of the mower. "Yonder, in the ravine's a well." Through the thick hazel bushes, tangled by the clinging grass, you drop down to the bottom of the ravine. Right under the cliff a little spring is hidden; an oak bush greedily spreads out its twigs like great fingers over the water; great silvery bubbles rise trembling from the bottom, covered with fine velvety moss. You fling yourself on the ground, you drink, but you are too lazy to stir. You are in the shade, you drink in the damp fragrance, you take your ease, while the bushes face you, glowing and, as it were, turning yellow in the sun. But what is that? There is a sudden flying gust of wind; the air is astir all about you: was not that thunder? Is it the heat thickening? Is a storm coming on? . . . And now there is a faint flash of lightning. Yes, there will be a storm! The sun is still blazing; you can still go on hunting. But the storm-cloud grows; its front edge, drawn out like a long sleeve, bends over into an arch. Make haste! over there you think you catch sight of a hay-barn . . . make haste! . . . You run there, go in. . . . What rain! What flashes of lightning! The water drips in through some hole in the thatch-roof on to the sweet-smelling hay. But now the sun is shining bright again. The storm is over; you come out. My God, the joyous sparkle of everything! The fresh, limpid air, the scent of raspberries and mushrooms! And then the evening comes on. There is the blaze of fire glowing and covering half the sky. The sun sets; the air near you has a peculiar transparency as of crystal; over the distance lies a soft, warm-looking haze; with the dew a crimson light is shed on the fields, lately plunged in floods of limpid gold; from trees and bushes and high stacks of hay run long shadows. The sun has set; a star gleams and quivers in the fiery sea of the sunset; and now it pales; the sky grows blue; the separate shadows vanish; the air is plunged in darkness. It is time to turn homewards to the village, to the hut, where you will stay the night. Shouldering your gun, you move briskly, in spite of fatigue. Meanwhile, the night comes on: now you cannot see twenty paces from you; the dogs show faintly white in the dark. Over there, above the black bushes, there is a vague brightness on the horizon. What is it?—a fire? . . . No, it is the moon rising. And away below, to the right, the village lights are twinkling already. And here at last is your hut. Through the tiny window you see a table, with a white cloth, a candle burning, supper. . . .

Another time you order the racing droshky to be got out, and set off to the forest to shoot woodcock. It is pleasant making your way along the narrow path between two high walls of rye. The ears softly strike you in the face; the corn-flowers cling round your legs; the quails call around; the horse moves along at a lazy trot. And here is the forest, all shade and silence. Graceful aspens rustle high above you; the long hanging branches of the birches scarcely stir; a mighty oak stands like a champion beside a lovely lime-tree. You go along the green path, streaked with shade; great yellow flies stay suspended, motionless, in the sunny air, and suddenly dart away; midges hover in a cloud, bright in the shade, dark in the sun; the birds are singing peacefully; the golden little voice of the warbler sings of innocent, babbling joyousness, in sweet accord with the scent of the lilies of the valley. Further, further, deeper into the forest . . .

the forest grows more dense. . . . An unutterable stillness falls upon the soul within; without, too, all is still and dreamy. But now a wind has sprung up, and the tree-tops are booming like falling waves. Here and there, through last year's brown leaves, grow tall grasses; mushrooms stand apart under their wide-brimmed hats. All at once a hare skips out; the dog scurries after it with a resounding bark. . . .

And how fair is this same forest in late autumn, when the snipe are on the wing! They do not keep in the heart of the forest; one must look for them along the outskirts. There is no wind, and no sun, no light, no shade, no movement, no sound; the autumn perfume, like the perfume of wine, is diffused in the soft air; a delicate haze hangs over the yellow fields in the distance. The still sky is a peacefully untroubled white through the bare brown branches; in parts, on the limes, hang the last golden leaves. The damp earth is elastic under your feet; the high dry blades of grass do not stir; long threads lie shining on the blanched turf, white with dew. You breathe tranquilly; but there is a strange tremor in the soul. You walk along the forest's edge, look after your dog, and meanwhile loved forms, loved faces, dead and living, come to your mind; long, long slumbering impressions unexpectedly awaken; the fancy darts off and soars like a bird; and all moves so clearly and stands out before your eyes. The heart at one time throbs and beats, plunging passionately forward; at another it is drowned beyond recall in memories. Your whole life, as it were, unrolls lightly and rapidly before you; a man at such times possesses all his past all his feelings and his powers—all his soul; and there is nothing around to hinder him—no sun, no wind no sound. . . .

And a clear, rather cold autumn day, with a frost in the morning, when the birch, all golden like some tree in a fairy-tale, stands out picturesquely against the pale-blue sky; when the sun, standing low in the sky, does not warm, but shines more brightly than in summer; the small aspen copse is all a-sparkle through and through, as though it were glad and at ease in its nakedness; the hoar-frost is still white at the bottom of the hollows; while a fresh wind softly stirs up and drives before it the falling, crumpled leaves; when blue ripples whisk gladly along the river, lifting rhythmically the scattered geese and ducks; in the distance the mill creaks, half hidden by the willows; and with changing colours in the clear air the pigeons wheel in swift circles above it.

Sweet, too, are dull days in summer, though the hunters do not like them. On such days one can't shoot the bird that flutters up from under your very feet and vanishes at once in the whitish dark of the hanging fog. But how peaceful, how unutterably peaceful it is everywhere! Everything is awake, and everything is hushed. You pass by a tree: it does not stir a leaf; it is musing in repose. Through the thin steamy mist, evenly diffused in the air, there is a long streak of black before you. You take it for a neighbouring copse close at hand; you go up—the copse is transformed into a high row of wormwood in the boundary-ditch. Above you, around you, on all sides—mist. . . . But now a breeze is faintly astir; a patch of pale-blue sky peeps dimly out; through the thinning, as it were, steaming mist, a ray of golden-yellow sunshine breaks out suddenly, flows in a long stream, strikes on the fields and in the copse—and now everything is overcast again. For long this struggle is drawn out, but how unutterably brilliant and magnificent the day becomes when at last light triumphs and the last waves of the warmed mist here unroll and are drawn out over the plains, there wind away and vanish into the deep, softly shining heights.

Again you set off into outlying country, to the steppe. For some ten versts you make your way over cross-roads, and here at last is the highroad. Past endless trains of wagons, past wayside taverns, with the hissing samovar under a shed, wide-open gates and a well, from one hamlet to another; across endless fields, alongside green hempfields, a long, long time you drive. The magpies flutter from willow to willow; peasant women with long rakes in their hands wander in the fields; a man in a threadbare nankin overcoat, with a wicker pannier over his shoulder, trudges along with weary step; a heavy country coach, harnessed with six tall, broken-winded horses, rolls to meet you. The corner of a cushion is sticking out of a window, and on a sack up behind, hanging on to a string, perches a groom in a fur cloak, splashed with mud to his very eyebrows. And here is the little district town with its crooked little wooden houses, its endless fences, its empty stone shops, its old-fashioned bridge over a deep ravine. On, on! . . . The steppe country is reached at last. You look from a hill-top; what a view! Round low hills, tilled and sown to their very tops, are seen in broad undulations; ravines, overgrown with bushes, wind coiling among them; small copses are scattered like oblong islands; from village to village run narrow paths; churches stand out white; between willow is bushes glimmers a little river, in four places dammed up by dykes; far off, in a field, in a line, an old manor house, with its outhouses, orchard, and threshing-floor, huddles close up to a small pond. But on, on you go. The hills are smaller and ever smaller; there is scarcely a tree to be seen. Here it is at last—the boundless, untrodden steppe!

And on a winter day to walk over the high snowdrifts after hares; to breathe the keen frosty air, while half-closing the eyes involuntarily at the fine blinding sparkle of the soft snow; to admire the emerald sky above the reddish forest! . . . And the first spring day when everything is shining, and breaking up, when across the heavy streams, from the melting snow, there is already the scent of the thawing earth; when on the bare thawed places, under the slanting sunshine, the larks are singing confidingly, and, with glad splash and roar, the torrents roll from ravine to ravine.

But it is time to end. By the way, I have spoken of spring: in spring it is easy to part; in spring even the happy are drawn away to the distance. . . . Farewell, reader! I wish you unbroken prosperity.

Sporting Adventures in the Northern Seas

JAMES LAMONT, ESQ., F.G.S.

Background

First Trip to Spitzbergen in 1858.—Find Schooner Yacht and light Gigs unsuitable.—Determine to go again in 1859.—Hire a suitable Vessel and Crew, and build two Boats.—Lord David Kennedy agrees to accompany me.—Contested Election delays our starting.—Result of Poll unfortunate alike for Walruses and Constituency.—Preliminary Trip to Guernsey.—Sail from Leith.—Steamer a little out in her Reckoning.—Dreadful Famine in Lerwick.—Gale.—Namsen Fiord and River.—Salmon Fishing.—Terry's Breech-loading Rifles.

In August, 1858, while cruising in my yacht the "Ginevra," of 142 tons, on the coast of Norway, I was induced, by the accounts I received of reindeer and other game to be met with in Spitzbergen, to make a trip across from Hammerfest to that country. It being late in the season before we got there, our stay was very short, and our sport was limited to killing a few reindeer, seals, and Brent geese, and to assisting in the harpooning of one or two walruses, in the boats of a sealing brig, which we fell in with amongst the ice. I however saw enough of Spitzbergen to convince me that wonderful sport, and of a most original description, was to be obtained there by anyone who would go at the proper season, with a suitably equipped vessel and proper boats, manned by a crew of men accustomed to the ice and to the pursuit of the walrus and the seal.

Although I have the honour to append the letters F.G.S. to my name, I make no pretensions to the character of a scientific geologist, but I was also very much impressed with the interesting field Spitzbergen affords to a votary of that noble science, and particularly with the strong evidence to be met with in support of the theory of the gradual upheaval of the land in that remote part of the world, and I was anxious to investigate further this interesting phenomenon.

I perceived on this occasion that nothing could be more utterly inapplicable for ice-navigation than a long fore-and-aft rigged schooner yacht, as in threading the intricate mazes of the ice there was no possibility of stopping her "way" to avoid collisions, as is done by backing the topsails of a square-rigged vessel, and her frail planking and thin copper were exposed to constant destruction from the ice. The dandified "ultramarine blue" painted gigs were also totally unsuited for the rough work of pushing in amongst the ice in pursuit of the seal and the walrus; indeed, it was very fortunate for us that we did not succeed in harpooning one of the latter mighty amphibiæ from the yacht's boats, for my subsequent experience of the strength and ferocity of these animals leads me to believe that he would infallibly have pulled us all to the bottom of the sea.

In the spring of 1859, therefore, I made up my mind to have another trip to Spitzbergen, and to go about it in a more systematic way; so early in the season I wrote to a gentleman in Hammerfest, who had been good enough to accompany me on my previous trip as an amateur pilot, requesting him to hire for me a small, stout *jagt*,* suitably planked, and provided with a square topsail and everything requisite for a summer's campaign against the feræ naturæ of the arctic regions; and including casks to stow their blubber in, as I expected to be reimbursed for at least a part of the heavy outlay these preparations entailed, by the proceeds of skins and oil. I also ordered two suitable whale- (or rather walrus-) boats to be constructed in Hammerfest, of a size slightly larger than those commonly used, so as to admit of an amateur sitting comfortably in the stern without his having necessarily to act as one of the boat's crew; and, finally, I desired my agent to engage two skilful harpooners, and men enough to man the boats and navigate the *jagt*—English sailors being almost as useless as the boats for this description of work.

On mentioning my projected expedition to a friend, renowned as a sportsman with the rifle and the spear on the plains of India, and telling him of the sport I expected amongst the icebergs of the North, he at once agreed to join me, and entered with heart and purse into the arrangements; and here let me state that, during ten years I have spent in travelling in different parts of the world, I have never fallen in with a pleasanter and more unselfish companion, or a keener and a braver sportsman, than Lord David Kennedy.

When we were nearly ready to start, and I was superintending the outfitting of my yacht at Southampton, I was most unexpectedly requested by the Liberal party of a Scottish county to become their candidate in the general election about to take place; so deeming it my duty to sacrifice my amusement to my country's good, I stayed the preparations for sea, and for the ten following days I was engaged in all the excitement of an electoral contest. The result, by a very narrow majority, proved unfortunate for the walruses, although perhaps the cynical reader may be disposed to add, "fortunate for the constituency," and I was once more at liberty to proceed on my intended voyage.

With the view of disposing of these interesting animals (captured young bears), I entered into correspondence with nearly every wild-beast-keeper and secretary of Zoological Gardens in the United Kingdom, but *as usual* the "British market was quite overstocked." There was a "glut" of bears in fact. It then occurred to me that I could not put them to better account than by turning them out in a large wood at home, and inviting my friends and neighbours to enjoy the Scandinavian diversion of a *skall;* but the probable difficulty of obtaining *beaters* occurred to me as *one* objection, and the possibility of being brought in for heavy *game damages* as *another;* so eventually I disposed of them to M. le Directeur of the Jardin des Plantes, in Paris, and I wish his Imperial Majesty joy of his purchase. I had the satisfaction of seeing them in that establishment some months later, considerably grown, but their naturally amiable

---

*A small sloop without a topmast; a rig very general amongst the Scandinavian coasters.

dispositions not improved by their being confined in one of the warm, dry dens used for the tropical Carnivoræ.

They did *not*, like the lion in the story, recognise and welcome their old shipmate with transports of joy.

In conclusion, I beg to direct attention to the following facsimile of an engraving executed by Lord David Kennedy on one of the cabin-beams of the "Anna Louisa," as it contains a concise summary of our game-list.

LORD DAVID KENNEDY
and JAMES LAMONT
Hired this Sloop
ANNA LOUISA not A 1.
In the Summer of the Year 1859
And killed in SPITZBERGEN
46 WALRUSES
88 SEALS
8 POLAR BEARS
1 WHITE WHALE
61 REIN-DEER
TOTAL, 204 HEAD.

N.B. In addition to the above we sank and lost about 20 Walruses and 40 Seals.

No one who has not tried it will readily believe how extremely difficult it is to shoot an old bull-walrus clean dead. The front or sides of his head may be knocked all to pieces with bullets, and the animal yet have sense and strength sufficient left him to enable him to swim and dive out of reach. If he is lying on his side, with his back turned to his assailant, it is easy enough, as the brain is then quite exposed, and the crown of the head is easily penetrated; but one rarely gets the walrus in that position, and when it so happens, it is generally better policy to harpoon him without shooting.

By firing at an old bull directly facing you, it is almost impossible to kill him, but if *half-front* to you, a shot just above the eye may prove fatal. If sideways, he can only be killed by aiming about six inches behind the eye, and about one-fourth of the apparent depth of his head from the top; but the eye, of course, cannot be seen unless the animal is very close to you, and the difficulty is enormously increased by the back of the head being so embedded in fat, as to appear as if it were part of the neck.

If you hit him much below a certain part of the head you strike the jaw-joint, which is about the strongest part of the whole cranium. A leaden bullet striking there, or on the front of the head, is flattened like a piece of putty, without doing much injury to the walrus; and we sometimes found that even our hardened bullets, propelled by five drachms of powder, were broken into little pieces, against the rocky crania of these animals.

Walrus-tusks are composed of very hard, dense, and white ivory. Their small size rendering them inapplicable for many ivory manufactures, they do not command nearly the price of elephant ivory, but they are in high repute for the manufacture of false teeth, and are also made into chessmen, umbrella-handles, whistles, and other small articles.

The upper lip of the walrus is thickly set with strong, transparent, bristly hairs, about six inches long, and as thick as a crow-quill; and this terrific moustache, together with his long white tusks, and fierce-looking, bloodshot eyes, gives *Rosmarus trichecus* altogether a most unearthly and demoniacal appearance as he rears his head above the waves. I think it not unlikely that the old fable of the mermaid may have been originated by their grim resemblance to the head of a human being when in this position.

There is one very striking peculiarity connected with the osteological structure of the walrus, which I do not recollect to have observed a mention of in any of the printed accounts of the animal. I dare not amplify this allusion, but I fancied that I should be the first to direct the attention of scientific men to the circumstance. On mentioning it, however, to my friend Professor M——, I found that he was quite aware of the peculiarity in question, and that it is well known to the students of comparative anatomy.

The cook went out this morning to officiate as harpooner *pro tempore*, and while darting the harpoon at a seal which Lord David had wounded, he threw his watch into the sea along with the weapon. The "Doctor" was so thunderstruck by this overwhelming misfortune, that he stood on the ice gazing into the depths of the sea, as if he expected the watch to float up again. The seal came up again (although the watch did not), and the cook so far recovered his presence of mind as to *spit* him this time, and then, to the great amusement of Lord David and the crew, he began to bewail the loss of his watch, which had been "such a good one, and had cost him no less than six dollars"; nor was he to be comforted, until Kennedy consoled him by the promise of another of equal value.

There is plenty of fine ice in sight to-day, but we have unknowingly drifted too far from the coast, where the water is too deep for walruses; as these animals cannot descend in more than about twenty-five fathoms, and they prefer fifteen or even ten fathoms. We discovered our mistake by getting a glimpse of the mountains of Hope Island, and immediately stood in to the westward towards the shore of Spitzbergen, now distant about twenty-five miles.

The Hunt is On

July, 1859—At 3 a.m. this morning we were aroused by the cheering cry of "Hvalruus paa Ysen" (walruses on the ice). We both got up immediately, and from the deck a curious and exciting spectacle met our admiring gaze! Four large flat icebergs were so densely packed with walruses that they were sunk almost awash with the water, and had the appearance of being solid *islands of walrus!*

The monsters lay with their heads reclining on one another's backs and sterns, just as I have seen rhinoceroses lying asleep in the African forests; or, to use a more familiar simile, like a lot of fat hogs in a British straw-yard. I should think there were about eighty or one hundred on the ice, and many more swam grunting and spouting around, and tried to clamber up amongst their friends, who, like surly people in a full omnibus, grunted at them angrily, as if to say "Confound you, don't you see that we are full." There were plenty more good flat icebergs about, but they always seem to like being packed as closely as possible for mutual warmth. These four islands were several hundred yards apart, and after feasting our eyes for a little on the glorious sight, we resolved to take them in succession, and not to fire at first, but the walruses had not been long enough on the ice to have got properly sleepy, and the discontented individuals in the water gave the rest the alarm, so that we only managed to secure four altogether.

Solomon, our untried harpooner, acquitted himself pretty tolerably on this his first fair trial, for he killed one out of the first herd, and two at a time out of the second, but on the latter occasion he as nearly as possible upset the boat by allowing one of the lines to run over the gunwale aft of the notches, at the bow: the boat most certainly would have been upset, had it not been that it was ballasted with the blubber of the one already killed; as it was, she was half filled with water, and Lord David and the crew were on the point of jumping out, when fortunately she righted again.

This herd consisted chiefly of cows and young bulls, and they then dispersed or got out of reach amongst the ice.

In the forenoon we discovered a huge bull, with fine tusks, by himself sound asleep on a small sloping piece of ice, and I went in Solomon's boat to attack him. The shape of the iceberg would not permit us to approach within stabbing distance of the ball, but as he was not more than five yards from the bow of the boat, I very foolishly did not fire, as I considered the harpoon a certainty, but to my utter disgust and astonishment, Solomon threw two harpoons one after the other, and missed the huge animal with both: the walrus awoke at the sound the second harpoon made on the ice, and was into the sea like a shot. The rest of the boat's crew were as much annoyed as myself, and anathematised the unhappy Solomon in every language spoken in Scandinavia. I believe I added some strongish expressions in English. We made up our minds to disrate Solomon if this occurs again, and to try another of the crew as harpooner instead of him.

14th.— North-east wind, thick fog, and hard frost, all the rigging encased with icicles. Hitherto all our skins, with the blubber attached, had been thrown into the hold "in bulk," but they have now accumulated so as to render it necessary that the blubber should be divided from the skins and stowed in the casks; we therefore take advantage of the fog to-day to perform this necessary, but unpleasant process; which is conducted as follows.

There is set up across the deck, immediately aft the hatchway, a sort of frame or stage of stout planks, about four feet high, and sloping down at an angle of about 60°, with the deck at the forward side: it is perpendicular aft, and at that side of it the two men who are to act as "Specksioneers" (blubber-cutters) take their stand, clad in oil-skin from top to toe, and armed with large knives, sharp as razors, and curved on the edge. The skins are then hoisted out of the hold and hung across the frame, two at a time, with the blubber side upmost; it is an operation requiring great dexterity to separate the fat from the skin, so as to remove the whole of it, and not to cut or shave the skin itself, but by a sort of *mowing* motion of the knife, which is held in both hands, from left to right, these men do it with great rapidity and neatness. As the blubber is peeled off it is divided into slabs of twenty or thirty pounds' weight each and thrown down the hatchway, where two men are ready to receive it and to slip it into the square bung holes of the casks; from its oleaginousness it soon finds its own level in the casks, and when full these arc fastened up. I ought to have mentioned that the skins of full grown walruses are always taken off the animal in two halves, being divided longitudinally down the back and the belly; the skins of calf walruses and seals are always left entire. Walrus hide is a valuable commodity, and sells for from two to four dollars per half skin, calves only counting for a half; it is principally exported to Russia and Sweden, where it is used to manufacture harness and sole leather; it is also twisted into tiller ropes, and is used for protecting the rigging of ships from chafing. In former times nearly all the rigging of vessels on the north coasts of Norway and Russia used to be composed of walrus skin.

When there is a superfluity of the article in the market I believe it is boiled into glue. It is from an inch to an inch and a half thick, very pliable in its green state, but slightly spongy, so that I should doubt the quality of the leather made from it.

The seal-skins mostly find their way to Scotland, where, I believe, they are made into what are known in the hosiers' shops as "dog-skin" and "Dundee kid" gloves. Their value in Hammerfest is from one to two dollars a skin.

The walrus has not nearly so much blubber, in proportion to his size, as the seal; thus a seal of 600 lbs. will carry 200 or 250 lbs. of fat; an ordinary walrus may weigh 2000 lbs., but his fat will not exceed that of the seal; a full sized old bull walrus must weigh, at least, 3000 lbs., and such a walrus will produce, if very fat, 650 lbs. of blubber, but seldom more than 500 lbs., which latter was, I think, about the maximum quantity yielded by the most obese of our victims. Neither does the fat of the walrus afford so fine an oil as that of the seal, but it is usual to mix them indiscriminately together, and the compound is always exported into Southern Europe under the name of seal-oil.

We begin to find some of these long, dreary, foggy days intolerably irksome, as our cabin is singularly ill-adapted for passing much idle time in; it is literally almost impossible either to sit, stand up, or lie down in it; it is only five feet high, except where a small dingy sky-light three feet square gives us the advantage of another foot; there is a "bunk" on each side of about 5½ × 2½—and one can hardly be said to be *lying down* in five and a half feet length; each bunk has a locker in front of it nine inches broad, and any one unfortunate enough to have to try, will find that any posture is preferable to *sitting* long on a locker nine inches in breadth, with a perpendicular back. The cabin from end to end between these lockers is about 7 × 4, but nearly half of this length is occupied by the angular projections forming the counter of the vessel, over which is the table, so that the space available for moving about, washing, and dressing, &c., is exactly four feet square. Behind the after end of each bunk is a small open space filled by a barrel of biscuits, jar of butter, canisters of tea, coffee, and sugar, magazine of powder, bags of shot, &c. &c. Our guns, pouches, and spare clothes hang on nails inside the bed places and in the corners. Aft amidships, in a slip of leather nailed to the wall, hangs a bottle of brandy—the sole stimulant we indulge in; and side by side with the more generous fluid is a bottle of chloride of lime with the cork out, for the purpose of mollifying, in some measure, the awful effluvium caused by the commingling of putrid walrus oil and bilge water—vain hope! Add to these little *agrémens* the fact that the thermometer averages 40° in the cabin, and I think it will be generally conceded that we are paying pretty clear for the pleasure of hunting walruses in the Arctic seas. I must not omit to mention that the cabin has *two* redeeming points, viz. there are no vermin, and the wood of which the beams and boarding is composed is of a very light and soft description, eminently adapted for "whittling" and engraving, and in these intellectual and scientific occupations we find a great resource. As for reading, it is next to impossible, for I defy anybody to read long sitting on a locker nine inches broad; also the bunks are too dark, and if we try to read in them, we generally go to sleep.

15th.—Wind round to the south-west, and mild. Summoned on deck at 5 a.m., a large herd of walruses being reported from the masthead. They were a long distance off, and were not visible from the deck; but, as it was dead calm, Isaac said we had better go up to them in the boats for fear of fog coming on again, or some other boats being before us; so we had our breakfast first, and then started with both boats full-manned. We had a pleasant row of four or five miles over calm water quite free of ice, and were cheered for the latter half of the distance by the sonorous bellowing and trumpeting of a vast number of walruses. We soon came in sight of a long line of low flat icebergs crowded with sea-horses. There were at least ten of these bergs so packed with the walruses that in some places they lay two-deep on the ice! There cannot have been less than 300 in sight at once; but they were very shy and restless, and, although we tried every troop in succession as carefully as possible, we did not succeed in getting within harpooning distance of a single walrus. Many of them were asleep; but there were always some moving about, who gave the alarm to their sleeping comrades by flapping them with their fore-feet, and one troop after another managed to scuffle into the sea always just a second or so in time to avoid the deadly harpoon. When there are so many together there is always a pretty fair chance of securing some by "jaging" them in the water, that is to say by perseveringly rowing after them as hard as possible, and keeping on in the same direction they appear to take when they dive; if there are calves in the herd they cannot go much faster than the boat, if so fast; also the calves must come up to breathe much more frequently than the old ones, and the whole herd generally accommodate their pace to that of the old cows with young ones. In all my sporting experience I never saw anything to equal the wild excitement of these hunts. Five pair of oars, pulled with utmost strength, make the boat seem to fly through the water, while, perhaps, a hundred walruses roaring, bellowing, blowing, snorting, and splashing, make an acre of the sea all in a foam before and around her. The harpooner stands with one foot on the thwart and the other on the front locker, with the line coiled in his right hand, and the long weapon in both hands ready balanced for a dart, while he shouts to the crew which direction to take, as he frequently, from standing upright in the boat, can see the walruses under water.

The herd generally keep close together, and the simultaneousness with which they dive and reappear again is remarkable—one moment you see a hundred grisly heads and long gleaming white tusks above the waves, they give one spout from their blow-holes, take one breath of fresh air, and the next moment you see a hundred brown hemispherical backs, the next a hundred pair of hind-flippers flourishing, and then they are all down. On, on, goes the boat as hard as ever we can pull the oars; up come the seahorses again, pretty close this time, and before they can draw breath the boat rushes into the midst of them: *whish!* goes the harpoon: *birr!* goes the line over the gunwale: and a luckless junger on whom Christian has kept his eye, is "fast!": his bereaved mother charges the boat instantly with flashing eyes and snorting with rage; she quickly receives a harpoon in the back and a bullet in the brains, and she hangs lifeless on the line: now the junger begins to utter his plaintive grunting bark, and fifty furious walruses are close round the boat in a few seconds, rearing up breast high in the water and snorting and blowing as if they would tear us all to pieces! Two of these auxiliaries are speedily harpooned in their turn, and the rest hang back a little, when as bad luck would have it, the junger gave up the ghost owing to the severity of his harpooning, and the others, no longer attracted by his cries, retire to a more prudent distance. But for the "untoward" and premature decease of the junger, the men tell me we should have had more walruses on our hands than we could manage. We now devote our attention to "polishing off" the two live walruses—well-sized young bulls—who are still towing the heavy boat with their two dead comrades attached as if she was behind a steam-tug, and struggling madly to drag us under the icebergs: a vigorous application of the lances soon settles the business, and we now with some difficulty tow our four dead victims to the nearest flat iceberg and fix the ice-anchor, by which, with the powerful aid of block-and-tackle, we haul them one by one on the ice and divest them of their spoils. Meantime Lord David's boat is carried past us at eight miles an hour in full tow of two enormous bulls, with his Lordship sitting in the stern like Neptune in his car, but holding in his hand, instead of the trident of the marine god, a much more effective weapon in the shape of a four-barrelled rifle.

While we were engaged in cutting up these walruses, there were at least fifty more surrounding the iceberg, snorting and bellowing, and rearing up in the water as if smelling the blood of their slaughtered friends and curious to see what we were doing to them now: they were so close that I might have shot a dozen of them, but as they would have been sure to sink before the boat could get to them, I was not so cruel as wantonly to take their lives. When the walruses were all skinned we followed the herd again with success, and when we left off, in consequence of dense fog suddenly coming on, we had secured nine altogether—a very fair morning's bag we thought.

The sloop by this time had got a breeze, and sailed up within fifty yards of us, which saved us a long row with our fatigued crews and heavy-laden boats. During this morning's proceedings, I realised the immense advantage of striking a junger first when practicable: this curious clannish practice of coming to assist a calf in distress, arises from their being in the habit of combining to resist the attacks of the Polar bear, which is said often to succeed in killing the walrus: if, however, Bruin, pressed by hunger and a tempting opportunity, is so ill-advised as to snap a calf, the whole herd come upon him, drag him under water, and tear him to pieces with their long sharp tusks. I am told this has been seen to occur, and I quite believe it.

The walrus is an inoffensive beast if let alone, but hunting them is far from being child's play, as the following sad story will show.

About ten days after the exciting *chasse* which I have just described, the skyppar of a small schooner, which was in sight, came on board to ask us for the loan of a gun, as he had broken all his, and he told us that a boat belonging to a sloop from Tromsöe had been upset two or three days before in our immediate vicinity, and one of the crew killed by a walrus. It seemed that the walrus, a large old bull, charged the boat, and the harpooner as usual received him with his lance full in the chest, but the shaft of the lance broke all to shivers, and the walrus, getting inside of it, threw himself on the gunwale of the boat and overset it in an instant. While the men were floundering in the water amongst their oars and tackle, the infuriated animal rushed in amongst them, and selecting the unlucky harpooner, who, I fancy had fallen next him, he tore him nearly into two halves with his tusks. The rest of the men saved themselves by clambering on to the ice until the other boat came to their assistance.

Upon another occasion, I made the acquaintance of the skyppar of a sloop, who had been seized by a bereaved cow-walrus, and by her dragged twice to the bottom of the sea; but without receiving any injury beyond being nearly drowned and having a deep scar ploughed in each side of his forehead by the tusks of the animal, which he thought did not wish to hurt him, but mistook him for her calf, as he floundered in the water.

Owing to the great coolness and expertness of the men following this pursuit, such mishaps are not of very frequent occurrence, but still a season seldom passes without two or three lives being lost one way or another.

16th.—Mem. "Johann" alias "Jack" to be second harpooner on trial, *vice* Solomon, superseded for incapacity: the latter bears his degradation with philosophy and equanimity worthy of his great namesake, and descends to the much less honourable position of line-holder; probably he is somewhat consoled for his loss of position by knowing that it will not affect his emoluments—having signed articles as harpooner at 20 dollars per mensem. To be a good harpooner requires great courage, activity, and presence of mind, and it is a common remark, that "not one man in a hundred is capable of ever becoming a good one." Jack has been six voyages to Spitzbergen, but has never acted as harpooner before; but being a cool, active, and energetic fellow, I think there is *the making* of one in him. Solomon never will be one as long as he lives.

Beautiful bright morning with west wind. We have beat back to the Thousand Islands during the night, as our people suppose that the great herds of walruses we saw have gone there. Ice very much dispersed since we were here before.

Dined upon stewed walrus veal—very good meat, and without the disagreeable fishy flavour of seal, but slightly insipid.

Saw no game all day, but one walrus in the water. Calm in the evening.

Catskill Mountains and the Region Around—Early Hunters and Their Adventures

REV. CHARLES ROCKWELL

The deep, dark, and widespread forests, the high, rough mountain cliffs, the wild ravines and caves of the Catskill Mountains, made them, from early times, a chosen and favorite resort of lynx, panther, wolves, bears, deer, and large and enormous snakes. A volume might be filled with the adventures of early hunters in this region, some of which I will here describe, as related to me by them and their children.

Among the most celebrated of these early hunters were the Piersons, of Kaatsban, the Hummels, of Blue Mountain, Benjamin Peck, of Palensville, and Frederick Sax, of Kiskatom, though he lived, in early life, near West Camp, in Saugerties. John Pierson would camp out alone, for two or three weeks at a time, on and near Roundtop, in Cairo, killing fifteen or twenty deer during the time. There was a large laurel swamp on the mountains, near the base of the South Mountain, where deer fed when snow was deep. Some would not eat their flesh when they fed on laurel, though others did. They were killed mostly from May or June until January. There was a great run or track for deer, near the upper end of the Cauterskill Clove, and along the ravine near the Falls, below the Laurel House. Hunters here, as elsewhere, had favorite stands, where they concealed themselves, and shot deer as they were driven past them by the dogs. Wolves used also to chase deer until they were overcome with fatigue, and then kill and eat them. Hence wolves and deer left this region about the same time, more than thirty years since, having from an early date been very numerous. The wolves were quite troublesome and destructive to domestic animals, so that it was often necessary closely to confine sheep, swine, and young cattle at night.

Benjamin Peck came to Palensville, from Litchfield, Connecticut, about the year 1796. He was brought up by his uncle, Paul Peck, who was a famous trapper and hunter, sometimes going as far as Canada in pursuit of wild animals, for the sake of their fur and skins. Benjamin Peck served in the army through all the Revolutionary War, having gone early to Boston, and was afterwards enlisted in the cavalry regiment of Colonel Sheldon, of Litchfield, and was with him on the Hudson River when Esopus was burned, our forces being then opposite the place, and wishing to cross over and relieve it, but they were prevented from doing so by two British ships of war, which were lying in the river. What he then saw and learned of the abundance of game in the mountains may have led him, at a later date, to remove here. From his son, of the same name, who came here with his father when seven years old, and is now living in Palensville, at the age of seventy-six, I learned the following facts:

The first year they were here Mr. Peck killed some seven or eight wolves, seventeen bears, and seventy-three deer, which he secured, besides others which were mortally wounded but fled beyond his reach. At first he practised what is called "still hunting," stealing on game unawares or watching for them where they passed along, without the aid of clogs. He soon procured a large and strong bear-trap with steel springs and sharp teeth like nails, with which he caught many bears, but did not use the log or fall-trap and cage, with which bears are still caught on the mountains. His steel trap he used without bait, in a narrow, rocky ravine, near the top of South Mountain, through which bears passed in coming down from the evergreen woods, near the summit of the mountain, where they had their dens, to the oak woods below, to feed on acorns. The rocky ravine through which the bears passed was so narrow that they could not well avoid getting in the trap.

One day while hunting north of the Clove, on the mountain, a deer came along heated and fatigued, pursued as he supposed by his dog; when, having shot it, and, as his custom was, having loaded his gun immediately, an immense wolf followed on the track of the deer, which he also shot. At another time Mr. Peck met a bear, with two cubs, which had seriously injured and driven off his dogs with the exception of one, which was very staunch and of an imported breed, which followed by scent, but more resembled a greyhound than a bloodhound. This dog he called away, when the bear made a rush upon him, when, waiting until she was about a foot from the muzzle of his gun, he shot her in the breast, and the ball passed through the whole length of her body, suddenly ending her days. Mr. Peck continued to hunt until he died, in Palensville, where his son now lives, in 1820, in the sixty-fourth year of his age.

Mr. Hezekiah Myers, aged ninety, hunted some in his early days, and was familiar with the hunting adventures of others. He was once with a hunting party on the mountains when the dogs drove a bear so near him that he could have struck him with an axe which he had in his hand; but as he had, besides this, only a pistol, he feared to strike him, though many of the old bear-hunters did not shrink from fighting a bear with an axe. To strike and wound a bear, without killing him, is, however, dangerous, as when thus enraged they are very furious. Nor is it safe to wait until a bear is as near as was the one shot by Mr. Peck, spoken of above; for should the gun miss fire, or only wound the bear, he might prove a troublesome neighbor.

Mr. William Travis, aged seventy-eight, a neighbor of Mr. Myers in Palensville, near the Clove, when sixteen years old, watched at night for a bear in a cornfield a little north of where Mr. Charles Teal now lives. He had done much injury to all the fields in the neighborhood; and hence all the neighbors watched in their respective fields at the same time, as he did not visit the same field two nights in succession. Near morning Mr. Travis heard a bear in the bushes, then he entered the field, and, rising up erect, snuffed the air to learn if any danger was near, and, bringing his paws together, drew before him the corn of two hills, one on each side of him, and began to eat. Mr. Travis rose twice before he dared to fire; but the third time shot him in the breast, when he turned back over the fence, groaning like a man. A Dutchman who was near him asleep, rose suddenly, sadly frightened, made a fearful floundering on the ground, declaring that he had shot a black man. Soon guns were heard in all directions, as the neighbors hastened where the first shot was heard. The bear, a large one was found in the morning in the mud, in the woods near by, where he had gone to check the flow of blood. Though badly wounded, it required several shots to kill him.

When Mr. Travis was living for a time in Lexington, west of the mountains, a neighbor and friend of his went to Shandaken, some twenty miles south, to keep school. One day, as some of his pupils went to drive the cows home from pasture, they found a large bear seated on the carcase of one of the cows, which he had killed, taking his supper from her flesh. The children gave the alarm, when the neighbors, who were together at a raising, took their guns—five rifles, and several shot-guns; and having by shooting so injured one of his legs that he could not move rapidly, they fired at him thirty-five times before they killed him. Mr. Travis had one of his tusks, which was larger than his thumb. When dressed, the four quarters weighed more than four hundred pounds.

Colonel Merchant Lawrence, who for many years lived where the family of the late Joseph Sax now reside, opposite the Dutch Church, at the foot of the mountain, and kept a public house there, tamed and raised several young bears, some of which he kept until three years old. His house was a favorite resort of sportsmen; and James Powers, Esq., a prominent lawyer in Catskill, now more than eighty years of age, told me that he used, after the labors of the day in his office, to drive out to Lawrence's, spend the night there, catch a fine string of trout from the meadow brooks near by, and then return to town in time for the business of the day. For several years Colonel Lawrence invited him and other friends to a New Year's supper of bear's meat, which they highly relished. From two sons of Colonel Lawrence, who live near me, and who from early life have been familiar with hunting, I have learned many facts with regard to early hunting adventures, and the habits of the bears tamed and fed by them when they were young. Tame bears do not commonly lie torpid in their dens the first winter of their lives, especially if they are in a public place, where there is much to excite them. This was true of bears kept by Colonel Lawrence; and Mr. Schutt, at the Laurel House, has a large young bear, which, during the whole of the winter of 1865–6, moved freely about. Some, however, sleep through their first winter.

As bears grow old they commonly become ugly and cross, the females being more so than the males. One of the bears kept by Colonel Lawrence, when a storm was coming on, would climb to the top of a high post to which he was chained, and howl loud and long, which always proved to be a sure sign of rain or snow. Sometimes these bears would be very kind and affectionate with those who trained and fed them, but fierce and savage when strangers approached them. As cold weather came on they became cross and sometimes dangerous. A son of Colonel Lawrence, and another man, once beat a furious bear of his on the head with clubs for half an hour, before they could subdue him; his head swelling up, and the blood running from his nostrils. Dens were commonly made for them by sinking part of a large hollow tree several feet in length in the ground, with an entrance to it at one end; but sometimes they dug dens for themselves in the side of a hill to the horizontal depth of ten or twelve feet.

One of the bears kept by Colonel Lawrence was quite a pet with his son Merchant, then fifteen years of age, who played freely with him; but, as is supposed, becoming cross with the approach of winter, and excited to fury by the smell of the blood of a squirrel on the pantaloons of the boy, he seized him by the leg, and tried to drag him into his den to devour him. This the boy prevented, by seating himself on the end of the log within which the bear was trying to draw him, where the beast fiercely gnawed his leg from the heel to the knee, until a smaller boy who was with him called the Colonel with his gun, and his wife with an axe, from the house for his relief. The father wished to shoot the bear; but the mother, fearing lest the boy might be injured by the shot, prevented him, and, beating the teeth of the bear with the axe, compelled him, for a moment, to loosen his hold on the boy, when he was hastily withdrawn, the bear rushing fiercely after him as far as his chain would permit him to do so. The bones of the leg were not injured, though portions of the tendon separated from the flesh.

Facts have been stated, showing how difficult it is to kill an old bear by shooting him, and hence the danger there is of waiting until they are quite near before shooting, lest, having wounded them, they should prove dangerous.

Colonel Lawrence, wishing to have an old bear of his killed, his son took a gun and shot him deliberately in the head. The bear gave little heed to the shot, and a younger son bantered his brother on being such a wonderful shot that he could not kill a bear with the muzzle of his gun close to his head, and told him that the bear cared so little about his shooting that if he should feed him he would eat as well as ever. This was warmly denied by the older son, when his brother brought some bread from the house which the bear quickly ate. A second shot, however, brought him to the ground. I have seen an ox shot several times in the head with a bullet before he fell. In such cases it is probable that the ball enters the head too high or too low to give a deadly wound.

One of my neighbors, aged seventy-four, relates among other things that one day while ploughing, he heard his two hunting dogs, and three belonging to Uncle Frederick Sax, barking on the side of the mountain above them. Mr. Sax went on the upper side of a high hemlock-tree, on which was a large bear, and the other man below it. As Mr. Sax aimed too low in shooting, he only wounded the bear in the fore leg, when, rushing quickly down from the tree, one of the dogs seized the bear by the throat, while bruin returned the compliment by firmly fixing his teeth in the skin of the dog's back; and thus, fiercely struggling, they rolled some ten rods down the steep side of the mountain, closely pursued by the other dogs and the man, until he twice struck the bear a heavy blow on the head with an axe, which killed him. So staunch and true, however, was the dog, that he did not loose his hold on the bear until he was dead; though the bear had, up to that time, held him in his teeth. This same man once very irreverently remarked to me that he was "no more afraid of a bear than of an old sow;" and he and other old hunters in this matter did certainly, at times, show their faith by their works. A tight hug by a bear is not, however, a thing to be lightly spoken of; and the way in which they thus embrace one, is not soon forgotten by those who have been favored with such a salutation.

The facts of which follow were stated to me late in June, 1866, by Frederick Layman, of Catskill, a nephew, if I mistake not, of Frederick Sax, the great bear-hunter; and who lived with him, in his mountain home, from the time he was eight years old until he was twenty. Mr. Layman is now sixty-eight years old, so that what is here related took place fifty years since and more. During the twelve years referred to above, Mr. Layman aided Uncle Frederick in killing thirty-five bears.

The first adventure they had together was south of Roundtop, in Cairo, as distinct from the high mountain in Hunter, of the same name, near where the Websters now live. A bear had made sad havoc with the corn in that neighborhood, and was tracked and treed by a dog, when Mr. Sax shot it through the leg, after which it ran a quarter of a mile. Another shot broke his back; when, sitting down, as the dogs rushed upon him, he knocked them, one after another, a distance of ten or fifteen feet with his paws. A third shot ended his days.

While hunting with Uncle Frederick in Winter Clove, they came upon three bears, in a den in the rocks, on a ledge some twelve feet high. They had no fair view of the bears; yet, after firing into the den twice, the noise and smoke drove the bears out, when a dog seized one of them, while another ran against Uncle Fred's legs, and he, with the two bears and the dog, all rolled down the ledge together—an adventure much more pleasant for one to tell of, or to hear, than to be engaged in. On pursuing these bears, one of them ran up a tree, half a mile distant from the den, and was shot; another was killed the next day, and the third escaped.

A bear was once caught in a trap, on the side of the mountain above Uncle Fred's, and Layman pursued him half a mile, leading his dog. As he fired at the bear, the dog broke loose from him, and, rushing upon the beast, bruin rose on his hind legs, and seizing the dog with his fore paws, was hugging him more closely than was either comfortable or safe for him, when, Layman coming up, seized the bear from behind by the nape of his neck, and pulled him over backwards. The bear then turning upon Layman, struck him with his claws in the palm of his hand, badly wounding and tearing it open, when the dog seized the bear and held him until Layman shot him.

On the side of the mountain, back of Nicholas Rowe's, a little northeast of where the tollgate on the road to the Mountain House now is, Uncle Frederick and Layman found a bear in a den. As he came out, Mr. Sax shot, and broke the under jaw of the bear, and Layman put a bullet in his head, but fired so low that it did not kill him. Uncle Fred, in a hand-to-hand fight with the bear, which was pressing hard upon him, while stepping backwards, hit against a fallen bush or pole, and fell upon his back, when the bear rushed upon him, and but for his broken jaw might have made quick work with him. The dogs, however, fiercely seized the bear, thus releasing Mr. Sax. The late Joseph Sax, who was working near by, having come up, Uncle Fred took his axe and with it killed the bear.

Frederick Layman used to hunt with Evert Lawrence, a son of Colonel Lawrence, spoken of above. South of the Cauterskill Clove they once treed a bear, when, both of them having fired at him, he fell from the tree, and, having run half a mile, he was stopped by the dogs. Layman loaded his gun, and was trying to get a chance to shoot the bear without putting the dogs in danger of being shot, when the bear suddenly sprang upon him, from an elevation of a few feet above him, threw him down under him, and would soon have ended both his hunting and his life had not one of the dogs seized the bear by the nose and two others in the rear, when Layman was quickly released, and, seizing his gun, shot him through the heart.

Uncle Frederick once shot a female bear just at night on the mountain back of his house, and, seizing her by the leg, dragged her home. The next morning her three cubs, several months old, having followed her trail down to near the house, were there treed by the dogs. The tree was cut down, when one of the cubs was killed by the dogs who had broken from their muzzles, while the other two were secured, one of them having been carried to the house in the checked woollen apron of Mrs. Sax, and, though it scratched her severely, she held it fast.

These two cubs were tamed and kept two or three years, one of them by Colonel Lawrence, at the hotel at the foot of the mountain, and the other by Mr. Peter P. Sax, about a mile north of the hotel and church. From the sons of Colonel Lawrence, and from Mr. Peter F. Sax, a nephew of Peter P., who lived with him when young, I had the facts which follow. Mr. Peter F. Sax was about twenty years old when the facts here spoken of took place, and is now sixty-four. He and one of the Lawrences referred to above were elders in the church of which I was pastor.

During the winter, from early in December until about the first of April, these bears were torpid in their dens, eating nothing, and when disturbed barely opening their eyes, without stirring unless they were forced to do so. They lay so still that they did not disturb the snow which fell on their chains, as the chains lay on the ground outside of their dens. The bear which Mr. Sax had, dug a den in the side of a hill near the house of a horizontal depth of about twelve feet, where he wintered. Mrs. Sax once in a measure forced him from his winter quarters, soon after he had retired there, to gratify the curiosity of some visitors, when so cross was he that he gave her a blow on her hand with his paw, the marks of which she bore with her to her grave, though he was very fond of her, and used to take food from her hands and her large pockets as he stood erect beside her. Peter F. Sax told me that he once tied a bone, with meat on it, on the end of a long pole, in winter, and thrust it under the nose of the bear, in his den, when he stupidly opened his eyes, but did not taste or touch it, though at other times he had a most greedy appetite for meat.

And now I come to a fact connected with the natural history of bears, of which I have never seen anything in books, but for the truth of which all the old hunters of the Catskill Mountains and the country around, and those connected with them, will solemnly vouch, as proved by their own personal observation, or the testimony of those whose veracity cannot be impeached, and the truth of whose statements no one who knew them well would ever question. And yet there may be those who would think it strange that an honest old Dutch dominie, of full size and mature age, should venture to tell as true what follows. My reply to such would be, that there always have been those in the world who doubt or deny the truth of what they themselves have never seen or known. A fool of this stripe, who said that he would not believe in what he had never seen, was very properly asked if he had ever seen his own back?

What I here refer to is that the second day of February of each year is known as "Bear's Day;" and that on that day bears wake from winter sleep, come forth from their dens, take a knowing observation of the weather for a few minutes, and then retire to their nests and finish their repose of some weeks or months—it may be longer. It is further claimed that if the sky is clear, the sun shining so that they can see their shadows, and the weather cold, when they thus come forth, they sleep quietly on until about the first of April, thinking that cold weather will continue thus long. On the other hand, if the weather is mild and cloudy, they look for an early spring, and often leave their dens; or if the water from the melting snow above them penetrates the earth, so as to wet them in their dens, they seek some new resting-place and home.

That bears do thus come forth from their dens the second day of February, is known by the tracks made by them that day at the mouth of their winter quarters, as also by observing the habits of tame bears, which, as in the case of the two named above, come forth on Bear Day, and, after wisely observing the weather some five minutes, retire again to rest. As several tame bears have been kept by those whom I know well, men of Christian principle, and entirely reliable, and after a careful observation in some cases for two or three successive winters of the same animals, as their testimony is uniform as to the fact that these bears did, each winter, thus come forth from their dens the second day of February, as described above, I cannot therefore question or doubt the truth of the statement here advanced. Thus much for Bear Day.

Since writing the above I met with the following, under date of February, 1867:

"The Weather at Cincinnati.—The 'Cincinnati Commercial' says that 'the old tradition that when, on the 2d of February, the ground-hog leaves his hole, and, seeing his shadow, returns to winter quarters, we may expect six weeks of severe winter weather, was determined, so far as this section is concerned, in favor of an early spring. The sky was overcast on Saturday; and the ground-hog, if he appeared at all, found that he cast no more shadow than the Dutchman who sold his to the Evil One.'"

The marmots, or woodchucks, are sometimes called ground—hogs, and so also are bears. Which are here meant, I do not know. The two tame bears spoken of above were killed at the same time, and their meat taken to market. The skin of one of them was sold for ten dollars in Albany, and stuffed, and is still in a museum there. Bears are seen here and there on the mountains every year, a few of which are killed; while, at times, they make free with sheep, calves, and swine. During the winter of 1865–6, a bear weighing three hundred and thirty-eight pounds when dressed was killed on Stony Clove; and one was shot by a grandson of Frederick Sax in October, 1866, the meat of which was eaten with a relish by those who had been familiar with such meat in their early days. The largest black bears in this region weigh, when dressed, from four hundred to five hundred pounds. Five or six bears were trapped or shot by hunters in and near Kiskatom in the fall and winter of 1866–7.

Traps for catching bears are made by hewing off the upper surface of logs to about one third of their thickness, thus making a floor seven feet long and three feet wide, with sides and an end of logs, some three feet high. There are two heavy logs lengthwise on the top, a low entrance, with two logs over it at one end. Within is what is called a figure four, or other spring, baited, by the falling of which the logs at the entrance come down, and the bear is thus caged.

In the autumn of 1857, bears trampled down and ate oats in a field near the lakes, just back of the Catskill Mountain House. They were tracked by Mr. Beach, proprietor of the house, and Old Thorp the Bear Hunter, as he is called, who lives there, along the ridge of the North Mountain, by the well-known marks which they make by rising on their hind feet and removing with their teeth a piece of bark from the sides of trees, when they wish to pass the same way again. It is said that along some of their paths, on the upper ridges of the Catskill Mountains, there are trees which have thus been entirely peeled some feet from the ground, and killed. A trap like the one spoken of above was built on the North Mountain, where its ruins now are, in which the old bears that troubled the oats were caught, while their young ones taken were near by.

It is a fact worth noticing that there are those who have a peculiar fondness for animals, and towards whom animals, both tame and wild, are strongly attracted. In one of the towns among the upper heights of the Catskill Mountains there is a Mrs. B—, who is peculiarly fond of animals, as they are also of her. She says that she is not afraid of any animal, and wild bears have come to her in the woods, and licked her hands. Domestic animals she sells; but will never have sheep, horned cattle, or swine killed on the farm, nor sold to butchers or drovers for slaughtering.

Her greatest favorites, however, are cats, of which she keeps twenty or thirty, each one having its own name and place for feeding. Wishing to spend a winter with friends in New England, some years since, she hired a man with a team to take her cats there, safely confined in a large box-cage, and with them a cow to furnish them with milk. While passing through the Cauterskill Clove, as the cats were noisy and troublesome, the man made an opening in their cage and let them all loose in the woods, much to the annoyance of their mistress when she learned of her loss.

Bears are very fond of wild berries, which grow in great abundance on the mountains, and are at times met with by those who are picking them. Some young ladies thus employed in the summer of 1865, a little north of and above the tollgate, on the way to the Mountain House, on looking up saw a bear near them, very politely standing upright, as much as to say, "I would take off my hat if I had one, and make you a low bow." They did not, however, wish for better acquaintance, and hurried down the mountain in double-quick time. One of them, a granddaughter of Frederick Sax, said that she would have taken a stick to him and driven him off, had not her companions left her alone in such bad company.

That the bears are not all dead yet, at least in the State of Maine, is evident from the following, published in the winter of 1866–7 under the heading of "Bears Killed:"

"Augusta, Me., January 10.—Returns received at the office of the Secretary of State show that during last year there were two hundred and sixty-five bears killed in this State. In Penobscot County alone there were one hundred and nine killed, and in the town of Lincoln forty-five.

"The returns show that there were only four wolves killed in the entire State during the year."

XII

The cougar or American panther, or painter, as this animal is often called, painter being a corruption of the word "panther," belongs to the feline or cat species, and is found from Patagonia, in South America, to the northern bounds of the State of New York. Its color on the back is reddish brown, with a lighter hue about the neck and the lower part of the body. Their whole length, including the tail, is commonly six feet or a little more, and they are the same with the Puma or South American lion. The jaguar, or American tiger, is somewhat larger and stronger than the panther, and is found from Paraguay, in South America, to the Red River in Texas. It has some seven stripes on each side, made up of a row of open rings, and with the panther is by furriers and by some naturalists held to be of the same species with the leopard, while others make them a distinct class.

Panthers were met with in the Catskill Mountains and the country around from the time of its first settlement,

Waking up in the early dawn, Levin tried to rouse his comrades. Vasenka, lying on his stomach, one stockinged foot thrust out, was so fast asleep that he could get no response from him. Oblonsky refused through his sleep to go so early. Even Laska, who slept curled up at the edge of the hay, got up reluctantly, lazily straightening and stretching her hind legs, first one and then the other. Levin put on his boots, took his gun and, carefully opening the creaking barn door, went out. The coachmen were sleeping by their carriages, the horses were dozing. Only one was lazily eating oats, scattering them all over the trough with its muzzle. It was still grey outside.

'What are you doing up so early, dearie?' the muzhik's old woman, stepping out of the cottage, addressed him amicably as a good old acquaintance.

'Going hunting, auntie. Is this the way to the marsh?'

'Straight through the back yards, past our threshing floor, my dear man, and then the hemp field—there's a footpath.'

Stepping carefully with her tanned bare feet, the old woman showed him to the fence of the threshing floor and opened it for him.

'Straight on and you'll hit the marsh. Our boys took the horses there last night.'

Laska gaily ran ahead on the path; Levin followed her with a quick, light step, constantly glancing at the sky. He did not want the sun to come up before he reached the marsh. But the sun did not tarry. The moon, which was still shining when he set out, now merely gleamed like bit of quicksilver; the morning star, which could not be missed earlier, now had to be looked for; the spots on the distant field, indistinct before, were now clearly visible. They were shocks of rye. Still invisible without sun's light, the dew on the tall, fragrant hemp, from which the heads had already been plucked, wetted Levin's legs and his blouse above the waist. In the transparent stillness of morning the slightest sounds could be heard. A bee whizzed past Levin's ear like a bullet. He looked closer and saw another, then a third. They all flew out from behind the wattle fence of the apiary and disappeared in the direction of the marsh. The path led him straight to the marsh. It could be recognized by the steam rising from it, thicker in some places, thinner in others, so that the sedge and some small willow bushes, like islands, wavered in this steam. At the edge of the marsh and the road, the boys and muzhiks who had spent the night with the horses all lay, having fallen asleep under their caftans before dawn. Not far from them, three hobbled horses moved about. One of them clanked its chains. Laska walked beside her master, looking about and asking to run ahead. As he walked past the sleeping muzhiks and came up to the first marshy patch, Levin checked his caps and let the dog go. One of the horses, a sleek chestnut two-year-old, saw the dog, shied, tossed its tail and snorted. The others also became frightened and, splashing their hobbled legs in the water, their hoofs making a sound like clapping as they pulled them from the thick clay, began leaping their way out of the marsh. Laska stopped, looking mockingly at the horses and questioningly at Levin. Levin patted her and whistled the signal for her to start.

Laska ran with a gay and preoccupied air over the bog that yielded under her.

Running into the marsh, Laska at once picked up, amidst the familiar smells of roots, marsh grass, rust, and the alien smell of horse dung, the bird smell spread all through the place, that same strong-smelling bird that excited her more than anything else. Here and there over the moss and marsh burdock this smell was very strong, but it was impossible to tell in which direction it grew stronger or weaker. To find the direction she had to go further downwind. Not feeling her legs under her, moving at a tense gallop so that she could stop at each leap if necessary, Laska ran to the right, away from the morning breeze blowing from the east, and then turned upwind. Breathing in the air with flared nostrils, she sensed at once that there were not only tracks but *they* themselves were there, and not one but many. She slowed the speed of her run. They were there, but precisely where she was still unable to tell. She had already begun a circle to find the place when her master's voice suddenly distracted her. 'Here, Laska!' he said, pointing in a different direction. She paused briefly, as if to ask if it would not be better to finish what she had begun. But he repeated the order in an angry voice, pointing to a water-flooded hummocky spot where there could not be anything. She obeyed him, pretending to search in order to give him pleasure, ran all over the hummocks and then went back to the former place, and immediately sensed them again. Now, when he was not hindering her, she knew what to do, and, not looking where she put her feet, stumbling in vexation over high hummocks and getting into the water, but managing with her strong, supple legs, she began the circle that would make everything clear to her. *Their* smell struck her more and more strongly, more and more distinctly, and suddenly it became perfectly clear to her that one of them was there, behind that hummock, five steps away from her. She stopped and her whole body froze. On her short legs she could see nothing ahead of her, but she knew from the smell that it was sitting no more than five steps away. She stood, sensing it more and more and delighting in the anticipation. Her tense tail was extended and only its very tip twitched. Her mouth was slightly open, her ears pricked up a little. One ear had got folded back as she ran, and she was breathing heavily but cautiously, and still more cautiously she turned more with her eyes than her head to look at her master. He, with his usual face but with his ever terrible eyes, was coming, stumbling over hummocks, and extremely slowly as it seemed to her. It seemed to her that he was moving slowly, yet he was running.

Noticing the special way Laska was searching, pressed flat to the ground, as if raking it with her hind legs in big strides, and with her mouth slightly open, Levin understood that she was after great snipe, and, praying to God in his heart that he would be successful, especially with the first bird, he ran to her. Coming right up to her, he began looking in front of him from his height and saw with his eyes what she had seen with her nose. In a space between two hummocks, close to one of them, he made out a great snipe. It was listening, its head turned. Then, fluffing its wings slightly and folding them again, it wagged its behind clumsily and disappeared round the corner.

'Flush it, flush it,' cried Levin, nudging Laska from behind.

'But I can't flush anything,' thought Laska. 'Where will I flush it from? I can sense them from here, but if I move forward, I won't be able to tell where they are or what they are.' Yet here he was nudging her with his knee and saying in an excited whisper: 'Flush it, Lasochka, flush it!'

'Well, if that's what he wants, I'll do it, but I can't answer for myself any more,' she thought and tore forward at full speed between the hummocks. She no longer smelled anything, but only saw and heard, without understanding anything.

Ten steps from the former place, with a thick creech and the swelling noise of wings peculiar to its kind, a single great snipe flew up. And lowing a shot it plopped down heavily, its white breast against the wet bog. Another did not wait but flew up behind Levin without the dog.

When Levin turned to it, it was already far away. But the shot reached it. Having flown some twenty yards, the second snipe suddenly jerked upwards and, tumbling like a thrown ball, fell heavily on to a dry patch.

'That'll do nicely!' thought Levin, putting the two plump, warm birds into his game bag. 'Eh, Lasochka, won't it do nicely?'

By the time Levin reloaded his gun and started off again, the sun, though still invisible behind the clouds, was already up. The crescent moon, having lost all its brilliance, showed white like a cloud in the sky; there was no longer a single star to be seen. The marshy patches, silvery with dew earlier, now became golden. The rustiness turned to amber. The blue of the grass changed to yellowish green. Little marsh birds pottered by the brook, in bushes glistening with dew and casting long shadows. A hawk woke up and sat on a haystack, turning its head from side to side, looking with displeasure at the marsh. Jackdaws flew into fields, and a barefoot boy was already driving the horses towards an old man, who had got up from under his caftan and was scratching himself. Smoke from the shooting, like milk, spread white over the green grass.

One of the boys came running to Levin.

'Uncle, there were ducks here yesterday!' he cried to him and followed him at a distance.

And in the sight of this boy, who expressed his approval, Levin took a double pleasure in straight away killing three more snipe, one after the other.

XIII

The hunters' omen proved true, that if the first beast or bird was taken the field would be lucky.

Tired, hungry, happy, Levin returned towards ten o'clock, having walked some twenty miles on foot, with nineteen pieces of fine game and one duck, which he tied to his belt because there was no room for it in his game bag. His comrades had long been awake and had had time to get hungry and have breakfast.

'Wait, wait, I know it's nineteen,' said Levin, counting for a second time the snipe and great snipe, doubled up and dry, caked with blood, their heads twisted to the side, no longer looking as impressive as when they flew.

The count was correct, and Levin was pleased at Stepan Arkadyich's envy. He was also pleased to find on his return that the messenger had already arrived with a note from Kitty.

'I am quite well and cheerful. If you are afraid for me, you may be more at ease than ever. I have a new bodyguard, Marya Vlasyevna' (this was the midwife, a new, important person in Levin's family life). 'She came to see how I am. She found me perfectly well, and we are having her stay until you come. Everyone is cheerful and well, so please don't you be in a hurry, and if the hunting is good, stay another day.'

These two joys, the lucky hunting and the note from his wife, were so great that the two minor unpleasantnesses that occurred afterwards passed easily for him. One was that the chestnut outrunner, evidently overworked the day before, was off her feed and looked dull. The coachman said she had been strained.

'She was overdriven yesterday, Konstantin Dmitrich,' he said. 'Of course, she was pushed hard those seven miles!'

The other unpleasantness that upset his good mood at first, but at which he later laughed a great deal, was that of all the provisions, which Kitty had sent with them in such abundance that it seemed they could not have been eaten in a week, nothing remained. Coming back from the hunt tired and hungry, Levin had been dreaming so specifically of pirozhki that, as he approached their quarters, he could already feel their smell and taste in his mouth, the way Laska could sense game, and he at once ordered Filipp to serve them. It turned out that there were not only no pirozhki but no chicken either.

'Quite an appetite!' said Stepan Arkadyich, laughing and pointing at Vasenka Veslovsky. 'I don't suffer from lack of appetite myself, but this is astonishing . . .'

'*Mais c'était délicieux.*' Veslovsky praised the beef he had just eaten.

'Well, nothing to be done!' said Levin, giving Veslovsky a dark look. 'Serve some beef, then, Filipp.'

'The beef got eaten. I gave the bone to the dogs,' Filipp replied.

Levin was so upset that he said vexedly:

'You might have left me at least something!' and nearly wept.

'Clean the game,' he said to Filipp in a trembling voice, trying not to look at Vasenka, 'and layer it with nettles. And fetch me some milk at least.'

Later on, when he had drunk his fill of milk, he felt ashamed at having shown vexation to a stranger, and he started laughing at his hungry anger.

That evening they hunted in yet another field, where Veslovsky also not several birds, and at night they returned home.

The way back was as merry as the way there. Veslovsky sang, then recalled with pleasure his exploits with the muzhiks who had treated him to vodka and said 'No offence,' then his night's exploits with the nuts and the farm girl, and the muzhik who had asked him whether he was married or not and, on learning that he was not, had told him: Don't you go looking at other men's wives; you'd best get one of your own.' These words especially made Veslovsky laugh.

'All in all I'm terribly pleased with our trip. And you, Levin?'

'I'm very pleased,' Levin said sincerely, especially glad not only that he did not feel the hostility he had felt towards Vasenka Veslovsky at home, but that, on the contrary, he felt the most friendly disposition towards him.

XV

The shooting place was not far away, across a stream in a small aspen grove. Nearing the wood, Levin got out and led Oblonsky to the corner of a mossy and marshy clearing that was already free of snow. He himself went back to a double birch at the other end and, leaning his gun against the fork of a dry lower branch, took off his caftan, tightened his belt, and made sure he had freedom to move his arms.

The old, grey-haired Laska, who had followed behind him, carefully sat down facing him and pricked up her ears. The sun was setting behind the large forest, and in its light the little birches scattered among the aspens were distinctly outlined with their hanging branches and buds swollen to bursting.

From a thicket in which there was still snow came the barely audible sound of water trickling in narrow, meandering streams. Small birds chirped and occasionally flew from tree to tree.

In intervals of complete silence one could hear the rustling of last year's leaves, stirred by the thawing ground and the growing grass.

'Imagine! You can hear and see the grass grow!' Levin said to himself, noticing the movement of a wet, slate-coloured aspen leaf beside a spear of young grass. He stood, listened, and looked down at the wet, mossy ground, at the attentive Laska, then at the sea of bare treetops of the forest spreading before him at the foot of the hill and the fading sky streaked with white clouds. A hawk, unhurriedly flapping its wings, flew high over the distant forest; another flew the same way in the same direction and disappeared. The birds chirped more loudly and busily in the thicket. An owl hooted not far away, and Laska gave a start, took several cautious steps and, cocking her head, began to listen. From across the stream came the call of a cuckoo. It cuckooed twice in its usual call, then wheezed, hurried and became confused.

'Imagine! a cuckoo already!' said Stepan Arkadyich, coming out from behind a bush.

'Yes, I can hear,' Levin replied, reluctantly breaking the silence of the forest with his voice, which he found disagreeable. 'It won't be long now.'

Stepan Arkadych's figure stepped back behind the bush, and Levin saw only the bright flame of a match, replaced at once by the red glow of a cigarette and blue smoke.

'Chik! chik!' clicked the hammers of Stepan Arkadyich's gun. 'And what's that cry?' asked Oblonsky, drawing Levin's attention to drawn-out yelping, as of a frolicking colt whinnying in a high voice.

'Ah, don't you know? It's a male hare. Enough talk! Listen, they're coming!' Levin almost cried out, cocking his gun.

They heard a high, distant whistling, and two seconds later, in the usual rhythm so well known to hunters, a second, a third, and after the third whistle came a chirring.

Levin cast a glance right, left, and there before him in the dull blue over the merging, tender sprouts of the aspen tops, a flying bird appeared. It flew straight towards him: the close, chirring sounds, like measured ripping of taut fabric, were just above his ears; the bird's long beak and neck could already be seen, and just as Levin aimed, red lightning flashed from behind the bush where Oblonsky stood; the bird dropped like an arrow and again soared up. Lightning flashed again and clap was heard; fluttering its wings as if trying to stay in the air, the bird paused, hung there for a moment, then plopped heavily to the marshy ground.

'Could we have missed?' cried Stepan Arkadyich, who was unable to see on account of the smoke.

'Here it is!' said Levin, pointing at Laska, who, with one ear raised and the tip of her fluffy tail wagging on high, stepping slowly as if she wished to prolong the pleasure, and almost smiling, brought the dead bird to her master. 'Well, I'm glad you got it,' said Levin, at the same time already feeling envious that it was not he who had succeeded in shooting this woodcock.

'A rotten miss with the right barrel,' Stepan Arkadyich replied, loading the gun. 'Shh . . . here they come.'

Indeed, they heard a quick succession of piercing whistles. Two woodcock, playing and chasing each other and only whistling, not chirring, came flying right over the hunters' heads. Four shots rang out and, like swallows, the woodcock made a quick swerve and vanished from sight.

The fowling was splendid. Stepan Arkadyich shot another two birds, and Levin two, one of which could not be found. It was getting dark. Bright, silvery Venus, low in the west, was already shining with her tender gleam behind the birches, and high in the east the sombre Arcturus already played its red fires. Overhead Levin kept finding and losing the stars of the Great Bear. The woodcock had stopped flying; but Levin decided to wait longer, until Venus, which he could see under a birch branch, rose above it and the stars of the Great Bear showed clearly. Venus had already risen above the branch, the chariot of the Great Bear with its shaft was already quite visible in the dark blue sky, but he still waited.

'Isn't it time?' said Stepan Arkadyich.

It was quiet in the forest and not a single bird moved.

'Let's stay longer.'

'As you wish.'

They were now standing about fifteen paces apart.

'Stiva!' Levin said suddenly and unexpectedly. 'Why don't you tell me whether your sister-in-law got married or when she's going to?'

Levin felt himself so firm and calm that he thought no answer could stir him. But he never expected what Stepan Arkadyich replied.

'She wasn't and isn't thinking of getting married, but she's very ill, and the doctors have sent her abroad. They even fear for her life.'

'What's that!' cried Levin. 'Very ill? What's wrong with her? How did she . . .'

While they were saying this, Laska, her ears pricked up, kept glancing at the sky and then reproachfully at them.

'Found a fine time to talk!' she thought. 'And there's one coming . . . There it is, all right. They'll miss it . . .' thought Laska.

But just then both men heard the piercing whistle, which seemed to lash at their ears, and they suddenly seized their guns and lightning flashed twice and two claps rang out simultaneously. The high-flying woodcock instantly folded its wings and fell into the thicket, bending the slender shoots.

'That's excellent! We shared one!' Levin cried out and ran into the thicket with Laska to look for the woodcock. 'Ah, yes, what was that unpleasant thing?' he recollected. 'Yes, Kitty's sick . . . Nothing to be done, very sorry,' he thought.

'Ah, she's found it! Good girl,' he said, taking the warm bird out of Laska's mouth and putting it into the nearly full game bag. 'I've found Stiva!' he cried.

Excerpted from *Catskill Mountains and the Region Around*

Phineas Finn

ANTHONY TROLLOPE

The Willingford Bull

Phineas left London by a night mail train on Easter Sunday, and found himself at the Willingford Bull about half an hour after midnight. Lord Chiltern was up and waiting for him, and supper was on the table. The Willingford Bull was an English inn of the old stamp, which had now, in these latter years of railway travelling, ceased to have a road business—for there were no travellers on the road, and but little posting—but had acquired a new trade as a Modern: adepot for hunters and hunting men. The landlord let out horses and kept hunting stables, and the house was generally filled from the beginning of November till the middle of April. Then it became a desert in the summer, and no guests were seen there, till the pink coats flocked down again into the shires.

'How many days do you mean to give us?' said Lord Chiltern, as he helped his friend to a devilled leg of turkey.

'I must go back on Wednesday,' said Phineas.

'That means Wednesday night. I'll tell you what we'll do. We've the Cottesmore to-morrow. We'll get into Tailby's country on Tuesday, and Fitzwilliam will be only twelve miles off on Wednesday. We shall be rather short of horses.'

'Pray don't let me put you out. I can hire something here, I suppose?'

'You won't put me out at all. There'll be three between us each day, and we'll run our luck. The horses have gone on to Empingham for to-morrow. Tailby is rather a way off—at Somerby; but we'll manage it. If the worst comes to the worst, we can get back to Stamford by rail. On Wednesday we shall have everything very comfortable. They're out beyond Stilton and will draw home our way. I've planned it all out. I've a trap with a fast stepper, and if we start to-morrow at half-past nine, we shall be in plenty of time. You shall ride Meg Merrilies, and if she don't carry you, you may shoot her.'

'Is she one of the pulling ones?'

'She is heavy in hand if you are heavy at her, but leave her mouth alone and she'll go like flowing water. You'd better not ride more in a crowd than you can help. Now what'll you drink?'

They sat up half the night smoking and talking, and Phineas learned more about Lord Chiltern then than ever he had learned before. There was brandy and water before them, but neither of them drank. Lord Chiltern, indeed, had a pint of beer by his side from which he sipped occasionally. 'I've taken to beer,' he said, 'as being the best drink going. When a man hunts six days a week he can afford to drink beer. I'm on an allowance—three pints a day. That's not too much.'

'And you drink nothing else?'

'Nothing when I'm alone—except a little cherry-brandy when I'm out. I never cared for drink—never in my life. I do like excitement, and have been less careful than I ought to have been as to what it has come from. I could give up drink to-morrow, without a struggle—if it were worth my while to make up my mind to do it. And it's the same with gambling. I never do gamble now, because I've got no money; but I own I like it better than anything in the world. While you are at it, there is life in it.'

'You should take to politics, Chiltern.'

'And I would have done so, but my father would not help me. Never mind, we will not talk about him. How does Laura get on with her husband?'

'Very happily, I should say.'

'I don't believe it,' said Lord Chiltern. 'Her temper is too much like mine to allow her to be happy with such a log of wood as Robert Kennedy. It is such men as he who drive me out of the pale of decent life. If that is decency, I'd sooner be indecent. You mark my words. They'll come to grief. She'll never be able to stand it.'

'I should think she had her own way in everything,' said Phineas.

'No, no. Though he's a prig, he's a man; and she will not find it easy to drive him.'

'But she may bend him.'

'Not an inch—that is if I understand his character. I suppose you see a good deal of them?'

'Yes—pretty well. I'm not there so often as I used to be in the Square.'

'You get sick of it, I suppose. I should. Do you see my father often?'

'Only occasionally. He is always very civil when I do see him.'

'He is the very pink of civility when he pleases, but the most unjust man I ever met.'

'I should not have thought that.'

'Yes, he is,' said the Earl's son, and all from lack of judgment to discern the truth. He makes up his mind to a thing on insufficient proof, and then nothing will turn him. He thinks well of you—would probably believe your word on any indifferent subject without thought of a doubt; but if you were to tell him that I didn't get drunk every night of my life and spend most of my time in thrashing policemen, he would not believe you. He would smile incredulously and make you a little bow. I can see him do it.'

'You are too hard on him, Chiltern.'

'He has been too hard on me, I know. Is Violet Effingham still in Grosvenor Place?'

'No; she's with Lady Baldock.'

'That old grandmother of evil has come to town—has she? Poor Violet! When we were young together we used to have such fun about that old woman.'

'The old woman is an ally of mine now,' said Phineas.

'You make allies everywhere. You know Violet Effingham of course?'

'Oh yes. I know her.'

'Don't you think her very charming?' said Lord Chiltern.

'Exceedingly charming.'

'I have asked that girl to marry me three times, and I shall never ask her again. There is a point beyond which a man shouldn't go. There are many reasons why it would be a good marriage. In the first place, her money would be serviceable. Then it would heal matters in our family, for my father is as prejudiced in her favour as he is against me. And I love her dearly. I've loved her all my life—since I used to buy cakes for her. But I shall never ask her again.'

'I would if I were you,' said Phineas—hardly knowing what it might be best for him to say.

'No; I never will. But I'll tell you what. I shall get into some desperate scrape about her. Of course she'll marry, and that soon. Then I shall make a fool of myself. When I hear that she is engaged I shall go and quarrel with the man, and kick him—or get kicked. All the world will turn against me, and I shall be called a wild beast.'

'A dog in the manger is what you should be called.'

'Exactly—but how is a man to help it? If you loved a girl, could you see another man take her?' Phineas remembered of course that he had lately come through this ordeal. 'It is as though he were to come and put his hand upon me, and wanted my own heart out of me. Though I have no property in her at all, no right to her—though she never gave me a word of encouragement, it is as though she were the most private thing in the world to me. I should be half mad, and in my madness I could not master the idea that I was being robbed. I should resent it as a personal interference.'

'I suppose it will come to that if you give her up yourself,' said Phineas.

'It is no question of giving up. Of course I cannot make her marry me. Light another cigar, old fellow.'

Phineas, as he lit the other cigar, remembered that he owed a certain duty in this matter to Lady Laura. She had commissioned him to persuade her brother that his suit with Violet Effingham would not be hopeless, if he could only restrain himself in his mode of conducting it. Phineas was disposed to do his duty, although he felt it to be very hard that he should be called upon to be eloquent against his own interest. He had been thinking for the last quarter of an hour how he must bear himself if it might turn out that he should be the man whom Lord Chiltern was resolved to kick. He looked at his friend and host, and became aware that a kicking-match with such a one would not be pleasant pastime. Nevertheless, he would be happy enough to be subject to Lord Chiltern's wrath for such a reason. He would do his duty by Lord Chiltern; and then, when that had been adequately done, he would, if occasion served, fight a battle for himself.

'You are too sudden with her, Chiltern,' he said, after a pause.

'What do you mean by too sudden?' said Lord Chiltern, almost angrily.

'You frighten her by being so impetuous. You rush at her as though you wanted to conquer her by a single blow.'

'So I do.'

'You should be more gentle with her. You should give her time to find out whether she likes you or not.'

'She has known me all her life, and has found that out long ago. Not but what you are right. I know you are right. If I were you, and had your skill in pleasing, I should drop soft words into her ear till I had caught her. But I have no gifts in that way. I am as awkward as a pig at what is called flirting. And I have an accursed pride which stands in my own light. If she were in this house this moment, and if I knew she were to be had for asking, I don't think I could bring myself to ask again. But we'll go to bed. It's half-past two, and we must be off at half-past nine, if we're to be at Exton Park gates at eleven.'

Phineas, as he went up-stairs, assured himself that he had done his duty. If there ever should come to be anything between him and Violet Effingham, Lord Chiltern might quarrel with him—might probably attempt that kicking encounter to which allusion had been made—but nobody could justly say that he had not behaved honourably to his friend.

On the next morning there was a bustle and a scurry, as there always is on such occasions, and the two men got off about ten minutes after time. But Lord Chiltern drove hard, and they reached the meet before the master had moved off. They had a fair day's sport with the Cottesmore; and Phineas, though he found that Meg Merrilies did require a good deal of riding, went through his day's work with credit. He had been riding since he was a child, as is the custom with all boys in Munster, and had an Irishman's natural aptitude for jumping. When they got back to the Willingford Bull he felt pleased with the day and rather proud of himself. 'It wasn't fast, you know,' said Chiltern, 'and I don't call that a stiff country. Besides, Meg is very handy when you've got her out of the crowd. You shall ride Bonebreaker to-morrow at Somerby, and you'll find that better fun.'

'Bonebreaker? Haven't I heard you say he rushes like mischief?'

'Well, he does rush. But, by George! you want a horse to rush in that country. When you have to go right through four or five feet of stiff green wood, like a bullet through a target, you want a little force, or you're apt to be left up a tree.'

'And what do you ride?'

'A brute I never put my leg on yet. He was sent down to Wilcox here, out of Lincolnshire, because they couldn't get anybody to ride him there. They say he goes with his head up in the air, and won't look at a fence that isn't as high as his breast. But I think he'll do here. I never saw a better made beast, or one with more power. Do you look at his shoulders. He's to be had for seventy pounds, and these are the sort of horses I like to buy.'

Again they dined alone, and Lord Chiltern explained to Phineas that he rarely associated with the men of either of the hunts in which he rode. 'There is a set of fellows down here who are poison to me, and there is another set, and I am poison to them. Everybody is very civil, as you see, but I have no associates. And gradually I am getting to have a reputation as though I were the devil himself. I think I shall come out next year dressed entirely in black.'

'Are you not wrong to give way to that kind of thing?'

'What the deuce am I to do? I can't make civil little speeches. When once a man gets a reputation as an ogre, it is the most difficult thing in the world to drop it. I could have a score of men here every day if I liked it—my title would do that for me—but they would be men I should loathe, and I should be sure to tell them so, even though I did not mean it. Bonebreaker, and the new horse, and another, went on at twelve to-day. You must expect hard work to-morrow, as I daresay we shan't be home before eight.'

The next day's meet was in Leicestershire, not far from Melton, and they started early. Phineas, to tell the truth of him, was rather afraid of Bonebreaker, and looked forward to the probability of an accident. He had neither wife nor child, and nobody had a better right to risk his neck. 'We'll put a gag on 'im,' said the groom, 'and you'll ride 'im in a ring—so that you may well-nigh break his jaw; but he is a rum un, sir.' 'I'll do my best,' said Phineas. 'He'll take all that,' said the groom. 'Just let him have his own way at everything,' said Lord Chiltern, as they moved away from the meet to Pickwell Gorse; 'and if you'll only sit on his back, he'll carry you through as safe as a church.' Phineas could not help thinking that the counsels of the master and of the groom were very different. 'My idea is,' continued Lord Chiltern, that in hunting you should always avoid a crowd. I don't think a horse is worth riding that will go in a crowd. It's just like yachting—you should have plenty of sea-room. If you're to pull your horse up at every fence till somebody else is over, I think you'd better come out on a donkey.' And so they went away to Pickwell Gorse.

There were over two hundred men out, and Phineas began to think that it might not be so easy to get out of the crowd. A crowd in a fast run no doubt quickly becomes small by degrees and beautifully less; but it is very difficult, especially for a stranger, to free himself from the rush at the first start. Lord Chiltern's horse plunged about so violently, as they stood on a little hill-side looking down upon the cover, that he was obliged to take him to a distance, and Phineas followed him. 'If he breaks down wind,' said Lord Chiltern, 'we can't be better than we are here. If he goes up wind, he must turn before long, and we shall be all right.' As he spoke an old hound opened true and sharp—an old hound whom all the pack believed—and in a moment there was no doubt that the fox had been found. 'There are not above eight or nine acres in it,' said Lord Chiltern, 'and he can't hang long. Did you ever see such an uneasy brute as this in your life? But I feel certain he'll go well when he gets away.'

Phineas was too much occupied with his own horse to think much of that on which Lord Chiltern was mounted. Bonebreaker, the very moment that he heard the old hound's note, stretched out his head, and put his mouth upon the bit, and began to tremble in every muscle. 'He's a great deal more anxious for it than you and I are,' said Lord Chiltern. 'I see they've given you that gag. But don't you ride him on it till he wants it. Give him lots of room, and he'll go in the snaffle.' All which caution made Phineas think that any insurance office would charge very dear on his life at the present moment.

The fox took two rings of the gorse, and then he went—up wind. 'It's not a vixen, I'll swear,' said Lord Chiltern. 'A vixen in cub never went away like that yet. Now then, Finn, my boy, keep to the right.' And Lord Chiltern, with the horse out of Lincolnshire, went away across the brow of the hill, leaving the hounds to the left, and selected, as his point of exit into the next field, a stiff rail, which, had there been an accident, must have put a very wide margin of ground between the rider and his horse. 'Go hard at your fences, and then you'll fall clear,' he had said to Phineas. I don't think, however, that he would have ridden at the rail as he did, but that there was no help for him. 'The brute began in his own way, and carried on after in the same fashion all through,' he said afterwards. Phineas took the fence a little lower down, and what it was at which he rode he never knew. Bonebreaker sailed over it, whatever it was, and he soon found himself by his friend's side.

The ruck of the men were lower down than our two heroes, and there were others far away to the left, and others, again, who had been at the end of the gorse, and were now behind. Our friends were not near the hounds, not within two fields of them, but the hounds were below them, and therefore could be seen. 'Don't be in a hurry, and they'll be round upon us,' Lord Chiltern said. 'How the deuce is one to help being in a hurry?' said Phineas, who was doing his very best to ride Bonebreaker with the snaffle, but had already began to feel that Bonebreaker cared nothing for that weak instrument. 'By George, I should like to change with you,' said Lord Chiltern. The Lincolnshire horse was going along with his head very low, boring as he galloped, but throwing his neck up at his fences, just when he ought to have kept himself steady. After this, though Phineas kept near Lord Chiltern throughout the run, they were not again near enough to exchange words; and, indeed, they had but little breath for such purpose.

Lord Chiltern rode still a little in advance, and Phineas, knowing his friend's partiality for solitude when taking his fences, kept a little to his left. He began to find that Bonebreaker knew pretty well what he was about. As for not using the gag rein, that was impossible. When a horse puts out what strength he has against a man's arm, a man must put out what strength he has against the horse's mouth. But Bonebreaker was cunning, and had had a gag rein on before. He contracted his lip here, and bent out his jaw there, till he had settled it to his mind, and then went away after his own fashion. He seemed to have a passion for smashing through big, high-grown ox-fences, and by degrees his rider came to feel that if there was nothing worse coming, the fun was not bad.

The fox ran up wind for a couple of miles or so, as Lord Chiltern had prophesied, and then turned—not to the right, as would best have served him and Phineas, but to the left—so that they were forced to make their way through the ruck of horses before they could place themselves again. Phineas found himself crossing a road, in and out of it, before he knew where he was, and for a while he lost sight of Lord Chiltern. But in truth he was leading now, whereas Lord Chiltern had led before. The two horses having been together all the morning, and on the previous day, were willing enough to remain in company, if they were allowed to do so. They both crossed the road, not very far from each other, going in and out amidst a crowd of horses, and before long were again placed well, now having the hunt on their right, whereas hitherto it had been on their left. They went over large pasture fields, and Phineas began to think that as long as Bonebreaker would be able to go through the thick grown-up hedges, all would be right. Now and again he came to a cut fence, a fence that had been cut and laid, and these were not so pleasant. Force was not sufficient for them, and they admitted of a mistake. But the horse, though he would rush at them unpleasantly, took them when they came without touching them. It might be all right yet—unless the beast should tire with him; and then, Phineas thought, a misfortune might probably occur. He remembered, as he flew over one such impediment, that he rode a stone heavier than his friend. At the end of forty-five minutes Bonebreaker also might become aware of the fact.

The hounds were running well in sight to their right, and Phineas began to feel some of that pride which a man indulges when he becomes aware that he has taken his place comfortably, has left the squad behind, and is going well. There were men nearer the hounds than he was, but he was near enough even for ambition. There had already been enough of the run to make him sure that it would be a 'good thing,' and enough to make him aware also that probably it might be too good. When a run is over, men are very apt to regret the termination, who a minute or two before were anxiously longing that the hounds might pull down their game. To finish well is everything in hunting. To have led for over an hour is nothing, let the pace and country have been what they might, if you fall away during the last half mile. Therefore it is that those behind hope that the fox may make this or that cover, while the forward men long to see him turned over in every field. To ride to hounds is very glorious; but to have ridden to hounds is more glorious still. They had now crossed another road, and a larger one, and had got into a somewhat closer country. The fields were not so big, and the fences were not so high. Phineas got a moment to look about him, and saw Lord Chiltern riding without his cap. He was very red in the face, and his eyes seemed to glare, and he was tugging at his horse with all his might. But the animal seemed still to go with perfect command of strength, and Phineas had too much work on his own hands to think of offering Quixotic assistance to anyone else. He saw some one, a farmer, as he thought, speak to Lord Chiltern as they rode close together; but Chiltern only shook his head and pulled at his horse.

There were brooks in those parts. The river Eye forms itself thereabouts, or some of its tributaries do so; and these tributaries, though small as rivers, are considerable to men on one side who are called by the exigencies of the occasion to place themselves quickly on the other. Phineas knew nothing of these brooks; but Bonebreaker had gone gallantly over two, and now that there came a third in the way, it was to be hoped that he might go gallantly over that also. Phineas, at any rate, had no power to decide otherwise. As long as the brute would go straight with him he could sit him; but he had long given up the idea of having a will of his own. Indeed, till he was within twenty yards of the brook, he did not see that it was larger than the others. He looked around, and there was Chiltern close to him, still fighting with his horse—but the farmer had turned away. He thought that Chiltern nodded to him, as much as to tell him to go on. On he went at any rate. The brook, when he came to it, seemed to be a huge black hole, yawning beneath him. The banks were quite steep, and just where he was to take off there was an ugly stump. It was too late to think of anything. He stuck his knees against his saddle—and in a moment was on the other side. The brute, who had taken off a yard before the stump, knowing well the danger of striking it with his foot, came down with a grunt, and did, I think, begin to feel the weight of that extra stone. Phineas, as soon as he was safe, looked back, and there was Lord Chiltern's horse in the very act of his spring—higher up the rivulet, where it was even broader. At that distance Phineas could see that Lord Chiltern was wild with rage against the beast. But whether he wished to take the leap or wished to avoid it, there was no choice left to him. The animal rushed at the brook, and in a moment the horse and horseman were lost to sight. It was well then that that extra stone should tell, as it enabled Phineas to arrest his horse and to come back to his friend.

The Lincolnshire horse had chested the further bank, and of course had fallen back into the stream. When Phineas got down he found that Lord Chiltern was wedged in between the horse and the bank, which was better, at any rate, than being under the horse in the water. 'All right, old fellow,' he said, with a smile, when he saw Phineas. 'You go on; it's too good to lose.' But he was very pale, and seemed to be quite helpless where he lay. The horse did not move—and never did move again. He had smashed his shoulder to pieces against a stump on the bank, and was afterwards shot on that very spot.

When Phineas got down he found that there was but little water where the horse lay. The depth of the stream had been on the side from which they had taken off, and the thick black mud lay within a foot of the surface, close to the bank against which Lord Chiltern was propped. 'That's the worst one I ever was on,' said Lord Chiltern; 'but I think he's gruelled now.'

'Are you hurt?'

'Well—I fancy there is something amiss. I can't move my arms; and I catch my breath. My legs are all right if I could get away from this accursed brute.'

'I told you so,' said the farmer, coming and looking down upon them from the bank. 'I told you so, but you wouldn't be said.' Then he too got down, and between them both they extricated Lord Chiltern from his position, and got him on to the bank.

'That un's a dead un,' said the farmer, pointing to the horse.

'So much the better,' said his lordship. 'Give us a drop of sherry, Finn.'

He had broken his collar-bone and three of his ribs. They got a farmer's trap from Wissindine and took him into Oakham. When there, he insisted on being taken on through Stamford to the Willingford Bull before he would have his bones set—picking up, however, a surgeon at Stamford. Phineas remained with him for a couple of days, losing his run with the Fitzwilliams and a day at the potted peas, and became very fond of his patient as he sat by his bedside.

'That was a good run, though, wasn't it?' said Lord Chiltern as Phineas took his leave. 'And, by George, Phineas, you rode Bonebreaker so well, that you shall have him as often as you'll come down. I don't know how it is, but you Irish fellows always ride.'

The Duke's Children—Killancodlem

ANTHONY TROLLOPE

Mr. Dobbes was probably right in his opinion that hotels, tourists, and congregations of men are detrimental to shooting. Crummie-Toddie was in all respects suited for sport. Killancodlem, though it had the name of a shooting-place, certainly was not so. Men going there took their guns. Gamekeepers were provided and gillies—and, in a moderate quantity, game. On certain grand days a deer or two might be shot—and would be very much talked about afterwards. But a glance at the place would suffice to show that Killancodlem was not intended for sport. It was a fine castellated mansion, with beautiful though narrow grounds, standing in the valley of the Archay River, with a mountain behind and the river in front. Between the gates and the river there was a public road on which a stage-coach ran, with loud-blown horns and the noise of many tourists. A mile beyond the Castle was the famous Killancodlem hotel which made up a hundred and twenty beds, and at which half as many more guests would sleep on occasions under the tables. And there was the Killancodlem post-office halfway between the two. At Crummie-Toddie they had to send nine miles for their letters and newspapers. At Killancodlem there was lawn-tennis and a billiard-room and dancing every night. The costumes of the ladies were lovely, and those of the gentlemen, who were wonderful in knickerbockers, picturesque hats and variegated stockings, hardly less so. And then there were carriages and saddle-horses, and paths had been made hither and thither through the rocks and hills for the sake of the scenery. Scenery! To hear Mr. Dobbes utter the single word was as good as a play. Was it for such cockney purposes as those that Scotland had been created, fit mother for grouse and deer?

Silverbridge arrived just before lunch, and was soon made to understand that it was impossible that he should go back that day. Mrs. Jones was very great on that occasion. 'You are afraid of Reginald Dobbes,' she said severely.

'I think I am rather.'

'Of course you are. How came it to pass that you of all men should submit yourself to such a tyrant?'

'Good shooting, you know,' said Silverbridge.

'But you dare not call an hour your own—or your soul. Mr. Dobbes and I are sworn enemies. We both like Scotland, and unfortunately we have fallen into the same neighbourhood. He looks upon me as the genius of sloth. I regard him as the incarnation of tyranny. He once said there should be no women in Scotland—just an old one here and there, who would know how to cook grouse. I offered to go and cook his grouse!'

'Any friend of mine,' continued Mrs. Jones, 'who comes down to Crummie-Toddie without staying a day or two with me—will never be my friend any more. I do not hesitate to tell you, Lord Silverbridge, that I call for your surrender, in order that I may show my power over Reginald Dobbes. Are you a Dobbite?'

'Not thorough-going,' said Silverbridge.

'Then be a Montacute Jones-ite; or a Boncassenite, if, as is possible, you prefer a young woman to an old one.' At this moment Isabel Boncassen was standing close to them.

'Killancodlem against Crummie-Toddie for ever!' said Miss Boncassen, waving her handkerchief. As a matter of course a messenger was sent back to Crummie-Toddie for the young lord's wearing apparel.

The whole of that afternoon he spent playing lawn-tennis with Miss Boncassen. Lady Mabel was asked to join the party, but she refused, having promised to take a walk to a distant waterfall where the Codlem falls into the Archay. A gentleman in knickerbockers was to have gone with her, and two other young ladies; but when the time came she was weary, she said—and she sat almost the entire afternoon looking at the game from a distance. Silverbridge played well, but not so well as the pretty American. With them were joined two others somewhat inferior, so that Silverbridge and Miss Boncassen were on different sides. They played game after game, and Miss Boncassen's side always won.

Very little was said between Silverbridge and Miss Boncassen which did not refer to the game. But Lady Mabel, looking on, told herself that they were making love to each other before her eyes. And why shouldn't they? She asked herself that question in perfect good faith. Why should they not be lovers? Was ever anything prettier than the girl in her country dress, active as a fawn and as graceful? Or could anything be more handsome, more attractive to a girl, more good-humoured, or better bred in his playful emulation than Silverbridge?

'When youth and pleasure meet, To chase the glowing hours with flying feet!' she said to herself over and over again.

But why had he sent her the ring? She would certainly give him back the ring and bid him bestow it at once upon Miss Boncassen. Inconstant boy! Then she would get up and wander away for a time and rebuke herself. What right had she even to think of inconstancy? Could she be so irrational, so unjust, as to be sick for his love, as to be angry with him because he seemed to prefer another? Was she not well aware that she herself did not love him;—but that she did love another man? She had made up her mind to marry him in order that she might be a duchess, and because she could give herself to him without any of that horror which would be her fate in submitting to matrimony with one or another of the young men around her. There might be disappointment. If he escaped her there would be bitter disappointment. But seeing how it was, had she any further ground for hope? She certainly had no ground for anger!

It was thus, within her own bosom, she put questions to herself. And yet all this before her was simply a game of play in which the girl and the young man were as eager for victory as though they were children. They were thinking neither of love nor love-making. That the girl should be so lovely was no doubt a pleasure to him;—and perhaps to her also that he should be joyous to look at and sweet of voice. But he, could he have been made to tell all the truth within him, would have still owned that it was his purpose to make Mabel his wife.

When the game was over and the propositions made for further matches and the like—Miss Boncassen said that she would betake herself to her own room. 'I never worked so hard in my life before,' she said. 'And I feel like a navvie. I could drink beer out of a jug and eat bread and cheese. I won't play with you any more, Lord Silverbridge, because I am beginning to think it is unladylike to exert myself.'

'Are you not glad you came over?' said Lady Mabel to him as he was going off the ground almost without seeing her.

'Pretty well,' he said.

'Is not that better than stalking?'

'Lawn-tennis?'

'Yes;—lawn-tennis—with Miss Boncassen.'

'She plays uncommonly well.'

'And so do you.'

'Ah, she has such an eye for distances.'

'And you—what have you an eye for? Will you answer me a question?'

'Well;—yes; I think so.'

'Truly.'

'Certainly; if I do answer it.'

'Do you not think her the most beautiful creature you ever saw in your life?' He pushed back his cap and looked at her without making any immediate answer. 'I do. Now tell me what you think.'

'I think that perhaps she is.'

'I knew you would say so. You are so honest that you could not bring yourself to tell a fib—even to me about that. Come here and sit down for a moment.' Of course he sat down by her. 'You know that Frank came to see me at Grex?'

'He never mentioned it.'

'Dear me;—how odd!'

'It was odd,' said he in a voice which showed that he was angry. She could hardly explain to herself why she told him this at the present moment. It came partly from jealousy, as though she had said to herself, 'Though he may neglect me, he shall know that there is someone who does not;'—and partly from an eager half-angry feeling that she would have nothing concealed. There were moments with her in which she thought that she could arrange her future life in accordance with certain wise rules over which her heart should have no influence. There were others, many others, in which her feelings completely got the better of her. And now she told herself that she would be afraid of nothing. There should be no deceit, no lies!

'He went to see you at Grex!' said Silverbridge.

'Why should he not have come to me at Grex?'

'Only it is so odd that he did not mention it. It seems to me that he is always having secrets with you of some kind.'

'Poor Frank! There is no one else who would come to see me at that tumbledown old place. But I have another thing to say to you. You have behaved badly to me.'

'Have I?'

'Yes, sir. After my folly about that ring you should have known better than to send it to me. You must take it back again.'

'You shall do exactly what you said you would. You shall give it to my wife—when I have one.'

'That did very well for me to say in a note. I did not want to send my anger to you over a distance of two or three hundred miles by the postman. But now that we are together you must take it back.'

'I will do no such thing,' said he sturdily.

'You speak as though this were a matter in which you can have your own way.'

'I mean to have mine about that.'

'Any lady then must be forced to take any present that a gentleman may send her! Allow me to assure you that the usages of society do not run in that direction. Here is the ring. I knew that you would come over to see—well, to see someone here, and I have kept it ready in my pocket.'

'I came over to see you.'

'Lord Silverbridge! But we know that in certain employments all things are fair.' He looked at her not knowing what were the employments to which she alluded. 'At any rate you will oblige me by—by—by not being troublesome, and putting this little trinket into your pocket.'

'Never! Nothing on earth shall make me do it.'

At Killancodlem they did not dine till half-past eight. Twilight was now stealing on these two, who were still out in the garden, all the others having gone in to dress. She looked round to see that no other eyes were watching them as she still held the ring. 'It is there,' she said, putting it on the bench between them. Then she prepared to rise from the seat so that she might leave it with him.

But he was too quick for her, and was away at a distance before she had collected her dress. And from a distance he spoke again, 'If you choose that it shall be lost, so be it.'

'You had better take it,' said she, following him slowly. But he would not turn back;—nor would she. They met again in the hall for a moment. 'I should be sorry it should be lost,' said he, 'because it belonged to my great-uncle. And I had hoped that I might live to see it very often.'

'You can fetch it,' she said, as she went to her room. He however would not fetch it. She had accepted it, and he would not take it back again, let the fate of the gem be what it might.

But to the feminine and more cautious mind the very value of the trinket made its position out there on the bench, within the grasp of any dishonest gardener, a burden to her. She could not reconcile it to her conscience that it should be so left. The diamond was a large one, and she had heard it spoken of as a stone of great value—so much so, that Silver-bridge had been blamed for wearing it ordinarily. She had asked for it in joke, regarding it as a thing which could not be given away. She could not go down herself and take it up again; but neither could she allow it to remain. As she went to her room she met Mrs. Jones already coming from hers. 'You will keep us all waiting,' said the hostess.

'Oh no;—nobody ever dressed so quickly. But, Mrs. Jones, will you do me a favour?'

'Certainly.'

'And will you let me explain something?'

'Anything you like—from a hopeless engagement down to a broken garter.'

'I am suffering neither from one or the other. But there is a most valuable ring lying out in the garden. Will you send for it?' Then of course the story had to be told. 'You will, I hope, understand how I came to ask for it foolishly. It was because it was the one thing which I was sure he would not give away.'

'Why not take it?'

'Can't you understand? I wouldn't for the world. But you will be good enough—won't you, to see that there is nothing else in it?'

'Nothing of love?'

'Nothing in the least. He and I are excellent friends. We are cousins, and intimate, and all that. I thought I might have had my joke, and now I am punished for it. As for love, don't you see he is over head and ears in love with Miss Boncassen?'

This was very imprudent on the part of Lady Mabel, who, had she been capable of clinging fast to her policy, would not now in a moment of strong feeling have done so much to raise obstacles in her own way. 'But you will send for it, won't you, and have it put on his dressing-table to-night?' When he went to bed Lord Silverbridge found it on his table.

But before that time came he had twice danced with Miss Boncassen, Lady Mabel having refused to dance with him. 'No,' she said, 'I am angry with you. You ought to have felt that it did not become you as a gentleman to subject me to inconvenience by throwing upon me the charge of that diamond. You may be foolish enough to be indifferent about its value, but as you have mixed me up with it I cannot afford to have it lost.'

'It is yours.'

'No, sir; it is not mine, nor will it ever be mine. But I wish you to understand that you have offended me.'

This made him so unhappy for the time that he almost told the story to Miss Boncassen. 'If I were to give you a ring,' he said, 'would not you accept it?'

'What a question!'

'What I mean is, don't you think all those conventional rules about men and women are absurd?'

'As a progressive American, of course I am bound to think all conventional rules are an abomination.'

'If you had a brother and I gave him a stick he'd take it.'

'Not across his back, I hope.'

'Or if I gave your father a book?'

'He'd take books to any extent, I should say.'

'And why not you a ring?'

'Who said I wouldn't? But after all this you mustn't try me.'

'I was not thinking of it.'

'I'm so glad of that! Well;—if you'll promise that you'll never offer me one, I'll promise that I'll take it when it comes. But what does all this mean?'

'It is not worth talking about.'

'You have offered somebody a ring, and somebody hasn't taken it. May I guess?'

'I had rather you did not.'

'I could, you know.'

'Never mind about that. Now come and have a turn. I am bound not to give you a ring; but you are bound to accept anything else I may offer.'

'No, Lord Silverbridge;—not at all. Nevertheless we'll have a turn.'

That night before he went up to his room he had told Isabel Boncassen that he loved her. And when he spoke he was telling her the truth. It had seemed to him that Mabel had become hard to him, and had over and over again rejected the approaches to tenderness which he had attempted to make in his intercourse with her. Even though she were to accept him, what would that be worth to him if she did not love him? So many things had been added together! Why had Tregear gone to Grex, and having gone there why had he kept his journey a secret? Tregear he knew was engaged to his sister;—but for all that, there was a closer intimacy between Mabel and Tregear than between Mabel and himself. And surely she might have taken his ring!

And then Isabel Boncassen was so perfect! Since he had first met her he had heard her loveliness talked of on all sides. It seemed to be admitted everywhere that so beautiful a creature had never before been seen in London. There is even a certain dignity attached to that which is praised by all lips. Miss Boncassen as an American girl, had she been judged to be beautiful only by his own eyes, might perhaps have seemed to him to be beneath his serious notice. In such a case he might have felt himself unable to justify so extraordinary a choice. But there was an acclamation of assent as to this girl! Then came the dancing—the one dance after another; the pressure of the hand, the entreaty that she would not, just on this occasion, dance with any other man, the attendance on her when she took her glass of wine, the whispered encouragement of Mrs. Montacute Jones, the half-resisting and yet half-yielding conduct of the girl. 'I shall not dance at all again,' she said when he asked her to stand up for another. 'Think of all that lawn-tennis this morning.'

'But you will play to-morrow?'

'I thought you were going.'

'Of course I shall stay now,' he said, and as he said it he put his hand on her hand, which was on his arm. She drew it away at once. 'I love you so dearly,' he whispered to her; 'so dearly.'

'Lord Silverbridge!'

'I do. I do. Can you say that you will love me in return?'

'I cannot,' she said slowly. 'I have never dreamed of such a thing. I hardly know now whether you are in earnest.'

'Indeed, indeed I am.'

'Then I will say good-night, and think about it. Everybody is going. We will have our game to-morrow at any rate.'

When he went to his room he found the ring on his dressing-table.

Chapter XL

'And then!'

On the next morning Miss Boncassen did not appear at breakfast. Word came that she had been so fatigued by the lawn-tennis as not to be able to leave her bed. 'I have been to her,' said Mrs. Montacute Jones, whispering to Lord Silverbridge, as though he were particularly interested. 'There's nothing really the matter. She will be down to lunch.'

'I was afraid she might be ill,' said Silverbridge, who was now hardly anxious to hide his admiration.

'Oh no;—nothing of that sort; but she will not be able to play again to-day. It was your fault. You should not have made her dance last night.' After that Mrs. Jones said a word about it all to Lady Mabel. 'I hope the Duke will not be angry with me.'

'Why should he be angry with you?'

'I don't suppose he will approve of it, and perhaps he'll say I brought them together on purpose.'

Excerpted from *The Duke's Children.*

Red Letter Days in British Columbia

LIEUTENANT TOWNSEND WHELEN

In the month of July, 1901, my partner, Bill Andrews, and I were at a small Hudson Bay post in the northern part of British Columbia, outfitting for a long hunting and exploring trip in the wild country to the North. The official map showed this country as "unexplored," with one or two rivers shown by dotted lines. This map was the drawing card which had brought us thousands of miles by rail, stage and pack train to this out-of-the-way spot. By the big stove in the living room of the factor's house we listened to weird tales of this north country, of its enormous mountains and glaciers, its rivers and lakes and of the quantities of game and fish. The factor told us of three men who had tried to get through there in the Klondike rush several years before and had not been heard from yet. The trappers and Siwashes could tell us of trails which ran up either side of the Scumscum, the river on which the post stood, but no one knew what lay between that and the Yukon to the north.

We spent two days here outfitting and on the morning of the third said goodbye to the assembled population and started with our pack train up the east bank of the Scumscum. We were starting out to live and travel in an unknown wilderness for over six months and our outfit may perhaps interest my readers: we had two saddle horses, four pack horses and a dog. A small tent formed one pack cover. We had ten heavy army blankets, which we used for saddle blankets while traveling, they being kept clean by using canvas sweat pads under them. We were able to pack 150 pounds of grub on each horse, divided up as nearly as I can remember as follows: One hundred and fifty pounds flour, 50 pounds sugar, 30 pounds beans, 10 pounds rice, 10 pounds dried apples, 20 pounds prunes, 30 pounds corn meal, 20 pounds oat-meal, 30 pounds potatoes, 10 pounds onions, 50 pounds bacon, 25 pounds salt, 1 pound pepper, 6 cans baking powder, 10 pounds soap, 10 pounds tobacco, 10 pounds tea, and a few little incidentals weighing probably 10 pounds. We took two extra sets of shoes for each horse, with tools for shoeing, 2 axes, 25 boxes of wax matches, a large can of gun oil, canton flannel for gun rags, 2 cleaning rods, a change of underclothes, 6 pairs of socks and 6 moccasins each, with buckskin for resoling, toilet articles, 100 yards of fishing line, 2 dozen fish hooks, an oil stove, file, screw-driver, needles and thread, etc.

For cooking utensils we had 2 frying pans, 3 kettles to nest, 2 tin cups, 3 tin plates and a gold pan. We took 300 cartridges for each of our rifles. Bill carried a .38–55 Winchester, model '94, and I had my old .40–72 Winchester, model '95, which had proved too reliable to relinquish for a high-power small bore. Both rifles were equipped with Lyman sights and carefully sighted. As a precaution we each took along extra front sights, firing pins and main-springs, but did not have a chance to use them. I loaded the ammunition for both rifles myself, with black powder, smokeless priming, and lead bullets. Both rifles proved equal to every emergency.

Where the post stood the mountains were low and covered for the most part with sage brush, with here and there a grove of pines or quaking aspen. As our pack train wound its way up the narrow trail above the river bank we saw many Siwashes spearing salmon, a very familiar sight in that country. These gradually became fewer and fewer, then we passed a miner's cabin and a Siwash village with its little log huts and its hay fields, from which grass is cut for the winter consumption of the horses. Gradually all signs of civilization disappeared, the mountains rose higher and higher, the valley became a canyon, and the roar of the river increased, until finally the narrowing trail wound around an outrageous corner with the river a thousand feet below, and looming up in front of us appeared a range of snow-capped moun-tains, and thus at last we were in the haven where we would be.

That night we camped on one of the little pine-covered benches above the canon. My, but it was good to get the smell of that everlasting sage out of our nostrils, and to take long whiffs of the balsam-ladened air! Sunset comes very late at this latitude in July, and it was an easy matter to wander up a little draw at nine in the evening and shoot the heads of three grouse. After supper it was mighty good to lie and smoke and listen to the tinkle of the horse bells as they fed on the luscious mountain grass. We were old campmates, Bill and I, and it took us back to many trips we had had before, which were, however, to be surpassed many times by this one. I can well remember how as a boy, when I first took to woods loaf-ing, I used to brood over a little work which we all know so well, entitled "Woodcraft" by that grand old man, "Nessmuk," and particularly that part where he relates about his eight-day tramp through the then virgin wilderness of Michigan. But here we were, starting out on a trip which was to take over half a year, during which time we were destined to cover over 1,500 miles of unexplored mountains, without the sight of a human face or an axe mark other than our own.

The next day after about an hour's travel, we passed the winter cabin of an old trapper, now deserted, but with the frames for stretching bear skins and boards for marten pelts lying around—betokening the owner's occupation. The dirt roof was entirely covered with the horns of deer and mountain sheep, and we longed to close our jaws on some good red venison. Here the man-made trails came to an end, and henceforth we used the game trails entirely. These intersect the country in every direction, being made by the deer, sheep and caribou in their migrations between the high and low altitudes. In some places they were hardly discernible, while in others we followed them for days, when they were as plainly marked as the bridle paths in a city park. A little further on we saw a whole family of goats sunning themselves on a high bluff across the river, and that night we dined on the ribs of a fat little spike buck which I shot in the park where we pitched our tent.

To chronicle all the events which occurred on that glorious trip would, I fear, tire my readers, so I will choose from the rich store certain ones which have made red-letter days in our lives. I can recollect but four days when we were unable to kill enough game or catch enough fish to keep the table well supplied, and as luck would have it, those four days came together, and we nearly starved. We had been camped for about a week in a broad wooded valley, having a glorious loaf after a hard struggle across a mountain pass, and were living on trout from a little stream alongside camp, and grouse which were in the pine woods by the thousands. Tiring of this diet we decided to take a little side trip and get a deer or two, taking only our three fattest horses and leaving the others behind to fatten up on the long grass in the valley, for they had become very poor owing to a week's work high up above timber line. The big game here was all high up in the mountains to escape the heat of the valley. So we started one morning, taking only a little tea, rice, three bannocks, our bedding and rifles, thinking that we would enjoy living on meat straight for a couple of days. We had along with us a black mongrel hound named Lion, belonging to Bill. He was a fine dog on grouse but prone to chase a deer once in a while.

About eight miles up the valley could be seen a high mountain of green serpentine rock and for many days we had been speculating on the many fine bucks which certainly lay in the little ravines around the base, so we chose this for our goal. We made the top of the mountain about three in the afternoon, and gazing down on the opposite side we saw a little lake with good horse feed around it and determined to camp there. About halfway down we jumped a doe and as it stood on a little hummock Bill blazed away at it and undershot. This was too much for Lion, the hound, and he broke after the deer, making the mountainside ring with his baying for half an hour. Well, we hunted all the next day, and the next, and never saw a hair. That dog had chased the deer all out of the country with his barking.

By this time our little grub-stake of rice, bannocks and tea was exhausted, and, to make things worse, on the third night we had a terrific hail storm, the stones covering the ground three inches deep. Breakfast the next morning consisted of tea alone and we felt pretty glum as we started out, determining that if we did not find game that day we would pull up stakes for our big camp in the valley. About one o'clock I struck a fresh deer trail and had not followed it long before three or four others joined it, all traveling on a game trail which led up a valley. This valley headed up about six miles from our camp in three little ravines, each about four miles long. When I got to the junction of these ravines it was getting dark and I had to make for camp. Bill was there before me and had the fire going and some tea brewing, but nothing else. He had traveled about twenty miles that day and had not seen a thing. I can still see the disgusted look on his face when he found I had killed nothing. We drank our tea in silence, drew our belts tighter and went to bed.

The next morning we saddled up our horses and pulled out. We had not tasted food for about sixty hours and were feeling very faint and weak. I can remember what an effort it was to get into the saddle and how sick and weak I felt when old Baldy, my saddle horse, broke into a trot. Our way back led near the spot where I had left the deer trail the night before, and we determined to ride that way hoping that perhaps we might get a shot at them. Bill came first, then Loco, the pack horse, and I brought up the rear. As we were crossing one of the little ravines at the head of the main valley Loco bolted and Bill took after him to drive him back into the trail. I sat on my horse idly watching the race, when suddenly I saw a mouse-colored flash and then another and heard the thump, thump of cloven feet. Almost instantly the whole ravine seemed to be alive with deer. They were running in every direction. I leaped from my horse and cut loose at the nearest, which happened to be a doe. She fell over a log and I could see her tail waving in little circles and knew I had her. Then I turned on a big buck on the other side of the ravine and at the second shot he stumbled and rolled into the little stream. I heard Bill shooting off to the left and yelled to him that we had enough, and he soon joined me, saying he had a spike buck down. It was the work of but a few minutes to dress the deer and soon we had a little fire going and the three livers hanging in little strips around it. Right here we three, that is, Bill, the dog, and myself, disposed of a liver apiece, and my! how easily and quickly it went—the first meat in over a week. Late that night we made our horse camp in the lower valley, having to walk all the way as our horses packed the meat. The next day was consumed entirely with jerking meat, cooking and eating. We consumed half the spike buck that day. When men do work such as we were doing their appetites are enormous, even without a fast of four days to sharpen them up.

One night I well remember after a particularly hard day with the pack train through a succession of wind-falls. We killed a porcupine just before camping and made it into a stew with rice, dough balls, onions and thick gravy, seasoned with curry. It filled the kettle to within an inch of the top and we ate the whole without stopping, whereat Bill remarked that it was enough for a whole boarding-house. According to the catalogue of Abercrombie and Fitch that kettle held eight quarts.

We made it the rule while our horses were in condition, to travel four days in the week, hunt two and rest one. Let me chronicle a day of traveling; it may interest some of you who have never traveled with a pack train. Arising at the first streak of dawn, one man cooked the breakfast while the other drove in the horses. These were allowed to graze free at every camping place, each horse having a cow bell around its neck, only Loco being hobbled, for he had a fashion of wandering off on an exploring expedition of his own and leading all the other horses with him. The horses were liable to be anywhere within two miles of camp, and it was necessary to get behind them to drive them in. Four miles over these mountains would be considered a pretty good day's work in the East. Out here it merely gave one an appetite for his breakfast. If you get behind a pack of well-trained horses they will usually walk right straight to camp, but on occasions I have walked, thrown stones and cussed from seven until twelve before I managed to get them in. Sometimes a bear will run off a pack of horses. This happened to us once and it took two days to track them to the head of a canyon, fifteen miles off, and then we had to break Loco all over again.

Breakfast and packing together would take an hour, so we seldom got started before seven o'clock. One of us rode first to pick out the trail, then followed the four pack horses and the man in the rear, whose duty it was to keep them in the trail and going along. Some days the trail was fine, running along the grassy south hillsides with fine views of the snowcapped ranges, rivers, lakes and glaciers; and on others it was one continual struggle over fallen logs, boulders, through ice-cold rivers, swifter than the Niagara rapids, and around bluffs so high that we could scarcely distinguish the outlines of the trees below. Suppose for a minute that you have the job of keeping the horses in the trail. You ride behind the last horse, lazily watching the train. You do not hurry them as they stop for an instant to catch at a whiff of bunch grass beside the trail. Two miles an hour is all the speed you can hope to make. Suddenly one horse will leave the trail enticed by some particularly green grass a little to one side, and leaning over in your saddle you pick up a stone and hurl it at the delinquent, and he falls into line again. Then everything goes well until suddenly one of the pack horses breaks off on a faint side trail going for all he is worth. You dig in your spurs and follow him down the mountain side over rocks and down timber until he comes to a stop half a mile below in a thicket of quaking aspen. You extricate him and drive him back. The next thing you know one of the horses starts to buck and you notice that his pack is turning; then everything starts at once. The pack slides between the horse's legs, he bucks all the harder, the frying pan comes loose, a side pack comes off and the other horses fly in every direction. Perhaps in an hour you have corralled the horses, repacked the cause of your troubles and are hitting the trail again. In another day's travel the trail may lead over down timber and big boulders and for eight solid hours you are whipping the horses to make them jump the obstructions, while your companion is pulling at the halters.

Rustling with a pack train is a soul-trying occupation. Where possible we always aimed to go into camp about three in the afternoon. Then the horses got a good feed before dark—they will not feed well at night—and we had plenty of time to make a comfortable camp and get a good supper. We seldom pitched our tent on these one-night camps unless the weather looked doubtful, preferring to make a bed of pine boughs near the fire. The blankets were laid on top of a couple of pack sheets and the tent over all.

For several days we had been traveling thus, looking for a pass across a long snow-capped mountain range which barred our way to the north. Finally we found a pass between two large peaks where we thought we could get through, so we started up. When we got up to timber-line the wind was blowing so hard that we could not sit on our horses. It would take up large stones the size of one's fist and hurl them down the mountain side. It swept by us cracking and roaring like a battery of rapid-fire guns. To cross was impossible, so we back-tracked a mile to a spot where a little creek crossed the trail, made camp and waited. It was three days before the wind went down enough to allow us to cross.

The mountain sheep had made a broad trail through the pass and it was easy to follow, being mostly over shale rock. That afternoon, descending the other side of the range, we camped just below timber line by a little lake of the most perfect emerald hue I have ever seen. The lake was about a mile long. At its head a large glacier extended way up towards the peaks. On the east was a wall of bright red rock, a thousand feet high, while to the west the hillside was covered with dwarf pine trees, some of them being not over a foot high and full-grown at that. Below our camp the little stream, the outlet of the lake, bounded down the hillside in a succession of waterfalls. A more beautiful picture I have yet to see. We stayed up late that night watching it in the light of the full moon and thanked our lucky stars that we were alive. It was very cold; we put on all the clothes we owned and turned in under seven blankets. The heavens seemed mighty near, indeed, and the stars crackled and almost exploded with the still silver mountains sparkling all around. We could hear the roar of the waterfalls below us and the bells of the horses on the hillside above. Our noses were very cold. Far off a coyote howled and so we went to sleep—and instantly it was morning.

I arose and washed in the lake. It was my turn to cook, but first of all I got my telescope and looked around for signs of game. Turning the glass to the top of the wooded hillside, I saw something white moving, and getting a steady position, I made it out to be the rump of a mountain sheep. Looking carefully I picked out four others. Then I called Bill. The sheep were mine by right of discovery, so we traded the cook detail and I took my rifle and belt, stripped to trousers, moccasins and shirt, and started out, going swiftly at first to warm up in the keen mountain air. I kept straight up the hillside until I got to the top and then started along the ridge toward the sheep. As I crossed a little rise I caught sight of them five hundred yards ahead, the band numbering about fifty. Some were feeding, others were bedded down in some shale. From here on it was all stalking, mostly crawling through the small trees and bushes which were hardly knee high. Finally, getting within one hundred and fifty yards, I got a good, steady prone position between the bushes, and picking out the largest ram, I got the white Lyman sight nicely centered behind his shoulder and very carefully and gradually I pressed the trigger. The instant the gun went off I knew he was mine, for I could call the shot exactly. Instantly the sheep were on the move. They seemed to double up bunch and then vanish. It was done so quickly that I doubt if I could have gotten in another shot even if I had wished it. The ram I had fired at was knocked completely off its feet, but picked himself up instantly and started off with the others; but after he had run about a hundred yards I saw his head drop and turning half a dozen somersaults, he rolled down the hill and I knew I had made a heart shot. His horns measured 16½ inches at the base, and the nose contained an enormous bump, probably caused in one of his fights for the supremacy of the herd.

I dressed the ram and then went for the horses. Bill, by this time, had everything packed up, so after going up the hill and loading the sheep on my saddle horse, we started down the range for a region where it was warmer and less strenuous and where the horse feed was better. That night we had mountain sheep ribs—the best meat that ever passed a human's mouth—and I had a head worth bringing home. A 16½-inch head is very rare in these days. I believe the record head measured about 19 inches. I remember distinctly, however, on another hunt in the Lillooet district of British Columbia, finding in the long grass of a valley the half-decayed head of an enormous ram. I measured the pith of the skull where the horn had been and it recorded 18 inches. The horn itself must have been at least 21 inches. The ram probably died of old age or was unable to get out of the high altitude when the snow came.

We journeyed on and on, having a glorious time in the freedom of the mountains. We were traveling in a circle, the diameter of which was about three hundred miles. One day we struck an enormous glacier and had to bend way off to the right to avoid it. For days as we travelled that glacier kept us company. It had its origin way up in a mass of peaks and perpetual snow, being fed from a dozen valleys. At least six moraines could be distinctly seen on its surface, and the air in its vicinity was decidedly cool. Where we first struck it it was probably six miles wide and I believe it was not a bit less than fifty miles long. We named it Chilco glacier, because it undoubtedly drained into a large lake of that name near the coast. At this point we were not over two hundred miles from the Pacific Ocean.

As the leaves on the aspen trees started to turn we gradually edged around and headed toward our starting point, going by another route, however, trusting to luck and the careful map we had been making to bring us out somewhere on the Scum-scum river above the post. The days were getting short now and the nights very cold. We had to travel during almost all the daylight and our horses started to get poor. The shoes we had taken for them were used up by this time and we had to avoid as much as possible the rocky country. We travelled fast for a month until we struck the headwaters of the Scum-scum; then knowing that we were practically safe from being snowed up in the mountain we made a permanent camp on a hillside where the horsefeed was good and started to hunt and tramp to our hearts' delight, while our horses filled up on the grass. We never killed any more game than we could use, which was about one animal every ten days. In this climate meat will keep for a month if protected from flies in the daytime and exposed to the night air after dark.

We were very proud of our permanent camp. The tent was pitched under a large pine tree in a thicket of willows and quaking aspen. All around it was built a windbreak of logs and pine boughs, leaving in front a yard, in the center of which was our camp fire. The windbreak went up six feet high and when a fire was going in front of the tent we were as warm as though in a cabin, no matter how hard the wind blew. Close beside the tent was a little spring, and a half a mile away was a lake full of trout from fifteen pounds down. We spent three days laying in a supply of firewood. Altogether it was the best camp I ever slept in. The hunting within tramping distance was splendid. We rarely hunted together, each preferring to go his own way. When we did not need meat we hunted varmints, and I brought in quite a number of prime coyote pelts and one wolf. One evening Bill staggered into camp with a big mountain lion over his shoulders. He just happened to run across it in a little pine thicket. That was the only one we saw on the whole trip, although their tracks were everywhere and we frequently heard their mutterings in the still evenings. The porcupines at this camp were unusually numerous. They would frequently get inside our wind break and had a great propensity for eating our soap. Lion, the hound, would not bother them; he had learned his lesson well. When they came around he would get an expression on his face as much as to say, "You give me a pain."

The nights were now very cold. It froze every night and we bedded ourselves down with lots of skins and used enormous logs on the fire so that it would keep going all night. We shot some marmots and made ourselves fur caps and gloves and patched up our outer garments with buckskin. And still the snow did not come.

One day while out hunting I saw a big goat on a bluff off to my right and determined to try to get him for his head, which appeared through my telescope to be an unusually good one. He was about half a mile off when I first spied him and the bluff extended several miles to the southwest like a great wall shutting off the view in that direction. I worked up to the foot of the bluffs and then along; climbing up several hundred feet I struck a shelf which appeared to run along the face at about the height I had seen the goat. It was ticklish work, for the shelf was covered with slide rock which I had to avoid disturbing, and then, too, in places it dwindled to a ledge barely three feet wide with about five hundred feet of nothing underneath. After about four hundred yards of this work I heard a rock fall above me and looking up saw the billy leaning over an outrageous corner looking at me. Aiming as nearly as I could straight up I let drive at the middle of the white mass. There was a grunt, a scramble and a lot of rocks, and then down came the goat, striking in between the cliff and a big boulder and not two feet from me. I fairly shivered for fear he would jump up and butt me off the ledge, but he only gave one quiver and lay still. The 330-grain bullet entering the stomach, had broken the spine and killed instantly. He was an old grandfather and had a splendid head, which I now treasure very highly. I took the head, skin, fat and some of the meat back to camp that night, having to pack it off the bluff in sections. The fat rendered out into three gold-pans full of lard. Goat-fat is excellent for frying and all through the trip it was a great saving on our bacon.

Then one night the snow came. We heard it gently tapping on the tent, and by morning there was three inches in our yard. The time had come only too soon to pull out, which we did about ten o'clock, bidding good-bye to our permanent camp with its comfortable windbreak, its fireplace, table and chairs. Below us the river ran through a canon and we had to cross quite a high mountain range to get through. As we ascended the snow got deeper and deeper. It was almost two feet deep on a level on top of the range. We had to go down a very steep hog-back, and here had trouble in plenty. The horses' feet balled up with snow and they were continually sliding. A pack horse slid down on top of my saddle horse and started him. I was on foot in front and they knocked me down and the three of us slid until stopped by a fallen tree. Such a mess I never saw. One horse was on top of another. The pack was loose and frozen ropes tangled up with everything. It took us half an hour to straighten up the mess and the frozen lash ropes cut our hands frightfully. My ankle had become slightly strained in the mix-up and for several days I suffered agonies with it. There was no stopping—we had to hit the trail hard or get snowed in. One day we stopped to hunt. Bill went out while I nursed my leg. He brought in a fine seven-point buck.

Speaking of the hunt he said: "I jumped the buck in a flat of down timber. He was going like mad about a hundred yards off when I first spied him. I threw up the old rifle and blazed away five times before he tumbled. Each time I pulled I was conscious that the sights looked just like that trademark of the Lyman sight showing the running deer and the sight. When I went over to look at the buck I had a nice little bunch of five shots right behind the shoulder. Those Lyman sights are surely the sights for a hunting rifle." Bill was one of the best shots on game I ever saw. One day I saw him cut the heads off of three grouse in trees while he sat in the saddle with his horse walking up hill. Both our rifles did mighty good work. The more I use a rifle the more I become convinced of the truth of the saying, "Beware of the man with one gun." Get a good rifle to suit you exactly. Fix the trigger pull and sights exactly as you wish them and then stick to that gun as long as it will shoot accurately and you will make few misses in the field.

Only too soon we drove our pack-train into the post. As we rode up two men were building a shack. One of them dropped a board and we nearly jumped out of our skins at the terrific noise. My! How loud everything sounded to our ears, accustomed only to the stillness of those grand mountains. We stayed at the post three days, disposing of our horses and boxing up our heads and skins, and then pulled out for civilization. Never again will such experiences come to us. The day of the wilderness hunter has gone for good. And so the hunt of our lives came to an end.

The Hunt for the Man-Eaters of Tsavo

LT. COL. J. M. PATTERSON, D. S. O.

Editor's Note: When assigned to help supervise the building of a Uganda Railroad bridge over the Tsavo River in east Africa in March, 1898, Lt. Col. J. H. Patterson, D. S. O., had little idea of the magnitude of the adventure upon which he was embarking. The site of the bridge, which is today a part of Kenya, became the scene of savage attacks by man-eating lions preying on the workers. Col. Patterson's stirring book, *The Man-Eaters of Tsavo*, remains in print to this day. The drama was also captured quite well in the film, *The Ghost and the Darkness*, starring Val Kilmer and Michael Douglas.

Unfortunately this happy state of affairs did not continue for long, and our work was soon interrupted in a rude and startling manner. Two most voracious and insatiable man-eating lions appeared upon the scene, and for over nine months waged an intermittent warfare against the railway and all those connected with it in the vicinity of Tsavo. This culminated in a perfect reign of terror in December, 1898, when they actually succeeded in bringing the railway works to a complete standstill for about three weeks. At first they were not always successful in their efforts to carry off a victim, but as time went on they stopped at nothing and indeed braved any danger in order to obtain their favourite food. Their methods then became so uncanny, and their man-stalking so well-timed and so certain of success, that the workmen firmly believed that they were not real animals at all, but devils in lions' shape. Many a time the coolies solemnly assured me that it was absolutely useless to attempt to shoot them. They were quite convinced that the angry spirits of two departed native chiefs had taken this form in order to protect against a railway being made through their country, and by stopping its progress to avenge the insult thus shown to them.

I had only been a few days at Tsavo when I first heard that these brutes had been seen in the neighbourhood. Shortly afterwards one or two coolies mysteriously disappeared, and I was told that they had been carried off by night from their tents and devoured by lions. At the time I did not credit this story, and was more inclined to believe that the unfortunate men had been the victims of foul play at the hands of some of their comrades. They were, as it happened, very good workmen, and had each saved a fair number of rupees, so I thought it quite likely that some scoundrels from the gangs had murdered them for the sake of their money. This suspicion, however, was very soon dispelled. About three weeks after my arrival, I was roused one morning about daybreak and told that one of my *jemadars*, a fine powerful Sikh named Ungan Singh, had been seized in his tent during the night, and dragged off and eaten.

Naturally I lost no time in making an examination of the place, and was soon convinced that the man had indeed been carried off by a lion, and its "pug" marks were plainly visible in the sand, while the furrows made by the heels of the victim showed the direction in which he had been dragged away. Moreover, the *jemadar* shared his tent with half a dozen other workmen, and one of his bedfellows had actually witnessed the occurrence. He graphically described how, at about midnight, the lion suddenly put its head in at the open tent door and seized Ungan Singh—who happened to be nearest the opening—by the throat. The unfortunate fellow cried out *"Choro"* ("Let go"), and threw his arms up round the lion's neck. The next moment he was gone, and his panic-stricken companions lay helpless, forced to listen to the terrible struggle which took place outside. Poor Ungan Singh must have died hard; but what chance had he? As a coolie gravely remarked, "Was he not fighting with a lion?"

On hearing this dreadful story I at once set out to try to track the animal, and was accompanied by Captain Haslem, who happened to be staying at Tsavo at the time, and who, poor fellow, himself met with a tragic fate very shortly afterwards. We found it an easy matter to follow the route taken by the lion, as he appeared to have stopped several times before beginning his meal. Pools of blood marked these halting-places, where he doubtless indulged in the man-eaters' habit of licking the skin off so as to get at the fresh blood. (I have been led to believe that this is their custom from the appearance of two half-eaten bodies which I subsequently rescued: the skin was gone in places, and the flesh looked dry, as if it had been sucked.) On reaching the spot where the body had been devoured, a dreadful spectacle presented itself. The ground all round was covered with blood and morsels of flesh and bones, but the unfortunate *jemadar*'s head had been left intact, save for the holes made by the lion's tusks on seizing him, and lay a short distance away from the other remains, the eyes staring wide open with a startled, horrified look in them. The place was considerably cut up, and on closer examination we found that two lions had been there and had probably struggled for possession of the body. It was the most gruesome sight I had ever seen. We collected the remains as well as we could and heaped stones on them, the head with its fixed, terrified stare seeming to watch us all the time, for it we did not bury, but took back to camp for identification before the Medical Officer.

Thus occurred my first experience of man-eating lions, and I vowed there and then that I would spare no pains to rid the neighbourhood of the brutes. I little knew the trouble that was in store for me, or how narrow were to be my own escapes from sharing poor Ungan Singh's fate.

That same night I sat up in a tree close to the late *jemadar*'s, tent, hoping that the lions would return to it for another victim. I was followed to my perch by a few of the more terrified coolies, who begged to be allowed to sit up in the tree with me; all the other workmen remained in their tents, but no more doors were left open. I had with me my .303 and 12-bore shot gun, one barrel loaded with ball and the other with slug. Shortly after settling down to my vigil, my hopes of bagging one of the brutes were raised by the sound of their ominous roaring coming closer and closer. Presently this ceased, and quiet reigned for an hour or two, as lions always stalk their prey in complete silence. All at once, however, we heard a great uproar and frenzied cries coming from another camp about half a mile away; we knew then that the lions had seized a victim there, and that we should see or hear nothing further of them that night.

Next morning I found that one of the brutes had broken into a tent at Railhead Camp—whence we had heard the commotion during the night—and had made off with a poor wretch who was lying there asleep. After a night's rest, therefore, I took up my position in a suitable tree near this tent. I did not at all like the idea of walking the half-mile to the place after dark, but all the same I felt fairly safe, as one of my men carried a bright lamp close behind me. He in his turn was followed by another leading a goat, which I tied under my tree in the hope that the lion might be tempted to seize it instead of a coolie. A steady drizzle commenced shortly after I had settled down to my night of watching, and I was soon thoroughly chilled and wet. I stuck to my uncomfortable post, however, hoping to get a shot, but I well remember the feeling of impotent disappointment I experienced when about midnight I heard screams and cries and a heartrending shriek, which told me that the man-eaters had again eluded me and had claimed another victim elsewhere.

At this time the various camps for the workmen were very scattered, so that the lions had a range of some eight miles on either side of Tsavo to work upon; and as their tactics seemed to be to break into a different camp each night, it was most difficult to forestall them. They almost appeared, too, to have an extraordinary and uncanny faculty of finding out our plans beforehand, so that no matter in how likely or how tempting a spot we lay in wait for them, they invariably avoided that particular place and seized their victim for the night from some other camp. Hunting them by day moreover, in such a dense wilderness as surrounded us, was an exceedingly tiring and really foolhardy undertaking. In a thick jungle of the kind round Tsavo the hunted animal has every chance against the hunter, as however careful the latter may be, a dead twig or something of the sort is sure to crackle just at the critical moment and so give the alarm. Still I never gave up hope of some day finding their lair, and accordingly continued to devote all my spare time to crawling about through the undergrowth. Many a time when attempting to force my way through this bewildering tangle I had to be released by my gun-bearer from the fast clutches of the "wait-a-bit"; and often with immense pains I succeeded in tracing the lions to the river after they had seized a victim, only to lose the trail from there onwards, owing to the rocky nature of the ground which they seemed to be careful to choose in retreating to their den.

At this early stage of the struggle, I am glad to say, the lions were not always successful in their efforts to capture a human being for their nightly meal, and one or two amusing incidents occurred to relieve the tension from which our nerves were beginning to suffer. On one occasion an enterprising *bun-niah* (Indian trader) was riding along on his donkey late one night, when suddenly a lion sprang out on him knocking over both man and beast. The donkey was badly wounded, and the lion was just about to seize the trader, when in some way or other his claws became entangled in a rope by which two empty oil tins were strung across the donkey's neck. The rattle and clatter made by these as he dragged them after him gave him such a fright that he turned tail and bolted off into the jungle, to the intense relief of the terrified *bunniah*, who quickly made his way up the nearest tree and remained there, shivering with fear, for the rest of the night.

Shortly after this episode, a Greek contractor named Themistocles Pappadimitrini had an equally marvellous escape. He was sleeping peacefully in his tent one night, when a lion broke in, and seized and made off with the mattress on which he was lying. Though rudely awakened, the Greek was quite unhurt and suffered from nothing worse than a bad fright. This same man, however, met with a melancholy fate not long afterwards. He had been to the Kili ma N'jaro district to buy cattle, and on the return journey attempted to take a short cut across country to the railway, but perished miserably of thirst on the way.

On another occasion fourteen coolies who slept together in a large tent were one night awakened by a lion suddenly jumping on to the tent and breaking through it. The brute landed with one claw on a coolie's shoulder, which was badly torn; but instead of seizing the man himself, in his hurry he grabbed a large bag of rice which happened to be lying in the tent, and made off with it, dropping it in disgust some little distance away when he realised his mistake.

These, however, were only the earlier efforts of the man-eaters. Later on, as will be seen, nothing flurried or frightened them in the least, and except as food they showed a complete contempt for human beings. Having once marked down a victim, they would allow nothing to deter them from securing him, whether he were protected by a thick fence, or inside a closed tent, or sitting round a brightly burning fire. Shots, shouting and firebrands they alike held in derision.

The Attack on the Goods-Wagon

All this time my own tent was pitched in an open clearing, unprotected by a fence of any kind round it. One night when the medical officer, Dr. Rose, was staying with me, we were awakened about midnight by hearing something tumbling about among the tent ropes, but on going out with a lantern we could discover nothing. Daylight, however, plainly revealed the "pug" marks of a lion, so that on that occasion I fancy one or other of us had a narrow escape. Warned by this experience, I at once arranged to move my quarters, and went to join forces with Dr. Brock, who had just arrived at Tsavo to take medical charge of the district. We shared a hut of palm leaves and boughs, which we had constructed on the eastern side of the river, close to the old caravan route leading to Uganda; and we had it surrounded by a circular *boma*, or thorn fence, about seventy yards in diameter, well made and thick and high. Our personal servants also lived within the enclosure, and a bright fire was always kept up throughout the night. For the sake of coolness, Brock and I used to sit out under the verandah of this hut in the evenings; but it was rather trying to our nerves to attempt to read or write there, as we never knew when a lion might spring over the *boma*, and be on us before we were aware. We therefore kept our rifles within easy reach, and cast many an anxious glance out into the inky darkness beyond the circle of the firelight. On one or two occasions, we found in the morning that the lions had come quite close to the fence; but fortunately they never succeeded in getting through.

By this time, too, the camps of the workmen had also been surrounded by thorn fences; nevertheless the lions managed to jump over or to break through some one or other of these, and regularly every few nights a man was carried off, the reports of the disappearance of this or that workman coming in to me with painful frequency. So long, however, as Railhead Camp—with its two or three thousand men, scattered over a wide area—remained at Tsavo, the coolies appeared not to take much notice of the dreadful deaths of their comrades. Each man felt, I suppose, that as the man-eaters had such a large number of victims to choose from, the chances of their selecting him in particular were very small. But when the large camp moved ahead with the railway, matters altered considerably. I was then left with only some few hundred men to complete the permanent works; and as all the remaining workmen were naturally camped together the attentions of the lions became more apparent and made a deeper impression. A regular panic consequently ensued, and it required all my powers of persuasion to induce the men to stay on. In fact, I succeeded in doing so only by allowing them to knock off all regular work until they had built exceptionally thick and high *bomas* round each camp. Within these enclosures fires were kept burning all night, and it was also the duty of the night-watchman to keep clattering half a dozen empty oil tins suspended from a convenient tree. These he manipulated by means of a long rope, while sitting in the hopes of terrifying away the man-eaters. In spite of all these precautions, however, the lions would not be denied, and men continued to disappear.

When the railhead workmen moved on, their hospital camp was left behind. It stood rather apart from the other camps, in a clearing about three-quarters of a mile from my hut, but was protected by a good thick fence and to all appearance was quite secure. It seemed, however, as if barriers were of no avail against the "demons," for before very long one of them found a weak spot in the *boma* and broke through. On this occasion the Hospital Assistant had a marvellous escape. Hearing a noise outside, he opened the door of his tent and was horrified to see a great lion standing a few yards away looking at him. The beast made a spring towards him, which gave the Assistant such a fright that he jumped backwards, and in doing so luckily upset a box containing medical stores. This crashed down with such a loud clatter of breaking glass that the lion was startled for the moment and made off to another part of the enclosure. Here, unfortunately, he was more successful, as he jumped on to and broke through a tent in which eight patients were lying. Two of them were badly wounded by his spring, while a third poor wretch was seized and dragged off bodily through the thorn fence. The two wounded coolies were left where they lay; a piece of torn tent having fallen over them; and in this position the doctor and I found them on our arrival soon after dawn next morning. We at once decided to move the hospital closer to the main camp; a fresh site was prepared, a stout hedge built round the enclosure, and all the patients were moved in before nightfall.

As I had heard that lions generally visit recently deserted camps, I decided to sit up all night in the vacated *boma* in the hope of getting an opportunity of bagging one of them; but in the middle of my lonely vigil I had the mortification of hearing shrieks and cries coming from the direction of the new hospital, telling me only too plainly that our dreaded foes had once more eluded me. Hurrying to the place at daylight I found that one of the lions had jumped over the newly erected fence and had carried off the hospital *bhisti* (water-carrier), and that several other coolies had been unwilling witnesses of the terrible scene which took place within the circle of light given by the big camp fire. The *bhisti*, it appears, had been lying on the floor, with his head towards the centre of the tent and his feet nearly touching the side. The lion managed to get its head in below the canvas, seized him by the foot and pulled him out. In desperation the unfortunate water-carrier clutched hold of a heavy box in a vain attempt to prevent himself being carried off, and dragged it with him until he was forced to let go by its being stopped by the side of the tent. He then caught hold of a tent rope, and clung tightly to it until it broke. As soon as the lion managed to get him clear of the tent, he sprang at his throat and after a few vicious shakes the poor *bhisti*'s agonising cries were silenced for ever. The brute then seized him in his mouth, like a huge cat with a mouse, and ran up and down the *boma* looking for a weak spot to break through. This he presently found and plunged into, dragging his victim with him and leaving shreds of torn cloth and flesh as ghastly evidences of his passage through the thorns. Dr. Brock and I were easily able to follow his track, and soon found the remains about four hundred yards away in the bush. There was the usual horrible sight. Very little was left of the unfortunate *bhisti*—only the skull, the jaws, a few of the larger bones and a portion of the palm with one or two fingers attached. On one of these was a silver ring, and this, with the teeth (a relic much prized by certain castes), was sent to the man's widow in India.

Again it was decided to move the hospital; and again, before nightfall, the work was completed, including a still stronger and thicker *boma*. When the patients had been moved, I had a covered goods-wagon placed in a favourable position on a siding which ran close to the site which had just been abandoned, and in this Brock and I arranged to sit up that night. We left a couple of tents still standing within the enclosure, and also tied up a few cattle in it as bait for the lions, who had been seen in no less than three different places in the neighbourhood during the afternoon (April 23). Four miles from Tsavo they had attempted to seize a coolie who was walking along the line. Fortunately, however, he had just time to escape up a tree, where he remained, more dead than alive, until he was rescued by the Traffic Manager, who caught sight of him from a passing train. They next appeared close to Tsavo Station, and a couple of hours later some workmen saw one of the lions stalking Dr. Brock as he was returning about dusk from the hospital.

In accordance with our plan, the doctor and I set out after dinner for the goods-wagon, which was about a mile away from our hut. In the light of subsequent events, we did a very foolish thing in taking up our position so late; nevertheless, we reached our destination in safety, and settled down to our watch about ten o'clock. We had the lower half of the door of the wagon closed, while the upper half was left wide open for observation: and we faced, of course, in the direction of the abandoned *boma*, which, however, we were unable to see in the inky darkness. For an hour or two everything was quiet, and the deadly silence was becoming very monotonous and oppressive, when suddenly, to our right, a dry twig snapped, and we knew that an animal of some sort was about. Soon afterwards we heard a dull thud, as if some heavy body had jumped over the *boma*. The cattle, too, became very uneasy, and we could hear them moving about restlessly. Then again came dead silence. At this juncture I proposed to my companion that I should get out of the wagon and lie on the ground close to it, as I could see better in that position should the lion come in our direction with his prey. Brock, however, persuaded me to remain where I was; and a few seconds afterwards I was heartily glad that I had taken his advice, for at that very moment one of the man-eaters—although we did not know it—was quietly stalking us, and was even then almost within springing distance. Orders had been given for the entrance to the *boma* to be blocked up, and accordingly we were listening in the expectation of hearing the lion force his way out through the bushes with his prey. As a matter of fact, however, the doorway had not been properly closed, and while we were wondering what the lion could be doing inside the *boma* for so long, he was outside all the time, silently reconnoitring our position.

Presently I fancied I saw something coming very stealthily towards us. I feared however, to trust to my eyes, which by that time were strained by prolonged staring through the darkness, so under my breath I asked Brock whether he saw anything, at the same time covering the dark object as well as I could with my rifle. Brock did not answer; he told me afterwards that he, too, thought he had seen something move, but was afraid to say so lest I should fire and it turn out to be nothing after all. After this there was intense silence again for a second or two, then with a sudden bound a huge body sprang at us. "The lion!" I shouted, and we both fired almost simultaneously—not a moment too soon, for in another second the brute would assuredly have landed inside the wagon. As it was, he must have swerved off in his spring, probably blinded by the flash and frightened by the noise of the double report which was increased a hundredfold by the reverberation of the hollow iron roof of the truck. Had we not been very much on the alert, he would undoubtedly have got one of us, and we realised that we had had a very lucky and very narrow escape. The next morning we found Brock's bullet embedded in the sand close to a footprint; it could not have missed the lion by more than an inch or two. Mine was nowhere to be found.

Thus ended my first direct encounter with one of the man-eaters.

The Reign of Terror

The lions seemed to have got a bad fright the night Brock and I sat up in wait for them in the goods-wagon, for they kept away from Tsavo and did not molest us in any way for some considerable time—not, in fact, until long after Brock had left me and gone on *safari* (a caravan journey) to Uganda. In this breathing space which they vouchsafed us, it occurred to me that should they renew their attacks, a trap would perhaps offer the best chance of getting at them, and that if I could construct one in which a couple of coolies might be used as bait without being subjected to any danger, the lions would be quite daring enough to enter it in search of them and thus be caught. I accordingly set to work at once, and in a short time managed to make a sufficiently strong trap out of wooden sleepers, tram-rails, pieces of telegraph wire, and a length of heavy chain. It was divided into two compartments—one for the men and one for the lion. A sliding door at one end admitted the former, and once inside this compartment they were perfectly safe, as between them and the lion, if he entered the other, ran a cross wall of iron rails only three inches apart, and embedded both top and bottom in heavy wooden sleepers. The door which was to admit the lion was, of course, at the opposite end of the structure, but otherwise the whole thing was very much on the principle of the ordinary rat-trap, except that it was not necessary for the lion to seize the bait in order to send the door clattering down. This part of the contrivance was arranged in the following manner. A heavy chain was secured along the top part of the lion's doorway, the ends hanging down to the ground on either side of the opening; and to these were fastened, strongly secured by stout wire, short lengths of rails placed about six inches apart. This made a sort of flexible door which could be packed into a small space when not in use, and which abutted against the top of the doorway when lifted up. The door was held in this position by a lever made of a piece of rail, which in turn was kept in its place by a wire fastened to one end and passing down to a spring concealed in the ground inside the cage. As soon as the lion entered sufficiently far into the trap, he would be bound to tread on the spring; his weight on this would release the wire, and in an instant down would come the door behind him; and he could not push it out in any way, as it fell into a groove between two rails firmly embedded in the ground.

In making this trap, which cost us a lot of work, we were rather at a loss for want of tools to bore holes in the rails for the doorway, so as to enable them to be fastened by the wire to the chain. It occurred to me, however, that a hard-nosed bullet from my .303 would penetrate the iron, and on making the experiment I was glad to find that a hole was made as cleanly as if it had been punched out.

When the trap was ready I pitched a tent over it in order further to deceive the lions, and built an exceedingly strong *boma* round it. One small entrance was made at the back of the enclosure for the men, which they were to close on going in by pulling a bush after them; and another entrance just in front of the door of the cage was left open for the lions. The wiseacres to whom I showed my invention were generally of the opinion that the man-eaters would be too cunning to walk into my parlour; but, as will be seen later, their predictions proved false. For the first few nights I baited the trap myself, but nothing happened except that I had a very sleepless and uncomfortable time, and was badly bitten by mosquitoes.

As a matter of fact, it was some months before the lions attacked us again, though from time to time we heard of their depredations in other quarters. Not long after our night in the goods-wagon, two men were carried off from railhead, while another was taken from a place called Engomani, about ten miles away. Within a very short time, this latter place was again visited by the brutes, two more men being seized, one of whom was killed and eaten, and the other so badly mauled that he died within a few days. As I have said, however, we at Tsavo enjoyed complete immunity from attack, and the coolies, believing that their dreaded foes had permanently deserted the district, resumed all their usual habits and occupations, and life in the camps returned to its normal routine.

At last we were suddenly startled out of this feeling of security. One dark night the familiar terror-stricken cries and screams awoke the camps, and we knew that the "demons" had returned and had commenced a new list of victims. On this occasion a number of men had been sleeping outside their tents for the sake of coolness, thinking, of course, that the lions had gone for good, when suddenly in the middle of the night one of the brutes was discovered forcing its way through the *boma*. The alarm was at once given, and sticks, stones and firebrands were hurled in the direction of the intruder. All was of no avail, however, for the lion burst into the midst of the terrified group, seized an unfortunate wretch amid the cries and shrieks of his companions, and dragged him off through the thick thorn fence. He was joined outside by the second lion, and so daring had the two brutes become that they did not trouble to carry their victim any further away, but devoured him within thirty yards of the tent where he had been seized. Although several shots were fired in their direction by the *jemadar* of the gang to which the coolie belonged, they took no notice of these and did not attempt to move until their horrible meal was finished. The few scattered fragments that remained of the body I would not allow to be buried at once, hoping that the lions would return to the spot the following night; and on the chance of this I took up my station at nightfall in a convenient tree. Nothing occurred to break the monotony of my watch, however, except that I had a visit from a hyena, and the next morning I learned that the lions had attacked another camp about two miles from Tsavo—for by this time the camps were again scattered, as I had works in progress all up and down the line. There the man-eaters had been successful in obtaining a victim, whom, as in the previous instance, they devoured quite close to the camp. How they forced their way through the *bomas* without making a noise was, and still is, a mystery to me; I should have thought that it was next to impossible for an animal to get through at all. Yet they continually did so, and without a sound being heard.

After this occurrence, I sat up every night for over a week near likely camps, but all in vain. Either the lions saw me and then went elsewhere, or else I was unlucky, for they took man after man from different places without ever once giving me a chance of a shot at them. This constant night watching was most dreary and fatiguing work, but I felt that it was a duty that had to be undertaken, as the men naturally looked to me for protection. In the whole of my life I have never experienced anything more nerve-shaking than to hear the deep roars of these dreadful monsters growing gradually nearer and nearer, and to know that some one or other of us was doomed to be their victim before morning dawned. Once they reached the vicinity of the camps, the roars completely ceased, and we knew that they were stalking for their prey. Shouts would then pass from camp to camp, *"Khabar dar, bhaieon, shaitan ata"* ("Beware, brothers, the devil is coming"), but the warning cries would prove of no avail, and sooner or later agonising shrieks would break the silence and another man would be missing from roll-call next morning.

I was naturally very disheartened at being foiled in this way night after night, and was soon at my wits' end to know what to do; it seemed as if the lions were really "devils" after all and bore a charmed life. As I have said before, tracking them through the jungle was a hopeless task; but as something had to be done to keep up the men's spirits, I spent many a wry day crawling on my hands and knees through the dense undergrowth of the exasperating wilderness around us. As a matter of fact, if I had come up with the lions on any of these expeditions, it was much more likely that they would have added me to their list of victims than that I should have succeeded in killing either of them, as everything would have been in their favour. About this time, too, I had many helpers, and several officers—civil, naval and military—came to Tsavo from the coast and sat up night after night in order to get a shot at our daring foes. All of us, however, met with the same lack of success, and the lions always seemed capable of avoiding the watchers, while succeeding at the same time in obtaining a victim.

I have a very vivid recollection of one particular night when the brutes seized a man from the railway station and brought him close to my camp to devour. I could plainly hear them crunching the bones, and the sound of their dreadful purring filled the air and rang in my ears for days afterwards. The terrible thing was to feel so helpless; it was useless to attempt to go out, as of course the poor fellow was dead, and in addition it was so pitch dark as to make it impossible to see anything. Some half a dozen workmen, who lived in a small enclosure close to mine, became so terrified on hearing the lions at their meal that they shouted and implored me to allow them to come inside my *boma*. This I willingly did, but soon afterwards I remembered that one man had been lying ill in their camp, and on making enquiry I found that they had callously left him behind alone. I immediately took some men with me to bring him to my *boma*, but on entering his tent I saw by the light of the lantern that the poor fellow was beyond need of safety. He had died of shock at being deserted by his companions.

From this time matters gradually became worse and worse. Hitherto, as a rule, only one of the man-eaters had made the attack and had done the foraging, while the other waited outside in the bush; but now they began to change their tactics, entering the *bomas* together and each seizing a victim. In this way two Swahili porters were killed during the last week of November, one being immediately carried off and devoured. The other was heard moaning for a long time, and when his terrified companions at last summoned up sufficient courage to go to his assistance, they found him stuck fast in the bushes of the *boma* through which for once the lion had apparently been unable to drag him. He was still alive when I saw him next morning, but so terribly mauled that he died before he could be got to the hospital.

Within a few days of this the two brutes made a most ferocious attack on the largest camp in the section, which for safety's sake was situated within a stone's throw of Tsavo Station and close to a Permanent Way Inspector's iron hut. Suddenly in the dead of night the two man-eaters burst in among the terrified workmen, and even from my *boma*, some distance away, I could plainly hear the panic-stricken shrieking of the coolies. Then followed cries of "They've taken him; they've taken him," as the brutes carried off their unfortunate victim and began their horrible feast close beside the camp. The Inspector, Mr. Dalgairns, fired over fifty shots in the direction in which he heard the lions, but they were not to be frightened and calmly lay there until their meal was finished. After examining the spot in the morning, we at once set out to follow the brutes, Mr. Dalgairns feeling confident that he had wounded one of them, as there was a trail on the sand like that of the toes of a broken limb. After some careful stalking, we suddenly found ourselves in the vicinity of the lions, and were greeted with ominous growlings. Cautiously advancing and pushing the bushes aside, we saw in the gloom what we at first took to be a lion cub; closer inspection, however, showed it to be the remains of the unfortunate coolie, which the man-eaters had evidently abandoned at our approach. The legs, one arm and half the body had been eaten, and it was the stiff fingers of the other arm trailing along the sand which had left the marks we had taken to be the trail of a wounded lion. By this time the beasts had retired far into the thick jungle where it was impossible to follow them, so we had the remains of the coolie buried and once more returned home disappointed.

Now the bravest men in the world, much less the ordinary Indian coolie, will not stand constant terrors of this sort indefinitely. The whole district was by this time thoroughly panic-stricken, and I was not at all surprised, therefore, to find on my return to camp that same afternoon (December 1) that the men had all struck work and were waiting to speak to me. When I sent for them, they flocked to my *boma* in a body and stated that they would not remain at Tsavo any longer for anything or anybody; they had come from India on an agreement to work for the government, not to supply food for either lions or "devils." No sooner had they delivered this ultimatum than a regular stampede took place. Some hundreds of them stopped the first passing train by throwing themselves on the rails in front of the engine, and then, swarming on to the trucks and throwing in their possessions anyhow, they fled from the accursed spot.

After this the railway works were completely stopped; and for the next three weeks practically nothing was done but build "lion-proof" huts for those workmen who had had sufficient courage to remain. It was a strange and amusing sight to see these shelters perched on the top of water-tanks, roofs and girders—anywhere for safety—while some even went so far as to dig pits inside their tents, into which they descended at night, covering the top over with heavy logs of wood. Every good-sized tree in the camp had as many beds lashed on to it as its branches would bear—and sometimes more. I remember that one night when the camp was attacked, so many men swarmed on to one particular tree that down it came with a crash, hurling its terror-stricken load of shrieking coolies close to the very lions they were trying to avoid. Fortunately for them, a victim had already been secured, and the brutes were too busy devouring him to pay attention to anything else.

The District Officer's Narrow Escape

Some little time before the flight of the workmen, I had written to Mr. Whitehead, the District Officer, asking him to come up and assist me in my campaign against the lions, and to bring with him any of his *askaris* (native soldiers) that he could spare. He replied accepting the invitation, and told me to expect him about dinner-time on December 2, which turned out to be the day after the exodus. His train was due at Tsavo about six o'clock in the evening, so I sent my "boy" up to the station to meet him and to help in carrying his baggage to the camp. In a very short time, however, the "boy" rushed back trembling with terror, and informed me that there was no sign of the train or of the railway staff, but that an enormous lion was standing on the station platform. This extraordinary story I did not believe in the least, as by this time the coolies—never remarkable for bravery—were in such a state of fright that if they caught sight of a hyena, of a baboon, or even a dog, in the bush, they were sure to imagine it was a lion; but I found out next day that it was an actual fact, and that both stationmaster and signalman had been obliged to take refuge from one of the man-eaters by locking themselves in the station building.

I waited some little time for Mr. Whitehead, but eventually, as he did not put in an appearance, I concluded that he must have postponed his journey until the next day, and so had my dinner in my customary solitary state. During the meal I heard a couple of shots, but paid no attention to them, as rifles were constantly being fired off in the neighbourhood of the camp. Later in the evening, I went out as usual to watch for our elusive foes, and took up my position in a crib made of sleepers which I had built on a big girder close to a camp which I thought was likely to be attacked. Soon after settling down at my post, I was surprised to hear the man-eaters growling and purring and crunching up bones about seventy yards from the crib. I could not understand what they had found to eat, as I had heard no commotion in the camps, and I knew by bitter experience that every meal the brutes obtained from us was announced by shrieks and uproar. The only conclusion I could come to was that they had pounced upon some poor unsuspecting native traveller. After a time I was able to make out their eyes glowing in the darkness, and I took as careful aim as was possible in the circumstances and fired; but the only notice they paid to the shot was to carry off whatever they were devouring and to retire quietly over a slight rise, which prevented me from seeing them. There they finished their meal at their ease.

As soon as it was daylight, I got out of my crib and went towards the place where I had last heard them. On the way, whom should I meet but my missing guest, Mr. Whitehead, looking very pale and ill, and generally dishevelled.

"Where on earth have you come from?" I exclaimed. "Why didn't you turn up to dinner last night?"

"A nice reception you give a fellow when you invite him to dinner," was his only reply.

"Why, what's up?" I asked.

"That infernal lion of yours nearly did for me last night," said Whitehead.

"Nonsense, you must have dreamed it!" I cried in astonishment.

For answer he turned round and showed me his back. "That's not much of a dream, is it?" he asked.

His clothing was rent by one huge tear from the nape of the neck downwards, and on the flesh there were four great claw marks, showing red and angry through the torn cloth. Without further parley, I hurried him off to my tent, and bathed and dressed his wounds; and when I had made him considerably more comfortable, I got from him the whole story of the events of the night.

It appeared that his train was very late, so that it was quite dark when he arrived at Tsavo Station, from which the track to my camp lay through a small cutting. He was accompanied by Abdullah, his sergeant of *askaris*, who walked close behind him carrying a lighted lamp. All went well until they were about half-way through the gloomy cutting, when one of the lions suddenly jumped down upon them from the high bank, knocking Whitehead over like a ninepin, and tearing his back in the manner I had seen. Fortunately, however, he had his carbine with him, and instantly fired. The flash and the loud report must have dazed the lion for a second or two, enabling Whitehead to disengage himself; but the next instant the brute pounced like lightning on the unfortunate Abdullah, with whom he at once made off. All that the poor fellow could say was: *"Eh, Bwana, simba"* ("Oh, Master, a lion"). As the lion was dragging him over the bank, Whitehead fired again, but without effect, and the brute quickly disappeared into the darkness with his prey. It was, of course, this unfortunate man whom I had heard the lions devouring during the night. Whitehead himself had a marvellous escape; his wounds were happily not very deep, and caused him little or no inconvenience afterwards.

On the same day, December 3, the forces arrayed against the lions were further strengthened. Mr. Farquhar, the Superintendent of Police, arrived from the coast with a score of sepoys to assist in hunting down the man-eaters, whose fame had by this time spread far and wide, and the most elaborate precautions were taken, his men being posted on the most convenient trees near every camp. Several other officials had also come up on leave to join in the chase, and each of these guarded a likely spot in the same way, Mr. Whitehead sharing my post inside the crib on the girder. Further, in spite of some chaff, my lion trap was put in thorough working order, and two of the sepoys were installed as bait.

Our preparations were quite complete by nightfall, and we all took up our appointed positions. Nothing happened until about nine o'clock, when to my great satisfaction the intense stillness was suddenly broken by the noise of the door of the trap clattering down. "At last," I thought, "one at least of the brutes is done for." But the sequel was an ignominious one.

The bait-sepoys had a lamp burning inside their part of the cage, and were each armed with a Martini rifle, with plenty of ammunition. They had also been given strict orders to shoot at once if a lion should enter the trap. Instead of doing so, however, they were so terrified when he rushed in and began to lash himself madly against the bars of the cage, that they completely lost their heads and were actually too unnerved to fire. Not for some minutes—not, indeed, until Mr. Farquhar, whose post was close by, shouted at them and cheered them on—did they at all recover themselves. Then when at last they did begin to fire, they fired with a vengeance—anywhere, anyhow. Whitehead and I were at right angles to the direction in which they should have shot, and yet their bullets came whizzing all round us. Altogether they fired over a score of shots, and in the end succeeded only in blowing away one of the bars of the door, thus allowing our prize to make good his escape. How they failed to kill him several times over is, and always will be, a complete mystery to me, as they could have put the muzzles of their rifles absolutely touching his body. There was, indeed, some blood scattered about the trap, but it was small consolation to know that the brute, whose capture and death seemed so certain, had only been slightly wounded.

Still we were not unduly dejected, and when morning came, a hunt was at once arranged. Accordingly we spent the greater part of the day on our hands and knees following the lions through the dense thickets of thorny jungle, but though we heard their growls from time to time, we never succeeded in actually coming up with them. Of the whole party, only Farquhar managed to catch a momentary glimpse of one as it bounded over a bush. Two days more were spent in the same manner, and with equal unsuccess; and then Farquhar and his sepoys were obliged to return to the coast. Mr. Whitehead also departed for his district, and once again I was left alone with the man-eaters.

The Death of the First Man-Eater

A day or two after the departure of my allies, as I was leaving my *boma* soon after dawn on December 9, I saw a Swahili running excitedly towards me, shouting out *"Simba! Simba!"* ("Lion! Lion!"), and every now and again looking behind him as he ran. On questioning him I found that the lions had tried to snatch a man from the camp by the river, but being foiled in this had seized and killed one of the donkeys, and were at that moment busy devouring it not far off. Now was my chance.

I rushed for the heavy rifle which Farquhar had kindly left with me for use in case an opportunity such as this should arise, and, led by the Swahili, I started most carefully to stalk the lions, who, I devoutly hoped, were confining their attention strictly to their meal. I was getting on splendidly, and could just make out the outline of one of them through the dense bush, when unfortunately my guide snapped a rotten branch. The wily beast heard the noise, growled his defiance, and disappeared in a moment into a patch of even thicker jungle close by. In desperation at the thought of his escaping me once again, I crept hurriedly back to the camp, summoned the available workmen and told them to bring all the tom-toms, tin cans and other noisy instruments of any kind that could be found. As quickly as possible I posted them in a half-circle round the thicket, and gave the head *jemadar* instructions to start a simultaneous beating of the tom-toms and cans as soon as he judged that I had had time to get round to the other side. I then crept round by myself and soon found a good position and one which the lion was most likely to retreat past, as it was in the middle of a broad animal path leading straight from the place where he was concealed. I lay down behind a small ant hill, and waited expectantly. Very soon I heard a tremendous din being raised by the advancing line of coolies, and almost immediately, to my intense joy, out into the open path stepped a huge maneless lion. It was the first occasion during all these trying months upon which I had had a fair chance at one of these brutes, and my satisfaction at the prospect of bagging him was unbounded.

Slowly he advanced along the path, stopping every few seconds to look round. I was only partially concealed from view, and if his attention had not been so fully occupied by the noise behind him, he must have observed me. As he was oblivious to my presence, however, I let him approach to within about fifteen yards of me, and then covered him with my rifle. The moment I moved to do this, he caught sight of me, and seemed much astonished at my sudden appearance, for he stuck his forefeet into the ground, threw himself back on his haunches and growled savagely. As I covered his brain with my rifle, I felt that at last I had him absolutely at my mercy, but . . . never trust an untried weapon! I pulled the trigger, and to my horror heard the dull snap that tells of a misfire.

Worse was to follow. I was so taken aback and disconcerted by this untoward accident that I entirely forgot to fire the left barrel, and lowered the rifle from my shoulder with the intention of reloading—if I should be given time. Fortunately for me, the lion was so distracted by the terrific din and uproar of the coolies behind him that instead of springing on me, as might have been expected, he bounded aside into the jungle again. By this time I had collected my wits, and just as he jumped I let him have the left barrel. An answering angry growl told me that he had been hit; but nevertheless he succeeded once more in getting clear away, for although I tracked him for some little distance, I eventually lost his trail in a rocky patch of ground.

Bitterly did I anathematise the hour in which I had relied on a borrowed weapon, and in my disappointment and vexation I abused owner, maker, and rifle with fine impartiality. On extracting the unexploded cartridge, I found that the needle had not struck home, the cap being only slightly dented; so that the whole fault did indeed lie with the rifle, which I later returned to Farquhar with polite compliments. Seriously, however, my continued ill-luck was most exasperating; and the result was that the Indians were more than ever confirmed in their belief that the lions were really evil spirits, proof against mortal weapons. Certainly, they did seem to bear charmed lives.

After this dismal failure there was, of course, nothing to do but to return to camp. Before doing so, however, I proceeded to view the dead donkey, which I found to have been only slightly devoured at the quarters. It is a curious fact that lions always begin at the tail of their prey and eat upwards towards the head. As their meal had thus been interrupted evidently at the very beginning, I felt pretty sure that one or other of the brutes would return to the carcase at nightfall. Accordingly, as there was no tree of any kind close at hand, I had a staging erected some ten feet away from the body. This *machan* was about twelve feet high and was composed of four poles stuck into the ground and inclined toward each other at the top, where a plank was lashed to serve as a seat. Further, as the nights were still pitch dark, I had the donkey's carcase secured by strong wires to a neighbouring stump, so that the lions might not be able to drag it away before I could get a shot at them.

At sundown, therefore, I took up my position on my airy perch, and much to the disgust of my gun-bearer, Mahina, I decided to go alone. I would gladly have taken him with me, indeed, but he had a bad cough, and I was afraid lest he should make any involuntary noise or movement which might spoil all. Darkness fell almost immediately, and everything became extraordinarily still. The silence of an African jungle on a dark night needs to be experienced to be realised; it is most impressive, especially when one is absolutely alone and isolated from one's fellow creatures, as I was then. The solitude and stillness, and the purpose of my vigil, all had their effect on me, and from a condition of strained expectancy I gradually fell into a dreamy mood which harmonised well with my surroundings. Suddenly I was startled out of my reverie by the snapping of a twig; and, straining my ears for a further sound, I fancied I could hear the rustling of a large body forcing its way through the bush. "The man-eater," I thought to myself; "surely to-night my luck will change and I shall bag one of the brutes." Profound silence again succeeded; I sat on my eyrie like a statue, every nerve tense with excitement. Very soon, however, all doubts as to the presence of the lion was dispelled. A deep long-drawn sigh—sure sign of hunger—came up from the bushes, and the rustling commenced again as he cautiously advanced. In a moment or two a sudden stop, followed by an angry growl, told me that my presence had been noticed; and I began to fear that disappointment awaited me once more.

But no; matters quickly took an unexpected turn. The hunter became the hunted; and instead of either making off or coming for the bait prepared for him, the lion began stealthily to stalk *me*! For about two hours he horrified me by slowly creeping round and round my crazy structure, gradually edging his way nearer and nearer. Every moment I expected him to rush it; and the staging had not been constructed with an eye to such a possibility. If one of the rather flimsy poles should break, or if the lion could spring the twelve feet which separated me from the ground . . . the thought was scarcely a pleasant one. I began to feel distinctly "creepy," and heartily repented my folly in having placed myself in such a dangerous position. I kept perfectly still, however, hardly daring even to blink my eyes: but the long continued strain was telling on my nerves, and my feelings may be better imagined than described when about midnight suddenly something came flop and struck me on the back of the head. For a moment I was so terrified that I nearly fell off the plank, as I thought that the lion had sprung on me from behind. Regaining my senses in a second or two, I realised that I had been hit by nothing more formidable than an owl, which had doubtless mistaken me for the branch of a tree—not a very alarming thing to happen in ordinary circumstances, I admit, but coming at the time it did, it almost paralysed me. The involuntary start which I could not help giving was immediately answered by a sinister growl from below.

After this I again kept as still as I could, though absolutely trembling with excitement; and in a short while I heard the lion begin to creep stealthily towards me. I could barely make out his form as he crouched among the whitish undergrowth; but I saw enough for my purpose and before he could come any nearer, I took careful aim and pulled the trigger. The sound of the shot was at once followed by a most terrific roar, and then I could hear him leaping about in all directions. I was no longer able to see him, however, as his first bound had taken him into the thick bush; but to make assurance doubly sure, I kept blazing away in the direction in which I heard him plunging about. At length came a series of mighty groans, gradually subsiding into deep sighs, and finally ceasing altogether; and I felt convinced that one of the "devils" who had so long harried us would trouble us no more.

As soon as I ceased firing, a tumult of inquiring voices was borne across the dark jungle from the men in camp about a quarter of a mile away. I shouted back that I was safe and sound, and that one of the lions was dead: whereupon such a mighty cheer went up from all the camps as must have astonished the denizens of the jungle for miles around. Shortly I saw scores of lights twinkling through the bushes: every man in camp turned out, and with tom-toms beating and horns blowing came running to the scene. They surrounded my eyrie, and to my amazement prostrated themselves on the ground before me, saluting me with cries of *"Mabarak! Mabarak!"* which I believe means "blessed one" or "saviour." All the same, I refused to allow any search to be made that night for the body of the lion, in case his companion might be close by; besides, it was possible that he might be still alive, and capable of making a last spring. Accordingly we all returned in triumph to the camp, where great rejoicings were kept up for the remainder of the night, the Swahili and other African natives celebrating the occasion by an especially wild and savage dance.

For my part, I anxiously awaited the dawn; and even before it was thoroughly light I was on my way to the eventful spot, as I could not completely persuade myself that even yet the "devil" might not have eluded me in some uncanny and mysterious way. Happily my fears proved groundless, and I was relieved to find that my luck—after playing me so many exasperating tricks—had really turned at last. I had scarcely traced the blood for more than a few paces when, on rounding a bush, I was startled to see a huge lion right in front of me, seemingly alive and crouching for a spring. On looking closer, however, I satisfied myself that he was really and truly stone-dead, whereupon my followers crowded round, laughed and danced and shouted with joy like children, and bore me in triumph shoulder-high round the dead body. These thanksgiving ceremonies being over, I examined the body and found that two bullets had taken effect—one close behind the left shoulder, evidently penetrating the heart, and the other in the off hind leg. The prize was indeed one to be proud of; his length from tip of nose to tip of tail was nine feet eight inches, he stood three feet nine inches high, and it took eight men to carry him back to camp. The only blemish was that the skin was much scored by the *boma* thorns through which he had so often forced his way in carrying off his victims.

The news of the death of one of the notorious man-eaters soon spread far and wide over the country: telegrams of congratulations came pouring in, and scores of people flocked from up and down the railway to see the skin for themselves.

The Death of the Second Man-Eater

It must not be imagined that with the death of this lion our troubles at Tsavo were at an end; his companion was still at large, and very soon began to make us unpleasantly aware of the fact. Only a few nights elapsed before he made an attempt to get at the Permanent Way Inspector, climbing up the steps of his bungalow and prowling round the verandah. The Inspector, hearing the noise and thinking it was a drunken coolie, shouted angrily "Go away!" but, fortunately for him, did not attempt to come out or to open the door. Thus disappointed in his attempt to obtain a meal of human flesh, the lion seized a couple of the Inspector's goats and devoured them there and then.

On hearing of this occurrence, I determined to sit up the next night near the Inspector's bungalow. Fortunately there was a vacant iron shanty close at hand, with a convenient loophole in it for firing from; and outside this I placed three full-grown goats as bait, tying them to a half-length of rail, weighing about 250 lbs. The night passed uneventfully until just before daybreak, when at last the lion turned up, pounced on one of the goats and made off with it, at the same time dragging away the others, rail and all. I fired several shots in his direction, but it was pitch dark and quite impossible to see anything, so I only succeeded in hitting one of the goats. I often longed for a flashlight on such occasions.

Next morning I started off in pursuit and was joined by some others from the camp. I found that the trail of the goats and rail was easily followed, and we soon came up, about a quarter of a mile away, to where the lion was still busy at his meal. He was concealed in some thick bush and growled angrily on hearing our approach; finally, as we got closer, he suddenly made a charge, rushing through the bushes at a great pace. In an instant, every man of the party scrambled hastily up the nearest tree, with the exception of one of my assistants, Mr. Winkler, who stood steadily by me throughout. The brute, however, did not press his charge home: and on throwing stones into the bushes where we had last seen him, we guessed by the silence that he had slunk off. We therefore advanced cautiously, and on getting up to the place discovered that he had indeed escaped us, leaving two of the goats scarcely touched.

Thinking that in all probability the lion would return as usual to finish his meal, I had a very strong scaffolding put up a few feet away from the dead goats, and took up my position on it before dark. On this occasion I brought my gun-bearer, Mahina, to take a turn at watching, as I was by this time worn out for want of sleep, having spent so many nights on the look-out. I was just dozing off comfortably when suddenly I felt my arm seized, and on looking up saw Mahina pointing in the direction of the goats. *"Sher!"* ("Lion!") was all he whispered. I grasped my double smooth-bore, which I had charged with slug, and waited patiently. In a few moments I was rewarded, for as I watched the spot where I expected the lion to appear, there was a rustling among the bushes and I saw him stealthily emerge into the open and pass almost directly beneath us. I fired both barrels practically together into his shoulder, and to my joy could see him go down under the force of the blow. Quickly I reached for the magazine rifle, but before I could use it, he was out of sight among the bushes, and I had to fire after him quite at random. Nevertheless I was confident of getting him in the morning, and accordingly set out as soon as it was light. For over a mile there was no difficulty in following the blood-trail, and as he had rested several times I felt sure that he had been badly wounded. In the end, however, my hunt proved fruitless, for after a time the traces of blood ceased and the surface of the ground became rocky, so that I was no longer able to follow the spoor.

About this time Sir Guilford Molesworth, K. C. I. E., late Consulting Engineer to the Government of India for State Railways, passed through Tsavo on a tour of inspection on behalf of the Foreign Office. After examining the bridge and other works and expressing his satisfaction, he took a number of photographs, one or two of which he has kindly allowed me to reproduce in this book. He thoroughly sympathised with us in all the trials we had endured from the man-eaters, and was delighted that one at least was dead. When he asked me if I expected to get the second lion soon, I well remember his half-doubting smile as I rather too confidently asserted that I hoped to bag him also in the course of a few days.

As it happened, there was no sign of our enemy for about ten days after this, and we began to hope that he had died of his wounds in the bush. All the same we still took every precaution at night, and it was fortunate that we did so, as otherwise at least one more victim would have been added to the list. For on the night of December 27, I was suddenly aroused by terrified shouts from my trolley men, who slept in a tree close outside my *boma* to the effect that a lion was trying to get at them. It would have been madness to have gone out, as the moon was hidden by dense clouds and it was absolutely impossible to see anything more than a yard in front of one; so all I could do was to fire off a few rounds just to frighten the brute away. This apparently had the desired effect, for the men were not further molested that night; but the man-eater had evidently prowled about for some time, for we found in the morning that he had gone right into every one of their tents, and round the tree was a regular ring of his footmarks.

The following evening I took up my position in this same tree, in the hope that he would make another attempt. The night began badly, as while climbing up to my perch I very nearly put my hand on a venomous snake which was lying coiled round one of the branches. As may be imagined, I came down again very quickly, but one of my men managed to despatch it with a long pole. Fortunately the night was clear and cloudless, and the moon made every thing almost as bright as day. I kept watch until about 2 a.m., when I roused Mahina to take his turn. For about an hour I slept peacefully with my back to the tree, and then woke suddenly with an uncanny feeling that something was wrong. Mahina, however, was on the alert, and had seen nothing; and although I looked carefully round us on all sides, I too could discover nothing unusual. Only half satisfied, I was about to lie back again, when I fancied I saw something move a little way off among the low bushes. On gazing intently at the spot for a few seconds, I found I was not mistaken. It was the man-eater, cautiously stalking us.

The ground was fairly open round our tree, with only a small bush every here and there; and from our position it was a most fascinating sight to watch this great brute stealing stealthily round us, taking advantage of every bit of cover as he came. His skill showed that he was an old hand at the terrible game of man-hunting: so I determined to run no undue risk of losing him this time. I accordingly waited until he got quite close—about twenty yards away—and then fired my .303 at his chest. I heard the bullet strike him, but unfortunately it had no knockdown effect, for with a fierce growl he turned and made off with great long bounds. Before he disappeared from sight, however, I managed to have three more shots at him from the magazine rifle, and another growl told me that the last of these had also taken effect.

We awaited daylight with impatience, and at the first glimmer of dawn we set out to hunt him down. I took a native tracker with me, so that I was free to keep a good look-out, while Mahina followed immediately behind with a Martini carbine. Splashes of blood being plentiful, we were able to get along quickly; and we had not proceeded more than a quarter of a mile through the jungle when suddenly a fierce warning growl was heard right in front of us. Looking cautiously through the bushes, I could see the man-eater glaring out in our direction, and showing his tusks in an angry snarl. I at once took careful aim and fired. Instantly he sprang out and made a most determined charge down on us. I fired again and knocked him over; but in a second he was up once more and coming for me as fast as he could in his crippled condition. A third shot had no apparent effect, so I put out my hand for the Martini, hoping to stop him with it. To my dismay, however, it was not there. The terror of the sudden charge had proved too much for Mahina, and both he and the carbine were by this time well on their way up a tree. In the circumstances there was nothing to do but follow suit, which I did without loss of time: and but for the fact that one of my shots had broken a hind leg, the brute would most certainly have had me. Even as it was, I had barely time to swing myself up out of his reach before he arrived at the foot of the tree.

When the lion found he was too late, he started to limp back to the thicket; but by this time I had seized the carbine from Mahina, and the first shot I fired from it seemed to give him his quietus, for he fell over and lay motionless. Rather foolishly, I at once scrambled down from the tree and walked up towards him. To my surprise and no little alarm he jumped up and attempted another charge. This time, however, a Martini bullet in the chest and another in the head finished him for good and all; he dropped in his tracks not five yards away from me, and died gamely, biting savagely at a branch which had fallen to the ground.

By this time all the workmen in camp, attracted by the sound of the firing, had arrived on the scene, and so great was their resentment against the brute who had killed such numbers of their comrades that it was only with the greatest difficulty that I could restrain them from tearing the dead body to pieces. Eventually, amid the wild rejoicings of the natives and coolies, I had the lion carried to my *boma*, which was close at hand. On examination we found no less than six bullet holes in the body, and embedded only a little way in the flesh of the back was the slug which I had fired into him from the scaffolding about ten days previously. He measured nine feet six inches from tip of nose to tip of tail, and stood three feet eleven and a half inches high; but, as in the case of his companion, the skin was disfigured by being deeply scored all over by the *boma* thorns.

The news of the death of the second "devil" soon spread far and wide over the country, and natives actually travelled from up and down the line to have a look at my trophies and at the "devil-killer," as they called me. Best of all, the coolies who had absconded came flocking back to Tsavo, and much to my relief work was resumed and we were never again troubled by man-eaters. It was amusing, indeed, to notice the change which took place in the attitude of the workmen towards me after I had killed the two lions. Instead of wishing to murder me, as they once did, they could not now do enough for me, and as a token of their gratitude they presented me with a beautiful silver bowl, as well as with a long poem written in Hindustani describing all our trials and my ultimate victory. As the poem relates our troubles in somewhat quaint and biblical language, I have given a translation of it in the appendix. The bowl I shall always consider my most highly prized and hardest won trophy. The inscription on it reads as follows:—

Sir—We, your Overseer, Timekeepers, *Mistaris* and Workmen, present you with this bowl as a token of our gratitude to you for your bravery in killing two man-eating lions at great risk to your own life, thereby saving us from the fate of being devoured by these terrible monsters who nightly broke into our tents and took our fellow-workers from our side. In presenting you with this bowl, we all add our prayers for your long life, happiness and prosperity. We shall ever remain, Sir, Your grateful servants,

Baboo Purshotam Hurjee Purmar, *Overseer and Clerk of the Works, on behalf of your Workmen.*

Dated at Tsavo, *January* 30, 1899.

Before I leave the subject of "The Man-Eaters of Tsavo," it may be of interest to mention that these two lions possess the distinction, probably unique among wild animals, of having been specifically referred to in the House of Lords by the Prime Minister of the day. Speaking of the difficulties which had been encountered in the construction of the Uganda Railway, the late Lord Salisbury said:—

"The whole of the works were put a stop to for three weeks because a party of man-eating lions appeared in the locality and conceived a most unfortunate taste for our porters. At last the labourers entirely declined to go on unless they were guarded by an iron entrenchment. Of course it is difficult to work a railway under these conditions, and until we found an enthusiastic sportsman to get rid of these lions, our enterprise was seriously hindered."

Also, *The Spectator* of March 3, 1900, had an article entitled "The Lions that Stopped the Railway," from which the following extracts are taken:—

"The parallel to the story of the lions which stopped the rebuilding of Samaria must occur to everyone, and if the Samaritans had quarter as good cause for their fears as had the railway coolies, their wish to propitiate the local deities is easily understood. If the whole body of lion anecdote, from the days of the Assyrian Kings till the last year of the nineteenth century, were collated and brought together, it would not equal in tragedy or atrocity, in savageness or in sheer insolent contempt for man, armed or unarmed, white or black, the story of these two beasts. . . .

"To what a distance the whole story carries us back, and how impossible it becomes to account for the survival of primitive man against this kind of foe! For fire—which has hitherto been regarded as his main safeguard against the carnivora—these cared nothing. It is curious that the Tsavo lions were not killed by poison, for strychnine is easily used, and with effect.* Poison may have been used early in the history of man, for its powers are employed with strange skill by the men in the tropical forest, both in American and West Central Africa. But there is no evidence that the old inhabitants of Europe, or if Assyria or Asia Minor, ever killed lions or wolves by this means. They looked to the King or chief, or some champion, to kill these monsters for them. It was not the sport but the duty of Kings, and was in itself a title to be a ruler of men. Theseus, who cleared the roads of beasts and robbers; Hercules, the lion killer; St. George, the dragon-slayer, and all the rest of their class owed to this their everlasting fame. From the story of the Tsavo River we can appreciate their services to man even at this distance of time. When the jungle twinkled with hundreds of lamps, as the shout went on from camp to camp that the first lion was dead, as the hurrying crowds fell prostrate in the midnight forest, laying their heads on his feet, and the Africans danced savage and ceremonial dances of thanksgiving, Mr. Patterson must have realised in no common way what it was to have been a hero and deliverer in the days when man was not yet undisputed lord of the creation, and might pass at any moment under the savage dominion of the beasts."

Well had the two man-eaters earned all this fame; they had devoured between them no less than twenty-eight Indian coolies, in addition to scores of unfortunate African natives of whom no official record was kept.

(*I may mention that poison *was* tried, but without effect. The poisoned carcases of transport animals which had died from the bite of the tsetse fly were placed in likely spots, but the wily man-eaters would not touch them, and much preferred live men to dead donkeys.)

Tige's Lion

ZANE GREY

Sportsmen who have hunted mountain lions are familiar with the details. The rock-ribbed ravines and spear-pointed pines, the patches of snow on the slopes, and the dry stone dust under the yellow cliffs with its pungent animal odor—these characterize the home of the big cat. The baying of the hounds, the cautious pursuit on foot or the long thrilling chase on horseback, ending before a dark cave or under a pine, and the "stand and deliver" with a heavy rifle—these are the features.

I have a story to tell of a hunt that was different.

The time was in May. With Buffalo Jones, the old plainsman, and his cowboys, I was camped on the northern rim of the Grand Canyon of Arizona, in what the Indians once named the Siwash. This heavily timbered plateau, bounded on three sides by the desert and on the fourth side by that strange delusive cleft called the canyon, is as wild and lonely, and as beautiful a place as was ever visited by man. Buckskin Mountain surmounts the plateau, and its innumerable breaks or ravines slope gently into the canyon. Here range thousands of deer and wild mustangs, and mountain lions live fat and unmolested.

On the morning of May 12, when Jones routed us out at five o'clock, as was his custom, a white frost, as deep as a light snow, clothed the forest. The air was nipping. An eager, crackling welcome came from the blazing campfire. Jim raked the hot coals over the lid of his oven. Frank and Lawson trooped in with the horses. Jones, as usual, had trouble with his hounds, particularly the ever-belligerent Tige.

Hounds in that remote section of Arizona retain a majority of their primitive instincts. Most of the time the meat they get they "rustle" for. So, taking the hard life into consideration, Jones' dogs were fairly well-behaved. Tige, a large-framed yellow bloodhound, was young, intractable, and as fierce as a tiger—whence his name. According to the cowboys, Tige was a cross between a locoed coyote and a maverick; in Jones' idea he had all the points of a great lion dog, only he needed his spirit curbed. Tige chased many a lion; he got tongue lashings and lashings of other kind, and even charge of fine shot; but his spirit remained untamed.

We had a captive lion in camp—one Jones had lassoed and brought in a few days before—and Tige had taken the matter as a direct insult to himself. Fight he would, and there was no use to club him. And on this morning when Jones slipped his chain he made for the lion again. After sundry knocks and scratches we dragged Tige to the campfire while we ate breakfast. Even then, with Jones' powerful grasp on his collar, he vented his displeasure and growled. The lion crouched close behind the pine and watched the hound with somber fiery eyes.

"Hurry, boys!" called Jones, in his sharp voice. "We'll tie up a lion this morning, sure as you're born. Jim, you and Lawson stick with us to-day. Yesterday, if we hadn't split, and lost each other, we'd have got one of those lions. If we get separated, keep yelling our signal."

Then he turned to me and shook his big finger: "Listen. I want you to hold in that black demon of a horse you're riding. He'll kill you if you are not careful. He hasn't been broke long. A year ago he was leading a band of wild mustangs over the mountain. Pull him in; hold him tight!"

"Which way?" asked Frank, as he swung into his saddle.

"I reckon it doesn't much matter," replied Jones, with his dry, grim chuckle. "We run across lion sign everywhere, don't we? Let's circle through the woods while the frost stays on."

We rode out under the stately silvered pines, down the long white aisles, with the rising sun tingeing the forest a delicate pink. The impatient hounds, sniffing and whining, trotted after Jones. They crossed fresh deer tracks with never a sign. Here and there deer, a species of mule deer almost as large as elk, bounded up the slopes. A mile or more from camp we ran over a lion trail headed for the mountain.

Sounder, the keenest hound we had, opened up first and was off like a shot. Tige gave tongue and leaped after him; then old Mose, with his short bark, led the rest of the pack. Our horses burst into action like a string of racers at the post. With Frank on his white mustang setting the pace, we drove through the forest glades swift as the wind.

"A hot trail, boys! Hi! Hi! Hi!" yelled Jones.

No need was there to inspire us. The music of the hounds did that. We split the cold air till it sang in our ears; we could scarcely get our breath, and no longer smelt the pine. The fresh and willing horses stretched lower and lower. The hounds passed out of sight into the forest, but their yelps and bays, now low, now clear, floated back to us. Either I forgot Jones' admonition or disregarded it, for I gave my horse,

Satan, free rein and, without my realizing it at the time, he moved out ahead of the bunch. Compared to the riders in my rear I was a poor horseman, but as long as I could stick on, what did I care for that? Riding Satan was like sailing on a feather in a storm. Something wild in my blood leaped. My greatest danger lay in the snags and branches of the pines. Half the time I hugged Satan's neck to miss them. Many a knock and a brush I got. Looking backward once I saw I was leaving my companions, and grimly recalling former chases, in the finish of which I had not shown, I called to Satan.

"On! On! On, old fellow! This is our day!"

Then it seemed he had not been running at all. How he responded! His light, long powerful stride was a beautiful thing. The cold, sweet pine air, cutting between my teeth, left a taste in my mouth, and it had the exhilaration of old wine. I rejoiced in the wildness of movement and the indescribable blurred black and white around me; in sheer madness of sensorial perception I let out ringing yells. It was as if I were alone in the woods; it was all mine, and there was joy of chase, of action and of life.

The trail began to circle to the southwest, and in the next mile turned in the direction from which it had come. This meant the lion had probably been close at hand when we struck his trail, and hearing the hounds he had made for the canyon. Down the long, slightly swelling slope Satan thundered, and the pines resembled fence-pickets from a coasting sled. Often I saw gray, bounding flashes against the white background, and knew I had jumped deer. I wondered if any of the hounds were at fault, for sometimes they became confused at the crossing of a fresher scent. Satan kept a steady gait for five miles down the forest slope, and then raced out of the pines into a growth of scrubby oak. I knew I was not now far from the rim of the canyon, and despaired of coming up with the lion. Suddenly I realized I was not following a trail, as the frost had disappeared in the open. Neither did I hear the baying of the hounds. I hauled Satan up and, listening, heard no sound.

"Waa-hoo! Waa-hoo!" I yelled our signal cry. No answer came: only the haunting echo. While I was vainly trying to decide what to do, the dead silence was sharply broken by the deep bay of a hound. It was Tige's voice. In another second I had Satan plunging through the thicket of short oaks. Soon we were among the piñons near the rim of the canyon. Again I reined Satan to a standstill. From this point I could see out into the canyon, and as always, even under the most exciting circumstances, I drew a sharp breath at the wonder, the mystery, the sublimity of the scene. The tips of yellow crags and gray mesas and red turrets rose out of the blue haze of distance. The awful chasm, eighteen miles wide and more than a mile deep, stretched away clear and vividly outlined in the rare atmosphere for a hundred miles. The canyon seemed still wrapped in slumber and a strange, vast silence that was the silence of ages, hung over the many-hued escarpments and sculptured domes.

Tige's bay, sounding close at hand, startled me and made Satan jump. I slid to the ground, and pulling my little Remington from the saddle, began hunting in the piñons for the hound.

Presently I sighted him, standing with his front paws against a big piñon. Tige saw me, wagged his tail, howled and looked up. Perhaps twenty feet from the ground a full-grown lion stood on branches that were swaying with his weight. He glared down at Tige and waved his long tail. He had a mean face, snarling, vicious. His fat sides heaved and I gathered he was not used to running, and had been driven to his limit.

"Tige, old boy, you're the real thing!" I yelled. "Keep him there!" For an instant I fingered the safety catch on my automatic. I did not much fancy being alone with that old fellow. I had already seen a grim, snarling face and outstretched claws in the air before my eyes—and once was enough! Still I did not want to kill him. Finally I walked cautiously to within fifty feet of him, and when he showed resentment in a slowly crouching movement I hastily snapped a picture of him. Hardly had I turned the film round when he leaped from the tree and bounded away. Knowing he would make for the rim and thus escape I dropped my camera and grabbed up the rifle. But I could not cut loose on him, because Tige kept nipping him, and I feared I might shoot the hound. Tige knew as well as I the intention of the lion and—brave fellow!—he ran between the beast and the canyon and turned him towards the woods. At this great work on the part of Tige I yelled frantically and dashed for my horse. Though the lion had passed close, Satan had not moved from his tracks.

"Hi! Hi! Hi! Take him, Tige!" I screamed, as the black launched out like an arrow.

On the open flat I spied Tige and his quarry, resembling yellow flashes in the scrub oak; and twice the hound jumped the lion. I swore in my teeth. The brave and crazy dog was going to his death. Satan fairly crashed through the thicket and we gained. I saw we were running along a cut-in from the main rim wall, and I thought the lion was making for a break where he could get down. Suddenly I saw him leap high into a pine on the edge of the forest. When I came up Tige was trying to climb the tree.

"Tige, old boy, I guess Jones had you sized up right," I cried, as I dismounted. "If that brute jumps again it will be his last."

At this moment I heard a yell, and I sent out three "Waa-hoos," which meant "Come quickly!" In a few moments Sounder burst out of the forest, then Don, then Mose. How they did yelp! I heard the pounding of hoofs, more yells, and soon Frank dashed into the open, followed by the others. The big tawny lion was in plain sight, and as each hunter saw him a wild yell pealed out.

"Hi! Hi! There he is! Tige, you're the stuff!" cried Jones, whirling off his horse. "You didn't split on deer trails, like the rest of these blasted long-eared canines. You stuck to him, old dog! Well, he's your lion. Boys, spread out now and surround the tree. This is a good tree and I hope we can hold him here. If he jumps he'll get over the rim, sure. Make all the racket you can, and get ready for work when I rope him."

Sounder, Mose, Ranger and Don went wild while Jones began climbing the tree, and as for Tige, he went through antics never before seen in a dog. Jones climbed slowly, laboriously, with his lasso trailing behind him, his brawny arms bare. How grim and cool he looked! I felt sorry for the lion.

"Look out!" called Jim. "Shore thet lion means biz."

"Jones, he's an old cuss, an' won't stand no foolin'," said Frank.

The old buffalo hunter climbed just the same, calmly and deliberately, as if he were unaware of danger.

Lawson, who was afraid of nothing on earth except lions, edged farther and farther from under the pine. The lion walked back up the limb he had gone down, and he hissed and growled. When Jones reached the first fork, the lion spat. His eyes emitted flames; his sharp claws dug into the bark of the limb; he began to show restlessness and fear. All at once he made a quick start, apparently to descend and meet Jones. We yelled like a crew of demons, and he slipped back a bit.

"Far enough!" yelled Frank, and his voice rang.

"Cut me a pole," called Jones.

In a twinkling Frank procured a long sapling and handed it up. Jones hung the noose of his lasso on it, and slowly extended it toward the lion. I snapped a picture here, and was about to take another when Jim yelled to me.

"Here, you with the rifle! Be ready. Shore we'll have hell in a minute."

Hell there was, in less time. With the dexterity of a conjuror Jones slipped the noose over the head of the lion and tightened it. Spitting furiously the lion bit, tore and clawed at the rope.

"Pull him off, boys! Now! Hurry, while the rope is over that short limb. Then we'll hang him in the air for a minute while I come down and lasso his paws. Pull! Pull!"

The boys pulled with all their might but the lion never budged.

"Pull him off, dang it! Pull!" impatiently yelled Jones, punching the lion with the pole.

But the powerful beast would not be dislodged. His long body lengthened on the limb and his great muscles stood out in ridges. There was something grand in his defiance and his resistance. Suddenly Jones grasped the lasso and slid down it, hand over hand.

I groaned in my spirit. What a picture to miss! There I was with a rifle, the only one in the party, and I had to stand ready to protect life if possible—and I had to watch a rare opportunity, one in a lifetime, pass without even a try. It made me sick.

The men strained on the lasso, and shouted; the hounds whined, quivered and leaped into the air; the lion hugged the branch with his brawny paws.

"Throw your weight on the rope," ordered Jones.

For an instant the lion actually held the men off the ground; then with a scratching and tearing of bark he tumbled. But Jones had not calculated on the strength of the snag over which he expected to hang the lion. The snag was rotten; it broke. The lion whirled in the air. Crash! He had barely missed Lawson.

In a flash the scene changed from one of half-comic excitement to one of terrible danger and probably tragedy. There was a chorus of exclamation, and snarls and yelps, all coming from a cloud of dust. Then I saw a yellow revolving body in the midst of furry black whirling objects. I dared not shoot for fear of hitting my friends. Out of this snarling melee the lion sprang towards freedom. Jones pounced on the whipping lasso, Frank and Jim were not an instant behind him, and the dogs kept at the heels of the lion. He turned on them like an exploding torpedo; then, giving a tremendous bound, straightened the lasso and threw the three men flat on their faces. But they held on.

Suddenly checked, the lion took a side jump bringing the tight lasso in connection with Lawson's flying feet. The frightened fellow had been trying to get out of the way. The lasso tripped him, giving him a hard fall. I tried to bring my rifle to bear just as the lion savagely turned on Lawson. But the brute was so quick, the action of the struggling men so confused and fast that it was impossible. I heard Jones bawl out some unintelligible command; I heard Lawson scream; I saw the flaming-eyed brute, all instinct with savage life, reach out with both huge paws.

It was at this critical instant that Tige bowled pell-mell into the very jaws of the lion. They began a terrific wrestling combat. The lasso flew out of the hands of Frank and Jim, but the burly Jones, like his great dog, held on. Tige and the lion, fighting tooth and claw, began to roll down the incline. Jones was pulled to his feet, thrown flat again and dragged.

"Grab the rope!" he roared.

But no one could move. Jones rose to his knees, then fell, and lost the lasso.

Hound and lion in a savage clutch of death whirled down, nearer and nearer to the rim wall of the canyon. As they rolled I heard to rend and tear of hide. I knew Tige would never let go, even if he could, and I opened up with the automatic.

I heard the spats of the bullets, and saw fur, blood and gravel fly. On the very verge of the precipice the lion stretched out convulsively. Tige clung to his neck with a grim hold. Then they slipped over the wall.

Silence for a long second—then crash! There came up the rattle of stones, silence for a palpitating second—then crash! It was heavier, farther down and followed by a roar of sliding stones. Silence for a long, long moment. Finally a faint faraway sound which died instantly. The lion king lay at the foot of this throne and Tige lay with him.

De Shootinest Gent'man

NASH BUCKINGHAM

Supper was a delicious memory. In the matter of a certain goose stew, Aunt Molly had fairly outdone herself. And we, in turn, had jolly well done her out of practically all the goose. It may not come amiss to explain frankly and aboveboard the entire transaction with reference to said goose. Its breast had been deftly detached, lightly grilled and sliced into ordinary "mouth-size" portions. The remainder of the dismembered bird, back, limbs and all parts of the first part thereunto pertaining were put into an iron pot. Keeping company with the martyred fowl, in due proportion of culinary wizardry, were sundry bell peppers, two cans of mock turtle soup, diced roast pork, scrambled ham rinds, peas, potatoes, some corn and dried garden okra, shredded onions and pretty much anything and everything that wasn't tied down or that Molly had lying loose around her kitchen. This stew, served right royally, and attended by outriders of "cracklin' bread," was flanked by a man-at-arms in the form of a saucily flavored brown gravy. I recall a dish of broiled teal and some country puddin' with ginger pour-over, but merely mention these in passing.

So the Judge and I, in rare good humor (I forgot to add that there had been a dusty bottle of the Judge's famous port), as becomes sportsmen blessed with a perfect day's imperfect duck shooting, had discussed each individual bird brought to bag, with reasons, pro and con, why an undeniably large quota had escaped uninjured. We bordered upon that indecisive moment when bedtime should be imminent, were it not for the delightful trouble of getting started in that direction. As I recollect it, ruminating upon our sumptuous repast, the Judge had just countered upon my remark that I had never gotten enough hot turkey hash and beaten biscuits, by stating decisively that his craving for smothered quail remained inviolate, when the door opened softly and in slid "Ho'ace"! He had come, following a custom of many years, to tale final breakfast instructions before packing the embers in "Steamboat Bill," the stove, and dousing our glim.

Seeing upon the center table, t'wixt the Judge and me, a bottle and the unmistakable ingredients and tools of the former's ironclad rule for a hunter's nightcap, Ho'ace paused in embarrassed hesitation and seated himself quickly upon an empty shell case. His attitude was a cross between that of a timid gazelle's scenting danger and a wary hunter's sighting game and effacing himself gently from the landscape.

Long experience in the imperative issue of securing an invitation to "get his'n" had taught Ho'ace that it were ever best to appear humbly disinterested and thoroughly foreign to the subject until negotiations, if need be even much later, were opened with him directly or indirectly. With old-time members he steered along the above lines. But with newer ones or their uninitiated guests, he believed in quicker campaigning, or, conditions warranting, higher pressure sales methods. The Judge, reaching for the sugar bowl, mixed his sweetening water with adroit twirl and careful scrutiny as to texture; fastening upon Ho'ace meanwhile a melting look of liquid mercy. In a twinkling, however, his humor changed and the darky found himself in the glare of a forbidding menace, creditable in his palmiest days to the late Mister Chief Justice Jeffries himself.

"Ho'ace," demanded the Judge, tilting into his now ready receptacle a gurgling, man-size libation, "who is the best shot—the best duck-shot—you have ever paddled on this lake—barring—of course—a-h-e-m-m—myself?" Surveying himself with the coyness of a juvenile, the Judge stirred his now beading toddy dreamily and awaited the encore. Ho'ace squirmed a bit as the closing words of the Judge's query struck home with appalling menace upon his ears. He plucked nervously at his battered headpiece. His eyes, exhibiting a vast expanse of white, roamed pictured walls and smoke-dimmed ceiling in furtive, reflective, helpless quandary. Then speaking slowly and gradually warming to his subject, he fashioned the following alibi.

"Jedge, y' know, suh, us all has ouh good an' ouh bad days wid de ducks. Yes, my Lawdy, us sho' do. Dey's times whin de ducks flies all ovah ev'ything an' ev'ybody, an' still us kain't none o' us hit nuthin'—lak me an' you wuz dis mawnin'." At this juncture the Judge interrupted, reminding Ho'ace that he meant when the Judge—and *not* the Judge and Ho'ace—was shooting.

"An' den deys times whin h'it look lak dey ain't no shot too hard nur nary a duck too far not t'be kilt. But Mister Buckin'ham yonder—Mister Nash—he brung down de shootin'est gent'man what took all de cake. H'it's lots o' d' members here whut's darin' shooters, but dat fren' o' Mister Nash's—uummppphhh—don't never talk t' me 'bout him whur de ducks kin hear. 'Cause dey'll leave de laik ef dey hears he's even comin' dis way.

"Dat gent'man rode me jes' lak I wuz' er saddle, an' he done had on rooster spurs. Mister Nash he brung him on down here an' say, 'Ho'ace,' he say, 'here's a gent'man frum Englan',' he say, 'Mister Money—Mister Harol' Money—an' say I wants you t' paddle him tomorrow an' see dat he gits er gran' shoot—unnerstan'?' I say, 'Yaas, suh, Mister Nash,' I say, 'dat I'll sho'ly do, suh. Mister Money gwi' hav' er fine picnic ef I has t' see dat he do my sef—but kin he shoot, suh?'

"Mister Nash, he say, 'Uh—why—uh—yaas, Ho'ace, Mister Money he's—uh—ve'y fair shot—'bout lak Mister Immitt Joyner or Mister Hal Howard.' I say t' mysef, I say, 'Uuummmpphhh—huuummmppphhh—well—he'ah now—ef dats d' case, me an' Mister Money gwi' *do* some shootin' in d' mawnin.'

"Mister Money he talk so kin'er queer an' brief like, dat I hadda pay clos't inspection t' whut he all de time asayin'. But nex' mawnin', whin me an' him goes out in de bote, I seen he had a gre't big ol' happy bottle o' Brooklyn Handicap in dat shell box so I say t' m'sef, I say, 'W-e-l-l-l—me an' Mister Money gwi' got erlong someway, us is.'

"I paddles him on up de laik an' he say t' me, say, 'Hawrice—uh—hav yo'—er—got anny wager,' he say, 'or proposition t' mek t' me, as regards," he say, 't' shootin' dem dar eloosive wil'fowls?' he say.

"I kinder studies a minit, 'cause, lak I done say, he talk so brief. Den I says, 'I guess you is right 'bout dat, suh.'

"He say, 'Does you follow me, Hawrice, or is I alone?' he say.

"I says, 'Naw, suh, Mister, I'm right wid you in dis bote.'

"'You has no proposition t' mek wid me den?' he say.

"S' I, 'Naw, suh, Boss, I leaves all dat wid you, suh, trustin' t' yo' gin'rosiry, suh.'

"'Ve'y good, Hawrice,' he say, 'I sees you doan grasp de principul. Now I will mek you de proposi-tion,' he say. I jes' kep' on paddlin'. He say, 'Ev'y time I miss er duck you gits er dram frum dis hu'ah bottle—ev'y time I kills er duck—I gits de drink—which is h'it—come—come—speak up, my man.'

"I didn' b'lieve I done heard Mister Money rightly, an' I say, 'Uh—Mister Money,' I say, 'suh, does you mean dat I kin d' chice whedder you misses or kills ev'y time an' gits er drink?'

"He say, 'Dat's my defi',' he say.

"I says, 'Well, den—w-e-l-l—den—ef dat's de case, I gwi' choose ev'y time yo' misses, suh.' Den I say t'm'sef, I say, 'Ho'ace, right hu'ah whar you gotta be keerful, 'ginst you fall outa d' bote an' git fired frum d' lodge; 'cause ef'n you gits er drink ev'y time dis gent'man misses an' he shoot lak Mister Hal Howard, you an' him sho' gwi' drink er worl' o' liquah—er worl' o' liquah.'

"I pushes on up nurly to de Han'werker stan', an' I peeks in back by da li'l pocket whut shallers off'n de laik, an' sees some sev'ul blackjacks—four on 'em—settin' in dar. Dey done seen us, too. An' up come dey haids. I spy 'em twis'in', an' turnin'—gittin' raidy t' pull dey freight frum dar. I says, 'Mister Money,' I says, 'yawnder sets some ducks—look out now, suh, 'cause dey gwi' try t' rush on out pas' us whin dey come outa dat pocket.' Den I think, 'W-e-l-l-l, hu'ah whar I knocks d' gol' fillin' outa d' mouf' o' Mister Money's bottle o' Brooklyn Handicap!'

"I raised de lid o' d' shell box an' dar laid dat ol' bottle—still dar. I say, 'Uuummmppphhh—hummmph.' Jus' 'bout dat time up goes dem black-haids an' outa dar dey come—dey did—flyin' low t' d' watah—an' sorta raisin' lak—y' knows how dey does h'it, Jedge?'

"Mister Money he jus' pick up dat fas' feedin' gun—t'war er pump—not one o' dese hu'ah new afromatics—an' whin he did, I done reach f' d' bottle, 'cause I jes' natcherly know'd dat my time had done come. Mister Money he swings down on dem bullies. Ker-py—ker-py-powie-powie—splamp-splamp-splamp—ker-splash—Lawdy mussy—gent'-mans—fo' times, right in d' same place, h'it sounded lak—an' d' las' duck fell ker-flop almos' in ouh bote.

"I done let go d' bottle, an' Mister Money say—mighty cool lak—say, 'Hawrice, say, kin'ly to examine dat las' chap clos'ly,' he say, 'an' obsurve,' he say, 'ef'n he ain' shot thru de eye.'

"I rakes in dat blackjack, an' sho' nuff—bofe eyes done shot plum out—yaas, suh, bofe on 'em right on out. Mister Money say, 'I wuz—er—slightly afraid,' he say, 'dat I had unknowin'ly struck dat fella er trifle too far t' win'ward,' he say. 'A ve'y fair start, Hawrice,' he say. 'You'd bettah place me in my station, so we may continue on wid'out interruption,' he say.

"'Yaas, suh,' I say. 'I'm on my way right dar now, suh, 'an I say t' m'sef, I say, 'Mek haste, Man, an' put dis gent'man in his bline an' giv' him er proper chanc't to miss er duck. I didn' hones'ly b'lieve but whut killin' all four o' dem other ducks so peart lak wuz er sorter accident. So I put him on de Han' werker bline. He seen I kep' de main shell bucket an' d' liquah, but he never said nuthin'. I put out d' m 'coys an' den creep back wid d' bote into d' willows t' watch.

"Pretty soon, hu'ah come er big ole drake flyin' mighty high. Ouh ole hen bird she holler t' him, an' d' drake he sorter twis' his haid an' look down. 'Warn't figurin' nuthin' but whut Mister Money gwi' let dat drake circle an' come 'mongst d' m 'coys—but—aw—aw! All uv er sudden he jus' raise up sharp lak an'—kerzowie! Dat ole drake jus' throw his haid on his back an' ride on down—looked t' me lak he fell er mile—an' whin he hit he thow'd watah fo' feet. Mister Money he nuvver said er word—jus' sot dar!

"Hu'ah come another drake—way off t' d' lef'—up over back o' me. He turn eroun'—quick lak—he did an'—kerzowie—he cut him on down, too. Dat drake fall way back in d' willows an' cose I hadda wade after 'im.

"Whilst I wuz gone, Mister Money shoot twice. An' whin I come stumblin' back, dar laid two mo' ducks wid dey feets in de air. Befo' I hav' time t' git in de bote again he done knock down er hen away off in d' elbow brush.

"I say, 'Mister Money, suh, I hav' behin' some farknockin' guns in my time an' I'se er willin' worker, shoe—but ef you doan, please suh, kill dem ducks closer lak, you gwi' kill yo' willin' supporter Ho'ace in de mud.' He say, 'Da's all right 'bout dat,' he say. 'Go git d' bird—he kain't git er-way 'cause h'its dead ez er wedge.'

"Whin I crawls back t' d' bote dat las' time—it done got mighty col'. Dar us set—me in one en' ashiverin' an' dat ole big bottle wid de gol' haid in de far en'. Might jus' ez well bin ten miles so far ez my chances had done gone.

"Five mo' ducks come in—three singles an' er pair o' sprigs. An' Mister Money he chewed 'em all up lak good eatin'. One time, tho' he had t' shoot one o' them high-flyin' sprigs twice, an' I done got halfway in de bote reachin' fer dat bottle—but de las' shot got 'im. Aftah while, Mister Money say—'Hawrice,' he say, 'how is you hittin' off—my man?'

"'Mister Money' I say, 'I'se pow'ful col', suh, an' ef you wants er 'unable, no 'count paddler t' tell you d' truth, suh, I b'lieves I done made er pow'ful po' bet.' He say 'Poss'bly so, Hawrice, poss'bly so.' But dat 'poss'bly' didn' git me nuthin'.

"Jedge, y' Honor, you know dat gent'man sot dar an' kill ev'ry duck come in, an' had his limit long befo' de eight-o'clock train runned. I done gone t' watchin' an' de las' duck whut come by wuz one o' dem lightnin'-express teals. Hu'ah he come—er greenwing drake—look lak' somebody done blowed er buckshot pas' us. I riz' up an' hollered, 'Fly fas', ole teal, do yo' bes'—caus' Ho'ace needs er drink.' But

Mister Money jus' jumped up an' thow'd him forty feet—skippin' 'long d' watah. I say, 'Hol' on, Mister Money, hol' on—you done kilt d' limit.'

"'Oh,' he say, 'I hav'—hav' I?'

"I say, 'Yaas, suh, an' you ain't bin long 'bout h'it—neither.

"He say, 'What are you doin' gittin' so col' then?'

"I say, 'I spec' findin' out dat I hav' done made er bad bet had er lot t' do wid d' air.'

"An' dar laid dat Brooklyn Handicap all dat time—he nuvver touched none—an' me neither. I paddles him on back to de house, an' he comes er stalkin' on in hu'ah, he did—lookin' kinda mad lak—never said nuthin' 'bout no drink. Finally he say, 'Hawrice,' he say, 'git me a bucket o' col' watah.' I say t' m'sef, I say, 'W-e-l-l-l, das mo' lak h'it—ef he wants er bucket o' watah. Boy—you gwi *see* some real drinkin' now.'

"Whin I come in wid d' pail, Mister Money took offin all his clothes an' step out onto d' side po'ch an' say, 'Th'ow dat watah ovah me, Hawrice. I am lit'rully compel,' he say, 't' have my col' tub ev'y mawnin'.' M-a-n-n-n-n! I sho' tow'd dat ice col' watah onto him wid all my heart an' soul. But he jus' gasp an' hollah, an' jump up an' down an' slap hisse'f. Den he had me rub him red wid er big rough towel. I sho' rubbed him, too. Come on in d' clubroom hu'ah, he did, an' mek hisse'f comfort'ble in dat big ol' rockin' chair yonder—an' went t' readin'. I brought in his shell bucket an' begin cleanin' his gun. But I seen him kinder smilin' t' hisse'f. Atta while, he says 'Hawrice,' he say, 'you hav' done los' yo' bet?'

"I kinder hang my haid lak, an' 'low, 'Yaas, suh, Mister Money, I don' said farewell t' d' liquah!'

"He say, 'Yo' admits den dat you hav' done los' fair an' square—an' dat yo' realizes h'it?'

"'Yaas, suh!'

"He say, 'Yo' judgmint,' he say, 'wuz ve'y fair, considerin',' he say, 'de great law uv' av'ridge—but circumstance,' he say, 'has done render de ult'mate outcome subjec' t' d' mighty whims o' chance?'

"I say, 'Yaas, suh,' ve'y mournful lak.

"He say, 'In so far as realizin' on anything 'ceptin' de mercy o' d' Cote—say—you is absolutely nonest—eh, my man?'

"I say, 'Yaas, suh, barrin' yo' mercy, suh.'

"Den he think er moment, an' say, 'Verrree—verree—good!'

"Den he 'low, 'Sence you acknowledges d' cawn, an' admits dat you hav' done got grabbed,' he say, 'step up,' he say, 'an' git you a tumbler—po' yo'sef er drink—po' er big one, too.'

"I never stopped f' nuthin' den—jes' runned an' got me a glass outa de kitchen. Ole Molly, she say, 'Whur you goin' so fas'?' I say, 'Doan stop me now ole 'ooman—I got business—p'ticler business—an' I sho' poh'd me er big bait o' liquah—er whole sloo' o' liquah. Mister Money say, 'Hawrice—de size o' yo' po'tion,' he say, 'is primus facious ev'dence,' he say, 'dat you gwi' spout er toast in honor,' he say, 'o' d' occasion.'

"I say, 'Mister Money, suh,' I say, 'all I got t' say, suh, is dat you is de kingpin, champeen duck shotter so far as I hav' done bin' in dis life—an' ve'y prob'ly as far as I'se likely t' keep on goin', too.' He sorter smile t' hisse'f!

"'Now, suh, please, suh, tell me dis—is you *ever* missed er duck—anywhar'—anytime—anyhow—suh?'

"He say 'Really, Hawrice,' he say, 'you embarrasses me,' he say, 'so hav' another snifter—there is mo', considerably mo',' he say, 'in yo' system what demands utt'rance,' he say.

"I done poh'd me another slug o' Brooklyn Handicap an' say, 'Mister Money,' I say, 'does you expec' t' *ever* miss another duck ez long ez you lives, suh?'

"He say, 'Hawrice,' he say, 'you embarrasses me,' he say, 'beyon' words—you overwhelms me,' he say. 'Git t' hell outa hu'ah befo' you gits us bofe drunk.'"

Some Tiger Stories

SIR RICHARD DANE

I shot my first tiger in the Kanker State in the Central Provinces in January, 1900, under the wing of a gentleman who had shot many tigers and had had much experience of the sport. The lesson, which I had taken most to heart, was that a long shot taken in the direction of the beat might drive the tiger back into the beat and lead to a casualty among the beaters. There were three tigers in the beat, a tigress and two three-quarter grown cubs. My machan had been tied in front so as to give me the first chance of a shot, and my mentor sat in a machan behind me, so as to shoot any animal which might escape me. My machan was badly tied, especially for a man shooting, as I do, from the left shoulder. The string bed, which formed it, was tied with one end facing the beat, and along the left of the machan there were tree trunks. On this side, therefore, I could fire only straight in front of me, but I was too inexperienced to recognise fully the unsatisfactory nature of the position, and settled myself in the machan without making any objection. As the beat proceeded the tigress appeared and stood on my left front, looking up apparently at one of the stops. She gave me as good a shot as I have ever had in a beat, as she was broadside on and quite motionless; but the distance was over 100 yards, and, being very anxious not to be the cause of any mishap, I decided to allow her to approach. Suddenly, with a "Wouf," she started off at a gallop to the left, passed instantly out of my fire zone, and I was compelled to look on helplessly as she passed the machan. She was fired at but missed by my mentor, and got clean away. One of the cubs followed, and I got in a shot at it, as it passed, but missed. The other cub gave me an easy shot, and I killed it. If I had shot the tigress we should probably have bagged all three, but I had correctly carried out instructions, and the instructions were absolutely sound. The line between success and failure, in big-game shooting, is a very narrow one.

I then shot a fine tiger in a beat in the Bustar State, killing him with a single shot as he walked fast through the bushes. I also killed a fine panther by moonlight, when sitting up over a kill, though the body was unfortunately not found until the skin was spoiled. On the whole, therefore, I did pretty well for a beginner in this expedition . . .

I then took part in a tiger-shoot with elephants in the Terai on the border of the Bahraich district of Oudh, in April, 1900, and my companions were Mr. Harrison, the Collector of the district, and Mr. A. Wood, the Manager of the Kapurthala Estates in Oudh. I had the elephant Chainchal on this occasion, and did pretty well. It was, I think, established that I put the first bullet into a tigress, which was subsequently killed by Harrison; but I made no claim for the skin, as the tigress was unquestionably knocked over and killed by him.

We then had a beat for a tiger which was fired at by both Harrison and myself, and badly wounded, and was eventually finished off by Wood. Both Harrison and myself were using black powder .500 Express rifles, but fortunately he had only wax in his bullets, and I had copper-tubes in mine. We both claimed the shot; and, as the result of a friendly discussion, it appeared probable that the successful shot was Harrison's. I therefore resigned the tiger with the best grace possible, and we were all round the carcass during the skinning operation, when Harrison's servant, who was groping in the inside of the tiger, held up something, saying, "What is this?" Examination showed that it was the copper tube of my bullet, making it clear that mine had been the successful shot, and the ownership of the tiger was accordingly transferred.

This tiger broke out of the beat and might have gone clear away before he was fired at; but the Maila nullah which we were beating, with its cool, shady trees and dense cane brake and a stream of water in the centre, was a favourite place for tigers in the hot weather, and the animal, sooner than face the burning heat of the sun at midday, returned to the nullah further on, and met with his death in consequence.

It is sometimes very difficult to decide who has fired the first successful shot, but, if the contending sportsmen are required to describe accurately the position of the tiger when they fired, a carefully conducted post-mortem examination, after removal of the skin, will generally disclose the truth. The excitement of a tiger-shoot is not, however, conducive to the frame of mind which is required for a judicial investigation, and heated arguments and disputes often result.

I shot a fine panther in the same beat as the tiger, and Harrison also shot a female panther. Two or three days afterwards Wood shot a good tigress. The bag, therefore, was very evenly distributed on this occasion.

My next tiger-hunt was in January, 1901, in the Patna State, which was, at the time, in the Central Provinces, but has now been transferred to Bengal. I had a female elephant to ride and a good native shikari with me, but no European companion, and the country we were hunting contained buffaloes as well as tigers. The first tiger we heard of was said to have eaten a certain number of bullocks and buffaloes and two men, and the Uriya villagers, who had suffered from his depredations, were naturally very anxious to have him killed. The first bullock we tied out was completely devoured, and the tiger was not in the beat. He killed again the following night, however, and dragged the carcass of the bullock from the road on which it was tied to a place within a few yards of the edge of the jungle in the direction of the village, and there lay up with it. A machan was tied for me, and the beat was lined up in the rice-fields, within a few yards—as appeared from a subsequent examination—of the tiger's resting-place. The first yell given by the beaters evidently startled the tiger, and before the beat had well started I saw him emerging from the jungle on my right at a fast trot. The stop either did not see him or was seized with panic, as he made no attempt to check him. I turned quickly on the machan and fired, and the tiger broke into a gallop and disappeared. Examination showed that the shot had passed under the tiger and struck the ground well beyond the place where he had broken into a gallop. It missed him, therefore, by a few inches only. The direction was good, and the elevation only was wrong.

This was a serious disappointment, but in the night the tiger, who was evidently a very ravenous brute, returned to the kill and dragged the remains to another hiding-place in the same jungle. The shikari wanted me to sit up for him, but I decided to have another beat. On this occasion the tiger emerged at a fast walk and gave me an easy shot, but on my wrong side. I hit him with the first barrel low down in the stomach. He gave a tremendous "Wouf," and went off at a gallop. I swung round on the machan and, as he was galloping off, made a good shot with the second barrel, and put a bullet into the centre of his back. When the beaters came up I descended and we began to look for blood. I knew that I had hit him with the first barrel, and the stop on my left said that he had answered to the second shot also. There was no blood, however, and a small piece of fat about the size of my little fingernail was the only trace of the tiger which could be found near the machan. The ground was most unfavourable, with clumps of bamboos at intervals and scrub jungle, as high as a man's waist, in between. There were, however, some trees. I sent for the riding elephant, and we advanced together, the elephant being a few paces in front, and I following on foot and keeping, as far as possible, a tree between me and the elephant, as I was doubtful of her staunchness. Before we had gone far the mahout declared that he heard the tiger growling, but I urged him to proceed, and we advanced a few paces farther. Then there was a roar, and the elephant swung round and bolted. I have never seen an elephant travel as she did on that occasion, and the mahout said afterwards that she had actually twisted his neck by the rapidity with which she swung round. It was, however, a case of "eyes front," and I stood waiting for the attack. Fortunately for me, the tiger did not charge, but retreated, attempting to escape.

The demonstration caused a general stampede, but after some time my attendants were reassured and returned. Mihtab Khan had, as he explained, laid hold of the shikari as he was retreating, but the shikari said that he had recently married a wife and was therefore obliged to take care of himself.

A protracted reconnaissance made from trees disclosed the fact that the tiger had gone, and in the bamboo clump, in which he was lying, there was a great pool of blood. The wounds had not bled until he lay down on the ground. This encouraged us all, and we started in pursuit, tracking the tiger by the blood which was now flowing. We followed him for a considerable distance into the open country, and there in a clump of bushes at the foot of a tree he lay up again. The Uriyas, as Indians often do, passed from panic to over-confidence, and I had the greatest difficulty in keeping them behind me. I had placed Mihtab Khan on the elephant, which followed along behind us, to give confidence to the mahout; and from the elephant Mihtab Khan and the mahout saw the tiger's ear move, as he lay in the clump of bushes. The shikari and I had passed within a few yards of him. We drew back and held a council of war. I had the black powder .500 Express, with which I had shot the other four tigers, and the shikari had a Lee-Metford. My idea was to give the Lee-Metford to Mihtab Khan and allow him to fire from the back of the elephant, and to shoot the tiger, as he rose, with the .500; but the mahout urged me to mount the elephant and shoot, and, as she was then standing very quietly, I decided to try this. The elephant, as I afterwards heard, would not stand a shotgun; but, when drawn back from the proximity of the tiger, she allowed me to mount without difficulty and then, under pressure from the mahout, she advanced and stood within 30 yards of the bushes. After some time I made out the outline of the tiger crouching in the bushes, and the elephant allowed me to take a steady aim. As soon as I fired, however, she swung round with amazing quickness; and, seeing that I must be thrown off, as I was merely sitting on the pad and my hands were engaged with the rifle, I jumped and landed on my feet, but fell back, cracking the stock of my rifle. I sprang to my feet with very creditable rapidity, but fortunately for me the tiger was done for. He staggered to his feet but did not leave the bushes, and a shot by the shikari finally laid him low. My shot from the elephant merely passed through the forearm and did him no appreciable injury, but the shot in the back, as he galloped off, had inflicted a mortal wound. The shot in the lower part of the belly also caused serious internal injury.

He was a young tiger, with a very good coat. The shikari thought he was too young to have commenced man-eating, but there did not appear to be any other tiger in the neighbourhood, and he was a very voracious animal. The view that only old or crippled tigers become man-eaters is only partly correct. Cubs, which have been brought up on human flesh, and which have repeatedly seen their mother attacking and killing human beings, must frequently take to the business when they begin hunting on their own account, especially if game is scarce in the place in which they reside, as was the case in the Patna State. Altogether, this tiger provided three successive days' entertainment. The rifle, though damaged, was not completely unserviceable, and I was able to go on shooting.

For some days after this excitement the elephant was decidedly mischievous. On the day following the death of the tiger she tried to catch hold of a native with her trunk as he ran past her; and on another occasion, after the mahout's wife had given her some bananas, she seized the woman round the waist with her trunk and lifted her up, but did not actually injure her. I was in the tent when this occurred, but, hearing a row, I came out and found the mahout abusing the elephant as only an Indian can.

She was, I think, the fastest and most comfortable elephant I have ever ridden, but she had a temper and was said to have killed several people. The mahout managed her well, but he told me that she had been the favourite riding elephant of the Raja of Bustar, and that, on one occasion, when the Raja had gone down to the river to bathe and had dismounted from the elephant, she suddenly seized a man and tore him in two. The Raja, as was said, fell off his chair with fright, and after this, not unnaturally, parted with the elephant. The mahout said that she had killed five or six people at different times after this, but that he had succeeded in reducing her to submission. On one occasion, as he said, he had tied her up for the night and lain down to sleep at a safe distance, but had omitted to remove out of her reach the lance, which is used to subdue a refractory elephant. In the night he felt something in his hair, and, after brushing at it ineffectually, awoke to find that the elephant had got hold of the lance, broken it in two, and was trying to twist one of the broken pieces into his hair so that she might be able to pull him over to her. I am not prepared to vouch for the truth of this story; but, if it were a lie, it was exceedingly well told, and I saw no reason at the time to doubt the man. He became quite excited at the reminiscence. He was certainly a good mahout, and behaved well on the day when the tiger was shot.

On any occasion on which I was left alone on the back of the elephant, after hearing these stories, I was always glad to see the mahout return; but my personal relations with the elephant were very satisfactory.

We then started to hunt a man-eating family, which were said to have eaten over twenty people between August and the time of my visit in January. There were a tigress and two well-grown cubs, and a tiger was said to join the party occasionally. These tigers had created a scare, and we had to tie out our own buffaloes. It was rather creepy work, but the shikari did this bravely enough. The last kill had occurred about eight days before we arrived on the scene, and the villagers had been too frightened to visit the place. I went there with the old man, who had been with the victim when he was killed, and saw the two bundles of wood which they were tying up at the time. Death appeared to have been instantaneous, as his companion said that the man, when seized, did not utter a cry. The drag was clearly visible in the grass, and, after following it for a few yards, we found the man's loin-cloth, and, farther on, the place where he had been eaten. We hunted for some days and tied out baits, but saw nothing of the tigers, which had for some reason or other left the neighbourhood. . . .

In April, 1901, I had another tiger-hunt in the Terai, on the border of the Bahraich district, with Mr. Faunthorpe, I.C.S., who was then the Collector, and Mr. A. Wood. We got no tigers in Nepal, and the expedition was in danger of being a complete failure, when we received news of a tigress which had killed in one day three head of cattle in a village in the Bahraich district, near the border. We moved camp to this place, and we found that the cover in which the tigress was lying, consisted of a triangular patch of high reeds on the border of a small lagoon. The line of elephants was formed at the base of the triangle, and the beat was a pretty and exciting one. Wood was with the line; I had the next position in front of the beat, and Faunthorpe was beyond me. The tigress was soon on the move, and we could hear her splashing in the reeds as she moved along the edge of the lagoon. When the line was half-way through the patch of reeds she charged the elephants with a roar and threw the line into confusion. With a little more courage she could have broken through and escaped, but her heart failed her and she retreated until she was pushed up into the very apex of the triangle. She might have escaped across the water, as this side of the beat was unprotected; but she would not face the open. At last, when driven into the extreme corner of the reeds, she rushed out on the side where we were all standing. Wood had a shot at her but missed, and she came straight for my elephant. Seeing the elephant, she declined the encounter, and swung round, and as she swung round I fired. A second later Faunthorpe's shot rang out. Our shots were so nearly simultaneous that he did not hear my shot, but I heard his. Two more shots were fired by Wood and myself at the tigress, as she was struggling in the grass; but these were misses. My shot struck the tigress in the heart, and Faunthorpe's shot struck her in the back near the shoulder as she was end on to him. I was using an Express and firing shell, and the others fired solid bullets; there was, therefore, no difficulty in identifying the different shots on this occasion. Our two shots were fired almost simultaneously, but Faunthorpe, seeing that my shot had killed the tigress, did not make any claim. I rode an elephant belonging to the Maharajah of Balrampur on this occasion, and she stood staunchly when the shots were fired though she was not highly tried.

In 1903–4, I had a run of ill-luck, taking part in three expeditions to the Terai, in the course of which no less than nine tigers and tigresses and two cubs were shot, and the only animal which fell to my lot was a large panther, which I shot over a kill.

On the first occasion, in April, 1903, the party consisted of Mr. A. Wood, the late Major Lumsden, I.M.S., Mr. Channer, the Divisional Forest Officer, and myself, and we hunted a portion of the Terai at some distance from the ground which we hunted during my first two expeditions. Major Lumsden rode the elephant Chainchal, and I was riding an elephant which was lent me by the Maharajah of Balrampur. Shortly after our arrival on the ground a good tiger was marked down in a very small patch of thick jungle on the bank of a small deep nullah, or stream, which was overhung with trees. The tiger had killed a chital, and dragged the carcass into the cover, and it was therefore a sure find. Lumsden was with the beat; Wood had the best place on the bank of the nullah at the end of the patch of cover; and Channer and I were among the trees on the opposite side of the nullah. The guns were, therefore, roughly speaking, at the four corners of a square with the corner, at which Wood was posted, projecting. The patch of jungle was very thick, and Lumsden was not thought to have any chance. Chainchal's mahout, however (Karim by name), was a very plucky, intelligent fellow, with very good vision, and while the elephants were trying to force their way into the patch of jungle, he saw the tiger standing in thick cover. Lumsden failed to see him until he moved. He then fired both barrels, but he had missed his chance, and the tiger rushed from the thicket and plunged into the water with a tremendous splash, swimming straight across to where I was posted among the trees on the other bank. An overhanging branch obscured my vision at the particular point at which the tiger was crossing; and, though I could see the water moving as he swam, I could not actually see his head. He was, however, making for the bank very near the place where my elephant was standing; and the shikari in the howdah behind me, who perhaps saw the animal, was adjuring me to shoot. Very unwisely, therefore, I fired. The tiger answered to the shot with a roar, and the bullet evidently struck the water very near him. My elephant then swung round so that I could not fire again, and, looking backwards, I could just see the tiger climb the bank behind me. Wood had a shot at him as he ascended the bank, but missed. The tiger then made off along the bank and ran right into Channer. Thinking he was trapped, he turned with a roar and plunged with another splash into the water, and swam back to the thicket in which he was lying at the outset. Owing to the overhanging trees, he was not visible after he sprang into the water until he reached cover. After some time he was beaten out again, and this time took the line he was expected to take, giving Wood a good chance. A shot near the head stopped him, and a second bullet finished him off. My shot was thought to have been a hit, but examination showed that it was Wood's tiger. This is the only occasion I can remember in which every member of a party had a fair chance in turn at a tiger. The beat also was one of the prettiest and most exciting in which I have ever taken part.

After this the shikaris reported that there were no other tigers in the vicinity of the camp, and went to some place at a considerable distance to look for tracks. We were reconciling ourselves to some hot days of waiting, but very soon after the shikaris had gone some herdsmen came in and said that a tiger had killed one of their buffaloes. We went to the place and found a recently killed buffalo; but the only patch of forest which was near the place had been fired, and, although it had apparently been too damp to burn well, some fallen trees were actually on fire. We tried a beat, and the tiger was there right enough. In shooting with elephants, there is very little danger to the beaters, and, as everyone is anxious to put the first bullet into the tiger, there is often some rather wild shooting. As the line advanced both Wood and I had shots. I fired without success at a movement in the high grass; and then the tiger, which was fairly cornered, broke with a roar into the open, a little to my left front. It was a grand spectacle, as the tiger showed up magnificently on the short green grass. With Chainchal, I should probably have got that tiger; but my elephant was not a good one, and I tried her rather severely. Leaning well out of the howdah, I waited until the tiger was close up so as to make sure of the shot; but, just as I was pulling the trigger, the elephant funked and swung round with a jerk, and the rifle went off in the air. By the time the elephant had been turned round the tiger had galloped some distance; shots fired at his tail by Wood and myself were unsuccessful, and he got clean away. It was very disappointing; but it was partly my fault, as I ought to have made allowance for the possibility of the elephant funking, and fired as soon as the tiger appeared.

The Terai, or moist alluvial land, lying between the branches of the mighty Gagra River, provides grazing in the hot weather for large herds of cattle and buffaloes. The grass is burnt in the spring, and at the end of April, the land is covered with short green grass. Tigers still abound in this part of India, and toll is taken of the herds. These grazing buffaloes will, as one of the herdsmen informed me, respond to a particular call announcing the advent of a tiger, and will charge *en masse* and drive the animal away; but young buffaloes, when detached from the herd, are not infrequently attacked and killed.

A tigress with three small cubs was then marked down in a dry ravine near a village. The tigress was in poor condition, and evidently found a difficulty in feeding her numerous progeny; and apparently she had taken up her quarters in the ravine on the chance of killing one of the village cattle, as there was no game in the vicinity. Wood was with the line of elephants on this occasion; Lumsden was on the left bank, and Channer and I were on the right bank of the ravine. The beat was up the ravine. Shortly after the beat started Wood, whose elephant was moving along the bed of the ravine, saw the tigress crouching on the sand, facing him at a short distance. He fired at her with a shotgun loaded with ball, and the shot passed through one of her ears, which was evidently cocked forward. Subsequent examination showed that the bullet drilled a small round hole, the edges of which were not even reddened with blood. It was a close shave, but the animal was quite uninjured and blood was not drawn. The tigress then appeared near Lumsden, who fired, and, as he subsequently said, knocked her over into the ravine. Very shortly after this she appeared on my side of the ravine. She walked quietly and quickly round a bush, and did not appear to be wounded, and I fired, hitting her with my Express on the near side, but rather far back. She disappeared into the ravine and wandered about there for a little time. Then Channer, who was shooting with a small-bore, high-velocity rifle, saw her and fired, and shortly after, she was seen to be dead. Two bullet-holes were visible in the skin, one a small one in the back near the neck, and the other a large one in the near side. Lumsden was quite confident that he had hit the tigress and knocked her over, and suggested that the large hole in the side was the hole of exit of his bullet. Both the other sportsmen thought that the tiger was Lumsden's, and Channer did not claim a hit. There was much blood in the ravine, but it was impossible to say from which wound it proceeded, and I therefore contented myself with pointing out that the hole in the side was the hole of my bullet, and did not claim the tigress and was not present at the post-mortem. The natives who skinned and cut up the tigress were told to produce the bullets, and mine was duly produced, and was admitted by Major Lumsden to be not his. His bullet, which was also an expanding one, was not found. On the following morning, when we were looking at the skin, Lumsden himself noticed a small round hole in the skin of the belly, but he was so convinced that he had shot the tigress that he did not give the matter much attention. I said nothing, but thought a good deal. It was clear to me that Lumsden had missed the tigress, and that I had put the first bullet into her, and that she had then been killed by Channer, whose bullet had entered the back and come out through the belly. I kept my conclusions, however, to myself, merely resolving that I would always be present at a post-mortem in the future. Poor Lumsden was a good sportsman, and was perfectly convinced that he had shot the tigress; but, as already said, a painstaking investigation is often necessary before it can be determined who has scored the first hit.

A forest officer of my acquaintance told me that on one occasion he had arranged a tiger-shoot for two military officers. One had, if I remember right, shot a tiger before, and the other had not. The tiger went first to the more experienced sportsman of the two, who fired at it. The tiger then went to the other man, who fired at it and killed it. Overjoyed at his good fortune, he chaffed his friend about his bad shot, and the other accepted the chaff. The forest officer, from curiosity, went along the route by which the tiger had approached the second machan, and found blood all along the track. But, where ignorance is bliss, it is folly to be wise; both the sportsmen were satisfied, and he left them in blissful ignorance of his discovery.

Major Lumsden shot two of the small cubs. The third must also have died, as they were much too young to hunt for themselves.

Our next hunt was an exciting one. A tiger was marked down in a thick bed of reeds in a swampy clearing in the middle of sal forest. We posted ourselves round the reeds, and the tiger broke out near the place where Channer was posted; but, as well as I remember, he did not, owing to some difficulty with his elephant, get a shot. As the tiger was disappearing into the forest Lumsden fired and put a bullet into him. There was very little blood, and it was uncertain how far the tiger had gone; but we formed a long line in the forest, with the elephants about 50 yards apart, and drove forward in the hope of rounding him up. I was on the extreme right of the line, and before we had gone far the mahout said that he heard the tiger growling. I heard him also and ought, perhaps, to have called a halt and sent for the others. I was afraid, however, that the tiger might escape, as he did not appear to be badly wounded, and was also, it must be admitted, very anxious to see a fine charge. The prospect of an encounter, therefore, was not unwelcome. I accordingly encouraged the mahout to proceed; and, as soon as we advanced, the tiger burst from some bushes at the foot of a tree in which he was lying and charged.

I have heard it said that a tiger always charges at a fast run. This one charged at a gallop. He was in the middle of a spring, with his forelegs stretched out in front and the hind-legs stretched out straight behind him, when I fired. Directly I fired, the elephant swung round so that I could not fire the second barrel, and the tiger pushed home the charge and seized her by the middle of the thigh. In the struggle that ensued I received a severe bruise on the forearm, but was not otherwise injured, though I was in great danger of being crushed, as the howdah was in constant collision with a tree or trees. The howdah, which was very strongly built, was much damaged. I was quite unable to shoot, and got down into the howdah and trusted for safety to the elephant. Presently she flopped down, and I thought the tiger had pulled her over, but apparently she sat down so as to pinch the tiger's head and make him let go. The manœuvre succeeded, as she shook him off, and then got up and bolted. She did not, however, go far, and the mahout recovered control and stopped her. Mihtab Khan, who was behind me in the howdah, seized a bough in the struggle, and, being a powerful man, swung himself up into a tree. He had a Lee-Metford rifle in one hand, and it was a fine acrobatic performance; but he made no attempt to fire at the tiger.

I then sent for the others, and Wood and Lumsden joined me. The tiger had retreated to the bushes from which he had charged, and lay there growling. We all advanced upon him together, but my elephant was badly shaken and would not keep in line with the other two. Wood saw, or thought he saw, the tiger, and fired the first shot, but the tiger made no response and continued his low growling. Lumsden then pushed forward on Chainchal, and saw the tiger lying on the ground, and put a bullet into his brain. There were two bullet-holes in his side, and his hind-leg was broken to pieces below the hock. My bullet had struck him in the flank and run down his hind-leg, as it was stretched out behind him in the gallop. But for this he would probably have sprung on top of the elephant, and might have pulled one of us out of the howdah, as he was in no way crippled and made a most determined charge. The elephant was badly mauled, but recovered under treatment. If she had not turned round, I might have finished off the tiger without difficulty with the second barrel.

This was the best tiger-shoot in which I ever took part, though in the matter of the bag I personally came off badly. My elephant did not serve me well, but in the first beat I made a bad error of judgment. I think, however, that I put the first bullet into one of the three full-grown tigers which were killed, and contributed materially to the death of another. I may possibly have transposed the order of one or two of the hunts, but the different events and scenes are still fresh in my memory.

On the next expedition the party consisted of Mr. Wood, Major Lumsden, and myself. Wood shot a tigress and a young tiger in a beat in which we were seated in machans, but I think these were the only two shots which were fired at tigers in the course of the expedition, which was comparatively unsuccessful and uneventful. . . .

On the next occasion on which I visited the Terai, the party consisted of Major Lumsden, Mrs. Lumsden, and myself; and Mrs. Lumsden, who was a very good shot, killed a tiger in fine style. The tiger had killed in a sandy nullah, and lain up with the kill in a small patch of thick cover under the high bank of the nullah. We were all posted in the forest facing the high bank in question, Lumsden on the right, Mrs. Lumsden, who was on Chainchal, in the centre, and I on the left. We took up our positions just in time, as the tiger, scenting trouble, tried to slink away before the beat commenced. He came towards Mrs. Lumsden, who hit him with her first shot with the Rigby-Mauser she was using, but missed him with the second, as he turned and dashed back into the beat. He soon appeared again on the same line, and Mrs. Lumsden fired, hitting him in the mouth. The bullet, however, merely broke one of the canine teeth, and was diverted. A shot in the head is often a very unsatisfactory one. The tiger then tried to slink out on the right, and Lumsden had two shots at him, hitting him with one and turning him back into the beat, but missing him with the other. He then broke out at a gallop between Major and Mrs. Lumsden; and the latter, with a well-placed shot, rolled him over. I was on lower ground, and, although I was not more than 100 yards distant from Mrs. Lumsden, I could not see what was going on.

The tiger had rather a small head, and was certainly wanting in spirit, as he made no attempt to take the offensive; but he was the largest tiger that I have ever seen shot, measuring between pegs fixed in the ground, at the head and tail, 9 feet 8 inches.

A day or two after this we had a beat for two young tigers in the very place in which Wood had shot the two tigers on the previous expedition; and, as before, we were posted in machans. Mrs. Lumsden had shots at the tigers, as they broke, but failed to stop them. We then formed a long line, and hunted them through the sal forest for some hours. Lumsden had a shot at one of them, a young tigress, which then passed me at a gallop. The distance, when I fired, was considerable, but the tigress passed me apparently unwounded. One of the two shots, however, was evidently a hit, as the tigress was seen shortly afterwards lying up behind a tree. I had a staunch but very slow elephant, and Lumsden reached the place before me and put a bullet into the tiger. One or two more shots were then fired to finish her off. I made no claim, as the tigress may possibly have been wounded by Lumsden's first shot, and he certainly gave her the *coup de grâce;* but the idea among the men was that I had put a bullet into her.

After the death of the tigress we sat unsuccessfully over two kills which had occurred in the forest until a late hour, and then had a long elephant-ride back to camp, arriving there long after dark. It was hot weather, and, for a lady, it was a wonderful exhibition of endurance. We got no more tigers; but I shot the panther already referred to in the course of this expedition.

I had also an interesting but most exasperating experience, when sitting up over a kill for a tiger. One of our buffaloes had been killed, and we had beaten the ground, but the beat was blank. It was decided, therefore, that I should sit up for the tiger on the chance of his returning to the kill. A machan was constructed, and a local shikari, who was with us, climbed into it. I ordered him out, but he pleaded very hard to be allowed to remain; and, as the kill was lying among bushes, I unfortunately thought that his hearing might be of use, and allowed him to sit with me. Before it was dark the tiger came, and the shikari, suddenly seeing him standing on some rising ground above the level of the machan, completely lost his nerve. He stammered out that the tiger had come, and threw his arms round me to turn me around to have a shot at it. The tiger of course saw the movement, or heard the noise and was off. I have always regarded it as creditable to my forbearance that I did not lay a hand on the shikari. . . .

In April, 1905, I made my last expedition to the Terai. The party on this occasion consisted of Mr. W.B.M. Bird, Mr. A. Wood, and myself. Major Fullerton, who had succeeded Major Lumsden as

Civil Surgeon of Bahraich, was also with us during part of the time. On this occasion I rode the elephant Chainchal, and had better fortune. Our shooting-camp was on the bank of the Rapti River; and we reached the camp on the 20th of April. In the afternoon of that day and on the 21st, we hunted without any definite information and without success, but on the 22nd, a tigress was marked down in some very thick cover. The first beat we had for her was unsuccessful, but she did not leave the place, and we beat the cover again on the following day from a different direction. I was on one side of the cover a little in advance of the line of elephants, and when the line had advanced for some distance the tigress came along the edge of the cover, quite near the elephant. She was not properly visible, and I was doubtful about firing; but the mahout, Karim, pointed in the direction in which the bushes were moving and urged me to shoot. I decided, therefore, to chance a shot and fired. The shot, by good fortune, struck the tigress near the root of the tail, and she turned and rushed in the direction of the beaters outside the edge of the jungle. Chainchal stood staunchly, and with the second barrel I broke the tigress's left shoulder as she charged past me. She then lay up under a bush in the cover, and with some difficulty I made her out from the howdah and finished her off. This tigress had a very beautifully marked skin, which makes a very handsome trophy.

On the next day a good tiger was marked down, and, having shot the tigress, I was put in what was supposed to be the worst place, at the end of the beat, Wood having the position on the side of the beat, while Bird was covering him. But fortune favoured me, and, as the line of elephants advanced, I saw the tiger's head in the jungle about 80 yards away. He was standing broadside on the Wood, and at no great distance, but was hidden from him by the bushes. Momentarily I expected to hear his rifle, but he did not fire, and the tiger remained standing with his head slightly turned, listening to the advancing elephants. I accordingly fired from a standing position in the howdah, aiming between the eyes. I made a good shot, the bullet striking the tiger between the nose and the left eye. Subsequent examination showed that the bullet, which was a shell from a .500 black powder Express, broke the palate, nearly severed the tongue, and tore off two big molar teeth, one in the upper and one in the lower jaw. The tiger probably would have died, but for the time being he was in no way crippled. For some seconds, however, he was knocked out of time; and, as nothing was visible, I hoped that I had killed him. He then got up and dashed out of the jungle at a gallop, mad with pain and rage. I failed to stop him; but, after galloping aimlessly about for some seconds, he passed near Bird, who knocked him over and then finished him, with two well-directed shots. As already said, a shot in the head or face often gives very unsatisfactory results.

On the 26th of April, Bird got his chance and shot a fine tiger, killing it with a single shot. He was using a double-barrelled .360 bore high-velocity rifle, and the tiger, with a bullet through his heart, galloped, apparently uninjured, for at least one hundred yards. Thinking he had missed, Karim urged Chainchal to speed to cut him off, and, just as an encounter was imminent, the tiger collapsed in his gallop, and fell stone dead in a small ditch. He lay in this ditch all limp and crumpled up, like a well-shot rabbit.

On the 28th, Bird shot a bear, which was marked down by the shikaris in a clump of bushes; and on the 30th of April, he shot a second tiger.

This tiger had apparently had a fight with another tiger, or with a bear, and had come off second best. He had lost one eye and was badly clawed about the body. When beaten out of the cover, in which he was lying, he broke at a gallop; but his blind eye prevented him from seeing Bird, whose elephant was standing in a fairly open place. The tiger therefore passed close to him, and was killed by a single well-placed shot.

On the 1st of May, Bird and I had a very interesting but unsuccessful sit for another tiger. The tiger had killed and eaten two or three of our buffaloes, but could not be located for the purposes of a beat. He was, evidently, a very cunning brute. One day the shikaris returned full of confidence, having marked him down in a very favourable locality, but he cleared out before we arrived and the beat was blank. We decided, therefore, to sit up over a live buffalo, which was tied upon the road upon which the other buffaloes had been killed. Our machan was well screened, having been tied in a thick leafy tree, but we could see only to our front, and could neither shoot nor see anything up the road behind us. The buffalo was tied about 20 paces from us down the road. There was no moon, but the night was clear, and the tiger came at about ten o'clock. I was dozing at the time, but Bird was watchful and heard him, and, at a touch from him, I took in the situation. The tiger stood for some time on the road to the rear of the machan, watching the buffalo, and then, as could be seen in the morning, lay down in the grass to our right, nearly parallel to the machan. Then he got up and walked round the buffalo, without showing himself; but apparently he was suspicious of a trap, and made no attack. The buffalo did not appear to be particularly alarmed, but kept head on to the tiger, and, as the tiger moved, the buffalo's head followed it round. After an hour or so, the tiger departed, and we sat there until the dawn without any further excitement. We heard spotted deer calling in the distance, and the tiger was apparently in pursuit of them.

I have heard it said, more than once, that a tiger will not kill readily a buffalo with a white blaze on his forehead. The one tied out had a white blaze, and this may have been the reason why the tiger would not attack. There certainly was no other cause apparent. I do not think the tiger could possibly have detected our presence, as we both sat very still and quiet, and the machan was well hidden.

Some days of waiting and unsuccessful hunting followed, but on the 6th of May, a tigress was marked down in the same cover in which I had shot the tiger on the 24th. Fullerton was given the best place, and had a good shot at the tigress, but unfortunately missed. I had two shots at her as she galloped away, but she broke out of the cover to my right and at some distance from me, and I failed to stop her.

This ended the hunt, and on the 7th of May, we struck our tents and started for Nipal Ganj on our return journey to Bahraich.

The Pickwick Papers

CHARLES DICKENS

Chapter VI

"PLEASANT, pleasant country," sighed the enthusiastic gentleman, as he opened his lattice window. "Who could live to gaze from day to day on bricks and slates, who had once felt the influence of a scene like this?"

"Hallo!" was the sound that roused him.

He looked to the right, but he saw nobody; his eyes wandered to the left, and pierced the prospect; he stared into the sky, but he wasn't wanted there; and then he did what a common mind would have done at once—looked into the garden, and there saw Mr. Wardle.

"How are you?" said that good-humoured individual, out of breath with his own anticipations of pleasure. "Beautiful morning, ain't it? Glad to see you up so early. Make haste down, and come out. I'll wait for you here."

Mr. Pickwick needed no second invitation. Ten minutes sufficed for the completion of his toilet, and at the expiration of that time he was by the old gentleman's side.

"Hallo!" said Mr. Pickwick in his turn: seeing that his companion was armed with a gun, and that another lay ready on the grass. "What's going forward?"

"Why, your friend and I," replied the host, "are going out rook-shooting before breakfast. He's a very good shot, ain't he?"

"I've heard him say he's a capital one," replied Mr. Pickwick; "but I never saw him aim at anything."

The old gentleman laid one gun on the ground, and loaded the other.

"Here they are," said Mr. Pickwick; and as he spoke, the forms of Mr. Tupman, Mr. Snodgrass, and Mr. Winkle appeared in the distance.

"Come along," shouted the old gentleman, addressing Mr. Winkle; "a keen hand like you ought to have been up long ago, even to such poor work as this."

Mr. Winkle responded with a forced smile, and took up the spare gun with an expression of countenance which a metaphysical rook, impressed with a foreboding of his approaching death by violence, may be supposed to assume. It might have been keenness, but it looked remarkably like misery.

"Very well. Shall I begin?"

"If you please," said Mr. Winkle, glad of any respite.

"Stand aside, then. Now for it."

The boy shouted, and shook a branch with a nest on it. Half a dozen young rooks in violent conversation, flew out to ask what the matter was. The old gentleman fired by way of reply. Down fell one bird, and off flew the others.

"Now, Mr. Winkle," said the host, reloading his own gun. "Fire away."

Mr. Winkle advanced, and levelled his gun. Mr. Pickwick and his friends cowered involuntarily to escape damage from the heavy fall of rooks, which they felt quite certain would be occasioned by the devastating barrel of their friend. There was a solemn pause—a shout—a flapping of wings—a faint click.

"Hallo!" said the old gentleman.

"Won't it go?" inquired Mr. Pickwick.

"Missed fire," said Mr. Winkle, who was very pale: probably from disappointment.

"Odd," said the old gentleman, taking the gun. "Never knew one of them miss fire before. Why, I don't see anything of the cap."

"Bless my soul," said Mr. Winkle. "I declare I forgot the cap!"

The slight omission was rectified. Mr. Pickwick crouched again. Mr. Winkle stepped forward with an air of determination and resolution; and Mr. Tupman looked out from behind a tree. The boy shouted;—four birds flew out. Mr. Winkle fired. There was a scream as of an individual—not a rook—in corporeal anguish. Mr. Tupman had saved the lives of innumerable unoffending birds by receiving a portion of the charge in his left arm.

To describe the confusion that ensued would be impossible. To tell how Mr. Pickwick in the first transport of his emotion called Mr. Winkle "Wretch!" how Mr. Tupman lay prostrate on the ground; and how Mr. Winkle knelt horror-stricken beside him; how Mr. Tupman called distractedly upon some feminine Christian name, and then opened first one eye, and then the other, and then fell back and shut them both;—all this would be as difficult to describe in detail, as it would be to depict the gradual recovering of the unfortunate individual, the binding up of his arm with pocket handkerchiefs, and the conveying him back by slow degrees supported by the arms of his anxious friends.

They drew near the house. The ladies were at the garden gate, waiting for their arrival and their breakfast. The spinster aunt appeared; she smiled, and beckoned them to walk quicker. 'Twas evident she knew not of the disaster. Poor thing! There are times when ignorance is bliss indeed.

They approached nearer.

"Why, what *is* the matter with the little old gentleman?" said Isabella Wardle. The spinster aunt heeded not the remark; she thought it applied to Mr. Pickwick. In her eyes Tracy Tupman was a youth; she viewed his years through a diminishing glass.

"Don't be frightened," called out the old host, fearful of alarming his daughters. The little party had crowded so completely round Mr. Tupman, that they could not yet clearly discern the nature of the accident.

"Don't be frightened," said the host.

"What's the matter?" screamed the ladies.

"Mr. Tupman has met with a little accident; that's all."

The spinster aunt uttered a piercing scream, burst into an hysteric laugh, and fell backwards in the arms of her nieces.

"Throw some cold water over her," said the old gentleman.

"No, no," murmured the spinster aunt; "I am better now. Bella, Emily—a surgeon! Is he wounded?— Is he dead?—Is he——ha, ha, ha!" Here the spinster aunt burst into fit number two, of hysteric laughter, interspersed with screams.

"Calm yourself," said Mr. Tupman, affected almost to tears by this expression of sympathy with his sufferings. "Dear, dear madam, calm yourself."

"It is his voice!" exclaimed the spinster aunt; and strong symptoms of fit number three developed themselves forthwith.

"Do not agitate yourself I entreat you, dearest madam," said Mr. Tupman, soothingly. "I am very little hurt, I assure you."

"Then you are not dead!" ejaculated the hysterical lady. "Oh, say you are not dead!"

"Don't be a fool, Rachael," interposed Mr. Wardle, rather more roughly than was quite consistent with the poetic nature of the scene. "What the devil's the use of his *saying* he isn't dead?"

"No, no, I am not," said Mr. Tupman. "I require no assistance but yours. Let me lean on your arm." He added, in a whisper, "Oh Miss Rachael!" The agitated female advanced, and offered her arm. They turned into the breakfast parlour. Mr. Tracy Tupman gently pressed her hand to his lips, and sank upon the sofa.

"Are you faint?" inquired the anxious Rachael.

"No," said Mr. Tupman. "It is nothing. I shall be better presently." He closed his eyes.

"He sleeps," murmured the spinster aunt. (His organs of vision had been closed nearly twenty seconds.) "Dear—dear—Mr. Tupman!"

Mr. Tupman jumped up—"Oh, say those words again!" he exclaimed.

The lady started. "Surely you did not hear them!" she said, bashfully.

"Oh yes I did!" replied Mr. Tupman; "repeat them. If you would have me recover, repeat them."

"Hush!" said the lady. "My brother."

Mr. Tracy Tupman resumed his former position; and Mr. Wardle accompanied by a surgeon entered the room.

The arm was examined, the wound dressed, and pronounced to be a very slight one; and the minds of the company having been thus satisfied, they proceeded to satisfy their appetites with countenances to which an expression of cheerfulness was again restored. Mr. Pickwick alone was silent and reserved. Doubt and distrust were exhibited in his countenance. His confidence in Mr. Winkle had been shaken—greatly shaken—by the proceedings of the morning.

"Are you a cricketer?" inquired Mr. Wardle of the marksman.

At any other time, Mr. Winkle would have replied in the affirmative. He felt the delicacy of his situation, and modestly replied, "No."

"Are you, sir?" inquired Mr. Snodgrass.

"I was once upon a time," replied the host; "but I have given it up now. I subscribe to the club here, but I don't play."

"The grand match is played to-day, I believe," said Mr. Pickwick.

"It is," replied the host. "Of course you would like to see it."

"I, sir," replied Mr. Pickwick, "am delighted to view any sports which may be safely indulged in, and in which the impotent effects of unskillful people do not endanger human life." Mr. Pickwick paused, and looked steadily on Mr. Winkle, who quailed beneath his leader's searching glance. The great man withdrew his eyes after a few minutes, and added: "Shall we be justified in leaving our wounded friend to the care of the ladies?"

"You cannot leave me in better hands," said Mr. Tupman.

Thinking Like a Mountain

ALDO LEOPOLD

A deep chesty bawl echoes from rimrock to rimrock, rolls down the mountain, and fades into the far blackness of the night. It is an outburst of wild defiant sorrow, and of contempt for all the adversities of the world.

Every living thing (and perhaps many a dead one as well) pays heed to that call. To the deer it is a reminder of the way of all flesh, to the pine a forecast of midnight scuffles and of blood upon the snow, to the coyote a promise of gleanings to come, to the cowman a threat of red ink at the bank, to the hunter a challenge of fang against bullet. Yet behind these obvious and immediate hopes and fears there lies a deeper meaning, known only to the mountain itself. Only the mountain has lived long enough to listen objectively to the howl of a wolf.

Those unable to decipher the hidden meaning know nevertheless that it is there, for it is felt in all wolf country, and distinguishes that country from all other land. It tingles in the spine of all who hear wolves by night, or who scan their tracks by day. Even without sight or sound of wolf, it is implicit in a hundred small events: the midnight whinny of a pack horse, the rattle of rolling rocks, the bound of a fleeing deer, the way shadows lie under the spruces. Only the ineducable tyro can fail to sense the presence or absence of wolves, or the fact that mountains have a secret opinion about them.

My own conviction on this score dates from the day I saw a wolf die. We were eating lunch on a high rimrock, at the foot of which a turbulent river elbowed its way. We saw what we thought was a doe fording the torrent, her breast awash in white water. When she climbed the bank toward us and shook out her tail, we realized our error: it was a wolf. A half-dozen others, evidently grown pups, sprang from the willows and all joined in a welcoming melee of wagging tails and playful maulings. What was literally a pile of wolves writhed and tumbled in the center of an open flat at the foot of our rimrock.

In those days we had never heard of passing up a chance to kill a wolf. In a second we were pumping lead into the pack, but with more excitement than accuracy: how to aim a steep downhill shot is always confusing. When our rifles were empty, the old wolf was down, and a pup was dragging a leg into impassable slide-rocks.

We reached the old wolf in time to watch a fierce green fire dying in her eyes. I realized then, and have known ever since, that there was something new to me in those eyes—something known only to her and to the mountain. I was young then, and full of trigger-itch; I thought that because fewer wolves meant more deer, that no wolves would mean hunters' paradise. But after seeing the green fire die, I sensed that neither the wolf nor the mountain agreed with such a view.

Since then I have lived to see state after state extirpate its wolves. I have watched the face of many a newly wolfless mountain, and seen the south-facing slopes wrinkle with a maze of new deer trails. I have seen every edible bush and seedling browsed, first to anaemic desuetude, and then to death. I have seen every edible tree defoliated to the height of a saddlehorn. Such a mountain looks as if someone had given God a new pruning shears, and forbidden Him all other exercise. In the end the starved bones of the hoped-for deer herd, dead of its own too-much, bleach with the bones of the dead sage, or molder under the high-lined junipers.

I now suspect that just as a deer herd lives in mortal fear of its wolves, so does a mountain live in mortal fear of its deer. And perhaps with better cause, for while a buck pulled down by wolves can be replaced in two or three years, a range pulled down by too many deer may fail of replacement in as many decades.

So also with cows. The cowman who cleans his range of wolves does not realize that he is taking over the wolf's job of trimming the herd to fit the range. He has not learned to think like a mountain. Hence we have dustbowls, and rivers washing the future into the sea.

PART III

Big Game

Luck of the Draw

LEE WULFF

I had my archery equipment and cameras with me when a sudden change in plans led me through St. John's in Newfoundland, and to a meeting with my old friend O. L. (Al) Vardy, the province's tourist director. Al lost no time telling me that the hunting film I'd made for him in 1939 had pretty well covered its audiences, and that he'd like a new one on moose and caribou. "Do you suppose you could build a film for us around the bow and arrow?" he asked.

Right then I wished that Fred Bear or some other top archer were with me, for while I can shoot a bow well enough to cluster arrows at twenty yards, the arrows begin to scatter when the target distance reaches out to forty or fifty yards.

I realized that if I were to be the archer in the film Al wanted I'd have to get very close to the game. Assuming that I could, I'd also need a cameraman who could ghost through cover with me, to be sure of getting both the animal and me in the picture when the moment came to release the arrow.

And of course I'd need all the luck in the world to combine the stalk of a well-antlered animal with a short shot in a sunlit clearing where the cameraman could record the kill.

It all added up to quite a challenge, and I readily accepted it.

Al arranged for a warden named Ron Callahan to go with me to act as cameraman, and also for Jack McNeill to be our guide. He got permission for me to take a caribou and a moose (normally the limit is one animal per hunter), and made plans for a camp to be set up in a good game area.

While the province's fish and game service uses planes for making big-game animal surveys, none was available for film work. The fact that I was traveling in my own seaplane was a big plus and a major factor in my decision to take on the job.

The season opened September 1, less than a week after I'd met Al, and, as luck would have it, by afternoon of that day we'd almost managed to film the essential sequences. Almost—but not quite.

We'd met—Ron Callahan, Jack McNeill, and I—on opening-day morning at a lumber camp where a supply road touches a lake, and by noon the tent was set up and Ron and I were ferrying in the last of our supplies. Our course led over fifteen miles of hilly country to the western side of a great basin draining down to Meelpaeg, a large and swampy lake.

When Al told me he'd send a warden to be my cameraman, I expected to meet a quiet man, bred of long, lone years in the bush. Ron Callahan didn't come much above my shoulder, wore an infectious grin, and had a sparkle in his eye. His girth was ample, but his legs were spindly.

At first glance I doubted that he could travel through blow-downs very far or very quietly, and my spirits fell when I learned that his camera experience was limited to a box model and that he'd never seen a live moose or caribou before the previous season.

My worry soon evaporated. Ron has amazing endurance, and though he often crawled under logs that I crawled over, not once during our hunt did I look for him but what he was in position. He quickly learned how to set and operate the cameras. Planning, making decisions on use of lenses and lens settings, framing, and duration of sequences were things we worked out together.

We were flying above an old cutover area when I looked down and saw a granddaddy moose. Bright sun flashed on his antlers, spread high and wide. His coat was dark, shadowed by alders and young birches. He stood motionless, listening to our engine. Ron saw him too and said, "Lord, what a head he's carrying." I was already looking for water.

A small pond glistened in the sunlight half a mile beyond, and I headed for it. From a high circle above the bull we looked over the terrain and made mental notes—the half-grown logging road that stretched toward him from the pond, the white birches clustered at a point where we should leave the road to work uphill, and the scattered birches, evergreens, and low bushes all about him.

A gliding spiral brought us down to three hundred feet. My first good look at those broad antlers and the high-held head told me the moose would be a good model. Then my eyes were on rocks, open patches of swampy grass, a leaning tamarack, a scrubby birch with yellow leaves, and half a hundred other little things I wanted to remember once we began to stalk.

Though most moose placidly hold their ground until a plane is almost on them, others spook easily. I let the ship swing toward the pond, but when the bull was well behind us I added power and climbed a few hundred feet to look the pond over. The water was peat-stained and typically dark, but I spotted what seemed to be a clear stretch and made the landing. The shores were overhung with brush and dead timber, and we got soaked to the hips when we slogged from the plane to solid ground.

From the air the earth looks like a map. But the pathways on it, so easy for the eye to follow from above, become a maze of small rises and shallows when you ease down among them. Where Ron and I should have turned left for the last hundred yards of our climb, we continued onward. That's how we missed the big bull's feeding spot.

The cutover was a mixture of small second growth, dead tops, down trees, and vines, with dead sticks crisscrossed everywhere. One man might travel through it with reasonable quiet, but two, one twenty paces behind the other, could scarcely manage fifty feet without making a warning sound. The brush was tall enough for a moose to hide in and thick enough to cut down a camera's field to almost nothing.

When I was certain we'd come too far, I climbed to the crest of a ridge and, standing atop a high boulder, decided to make for a certain twisted birch. With all the noise we'd made I had little hope that the bull would still be around. But my bow was ready, my feet paused at each step, and my eyes were searching every thicket. I should have seen him but I didn't. I heard him first—behind me, then abreast of Ron, who whistled.

I could see him, camera in position, but the bull was hidden. I heard the sucking sound of hooves being lifted from soft earth, saw a flash of antlers above the leaves, and caught a glimpse of a dark shoulder and a back. Branches cracked and leaves swished—then silence. I must have passed within twenty-five feet of that bull. If my eyes had been able to ferret out his form, I would have had a standing shot at that distance.

But it was wrong, all wrong. Even if I'd seen him and Ron had lined up the camera, it wouldn't have made a movie. The moose would have been hidden and the camera's field couldn't possibly have taken in both of us. What had seemed like an excellent chance for pictures had been no chance at all. At best we would simply have had a kill.

I knew for certain now that trying to make a film through casual stalking was a daydream. We'd have to work out a campaign combining the best available sun, wind, distance, timing, and action. I despaired of doing that with a moose, for in early September—before the rut—most of them are in timber, feeding little, loafing, often lying down. Caribou are more likely to be out in the open at this season, so it seemed logical to turn our attention to them.

Jack McNeill is an old-timer. In his seventy years he's seen caribou herds cover Newfoundland's great marshy basins and cross the roads in endless processions. He can remember when the caribou were almost wiped out, when there were no moose on the island, and when the first of the great-antlered bulls began to spread downward into the central part where he did his trapping and timber work. Jack knows the caribou's habits and the animal's time-worn trails.

After we'd unloaded the aircraft at the campsite, Ron and I changed to dry socks and trousers while Jack made a fire under a couple of cans of beans. We were ready to go when the sun was still two hours high. Jack led us to a sag in a timbered ridge where the woods necked down to a fringe and a great open marsh spread out on either side. A caribou trail leading from one side of the marsh to the other was deeply cut and there was fresh sign on the brown soil. We hid in cover to the west of the trail where any crossing animal would come within arrow range, and waited while the sun sank slowly toward the treetops.

When I'd made the film Al Vardy had spoken about, a trained cameraman and two guides had been with me and I'd carried a rifle instead of a bow. Even so, we'd had our troubles. Weather tied us up for days. One stag spooked before the camera could get into action. Well-trodden caribou trails proved endlessly empty. It took us ten days to get the caribou we wanted, and we'd had every conceivable advantage. Al said the caribou herd had about doubled since then, but that still didn't make the odds too good.

We'd had much the same trouble with the moose section of the old film. We'd found big bulls in thickets where a bullet could penetrate but where the camera couldn't do its work. That hunt also lasted ten days. Time dulls the memory, and in speaking with Vardy I'd forgotten many of the old problems we'd run into. As we waited now, they came back to mind.

The tall spruces were sending long shadows across the marsh when Jack motioned for quiet. A caribou came lazing along a few paces at a time between mouthfuls, taking longer pauses occasionally as he grazed more seriously. It took him fully fifteen minutes to cross the field. By that time the entire valley lay in shadow.

He was a small stag, a two-year-old, and his velveted antlers were short and slim. His brown sides shaded to slate gray and to white at his belly, and white shone at his neck and below his stubby tail.

I wormed my way forward and then raised to a full stand as the stag drew abreast. Cradled against the flexed bow lay an arrow, its nock in the string at my chin, broadhead touching a left-hand finger at the grip. Ron, behind me, was on one knee, sighting the camera. My grip held firm, for the draw was for practice so that Ron would know what to expect when the right moment came.

The caribou sensed the movement and turned to see the tensing of the bow. The draw was hardly made before he was in full flight. He was out of sight in seconds.

It's easy for a guide to remember a hundred caribou kills and forget that many were not in sunlight or within reach of an arrow. It's also easy to remember opportunities when open seasons were long and caribou were everywhere. But it's hard for a guide to realize how accurately placed both archer and cameraman must be and how swift and sure each must perform in filming a kill. The cameraman must always have the sun at his back, regardless of wind direction. He must be far enough away to show both hunter and his game in his lens, yet close enough for the images to be sharp and clear. He must move quietly, start his camera before the action starts, and not stop the camera before the action is complete. However great the difficulties may be for a solo hunter, for a camera-hunter team they're increased a hundredfold.

That night mist closed in over the lake just before dawn. Low clouds swept up the valley hiding the hills across the pond and blotting out the sun. But about an hour after breakfast patches of blue sky showed. Ron and I put our gear aboard the plane and climbed up to look over the country, leaving Jack to spend his day scouting around camp.

The land rises ever higher from Meelpaeg Lake to Annieopsquotch Mountains and Harpoon Hills. Near Meelpaeg there's swamp, pond, and rocky outcrop, but little timber. As the land lifts, the open marshes grow larger and scattered patches of timber appear. Still higher, the timber fills in to almost solid forest, broken by small marshes, a few rocky ridges, olakes, and ponds. There are no roads, no signs of human habitation in more than a thousand square miles.

We saw a doe and fawn caribou before we'd flown a mile. They stopped grazing long enough to watch our shadow pass them. Ten minutes later we saw a half-submerged cow moose, one with a calf.

Two casks of aviation gasoline should have been waiting for me at the logging camp where we'd met, but none had arrived. So to get some we took a winding course to the airport at Buchans, some thirty miles away.

While there we talked with a mining company's seaplane pilot. He reported seeing a herd of more than a thousand caribou near Newfoundland's southern shore, a little over a hundred miles away. He'd seen them earlier in the summer and had landed on a pond amid the herd. They walked by him on both sides, only a few yards away, when he climbed a rise to watch. The area was near the headwaters of LaPoile River. With my plane's main tanks and auxiliary filled, we took off toward LaPoile.

We flew till we could see the Gulf of St. Lawrence in the distance, then crisscrossed a rocky plateau that lay between there and LaPoile. We counted twelve caribou in that area, but none had decent antlers. We found no sign of the herd that roamed there a month before. On the way back, after more than five hours in the air, we swung along the shady side of the Annieopsquotches and straightened away toward Meelpaeg.

Suddenly there was game all around us. A small-homed bull and a cow moose stood in an open glen beside a brook, and farther on were two cows and a calf. At Blizzard Pond we saw a light spot on a grassy slope and made out a well-antlered stag lying less than a quarter of a mile from the pond's edge.

We set down on the rippling waves like a gull and idled up to the shore. The half-down sun shone clearly. Swiftly we tied the plane to tree stumps, and with bow, quiver, and cameras began our stalk.

We were downwind and the sun was at our backs. As we approached I moved ahead to some evergreens at the forest's edge and scanned the field. It was empty. There was no sign of the caribou, but I was certain he could neither have heard nor scented us. We waited and watched for some minutes.

Then we moved into the open and onto higher ground. As I scanned the field's far boundary I saw horns projecting above the yellow marsh grass some eighty yards beyond a gully. We put a tree between the horns and us and moved closer.

Though I had cover up to about eighty yards, I chose to see how much closer I could get by crawling in the grass. It was wet crawling. The water soaked through my clothing, and wet moss brushed my face.

I inched along till I came, unknowing, to a gradual drop sloping more steeply toward the stag. The low grass hid both stag and slope from me until I came into his vision. He saw me, and started to rise. I jumped to my feet and drew the bow, but the stag wheeled away. My broadhead streaked through the arch of his antlers, passing just above his back.

Halfway across the marsh he stopped and turned to stare at me and then at Ron, who had come up from behind. We stood and watched him start to feed. He lifted his head from time to time to look at us, but apparently felt safe at that distance. There was no way I could get close enough for another shot, so we picked up our gear and went back to the plane.

We were tired and hungry when we reached camp, but at least the day's scouting had turned up one good chance. A sunny tomorrow might well bring us more luck, as we saw it then. There was good news at camp, too. Jack had seen a fair bull moose come out on the shore across the pond, and he'd also spotted three caribou and found fresh tracks of others in the marshes behind camp.

The third day began with splatters of rain, but Jack's report of caribou activity near camp encouraged us to weatherproof ourselves and our equipment and go scouting the nearby ridges. We settled in the lee of a small woods where we could watch the far side of the valley, and waited.

Within an hour the drizzle all but stopped and the ceiling rose to more than five hundred feet. Visibility was good, though for effective work with 16 mm. color film nothing equals sunlight. Without direct sun, lens openings must be wide, and as a result less of the field is in focus. The color is less brilliant, the shadow contrast poor. Drops of water may fall on the lens, causing blurs. Yet, no matter how slim the chance or how great the obstacles, when taking a hunting film it always makes sense to have the equipment ready. We might have only one more chance in another two weeks, and to miss it could mean a clean bust.

Jack sighted a caribou stag about three-quarters of a mile off. He was slowly feeding along a course that looked as if it would bring him between us and the lake. We watched for twenty-five minutes.

Then Jack explained that we could see only the base of what was actually a great L-shaped field. He thought the animal might proceed along a stretch of meadow hidden from us, and perhaps on through a narrow opening into still another field. We faded back into the timber and set about to reach the top of the L.

The trees in the woodland Jack led us through were far enough apart to make travel quiet and easy, but an overhang of wet branches soaked us above the waist, while the low bushes soaked us to our hips. But when Jack finally led us to the edge of the timber our discomfort was forgotten. The stag was feeding placidly a quarter of a mile away.

When the plastic cover had been taken off my quiver, the camera brought out of its waterproof wrappings, and everything else O.K.'d, Jack settled himself to watch. Ron and I edged toward a point of trees that would provide cover well into the field.

The two hundred yards from the last low spruce to the feeding stag diminished slowly as the animal came on. His horns were wide and fully in velvet. The brow horns were paired and gave the effect of a massive, well-balanced head. I judged him for about thirty points, but what he lacked in points he more than made up for by his appearance of solidity and strength.

When the distance had narrowed to not much over a hundred yards, the stag fed for a long time, then lay down. His head was quartering away from us, and unless we frightened him by a noise, or the wind shifted, or some sixth sense warned him of danger, there was a chance that I could get fairly close. Ron and I checked the camera settings against the light reading, and I started moving forward at a half crouch.

I knew that the soft, swampy earth would make a sucking sound if I put my weight on one foot too long and then tried to lift it, and also that the grass would swish if I moved too fast. At any point a stick might snap if I stepped on it. My eyes swept from the ground to the stag and back to the ground again. I moved forward, step by step.

A patch of sunlight swept over me, and I stood stock-still. Unless action took place in the more prevalent overcast, the lens settings we'd fixed would be wrong. The caribou's head stirred, and he lifted it to test the wind. When it clouded up again I moved ahead. Seventy-five yards is a long way for a hunter to travel in the open toward a wary animal. It gave me a feeling of nakedness, and I kept thinking that the animal should at least be able to sense my presence even though he couldn't see me. My muscles were tight and my nerves were tense when my right foot sank to the ankle in soft earth. There was no avoiding the sound of air rushing in to fill the hole, though I put my right hand to the grass to help me withdraw my foot slowly. I could see another patch of sunlight coming.

The horned head swung my way and the stag's muscles rippled for the rise. I straightened, drew the bow, and released my arrow almost in a single motion as the stag came to his feet. By the time I'd fitted the second arrow to the bow he was seventy yards away, going swiftly but in halting strides. The arrow had penetrated his chest cavity, and I knew the wound was mortal.

Then the sunlight poured down. I could only hope the exposure guess, made in advance of the actual shooting, was good enough. Then I started worrying about Ron. Had he started the camera too soon and run out before the action was over? Had his sighting brought both of us into the field? Had he left the lens settings unchanged? He quickly assured me that everything had gone off O.K., and the processed film we previewed later bore him out.

The stag was dead when we found him. Then, using the same clouded light, we built up the story of the stalk to the point of the kill, and continued it through the packing of the head and meat back to camp. The background of a hunt can be filmed easily enough, but there's no substitute for the actual striking of the arrow.

We still had ten more days to hunt. As a hedge against the possibility of the film's loss or failure, we decided to go right after a bull moose. If we could bring it off, we'd have the certainty of at least one good kill and perhaps a double-header—a complete bow-hunting coverage of both animals.

The number of mature bull moose taken by modern archers can probably be counted on one's fingers. Bow-shooting Indians, with no seasons to hinder them, occasionally killed moose bogged down in deep snow, but today's archers, hunting moose during open seasons, truly have their work cut out for them.

When the rut is on and the bulls are moving, it's easy enough to see one. But in September's first weeks the bulls are still lazy. A rutting bull can be called in for a shot, but a drowsy bull, heavy with fat, must be found before he can be stalked. Nine out of ten of them stick to the deep woods.

Our best chance of locating a bull was from the air in the Meelpaeg basin. Since my plane carries only two persons, Ron and I hunted while Jack scouted close to camp for a bull whose habits he could observe and whose routine would permit a planned ambush.

Ron and I found that game would come out of the woods periodically, and that in as short a time as fifteen minutes an apparently empty area would have several animals in it.

Several times we made long stalks only to find the bulls gone or so well hidden that we couldn't find them. We spotted at least a dozen animals placidly feeding in areas too far from suitable landing water for us to attempt to reach them.

A week passed and the weather was holding mostly fair when we saw a pair of big bulls lying in a small meadow flanked by rocky ridges. The field was in an area where an old burn and strong winds had taken out all but scrub trees and spilled blown-downs over the half-covered rocks.

We landed on a nearby lake and secured the plane. Our approach brought us out on a great boulder overlooking the glade. One bull was on his feet, stretching to reach a young birch. He soon settled back. Both animals were in their prime, well-fed, heavy, and strong. Their antlers were massive and still in velvet. Typical with Newfoundland's bulls, their palms spread upward rather than outward. One bull faced us, the other faced away, and the distance was over a hundred yards.

Ron readied the camera and then ducked down at the rear of the boulder and waited. I worked down the hidden side of the ridge, then swung around to try an approach across the level meadow. The only cover consisted of some small and feathery larches.

When I knew that only half a dozen steps would bring the two bulls into sight, I became aware of movement just ahead of me. For an instant I thought one of the moose had decided to travel or that both had spooked. Then a doe caribou followed by a fawn walked from behind the low bushes and headed toward the moose.

The setup had been complicated enough without the caribou. Now a stray gust of wind could take my scent to them where they'd stopped less than thirty feet away. The caribou moved on into the meadow.

One bull let out a guttural rumble. A few seconds later doe and fawn returned as they had gone, their eyes ahead, failing to notice me. When I could move forward again both bulls were on their feet and looking in my direction, but in five minutes they settled down in the grass. Only by walking across thirty yards of clearing, in full view of one bull, could I reach the far side of the meadow where low cover might hide me.

If they had time to wait, so did I. The sun was high. Ron was comfortable on his perch. The minutes ticked away. Finally the bull facing my way shifted his head.

I moved swiftly across the opening, then more slowly behind a screen of larch branches. I glanced up from time to time to see Ron's head partly exposed atop the big rock. Finally I was within forty yards of the nearest moose.

Two spindly larches stood between us. Through their lacy branches I could make out a bulky form and the spread of great palms, but I took time to study the situation. Stalking two animals is many times more difficult than stalking one. One or the other, or both, might discover me or decide to move. I went to my belly and crawled to the feathery larches.

I nocked an arrow as I rose to draw, and I could hear and see the bulls rising to face me. For an instant the near bull stood still, startled and alert, big as a horse, and topped by towering antlers. My arrow struck him with a solid *chunk*, and he whirled out of sight. The second bull, also dark and heavy, vanished in timber sixty yards away. Without setting another arrow to the bow, I raised my hand to Ron on the rock. I was sure my arrow would kill.

Half an hour later I was ashamed of that vain gesture. We picked up the arrow's shaft where the bull had first staggered through the branches. It had snapped cleanly at the head. The depth of blood on the shaft was only five inches.

We found blood on the trail only where the bull had brushed against fallen or dry timber with his left shoulder. The truth was plain. At thirty feet I'd driven a shaft directly into his shoulder, into the heavy bone blocking off his chest cavity. Foolishly, I'd centered my aim on the usually vital area, thinking of deer and light-boned animals, of the certainty of a hit, of anything but heavy moose bones. I should have shot at the neck, fully exposed as the animal stood quartering toward me. Second thought told me that no arrow could penetrate the chest cavity at that angle. It was a lesson learned the hard way. In shooting an arrow into a heavy-boned animal's vital organs, aim from the side or rear.

After we lost the moose trail we cruised over the area for hours in the plane, but we never saw either bull again. I'm convinced that my arrow gave its victim little more than a sore shoulder. The embedded point would work its way out or the flesh would heal over it.

The hunt might well have ended then had it rained, for the chances of downing a moose seemed slimmer than ever; but, surprisingly, two more good days followed. From our seats in the sky we sighted a bull's shining horns as he fed atop a ridge.

Oddly enough, the stalk was again complicated by roaming caribou, this time a stag, a doe, and a fawn. We came on them suddenly and feared they'd spook the moose, but they passed us by. When we finally topped the ridge and found the bull, he was ambling slowly down the slope and away from us. Then he lay down.

The setup was perfect—sun was high, sky clear, wind blowing in little gusts that would hide all but a careless footfall. The stalk could be made with the sun behind me and with enough cover to get within twenty-five feet of him. Meanwhile Ron could perch on a bush-topped rock not sixty yards away and take his movie sequences while I crept forward on my belly.

All this was done. I rose from behind the last evergreen and drew and loosed an arrow that drove swiftly, straight, and hard into his vitals, cutting a corner of his heart before he was aware that I existed. Ron started the camera when I drew the bow and kept it going as the great bull reared up and moved crazily out of our sight. We found him, stone dead, three hundred yards away.

It was dream stuff, except for the solid satisfaction of having moose steaks broiled over coals, for the antlers strapped to my pontoon fittings, and for the viewing of the processed film in which those moments come alive again. The 1939 film shows a dark-haired young hunter killing a caribou and then a moose, each with a single bullet. The new one shows the same man, now gray-haired, kill as good a stag and a better bull, each with a single arrow.

If I were required to duplicate that film, I'd want at least five seasons' leeway to do it—and I'd want Ron Callahan along with his luck, his work, and his prayers.

Reprinted with permission of Joan Wulff.

Ode to Billy Joe

NORMAN STRUNG

Billy Joe . . . the first time I saw him was on a high, windy ridge so far away that rocks the size of a room appeared to be pebbles. Even through 7x35 binoculars he was a pinpoint of white, but he was an unmistakable mountain goat—huge, with slow, lumbering movements that broadcast a supreme unconcern for time and circumstance. It was almost as if he knew his grace, and glorified in pure being.

It was our first year together in Montana, my wife and I. She wasn't my wife then. Sil had joined me in Montana the year after I started school there, partly because we were in love, but, in a greater sense, because we both perceived a choking future in New York City. She wanted out as I wanted out, and it was one of those things that classify as "life's opportunities."

We were there, just at the edge of timberline, dog-tired and cranky with each other because my '56 DeSoto had grounded out at the piddling beginnings of an abandoned logging road. We had to walk from there, up, up, ever up over endless switchbacks. If we tried to cut them short, we ran into a waist-high tangle of logging slash too high to step over, and too low to crawl under.

We carried crude, wood packboards to take the meat out. They were loaded with a canteen, 50 feet of three-eighths-inch manilla hemp, a box of shells and binoculars. After we reached the timberline, and saw the distance between us and Billy, we said the hell with it and went back to the car. It was already noon, and we were tired from having spent a restless night sleeping on car seats.

We planned to return the next week, but that Friday 12 inches of snow fell in the valleys above 4000 feet. Billy lived up around 10,000 feet. That weekend we learned the hard way that you can't jockey a '56 DeSoto up a logging road with no snow tires and two feet of snow, however lofty your ambitions.

The next year was different—a better-prepared time. We bought a small A-wall tent, cots, and a pickup truck. Its traction wasn't much better than the DeSoto, but it had plenty of clearance for the high-crowned road, and it took us within two miles of the timberline.

We made a base camp, and daily walked the five miles that took us into goat country. It was a beautiful walk, up a flat valley floor soft and spongy with duff, past raucous waterfalls, then straight up a lung-thumping climb we called "Coronary Hill". At the top of that hill you could turn around and see forever—the Bridger Mountains, the patchwork of valley farms by the Shields River, and, ahead of us, towering cliffs of granite and scree. They were dizzying heights and heady days, a week's worth of walking in an awesome land of boulders that seemed monuments.

We spent a good part of each day glassing from a windy outcropping.

"There . . . is that him?"

Four glass eyes cut a talus slope into grids.

"You mean that white thing next to that gnarled pine?"

"Yes."

"No, just the sunglare off a whitish boulder."

"Dammit . . . I thought we'd found him!"

Then we'd glass some more. But it wasn't lonely or dull. In the morning sun, frost relinquished its adhesive grip, and the clatter of rocks confirmed that drops of water humble the majesty of mountains.

Coneys scrambled in the sun, and we found their tiny haystacks among the loose flakes of rock. How such small, delicate rodents could tough out eight months of iron cold amazed us, particularly when we found that coneys die from fright if you hold one in your hand, however gently.

Our evenings were a cozy retreat from the cold winds that were building in the hollows and crannies of the Crazy Mountains. As we walked back to camp they were a constant warning at our backs, swirling down the canyons, affirming that winter would soon sift down from the peaks and that it was a force to be reckoned with up there. But ahead lay a warm campfire, and a meal of grouse or trout gleaned from our day in the mountains. An "unsuccessful" hunt? Not on your life. And besides, we had seen him again.

It was on the last day of our week. Classes were beginning at the university, and Sil was to begin a job—feeding rats in the psychology laboratory if memory serves me right.

We were glassing those same slopes—a tapestry of grassy swales and rocky corridors we'd decided was prime mountain goat habitat—when we heard another mini-rockslide at our backs. But it was different from the hundred-odd we'd known—tinkling, delicate, and not of the primal force to which our eyes and ears had been witness.

We turned simultaneously, and there, 300 yards away, standing on an outcrop framed by gnomish trees, stood Billy. He was there for just an instant . . . too short a time for me to pick up my rifle, and get a decent bead, and I've been told I'm a very quick shot. Yet, it was a long enough span of time for the picture of him to still register perfectly in my mind: the shiny black horns, the long guard hairs that made his massive chest so huge it appeared malformed, and even his sparkling eyes looking down on us with just the mildest concern. Then he was gone. We saw him a minute later for an equally short time, crossing the rocky rubble under a sheer cliff. I wanted him, but the shot was too chancy—a .358 Winchester is not a 500-yard gun. He disappeared up a chimney, not running like a deer, but moving with the powerful grace of a plow horse. I was shaking, just as I had been when I shot my first deer. Goat fever. The winds of winter blew hard at our backs as we slid down Coronary Hill that evening.

The next year was different . . . in many ways. Sil and I were married, Sil had twisted her ankle in the process of building our log cabin, and I was convinced the only way to get Billy was to live with him. In early September, a friend who shared my love of guitar strummin', banjo pickin', and country bluegrass music happened to drift through Bozeman. We played a few licks, sipped a scotch or two, and our conversation turned to Billy. "Sure," Ken said, "I'd love to go along and watch."

It was all pretty primitive by modern backpacking standards: Army rucksacks of the upside down "T" design that pulled your shoulders down and back and leveled the load hard on your hips, a plastic dropcloth for cover, and glass jars of peanut butter and jelly in case we got tired of cheese macaroni and bouillon cubes. But it was a camp we could take with us. We were going up high for four days to live near the top of the world.

Goat season opened September 15th that year, and on the morning of the fourteenth we set out, stopping by the cliffs of Bridger Canyon so I could sight in my new .270, yet another addition to my growing expertise. The tight spot in that canyon, the place where the cliffs were straight and a perfect backstop, is in a strange "S" curve, and the wind that blew steadily and knife-edged through that rock contortion seemed ill. I'd lived in Montana for four years and was beginning to know its caprice. Something wasn't right.

That same sense of foreboding gnawed beneath my wool shirt when we stopped to photograph the Crazies from the Shields River Bench. What a range they are! Not the tallest in Montana, but they rise from a low floor to 11,000 feet, and seem unconnected to the rest of the Rockies; a mighty surge of rock, peak and cliff that's just out there in the prairie for the purpose of warning people coming from the East that, "this is just a little piece of what lies beyond!"

There are tales connected with how the Crazies were named. One is that a madwoman wandered around their peaks and crags for several years. Another is that the drainages are a crazy pattern of switchbacks and turnarounds where it's very easy to get lost. They were also a sacred place to the Crow Indians. The place of the Vision Quest, where Crow boys fasted for days on a mountaintop until they received a vision that would guide them through life. To the Crow, the Crazies were an important part of becoming a man.

The wind blew hard and unrelenting into our faces as we looked at the mountains from afar. It came from the east. Not gusty or puffy, just steady, and it was cold. That's a funny thing about that country.

I doubt that the cold would have registered on a thermometer. It would have read around 65 degrees that day, but there was a skin-perceptible message in it that mechanical yardsticks can never record. I sensed it, but machines had predicted five days of Indian summer.

We joggled and bounced into the canyon, and when we reached the jump-off spot things seemed better. A few puffy clouds drifted overhead, but the wind had died and the sun felt warm on our backs. We shouldered our packs and began winding our way into Billy's country.

The walk up the flattish valley floor wasn't too bad; a little sweat, some hard breathing, but the effort felt good in my legs and my lungs. Then we came to Coronary Hill.

There is a saying that goes: "Wise men climb a mountain one step at a time;" that if all you have in your head is the top, the mountain will prove insurmountable. I began the climb with the right attitude, but as the pitch increased and the muscles in my legs pulled to the straining point, getting to the top was all I thought of. The heavy, unbalanced pack was more than uncomfortable weight. Twice, while pausing to catch my breath, I wobbled off balance and my legs went out from under me. Then we cut to the right, off the trail and up a steeper slope slick with browning summer grass. The little outcrop and grove of gnarled trees from where we'd seen Billy the year before waited up there. And a little spring where deer often watered. The climb became a series of hand-holds and knee-crawls, every five steps demanding a rest. When we got to the top I threw down my heavy pack and gazed into nothing for a long while. I was exhausted.

My clothes were soppy with perspiration, but the wind was cooling me down. The wind. It blew very hard up there, coming in great, bowling gusts of plus-40. It's said that a combination of hard, unrelenting wind and isolation is sufficient to drive people mad, and I could see why. The wind up there was more than unpleasant, it was brutal.

At that point. I would have been glad to roll out my sleeping bag and collapse, but we needed shelter. Ken and I set about building our tent.

It was six-mil plastic, very light, stretched across nylon parachute cord. We pitched it quite professionally, using pebbles bunched inside the material for strong tie-downs, but the wind grew stronger, snapping and buffeting the tent even in the lee of the hollow where we'd pitched it. It groaned through the trees at 50 miles an hour, and the clouds grew ominous. They were banked up on the other side of the mountain range as if they were dammed by the tall peaks. But the dam wasn't holding. Thin, smoky fingers of clouds were spilling over the top, not flying by overhead, but sifting down into the valley below us. It was getting dark fast. The wind gusted to 55 and one of our careful tie-downs let go, whiplashing in the wind.

"I don't like this, Ken," I said.

"I don't either, but what can we do?"

"Go back down to the valley and come up again in the morning. This tent will never hold up here, and there's a very bad storm building."

We cached many of our canned goods, packed up what was left and picked our painful way down the hill. When we got to the valley floor, it was dark, but the thick pines broke the force of the wind. It roared overhead, trunks whipped back and forth; but close to the spongy duff things seemed nearly calm by comparison. We pitched the tent by firelight, ate a candy bar and fell into an exhausted sleep. I have no idea how hard the wind blew by the crags and peaks of the high country that night; 100 miles an hour doesn't seem beyond reason. I do know that I awoke several times to hear it roaring like a freight train. Twice I heard trees go down very close to our tent.

I awoke the next morning cold and cramped, and so close to Ken you couldn't have slid a matchstick between us. It was damp and ghostly quiet. I tried to back away and felt strong-but-gentle pressure on my back. Sleep-fogged, I panicked . . . sudden claustrophobia.

"What the hell . . ."

We both sat up, our heads supporting the low, icy roof of the sagging tent. The top was plastic grey, the sides white. I looked out the front flap; a foot-and-a-half of snow had fallen during the night, and it was still coming down.

Did you ever look for an elusive, white mountain goat in a snowstorm? I never did find Billy that year.

The next goat season appeared more promising. Perhaps because of the heavy, early snow of the previous year, the Fish and Game Department scheduled a September first opening. It was promising, too, in terms of my growing professionalism. I now had an aluminum frame pack, a mountain tent, freeze-dried foods, and three people to help me pack out meat. Sam Curtis, a poet; Wes Sommer, a teacher; and Kit Langan, a high school student, wanted to go along and see the country where Billy lived.

The walk up Coronary Hill was much easier with a pack trimmed to 35 pounds. The weather was gentle and summer-like, and we pitched camp in a neat cluster of tents, within throwing distance of the spring. From the very first step, it had all the signs of a good trip for everyone but Kit. His feet blistered badly in his new boots. But for the rest of us, things seemed right and indeed they were. That year marked the closest I ever came to Billy.

On the second day, Sam and Wes pushed on up the valley, while I watched with binoculars, toward the great clamshell mountain that marked the highest peak in the range. It was just an exploratory walk, but they came back excited about the country they'd seen.

"Come with us tomorrow." Wes said. "There's gotta be some goats up in that basin."

I didn't have much faith in Wes' judgement; he'd never shot a deer before, much less a goat. But their glowing descriptions of country I'd yet to see sparked a sense of adventure in me. I didn't plan to see Billy, but we went up there anyway.

The head of Cottonwood Creek was a huge basin, with a half-dozen deep-cut canyons tunneling down into it. The walls and slopes that dished up to jagged skylines must have encompassed ten square miles, yet I could count on my fingers the number of trees that held tenuous root. It was all grey cliff, rock, rubble and, except for the grassy floor and small stream where we walked, sterile in appearance. Not sterile in a negative sense, but rather, in terms of an exquisite cleanliness and freshness. The air was sharp and light.

Wes was first to see Billy, halfway up the slope of one of those twisted canyons, and my judgment about his hunting knowledge had been right. "Hey," he said, "Is that a mountain goat?"

Mountain goat indeed! The animal lumbered from left to right, moving slowly, the nape of his neck rolling from side to side like a grizzly bear's. His horns curved gracefully back over his head and were visible at 1,000 yards. That wasn't just a mountain goat, it was Billy!

"Don't move," I whispered. "Talk low. Don't let him know we're here."

We crouched behind a great, square boulder, while I watched his movements with lightweight binocs. He was about to disappear behind an outcrop when he stopped, turned around twice like a dog, and lay down.

"We've got him!" I said.

We traced the path I'd take. Up a boulder-strewn slope of scree to the edge of the outcrop, then pop around to confront Billy. He was no more than 150 yards from the outcrop. I marked and recorded the precise feature of the rock formation that would have me slightly above him. It was set.

Wes and Sam grew small below me as I picked my way across tottering boulders. "Keep your breath . . . don't clunk rocks. Above all, don't break your leg!" I stopped and rested several times. Looking back. I saw icy-blue gems of glacial lakes I had never known were there, and a huge snowfield at the base of the clamshell mountain. Then another 50 yards and a rest. The air was extremely thin at that elevation. I could feel the giddiness and the thumping in my temples.

Things went right. I made not a sound on my stalk, and had reached the outcrop exactly where I'd planned to be. I rested, sizing up the route that would carry me around.

A good rock ledge started me off, but it gradually got narrower and narrower, then began to cleave into fist-sized squares of frostwork that were a sure sign of rotten rock. I looked down, and sharp-edged boulders glared up from 50 feet below. A mountain goat might make it, but I backed off, frustrated. Ten more feet and I would have had my shot.

I recalled that the outcrop below me had appeared to be some sort of dike—an intrusion of hard rock between layers of soft rock that wear away first, leaving a standing wall. The dike had risen clear to the top of the mountain, joining the peak at an impassable cliff. The only way to go was down and around on the flakes of rock at the base of the outcrop.

When you're walking uphill, it's relatively easy to be quiet. Your footfalls rest lightly at first, then gradually increase the pressure underneath them as you slowly shift your weight and rise. Going downhill is a much more difficult proposition; your foot, and the weight it supports, tends to come down all at once and hard. I knew this. I also knew I'd come out below Billy. He now had the advantage.

I walked on eggs, descending next to that moss of rock, using hand holds to cushion the impact of my step. I made it down 20 yards without a sound. With only another ten to go, things began to slip. My step was quiet enough, but the slab of scree upon which I stood was unstable. It rocked, I lost the knife-edge of perfect balance, and, in regaining it, kicked loose a tiny slide. The rocks tinkled down.

There was no question: Billy would be on his feet and moving. I hurried down the remaining slope, not caring about noise now, just angling to get into position for a shot before he disappeared inside some cleft in the mountain. I rounded the base of the outcrop and saw him, making his way back along the same path he'd taken to his bed. He was at 200 yards and running; a prone position was impossible. I squatted and tracked him with the scope.

The roar of the rifle echoed among the ridges and monuments of the Crazies.

The crack of the second shot found Billy whirling wildly. A hit! The goat turned twice around. "It must be a shoulder!" I thought. He began to run the other way . . . toward me.

"This will be it. I've got him. Now!" I tracked him again and fired.

Then Billy was gone, lost in the concussion of the shot and the wisp of smoke that drifted from the tip of my barrel.

I grinned as I slipped three more shells into the magazine. My hands were shaking—goat fever again. "Don't get excited, give him time to lie down."

Far below me I could see Wes and Sam working their way up the tricky slope.

I was sure I had my goat, yet there was one little doubt chipping fragments from my mass of confidence. I had seen no blood on Billy's coat. None as he whirled, and, most significantly, none as he came back toward me. The exit hole of the bullet—if it did exit—surely should have left a massive wound. I marked the spot carefully where I'd last seen Billy, and waited for Wes and Sam.

When they arrived, we walked over to the place. It was another one of those damnable chimneys that ate up mountain goats. The fine color change of freshly overturned scruff and scrabble was there to prove Billy had taken this route, so I told Sam and Wes to wait and went up the chimney. At every ledge and potential resting spot, I expected to come upon the dazzling white of Billy's hide, and every place was a disappointment. More telling, there was not a scrap of hair or drop of blood along the entire route. After 50 yards of climbing I ran into a cliff that was impassable . . . unless you were a mountain goat.

I returned with the sad news, and we went over to the place where I thought I'd connected. We couldn't find the spot precisely; no place I could point to and say. "There is where he whirled." The talus was all too look-alike. But I surely knew the general area by back-sighting with my rifle, and we combed that 50-foot-diameter circle for an hour. Like the chimney, there wasn't a sign of a hit.

I was very troubled that night, for when you've hunted enough, you get a feeling when you connect. It's intuitive, but it's usually right. I had that feeling about Billy, and I wouldn't let him go unclaimed. I climbed back up that steep slope the next day and spent another three hours combing the theater of our play. I found the haystacks of Coney, but no hair of Billy. I was beginning to believe I'd missed after all.

That night helped, too, and as a matter of fact, it was the night Billy was christened. When we got down to the truck, another party of hunters were camped there. They asked about our luck and we told them.

"You saw him, huh?" one lean and grizzled cowboy drawled. "People been after that goat for ten years. That's ol' Billy. Don't worry, he's just outfoxed you like he's done everybody else."

"Yep," Sam drawled in gentle imitation on the way home, "Ole Billy Joe. Got a hunch he'll be around for a few years to come . . ." Henceforth that goat and that goat alone has been Billy Joe, Billy for short.

Wes left the next year for a teaching position at another university. I took a teaching position at Montana State. Sam was still around, and our tales of the high country persuaded another compadre to join us. Walt Hodges was a photographer who'd never been up there and wanted to record the experience on film. We packed in the day before the September first opening.

This time we were to push further yet: right up to the base of the clamshell mountain where I'd seen a beautiful glacial lake. In addition to our camping gear and rifle, we also brought some trail rods and lures.

We got there when it was still light, with peach-colored rays of the setting sun falling on the clamshell mountain. In no time we had the makings of a cutthroat trout supper. We ate with fork and fingers, recounting tales of Billy Joe, and inhaling deeply of the clear air and the gentle mountain evening around us. Tomorrow the hunt would begin all over again.

We spent the entire day glassing and walking, discovering new canyons and crannies, marvelling at the abstract formations of rock. And we found a second fishing lake, this one holding brookies.

We sat down to make supper and sip from Sam's flask of bourbon at about 6:30. The sun was casting long shadows, turning the mountainside pink and blue, when Sam saw him once again.

He was ambling along the headwall opposite the clamshell mountain at the same roll-shoulder gait I'd learned to recognize. I flipped my glasses to my brows; for sure, it was Billy. Then he lay down for the night.

I began climbing the next morning, marking his position by the ragged, yellow peak above him, using terrain to mask my approach. Sam could watch the whole stalk from camp, and he agreed to signal if Billy began to move. I climbed most of that morning, trying to get close to his position from a dozen different directions, but was stopped cold each time by a cliff, a dike, or a route that would carry me into Billy's view. Even an approach from above was impossible; he lay on a rock ledge under a slight overhang.

I returned to camp, and Sam and I watched Billy for the rest of the day while we fished for cutthroat trout. He got up to feed in the afternoon, but didn't move more than 50 yards from his bed. The next morning he was gone, and we never saw him again.

That was the last time I hunted Billy. Because of increased population in the state, or more out-of-state hunters, or some reason I can't fathom, I haven't drawn a special goat-permit for the Crazy Mountains since then. I have gone back in the summers to fish the lake at the foot of the clamshell mountain, and I've seen him once or twice: those same horns, that same massive chest, his lumbering gait and magnificent unconcern.

I apply for a permit each year, and I'm sure one of these times, the blinking face of the computer will smile my way, and I'll get another crack at Billy Joe. Then maybe things will go my way.

Yet, on misty-blue winter nights, when drifting snow curls smoke-like around the corners of my cabin, I find myself drinking deeply of strong whiskey, and toasting his everlasting good health.

Reprinted with permission of Silvia Strung.

A Day Out

CHRIS MADSON

The sound filtered slowly down through the layers of sleep, and I contemplated it awhile with what little consciousness I had, wondering whether it was part of the dream or something from the outside. It held steady under my attention, not very dream-like, until it seemed real enough to be worth investigating. I drifted back up into the real world and opened one eye.

Waking up in the cabin in the wee hours of the morning is always a little disorienting. The blackness is nearly perfect—it's hard to tell whether you're looking at the room or the back side of your eyelids. At last, I picked up a few cues to locate myself. Over in the direction of the wood stove, Kuntz started snoring, and in the cot next to mine, Obie stirred in his sleeping bag. The chill in the darkness settled onto my face like snow.

I sorted through the small noises in the night, for the one that had roused me. In a moment, it came again, the quick soft concussion of wind against the glass of the invisible window and the rattle of sleet on the roof. I shivered in the warmth of the down bag and tried hard to be thankful for the change in weather as I drifted off again.

The alarm came a couple of hours later. I groped for it on the windowsill, killed it, and rose up on one elbow, the first step to dragging myself out of bed. Somebody's feet hit the floor, and I could hear the steps across the room toward the kitchen. Then the "plunk-plunk-plunk" of a Coleman lantern being pumped, the hiss of compressed gas, and the pop and roar as light flooded through the cabin.

Obie put the kettle on the stove and limped back to bed.

"Snowing," he said.

"Sounds like the wind's gone down, though," I offered. "Should be a good day."

"Mmmm," Obie commented with about as much enthusiasm as I felt.

The Professor swung his legs over the edge of his cot and put his feet gingerly on the deck. "Time for the other boots," he said to himself; then, as he ransacked his duffle bag for moleskin—"Whatayou nimrods want for breakfast?"

The smell of antelope sausage and pancakes infused the cabin with a new sense of purpose. While the Professor put the finishing touches on breakfast, I built sandwiches; Obie and Kuntz fussed with equipment, and Cosetti sat at the kitchen table, intent on swathing both his feet with band-aids.

Kuntz eyed these proceedings with amusement. "You need another partner, Cosetti," he commented. "The Professor's gonna wear your feet off to the knees."

"Yeah," Cosetti grinned, "but he gets results."

Kuntz shook his head with a show of pained tolerance.

"He doesn't play fair, though. Just walks 'em 'til they surrender. They all draw straws to see who's gonna give himself up for the good of the herd. Hardly sporting."

"Jealousy," the Professor commented without looking up from the frying pan.

We sorted out the day over the second stack of flapjacks. The Professor and Cosetti had decided to start on North Crockett Ridge—not even the Professor knew where they would end up. Kuntz had it in mind to look at the south side of Horse Creek Basin, and Obie and I were bound for opposite sides of Lava Rim. With the breakfast dishes out of the way, the time had come. I stuck an extra pair of socks into my pack next to my lunch, wished the crowd luck, and stepped out into the last of the night.

The wind had faded almost to nothing, and a light sifting of snow settled down out of the pines. There was a faintly luminous quality to the darkness, a sign that the clouds were very low, which was hardly surprising with two inches of fresh white on the ground. The cold cut right to my skin—nothing half an hour of walking wouldn't cure but a stern test of resolve at 6:00 in the morning. I thought about grabbing another layer, then cancelled the thought and headed for the timber.

With the overcast, it would be a solid hour before there was light enough to shoot by, which was alright since I needed nearly that long to get the breakfast table conversation out of my system. Bit by bit, I could feel the silence of the predawn settling into my head. Where I was going started not to matter; where I *was* from second to second began to be the issue. The unique background of tiny sounds emerged—the drip of meltwater from the branches overhead; the small, inanimate creaking and crackling of twigs settling under the weight of the snowfall; the breeze stirring the treetops; my boots packing the snow; my breath; the tiny seashell rushing of blood in my ears. With any luck, there would be another sound sometime during the day, the difference almost impossible to describe, yet recognizable, the nuance of purpose behind it. The dainty, almost imperceptible stirring of 500 pounds of bull elk in the deadfall. No matter how many times I had heard it, that sound never failed to amaze me with its smallness.

The light came on by slow degrees. As I broke out onto the edge of Duck Lake, it occurred to me that I could see across it, that it was time to chamber a round. The clouds were snarled in the treetops across the lake, and the snow fell like down, settling on the huckleberry leaves with a faint rustling. I could feel the weight of my wet Malone pants beginning to gather at my belt. Of course, the sensible thing to have done was put on rain pants as soon as I left the cabin.

"Except I can't stand the noise," I thought. And, anyway, you could almost convince yourself that sopping wool pants are comfortable if you worked at it. "Just a good thing they aren't Levi's—I'd be freezing to death."

I was almost around the lake when I struck a trail. The little ridge of snow in the middle of the first track stood up crisp and sharp; the place in the bottom where the snow had been packed thin was dark with moisture but hadn't melted through. No fresh snowflakes there. Worth following.

The trick, of course, was to see them before they saw you. Easily said. Somewhere out there in that tangle there were four cows with a bull trailing along behind. Five sets of eyes and ears, five very suspicious natures. They had played some version of this game every day of their lives and were on a long winning streak. I was an amateur.

The internal coaching started. Check every line of sight through the trees. Hard to tell how far you can see down those little corridors, forty yards, maybe fifty or sixty now and then. They won't be in a clear spot where you can see them. Look hardest where it's hardest to see. Keep an eye out behind—they may loop around to look at their back trail. Listen. A cracked twig with some life in it. Pine squirrel. You knew that; the sound was too big for an elk. Suddenly, the heavy musk in the air. Elk scent. Must be close. Must be. Anyway, they can't hear you moving. You can't even hear you. Moving slow, though. You suppose they're walking this slow? Maybe they'll bed down. Maybe not.

There was no sign of the passage of time in the overcast, only the dripping timber and the snow, thinning slowly as the temperature eased upward. The tracks began to fade. Always seemed like a simple job to track an elk until it came down to the tracking. What with the underbrush and deadfall, it was hard to find marks even in good tracking snow. As the snow slowly faded away, I found myself watching the ground more than I was watching the woods, an excellent way to bump into the bunch before I saw them. At last, the marks disappeared into a thick patch of huckleberry, and I could see it was no use.

The focus on the moment suddenly evaporated, and I realized I was hungry. A check of the watch showed close enough to noon.

Six hours on that bunch. Out about seven miles from camp. Over this direction, that's seven miles from the nearest Forest Service trail, too. And it's past time for lunch.

I picked a log that looked almost dry and sat down. The menu for the day was a blue grouse sandwich, one of the world's great unknown delicacies, and a Mound's bar. When I'd finished, I pulled out the dry socks, another of the world's great luxuries, and gave my feet a little attention. The boots had kept the water out below, but the incessant runoff down the pants had finally found the tops of the first pair of socks. I poured half a cup of water out of each boot, wrung out the used socks, and put on the new ones. Both feet were appreciative.

"Least I can do, guys," I thought down their way. "We've got about ten miles more to do before we get back to camp." Hearing no cries of outrage, I laced up and headed into the afternoon.

As it turned out, the afternoon held no elk for me. I took some encouragement from an encounter toward evening when two huge bull moose drifted within thirty yards of me, so close I could hear the rumbling of their guts processing the day's browse. Neither of them saw me, smelled me, or heard me as I slipped away.

"If I can do that with moose," I thought, "I ought to be able to get within rifle range of a bull elk." The elk, however, were not inclined to give me the chance.

In the middle of the day, the snow had changed to sleet, then a light rain. The silver of the day faded into shades of gray and black as the last snow soaked into the ground, and night came by slow degrees.

Every season, the little discoveries happen again. As the darkness deepened, I was surprised as I had been surprised so many times before at how the human eye accommodates itself to night. I played the rods-and-cones game as I picked my way, looking away from where I wanted to go so I could see what was there, and it occurred to me that there was some deeper significance in the exercise if I would only stop walking a minute and consider it. Not too much later, I caught a shin on a dry stub sticking out of a spruce log and decided to give up the philosophical inquiry for the more useful illumination of a flashlight.

It was about eight when I suddenly broke out of the timber onto the gravel road. Only a mile left on even terrain. I turned off the flashlight and forced my legs back to lengthen the stride, the rain still pattering down on my hood, mixed now with sleet and an occasional sloppy flake. A walking tune began running through my mind. "Gray skies all of them gone; nothing but blue skies all day long . . ."

There is a special, bittersweet lonesome in the last mile of the day. Out before light, back after dark, a long day in the black timber beyond the reach of humanity, with only the tiny voice in your head to break the white-hot focus on each second, each sound, sight, and scent. And so I swung along at a good pace through the night, savoring this last moment and looking forward to ending it.

At last, I saw the buttery light winking in a distant window, and in five minutes, I pushed open the door. The warmth of the room was mixed with the thick, rich smell of browned meat and cooked onions.

"Thought you might have decided to spend the night out," the Professor commented sarcastically. "Being such a beautiful evening." Then, after a significant pause, "Fresh tenderloin on the back of the stove."

Stowing my rifle on the woodpile, I shed my raincoat, then turned back to the kitchen.

"So, whose tenderloin is it?"

"The elk's, of course," the Professor smirked.

Obie came to my rescue. "Cosetti's. Nice bull, too." I looked over to Cosetti in the corner. A face etched with the effort of a long, hard day and a smile like a three-year-old with a handful of candy. I loaded a plate with fresh elk, onions, cottage fries, and salad, perhaps the best meal that was served west of the Mississippi that night.

"Well, come on; let's hear the tale."

It was half an hour in the telling, wandering like a hunter's track out into the dark wilderness around us, past the private landmarks known only to the camp—the Rintimacki wallow, Langston's grizzly place, the spot where the Professor killed the big bull. Seventeen miles it went, almost around to the country I'd been hunting. The Professor had finally cut tracks in a patch of snow on a north-facing ridge, just enough trail to give him a feel for where they were going. After an hour of tracking and guessing, they had heard clattering in the timber up ahead, two bulls mixing it up on the other side of a low ridge. The Professor motioned Cosetti to sit down, then cow-called. Both bulls came at a trot. Cosetti took the bigger one with a neck shot at forty yards.

"It was something, let me tell you!" His eyes were wide again, as he looked out the window into the night, still seeing the two bulls coming through the trees. The excitement of that moment carried the conversation for another thirty minutes or so while Obie took my shift on the dinner dishes and I wiped down my rifle.

With the story well told and congratulations passed around, talk turned to plans for the next morning. There was guarded optimism. We had narrowed the possibilities to a reasonable number. All we had to do was keep at it. The strategy session ended as we all crawled into our sleeping bags. Obie shut down the lantern, and I watched the yellow flames play around the mantles as the light flickered and faded out.

I stared into the darkness and absorbed the luxury of being horizontal in a nest of down. On the windowsill, the invisible alarm clock ticked off the seconds of the night against the silken background of the north breeze in the tops of the pines outside, a fitting lullaby for a cabin full of worn-out elk stalkers.

As I waited for the ache in my legs to subside, I considered my luck. The place and the moment were humble enough by any standards of the outside world, but they had an intrinsic value that was beyond price. It all had to do with the quality of the effort spent getting here. The occupants had earned their berths on the cots around the room. And, tomorrow, they would earn them again. Beginning about 4:00. Just a little rest first. The ticking of the clock slowly faded, and I settled down to savor the last simple pleasure of the day, the sleep that only twenty miles in the timber can bring. My feet figured they had earned it.

The Elk from Hell

PETER FIDUCCIA

I have stalked after big game across North America for forty-five years. During this time, I have come to understand *real* hunting involves a lot of personal endurance, a lot of planning, some suffering, and, on some hunts, a large dose of pain and humility.

Take the time I was elk hunting on Saddle Mountain in Crawford, Colorado. I spotted a mature bull elk standing in an open park (us Easterners would call it a field or clearing), high on a mountain just above the tree line. Being a 'real man' of a hunter, I immediately started my steep ascent up the mountain to intercept the bull. As I reached about 8,000 feet hours later, I realized two things didn't make sense. The first was that against all odds, the bull was still standing in the same place that I originally spotted him! In fact, he was glancing down at me and the corner of his lip appeared to be curled upward—and looked a lot like an offhand smirk to me. The second was that the bull seemed to be tapping his right hoof as if to imply his impatience with my ascent! I should have turned around right then and there. But as any elk hunter can attest, a big bull is worth some hard work—and weirdness.

As I crested the next ledge, I was at 9,000 feet. For a hunter from the East this is not good. My eyes were bulging from their sockets, my lungs felt as though something was crushing them, my knees were hurting, and I was drooling saliva mixed with blood from the corner of my mouth. Oh yeah, and from my ears, too. But being a *real* hunter, I pressed upward and onward toward the elk—which, oddly, had only moved an equal distance from me when I was at the 8,000-foot height.

As I clawed and scratched my way up a rocky outcropping that I had fallen backwards on several times, I reached the 10,000-foot mark of the mountain. I knew this because I could see the underbellies of passing aircraft and clearly read the numbers on the wings. Upon standing up, I could also plainly see the impressive bull standing broadside only 50 yards in front of me. Wobbling from exhaustion, I tried to quickly un-shoulder my rifle, but the rifle strap got caught on a tiny tip of bone poking out of my shoulder and was jerked out of my grip and fell to the ground.

In disbelief, I watched as the bull arrogantly walked off into the timber occasionally glancing back at me while hissing like a snake. "Do elk hiss?" I thought. Nah. I foolishly followed him into a patch of dark timber as I tried to remove the dirt from my scope. Obviously, I hadn't yet realized that this was all part of a devious plan devised by a wretched and evil animal. Oh, you don't believe such animals exist, huh? Then you probably have never read Moby Dick and what he did to Captain Ahab have you?

Once in the timber, the very dark and forbidding timber, the bull paused and slowly shook his head from side to side showing off his set of 7x7 antlers. As any bull elk hunter understands, that is all that it took for me to make my next mistake and continue to press on after him. But first, I had to remove the sharp branch that I hadn't seen in the dark timber and was now sticking out of my forehead. I wiped the blood from my right eye and the scope and moved slowly and deeper into the conifers.

Exiting from the timber I noticed the sun was lower—much lower than when I entered it a few hours earlier. Standing on a wobbling ledge, I briefly caught sight of the devil bull as he turned and headed down into a thick patch of aspens. As I stood there glassing him, the ledge crumpled under my feet and I plunged twenty feet to the rock strewn earth below landing on countless small and very sharp rocks.

Softly crying, I made a blood-wrenching scream (albeit under my breath as to not scare off the bull). As I stood up I noticed my hunting pants were torn around my left knee. I tried to fold the loose patch back into the pants but my swollen, bleeding kneecap prevented me from doing so.

Holding my &*%$ kneecap with one hand and hopping along, I now I wanted to place the *7#& crosshairs on this hideous bull more than ever. The hunt had developed into a plan of revenge and a burning desire to see the bull absorb the full impact of my 180-grain Silvertip. But first I had to try free my jammed bolt back into shape. Absurdly, the bull waited 75 yards below me until I got the bolt to work freely again.

Again, hobbling and staggering I made my way toward the shimmering aspens. Now there were two things flickering, the quakies and my life. But being a real-man of a hunter I was undaunted. As I broke free of the aspen patch I could see the bull crossing below me through a patch of slide rock.

Since I couldn't carry the rifle over my injured shoulder, it was now at the ready. As I slowly and painfully brought it up to my face, I realized I had to wipe the dry blood from my eye in order to clearly see through the scope. Just then, the slide rock beneath my feet began to roll like millions of marbles and down I went. I slid, rolled, tumbled, and then slid some more down the mountain and under the belly of the bull who had uncannily open his legs just wide enough to let me pass through!

As I got up and removed a stone from the muzzle of my rifle and picked up my hat, gloves, and my front tooth—I realized I wasn't as upset as I should have been. Why should I be? I could clearly see that my fall helped me to quickly gain ground on the big bull that now stood a hundred steps above me.

I raised my rifle—or what was left of it, and aimed at the bull. I instantly realized he was much higher than I originally thought and I had to quickly raise the rifle to a much higher angle. As I lept up from cartwheeling down the slope, I felt that Lady Luck had smiled on me again. She provided several small but painfully hard evergreen trees that aided in stopping me from cart-wheeling all the way to the bottom of the mountain. I thanked her but I cursed the wicked bull as I plucked dozens of sharp pine needles from my lips, cheeks and skull. Oh, and some small twigs were sticking out from all parts of my now numb body.

I was going to kill this elk, but not before I carefully checked my entire body to see if I had missed any unnoticed cuts, bruises, bleeding, protruding bones, or additional missing teeth. I only found one small, tiny branch sticking out of my ear. Actually, only part of one sticking out of my ear—the rest of the branch had broken off inside my ear. I could see the bull bugling, but for some reason I couldn't hear him well. At that moment I was inspired to call out loud enough for the elk to hear me, "Now you've asked for it, you brainless jerk!"

With that, I entered the dark forest known to every elk hunter as black forest. So dense is this woods that it doesn't allow sunlight to penetrate its branches. I mean it is r-e-a-l-l-y dark inside—darker than the black timber earlier. Darker than a witch's heart and that's dark. You're getting the idea, right?

Not long after entering the dark forest, I couldn't find hide nor hair of the bull. An hour later I had to admit to myself that I was lost. I looked for my compass, but quickly realized it was in my backpack that fell free when I cart-wheeled down the mountain earlier. I'm a knowledgeable hunter and so I knew it was important for me to gather some firewood—especially since I didn't have any food or water, or matches to make a fire. Yup, they were in the backpack too. It was going to be a long night, but that would give me plenty of time to think about how I was going to kill the bull in the morning!

As I sat in the cold, dark night I heard the eerie bugle of a mature bull elk. The bugle sounded like no other I had ever heard before—in fact, it sounded more like laughter than an elk bugle—but that may have been because my eardrum was punctured. I comforted myself by humming a few bars of the song that goes, "Whenever you feel afraid, just hold your head erect." Just then, I heard the snap of a twig and the unmistakable growl of a hungry grizzly bear followed by what I was positive now was indeed the laughter of an elk . . .

Reprinted with permission of the author. Go to www.deerdoctor.com for information on Peter Fiduccia's books and videos.

The Trouble With Goats

DIANA RUPP

"The trouble with goats," said Ryan Damstrom, "is you have to kill them where they live."

Ryan, a thirty-year-old veteran sheep and goat guide, made the comment cheerfully and mostly for my benefit, since he moved up and down mountains almost as easily as his quarry. He had set up his spotting scope atop a snow-covered boulder and he rested a gloved hand atop it as he spoke, studying the peak that loomed above us. Shin-deep in snow beside the boulder, clutching my binocular, I let my eyes travel up the spruce-timbered slope, then on up the open, snow-blanketed face that loomed above timberline to a small cave nestled in the base of a sheer rock cliff that jutted straight up to form the peak of the mountain.

In the mouth of that cave lay a mountain goat. It looked relaxed, with one front leg tucked beneath its body and the other outstretched as it chewed its cud and calmly surveyed its breathtaking world from an elevation of some nine thousand feet. In choosing the little cave—not much more than an overhang of rock—for its midday bedding spot, the billy had claimed the best location on the mountain. Not only did it have protection from the wind that knifed across the peak, but the goat could see anything approaching from below, and only another mountain goat, or perhaps Sir Edmund Hillary, could possibly approach from above.

Ryan, outfitter Anna Fontana, and I had ridden some two and a half hours out of our snug log-cabin wilderness camp in southeastern British Columbia that morning, blessedly gaining a great deal of elevation on horseback. The snow from yesterday's storm lay heavily on every branch and leaf. Each time my horse, Laredo, brushed a limb, small avalanches would cascade silently over his mane, across my jacket, and occasionally down the back of my neck.

We rode to the shoreline of a mountain lake whose crystal waters perfectly reflected the snowy grandeur of the Canadian Rockies, and I was so taken with the Christmas-card scene that I nearly forgot to look for goats. Fortunately, Ryan and Anna were not so easily distracted, and they thoroughly scanned the white peaks for white goats as I juggled camera and binocular. We were miles from any road, and the small sounds of the camera shutter and the saddle leather creaking on the backs of the dozing horses were swallowed instantly in the cavernous silence of the snow-blanketed wilderness.

Since we didn't spot any goats from the lake shore, we mounted up again and rode around the lake to where we could see the peaks from another angle. There was no apparent trail and the brush was thick along the shoreline. Ryan's long beard was powdered with white by the time we pulled up at the bottom of a ravine and slid to the ground. It was as far as we would ride; from here, the topography angled steeply upward.

I hadn't even finished tying Laredo to the nearest tree when Anna, already glued to her binocular, said, "There's a goat up there in that cave."

I swapped my down jacket for windproof fleece, lightening my clothing for the climb as much as I dared. We left the extra gear with the horses and hiked through the snow to the top of a bluff where Ryan set up his spotting scope to take a better look at the billy. As we glassed, he hatched a plan: he figured that if we climbed up to the timberline, we might be able to get a 300-yard shot at the goat from just inside the cover of the last line of trees. I looked at the mountain again and thought of the slog we'd had through the snow just to climb this little bluff, only a few hundred yards from the horses. But I'd certainly entertained no illusions when I booked this hunt; I knew full well that no mountain goat hunt is easy, for the very reason Ryan had just articulated so succinctly.

Although I had come prepared for any weather, I really hadn't expected snow on this hunt. October was not even a week old, and just two days earlier we'd ridden into our backcountry camp on a warm autumn afternoon. But then we'd spent twenty-four hours snowbound in the cabins as visibility on the peaks deteriorated to zero and winter arrived with a vengeance.

Anna, her blonde hair covered by a warm fleece watch cap, smiled at me over her binocular. Grinning back, I couldn't help but appreciate her deep attachment to this area of southeastern British Columbia where her late husband, Bob, started the well-respected Elk Valley Bighorn Outfitters some twenty-seven years ago. Anna is a savvy organizer who possesses a vast knowledge of the country and its game thanks to her former profession as a provincial wildlife biologist, which she left some years ago to work full-time with Bob in the hunting business. Following Bob's death in 2004, she took over the outfit and runs it ably. Her guide area holds not just striking scenery but also some of the finest and most diverse big-game habitat in the world. We'd already seen a big bull moose, herds of elk, a dozen mountain goats, several mule deer, Rocky Mountain bighorns, and a young grizzly that strolled through our camp during the snowstorm. But what had really brought me to this stunning area was the fact that these mountains hold the densest population of mountain goats found anywhere in North America. After only a few hours of searching, we'd already spotted the billy we were looking for.

Despite the fact that it was only our first full day of hunting, we didn't even consider not stalking the goat. I'd already seen how things worked in the mountains this late in the year: If we were unlucky, another snowstorm or even heavy fog could shut down our hunting for the remainder of the week. In this country, you have to make the most of the days you're given. In other words, hunt goats while the sun shines.

Moments later, Ryan packed up his spotting scope and was making tracks through the spruce timber. I slung my Sako Finnlight .280 across my back and followed, staying in the trail he broke as Anna followed right behind.

I pushed myself, determined to stay up with Ryan, taking advantage of small trees and branches to pull myself up the slope when I could. I hadn't been working out all summer for nothing. Soon my insulated gloves were soaked with sweat, and I switched to wool ones, which quickly became caked with snow. I could have used a drink of water, but the tube from the water bladder in my daypack had long since frozen solid. I stuffed the bite valve down my shirt, where it thawed just enough to give up a drop or two of liquid and quickly re-froze. I concentrated then on the climb, trying to think about only one step at a time to avoid being intimidated by the mountain. More than an hour later I started to see glimmers of light through the spruce boughs ahead. We were approaching timberline.

Ryan paused and knelt in the snow. I dropped down beside him and we both looked up. A few dozen yards ahead of us, the trees ended and the snow-covered, open face of the mountain slanted steeply up toward the sheer rock cliff. I couldn't quite see the cave.

"I can't see that goat from here," Ryan whispered, "but we should get into a spot where we can get a shot just about any time." I nodded and followed as he continued uphill, making sure to stay right on his heels.

The trees thinned without giving us a view of the goat. Ryan paused at the last tree, glassed carefully, and then moved out onto the open face. It was like stepping through a doorway from a dim room into daylight. In a few steps we left behind the shelter of the tall spruce and lodgepole and found ourselves on a steep, exposed slope. Here, the snow was a blessing; knee-deep now, it anchored me on what would have otherwise been slippery, treacherous footing. The wind blasted into my right cheek, driving sand-size particles of snow before it.

With every step, I felt the vista opening up, and, even at the risk of falling behind Ryan, I had to pause and glance over my shoulder. I was rewarded with a goat's-eye view of the world: The lake we'd ridden around lay far below like a black jewel, surrounded by glistening white, knife-edged peaks that seemed to stretch to the far corners of the world. The vista sent a surge of joy through me. I took a deep breath and pushed on, catching up with Ryan at a lone, wind-blasted, six-foot spruce tree that was somehow clinging to life on the open face.

We could see the cave now, a dark, empty opening in the cliff face almost directly above us. It was like looking up a wall at a small hole where a mouse might live. But Ryan was shaking his head in puzzlement.

"The goat's not there," he said. "He's moved. Maybe he crossed over the ridge to join those nannies we saw earlier. If we go on up the ridge, we should be able to roll over the top and take a look."

I almost never question a guide, but I couldn't shake one nagging doubt. "Isn't it possible," I suggested, "that he's still tucked inside the lip of the cave, and we just can't see him because we're looking straight up?" The smooth, apparently trackless snow in front of the cave was also bothering me.

But Ryan shook his head again. He was convinced the goat had moved. "I don't think he's there, or we'd be able to see him from here. Let's go take a look over that far ridge."

That meant continuing the dizzying trek across the open face, but my drive to kill a goat, wherever it might be, was overpowering. "OK, I'm right behind you," I said. And I was, for about fifty yards. But the high-altitude walk through the knee-deep snow was starting to take its toll, and I began to lag a bit.

Unknown to me, Ryan was mulling over my remark about the goat possibly still being in the cave, and, on a whim, he decided to get closer just to make sure. Even if the goat wasn't there, he figured we'd look for tracks leaving the cave, which would tell us which way it was heading. So he took a sudden 45-degree turn upslope. I was about fifteen feet behind him, concentrating too hard on my footing, when Ryan suddenly shouted something about a goat and wanting me to shoot it.

Glancing up, I saw the billy less than fifty yards away and looking positively enormous, making its way slowly across the base of the sheer rock cliff, just starting to angle upward. Ryan was directly between me and the goat—a problem, but I had a more immediate one: my rifle was still slung across my back.

I dropped to my knees in the snow and clawed my way out of the sling, then ripped off the scope caps. Ryan, realizing he was in my line of fire, tobogganed back down the slope, skidding to a stop beside me in a puff of snow. Trying to shoot straight uphill played havoc with my kneeling position, so I leaned against Ryan to steady myself, looked through the scope, and saw . . . nothing.

I stared at the scope in disbelief—the lenses were covered with condensation that had formed inside the scope caps, but I still should have been able to see through them. As I wiped frantically at the scope, Ryan reached over and calmly turned the magnification down from 8 to 2.5. I cursed my rookie mistake but quickly cleared my head. I got steady again, and now found the goat easily in the scope, a bright white target against the brown cliff, climbing slowly and deliberately—confident, no doubt, that nothing could follow.

And almost nothing could—except a bullet. My first hit was solid, right behind the shoulder, but I saw no reaction from the goat. I cranked the bolt and immediately put a second shot right beside the first; the billy, now having trouble with its footing, turned directly away, and I finished with a Texas heart shot. At that, the goat sagged, dropped, and rolled gently some ten yards down to the base of the cliff.

Ryan roared with glee, we high-fived, and he rushed up the slope to examine the trophy. I unloaded my rifle, gathered my gear, and stood up as the adrenaline drained away, surprised to discover that my legs were shaking and the wind had a frigid edge I hadn't noticed before. Anna, who had waited at timberline, shouted congratulations from below and started up to join us.

I made my way up to Ryan and the goat, stopping briefly to peer into the goat's snug little cave, where it had been all this time. I noted with interest that when the goat had spotted us, it hadn't panicked—it was used to danger coming from below, and apparently had supreme confidence in its ability to climb out of harm's way.

"It's a great goat," Ryan enthused when I got to him. Its jet-black horns were almost perfectly matched; back at camp, we'd measure them at 9¼″ with 5½″ bases. The annular rings told us the billy was eight and a half years old. But I was most thoroughly taken with its lush coat—the white fur was beautiful and luxuriant, longer and softer than the finest sheepskin.

I dug myself a shelf of snow so I could sit with my goat on that precarious perch, bury my cold hands in its fur, and finally take the time to study the tremendous view that the goat had surveyed for most of its lifetime. The unpredictable weather in the mountains made itself felt: One minute the sun shone, and the next a miniature gale swirled snow around us. My face was so cold when I grinned for photos I felt as if my cheeks might crack. While Ryan skinned the goat, palm-size chunks of ice cracked off the cliff above, clattered down, and pelted us.

When the work was finished, we stuffed the goat hide in Ryan's pack and I loaded his spotting scope and other equipment in my own. Anna gave the skinned carcass a boot and sent it rolling down the mountain. Ryan and Anna caromed happily after it, and I butt-tobogganed after them at a somewhat more cautious pace. We stopped at the bottom to quarter the goat in preparation for lashing the meat behind our saddles, and when we finally reached the horses late in the afternoon, we were still giddy with success. I found to my embarrassment that my legs, which had so faithfully carried me to the top of the mountain, suddenly lacked the strength to propel me into the saddle. I had to lead Laredo to a fallen log and crawl awkwardly onto his back, much to the amusement of my companions.

The trouble with goats may be, as Ryan said, having to hunt them where they live. But up on the high, lonely peaks the goat calls home, a hunter experiences not just the thrill of pursuing a worthy quarry and the satisfaction of meeting a physical challenge, but the pure joy of spending a few hours in one of the world's harshest and most beautiful places. It's well worth the trouble.

Excerpted from *Sports Afield* magazine. Reprinted with permission of the author.

Father-Son Alaska Bear Adventure

TED NUGENT

I could see the threatening yellow-white canines with each drooling, audible chomp of his powerful predator jaws. His broad, massive black head swung methodically, beady eyes drilling into my soul at a scant fifteen yards. The cathedral of majestic old growth firs allowed just enough sunlight to slice into our primeval standoff-zone to provide a surreal, shadowy, even mystical eeriness to this boreal wilderness stage. I was at once engulfed and owned by the here and now, yet somehow strangely out of body, beyond history. Time stood still, and so did I. The Detroiter inside emboldened me to nerve it out. Afterall, I jammed with the mighty Funkbrothers of Motown, so big, tough black guys didn't scare me. In fact, they're my friends, good friends actually, and I felt quite at home in such a setting, thank you. Except, this time, this big black guy didn't want to share R&B guitar licks with me. I felt other, more powerful life and death dynamics alive and about, even palpable here in the Alaskan wilderness of Prince of Wales. The majestic, mature black bear alpha boar now took another few swaggering steps toward me. I held my ground. It was truly the essence of life. The powerful spirit of brother bear was now a part of me. The brisk wind was a prayer for the wildthings, the delicious Alaskan air protein for my soul. Was I alive or in a hunter's dream? The moment of truth was here and now. Tooth, fang and claw in all its perfection. I was about to implode. Beautiful.

Just behind and over my right shoulder was my best hunting partner and son, Toby, vidcam rocking, capturing on digital tape the timeless encounter of man and beast. Not just predator and prey, mind you, but the elevated intensity of dominant predator facing dominant predator, a classic standoff of metaphysical proportions on a chunk of sacred wildground; the Last Frontier of not just Mother Earth, but far beyond into the spiritual sphere of dreams. At the time, I was not conscious of Toby and our friend Steve Sims at my side, but it was a certainty that Steve already had his Glock 10mm at the ready with bear-whomping 200 grain CorBon Penetrators ready to rock. Nonetheless, this huge bruin was so close now, that his notoriously explosive charging speed was a moot point, unstoppable in any situation, but hopeless with his high-ground advantage before me. My trusty bow and arrow felt absolutely feeble considering the possibilities. Fred Bear crouched behind a huge boulder on a beach, the world record Brown Bear right there coming on at spitting distance. Do you see it? I do. It was scrumptiously inebriating, intoxicating, at once sensually invigorating. This is how smart people get high: stoned but dangerously in tune, at the very peak of readiness. We were rockin bigtime. Now what?

Having just celebrated my other favorite rite of spring with a beautiful Texas Rio Grande wild turkey in the bag, bear hunting with my son in America's number-one biggest state was the perfect next logical step for the thrilling season of renewal. And where better than Alaska with the Sims tribe, on the crystalline frigid waters of the Prince of Wales archipelago. Connecting in Seattle, Toby and I flew into Ketchikan and then on to remote Craig where we skiffed across the placid bay to the Sim's Eldorado fishing trawler for a week in the pristine wilderness of the 50th State. Bear heaven for sure, as Steve, Gary and Mike Sims celebrate a family tradition of spiritual renewal and great escape that all brothers oughta. With God smiling down upon us, the warm, sunny, clear weather was out of the ordinary but heartily welcomed by all as we cruised across the brilliant calm waters, snacking on incredibly delicious, freshly harvested King and Dungeness crabs fit for a king. God, I love America.

The Eldorado is a fine, sturdy, 58-foot commercial fishing boat, set up to comfortably accommodate the happy-go-lucky eight-man bear hunting party for the month. With experienced professionals on board, this may very well be the most independent vessel on the waters of wild Alaska a guy could ever dream of. Toby and I were in awe of the beauty and ruggedness of it all, more than ready to give it our best mountain man shot. The Spirit of the Wild indeed.

An Alaskan resident, Mike Sims knew the ropes well for such a wild outing, and ably assisted by BloodBrothers Kevin Miller and Jimmy Ford, true wilderness Natty Bumpo, Jeremiah Johnsons if ever there were, we knew we were in the hands of master outdoorsmen and in for one hell of a dream excursion. And so it was as we headed into a stunning, sheltered cove amongst the timbered islands, beaching our skiff as Toby, Steve and I entered the wildzone, cocked, locked and ready to rock, doc. Spirits soared on high.

Steve had barely left the gravel beach and stuck his head into the canopy of the towering conifers when his hand flashed up and he hissed, "BEAR! BIG BEAR!" Toby snapped the vidcam into record and I peeked into the shadows to see a huge black blob with eyes, staring back at us from the darkened depths only 30 yards ahead. Surrounded by gigantic old-growth timber and remnant giant stumpage from time immemorial, the great black bear peered at the strange threesome of unidentified intruders. Clearly this old boy had never laid eyes on such creatures and was unafraid, even bold. I pussyfooted forward as I loaded an arrow onto my bowstring, already committed to killing this beast. Hearts were a-pumpin', adrenalin was a-dumpin', spirits a-thumpin', well into the ultimate wildzone. And on he came, slow but sure. And I responded in kind, moving closer to the mighty killing machine, closing the distance well within the dangerzone. He paused every few bowlegged steps, mouth dripping saliva, killer canines aglow with digestive spittle. I froze. He was now only 20 yards out, slightly quartering towards me, looking bigger by the minute. With a huge, wide head, and his broad, heavy belly-dragging torso, I knew I was looking at one great bear.

He plodded behind a huge stump and sat back on his haunches for further scrutiny, adding as much drama and excitement to the hunt as can be imagined. I took another silent step forward and stood at the ready. The amazing video footage clearly shows his overt cockiness and domineering scowl as he moved closer now, at only fifteen yards uphill through a screen of brush and fresh green spring forest growth. I drew my bow and looked at his hulking chest behind the massive shoulder and let fly. I shot too fast, my entire, long archery life lessons of control and discipline destroyed by the electricity of it all as the deadly projectile zinged harmlessly over the monster's back, sticking hard into a tree beyond.

Damn! The hoary black locomotive lurched instantly and vanished into a slight depression as I yanked another arrow from my quiver and dashed up the incline to see him slowly walking beneath giant deadfalls. Instinctively my 2nd arrow came back unto itself and was gone across the 20 yard gap right now. My glowing Lumenok lighted arrow nock showed the mystical flight of my arrow like a laser-beam as it punched hard into the rear ribs, angling forward into the beast's life giving vitals.

Oh baby! How sweet it is! I'd rather be lucky than good anytime. Thank you, Lord. Youdaman!

Breathless, Steve and Toby now joined me at the crest of BearHill, and we gushed with the excitement that only bear hunters on the ground, face to face with such a beast can possibly understand. It was Nugent partytime if ever there was. Toby was not able to crest the hump with me in order to film the second shot, so I reviewed the spine tingling details with my

BloodBrothers as we strategized our next move. Steve wisely advised we back off and wait to investigate my hit, but I just had to check out the main trail on which the bear had vanished to see if there was any blood at all. And there was. Good blood and tracks of a scrambling beast.

With vidcam rolling behind me, I crawled into the jungle tunnel, pushing my own Glock 10mm ahead of me, radar on commando feeding frenzy mode. We had only crawled a few yards, Steve right on my heels, when Toby gave a slight whistle, pointing high up into the treetops ahead. At once, all three of us saw the huge black lump 30 feet up, 30 yards ahead, and I swung up my pistol instinctively. The Glock barked three series of rapid double taps, the huge bruin tumbling out of the towering spruce in a spectacular black swandive from heaven. It was amazing. He slammed back to the good mother earth with a shattering thump, and lay still. All was silent. We were breathless and stunned. Then the celebration dance began. In respect for the astonishing beast and the thrills he had provided us, intense celebration erupted in the jungle. In the jungle, baby.

He was stunning. Glistening, rich, thick, luxurious blue-ebony hide in its prime from a long winter's nap, we had us a black bear of a lifetime. Nearly five-inch pads with long, black claws and a skull that would go over 20 inches, this springtime blackie would weigh over 400 pounds and provide a gorgeous rug to rival the fun factor of the hunt. Just a day prior, a native Alaskan woman named Nina had introduced herself and her daughter to Toby and me at the Narrows Inn in Ketchikan, giving us a sacred gift of an Alaskan eagle feather as a token of spiritual good luck. The spirit of the mighty eagle had indeed stood with us in that chunk of Alaska, and an eagle-bear ceremony was at hand. Great footage of the emotional setting was captured for our Spirit of the Wild TV show, and more than a roll of film captured photos of which powerful memories will be shared with all our family and friends.

Back at the Eldorado, we hoisted the huge bear onto the deck with the big fishing crane, and memories of those amazing films of Fred Bear doing the same thing with Ed Bilderback on the Valiant Maid came gushing back. We felt at one with nature in all her tooth, fang and claw perfection. Dining on fresh crab, shrimp and halibut that night, reviewing all the thrilling details of our day, took on a life of its own. We were absolutely there, but also hovering overhead, the adventures of family, friends and explorers of this great land before us flashing by like visions of eternity. It was wild, and we all cherished it as wild as it gets in wild Alaska in the springtime, starting all over again.

For more thrilling outdoor adventures in Ted's book *Bloodtrails II—The Truth about Bowhunting*, or to book the ultimate hunt with Ted, call 800-343-4868 or visit www.tednugent.com.

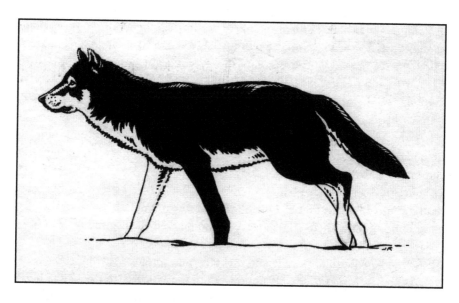

Wolf Hunters

CHRISTOPHER BATIN

If looks could kill, then the wolf was ripping me apart, limb by limb.

At 40 yards, its hungry yellow eyes fed ravenously on every blink and breath I took. Yet it was the sharp bite of those black pupils that pierced through to my very core.

Never have I been so intensely scrutinized. The gaze of a deer or an elk envelops you superficially like lightly falling snow. Their eyes mirror thoughts of escape, or uncertainty at what they see.

Not so with this wolf. Its riveting gaze mirrored something far more unnerving: predatory intelligence. Those two eyes blazed with the intensity of firestorm that viewed me as both predator and prey. I, too, was facing the most challenging prey of all: another predator. At the thought, my spine and arms tingled with excitement.

It boiled down to which predator would blink first.

The wolf's wedge-shaped head dropped slightly to keep me in focus between spruce branches. Easing the rifle to my shoulder, I kept my gaze on the wolf and became semi-aware of the world around me. Our boat bobbed slightly in the slow current of western Alaska's Innoko River. Through my peripheral vision, I could see my moose hunting partners looking downriver and to the other side, oblivious to the trophy on the left bank. There could be no sudden move or speaking to gain their attention.

The wolf was as solid as the massive spruce trees that surrounded it. It stood three feet high at the shoulder. Its muzzle pointed toward me like a broadhead lance loaded in a catapult. How many times had that snout and those two-inch canines clamp down on the those of a 1200-pound bull moose? The wolf would use its 110 pounds and six feet of body as an anchor to keep the moose from rearing up and slashing away defensively with its axe-like front hooves. If the wolf can hang on long enough, the remainder of the pack hamstrings the moose. Within seconds, the wolves begin eating the moose alive.

I eased up the rifle and found the wolf in my scope.

"Wait! Don't shoot!" the other hunter in the boat hissed as he saw the wolf. I eased off the trigger squeeze. He swung around and scrambled for his rifle, breaking my gaze. I blinked. The wolf had vanished. I did not see the wolf turn and run. Neither a leaf rustled, nor twig move to indicate its presence. I gritted my teeth and engaged the safety, while searching the spruce thickets for a sign of those blazing yellow eyes. Nothing.

The other hunter was a greenhorn who wanted a wolf, but didn't want to pay the price of constant vigilance. We both returned home, empty handed. I cherish the moment because to this day, that experience was my closest encounter with an Alaska wolf. It also marked the beginning of my 28-year apprenticeship as an Alaska wolf hunter.

Wolf hunters are tough, both physically and mentally, and for good reason.

Like the predator he pursues, the wolf hunter is often as reviled and hated as he is praised and honored. Many despise him because he is killing a symbol of their idea of wilderness. On the other hand, ranchers, hunters and victims hail him as a hero, feed him dinner, and learn from him. This human in wolf's clothing helps keep Nature's most efficient canine predator check.

Wolves and wolf hunters were once widespread across the United States. Our history is earmarked with the bloody annotations of wolves attacking humans as well as killing countless deer, elk, pets, and livestock. The need for wolf control was as real at times as it was imagined.

Today, wolves and American civilization have difficulty co-existing. As with snowshoe hares and lynx cycle, when the hares drop in numbers, the predators also disappear. Likewise, the wolf hunter today in the Lower 48 is as scarce as the wolf. An occasional obituary will list the deceased as "wolf hunter." Among sourdoughs, this title is the equivalent of a Ph.D. in outdoor skills and survival, hunting strategy and ruggedness of spirit.

Wolf hunters still thrive in Alaska, however, and Richard Gardner is living proof that ruggedness is a prerequisite for the chase. Growing up in Ohio, he moved to Alaska over two decades ago. Each winter, this 43-year-old father of two spends several months running over hundred miles of marten traplines and hunting wolves in the glacial ravages of Alaska's Delta River and Black Rapids Glacier area. The wind-chill factor in this windy hell can remain at 50 below for days at a time.

Several years ago, he telephoned and asked if I could break away for a week. He had just finished snowshoeing 20 miles into town. The snowmobile he had been riding had blown an engine, and the other machine he was using at his cabin 50 miles inland had busted a ski. He needed someone to travel with him, repair both and bring them back. The next day, we were both heading into the Alaska wilderness on his last, remaining snowmobile.

About 40 miles in, he showed me a windswept portion of the Delta River. The site was unsettling, because through the crystal clear ice at our feet, you could see the current tumble over boulders beneath us. It was here that Gardner related his tale:

"I could see where the wolves had been chasing moose along this section of river, so I was following their tracks when the ice began to crack. It was 34 below, so I knew the ice was safe for travel. The ice continued to crack and boom. I noticed an upswelling of groundwater, and observed the ice wasn't very thick below me. But it was too late."

He explained how his snowmobile suddenly broke through the river ice, immersing him to his waist. The river water immediately froze on his jacket and sleeves. He fought off the sudden numbness and scrambled to work the track onto the broken slabs of floating ice. He revved and pushed his machine out of the river, before clawing his way out of the icy water. He rolled in the snow to absorb the extra water, and, with numbed fingers, built a fire and dried out. He kept hunting and trapping the area and eventually returned home that season with two wolves.

That's wolf-hunter tough.

Alaska's 40,0000 wolves make it the last bastion for wolf hunters. Don't confuse today's wolf hunter with the aerial hunters of the past or those who have used poison to take their prey. The new generation pursues wolves the old-fashioned way: from the ground. And a mid-winter wolf hunt is one of the toughest hunts in North America.

Wolf hunters endure—almost relish—the raw adversity of a winter wolf hunt because of its unpredictable and varied hunting environments. I've accompanied wolf hunting guides across hundreds of miles of wilderness, hanging on to a sled that bucked and darted across the frozen tussocks like an iron bronco. We've kept food and water under snowmobile cowlings to keep them from freezing rock solid in 30-below temperatures. I've weathered winter storms in old trapper shacks as the green and red curtains of northern lights blazed overhead. I've read the names and kills of hunters dating back 60 years, carved into the cabin walls. I've dug up C-rations buried in the thick, sawdust floor of these cabins, and read yellowed books from the 1930s, running my fingers over their pencilled annotations in the side margins. The wilderness environment, and its history, are integral parts of winter wolf hunting.

Those who desire more hunting time hunt wolves in the spring and fall. I recall one Alaska caribou hunt where I had a rare opportunity. Like mosquitoes hovering just out of reach, two wolves kept just outside the 150-yard safety buffer of several hundred migrating caribou.

The pair snuck through the timbered fringe, waiting for a chance to take a wayward or careless animal. I positioned myself to take the 200-yard shot without spooking or hitting the caribou that surrounded me. In addition to the wolf eyes always on the prowl for potential danger, there are thousands of caribou eyes watching for the slightest movement within their safety zone. Spook the prey, and you spook the predator. As the wolves stopped a marshy clearing, I fired. I still don't know if the single shot spooked the caribou, or if it was me running up to my trophy as excited as a schoolboy heading home to his first day of summer vacation.

Most wolves are taken incidentally to hunting other species. I accompanied Mike Lencoski a moose hunt when he took a handsome black wolf while floating in a remote Alaska river. His hunting partner, Steve Armington, bagged an equally rare trophy, a wolverine, while hatching over a moose gut pile. There was no great lead into most wolf hunts. The animal suddenly appears, and you shoot. Such "luck" can occur on do-it-yourself hunts, but usually requires the local knowledge of a registered guide.

Only a handful of Alaska wolf-hunting guides specialize in hunting wolves. Don't expect to meet any members of this elite, yet prestigious group at fancy corporate banquets or tea parties. Look for them in single-light café in remote Alaska villages, or huddled around oil heaters in aircraft hangars, waiting for those few precious hours of daylight to fly to their hunting camps. Insulated bibs and bunny boots make their already husky physique even more intimidating. Weathered by extreme cold and sun, their leathery brown faces peer out of parka ruffs lined with wolf or wolverine, the only fur that their breath will not freeze. This eclectic bunch only socializes with wolf hunters or trappers. The reason for this preference is easily understood. Few others are found in Alaska's February winter wilderness in sub-30-below temperatures.

Why Hunt Wolves?

A wolf adheres to a singularity of purpose: to kill. And killing is a means to an end: food for itself and the pack. A wolf that doesn't kill is akin to a human who doesn't think: both are immediately destined for extinction. A wolf is Nature's perfect predator—often more cunning than man.

Wayne Heimer has hunted wolves off and on as a Dall sheep biologist with the Alaska Department of Fish and Game. One April, before the grizzly bears emerged from hibernation, Heimer was required to shoot five Dall sheep ewes that would be later sent to a laboratory or analysis. He harvested the animals and stacked them on a mountaintop for helicopter pickup before returning to his alpine camp. Heimer sensed something was wrong that night, out couldn't finger the problem. The next morning he awoke and jumped a black wolf. By the time he removed the rifle from his pack and fired, the wolf was passing 400 yards. Heimer missed. He knew why the wolf was there and looked for others, but they too were long gone. It was too late anyway.

"The pile of sheep had disappeared," he said. "There was no meat. Nothing but hair and a few gnawed-on skulls. Four hundred pounds of sheep consumed overnight.

"A wolf will kill anything: the strong, the weak," says master guide Jim Bailey, a veteran wolf hunter. He watched a wolf pack consume an entire frozen moose in less than a week. He has also seen wolves defer to brown bears feeding on moose, preferring to wait their turn at scavenging, rather than risk losing their lives.

The Call of the Wild

Wolf hunter Sid Cook was investigating an area of Prince of Wales Island, where evidence indicates that a hunter was probably attacked and eaten by a pack of wolves, yet the evidence was inconclusive. Cook, a lifelong Alaskan, said he was in the same area when a pack of wolves surrounded him.

"When wolves are so close and start howling, to communicate to each other, they sound fake," he said. "The echo, the reverberation isn't there. But they were wolves, holding just in the timber, surrounding me as I walked through the trees. They were howling and yapping to each other, communicating as hunters. I loaded my rifle and prepared for an attack, but suddenly, the wolves disappeared. It was as frightening as it was eerie."

I know the feeling, having stood my ground against wolves years ago when I bagged my first caribou. My hunting friends J. W. Smith and Kristin Melby had heard the wolves howl after I shot the animal in late afternoon. As the sun was setting over the north Pacific, they had to head down to base camp, but promised to return the next day with the aircraft. I wasn't about to leave my trophy or the meat. They handed me an orange, some snacks, and an extra jacket. The wolves smelled the fresh meat, and moved in close, but stayed out of sight in the alder brush. That night, the wind picked up to about 20 mph, which made hearing difficult. I hauled the meat to a gully, where I built a fire from brush. The wolves continued to howl through the first portion of the evening, before becoming silent.

It is the not-knowing that is nervewracking when watching a pile of fresh meat. I huddled over my fire, feeding it pencil-sized sticks. Sleep had eluded me for much of the night, and dawn finally arrived. My friends flew back and landed on the ridge top, and said they had seen no sign of wolf in the area. But then again, there was neither any sign of the caribou gutpile and bones at my killsite on the nearby ridge.

Wolf hunters generally have at least one wolf rug, mount or tanned hide in their possession. I have a wolf rug hanging in my library den. This is a fitting locale, as the wolf bespeaks intelligence, and yet is as elusive as wisdom. I often think of the positive qualities that make it a wolf: its social tolerance, perseverance, patience, and adaptability. In many ways, the wolf is a fitting role model for humans, as well as a reminder of our own limitations as hunters. Wolves are better equipped than men to kill prey. Wolves can run faster and better withstand severe cold. All men have going for them is intellectual capacity. Unfortunately, many hunters don't make full use of it. Wolves do. Only if it competes with humans for prey do we view a wolf as a pest that needs to be controlled. Wolves must be kept in check it we are to maintain healthy game populations for subsistence, sport hunting and wildlife viewing, as well as stocks of domestic animals and pets.

Try wolf hunting this season and see if you are wolf-hunter tough. The spur, the tonic that initially creates a wolf hunter is to hear the unmistakable call of a lone wolf. Indeed, this "call of the wild" is a simple, yet complex communication of one predator speaking to another: the language of hunters that only another hunter can truly understand. Nodding one's head in respect to the call is all a wolf hunter can do, and perhaps recall a few lines from Robert Service's "Heart of this":

"I have clinched and closed with the naked North, I have learned to defy and defend; Shoulder to shoulder we have fought it out, yet the Wild must win in the end." Alaska wolf hunters ensure the wild does win. As humans fail to domesticate wild adult wolves, so does city life fail to domesticate the human hunter. Each hunting season, we each answer the call of the wild, just as the wolf does each day when stalking its prey. We know and accept that there is no taking the thrill of the hunt out of either of us.

As a result, any wolf hunter worth his bacon and beans would never advocate altogether eliminating the wolf from its wilderness environment. His desire is not only out of respect for the wolf and the hunt, but also for a greater purpose that Henry David Thoreau sums up best:

"For in wildness is the preservation of the world."

Christopher Batin is a resident of Alaska, and editor and publisher of Alaska Hunter Publications. He is also the author of the award-winning book, *Hunting in Alaska: A Comprehensive Guide*, which includes a detailed chapter on how to hunt Alaska wolves.

Night of the Brown Bear

CHRISTOPHER BATIN

Have you looked over your shoulder lately? There is a beast that lives in the rural forests, a beast that often watches you without you knowing; perhaps as you fish a stream, or maybe as you hunt birds in the local forest. This beast has stalked and killed sportsmen, ambushing them when they least expect it. And there's one out there now, waiting for you, as you head out on your hunting trip with friends.

You don't recognize the visible and invisible signs as you drive the gravel road to the forest campground: the remains of a moose that died months ago from winter starvation; a poor berry season; your bullheadedness in taking a shortcut through the dense brush rather than the trail to the campsite. Maybe it's the music blaring away through the headsets that will change your destiny. Enough. Separately, they are unrelated elements of historical insignificance. Unrelated until the Hand of Fate, and your complacency, lead you from the city and all its safeguards and place you onto the path that leads into the Night of the Brown Bear.

As you walk through the wilderness, too impatient to wait for your hunting buddies as they gear up, know this: what you're about to experience is a horror so intense that it can mentally and physically scar you for life—that is, *IF* you manage to live through it. Hundreds of people have been maimed and/or killed by brown bear. The numbers are not great. But when you are one of those numbers, it is one too many.

Non-aggressive encounters of camp robbing and stalking are frightening enough. Brown bears have different reasons for killing. Some are rogues who are afraid of nothing, not even man. Others are predators, stalking anything that moves in the night, including hunters. A brown bear is so strong that it can snap the neck of an 800-pound moose with one swipe. These become territorial bears, and will attack and maim unsuspecting humans and other bears who get too close to their kills. And of course, there are always those bears that attack just because they are plain, outright mean. You're about to walk into a bear that is all four.

The bear sways slowly in the brush, nose twitching as it guards a rotting moose carcass. Its eyes pierce the darkness, waiting, watching for the source of the footsteps. As you approach, the boar drops his head, and pooled-up saliva oozes out in bubbly strands and globs onto rotting alder leaves. As your music blares away through your headsets, you never hear the explosion of brush, or see the 1,200 pounds of rippling muscle and hide traveling toward you at 30 mph. The impact slams you into the ground, leaving you breathless. Arms flail in a confusing mix of fear, shock, and defense. You twist with superhuman strength to escape, but to no avail. A shroud of suffocating, stinky wet fur jams into your mouth and nose. You jerk your head sideways and suck in a deep breath . . . and scream. Your mind floats around in a void of confusion as an eight-inch paw hits your head with the power of a bat smashing out a home run. Neck vertebrae crack; an eardrum ruptures. Even in deafness, there is no deliverance from the angry roars that echo again and again inside your head. The explosive growls in your face reek of rotting moose guts, and cause your stomach to convulse.

The foot pad holding you down is as heavy and coarse as a column of pot-marked concrete, and just as cold. The three-inch claws grate your skull and continue downward, gouging out chunks of flesh and muscle from your chin and shoulder. You squirm and flail away with your arms to escape the pain. Your eyes bulge out of their sockets as another paw swats you in the back of the head. Claws recoil violently, ripping off half your scalp. Two-inch-long canines stab repeatedly into your face, neck and skull. You feel the bones of your nose and cheekbone crunch like a flimsy soda can. A torrent of blood rushes down your throat, and the terrorized scream that formed seconds earlier becomes nothing more than a raspy gurgle. Time loses all meaning.

Only now do you know what true terror is. There are no switches to turn off the horror. Closing your eyes won't make it stop. Your last thoughts before unconsciousness overtakes you: "Why me? If only I had another chance, if only I had known!"

Each heartbeat drags out for months; a breath seems to come every few years. Then blackness.

For now, the bear leaves your limp, broken body to check the moose carcass. Now it has two food sources to protect. As the northern lights glow an eerie green overhead, the only movement left is the slowing pulse of your blood, streaming into the sand.

"Good. You're coming around. Here, drink this cup of hot Labrador Tea. I'll stoke the campfire with this driftwood while you get oriented.

"You're in my Alaska brown bear survival camp. Found you off the main trail. You must have slipped and hit your head on a rock. Glad I found you when I did, 'cause you don't wanna be walking around alone out there again, being new to the area and all. Especially tonight. See that moon and the way those northern lights are blazing away overhead? Night of the Brown Bear. If you listen carefully to my words, you'll have a second chance to do it right. Ignore my advice and anything can happen on a night like this. If you ain't a bit scared, you're either a damn liar or too ignorant to know any better. I believe it's the latter.

"Bear-mauling victims—at least those fortunate to have lived through some of the horrors you've just experienced—often admit they failed to implement one or more precautionary measures that might have prevented the bear attack. I'll share these with you later. For now, remember this: A bear's *reaction* is often the result of man's *inaction* in properly planning checks or procedures when traveling in bear country.

"You can leave if you want, but here's the bottom line: You're in the heart of the world's greatest concentration of brown bear. Around these parts in Alaska, biologists figure there's a bear for every square mile. About 3,000 in all I'm told. Seems there's twice that many at times. But you'll find out for yourself soon enough. You're here for one reason: to listen, and learn the secrets of stayin' alive in this country. I'll stay with you 'til morning. After that, I'm done with ya, and you take responsibility for your own path through the Night of the Brown Bear.

"Yes, I'm a real-life person. I've been hunting and traveling Alaska bear country goin' on 33 years now, and here's a fact I'll share with you before you ask. Yes, I've had my share of frights and close calls with brown bears, mostly because I didn't have someone teach me what you're going to learn here tonight. I learned the hard way, which can be downright painful if you ain't too smart or lucky. Never been much on brains in my youth, if you add up all the stupid things I've done and gotten away with. Guess I'll just hafta credit my survival to luck."

"Stoke that fire, friend, before those bears creep in on us!"

"So, you thought you could steal the fruits away from Mother Fear, without paying the obligatory price of an embrace, huh? You can only cheat fear for so long, friend, getting your jollies by watching those movies or playing video games of overpowering ghastly ghouls and werewolves. Ha! Such exercises are not only ineffective, but also childish and self-deceptive. Here's why:

"Hollywood horrors offer fail-safe protection: or, the thrill without the spill—your blood, that is. You can find sanctuary by closing your eyes. Afterwards, your subconscious *knows* that the appearance of the ending movie credits guarantees your safe passage back to the lobby. The wispy, green tendrils of evil spirits oozing out of the filmstrip are neutralized. Zombies have lost their power to bury people alive. Werewolves have no fangs and claws to maim and injure. When you embark on a journey through the Night of the Brown Bear, you enter *the Threshhold of Truth!* People have been buried alive by bears. And a single swipe of a bear paw can bleed you dry in minutes. This is real-life danger that doesn't disappear when you close your eyes.

"Territorial and rogue bears can and will kill you. They stink of rotting salmon and festering battle scars. Decaying teeth often fuel nasty dispositions. Never trust any bear, especially a rogue that approaches you at night! These bears usually exhibit no fear toward humans, a species they view as an easily overpowered and insignificant obstacle to the comforts of a full belly and dominance.

"Throw a couple of logs on the campfire, friend, to take off the chill you're feeling, and turn the Coleman light to full. The fear you felt on your initial journey through the Night of the Brown Bear is natural. Fear is the check, and balance that keeps you in tune with your environment and out of the hospital. But learn to control it, because as the wolf somehow senses the presence of the maimed and crippled in a herd of caribou, so too are brown bears able to sense fear in humans, which often triggers the instinct to attack.

"Listen to me and the experiences others have had, and hopefully these true-to-life stories will help you become a believer, rather than a victim, of the Night of the Brown Bear.

"Leave the city and most of its social trappings behind when you enter the wilderness, or they will eventually contribute to your demise. The leeches of ambivalence and complacency thrive in the pond of urban life. You'll never know when they'll attach themselves to your subconscious mind, but they always do eventually. They suck the lifeblood of adaptive and strategic reasoning from your psyche, leaving your survival instincts too anemic to see the dangers of brown bear country, let alone cope with them.

"These debilitating symptoms are obvious. In bear country, hunters often behave like kids at a carnival, so caught up in all the wonderful sights and smells of hunting camp that they fail to first see, then interpret, the danger of a lightning storm flashing overhead. Likewise, they walk through bear country with the same ambivalence to the dangers of their environment. Sound familiar? Your physical eyes may see the obvious path, but your mind's eye is drawing up plans on how to celebrate your pal's first blacktail deer. You see, the brown splotch to the right, but you don't see them as two cubs playing in the blueberry bushes with an irate sow approaching from behind.

"You want to know what the least-recognized, yet most viable danger of camping in bear country is? Modern tents provide excellent protection from the ravages of typhoons and battering hailstones. That's what they were designed for. Yet "the safety of your tent" is an oxymoron when a tent is viewed as an effective deterrent to inquisitive or rogue brown bears. I view a tent in brown bear country as nothing more than wrapping material for a human burrito encased in a fluffy Hollofil center. While a tent offers slightly greater deterrent to inquisitive brown bears than say, sleeping in the open, your blind-faith acceptance of it as a "Hands-Off-Or-Else" fortress is nothing more than a manifestation of the Ostrich Syndrome: a compulsiveness to hide your head in a sleeping bag, feeling confident the danger will not find you. Camp long enough in brown bear country and the danger *will* find you, as Myles Tenbroeck discovered with friend John Firneno in July, 1998.

"The two men were fishing for salmon on a remote boat-accessible-only tributary of southcentral Alaska's Talkeetna River. Leaving the other anglers and their tents camped at the creek mouth, they hiked several hundred yards upstream and found solitude, a good fishing hole, and a sandbar to pitch their tent.

"Myles was a four-year veteran of Alaska Army Airborne ROTC. Trained to be tough. Composed under pressure. Resilient to adversity under a variety of Alaska conditions.

"The pair pitched their tent in the open, away from obvious bear trails. They stored their food in a bearproof food bag hung in a tall spruce, and cooked their meals 50 yards from their tent. After a day of good salmon fishing, and seeing no bears, they called it a night.

"At 3 a.m., Alaska's waning midnight sun resembles a flickering candle: there's just enough light to see, yet it is dark enough to cast eerie shadows.

"Growing up on the south side of Chicago, Myles said John always had a hard time sleeping when he knew bullies and thieves were around. And from the looming size of the shadow eclipsing the tent, he realized that perhaps the biggest bully of his life was about to pay them a visit.

"He nudged Myles once. Twice. Lifting his head off his makeshift backpack/pillow, Myles blinked several times, and looked at John in a quizzical daze. Suddenly, five claws punch through the sidewall of their tent, stopping less than six inches above Myles' head. Reaching the bottom of the tent, the claws skewered Myles backpack with the force of a gaffer impaling a fish. The bear's hairy front leg recoiled like a snap trigger, and the pack disappeared through the hole. In disbelief, Myles realized that his head had been on that pack a mere seconds earlier.

"It was time for action. Just as Myles eased forward to stick his head through the gaping hole to confirm a visual OK to exit, the bear plunged its head into the tent, its twitching nose stopping inches from Myles' face.

"John watched in silent horror. All he could think was how he was going to explain to Myles' mother why her son's body didn't have a head on it anymore.

"The bear immediately recoiled in a snort of spray as Myles back-pedaled in a flurry of shouts and obscenities. Caught up in the effects of adrenaline rush, he pulled on a stocking cap, slipped into his Army boots and grabbed his 9 mm semi-auto. Scurrying out of the tent, he quickly relieved himself before charging into the brush to retrieve his backpack. John grabbed a shotgun and vowed to save his friend from what he viewed as an irrational, impulsive response. The sight of Myles running into the brush, waving a 9 mm in one hand and clothed only in a stocking cap, boots, and boxer shorts emblazoned with bright red hearts was a frightful, yet hilarious sight. Seconds later, Myles emerged from the brush with his pack that the bear had dropped in his escape. They duct-taped a trash bag over the hole, and went fishing.

"At about 3 a.m. the next evening, John shook Myles awake again. Both watched the entrance to their tent in wide-eyed amazement after they heard a couple of shotgun blasts fired at the creek mouth camps. Twenty seconds later, Myles and John watched several bears stampeding through the water and darting through the brush. More shots rang out, then quiet. John remained wide-eyed until about 7 a.m., when he again shook Myles awake. He stopped shaking when he glanced back outside and found his nose within inches of a brown bear that pretty much filled the vestibule of their tent, with plenty of bear left over to come inside. When Myles sat up the bear spun on its heels and left. With enough bear adventures for one season, the pair packed up their camp later that day and returned to Fairbanks.

"Unlike their comic counterparts, Alaska bears often ignore picnic baskets when there are coolers of food or deer meat to steal, and the bigger they are, the better. While fishing in the Susitna Drainage one evening, Mark Ubanic woke up with a start, and watched bewilderedly as a massive brown bear chewed into the end of a five-foot-long cooler. The teeth punctured the hard plastic as if it were butter, but the lid wouldn't budge. A powerful death-grip bite, followed by a massive headshake, also failed to dislodge the contents.

"Not bringing a cooler with him, Mark realized he was witness to a theft and a breaking (and soon-to-be entering) crime scene. Mirth turned to caution as another bear appeared. He watched the bears work over the cooler. Like tag-team wrestlers, one rested while the other chewed off bits of plastic. A third bear soon joined the fracas, and slammed its body into the cooler several times. Obviously irate, the bear sprung into the air and body-slammed the cooler with all its weight. Soon after, the grunts, warning growls and sloppy and furious chomping signaled the cooler had popped open as the bears gorged on the feast. Mark soon heard, but dared not look to confirm, that some bears were becoming increasingly angry over sharing. The first bear to be chased off looked around and gazed into Mark's tent. Mark froze, then suddenly breathed a sigh of relief when the owner of the cooler charged up the trail, shouting, waving his arms and yelling. The bears scattered to the four woods with various foodstuffs.

"While bear encounters like these make us wipe our brow and pat ourselves on the back for being true survivors, there is no comparing them with those victims of bear attacks who have been maimed . . . or have never emerged from their journey through the Night of the Brown Bear.

"In 1996, world-famous brown-bear photographer and author Michio Hoshino was photographing bears with a film crew on Russia's Kamchatka Peninsula. In the early morning hours, a rogue bear dragged Michio from his tent and killed him before dragging him off a short ways into the brush. The bear was quickly hunted down and dispatched, but it failed to bring Michio back. Michio made a decision to venture into the Night of the Brown Bear. In its darkness, he dared to walk too close to the edge, and slipped.

"The Night of the Brown-Bear is many things, but it is not a single face of a bear or any one incident that can be described. Rather, it is a conglomerate of concerns, a melting pot of very real dangers, shortcomings, hazards, and personal fears, that when combined, form a different face of terror for every man.

"Identify your ultimate fear before venturing into the night. It will help identify your strengths and weaknesses. Some express a hysteria-like concern in not knowing how to protect their children from a brown bear that ran down and killed a King Cove, Alaska boy. Others fear an attack while sleeping in their hunting tent. Others still are afraid of being eaten alive—all of which, although rarely, have happened.

"Even a log cabin often proves to be an ineffective sanctuary. Guide Jim Bailey tells of how a brown bear destroyed his bear-proofed hunting cabin, ripping the door off its hinges, demolishing furniture, biting into pans and utensils before leaving a ring of fur on the jagged edges of a window it probably broke on its way out. Bailey figures the bear smelled what might have been food crumbs that fell into the cracks of the cabin floor, because his floorboards were pried up, with the edges chewed and appeared to be licked clean.

"If you are to survive an encounter with a brown bear, start now by learning how to selectively purge your civilized conditioning. For good reason, our laws encourage us to settle disputes of injuries, thievery or property damage through a mediator or the courts. Brown bears don't recognize this authority, and survive by dominating territory. We fall into peril when we don't reprogram our subconscious prior to entering the field. Society embraces kiss-and-make-better solutions to cure the anethemic hemorrhaging of our follow-the-herd programming. Social change has embraced the concept of consolation awards for 'Worst Costume' or 'Last Place Finish.' Living in an environment that rewards failure, weakens your focus, and dissolves your will may be acceptable in suburbia, but not in the wilderness! *Eliminate* such programming if you wish to survive the Night of the Brown Bear! The prescription for your survival health and welfare is *The Highlander* theme: 'There can be only one!'

"For this is the only law you must adhere to during your darkest hours of trial: you *will* be the one left standing. But it takes time to train yourself to overcome the paralyzing grip of failure and react with physical precision. Commit now to do whatever it takes to ready yourself. If a hungry, 1100-pound boar decides to strong-paw itself into your hunting tent, expect no help from the cavalry, police, or even your friends. Once trained, you will have the skills to respond immediately to Nature's involuntary summons and dominate the Wilderness Court of DLP: Defense of Life and Property. Within seconds, you must transcend above your victimized state and become judge, jury and if necessary, executioner. You will triumph. Without practice, the resulting consequences of error or indecision in any of these areas can kill you.

"I've had my own experiences with DLP and these rogue raiders. On one trip, I was hunting black-tail deer and elk from an old trappers cabin on Afognak Island with two friends. Winter and freezeup arrived early; salmon runs were poor; and the bears, hungry. At least our deer would be safe, as brown bears don't climb trees. Or so we thought.

"One by one, our deer disappeared from the massive branches of a huge spruce. In our cabin, we'd hear the dull thuds of frozen deer dropping 20 feet to the forest floor. Rushing out with rifles in hand, we'd find no night marauder: only hair, claw marks and deeply gouged and missing bark indicating how the bear had clawed up the tree, reached out and slashed down each deer.

"As we bagged more deer the following days, the bear stole and ate each one. The bruin was much craftier now, knowing we were watching and avoiding our efforts to bag him. When the storms hit, we'd never hear the bear. Just see the remnants of deer hide or hair the next morning when we awoke. One evening, angered and frustrated that our deer were gone, and having nothing to sit up all night to protect, we settled in for a good night's sleep.

"Shortly before midnight, John awoke to his side of the cabin shuddering and stovepipe rattling. John shouted at the top of his voice, his words red-hot needles searing my subconscious. Emerging from deep sleep, I couldn't see in the blackness, and assumed the bear had broken into the cabin and was attacking John. I grabbed my rifle and rolled off the top bunk. I dropped through the blackness to the floor, landing on my feet and ready to defend.

"Waving flashlight beams and three-second mini-novas of strike-anywhere matchheads revealed no bear inside the cabin. With rifles ready, we ventured into the howling wind for a sign of what happened. The ends of the 12-inch cabin logs, sturdy, yet slightly soft from years of weathering, were sheared off the main logs of the cabin. Others above it were gouged by claws. The bear had attempted to climb onto the roof, possibly to get at and eat a small piece of frozen deer tenderloin the cook had saved.

"Soon the once-a-night visits became several times a night. Such fearless attacks were potentially dangerous, especially when sleep-groggy hunters stagger out the cabin door at all hours to relieve themselves.

"Desperate, we devised a workable plan. We tied a string to a game bag that held the last remaining scraps of our deer. We ran the string through a hole in the cabin door, and tied on a series of empty soda cans. Sitting on empty five-gallon pails, we hovered over the cans, waiting in silence, fighting off the urge to sleep. About 10 p.m., the cans crept ever so slowly toward the door. They twitched again, then clicked together. We were ready.

"In the narrow penlight beam, I could see John ready the huge, wide-beam flashlight. Rick slipped off the safety on his .338. I stood ready with my .338 and headlamp. We all nodded in unison that we were ready. John cracked open the cabin door and flicked on the flashlight. The white beam caught the brownie full-form and Rick's .338 hit its mark. Pulling on our fleece clothing, we ventured out into the 15-below temperatures and 20-mph winds, finding the bear less than 30 yards from our cabin. The 8-footer was layered with fat and showed no evidence of starving.

"It's easy to understand why bears like tent camps. Looking at a campground from the air, the brightly colored tents and coolers resemble colored hors d'oeuvres, arranged in appetizing fashion and surrounded by a decorative garnish of forest.

"Friend J. W. Smith ran a *hunting and fishing camp* on the Alaska Peninsula, the heart of brown bear country. His dozen tents are pitched within 100 yards of the best sportfishing as well as bear-viewing spots. But don't look out on the flats for the bears, but rather, in camp. Some of the problems J. W. Smith has learned to live with:

"Meal preparation often requires a guide to grab a shotgun and, while shooting into the air, chase the bears out of the cook tent.

"Throughout dinner, newly arrived guests watch wide-eyed as a guide would suddenly excuse himself, grab a shotgun, and rush outside, shooting into the air, followed by a round of expletives.

"Inside the Quonset-hunt dining tent, clients indulge in to-the-rim refills of fine Cabernet to help calm their nerves for the inevitable hike back to their sleeping tents. J. W. claimed never to have lost a client to a bear.

"Sometimes Smith becomes what the guides call 'unbearable.' Once while taking an afternoon nap in his tent, Smith awoke with a start to find a bear sniffing around his head. The bear's salmon-fattened, rotundo body plugged the tent as tightly as a cork in a wine bottle. Smith gave the bear a strong right cross, which sent it scurrying for cover. Sometimes you just gotta stand your ground and fight back.

"The Night of the Brown Bear also has a lighter side, ranging from bear jokes to black humor. For instance, be wary of a hunting buddy who wears sneakers and carries a .22 for bear protection. Why? Because if you can't outrun your buddy, he'll shoot you in the foot with the .22 to slow you down, so he can outrun you. (From what I'm told, the lighter caliber doesn't inflict much damage, and imparts a hop-along, crippling effect, which the bears seem to prefer.)

"Of course, here's an instance I heard about on the incorrect use of pepper spray. A newly arrived soldier to Alaska purchased some pepper-spray bear repellent. According to hospital personnel, the soldier stated that immediately before departing on a fishing trip, he perhaps took the term 'bear repellent' a bit too literally. He assumed the application was the same as with insect repellent. He sprayed his face and neck with the 'bear repellent,' and immediately realized the severity of his mistake. The moral of the story? Let the bears pepper their own soldier steak!

"Ah, look, the first rays of morning. Before you depart, friend, on your hunt, let me share with you a few words that have kept me and quite a few of my fellow brown bears alive from hasty, impulsive mistakes made by either side. Shocked to hear that? Don't be. Honorable warriors respect their adversaries, and after being thoroughly trained in battle or survival, the ultimate goal of any warrior-survivor should be peace.

"The phrase is from Sun Tzu, an ancient Chinese strategist and military tactician. I've taken the liberty to modify it slightly in recognition of you being made an honorary graduate of the Night of the Brown Bear:

"'You do not have to possess sharp eyes to see the sun and the moon, nor does it take good ears to hear the thunderstorm. Wisdom in brown-bear country is not obvious. You must see the subtle and notice the hidden to emerge victorious.'"

"As you walk through the Night of the Brown Bear, feel the wilderness with more than just your hands. Look with more than just your physical eyes; look with the eyes of your soul, and hear the bear and its environment speak to you of its dangers, as well as its wonders. Do this, and I guarantee you'll avoid most if not all hazardous or life-threatening brown-bear encounters.

"Speaking of communication, the twitch in my fishing arm tells me we should grab those fly rods, and amble down to my favorite salmon hole before the bears do. Your blacktail deer can wait, as these late-run silvers are so much fun this time of year. And who knows? Perhaps if we're lucky, and we sing as we go, we'll discover that we're too late and find a salmon flopping around for us in the middle of the trail!"

Christopher Batin is a resident of Alaska, and editor and publisher of Alaska Hunter Publications. He is also the author of the award-winning book, *Hunting in Alaska: A Comprehensive Guide*, which includes a detailed chapter on how to hunt Alaska wolves.

Living on Tundra Time

J. SCOTT RUPP

The question was not if I was going to fall into the lake but rather how spectacularly. Perched precariously on two rocks several yards from shore—one foot on one rock and one foot on the other—I gave the freighter canoe a gentle shove-off for Cliff White's return to camp. Now, with the shore behind me, my rifle in hand and pack frame and fully loaded daypack on my back, I had to get turned around somehow.

I was halfway through the turn when I went in, plunging waist-deep into the cold Arctic water. Hell of a way to start the day. Cliff called over to ask if I wanted to head back to camp and change into dry clothes, but I waved him off and waded toward the bank.

There were three bull caribou somewhere on the ridge above me, and it was the fourth day of a five-day hunt in northern Quebec—a hunt that had been highly rewarding but also highly unsuccessful from a tag-filling point of view.

Once ashore, I set off at a brisk pace for the top of the ridge where I hoped to intercept the bulls. I was breathing heavily by the time I neared the crest, and I began to angle to the right in hopes of getting in front of and above the caribou. Fortune was with me. As I crossed the top, hunching over as low as I could go to minimize my silhouette, I spotted antler tops bobbing just over the rise.

Crab-walking forward a few yards, I got a glimpse of the antlers and backs of two bulls feeding on lichen about 50 yards away. Then the rack of the trio's third member glided into view. Now here was a winner—the best set of antlers of any bull I'd seen in three hard days of hunting. Just that suddenly, before I could move into position for a shot, all three bedded down. The wind direction and our relative positions on the hilltop left me only one choice: get on my belly, flatten out like a pancake and crawl.

Hunting out of Arctic Adventures' Lake Ikirtuuq camp last year was a kind of busman's holiday for me. While it's been my pleasure to partner up with some of the best hunters and guides in the country, I longed for a chance to go solo for a few days—just take a pack and some food and roam at my own pace.

And where better than northern Quebec to do it? I've loved the far north ever since I first set foot in it, and I was especially impressed by the Lake Ikirtuuq area. The region, about an hour's flight out of Kuujjuaq and situated at the southernmost edge of the southern Arctic, features gently rolling topography dotted with myriad lakes large and small.

There aren't many trees to speak of—mostly stunted, hardy spruces mixed in with patches of knee- to waist-high willows growing on lake fringes and in small ravines. The rest of the vegetation is low-growing ground cover, including the lichens on which the caribou feed. If you look closely you'll also discover tundra blueberries. They have a tart sweetness to them, as do the cloud berries, which glow an electric salmon color.

At first glance it seems a desolate place, but the tundra is home to wildlife other than caribou. One morning, as I lay prone in a big rockpile while glassing a small group of caribou, a grayish-brown, furry head with two pointy ears popped up behind a rock a few yards in front of me, and a pair of inquisitive eyes bored into mine. The Arctic fox, its coat partway through the transition to winter white, stared at me for a few seconds, darted a short distance to the left, stopped to stare again, then disappeared.

Lake Ikirtuuq is also far north enough to play host to considerably larger fauna. There are occasional muskox sightings, and the week before our crew arrived, a bush pilot had spotted and photographed a polar bear less than 15 miles from our camp. More than once I turned to check my back trail to ensure no massive white form was striding across the tundra, coming for me.

Few places offer the chance to stare into a blue sky devoid of jet contrails and to watch the majesty of the northern lights or the specter of a giant moon rising in the distance—its brilliant clarity unspoiled by air pollution.

And then there's the hunt itself. In my judgment there's nothing more fun to hunt than caribou. In most places you get two tags, which means you can fill the freezer with one bull then hunt for a trophy, if that's your pleasure.

With any luck there are enough caribou around so you're constantly seeing small or large herds, bachelor bands or solitary bulls. You can wait at likely crossings or walk and glass, depending on your druthers.

And while judging caribou is no easy task, I find it fascinating to compare all the different antler configurations caribou carry, and I was excited at the prospect of another crack at hunting them.

When our float plane's skids hit the water at Lake Ikirtuuq, the rain was just getting cranked up. There were still a few hours of light left, though, and several of us, eager to start hunting, decided to brave the weather. I climbed the ridge behind camp and dropped down the other side, finding the boat Cliff and his guides had rigged with a pulley to cross a rushing creek.

I stepped gingerly into the white Zodiac-looking craft and laid my rifle against the bow before reaching up to pull on the nylon rope above my head. The boat swung gently in the current as I pulled it across, and I beached it on a large, flat rock on the far side.

Pushing through 50 yards or so of waist-high willows, I emerged onto the open tundra and hiked uphill a ways before plopping down to do some glassing—which turned out to be pretty much out of the question. Horizontal rain drove into the objective lenses of my binoculars and speckled and splatted onto my glasses. I sat there anyway, reveling in the relative misery of an Arctic rainstorm.

The next day, outfitting myself like some kind of flatland Sherpa, I crossed the creek again and embarked on a daylong loop I'd planned the night before.

Caribou weren't in short supply. Nearly every vantage point I hiked to afforded a look at a small herd or two, and at lunchtime I stalked a solitary bull just for fun—closing to within 50 yards and then letting him pass by, none the wiser about my presence.

There was a narrow, crescent-shaped lake on the back side of the first ridge I crossed, and I moved northwest along it, staying high enough for a good view while keeping myself out of the lees where thousands, perhaps millions of white-footed blackflies waited to swarm any warm-blooded passersby.

By early afternoon I'd looked over maybe 100 caribou, but I had made the decision at the start of the trip to kill just one good bull, and none of the ones I'd seen made that grade. Then, as I neared the tip of the lake, I spotted two pale bulls rounding the lake and heading more or less in my direction. A quick inspection with the Leica Trinovid binoculars told me they were worth getting closer to.

The bulls swung left into a wide, shallow drainage and began moving perpendicularly to me. The fact is that you can't catch caribou, but I judged their angle of travel and figured I could head them off. Jog became trot became sweaty, heavy-breathing run. Maybe Carl Lewis could have caught them, but I could not—although, in my defense, I'd like to see Mr. Lewis try sprinting across the tundra wearing boots and a pack and carrying a rifle.

As afternoon passed into evening, I made my way back to camp. It took a while to navigate around all the small lakes and swampy spots, but eventually I came to the little boat and pulled myself across.

The next day I retraced my route back to the tip of the lake. It seemed like a logical spot for caribou to cross, and on the far side was a tall ridge—the highest in the area. My plan was to watch the end of the lake for a while, and if nothing happened I'd set out for the top of the ridge.

The morning passed slowly, the caribou sightings few and far between. One bull worked his way along the far shore before walking into the lake and swimming across. From my distant vantage point all that was visible was the bull's rack, gliding gently across the shimmering water like some ancient mystic ship.

At noon I wolfed down a carbohydrate bar, filled the water bladder of my daypack from a small pyramid-shaped pond and set off for the ridge. I expected the hike to take an hour, but it stretched to two before I gained the top and looked down the back side. The optimist in me was hoping for a vast herd of caribou that stretched for miles; the realist got five cows and a couple of calves.

That night I hatched a new plan. My fellow hunters were having mixed success, but it seemed the far side of the lake on which our camp sat was producing the best action. I decided to hunt my way around the northern half of the lake.

It was as good a plan as any, but by lunchtime I was having doubts. For the first time in days I was coming up completely empty—no sightings at all. Then I crested a far ridge and found them. It wasn't exactly a honey hole, but there were perhaps 50 to 75 caribou in several small groups spread across a valley floor for about a mile.

The wind was blowing a full 30 mph, with higher gusts, and I lay down next to a rock that was about as long as my body but only a foot high. It would have to do. As the wind ripped above me, I glassed the valley and waited to see if anything big would turn up. Nothing did, and with the end of the day approaching I began the long trek back to camp.

Heartened by what I'd seen, I asked Cliff if he'd ferry me across the lake the next day, figuring to start from that last glassing point and push into the valley—and cross it if necessary. The next morning, as I stepped out of my cabin, rifle in hand and ready to go, Cliff called for me to come look through the spotting scope trained on the ridge across the lake. I got there just in time to see the three bulls disappear over the top. With more than a little excitement, I hustled down to the big canoe for the short trip across.

Now I was lying within 50 yards of the trio. I could see just the two smaller ones to my left, only their antlers and ears visible, and I'd pretty much low-crawled past them when I saw antlers coming dead ahead. The big bull walked into view at 40 yards, stopped and stared at the strange creature on the ground before him.

The bull was quartering on, and it was a simple matter to move the Sako Finnlight .280 into position, place the crosshairs of the Weaver Grand Slam on the point of his near shoulder and squeeze the trigger.

The shot sounded small and hollow at such close range, and the bull took a step back and a few unsteady sidesteps to the right. I'd already worked the bolt and was ready to deliver another shot when he fell to the ground with a thud.

I recovered the Federal 150-grain Nosier Partition easily; it was protruding through the hide just shy of the far hip in a perfect mushroom. I rolled the bull onto his stomach, set my camera on top of the daypack and spent an exhausting 45 minutes taking photos. I'd hit the self-timer, run to the bull and struggle to lift his head into position before the shutter fired, then trot back to the camera to do it again.

Eventually I broke out the knives and the sharpening stone. I skinned out one side, and after a bit of trial and error located the ball socket that allowed me to separate the rear quarter without nicking the entrails. All the while, the bull was swelling like a Macy's Thanksgiving Day Parade float as the gases from his digestive system built up. The rest of the work went smoothly, and soon I was lashing meat bags to the pack frame and hauling a load down to the lake shore.

At the start of the second and last trip, I radioed the camp for someone to come pick me up, and by the time I got down to the water's edge, I could see the freighter canoe kicking up a white wake as it headed across.

"Hey, you got one!" the guide called as he cut the engine and eased toward the rocks. "And all butchered and packed out. You're all right!"

Yes, I did feel all right.

This story originally appeared in *Petersen's Hunting*, July 2005; reprinted with permission of the author.

Two Bulls

E. DONNALL THOMAS, JR.

The elk of a lifetime reminds us that the value of the hunt cannot be measured in inches.

Wind is the most capricious element the bowhunter faces in the field. It cannot be controlled or disguised, and game animals detect the scent it carries with an acuity we can scarcely imagine. Since we are largely at its mercy, the best approach to a fickle wind is often a judicious retreat. All successful hunters must eventually learn that lesson, especially those ambitious enough to do their hunting with traditional archery tackle.

That's why I spent days waiting for a southwest wind to follow the elk down the coulee as they moved from the bedding cover to the little spring. Southwest winds are common in my part of Montana, but the weather had pushed steadily out of the northwest all week. Northwest was close, but it wasn't close enough, not for the big herd bull and his harem of jittery cows. After all the scouting I had done, I wasn't taking any chances. I was the only member of this cast of characters who knew that an elk hunt was taking place, and since I wasn't going to let a treacherous puff of wind cost me that advantage, there was nothing to do but avoid the area until conditions changed. Patience and planning may not enjoy the appeal of more aggressive hunting tactics, but sometimes that approach is just what it takes to get the job done.

Now, the wind was finally right. Warm autumn colors spread across the hills as I hiked up the draw and settled into my blind near the edge of the spring. Fresh elk tracks punctuated the mud in front of my hiding place, and the willows bore fresh scars from heavy antlers. With the wind in my face at last, this was the night to kill the herd bull . . . if the elk came down this coulee instead of one of a dozen others, and if they arrived during shooting light, and if the cows didn't detect me first. Suddenly, the litany seemed all but overwhelming.

My blind was a simple affair cobbled together from brush and a strip of camo netting. Squatting inside, I noticed the freshly killed remains of a sharptail left behind by a hawk. I started to discard them, but then I hesitated. There was no reason why two predators couldn't share the cover. Finally, I nocked an arrow, checked my shooting lanes, and fussed over a few stray twigs and branches until I was sure there was nothing left to deflect a shaft.

Then there was nothing left to do but wait.

Although unfavorable winds had kept me away longer than I wanted, it had scarcely been an uneventful week. Little wonder; for serious Montana bowhunters, there is hardly ever an uneventful week in September.

My only regret was that I hadn't been there when Joe killed his bull. Joe is the teenage son of long-time hunting partner Ray Stalmaster, and while he has accumulated a record of success that most archers twice his age might envy, a big elk had always eluded him. He deserved a good bull, and I was sorry I hadn't been there when he finally killed one.

And he had taken his bull with class. Joe was working his way down a long draw when he heard the first bugle on the ridge above him. Hustling ahead in order to pick up some more of the wind, he kept track of the bull's progress with his ears as their two paths slowly converged. Finally, he came to the edge of an open meadow and realized that he was going to meet his quarry without the benefit of cover.

But there was a lone pine tree in the middle of the clearing. Thinking quickly, Joe climbed up into its lower branches. When he finally saw the bull emerge from the timber, he cow-called and the bull charged the source of the sound. Joe's longbow sent his arrow down from the tree and through the elk's heart, and he watched it collapse in plain sight barely fifty yards away.

Imaginative tactics, good shooting, and a clean kill . . . bowhunting doesn't get much better than that. And to top all this off, the bull was a heavy, symmetrical seven point, the kind of animal most elk hunters will do without for a lifetime. Joe was modest, Ray was proud, and everyone was happy. For a while, it seemed as if the season had given us all that we could ask of it, but I still had an elk tag in my pocket, and the memory of all that fresh sign around the wallows just wouldn't go away.

Nestled in my blind, I watched a herd of antelope cross the head of the coulee half a mile to the west. A marsh hawk worked the tall grass on the other side of the spring, feinting, towering, and finally moving on. I wondered if this was the other hunter whose meal I had so recently interrupted, and if so, what his attitude might be toward my intrusion. Through it all, the wind held steady from the direction of the setting sun. All I needed to convert a beautiful evening into an elk hunt was some elk.

And suddenly they were there, a dozen harried cows stampeding down the draw toward the spring. It didn't take long to determine the source of their agitation. A piercing bugle rose above the sound of the breeze, ending in a resonant grunt that seemed to shake the earth. When the bull finally trotted into sight at the rear of the column, I didn't need my binoculars to know that I was coming face to face with the king of the mountain himself.

In fact, events were moving a lot faster than I wanted. An enthusiast of controlled, deliberate archery, I had envisioned lots of time to make sure the end game went according to plan, but the elk had other things in mind. Flush with the imperatives of the rut, the bull was bugling incessantly and charging his cows like an overworked sheep dog trying to keep track of too many sheep. Suddenly, cow elk were scattered everywhere. Matters were getting out of hand.

With the bull still over a hundred yards away, the lead cow was already behind me, bearing down on my scent line with the determination of an impending train wreck. One alarm bark from her and the hunt would be over, and I suddenly saw all those hours of restraint flicker like a candle in the wind. Cow-calling was pointless; I was surrounded by naturals squealing their heads off. But if I could convince the herd bull that an intruder had worked his way into his harem of cows . . .

Although bugling is widely regarded as the essence of the archery elk hunting experience, I don't bugle a lot any more. Calling always involves an exchange of information, and when elk are heavily hunted, that exchange may well work to the hunter's disadvantage. Furthermore, in my own ornery way I've come to regard the elk bugle as one of the most overused (and frankly abused) tools in the field. I guess I've just seen too many novices bugling from the back of four-wheelers, which makes the whole process loose its charm.

But there are still times to bugle, and this was one of them. I licked my diaphragm call into my mouth and gave the evening air my best. At the sound of the challenge, the herd bull went berserk. I came to full draw as he closed on a dead run, and when he hesitated at five yards, my recurve sent an arrow crashing into the sweet spot right behind his shoulder.

Sometimes patience and planning have their rewards.

Darkness had fallen by the time I finally walked up to the dead bull, and my elation was tempered by the demands of field-dressing the huge animal by myself while struggling with a flashlight and trying to avoid cutting off one of my own fingers deep in the elk's body cavity.

I didn't really appreciate just how big the antlers were until my wife Lori, my friend Tim Conrads, and I returned early the next morning and I ran my hands over them in the daylight. The bases were massive, the brow tines sweeping. The crowns were adorned with a scattering of extra points, adding up to nine total on one side and seven on the other. The main beams were black with pine pitch, but the tip of each point was polished to a perfect, ivory white. I've looked over a lot of elk in my time, but I finally realized that I had just killed one of the most striking bulls I've ever seen.

News of this kind travels fast in a small town, especially a small town full of bowhunters. By the time the quarters were hanging safely at the meat locker, friends were arriving at the house to take a look at the antlers. Fresh from school, young Joe Stalmaster was one of the first.

Suddenly, I realized that I might have inadvertently diminished the impact of his own earlier accomplishment. I am not a competitive hunter and neither are any of my friends. No one in our company keeps score. But it was still hard to believe that Joe wasn't feeling some sense of deflation as he studied those massive antlers.

Then I realized that something had been bothering me all night. The fact was that I had killed my bull from a stationary ambush, from which a large measure of the elk hunting experience had been missing: the lung-burning pace of the chase up the mountain, the fluid geometry of eyes, noses, and wind during the course of a long stalk. There wasn't anything wrong with the way I had killed the bull. I had interpreted the sign accurately, made a good critical decision, and shot well when the opportunity came. Even so, the kill suffered from what I would have to call the absence of perfection. Joe's hunt had been pure; mine was the trout taken on a Wooly Bugger instead of a dry fly, the jump-shot mallards rather than the limit taken over decoys. There was just no way around it.

Reading Ted Kerasote's excellent book *Bloodties*, it was hard for me to avoid the impression that Kerasote was taking all of this a bit too far in his own discussion of elk hunting.

Lighten up, I wanted to say: hunting is a natural, instinctive activity, and we don't have to anguish over its conduct quite that much. Now, perhaps I was doing the same thing. I have been drawing finer and finer lines throughout my own years in the field, beginning with the decision to hunt only with the bow, and extending to the commitment to limit myself to traditional archery tackle. Just how finely do these lines really need to be drawn?

"It's a beautiful bull," Joe finally said, interrupting my reverie. "And it's sure a lot bigger than mine." The smile on his face denied all possibility of envy.

"It's bigger," I agreed. "But yours was better."

And then I told him why.

Reprinted with permission of the author. To order his books, go to www.donthomasbooks.com.

In the Heat of the Rut

GREG RODRIGUEZ

"Greg, I had a cancellation on one of my moose hunts and I would really like you to come." The voice on the phone was that of Shane Black, co-owner of B.C. Safaris. "The rut should be going strong that week and I'm pretty sure you'll take a nice bull."

I'd always wanted to hunt moose, so I started looking for flights on the internet before I hung up the phone. But I had no idea of the adventure that lay in store. A mere two months after that phone call I was experiencing the odd sensation of my first-ever floatplane landing as the Beaver touched down on the surface of a lake near Black's moose camp in far northern British Columbia.

On our first day, after verifying that my rifle had survived the flight intact, I paddled off in a canoe with Jason Strout, one of Shane's guides, to see if we could get lucky while the rest of the crew finished packing for the next day's ride to spike camp. We paddled for about an hour to the end of a long, narrow lake that had been carved by glaciers eons ago. The icy water was smooth as glass. As we paddled along, enjoying the scenery, I felt my body begin to take on the pace of my majestic surroundings. Our strokes began to take on a smooth, comfortable rhythm, and, in seemingly no time at all, had carried us to the end of the lake where we climbed a hill to get a view of the surrounding area.

The short climb through the buck brush proved to be far more difficult than it looked. The brush grabbed at me like the tentacles of a thousand octopi, which made each step a major undertaking. When we reached the top, we took a few minutes to catch our breath before Jason started cow-calling. It didn't take long to figure out that that Shane's prediction was correct: the rut was in full swing. Five minutes into the first calling sequence, we saw a young bull emerge from the brush in front of us. It slowly circled to our downwind side, looking for love. I was so focused on snapping photos of the young bull that I almost didn't hear Jason's whispered warning.

Another bull was working his way behind us. This one was coming quickly, grunting and breaking branches along the way to warn off the younger bull. It grunted again, sounding as if it were right on top of us, but the brush was so thick it would be in our laps before we saw it. We wouldn't have the luxury of passing up the shot at that point, so Jason grabbed our stuff and hissed, "Run!"

We slipped and skidded down the hill, looking up just in time to see a huge bull barreling in, snapping branches and foaming at the mouth. The moose skidded to a stop when it saw us and disappeared as quickly as it came, but the image of that ornery old Bullwinkle charging through the trees is one I will not soon forget.

We tried calling unsuccessfully from one more location before paddling back towards camp. Halfway back, we saw yet another bull on the bank. This one was rubbing its wide, heavy antlers on a poplar, snapping branches, and grunting deeply. There must have been a cow nearby, but we didn't look—we were too busy trying to decide if we should take this fine bull on the first day or refuse this obvious gift from Diana and hold out for something bigger. Ever the optimist, I elected to pass.

The old bull kept its head down while it worked over a small bush with its antlers, so I asked Jason to grunt to get the moose to look up so I could snap a photo. But when Jason grunted, the bull charged us with a speed and determination that belied its oafish appearance. I dropped my camera in the boat and reached for my rifle while Jason paddled furiously backward. Luckily, Jason's strokes, combined with the massive wake of the bull's charge, carried us far enough away from the bank that the bull stopped short, apparently content to have driven us away. It was an awe-inspiring encounter that further served to remind me just how dangerous rutting moose can be.

Lucky Camp

For the next morning's ride to our spike camp, I was assigned a sure-footed little buckskin mare named Banjo. We saw several groups of moose on the way in, one of which was led by an ancient bull. It was massive, but its magnificent paddles carried only remnants of the points it had surely worn in seasons past. I had won the coin toss at base camp, so the decision was mine. I thought long and hard before offering the opportunity to Nick Kemp and Rick Brown, the other two hunters with us. I am sure the sight of that big bull's antlers moving through the brush gave them pause, but they decided to wait until we reached fly camp, too. It was a tough decision. Only time would tell if it was the right one.

Situated in a stand of trees with scenic vistas and a beautiful creek, our pretty little camp just *felt* lucky. We all pitched in and finished setting it up just as the last rays of the sun faded beyond the distant peaks.

We sat around a little wood stove trying to stay warm and discussing strategy with our guides. We were excited about our prospects, but the long ride had taken its toll, and the conversations soon faded as we dozed off, one by one, despite the fact that it was so cold in our tent that we could see our breath as it rose towards the ceiling.

The camp was abuzz the next morning as we scurried about, saddling horses and preparing gear. We had a quick planning session to make sure everyone knew where to go and then mounted up for the ride to our assigned hunting area. Just twenty minutes from camp, we saw four cow moose. Shane felt there had to be a bull around them, so we decided to set up on a nearby hill to glass and call.

We tied our horses and did our best to sneak up the hill, fighting the brush every step of the way. The cows knew we were there but they didn't seem threatened by our presence. We took a few minutes to settle in and then the waiting began. Shane would call for a few minutes, then we would glass for a while, then he would call again. The hunting was much slower paced than I expected, but there were now three different groups of cows nearby, so Shane was determined to stay put.

"Trust me," he said. "We'll shoot a bull here today."

Two hours after we set up, we heard several shots in the distance. Soon, Shane's radio beeped and we heard the good news—Rick had taken a nice moose. We radioed our congratulations. Thirty minutes later, four more shots rang out from the opposite end of the valley, and shortly afterward, the radio confirmed that Nick had scored on a record book bull. After all the excitement, Shane and I decided to break for lunch since he figured the moose would likely bed down in the middle of the day. Our time would come.

Jason radioed again while we were eating lunch and asked if we could help them find Rick's moose—they were having trouble locating it in the six-foot-high buck brush where it had dropped. We returned to the horses, saddled up, and rode in their direction but they found Rick's moose before we reached them. Since we were close, we joined them anyway to congratulate the hunter and admire the moose. We found Rick ecstatic with his big bull and his 260-yard shot, which he made from 15 feet up a swaying poplar.

We helped them quarter Rick's bull, and when we finished, it was prime time. We got back on our horses and headed back the way we'd come, stopping near our morning vantage point. Again we fought the buck brush to gain a peak near where we'd been that morning, then settled in to call for the last, golden hour of the day.

Jason joined us, calling with his megaphone-style call from the hilltop. We hoped the louder call would reach the bull that Shane felt sure was hiding in the distant timber. Shane and I glassed while Jason called, and it wasn't long before Shane hissed, "There's a huge bull coming out of the tree line at the end of the valley."

We weren't sure if it was just a coincidence or if the bull was really responding to the call. Daylight was fading fast, so everything had to work out perfectly for us to get a crack at that bull. The moose was coming towards the call, but not quickly enough. It wouldn't make it to our position before dark, so Shane and I decided to run to the next hill in an effort to intercept it. We donned our packs and raced down the hill, leaving Jason in place to keep the moose's attention focused away from us.

The next hill was taller and steeper than the one we had just descended, and the buck brush was thicker. I climbed as fast as possible, fighting the buck brush every step of the way. My legs and lungs were burning when I reached the top, but Shane told me to stay low and hurry. I knew the moose was close, and there was no way I just made that climb for nothing, so I took a deep breath and ran the last fifty meters, crouching as low as possible.

When I plopped down behind a tree at the top, I could see antlers snaking their way through the brush.

The bull was ambling towards us, moving steadily but not rushing, its attention focused on the distant hill where Jason was calling. I could track the bull's movements by its antlers, which towered over the brush and shone brightly in the setting sun. Our plan appeared to be working, but the moose was still too far away to shoot.

I kept looking ahead, trying to predict the bull's line of travel and hoping it would find a clearing, but there were only a few small openings. That's when I noticed the small creek that ran perpendicular to the hill. As long as the moose didn't climb the ridge opposite me, it would have to cross that creek somewhere, so I rested my .375 H&H in the crotch of a tree, trained the scope in the direction of the creek, and hoped for the best.

The bull's pace never wavered, and soon it was at the creek. "How far?" I asked.

"Three hundred and sixty-eight yards," Shane replied. "Can you make the shot?"

"Yes," I replied as I lined the crosshairs up on the bull's foreleg, accounted for the distance, and slowly squeezed the trigger. I felt good about the shot, and was surprised when it missed cleanly. I quickly worked the bolt, and as I did, I noticed that somehow the lever on my rear scope mount had come loose.

I quickly tightened the lever, held the same sight picture and squeezed off another shot. I was rewarded a second later with the sound of a solid hit. The moose stumbled out of the creek and I shot again, then once more as it turned away. That final 300-grain Trophy Bonded bullet dropped the moose, and just like that, we had done something that had never been done before in the history of B.C. Safaris—three hunters had taken three trophy moose in a single day.

I reached down to pick up my empty cases and caught sight of something else. The discarded peels of the orange I had eaten at lunch were on the ground right next to them. I remembered Shane's words from earlier that morning—that if we were patient, we would take a bull from this spot.

Grinning, Shane pointed out that had I just stayed there, I would have saved myself the arduous fight through the brush and the hard work on Rick's moose.

That night, we hunters sat by the fire—three friends who had been perfect strangers just seven days before—laughing, joking, and re-telling our hunting stories. We sat there until the last ember burned and the last tendril of smoke rose up toward the heavens and disappeared in the clear, cold air. Then we padded off to our bedrolls to dream of hunts past and hunts to come, and to relive that magical day when three hunters took three fantastic bulls in the heat of the rut.

Reprinted with permission of the author. To book a hunt through Greg Rodriguez's hunting agency, go to www.mbogo.net.

PART IV

Small Game

A Word Concerning Rabbit Hunting

GROVER CLEVELAND

Some hunters there are, of the super-refined and dudish sort, who deny to the rabbit any position among legitimate game animals; and there are others who, while grudgingly admitting rabbits to the list, seem to think it necessary to excuse their concession by calling them hares. I regard all this as pure affectation and nonsense. I deem it not beneath my dignity and standing as a reputable gunner to write of the rabbit as an entirely suitable member of the game community; and in doing so I am not dealing with hares or any other thing except plain, little every-day plebeian rabbits—sometimes appropriately called "cotton-tails." Though they may be "defamed by every charlatan" among hunters of self-constituted high degree, and despised by thousands who know nothing of their game qualities, I am not ashamed of their pursuit; and I count it by no means bad skill to force them by a successful shot to a topsy-turvy pause when at their best speed.

These sly little fellows feed at night, and during the day they hide so closely in grass or among rocks and brush that it is seldom they can be seen when at rest. Of course, no decent man will shoot a rabbit while sitting, and I have known them to refuse to start for anything less than a kick or punch. When they do start, however, they demonstrate quite clearly that they have kept their feet in the best possible position for a spring and run. After such a start the rabbit must in fairness be given an abundant chance to gain full headway, and when he has traversed the necessary distance for this, and is at his fastest gait, the hunter that shoots him has good reason to be satisfied with his marksmanship. I once actually poked one up and he escaped unhurt, though four loads of shot were sent after him.

In the main, however, dogs must be relied upon for the real enjoyment and success of rabbit hunting. The fastest dogs are not the best, because they are apt to chase the rabbit so swiftly and closely that he quickly betakes himself to a hole or other safe shelter, instead of relying upon his running ability. The baying of three or four good dogs steadily following a little cotton-tail should be as exhilarating and as pleasant to ears attuned to the music as if the chase were for bigger game. As the music is heard more distinctly, the hunter is allowed to flatter himself that his acute judgment can determine the route of the approaching game and the precise point from which an advantageous shot can be secured. The self-satisfied conceit aroused by a fortunate guess concerning this important detail, especially if supplemented by a fatal shot, should permit the lucky gunner to enjoy as fully the complacent pleasurable persuasion that the entire achievement is due to his sagacity, keenness and skill as though the animal circumvented were a larger beast. In either case the hunter experiences the delight born of a well-fed sense of superiority and self-pride; and this, notwithstanding all attempts to keep it in the background, is the most gratifying factor in every sporting indulgence.

Some people speak slightingly of the rabbit's eating qualities. This must be an abject surrender to fad or fashion. At any rate it is exceedingly unjust to the cotton-tail; and one who can relish tender chicken and refuse to eat a nicely cooked rabbit is, I believe, a victim of unfounded prejudices.

Why, then, should not rabbit hunting, when honorably pursued, be given a respectable place among gunning activities? It certainly has every element of rational outdoor recreation. It ministers to the most exhilarating and healthful exercise; it furnishes saving relief from care and overwork; it is free from wantonness and inexcusable destruction of animal life, and, if luck favors, it gives play to innocent but gratifying self-conceit.

Let us remember, however, that if rabbit hunting is to be a manly outdoor recreation, entirely free from meanness, and a sport in which a true hunter can indulge without shame, the little cotton-tail must in all circumstances be given a fair chance for his life.

Going After the Varying Hare
in Vermont's Snow Woods

NELSON BRYANT

It was cold, about six below zero. Deep in the woods, I was out of the wind, however, and comfortable even though standing still as I listened to the muffled baying of our beagle, Champ, who was plowing through the snow on the trail of a varying hare.

Champ was in the interior of a thick and extensive plantation of young spruces near Weston, on the northeastern edge of the Green Mountains. The plantation was too dense for a hunter on snowshoes to enter, so I was stationed on its outskirts waiting for the hare, or snowshoe rabbit, to emerge. Some distance away, also on the outskirts, were my companions—Bart Jacob of Winhall, Vermont, the dog's owner, and Niles Oesterle of Bennington, Vermont.

A vagrant gust of wind shot through the top of the tall spruce under which I waited, sending down a sparkling cascade of snow. The dog's voice rose and fell, and I tried in vain to pinpoint its location. I was unable to do so because on a similarly cold day more than thirty years ago, in the Battle of the Bulge, a German artillery shell exploding close by had ruined the hearing in my right ear. Receiving impulses from only one ear, the brain's computer cannot zero in on the direction of sound. So handicapped, I had no recourse but to remain where I was, hoping the rabbit would come my way.

I also knew that when there are several rabbits in a cover, some of the animals not being directly pursued by the beagle often move away from the sound of the chase, and sometimes in the course of a day's hunt these so-called "strays" provide most of the action. A half-hour after the dog had jumped the first rabbit, one of my companions fired twice, and in the hour following I heard two more shots. During all this the dog kept baying, so it seemed clear that either the hares had been missed entirely or strays had been taken. Ten minutes after the last of these shots, however, the dog fell silent, and I heard Jacob calling to me to come over to where he was. I shouted back that it would be simpler for him to come to me, and soon he and Oesterle appeared carrying three rabbits, Champ on a leash.

"I don't think Champ should hunt anymore," Jacob said. "He's got a sty on his eye, and he's cut it open."

The two hares shot by Oesterle had both been strays. Jacob's had not.

"I could have gotten a stray early in the hunt," Jacob said, "but I let it go. I often do this, because when the rabbit being chased finally is shot, I'll recall where I saw the stray and so will know where I can immediately put the dog on a fresh track. Of course, you can't always be sure you've got a stray coming at you.

"When I do shoot a rabbit I leave it there until the dog arrives—if he's going to arrive—because Champ enjoys finding something at the end of the line."

In the Northeast at the end of deer hunting (before the turn of the year) and waterfowl hunting (just after the turn of the year), cottontail and snowshoe rabbits are just about the only game that may still be sought. The larger and more athletic varying hare is a more challenging species to hunt than the cottontail rabbit, because the former runs faster and ranges wider, and because hunters usually follow it on snowshoes. Sometimes a few inches of new powder snow will cover a crust strong enough to support a man wearing only boots, but this does not happen often.

The snowshoe rabbit itself is not troubled by any snow conditions, because in fall the soles of its feet develop a heavy growth of hair that, coupled with its huge hind feet, serve as "snowshoes."

This hare adapts to winter in another way as well: in the fall its brown summer pelage begins to change to white, and the transformation continues until the only dark fur left is on the tips of its ears. The change is brought about by the shortening of daylight and will occur even if the days are warm and without snow. The reverse shift occurs in spring. Each alteration takes about eight weeks.

Deer hunters in the bare woods of November are well aware of the varying hare's pelage change. The snow-white animals show up for incredible distances in the brown woods. Indeed, late fall is just about the only time that the hunter without a dog will have any success going after snowshoe rabbits, for when they are sitting motionless in the snow they are nearly impossible to spot.

In New York State and northern New England the varying-hare breeding season begins near the end of February. The gestation period is thirty-seven days, and the latest litters—three litters a season seem to be the average—may be born as late as early October. The litter size varies from one to six, and the leverets, young hares, are born with full fur and eyes open, alert and able to walk and hop. Varying hares do not build nests; the female simply makes a depression on the forest floor.

Varying-hare populations dropped precipitously in all but the remotest regions of the Northeast when it was settled and land cleared for agriculture. Now, with farm land reverting back to woods in many places, good hare habitats are being created.

Varying hares require dense stands of conifers—spruces seem to be most favored—from 6 to 16 feet high as their base cover. They emerge from this base area at night to forage for food—a wide variety of plants, and buds of trees and shrubs—and during this foraging they use taller stands of conifers as avenues of travel. They dislike open spaces, and research has shown that even a two-lane highway is an effective barrier to them. The desire for overhead cover is undoubtedly born of a fear of attack from the air.

Once in a while, however, you will note where hares seem to lose some of their caution. Not far from where we hunted, near an abandoned beaver pond, I found a set of hare tracks in the open, in a gully beside a logging road. The tracks went west until they encountered another set coming from the opposite direction. The two animals had met and cavorted in the snow for a while, and then one had plunged across the open road into the alder swamp beyond. The onset of the mating season almost certainly accounts for this exuberant behavior.

Only a few weeks are now left for snowshoe-rabbit hunting in Vermont. But Jacob said, as we shuffled up the last hill toward our car, that the final week of the season was often the best time, for, among other things, the warmer weather makes it easier for the dog to follow the scent.

Whether in January or March, however, varying-hare hunting has a singular appeal to those who like the woods to themselves. The deer-hunting hordes have departed, and one will usually go all day without seeing anyone save those in his own party. Sometimes the silence will be shattered by the snarl of a snowmobile, but the operator of this machine usually runs well-defined trails or logging roads, and a snowmobile cannot negotiate much of the thick cover the hare hunter must visit. Also, though one sometimes encounters cross-country skiers or snowshoers wandering through the trackless, snow-filled woods, most of them congregate at various skiing centers and dutifully pursue one another along marked courses.

Deep in a stand of young spruces, waiting for the sharp yelp of the beagle to signal that the chase has begun, one revels in a white silence broken only by the thumps of snow that have slid from heavily laden branches or the cheerful cries of chickadees that cannot resist a close inspection of the intruder in their domain.

Then, when such a hunt is done, some closing ritual is proper. In our case, as we lounged in the brilliant midafternoon sunlight, the ritual involved a few bottles of imported beer and a batch of fat oysters I had brought with me from Martha's Vineyard. Having spread a burlap bag on the hood of Jacob's car, I shucked the bivalves open, and Jacob, who is a partner in the Tabusintac camps, a hunting and fishing lodge in New Brunswick, pronounced them as good as those from Tabusintac Bay.

Eating raw oysters in the mountains is always a special experience; they seem particularly precious so far removed from the ebb and flow of the tide.

Our little feast done, we drank a toast to Champ, who had done remarkably well on a cold day, and as we parted my companions invited me to join them in Vermont's forthcoming spring season for wild turkeys.

Squirrel Hunting: The Making of Young Hunters

JIM CASADA

A great American sporting scribe, Archibald Rutledge, once suggested that the ideal solution to so-called father-and-son problems lay in teaching boys to be hunters. Referring to his experiences with his three boys and his determination to do his best by them, "I decided primarily to make them sportsmen, for . . . To be a sportsman is a mighty long step in the direction of being a man." Old Flintlock, as friends and family knew him, believed that hunting was the finest legacy a father could leave his offspring. It is my fixed conviction, he argued, that if a parent can give his children a passionate and wholesome devotion to the outdoors, the fact that he cannot leave each of them a fortune does not really matter. They will always enjoy life in its nobler aspects without money and without price.

If one agrees with Rutledge's philosophy, and I suspect that anyone with much experience afield would readily concur, the next logical question focuses on appropriate steps to take in the shaping and molding of a hunter. This involves many considerations: gun safety, sporting ethics, woodsmanship, marksmanship and the like. One of the finest ways to address all these matters while giving a youngster plenty of opportunities for action and every likelihood of a lifelong love of sport is through squirrel hunting. The sport runs as a bright thread through the fabric of American history. Hardy frontiersmen sharpened their shooting eyes and secured food for the table through hunting bushytails. The animals were incredibly abundant, thanks in large measure to vast forests dominated by that now-vanished giant, the American chestnut. The standard practice was to "bark" squirrels. This involved choosing a bushytail perched on a low limb or near the base of a tree as one's target, then firing into the bark immediately beneath the animal. Accurate shots would stun or kill the squirrel with flying bark. This sensible practice had dual merits—no meat was damaged and the hunter could retrieve his lead bullet to be melted down and recast.

Such hunting required superb marksmanship combined with equally adept woodsmanship, and it was accomplished in these skills have played a key role in American wars from the Revolution right down into the modern era. For example, the Overmountain Boys, a group of highly skilled hunters whose efforts proved vital in defeating British forces at the pivotal Revolutionary War battles of Cowpens and Kings Mountain, came from the Appalachian backwoods of what today are parts of Tennessee and Kentucky. Moving through the woods like wraiths and firing with the same deadly accuracy they employed when squirrel hunting, they proved an elusive and deadly foe that left the Redcoats in disarray.

Jumping ahead to World War I, America's most decorated civilian soldier, Alvin Cullum York, a quiet country lad who had grown up hunting, braved the deadly killing fields of the Western Front and single-handedly killed 25 Germans, captured 132 more, and took 35 enemy machine guns. In the same conflict, staunch mountain lads who had hunted squirrels and roamed hardwood forests from boyhood formed the heart of the 117th Infantry that stopped German forces at the critical Battle of the Bulge. More recently, a man of my personal acquaintance who learned his shooting savvy and fieldcraft through countless days spent in the late autumn and winter woods saw three tours of duty in Viet Nam. For the first two he served as a sniper and the third one found him training other snipers. He is, quite simply, the finest woodsman I have ever known. Interestingly enough, he still ranks squirrel hunting as one of the sports he enjoys most. Individuals such as these—and there were countless others—were able to perform their daring deeds and earned the lasting gratitude of their country thanks to the fact that they possessed special skills. These skills included stealth, keen eyesight, a knack for hearing and immediately identifying woodland sounds, and appreciation of the habits and preferred habitat of the animals they hunted, superb marksmanship and the ability to remain perfectly motionless for extended periods of time. In short, they were woodsmen of the first order, and their woods-wise attributes were a direct product of long, patient hours spent hunting squirrels.

Today the sport has faded from the popularity it once enjoyed (as recently as 1960 squirrel hunting ranked as the most popular type of hunting in almost two dozen states), thanks in no small measure to the remarkable comeback stories of wild turkeys and the white-tailed deer. Nonetheless, squirrels remain incredibly abundant over much of the country, and that consideration, together with the tidbits of history noted above, suggest that squirrel hunting is an ideal way to mold and make a young hunter.

A youngster whose sporting apprenticeship involves a lot of squirrel hunting will learn much about the woods, for becoming consistently successful in the sport requires precisely the same abilities that will serve one well with bigger, more elusive quarries such as turkeys or deer. Moreover, with proper exposure, the youthful hunter will soon realize that he is involved in an ongoing learning process that will continue as long as he takes to the fields and woods. The dean of American camping, Horace Kephart, summed matters up nicely when he stated: "In the school of the outdoors there is no graduation day."

An ideal way to get a budding hunter started in the sport is with some pre-season forays into the autumn woods where he is an observer rather than hunter. It is easier to move through the forest unseen and unheard at this time of year, thanks to the fact that hardwoods still retain their leaves. This means squirrels are less likely to spot you at a distance. It also makes for quieter movement than is likely to be the case once dry leaves cover the forest floor, and at this season the tell-tale sights and sounds of dropping nuts or shaking limbs are a big help in locating the treetop tricksters. Some basic lessons regarding nut cuttings ("sign"), the location of nests and den trees, and general observations of squirrel behavior will be a real plus once actual hunting takes place. Ideally a mixture of still hunting and stalking should be employed once the apprentice actually goes hunting, and it might be best to take a youngster a few times as an observer and "helper" before putting a gun in his hand. Recollections of my first hunt when I actually carried a gun, a borrowed .410, remain as warm as that late October morning was cold. Seated shoulder-to-shoulder with my father, we watched and waited as the sun turned a heavy frost into a woodland sparkling with diamonds. Then, as the woods began to come alive, a nearby sound caught my attention. Carefully and slowly turning my head, as I had been taught, I spied a big old boar bushytail easing down the side of a shagbark hickory. "Ease your gun up and remember to squeeze the trigger when you're on him," Dad said. Moments later he was giving me a proud pat on the back as we admired my first squirrel. For me, as I suspect is true for countless others of my generation, the moment remains a magic one, transcended only by the day when I shared a similar experience with my daughter.

Those are the sort of memories (and training) every youngster deserves. A good introduction to still hunting comes by taking a position in close proximity to a mast-laden hickory or a grove of oaks, while old logging roads, ridge tops and river bottoms all lend themselves to effective stalking. As a rule, particularly if you have done a bit of homework in advance, action will be frequent enough to satisfy the sometimes short attention span of eager youngsters, and it is always important to remember that fun, along with safety, comes first and foremost. Make sure the hunt is enjoyable and there is every likelihood that you will be making a sportsman for life.

There is no set age at which a boy or girl is ready for their first gun, but usually it is somewhere between the ages of nine and twelve. Strict attention to sporting ethics should be a part of the educational process, and that means focusing on taking clean shots, shooting accurately and cleaning and eating the kill. Of course, once the ravenous appetites of youth have sampled the delights of dishes such as squirrel and dumplings, the latter will become a welcome part of the experience.

In time, the young hunter should reach a point where he can venture into the woods along or at least separate from his adult mentor when they go hunting. If possible, it is a good idea to include some hunting with a dog as a part of the overall introduction to squirrel hunting. A boy with a capable canine companion will know joys beyond compare. Make it a point to relive each hunt afterwards, quietly discussing what was observed and learned. Work in exposure to finding one's way in remote terrain, and while afield pay attention not only to squirrels and squirrel sign but other evidence of wildlife—deer trails, rubs or scrapes; turkey droppings or scratching; or maybe something as simple as eating a few sticky, sweet persimmons, picking frost-nipped pawpaws, or gathering black walnuts to be cracked later.

What you are doing, after all, is shaping a member of the next generation of hunters, and though we too seldom think of it in that light, being a part of that process is an awesome responsibility. Properly done though, the education of a youthful sportsman is as rewarding as it is important. You will reap a deep sense of inner satisfaction through knowing, as Archibald Rutledge put it in his inimitable fashion, that you have given a youngster a gift—hunting—that "inculcates patience, demands discipline and iron nerve, and develops a serenity of spirit that makes for long life and a long love of life." Those are qualities all of us would like for our offspring to possess, and one of the finest ways to make this happen is through providing them with an apprenticeship in squirrel hunting. Savvy in the ways of the wilds and trained in the school of the woods, the young Nimrod will have acquired skills that bring ample rewards throughout all his years.

Shotgun Versus .22 Rifle for Squirrels

The decision on whether to use a shotgun or a .22 when hunting squirrels is to a certain degree a matter of personal preference. Each has its special attributes as well as shortcomings. A shotgun makes sound sense when leaves are still on the trees and getting a full view of a bushytail can be problematic. Similarly, a scattergun has obvious advantages when dealing with a fleeing squirrel or one busily scurrying along a limb or the forest floor. A .22, on the other hand, places more of a premium on marksmanship (something that should certainly be stressed to young hunters), and a properly placed shot between the shoulders or in the head leaves the meat undamaged. Also, longer shots are possible with a rifle, and unlike the situation with a shotgun, you only need to see a small part of the squirrel (its head) to take a telling shot. When hunting in pairs, especially if you are using a dog, it makes sense for one hunter to carry a shotgun and the other a .22. That way you are ideally equipped to deal both with squirrels that hide high up in a tree and those that decide to light a shuck for the next county.

Different Tactics for Hunting Squirrels

A wide variety of tactics can be used to good effect when hunting squirrels. Whenever possible, it is a good idea to expose beginners to all of them. Here's a brief listing of the most popular techniques.

*Still-hunting. Probably the most popular approach to squirrel, still-hunting involves getting comfortably situated in a prime spot, such as near a den tree or in an area where mast is plentiful, and waiting for squirrels to appear. It is vital to keep still and remain constantly alert.

*Stalking. This involves easing through the woods looking and listening for your prey. It is best accomplished when leaves are still on the trees or when a recent rain makes near-silent movement through the woods possible. Old logging roads through forests are ideal for this approach.

*Hunting in pairs.

*Hunting with dogs.

Some Thoughts on Safety

When I first started squirrel hunting, my father rationed out shells to me one at a time. Once he decided I was ready to be in the woods by myself, maybe over the next ridge from him, that practice continued.

Never mind the fact that my gun was a single-shot .22, he knew that having only one shell would make me select my shot with great care. He explained this in detail, strongly hinting that to fire a shot and then sneak back to him asking for another shell without a squirrel in hand was something that just shouldn't happen. There were misses, but not many of them, and all the while I was learning the vital lessons of careful shot selection and making absolutely sure of one's target. All of this was accompanied by plenty of common sense instruction in gun safety. There was also one period of painful probation when I had the first gun of my own, a little .410, taken away for a time after getting caught crossing a fence without unloading it. You will have to decide how best to approach issues of gun safety, appropriate respect for the quarry, and related issues, but they should be an integral part of the hunting experience from the outset.

Reprinted with permission of the author. Jim Casada has written or edited more than forty books. Readers can order his books by going to his website, www.jimcasadaoutdoors.com. His website offers a free monthly e-newsletter.

Daybreak

RON ELLIS

I can never remember being late for a hunt. We may have been late for everything else in our lives, but we were never late for opening day. Maybe once or twice we were delayed in getting away from home so that we found ourselves hurrying along, in a race with the sun to reach the ridge top. But we always made it on time, with the Mercury rolling to a stop where the road ended, right in front of the old two-story white frame house with the big front porch that the Morgan boys called home. We sat there listening to the soft ticking of the Mercury's engine as it cooled down after the long run upriver. The woods, stretched out along the spine of the ridge that ran for more than a mile to the east, straight to the town of Persimmon Gap, were still black smudges against a developing gray sky, floating out there above Mercury on the hood. There was no mistaking the sound or the feel of it all.

Often, Stony's voice greeted us from out of the darkness. He would have seen our headlights coming down the road as he sat there on the front porch in the dark smoking his first cigarette of the day and sipping a cup of thick black coffee.

"Mornin', boys," he would yell. "Thought you might be up today. Good wet day to hunt." He would leave the porch and make his way through the grass to the car in the darkness, juggling a big white coffee mug in his left hand, and extend his free hand to Dad. They would shake and then Dad would pour himself a cup of coffee from the red thermos. They would both lean against the car and talk some in low voices and sip at their coffee and smoke, until Stony decided it was time to let us go.

"The light's comin' fast. You'd best be gettin' in the woods. Don't let me keep you. Come up to the house before you go. Sherm'll want to see you." He would retrace his steps to the house and retreat through the screen door into the rectangle of yellow light that was the kitchen. The last sound was of the screen door slapping shut against the doorframe, the big spring resonating in the dark.

In the car trunk—we called it the "boot" in those days—Dad kept the shotguns in green canvas cases: a pair of sweet little .410 pumps—a Sears Roebuck Ted Williams model for me and Dad's dream gun, a Winchester Model 42. The guns were stored on top of a big cardboard box, which was neatly filled with the important things we would need for the day's hunt: boxes of shotgun shells, canvas shell vests, the dependable Army canteen snug in its worn and faded green canvas sleeve, extra socks, olive drab cotton bandanas, cigars, and Snickers bars.

The taking of the gear from the trunk was done with a great deal of ceremony. Dad poured himself another cup of coffee from the thermos, lit a cigarette, and then stood quietly for a few moments just studying the darkness and listening. Though I was close by, I suspect he was, during those brief moments, very much alone with his memories and with familiar sounds and voices I could not hear. We spent some time loading our vests with shells—green Remington shells for me and blue Peters hulls for Dad—and taking care in assembling the rest of our equipment. We sprayed the tops of our green canvas caps and the cuffs of our pants and shirts with insect repellent, as much to discourage ticks, or so we thought, as the mosquitoes. Dad finished his last cup of coffee and another cigarette as we stood there in the dark.

We traded shotgun shells, without fail, before going into the woods on every hunt. It was a good luck ritual, a wish for a successful and safe hunt. We placed the "good luck shells," which is what Dad called them, into the magazines of the .410s and shucked them into the chambers, the little guns clicking and throwing metallic echoes into the hills that came back to us in the dark. And then we were ready.

We went into the big woods behind the barn by crossing through a low-hanging barbed wire fence that was just three loose rusting strands stretched between a fence post on the right and a head-high tree limb attached to an old hay barn on the left. This limb had been cut from the Osage orange trees that grew along the pasture on the river side of the woven-wire fence and it had been worn smooth by much handling over the years. The height and the position of the wire remained constant year after year, and once there was white deer hair wedged between the barbs. It was satisfying to know a deer had traveled through those woods, stopping at the fence, as we always did, listening and studying the woods ahead, testing the air, and then crossing the wire and leaving a tuft of hair, the only sign of its passing. Once we passed through the wire, the trip home seemed complete. We could begin to seriously hunt, focusing our attentions on the woods and listening for the whoosh! of sweeping tree limbs as squirrels made their way from den trees to feeding areas.

We stood perfectly still in the darkness listening to rainwater dripping from the trees and watching for light on the eastern horizon. We speculated, in whispers, on how many squirrels we might see and wondered if we would be lucky enough to have the river fog blanketing the ridges to hide our movements until well after first light. The fog up there hung close to the ground out in front of us. Coming up from the meadows below we heard the stuttering rhythm of cowbells as the animals grazed along through the steep pastures. I stood perfectly still and listened and wished again that nothing here would ever change and that this moment I lived for all year long would remain as sweet as it was for as long as I needed it. It was exciting, always, to see the day developing, like a photograph appearing in the white of the developer tray, glimpses of light and distorted black blobs at first, and then the whole image taking form out of a crack of light tracing the treeline to the east.

Then we heard the squirrels jumping through the rain-soaked foliage as they left their den trees—large, brooding beeches down below us, their lightning-struck tops jutting up like broken, decaying teeth—and then moving along a network of limbs, "traveling" is what we called it, toward the nut trees. We could see the squirrels as they came closer, jumping from tree to tree, bridging the sometimes incredibly long distances between the trees with their outstretched bodies, and then becoming specks, just dark silhouettes, moving silently along through the tops of the tallest trees. We waited to see which direction they were headed, trying to determine the trees they might be feeding in before we moved along the trail any further. At this point in the hunt, I always imagined Daniel Boone standing there on the same ridge, squirrel rifle in hand, waiting to "bark" a squirrel from a hickory limb at fifty paces with a musket ball. I had heard the old timers say during their front porch story sessions at the Persimmon Gap General Store that "Boone damn sure had hunted up in those woods." I believed it, too, because I was sure I could feel the ancient rhythms and detect another presence in the woods. The old timers said it was so and that it had been told to them when they were young by the old folks who knew about these things.

In August the squirrels were mostly feeding on hickory nuts in Cogan's Woods, which was filled with old shagbark hickories along the ridge tops and fence lines, and with slender tight-barked pig nut hickories in greater numbers along the flats and at the edges of clearings. The larger nuts of the shagbarks made loud soft thumps in the earth when dropped from the highest limbs of the tallest trees by feeding squirrels, a cherished sound, one that was heard in the ears long after the season had closed, especially in winter when snow-muffled dreams were filled with the expectations of the coming season. When "cutting a nut," the squirrel's teeth, long incisors capable of reducing the tough husks of hickory nuts to fine litter, made a familiar squeaking sound that never failed to put smiles on our faces. When we heard it, we listened more intently and tried to mark the exact tree where the squirrels were feeding. Once located, we moved on, with greater care and concern for where we placed our feet.

I always followed in Dad's boot tracks in the early days. It seemed I spent more time watching his back and trying to guess when he would stop so I would not stumble over his feet and make enough noise to run off all the squirrels in all of Belden County. He always had a smile on his face when he had located the feeding areas. He would turn toward me and point his right index finger toward his ear, pretend to cut a hickory nut, and then point up toward the trees ahead of us. His next motion would be a finger placed silently before his lips, finished off with a grin and, likely as not, his hand fishing for a smoke in his shirt pocket. Dad often smoked a big black Ibold cigar on these hunts, and its heavy strong smoke drifted back over his shoulder and across my brow, lingering and said it was so and that it had been told to them when they were young by the old folks who knew about these things.

In August the squirrels were mostly feeding on hickory nuts in Cogan's Woods, which was filled with old shagbark hickories along the ridge tops and fence lines, and with slender tight-barked pig nut hickories in greater numbers along the flats and at the edges of clearings. The larger nuts of the shagbarks made loud soft thumps in the earth when dropped from the highest limbs of the tallest trees by feeding squirrels, a cherished sound, one that was heard in the ears long after the season had closed, especially in winter when snow-muffled dreams were filled with the expectations of the coming season. When "cutting a nut," the squirrel's teeth, long incisors capable of reducing the tough husks of hickory nuts to fine litter, made a familiar squeaking sound that never failed to put smiles on our faces. When we heard it, we listened more intently and tried to mark the exact tree where the squirrels were feeding. Once located, we moved on, with greater care and concern for where we placed our feet.

I always followed in Dad's boot tracks in the early days. It seemed I spent more time watching his back and trying to guess when he would stop so I would not stumble over his feet and make enough noise to run off all the squirrels in all of Belden County. He always had a smile on his face when he had located the feeding areas. He would turn toward me and point his right index finger toward his ear, pretend to cut a hickory nut, and then point up toward the trees ahead of us. His next motion would be a finger placed silently before his lips, finished off with a grin and, likely as not, his hand fishing for a smoke in his shirt pocket. Dad often smoked a big black Ibold cigar on these hunts, and its heavy strong smoke drifted back over his shoulder and across my brow, lingering and mixing with the heavy dampness in the morning air. I could see the smoke and watch the paths it took on the air currents, and it was easy to see how scent could travel in so many different directions in the woods.

Walking the trails in silence was a skill not easily learned, particularly in those years when drought made the leaves so dry and crumbly it was as if we were trying to sneak along on a bed of potato chips. These trails we traveled had known, no doubt, the cautious, careful steps of Indian moccasins. As a kid of the 1950s, I was more than familiar with the Indian's legendary stealth. This was something known to every boy in Kentucky, whether from the many tales told to us by our parents and grandparents, or through the TV exploits of Fess Parker as the legendary pioneers Davy Crockett and Daniel Boone. It was known, too, in local legends that these same trails, which offered commanding views of the Ohio River and the valley below, had served as travel routes for parties of Indians, primarily Shawnee from north of the river, during incursions into the "dark and bloody ground," as "Caintucke" was sometimes called back then, to hunt or to slow the influx of settlers floating down the Ohio in flat boats to reach river ports to the west.

We drank silently of the sounds and smells of the country we had dreamt about and yearned for so many nights down river. I loved the fresh smell and look of the woods, especially after a morning rain, with the newly washed grasses of the fields a brilliant green and the abandoned rusted farm equipment shoved tight against the tree line, as if resting in the shadows that ran out from the woods and traveled into the meadows and lipped away over the ridge to the railroad tracks and the river below. We stood there for as long as it took us to feel satisfied, and then we moved farther into the woods through a passageway of wet foliage and emerged beneath a dripping canopy of hickory, wild cherry, and maple.

Dad was a sentimental man with a great heart. His whole life, or so it seemed to me, was an honest attempt to illuminate for me some of the best things in life, at least as he saw them, those little things in a person's life that went mainly unnoticed and unappreciated by so many people. He loved to point out the names of the trees and plants we encountered in Cogan's Woods. There were many, and he knew most of them: ginseng, staghorn sumac, wild grapes, ferns, beech, ash, wild cherry, poplar, hickory, blackberry and raspberry canes, Devil's toothbrush, persimmon trees, and paw paw patches, to name a few of his favorites. His eyes danced when he talked about the plants and the trees and about the people he had shared these woods with over the years. I was injected with his enthusiasm for the telling, and I listened with my heart.

On one particularly wet morning, the squirrels were cutting on large green hickory nuts—the kind with deeply etched lines that quarter the husks and that smell so strongly of wet greenery in the damp morning air—and we could hear them making all this noise from a long way off. As we crept closer, I saw that the top of the largest hickory was "alive" with squirrels. The highest branches of the tree scratched at the sky and stood in a group of three old shellbarks—their bark old and loose, peeling away from the trunk and turning up at the ends. I counted five gray squirrels before they began crossing through each other and jumbling up the count, just one short of that mythical limit I was always chasing.

Those squirrels were cutting so furiously that the hull litter sounded like a fine rain coming down through the hickory's broad green leaves.

"It's raining," Dad said, a big grin on his face. "You ready?"

"Sure," I said, smiling back. I thought that surely he could hear my heart beating through my shirt and shell vest.

"We'll split up and cover both sides of the tree. You on the right over there and me over here."

"Shoot the lowest one first?" I asked.

"Always. But make sure it's high enough off the ground to be safe. Higher . . ."

". . . than a tall man's head topped with a top hat," I said, finishing one of his favorite rules.

Dad smiled and raised the thumb of his right hand. The woods were noisy now. A blue jay squawked in the top of a beech tree, a church bell rang in Persimmon Gap, and a rooster crowed from across the river.

The squirrels were so busy with their feeding that we slipped through the woods and were almost on top of them before one of them saw us and began barking, cracking its tail furiously, while hanging on the side of the biggest hickory. He was up high enough to offer a safe shot. He left the tree on my side and the .410 pump went to my shoulder and at the shot he tumbled out of the sky in the middle of a leap, hitting the earth just after the slender blue paper hull, my "good luck shell," was ejected into the leaves. The rest of the squirrels scattered and either attempted to leave the tree or to hide, flattening their bodies out along the limbs, almost becoming the bark, their skin pressed so tightly to it. Dad took the next one as it leapt from the very top of the tree, its body crumpling short of the freedom offered by the nearby limbs of another hickory. The third one decided to hide. He killed that one as it hunched in the crotch of two large limbs, thinking it would go undetected so silent was it, except for the movement of its tail, the very edges of the downy fur ruffling ever so lightly in the morning breeze. It was enough.

The fourth one popped around my side of the tree. I made a quick shot that surprised both me and the squirrel, as the young gray dropped and lay motionless at the base of the tree. I pumped another shell into the chamber and missed one as it ran out a low limb headed for the safety of a nearby oak. He leapt from the side of the oak and ran out through the leaves down over the hill. I heard him bounding off in the dry leaves—never stopping, never looking back. Then there was a strange stillness, the kind of quiet that comes after so much noise and commotion in once quiet woods.

We gutted the squirrels with our pocketknives and poured water from the canteen into the exposed cavities and wiped the red muscled meat with folded paper towels. We threaded the squirrels onto our brass laundry pins and snapped them to our belts. The squirrels hung down and bumped against the front of our legs, staining our pants with flecks of dark red. We buried the towels with the entrails in the loose soil in the woods and covered the place with downed tree limbs.

"This is a good feeling," Dad said. "Yet, I always want to put them back in the trees so that I can come back another day and find them just the way we found them today." He picked up his beloved Winchester and slipped two fresh Peters shells into the magazine. He checked the safety and cradled the shotgun in the crook of his left arm. From his pants pocket he pulled out one of the spent shells, the green Remington "good luck shell" I had given him that morning, and rubbed it between his thumb and forefinger. As always, he held it to his nose and sniffed at the powder residue, as if by doing so he could keep the recent memory close, a reminder of a good day with its bittersweet moments.

"Let's sneak into the Grove," Dad whispered. He pocketed the shell and bent under a low-hanging limb of a young hickory that was heavy with the morning's rain. Water ran off the leaves and an orange spider clung to the center of its web, which was dotted with hundreds of tiny clear beads of water. Dad pushed the limb aside and held it back for me to pass, then returned it to its former position. I looked back at the spider and saw that it was making repairs to the web, which had been damaged with the bending of the limb. The spider continued to work and we slipped along the wet path, our eyes raised to the first light raining down through the tallest trees.

Excerpted from *Cogan's Woods;* reprinted with permission of the author.

New Wilderness

DAVID FOSTER

Dad called. "Let's go up to the home place. Bag some squirrels."

The home place is only that. A place. A weedy knoll on a hillock, about a mile down two overgrown ruts from State Highway 85. Dad was raised here while his father sharecropped for old man Minter. The family lived in a rickety, worn wood house that slouched heavily on its field-stone foundation beneath two spreading oaks. The oaks are still there. The house seems to have dissolved. Piece by piece stolen away by neighbors in search of fix-it wood or nature in search of rot. Even the field stones are gone, stickery weeds and stunted young oaks starved for sunlight taking their place.

We parked under the oaks and followed a deer trail down through the pines toward a stand of old, tall hardwoods dad called the "woodlot." It was Dad's favorite place to hunt squirrels. Had been for almost 70 years, wars and school and stints in distant cities notwithstanding.

"We hunted squirrel a lot when I was a boy," he said as we walked. "Papa didn't like it though. Preferred we shot rabbit. More meat on a rabbit. We'd find 'em in the bed and try to shoot their noses off. Squirrels were more fun. Smarter. Harder to hit. Harder to kill. You had to shoot straight. You only got three cartridges for a yard egg. You waste 'em and you could get a whipping. Meat hunting and Papa's belt led you to shoot straight. Real straight."

Sharecropping meant that old man Minter got two-thirds of whatever cotton Dad's dad grew. Some years they shared some corn as well. The other third was given over to various other holders of debt who would then extend just enough new debt to get the family through the winter so they could start all over again.

My dad remembers those years as good ones. I couldn't imagine it any other way myself. Life out here, in this game rich wilderness, had to have been good, farming aside, of course. Maybe better than good. I said so.

Dad smiled. "Wasn't a wilderness then. This was a community. This pine thicket was the close-in field. The far field was on the other side of Sweetwater Creek. The woodlot was the only real forest for miles. Back then this was all cotton fields and houses in every direction. Twenty or thirty families.

"The Minters lived down on what's now 85. Big three-story house. Handsome place. Over across the highway, which in those days was the farm road we drove in on, lived the Dukes. I took a shine early on to Eunice Dukes and her daddy never trusted me much after that. Some folks whose name I forget lived down in the hollow there and Lisbon Baptist Church was up on the other side of the hill. I remember when it burned.

"Over where the road crosses the creek, Sam Nations—your grandma got him confused with damn nations—had a white-washed two-story house. Heard my first radio program there. Jack Dempsey fight. Battery operated radio. Delcos, they were. I helped string the antenna.

"Lots of folks here then. You stand up here in the field and you heard kids playing, mules bellowing, folks shouting across the field."

It was hard to believe. From the homeplace back to Fayetteville there is hardly a house. Only rolling woodlands punctuated by a few pastures. Now the land is subdivided by deer hunting clubs instead of cotton fields.

"We lived here until '24. That's when the boll weevil moved in and we moved out. Mother nature, she just took the whole place back over. Gave it up to the critters. More game here now than we ever saw."

"Lots of squirrels," I said.

"That ain't the start of it. Deer. And turkey. Folks had long since killed them all when I was a kid. Deer are pests now. Back then, a deer would have been a godsend. Lord what your grandma would have given for a deer. Or a turkey. Best of all a turkey." Dad laughed. "Of course, we'd never seen a turkey, so if one came up it woulda probably scared us to death. No, squirrel and rabbit were pretty much the menu."

We shot four squirrels that day. Enough for dumplings. Dad got three with his old Stevens, as he sat at the base of a tall sweetgum. He mumbled once about what a pretty girl Eunice Dukes was. I couldn't help but think it must have been the best of both worlds, being my dad there under that tree, dead in the middle of his two favorite places: the old community and the new wilderness.

The Rabbit Runners

T. EDWARD NICKENS

"I don't like to hunt with a hungry man," Dungee Taylor says. He's a bull-sized fellow, bald, with one foot in the briers and a grin on his face, but I can read between the lines. His comment is both a statement of fact and an admonition: don't shoot too soon. Let the dogs have their fun. After all, that's the point of turning out 14 finely tuned beagles with a single thing on their minds—finding every rabbit on this patch of the planet.

"We're not out here to shoot everything we see," Taylor sings out. "We just want to teach these dogs how smart a rabbit really is." And with that, both feet go into the briers, and 240 pounds of denimclad rabbit hunter disappear into the tangled brambles along North Carolina's Neuse River.

As I fight through curtains of thorny smilax and blackberry, the beagles worm through briar so thick a breeze couldn't sneak through—an entire dog pack reduced to white-tipped tails senmaphoring in the brush. Good rabbit dogs rely on their eyes as much as their noses. At times I can see them looking for game; they burrow their snouts into every nook and cranny, then suddenly their heads are up, eyes dissecting the thicket for any sign of a rabbit. I can hear their heavy snorting as they siphon the air for scent.

They're hot onto something, but it seems to me that they've covered every inch of ground to no avail. Then Cassie, Taylor's "A-number-one jump dog," suddenly pushes a bunny from its bed not 10 feet from my bootlaces. Cassie opens up with a bawling cry. In seconds the rest of the pack honors the find, rushing to the hot scent. Rip booms out a guttural bass line of affirmation. PeeWee and Blondie add their high-pitched "chop" to the chorus. The pack is off, and the race is on.

Rabbit hunting with beagles is a coast-to-coast American tradition. From the alder thickets of the Northeast Kingdom of Vermont to the Mojave Desert scrub, from Dixie's swamp woods to the Midwest's endless farms, the sport assumes the vernacular character of whatever field it's played on. It can be done with one dog or a large pack. But a few things hold, no matter the region. Rabbit hunting is a congenial pursuit, commonly undertaken by a small group of hunters whose connections to each other cross multiple generations. It demands a chess player's logic and a gunslinger's reflexes.

Square off with a wild rabbit, and the deck is firmly stacked against you. Cottontails can exhibit blazing speed—they run up to 35 mph—and when that's not enough of a safety margin, they call on agility, camouflage, and an impressive capacity for strategic thinking. Rabbits feed mostly at night, and dawn finds them slinking into the thickest, gnarliest brier-thatched cover they can find. On cold days they seek a sunny, south-facing slope. There they hollow out a small bowl-shaped nest called a *form* and hunker down until dark.

The one chink in the rabbit's armor, however, is its well-known habit of circling back to the very patch of ground where it was jumped. A prize rabbit dog—using its extraordinary sense of smell—can pinpoint the loafing bunny, startle it to a chase, and ultimately run it past the hunter on stand.

Of course, a lot can happen between the first bawling cry of a beagle and the crack of a shotgun, and Taylor has seen it all. Now 49 years old, he learned to rabbit hunt under the eyes of his grandfather, who would place him against a sturdy tree so the recoil of a 12-gauge wouldn't knock the six-year-old boy down. "I just fell in love with it," Taylor recalls.

The Taylor family is still known for its love of beagle packs, and Dungee's father, Edward, and uncle Bill still hunt with him. "Growing up," his uncle Bill tells me, "we were hunting for the pot. And we hunted rabbits, coons, possums, and any bird big enough to clean." Days spent behind a mule and plow were followed by nights chasing dogs through the big woods, and the dogs were in the game for more than sport, too. "Back then the dogs were poor—hungry all the time—and they would run the daylights out of anything, yes, sir," Bill says. He grins behind dark sunglasses, his smile turning the corners of trim lambchop sideburns. The beagles weren't the only ones with limited resources. "We didn't hardly have any shells. We used sticks, rocks, whatever we could to save those shells. The dogs would run 'em so hard, they'd go into holes, and that's what you wanted them to do. We'd just dig them up."

These days, of course, running bunnies with beagles has more to do with the hunt and the hound music than filling an empty belly, and modern rabbit hunters have definite—and differing—ideas about what makes a good dog tick. Some dogs are particularly adept at scent trailing once a rabbit hits the road; others make a name for themselves through an ability to find and jump rabbits from the bed. When a rabbit changes course dramatically, some dogs naturally tend to hunt back and forth for the new scent trail. Others stay on the track, noses glued to the ground, and take longer to decipher the mystery.

With hounds in pursuit, a rabbit first pours on the speed to gain ground and a little bit of thinking room. That's when the fun begins. Cottontails are notorious for their cunning when chased, and their daring tricks to throw off the dogs are legendary. "I've seen them do crazy things," Taylor tells me as we break through the thicket to find a clearing for a stand. "Those rabbits will run full bore for a few hundred feet, then hop to the side and squat down tight as the dogs race by just a hand's width away." A rabbit on the run will suddenly spin 180 degrees, step to the side of its trail, and come running right back at a pack of tonguing dogs too intent on scent to notice the bunny. "He'll lick his feet real good to clean them off, then slip through the woods to sit up by some tree, and the dogs will never find him," Taylor says. Swamp rabbits will lie underwater alligator-style, with only their eyes and noses above the surface. Cottontails squirt through hollow logs, then hop to the top of the fallen trunk and head the other way.

Of course, it's not a dog's game alone. After the first few hours of daylight, the scent trails laid by feeding bunnies diminish, and hunters can jump as many rabbits as the beagles. "You've got to get in there with them," Taylor says. He kicks every downed treetop and hummock of grass. Rabbits will hide in culverts, drainage pipes, tree hollows, and ground burrows. He pokes and prods the shadows and looks for droppings and cuttings—shoots of greenbrier and blackberry cleanly snipped off at a 45-degree angle, showing that a bunny was snacking in the neighborhood.

They say a man's dogs are a reflection of him, and that's clearly the case with Taylor, who owns a moving company in Durham, North Carolina. "I just can't stand still. I've got to be moving, got to be moving, all the time," he says, each sentence a volley that chases the one before. "And that's how my dogs are. I want them pushing that rabbit. Don't give him too much time to think and duck those dogs. When they run like that, you don't hear nothing but sweet music."

At the moment, the music means a rabbit is headed my way, and fast. I take up a stand at the intersection of two trails. Robert Steed, Taylor's boyhood friend and hunting partner, is 40 yards away. "That rabbit comes running at you," he hollers, "you shoot at the ground in front of him, you hear?" I nod.

The dogs are in full cry, baying like a dozen cars locking up the brakes, moments before impact. When the rabbit squirts out of the brambles, it gives me a glancing look, then leaps across the trail. My shotgun bead points at an empty spot in the woods. Now the bunny takes two hops and spins like a top. It nearly runs over Steed's feet, ducks into the brambles, and is gone.

There will be more rabbits to come, and a few that aren't so lucky. But for now we haven't fired a shot, and all we can do is grin.

"That rabbit, now, he's a smart one," Taylor says, wiping the sweat from his brow as Rip, Brenda, LaVerne, and the gang go tearing off again. "Don't think he ain't."

Reprinted with permission of the author and *Field & Stream Magazine.*

PART V

Upland Birds

The Sundown Covey

LAMAR UNDERWOOD

Nobody ever used that name, really. But it was the covey of bobwhite quail that we always looked for almost with longing, as we turned our hunt homeward in the afternoon. By the time we came to that last stretch of ragged corn and soybean fields where this covey lived, the pines and moss-draped oaks would be looming darkly in the face of the dying sun. The other events of the afternoon never seemed to matter then. Tired pointer dogs bore ahead with new drive; we would watch carefully as they checked out each birdy objective, sure that we were headed for a significant encounter before we reached the small lane that led to the Georgia farmhouse. I always chose to think of those birds as "the sundown covey," although my grandfather or uncle usually would say something like "Let's look in on that bunch at the end of the lane." And then, more times than not, the evening stillness would be broken by my elder's announcement, "Yonder they are!" and we would move toward the dogs on point—small stark-white figures that always seemed to be chiseled out of the shadowy backdrop against the evening swamp.

There's always something special about hunting a covey of quail that you know like an old friend. One covey's pattern of movements between fields and swampy sanctuaries can be an intriguing and baffling problem. Another may be remarkably easy to find, and yet always manage to rocket away through such a thick tangle that you've mentally colored them *gone*, even before your finger touches the trigger. Another might usually present a good covey shot, while the singles tear away to . . . the backside of the moon, as far as you've been able to tell. My best hunts on more distant but greener pastures somehow have never seemed as inwardly satisfying as a day when a good dog and I can spend some time on familiar problems like these. Give me a covey I know, one that has tricked me, baffled me, eluded me—and by doing so brought me back to its corner of the woods for years.

In this sense, the covey we always hunted at sundown was even more special. As the nearest bunch of birds to the house, it was the most familiar. Here, trembling puppies got onto their first points. A lad learned that two quick shots into the brownish blur of the covey rise would put nothing into his stiff new hunting coat. A man returning from a war saw the birds running quick-footed across the lane and knew that he really was home again. The generations rolled on through times of kerosene lamps and cheap cotton to Ed Sullivan and soil-bank subsidies. And that same covey of bobwhites that had always seemed a part of the landscape still whistled in the long summer afternoons and hurtled across dead cornstalks that rattled in the winter breezes.

The hunters who looked for that covey and others in the fields nearby disciplined themselves never to shoot a covey below six birds. That number left plenty of seed for replenishment, so that every fall the coveys would again number fifteen to thirty birds, depending on how they had fared against predators.

Eventually, all that acreage moved out of our family. My visits to those coveys became less frequent as I necessarily turned toward education and then fields of commerce that were far away. But even during some marvelous quail-hunting days in other places, I often longed for return hunts to those intriguing coveys of the past. Would the swamp covey by the old pond still be up to their usual trick of flying into the field in the afternoon? Where would the singles from the peafield covey go now? Would the sundown covey still be there?

Finally, not long ago, the opportunity came for me to knock about a bit down in the home county. Several hunts with friends seemed as mere preludes to the long-awaited day when I got a chance to slip away alone to the old home grounds.

A soft rain had fallen during the night, but when I parked the truck by a thicket of pines just after sunrise, a stiff breeze had started tearing the overcast apart, and patches of blue were showing through the dullness. Shrugging into my bird vest, I ignored the shufflings and impatient whines that sounded from the dog box and stood a moment looking across a long soybean field that stretched toward a distant line of pines. I was mentally planning a route that would take me in a big circle to a dozen or so familiar coveys, then bring me to the sundown covey in the late evening. I unlatched the dog box, and the pointer, Mack, exploded from the truck and went through a routine of nervous preliminaries. I did the same, checking my bulging coat for shells, lunch and coffee. Then I clicked the double shut and stepped into the sedge alongside the field, calling: "All right, Mack. Look around!"

The pointer loped away in that deceptive, ground-eating gait that was his way of going. At age four, he had not exactly developed into the close worker I had been wanting. His predecessors who had run these fields in decades before were big-going speedsters suited to those times. Controlled burning and wide-roaming livestock kept the woodlands open then. Now most of the forests were so choked with brush and vines that wide-working dogs brought a legacy of frustration. Mack was easy to handle but tended to bend out too far from the gun unless checked back frequently. I really hated hearing myself say "Hunt close!" so often, but I hated even worse those agonizing slogging searches when he went on point in some dark corner of the swamp a quarter-mile from where I thought he'd been working.

The sun was bright on the sedge and pines now, and the air winy-crisp after the rain. Mack was a bouncing flash of white as he worked through the sedge and low pines. Once he started over the fence into the field, but I called him back. I wanted him to keep working down the edge. While the bean field seemed a tempting place to catch a breakfasting bevy, the cover bordering it offered much better chances—at least three to one, according to the quail-hunting education I had received here as a youngster. I could still imagine the sound of my grandfather's voice as he preached:

"Never mind all them picturebook covey rises in those magazines you read. It's only now and then you'll catch these old open coveys in the open. Birds once had to range wide and root for their keep. Now all the work's done for 'em. Combines and cornpickers leave so much feed scattered in the field the birds an feed in a few minutes, then leg it back into the cover. That's where you want to work. First, if they haven't gone to feed, you're likely to find 'em. If they've walked into the field, the dog'll trail 'em out. If they've already been into the field and fed, you'll still find 'em. Only time you'll miss is when they've flown into the field and are still there."

I had seen this simple philosophy pay increasing dividends as the years wore on. As the cover became thicker and the coveys smarter, the clear covey shot had become a rare, treasured experience. To spend a lot of time working through the fields was to be a dreamer of the highest order.

Still in the cover, we rounded the end of the small field and headed up the other side. I was beginning to feel the bite of the day's first disappointment; Mack had picked up no scent at all. Where were they? This covey had always been easy to find. Maybe they had been shot out, I thought. Maybe the whole place has been shot out.

I decided to play out a hunch. I pulled down a rusty strand of fence and stepped out into the field. Mack leaped the wire and raced away at full gallop. Far downfield he turned into the wind and suddenly froze in one of the most dramatic points I've ever seen. I knew he was right on top of those birds, his body curved tautly, his tail arching. "Oh ho!" I said aloud. "So you beggars *did* fly to the field."

My strides lengthened and became hurried. I snapped the gun open and checked the shells in an unnecessary gesture of nervousness. Normally steady hands seemed to tremble a little and felt very thick and uncertain. My heartbeat was a thunderous throb at the base of my throat.

My tangled nerves and wire-taut reflexes scarcely felt the nudge of a thought that said, "Relax. You've done this before." The case of shakes I undergo every time I step up to a point makes it difficult to attach any importance to that idea. Covey-rise jitters are known to have only one cure: action.

On my next step, the earth seemed to explode. The air was suddenly filled with blurry bits and pieces of speeding fragments, all boring toward the pines that loomed ahead. I found myself looking at one particular whirring form, and when the stock smacked against my face, the gun bucked angrily. The brown missile was unimpressed. He faded into the swamp, along with a skyful of surviving kinsmen. My loosely poked second shot failed to drop a tail-ender.

Mighty sorry gathering up of partridges, I thought, using the expression that was my uncle's favorite on the occasions when we struck out on a covey rise. "Sorry, boy," I called to Mack, who was busy vacuuming the grass in a futile search for downed birds.

My elders would have thought that bevy's maneuver of flying out to the field was the lowest trick in the book. But now the practice had become so typical among smart southern Bobs that it was hardly worth lamenting.

I called Mack away from his unrewarding retrieve and headed after those singles. The woods ahead looked clear enough for some choice shooting if I could keep Mack close.

Thirty minutes later I emerged from those woods a frustrated, angry man. My estimate that the birds had landed in the grassy, open pinelands was about two hundred yards wrong. Instead they had sailed on into one of the thickest, darkest sweet-gum swamps I've ever cursed a bird dog in. It took Mack all of fifteen seconds to get lost, and when I found him on point after ten minutes of searching I proceeded to put the first barrel into a gum tree and the second into a screen of titi bushes. Then the heebie-geebies really took over as I walked over two separate singles that jumped unannounced. Finally, Mack pointed again, but as I fought through the tearing clutches of briers and vines to get to him, I bumped another single, which I shot at without a glimmer of hope. That action caused Mack to take matters into his own hands and send the bird he was pointing vaulting away through the trees. Then followed a lot of unnecessary yelling, and we headed for the clear.

I should have known better. Single-bird hunting in that part of Georgia had become a sad business. Now I was discovering that my old hunting grounds were in the same shape as the rest of the county. If you were going to mess with singles, you had to wait for the right type of open woods. Most were just too thick to see a dog, much less a six-ounce bird. The day's shooting was certainly not going to follow the patterns of the past when it came to singles. I would have to wait until I got a bevy scattered in a better place.

We cut away from the field into a section of low moss-draped oak trees. Mack ranged ahead, working smartly. My frustrations of the first covey slipped away as I began considering the coming encounter with the next set of old friends. This covey, if they were still in business, would be composed of dark swamp birds that lived in the edge of the creek swamp but used this oak ridge to feed on acorns during early mornings and late afternoons. They were extremely hard to catch in the open, sometimes running for hundreds of yards in front of a dog on point. But what a sight they always made as they hurtled up among the moss-draped oaks on the lucky occasions when we did get them pinned nicely.

This oak ridge was fairly open, so I let Mack move on out a little bit. When he cut through one thickish cluster of trees and did not come out right away, I knew he had 'em.

Incredible, I thought. *The first two coveys are still here, and we've worked 'em both.* Then the words turned into brass in my mouth as I eased up to the dog and past him. The thunderous rise I had been expecting failed to occur. I let Mack move on ahead to relocate. Catlike, he crept through the low grass for a few yards, then froze again. I moved out in front once more, and still nothing happened.

Then, suddenly I heard them. Several yards out front the dry leaves rustled under the flow of quick-moving feet. The covey was up to its old trick of legging it for the sanctuary of the swamp.

I hurried forward, crashing through the briers. Just ahead, the low cover gave way to a wall of sweet-gum and cypress that marked the beginning of the swamp. Too late! I caught the sound of wings whirring. The birds had made the edge and were roaring off through the trees. They seemed to get up in groups of two and three. I caught an occasional glimpse of dim blurs through the screen of limbs and snapped a shot at one. Leaves and sticks showered down as Mack raced forward. Seconds later he emerged from the brush carrying a plump rooster bobwhite.

Had you seen me grinning over that bird, you might have thought I hadn't scored in five years. But the shot seemed mighty satisfying under the conditions. A few moments like this could make the day a lot more glorious than a coatful of birds ever could.

Now we followed an old lane that led down across the swamp and out beside a tremendous cornfield surrounded by pine and gallberry flats. I expected to find a couple of coveys here—and did, too, as the morning wore on in a succession of encounters with my old friends. A heart-warming double from a bevy Mack pinned along a fence row was followed by a succession of bewildering misses when we followed the singles into an open gallberry flat where I should have been able to score. Then we had the fun of unraveling a particularly difficult relocation problem when Mack picked up some hot scent in the corn but could not trail out to the birds. The edge of the field sloped down a grassy flat to an old pond with pine timber on the far side. I just knew those birds had flown across that pond to the woods to hole up for the day. When I took Mack over he made a beautiful point, standing just inside the woods. I wish I could always dope out a covey like that.

We spent the middle of the day stretched out on the grass on the pond dam. The sandwiches and coffee couldn't have tasted better. The sun was warm, and crows and doves flew against the blue sky. I thought about old hunts and old friends and couldn't have felt better.

In the afternoon we had a couple of interesting pieces of action, but failed to find some of my old neighbor coveys at home. My thoughts kept reaching ahead to the late-afternoon time when I would near the old now-deserted house by the lane and see the sundown covey again. Surely they would still be there. After all, we had been finding most of the old coveys. Who says you can't go home again? Who's afraid of you, Tom Wolfe?

The sun was dipping toward the pines and a sharp chill had come on when I skirted the last field and entered a stretch of open pine woods where I was counting on finding the covey of birds that I had carried in my mind all my life. Before I had gone fifty yards I came on something that shocked me as though I'd walked up on a ten-foot rattlesnake. A newly cut stake had been driven in the ground, and a red ribbon tied to the top of it. Farther on there was another, then another.

I had known that the new Savannah-Atlanta-Super-High-Speed-Interstate-Get-You-There-Quick-Highway was to pass through this general area. But surely, a couple of miles away. Not here. Not right here.

Gradually, my disbelief turned into anger. I felt like heading for the car right then and getting the hell out of there. Then suddenly three shots boomed in the woods some distance ahead.

Well, it was apparent that the sundown covey was still around. But an intruder had found them. I decided to go on up and talk to whoever it was. Actually, he probably had as much right to be here as I did now. I couldn't believe he was a regular hunter on this land, though. The coveys I had been finding all day were too populous with birds to be gunned heavily.

I walked slowly through the pines for a few minutes without spotting the other hunter. Then his gun thudded again, this time from farther down in the swamp. He's after the singles now, I thought. I called in Mack and waited there opposite the swamp. The other fellow would have to come out this way.

During the next few minutes two more separate shots sounded. The sun sank lower, and the breeze blew harder in the pines. Finally, I heard the bushes shaking and a man came out of the cover. When Mack started barking he spotted me and headed my way. As he came up I saw that he was young, carried an automatic and wore no hunting coat. He had some quail by the legs in his left hand.

"Looks like you did some good," I said.

"Yea, I got six."

"Where's your dog?" I asked.

"Oh, I don't have a dog. I spotted a covey crossing the road down there by the lane. I had the gun in the truck, so I went after 'em. Got three when I flushed 'em and three more down in the branch. Tiny little covey, though. I don't think there were more than six when I first flushed 'em. I imagine people been framin' into this bunch all the time." My heart sank when he said that. I didn't know what to say. He paused a minute, looking at Mack. "That's a nice dog. He any good?"

"Fair," I said. "Maybe you shouldn't have done that."

"What?"

"Shoot a small covey on down that way."

"Don't mean nothing. There's always a covey of birds along here. Every year. But there won't be for long. Interstate's coming through."

"Yea," I said slowly. "I see it is."

"Well, I gotta run. That's sure a nice-looking dog, Mister. See you around."

I watched him walk away. Then I leaned back against a pine, listening to the swamp noises. The wings of a pair of roost-bound ducks whispered overhead. An owl tuned up down in the swamp. Somehow I kept thinking that I would hear some birds calling each other back into a covey. Perhaps two or three had slipped away unseen from the roadside.

The night pressed down. Trembling in the cold, I started for the truck. Orion wheeled overhead. I started thinking about some new places I wanted to try. But never again did I hear that flutelike call that had sounded for me from that swamp so many times before.

Bobwhites in the Shinnery

GEOFFREY NORMAN

"You gotta make it," Ted said.

"I don't know . . ." I said into the phone.

"It's the kind of quail hunting you dream of. You'll think you've died and gone to heaven."

It wasn't the best image he could have used. And he seemed to realize it.

"Really, man," Ted said, more soberly. "After what you've been through, hell, you owe it to yourself."

It is always hard to turn down an invitation to do a little quail hunting, but I had prudent reasons for saying "No." I was only a couple of months past a little "minor" surgery that had turned into a major medical event. My heart had stopped—"cardiac arrest," they'd called it—while I'd been in the recovery room. The people attending to me had been quick to slap the paddles on my chest and shock my heart back into normal rhythm, and I am profoundly grateful for their professionalism, which prevented any permanent damage. Still . . .

All this had occurred at the end of the summer, so, naturally, one of my first concerns was that I'd be laid up during hunting season. But I'd rallied pretty quickly and had gone out after grouse and woodcock around home a few times since my scare and was fine. No trouble walking or climbing hills. I'd been in pretty good shape to begin with, and now I had a little metal box implanted in my chest that would shock me, automatically, if there were another arrest. The doctor who had put it in said he would bet money. The box felt strange, resting there under the skin just below my left shoulder. Strange and reassuring at the same time.

Even so, the doctors wanted me to stay close to home—which was Southern Vermont—for at least the first three months after what they liked to call "the event." And I was inclined for the first time in my life to accept? medical advice.

"Wild birds," he said. "Twenty coveys a day. Sometimes more."

"Where is it again?"

"Oklahoma. Not far from Amarillo. You fly into Oklahoma City, and I'll pick you up. We stay at a motel in Elk City."

"I don't know . . ." No matter how I stretched it, flying off to Oklahoma to hunt birds did not qualify as "sticking close to home."

"It's opening weekend," Ted went on, and I knew the voice of temptation in all its Biblical force. "Todd has whole sections of land leased up."

"I hear you."

"Wild birds," he said again. He knew my weakness—not just mine, any bird hunter's. And he was mercilessly exploiting it.

"What about dogs?" I said. Birds are not the only essential in bird hunting.

"Todd has a line on some that he says are pretty good. But I was hoping you'd bring Jeb." I could tell by Ted's tone that he knew he'd made the sale.

"He's never been to Oklahoma."

"Well, we need to fix that. I'm sure he'll find it to his liking."

"OK," I said, sounding like a man who just didn't have any alternative. "You talked me into it."

Getting ready to go was easy enough. The hard part was convincing my wife that I'd pace myself, quit if I started feeling bad, get plenty of sleep, watch what I ate and drank, and so on, and so on . . . I packed the necessary gear for me and for Jeb, my pointer who had just turned 12 but still had plenty of drive. Brush pants and boots for me. Leather booties for him, to guard against the sand spurs. Dog bowl, shock collar (which I seldom used any more), pad medication, vest, shotgun and so forth. We left in plenty of time to catch the plane, which meant four hours before departure. One and a half to get to the airport, and the balance for everything we had to deal with before departure. Halfway to the airport, I pulled over and gave Jeb a pill: a tranquilizer that a vet had prescribed. Although he is great on the highway—loves road trips—Jeb is not down with flying. If he is not sedated, he will howl from the time he goes into the traveling crate until he is rescued at the baggage claim. On one flight, everyone on the plane could hear him crying right up until the engines spooled and drowned out the noise. When we landed and the pilot cut the power, we could hear him again. He may have been howling through the entire flight. Other passengers looked at me with expressions of either pity or disapproval. Pity for the dog, no doubt. Disapproval for his cruel master.

We'd flown several times since that trip, and the tranquilizers had seemed to do the trick. When he went off in his crate with my duffel and my shotgun case, Jeb was lying down with his eyes closed.

"See you in Oklahoma City, bud," I said.

He didn't answer.

I went on up to the security checkpoint, where I notified one of the agents that I had an implanted device and endured my first pat-down search. *One more thing to get used to*, I thought.

It was late afternoon when we landed. Ted met me at baggage claim.

"You look pretty good for a man who's had a heart attack," he said.

"Kind of you to say."

"Don't mention it. Where's old Jeb?"

"He'll be coming along," I said. "He's the real reason you invited me on this trip, right? You didn't need me; you needed my dog."

"Well, hell, *of course* that's the reason. Don't tell me you were confused about that."

Ted has a weakness for pointers, and he was between dogs. Also, he'd hunted with Jeb before and liked his style, which might be characterized as "confident." Maybe even "aggressive." Ted also admired Jeb's sense of mischief. He'd witnessed some of his stunts, including the time Jeb charged into a packrat den and emerged with a full-grown skunk.

We recovered my bag, my gun and my dog.

"Three for three. Not bad," Ted said. He opened the door to the dog box when we were outside on the airport curb.

"Well, hello, Jeb. How's my man?"

Jeb emerged, shakily, and found a small shrub that served as a tree.

"*He* acts like the one who had the heart attack," Ted said.

"Don't worry," I said. "He'll be fine in the morning."

We drove west into the sunset. The highway was flanked by hard-looking rangeland where cattle grazed and the occasional oil pump worked monotonously away. The motel was expecting us, and because there were no signs saying pets were not allowed, I assumed they were. I made a bed for Jeb on the floor of my room and left him there while Ted and I joined another man, named Jeff, who would be hunting with us. We were in the dining room when Todd Rogers arrived.

An oil-field hand by profession, Todd had been moonlighting as a guide for turkey and deer hunters when he got the inspiration to branch out into quail. He negotiates with ranchers for hunting rights to their land and then takes hunters out for a fee. We were his first clients of the season.

Todd was lean, built like a rodeo cowboy and stingy with words. But friendly. He shook hands and made sure he had all of our names; then he told us that he'd been around that week checking on the places we'd be hunting.

"There's birds," he said. "Plenty of them. It's supposed to be hot tomorrow. But no wind. So that's good."

He stayed around for a beer, and we asked a few questions. After he left, we ordered dinner.

"You check out the parking lot of this place?" Jeff said.

"What about it?" I said.

"Well, it's the biggest motel in town, and there are two kinds of vehicles. Trucks that belong to Halliburton or one of the other drilling companies, and SUVs pulling trailers that are full of bird dogs. I saw one with Georgia plates."

"Opening weekend in Oklahoma," Ted said. "Some guys will crawl out of bed after a heart attack and come all the way from Vermont with a 12-year-old dog just to be here for that."

"Can you imagine?" Jeff said.

"Gentlemen," I said, "in the morning the invalids and the old dogs are going to shine. Just you watch."

It was about two hours after sunrise when we parked at the junction of two section roads next to a stock tank and an old windmill. The ground in front of us was covered in tall, tawny grass that Todd called "love grass." This flat, open stretch ran for a half-mile or so and then rose to a slight ridge covered with scrubby-looking stuff that I took for oak or maybe locust.

When I asked, Jeff said, "It's called 'shinnery.'"

"Beg pardon?"

"Shinnery. That means thick, worthless little stuff that will tear up your clothes and scratch your face and turn you every way but loose once you get in it."

"No particular tree then?"

"Nope."

"Just shinnery."

"You got it."

Todd had ridden out with another man, Roger Slife, who raised pointers and had brought a couple of his best dogs. They asked if I'd rather start out hunting Jeb by himself.

"Nope," I said. "We aren't proud—neither one of us—and we need all the help we can get."

So we crossed a fence and got started. Three hunters, two guides and two pointers. And in less than 15 minutes Todd said, "I believe we got us a point."

My legs weren't even limber yet, but my pulse picked up the way it always does when I see dogs on point. My heart, anyway, was in fine shape.

No way to say which dog had located the birds and which was backing. They may have located the covey more or less simultaneously from different angles. Anyway, they both were staunch, noses aimed at the same point in the undifferentiated grass. Jeff, Ted and I fanned out and walked in briskly.

The birds hadn't dispersed very much from their tight roosting formation, so they seemed to come up in a single ball and then angle off in separate trajectories, desperate to put some space between themselves and whatever had provoked their flight. It happened with the usual startling suddenness, and I shot before I was ready and while the birds were still in range. My typical opening salvo.

But *damn*. We weren't 200 yards from the truck, and already we were into birds.

"I believe I'm going to be glad I came," I said to Ted.

By midmorning we were halfway to our limits, the sun was up and bearing down hard, and we were stuck in the shinnery chasing singles. It was hard on the hunters and the dogs. Some of the thickets seemed to swallow us, and we would have to push through them by main force with our guns held tightly across our chests at port-arms. Sometimes a bird would get up, almost at our feet, or behind us. No chance. None at all.

Still, we were having a wonderful time. The country seemed epic by bird-hunting standards. We had walked for more than three hours and never cut a road, crossed a fence or bumped into another hunter. The dogs had found 10 coveys and made good points on most of them, even though scenting conditions were anything but ideal.

"I believe I heard the noon whistle," Ted said after we'd broken out of the shinnery and given up on the singles.

I checked my watch. It was a little after 11.

"Me, too," I said.

The dogs went along with the ruse. They were hot and tired, too. Especially Jeb, whose age was beginning to show.

We watered both dogs lavishly when we got back to the truck and drank canned sodas while we stood around and replayed the morning. No one was in a hurry to get on with the next thing. It felt good not to be moving.

We drove to a barbecue place where the ribs had been slow-cooking for so long they almost fell off the bone when you picked them up in your greasy fingers. The fried okra was also excellent.

"Can you imagine what your doctor would say about this lunch?" Ted said.

"What he doesn't know won't hurt him."

With great restraint and self-righteousness, I passed on dessert.

We scattered a flock of turkeys on the way into the next section we would be hunting. We lost sight of them as they sailed off toward a little rise grown up in shinnery.

"Pretty," Jeff said.

"Yeah," Todd said. "I believe I'll see them again in the spring."

Jeb was tired, but when I tried to leave him in the truck and hunt with Roger's fresher, younger dogs, he began howling like he was being put on an airplane. Without sedation.

"All right," I said, and opened the dog box. It's hard to deny a willing bird dog. The drive is so pure you feel like it's cruel *not* to let him do what is in his blood.

It won't kill him, I thought. The worst thing that could happen is . . . we'd have a tired, useless dog in the field with us.

I was wrong about that. But it came later.

The afternoon was better than the morning. It seemed like we were never out of birds. As soon as we had finished with the singles from one covey rise and decided to move on, the dogs would go on point and we would be into another covey. It may, actually, not have been *that* good, but it was about as good as I'd ever had it.

The day had cooled some, and even though they were tired, the dogs put on a good show. We even got a little comic relief when Jeb went on point 300 or 400 yards ahead of us in the middle of a field grown up in love grass.

"Strange place for a covey to be this time of day," Todd said.

"He's tired," I said. "Probably false-pointing so he can rest."

But Jeb held the point until, finally, I had to honor it. It was a long walk, and the love grass grew in clumps, so the footing was tricky. I called to Jeb a couple of times, but he stayed staunch.

"I can't believe you're making me come all this way for a false point," I said. I almost could touch him, and no bird had flown. "Let's go hunt birds."

About that moment a turkey came out of the grass 20 steps ahead of us. Jeb watched the turkey until it had set its wings and was sailing away in the distance. Then he turned his head and looked around at me. I'd seen the look before.

"My bad," I said. "I apologize. Now let's go hunt some of those *little* birds."

We quit a little before sunset, three or four birds short of a limit and wearily happy with the results of the day. We stood around the bed of the pickup in the cooling evening air. There was some canned beer on ice, and no pretentious microbrew has ever been so gratefully gulped down.

"Tomorrow should be better," Todd said.

"I don't see how it could be," Ted said.

"Not so hot. Dogs will work better."

"I'm not arguing."

We drove back to the motel, where I fed Jeb. He stayed awake just long enough to clean his bowl, and then he lay down on the bed I'd made for him and dropped into a deep, almost comatose sleep.

"Rest up, Bud," I said. "You get to do it again tomorrow."

He didn't move when I left or when I came back from a robust Mexican dinner and fell into an equally deep sleep.

Good as Saturday had been, Sunday was even better. It was cooler and there was some wind. We were all—men and dogs—a little slow getting started, but we warmed up quickly and got down to business and began to see those things that linger in a bird hunter's memory between seasons: clean doubles on a covey rise, birds staunchly pointed and backed, flawless retrieves. The country stretched out ahead of us, flat and uncluttered, so we could watch the dogs work, and it was, as it always is, a heart-stopping moment when one of them hit a point and firmed up on it.

"Look at that."

"Nothing prettier."

The morning passed quickly. After lunch Jeb was so worn out that I tried, again, to leave him behind. Nothing doing.

"Dog has plenty of want-to," Todd said.

Which is about as high a compliment as you can pay another man's dog.

Jeb had a hard time keeping out from underfoot, but it didn't make any difference. There were plenty of birds, and he still had enough in the tank to find them. With an hour of daylight left, we were three birds short of limiting out.

"I've got another place," Todd said. "Close to here. Let's run over there and see if we can find one more covey."

I had to lift Jeb down from the bed of the truck, but he insisted on coming.

"He'll be OK," Ted said. "He's got all winter to rest."

The last covey we needed was tight in a corner of a big field with dense shinnery on two sides. The light had changed, the air was much cooler, and it felt like November on the plains. The dogs stood their ground as we approached and then walked by them. The covey got up and flew toward the shinnery, framed against the orange sky. We all shot, and three birds fell.

"How many coveys did we flush in two days?" Ted said. We were standing around the bed of the pickup, getting after some beer.

"I'm not real good with numbers," I said. "More than enough to make me want to come back to Oklahoma."

"We ought to do it again, then," Jeff said. "Next year."

So we made the date, right there, on the side of a clay road while we drank the last of the beer and watched a little buck slip out of the shinnery and into the field where we'd just put up the last covey.

"You think old Jeb will still be up to it then?" Ted said.

"Count on it," I said. "Unlike me, he's indestructible."

I'd been thinking that all weekend, but as it turned out, neither of us was.

Jeb was too tired to eat when we got back to the motel. This was something I'd never seen before. He'd eaten every evening of his life, and if I'd been late getting around to feeding him, he'd let me know about it. He'd still eaten his supper after I'd pulled 50 porcupine quills from his tongue, gums and face and thought he'd need to sleep it off. No way, he'd indicated firmly—by barking—he'd wanted his groceries.

But those two hard days in Oklahoma had put him off his feed. I felt the old twinge of admiration and regret. He was a 12-year-old dog, but he wasn't ready to quit yet. Nothing wrong with *his* heart.

He didn't eat in the morning, either. And he slept in his crate all the way to the airport. I thought about skipping the tranquilizer this time, but it was going to be a long flight and I didn't want him to be distressed. A tough call.

I broke a pill in two and gave him half the usual dose. He was sleeping when the crate disappeared into the baggage-handling area.

An hour later I was waiting at the gate to board the plane when I heard myself being paged. I went to the desk, where a man from the airline asked me gently if I had checked a dog for travel on this flight.

"Yes," I said. And thought . . . *Dead.*

"Did you medicate him?"

"Yes," I said. "He's not good with flying."

"Well, he's barely responding to the handlers, and I took a look at him. If he were my dog, I wouldn't put him on this flight. I'd wait until he's more alert. But we still have a few minutes. Maybe you'd like to come see him yourself."

He led the way down into a busy area with concrete floors where the baggage was sorted. Jeb's crate was by itself in a corner. I opened the door and looked in.

Jeb was lying in a ball, with his face toward me. He didn't open his eyes when I said his name. Or when I put my hand on his flank. It rose, just slightly, and I could tell he was breathing. But it seemed like a long time between breaths.

"I'm sorry, old buddy."

So Jeb and I spent the entire day in the Oklahoma City airport. He slept all morning. By noon he was opening his eyes and drinking a little water. In the middle of the afternoon I took him outside to a small patch of grass, and we lay there together. Cars went by, and the people inside looked at us and tried to figure what we were about.

"You feeling a little better, old man?" I said.

I rubbed his ears, and he finally managed, feebly, to wag his tail.

"You're going to be OK," I said, with the same kind of relief I'd felt when the doctor had said the same thing to me.

"We'll be back out hunting birds in a day or two."

We left on the last possible flight that night.

I cursed myself for an idiot all the way home, and I tried to ease the guilt by feeding Jeb some hamburger when we got back to Vermont. He had his appetite back and cleaned his bowl. I gave him some more. He ate that too, and then he went to his familiar spot in front of the woodstove. He plainly felt better. But it was nothing compared to my sense of relief.

In a few days I was remembering the better parts of our trip to Oklahoma, and I like to think that Jeb was, too. And I was thinking a lot about something that might be called the "law of diminishing opportunities." Time passes, and we all get older. Dogs and men. Next time Ted calls, I won't ruminate and equivocate and wait to be talked into doing what I want to do.

As for opening day in Oklahoma ... I'm there. Me and Jeb. Long as our hearts hold out.

Showing the Way

CHRIS MADSON

"Well, I'm about to make your life more complicated."

Bill pushed back from the table after his second plate of stew and grinned. "How are you fixed for dogs?"

He knew, of course. Britt, my old male, was snoozing in his dog box, marshalling his energy for next day. Bill was the reason Britt and I had gotten together. He had called me when the litter was whelped, and eight weeks later, I'd made a 500-mile drive to check the pups. The dam was a beauty, with dual champion credits for three generations on each side of her pedigree. About all that could be said for the sire was that the A.K.C. certified him as pure Brittany. He was tall and rangy for a Brit, and he looked as if a pit bull had sneaked into his mother's kennel at a particularly delicate time.

Still, pretty is as pretty does, as the Kansas farm ladies say. Both sire and dam were superb quail dogs, the pride of a small-town banker who had the run of farms in three counties and spent more time minding the birds than computing compound interest. Bill had followed the careers of all the pups in the first two litters this pair had made, and he swore there wasn't a bad dog in the bunch.

I had my pick of the males in the third litter. There were five, as I recall, all of them as cute as eight-week-old puppies always are, a wriggling mass of warm tongues and floppy ears, led around already by inquiring pink noses. When I patted the ground and mouse-squeaked, one little male kept wobbling over to see me. Bold and curious for such a youngster, he had an interest in humans as well as other dogs, so we went home together.

I would like to believe that my flawless training brought out the best in him, but it would be fairer to say that he was talented enough to overcome the obvious shortcomings of his handler. We started on pheasants, but before he was through, he hunted bobwhites and cottontops, chukars and huns, sage grouse, sharptails, blues, and ruffs. When the water wasn't too cold, he retrieved mallards, and one November afternoon, he chased a crippled Canada goose a quarter of a mile over a Wyoming marsh and brought him to hand while my daughter and I watched. After eleven years, he was still following that unerring nose wherever the birds led, a little slower but no less enthusiastic.

Bill waited for me to bite.

"Alright, alright. What've you got?"

"I was talking with Jim the other day. He says the daughter of one of your dog's littermates just had a litter of her own. Nine weeks old next Tuesday."

"Geez, Bill."

"I know, I know—there's never a good time to start another dog... But, you know, we're driving right past there tomorrow. Jim wants to look 'em over."

"Well," I granted, "spose there's no harm in looking."

We met Jim the next morning, his pick-up loaded with a homemade dog box and a little female Brittany, rock hard from a season of bird hunting. Since I was heading the other direction at the end of the day, I followed in my own rig, Britt standing at the back window, whining softly.

Ten miles out of town, we pulled into a farm yard. The master of the spread had gone to pick up some lumber, but his wife told Jim to take us out to the kennel anyway. As we walked across the lawn toward the kennel, the dog house emptied out, the female watching us with just a touch of concern while nine puppies fell over each other on their way to the gate.

"I'm interested in one of these myself," Jim said as we squatted among the pups. "Let's take a couple along with us and see what they think of the cover."

I looked hard at Bill, and he held up his hands, grinning. "No obligation."

So we scooped up two likely looking young ladies, loaded them in the third kennel in the truck, and drove off into a calm, bright January morning that was just beginning to thaw around the edges—a perfect quail day.

Forty minutes later, we pulled onto a faint two-track that left the gravel just shy of the bridge over a little creek lined with elms and sumac. Like most streams in the Kansas Flint Hills, this one ran over a limestone bottom, spring-fed and crystalline, home to clouds of darters and a thriving population of spotted bass. It wound through the soft-shouldered hills, disappearing into groves of oak and walnut, then out again past slopes of Indiangrass and bluestem, a sampler of tawny yellow and burgundy in the low winter light. Along the creek bottom, there was just enough milo and corn stubble to sweeten the place for quail.

We uncased guns and headed north along the creek, leaning on the dogs for direction. They meandered through the stubble, crossed the creek, and worked west through a patch of timber, coming at last to a stand of grass and forbs at the top of the hill. Jim's female pointed hard where the trees gave way to a patch of sand plum on a south-facing bank. I stopped Britt to honor. Bill swung in on one side, and before anybody could set tactics, the covey exploded. I was too far away to shoot, so I could savor the sight of two exceptional gun hands working a covey. Neither man seemed to hurry—the guns came up in a fluid arc; there was a flurry of shots, and the dogs started their retrieves. Four birds on the first rise.

We hunted the singles of that covey with no success; the covey had blasted back through the timber, so it was hard to get a mark on any of the birds. As the morning wore on, we worked through one exceptional quail covert after another without finding any more quail. Around one, we circled back to the truck.

Bill had sandwich fixings and some hot chocolate, which went down well in the cool shade down by the creek. After we had eaten, Jim crawled into the back of the pick-up and opened the second kennel.

"Let's take a look at you girls."

He scooted off the tailgate with a wiggling Brittany in one hand. Released in the milo stubble, she immediately began snuffling over the ground. I went over to the field edge and cut a sumac wand about five feet long.

"Mind if I borrow a wing?" I asked Bill. He smiled and handed me one of the quail. I broke a wing off close to the body, stripped the lace out of one of my boots, and tied the wing to one end. I knotted the other end to the stick.

"Here, little one." I flipped the wing out on the ground and twitched it a couple of times, luring the pup out of the field. She scrambled over to the feathers and pounced, falling on her chin and somersaulting over the wing.

Bill shook his head. "First time away from mama. You have to give her high marks for confidence."

I flipped the wing back down on the ground, and the puppy flounced after it again. Jim grinned.

"You know, sometimes I think they don't really have a brain. Just a bird flittering around between their ears. Listen, these are both fine little dogs. If you want one, you pick it. I'll take the other one."

I scooped up the puppy and kneaded one of her ears while she chewed on my thumb with needle teeth.

"Yes, you ARE a mighty hunter," I told her. "But why don't you give us a chance to look at your sister." I crawled into the pick-up bed and swapped dogs.

The second infant was just as bold as the first. I turned to pick up my wing and pole, and when I looked back, she was already thirty yards down the creek bank, nose to the ground, stub tail vibrating. I squeaked at her and flipped the wing down on the ground. She pattered back with her head up, trying to figure out why she cared about the twitching feathers. As she came up, I let the wing settle. She slowed, took one more step … and froze, one forefoot in the air. It's a tricky thing for an eight-week-old to balance on just three feet, but she managed, wobbling a little as she watched the wing for any sign of motion. I dragged the wing a foot, and she pounced, missing it. Then I laid it out again, and she pointed again.

I glared at Bill. "This is your fault," and I picked up the pup, holding her freckled nose about an inch from mine. "Sweetie, I think you're gonna have to come back to Wyoming with me."

We loaded the puppies back into the truck and took one long swing through the afternoon. We found two more coveys there. Jim's little lady found one on the edge of a stand of bluestem and held it for two minutes while we scrambled to catch up. Then Britt pinned a second bunch at the head of a brushy swale. He was tired, but the point was high and stylish. The rise surprised me, as it always does, and I rushed the shot, wing-tipping a bird that fell into the thicket, out of sight. Britt disappeared into the brush and emerged a long minute later, a male bobwhite cradled gently in his mouth, bailing out the boss as he had so many times before.

We got back to the vehicles just as the sun dropped over the tall prairie ridge to the west. I cased my gun, boosted the old man into the back of the Trooper, and poured some water for him. He sniffed the bowl, then climbed into the back seat with a grunt, and curled up in a tight ball.

"How do you want to do this?" I asked Bill as I walked back to Jim's truck.

"Well, if you want to write a check, Jim can take it back. They'll send you the papers." Bill smiled again. "She IS a likely looking pup."

I took out my check book.

"Do me a favor, Jim?"

"Sure."

"Tell them not to cash this for a few days. I wasn't planning on doing any dog buying on this trip." He grinned. "I can do that."

Bill apologized for the ten coveys we hadn't found, and I assured him that good company is better than good shooting—although I was hoping we could combine the two some day. We shook hands and promised to make another rendezvous next season. Then Jim got into his truck and handed me the pup.

"Good luck with this one. She'll do well."

And with that, they headed east.

I made a nest of my hunting coat and down vest in the back of the car where a puppy's accident would be easiest to clean up. It was going to be a long drive—without a kennel for the youngster, I wasn't going to have the luxury of a motel room or a snooze in the back of the vehicle. So eleven hours back to the house. I settled in behind the wheel and pointed west.

There was a scrabbling in the back. In the rear view mirror, I saw a freckled nose poke up over top of the back seat. After a minute's struggle, she tumbled onto the seat with Britt. Charmed to find a parental figure, the little one stuck her nose out to get acquainted. There was a low growl, and the puppy decided this was not her mother. She scrambled up onto the console and fell into my lap.

"Well, if you're gonna ride up here, you better use the other seat." I scooted her over, and she stretched out as if she had been born there. As the miles flowed by, I could hear the old man snoring in back, a veteran of many hunts who had given everything he had to give one more time. Next to me, his niece slept the deep, untroubled sleep of the very young. Now and then, she snuffled and her feet twitched as she chased birds she did not yet recognize through fields she had not yet seen, her mind and heart running true in an ancient course. Youth and experience, promise and perfection.

And it occurred to me that they were not only better than I was at this game; they were better than I could ever hope to be. Ultimately, the proof of the hunt lies, not in bag limits or shells burned, but in the quality of the effort we make. It is a matter of focus and dedication, a commitment to a tradition that is older than mankind itself. Over the millennia, our dogs have led us in the chase, and things haven't changed much in all that time. For those of us who care about hunting, they show the way still.

Quail in the Thorned Land

MICHAEL MCINTOSH

South of San Antonio, the big country begins to narrow between the Gulf and the Rio Grande. Or so it shows on the map, shaped by two waters and veined with twisty rivers. But on the land itself, water and confinement hold little sway. It is a festival of sky and light and space, as if the territory refuses to recognize the diminishing boundaries of its map.

In the west, the Brasadera—the black-brush country—flows mile after mile toward Mexico. Gulfward lies open grassland dotted with mottes of oak and manzanilla. It is by turns a landscape stark and hard-bitten, delicate and lush, home to the rattlesnake and javelina, white-tail and razorback, jackrabbit, turkey, bobcat, and cougar.

And quail. It's a far cry in looks from Midwestern grainfields or the pine woods and broomsedge of the South, but this southern spur of Texas, shaped like the tip of a stout blade, is quail country to steal a hunter's heart.

As game birds go, quail are my oldest friends. I suspect I've traveled more linear miles in behalf of pheasants, but along the contours of the heart, which is the mileage that really counts, quail have taken me farther than any. Put me down in some quaily place with a few dogs and good friends, and you will find me a happy man. Make it a place I've never been before, let me explore it with those who know it well, and you will find me an extremely happy man. Add in the astonishing diversity of both land and game you'll find in south Texas, and the feeling borders on delirium.

In all the knocking around I've done to spend time in the company of quail, south Texas took a long time getting onto the itinerary. I don't know why, especially since the shooting there borders on legendary proportion. But the older I get, the more convinced I am that the really good things come along only when the time is right to appreciate them. So I was forty years into my life as a quail hunter when I finally got there.

"The thing about Herradura," David Gregory said, "is you'll find as many blue quail as bobwhites." We were rolling out of San Antonio just on the trailing edge of sunrise, southbound for Cotulla and the cut-off leading east into what is mostly blank space on the map. In fact, except for Interstate 35 and a few villages scattered along it, the map shows precisely seven highways and two towns in all of La Salle County, an area of just over 1,500 square miles. My kind of place. Knowing from experience that Brother Gregory does not overestimate the quality of the shooting he books, I figured Herradura Ranch would be my kind of place, too.

And then there were the blue quail he talked about. In the field guides, they are scaled quail; in local parlance cottontops; in scientific circles *Callipepla squamata;* in my hunting life to that point, merely a wraith. I'd had some momentary brushes with them in Mexico, first in Nuevo Leon and later in Sonora, but only so brief as a flush and a couple of wild, fruitless shots. According to one guide to North American birds, obviously not written by a quail hunter, blues are gregarious and therefore usually found in flocks; as a rule, moreover, a blue quail "seldom flies, preferring to run."

In the rhetoric classes I used to teach, we called this "understatement." In practice, when you're on the ground with a covey close by, you'd call it any number of things, most of which are unfit for tender ears. One leathery old south-Texas hunter told me, "Best way to handle a cottontop is shoot 'im on the ground, and then go stomp the little bastard flat before he gets up and runs off."

The ways they interact with the environments where they live are key factors in determining which birds are game and which birds aren't. For some, the environment is a factor all its own. Woodcock hunting is that way, and so is the business of ruffed grouse. Their habitat can be frustrating. So can blue quail habitat, but as if to add even a bit more edge to the sport, it can also kill you.

Unlike bobwhites, who are considerate enough to live in places reasonably comfortable to a hunter, blue quail hang out in the brush, and if you want to make medicine with them, you have to hang out there as well. Now, in most places, "brush" can be anything from doghair popple to an understory thick with shrubs, vines, and creepers. It can be unpleasant, especially if it owns a quotient of blackberry, but it seldom is truly miserable. In south Texas, however, as in Mexico, "brush" means black brush, and the only black brush pleasant enough to be miserable is a patch that's been chopped, burned, bulldozed, and buried.

Black brush is vegetation with character and a streak of villainy. Mesquite and huisache make up the heart of it, but the full depth of its character (and most of the villainy) comes from an incredible variety of smaller, thorn-bearing plants, each in its way capable of drawing blood, inflicting pain, or both. In the black brush lurks prickly pear and Spanish dagger, devil's head and wild currant and a whole array of things known mostly by their Spanish names—*coma* and *brasil* and *clepino, retama, retama chino, junco, granjeno*, and most vicious of all, *tasajilla. Tasajilla* is sometimes called rat-tailed cactus, which comes close enough to describing the slender green branches, but words can scarcely capture its long, needly spines, so sharp that even one feels like a jolt of electricity and so numerous that the whole plant seems to swarm at the merest touch—which is why *tasajilla* is also called jumping cactus.

At the edges where it meets the grassland, the black brush is open enough to stroll through without great difficulty. Leave the edges, though, and it's a different world. J. Frank Dobie, the great Texas historian and writer born in the Brasada, once described black brush as "too thick to cuss a cat in," which is about right. But it's wonderful game cover and definitely not too thick to cuss a quail in. Down at ground level there's plenty of running room, and the quail, blues especially, use it to full advantage.

Given all this and a bird that would rather use its legs than its wings, you might wonder why anyone in his right mind would bother. Actually, no one would, or at least no more than once, if the only way to hunt were simply to strike off cross-country, flogging brush that's capable of flogging you right back even when you're wearing chaps tough enough to be almost bulletproof. The country's too big for that sort of thing anyway; at 15,000 acres, Herradura is a modest-sized spread by local standards.

So you hunt from vehicles, in keeping with the fine old quail-shooting tradition practiced all across the South. In Georgia or Tennessee or Mississippi, this would be a rubber-tired democrat wagon and matched team of mules; in Texas it's a pickup custom-fitted with high seats, gun scabbards, and dog boxes.

And you hunt the edges—the ranch roads and the *senderos*, which is the local name for any clearing, natural or man-made. At Herradura, the ongoing management plan has created a vast network of *senderos* through the brush, providing the multiple benefits of access for hunting, more places for the birds to dust and feed, and in general more of the sort of edge habitat quail love so well. To say that it's been successful is to understate the case. I suppose you could keep count of the covies, though on a typical day you'll need more than both hands and both feet to do so, and at that level of quail hunting numbers hardly matter.

At any level, quail hunting is a triad, a seamless weave of hunter, bird, and dog. All upland bird hunting is that way to me. I know it's possible to hunt quail without a dog, because I've done it, but it's only a partial equation, missing some vital component, incomplete. Having been a lifelong foot hunter, I can't think of many pleasures more complete than rambling the countryside to the sound of dog bells—unless perhaps it's riding perched on a high-seat or bumper-rig, slowly cruising a dusty ranch road, flanked by a brace of dogs coursing the grass and the brushy edge. If I were inclined to submit my carcass to a funeral procession, that's the kind of hearse and cortege I'd want.

You'll hear it said that no dog but an English pointer is worth a hoot in the Texas brush; that setters are too thin-skinned, too delicate, too long-coated or short-winded, or too something-else to function in the heat and the cactus. The problem is, no one has bothered to tell this to David Schuster's setters, so they go out day after day, cover the ground, find covies and point singles as if they didn't know any better. David, who is the manager at Herradura and a dog man of the first water, keeps a few pointers in his kennel as well—most notably a big, brush-scarred old campaigner named Hank who paces himself like a marathon runner and seems to know every trick a blue or a bob ever thought of pulling—but the setters are the stars of the show.

Dogs wear down quickly in this warm country, even in January. Two brace is the minimum staff; three's better, worked on half-hour rotations with a long drink and an hour's rest between. For a handler, it's a continuous balancing act, trying to give the dogs full opportunity to show their stuff while at the same time conserving their energy.

For a hunter, shooting over the Herradura dogs is a delight. In the course of two full days, one young dog got over-antsy with a covey of bobwhite just one time. You can't ask for better dog work than that—nor, what with covey after covey of bobs on the broad prairies, better opportunities to enjoy it.

Handling blue quail is no mean feat for a pointing dog, because the little guys just won't sit still. If you can get them to flush and scatter a bit, the singles and pairs are more inclined to hold, but the classic scenario of easing in past the dogs and putting up a covey just doesn't happen with blues. Instead, it turns into a footrace the moment the dog strikes a point. If you don't push them hard, they simply run off, and if they do flush, you won't know exactly where they'll come from—except it won't be underfoot. As all this happens in the brush, trying to move fast through a world of thorns with one eye cocked for birds and the other searching for the next safe step gets to be a complicated little exercise, sort of like chasing bees while wading through porcupines.

Having thought about it since, I wonder if a man couldn't do himself a treat by hunting blues with two dogs, one of pointing breed and a small, nimble, well-schooled flusher to circle in and make 'em fly. I don't know whether anyone has tried this, but if you do, I'd be interested to know if it works.

Once in a while, in just the right place, blue quail can turn from demons to darlings, and after dragging us through the brush to make sure we paid our dues, David Schuster led us to the gate of heaven.

Not that it looked very heavenly—a fencerow-wide strip of scrub and cactus with a hundred yards or more of grass, sorghum and wildlife plantings on one side and a narrow, grassy on the other, leading off to the brush. Landscapewise, you wouldn't give it a second look, and even then you wouldn't necessarily recognize it as a splendid piece of habitat management. But it is. The blue quail move out of the brush to feed and use the fencerow strip for cover; flush them and they head back for the brush, crossing the *sendero*.

We were just three guns, David and Theresa Gregory and I. David took the far side of the fencerow, leaving the *sendero*—and, bless him, the best of the shooting—to Theresa and me. I moved out toward the edge of the brush to give Theresa first crack at the flushes, in part because I was raised on the concept of *ladies first* and partly because Theresa gets such a charge out of quail hunting that watching her is as much fun as the hunting itself.

I couldn't begin to tell you how many birds were in that little strip. Hundreds, easily. Blues being blues, they went sprinting down the row, flushing far ahead in knots of ten or a dozen, winging out across the *sendero* and pitching into the brush. I doubt we shot at even one percent of the birds we saw, but we got plenty of shooting nonetheless, because enough of them sprang up inside the gun, as the English say, to keep us busy. The dogs kept pointing and repositioning in a steady buzz of wings and the whomp of Theresa's 20-bore double.

It's the only time in my life I ever pass-shot quail. By the time they got out where I was they were hammering on at top speed, crossing left to right, some still climbing, others slanting toward the brush. It was like a driven-partridge shoot turned ninety degrees, and it was wonderful.

The fencerow and *sendero* stretch on for at least a mile. The farther we went, the more it seemed that every blue quail on this end of the ranch must surely be in there. But then, going over to pick up a dead bird near the brush, I spooked up a big covey that no doubt had paused on its way to the cover-strip to let us pass by. There was no telling how many had already moved in behind us. I'm sure we could've had another good round of shooting had we chosen to work the same cover going back.

But it was late in the day, and we were near enough to filling our daily limits that a few more birds wouldn't matter. David Schuster had brought the truck around to pick us up, and there was water for the dogs and cold drinks that came out of the cooler with chips of ice sliding off the cans, and my knees were just to the point of being pleasantly achy.

But first we had to have the daily lesson to prove that the only ultimately predictable thing about quail is their unpredictability. The fencerow ends with one low bush growing in a thick patch of grass no larger than a washtub. And while the four of us stood there talking, not twenty feet away, one of the little setters came loping by, swing around as if lassoed by the nose, and locked up solid on that swatch of grass.

We looked at this, then at one another, and came to an instant consensus: Surely a blue wouldn't sit there so long with all of us so near. Surely. But something clearly was there, so I walked over and kicked the bush. Exit one blue quail brushwards, in a powerful hurry. It's one of the pair I brought home for the taxidermist.

There is a certain moment in a quail-hunting day when time comes to a halt. It lies on the cusp between the hard-edged memory of wings and the anticipation of a warm shower and the cold, sharp taste of whiskey. It sounds like the sigh of a tired dog nestled in thick straw, and in south Texas it is the color of darkening land under a sky washed in outlandish pastels.

I was leaving Herradura next day, so I rode the high seat to get a last long look. As we rolled slowly down the ranch road toward the highway, the moment of suspended time broke and the brush country turned toward night. A pyrrhuloxia, the little Southwestern songbird that looks like a cardinal who had a parakeet for one of its grandparents, darted in front of us, heading for a roost in some mesquite or *hui-sache*. The javelinas were beginning to stir, mincing out of the brush on their impossibly tiny feet, stiff-necked and ill-tempered. I had earlier found the skull and jawbone of one of their kin, bleached white and clean and still bearing its quartet of sharp, pointed, two-inch tusks. Now, wired together and looking appropriately ferocious on the sitting-room mantel, it reminds me of the day and the country and quail among the thorns.

In Fields Near Home

VANCE BOURJAILY

Any autumn. Every autumn, so long as my luck holds and my health, and if I win the race. The race is a long, slow one that has been going on since I started to hunt again. The race is between my real competence at hunting gradually developing, and, gradually fading, the force of the fantasies which have sustained me while the skills are still weak. If the fantasies fade before the competence is really mine, I am lost as a hunter because I cannot enjoy disgust. I will have to stop, after all, and look for something else.

So I shan't write of any autumn, or every autumn, but of last autumn, the most recent and the most skilled. And not of any day, but a particular day, when things went really well.

7:45 No clock need wake me.

7:55 While I am pulling on my socks, taking simple-minded satisfaction in how clean my feet are from last night's bath, relishing the feel against them of heavy, close-knit wool, fluffed and warmed and freshly washed, the phone rings downstairs. I go down to answer it, stocking-footed and springy-soled, but I am not wondering particularly who the caller is. I am still thinking about clean feet and socks. Even 20 years after infantry training, I can remember what it is like to walk too far with wet lint, cold dirt, and calluses between the flesh and the matted stocking sole, and what it is like to long for the sight of one's own unfamiliar feet and for the opportunity to make them comfortable and unrepulsive.

It is Mr. Burton on the phone.

"Hello?"

"Yeah. Hi, Mr. Burton."

"Say, I've got some news. I called a farmer friend of mine, up north of Waterloo last night. He says there're lots of birds, his place hasn't been hunted for a week."

"Uh-huh."

"I thought we'd go up there instead."

Mr. Burton is a man in his late 50s whom I've known for two or three years. He took me duck hunting once, to a privately leased place, where we did quite well. I took him pheasant hunting in return, and he has a great admiration for my dog Moon. He wants his nephew to see Moon work. The kid has a day off from school today.

But: "The boy can't go after all," Mr. Burton says. "His mother won't let him. But say, I thought we might pick up Cary Johnson—you know him don't you? The attorney. He wants to go. We'll use his car."

Boy, I can see it. It's what my wife calls the drive-around. Mr. Burton will drive to my house; he will have coffee. We will drive to Johnson's house. We will have coffee while Johnson changes to different boots—it's colder than he expected. Johnson will meet a friend who doesn't want to hold us fellows up, but sure would like to go if we're sure there's room. We will have coffee at the drugstore while Johnson's friend goes home, to check with his wife and change. It will be very hot in the drugstore in hunting clothes; the friend will phone and say he can't go after all. Now nothing will be holding us up but the decision to change back to my car, because Johnson's afraid my dog's toenails will rip his seat covers. Off for Waterloo, two hours away (only an hour and a half if Mr. Burton knew exactly how to find the farm). The farmer will have given us up and gone to town. Now that we're here, though, we will drive into town to the feed store, and . . .

"Hell, Mr. Burton," I say. "I'm afraid I can't go along."

"Sure you can. We have a date, don't we?"

"I'll be glad . . ."

"Look, I know you'll like Johnson. That's real hunting up there—I'll bet you five right now we all get limits."

I will not allow myself to think up an excuse. "I'm sorry," I say. "I'll be glad to take you out around here." I even emphasize you a little to exclude Johnson, whoever he is.

"I pretty much promised my farmer friend . . . Oh, look now, is it a matter of having to be back or something?"

"I'm sorry."

"Well, I told him we'd come to Waterloo. There are some things I have to take up to him."

Not being among the things Mr. Burton has to take to his farmer friend, nor my dog either, I continue to decline. Hot damn. Boy, boy, boy. A day to myself.

Ten months a year I'm a social coward, but it's hard to bully me in hunting season, especially with clean socks on.

8:05 Shaving: unnecessary. Shaving for fun, with a brand new blade. Thinking: Mr. Burton, sir, if your hunting is good, and you

```
get a limit of three birds, in two hours . . . . . . . . 2
& it takes two hours' driving to get there. . . . . . . 2
& an hour of messing around on arrival . . . . . . . 1
& an hour for lunch . . . . . . . . . . . . . . . . 1
& two hours to get back and run people home . . . . . 2
                                                    ___
                                                     8
```

you will call it a good hunt, though the likelihood is, since you are no better shot than I, that other men will have shot one or more of your three birds. There is a shoot-as-shoot-can aspect to group hunts; it's assumed that all limits are combined, and it would be considered quit boorish to suggest that one would somehow like to shoot one's own birds.

Thinking: suppose I spend the same eight hours hunting, and it takes me all that time to get three pheasants. In my eccentric mind, that would be four times as good a hunt, since I would be outdoors four times as long. And be spared all that goddamn conversation.

Chortling at the face behind the lather: pleasant fellow, aren't you?

Thinking: God I like to hunt near home. The known covert, the familiar trail. And in my own way and at my own pace, considering any other man's. Someday I'll own the fields behind my house, and there'll be nothing but a door between me and the game—pick up a gun, call a dog, slip out. They'll know where I've gone.

Thinking as I see the naked face, with no lather to hide behind now: I'll take Mr. Burton soon. Pretty nice man. I'll find him birds, too, and stand aside while he shoots, as I did for Jake, and Grannum, and that short guy, whatever his name was, looked so good. Moon and I raised three birds for him, one after another, all in nice range, before he hit one. Damn. That's all right. I don't mind taking people. It's a privilege to go out with a wise hunter; a pleasure to go out with one of equal skill, if he's a friend; and a happy enough responsibility to take an inexperienced one sometimes. Eight or 10 pheasants given away like that this season? Why not? I've got 12 already myself, more than in any season before and this one's barely 10 days old. And for the first time, missed fewer than I've hit.

Eggs?

8:15 Sure! Eggs! Three of them! Fried in that olive oil, so they puff up. With lemon juice. Tabasco. Good. Peppery country sausage, and a stack of toast. Yes, hungry. Moon comes in.

"Hey, boy. Care to go?"

Wags.

"Wouldn't you just rather stay home today and rest up?"

Wags, grins.

"Yeah, wag. If you knew what I said you'd bite me."

Wags, stretches, rubs against me.

"You'd better have some breakfast, too." I go to the refrigerator. Moon is a big dog, a Weimaraner, and he gets a pound of hamburger mornings when he's going to be working. I scoop out cold ground meat from its paper carton, and pat it between my hands into a ball. I roll it across the floor, under his dignified nose. This is a silly game we play; he follows it with his eyes, then pounces as if it really were a ball, trapping it with a paw. My wife, coming in from the yard, catches us.

"Having a game of ball," I say.

"What is it you're always telling the children about not making the same joke twice?"

"Moon thinks it's funny."

"Moon's a very patient dog. I see you're planning to work again today."

I smile. I know this lady. "I really should write letters," I say.

"They can wait, can't they?" She smiles. She likes me to go hunting. She's still not really convinced that I enjoy it—when we were first married I liked cities—but if I do enjoy it, then certainly I must go.

Yes, letters can wait. Let them ripen a few more days. It's autumn. Maybe some of them will perish in the frost if I leave them another week or two—hell, even the oldest ones are barely a month old.

8:45 I never have to tell Moon to get in the car. He's on his hind legs, with his paws on the window, before I reach it. As I get in, start the car, and warm it up, an image comes into my mind of a certain hayfield. It's nice the way this happens; no reasoning, no weighing of one place to start against another. As if the image were projected directly by the precise feel of a certain temperature, a certain wind strength—from sensation to picture without intervening thought. As we drive, I can see just how much the hay should be waving in the wind, just how the shorter grass along the highway will look, going from white to wet as the frost melts off—for suddenly the sun's quite bright.

8:55 I stop, and look at the hayfield, and if sensation projected an image of it into my mind, now it's as if my mind could project this same image, expanded, onto a landscape. The hay is waving, just that much. The frost is starting to melt.

"Whoa, Moon. Stay."

I have three more minutes to think it over. Pheasant hunting starts at nine.

"Moonie. Quiet, boy."

He is quivering, whining, throwing his weight against the door.

I think they'll be in the hay itself—tall grass, really, not a seeded crop; anyway, not in this shorter stuff that grows in the first 100 yards or so along the road. Right?

8:58 Well. Yeah. Whoa.

The season's made its turn at last. Heavy frost every morning now. No more mosquitoes, flies. Cold enough so that it feels good to move, not so cold that I'll need gloves: perfect. No more grasshoppers, either. A sacrifice, in a way—pheasants that feed on hoppers, in open fields, are wilder and taste better than the ones that hang around corn.

The season's made its turn in another sense—the long progression of openings is over: Rabbits, squirrels, September 15. Geese, October 5. Ducks, snipe, October 27. Quail, November 3. Pheasants, November 10. That was 10 days ago. Finally, everything that's ever legal may be hunted. The closings haven't started yet. Amplitude. Best time of the year. Whoa.

8:59: Whoa! Now it's me quivering, whining, but I needn't throw my weight against the door—open it. I step out, making Moon stay. I uncase the gun, look at it with love, throw the case in the car; load. Breathe cold air. Good. Look around. Fine.

"Come on, Moonie. Nine o'clock."

9:00 I start on the most direct line through the short grass, toward the tall, not paying much attention to Moon, who must relieve himself. I think this is as much a matter of nervous tension as it is of regularity.

"Come on, Moon," I call, keeping to my line. "This way, boy."

He thinks he's got a scent back here, in the short grass; barely enough for a pheasant to hide in, and much too thin for cold-day cover.

"Come, Moon. Hyeahp."

It must be an old scent. But he disregards me. His stub of a tail begins to go as he angles off, about 30 yards from where I am; his body lowers just a little and he's moving quickly. I am ignorant in many things about hunting, but there's one thing I know after eight years with this dog, if you bother to hunt with a dog at all, believe what he tells you. Go where he says the bird is, not where you think it ought to be.

I move that way, going pretty quickly myself, still convinced it's an old foot-trail he's following, and he stops in a half-point, his head sinking down while his nose stays up, so that the gray neck is almost in a shallow S-curve.

A cock, going straight up, high, high, high. My gun goes up with him and is firm against my shoulder as he reaches the top of his leap. He seems to hang there as I fire, and he drops perfectly, two or three yards from where Moon waits.

"Good dog. Good boy, Moon," I say as he picks the heavy bird up in his mouth and brings it to me. "Moonie, that was perfect." The bird is thoroughly dead, but I open my pocket knife, press the blade into the roof of its mouth so that it will bleed properly. Check the spurs—they're stubby and almost rounded at the tip. This year's pheasant, probably. Young. Tender. Simply perfect.

Like a book pheasant, I think, and how seldom it happens. In the books, pheasants are said to rise straight up as this one did, going for altitude first, then pausing in the air to swing downwind. The books are quite wrong; most pheasants I see take straight off, without a jump, low and skimming, curving if they rise much, and never hanging at all. I wonder about evolution: among pheasant generations in this open country, did the ones who went towering into the air and hung like kites get killed off disproportionately? While the skulkers and skimmers and curvers survived, to transmit crafty genes?

"Old-fashioned pheasant, are you? You just set a record for me. I never dreamed I'd have a bird so early in the day." I check my watch.

9:15 The device I was so hopeful of is not working out too well. It is a leather holder that slides onto the belt, and has a set of rawhide loops. As I was supposed to, I have hooked the pheasant's legs into a loop, but he swings against my own leg at the knee. Maybe the thing was meant for taller men.

"Moon. This way. Come around, boy." I feel pretty strongly that we should hunt the edge.

The dangling bird is brushing grass tops. Maybe next time I should bring my trout creel, which is oversized, having been made by optimistic Italians. No half-dozen trout would much more than cover the bottom, but three cock pheasants might he nicely in the willow, their tails extending backwards through the crack between lid and body, the rigidity of the thing protecting them as a game bag doesn't.

"Moon. Come back here. Come around." He hasn't settled down for the day. Old as he is, he still takes a wild run, first thing.

I'm pretty well settled, myself (it's that bird bumping against my leg). Now Moon does come back into the area I want him in, the edge between high grass and low; there's a distinction between following your dog when he's got something and trusting him to weigh odds. I know odds better, and here is one of those things that will be a cliché of hunting in a few years since the game-management men are telling it to one another now and it's started filtering into outdoor magazines: the odds are that most game will be near the edge of cover, not in the center of it. The phrase for this is "edge factor."

"Haven't you heard of the edge factor?" I yell at Moon. "Get out along the edge here, boy." And in a few steps he has a scent again. When he's got the tail factor going, the odds change, and I follow him, almost trotting to keep up, as he works from edge to center, back toward edge, after what must be a running bird. He slows a little, but doesn't stops; the scent is hot, but apparently the bird is still moving. Moon stops, points, holds. I walk as fast as I can, am in range—and Moon starts again. He is in a crouch now, creeping forward in his point. The unseen bird must be shifting: he is starting to run again, for Moon moves out of the point and stars to lope: I move, fast as I can and still stay collected enough to shoot—gun held in both hands out in front of me—exhilarated to see the wonderful mixture of exuberance and certainty with which Moon goes. To make such big happy moves, and none of them a false one, is something only the most extraordinary human athletes can do after years of tanning it comes naturally to almost any dog. And that pheasant there in front of us—how he can go! Turn and twist through the tangle of steam stems, never showing himself, moving away from Moon's speed and my calculations. But we've got him—I think we do—Moon slows, points. Sometimes we win in a run down usually not usually the pheasant picks the right time, well out and away, to flush out of range—but this one stopped. Yes. Moon's holding again. I'm in range. I move up, beside the rigid dog. Past him. WHIRR-PT. The gun rises, checks itself, and I yell at Moon, who is ready to bound forward:

"Hen!"

Away she goes, and away goes Moon, and I yell: "Whoa. Hen, hen," but it doesn't stop him. He's pursuing, as if he could get up enough speed to rise onto the air after her. "Whoa." It doesn't stop him. WHIRRUPFT. That stops him. Stops me too. A second hen. WHIRRUPFT. WHIRRUPFT. Two more. And another, that makes five who were sitting tight. And then, way out, far from this little group, through which he must have passed, and far from us, I see the cock—almost certainly the bird we were chasing (hens don't run like that)—fly up silently, without a cackle, and glide away, across the road and out of sight.

9:30 "There's got to be another," I say to Moon. A man I know informed me quite vehemently a week ago that one ought never to talk to a dog in the field except to give commands; distracts him, the man said, keeps him too close. Tell you what, man: you run your dogs your way, and I'll run my dog mine. Okay?

We approach a fence, where the hayfield ends; the ground is clear for 20 feet before the fence line. Critical place. If birds have been moving ahead of us, and are reluctant to fly, this is where they'll hide. They won't run into the open. And just as I put this card in the calculator, one goes up. CUK CUK CUK, bursting past Moon full speed and low, putting the dog between me and him so that, while my gun is ready, I can't shoot immediately; he rises only enough to clear the fence, sweeping left between two bushes as I fire, and I see the pellets agitate the leaves of the right-hand bush, and I know I shot behind him.

Moon, in the immemorial way of bird dogs, looks back to me with what bird hunters who miss have immemorially taken for reproach.

We turn along the edge paralleling the fence. He may not have been the only one we chased down here—Moon is hunting, working from fence to edge, very deliberate. Me too. I wouldn't like to miss again. Moon swerves to the fence row, tries some likely brush. Nope. Lopes back to the edge, lopes along it. Point. Very stiff. Very sudden. Ten yards, straight ahead.

This is a beautifully awkward point, Moon's body curved into it, shoulders down, rear up, head almost looking back at me; this one really caught him. As now we'll catch the pheasant? So close. Dog so steady. I have the impression Moon's looking a bird straight in the eye. I move slowly. No need for speed, no reason to risk being off balance. Let's be so deliberate, so cool, so easy. The gun is ready to come up—I never have the feeling that I myself bring it up. Don't be off balance. He'll go now. Now. Nope—when he does, I try to tell myself, don't shoot too fast, let the bird get out a little, but I'm not really that good and confident in my shooting. Thanks be for brush loads. Ought to have them in both barrels for this situation. Will I have to kick the pheasant out? I am within two steps of Moon, who hasn't stirred except for the twitching of his shoulder and haunch muscles, when the creature bolts. Out he comes, under Moon's nose, and virtually between my legs if I didn't jump aside—a rabbit, tearing for the fence row. I could recover and shoot, it's an easy shot, but not today; I smile, relax, and sweat flows. I am not that desperate for game yet.

I yell "Whoa" at Moon, and for some dog's reason he obeys this time. I should punish him, now; for pointing fur? But it's my fault—sometimes, being a one-dog man, I shoot fur over him, though I recognize it as a genuine error in bird-dog handling. But with the long bond of hunting and mutual training between us (for Moon trained me no less than I did him), my taking a rabbit over him from time to time—or a mongoose, or a kangaroo—is not going to change things between us.

In any case, my wife's never especially pleased to see me bring a rabbit home, though the kids and I like to eat them. I pat Moon, who whoaed for the rabbit. "Whoa, big babe," I say softly. "Whoasie-posner, whoa-daboodle-dog, big sweet posner baby dog . . ." I am rubbing his back.

10:40 Step out of the car, look around, work it out: the birds slept late this morning, because of the wind and frost, and may therefore be feeding late. If so, they're in the field itself, which lies beyond two fallow fields. They roost here in this heavy cover, fly out to the corn—early on nice mornings; later, if I'm correct, on a day like this. When they're done feeding, they go to what game experts call loafing cover—relatively thin cover, near the feeding place, and stay in it till the second feeding in the afternoon; after which they'll be back here where they started, to roost again.

The wind is on my left cheek, as Moon and I go through the roosting cover, so I angle right. This will bring us to where we can turn and cross the popcorn field, walking straight into the wind. This will not only be better for Moon, for obvious reasons, but will also be better for shooting; birds in open rows, hearing us coming, can sail away out of range very fast with the wind behind them. If it blows towards me, they'll either be lifted high, going into the wind, or curve off to one side or the other.

The ragweed, as we come up close to it and Moon pauses before choosing a spot at which to plunge in, is eight feet high—thick, dry, brittle, gray-stemmed stuff that pops and crackles as he breaks into it. I move a few feet along the edge of the draw, shifting my position as I hear him working through, to stay as well in range of where he is as possible. I am calmly certain there's a bird in there, even that it's a cock. I think he moved in ahead of us as we were coming up the field, felt safe when he saw us apparently about to pass by, and doesn't want to leave the defense overhead protection now.

But he must. Moon will send him up in a moment, perhaps out the far side where the range will be extreme. It will be a long shot, if that happens, and Moon is now at the far edge, is turning along it, when I hear the cackle of the cock rising. For a moment I don't know where, can't see him, and by the time I do he's going out to my right, almost back towards me, having doubled away from the dog. Out he comes, already in full flight and low, with the wind behind him for speed. And yet I was so well set for this, for anything, that it all seems easy—to pivot, mounting the gun as I do, find it against my cheek and the bird big and solid at the end of the barrel, swing, taking my time, and shoot. The bird checks, fights air, and tumbles, and in my sense of perfection I make an error: I am so sure he's perfectly hit that I do not take the second shot, before he falls in some waist-high weeds. I mark the place by keeping my eye on a particular weed, a little taller than the others, and walk slowly, straight towards it, not letting my eye move away, confident he'll be lying right by it. Moon, working the ragweed, would neither see the rise nor mark the fall and he comes bounding out to me now, coming to the sound of the shot. I reach the spot first, so very carefully marked, and there's no bird there.

Hunters make errors; dogs correct them. While I am still standing there, irritated with myself for not having shot twice, Moon is circling me, casting, inhaling those great snuffs, finding the ground scent. He begins to work a straight line, checks as I follow him, starts again in a slightly different direction; I must trust him, absolutely, and I do. I remind myself that once he trailed a crippled bird more than half a mile in the direction opposite from that in which I had actually seen the bird start off. I kept trying to get him to go the other way, but he wouldn't; and he found the pheasant. It was by the edge of a dirt road, so that Max Morgan and I could clock the distance afterwards by car speedometer.

Our present bird is no such problem. Forty feet from where the empty shell waves gently back and forth on top of the weed, Moon hesitates, points. Then, and I do not know how he knows that this particular immobile pheasant will not fly (unless it's the smell of fresh blood), Moon lunges. His head darts into matted weeds, fights spurs for a moment, tosses the big bird once so that he can take it by the back, lifts it; and he comes to me proudly, trotting, head as high as he can hold it.

11:00 Iowa hunters are obsessed with corn. If there are no birds in the cornfields, they consider the situation hopeless. This may come from the fact that most of them hunt in drives—a number of men spread out in line, going along abreast through standing corn, with others blocking the end of the field. My experience, for I avoid that kind of hunt every chance I get, is quite different; I rarely find pheasants in cornfields, except along the edges. More than half of those I shoot. I find away from corn, in wild cover, and sometimes the crops show that the bird has not been eating grain at all but getting along on wilder seeds.

But as I start to hunt the popcorn field, something happens that shows why driving often works out. We start into the wind, as planned, moving down the field the long way, and way down at the other end a farm dog sees us. He starts towards us, intending to investigate Moon, I suppose. I see him come towards the field; I see him enter it, trotting our way, and the wind carries the sound of his barking. And then I see—the length of a football field away, reacting to the farm dog—pheasants go up; not two or three, but a flock, 12 or 14, and another and another and another, cocks and hens, flying off in all directions, sailing down wind and out of sight. Drivers and blockers would have had fast shooting with that bunch—but suppose I'd got up? Well, this gun only shoots twice. And, well again, boy. Three's the limit, dunghead. And you've got two already.

11:30 Two birds before lunch? I ought to limit out, I ought to limit out soon. And stop looking for pheasants, spend the afternoon on something else. Take Moon home to rest, maybe, and know that the wind's going down and the sun's getting hot, go into the woods for squirrels, something I like but never get around to.

Let's get the other one. Where?

We are walking back to the car, the shortest way, no reason to go through the popcorn field after what happened. Where? And I think of a pretty place, not far away.

11:45 Yes, it's pretty. Got a bird here last year, missed a couple, too, why haven't I been here this season? It's a puzzle, and the solution, as I step the car once more, is a pleasure: I know a lot of pretty places near home, 20 or 30 of them, all quite distinct, and have gotten or missed birds at all of them, one season or another.

There are no pheasants this time, only signs of pheasant: roosting places, full of droppings. Some fresh enough so that they were dropped this morning. A place for the next windy morning: I put that idea in a safe place and move back, after Moon—he's pretty excited with all the bird scent, but not violently; it's not that fresh—towards the fence along the soybean field. We turn from the creek, and go along the fence line, 20 or 30 feet out, towards an eight-acre patch of woods where I have often seen deer, and if I were a real reasoner or a real instinct man, not something in between, what happens would not find me unprepared. Moon goes into a majestically rigid point, foreleg raised, tail out straight, aimed at low bushes in the fence row. I hardly ever see him point so rigidly without first showing the signs he gives while the quarry is still shifting. I move in rather casually, suspecting a hen, but if it's a cock rather confident, after my last great shot, and there suddenly comes at me, buzzing angrily, a swarm of—pheasants? Too small—hornets? Sparrow? Quail! Drilling right at me, the air full of them, whirring, swerving to both sides.

Much too late, surprised, confused—abashed, for this is classic quail cover—I flounder around, face back the way I came, and pop off a pair of harmless shots, more in valediction than in hope of hitting. Turn back to look at Moon, and up comes a straggler, whirring all by himself, also past me. There are no easy shots on quail, but I could have him, I think, if both barrels weren't empty. He's so close that I can see the white on neck and face, and know him for a male. Jock though I am, at least I mark him down, relieved that he doesn't cross the creek.

Moon works straight to the spot where I marked the straggler, and sure enough he flushes, not giving the dog a chance to point, flushes high and I snap-shoot and he falls. Moon bounds after him and stops on the way, almost pitching forward, like a car when its brakes lock. Another bird. Ready. I hope I have my down bird marked. Careful. *Whirr*—I damn near stepped on him, and back he goes behind me. I swing 180 degrees, and as he angles away have him over the end of the barrel. As I fire, it seems almost accidental that I should be on him so readily, but it's not of course—it's the one kind of shot that never misses, the unplanned, reflexive shot, when conditioning has already operated before self-consciousness could start up. This quail falls in the soft maple seedlings, in a place I won't forget, but the first one may be hard.

He's not. I find him without difficulty, seeing him on the ground at just about the same time that Moon finds him too. Happy to have him, I bring Moon back to the soft maple seedlings, but we do not find the second bird.

12:30 Lunch is black coffee in the thermos, an apple and an orange, and the sight of two quail and two pheasants, lying in a neat row on the car floor. I had planned to go home for lunch; and it wouldn't take so very much time; but I would talk with my family, of course, and whatever it is this noon that they're concerned with, I would be concerned with. And that would break the spell, as an apple and an orange will not.

12:45 Also

1:45 and, I'm afraid

2:45 these hours repeat one another, and at the end of them I have: two pheasants, as before: two quail; and an afterthought.

The afterthought shouldn't have run through my mind, in the irritable state that it was in.

The only shots I took were at domestic pigeons, going by fast and far up, considered a nuisance around here; I missed both times. But what made me irritable were all the mourning doves.

There are doves all over the place in Iowa, in every covert that I hunt—according to the last Audubon Society spring census at Des Moines, doves were more common even than robins and meadow larks. In my three hard hours of barren pheasant hunting, I could have had shots at 20 or 25 doves (a game bird in 30 states, a game bird throughout the history of the world), and may not try them. Shooting doves is against the law in Iowa. The harvesting of our enormous surplus (for nine out of 10 will die before they're a year old anyway) is left to cats and owls and—because the dove ranges get so crowded—germs.

Leaving the half-picked cornfield, I jump yet another pair of doves, throw up my gun and track them making a pretended double, though I doubt that it would work.

Three hours of seeing doves, and no pheasants, has made me pettish, and perhaps I am beginning to tire.

A rabbit jumps out behind the dog, unseen by Moon but not by me. At first I assume that I want to let him go, as I did the earlier one; then he becomes the afterthought: company, dinner—so you won't let me shoot doves, eh, rabbit? He's dead before he can reach cover.

3:00 Now I have only an hour left to get my final bird, for pheasant hunting ends at four. This is a symbolic bird: a good hunter gets his limit. At noon it seemed almost sure I would; suddenly it's doubtful.

I sit in the car, one hand on Moon who is lying on the seat beside me. We've reached the time of the day when he rests when he can.

3:10 On my way to someplace else, I suddenly brake the car.

"Hey, did you see that?" I am talking to Moon again. He has a paw over his nose, and of course saw nothing. I look over him, eagerly, out the window and down into a big marsh we were about to pass by. We were on our way to the place I'd thought of, an old windbreak of evergreens near an abandoned farmhouse site, surrounded by overgrown pasture, and not too far from corn—It's an ace in-the-hole kind of place for evening shooting, for the pheasants come in there early to roost; I've used it sparingly, shown it to no one.

Going there would be our best chance to fill out, I think, but look: "Damn, Moon, snipe. Snipe, boy, I'm sure of it."

On the big marsh, shore birds are rising up and setting down, not in little squadrons like killdeer—which are shore birds about the same size, and very common—but a bird here, a bird there. Becoming instantly invisible when they land, too, and so not among the wading shore birds. I get out the glasses and step out of the car, telling Moon to stay. I catch one of the birds in the lenses, and the silhouette is unmistakable—the long, comic beak, the swept-back wings.

"You are snipe," I say, addressing—well, them, I suppose. "Where've you boys been?"

Two more whiz in and out of the image, too quickly to follow, two more of my favorite of all game birds. Habitat changes around here so much from year to year, with the great fluctuations in water level from the dam, that this marsh, which was full of snipe three years ago, has shown none at all so far this year. What snipe hunting I've found has been in temporarily puddled fields, after rains, and in a smaller marsh.

"I thought you'd never come," I say. "Moon!" I open the car door. "Moon, let's go." My heartiness is a little false, for snipe are my favorite bird, not Moon's. He'll flush them, if he must, but apparently they're distasteful to him, and when I manage to shoot one, he generally refuses even to pick it up, much less retrieve it for me.

Manage to shoot one? Last year, on the first day I hunted snipe, I shot 16 shells before I hit my first. That third pheasant can wait there in the hole with the other aces.

Remembering the 16 straight misses, I stuff my pockets with shells—brush loads still for the first shot but, with splendid consistency, high-brass 7½s for the second, full-choke shot. I won't use them on a big bird, like a pheasant; I will on a tiny bird, like a snipe. The snipe goes fast, and by the second shot you need all the range you can get.

I should have hip boots now. Go back and get them? Nuts. Get muddy.

Down we go, Moon with a certain silly enthusiasm for the muskrats he smells and may suppose are now to be our quarry. I see that the marsh water is shallow, but the mud under it is always deep—thigh-deep in some places; the only way to go into it is from hummock to hummock of marsh grass. Actually, I will stay out of it if I can, and so I turn along the edge, Moon hunting out in front. A snipe rises over the marsh at my right, too far to shoot at, scolding us anyway: *scaip, scaip*. Then two more, which let the dog get by them, going up between me and Moon—a chance for a double, in a highly theoretical way, I shoot and miss at the one on the left as he twists low along the edge. He rises, just after the shot, going up in a tight turn, and I shoot again, swinging up with him, and miss again.

At my first shot, the other snipe—the one I didn't shoot at—dove, as if hit. But I know he wasn't; I've seen the trick before. I know about where he went in, and I decide not to bother with Moon, who is chasing around in the mud, trying to convince himself that I knocked down a pheasant or something decent like that.

I wade in myself, mud to ankles, mud to calves, up to the tops of the low boots I'm wearing; no bird? What the hell, mud over the boot tops, and I finally climb a hummock. This puts up my diving snipe, 10 yards further out and scolding, but the hummocks are spaced too far apart in this part of the swamp so there's no point shooting. I couldn't recover him and I doubt that Moon would. I let him rise, twist, swoop upwards, and I stand as still as I can balanced on the little mound of grass; I know a trick myself. It works; at the top of his climb the snipe turns and comes streaking back, 40 yards up, directly overhead. I throw up the gun for the fast overhead shot, and miss.

I splash back to the edge and muck along. A snipe goes up, almost at my feet, and his first swerve coincides with my snap shot—a kind of luck that almost seems like skill. Moon, bounding back, has seen the bird fall and runs to it—smells it, curls his lip and slinks away. He turns his head to watch me bend to pick it up, and as I do, leaps back and tries to take it from me.

"Moondog." I say, addressing him severely by his full name. "I'm not your child to punish. I like this bird. Now stop it."

We start along again, come to the corner where the marsh dies out, and turn. Moon stops, sight-pointing in a half-hearted way, and a snipe goes up in front of him. This one curves towards some high weeds: I tire and miss, but stay on him as he suddenly straightens and goes winging straight out, rising very little. He is a good 40 yards away by now, but he tumbles when I fire, and falls on open ground. It takes very little to kill a snipe. I pace the distance, going to him, and watch Moon, for Moon picks this one up. Then, when I call to him to bring it, he gradually, perhaps sulkily, lowers his head and spits it out again. He strolls off as if there were nothing there. I scold him as I come up, but not very hard: he looks abashed, and makes a small show of hunting dead in a bare spot about 10 yards from where we both know the snipe is lying I pick up the bird, and tell Moon that he is probably the worst dog that ever lived, but not in an unkind voice for I wouldn't want to hurt his feelings.

This a pleasanter area we are crossing now firm mud, patches of swamp weeds, frequent puddles Moon, loping around aimlessly, blunders into a group of five or six snipe at the far side of a puddle, and I put trying to get a double out of my mind; I try to take my time: pick out an individual, follow him as he glides toward some high reeds and drop him.

Now we go along, towards the back of the marsh, shooting and missing, hitting just twice. One shot in particular pleases me: a snipe quite high, in full flight coming towards me. I shoot, remembering a phrase I once read: "A shotgun is a paint brush." I paint the snipe blue, to match the sky, starting my brush stroke just behind him, painting evenly along his body, completing the stroke about three lengths in front where I fire, and follow through. This is a classic shot, a memorable one, so much so that there are just two others I can put with it—one on a faraway pheasant last year, one on a high teal in Chile. The sky is all blue now, for the snipe is painted out of it and falls, almost into my hand.

It is just 3:55.

There is magic in this. The end of the legal pheasant hunting day is four o'clock.

4:00 Just after the pheasant, I kill another snipe, the sixth. He is along the stream, too, and so I follow it, awed at the thought that I might even get a limit on these. But on the next chance, not a hard one, I think too hard, and miss the first shot, as he twists, and the rising one as well.

We leave the watercourse for a tiny marsh, go back to it (or a branch) through government fields I've never crossed before, by strange potholes and unfamiliar willow stands. We flush a woodcock, cousin to the snipe, but shooting him is not permitted here. We turn away in a new direction—snipe and woodcock favor different sorts of cover. And sometime along in there, I walk up two snipe, shoot one very fast, and miss a perplexing but not impossible shot at the other, as he spirals up.

"There he goes," I think. "My limit bird." He flies into the east, where the sky is getting dark; clouds have come to the western horizon and the sun is gone for the day, behind them.

5:03 In this remnant of perfect habitat, the sky is empty. It is five minutes till sunset, but it is dusk already, when my last snipe does go up, I hear him before I see him. I crouch down, close to the ground, trying to expand the area of light against which he will show up, and he appears now, winging for the upper sky; but I cannot decide to shoot, shouldering my gun in that awkward position. And in another second it is too late, really too late, and I feel as if the last hunter in the world has let the last snipe go without a try.

I straighten up reluctantly, unload gun, and wonder where I am. Suddenly I am tired, melancholy, and very hungry. I know about which way to go, and start along, calling Moon, only half lost, dragging a little. The hunting is over and home an hour away.

I think of quail hunting in Louisiana, when we crouched, straining for shots at the final covey, as I did just now for the final snipe.

I find a little road I recognize, start on it the wrong way, correct myself and turn back along it. A touch of late sun shows now, through a rift, enough to cast a pale shadow in front of me—man with gun—on the sand road.

We were on an evening march, in some loose company formation, outside of training camp. We were boys.

I watched our shadows along the tall clay bank at the side of the road. We were too tired to talk, even garrulous Bobby Hirt, who went AWOL later and spent two years, so we heard, in military prison. He was a boy. We all were. But the helmeted shadows, with packs and guns in silhouette, were the shadows of soldiers—faceless, menacing, expendable. No one shadow different from the other. I could not tell you, for after training we dispersed, going out as infantry replacements, which of those boys, whose misery and defiance and occasional good times I shared for 17 unforgotten weeks, actually were expended. Several, of course, since statistics show what they do of infantry replacements. Statistics are the representation of shadows by numbers.

My shadow on the sand road is of a different kind. I have come a little way in 19 years, whatever the world has done. I am alone, in a solitary place, as I wish to be, accountable only as I am willing to be held so, therefore no man's statistic. Melancholy for the moment, but only because I am weary, and coming to the end of this day which, full of remembering, will be itself remembered.

Moon is beside me, tired now too, throwing his own pale dog-shadow ahead. And the hunter-shadow with him, the pheasant hanging from the hunter's belt, sniper bulging in the jacket—the image teases me. It is not the soldiers, but some other memory. An image, failing because the sun is failing, the rift closing very slowly. An image of. A hunter like. A dream? Not a dream, but the ghost of a dream, my old, hunter-and-his-dog-at-dusk dream. And the sun goes down, and the ghost with it, and the car is in sight that will carry us home.

Intelligence

DATUS PROPER

During the next week, Trooper and I healed all six feet while I applied my head to the problem. That dog was a great recuperator. From Sunday through Wednesday he slept under the kitchen counter, except when my wife rolled him over and reminded him that he ought to go out and kill some shrubbery. By Thursday he was up in the morning and asking if I was headed for the office or someplace worthwhile. By Saturday he could make a standing long-jump into the rear of the wagon. And by then I was ready for some head-hunting, which was intended to work better than foot-hunting

    I pretended to be in Ireland. Irish birds cope with a paucity of good protective cover, fields grazed bare, and 5 million Irishmen devoted to roast pheasant. Sounds like parts of America in the bad new days. In Ireland my friends had concerned themselves with intelligence, so that is how Trooper and I set about doing it to the recently scarce pheasants of the New World. We could hardly do worse than we had by roaming where a free spirit beckoned.

    By "intelligence," I do not refer to the brain cells, though Trooper had those, too. (For instance, he had quickly perceived that pheasant tastes good, and nothing would persuade him that it was wrong to have a little chew.) No, by intelligence I mean the kind of information collected by the Department of Dirty Tricks about our opponents overseas. In the easy old days, my approach had been to get hunting permission in several places before the season, then hunt wherever it felt good. It worked when there were lots of birds and few hunters, but not vice versa.

In Ireland, Ned Maguire would tell me of a conversation with Mrs. Murphy after the Mass. She had heard a cock crowing during a picnic at Roundwood. Right: let's get the dog and have a look. Sometimes we found what we were looking for. We never found more than one, but chasing it was more fun than shooting an easy limit, and more meritorious. You do not want to shoot many of the clever ones. Inflation depreciates the currency of emotion.

The Irish gave me a new way of looking at brown trout, gray partridges, and red grouse; and no Irishman was ever heard to suggest that pheasants occupy a lower pedestal than any of these. At the Irish dinner table, the pheasant sits above the salt with the woodcock. An old cock pheasant is, perhaps, the toughest to hunt of the lot.

It did not hurt that the Irish shared my passion for pointing dogs—which they considered the most practical way to convey bird from hedgerow to table. Trooper was not with me there, but we'd turn loose Ned's English setter, Paddy's Irish setter, Bryan's dropper (pointer-setter cross), or Liam's shorthair. The dog would take a quick run around all four sides of a field. We'd wait and, if the dog came back, go through the gate to the next field, and the next, and a dozen more. We'd hike five miles while the pointer ran fifty and found the pheasant that someone had told us to look for in one of them. When the point came, the fellow who was not the handler (me) would discover that he could, after all, get through a hedge made for turning dairy bulls. I'd get more scratches than birds. Still, during the season, the rope in the coal shed usually had something hanging from it, aging: a pheasant.

One cock pheasant.

Singular Hunting

The idea is not to look for pheasants, plural and abstract, but pheasant: a singular, particular, concrete cock pheasant. You have to find them one by one, not collectively. Consider it a kind of big-game hunting—not a ridiculous comparison, these days. While pheasants were decreasing, deer were increasing, and now I can usually shoot one for venison in an hour or so. A good buck still takes intelligence, and so does a cock pheasant.

You might spot one from your car, especially early and late in the days before the season opens. Take binoculars. The cock is not as wary of cars as of people on foot, but he is more shy than he was in 1945 or 1969. You will do better exploiting his tragic flaw: He talks too much. The cackling decreases, but does not cease, as the days get shorter. It goes on even during the late season. Mostly the rooster brags to the neighborhood in early morning and late evening, when hunters are drinking coffee or putting ointment on blisters. He is most likely to blow his cover one-half hour before sunrise. If you are listening, you can wait till the legal shooting time, then go out and amputate his reveille.

Of course, if you live two hours' drive from the hunting, arrival before sunrise means getting up early in the morning, or perhaps late at night. You could talk instead to the fellow who lives there: the farmer. He, as you might expect, knows something about musical performances on his acres. He may share the knowledge—and the hunting—with a solitary hunter who looks as if he can be counted on to stay out of standing crops: farmers are extra-wary of hunters who come by the van-load.

During that Pennsylvania November, one farmer told me that he had heard a cock crowing behind the house the evening before I stepped into the field carelessly, figuring that the bird had moved on, and flushed it within ten feet. Pheasants love dirty tricks. This one found out that I can shoot my old double 12-gauge pretty fast. On the other hand, a repeater might have allowed me to miss five times instead of two, earning some sort of award for nonexploitative use of the environment.

At least the intelligence was good.

Where They Aren't

In heavily hunted country you may be surprised, on the dawn patrol, to find how many pretty places have no cocks. Trooper and I almost stopped hunting on land that was not posted—my favorite old coverts. In places where hunters could just jump out of their cars and get going, the birds departed early in the season and did not return till it was over. I had no special private access but spent some time knocking on doors. It was much less fun than hunting. I felt like an encyclopedia salesman, but encyclopedia salesmen presumably sell the occasional encyclopedia. I got permission to hunt in the occasional place that had birds.

When the Pennsylvania season ended, Trooper and I went south of the Mason-Dixon line, into Maryland, and hunted for six more weeks. It was a pattern that we had followed for years. In 1982, however, we found more pheasants south of Pennsylvania for the first time. Maryland had become, in effect, all posted property. A new law made it illegal to hunt except by written permission from the landowner—with high fines and no excuses. It hurt. Then it improved the sport. What impressed me most was the discovery that Mennonite farms had no pheasants even in Maryland. The Mennonites, bless their souls, would sign anybody's permission slip, and everybody knew it, including the pheasants, which moved out.

Posted signs meant the end of hunting in the free old way. I'd rather take a trip in back in time than anywhere else, but the change saved hunting near Washington. Most of us hunters thought of the problem as finding birds. The bigger problem was escaping from people.

Cover

But there was still the matter of hunting in the right cover, because cocks were nowhere abundant, and they did not spend all day at the site of their reveille.

One of the most useful bits of intelligence was that pheasants were no longer in standing corn. Hunters have been slow to cope with this atrocity. Pheasants and corn used to go together like apple pie and cheese, love and marriage, horse and carriage. The biggest losers have been hunters without dogs, who could flush birds from corn more easily than from most other cover. I do not mean that pheasants now dislike corn: they feed on broken ears lying around after harvesting, and before that they run into standing corn when pushed. But they do not dawdle there. The problem seems to be that herbicides have killed off the grass and weeds in "no-till" corn. It was the undergrowth that pheasants used to like, more than the tall stalks. Check a cornfield in the snow now and see how scarce tracks are. Even the mice have left.

Half a dozen farmers gave me the same story: they had just harvested forty acres of corn (or thirty, or a hundred) and hardly a pheasant had flown out of it. Bobwhites were even more scarce. Pheasants were still around, but less of them, and elsewhere.

Elsewhere turned out to be big fields—the bigger the better—ungrazed and overgrown. Call it grass, in shorthand. More precisely, it is herbaceous cover: grasses, forbs, legumes, annuals with lots of seeds. Later in the eighties, the Conservation Reserve Program would give us the best of all: fields of tall, stiff grasses that would not mat down even in the winter. But there were some good places even in 1982. Old, unmown hayfields were best.

Stream-bottoms and swamps were worth hunting too, but not quite as good. This may seem surprising. Wet cover is where most hunters go when the birds get scarce, but then most hunters do not have pointing dogs. Pheasants want to be (1) where the hunter is not and (2) where he will have trouble cornering them if he follows. Swamps may have edges of some kind where the bird can be forced to fly: edges where reeds meet water or cattails meet thinner cover. In a big field with the right cover, a cock can dodge a human forever without being herded to an edge.

Pheasants prefer ground-cover of a certain density. (Always have, I suppose, though the corn fooled us.) Inside, they want tunnellike paths just big enough for an agile bird. A dog (or a fox) is taller, so he has to waste energy pushing through heavy vegetation. A hawk cannot see down through it. A cock pheasant, however, can jump out with one push of those springy legs. He likes that better than brush that tangles his wings. (I have seen him get stuck.)

Ideally, the cover should come somewhere between a hunter's knee and his waist. Of course you have seen pheasants in lower stuff. Wouldn't surprise me to hear that a cock had escaped unseen across a billiard table, but he'd rather improve the odds.

During the rest of the three-month season, Trooper got me a pheasant every Saturday. One would have been more than enough to make the world fit to live in for the rest of the week. It was hard to convince Trooper that we should quit in the morning, though, so most Saturdays we wound up with our limit of two by sundown. Two cocks are almost an embarrassment of riches. I would have felt better hiding them and pretending that we had been skunked. For proper aging, however, birds must cool and dry quickly. The only place with good air circulation was the top of Trooper's mesh cage.

Trucks on the interstate highway would slow down while drivers peered inside the station wagon at those birds. The boys from the service station would stand around, hoping that I would reveal the hot spot. My wagon's odometer was going around for the second time, but the folks in new Mercedes had to wait while my windshield was washed and my oil checked twice.

If you want to find what pheasants mean to the American people, try carrying a couple of them around in full feather one January day. It is like traveling in July with a very pretty lady wearing less plumage. Observe: you, personally, are invisible, because everyone is watching your symbol. You want to know what the real national bird is? It's not the bald eagle, nor yet Benjamin Franklin's wild turkey. The people have chosen. They vote with South Dakota.

From *Pheasants of the Mind*. Reprinted with permission of Anna Proper.

Autumn Quarter

E. DONNALL THOMAS, JR.

There are only two times of year in Montana: bird season and all the rest.

September

Silence and an expanse of empty spaces. Isolated by the approaching sunrise, brilliant Venus stands alone above the eastern horizon, her fellow stars and planets banished by the light for yet another long Indian summer day. I can feel a suggestion of fall in the last of the pleasant overnight chill, but the crunch of dry grass underfoot and the awakening buzz of insects remind me at once that it will not last for long. This early in the season, it's important to reach the field at first light, while it's cool enough to hike comfortably and good scenting conditions still prevail. Midday belongs to mad dogs and Englishmen, and the Labs and I fail to qualify on either count.

Conceding a bit of discipline to their enthusiasm, Sonny and Jake boil out of the back of the truck as soon as the tailgate opens, but it's not the time or the place to correct them. Their only fault lies in their eagerness to hunt and I'll trade proper attitude for proper manners any day, in dogs as well as people. Together—more or less—the three of us set off toward a shallow coulee dotted with clumps of buffaloberry. This is natural, unspoiled sharptail habitat, and the size and splendid emptiness of the cover ahead would provide reason enough to be here even if I didn't carry a shotgun over my shoulder and a hunting license buried somewhere deep inside my pocket.

Although generally a sociable person, I've always enjoyed hunting early season sharptails alone, or at least with no company other than the dogs'. Practically unchanged since the days of Lewis and Clark, real prairie bird cover invites the kind of introspection that develops best away from the distraction of human voices. And when you've been at this as long as I have, you go for the feel of the country as much as for the heft of the birds in the game vest at the end of the day. All of which provides at least an attempted explanation for the peculiar emotional ambience I experience as the dogs approach the first cluster of brush: *alone without feeling lonely*, or something like that.

Still too young to appreciate Sutton's Law, Jake expends futile calories cutting wide circles through the grass. Sonny knows better, and as we close within shotgun range of the brush he picks up his tail and wades into the cover, leaving me with nothing to do but stand at port arms and wait. In the best of all possible worlds, this kind of effort would earn the dog the reward of a flush and a retrieve or two, but nature has always been an indifferent accountant and the morning air remains silent despite his determined labor down in the thorns.

But Sonny and I know this much even if Jake does not: *send enough Labrador retrievers into enough good bird cover and something's gonna happen.* You can take that adage to the bank, and half a mile farther up the coulee, sure enough. With a faint suggestion of a breeze in our faces, Jake picks up a whiff of something that sends him into the brush right along with Sonny. That serves as my cue to scramble to the uphill side of the cover where I can see well enough to shoot anything that emerges. The sound of wings comes first as the grouse fight their way upward through the tightly woven branches. Then they're chuckling their rich, reedy alarm calls and spilling over the top of the foliage like popcorn exploding from an overheated pan. The shooting that follows isn't hard shooting but it's good shooting, the kind that makes you appreciate the birds as something more than targets with feathers, and when it's done there's a bird for each dog.

Perhaps nature knows how to keep score after all.

October

There's a real edge to the air now, a bite that reminds you where your nose ends and the rest of the world begins. Here along the creek bottom, the year's first hard frosts seem to have set the foliage on fire. The drab early season earth tones have yielded to a riot of pastels: crimson, orange, and magenta, shades that fix the place and time immediately in the hearts of those who have been here before. It's pheasant season on the high plains, and a special kind of urgency prevails. For the faithful, pheasant season never comes quickly enough, and once it's there at last, it turns out to be as hard to hold as mirage water.

Our new quarry seems to reflect the visual changes in the terrain. All muted grays and browns, the sharptails and Huns that defined the early season seemed designed to blend into their surroundings without attracting attention. Cock ring-necked pheasants, on the other hand, serve as a study in self-promotion: garish bursts of color ready to explode from the brush in front of the dogs like advertisements for themselves. While grouse and partridge basically seem to want to get along, pheasants act like they're daring you to do something about them, and believe me, we'd like to.

If only it were that simple. In fact, wild pheasants back up their brash first impressions with cunning and tenacity unique among all upland birds. Hunting them successfully requires a level of perseverance ordinarily reserved for big game. Among their real enthusiasts, those qualities count for even more than the excitement of the flush or the appeal of pheasants on the table. You hunt them for the same reason you accept any challenge, and there's an edginess to the process no other western game bird can evoke.

Because so many of our friends understand this point of view, October has become the social part of hunting season around our house. The long, solitary walks through the sharptail cover lie behind me now, replaced by a pleasant swell of company. And I feel no regrets. Pheasants are what you do with friends just as surely as grouse are what you do alone, partly because of the demands of strategy and partly because of the essential human need to share both the triumph and despair pheasants alone arouse.

And so we form quite a crew as we head toward the brambles along the creek bottom: me, my wife Lori, three old friends from out of state, and enough dogs to populate a kennel. As an outdoorsman who appreciates his solitude, I ordinarily might bridle at this kind of production, but not today. The cover ahead looks big enough to swallow us all, and there will have to be some teamwork down there in the stickers if we are to prevail. Besides, pheasants are on the menu back home tonight, and autumn is no time to begin a diet.

Our strategic objective is to push the creek bends back and forth toward one another in a series of pincer movements, trapping running birds between dogs and open water and forcing them into the air, hopefully within shotgun range of somebody. Given our visitors' lack of familiarity with the cover, it takes a certain amount of discussion to get all this worked out, but finally everyone winds up where they need to be and it's time for me to wade into the cover with the dogs. Mornings like this remind me why I've always resisted the occasional urge to involve myself in the guiding business. Pushing pheasant cover for friends is one thing, but if I were doing this for money, there would have to be a hell of a lot of it.

I've never warmed to the habit of wearing brush pants in the field. As a bowhunter, I feel an instinctive aversion to noisy clothing and brush pants always seem to drag at my legs when I really want to cover some miles in search of birds. Now as I tack back and forth through the brush behind the dogs, thorns slap against my unprotected thighs to remind me of my hubris. To make matters worse, the beavers have been busy over the summer and gnawed willow butts stud the ground like punji stakes. While I know better than to take any of this personally, all these slings and arrows are certainly enough to whet the appetite. Halfway to our rendezvous with the creek, I want the cover to produce some birds with a sense of longing I haven't felt . . . well, since last pheasant season.

I've lost track of everyone else's dogs, which is probably just as well. Hunting wild pheasants isn't the kind of thing dogs can learn in school, and Sonny, Jake and I have worked things out together in a manner only experience can teach. As the high bank on the creek's outside bend appears over the top of the brush, I can feel the dog's intensity begin to gather as they work the scent through the cover ahead. There will be pheasants, it seems. Our job is not to let them embarrass us.

The angry cackle that accompanies the first rise identifies the bird as a rooster, but somehow the pheasant splits the defense and escapes downstream without offering anyone a shot. A second bird tries to cut back against the grain behind me, but when he finally flushes I'm too tangled up in the brush to raise my shotgun. Finally someone fires up ahead, but I'm too far down in the willows to appreciate the result. The sound of the shot signals an end to all restraint on the pheasants' part. Still unable to see much of anything, I am reduced to following the course of events with my ears: wings, cackles, another shot, silence. For a moment, that is all.

"Well?" I inquire expectantly as I emerge at last from the cover.

"Dick has one bird down," Lori announces from the top of the bank, and suddenly there is Sonny with a mouth full of rooster to prove it.

"How many roosters were there?" I ask, far from certain that I really want to know.

"Lots," Lori acknowledges with a laugh.

"Dozens," someone else confirms.

Of course I knew as much, and as I toss our one dead bird up the bank to Dick its weight feels insubstantial compared to what might have been. But the only event that can really ruin a good day of pheasant hunting is an easy limit, and as we turn up the coulee and proceed onwards toward our next appointment with the thorns, we all feel an indescribable lightness in our hearts.

November

The colors have deserted the landscape now, gone south, it seems, right along with the teal and the meadowlarks. The remains of the year's first real snow cover the mountains behind town and a mantle of high clouds above the western horizon promises more to come. Our guests have left and the house feels as quiet as the brooding countryside beyond. Hunting season has entered the home stretch and the sense of impending loss feels palpable. The idea is to squeeze every possible drop from what remains.

The circle of the hunting's pace has turned round again, from simplicity to spectacle and back to simplicity once again. The seasons' advance has brought the mallards down from the north and the cold has concentrated them along the creek. With little more than an hour remaining between the office and the end of the day, I barely have time to change clothes, round up a few decoys, and head to the nearest open water I know. With a bit of luck, that will do.

This afternoon, I'm making the effort for the dog more than for myself. This has been young Jake's coming-out season. He's finally found a place for himself in the kennel's hierarchy. While he's still no match for Sonny's guile in upland cover, he's defined his role in the duck blind, and I want to be sure he remembers it during the long, quiet months ahead.

Like all kids, Jake has trouble waiting patiently, and as we crouch behind the fallen cottonwood and watch the decoys circle lazily in the backwater it's all I can do to keep from swatting him. While Sonny would sit quietly and scan the sky, his heir-apparent fidgets constantly and his intemperance almost proves enough to ruin the evening. But suddenly a lone drake mallard is circling high overhead, and once he finally sets his wings and makes what proves to be a fatal commitment to land, it's show time.

It's really impossible to appreciate a determined Labrador retriever's water entry without seeing it firsthand. I'm certainly not about to do it justice through the printed word. At the sound of the dead duck hitting the creek and my command to *Fetch!*, Jake morphs from a bundle of unfocused adolescent energy into a furry yellow vector full of more purpose than most people would ever imagine possible in a dog. As he leaps down the bank, I dodge the geyser of spray and experience a realization.

Water is his element. This is where he belongs. Technically there isn't much to the retrieve, but Jake makes something of it anyway: an operatic spectacle fueled by passion and desire. This kind of performance is impossible to define by any number of dead birds collected. Like most of life's great performances, the opportunity to enjoy a front row seat speaks for itself in the end.

By the time I've gathered the decoys and started back toward the vehicle, the air overhead is spitting snow. Like a less than entirely welcome house guest, winter feels as if it has come to stay. The warm brown fields we hunted in September might as well belong to the landscape of another continent, if not another planet. September, October, November: three discarded pages on the calendar cannot begin to suggest the complexity of all that has taken place. There's nothing left to do but haul the memories home like the decoys in the bag and store them for another year.

Autumn quarter. It's why we live where we do.

Reprinted with permission of the author. To order his books, go to www.donthomasbooks.com.

First Grouse

WILLIAM G. TAPPLY

"Children," my father liked to say, "should be seen and not heard."

It was something I tried hard to be good at. I made a special point of being seen, because I didn't want to be overlooked. So when my father rose before dawn on those Saturday mornings in October and November, I got up, too. I helped lug the gear up from the cellar and set it out on the back porch—the leg o' mutton shotgun case, my father's big duffel bag, the wicker lunch basket, and the canvas bag that held boxes of shells, topographic maps, the dog's belled collar, cans of horsemeat, and rags pungent with Hoppe's.

In the kitchen, my father worked over the black skillet where the bacon sizzled and spat. When his partner arrived, I sat with the men at the cramped table watching the suburban sky brighten over the back yard. My father's partner called himself Grampa Grouse. My father called him Grampa, and I was expected to, also. Grampa Grouse was white-haired, rosy-cheeked, and jolly, always bubbling with enthusiasm—my vision of Santa Claus—and he loved to tell extravagant stories about partridge and the dogs and men who hunted them.

I ate with the men, and the dogs waited under the table. Grampa Grouse slipped crusts of toast and strips of bacon to them, and when the men pushed back their chairs and lit their pipes, the dogs' tails began to thump against the floor, and then they uncurled themselves and scratched and skidded across the linoleum to the back door and began to whine and bump their noses against it.

That, in turn, signaled the men to get up from the table. "The dogs need to bust their boilers," Grampa Grouse would say, and he'd let them into the back yard. My father would kiss my mother and clap my shoulder. And then the two men would leave.

On Sunday night I would meet them at Grampa Grouse's wagon when it pulled into the driveway. I'd help my father lug in the gear and the dead birds, and then I'd watch while he cleaned them at the kitchen sink. My job was to swab out the barrels of my father's shotgun and rub it down with an oily rag. I performed this important job with care. I knew my father would peer through the barrels and look for fingerprints on the metal, and I understood that cleaning a shotgun properly was one step toward shooting it.

I didn't really mind being left behind. My day would come. I knew that.

I imagined it would be a dramatic moment, like getting married or having my first drink of whiskey. There would be a speech about the serious nature of firearms and adult responsibility and the honored ceremonies of grouse hunting, and how being seen and not heard was important for men as well as boys.

When it actually happened, though, the moment could have almost slipped past without being noticed. One Friday evening in the October after I turned eleven, my father looked up from his newspaper and said, "Want to come with us tomorrow?"

I rode in the back seat for the two-hour drive into New Hampshire. My father and Grampa Grouse talked about business and politics and foreign policy, about men and bird dogs who had died, subjects not selected for my interest, but not censored because I was in the back seat, either. They included me, I understood, by not excluding me.

I was not allowed to carry a gun on this my first grouse hunt, of course. "Walk directly behind me," my father instructed me while we laced on our boots at the first cover. "Stay close to me, and keep your eyes and ears open. When a bird flushes, fall flat to the ground. If you can't do that, you'll have to stay in the car."

Grouse covers, I quickly learned, were thick, hostile places, nothing like the Aden Lassell Ripley watercolors that hung in my father's den. Grouse covers were hilly, rocky, brushy, muddy hellholes where hunters had to wade through juniper clumps and claw through briar patches and clamber over blowdown. I struggled to keep up with my father. Sometimes saplings snapped back against my face and made my eyes water.

Once my feet got tangled and I fell. Before I could scramble to my feet, my father stopped and looked back at me. "You've got to keep up," he said.

"I tripped," I said. "It's hard walking."

"You can go back to the car if you want."

"I'm okay."

The first time a grouse flushed, I watched my father's gun snap up and shoot into the thick autumn foliage. The gun seemed to react on its own, independent of the man who carried it. I never saw the bird. I only heard the sudden, explosive whirr.

"Well?" called Grampa Grouse from somewhere off to the right.

"Nope," called my father. "Dog busted him."

Then he turned and looked at me. I was standing there right behind him. "I told you to fall to the ground when a bird gets up," he said.

"I heard the noise," I said. "I didn't know . . ."

"That was a grouse. That's the noise they make when they flush. You've got to go to the ground."

"Okay," I said. "I understand."

I learned that grouse hunting involved miles of hard walking, a great deal of yelling at the dogs, frequent shooting, and not much killing.

The day was warm and I soon grew tired. The part I liked best was returning to Grampa's wagon after each cover. There the men would pour coffee for me from a big steel Thermos. The coffee was cut with milk and sweetened with sugar. I had never tasted coffee before that day. It wasn't whiskey, but drinking coffee for the first time nevertheless seemed important to me.

Many grouse flushed that morning, and I quickly learned to fall to the ground at the sound. When my father finally shot one, he turned and said, "Did you see that?"

"Of course not," I said. "I was lying on the ground."

He smiled.

We ate lunch by a brook in the woods. Thick corned beef-and-cheese sandwiches between slices of bread my mother had baked. Big wedges of applesauce cake, my mother's secret recipe. More sweet coffee. I grew drowsy. My legs ached.

After a while, Grampa Grouse unfolded himself, stood up, and stretched. "Better get a move on," he said. "Don't want to get all bogged down."

It grew cloudy and cooler in the afternoon. A soft rain began to sift down from the gray sky, and the woods were silent except for the tinkle of the dogs' bells and the occasional whistles that my father exchanged with Grampa Grouse. My pants soaked up rainwater from the brush. I found myself stumbling. I hoped it would be over soon. I plodded along behind my father, my eyes on the ground so I wouldn't trip and fall again.

We were moving through an old apple orchard. It grew thick with juniper and thornapple and popple and alder. A blanket of small, hard Baldwin apples carpeted the ground under the trees. They cracked under my boots. The woods smelled sweet with their ripe aroma.

Suddenly my father stopped. "Look!" he hissed.

I peered along his pointing arm and saw the big bird perched on the lowest limb of a gaunt old apple tree. One of the dogs stood directly underneath, looking up. The grouse craned its neck, peering down at the dog.

My father pressed his shotgun into my hands. "Shoot him," he said.

I had fired my father's shotgun just once in my life. I'd shot it at a rusty old oil drum. The oil drum had disintegrated. My father had said, "Good shot," but I understood it had nothing to do with marksmanship. This had been a lesson about the power of shotguns.

I pressed the gun against my shoulder, aimed it at the grouse in the apple tree, and tugged at the trigger. Nothing happened.

"The safety," my father whispered. "Quick."

I remembered. I thumbed off the safety, set the bird over the barrels, and pulled the trigger. The gun sounded louder than I remembered from shooting at the oil drum. The grouse fell from the tree.

"Hey!" my father said. "You got him. Good shot."

The dog came trotting in with the dead grouse in his mouth. My father took it from the dog, stroked the bird's feathers, then handed it to me. "Your first grouse," he said. "Congratulations."

I carried the grouse by its feet through the rest of the cover. When we got back to Grampa Grouse's wagon, my father took a picture of me. Grampa punched my shoulder and called me Nimrod.

The men tried to act as if my first grouse was a big triumph, but I understood that hitting a sitting grouse with a shotgun was no great feat. No different from shooting an oil drum, really. Something any boy could do. I also understood, because I'd been paying attention that day, that the men shot only at flying grouse.

Being seen but not heard, of course, I did not share this understanding with my father and Grampa Grouse.

After that day, I accompanied my father almost every autumn weekend, and when I turned thirteen, my father gave me my own shotgun, a single-barreled Savage 20-gauge with a thumb safety.

Being seen and not heard, I had come to realize, enabled me to learn a great deal. I absorbed what the men said—from the back seat and in grouse covers and while eating lunch alongside brooks and in hotel dining rooms. I watched what the dogs did and the paths my father took through the woods, and I noticed the kinds of places where grouse hid.

Now, carrying my own shotgun and walking my own routes through covers, I found I had a good instinct for grouse. My father and I and Grampa Grouse worked as a team, pinching birds between us so that one or the other of us would get a good shot.

There were a lot of grouse in the New England woods in those days, and I had my share of chances. My father had told me that having a single-shot gun would make me a better marksman, but it didn't work out that way. I had quick reflexes, and soon my Savage was coming to my shoulder and my thumb was flicking off the safety and I was pulling the trigger without any conscious thought. I shot often. I took crossing shots and straightaway shots and odd-angled shots at flying grouse. I learned to shoot through the leaves where I thought a grouse might be headed, and sometimes I shot at the sound of the flush when all I saw was a quick blur.

I never once hit a flying grouse.

"Keep shooting," my father counseled. "You can't hit what you don't shoot at. It'll happen. The good old law of averages, right?"

A couple of times I broke my private vow and shot a grouse out of a tree or off a stone wall. I did it out of anger and frustration at my own incompetence, and even when my father congratulated me on bagging a bird, I found that it gave me no satisfaction whatsoever. Men, I knew, did not shoot sitting grouse.

So for the entire season of my thirteenth year and most of the next one, too, I kept my wingshooting streak alive. I shot often and missed every time.

When we hunted with other men, neither my father nor I mentioned my perfect record, the fact that I had never once downed a flying grouse. Since everybody missed grouse far more often than they hit them, nobody except my father knew my secret.

I understood that shooting grouse out of the air was not really the main point of grouse hunting. I liked figuring out where a grouse might be, sneaking up on it, planning how I'd get a shot when it flushed, or if I didn't, one of the other men would. I liked watching the dogs work. I liked the New England woods in the fall, the way the melting frost glistened on the goldenrod early in the morning and the way Baldwin apples smelled when the ground was blanketed with them. I liked riding in the back seat with the dogs, listening to the men talk, being seen and not heard.

But I had never shot a flying grouse. That single fact separated me from the men. Shooting a few from trees or stone walls didn't count. Boys did that, but not men.

On the final weekend of that year's grouse season, my father and I traveled to a new area. We hunted with three old friends of his, men I had never met.

These men included me in their conversations and treated me like a man. They had not known me when I plodded through grouse covers in my father's footsteps. They had not witnessed my first grouse, shot out of a tree. They didn't know that I had never shot a grouse on the wing. I spoke when spoken to, and otherwise continued to be seen and not heard.

We found very few grouse on Saturday. Two of the men missed hasty shots. I never saw a feather, never even had a chance to shoot and miss.

Sunday, the last day of the season, was one of those dark, bitter, late-November New England days. Winter was in the air. Heavy clouds hung over the leafless woods, and now and then a few hard little kernels of snow spit down from the sky. We hunted hard all morning and never flushed a grouse. At lunch the men talked about calling it a season and getting an early start for home.

But one of them said he had a secret cover we ought to try first, and the others agreed, although I noticed their lack of enthusiasm.

The birdy part of the cover lay at the end of a long tote road that twisted down a hill through a mixture of pine and poplar. The men and I trudged along with our shotguns at our sides while the dogs, who seemed to have lost their enthusiasm, too, snuffled along ahead of us.

Suddenly the man in front stopped and raised his hand. "We got a point," he whispered.

I looked, and under an apple tree at the foot of the hill, I saw the dog stretched out.

"There she is!" hissed the man a moment later, and I saw her, too—a grouse pecking fallen apples about fifteen feet from the dog's nose.

We stood there in the path for a minute, just watching, the dog staunch on point, the grouse oblivious, pecking apples, taking a step, bending to take another peck.

Then one of the men touched my shoulder and said: "You take her."

I caught my father's eye. He nodded. So I stepped forward, gripping my Savage single-shot at port arms, and approached the place where the dog was still on point.

The grouse had wandered into the thick undergrowth, and for a minute I couldn't see her. Then I did. She had stopped and twisted her neck around to look directly at me. I stood there, staring back into her intelligent, glittery eyes.

From behind me, one of the men said, "Go ahead. Shoot her. Quick, before she flies."

I raised my gun to my shoulder and aimed at the bird. The grouse kept peering at me.

Then I lowered my gun. I couldn't do it. Shooting this grouse on the ground would prove nothing, and I felt that I had something I needed to prove.

Boys, I thought, shoot grouse on the ground. Men only shoot them when they're flying.

I'd miss, of course. I always did. So what? Better to miss like a man than kill a grouse like a boy.

Then the grouse ducked her head, scuttled deeper into the brush, and disappeared from sight. I stepped forward, paused, took another step.

The grouse exploded, practically from under my feet. She rose, then suddenly angled toward the left. I have no memory of my gun coming up, my thumb flicking off the safety, my finger pulling the trigger.

But I heard the muffled thump of the bird hitting the ground and the quick flurry of wingbeats, and then I heard the men behind me shouting.

A moment later the dog brought the grouse to me. I took her in my hand, smoothed her feathers, tucked her into the pocket in the back of my vest, and walked back to where the men were standing. I was surprised that I felt no particular elation.

"Good shot," said one of the men. "Nice goin'," said another, and I caught the tone I'd hoped for in their voices: It had been a good shot, not a spectacular one, they were saying. It was a shot that grouse hunters often miss but sometimes make, and I had done well.

There was no exaggerated celebration, as there might have been had they known that I had never before shot a grouse out of the air, and that was exactly the way I wanted it.

I glanced at my father, begging him with my eyes not to reveal my secret. My father nodded once, then turned to the other men. "So," he said, "is the rest of this cover worth hunting?"

Reprinted with permission of the author. To order his books, go to www.williamgtapply.com.

Spiller Country

WILLIAM G. TAPPLY

Three or four times a year I take my old friend's shotgun from my gun cabinet, break it apart, check it for rust, and give it a good cleaning. It's a Parker 20, VH grade, a nice gun—beautiful, in fact—and perhaps modestly valuable. It looks like it's been hunted hard, and it has. Its bluing is worn shiny around the breech and at the ends of the barrels, there are dents in the stock, and the recoil pad is beginning to crumble. I've never bothered to have it appraised. It's not for sale, so why bother, although men who know its provenance have offered me what I'm sure is ten times what a shrewd gunsmith would pay.

I fit it together, snap it to my shoulder, trace the hard flight of a grouse cutting across the wall of my den, and remember all the birds it's shot—and all those I've missed with it. Then I sit back, lay the little Parker on my lap, close my eyes, and indulge myself in a moment of nostalgia—for the days when I tromped the uplands with Burt Spiller, and for the days when ruffed grouse prospered in Spiller country.

According to my father's meticulous journals, I hunted with Burton L. Spiller for the first time on November 10, 1951. Well, I didn't actually hunt in those days. I was eleven, too young to carry a gun in the woods. Instead, I followed at my father's heels all day—through briar and alder and mud, up hill and over stone wall and around blowdown. I didn't mind. Grouse hunting in those days was exciting enough even if you couldn't shoot.

One English setter, two men, and one boy flushed 23 separate grouse that November day in Burt's string of southern New Hampshire covers. Burt, who was sixty-five, walked the field edges and shot one of them with his sleek little Parker. My father dropped three.

Dad's journals suggest that was an average day back then.

In the 1955 season we became a regular threesome. At nine every Saturday morning, Dad and I pulled up in front of Burt's white frame house in East Rochester. A leg o' mutton gun case, black lunch pail, and pair of well-oiled boots were already lined up on the porch, and when Dad tooted the horn, Burt came out, waved, and lugged his gear to the car. "Hi," he always grinned. "I've been expecting you. It looks like a wonderful day."

Burton L. Spiller was born on December 21, 1886, the right time—in Portland, Maine, the right place.

The nineteenth-century Maine farmers had opened the land. They moved rocks to clear pasture-land and piled them along the edges to make Frost's "good fences." They planted apples—Baldwins and Gravensteins, Northern Spies and Russets and Pippins. Second-growth birch and popple and alder and hemlock pushed in when the farms were abandoned. Just about the time young Burt was old enough to carry a shotgun into the woods, classic grouse cover was everywhere. No wonder Burt Spiller became a partridge hunter.

He blasted his first grouse off the ground with his father's 10-gauge duck gun when he was seven. "Many, many times I have stood as I stood then," he wrote in "His Majesty, the Grouse," his first published story, "but there has never been another grouse—or another thrill like that one. The kick is still there, as I presume it still is in the old 10-gauge, but—well—we are a little harder around the heart and shoulders than we were then."

A year later the Spillers moved down the seacoast to the little hamlet of Wells, and young Burt's lifelong love affair with the ruffed grouse was sealed. "Other boys of my acquaintance might content themselves with slaying elephants and lions and other inconsequential members of the animal kingdom," he wrote, "but I wanted none of that . . . Nothing but the lordly pa'tridge would satisfy me."

Eventually Burt bartered his bicycle and his watch for a 16-gauge double and "began to kill grouse regularly on the wing. I used the word 'regularly' advisedly," he wrote, "for the regularity was truly astounding. I shot a bird and killed it. Then I shot at forty-nine more and missed ingloriously. Then I killed another."

When he was a young man, he teamed up briefly with a pair of market hunters, an experience that steeped him in grouse lore and sharpened his wingshooting eye. But eventually he recognized "the difference between a sportsman and that reprehensible thing I was becoming . . . . [so] I bought a bird dog and became a sportsman."

In 1911 Burton Spiller married and settled in East Rochester, New Hampshire, where he lived out the rest of his life. He was a blacksmith and a welder, and during the Great War he built submarines at the Portsmouth Naval Shipyard. He raised and bred prize-winning gladioli. He carved violins and made hunting knives. He hunted—not just grouse and woodcock, but ducks and deer, too—and he fished for brook trout and landlocked salmon.

And although he was pretty much self-educated, he began to write, working nights on his old Oliver typewriter. He sold "His Majesty, the Grouse" to *Field & Stream* in 1931. It was the first of 53 Spiller stories that magazine would print. The last was "Grouse Oddities," in 1967, when Burt was 81.

Between 1935 and 1938 the Derrydale Press published a Spiller book a year—all numbered, deluxe editions limited to 950 copies. First came the classic *Grouse Feathers*, then *Thoroughbred* and *Firelight* and *More Grouse Feathers*. All have been reprinted one time or another. Those original Derrydales are treasures.

Around that time, someone dubbed Burt "the poet laureate of the ruffed grouse." The name stuck, as it should have.

In 1962 *Drummer in the Woods*, a collection of previously-published grouse stories (mostly from *Field & Stream*), appeared. Burt also wrote a boy's adventure yarn called *Northland Castaways*, and in 1974, the year after he died, *Fishin' Around*, a collection of his low-key fishing stories, appeared.

I guess at one time or another while the two of us were eating my mother's applesauce cake by a New Hampshire brook or bouncing over a dirt road between covers or trudging side-by-side down an overgrown tote road, Burt told me most of his stories. Whenever I reread a couple of them, as I do every time I take out the old Parker, I can hear Burt's soft voice, see the twinkle in his eye, and feel his finger poking my arm for emphasis.

In 1955, when I began hunting regularly with him, Burt was already 69 years old. He was a small, wiry, soft-spoken man, old enough to be my father's father. I called him "Mr. Spiller," as I'd been taught. But on the first morning of our first hunt he put his hand on my shoulder and said, "Burt, please. Call me Burt. When a grouse gets up, you can't go yelling 'Mark! Mr. Spiller!' now, can you?"

I never heard him raise his voice, curse even mildly, or criticize or poke fun at any man or dog. He was a devout church-going family man who did not hunt on Sundays, even though it was legal in New Hampshire, or drink alcohol, but he was neither pious nor self-righteous.

A good joke, for Burt, was a joke on himself. His favorite stories were about the grouse that outsmarted him and the times he got lost in the woods.

He wore an old-fashioned hearing aid, the kind that plugged into his ear with wires running to the battery in his pocket. "I can hear pretty well," he told me cheerfully, "but sometimes I have trouble picking up the direction." It had to have been a terrible handicap for a grouse hunter, and it probably accounted for the fact that even in those years when partridge were bountiful in his covers, many a day passed when Burt never fired his gun.

When he saw a bird, though, his swing was as silky as I guessed it had been fifty years earlier. Once he and I were trudging side-by-side up the old Tripwire woodsroad on our way back to the car. Our guns dangled at our sides, and we were talking and admiring the way the October sunlight filtered through the golden foliage of the beeches that bordered the roadway and arched overhead. Dad and the dog were working their way along parallel with us somewhere far off to the left.

Suddenly Dad yelled, "Mark! Your way!"

A moment later a grouse crashed through the leaves and rocketed across the narrow road in front of us. It didn't make it. Burt's Parker spoke once, and the bird cartwheeled to the ground.

It was a spectacular shot.

Burt picked up the stone-dead partridge and stroked its neck feathers. Then he looked up at me. He shook his head and smiled apologetically. "Sorry," he said. "I should have let you take him."

He knew, of course, that the odds of my shooting that grouse were exactly the same as his own when he'd been my age: about one in fifty. But that was Burt.

I was young and eager, and I tended to measure the success of a day's hunting by the heft of my game pocket. I learned how to hit flying grouse the old fashioned way—by shooting often and relying on the law of averages—and as much as I missed, and as much as I expected to miss, I still tended to kick stumps and grumble and sulk when it kept happening.

Burt used to tell me, "Just keep shootin'. You can't hit anything if you don't shoot. And always remember: every time you hit a flying grouse is a good shot."

I noticed that he never grumbled or sulked when he missed, although, to be accurate, he didn't seem to miss very often. Even on those days when birds were scarce, and it rained, and the dog behaved poorly, and nobody got any shots, Burt always had fun. Afterwards, when we dropped him off at his house, he always smiled and said the same thing: "A wonderful hunt. See you next week."

Gradually I learned to say the same thing at the end of every day—"A wonderful hunt"—and mean it. Burt taught me that.

He was moving a lot slower in 1964, and although he still wore the old hearing aid, he didn't seem to pick up sounds as well. Burt was 78 that year. But he still greeted us the same way when we picked him up in the morning: "Hi. I've been expecting you. It looks like a wonderful day."

On the second weekend of the season after we laced on our boots at our Bullring cover for the day's first hunt, Burt said, "Uh, Bill? Can I heft your gun?"

I handed him my cheap Savage single-shot.

He threw it to his shoulder. "Comes up nice," he said. "Mind if I try it?"

"Sure," I said, though I couldn't understand why he'd want to.

"Here," he said. "You better take mine." He handed me his slick little Parker.

I carried Burt's gun through the Bullring, and he carried mine. I recall missing a couple of woodcock with it. Burt, straggling along the fringes of the cover, had no shots.

At our next stop, Burt picked up the Savage. "Never got to fire it back there," he said. "Mind if I try again?"

And so Burt lugged my gun around that day while I carried his Parker, and Dad's journal reports that I ended up shooting a woodcock, while Burt never dirtied the barrel of that Savage.

When we dropped him off, he said, "Why don't you hang onto that gun if you want to."

"Well, sure," I stammered. "I mean, I'd love to."

He smiled and waved. "A wonderful hunt, wasn't it?"

The next week when we stopped for Burt, it was my Savage that stood on his porch alongside his lunch pail and boots, and he carried it all day while I toted the Parker. And nothing was ever again said about it. We had swapped guns, and Burt had managed to accomplish it his own way, without ceremony. He never even gave me the chance to properly thank him.

I know for certain that Burton Spiller shot only one more grouse in his life, and it happened a couple of weeks after we'd exchanged guns. He was following a field edge while Dad and I were slogging through the thick stuff, and a bird flushed wild and headed in Burt's direction. Dad screamed, "Mark! Burt!" and I could hear the frustration in his voice, knowing that Burt probably couldn't hear him and wouldn't hear or see the bird.

But a moment later, from far off to our right, came a single shot.

We hooked over to the field and emerged behind Burt. He was trudging slowly up the slope, my gun over his right shoulder and a grouse hanging by its legs from his left hand.

Burt Spiller shot his last partridge with my gun.

The following Saturday—October 31, 1964—sometime in the morning, Burt fell. He never complained—didn't even tell us when it happened—but by the middle of the afternoon he had to call it quits.

He was still hurting the next week and the week after, and then the season was over.

Burt Spiller had hunted grouse for the last time.

During the next decade, Dad and I visited him periodically. He always had a smile and wanted to hear about the hunting. He continued to write stories and raise gladioli right up to his death on May 26, 1973.

A few months later, the old Savage came back to me with Burt's instruction: "For Bill's son."

Dad and I continued to hunt Spiller country for the next several seasons. Then one October we found a power line had cut the heart out of Schoolhouse. The next winter, Bullring became a highway cloverleaf and a Stop & Shop parking lot took the upper end of Tap's Corner. A couple of years later, the dirt road to The Old Hotel got paved over, and pastel-colored ranch houses sprouted up along both sides.

Burt's covers, those that remained, changed, too. Mankiller and Tripwire just didn't look birdy anymore. The hillsides that had once sprouted thick with juniper and birch whips and head-high alders grew into mature pine-and-hardwood forests, and after a while we stopped hunting Spiller country altogether.

Anyway, it would never be the same. It always seemed as if we'd forgotten the most important stop of all—at the white frame house in the village of East Rochester, where Burt would come to his door on a Saturday morning, grin and wave, lug his gear to the car, and say, "Hi. I've been expecting you. It looks like a wonderful day."

Reprinted with permission of the author. To order his books, go to www.williamgtapply.com.

Vermont Bird Hunt Ended Successfully

NELSON BRYANT

A full moon had risen above the valley through which 20 Mile Stream Road wanders. Two wraiths fluttered past my truck's windshield, appearing and disappearing before I had time to slow. They were woodcock moving south ahead of the cold weather, and seeing them seemed to augur well for the two-day grouse and woodcock hunt that lay ahead.

My destination was the home of Russ and Ann Carpenter, and the directions for reaching it were reassuring to one who feels confined if the nearest neighbor's house is within earshot. "Take Twenty Mile Stream Road out of Proctorsville," Mr. Carpenter had said over the telephone. "Go north on it for several miles until it turns to dirt. Go a few miles more, turn right off it on Newton Road, go up the hill and our house is the last one."

Living at the end of the road on a remote, wooded hillside in Vermont suits Mr. Carpenter, an accomplished outdoorsman and gunsmith and a contributing editor to the *American Rifleman*. A big, friendly man, he came out to meet me as I pulled into his dooryard. A few minutes later I was beside the woodstove in his log home, coffee in hand and a trio of Brittany spaniels soliciting my caresses.

The dogs deserted me upon the arrival of the two other members of our hunt, Bob Elman of Stewartsville, New Jersey, and John Falk of South Salem, New York.

The temperature went well below freezing that night, and by dawn a near gale was blowing out of the northwest, filling the woods with sound.

We began hunting in excellent grouse cover, a mixture of hardwoods and conifers often interspersed with abandoned apple orchards. Some of those trees were festooned with well-formed fruit, and I marveled that this could happen after a half century or more of neglect.

Apples and fall hunting are intertwined. I never pass such trees without sampling the fruit, which has a bittersweet flavor, one that suits my mood in autumn more than in any other time of year—moving me alternately to pleasure and sadness. One moment I am delighting in the crisp, cool weather, the smell of wet leaves, and the apples, beechnuts and acorns underfoot. The next moment, I am grieving over summer's short stay.

Grouse are also fond of apples, and in less than a half hour, Mr. Carpenter's seven-year-old Brittany bitch, Muffin, was becoming decidedly birdy as she worked her way through an old orchard.

Twice she went on point and twice the grouse she had located took wing before we could move within range, a phenomenon that is called flushing wild. Grouse tend to do this on windy days because, one assumes, they cannot accurately pinpoint the noise made by an approaching hunter. There were other occasions on that day when one or more of us thought we heard a grouse taking off, but we could not be sure. That was particularly true when Mr. Carpenter and I were involved because both of us have lost a great deal of hearing, largely the result of too much target shooting in an era when there was little or no awareness of the need for hearing protection.

Although no shot was fired for the first two hours, Muffin worked superbly the entire time, ranging back and forth in front of us, neither too close nor too far. Most upland bird hunters put a bell on their dog's collar. This serves two purposes: it helps the hunter keep track of his animal when it is in thick cover, and when it stops tinkling, it lets the hunter know that the dog is motionless and on point.

Shortly after midday, our host bagged a woodcock that flushed out of an alder swamp as the three of us stood talking on a dirt road. I was the first to see that bird coming but could take no action because I was stuffing my pipe with tobacco. We harvested only one more woodcock that day and found none the next.

A short while later, Mr. Elman was embarrassed when he missed, with both barrels, a grouse that flew across that same road. Any grouse hunter worth his salt has to kick himself under such circumstances, because the birds are rarely seen without trees or thickets intervening.

The temperature was less than 20 degrees the following morning, some of the upper trails of two nearby ski areas were filled with manmade snow and the wind had abated only a trifle. Because woodcock were so scarce, we focused on grouse habitat.

We put up ten grouse that morning—two of them were probably birds flushed a second time—but shot at only two and bagged none.

Early in the afternoon, we came down out of the hills and repaired to a coffee and doughnut shop in Ludlow to plan our strategy for the remaining three hours of daylight. Mr. Elman and I, in my truck, would follow the others in Mr. Carpenter's truck. I failed in that mission and Mr. Elman and I wound up in a gas station wondering what to do. Up to that point, I hadn't fired a shot on either day and had decided, after losing our guide, that I was doomed to a birdless hunt. Because we were unfamiliar with the area, Mr. Elman suggested that the only thing we could do was return to one of the locations we had visited that morning.

"Wouldn't it be great," he said, "if we could pick up a grouse on our own without the dog?"

We reached the spot with perhaps fifteen minutes remaining before the sunset hunting curfew. The valley was deep in shadow; under the white pines where we entered, the woods' darkness was at hand. I had chosen that spot because I had seen two of the grouse we had put to flight earlier in the day head in that direction. We were less than 100 yards from our starting point when a grouse burst forth before me and flew straight away—more phantom than bird—into the gloom. My first shot was high and to the left, but the second was on target and the bird fell, killed instantly. I found it breast up on the dark forest floor and gave it to Mr. Elman, who has less opportunity to hunt than I do.

Targeting the Thunder-Maker

ROBERT F. JONES

Some upland wingshots I know spend their spring months engaged in such lesser outdoor activities as trout fishing, turkey hunting, running white-water rivers, gardening or even (for shame!) playing golf. Not I. From mid-April to early May you'll find me at dawn prowling the vernal woods of southwestern Vermont or walking the adjacent dirt roads, rain or shine, listening for the sound of distant thunder. Spring, after all, is the prime drumming season for ruffed grouse.

As the late Gordon Gullion—who knew more about *Bonasa umbellus* than any other researcher of the 20th Century—wrote in *Grouse of the North Shore*, "Fishermen working a favorite trout stream in the spring often hear the drummer's roll from nearby hillsides. Canoeists drifting down a river on a midsummer afternoon may hear an occasional drum from the bordering woodlands. In the fall, hunters waiting quietly for a wary whitetail frequently hear the distant drumming of the male ruffed grouse. Midwinter drumming is infrequent, but occurs from time to time. It is not often heard, but the unmistakable marks [of the drummer's wings] can be found on snow-covered logs in January and February." Yet the peak of drumming activity comes "as the snow melts in the spring and the breeding season approaches."

I'm not out there listening to drummers for the sheer, heartwarming, aesthetic experience of it. To my ear, a drumming grouse is nowhere near as mellifluous as a "singing" woodcock or a gobbling wild turkey. And just being out at dawn during April in Vermont can make for a wet, muddy, bone-chilling morning. Even if the sky is clear and the sun has some strength to it, that only provokes the black flies to chow down more greedily. But for the dedicated grouse hunter, these excursions are worth the discomfort. If you know where a cock grouse is drumming in springtime, you know he'll be in the same general vicinity five or six months later, come bird season. And if his drumming has managed to secure him a mate or two, there'll be plenty of naïve young grouse wandering the woods as well.

Though spring drumming serves as an advertisement for hen grouse to "come and get it," the most important purpose of sounding the thunder is to warn all other male grouse within hearing to keep clear of the drummer's turf. This is usually a chunk of woods about eight or ten acres in area. As Gullion notes, "In contiguous, good ruffed grouse habitat, drumming males are often spaced quite evenly, about 148 to 159 yards apart. . . ." I've never found them that close together, but if your spring scouting expeditions are profitable and local habitat is good, you may hear as many as three or four drummers sounding off almost simultaneously. Under the right conditions—a cold, windless, slightly misty morning—a drummer can be heard as far as a half-mile away, though a quarter-mile is more often the case in the dense woods ruffs prefer. Heavy spruce or fir cover muffles the sound even further.

During the spring drumming season, cock grouse sound off for five to eight seconds per drum roll, and the riffs are almost always spaced four minutes apart.

Gullion writes, "The drumming sound is made by the bird leaning back on his tail and striking his wings against the air violently enough to create a momentary vacuum, much as lighting does when it flashes through the sky. . . . Contrary to some of the tales one hears, the male grouse does not beat on a log with his wings, nor does he peck the log to drum."

Though the classic drumming scene, beloved of 19th-century artists, pictures a cock grouse standing tall on a massive, hollow, moss-covered blowdown in thick, primeval woods, it turns out that today's grouse don't even need logs to drum on. Gullion, during his 33 years of study (1958 to 1991) in the Cloquet Forest of northeastern Minnesota, found them playing Gene Krupa on boulders, woodpiles, exposed road culverts, the roots of trees, mounds of bare dirt "and even the snowbanks along roadways." Here in interior New England I often find them drumming atop old stone walls where former pastures have reverted to aspen groves. The frayed, molted wing feathers on or near the walls confirm that these are indeed drumming sites.

There's often a kind of ventriloquial quality to a grouse's drumbeat. This is especially true in the steep, hilly, wooded country that characterizes most good New England grouse coverts. What's more, ruffs sometimes change position while drumming on their log or stone wall or boulder, turning a complete 180 between drum rolls. This can throw off the listener's sense of the drummer's location by as much as 30 to 45 degrees. Still, if you wait patiently for perhaps a half hour—say seven or eight solos, quietly changing position from time to time—you can usually zero in on the drumming site. Approaching it is another matter.

Gullion found that at Cloquet, "good drumming sites are quite predator-proof." This clumsy, two-legged predator can second that conclusion. During my first bird season in Vermont I spent many a grouseless morning trying to sneak up on and bushwhack a drummer that had the nerve to sound off not a hundred yards from my house. For some reason this bird was drumming as if it were springtime—which they'll do. I once heard a ruff, maybe this same one, drumming his wings off at midnight on New Year's

Eve, under a full moon that turned the snowy meadow behind my house into a reflecting shield that almost made me wince. He kept it up until moonset, at 5 a.m.

My "house grouse" was brazen, to say the least. This was in the early years of my great black Lab Luke, and the grouse drove both of us nuts. Time after time we tried to flush the thunder-maker, pussy-footing up on his drumming site like a couple of scalp-hunting Apaches, but whenever we got to the knoll where he worked his tympanic magic, he was gone. We never heard him flush. He just walked off into the woods as silent as a ghost. Ten or twenty minutes later we would hear him sound off again from one of his subsidiary drumming logs. His primary log, a wind-toppled white pine, was anchored by a big ball of roots and dirt. Gullion calls this a "guard object," and male grouse are "partial" to such blowdowns. "On this sort of site," he says, "the bird will usually select a drumming stage on the trunk about three to five feet from the root mass [which] provides protection against predation for as much as an eighth to a quarter of the horizon." Luke and I always seemed to approach the bird from the wrong quarter. When we finally wised up, we tried to outflank the bird, coming in from a different direction that took us through heavy young aspen whips and up a steep hill. By the time we got up there, of course, he was always long gone.

"In spite of the drumming [which alerts predators] and the amount of time that a male grouse may spend on his log," Gullion says, "he is probably more secure there than at any other time in his life. We have never seen evidence of predation at a log that was in really good cover." Tell me about it.

Of course, man is only a minor predator on the ruffed grouse. Bobcats, lynx, foxes and coyotes are far more successful at procuring a pa'tridge supper. But the raptors do even better. Great horned owls, gray owls, barred owls and goshawks cut a wide swath through grouse populations, particularly during snowless winters. If the snow is deep enough, grouse can burrow into a drift to spend the night, but in an open winter they must roost in the trees, making them easy pickings for night-hunting owls. And during daylight hours, most of which grouse spend feeding, often popping buds and catkins from various trees (primarily aspen), they are vulnerable to attack by goshawks. Indeed, Gullion remarks, "goshawk" could very well be a contraction of the words "grouse hawk," so successful are these big blue-gray accipiters at snagging ruffs.

You would therefore think that a male grouse would be a damned fool to announce his presence from his drumming log and stay there for more than an hour a day. But drumming logs are chosen care-fully. They're usually surrounded by a thick growth of brush or saplings. "This should extend at least three feet above the level of the log," Gullion writes, "and more often 15 or 20 feet. At preferred sites the density of hardwood saplings is usually in the range of 3,000 to 7,000 stems per acre." Mighty thick stuff. Brush surrounding drumming sites is even denser—close to 10,000 stems per acre. "This vertical cover," Gullion continues, "should have a fairly even distribution around the drumming [log] to provide optimum protection for the male. The drumming male also needs a clear escape route from the log, a path where there are few branches or stems to impede rapid movement by a fleeing bird."

No wonder Luke and I could never flush the house grouse. But trying to do so produced some good shooting despite our frustrations. The knoll where the drumming log lay looked down on a piece of wet ground that harbored plenty of woodcock. A half-dozen times during our stalks we flushed young grouse-of-the-year feeding in the vicinity, and I managed to scratch down two or three of them. So all was not in vain.

The following spring I managed to catch a glimpse of my nemesis. More than a glimpse. I left Luke at home one morning and crawled on my hands and knees up to the knoll. It was just getting light, and the ground was so damp that no leaves or twigs crackled as I stalked closer and closer to the thunder-maker. He was drumming every four minutes—hot, hectic flurries like a chain saw starting—and I timed my movements to coincide with his riffs. He was really fired up now, so into it that he'd lost his fear of man. Gullion on a number of occasions got so close to drumming grouse that "they would step onto an opened hand and allow themselves to be lifted above the ground, but they would not allow another hand to be brought close to them; they would not tolerate being restrained in any manner. . . . On several occasions when the moon was full, using a headlamp, I have snuck close enough to touch drummers on their logs."

Well, I have yet to "count coup" on a drumming grouse. But on that spring morning I finally saw one in action. From 10 yards away, lying flat on my belly in the wet leaf mold, I watched him tilt his fanned tail back, erect his ruff and sound off with a blur of wings—*bup, bup, bup, vrooooom!* I watched him drum for nearly a half hour. Finally he spotted me, dropped backward off his log and high-tailed it—God knows where.

The following fall I left him alone and hunted other coverts.

Reprinted with permission of Louise H. Jones.

No Woodcock—but Nothing to Grouse About, Either

GEOFFREY NORMAN

The gaudy red leaves of the early foliage season were down, and the worn old hills of Vermont were in yellow and gold from the last holdouts that refused, stubbornly, to fall. These were mainly ash and aspen, and they gave things a stately and vaguely melancholy look. You could feel the season, and another year, coming to an end.

But this was best time to be in the New England woods if you are a bird hunter. Earlier, the leaves were still thick enough to provide concealment for the birds, even those that flushed in range, startling you with the explosive sound of their wings. And now, in November, the weather has begun to change, and while you might hunt when the temperature is near freezing and the wind is making it feel even colder, it is a lot more pleasant when you can go in your shirtsleeves. But if your timing is right, you might catch a flight of woodcock on a gorgeous autumn day in October.

These "flight birds" were migrating down from their nesting areas in Canada to their winter grounds, some of which are as far south as the Louisiana bayou country. Woodcock fly at night, so the hunter should get out early in the morning to the aspen and alder covers where he knows they like to lay over. The birds rest and feed in these places, using their long, needle-shaped beaks to dig for earthworms. If you get into a place where a flight has come in, you can see the droppings on the ground—hunters call this "chalk"—and find enough birds to fill your limit of three in a couple of hours or less.

Woodcock are easy on dogs. They give off a lot of scent and they hold very tight. Even an average dog can perform like a star in a cover that is full of flight birds. Many hunters will tell you that, for this reason, the woodcock is their preferred bird. They are also coveted by people with a taste for game. Woodcock are strong fliers with—shall we say—a rich diet. The flesh is dark in appearance and taste, which suggests some kind of exotic and vastly improved liver. My daughter. Hadley, prizes woodcock over anything that can be put on the table.

One Sunday last year she came home for the weekend and almost missed the bus back to school when we stayed too long in a cover. There were some flight birds, but I couldn't seem to hit them when they flew. I finally got my limit and barely had time to draw and pluck the birds and pack them in a small cooler before she left for Boston, where her roommates said no thanks—they'd stick with chicken. She ate all three birds herself and called home to tell me about it.

So we were hopeful on a recent Sunday morning when we went out to one of our favorite places. The only concern was the weather. It had been unseasonably warm, and the conventional wisdom among bird hunters is that you need a cold front to push the birds into migrating. Like a lot of hunting lore, the validity of this one is suspect. It seemed just as likely that the birds' migrating instinct would be triggered by shorter days and less sunlight.

We parked the truck and walked up a dirt road to one of those long flats on the top of a hill that had once been under cultivation. But Vermont is not congenial to farming, and on the hill's 200 acres, the only signs of human occupation were a few crumbling stone walls, poignant reminders of just how much labor had gone into a failed enterprise. There were a few sturdy old apple trees in one corner of the piece, but we decided to hunt this part later, for grouse, and went straight to a low spot that had been good to us in the past. We had to wait for Jeb to take a couple of warm-up laps, somewhere out of sight, while I yelled, pointlessly, for him to settle down and get to work.

"Same old Jeb," Hadley said. Every season, we think he will have matured and settled down. He is eight, on the backside of a pointer's prime, but shows no inclination to grow up or slow down. Eventually, he arrived, muddy and ready to hunt.

"Where the hell you been?" I said. He gave me a look, then headed for the alders and aspens and dove right in. Hadley and I picked our way through the thick cover. I looked for chalk and didn't find any. Jeb hunted carefully but never stopped moving. We spent an hour in the low spot and never flushed a bird.

"If they aren't here," I said, "then they must still be in Canada. And that's too far to drive."

We had a couple of hours, still, before we had to be back at the house to deal with other things. So we gathered Jeb up and got him headed in the direction of the old apple trees. This ground, too, was barren. We moved on to another part of the cover where there were some fox grapes, which grouse will eat, and thorn apples, which an expert hunter and naturalist I know claims are their preferred food.

The ruffed grouse is a resident. He does not migrate and he doesn't ever get very far from his home territory, probably flying less in his lifetime than a woodcock does in two or three days. He likes very thick cover and uses his camouflage and his legs to avoid danger, getting airborne only as a last resort. Grouse are exceedingly wary. A mature bird that has been hunted and survived the experience often seems to have learned from it. I have heard them flush, at a distance, when they heard a car door slam. They seldom hold for a dog, and when they run and the dog follows, they get up out of range. If they do hold, it is generally in exceedingly tight cover so that when they fly, you have a hard time getting a clear shot.

When we reached the thorn apples, Jeb was already on point. Hadley and I went in slowly, on either side of him, and when the bird got up, I had a shot.

To my vast surprise, I made it. Jeb retrieved the bird and Hadley said, "Way to go, Dad. You the man."

We kicked up two more birds, out of range, before it was time to head for the truck. On the way out, we crossed a clearing that looked out on the valley that ran east and west as far as we could see. We could make out the peaks of the Adirondacks on the horizon. The valley was carved neatly into small farms and fields, and at one end there was a little town with an austere white church at its center. The hills on the opposite side of the valley were dappled in gold and yellow.

"Hey, Dad." Hadley said, "Is this beautiful or what?" Beautiful, I agreed.

Also fleeting. But I didn't mention that.

From the *Wall Street Journal*, November 7, 2001. Reprinted with permission of the author.

Convert

RON ELLIS

We were so taken with bird hunting back when we first discovered it that we suspected magic must somehow be involved to weave such an enchantment. It was especially so when the three of us, good friends and longtime hunting partners, took a week to travel north out of Kentucky and Ohio to follow our young dogs through storied grouse cover "up in Michigan."

The October woods that season were perfect. The canopy formed by the hardwoods bordering the pines and tamaracks was quilted with intense colors, the light passing through them so pure and perfect we believed it must surely flow from a holy source.

We hunted for two days with a guide in that grand bird country and found a good many grouse. We killed only a few since most of the birds flushed from clear-cuts so dense we had to thread our guns through a spidery-maze of branches just to be prepared to imagine a shot, much less actually take one.

We reached the best spots by traveling nameless sand tracks that carried us deeper into the country. Along these roads we explored some low ground, looking for birds in places where shadows spilled out of the swamps and mixed nervously with the splashy, vibrant colors of the uplands. Edge cover, holy ground for sure, a place where grouse could be found.

While searching for grouse we unexpectedly discovered woodcock. They were clustered together in great numbers along tiny streams that threaded through patches of twisted alders, their exposed roots clumped up on ground that was mossy and soft and mostly open beneath a low canopy. Much later we learned we had stumbled upon a classic "flight of woodcock," or a "fall of woodcock," a description that seems more magical, more precise and wonderful, when attempting to describe the mysterious comings and goings of this magnificent little bird.

But we were younger then and only had eyes for the quick, flashy grouse. The little tawny-colored migrants with the upside-down brains, their secret ways and mystical charms still foreign to us, had yet to become an obsession. While my strongest affections were still showered on the grouse, Lady, my orange-and-white Brittany with the smiling eyes, preferred the diminutive woodcock, from the very first time she found one hunkered in that strange scent cloud out in front of her pink nose. After discovering them she'd nearly wiggle her stubby tail out of its socket when one was near, while grouse just made her pull a routine point, the tail twitching a bit, the scent imparting no particular emotion to her motion.

Much later we learned we had stumbled upon a "fall of woodcock," a description that seems more magical, more precise and wonderful when attempting to describe the mysterious comings and goings of this magnificent little bird.

On the third day we hunted without a guide. It was late in the afternoon when we pulled the Volkswagen van off one of those disappearing sand tracks and headed into a piece of cover that was so birdy we could almost smell the grouse. With high expectations and an eye on the lengthening shadows, I followed Lady through that perfect thicket, without so much as a flush, and came out into an overgrown meadow on the opposite side.

At the far end of the open ground we passed quietly through a long-abandoned homesite bordered by a windbreak of weathered pines. Just beyond stood a small grove of hardwoods, the ground sloping slightly upward toward its center. The light that fell out of those trees was made up of columns of pale, dusty yellow filtered through an intense quiet, and the earth was soft there, with a clear, cold-water seep murmuring nearby.

The air was thick with the promise of birds.

Lady hit scent and danced her careful dance to show me birds were near. She twisted her butt about and drifted nearly stiff-legged with the scent, until just inside the grove, she pointed—an intense, low-to-the-ground point on the downhill side of a large rock.

Not wanting to spoil the moment, I moved quietly to her; no unnecessary sounds, no yelling of "Point!" to my companions. I was alone with my dog, partners in a perfect stillness, as I walked straight into the cover past her point, my eyes raised to a single opening in the trees.

The woodcock flushed from under Lady's nose and spiraled straight up through an autumnal canopy of many colors that were as memorable as those that danced through the stained-glass windows and spilled onto the stone floors of the cathedral where I attended mass as a child. There was the familiar motion of the twenty-gauge, and at the shot, russet feathers drifted against the evening sky. It was as close to the perfect bird-hunting experience as I had ever imagined—the place, the point, the shot—as the intoxicating scent of spent powder, mixed with Hoppes No. 9, swirled back ahead of the returning dog, like incense in the October quiet.

Lady dropped the bird close to me (a rarity). I picked it up and brushed the leaves and twigs from its feathers, and then held it in both hands. I marveled at the woodcock's markings and subtle colors—the solid body of taupe mixed with reddish hues, dark brown, black and delicate washes of blue—before placing it in my coat. Then I broke open the gun, took a great whiff of the spent shell and lit a cigar, all the while searching for an appropriate comparison for what I was feeling.

In the end, with the sun sliding down the horizon and the cigar smoke drifting to the heavens, I decided that it felt just like religion, but without the guilt that so often accompanied the experience in my youth. Being in the spirit of things, I offered thanks, called the dog and went in search of more woodcock.

A fresh convert knows no limit to his fervor.

Green Eyes

MICHAEL MCINTOSH

"Goodbye, Miss October," Scotty said and laid the calendar page reverently on the fire.

Mac laughed. "A one-track mind," he said. "Pitiful." But he, too, watched solemnly as the paper flared and blackened, leaving a momentary cameo at the center, where a stylish setter watched two woodcock rise against a screen of slender aspens.

"You're also three days early," Mac said, "Unless I've managed to lose track of time altogether."

"So I'm fickle," Scotty said. "Miss November's no slouch, either." He hung the calendar back on its nail by the kitchen door. "Never could resist brown eyes."

The eyes in question gazed soulfully over a dead mallard.

Tom came in through the kitchen with an armload of firewood and glanced at the calendar. "Handsome Labrador," he said. "Is it November already?"

"Only to the fickle," Mac said.

Tom dumped the logs in the woodbox, chunked a fresh bolt of oak onto the fire, kicked off his unlaced boots, and slid a chair close to the hearth. "Scotty, you're the only man I know whose favorite pinups all have wet noses and like to drink out of puddles."

"Funny, Sarah says the same thing," Scotty mused. "I suppose I'd change my mind if your average pinup type knew the difference between a vent rib and a nailfile."

"Meeting a woman who hunts can be more of a shock than you might imagine," Tom said. "I met one once, and I've never been the same since.

"It was one of those days that makes every trite, goofy thing ever written about October seem like the grandest poetry. It had poured rain for about three days and then turned clear. The English brew a special run of ale in October—delightful stuff, winey as an overripe apple. Well, the air was like that. What leaves were left had all gone gold, and the tamaracks were bright, blazing yellow. It was the sort of day you can't even think about without getting as sappy as a kid on a first date.

"I was basically a kid myself, barely two years out of the University, the ink hardly dry on my diploma. I'd moved back here after a few miserable months in a big law firm in Minneapolis—which was long enough to find out that big-city life wasn't for me. I was working hard to put together a practice in Tamarack, hunting when I could, which wasn't very often.

"But I got one whiff of the air that morning and decided it was no day for wills and land titles or any such dusty stuff. So I packed up my gun, put Jericho in the car, and took off.

"We poked through a couple of coverts and flew a few grouse. I got a good shot at one that Jericho pointed beside an old log road, and by late morning I was feeling about as good as any young fellow has a right to feel.

"We had our lunch under a big oak by a pasture, lazing in the grass and watching a hawk. I had a mind to spend the afternoon in a covert about a mile to the west, one I hadn't been in since I was a kid, and decided to walk cross-country instead of driving around to it. I'd never been in the center of that section, didn't have a clue if there was any cover in it, but it seemed like a good day to find out.

"We crossed a couple of hills and came down to a little stream. I could see some gray dogwood on the other side, figured there might be a grouse or two close by, so it didn't surprise me when Jericho went on point in the tag alders. When I got up closer, though, I could see he wasn't pointing. He looked like he was honoring, which struck me as odd, since I was by myself and had only the one dog.

"But that's exactly what he was doing—backing a little setter that was dead serious about something at the base of an alder clump.

"I looked around, didn't see anybody, and stood there not quite sure what to do next. The little setter was wearing a collar and bell and looked well cared-for. I'd just about decided to flush whatever she was pointing and see if she had a tag, when a voice out of nowhere said, 'That's a picture to put on a calendar.'

"I almost jumped out of my boots, it startled me so. I turned around and there she stood, next to a popple tree, smiling.

"Lads, I will take that picture to my grave. I can't begin to tell you all the things that whirled through my mind in those few moments. I'm not even sure it was a few moments. Time simply stopped moving.

"I was looking into a pair of eyes the most brilliant, astonishing green I ever saw, looking at a face framed in dark, curling hair, all lit by a smile I couldn't describe if I tried for the rest of my life. And I have.

"For one completely irrational instant I imagined her on horseback, galloping over the moors of Scotland, all tumbled hair and flashing eyes, some wild, fey spirit whose name would be Dierdre . . . don't even ask where all that came from.

"Actually, I just stood there gawping. How long, I don't know, though she was still smiling when I gathered up enough of my wits to notice that she was carrying a gun.

" 'Uh . . . I . . . uh . . . your, uh, dog.' I said, or something equally inane. She kept smiling at me as if I hadn't said anything, which was basically the case. She was looking at the dogs. The little setter was still on point, and Jericho was still honoring, waving his tail slowly from side to side. 'Bird,' I said, with what I imagine was a grin you don't often see outside an asylum.

"She turned those green eyes on me again and I thought my legs would give out. You know, we have a pair of ligaments behind our knees that respond to emotion—fear, panic, relief, any really powerful feeling. Right then, mine were twanging and jittering like guitar strings. She said, 'I hate to break up such a lovely picture, but she's just a youngster and probably won't hold that point much longer.'

"She might as well have spoken in some ancient tongue for all I could do to reply anything but '*Awp.*'

"She walked past Jericho and up to the little setter. A woodcock twittered up from behind the alders, and she took one step to the side, swung her gun, and dropped it neatly.

" 'Fetch, Nellie,' she said. Nellie darted out and started nosing after the bird. Jericho trotted along behind her, and I sat down on a log to see if I could get my knee-joints reconnected to my brain.

"By the time Nellie fetched the woodcock and her mistress had it stowed in her vest, I was more or less in control of most of my senses—at least enough to have a look at the rest of this enchanting woman. In those benighted days, every female younger than your grandmother was universally referred to as a 'girl.' This one was young, but she was no girl. She was tall and slender, and neither the fawn-colored shirt nor the brush pants nor the canvas vest obscured the fact of a decidedly womanly body underneath. She was carrying a 20-gauge Fox gun, wearing Bean boots and a tweed hat, and I was losing my mind.

"She walked over to me, peeling off her glove, held out her hand and said, 'I'm Caroline Fitzgerald.' So much for Dierdre. I took her hand and said what I thought was my name, adding, 'We've never met.' I'd been away a few years, but I'd never forget a stunner like her.

"If she was impressed by my grasp of the obvious, she didn't say so. Instead, she laughed, a musical sound that made my blood hiss and tingle. 'I live in St. Paul,' she said. 'We're here for the fall.'

"I had no idea whether 'we' meant a husband, a family, or the Marine Corps Band, and she was still wearing a glove on her left hand. So, with all the subtlety I could muster, I gave her another of my now-patentable stupid grins and said, 'We?'

" 'My parents and I. My father bought this land a few years ago, as a summer place.' She breathed another throaty laugh. 'He thinks it's only a mite less remote than the Arctic Circle. I think it's lovely.'

"I stopped myself from saying something irretrievably dopey and said something only moderately dopey instead. What, I don't remember. I do remember stammering an apology for trespassing and received a charming assurance that I wasn't likely to be jailed for it. Jericho, who was old enough to stick around when I wasn't moving, had lain down to wait. Nellie, from the sound of her bell, was somewhere upstream, no doubt searching for more woodcock. Caroline asked if I'd care to join her.

"In those days, woodcock were not my favorite sport. I was a grouse hunter, dyed-in-the-wool. But if Caroline Fitzgerald had invited me to shoot grasshoppers or aspen leaves, I'd have accepted happily.

"Much of that afternoon is a blur to me now. It was a blur to me then, actually, except for Caroline. I couldn't take my eyes off her—which made the hunting sort of a rough go. It's a wonder I didn't break my fool neck. At least she had the good grace not to laugh out loud.

"That alder run was stiff with woodcock, and before long I began to see that Caroline Fitzgerald was remarkable for more than just her incredible eyes. It's rare enough to come across a woman who hunts and rarer still to find one who hunts as if it's the most natural thing in the world. Most of them either act as if they'd really rather be doing something else, or they go about it with a kind of bloodthirsty aggressiveness that isn't becoming even to a man.

"But not Caroline. She was neither clumsy nor hesitant nor one of the guys. She was just a woman who clearly enjoyed what she was doing.

"She had a sure, gentle touch with her dog, which, she told me, technically was her father's, though she and Nellie had sort of adopted one another as favorite companions. She was a good shot, not spectacular, but good, and she handled her little Fox with the same natural grace that she did everything else.

"Once, I flushed a 'cock that flew straight toward her and dropped down right at her feet. When it flushed again a few moments later, she let it go without firing, though I knew she had an open shot. She told me later that when it realized she was standing there almost at arm's length, it fanned its tail and strutted like a little turkey cock before quitting the scene. 'Any bird with that kind of audacity deserves a break,' she said.

"It's the sort of thing that only another bird hunter understands, and it raised Caroline Fitzgerald another notch or two in my estimation—if that was possible.

"She filled her limit about three o'clock. I had two or three, and I was so befuddled by her that I wasn't shooting well at all, so I didn't mind quitting. We found a sunny log and sat talking while the dogs dozed. We told each other the sort of life-history things that people exchange at such times, though I'm afraid I did most of the talking. She had a fine way of putting you at ease.

"Finally, she thanked me for a pleasant afternoon and said that perhaps we'd meet again. I was prepared to do almost anything to make sure that happened, so I asked if she'd care to join me in a couple of coverts I knew. She said yes, and after arranging to meet at her father's house the following day, she gave me one last smile, whistled for Nellie, and struck off into the woods.

"Jericho and I turned back the way we'd come. Before we got to the car, we moved at least four more grouse, two of which were such wide-open shots that Jericho got miffed with me when I blew them both. Actually, I don't even remember pulling the triggers, and I wouldn't have bet a brass nickel on being able to hit the ground with my hat. All I could see were Caroline Fitzgerald's eyes.

"Next morning, I found the house where the elder Fitzgerald evidently intended to spend his golden years—a newly built log edifice only a bit smaller than the Minnesota Supreme Court building. Caroline's father was a railroad man with a taste for sport and more than enough ready cash to satisfy any urges he might have. He was tending to some business in Duluth that day, but I met Caroline's mother, a charming lady who owned somewhat less intense versions of Caroline's green eyes, and spent a few minutes marveling at the gymnasium-sized living room, all built of native timber and stone. The place still stands, by the way, though it's a resort now.

"I'd spent much of the previous night trying to collect myself into a state that might be a bit more poised than the uproar I'd felt the day before. Naturally, I got things off to a fine start by trying to drive off in high gear instead of low, but if she saw anything unusual about lurching and chugging down the lane, she didn't mention it. I finally got the transmission and my blood pressure under control, and we set out in earnest, Jericho and Nellie perched in the back seat like a couple of shaggy chaperones, Caroline relaxed and chatty beside me.

"She was wearing a plaid shirt that was mostly green and dark red, and the colors made her eyes fairly glow. She'd gathered her hair into a braid and pinned it up at the back; uncovered by her hat, it showed auburn highlights in the sun. It's a good thing there isn't much traffic on the back roads hereabouts, because it was all I could do to keep the car between the ditches. She seemed to have no notion at all of how extraordinarily beautiful she was. But then, I was aware of that enough for both of us.

"In the first covert, Jericho nailed a grouse not ten minutes from the car. I offered Caroline the flush, but she declined, saying that such a good omen deserved a better shot than she. Considering my track record since meeting her, I was not inclined to consider myself a candidate. Jericho probably would have laughed out loud if he hadn't been busy at the moment. Still, the red gods are not without a sense of pity, it seemed. I killed the bird stone dead with the first barrel.

"And that seemed to break the jinx. I didn't lose any appreciation for the way Caroline looked or sounded or moved, but I suddenly found myself able to function like a relatively normal adult.

"I don't think I've ever enjoyed hunting more. Once we got into the alder bottoms, we found woodcock everywhere. Something magical seemed to happen. I never was the sort of crash-ahead type who hunts as if he's going for a record in the obstacle course, but I've always liked to get right into the thick of things for grouse—still do, as you know. It's still the most satisfying way to hunt grouse, but that day I truly discovered woodcock.

"I discovered a degree of finesse and elegance and grace that simply isn't available from any other bird. I'd always thought of woodcock as rather bumbling, hapless little things that never seemed quite connected with a hunter. Go after a smart old grouse and you immediately strike up a relationship with it—the two of you start acting and reacting to one another as if you're the only living things on earth.

"The same thing happens with woodcock but in different ways, more subtle. Woodcock touch a gentler emotion, one that runs just as deep as any other but vibrates with a softer resonance. A grouse can be anything from a saxophone to a bugle. A woodcock is always a cello.

"Next time you're dressing birds in a mixed bag, notice that a woodcock's heart is almost as big as a grouse's, even though its body is far smaller. That ought to tell you something. I didn't think of all these lofty metaphors that morning, of course, but I certainly felt them. As I said, it was magical.

"Even the dogs seemed to feel it. Some of Nellie's sweet nature rubbed off on Jericho, and he comported himself in a more gentlemanly way than usual. At one point, Caroline asked me to help refine Nellie's back-pointing work, which already was better than you'd expect of a dog her age. She'd had some early training from a professional, but Caroline told me she wanted to do the finishing herself.

" 'Did you train Jericho?' she asked. 'He's a fine hunter.'

" 'I did, but most of what he knows has come from experience. I've always liked working with dogs but I'm no professional.'

" 'Experience has its lessons,' she said. 'And we learn them if we're lucky.' She looked at me with suddenly serious eyes. 'You're a lucky man, Tom, to be here where you really want to be and to do what pleases you. That may be worth more than you imagine.'

"There was a strangely hard edge to her voice, and it set me back. Before I could say anything, she turned away and started off after the sound of the dog bells.

"What she'd said kept running through my mind. I'd never thought of myself as lucky or unlucky, certainly not in coming back to Tamarack. That was a decision that had nothing to do with luck, so far as I could see. It was simply a choice between being a big-city attorney or a country lawyer. It seemed perfectly clear-cut to me, but my word, there's nothing like the certainty of youth. Only later did I realize she was right.

"Caroline seemed quieter, more thoughtful. We hunted on, circling back to the car, not saying much. She'd made a lunch for us, and I'd already picked the place where I wanted to go. The old Petersen place was my favorite even then, and I wanted Caroline to see it.

"You know how the Petersen looks on a fine October day. It didn't look much different then. The old house hadn't been deserted as long and naturally wasn't as weathered as it is now, and the timber on the far hill was younger and thicker. But the meadow and the stream and the beaver pond and the pine grove by the house were all there. It seemed fitting to take the most beautiful woman I'd ever met to the most beautiful place I knew.

"We unpacked the lunch basket under a big Norway pine at the end of the grove and sat where we could look down the meadow toward the stream and the woods beyond. The meadow was rank with grass still summer-green, rippling in the breeze. I don't recall what we ate—pine cones and thornapple twigs, for all I knew, or cared. To be there was as complete a measure of contentment as I could imagine. She was still subdued, but that's what the Petersen place does to you anyway. I figured she'd say what was on her mind when she felt like it.

"I turned back from looking to see where the dogs were and found her staring at me, solemn as a judge.

" 'Tom,' she said, 'there's something I want you to know about me. We don't know each other, really, but I think you'll understand what I have to say. I've never said it to anyone. It's only now, in fact, that I'm able to explain it to myself. I'm engaged to be married.'

"Well. There it was. No great surprise, I suppose, but I felt as if I'd swallowed a chunk of ice the size of my fist. At that moment, I couldn't have said a word if you'd held a gun to my head.

" 'I am betrothed to a pleasant young man with a good future,' she went on after a moment. 'The right pedigree, old St. Paul family—well-connected, I believe the phrase is. We've known each other for years, the same social circles, you know.' She enunciated the words carefully, ironically. She looked out over the meadow and turned her eyes back to me.

" 'He's a decent fellow and I do care for him. Which will make it all the more difficult to tell him that I'm not going to marry him.'

"I realized I was holding my breath and let it out.

" 'You have no idea what it's like to be a woman.' She had me there. I shook my head. 'In some ways, it's not much different from being a dog, except a dog doesn't know it's a piece of property to be bought, bartered, or given away. Most women don't, either, or aren't willing to admit it.' She smiled a sweet, sad smile. 'This doesn't make much sense, does it?' I shook my head again.

" 'Tom, I'm engaged to be married because that's what I'm supposed to do. At a certain point, everyone assumed Charles—that's his name—would ask me to marry him: our friends, his parents, my parents, Charles, even I. And of course if he asked, I'd accept. Well, he did, and I did, and everyone was pleased, and there were engagement parties and announcements and everything that's part of the process of transferring ownership of a woman from one man to another. I don't suppose you studied that sort of thing in law school, but it's all quite a standard process. That was ten months ago. The wedding is to be three days after Christmas. But it isn't going to be.'

"She picked up an apple and turned it over and over in her hands. 'Why not?' I asked.

" 'I don't remember exactly when I realized that I'd made all sorts of decisions without making any choices. Perhaps it was when I really began to see what was in store for me. I began to see that I was about to take up my mother's life and her mother's life and the lives of all the married women I know. My father, obviously, is quite wealthy; so are all his friends, and so are all my friends. The men spend their lives getting richer. The women are sedate and cultured, managing households and the upbringing of children, taking a genteel interest in the arts and in such worthy causes as don't threaten the world they live in.'

"She stopped for a moment, her eyes glistening. 'The more I thought about it, the worse it made me feel—unhappy and frightened and angry. I don't want to be some pampered pet on a velvet rope, living a serene and useless life.

" 'Spending the fall here was my idea. I could've stayed in St. Paul. But I insisted on coming, to get away and think. A week after we got here I took off the ring Charles gave me. I told my mother it was because I didn't want to lose it outdoors. Tonight, I'll tell her the real reason. They'll both be quite upset, partly because they truly want me to be happy, but partly, too, because it's going to be very awkward for them to have a daughter who'd do such a scandalous thing as break an engagement. It's going to ruin their round of holiday parties this year. But that will have to be as it will be.'

"She shot me a suddenly mischievous look and said, 'Part of this is your doing, you know.' I started to apologize, but she stopped me. 'Not what you think. Don't you see, Tom? You did what I want so much to do. You set your life on a course of your own choosing. You followed your heart instead of surrendering to a life that would, in time, give you everything you wanted except happiness. And your heart led you back here. And you know, you were right.'

"I said, 'Caroline, everything you say is true. I can't pretend that I really know how you feel about … all this. You said so yourself: I have no idea what it's like to be a woman. In fact, I never even *thought* of it until now. But I do know what it is to give up the certainty of comfort for the hope of being truly happy. It was the right choice for me, and I wish no less for you.'

"She leaned over and kissed me on the cheek, said 'Thank you,' and started gathering up the remains of our lunch. 'Show me the rest of this beautiful place. I need to stretch my legs.'

"At the moment, I felt a need to stretch my head. My mind was fairly tumbling with all she'd said, things as alien to my experience as the far side of China, yet things so clearly real that it was impossible not to recognize them.

"Guessing that she'd like some time to herself, I suggested we split up to hunt the stream coverts. I'd cross over above the beaver pond and take the far side, and she could go through the alders below the house. We'd meet below the beaver dam where it's easy to cross the stream and then go back through the woods together. She agreed. We put the lunch basket in the car and set off.

"The rain had sent the creek running full, and I had to go way upstream to find a crossing. Once over, I ambled along, not really hunting, my mind too full of Caroline to pay much attention. I walked right up on Jericho on point and flushed the bird before I even knew he was there. He gave me a disgusted look and went on downstream. I heard one shot from Caroline's direction and figured she'd found a bird.

"I was about a hundred yards above the beaver dam when I heard a dog start shrieking. It was coming from about where Caroline should have been by then, and the first thing I thought was that Nellie had run into a porcupine. I beat through the brush as fast as I could, thinking to wade the stream below the dam, cursing porcupines and bad luck in general. When I got free of the brush at the end of the dam, what I saw stopped me cold.

"It wasn't Nellie screaming. It was Jericho. And there wasn't any porky. The damn fool had run out onto the beaver dam; I guess he'd decided to go with somebody who was really hunting. In those days, the dam wasn't quite as big as it is now, but it was big enough to stop a lot of water. The rain had raised the pond to spill-over, and the center of the dam was starting to wash out. Water was pouring through a three- or four-foot gap, and Jericho had tried to jump across or swim around it or something. In any case, he got his leg fast in the sticks, and he was caught. It was all he could do to keep his head out of the water, and every time he slacked off, the current pulled him under. He was a big dog, strong as a moose, but he couldn't hold out forever.

"Then I saw Caroline.

"She was on the dam, heading toward Jericho and having a hard time keeping her feet. You know what trying to walk on a beaver dam is like, even when you're going slow. I was afraid she'd get her own foot caught. I had no notion whether she could swim. I had visions of her disappearing under the water and never coming up, and I felt such a stab of fear that I could scarcely catch my breath. I shouted to her, but she didn't seem to hear, so I started shucking off my vest.

"Just as I started out on the dam myself, she got to the middle, grabbed hold of a branch, and leaned out to Jericho. He was about done in. She caught his collar and gave a heave that would've taxed the strength of any man. And she pulled him free.

"Then everything changed to slow-motion. She lost her grip and hit the water, and the two of them tumbled through the gap and out of sight.

"For about three seconds, I'm sure my heart stopped dead still. The downstream side was mostly marsh, but there was a fair-sized pool in the main channel, and the water spilling through had turned it into a cauldron. I was sure I'd find them both dead.

"I scrambled down the back side of the dam and started floundering through the mud and rushes, sinking in to my knees. It was like trying to swim through honey. I couldn't see or hear anything except rushing water and my own slogging around. My lungs felt like I was breathing fire. It seemed forever before I got to a hummock, climbed onto it, and stood up.

"I saw nothing but rushes and marsh grass and cattails. If I'd had the breath, I'd have screamed in sheer anguish. Then I caught a flash of white through the grass and saw Jericho about twenty yards away, hauling himself up onto a hummock of his own. I shouted Caroline's name, and then again. When I heard her shout back, 'Over here,' my knees went so watery that I almost went headfirst into the mud.

"I got to her just in time to give her a hand out of the stream. She was bedraggled as a drowned cat, her hat gone, hair undone and plastered to her face. But she was smiling, her green eyes flashing. I felt some vital connection in me break and reform. I hugged her until she gasped for breath.

" 'I didn't know if you could swim,' I said after a moment.

"She pushed back her wet hair and grinned. 'Even children of the idle rich manage to learn a few useful skills, you know. Where's Jericho?'

"I whistled and heard his bell, whistled again to give him the direction, and presently we could see the rushes waving as he made his way to us, limping and as wet as Caroline but otherwise undamaged. The three of us slogged our way out of the marsh, gathered up Caroline's gun and vest, and walked to the meadow. Nellie, who had watched it all from the edge of the woods, lay down next to Caroline, and for a long time no one said anything.

"She lay in the grass, eyes closed, breast rising and falling as her body absorbed its adrenaline. I wanted to hold her and say things that probably would have embarrassed us both a day later. Instead, I told her to wait there and waded back through the marsh—I wasn't likely to get any wetter or muddier no matter what I did—and collected my own gun and vest.

"When I got back, she was kneeling beside Jericho, gently flexing his leg and making soft sounds to him.

" 'Nothing's broken, as far as I can see,' she said, 'but he's probably going to be gimpy for a few days.'

" 'He'll have plenty of company,' I said. 'Let's get you home to dry out.'

" 'Tom, wait. Sit down here a minute.' I did. 'This has been quite a day, all in all, and in an odd sort of way, I think I owe you my life.' She held up her hand. 'No, don't say anything. I didn't come anywhere near drowning, though I could have. But that's not what I mean. Just being with you and being able to tell you all the things I've told you has been like a reprieve, a freedom I'd almost given up hoping for. You're a sweet man, Tom, and I'm very fond of you.

" 'If this were a fine romantic story instead of real life, we'd probably have sworn undying love right there in the mud when you pulled me out. We were both frightened enough. But we've also lived enough to know that's not how it happens—not that the feelings wouldn't have been real; they just wouldn't have been the feelings we thought they were. I've already made one nearly awful mistake, and I'd be foolish not to learn from it.'

" 'This all sounds like good-bye,' I said.

"She smiled. 'No, Tom, it isn't good-bye at all. It's only to say that whatever happens from now on will be for the right reasons—or at least the best reasons I can find. I'll have to go back to the Cities for a while, to face some unfinished business, but I won't be gone long. And then I'm coming back here. I think there's a lot of lovely territory to explore here. I'd like to know it all better.' "

The fire was only a mound of glowing embers where a few flickers of flame licked up. Mac and Scotty were sunk deep into their chairs. The dogs sprawled snoring on the hearth rug. A faint night wind muttered in the pines beyond the windows.

Tom drained his glass.

"Lord, lads, you should've muzzled me an hour ago. I must get myself home, though Caroline will be long asleep. Let's meet in the village for breakfast. I think tomorrow might be a good day to see if there are any woodcock at the Petersen place."

What's Worth Saving

CHRIS MADSON

It is a landscape that has been tamed. The wheat stubble stretches out to the horizon over the gentle swells of the high plains, punctuated now and then by a farmstead or, more often, a long-abandoned school house or barn with empty window frames and clapboards weathered to a dove-soft gray. Down below, the course of the old Missouri with its buffalo bones and keelboat wrecks winds unseen under the blue expanse of Lake Sakakawea. The fierce, feral history of this place has been buried by the plow or drowned.

And yet it still feels wild. It is still empty country. If you were to break down on one of these roads, it might be a ten-mile walk to the nearest telephone or a two-hour wait for the first passing pickup. It may be a mile between fences. In late October with the first northers gathering on the horizon, the skiers and fishermen have winterized their boats and stored them away, leaving the lake to a few private weeks with sun and breeze before freeze-up.

There is something else here as well. The face of the land is easily changed—the wild herds and the people who followed them, the river, the prairie sod were all formidable obstacles, but they were rooted in place, fixed targets. Eventually, they had to yield to the immense mechanical advantage of the technology brought to bear on them. But this place has an essence that has survived domestication. It floats on the wind like cottonwood down, delicate, transient, always just beyond the reach of our machines and ambitions, settling lightly in places where it is not disturbed.

Standing on the edge of the wheat looking down 300 feet or so to one of the arms of Sakakawea, I see what's left of the old times. These are the Missouri breaks, the hills and ravines that are too steep to plow, too tall to flood. They're covered by the northern prairie's version of savannah. The south-facing slopes support a lush stand of native grasses—I see sideoats grama and little bluestem along with the dried heads of coneflower and gayfeather. The north-facing slopes trend down into think stands of shrubs standing knee- to chin-high. The snowberries are thick, and the buffaloberries are bending over with loads of scarlet fruit. In the bottoms of the ravines, there are clumps of hawthorn, gray screens of branches tinted with a wash of hot pink—a bumper crop of fruit like tiny crab apples.

Meg surveys the scent along the field edge while I plot a strategy. There will be birds here. The sharptails could be anywhere; the pheasants are likely to be tight in the woody cover close to the wheat. I decide to take a compromise course, fifty yards into the grass, then upwind along the wheat. Meg has finished her fresh-out-of-the-car ricochet and settles down to hunt ahead of me.

We hunt a mile with great expectations. Every hundred yards, there's an other promising corner of cover—a clump of buffaloberry; a grassy rock pile; the head of ravine choked with hawthorn, ragweed, and burdock. All good-looking spots; none of them with birds. It's testament to the harshness of this country. In spite of the apparent wealth of food and cover, there's a limit to how many birds this cover will support. Seems a little strange right now, I think; probably wouldn't if I were here in February.

A cool front is passing. The sky is tangled with clouds, and now and then, there's a patch of blue and a shaft of afternoon sun. I'm watching one of the patches play over the surface of the lake a couple of miles away when I become aware of a chuckle at the head of the next ravine. A sharptail. The usual quiet rise and rub-it-in call. I run toward the spot, hoping to catch a second bird, but all four have gotten out ahead of me.

It's the first sign that we've come to the right spot. On the next grassy rise, two more grouse flush wild, then another three. I take a fifty-yard shot and miss. The disappearing bird chuckles. Frustration sets in.

Four more birds out of the head of the next ravine. Two more out of the grass beyond. Another long shot. Another miss. The grouse gods don't seem inclined to give up anything easy. And then, a careless single flushes out of the stubble edge, thirty yards out instead of forty-five. The sixteen-gauge speaks, and the birds hesitates in the air, then fights to control the fall. Meg makes a seventy-yard retrieve, and the expedition seems more worthwhile.

Half a mile farther on, I angle out into the sparse snowberry on a north-facing slope and find myself in the middle of a stand of bittersweet. Where I grew up on the breaks of the Mississippi, bittersweet is a robust vine that climbs its way into small trees—here it's a single spindly stick mixed with other shrubs. Still, the berry is unmistakable—a yellow-and-orange fruit like a tiny Japanese lantern.

It is a sign of advancing years, I suppose, but I find memories pursuing me more these days than they once did. Dad used to suspend our bobwhite hunts when we came on a canopy of bittersweet twined into the edge of a patch of timber. I had the honor of shinnying up the trees and doing the cutting. Dad collected the harvest carefully and eased the cut branches into his game pocket. Mom valued the sprigs even more than the quail we brought home. The harvested vines went up around the dining room wall for the holiday season. To this day bittersweet means Thanksgiving to me.

Dad passed on twelve years ago, leaving me the sixteen-gauge in my hand and an incomparable legacy of good times in wild places. A quail hunt long past comes back to me over the years, a warm recollection, a hard, hard loss. A bittersweet moment.

A patch of sun drifts across the grass and moves on, leaving the breaks around me in the flat gray light of late afternoon. Time to head back.

We drop down the slope a hundred yards or so and take the contour where the prairie blends into the shrubs. Meg works close and careful in the best kind of collaboration. She's beginning to understand the lay of this new kind of cover and the birds living there—I don't have to make a sound to direct her.

Another pool of sun drifts across the broad prairie hillside in front of us, and the grass turns tawny with strokes of wine-colored bluestem scattered through it. Meg comes up on a low stand of buffaloberry and points hard. I step up to the edge, and five sharptails jump. The straightaway crumples with the first shot, and I swing hard to catch the crossing bird, without success. Meg has already disappeared into the bushes far below me and, after a couple of minutes, emerges again with the bird in her mouth and one wing across her eyes.

It's the last good chance we have on sharptails. We see half a dozen more as we work back over three or four miles of the breaks, but they all flush wild. The clouds have thickened again, and in the deepening twilight, geese and mallards start lifting out of some secluded bay headed for feed. Waves of them pass overhead, talking back and forth as they survey the options for supper.

We bump two whitetails out of their beds in the head of a ravine. The forkhorn stops on the edge the wheat forty yards away to take a second look; the eight-point has played this game before—he ducks behind a thick stand of hawthorn before he checks the source of the disturbance.

Then Meg pokes her nose into a buffaloberry patch, scattering the usual collection of juncos and sparrows, and a blur of movement streaks over my shoulder, nearly hitting one of the little birds. After the miss, the form sweeps upward thirty yards or so and suddenly suspends itself over the dog. It has the sleek aerodynamics of a falcon, and judging from its size, I figure it must be a kestrel. I'm wrong. The bird circles around us, showing its tail, then swings downwind to watch us again. A merlin. This is a new life bird for me. Trim, unafraid, a complete master of the air, the falcon follows us for ten minutes, waiting for us to shake more songbirds out of the cover. After two more unsuccessful stoops, it wheels and disappears.

As we cover the last of the hills back to the truck, I find myself pondering the wealth of the day. Maybe thirty grouse, several thousand geese and ducks, a couple of bucks, a wild falcon, the endless kaleidoscope of prairie grass and sky—what is this afternoon worth? Generations of hunters before me have named the price and currency. The Teddy Roosevelts and George Bird Grinnells, the Aldo Leopolds and Ding Darlings, the Herbert Stoddards and Paul Erringtons spent their lives to preserve such places, such days, then passed them on to me.

Up ahead, I see the shelterbelt that runs along the two-track where my truck is parked. The light is fading slowly toward night, and the quiet of the coming evening is gathering in the shadows. Meg, still hunting, disappears into the kosha edge, and I hear the oddly sharp slap of a primary on a weed stalk. A rooster pheasant jumps between two stunted cottonwoods. There's an eight-foot window in the branches; no time to think; snap shot, and the rooster disappears into the jungle of weeds. Even if I hit him, there's no way I can find him. Then the sound of movement in the cover. Meg.

As she steps out of the weeds, the sun drops into one last crack in the clouds, and the landscape is drenched in the rich butterscotch light of a high plains sunset. The bird glows like molten copper as she drops it in my hand while the last breeze of the day sighs through the branches and comes to rest. For a long breath, it seems as if time has paused. And it occurs to me that Dad must be somewhere close by.

Smiling.

PART VI

Waterfowl

The Old Brown Mackinaw

GORDON MACQUARRIE

When the President of the Old Duck Hunters' Association, Inc., died, the hearts of many men fell to the ground.

There was no one like Mister President. When the old-timers go there is no bringing them back, nor is there any hope of replacing them. They are gone, and there is a void and for many, many years I knew the void would never be filled, for this paragon of the duck blinds and the trout streams had been the companion of my heart's desire for almost 20 years.

I made the common mistake. I looked for another, exactly like Hizzoner. How foolish it is, as foolish as it is for a man to try to find another beloved hunting dog, exactly like the one that's gone.

In the years after Mister President's death I fished and hunted more than before, and often alone. There was a great deal of fishing and hunting, from Florida to Alaska, before a man came along who fit the role once occupied by Mister President. This is how it was:

I was sitting in the ballroom of the Loraine Hotel in Madison, Wisconsin, covering the proceedings of the unique Wisconsin Conservation Congress. I became aware that a man carrying one of the 71 labels for the 71 counties of the state was eyeing me.

He held aloft the cardboard label "Iowa" signifying that he was a Big Wheel in conservation from that western Wisconsin county. He looked like Huckleberry Finn and he grinned eternally. One of the first thoughts I had about him was that he probably could not turn down the corners of his lips if he wanted to.

Each time I glanced at him his eye was upon me. This sort of thing is unnerving. Once he caught my eye and held it and grinned harder. I grinned back, foolishly. The beggar burst out laughing. I felt like a fool. He knew it and laughed at me.

Let me give you the picture more completely. In that room sat more than 300 dedicated, articulate conservationists. They were framing, no less, the fish and game code of this sovereign state for an entire year. Not in silence, you may be sure.

Up at the front table on the platform, as chairman of the Congress, sat Dr. Hugo Schneider of Wausau, with a gavel in one hand and—so help me!—a muzzle-loading squirrel rifle in the other. Each time Robert's Rules of Order seemed about to go out the window, Doc would abandon the gavel and reach for the rifle.

In this delightful pandemonium, in this convention of impassioned hunters and fishers and amidst the shrieks from the wounded and dying delegates, Wisconsin evolves its game and fish laws. And if you can think of a more democratic way, suggest it. We may try it.

At one point in the milling commotion and confusion, I saw my grinning friend slip to the floor and on his hands and knees start crawling toward me. By this manner of locomotion he managed to evade the baleful eye and subsequent vengeance of Dr. Schneider, and he crawled up to my chair and handed me a scribbled note. Then still on his hands and knees, he crawled away. The note read:

I've been reading your drivel for years. See me after school if you want to get some good partridge hunting.
Harry

Since then I suppose I've "seen him" a thousand times—on trout streams, on lakes, in partridge cover, in the deer woods, in the quail thickets, and yes, in the August cow pastures where the blackberries grow as long as your thumb, and in the good September days when you can fill a bushel basket with hickory nuts beneath one tree.

No outdoor event of its season escapes Harry. He is lean and fiftyish. He is a superb shot. He ties his own flies, one a black killer with a tiny spinner at the eye made from special light material he begs, or steals from dentist friends. On a dare, once he shinnied up a 12-foot pole and came back down headfirst. Once he made me a pair of buckskin pants. All in all, an unbelievable person.

How natural then, just this last October, that we should rendezvous, not in Iowa County—we save those partridge until December—but at the ancient headquarters of the Old Duck Hunters' Association, two whoops and a holler north of Hayward, Wisconsin.

I got there first. This is not hard for me to do when going to this place. Some things do not change and this is one of those things. It's exactly like it was before the atomic age. On that particular day, late October's yellow shafts were slanting through the Norways on the old cedar logs of the place. A chipmunk which had learned to beg in summer came tentatively close, then scurried away, uncertain now.

All was in order, down to the new windowpane I had to put in where a partridge in the crazy time had flown through. The label was still pasted to the tiny square of glass. I must scratch it off someday but there is always so much to do at places like this.

I went to the shed at the rear to check decoy cords and anchors. When you open this shed door one of the first things to catch your eye is a brown, checked-pattern mackinaw, about 50 years old, I guess. It belonged to the President of the Old Duck Hunters. I like to keep it there. It belongs there.

Flying squirrels had filled one pocket of the mackinaw with acorns. They always do that, but these avian rodents, so quick to unravel soft, new wool for nests, have never chewed at the threadbare carcass of Mister President's heroic jacket. Perhaps this is because the wool, felted and tough, has lost its softness and flavor.

I launched a boat, readied a smaller skiff and screwed the motor on the big boat. I fetched three bags of decoys down the hill and placed them handy. I put an ax—for blind building—in the boat with other gear, and when I got back up the hill to the cabin Harry was there.

On the way—a 300-mile drive—he had hesitated, he said, long enough to slay two pheasant roosters.

"I see," he said, "that you have been here an hour and have killed 'ary a duck or partridge." He explained that he had felt my auto radiator—"She's cooled only about an hour." This man operates like a house detective. I explained that in the remaining hour and a half of daylight I would prepare him a kingly supper.

"An hour and a half of daylight!" He flung two skinned pheasants at me, dashed to his car and returned, running, bearing fishing tackle.

"D'ja soak the boat?" he cried as he passed me. I doubt if he heard my answer for he was soon down the hill and nearing the beach when I replied. Within two minutes he was trolling.

The man never lived who could fill up each moment of a day like this one. Nor was there ever a one who could, once the day was done, fall asleep so fast. He goes, I am sure, into a world of dreams, there to continue the pursuits of fish and game, man's life's blood—well, his, anyway.

I lit the fireplace. No need for the big steel stove, or was there? Late October weather in the north can be treacherous. I laid the big stove fire, to play safe. The provident Harry had made getting supper easy. You take two pheasants and cut them up. You save the giblets. You steam some wild rice for an hour. . . .

It was long after dark when Harry returned. He had a 7- or 8-pound northern and a walleye half as big—"If we're gonna be here for four days, somebody around here has got to bring home the grub."

I set the table fast for fear he would fall asleep. He stuffed himself with pheasant and wild rice and mentioned that he must not forget to tell his wife how badly I treated him. Then he collapsed on the davenport before the fire, and in one yawn and a short whistle he was gone. I washed the dishes.

No, he is not a shirker. Before sleep afflicts him he will kill himself at any job which needs doing, especially if it pertains to hunting and fishing. To prove his willingness for the menial tasks, I recall a deer camp one night when one of the boys brought in a 300-pound bear—dragged him right through the door and dropped him at Harry's feet.

Harry was wiping the dishes, clad only in a suit of new, red underwear. He had sworn to be the first man in that camp to bring in important game, and because now he obviously had not, he turned, dishcloth in hand, eyed the bear casually and remarked:

"Johnny, that's a mighty nice little woodchuck you got there."

Even when I turned on the radio for a weather report he did not awaken. His snores, wondrously inventive, competed with the welcome report of changing and colder weather. Outside the wind was coming along a bit and it was in the northwest. But mostly it was the warm wind hurrying back south ahead of something colder at its back.

Iowa County's nonpareil was bedded down in the far room where his snores joined the issue with the rising wind which keened over the roof. A good fair contest, that.

When I arose I had to light the big heater for the weather had made up its mind. No snow, but a thermometer at 26 degrees and a buster of a wind. I hurried with breakfast because I thought we might have to build a blind on Posey's point. That point, the right one on this day, had not been hunted in the season. When I mentioned the reason for haste he explained:

"Man, I built that blind yesterday. You think I fooled away three hours just catching a couple fish?"

It is not possible to dislike a man like that. Furthermore, I knew this blind would be no wild dove's nest, but a thing of perfection, perfectly blended with the shore line.

A lot of people in this country think the Old Duck Hunters are crazy when they hunt this lake. We carry so many decoys that we have to tow them behind in a skiff. Fifty is our minimum, half of them over-sized balsas, and a scattering of some beat-up antiques more than 120 years old, just for luck.

Settling himself for some duck blind gossip, Harry began, "I was down on the Mississippi at Ferryville last week. Mallards all over the—"

"Mark!"

A hundred bluebills, maybe twice that, who knows, came straight in without once swinging, and sat. We never touched a feather as they rose. I have done it before and I'll do it again and may God have mercy on my soul.

"This," said Harry, "will become one of the greatest lies in history when I tell my grandchildren about it. I am reminded of Mark Twain. When Albert Bigelow Paine was writing his biography and taking copious notes, he once remarked to Twain that his experiences and adventures were wonderful copy.

" 'Yes, yes,' replied Mr. Clemens. 'And the most remarkable thing about it is that half of them are true.'"

He then set his jaw and announced he would kill the next three straight with as many shots. This he did, for I did not fire. While I was retrieving them in the decoy skiff, another bundle of bluebills tried to join those giant decoys and were frightened off by me. Walking to the blind from the boat, I saw Harry kill a canvasback.

He was through for the day and not a half hour had passed. Many Badgers will remember that late October day. Ducks flew like crazy from the Kakagon sloughs of Lake Superior to sprawling Horicon marsh, 300 miles away. Only one other day of that season beat it—Wednesday, November 2.

Harry cased his gun and watched. I cannot shoot like Harry, but getting four ducks on such a day was child's play. Many times we had more divers over our decoys than we had decoys. It was pick-and-choose duck hunting. I settled for four bullneck canvasbacks.

Back at the cabin we nailed their bills to the shed wall, and over a cup of coffee Harry said the divers we'd seen reminded him of the "kin to can't day." Then, he explained, the law let a man shoot the whole day through from as soon "as he kin see until the time that he can't see." I knew a place, Oscar Ruprecht's sugar bush, and we drove the eight miles to it.

This chunk of maple is on an island of heavier soil in an ocean of glacial sand, grown to pines. If its owner had the equipment he could tap 5,000 trees. Many know it and hunt it. We separated, for we are both snap shooters, or think we are.

The plan was to meet on a high, rocky bluff where the river Ounce passes by below, on its way to the Totagatic. Here was no dish like that easy duck blind venture. These were mature, hunted ruffed grouse, all the more nervous because the wind was high. On one of the tote trails where Oscar's tractor hauls the sap tank I missed my first bird, then missed two more.

A half mile to my right two calculated shots sounded, well spaced. Perhaps a double. Ah, well ... My fourth bird was as good as dead when it got out of the red clover in mid-trail and flew straight down the road. I missed him, too.

Three times more, and later a couple more times Harry's gun sounded. Then two birds flung themselves out of the yellow bracken beside the two-rut road and I got one. When I was walking over to pick it up, a third pumped up and I got it.

It was noon when I got to the high bluff. Deer hunters with scopes on their rifles love this place. From it they overlook almost a half mile of good deer country in three directions. My sandwich tasted good. I lit a little friendship fire and thought about other days on the river below me. It's a pretty good trout stream for anyone who will walk in two miles before starting to fish.

Harry came along. He'd been far up the valley of the Ounce, bucking fierce cover—no sugar bush tote trails in there, only deer trails. But he had five grouse. We hunted back to the car, and in his presence I was lucky enough to kill my third bird.

It was around 2 p.m. when we pulled into the cabin. My Huckleberry Finn who I have seen, on occasion, whittle away at a pine stick for 20 minutes without doing anything but meditate, was a ball of fire on this day. He tied into the ducks and partridge. When he had finished cleaning them his insatiable eye fell upon the woodpile.

You can spot those real country-raised boys every time when they grab an ax. They know what to do with it. No false moves. No glancing blows. In no time he had half a cord of fine stuff split and piled for the kitchen range and he went on from that to the sheer labor of splitting big maple logs with a wedge for the fireplace.

He spotted my canoe and considered painting it, but decided it was too cold, and anyway, it had begun to snow a little. Then he speculated about the weather, and when I said I wished I had a weather vane on the ridgepole, he went into action.

He whittled out an arrow from an old shingle, loosely nailed it to a stick, climbed to the roof and nailed it there firmly. I suppose that if I had mentioned building an addition to the back porch he'd have started right in. He came down from the roof covered with snow and said he wished he hadn't killed those four ducks in the morning, so he could go again.

"But, let's go anyway," he suggested. "No guns. Put out the decoys and just watch 'em."

Out there on the point the divers were riding that wind out of Canada. Scores of them rode into and above the decoys. Posey, the owner of the point, came along for a visit and decided we were both crazy when he saw what we were doing. Nevertheless, we had him ducking down as excited as we were when a new band of bluebills burst out of the snow. Only in the big duck years can a hunter enjoy such madness.

Our shore duty at dark that night involved careful preparations against the storm. We pulled up the boat and skiff higher than usual and covered everything with a weighted tarp.

Walking up the hill, I considered how nice it was to have one of the faithful, like Harry, on the premises. He should have been bone tired. Certainly I was. But before I relit the big heater he took down its 15 feet of stovepipe, shook out the soot and wired it back to the ceiling. He carried in enough wood for the remaining three days, stamping off snow and whistling and remembering such tales as one hears in all properly managed hunting camps.

He spied a seam rip in my buckskin pants and ordered me to take them off. While he mended them he complained bitterly about such neglect on my part—"There's nothing wrong with the workmanship on these pants."

He had made them himself, two months before, from two big chrome-tanned doeskins. He just walked into my house one night with a gunny sack containing the skins, a piece of chalk and some old shears his wife used for trimming plants. He cut the pants out, fitted them to me and took them to the shoemaker's shop where he sewed them up and affixed buttons. I never in my life wore pants that fit so well.

This man should have been born in the same time as a Kit Carson or a Jim Bridger. Turn him loose anywhere in his native heath, which is Wisconsin, and, given matches, an ax, a fishhook and some string, he'll never go hungry or cold.

He is a true countryman, a species almost extinct. Each day of the year finds him outdoors for at least a little while. In trout season he hits the nearby streams for an hour or two around sunup. His garden is huge and productive. In the raspberry season you may not go near his home without being forced, at gun point if need be, to eat a quart of raspberries with cream.

He represents something almost gone from our midst. He knows the value of working with his own hands, of being eternally busy, except when sleeping. His last act that snowy evening was to go to his car and return with a bushel of hickory nuts. He set up a nut-cracking factory on a table, using a little round steel anvil he had brought for busting 'em. He had a pint of hickory nut meats when I put the grub on the table.

He almost fell asleep at the table. Then he yawned and whistled and looked out the door and said he was glad it was snowing hard—"Don't shoot at anything but cans in the morning." He flopped on the davenport and was gone to that far-off land where no trout of less than five pounds comes to a surface fly and the duck season runs all year.

I tidied up and washed the dishes. I smelled the weather and smoked a pipe. The fireplace light danced on the big yellow cedar beams. The snow hissed against the window. The President of the Old Duck Hunters' Association should have been there.

Maybe he was. At any rate, I went out to the shed and took the old brown mackinaw off its nail and brought it in and laid it over Harry's shoulders. It looked just fine there.

From *Stories of the Old Duck Hunters.* Reprinted with permission of Willow Creek Press. Readers interested in books by Gordon MacQuarrie should go to www.willowcreekpress.com.

"Pothole Guys, Friz Out"

GORDON MACQUARRIE

The president of the Old Duck Hunters' Association, Inc., hauled up in front of my house in the newest, gaudiest automobile which had to that date, turned west off Lake drive onto East Lexington boulevard.

It seemed that even the gray squirrels among the boulevard beeches were impressed by the stream-lined vehicle, if not by the inelegant driver, Hizzoner himself, in a flannel shirt and battered brown hat.

I saw him coming for two blocks for I had been expecting him. The village hall and police station are his landmarks. He made a horseshoe turn around the end of the boulevard, slid into the curb and yelled for all to hear:

"The minute I saw the jail I knew where to find you!"

Leaf-raking brethren of the chase leaned on their implements and yipped. The Old Man freed himself from his imposing machine and studied a Schnauzer dog which had arrived with a band of kids to investigate the new automotive device. *Anent* the dog, Mister President demanded:

"Is that a dog or a bundle of oakum?" He is congenitally allergic to all but the hunting breeds.

In due course he came inside. He'd driven the dealer's model superduper up from the factory and was stopping on the way by prearrangement to rescue me from the city's toils.

"Going through Chicago," he explained, "every cop on Michigan avenue made the same mental note as I drove by—'roughly dressed man in brand new auto.' If the police come, my identification papers are in the glove compartment."

He had climbed into his old hunting clothes for comfort in the long drive.

Later in the evening we loaded the car with decoys, shell boxes, duffel bags and in the early morning while the household slept the Old Duck Hunters' Association crept away.

The elements had descended. Streets were semi-granite with frozen sleet.

"Just what the doctor ordered," Mister President exulted. "If it's freezing down here, it's frozen up there."

Daylight came on the feet of snails but long before then the Old Man bade me halt on the slippery road. With the tire gauge in one hand and a flashlight in the other he let ten pounds of air out of each tire. After that we got along faster.

At Portage, Wis., the President was happen than ever, for snow was falling. We had breakfast and went on. North of Tomah the sleet was gone from the road and dry snow was whipping across the concrete. We re-inflated the tires and pushed on. At Chippewa Falls, crossing the big bridge, visibility up and down the Chippewa river was 200 yards.

Hizzoner nodded in the seat beside me. He was asleep and snoring at Spooner. The snow and the wind increased. The footing for tires was perfect, thanks to the built-up highway over which dry flakes rolled in sheets. Mister President awoke at Minong while a man by the name of Andy Gorud filled the tank.

"Is that it, Andy?" the Old Man asked. For answer Andy took us to his back porch and exhibited a possession limit of snow-sprinkled redheads. Andy said indeed this was it, but if the weather kept up it might drive every duck out of the country before morning.

"Bosh!" said Mister President. "Only the shallow lakes and potholes will freeze. The ducks'll have to wet their feet in big water tomorrow morning."

Such a man, that Andy. Once he walked two miles in the rain with a heavy jack to hoist us up and put on our chains.

The snow kept up. At Gordon we turned off. The Old Man was wide awake now.

"She's a good un," he said, watching the county trunk. "Come so quick they haven't got all the snow fences up. If you see a drift back up and give 'er tarpaper."

Tarpaper was required in several places. I complimented him on the power under the hood of his newest contraption but he was not enthusiastic—"They're all too low, no good in a two-rut road. They're making them so low pretty soon you can use a gopher hole for a garage."

It grew dark. The driving flakes stabbed at the windshield. By the time I was ready to turn off the county trunk onto the town road the Old Man had demanded the driver's seat. He knew that the in-road would be well filled with snow. I protested but he said I could drive "the day you learn your driving brains are in the seat of your pants."

There were a few spots on that narrow road between the jack pines where we barely got over the rises. The car was pushing snow 12 inches deep when we stopped at the top of the last hill.

We went ahead and got a fire going. When I got to the cabin with the first load the fireplace was roaring and he was coaxing the kitchen range to life. By the time I had hauled in the last of the gear and shoveled the snow off the stoop he had water hot enough for tea. While we ate supper the temperature slid from 28 to 24.

We hauled in wood, broke out blankets and took a hooded motor from the shed down through the snow to the lake. We took a boat off its winter roost and set it handy by the edge of the tossing lake. We brought down guns and decoys, put them in the boat and covered everything with a canvas tarp. Then there was time to size up the night.

It was a daisy. There was snow halfway to the knees on the beach. The flashlight's circle revealed a black, tossing lake. From the hill at our backs the wind screamed down through the pine trees.

"How'd you like to be a field mouse on a night like this?" Hizzoner reflected.

We went back up the hill. The last thing Mister President did was study the thermometer. I heard him say, "She's dropped to 22 and it's only 8 o'clock." After that the fireplace crackled, the wind cried, the blankets felt awfully good . . .

In the morning there wasn't a breath of wind. Of course he was up before me, useful and belligerent. Everything was ready, including the country smoked bacon. I started to open the door to inspect the thermometer and he announced, "Fifteen about half an hour ago."

I studied him jealously as I have often. There he was, 30 years older than I, tough as a goat, alert as a weasel. He'd just finished an exhausting business trip. Forty-eight hours before he had been 600 miles from this place. He ate six eggs to my four, eyeing me with the indulgent authority a bird dog man feels for a new pup.

"The hell with the dishes and put on all the clothes you've got," he directed.

The lake in the darkness held an ominous quiet, like a creature which had threshed itself to exhaustion. We flung off the tarp with one flip to keep snow off gear, slid in the boat, screwed on the motor and roared out.

We were afloat on blackness, rimmed with the faint white of snow on the shores. Mister President huddled in the bow in the copious brown mackinaw, its collar inches above his ears. He fished in pockets and drew on mittens and when his hands were warmed he fished again and presently a match glowed over the bowl of his crooked little pipe. I saw that he was grinning, so I throttled the motor and yelled, "What's the joke?"

"No joke," he came back. "Just a morning for the books."

The run to this place requires about 30 minutes. Dim landmarks on shore were illuminated just enough by the snow. We cut wide around the shallow point bar and went south for the shallow end of the lake. The Old Man has bet that he can, blindfold, land an outboard within 100 yards of the shallow bay point from our beach. There are no takers.

A little daylight was making as I cut the speed and turned toward the shore. The President said. "Go back down the shore further from the blind. The boat'll stand out against the snow like a silo." We beached 200 yards from the point.

There was plenty of time. When the Old Man is master of ceremonies you get up early enough to savor the taste of morning. And what a morning! Just once in a coon's age do the elements conspire with latitude to douse North Wisconsin with snow of mid-winter depth in October. It is a very lovely thing. We toted up the gear to the blind. I was impatient to get out in the shallows in my waders and spread decoys. The Old Man detained me.

"I suppose," he said, "that when a man quits liking this it's time to bury him."

He was determined to size up the morning, and he did size it up. Between hauls on the blackened brier he continued, "Once before I saw this point just as pretty. Back in 1919. Just about the same depth of snow, same old lake black as ink, trees ag'in the sky . . ."

I had paused to honor his rhapsody, so he snorted, "Get them boosters out there, dang yuh, while I rebuild the blind!"

Rebuild it he did, pausing now and then in the growing light to tell me where to place the next decoy. In the blind I found he had the rough bench swept off, the blind repaired and a thermos of coffee at hand. He sat on the right side of the bench and both our guns, his automatic and my double, were held away from the snowy wall of the blind by forked sticks. It was unmercifully cold for sitting. He explained his thesis for the day—

"The potholes chilled over in the night. The ice crep' out from shore. The ducks huddled up, getting closer and closer as the ice reached for 'em. First good daylight they'll look around at each other and say, 'Let's go. This place is getting too crowded.'"

"You don't suppose they've all left the country?" I ventured. There was scorn in his reply.

"The best ducks stay 'til the last dog's hung."

A burst of bluebills went over and planed into the lake, far out.

"They were up awfully high for cold weather ducks," I said. "I'm afraid if they move they'll go a long ways today—if there are any left around."

"They'll be lower," he said.

A pair dropped in from in back of us. It was apparent they'd come in from any quarter in the absence of wind. I reached for the gun and slid out a toe to kick my shellbox. The Old Man put a mittened hand on my right knee. I could feel his fingers squeeze through leather and wool. Following his eyes I saw what he saw.

They were at the left, about a hundred ducks, an embroidery of ducks, skeined out in a long line with a knot at the head. We crouched down and the Old Man whispered:

"Pothole guys, friz out. Might be from Minnesota. Maybe Ontario. They'll swing and size 'er up and the whole dang bundle will—"

Swi-i-i-ish!

While we had watched the mid-lake flock fifty or so had slid into the decoys, bluebills everyone. The President from his corner eyed me and whispered, "Flyin' high, did you say? No, don't shoot! We're gonna have fun."

The mid-lake flock swung in, decoyed by their confident cousins. The President of the Old Duck Hunters' grinned like a schoolboy. He was on his knees in the trampled snow, close against the front wall of the blind. So was I and he was laughing at me. Fifty ducks sat in the decoys, another hundred were coming in, and the Old Man said to me:

"Hold out your hand so I can see if you're steady."

At the moment that the landed birds were flailing out the incomers were tobogganing in with their wing flaps down. The Old Man arose and shouted:

"Hello, kids!"

His deliberateness was maddening. I emptied the double before he brought up his automatic. I reloaded and fired again and he still had a shell to go. He spent it expertly on a drake.

Then the ducks were gone and I was trying to stuff a round brass match safe into the breech and the Old Man was collapsed on the bench, laughing.

"Up high for cold weather ducks!" he howled.

There were seven down, two far out, and as I raced back for the boat Mister President heckled, "Wish I had that East Lexington boulevard Snootzer here and I'd learn him to be a dog!"

As I rowed out for the pick-up he shouted across the water, "Do you get a bottle of turpentine with every Snootzer you buy?"

As he had predicted, it was a day for the books. The clouds pressed down. They leaned against the earth. No snow fell but you knew it might any minute. There were not just clouds but layers of clouds, and ramparts and bastions and lumps of clouds in between the layers.

We sat and drank coffee. We let bluebills sit among the decoys. That was after Hizzoner decreed, "No more 'bills. Pick the redheads if you can. If you miss a mallard I'll kill yuh."

The quick dark day sped by. To have killed a hundred diving ducks apiece would have been child's play. Canvasback, whistlers, mergansers, red heads, and bluebills by the hundreds trouped over the hundred-year old decoys which are the sole property of the Old Duck Hunters' Association.

"I'd give a lot for a brace of mallards to color up the bag," he said.

The Lady Who Waits for Mister President likes mallards.

Be assured, mallards were present, as well as those dusky wise men, black ducks. They would swing in high over the open water and look it over. They did not care for any part of our point blind in the snow.

"Wise guys," Mister President said. "They see the point and two dark objects against the snow in the blind, and one of the objects wiggling all over the place. That'll be you."

We went back to the boat and fetched the white tarpaulin. He threw it over the top of the blind and propped up the front of it with cut poles. The tarp erased us from above and seven laboring mallards swung closer. Before throwing off the tarp, Mister President whispered: "Slow down sos'te to nail 'em."

Back went the tarp. I missed a climber, then crumpled him. Hizzoner collected three. He just spattered them. Because these were for the Lady Who Waits.

We picked up and hauled out, raising rafted diving ducks in the long run back.

We hoisted the boat onto its winter trestles, upside down, to let it drain and dry. We put the gear beneath it and slung the tarp over it. We went up the hill and stirred the fires.

I got supper. I worried about the super-duper on the hilltop at the road's end but he said he had drained it. I lugged in more wood and heaped up the fireplace.

He said in the morning we might have to break ice to get out from shore. He said, "We might not see much more than whistlers." He said to steep the tea good. He said not to forget to climb down the well and open the bleeder on the pump "because she's going to really drop tonight." He said he thought he'd "take a little nap 'fore supper." And finally he said:

"Draw them mallards, will yuh, son? She likes 'em drawed."

From *Stories of the Old Duck Hunters*. Reprinted with permission of Willow Creek Press. Readers interested in books by Gordon MacQuarrie should go to www.willowcreekpress.com.

The Wings of Dawn

GEORGE REIGER

Outsiders call us sadists or masochists; sometimes both. Others—mostly ourselves—describe our activities in romantic, even heroic, terms. We take ourselves very seriously and tend to forget that much of duck and goose hunting is fun and sometimes ridiculous.

For two days last season, I scouted a piece of salt marsh where several black ducks and mallards appeared to be in residence. I decided to go in the next day at dawn with my layout boat to try to decoy a limit. All night long, a northeast wind pushed the ocean through the inlets and over sod islands so that by first light, with my retriever tucked between my knees and myself tucked horizontally into the 9-foot punt, the tide began to float the boat off the point where I had hidden her.

I worried lest the boat's rocking would alarm ducks and wondered whether the brisk breeze wouldn't blow the punt completely clear of the reeds. I sat up, took one of the oars, shoved it hard down into the mud, and tied the painter to it. Now let her blow!

A half hour passed with no ducks to the decoys. Geese were fly high overhead, and ducks were trading in the distance. But the storm tide had lifted the boat well above the grass, and little white-capped waves slapped the hull and rocked my half-dozen decoys.

I was on the verge of packing it in when a pair of black ducks appeared low over the marsh obviously looking for company. I squiggled lower, hissed at my dog to stay down, and watched the birds approach from under the brim of my cap. My face was blackened, my pale hands were gloved, and only the stark bar of blued metal and wood resting across my camouflaged chest would spark the birds' suspicions.

Ordinarily they should have come straight in. But with all the marsh under water, they were wary of the curious "log" bumping near their rock-and-rolling buddies. Something wasn't right. They decided to swing by, look the situation over, and think about it.

"Just one," I pleaded. "Just one would make a perfect day. But, Lord, wouldn't a double be sweet!"

The ducks were gone half a minute. Then I noticed them to my right, flying wide of the decoys, but lower. When they turned upwind, no more than ten feet off the water, I knew they were coming—100 yards, 90, 80, 70 . . .

When the birds were less than 60 yards away, the oar suddenly pulled from the mud, surged into the air, slammed down on my head, startled the dog into jumping overboard, and the boat shipped a barrel of icy water that poured in like electricity around my crotch. I watched the black ducks blow away: 150 yards, 200, 300 . . . Then the sky broke loose and sleet obliterated the scene.

With the punt drifting away from the decoys, the dog paddling and whimpering in circles around me, and freezing water sloshing around my hips every time I made the slightest move, I did what any sane man would do: I laughed. I laughed and cussed and laughed again at all the follies of our magnificent recreation.

Halfway through the season, I left a dozen decoys out overnight in a pond. When I returned at dawn, I found two teal missing from the rig. Considerable searching turned up only one where an otter had pulled the bird—dragging the line and weight behind it—30 yards from the edge of the water. Somehow this otter, or a companion—the busy, back-and-forth tracks of otter never make such things clear—had contrived to carry off the other decoy to do with it what only an otter can tell.

I was fascinated; I was charmed. What a bizarre fate for a teal drake facsimile: that it becomes an otter's plaything. When I told one of my neighbors about the experience, he snorted and asked if I had shot enough ducks that day to make up the loss. But then, this man doesn't pretend to be a sportsman.

Two Washington, D.C., friends came down to share a seaside outing with me. An hour after dawn I was looking behind the blind and out to the ocean when I spotted a pair of puddle ducks coming down the coast. I provided the following, over-the-shoulder commentary for my companions:

"They're not too high—They should see the decoys—They have seen the decoys!—They're coming lower—They're going to circle—You should see them by now—They should be right over you—Why doesn't somebody shoot?!"

I turned and found both my companions peering around their end of the blind trying to see where I had been looking. No one was minding the store out front.

"Where are the ducks?" they whispered.

I looked up and saw a pair of gadwall hovering and staring down at me with something approaching bemusement.

"There!"

Guns began blazing and seven shots later we had one of the two birds.

"All right, guys, no more Gong Shows. Each person watches a different direction, and we'll use compass points to indicate where the birds are."

"Good idea," said Paul. "That's south."

"No, that's east."

"South."

"Paul, I live here; that's east."

"You're both wrong," announced Mel, uncapping a tiny compass he had tucked among his spare shells. "That's eastsoutheast."

Debating the fine points of the compass kept us busy until a goldeneye buzzed over the decoys without a shot being fired. We then decided to wrap up the compass conversation and concentrate on duck hunting. We compromised by calling "south" and "eastsoutheast," east and boxed the rest of the imaginary compass card accordingly. Going through the drill made us feel better. It was as though we had actually learned something—as though this time we were prepared for any and all contingencies, even though experience indicates that each fiasco in waterfowling is somehow unique and unforeseeable.

Suddenly we heard the distant murmur of geese.

"North," said Mel, "and coming this way!"

"More like northwest," said Paul, "and the wind will carry them wide."

"Start calling," I ordered. "And stay back in the blind. We don't want to spook them while trying to get a look."

The sound of Canada geese carries a long distance under most any atmospheric condition. Biologists suspect the birds may use their calling to echolocate their way through fog. When Canadas are flying downwind toward a tries of expectant hunters, the honking seems to come from a public address system mounted on the roof of the blind—even when the birds are still half a mile away.

But this time there was no rubber-necking. This time we were ready. My companions and I scrunched into the corners of the blind and matched yelp for yelp the calling of the geese behind us. We didn't go into action until we saw a wingtip flash about 30 yards above the edge of the plywood roof.

"NOW!"

Mel and Paul leaped up and did an audition for a movie called *Abbott and Costello Go Hunting.* Paul stepped on Mel's foot, and Mel recovered his balance by knocking Paul back into the corner. Then, swinging on the nearest bird, which look as large as a bomber, Mel squeezed the trigger of his empty gun. He had forgotten to reload after the gadwall farce.

Meanwhile I had somehow contrived to insert the thumb tang on the bolt of my semi-automatic shotgun through a hole in my right glove and couldn't get my hand free. My frantic gyrations and furious oaths brought the dog around to the entrance of the blind where he peered in to see what was going on.

A dozen geese flew by unscathed, but our imprecations quickly turned into such uproarious laughter it took still another missed opportunity to sober us up. No, we hadn't been drinking. And we did quite well when we finally got organized. Funny though: I don't remember those details half as well as the foolish way we began.

How do you explain waterfowling to anyone who does not share your faith? How can you even describe events to those who care but were not there?

With my final shot last season, I killed a black duck. That is a simple statement of fact. But those few words mask a range of sensations which could not be duplicated with a sound-and-light replica of the outing.

This is because you'd have to know my dog is old and that day lame, and I wanted to get his mind off his hurt by doing something he loves and does well: jump shooting. You'd also have to know that I had watched half a hundred black ducks angle down in the afternoon mist toward a series of meanders in two drains of the high marsh, and despite a following wind which blew every crunch of spartina grass underfoot ahead of us to spook the wary birds, I was confident that eventually Rocky and I would find an elbow of water to which we could turn upwind and find an unsuspecting duck.

You'd have to hear the whispering wings of birds in the air, and see how I'd periodically squat, less with the hope of having a shot, than to pause and watch the panorama of waterfowl returning to the evening marsh. You'd have to see the pair of mallards pitch to a pond several hundred yards away, and know that because I'd rather kill one of these interlopers of the salt lands than a native black duck, I made a special effort to reach the alert drake and his oblivious hen. You'd see the mallards sitting close by the opposite shore and then noisily flushing out of range. You'd watch Rocky and me turn back to our original course, and when we were 75 yards away, you'd glance back in time to see a solitary black duck take to the air a few feet from where we'd stood while contemplating the fleeing mallards. You'd hear me chuckle and tell my dog that I hoped the crafty bird lived another decade, and you'd see Rocky look up as if he understood every word.

Other ducks were getting up in the mist, but only a few were at extreme range, and you'd know that once the gun was fired, every bird in the marsh would be up and gone. So you wait with me for the shot that can't be missed.

You'd watch me come to a deep, unwadable creek, and while I look for a possible ford, two black ducks leap up from the other side. Despite the fact you are hunting them, the sudden rise of a pair of ducks is always a strangely unexpected event.

You are behind my eyes as I fire at the farthest bird in an attempt to score a double, miss, swing on the nearest, and kill it with a charge of steel 2s. While Rocky swims the channel to retrieve the fallen bird, you let the sight and sound of dozens of ducks rising from all parts of the darkening marsh and the cold mist on your cheek saturate your senses.

My watch tells me there are still seven minutes left in the season. But my day, my year, is done. I turn back toward the distant blind and calculate that in a narrow, ten-square-mile band of salt marsh, I am the only human being, and the proud, head-high sashaying dog striding before me with a black duck in his mouth is all the human companionship a waterfowler needs.

An oar, an otter, a tangled glove, and a last-chance duck. These are the memories of waterfowling. These are the words and experiences we seek to recover or revise each time we return to the marsh. If we weren't dedicated, we would not suffer the small tribulations surrounding our recreation. And it is this dedication—call it "obsession" if you like—that provides hope for the future.

Thousands of years ago, men crouched at the edge of ponds to fling their stones and arrows at ducks and geese lured by crude facsimiles of themselves. So long as waterfowl and men exist, we will hunt the wings of dawn.

Waterfowling's Final Frontier

TOM HUGGLER

The late Al Davis of Columbiaville, Michigan, lived to hunt ducks. Davis worked the second shift at an auto factory in nearby Flint so he could be in the marsh on Saginaw Bay or on the flats of Lake St. Clair a hundred miles from home before dawn the next morning. When sleep deprivation took over—as it always does with rabid waterfowlers—Davis would float rivers close to home in his aluminum canoe, but he never fell asleep at the paddle. He left that task to me.

One such trip occurred years ago on a day deep into October when Davis and I floated the Flint River from his 16-foot Smokercraft. I sat cross-legged in the bow, a 20-gauge double barrel across my knees, and tried to keep a wary eye open for ducks as Davis kept the canoe on course with deft paddle flicks from the stern.

But I found it hard to concentrate on duck hunting that morning. Five minutes from the parking lot was time enough to drown out road noise, and soon I had put telephones and typewriters out of my mind. Adding to my reverie were gold and red maple leaves that swirled in the brown current and pockets of fog that curled like campfire smoke above the bubbling stream. The patchy fog, in particular, rendered a dreamlike atmosphere to the morning, and it was fitting to think back to earlier times when this same river had borne me along as a schoolboy trapper and fisherman.

I thought about the wood ducks, herons and deer that were in such short supply here when I was a kid but that were much more plentiful now. I thought about the sandbars where we camped, the bonfires that sputtered all night, the bullheads and mud puppies we snaked from the dark stream. I got so wrapped up in remembering things of the past that it seemed entirely possible that the man in the stern, moving us along with silent, steady strokes, was not my friend at all but rather my dad. I was 13 again, legs shivering in hip boots, eyes watering from the November wind in my face, the mug of cocoa (now coffee) cradled between my hands growing tepid too fast.

A beaver swimming nearby cracked the water with its tail like a pistol shot and then dived. Al's 90-pound yellow Lab, John, leaped from the canoe as though fired from a slingshot, and my heart jumped into my throat. Somehow Davis kept the canoe from flipping and then ordered John back into the boat.

Five minutes later I missed the first pair of wood ducks—a colorful drake and a hen with white eye patch. They scuttled down the bank, leaped into the river and were aloft before I could react.

"You gotta be quick," Al reminded me. "Keep your gun halfway up on the turns. Pretend you're a kid playing with marbles, hunching over the ring. Steady and ready—that's the key to float hunting."

When we switched places, the edgy birds seemed to become more concentrated. Singles and pairs that we spooked rocketed downstream to join other ducks, and during the last mile of our float we were putting as many as a dozen woodies in the air at once. I had never before experienced such a spectacle of color—the autumn sun bouncing off the drake's burnished colors of red, white and purple. Al shot his two-bird limit, and then I scored twice, too.

"Rivers are the final frontier for duck and goose hunters," he used to say, "because nobody hunts 'em."

That experience and others opened my eyes to the enormous potential awaiting waterfowlers. Rivers are the earth's arteries, and the blood supply seems inexhaustible. North America is home to thousands of streams. More than 450 pour into the Great Lakes alone. Michigan has 36,000 miles of navigable waterways. Many of these, as well as flows throughout the country, are ideal for float hunting because ducks and geese use them for migratory corridors and to rest and feed in spring and fall. Geese often nest on islands and along points, and puddle ducks in particular like the bayous and pool areas formed by oxbows and switchbacks. Heavy rainfall that sends rivers over their banks flood the timbered bottom lands that wood ducks and mallards find so attractive. Thousands of local puddlers including teal, pintails and black ducks raise their families on these waterways and sometimes never see a human being until they migrate south in the fall.

Rivers may provide the only wet habitat for miles around. Last January, for example, I hunted the North Platte River at Scottsbluff, Nebraska, where some 80,000 to 100,000 mallards and 60,000 Canada geese overwinter. Although we hunted successfully over decoys from stationary blinds along the river, many times I wondered aloud to my friends how much fun it would be to float this river—to jump scads of mallards around every bend. We never found out. I doubt if anyone else ever has either.

I like a canoe for negotiating the smaller streams I favor because the craft are light, quiet and easy to handle in tight spots. Some hunters I know use duck boats designed for marsh hunting, and these are fine, too, except for the weight difference. The disadvantage of using a heavy boat shows up right away if you must drag it over logs or pick it up on a portage, a task to expect when floating the small waterways.

Aluminum or wooden fishing boats also tend to draw too much water and bog down in small streams; however, they are safer for hunters not familiar with canoes. A 14- or 15-foot canoe is large enough for one hunter; for two people use a canoe that is at least 16 feet long. During the excitement of a hunt, a crowded canoe can tip with little or no warning.

Only the bow hunter should shoot. The stern paddler should keep his gun unloaded and his mind on keeping the canoe upright. When a bevy of mallards suddenly bursts from the river, the stern hunter may be tempted to join the action but he can't if his gun is unloaded. The partners can switch off from time to time—as Davis and I used to do—so both have the chance to shoot.

As kids we once narrowly escaped a hunting accident. A friend and I were floating a wide, sluggish river when suddenly we jumped a small flock of teal in some pocket water around a sharp bend. I got off a couple rounds when my friend's gun suddenly exploded, practically in my ear. I momentarily lost my sense of balance, and my ears rang for hours. I could easily have been killed. That was the day we vowed to arm only the bow hunter.

Puddle ducks that use rivers all season long—and even unsophisticated diving ducks in the late season—are usually smart, and getting close enough for flushes within range requires patience and stealth. With geese it is even more difficult to drift within killing distance. Although the birds may never have been shot at, they have used their wits to survive the predators that haunt most waterways—everything from snapping turtles and big fish to coyotes, eagles and large owls. By early fall, waterfowl that have survived the dangers associated with growing up on a river, are plenty wary. The area where they live may actually contribute to their vigilance because field of vision is limited along a heavily wooded waterway. I don't think I've ever encountered a stupid small stream duck.

To stalk them successfully, hunters must lie low in their canoes and remain motionless, especially when approaching a bend. Negotiate these bends on the faster, deeper water of the outside turn, and stay alert even if you see nothing. Many times while entering a straight, open stretch of stream that seemed empty of life, I've stretched my muscles only to have ducks blow up from behind a debris pile or storm-toppled tree.

Camouflage clothing that blends in well with the river environment is important. Consider sanding shiny canoe paddles and then shellacking them with a non-gloss coating or painting them a dull, dead-grass color. On bright days the sun will glint off gun barrels and bright canoe paddles with all the flash of a welder's torch and give downstream ducks a distant early warning. Another tip: you can deaden noise in the boat by applying carpeting remnants to the floor. A friend of Al Davis's used to slit a section of old garden hose and snap it to the gunnels of his aluminum canoe to cut down on noise.

To my mind, aluminum craft are too noisy. The boat I use today is a 16-foot Old Town Discover canoe made of fiberglass. Camouflaging the canoe with branches or leaves to make it look like a big log knocked into the stream by a storm can help in those few places where hunting pressure has made water-fowl more wary than normal.

For some reason, some jumped ducks fly upstream right at the boat to offer easy passing shots. This phenomenon is especially true of migrating bluebills, goldeneyes, bufflehead and other divers, which sometimes flock to rivers to escape hunting pressure on the big water.

Not much equipment is needed to hunt waterfowl from canoes. Choose a personal flotation device in camo pattern as part of your overall clothing. I like to wear chest waders and keep a rain parka or

Gore-tex coat for sudden downpours. The waders are useful for getting in the stream in tight places, too. I carry a dry change of clothes in a plastic bag. In recent years my cellular phone in a small, waterproof bag goes everywhere with me for the assurance it provides in event of an emergency.

Consider packing a few decoys and setting up in early morning or late afternoon on a point, island or calm stretch. Puddlers often take to the air at such times and can be suckered into range with the right combination of calling and decoying. Michigan's Cass River between Caro and St. Charles flows through state game areas, some of which have large numbers of Canada geese. Setting up a half-dozen silhouette decoys along a certain sandbar that geese fly over enroute to feeding zones has worked two of the three times we tried the tactic. The only time it failed was when the geese changed their flight plan for reasons we never figured out.

"I swear I heard a duck stretch his wings," whispered Al Davis, as he hunched lower in the bow. Dense fog wafted from the mud-colored water as our canoe sliced quietly downstream while I corrected course with a paddle turn here and there from my seat in the stern.

Three feet above the stream, the bright, early October sunshine fought to penetrate a dense fog that blanketed the stream like wet wool. That morning we were floating Shiawassee River for puddlers and hoping the fog would allow us to creep close to resting ducks. Suddenly I heard the sound of a duck running on water, trying to get airborne. The wet smacks of webbed feet gave way to frantic quacking, and then a drake mallard, emerald head as polished as a billiard ball, punched up for the open sky. Al dropped him, cleanly, with a single shot from his 12-gauge pump.

A River Never Sleeps wrote Roderick-Haig-Brown, but I often do, especially when I'm carried along by water that passes this way once. The way I look at it, nothing out there is more graceful than a river, and fluidity is everything. But on this dreamlike morning sleep was impossible. After all, it was my turn in the bow.

Hunting from an Unusual Blind

NELSON BRYANT

Although the excuses offered by waterfowlers who fail to shoot their limit of birds are as plentiful as pinfeathers on a young duck, I have one that is, I believe, without precedent.

Whit Manter of this town and I bagged only four Canada geese instead of the ten allowed us because our blind was an outhouse.

Those who have never hunted out of an outhouse cannot appreciate what a handicap such a hiding place presents, but before I expand on this I should explain why we were using it.

The structure is smack-dab in the middle of a farmer's field adjoining a salt pond. There is a conventional blind on the pond's shore, but we were not in it because the geese have of late been settling down in the middle of the field no matter how many decoys were spread about the shorefront location. That the pond has been frozen solid for the past couple of weeks probably has something to do with this.

The alert reader might also wonder why an outhouse is situated on a windswept plain. It was put there, held upright against northeast gales by two iron fence posts driven into the earth, to accommodate those who attend the annual picnic of the town's volunteer fire department.

Arriving there forty-five minutes before daylight, Whit and I set out two dozen oversized shell decoys. Bogus birds of this genre weigh very little and their heads and necks are detachable, making it possible to stack as many as a dozen bodies together for transportation and storage.

We missed our first chance of the day when a lone goose came in low over the pond, remaining silent and unseen until it was too late, just as we finished arranging our rig. Our guns were leaning against the outhouse six feet away, so all we could do was stand motionless while the bird set its wings and landed about 35 yards away. The instant I made a move toward my gun, it departed.

We regarded that as a good omen, even though the day was far from ideal for goose hunting, with bright sunshine and only a whisper of wind from the west.

Half an hour later, we got a taste of what lay ahead when a flock of fourteen geese appeared in the distance. We entered the outhouse from whose interior Whit began calling them. I have neglected to mention that although the structure was a good-sized two-holer, it was divided in half by a wooden partition, making it impossible for us to see each other unless we stuck our heads out of our respective open doorways. The geese were coming from the blind, or back side, of the building, so all we could do was to listen for their approach.

Their clamoring grew louder and a moment later we saw their shadows as they passed directly overhead, well within range. From the twilight of our cubicles, we watched them circle until they were once again out of sight behind us. A muffled consultation through the partition wall resulted in an agreement to go for them if they came that close the second time around.

When their shadows appeared once more, we jumped out of our hiding places and shot one bird each, and at the sound of our guns, five that had already landed out of sight on the other side of the outhouse took wing and were out of range before we could fire.

Before we could pick up the downed birds, we saw another flock of about twenty birds approaching and darted back into our lairs.

Thinking of what had happened only two minutes before, I tapped on the partition to get Whit's attention and told him that this time around I would await his signal to leap forth.

Being more than three decades younger than I, his hearing is acute, and I thought that he might be able to better estimate the moment of truth.

Once again, the honking of the geese drew near. Whit cried, "Now!" He stepped outside and fired twice, dropping one. I lurched forth too late to do anything, my gunning coat having caught on the edge of the door.

The lack of wind was also adding to our problems. Had there been a stiff breeze, the geese that did respond to our decoys and our calling would not have been so indecisive.

Whit remarked that if we had a brace and bit, we could drill peep holes in the back of the outhouse. We could also have shot peep holes in it, but declined that gambit because the structure wasn't ours. We decided that our best bet was to remain inside until the birds landed. Even though we wouldn't know their exact location, that would we reasoned, give us an extra second or so to spot, flush and shoot them.

Three or four times after that decision, small flocks of geese, always gabbling incessantly, came in to look at our rig, then became indecisive and left. On each occasion, had there not been a roof over us, we would have been able to fill our limits. The five-bird daily limit applies during Massachusetts's experimental coastal region season for Canada geese, which began January 21 and ended at sunset February 5. Canada geese have proliferated in the Northeast during the past decade and in some areas have become a nuisance, raising havoc with crops and golf courses.

Sticking to our game plan, Whit and I lurked within the outhouse as long as birds were visible. Between eight-thirty and nine the flights stopped and we were about to call it quits when a huge flock of about three hundred geese appeared more than a mile away in the west. The flock began to break up into smaller groups, and one of about thirty headed our way. They came to us, talking with great animation, then flew away. As I peered out the doorway, I had the feeling that the departing flock was a little smaller than it should have been.

"I think," I whispered to Whit, whose head emerged from his half of the building, "that a few of them are on the ground behind us."

I eased my head around the corner of the building and four geese were on the ground about 40 yards away. I eased back, reported my finding to my companion, who said, "Go ahead. I'll come around behind you."

The birds were nervous and jumped the instant I stepped around the corner. I shot one and could have shot another if I had remembered to pump a fresh shell into the chamber of my new gun, a slide-action repeater with which I am unfamiliar. Whit had no chance to fire.

As we were picking up the decoys, five Canada geese accompanied by one snow goose came in, and even though we were standing in the open, our guns 30 yards away against the building, they circled us several times, often within range.

The outhouse caper seemed a poor way to end the season, so the next day I went forth with my brother Dan to a field where we quickly put up a blind of camouflage netting against a wire fence, set out twenty decoys, and in two hours had our ten birds.

Guided to the Waterfowl

NELSON BRYANT

When the first duck, a green-winged teal, streaked by shortly after dawn, I was not ready for it, being engaged in lighting my pipe.

"Shoot," our guide, Bob Hester, had said, and the others with us, Jerome Robinson, of Canaan, New Hampshire, and Joel Arrington, of Raleigh, North Carolina, could not respond because the bird was off my end of the blind.

"I'm sorry, Bob," I said. "It takes me a while to get used to a new situation and my pipe is an essential ingredient in that adjustment."

He regarded me with a vaguely troubled air. Waterfowl guides encounter an incredible variety of personalities in their clients, ranging from the fellow who shoots at every duck that goes by, even if it is out of range or more properly the target of one of his companions, to the man who seems unable to pull the trigger.

Mr. Hester was also worried, I think, about my armament, a 20-gauge over-and-under chambered for 3-inch shells and bored, improved and modified. For the uninitiated, a shotgun of this genre is quite properly considered a quail or grouse gun, being a little small and choked too loose for some water-fowling.

There was a time when I went after duck and geese with a full-choke 12-gauge or even the larger 10-gauge, but in recent years I have given all my modern shotguns, save the 20-gauge, to my sons. The 20 is perfectly adequate for decoying ducks and geese; a person only has to remember to pass up any shot over 40 yards. When flight shooting, it is a handicap because at least half the birds are passing at more than 40 yards.

My only exception to using the 20-gauge occurs when I go snipe or rabbit hunting with a little 28-gauge side-by-side muzzle-loading double, or waterfowl hunting with a 12-gauge muzzle-loading double.

This penchant for muzzle-loading shotguns (and rifles) is, I rather imagine, a way of easing into that time of life that moves many men to savor the pre-kill ritual of the hunt as well as the final act. Nearly all of us go through a period when shooting a limit of birds is a near obsession, but almost inevitably there comes a time when a brace of ducks for a well-planned dinner is utterly satisfying.

A short while after the teal escaped unscathed, I put Mr. Hester's doubts to rest, making a nice shot on another teal, and throughout the morning we performed in creditable fashion, taking seventeen birds, including teal, pintails, a mallard and one shoveler.

We were hunting out of Mr. Hester's Mattamuskeet Inn, which is located just east of Route 94 on the north shore of Lake Mattamuskeet, and our blind was in one of four flooded impoundments created by Mr. Hester, who is also a farmer.

Mr. Hester started building these impoundments, which range from 18 to 235 acres in size, about six years ago. The impoundments are planted with food many waterfowl crave, including sorghum and millet.

The low-lying area around Lake Mattamuskeet—most of the lake and its shoreline is within a national wildlife refuge—lends itself to the impoundment concept. Building impoundment areas and flooding and planting them is an expensive endeavor, but if they are properly hunted—not pounded every day—excellent water-fowling can result.

Mr. Hester runs a first-rate enterprise. He has fifty-eight blinds in all—eleven on the impoundments, five in areas of the lake open to shooting, two floating blinds in nearby Pamlico Sound and the remainder field blinds. He and his guides are expert at decoy layouts and calling and remain affable and eager after weeks of rising at four a.m.

Both the impoundment blinds and the stake blinds in Lake Mattamuskeet that my friends and I visited are also ideal for photographing waterfowl and in all instances it was possible for a man to set up with a telephoto lens in a "hide" of his own a hundred yards, or less, away.

The stake blinds—one wears waders to reach them—in the lake are also excellent locations from which to observe and photograph (the birds are protected) whistling swans. Approximately one-fifth, amounting to perhaps twenty thousand, of this continent's population of these magnificent birds winter on Mattamuskeet after journeying thousands of miles from the Northwest Canadian Arctic.

Canada geese are also present, as are a wild variety of puddle ducks and even diving ducks, including scaup. The lake is about 18 miles long and six miles wide and most of it is less than waist deep. There are various theories about how Mattamuskeet was formed, one being that it was caused by a fire burning down through peat. There were various plans to drain and farm the lake early in this century, but they were abandoned and it became a refuge in 1934.

Mr. Hester, as his impoundment-building indicates, is interested in improving the hunting opportunities in the area. He is also interested in the birds themselves.

One evening during our stay there we accompanied him to nearby Engelhard where a dinner, raffle and auction was held to raise money in an attempt to bolster the small population of blue geese, about 1,500, that have historically wintered on Lake Mattamuskeet. The endeavor, currently being led by Mr. Hester and Ben Simmons, Jr., of Fairfield, involves raising breeding pairs of the birds on land around the lake already leased for that purpose.

Sea Geese & Desert Whales

ROBERT F. JONES

Toward sundown the geese began moving. We could see wedges of them sweeping down the desert shoreline, circling and settling in the shallow, reed-grown water of the shoals. Their soft voices came over the water to us on the sea breeze—a quiet, querulous *rouk, rouk, rouk*. They were Pacific black brant—*Branta bernicla nigricans*—some of the smallest geese in the world but incredibly fast, strong and dodgy targets on a gusting wind. Brant are about the size of black ducks and just as delicious, with dark heads and necks ringed by an inconspicuous white collar. They take a lot of killing. This evening we were racing across the lagoon to one of the unoccupied shoals in a small, aluminum-hulled panga, the outboard at full throttle, hoping to get in position among the reeds before the first flight arrived. My eyes were on the birds when it happened. . .

Suddenly the water to starboard erupted, as if someone had triggered a bottom mine, and a huge gray monstrosity scabbed in patches of orange and yellow surged into view not an arm's length away. It rose from the water to a height of perhaps ten feet and stared at me with one small, piggy eye. Then it opened its long, ugly maw and clapped its jaws. It had bad breath.

The monster was a California gray whale, aka devilfish, scrag whale, mussel-digger or desert whale, and the cow's sudden appearance scared me silly. But she was only "spyhopping," poking her huge barnacle-laden head out of the water to see who was making all that racket topside in this, her preferred calving area. We were in Bahía La Magdelena, on the west coast of Baja California, one of three Mexican lagoons where gray whales spend their winters bearing and rearing their young. The whale's unexpected appearance was only one of many surprises on that strange expedition.

Mag Bay, as it's more popularly known among gringo sportsmen, is about 30 miles long by 5 to 10 wide—a huge, nutrient-rich lagoon protected from the strong, steady onslaught of Pacific rollers by two long barrier islands, Magdalena and Santa Margarita, which consist almost entirely of white and dunes. Its deeply notched shoreline offers plenty of beaches, inlets, marshes and mangrove swamps, most of which serve as sanctuaries to wintering waterfowl. But Mag Bay's shallow, food-rich waters offer world-class light-tackle angling as well. I traveled there often in the mid-1970s. There are swank resorts on Mag Bay nowadays, but back then we usually roughed it on a tugboat anchored off Puerto L'pez Mateos, paying a few pesos a day for our lodging and running out at dawn in the skiff to shoot ducks and brant, then fishing the *esteros* all day for snook, corvina, halibut, leopard groupet and spotted bay bass. It was hot work on the water, and sometimes we cooled out at midday by diving for *langosta*—rock lobster. At dusk we would hit the brant again.

Mexico's Mag Bay is home to Pacific brant—as well as California gray whales.

Both the fishing and lobstering were good, but the brant and the gray whales were out of this world. Both critters show up in Mag Bay sometime in January and for the next three months claim it as their playground. It's a sight to behold. Adult gray whales, which can grow to 50 feet long and weigh up to 35 tons, are the mottled color of a well-worn truck tire (though albinos are not uncommon). The body is usually covered with white, yellow, or orange patches of barnacles and whale lice, particularly on top of the head, around the blowhole and on the forward part of the back. The gray's head is narrow and arched along the upper surface, giving it a conical shape. The mouth is rimmed on each side with 130 to 180 relatively small baleen plates, which serve as strainers in which the whale gathers its food (mainly tubeworms, mollusks and shrimp). Primarily a bottom feeder, it can dive to 395 feet, but the gray prefers much shallower water. While feeding it stirs up clouds of sediment from the seabed—gigantic discolorations that resemble bonefish "muds" and can cover many acres. A feeding whale filters this mud through its baleen plates, on which shrimp, tubeworms and amphipods collect for later eating. These big muds attract gamefish, eager to pick off anything edible that's escaped the whale's jaws, and we quickly learned to fish the edges of them—often with great success.

Three distinct populations of gray whales once existed. A North Atlantic subspecies was hunted to extinction around 1700; a Korean population in the Northwest Pacific was fair game until 1968 and is now rare; the third group, the California gray of the Northeast Pacific, is doing well for now.

Before whalers discovered their breeding grounds, there were somewhere between 15,000 and 24,000 gray whales in the Pacific, and though whaling was legal, the killing of them was not widespread. Then in 1857 Captain Charles Scammon discovered the Baja lagoons where California grays went to calve. The shallow water of the lagoons made the grays easy prey for whalers. This was classic Moby Dick whaling, with lookouts shouting "Thar she blows!" and long chases in oar-powered whaleboats before the harpoons were hurled.

But the shallow waters of the hunting ground led to casualties among the whalers. A harpooned gray whale, unable to sound as it would in mid-ocean, might turn on the boat that was plaguing it, smash it to bits, then flail the floundering boat crew to death with its broad, heavy flukes. One whale even chased a harpooner clear up onto the beach, scooting along after the terrified tar on its long, powerful pectoral fins.

Still, it was an uneven match, and by 1898 the gray whale population had shrunk to only 2,000. When factory ships and cannon-propelled harpoons with explosive heads came into use in the 1920s, the game was nearly over. By the early 1940s gray whales were close to extinction. Then in 1946 the International Whaling Commission was formed and passed laws prohibiting the killing of gray whales. Nature recovers fast with half a break. By 1983 there were 16,000 whales in the Pacific, and nine years later the population was more than 20,000. The whale population is still growing today.

The warm, shallow "nursery" lagoons of Baja California are perfect for gray whales to have their calves, which measure about 15 feet long at birth and weigh some 1,500 pounds. Another female gray, called an "auntie," usually serves as a kind of cetacean midwife during this gargantuan labor process. The newborns immediately start suckling. A mother whale's milk is 53-percent fat—10 times richer than a dairy cow's milk—and the calf will need every bit of this fat to build up blubber for the long trip north. These whales are well traveled, covering 12,000 miles in an annual round trip from their Arctic feeding grounds in the Beaufort, Bering and Chukchi seas to the Baja breeding grounds. By the time the whales leave the lagoons in March for their return voyage, the calves are nearly 20 feet long and have doubled their weight.

Grays are the most active of all large whales, spyhopping, lobtailing and breaching all over the Bay. They displace a lot of water. We were frequently drenched when they rose without warning beside the boat and splatted the water with their massive tail flukes.

Just as surprising were the brant, which initially pitched to our crudely painted Clorox-bottle decoys with kamikaze-like abandon. After the first couple of days, however, it was almost impossible to toll them within gun range. Quick studies, indeed.

Yet according to the waterfowling literature I'd read, brant, along with buffleheads, are the easiest waterfowl to hunt—reasonably predictable in their daily habits and simple to decoy. "Both birds like to get shot," one authority writes, "and if you miss will often return to give you another chance, although both do seem to get tired of getting killed late in the season." *Maybe that's it*, I thought. *These birds have run a gauntlet of gunners from their summer breeding grounds in the high Arctic clear down to the Baja, and of course they've wised up en route.* But then I read that most Pacific brant fly nonstop from southeastern Alaska or British Columbia to the west coast of Mexico—a distance of at least 3,000 miles—at an altitude of 750 feet over the open sea. Not many hunters could be banging away at them on such a flight path.

Black brant, a bird of circumpolar distribution, are probably the fastest geese in the world. Back in 1965 an ornithologist named Arthur Skogman Einarsen clocked the birds at speeds of 62 mph—more than half again as fast as Canada geese, which top out at 36 to 40 mph. Small and agile, brant have a much faster wingbeat—three or four per second—than their larger Canadian kin. They're true sea geese, spending nearly all their lives on or over salt water and breeding clear around the Arctic Circle. Their preferred food is eelgrass (*Zoster marina*), but in 1931 a mysterious fungus destroyed most of the eelgrass on both sides of the Atlantic. Within a few years the Atlantic brant (*Branta bernicla hrota*) suffered a near-total population collapse. Where once they wintered in the Chesapeake region by the tens of thousands and old-time market gunners used to sell them for 50 cents apiece, nowadays you're lucky to see a few hundred in a bunch. What's worse, from the gourmet's standpoint, is that the Atlantic brant that have survived have done so by feeding on sea lettuce (*Ulva lactuca*), a leafy alga rich in iodine and iron that imparts a rank flavor to the birds' flesh. But as we saw and tasted at Mag Bay, the Pacific brant, which still have plenty of eelgrass to feed on, are not only abundant but as succulent as ever.

My gunning and angling companion on this trip was a childhood buddy named Harry Lenartz, who'd grown up to become one of California's most successful ophthalmologists. My most vivid memory of the Mag Bay adventure was the finale of that day when the spyhopping gray whale nearly capsized us. We made it to the shoal just minutes before the brant arrived. Our Mexican boatman debarked the two of us in waist-deep water, then raced back out to sea so as not to spook the brant. We waded ashore with shotguns and shell boxes held high over our heads, like Marines invading Tarawa. Harry sloshed fast and low across the shoal and hunkered down in the reeds. I found a flat rock only slightly submerged and sat down on it—only to feel the sting of a sea urchin's spines in my butt. I stifled a heartfelt scream. I had to. The birds were coming.

No decoys this time and no goose calls. We trusted to faith. And it worked. The brant circled us only once then committed—cupping in against the wind, tilting crazily from wing to wing, black against the hard blue desert sky, and chuckling to one another—*rouk, rouk, rouk!*

I dropped two with my first shot, another with the second barrel. Harry's gun banged flat downwind of me and I caught the flash of falling birds out of the corner of my eye. I then looked over just in time to see him stand, swing and take the prettiest triple I've ever seen. Three birds with one shot—all killed stone dead—directly overhead. They splashed all around him.

"Hey, Bob!" Harry yelled, grinning against the wind. "It's raining *Branta bernicla!*"

And with that, a gray whale rolled in the channel between us and the mainland, flagging its flukes in the sunset.

We ate well that night.

Reprinted with permission of Louise H. Jones.

PART VII

Turkey Hunting

That Twenty-Five-Pound Gobbler

ARCHIBALD RUTLEDGE

I suppose that there are other things which make a hunter uneasy, but of one thing I am very sure: that is to locate and to begin to stalk a deer or a turkey, only to find that another hunter is doing precisely the same thing at the same time. The feeling I had was worse than uneasy. It is, in fact, as inaccurate as if a man should say, after listening to a comrade swearing roundly, "Bill is expressing himself uneasily."

To be frank, I was jealous; and all the more so because I knew that Dade Saunders was just as good a turkey-hunter as I am—and maybe a good deal better. At any rate, both of us got after the same whopping gobbler. We knew this turkey and we knew each other; and I am positive that the wise old bird knew both of us far better than we knew him.

But we hunters have ways of improving our acquaintance with creatures that are over-wild and shy. Both Dade and I saw him, I suppose, a dozen times, and twice Dade shot at him. I had never fired at him, for I did not want to cripple, but to kill; and he never came within a hundred yards of me. Yet I felt that the gobbler ought to be mine; and for the simple reason that Dade Saunders was a shameless poacher and a hunter-out-of-season.

I have in mind the day when I came upon him in the pine-lands in mid-July, when he had in his wagon *five* bucks in the velvet, all killed that morning. Now, this isn't a fiction story; this is fact. And after I have told you of those bucks, I think you'll want me to beat Dade to the great American bird.

This wild turkey had the oddest range that you could imagine. You hear of turkeys ranging "original forests," "timbered wilds," and the like. Make up your mind that if wild turkeys have a chance they are going to come near civilization. The closer they are to man, the farther they are away from their other enemies. Near civilization they at least have (but for the likes of Dade Saunders) the protection of the law. But in the wilds what protection do they have from wildcats, from eagles, from weasels (I am thinking of young turkeys as well as old), and from all their other predatory persecutors?

Well, as I say, time and again I have known wild turkeys to come, and to seem to enjoy coming, close to houses. I have stood on the porch of my plantation home and have watched a wild flock feeding under the great live-oaks there. I have repeatedly flushed wild turkeys in an autumn cornfield. I have shot them in rice stubble.

Of course they do not come for sentiment. They are after grain. And if there is any better wild game than a rice-field wild turkey, stuffed with peanuts, circled with browned sweet potatoes, and fragrant with a rich gravy that plantation cooks know how to make, I'll follow you to it.

The gobbler I was after was a haunter of the edges of civilization. He didn't seem to like the wild woods. I think he got hungry there. But on the margins of fields that had been planted he could get all he wanted to eat of the things he most enjoyed. He particularly liked the edges of cultivated fields that bordered either on the pinewoods or else on the marshy rice-lands.

One day I spent three hours in the gaunt chimney of a burned rice-mill, watching this gobbler feeding on such edges. Although I was sure that sooner or later he would pass the mouth of the chimney, giving me a chance for a shot, he kept just that distance between us that makes a gun a vain thing in a man's hands. But though he did not give me my chance, he let me watch him all I pleased. This I did through certain dusty crevices between the bricks of the old chimney.

If I had been taking a post-graduate course in caution, this wise old bird would have been my teacher. Whatever he happened to be doing, his eyes and his ears were wide with vigilance. I saw him first standing beside a fallen pine log on the brow of a little hill where peanuts had been planted. I made the shelter of the chimney before he recognized me. But he must have seen the move I made.

I have hunted turkeys long enough to be thoroughly rid of the idea that a human being can make a motion that a wild turkey cannot see. One of my woodsman friends said to me, "Why, a gobbler can see anything. He can see a jaybird turn a somersault on the verge of the horizon." He was right.

Watching from my cover I saw this gobbler scratching for peanuts. He was very deliberate about this. Often he would draw back one huge handful (or footful) of viney soil, only to leave it there while he looked and listened. I have seen a turkey do the same thing while scratching in leaves. Now, a buck while feeding will alternately keep his head up and down; but a turkey gobbler keeps his down very little. That bright black eye of his, set in that sharp bluish head, is keeping its vision on every object on the landscape.

My gobbler (I called him mine from the first time I saw him) found many peanuts, and he relished them. From that feast he walked over into a patch of autumn-dried crabgrass. The long pendulous heads of this grass, full of seeds, he stripped skillfully. When satisfied with this food, he dusted himself beside an old stump. It was interesting to watch this; and while he was doing it I wondered if it was not my chance to leave the chimney, make a detour, and come up behind the stump. But of course just as I decided to do this, he got up, shook a small cloud of dust from his feathers, stepped off into the open, and there began to preen himself.

A short while thereafter he went down to a marshy edge, there finding a warm sandy hole on the sunny side of a briar patch, where he continued his dusting and loafing. I believe that he knew the stump, which shut off his view of what was behind it, was no place to choose for a midday rest.

All this time I waited patiently; interested, to be sure, but I would have been vastly more so if the lordly old fellow had turned my way. This I expected him to do when he got tired of loafing. Instead, he deliberately walked into the tall ranks of the marsh, which extended riverward for half a mile. At that I hurried forward, hoping to flush him on the margin; but he had vanished for that day. But though he had escaped me, the sight of him had made me keen to follow him until he expressed a willingness to accompany me home.

Just as I was turning away from the marsh I heard a turkey call from the shelter of a big live-oak beside the old chimney. I knew that it was Dade Saunders, and that he was after my gobbler. I walked over to where he was making his box-call plead. He expressed no surprise on seeing me. We greeted each other as two hunters, who are not over-friendly, greet when they find themselves after the same game.

"I seen his tracks," said Dade. "I believe he limps in the one foot since I shot him last Sunday will be a week."

"He must be a big bird," I said; "you were lucky to have a shot."

Dade's eyes grew hungrily bright.

"He's the biggest in these woods, and I'll git him yet. You jest watch me."

"I suppose you will, Dade. You are the best turkey-hunter of these parts."

I hoped to make him overconfident; and praise is a great corrupter of mankind. It is not unlikely to make a hunter miss a shot. I remember that a friend of mine once said laughingly: "If a man tells me I am a good shot, I will miss my next chance, as sure as guns; but if he cusses me and tells me I'm not worth a darn, then watch me shoot!"

Dade and I parted for the time. I went off toward the marsh, whistling an old song. I wanted to have the gobbler put a little more distance between himself and the poacher. Besides, I felt that it was right of me to do this: for while I was on my own land, my visitor was trespassing. I hung around in the scrub—oak thickets for awhile; but no gun spoke out, I knew that the old gobbler's intelligence plus my whistling game had "foiled the relentless" Dade. It was a week later that the three of us met again.

Not far from the peanut field there is a plantation corner. Now, most plantation corners are grave-yards; that is, cemeteries of the old days, where slaves were buried. Occasionally now Negroes are buried there, but pathways have to be cut through the jungle-like growths to enable the cortege to enter.

Such a place is a wilderness for sure. Here grow towering pines, mournful and moss-draped. Here are hollies, canopied with jasmine-vines; here are thickets of myrtle, sweet gum, and young pines. If a covey of quail goes into such a place, you might as well whistle your dog off and go after another lot of birds.

Here deer love to come in the summer, where they can hide from the heat and the gauze-winged flies. Here in the winter is a haunt for woodcock, a good range (for great live-oaks drop their sweet acorns) for wild turkeys, and a harbor for foxes. In those great pines and oaks turkeys love to roost. It was on the borders of just such a corner that I roosted the splendid gobbler.

It was a glowing December sunset. I had left the house an hour before to stroll the plantation roads, counting (as I always do) the number of deer and turkey tracks that had recently been made in the soft damp sand. Coming near the dense corner, I sat against the bole of a monster pine. I love to be a mere watcher in woodlands as well as a hunter.

About two hundred yards away there was a little sunny hill, grown to scrub-oaks. They stood sparsely; that enabled me to see well what I now saw. Into my vision, with the rays of the sinking sun gleaming softly on the bronze of his neck and shoulders, the great gobbler stepped with superb beauty. Though he deigned to scratch once or twice in the leaves, and peck indifferently at what he thus uncovered, I knew he was bent on roosting; for not only was it nearly his bedtime, but he seemed to be examining with critical judgment every tall tree in his neighborhood.

He remained in my sight ten minutes; then he stepped into a patch of gallberries. I sat where I was. I tried my best to be as silent and as motionless as the bodies lying in the ancient graves behind me. The big fellow kept me on the anxious bench for five minutes. Then he shot his great bulk into the air, beating his ponderous way into the huge pine that seemed to sentry that whole wild tract of woodland.

I marked him when he came to his limb. He sailed up to it and alighted with much scraping of bark with his No. 10 shoes. There was my gobbler poised against the warm red sky of that winter twilight. It was hard to take my sight from him; but I did so in order to get my bearings in relation to his position. His flight had brought him nearer to me than he had been on the ground. But he was still far out of gun-range.

There was no use for me to look into the graveyard, for a man cannot see a foot into such a place. I glanced down the dim pinewood road. A moving object along its edge attracted my attention. It skulked. It seemed to flit like a ghostly thing from pine to pine. But, though I was near a cemetery, I knew I was looking at no "haunt." It was Dade Saunders.

He had roosted the gobbler, and he was trying to get up to him. Moreover, he was at least fifty yards closer to him than I was. I felt like shouting to him to get off my land; but then a better thought came. I pulled out my turkey call.

The first note was good, as was intended. But after that there came some heart-stilling squeaks and shrills. In the dusk I noted two things; I saw Dade make a furious gesture, and at almost the same instant the old gobbler launched out from the pine, winging a lordly way far across the graveyard thicket. I walked down slowly and peeringly to meet Dade.

"Your call's broke," he announced.

"What makes you think so?" I asked.

"Sounds awful funny to me," he said; "more than likely it might scare a turkey. Seen him lately?" he asked.

"You are better at seeing that old bird than I am, Dade."

Thus I put him off; and shortly thereafter we parted. He was sure that I had not seen the gobbler; and that suited me all right.

Then came the day of days. I was up at dawn, and when certain red lights between the stems of the pines announced daybreak, I was at the far southern end of the plantation, on a road on either side of which were good turkey woods. I just had a notion that my gobbler might be found there, as he had of late taken to roosting in a tupelo swamp near the river, and adjacent to these woodlands.

Where some lumbermen had cut away the big timber, sawing the huge short-leaf pines close to the ground, I took my stand (or my seat) on one of these big stumps. Before me was a tangle of undergrowth; but it was not very thick or high. It gave me the screen I wanted; but if my turkey came out through it, I could see to shoot.

It was just before sunrise that I began to call. It was a little early in the year (then the end of February) to lure a solitary gobbler by a call; but otherwise the chance looked good. And I am vain enough to say that my willow box was not broken that morning. Yet it was not I but two Cooper's hawks that got the old wily rascal excited.

They were circling high and crying shrilly over a certain stretch of deep woodland; and the gobbler, undoubtedly irritated by the sounds, or at least not to be outdone by two mere marauders on a domain which he felt to be his own, would gobble fiercely every time one of the hawks would cry. The hawks had their eye on a building site; wherefore their excited maneuvering and shrilling continued; and as long as they kept up their screaming, so long did the wild gobbler answer in rivalry or provoked superiority, until his wattles must have been fiery red and near to bursting.

I had an idea that the hawks were directing some of their crying at the turkey, in which case the performance was a genuine scolding match of the wilderness. And before it was over, several gray squirrels had added to the already raucous debate their impatient coughing barks. This business lasted nearly an hour, until the sun had begun to make the thickets "smoke off" their shining burden of morning dew.

I had let up on my calling for awhile; but when the hawks had at last been silenced by the distance, I began once more to plead. Had I had a gobbler-call, the now enraged turkey would have come to me as straight as a surveyor runs a line. But I did my best with the one I had. I had answered by one short gobble, then by silence.

I laid down my call on the stump and took up my gun. It was in such a position that I could shoot quickly without much further motion. It is a genuine feat to shoot a turkey on the ground *after* he has made you out. I felt that a great moment was coming.

But you know how hunter's luck sometimes turns. Just as I thought it was about time for him to be in the pine thicket ahead of me, when, indeed, I thought I had heard his heavy but cautious step, from across the road, where lay the companion tract of turkey-woods to the one I was in, came a delicately pleading call from a hen turkey. The thing was irresistible to the gobbler; but I knew it to be Dade Saunders. What should I do?

At such a time a man has to use all the headwork he has. And in hunting I had long since learned that that often means not to do a darn thing but to sit tight. All I did was to put my gun to my face.

If the gobbler was going to Dade, he might pass me. I had started him coming; if Dade kept him going, he might run within hailing distance. Dade was farther back in the woods than I was. I waited.

No step was heard. No twig was snapped. But suddenly, fifty yards ahead of me, the great bird emerged from the thicket of pines. For an instant the sun gleamed on his royal plumage. My gun was on him, but the glint of the sun along the barrel dazzled me. I stayed my finger on the trigger. At that instant he made me out. What he did was smart. He made himself so small that I believed it to be a second turkey. Then he ran crouching through the vines and huckleberry bushes.

Four times I thought I had my gun on him, but his dodging was that of an expert. He was getting away; moreover, he was making straight for Dade. There was a small gap in the bushes sixty yards from me, off to my left. He had not yet crossed that. I threw my gun in the opening. In a moment he flashed into it, running like a racehorse. I let him have it. And I saw him go down.

Five minutes later, when I had hung him on a scrub-oak, and was admiring the entire beauty of him, a knowing, cat-like step sounded behind me.

"Well, sir," said Dade, a generous admiration for the beauty of the great bird overcoming other less kindly emotions, "so you beat me to him."

There was nothing for me to do but to agree. I then asked Dade to walk home with me so that we might weigh him. He carried the scales well down at the 25-pound mark. An extraordinary feature of his manly equipment was the presence of three separate beards, one beneath the other, no two connected. And his spurs were respectable rapiers.

"Dade," I said, "what am I gong to do with this gobbler? I am alone here on the plantation."

The pineland poacher did not solve my problem for me.

"I tell you," said I, trying to forget the matter of the five velveted bucks, "some of the boys from down the river are going to come up on Sunday to see how he tastes. Will you join us?"

You know Dade Saunders' answer; for when a hunter refuses an invitation to help eat a wild turkey, he can be sold to a circus.

Ben Franklin Talked Turkey, to No Avail

NELSON BRYANT

Those who sally forth May 1, shotgun in hand, for the opening of New York State's turkey season would not be doing so if Benjamin Franklin had gotten his way.

Mr. Franklin had sought to have the wild turkey declared this country's national bird, a classification that would have undoubtedly afforded it total protection.

A sagacious man, Mr. Franklin was not off base in his desire to have the turkey so honored, for it is a bird of the American wilderness, one that ranged over most of this country and whose populations—there are four major species native to this country—in pre-Columbian days have been estimated at more than ten million. Pursued insatiably both for home consumption and for sale, it was virtually extirpated from this country by the latter part of the last century. Destruction of mature hardwood forests—its preferred habitat—was also a factor in this. By 1850, there were no wild turkeys at all in New England and New York State and only a few scattered flocks in Pennsylvania.

A few decades ago, state fish and game departments began paying attention to the wild turkey. It has been restored to its former range and, in a few instances, to states outside its historical territory. The fundamental technique for this is live trapping with nets and transfer to a new area. New York began its turkey trapping and transfer program in 1959, using birds that had strayed into the southwestern part of the state from Pennsylvania.

It was not uncommon for a hunter to bag a couple of dozen birds in a day's hunt in the early part of the last century. In Arlie Schorger's *The Wild Turkey: Its History and Domestication,* there is an account of two men in Scotland County, Missouri, who killed 132 turkeys with their rifles in one day while husking corn. This could not happen today. The huge flocks—sometimes in the thousands—no longer exist, and the birds that now range our woodland are, for the most part, incredibly wary.

It is possible for a spring season turkey hunter with no previous experience to bag a gobbler, but this is a rare occurrence. To be assured of even a fair chance of success, one must learn how to locate the birds—in spring hunting, this means finding the places where gobblers roost—and how to call them in.

As in other states, New York's spring turkey hunt is aimed at the male birds, also called toms or gobblers. The most obvious difference between the sexes is the beard protruding from the chest of the male, although a few females are so adorned.

Hunters may take only bearded birds in spring. Shooting hours are from thirty minutes before sunrise to noon. This timing affords protection to the hens, most of which are on their nests during that period.

Having the spring season coincide with the nesting and incubation period also aids the hunter. With most of the hens in his range impregnated, a gobbler—his procreative ardor still aflame—is hard-pressed to find a receptive female.

The typical hunter—wearing full camouflage—is in the woods long before dawn. Ensconcing himself in a likely spot—sometimes nothing more than a hollow on a mountainside—he begins to make the sounds of a lovelorn hen. There are a variety of commercially available calls one may use for this, and one of the most effective and easiest to master is the swinging-lid box call. Some accomplished hunters switch to a diaphragm—or mouth—call for the closing moments of the game because it leaves their hands free to handle their guns.

There are occasions when less than half an hour passes between the time a gobbler first responds to the hunter's blandishments and when he comes within shotgun range, but that is uncommon. More often than not, hours pass while the tom closes in, circling, pausing and even retreating. Turkeys have incredibly good eyesight and first-rate hearing, and it may be that a wary gobbler has seen something that troubles him or that the hunter has sounded a sour note.

During this approach period, the hunter must remain motionless except when he eases around to face the direction from which the bird is coming. In the final minutes, the gobbler can usually be heard strutting through the leaves.

A prolonged wait can be surprisingly difficult. On one turkey hunt more than a decade ago, my companion shot the gobbler, then lay writhing on the ground with a cramp in his leg shrieking for me to make sure the bird was dead.

The best way to learn how to go after spring turkeys is to go out with an experienced hunter, but one can teach oneself, or at least speed up the learning process, by reading books on the subject and by listening to records of turkey calling.

New York state also permits the use of decoys, either full-bodied or silhouette, and these often work very well.

Only shotguns may be used, and the shot size may be no larger than No. 2 and no smaller than No. 8. A more realistic shot size requirement would be from BB's through No. 6, but there are bizarre shot-size and caliber restrictions in the hunting regulations of almost every state.

Spring turkey hunting is allowed in all of New York state save Long Island. A map and description of the spring turkey hunting area is provided each hunter when he applies for his $2 turkey permit at license-issuing agencies or regional offices of the state's Department of Environmental Conservation. One must, of course, have a hunting license in order to obtain a permit.

The Central Character

TOM KELLY

We now have come to the central character of the work, the reason we are all here, the turkey himself. I will spend only a modest amount of time in discussions of food and habitat, the specifics of his life cycle, population dynamics, etc, etc. Every bit of this either has been done or is being done by competent biologists, and there are literally thousands of words in print about almost every aspect of a turkey's life and habits. Since this essay is designed to be a manual for the beginning hunter, I will spend very little time in statistics but will concentrate on the probable reaction of turkeys to various stimuli or, to put it more simply, why does he act like he does, and what can you do to get him to do what you want, rather than simply accepting what he does as gospel and trying to fit your actions around his.

A lot of turkey hunting follows just this line of endeavor and has been following it for some time. The hunter makes no real effort to adjust the movement of turkeys. He tries to find out what the turkey wants to do, goes to one of the places the turkey usually visits in doing this, and waits for the quarry to arrive. The only method he uses to get the turkey to react to a situation is to use bait.

Back in my vanished youth, before the advent of television, nearly every kid of my acquaintance went to the cowboy movies on Saturday afternoon. A kid got in for a dime, most of the Saturday afternoon shows were double features, and many of them had one of the episodes of a 15 chapter serial that was shown between the movies. Usually the serial was not a western, although when it was, you got a solid three hours of the old west. None of the westerns, known to us locals as cowboy shows, bothered their heads with any smidgen of deep sociological drama, or boy-girl relationships. The love interest was usually between the hero and his horse. There was always lots of gunfire, fist fights in saloons, stagecoach robberies, cattle stampedes, and Indian uprisings. Plots were pretty straightforward and familiar. In fact, Republic Pictures, a Hollywood studio that made a great many of these horse operas, had a particular outcropping of rock in one of its locations that was shown so often it became familiar, and every kid in the theater recognized it.

Posses galloped past these rocks. Indians attacked wagon trains in the flat just below them. The hero and his second lead often hid behind this same old set of rocks to fight off the assault of the bad guys while they waited for the arrival of the U.S. Cavalry.

In addition to a similarity of scenery there were a good many instances where situations seen in one epic repeated themselves in another, repeated themselves to the extent of using the same familiar names.

In story after story, after the bad guys had robbed the bank, or rustled the cattle, or burned down the ranch house leaving the rancher wounded in the shoulder and his daughter crying and wringing her hands, there would be a scene in front of the Sheriffs office, which was always a door or two down the street from the saloon.

The scene always featured the formation of the posse. The posse may have been officially led by the Sheriff but it always placed itself under the tactical command of the hero, and the final line in nearly every formation process, the last thing said before the posse galloped off in pursuit in of the outlaws, was,

"We'll cut 'em off at Eagle Pass."

Until very early in the 1950s, most of the turkeys killed in the States of Alabama and Mississippi, were killed the same way. The hunters cut the turkeys off at Eagle Pass and ambushed their ass after they got there.

The rocks were not like the Republic Pictures rocks as seen on consecutive Saturday afternoons, and the ambush weapons were not single-action Colt 45s, that shot three-inch, six-shot groups at 200 yards, like the Colts used in Republic Pictures did, but the tactical principles were identical.

Almost all deer hunts in those days were driven hunts, with a collection of eight to ten drivers, a couple of dozen hounds, and up to forty or fifty standers spaced along the boundary of the property being hunted. All the standers were armed with shotguns, rifles of any caliber were expressly forbidden, and the hunt master's instructions before the drive specifically instructed the standers to shoot buck deer, turkey gobblers, and wildcats. Most standers kept one barrel loaded with buckshot and one with 5s or 6s, and it is very likely that seventy-five percent of the legal turkeys killed in the two states between 1925 and 1955 were killed on deer drives.

A lot of turkeys were killed at baited trenches, because the chufa patch, the present day legal equivalent of baiting, had not yet been invented, so many blinds were built in pea fields, and near feed lots or catch pens. But what it all really amounted to was that part of the party lay in ambush at Eagle Pass while the other part drove the turkeys to it, or by a judicious use of bait, artificial Eagle Passes were created and the guns simply lay in ambush there and waited for the turkeys to arrive.

The principles of scattering fall turkeys and calling the drove back together, or the art of calling gobbling turkeys from the roost in the Spring were known, but they were considered prohibitedly difficult. There were not many turkeys to begin with, it was felt that every succeeding year there would be less, and the general consensus was one of, "I better get mine while the getting's good."

Even now, years after re-establishment has occurred, a lot of the same kind of thing still goes on.

There are still turkeys being killed from car windows. There are still blinds built at the edge of chufa patches, blinds being occupied from 1:00 P. M. until sundown by people who yelp once every thirty minutes. There are still boats running the river, trying to find turkeys on sand bars, and then beaching the boat on the bar, leaving the motor running, and the occupants going over the bar and through the willows, in line abreast with guns at high port. Turkeys are going to be ambushed and turkeys are going to be surrounded, and rushed. There will always be corners cut, and people willing to cut them.

The reason for most of this is that turkey hunting is such a solitary and private sport—a turkey killed on the fair and square is such a difficult trophy—that many people are willing to make unfortunate arrangements. And because of this signal lack of witnesses, when you are standing at the tailgate of the truck, or the boat landing, or on the steps of the clubhouse in front of the photographer, the bystanders are going to have to take your unsupported word as to what the dead turkey was doing when you shot him.

There is a set of thought processes that are all too prevalent, and a segment of society in existence, that simply have to make a four-star production out of a piece of luck. Every turkey some people bring in has to have been a classic. A duel between Holmes and Moriarty, or a combination of Horatius at the Bridge and the Charge of the Light Brigade.

Most of the time a person who specializes in these epics is going to get away with it, but there will be instances where they won't. Let me lay on you a true story, now forty-some years old, and all the participants but me have gone to that great roost tree in the sky. It is the story of a man's first turkey and I would not be telling it now except for the fact that it may help drive home a point, both the man and the turkey protagonists are dead and can remain nameless, and I am the only surviving witness.

It was in the first week of the spring gobbler season and I was hunting in the company of a man I had known for some years. The individual was a good hunter of other game but was very new to turkeys. He was, as well, one of those people who have trouble moving about and finding his way in the woods and no matter what questions you asked later, you could never find out from his answers exactly where he had been and what he had seen.

When you had agreed to meet back at the truck at such and such a time he was generally a little late, but he was forever coming from a strange direction and you could never get out of him where he had been and why he was approaching from north of the road when you both had agreed where he and you would hunt and he had chosen to go south of the road.

On this particular morning I had heard a turkey gobble north of the creek on my side, after we had separated. I had gone to the turkey and set up and at the first yelp he gobbled back, and then never made another sound. I gave him the obligatory twenty minutes and then added another ten minutes for lagniappe, and then I decided he had seen something else and flown down to it, although I had not heard him leave the limb. I got up, moved a hundred yards or so in the direction of where he had been when I first heard him gobble, picked a place and sat down, and decided to spend a little time there.

I cannot say that it happens all that often, but sometimes a turkey will fly down, go off in one direction, and then for some unknown reason turn around and come back. I really don't know what causes him to do it, there is even a strong possibility in my mind that it may not be the same turkey, but when you have no other prospects, it is worth spending another twenty or thirty minutes on speculation. After all, he went away, you seem to have lost, you can't lose no loster, and it is sort of like desperation passes to the back of the end zone in the last two seconds.

The second time I yelped, a turkey yelped back that sounded as if he were some two hundred yards east of where I sat. The yelping was coarse enough to have come from a young gobbler but I could not be positive, and many turkeys yelp so much alike that I cannot always tell hens from gobblers. He yelped back three or four times over the next thirty minutes, as best I could tell from exactly the same place, and I became convinced he was a young gobbler still in the tree, willing to answer but unwilling to walk over there and see what was going on, for fear that he might run into an old gobbler whose irritation threshold would be breached by his appearance.

Young gobblers in the spring have a tendency to do this. They are interested, interested enough to answer, sometimes several times. They are generally unwilling to walk over to where you are to explore who you are, and often, if they do come, they will fly over and stay up in a tree after they get there. I have seen one sit in a tree for more than an hour doing just that.

I think they are trying to cover both bases. They can satisfy their curiosity on one hand and stay out of harm's way on the other, in case there is an old gobbler accompanying the turkey hen doing the yelping. They consider it to be a risk-free form of reconnaissance.

In this particular case, I heard the turkey leave the tree. He flew towards me from the northeast and alighted in a tree about 200 yards to my right front. The second he stopped, almost before he could get his wings folded, there was a single shot and somebody rolled him off the limb. I suspected I knew who it was, but I took the time to go back to my original position to make sure I had left no piece of equipment there, and then worked my way back to the car.

My friend was there, with a twelve-pound yearling gobbler that hadn't been dead long enough to get stiff, and a recitation of moves, counter moves, position changes and tactics worthy of C. L. Jordan himself, on one of his better days. It was a saga that approached epic proportions, and if you had not known better, you would have been hanging on every word in breathless anticipation.

The trouble was that I knew better because I knew exactly what had happened, and had been prepared to tell him so as soon as I had finished with my congratulations. He never gave me a chance. He launched into his story before I could finish saying, "This is great, Chuck, I'm glad you got one."

I never did bring up the question of why he was north of the creek when we had agreed he would stay south of it. Robinson Creek at that point is about ankle deep and eight feet wide, but is clearly visible.

I never questioned the breathtaking accounts of gobble and double gobble, of strut and drum, of coming in and going back, none of which I heard, just as I had heard none of his calling which had caused the turkey to turn and come in at the final call. All of which constitutes highly unusual behavior patterns and uncharacteristic actions for a twelve-pound yearling gobbler with button spurs and a three-inch beard. A bird that had the distinctive four or five feathers that stick three inches beyond the rest of the tail feathers, like every other twelve-pound jake in Monroe county. A bird that had yelped three times in the last forty minutes, and a bird that I seen him shoot out of a tree fifteen minutes ago.

What I did feel was a distinct pang of envy at the level of creative skill required to be able to come up with an Odyssey equal to the one I was hearing, in the fifteen minutes of time he had available for its composition.

American literature is poorer because of his passing.

The point of this little trip down memory lane is to leave you with a word of warning—not advice, mind you—simply a note for self-preservation. As you begin the business of hunting alone, you will find that it is pretty much like I said earlier. Nobody but you will be there at the demise of the turkey, so your report of the encounter becomes the only verifying evidence.

I am aware that a beginning hunter comes under a degree of pressure, largely pressure that he brings on himself. You have spent all this beginning apprenticeship in the company of someone else, or, if you have undertaken to teach yourself the business with no help at all, you finally get to a point where you begin to feel that a degree of success is mandatory. Unless you want people to believe you are a complete klutz, then it becomes mandatory for you to have a success every once in a while. None of this is unusual, you have assessed the situation correctly, and in the beginning you take them any way you can get them. Everybody understands how these things go and almost nobody is going to confront you with questions and accusations.

There is no intention on my part to insist that every story you tell be restricted to matters of petrified truth with no embellishment. There is an old story that it is a poor piece of cloth that cannot be improved with a touch of embroidery.

But you ought to keep things within the realm of reason.

Take every lucky turkey that circumstances offer you. This means you are going to get some turkeys you did not earn, but, on the contrary, you are going to be shut out of a great many turkeys that you did earn, but that unfortunate circumstances conspired to deny you that final opportunity to pull the trigger. Some of these denials will be your fault, some of them will not.

Just remember to keep the thing believable, be it bad luck or good.

A first turkey, like the one in the story above, does not require that you make the call-up and terminal shot rival Pickett's charge at Gettysburg in pure melodrama. It would have been far more appropriate for the man in this instance to simply say, "The damn thing just flew up and lit in a tree and when he did I rolled him out. I had been calling for thirty minutes but I honestly don't know whether he came to my calling or not."

I knew he had not been calling for thirty minutes, but I would have been willing to give him the benefit of the doubt. Maybe he had been calling softly and I had missed it.

It doesn't matter. The turkey lies in the back of the truck and the score is now Turkeys 234, Hunters 1. Every old turkey hunter in the world will understand. All the decent human beings among them will approve.

The first turkey you shoot alone—what the hell, the first two dozen turkeys—can come any way they want to. After that point you are supposed to be largely grown up. At that point, it is expected that you should stop cutting corners, turn in your acolyte's badge, apply for journeyman papers, and become a decent, law-abiding member of the lodge.

I never told the story you just read before now, because I had to wait for one of the principal characters to pass on so that he would not be embarrassed. The fact that I heard the turkey as well as my friend, and saw him light in the tree before the shot, simply solidified it. All those comments about the turkey gobbling and double gobbling and going away, and coming back, would ring falsely to an old hunter.

Jakes gobble very seldom. Those that do are just learning how, are uneasy in doing it, know that an old gobbler who hears them is apt to come over there and teach them the error of their ways, and the whole set of particulars in this first kill, as reported, was out of context.

This man cheated himself, because he told a lie about his first turkey, and that first one, the first one that you do for yourself, not one that someone has presented to you, is an event to be cherished and needs no embellishment.

Understand now, I am not against lies per se. All turkey hunters lie. As one, you are just as entitled to stretch things as any other member of the lodge. If you choose, you can make yourself more of a hero in the affair than you really were, but you have to remember the hallmarks of an artistic lie.

An artistic lie is well-documented, believable, possible, and the liar should not be the hero in the affair. He can share that glory if he chooses, but he cannot be the sole owner.

Before you disregard this piece of advice as out-of-hand drivel you should remember one thing. In this particular matter you should be aware that you are listening to an expert in the field.

Excerpted with permission from the author's newest book, *A Fork In the Road*. To order a copy, go to www.tomkellyinc.net.

The Turkey Cure

SYDNEY LEA

By now, nearly every time I walked down to let my pointers out, I flushed the broad-wing hen who nests in the same white pine each spring. She's always been a sort of genie of renewal, and the life force in me surges to regard her tail in flight, the severity of its black and white bands somehow metaphorizing the distinction between seasons. Dark winter, bright spring.

This year, thanks to last autumn's bountiful mast, the chipmunk and red squirrel populations seem to have grown threefold, a great thing for a hawk, of course, and for all the other predators—fox, coyote, fisher, and so on—whose energy has thrilled me from boyhood. And yet this time around, such tokens of regeneration, and others—loosing of freshets, budding out of broadleafs, sweet ruckus of peepers, patrol of kingfishers—none of these quickened me as before. My tendency to foist poetic readings onto nature, however irresistible, struck me as more than ever inaccurate in its willfulness.

Perhaps the suicide, a year back, kept me down like this, as it had all through the winter. The beautiful boy, my oldest son's bosom friend, had fallen into a contemporary trap, the one called crack, and ended in a California closet, a cheap belt for a noose. But if that horror proved a central motive for my long depression, I might have chosen from a myriad: the obscene death by cancer, say, of my father-in-law, too weak at the last even to cough for himself. A brilliant, handsome, volatile man, he'd stuck to being a journalism professor, loathing the job for the final decade, waiting out retirement age, at which he was diagnosed all but instantly. No time for his many writing intentions, none for the book-length thing on that Canadian copper mine, the history, sociology, mythology of its region, which he'd never visit after all.

Or I could batten on my mother's life-threatening aortal operation, from which she recovered, but which forecast the closing of a crucial cycle: she who'd borne would leave me. Years before the surgery, I'd had an odd vision, whether in sleep or awake I still can't say. Standing on the cobbly stoop of my Maine hunting camp, I looked upward and beheld the heavens' vault sealing itself like a womb after birth, so that it couldn't recur, the dream of reentry that all through life any child will crave when otherwise comfortless.

Closed out. The world blank as a sheet of paper, as the sheet unmarked by my wife's father. In which blank realm my role would be to evaluate students' poems and fictions, not to write any more of these myself, not to write anything at all. Rather, I'd continue to fetch and carry my kids, but would be no proper father, down in the mouth all day and night; no proper husband, either, to the woman too good for me by half, who deserved worship, probably, but at the least some friendship. My agenda? Do dishes. Cook so-so meals by the hundred. Watch the years mount: the yellow leaves of spring apparently stained overnight to those other yellows of autumn; the hare gone white from brown in a blink; warbler ceding to snowbird. Watch my body slump. Fifty would be sixty would be seventy. Tomorrow.

Attending all this, a changed prospect on the hunt. I'd long considered myself, particularly, one of the better grouse men I knew, but by virtue of a chainsaw accident that radically cut my leg and my woods time in the preceding fall and by virtue of a rock-bottom bird population in the past few years, the tasty little monuments to success lay more and more seldom in the freezer. It was also hard to make a young dog under these circumstances, and a made dog has forever been an even more important sort of monument.

In short, I was beginning to surmise that my skills in this formerly sacramental portion of existence were dying, like men and women all around me. If there'd been a time when I was one to whom—as a student of the great Aldo Leopold marveled about him—"the game just seemed to come," that time was fled.

The blank—and the random. Absences and murderous presences. Death as multifold, a gang of thugs who killed by hanging or by instilling mortal illness, who invited the potentially lethal scalpel. Death, whose many incursions seemed perfectly analogized by the awful crop-pings-up of so-called development in my hunting grounds. Such grounds, or so in my vanity I'd for decades imagined, belonged to me. To me and my dogs. Me and my prey. Me and my friends, so many of them either perished now or diminished or otherwise moved on, out of my ken.

The first morning of Vermont's turkey season, I had practically to horsewhip myself out of bed, sensing my failure before the fact, anticipating my fatigue, which would set in by noon and put me behind in my journeyman jobs. I'd have held such tiredness in contempt, of course, in naive youth, when a duck blind at dawn segued into seven hours afield behind a pair of gun dogs and then into an evening's carousing till the small hours.

The hardwoods did look beautiful at the top of the first ridge, their leaves pastel, their every storey melodious with migrants. The abandoned twitch roads were so thickly clotted by bluets as still to seem snow-covered. Black duck and mallard croaked in the spring pools. Wake-robin already showed in wet gullies.

There was also a lovesick barred owl chanting not far off. No turkey answered that owl's call, however, nor my own imitation of it. For a month, there'd been sign all over the four good ridges I meant to roam that opening morning: I'd seen a gobbling jake within a hundred yards of my house; I'd heard other gobblers on the west side of the pond that bisects my property. But on that day, no response. None, that is, save the owl's. Defying its reputation for wisdom, the bird luffed in over my head, perched a spell in a sick butternut, went out disenchanted. And so, given the late drift of my spirits, it was easy, too easy, to construct crude allegory: the world had ceased answering me . . . or had come to answer in inappropriate ways.

I trudged home well before the law said I had to.

Work and parenthood conspired to keep me off those ridges for another ten days. Or so I told myself. In fact, I felt the depressive's gratitude for such impediment, which freed me to moan with self-pity over being thus deprived but left me with no obligation to take up the thing I was deprived of. The best of two bad worlds.

And yet at length I *did* feel some sort of obligation once more to mount the hills. A better self (inside this worse) had retained some of an old and glorious hope, in however ghostly a guise. And the better self had its reasons: immediately on reaching the granite dune that caps the first ridge, I was greeted with a gobble. The call must instantly have obscured my melancholies, since I don't remember their weight in the ensuing hour. I do remember surveying the terrain around me, simultaneously judging with my damnably poor, gun-shot ears the location of the tom. I would need to drop to his elevation if I hoped to call him in.

Well, I knew the country if anyone did. I turned directly away from the gobble, which now came with a heartening frequency, doglegged to a twitch road that ran under a knoll to the west, and then crept back, the knoll covering me till the road petered out by the white oak stand in which I guessed my turkey strutted. The guess was pretty close: he was on the woods' far margin, some two hundred yards from where I quickly set up, my back to a lichened slab, my right foot pointed in his direction, the Browning on my cocked left knee, the veil slipped over my face.

I decided for a start to try no more than a soft, whimpering chirp. It was early, the sky not yet even pearlescent. The turkey yammering right back at me (or so I thought), I whiffed an ozonic scent that I needn't describe to any hunter of wary game; my heart beat in a full, shirt-stretching cadence, and—despite the chill of a northcountry dawn—sweat drops formed on my cheekbones. I slightly lessened the crook of my left leg, to see if it would hold more still in a different position. It did.

Everything perfect. And yet, rather than coming my way, the tom kept working south, meanwhile moving up an elevation. I was patient. I didn't over-call or hasten to relocate. Minutes passed, the bird's cackle fading by degrees, before I made myself take stock of the land again. At last I stood, then circled back to the east, for I knew another hill-hidden trail, the beat of deer and occasional moose, that would provide quiet and easy travel and would put me back on top, about parallel, I believed, with where the turkey now sang.

Again and again I established myself at what appeared ideal places. Again and again I heard the quarry's noise dim, always to the south. So in fact, and in honesty: there *were* moments when my mopery returned; everything, I told myself, was right about this chase . . . except that I didn't have the requisite skills to end it the way I meant to end it. But I rallied from these instants of despair: I had enough experience to realize that were the problem only in my calling, this tom would long since have spooked, long since have quit gobbling.

In time I judged the problem lay in the bird's already having a hen, and likely more than one. If I were to get a look at him, then, it would be by way not of deception but of ambush. Unable to turn him, I'd need to head him off.

Most of the ridges on my property run more or less north and south, but one is perpendicular to these. It occurred to me that—turkeys so often describing a circle in their morning rambles—this tom and his coterie night well come to that odd ridge out, turning east along it to regain the highest ridge of all, the one where they'd probably roosted. If that bet proved right, the bird would have to travel an almost knife-thin granite strip some hundred yards above the south end of the pond. A good lie for me, then.

The turkey cries suddenly seemed to be moving more quickly, which meant I must get to that strip in a hurry. I dogtrotted to the edge of the ridge, then all but skied down, so abundant were the oak nuts on that flank despite the ardor of the winter deer herd and of spring's rodents. Now and then I felt slight, brief burnings above my left kneecap: adhesions popping under the ugly scar from my Labor Day accident. But this discomfort left me unalarmed: my mind set on being where I needed to be, I even believed (I still think rightly) that the breach of those adhesions would do me nothing but good, would help turn me loose. And in fact, hitting the bottomland, I broke into a run that felt less awkward and leaden than it had for months. A single hooded merganser, sojourning on his way to the Ungava, made to fly as I coursed by, but then elected simply to dip underwater till I was past. I might thus see him again on our pond, little clown, a notion that filled me with strange delight.

Glancing back, I noticed that the morning mist over the water had somehow and abruptly become general, the world gone soft-edged in fog. The top of the scarp I'd just tumbled down had vanished, along with all but the lowest others, into cloud. A mix of that wetness and the sweat of exertion fogged my glasses, which would have to be clear by the time the tom—please, God!—came into view. So I yanked them off and held them in my hand like a baton as I raced onward.

My breath came with surprising ease. "Not bad for an old guy," I whispered to myself, feeling my cheek muscles tauten in a grin. Well behind me, I heard my bitch Sue let out a single, houndlike howl from her kennel, nothing in it to alarm a gobbler. Indeed, I thought I heard the gobbler answer to that wail, and persuaded myself that the answer came from exactly the right quarter, not far west of where I meant soon to arrive. I envisioned the bird as I ran: he'd be coming out of the hornbeam grove just now, stepping into the high hemlocks, his snood turgid and scarlet, his tail clenching and unfurling, his hens fossicking all about.

And before long, he'd reach that granite pathway.

The fog was everywhere now, but it showed itself in weird little pilasters, as if each had wandered off the pondwater and were walking the land in a company of its familiars—thin, benign ghosts.

You'll imagine me single-minded, as I imagined myself. But in recall, there seems to have been so much to *notice*: by the pond's standpipe, a clump of shoots that in a month or so would bend with the weight of wild iris; above, daylight's first vulture, which hadn't been there and now suddenly was, languidly sliding the updrafts by the ridge I was bound for; a few stubborn gray frogs yet droning at each other, bank to bank; the woods' smell, like chamois.

My boots left prints in the bluets. Again I thought of snow as I studied the earth rolling under me. At last, hearing the turkey rattle the air in that hemlock grove, I started to climb; by now, the illusion of infinite stamina was unraveling: my legs ached, and my breaths were like sobs. Yet I went on, hiking now, to be sure, not running. So much—a world, it seemed—depended on the next few minutes.

The gobbler could not have been more than a few hundred yards away when I reached the top of the ridge. There I discovered, as if placed by providence itself, a tub-sized depression in the granite apron. I scooched into it, then sprawled prone: there was even a cleft in the rock, like the archer's slit in a medieval turret, through which I could see 180 degrees, and through which, fate willing, I'd be able to shoot.

The turkey remained as persistent in his call as he'd been since first I heard it, and he was, no doubt about it, headed my way. I slipped my eyeglasses back on, pulled down the veil, then cursed mutely: once more the ambient fog and my own sweat clouded the lenses so that I could see nothing.

A blank.

I reached up under the veil with my gloved right hand, rubbing a small circle on either side. Within seconds these circles clouded again. The bird's gobble was louder by now than my thoughts. I drew the glasses to the tip of my nose and squinted over them, but I was too blind that way. The cruelty of my circumstance seemed incredible.

And then a cold breeze kicked up. Some may doubt me, may think this all sounds too scripted. I cannot prove a thing, for I was the lone human in that place; I merely know what I know, and I know that such a wind arrived, can all but feel it again as I carry on here.

My vision went clear . . . and the gobbler quit calling.

Long, long minutes yawned. I imagined the tom, with those eyes, that beggar comparison, to have seen through the rock-cleft where I lay, to have seen me fuss with my misted lenses, to have scooted off with his hen or his harem, not to reappear. My gloom, however, had evidently and patiently been awaiting its chance to reappear; it stole, as always, first into my gut, from where it would soon make its climb—more deliberate than my own one at dawn—into such parts of me as harbor the spirit. I lay there helpless.

There seem to be (who knows why?) bountiful moments in one's life that one doesn't have to deserve. That foggy morning well behind me now, I think back on a bright boy's terrible self-murder, and how badly I responded on hearing of it; I think of the brusqueness with which I greeted my wife's uncountable acts and words of kindness to me; of how dully I observed the innocence of my smaller children, the decency of my older; of the unacknowledged splendors of the earth and air and water among which I'd long dwelled; of my fine physical fortune, which I have taken too often for granted.

The depression I'd felt for the protracted interlude leading up to that hunt now seems to have been so easy, so self-indulgent!

Tall as a man, a bird walked forth, stirring the mist with his bulk, silent—behind him, slightly smaller, an apparently endless procession of hen turkeys. I saw them all through the chink in my granite enclosure. My gun barrel rested on a spur of rock, parallel to the pungent, pine-spilled ground. The tom had grown cautious, as a tom will uncannily, unaccountably, do in such moments. Yet he continued to pick his way toward me, lifting and gingerly replacing each foot, almost in the manner of a heron.

The turkey at last intersected with the lane my shot would take, his beard thrust forward like a bowsprit, lucent with silver dew. He stretched his neck and cocked his head northward. I squeezed the trigger, and he collapsed.

I thumbed back the safety and jerked to my feet, rushing to the spot. As I ran, I found myself expecting no sign of a bird—expecting to awaken, that is, from a dream whose untruth would leave me weeping on that shoulder of stone.

But there the bird did lie, in all his gorgeous giantism. An impossibility, but there indeed he lay. I put the shotgun aside, leaned over, grasping a horny shin with each hand. At my touch the gobbler came back to life, his great wings pistons, his whole frame pumping to reach the catastrophic cliff face just beyond us, down which he would surely hurl himself, never to be found. I held tight to him, my heels hopelessly digging for purchase in the granite. It was like trying to arrest the motion of some machine gone weirdly autonomous.

I now look back upon that desperate wrestle as a necessarily absurd, and comic, chapter in all this. What must I have looked like? A man of two hundred pounds and more being drawn by the will of a wild thing, even in death, toward unseemly conclusion.

But at length I prevailed.

They are hard things to explain to a non-hunter, let alone to an anti-hunter—the recognitions that came to me on that morning. I recognized, say, that the whole ritual had realized itself on my land; indeed, the kill transpired at a distance of no more than three hundred yards from the warm house in which I live.

I live, too, in a country so rich that the thousands of its citizens who have no houses—never mind land—constitute a national disgrace.

Perhaps I'm less a hunter than once I was; but on that spangled ledge it struck me that I did have some skills left anyhow. Maybe my fiftyish body was, as I earlier put it, slumping; but I had gotten to my vantage largely on the run. Nine months earlier, I'd sawn my left quadricep to the bone: two inches lower lay the kneecap; four inches rightward lay the femoral artery; I'd gotten off with three days in a hospital bed, four weeks of crutches, a spectacular and story-laden cicatrice the only residue of the whole ordeal.

I was so well married and so well childed that then as now I could find no adequate words to express my good fortune. But subsuming all these omens of my rare welfare, all these recognitions, is what I can only call a spiritual truth. I will abuse it, as I have done before, as any pilgrim must, but there it was.

Is.

My mother, like Breck the suicide, like Amico the cancer victim, must die, soon or late. As must I. As must every last one of us. And yet for a moment and much more a truth shone clear: be receptive and you will receive.

I felt, I feel, a great *gratitude* to a certain wild turkey. Again the anti-hunter winces, no doubt. And yet, walking down that steep ridge, the luminous body slung over my shoulder in all its heft, I recalled, as I do now, the perfection of that bird's coming to me. I had done something right, and my prey had therefore obliged me. What had been random was for a spell at least coherent.

It was not, however, a bird alone that came to me. The very world, however slight my worthiness for such a miracle, had come as well.

Reprinted with permission of the author. Originally published in *The Southern Review*.

Ol' Ben

J. WAYNE FEARS

Wild-turkey hunters know that every hunt on which you work a gobbler becomes a great hunting memory. Whether the bird is taken or not is really of little consequence as the years roll by.

But in the same vein, experienced spring gobbler hunters also know there are some gobblers which seem ghostlike. These are almost supernatural birds which seem to know what we're going to do before we do it. These challenging toms are the ones we'll always remember as the "great gobblers."

Those special gobblers always seem to earn a name, and one of my most memorable was a gobbler I, and several other hunters, tagged "Ol' Ben."

Ol' Ben was a bully, lover, and control freak, all wrapped up into one gobbler. This bird controlled all the turkey activity in a large hardwood bottom in the bend of the Tombigee River in Alabama. So the name we gave him, Ol' Ben, seemed to fit.

Just prior to the opening of the spring turkey season that year, there were four gobbling birds in the river bend, but when Ol' Ben took to gobbling, all the others stopped. There was little doubt Ol' Ben was a mean, tough boss gobbler.

During the first two weeks that season I was hunting another area, but the difficulty my friends were having with Ol' Ben made me switch hunting areas to concentrate on him alone.

The first couple of mornings I tried to set up on Ol' Ben were blown due to my lack of knowledge of the terrain. Both mornings I got the old boss tom to gobble at first light with a crow call, but each time there was a deep creek separating us. That spring we had lots of rain and the flat bottoms were flooded in many areas.

On the third morning, I waded water up to my chest to get on the same side of the slough Ol' Ben was on. The gravelly-voiced old boy had about 20 hens roosting in trees near him, and I couldn't get any closer than 150 yards.

Nothing I did that morning worked. My best yelps, cackles, and clucks only caused him to double-gobble. When time came for him to fly down, he headed to the west towards the river with his harem of hens. My attempt to cut him off was foiled by more deep water.

All I could think about was how to outsmart Ol' Ben. Sometime during fretting and fussing, an idea occurred to me—why not try to confuse Ol' Ben? I could approach his roosting area from the river to the west. Then, if he flew down the same direction he had that morning, I would be set up in his line of movement to call to him. I planned to use a different turkey call that would sound like a new hen.

Then, if I could get another hunter to wade into Ol' Ben's roosting area from the east and set up using a gobble box, the gobbler might fly down to fight the intruder. Between an intruding gobbler and a new hen Ol' Ben might make a mistake.

I called a fellow wildlife biologist and master turkey hunter, Nathan Connell, and told him my plan. He was game to try this well-known gobbler.

Long before dawn the next morning, we were each wading deep water, working our way into position. This time I took advantage of the darkness and moved to within 100 yards of the tall water oaks where the boss gobbler had been roosting. I had a long wait sitting at the base of a large hickory in wet leaves.

As the first red birds started calling, I heard the soft tree yelps from several nearby trees; the hens were stirring. Then, Ol' Ben rocked the woods with a resounding gobble. He was on the same limb he had been on the morning before. It was hard to sit there and not yelp to him, but Nathan and I had agreed not to do anything until Ol' Ben was ready to fly down.

The waiting seemed like an eternity as I watched several hens nervously move around on tree limbs almost directly over my head. Ol' Ben gave one of his best performances that morning, breaking the stillness with double-gobble after double-gobble.

As the sun rose in the east, two hens flew down almost at my feet. Then three more sailed over my head, landing behind me and yelping loudly.

Just as the hens flew over my head, I heard Nathan rattle his gobble box some 200-plus yards out in front of me. I thought Ol' Ben would burst his voice box as he instantly answered with a loud gobble. Nathan came back with a double-gobble. This was too much for Ol' Ben. He flew from his roost and landed somewhere—out of sight—to my right front. When he hit the ground, he gobbled six times.

Then, I got into the act. I gave a loud series of yelps with my mouth call. Ol' Ben gobbled back before the last yelp ended.

He was walking fast 75 yards in front of me. Then Nathan gave a double gobble, and the boss gobbler did an about face, gobbling continuously as he started back toward Nathan.

Just then, a hen flew down from a tree to my right and hit the ground at my feet, ran straight at me and crashed into my ribs! She flew off, putting like crazy, but Ol' Ben was too upset to pay heed. For the next five minutes he would walk toward Nathan, and when I would yelp back, he'd walk toward me.

All at once, the sound of a new hen won out, and he started trotting directly to me. The shot was anticlimactic. It had been one of the most exciting mornings I had ever enjoyed as a hunter. Ol' Ben weighed only 14 pounds and had few feathers on his bottom side. He had been a busy gobbler! His spurs were one inch long and he sported an 11-inch beard.

The following week my friends told me that seven toms were gobbling in the same area. Ol' Ben truly had been a boss gobbler.

Reprinted with permission of the author. The author's many books are available on his website: www.jwaynefears.com.

A Successful Fall Hunt

JOHN MCDANIEL

The dark hills are silhouetted against the slightly lighter sky as I pull onto the logging road. This leg of the trip is rough, and I brace myself in the seat as the bouncing headlights cut through the trees. Finally, I reach the area from which the hunt will begin. Stepping from the jeep, I am greeted by the cool air of the mountain. I close the door of the big vehicle with care. I hate the loud, metallic sounds the latch produces. Despite the lack of light, I am comfortable and relaxed as I set out on the familiar trail. My clothes fit perfectly, the gun is familiar, and the boots have logged one hundred miles on this mountain. The smells of the November woods, the strength of my body, and the expectations of the day surge through me. Damn, it's great to be on the mountain!

I walk through the dark woods towards the big hardwoods near the head of the little cove. I saw fresh sign in the area two days before, and if I am lucky. . . . As dawn comes, I listen for the sounds of birds leaving their roosts. No such sounds are forthcoming. I begin the arduous search for the flock. There are no shortcuts. I go up and over ridges, and down into basins, and along small streams. I discipline myself to approach each ridge with caution and to search each cove with the bright binoculars. My legs begin to ache, and despite the forty-degree temperature, sweat rolls down my face. I have hunted hard and am satisfied with the morning.

There is no time for the grouse hunter's relaxed lunch on the tailgate of a station wagon. There is no time to play with the warm and happy Brittany after lunch. The turkey hunter opens his meager lunch on a high, hardwood ridge overlooking a spring. You are still turkey hunting. You need every minute, every day, if you want to be able to kill them with the consistency that separates the turkey hunter from the good old boy who blundered into them.

After lunch, I plan the hunt for the afternoon. It is warmer. I decide to work down along an ample stream that drains the large mountain to my north. It is almost three when I finally reach the valley. I bend to drink from the small stream, confident that there is no threat of pollution here, back from the roads, the cattle, the quail, and the quail hunters. Drinking from clear streams is one of the fringe benefits of turkey hunting. After a brief pause, I continue to hunt.

The small circle of earth, devoid of leaves, sends a shiver through my body. My entire body tightens as I inspect the sign—fresh! The scratching indicates a large flock. I move quickly, aware that the birds may be within one hundred yards. My body drinks the adrenalin and I acquire new strength. Turkeys! I pause and hear them raking the leaves in front of me. There is no question about the rhythmic sound the large birds make as they scratch in the cluttered forest floor in search of mast. I judge them to be seventy-five to one hundred yards downstream. I move carefully. The knowledge that I will get close to them increases the thrill. The laurel opens a bit, and I see them. Several of the sleek, great birds are by the bank of the stream. My mind races as I assess the situation. Am I close enough to rush? Would it be better to try to circle in front of the feeding flock? Have they sensed my presence? The quick putt-putt alarm call answers my question.

I throw myself toward them. The sprint is the infantryman's rush, hampered by equipment, the mobility of the arms restricted by the heavy gun. I rushed this way once, not long ago, carrying an M16. There was no more effort expended than there is now. The birds lift their heads quickly. They are trans-fixed in concerned inspection, the big eyes having focused on the awkward predator and the small brain translating the image as a threat. They leap into flight. The flush of one turkey is impressive; the flush of a large drove is pandemonium. Birds I had not seen materialize, and the six become twenty. All are airborne at the same time. Sometimes, one turkey will respond more slowly than the rest. Not this time. The flight is not graceful; yet in a very short time, a very large bird climbs through mature trees and is out of range. Incapable of any more productive action, I watch as the turkeys fan out in flight, each seeking its own path of escape. The surprise and the dense cover has resulted in effective dispersion of the drove. Scattered!

The turkeys gone, I sit down to collect myself and plan a strategy for the next episode. I check my watch. It is 3:30. I doubt if they will try to get back together before sunset; however, I will wait just in case. I construct a blind in the precise spot from which the drove flushed. I climb into the blind, allow my tired body to sink into the cool soil, and wait. Sunset comes quickly, and there is no indication that there is a wild turkey within five hundred miles. I awkwardly step out of the blind for the long walk back to the jeep. As I begin the descent, my mind drifts to the scattered young turkeys on the mountain, eager for the companionship the drove offers. Tomorrow should be the day!

Nell listens to her turkey hunter/husband's story and asks with a smile, "You wouldn't be going up there tomorrow, would you?" I smile back.

Despite the nine o'clock bedtime, I am numb as I grope through the room at 4:30 a.m. The anticipation of the scattered flock helps offset the fatigue, and I move to the kitchen with determination, if not grace.

A relatively short ride in the Jeep, a long climb through the dark woods, and soon I am in the small blind. I ease myself into a comfortable position and wait for dawn.

Light comes, and I pull my body together against the now-penetrating cold. I am tight with antici-pation, because I am sure there will be turkeys calling on the mountain. The wait is short. The call is clear and unmistakable. It is the high-pitched whistle of the young turkey. The thrill of hearing the bird is tremendous. The challenge of making a good call is heightened by the knowledge that if you succeed the young bird will probably come running. The hours of practice with the call, and the successful attempts in the past, give me confidence. I put the small diaphragm caller on my tongue and place it against the roof of my mouth. I prepare my throat and mouth and then bring five quick bursts of air from my lungs. The young turkey answers immediately, and I sense an urgency in its call. I prepare to respond, but the call of another turkey, also below me but farther to the right, interrupts my preparation. I answer, and both turkeys scream back with eagerness. The bird to the right calls again, and this time he sounds perceptibly closer. I call back and try to interject a sense of panic and urgency in the notes.

It is always such a great thrill to hear the bold, loud calls. The second bird that answered is now coming steadily toward me, and I shift my position in anticipation of his arrival. A dense clump of laurel will prevent me from seeing the turkey until he is within seventy yards of the blind. I wait, trying to control the now rapid beating of my heart. I listen intently to the bird's call, and I pick up the character-istic deep yelps with which the young gobbler terminates his key-key call. At a range of what I guess to be a hundred yards, the bird lets out a series of loud whistles. I push the gun forward until the blue rib and the tiny bead of silver are superimposed on the tangle of laurel. I focus on the small bead, and the laurel blurs into an impressionistic pattern of color. I hear the distinctive two-footed gait as he comes. His approach is anything but stealthy. He comes boldly, sounding like a quick-footed man in the leaves. I move the safety off. I search frantically, as the sound of his approach makes it impossible to believe he is not in sight. The first visible indication of his presence is a flash of black to the right of the spot upon which I have concentrated my attention. I adjust my body position slightly and look down the rib of the shotgun. At fifty yards, the entire bird is visible, his body iridescent in the now higher sun. The turkey comes boldly toward me. The long legs reach forward, and the bright eyes burn with intensity. The tiny silver bead enters the bright picture, and I place it under his head. The bird continues to stride toward me. He is close enough. I feel the gun jar in my hands before there is any distinct decision to shoot. After the instant blur, produced by the heavy recoil, I refocus my eyes and see the broad, red-brown tail fanned gracefully in the air. It is enough. I jerk myself from the confining blind and run, on cramped legs, to the dying turkey.

I am pleased to find the bird has been killed cleanly. Tiny points of bright red blood mark the large, blue head, providing vivid testimony to the effectiveness of the small shot. I inspect the wounds and then look at the entire bird. The myriad feathers shine in the bright sun. As always, I am particularly impressed by the size of the bird's eyes. I sit back and enjoy the warm satisfaction of the moment.

Turkeys can be killed by chance, but when they are killed consistently, it is not due to chance. I inspect the bird and relive the episode. I particularly cherish these calm moments. I celebrate my victory with a can of Coke I carry in my pack for the occasion. I reflect on the accomplishment and I am unashamedly proud. I give humble thanks for being provided with the opportunity. I admire the wonderful bird. I enjoy my own company. Finally, I place the turkey's legs together, grasp them tightly in my right hand, swing him over my shoulder, pick up the shotgun and head down the slope.

I never have much trouble carrying a turkey out of the woods. I've killed a few large ones—one that weighed in excess of nineteen pounds—but the walk out has always been easy. The joy of victory is a great equalizer for fatigue. I move easily through the woods with the large bird on my shoulder. As I leave the woods, I transfer the turkey to my other shoulder and head down the logging road toward the Jeep. I can't wait to take the bird back to Nell.

I hear the pick-up struggling up the road before I see it. It lurches into view, its metallic colors and harsh noises an obscene intrusion on the serenity. Three large men struggled to stay in their seats as the vehicle fights up the difficult slope. As I move to the side to let them pass, I pull the turkey up a little higher and try to appear nonchalant. The hunters don't pass. Three heavy men descend from the still-moving car to see my bird. They wear new camouflage gear, and their guns are handsome. None has ever killed a turkey. They too are free to hunt turkeys for the first week of the season. The fatigue of one-and-a-half days of turkey hunting is visible in their faces. The men press close to examine my young gobbler. There is awe in their eyes as they inspect the beautiful bird. They ask the inevitable questions and then squeeze back into the pickup, their spirits and strength renewed. I watch their heads bob in animated conversation as the pickup surges up the road. I tell them exactly where I had encountered the turkeys. They are confident, too confident. As I watch the awkward vehicle struggle, I smile to myself. Somehow, I know that my turkey will be the only one taken from the drove on this still-young fall day.

Reprinted with permission of the author and Amwell Press.

Turkey Hunters

JOHN MCDANIEL

The turkey selects turkey hunters. The process has selected men who enjoy a blend of physical toughness, intelligence, and determination. The great turkey hunters I know laugh when I suggest that they write about the bird they chase. One is a native West Virginian who speaks with a soft mountain accent. He lives to hunt wild turkeys. His occupation, that of a forester, allows him to be close to these birds he loves. During last year's spring season James had twenty possible calendar days for hunting. He hunted on eighteen. On each of those mornings, he was up at two-thirty to face the demanding hills of eastern West Virginia. He is an accomplished caller and splendid shot. Last spring, he failed to kill a gobbler. He was neither surprised nor distraught.

In many small mountain communities, the respect the turkey hunter earns cuts across sub-cultural boundaries based on sex. I have heard the proud wife or mother say, with unusual boldness, "James hunts nothing but turkeys; he doesn't fool with anything else." Mountain women boast of men who kill turkeys regularly.

Wherever he is and in whatever cultural situation he lives, the turkey hunter is in a class by himself. He enjoys this status in both the warm den of the prestigious hunting club and in the drab barbershop in the bleak Appalachian town. One is not a turkey hunter by virtue of killing a turkey or even a few turkeys; on the contrary, turkeys fall to deer hunters and squirrel hunters with a regularity that disturbs turkey hunters. One acquires the status of turkey hunter by demonstrating consistent success. To achieve this measure of success, a degree of specialization must be developed. It is nice to talk of how in May one can hunt turkeys in the morning and fish for trout in the afternoon; however, if you expect to kill your gobbler regularly in the spring you will fish very little. You must invest full days for consistent success with spring gobblers. The season may end at 11 a.m., but you have to scout in the afternoons and practice your calling in the evenings. In addition, the 2:30 a.m. alarm will dampen the enthusiasm with which one awaits the 3:30 p.m. hatch of mayflies. The turkey asks a lot. The successful turkey hunter pays his dues.

Turkeys demand the development and maintenance of stamina in the hunter. I have hunted turkeys with accomplished college athletes and they have suffered under the strain. If you wonder what the rigors of a sheep hunt are like, try a turkey in the rugged ridges of our Appalachian states. If you kill grouse with your legs, you kill turkeys with your heart.

The grouse hunter will, with accuracy, state that his bird also demands dedication and hard work. The distinguishing element is the level of patience required. The grouse hunter often hunts for a long time between flushes but he rarely goes days without seeing a bird. The best turkey hunter anticipates days without encountering game. He develops the quiet dedication of the salmon fisherman. Both men are addicted to the pursuit of the difficult. The nature of the game, be it salmon or turkey, provides one with the strength to face the incredibly long periods between contact with the quarry. The turkey hunter can appreciate the sense of satisfaction and fulfillment that the salmon specialist feels after having fished a stream well without moving a fish. Does even the most avid grouse hunter reflect with satisfaction on a day when no bird is flushed? I submit that this difference is a measure of the status of salmon to other fish and the wild turkey to other birds, even grouse.

One of the most important skills, the art of calling the wild turkey, was first practiced by the American Indian hundreds and even thousands of years ago. Today, nothing indicates a turkey can be fooled more easily; on the contrary, there are those who would suggest the challenge has increased with greater hunting pressure. Despite what the salesmen of turkey calls may state, it is not easy.

The turkey will not be consistently harvested by poor shooters. The vulnerable parts of the bird are small. If you use a shotgun, the turkey will teach you the modest range at which such a weapon is lethal. If you read about eighty-yard turkey guns, the piece was written by someone who doesn't know how difficult a turkey is to kill. You can quote pattern densities all day but any turkey that is over sixty yards from the shooter has a good chance of surviving a shot regardless of gauge, choke, load, or shot size. With a rifle, you have to be able to shoot accurately to kill turkeys. The modest skill that has been developed by many efficient deer hunters is just not adequate.

If turkey hunters, as a group, have a weakness it is a proclivity to avocational arrogance. The respect the turkey hunter allocates to hunters of other games is measured. Deer hunting is perceived as an activity best suited to adolescents, the infirm, the fat, and the old. In response to the question, "Why don't you hunt deer?" a wiry turkey hunter raised his light blue eyes to the interrogator and said:

Any fool can kill a deer every year. He just finds himself a trail, sits down and, sooner or later, some impatient fellow from the city will chase one up the trail. The deer won't see the boy and the deer's mind ain't quick enough to convince him what to do about that boy's smell. So, the deer gawks at the smell and stamps his feet at it. Now if that good old boy don't get too nervous he will fill the scope up with the body of the deer and kill him.

A turkey hunter, don't you see, he goes out and *hunts* a turkey. He don't depend on tree stands, or drives, or city fellows to push a half-blind animal to him. A turkey hunter has to be *smart enough* to know where the flock will be, *tough enough* to get close to scatter the birds, *clever enough* to put his blind in the right place, and *talented enough* to call a bird up. Now, after he has done all that he better know how to sit *still* and be patient. Finally, when that bird is there, he better shoot *straight* and *quick* because a turkey's head and neck are small and even a young one won't stand there gawking at you and stamping his feet.

Portrait of a Turkey Hunter

James is a turkey hunter. In his part of West Virginia, no sentence says more about him. James is not a member of the N.R.A., he belongs to no hunt club, he subscribes to no outdoor journals, he does not hunt turkeys for human companionship. The loud, crowded, aggressively masculine hunt camp is as uncomfortable to him as an urban bar.

James lives to hunt turkeys. His is the legacy of the hunter that historians say helped shape the nation's character and that anthropologists argue helped establish the path of human evolution.

James has been captured, perhaps seduced, by both the challenge that the wild turkeys present and the comfort he derives from being embraced by those wild areas the turkey inhabits. James knows he is good at hunting turkeys and he is proud of it. He takes great satisfaction from the fact he is the best turkey hunter in Randolph County. He is neither a hermit nor a recluse. His tax statement says that he is a forester. In fact, he is a turkey hunter who works as a forester because his culture does not subsidize hunting. He works hard as a forester. Unfortunately, the diligent performance of his job provides less satisfaction and less public acclaim than that which accrues from his exploits as a superb turkey hunter.

James lives for November and April. During November, his days average eighteen hours in length. He gets no overtime—he asks for none. He eats, sleeps, and hunts. On many occasions he sleeps and eats only enough to be able to hunt. In the spring, turkeys begin to gobble at 4:30 a.m. To be in position at the top of a 3,000-foot ridge, you have to wake at 2:30. I know; I've hunted with James. The season is thirty days in length. He rarely misses more than a day. The last day of the spring season he will look like the GI after Anzio or one of Napoleon's boys on the road back from Moscow. He will have hunted to the edge of exhaustion. He occasionally falls over that edge.

He enjoys the fact that turkeys are tough. In James' words, he appreciates the fact "they make you bleed a little." Have you ever tried to climb up a mile-long, 60-degree slope in 70 degree April heat, bearing thirty pounds of clothes and equipment? Your legs cramp, your body aches, you wonder what the strain will do to a forty-year-old heart. You slip, and the equipment pounds you onto the sharp limestone and you grunt with very real pain. You get a sick feeling as you look up at the dark and distant ridge. Finally, you reach the ridge, find the tree, and sink into the cool ground. You let your body collapse and you feel your heart still struggle with the strain imposed by the climb. You look over the now-lighter valley. You are proud of the perspective. You smile at James. He smiles back. This is the essential companionship of human hunting. Two men attempting something difficult together. Two friends who respect each other and celebrate each other's success, and are sensitive to each other's failures. This is not the raucous companionship of the deer camp where petty jealousy and envy turn cooperation into meaningless competition.

The gobble makes the climb inconsequential. Myriad years of human evolution have provided James with the mind and body to respond to the gobble. Instantly, he is alert and capable. He registers the distance to the bird and plans the attack with skill and speed. Gentle, soft-spoken, James is transformed into the most effective predator in the animal world. He runs toward the bird with agility and determination. His mind weighs all the necessary information. How far is the bird? How old is he? Where would it be best to call from? Is he still on the roost? His brain is James' greatest physical asset. The brain evolved in response to the need to perform such tasks.

James knows what it takes to kill turkeys regularly. He derives a sense of self-worth from his hunting success. They can call him lucky but he knows better. He has confidence in himself and knows that luck does not put his turkeys on the ground. His success and the reputation which accompanies it are based exclusively on his competence. Dress, articulateness, wealth, formal education, social position, or being an effective braggart have no relevance to his success. His accomplishments are earned and they are meaningful to his reputation. This is not killing a deer blinded by fear of an army of hunters. James knows the men of hunting camps are not efficient hunters. He encounters them occasionally. They are either sitting in trees in silent ambush, incapable of more skillful hunting, or they barge through the woods, loud, laden with sidearms and huge knives; an obscene parody of the efficient and proud human hunter.

Turkey hunting selects against the incompetent. Oh, the incompetent will enjoy occasional success but they are not capable of consistent success under fair conditions. In most cultures, only the consistently successful hunters are allocated the respect of their peers. James avoids the incompetent in the woods. They are dangerous.

I sat with James once and listened to a man call at James with his recently purchased box call. The man was very excited because he was sure James' call had been a turkey. I thought it was funny. James wasn't amused. "That boy may fire a shot up here after a while. Then he will go back to his camp and say he called one up close. They've shot at me a time or two. I wish these hills were even steeper so that we could get away from all of them all the time."

A day with James will provide a better testimony to the skill of human hunters than watching a movie of bushmen killing a giraffe in the Kalahari Desert. Have you ever heard a really good turkey hunter run a call? I don't like to watch James when he calls. He goes into himself. The blue eyes focus on something distant. The tone is unbelievable. He sounds exactly like a turkey. No better testimony can be made to the skill of human hunters than to hear a good one with a call.

James does not take the killing of turkeys as being secondary to some mystic experience of relating to the woods. James loves to *kill* turkeys. He talks about the times he has called birds up and not killed them.

"I don't know why, but it's not the same. You know the time you took those photographs of the birds. It just wasn't the same. I like to be looking down the rib of the old Ithaca. I call better. You know I love my turkeys and I've passed up killing hens and young birds. But most of all I enjoy killing them. It hasn't diminished at all. I still like to carry them out of the woods."

James is a wonderful woodsman and when in the woods he is not oblivious to other creatures. I have watched him as he enjoyed the frolicking of young squirrels. He does not kill to answer some twisted need.

One summer evening when riding up to the mountain to search for young turkeys, we encountered a huge timber rattlesnake on the side of the road. James backed up to look at the snake and the rattler came for the big four-wheel drive vehicle. James said, with obvious admiration and respect, "This truck is a thousand times bigger than he is but that boy is standing his ground." It would have been easy to kill the snake and it would have made the local newspapers. James never considered killing it.

James' turkey gun is a 10-gauge Ithaca double he bought at a hardware store in Elkins, in 1936. He had seen one a man from New York had brought to hunt turkeys with and the hardware store owner ordered a similar gun. He has killed 118 turkeys with the gun. "Don't figure how many birds that works out to a year because it might be a bird or two over the limit," he once said with a smile. The gun fits the man. It is a credit to American ingenuity and craftsmanship.

The gun is not as pretty as a Purdey but this is an American gun. It was made for honest, decent men who were not born of noble lineage. When its price tag was $100 the Purdey sold for $1000. It is a testimony to the democratic nature of American hunting. The 10½-pound gun is a collector's item—like its owner, it is authentic. It is a reminder of a period when fine American shotguns were made by hand, by men who cared.

It's interesting that the few great turkey hunters I know are armed with old Model 12 Winchesters, Browning automatics made in Belgium, L. C. Smiths, big Parkers, and pre-1964 Model 70 Winchesters in 22 Hornet. These guns were made for people like James. The semi-wild preserves select for impressed checkering, plastic butt plates, stamped metal and men who have been weaned on preserves and plastic guns.

James exists—right now he is probably working with his calls. The big Ithaca, carefully cleaned, hangs in his modest home.

In other sections of this county, proud guns hang waiting to be used by capable men and women. Their hunting knowledge and competence will match that of any rich German in the Black Forest. These hunters provide proof of the fact that contemporary hunting still requires the development of skills and capabilities. Hunting for these Americans provides enjoyment, satisfaction, and fulfillment.

Reprinted with permission of the author and Amwell Press.

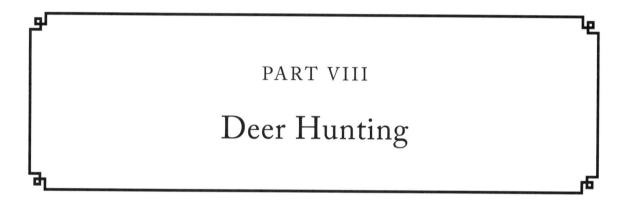

PART VIII

Deer Hunting

Trail's End

SIG OLSON

It was early morning in the northern wilderness, one of those rare, breathless mornings that come only in November, and though it was not yet light enough to see, the birds were stirring. A covey of partridge whirred up from their cozy burrows in the snow and lit in the top of a white birch, where they feasted noisily upon the frozen brown buds. The rolling tattoo of a downy woodpecker, also looking for his breakfast, reverberated again and again through the timber.

They were not the only ones astir, however, for far down the trail leading from the Tamarack Swamp to Kennedy Lake browsed a big buck. He worked his way leisurely along, stopping now and then to scratch away the fresh snow and nibble daintily the still tender green things underneath. A large buck he was, even as deer run, and as smooth and sleek as good feeding could make him. His horns, almost too large, were queerly shaped, for instead of being rounded as in other deer, they were broad and palmate, the horns of a true swamp buck.

The eastern skyline was just beginning to tint with lavender as he reached the summit of the ridge overlooking the lake. He stopped for his usual morning survey of the landscape below him. For some reason, ever since his spike-buck days, he had always stopped there to look the country over before working down to water. He did not know that for countless generations before him, in the days when the pine timber stood tall and gloomy round the shores of the lake, other swamp bucks had also stopped, to scent the wind and listen, before going down to drink.

As he stood on the crest of the ridge, his gaze took in the long reaches of dark blue water far below him; the ice-rimmed shores with long white windfalls reaching like frozen fingers out into the shallows, and the mottled green and gray of the brush covered slopes. His attention was finally centered on a little log cabin tucked away on the opposite shore in a clump of second growth spruce and balsam. Straight above it rose a thin wreath of pale blue smoke, almost as blue as the clear morning air. The metallic chuck, chuck of an axe ringing on a dry log, came clearly across the water, and a breath of air brought to him strange odors that somehow filled him with a vague misgiving.

He was fascinated by the cabin and could not take his gaze from it. On other mornings, it had seemed as much a part of the shoreline as the trees themselves, but now it was different. A flood of almost-forgotten memories surged back to him, of days long ago, when similar odors and sounds had brought with them a danger far greater than that of any natural enemy. He rubbed the top of a low hazel bush and stamped his forefeet nervously, undecided about what to do. Then, in a flash, the full realization came to him. He understood the meaning of it all. This was the season of the year when man was no longer his friend, and it was not safe to be seen in the logging roads or in the open clearings near the log houses. He sniffed the air keenly a moment longer, to be sure, then snorted loudly as if to warn all the wilderness folk of their danger, and bounded back up the trail the way he had come.

Not until he had regained the heavy protecting timber of the Tamarack Swamp, north of Kennedy Lake, did he feel safe. What he had seen made him once again the wary old buck who had lived by his cunning and strength through many a hunting season. Although he was safe for the time being, he was too experienced not to know that before many days had passed, the Tamarack Swamp would no longer be a haven of refuge.

As he worked deeper into the heavy moss-hung timber, he stopped frequently to look into the shadows. The trail here was knee-deep in moss and criss-crossed by a labyrinth of narrow rabbit runways. Soon his search was rewarded, for a sleek yearling doe met him at a place where two trails crossed. After nosing each other tenderly, by way of recognition, they began feeding together on the tender shoots of blueberries and still green tufts of swamp grass underneath the protecting blanket of snow.

All that morning they fed leisurely and when the sun was high in the heavens, they worked cautiously over to the edge of the swamp. Here was a warm sunny opening hedged in by huge windfalls grown over with a dense tangle of blackberry vines. They often came here for their afternoon sunning, as the ice-encrusted ovals in the snow attested. Leaping a big windfall that guarded the entrance to the opening, they carefully examined the ground, then picked their beds close together. There they rested contentedly with the warm sun shining upon them, little thinking that soon their peace would be broken.

The snow had fallen early that autumn and good feed had been scarce everywhere, except in the depths of the Tamarack Swamp, where the protecting timber had sheltered the grass and small green things. The plague had killed off most of the rabbits, and the few that survived were already forced to feed upon the bark of the poplar. The heavy crust, forming suddenly the night after the first heavy snow, had imprisoned countless partridge and grouse in their tunnels. As a result, small game was scarce and the wolves were lean and gaunt, although it was yet hardly winter. The stark famine months ahead gave promise of nothing but starvation and death, and the weird, discordant music of the wolf pack had sounded almost every night since the last full moon.

The swamp buck and his doe had not as yet felt the pinch of hunger, but instinct told them to keep close to the shelter of the Tamarack Swamp, so except for the morning strolls of the buck to the shore of Kennedy Lake, they had seldom ventured far from the timber. They had often heard the wolf pack, but always so far away that there was little danger as long as they stayed under cover.

Several days had passed since the buck had been to the shore of Kennedy Lake. As yet the silence of the swamp had been unbroken except for the crunching of their own hooves through the icy crust on the trails, and the buck was beginning to wonder if there was really anything to fear. Then one day, as they were again leisurely working their way over to the sunning place in the clearing, they were startled by the strange noises far toward the east end of the swamp. They stopped, every nerve on edge. At times they could hear them quite plainly, then again they would be so faint as to be almost indistinguishable from the other sounds of the forest.

The two deer were not much concerned at first. After satisfying themselves that there was no real danger, they started again down the trail toward the clearing. They could still hear the noises occasionally, but could not tell whether they were coming closer or going further away.

Then just as they neared the edge of the swamp, the sound of heavy footsteps seemed suddenly to grow louder and more distinct. Once more they stopped and stood with heads high, ears pricked up, listening intently. This time they were thoroughly alarmed. Closer and closer came the racket. Now they could hear distinctly the crunching of snow and the crackling of twigs, and then the whole east end of the timber seemed to be fairly alive with tumult, and the air reeked with danger.

The buck ran in a circle, sniffing keenly. The same scent that had come to him from the cabin now rankled heavily in the air, and he knew the time had come to leave the shelter of the Tamarack Swamp. He hesitated, however, not knowing which way to turn. Back and forth he ran, stopping now and then to paw the ground, or to blow the air through his nostrils with the sharp whistling noise that all deer use when in danger.

A branch cracked sharply close at hand, and the scent came doubly strong from the east. With a wild snort the buck wheeled and led the way toward the western end of the swamp followed closely by the doe. Their only hope lay in reaching a heavy belt of green hemlock timber which they knew was separated from the western end of the Tamarack Swamp by a broad stretch of barren, burned-over slashing. As they neared the edge of the swamp they stopped, dreading to leave its protection. From where they stood they could see the dark wall of timber half a mile away. A brushy gully ran diagonally toward it across the open slashing, offering some protection, but the hills on either side were as stark and bare as an open field.

Again came the crack and crunch, now so close that the very air burned with danger. It was time to go. They bounded out of the timber, their white flags waving defiance, and were soon in the brush gully, going like the wind. Just as they sailed over a windfall, the buck caught a glimpse of something moving on a big black pine stump on top of the ridge to their right. Then the quiet was shattered by a succession of rending crashes, and strange singing and whining sounds filled the air above them.

Again and again came the crashes. Suddenly the little doe stopped dead in her tracks. She gave a frightened baa-aa-a of pain and terror as the blood burst in a stream from a jagged wound in her throat. The buck stopped and ran back to where she stood, head down and swaying unsteadily. He watched her a moment, then, growing nervous, started down the trail again. The doe tried bravely to follow, but fell halfway across a windfall too high for her to clear. Again the buck stopped and watched her anxiously. The snow by the windfall was soon stained bright red with blood, and the head of the little doe sank lower and lower in spite of her brave efforts to hold it up.

Hurriedly the buck looked about him. Several black figures were coming rapidly down the ridge. He nosed his doe gently, but this time she did not move. Raising his head he looked toward the approaching figures. Danger was close, but he could not leave his mate.

A spurt of smoke came from one of the figures, followed by another crash. This time the buck felt a blow so sharp that it made him stumble. Staggering to his feet, he plunged blindly down the gully. His flag was down, the sure sign of a wounded deer. Again and again came the crashes, and the air above him whined and sang as the leaden pellets searched for their mark. The bark flew from a birch tree close by, spattering him with fragments. In spite of his wound, he ran swiftly and was soon out of range in the protecting green timber. He knew that he would not be tracked for at least an hour, as his pursuers would wait for him to lie down and stiffen.

He was bleeding badly from a long red scar cutting across his flank, and his back trail was sprinkled with tiny red dots. Where he stopped to rest and listen, little puddles of blood would form that quickly turned bluish black in the snow. For two hours he ran steadily, and then was so weakened by loss of blood that at last he was forced to lie down.

After a short rest, he staggered to his feet, stiffened badly. The bed he had melted in the snow was stained dark red from his bleeding flank. The cold, however, had contracted the wound and had stopped the bleeding a little. He limped painfully down the trail, not caring much which direction it led. Every step was torture. Once when crossing a small gully, he stumbled and fell on his wounded leg. It rested him to lie there, and it was all he could do to force himself on.

While crossing a ridge, the wind bore the man scent strongly to him, and he knew that now he was being trailed. Once, he heard the brush crack behind him, and was so startled that the wound was jerked open and the bleeding started afresh. He watched his back trail nervously, expecting to see his pursuer at any moment and hear again the rending crash that would mean death.

He grew steadily weaker and knew that unless night came soon, he would be overtaken. He had to rest more often now, and when he did move it was to stagger aimlessly down the trail, stumbling on roots and stubs. It was much easier now to walk around the windfalls than to try to jump over as he had always done before.

The shadows were growing longer and longer, and in the hollows it was already getting dusk. If he could last until nightfall he would be safe. But the man scent was getting still stronger, and he realized at last that speed alone could not save him. Strategy was the only course. If his pursuer could be thrown off the trail, only long enough to delay him half an hour, darkness would be upon the wilderness and he could rest.

So waiting until the trail ran down onto a steep ravine filled with brush and windfalls, the buck suddenly turned and walked back on his own trail as far as he dared. It was the old trick of back tracking that deer have used for ages to elude their pursuers. Then stopping suddenly, he jumped as far to the side as his strength would permit, landing with all four feet tightly bunched together in the very center of a scrubby hazel bush. From there, he worked his way slowly into a patch of scrub spruce and lay down, exhausted, under an old windfall. Weakened as he was from loss of blood and from the throbbing pain in his flank, it was all he could do to keep his eyes riveted on his back trail, and his ears strained for the rustling and crunching that he feared would come, unless darkness came first.

It seemed that he had barely lain down, when without warning, the brush cracked sharply, and not 100 yards away appeared a black figure. The buck was petrified with terror. His ruse had failed. He shrank as far down as he could in the grass under the windfall and his eyes almost burst from their sockets. Frantically he thought of leaving his hiding place, but knew that would only invite death. The figure came closer and closer, bending low over the trail and peering keenly into the spruce thicket ahead. In the fading light the buck was well hidden by the windfall, but the blood-spattered trail led straight to his hiding place. Discovery seemed certain.

The figure picked its way still nearer. It was now within 30 feet of the windfall. The buck watched, hardly daring to breathe. Then, in order to get a better view into the thicket, the hunter started to climb a snow covered stump close by. Suddenly, losing his balance, he slipped and plunged backwards into the snow. The buck saw his chance. Gathering all his remaining strength, he dashed out of his cover and was soon hidden in the thick growth of spruce.

It was almost dark now and he knew that as far as the hunter was concerned, he was safe. Circling slowly around, he soon found a sheltered hiding place in a dense clump of spruce where he could rest and allow his wound to heal.

Night came swiftly, bringing with it protection and peace. The stars came out one by one, and a full November moon climbed into the sky, flooding the snowy wilderness with its radiance.

Several hours had passed since the buck had lain down to rest in the spruce thicket. The moon was now riding high in the heavens and in the open places it was almost as light as day. Although well hidden, he dozed fitfully, waking at times with a start, thinking that again he was being trailed. He would then lie and listen, with nerves strained to the breaking point, for any sounds of the wild that might mean danger. An owl hooted over in a clump of timber, and the new forming ice on the shores of Kennedy Lake, half a mile away, rumbled ominously. Then he heard a long quavering call, so faint and far away that it almost blended with the whispering of the wind. The coarse hair on his shoulders bristled as he recognized the hunting call of the age-old enemy of his kind. It was answered again and again. The wolf pack was gathering, and for the first time in his life, the buck knew fear. In the shelter of the Tamarack Swamp there had been little danger, and even if he had been driven to the open, his strength and speed would have carried him far from harm. Now, sorely wounded and far from shelter, he would have hardly a fighting chance should the pack pick up his trail.

They were now running in full cry, having struck a trail in the direction of the big swamp far to the west. To the buck, the weird music was as a song of death. Circling and circling, for a time they seemed to draw no nearer. As yet he was not sure whether it was his own blood-bespattered trail that they were unraveling, or that of some other one of his kind. Then, suddenly, the cries grew in fierceness and volume and sounded much closer than before. He listened spellbound as he finally realized the truth it was his own trail they were following. The fiendish chorus grew steadily louder and more venomous, and now had a new note of triumph in it that boded ill for whatever came in its way.

He could wait no longer and sprang to his feet. To his dismay, he was so stiffened and sore, that he could hardly take a step. Forcing himself on, he hobbled painfully through the poplar brush and clumps of timber in the direction of the lake. Small windfalls made him stumble, and having to walk around hummocks and hollows made progress slow and difficult. How he longed for his old strength and endurance. About two-thirds of the distance to the lake had been covered and already occasional glimpses of water appeared between the openings.

Suddenly the cries of the pack burst out in redoubled fury behind him, and the buck knew they had found his warm blood-stained bed. Plunging blindly on, he used every ounce of strength and energy that he had left, for now the end was only a matter of minutes. The water was his only hope, for by reaching that he would at least escape being torn to shreds by the teeth of the pack. He could hear them coming swiftly down the ridge behind him and every strange shadow he mistook for one of the gliding forms of his pursuers. They were now so close that he could hear their snarls and yapping. Then a movement caught his eye in the checkered moonlight. A long gray shape had slipped out of the darkness and was easily keeping pace with him. Another form crept in silently on the other side and both ran like phantoms with no apparent effort. He was terror-stricken, but kept on desperately. Other ghost-like shapes filtered in from the timber, but still they did not close. The water was just ahead. They would wait till he broke from the brush that lined the shore. With a crash, he burst through the last fringe of alders and charged forward. As he did so, a huge gray form shot out of the shadows and launched itself at his throat. He saw the movement in time and caught the full force of the blow on his horns. A wild toss and the snarling shape splashed into the ice rimmed shallows. At the same instant the two that had been running alongside closed, one for his throat and the other for his hamstrings. The first he hit a stunning blow with his sharp front hoof, but as he did so the teeth of the other fastened on the tendon of his hind leg. A frantic leap loosened his hold and the buck half-plunged and half-slid over the ice into the waters of Kennedy Lake. Then the rest of the pack tore down to the beach with a deafening babble of snarls and howls, expecting to find their quarry down or at bay. When they realized that they had been outwitted, their anger was hideous and the air was rent with howls and yaps.

The cold water seemed to put new life into the buck and each stroke was stronger than the one before. Nevertheless, it was a long hard swim, and before he was halfway across, the benumbing cold had begun to tell. He fought on stubbornly, his breath coming in short, choking sobs and finally, after what seemed ages, touched the hard sandy bottom of the other shore. Dragging himself painfully out, he lay down exhausted in the snow. All sense of feeling had left his tortured body, but the steady lap, lap of the waves against the tinkling shore ice soothed him into sleep.

When he awoke, the sun was high in the heavens. For a long time he lay as in a stupor, too weak and sorely stiffened to move. Then with a mighty effort he struggled to his feet, and stood motionless, bracing himself unsteadily. Slowly his strength returned and leaving his bed, he picked his way carefully along the beach, until he struck the trail, down which he had so often come to drink. He followed it to the summit of the ridge overlooking the lake.

The dark blue waters sparkled in the sun, and the rolling spruce covered ridges were green as they had always been. Nothing had really changed, yet never again would it be the same. He was a stranger in the land of his birth, a lonely fugitive where once he had roamed at will, his only choice to leave forever the ancient range of his breed. For a time he wavered torn between his emotions, then finally turned to go. Suddenly an overwhelming desire possessed him, to visit again the place where last he had seen his mate. He worked slowly down the trail to the old Tamarack Swamp and did not stop until he came to the old meeting place deep in the shadows where the two trails crossed. For a long time he did not move, then turned and headed into the north to a new wilderness far from the old, a land as yet untouched, the range of the Moose and Caribou.

Three Men and a Buck

WILLIAM A. MILE

The whole thing happened because Doc had a friend who owned a farm in upstate New York, in the foothills of the Adirondacks. Here he had retired to the placid life of reading and checker-playing. That is, most of his time was spent that way. The rest of the day was spent chasing deer out of his young orchard. That's the way the story came to us.

Now the mere mention of venison seems to rouse the sporting instinct. The pulse quickens; the fountain of youth starts bubbling. Even the most serene individual will prick up his ears. It's like a bugle call to an old war horse. Must be a throwback to our pioneer forbears.

Anyway, it was the origin of the most incongruous foursome that ever responded to the call of the wild. There was Jim, a surgeon of great repute in the greatest city; Joe, a dentist who asked and received better than ten dollars an hour for his labors; Sam, an undertaker, who, contrary to tradition, was fat and jolly and as full of jokes as a hound dog is of ticks. And a magazine publisher. I was the publisher.

How we ever got together for a deer hunt remains a mystery to this day. We had nothing in common. We were, indeed, members of the same club—but all for different reasons. However, just the suggestion of venison seems to make strange bedfellows.

Jim started it all at the round-table lunch at the club when he passed around a letter from his retired friend in the Adirondacks. It wasn't much of a letter, as I recall. Merely the suggestion that Jim come up and help dispose of some of the deer that were chewing up the young fruit trees. So the four of us looked at one another and asked: "Why not?" Sam, the undertaker, was more candid. He still maintains that he went along solely for business reasons.

The outfits that were lugged aboard the Adirondacks Special at Grand Central Terminal a couple of weeks later were just as much mismated as we were. That is, all but Sam's. All he brought was an overnight bag, which held a gallon jug and a change of underwear. Sam said the jug contained embalming fluid. It did. It was four-year-old applejack—also known as Jersey lightning. It has other names too, that are just as apt as the drink is effective.

The treasure in Jim's outfit was a sheep-lined trench coat that reached below his knees—just the right length to entangle the leg action. Joe simply brought his oldest clothes and a borrowed Winchester. My rig was fairly complete, with duffel bag, hunting togs, shoepacs with no heels. The shoepacs were a mistake. My gun was an 8 mm Sauer-Mauser that immediately got a lot of examining and required a lot of explaining.

When we tumbled out of the sleeper on a cold November morning, the temperature was well below freezing. There was nothing in sight but the platform and a horse-drawn stagecoach. Funny how some Adirondack villages are located so many miles away from the railroad, and use train stops in the wilds. The ten-mile ride before breakfast over slippery mountain roads took a couple of hours, and during the ride Sam's supply of embalming fluid was appreciably lowered. State troopers stopped us en route to check our licenses, which luckily were in order, though one of the troopers took plenty of time to examine the Sauer-Mauser.

It was still early in the morning, according to city standards, when we arrived at the farm. Just seven o'clock. Breakfast was waiting, for we were expected. Now, if you've never sat down to an Adirondack farm breakfast on a cold November morning after a two-hour ride—man, you've missed something. That meal alone was worth the price of the whole trip. Fried cakes (flapjacks to you), real maple sirup, country sausage homemade from home-grown pigs, fried eggs by the dozen, sizzling bacon, fried ham, and country-fried potatoes—and coffee in what looked like a lumber-camp coffeepot.

That was the assortment. The quantity was even larger. But it wasn't too much. Four healthy appetites can do wonders to such a meal. But what a far cry it was from our usual orange juice, toast, and coffee, with which we started the day's work back in the city!

Even the irrepressible Sam finally called quits, though he did try to kiss Sally, the dusky cook, from sheer gratitude. He stopped only when she said: "Ah declares, Mistuh Sam, ef yuh don't quit dat monkeyin', Ise gonna souse yuh with dis yere dishwater." But she was pleased by his enthusiasm just the same. From then on, he was her favored "chile."

The two natives who were to do the "guidin" arrived shortly after breakfast. They were an odd pair. Lou was about six feet four, looking a lot as Lincoln must have in his rail-splitting days, and with just as dour a countenance. Jules, his partner, a French-Canadian, was at least a foot shorter, and as round and chubby as Lou was tall and lean.

We were late in getting started. Much too late, as we found out afterward. But then we found out lots of other things too. Same decided that he would stay at the farm, and no amount of persuasion would make him change his mind. "Nope," he said, "I'm tired already, and it's too soon after eating. I'll just wait here until you fellows get back—one way or another. You may need me. Besides, Sally's going to bake me an apple pie."

That was that. The three of us got off finally, sometime after nine o'clock, with two guides leading the way. There was a bit of misgiving, however, for Sam's remarks, jokingly made as they were, stuck in our minds. The pace set by Lou and Jules should have been warning enough. But we were all mature men in fair physical trim. We had knocked around plenty—and had taken plenty of knocks. So the pace was a challenge which we accepted. It never occurred to any of us then that we were getting the works. But we were. The snow was just a couple of inches deep—just a fine tracking snow, according to Lou. The first mile or so across the pasture that led to the edge of the woods, passed without any particular discomfort, though it wasn't exactly a Sunday stroll.

It was not until we were in the woods, headed up the mountain, that the first sign of trouble appeared. Jim's knee-length sheep-lined coat began to get in its fine work. If there was any trail, it to had been carefully avoided. Climbing through down timber is a tough job at the best. In such a rig, Jim had trouble aplenty. He was sweating profusely and cussing more profusely—when he had breath enough to cuss. I offered to take his gun, but he wouldn't hear of it. It was just as well. My heel-less shoepacs worked satisfactorily crossing the flat pasture land. Upgrade in the woods was another story, and I found myself slipping back two steps for every one I advanced. They were of no help climbing in and out of ravines, of which there seemed to be plenty.

Somewhere up ahead, Lou and Jules had disappeared. It was an easy matter to follow their trail, but we were falling far behind the pace. I lost count of the number of times we stopped for a breather, but there were many of them. Joe, the dentist, wasn't doing so badly in his outfit of old clothes. His footgear was most unorthodox, for a well-rigged Nimrod—just a pair of overshoes or arctics over his city shoes—but they were mighty effective and I would gladly have swapped my shoepacs for them.

It was nearly noon when we reached the ridge from which we were to hunt. It wasn't much of a mountain, according to Western standards—just a mere three or four thousand feet. For us it was too much, particularly as we had found every ravine and had climbed over or under every piece of fallen timber on the way up. Lou and Jules were waiting for us, calmly smoking their pipes, their backs resting comfortably against a tree trunk. Apparently it had been just a nice morning jaunt to them. They eyed us speculatively but said nothing. We gave it right back to them with suspicion added, but we too, said nothing. We couldn't. There wasn't breath enough.

Maybe fifteen minutes passed in silence. Darn taciturn, these natives. Then Lou outlined the plan of campaign. It was simple enough, and sounded logical. The three of us were to be placed on separate stations or posts about a quarter of a mile apart, where each of us could get a good view down each side of the ridge. Lou and Jules were to separate, each taking a side of the mountain and working up again from the bottom. The idea was, any deer lurking in the thickets would be jumped by one or the other of them and would head up the mountain, crossing our line of posts, so that one of us might get a shot. Yes, it seemed logical enough then. None of us figured that the noise we'd made coming up the ridge had probably scared every deer—if there ever were any—clear into the next county. All we had to worry about was not to take a shot at each other.

So off we went with Lou to take our respective posts. Joe was dropped first, by a nice round stump, and with a clear view in all directions. Jim was next. He drew an outcrop of rock that also gave him an unbroken view. On we went up the ridge to the very end. Below was an almost sheer drop of several hundred feet. This was my station—also with a nice rock outcrop. South of me were my two companions, perhaps a quarter and half a mile away respectively. They were in plain sight when they stood up. If they sat down there was nothing but the mountain ridge with its sparse covering. Off in the distance were more ridges, more ravines, and more mountains.

Lou left me without a word and departed down the mountain. No final word of instruction. No warning of any kind. No suggestion of when he'd be back. He just went. And then silence. Nothing moved or made a noise except as a vagrant breeze occasionally rustled a dead leaf. I slipped the cartridge clip into the Mauser and waited. Fifteen minutes passed—then a half hour. Nothing happened. Nothing stirred.

To the south, I could see Jim and Joe, equally alert, like two sturdy outposts ready to go into action at the first opportunity. And so we passed the first hour. That was about as long as the alertness lasted. I found a sheltered nook against the rock outcrop and settled down with my back against it. I wanted to smoke, but didn't dare, for fear the tobacco aroma would reach the keen nostrils of some soft-footed deer. That was all I remembered for some time. The utter stillness covered me like a blanket—and I slept.

When I awoke the sun was well down in the southwest. My wristwatch said three-thirty, so I got up and stretched. Not a sign of Jim or Joe. I tried a cautious yell to attract Jim's attention. No response. That was too much. Picking up my rifle, I made my way to Jim's post. He was there right enough, but sound asleep. The snow was littered with cigarette butts. If he had thought the tobacco odor might reach the deer, he didn't care about it. I stirred him with my foot. He roused with a sleepy "Hello—what's up?"

Joe popped up on his stump and we waved for him to join us. He hadn't been asleep, he said, and produced a nicely carved cane whittled from a handy bush as proof. So we held a council of war. The sky was thickening fast. Clouds had come up from nowhere, and the sun had disappeared. It was colder. There was a distinct smell of snow in the air.

Whatever decision we might have reached eventually was postponed by a bedlam of noise from down the mountain—loud yells and much baying of hounds. Lou and Jules had jumped a deer. Jim lost his lethargy immediately, as Joe and I sprinted for our opposite posts. At last we were to get some action. Back at the rock outcrop I waited. If I examined the action of my Mauser once, I did a dozen times. I wondered if I would get buck fever.

The noise was getting closer, but the baying of the hounds had stopped except for an occasional yelp. It was beginning to get dark, and the snow started—big flakes, they were, that made for poor visibility. But I was all set for a quick snap shot if necessary.

Suddenly all noise stopped; then from out of the silence came the single sharp crack of a rifle. I looked toward Jim and Joe. They were alert but barely visible. Neither of them had shot—the report was more to the west of them. Lou or Jules. Maybe they had missed, and I might get a running shot. I knew that the deer would be getting away fast, if he could get away at all. So I waited, nerves tense. Nothing appeared. A crashing in the underbrush at my right focused my attention there. It was followed by a loud "Hello, thar" that brought my rifle down. Out from the brush came Lou, followed by Jules, who let out a loud bay as he appeared. So Jules was the baying hound. Jules carried a nice plump snowshoe rabbit. So that was the deer!

"Well, too bad you boys didn't get no shootin'. Guess they ain't no deer amovin' today." It was Lou. "Well, we might git one in the swamp on the way out," he continued, "but we gotta git agoin'. It's gittin' dark, and acomin' on to snow." And with no further word he and Jules started off. If the pace had been fast for us coming up the mountain, it was as nothing at all to the rate going down. Lou's long legs just reached out in four-foot strides. Jules, shorter geared, with legs fairly twinkling, looked like a small boy being led to the woodshed by an irate father. We picked up Jim and Joe with a curt "Come on, we gotta git." We did—and how!

But lo—a miracle. Going up that darn mountain we had the toughest kind of going. In and out of ravines, over and under logs and down timber that had pulled our corks. Now Lou had found a perfectly good wood or tote road that was a boulevard by comparison, and down which he fairly flew.

If my shoepacs had given me trouble going up, that trouble was doubled on the way back. I had absolutely no traction. I lost count of the number of times that I sat down, sometimes gracefully like an adagio dancer, but more often suddenly, and with a jar that shook my back teeth. The fast pace set by the guides, the snow, and fast-approaching darkness made it worse. We had been jobbed. I was sure of it. Somehow we reached the bottom.

The ground flattened out and I greeted it with a welcome sigh. Too soon. A little farther along, just as I'd begun to hit my stride, one foot sank down about six inches, and I nearly pitched on my face. A swamp. The rest was nightmare. Every few steps, one foot or the other would sink into the half-frozen bog until it seemed there would be no ending. There was. I fetched up suddenly against the man ahead. Forward progress had ceased. What now? Just a beaver dam to be crossed!

If you've ever crossed a beaver dam in shoepacs, in snow and darkness, carrying a rifle like a balancing pole, it's an experience you won't ever want to repeat. On one side, a pond covered with slush ice and deeper than you cared to think about; on the other side, rocks, and darkness with somewhere a brook trickling. There was little choice. Just a thorough wetting one way, and a broken leg the other. If I had any leaning at all, it was definitely toward the wetting.

Somehow we all made it safely. Lou led the way. He can have that credit for what it's worth. Jules brought up the rear—to fish us out from one side or the other, I suppose. Yes, we made it, but I wouldn't tackle it again for all the deer in the woods.

"You boys did all right," said Lou from somewhere out of the darkness ahead, as we trudged down the road toward the farmhouse, whose lights faintly shone in the distance. Nobody answered. What was there to say? What we thought was something else again. And so we got back to the farm—silently and in single file.

Our entrance into the farmhouse was made with no exuberation. Sam was playing checkers with our host. The half-emptied jug of applejack sat conveniently on the floor by his chair. "All back safe, eh? That's good," he said, as if he didn't mean it. "Any luck?"

Our silence gave him the answer. "Too bad," he continued. "Here, take a shot of apple and you'll feel better."

There was a smirk on his face that I didn't fancy. He had a look like the cat that ate the canary. Was he responsible for our ragging? I wondered, as I reached for the extended glass. But no. That couldn't be. Sam didn't know either Lou or Jules. He'd never seen them before. What was it? Something was in the air.

Then Sally stuck her head in through the kitchen doorway and announced: "Supper's gwine be ready in a shake, gemmun. Yo better git yosef cleaned up." And back she went into the kitchen with a chuckle.

The wash bench was out back of the kitchen. Jim was the first to reach it . . . a wild yell from him brought us all running.

Out back of the woodshed, strung up by his horns, was a nice plump spike-horn buck. So that was the Ethiopian.

Then the story came out. Sally had spied the young buck in the orchard behind the barn. She had told Sam, who quit his checkers and applejack long enough to borrow a rifle from our host, then meandered out and shot the buck—not a hundred yards from the house.

That's all there was to it. But it was too much for Lou and Jules. They disappeared into the darkness with a well-emphasized "GOOD NIGHT!"

Some day, though, I'm going on another deer hunt. And when I do, there'll be no climbing mountains, clambering through ravines, or crossing beaver dams. I'm just going to get a bag, and a jug—and follow Sam's system.

The First Snow of Autumn

NORMAN STRUNG

Last fall was one of the driest on record in the West. Arrowleaf crackled underfoot like rice paper, temperatures that should have hovered close to freezing hit 60 every day, and meadowlarks were still warbling in November.

It didn't feel like big-game season, and I didn't feel like hunting; but deer and elk represent sustenance as much as sport to my wife and me, and the weather patterns that caused the drought showed no signs of abating.

Two, perhaps three, times a week I would course the mountainsides that rise above our cabin and return sweaty, discouraged, and emptyhanded. The sighting of so much as a doe was cause for celebration; the woods seemed barren, boring, and without promise.

Then, one mid-November night it snowed. It was not a heavy fall, but upon awakening that morning, there was a palpable change in the air. It smelled swept-clean and new, and for the first time that season I felt the electricity of anticipation. When I struck the woods there was a new snap to my step.

I crossed my first trail at sunrise, and a half hour later I had four muley does and fawns in my sights. They were feeding beneath a big Douglas fir on a south-facing slope, and they never saw me. I left them and went over the ridge, striking the trail of a good-sized herd a mile away.

When I caught up with the deer, they were bedded down at the head of a black coulee. A doe jumped up, and led eight does and fawns by me. They passed one by one between a gap in the timber like sheep jumping a fence. A forkhorn brought up the rear, and I considered taking him, but declined. I wanted a heavier animal.

It's not the amount of early snow but its mere presence that gives the deer hunter a new advantage.

As noon approached, my legs began to tire. I turned homeward, working downslope on a gentle incline that led me over a series of terraces and through dark pine hollows. I slipped up on two other skinheads who never knew I was there and killed a four-pointer where the forest met the canyon floor.

On that one day I had seen more deer than during the previous three weeks of hard hunting. The temptation is to owe their sudden appearance to migration, but snow depths were insufficient to create the kinds of conditions in the high country that would force game into the lowlands. The deer had actually been around all season long; it just took a little snow for me to see them.

There are both physiological and psychological reasons why this happens. Most important is the effect the first snow of the year has upon a deer's perception of critical zones.

Most deer develop a sixth sense regarding how close they will allow a human to approach before becoming evasive. This critical zone amounts to a circle of terrain, and its diameter varies with the kind of cover they inhabit—the thicker the vegetation, the tighter the circle. Critical zones are largely determined by a visual limit called the forest curtain. This is the distance you and they can normally see into the forest. It is not a wall, but more like a veil, a gauzy haze of brush and trees. At the inner limit of the curtain you can see objects clearly. At its outer limit everything is obscured. However, between those two points, a sharp eye can usually pick out the ill-defined form of a deer.

Perhaps taught by the actions of older deer, or by signals of human recognition—hunters or hikers staring, pointing, yelling, making excited motions, or shooting—deer learn at what point within that curtain it is safe to watch a walking hunter without being seen. Snow, because it reflects flat light into the darkest woodland corners, and because of the contrast it provides, moves the forest curtain back. But deer don't realize that at first—remember, the animals have spent six to eight snow-free months with the woods on their side, warned by sounds and scents and hidden in dappled shadow patterns—and as a result, they stay put and are easier to spot.

Even light snow cover can short-circuit a deer's early warning system: it muffles and absorbs the sound and shock of footfalls, helps cover and diffuse human scent, and silhouettes the deer's telltale outline. All in all, the first snow of autumn brings a dramatic change in a deer's environment that the animal is unprepared to cope with and that makes it much easier to hunt.

On the other side of the prey/predator relationship, snow has a positive effect on hunters and their habits. Perhaps the visual change wrought by a blanket of white suggests to our subconscious that the slate has been wiped clean. Perhaps it is the invigorating effect of cold, crisp air. Whatever the reason, the sight of fresh snow seems to call up a new reserve of human energy and resolve. You are more eager, more confident, and as a result, you hunt harder.

Tracks play a part, too. Not so much because they lead directly to game, but because a fresh track is incontrovertible evidence that a deer passed that way recently and that it is somewhere nearby. Cutting tracks pumps you up psychologically. It keens your senses and forces all of them to focus upon one thing—serious hunting—and that edge often accounts for the difference between success and failure.

I remember one particular fall—back when I was a guide and outfitter—when the weather conditions were similar to those I experienced last year. Indian summer lingered like a curse, and except for the flurry of activity that always occurs on opening day, the meatpole behind camp held neither elk nor deer week after week.

Many times watching a football or baseball game, I have sensed a lack of spirit on the part of the losing team. It is not an identifiable fault or flaw, just a kind of negative aura that hangs over the heads of the players and the way they execute their parts. An equivalent dark cloud hung over my clients every day we went up into the mountains, an overbearing sense of "the game is already lost."

Then one morning we awakened to three inches of snow that had flurried in during the night. I can still recall stepping out of my tent to greet that day. The scattering clouds were tinted pink by the first rays of the rising sun and they wreathed the distant peaks like cotton candy. Snow clung to every branch and bough so lightly that it seemed a sharp breath would blow it all away. Suddenly it was a whole new ball game.

Like a key play that sparks a rally, you could feel a change at the breakfast table. Conversation was more animated, everyone ate with more gusto, and where clients had lingered over their coffee before, they now left the table to get suited up immediately.

The presence of tracks urged them deeper into the timber that day. They complained less about being winded and tired. They went the extra yard, and that afternoon we shot a fine muley buck, then a spike elk the next morning, and the rest of the week went well.

Although a fresh snowfall is a powerful ally, hunters do need to adapt to some of the changes it brings about. It's always a good idea to use binoculars when big-game hunting, but it's a virtual necessity when there's new snow.

Clinging to boughs, branches, and the trunks of fallen trees, cottony snow combines with the forest tones to create the illusion of an animal—the right balance and shape of white, brown, gray, or buff that suggests things like the white throat patch on a whitetail or muley, or the butt of an elk. With a pair of binoculars, these illusions can be sorted out quickly. Before I got that figured out, I spent a lot of time stalking stumps or, more embarrassing, watched the object I had positively identified as a blowdown get up and run away.

Wool pants, recommended hunting apparel because they are quiet, are a must when hunting in snow. Every other material forms ice around the cuffs, which then whiff and wheeze as you walk, warning every creature within earshot. Wool stays supple and soft.

Lastly, I have found that game learns to adjust quickly to the changes brought about by the first snow: the harder they are hunted, the sooner they extend critical zones to encompass the new forest curtain. Hunting the same area with no competition, I figure I have four days before the deer move farther back into the brush. In heavily hunted areas, I've seen them do it the second day.

When that happens, if I have the gift of time, I hang up my rifle until a truly severe storm blows in from the north, with all the physical stresses attendant to knee-deep snow and bitter cold. That kind of a snow changes game habits once again, and in other ways. But that is yet another story.

Reprinted with permission of Silvia Strung.

Hunting with Lady Luck

NORMAN STRUNG

Although the annals of outdoor literature are clogged with the sweet smell of success, if the truth be told, the great majority of big-game hunts are tinged with the scent of skunk. Whether you are after deer, antelope, or elk, when you embark on an essentially public opportunity where everyone has a fair crack at game, it is rare not to spend long, hard hours, slogging through snow and mud, before you see so much as the flicker of a white tail or the buff-colored butt of a wapiti winking at you through the timber. The Daniel Boones among us notwithstanding—and I haven't met one yet—the average hunter pays his dues for every head of big game the same way that dues are exacted in other pursuits.

It is that cold fact that runs through my mind every dim morning I set foot in the woods, yet like a carrot on a stick, or a bone suspended just out of reach of a salivating dog, I am also urged on into the dark prospects ahead by the singular memory of one incredible weekend, when *everything* went right—with one small exception.

It began normally enough: at the ranch home of an old friend, among the company of old friends and ranchers and hunters, a weekend visit for my wife and I that just happened to coincide with the end of deer season, crops in at long last, cattle weaned and in winter pastures, and more than enough hay to last until spring. It was one of those rare times when men of the soil were actually caught up with everything that needed doing, and the concept of simply relaxing being as foreign to them as a map of the New York City subway system, they were just itching to find something else to do.

Eli sized up the situation. "Hell, there's enough of us here to have a whale of a drive on Franny's Island. Let's go hunting in the morning."

Franny's Island was an impenetrable tangle of willow and wild rose in the Yellowstone River. It hid huge whitetails, or at least that's what things like tracks and scat piles suggested, but pinning them down in that jungle was like catching a greased pig in a cactus patch.

"Sounds good to me," Carroll chimed in. "We get all these guys pointed in the same direction, we might do some good."

Al, Deek, Harvy, and Harlan nodded in approval, Harlan adding, "There's been some real soakers feeding in my beet field, and I'll bet they're holin' up on Franny's Island during the day."

So the plans were made. We would meet at Carroll's house for breakfast at five, then proceed to the island. Four of us would take a stand, and four of us would drive.

A raging red sunshine was just beginning to spread across the eastern sky as we trudged across the wide, shallow slough that separated Franny's Island from the mainland. It was a hunter's morning: cold and still. Breath vapors hung in the air like smoke, and you could hear cows bellowing for their calves three miles away. Over coffee we'd divvied up the details; Eli, Carroll, Sil, and I would drive while Harvey, Harlan, Deek, and Al would take stands on the lower end of the island.

"There's an old fallen snag tree at the edge of the slough," I had said, "with a deer trail like a highway underneath it. Somebody cover it, because I'll bet that's where they'll come boiling out."

The task before the drivers was simple and straightforward: form up in a relatively straight line, try to keep track of one another, and wade through the prickly patches of primrose and willow where deer loved to bed down. If you jumped a deer and could tell its sex, you bellowed out "doe" or "buck." If you only heard its retreating hoofbeats, you yelled "deer."

Franny's Island is typical of the landforms common to moderately swift Western rivers. An overstory of cathedral-like cottonwood and box elder presides over a bottomland of brush that grows thicker and thicker as you approach its downstream limits. At first the walking was easy, the clawing brush growing in isolated patches that were seldom more than waist-high. I heard Eli yell "Doe and fawn," then laughed as the pair very nearly ran over me, their liquid eyes wide as saucers when they recognized me at a distance of about 10 feet.

Gradually the brush grew denser. The other drivers became glimpses of orange, and in places I had to duck-walk to follow the deer trails that tunneled through thickets. Soon I was on my hands and knees, the morning sun the only beacon by which I kept from becoming totally disoriented.

From that low vantage, I began to notice all those signs that point toward a very big buck very much in rut; scrapes musky with the scent of urine, pellets of scat the size of marbles, and fresh rubs at the base of the biggest willows. Then the trail led into what I can only describe as a series of deer nests; rooms formed within the densest willows by nature or intent, replete with beds in the soft duff, and a roof of twined branches that blotted out the sun and probably did a good job of shedding rain and snow. It was a storybook setting: the perfect lair for a trophy buck, yet how often before had such sign proved to be fruitless novelties?

Suddenly the brush to my right exploded. I can use no other word to describe it. It was not the sound of a deer rising to its feet and dashing off, but more like a big cock pheasant trying to rattle into the sky through bone-dry standing corn. I couldn't see what made the noise, but given the crackling and crunching that was fast receding, it had to be big. I made a wild guess, and hollered "Deer . . . deer!"

In 30 seconds, the first shot rang out, then another, and another. From their location it was obvious the buck had struck out for the tip of the island, had run into the posters, and was now heading south for the mainland. I cannot say how many shots were fired: five? six? But the last one was plainly the last, the *plop* of a hit hanging in the still air like a word of confirmation.

Next to downing a big buck of your own, the most thrilling part of a deer hunt lies in the speculation that occurs between the sure knowledge that a companion has scored and coming upon the animal. Buck, doe, points, spread, weight, circumstances surrounding the kill?

When I found my partners, they were squatting around a four-by-four whitetail. Not only did it carry a set of antlers that took your breath away, but it was also big in body, and so gray and grizzled with age, that at a distance, I mistook it for a mule deer. It had emerged from the island exactly where I predicted it would, and the buck had fallen to a shot from Al's rifle. Remarkable too, was that he had crossed the slough before expiring, obviating the need for a long drag over dry, sandy ground or a boat launched down an eight-foot bank to get him to the mainland. From where he lay, it was less than 50 yards to a farm road and a waiting pickup.

In an hour we were back at Eli's ranch. The deer weighed in at 172 pounds field-dressed, and Al was delighted. It was the biggest whitetail he'd ever shot, and he already had chosen the place in his home where he'd hang the head.

Al was done for the season, but the rest of us still had the hunting bug. After lunch, half the party elected to shoot pheasants, but Eli ushered Carroll and me into his pickup.

"The hired man says he's been seeing a real soaker of a muley over by the Sarpy Breaks. Let's take a drive over there to see if we can't find him."

The chances of finding an earmarked deer in the Sarpy Breaks are about the same as finding an honest man at a liars' convention. It is a tumbledown jackpot of juniper, sandstone cliffs, and ponderosa pine, where a big population of muleys move around like ghosts, and where there are many spots so remote that you just don't shoot a deer in them, and if you do, you bring a frying pan and eat it there. Rather, a hunt over at Sarpy is a chance to see wildlife along the way, to catch glimpses of breathtaking scenery and the glory of a prairie sunset, and maybe, just maybe, luck into a nice buck. But running down a particular deer a hired man saw? Never.

Pickup hunting is the most logical way to work out the Breaks, and by that I do not mean running down deer and shooting them from a pickup. Rather, you drive out on long points and ridges and glass the vastness below you for some sign of a bedded deer that can be stalked, or use the pickup to drop off drivers who work up coulee bottoms while you double back to pick them up, acting as both chauffeur and poster. It's the only practical way to hunt a country that is measured by square miles rather than acres.

We had driven out on two ridges when Eli brought the pickup to a halt on a long finger of land transected by a fence. Below us lay a tortured drainage of ravines and washes, buckbrush and tall timber on the north-facing slopes. To our right, just over the brow of the hill, we saw the top of an old dead snag tree. Then the tree got up and looked at us.

I cannot begin to estimate the number of deer that Eli and Carroll have shot between them. It is enough to say that they are among the coolest and most collected hunters I have known. Yet it is testimony of the nerve-jangling excitement that arises at the sight of a truly large deer in all of us that both men came totally unglued. Simultaneously, Caroll blurted, "I can't get out of the pickup truck," while Eli kept stepping in and out of the truck, hitting he ground, then jumping back in to apply the brakes. Carroll's gun had become lodged across the truck door and in that moment that demanded swift action, he couldn't figure out how to disengage it, but kept pushing against it, trying to get out. Eli simply hadn't considered putting the truck in park or shutting the engine off. Every time he stepped out, it would roll forward.

The grandfather muley watched all this with mild amusement, then was off like a shot. Carroll finally got his gun unwedged, and Eli had covered enough ground to run the pickup into the restraining fence, where it at last stopped, but Carroll groaned again, "Can't get the gun to shoot!" as he squeezed the trigger until his knuckles turned white.

This was because the bolt was open, a standard safety practice we have all observed since the day we met. By the time everyone got it all together, the muley was long gone, without a shot having been fired.

All of us have heard tales about dumb muleys: how they stop and look back and such, and it's rather true of young deer. Every trophy-class muley I have ever seen, however, was every bit as smart as a white-tail, tucking his head low and running like the wind until he had put several miles between hunter and hunted. So I greeted Eli's suggestion that we fan out and circle around the ridge with some degree of skepticism.

Then, just as the sun set and darkness began to creep over the land, I heard one shot boom out so close that I thought I felt the concussion. Eli had surprised the very same deer, which was evidently watching me from the dense shadows of a big pine. It wasn't 200 yards from where we had first seen it, and we backed the pickup right up to the carcass. It was a magnificent four-by-four, with a high rack of dark, rich chestnut. At the weighing-in ceremonies that evening, he tipped the scales at 210 pounds!

Dinner was a celebration that night. The pheasant hunters had done well, and Eli allowed as how his deer was the biggest muley to come off the ranch, he would mount it. But there were still a lot of unfilled tags, and tomorrow was the last day of deer season. "Let's try Franny's again in the morning . . ."

The possibility of downing another big buck never even crossed my mind. But given all the sign on Franny's Island, there was surely a butterbuck or two around—some tender young three- or four-point with spindly tines that would put meat in the pot.

I again elected to drive, but Sil took a stand in the same place Al had been. To my utter amazement, the morning proved a carbon copy of the day before. I put a deer up while crawling through the same bower of brush, and Sil shot it as it broke for the mainland. But this one had the uncommon decency to scale that eight-foot bank and come to rest between two logs in an attitude of repose that permitted evisceration with surgical precision. It died ten yards from the road and pickup access. Someone in the party grumbled to Sil, "Next time, can you put him in the bed of the pickup?"

The buck's headgear was every bit as massive as Al's deer, but it wore five perfect points on a side. It is something of a cliché to call a big buck a "mosshorn," but indeed, this one was. The knobby burls at the base of its antlers were green in the pocks, though I couldn't tell if it was vegetable matter deposited in the process of rubbing or if it really was moss. The deer weighed 178 pounds, and it was the largest in weight and antler size that Sil has ever shot. It adorns the wall above her office desk in our home.

Three trophies in a day and a half, deer that behaved by the books, and an extra kiss from Lady Luck that put each of them close to a pickup. It was surely the most perfect hunt in my life, marred by only one thing: I don't have the slightest idea why, nor what it was that we did right, and in the absence of such knowledge, I doubt we can make such magic ever happen again.

Reprinted with permission of Silvia Strung.

A Flintlock in the Rain

LIONEL ATWILL

I came upon the archaic world of blackpowder a year ago at a hunting trade show in Houston. I was frazzled from stalking concrete aisles and in vile humor, affronted by the trash I had seen hawked under the banner of outdoor sport: saw-toothed survival knives, SWAT team web gear, drum-fed shotguns for home defense. In a search for an exit, I came across a small booth displaying flintlock rifles that so caught my eye, I forgot my vitriol and simply stood and stared, moonstruck.

I haven't reacted to guns that way since I was 12 and spent nights under the covers reading Guns Magazine with a flashlight. Those flintlocks had full stocks of curly maple, rich brown barrels and burnished brass fittings. Their workmanship was admirable, but what distinguished them was their lines. They had a subtle grace that made them particularly pleasing. "Pick one up," said a man in a blazer, and I did. The gun balanced and pointed and held steady and swung quite perfectly. I lusted for one of those guns.

The man in the blazer smiled. He had seen this infatuation before, and he appreciated it, for he was both designer and builder of the guns. We chatted for a while and hit it off so well that when I walked away he promised to send me one of his flintlocks; I promised to take him on a deer hunt in the Adirondacks. We kept those promises. In so doing I learned a lot about blackpowder—more, certainly, than just the mechanics of the shot. The man in the blazer learned something about the big north woods. And we both learned a bit about the sound of *pffft*.

Initially, I was attracted to the simplicity of those rifles. At least I felt that way until I looked beyond lines and function to the abstruse world of contemporary blackpowder shooting. I bought a fat paperback, one of those "everything you want to know" books, and found chapters on the most esoteric subjects: pillow ticking versus linen patches; cast versus swaged balls; moose milk versus bear fat as a lubricant. The author spoke of working up to that perfect combination of powder, patch and ball with analytical techniques out of a physics lab. And the section on accoutrements read like a Revolutionary quartermaster's inventory: jags, worms, ramrods, starters, possibles bag, powderhorn, pick, primer, flint knapper—on and on. No wonder frontiersmen died early, I thought; they fell to terminal hernias from carrying so much stuff.

When the flintlock arrived, I was thoroughly intimidated, but then a letter fell out of the box, a letter from the man who made the gun. This, in part, is what it said: "I would suggest you start with a .490 ball (the rifle is 50 caliber), a .20 patch and 70 grains of FFFg blackpowder. I would take the powder charge up at five-grain increments to 100 grains. You should find a cloverleaf group somewhere in there .... Also, sometimes these guns are a little funny about cleaning, in that you may have to run a patch through about every third shot or so to make them group."

That struck me as terrifyingly simplistic. I had read so much about analyzing spent patches, chronographing balls and scouring between shots that when this man told me, in effect, to stuff it and shoot it, I panicked. What kind of patch should I use, and should it be precut or cut on the muzzle? What about lubricants? Cast balls? Swaged? Should I take the gun apart and scrub it with hot water? Would a cycle through the dishwasher help?

My reaction, you see, was typical consumer overload. I called the rifle's father. For lubricant, he used spit; worked okay for the old-timers. Wouldn't take the gun apart; no, just swab it out with cleaner and a half-dozen patches. "If had to take a rifle apart every time I shot," he said, "I'd never fire one."

Then he told me a story that summed up his feelings for flintlocks. He and a friend went on an antelope hunt in Wyoming. His friend dropped a nice buck. They tossed most of their gear into the truck, which a rancher friend was driving, and set out to gut the kill. The rancher said he had to go to town but would be back in an hour, and took off.

As soon as the truck disappeared, the antelope got up and stumbled off. In 100 yards it lay down, but when the two hunters approached, it stumbled off again. This continued until antelope and hunters had traveled nearly a mile. The animal, although seriously wounded, was showing no signs of giving up the chase.

The guy who shot the buck had his gun but not his possibles bag, the pouch in which blackpowder hunters carry gear. My friend didn't have a thing with him—except an idea. He looked in his pocket and, sure enough, in the fluff and lint was a smidgen of powder, dribbles from a powderhorn he had carried there. He pinched up the powder and dropped it down the barrel of his friend's gun. He saved just enough to prime the pan. Then he looked around the ground for a 50-caliber rock. He found one, patched it with a piece of his shirt, and rammed it home. So armed, his friend stalked the antelope and killed it—or rocked it to death.

"Always some way to get one of these guns to go off," he said. "One of the things I really like about flintlocks is that you can look at one and understand it, everything about it. A flintlock is pure, simple function, and its beauty evolved from that simplicity. That, and the fact that without too much trouble you can get one to shoot pretty good against a modern rifle, make a flintlock special."

I would soon agree. Behind my house I paced 50 yards and rigged a shooting bench out of cinderblocks and a board. With my blackpowder book and my mentor's letter beside me, I poured a measure of powder. I started the ball (swaddled in mattress ticking) down the barrel with a short dowel. When it was level with the muzzle, I cut off the excess fabric, and with that slice of the knife I traveled back 200 years, back through a hundred paintings and drawings I had seen of frontiersmen doing the same thing. The twist of the wrist that turned the knife that sliced the cloth was nearly instinctive and very pleasant. I rammed the ball home, settled into the bench, primed the pan, set the trigger, cocked the hammer, cuddled up to the stock, sought out the sites, settled on the target, sighed, and fired.

It took me 20 minutes to recover, clean up, and reload after that first shot. When I had fired two more times, I checked my target. The cloverleaf was not there. What appeared on the target was a mild case of measles. I followed my mentor's advice and increased the charge. The second group was an improvement; the third fit in a two-inch circle.

I drew out that ritual several more days, one group after another at five-grain intervals, until I pumped three balls into the target so close to one another that the cloverleaf appeared. I can't shoot that well; never have. But I did.

Suddenly the gun took on mystical proportions. Pouring the powder down the barrel and ramming the ball home and fiddling until the cloverleaf appeared put life into that rifle, made it organic to the hunt. I felt a closeness to it, too, the way one feels to a friend rather than to a tool.

That feeling of partnership (reflected, perhaps, in the frontiersman's habit of naming his gun) is one of the reasons people like blackpowder, I came to believe. A sense of history is another, the notion that a window to the past is opened through an act—loading and shooting a flintlock—that men of the 20th century can share with men of the 18th. And there is the simplicity of the sport (if we do not approach it with the contemporary need to quantify and qualify). There are no secrets in the mechanism of a flintlock, no magic of design. The flint strikes the steel frizzen, hot bits of metal shower into the prime, sparks explode upward and outward and through the touchhole, the main charge ignites, gasses expand, and a ball—or a rock—heads toward game.

The maker of that gun, Ted Hatfield, lives in St. Joseph, Missouri, a town that was once the springboard to the West. Ted's name draws smirks because Hatfield conjures up a picture of a feuding hillbilly with a pointy hat and a backyard still. Truth be told, Ted is one of those Hatfields, and although he doesn't wear a pointy hat (in public, at least), he does bottle up some smooth corn liquor in stoneware jugs (quite legally, I must add).

Ted flew from Missouri to Vermont, where I live, with an aluminum case about a flintlock long and an appetite for a north-woods white-tailed deer. I picked him up at the airport and brought him home to a pile of red meat and a bottle or two of wine the same color. That is a nice ritual on the day before a hunt.

We were out of the house at dawn. Down at the general store we met BJ, my hunting partner on many an exploit, and Davey Hicks, a pal who sells guns, buys fur, and trades in ginseng, antlers and bear gallbladders—a country commodities speculator, you might say—and headed north and west to the center of the Adirondacks.

The Adirondacks embrace six million acres in northern New York, more than a third of which is state land. Much of that public holding is designated wilderness, zoned and restricted to ensure that those qualities that make country wild are preserved—forever, one hopes. For people who have never seen the Adirondacks, it is hard to believe such unspoiled land exists so close to the urban sprawl of the East Coast. But it does. I have roamed a good bit through America's wilds, and my touchstone for wilderness, my standard for comparison, has always been the Adirondacks.

I planned to take Ted and crew into an area I had fished and hiked for many years. The trip would mean a lengthy drive and nine miles of canoeing—upstream. That plan changed the day before we left, when I spoke with a friend who told me of a new acquisition by the state, a large section of land that had never been open to public hunting, land surrounding a superb waterway—a river and lake. Loons, beavers, otters, ospreys—the indices of wilderness were there, said my friend, so I changed our plans. The drive and the paddle would be shorter. And the hunting, I believed, would be better. That decision, like most made at the 11th hour, was a trifle flawed.

We drove all morning, stopping in every hardware store we passed for last-minute necessities. We launched our canoes, chockablock with gear, in midafternoon, and paddled up a meandering river that took us and our flintlocks back in time.

The river was deep in shadows when tired backs and sore arms told us the time to camp had arrived. We headed for shore and a bureaucratic catch-22 of ponderous perplexity.

At our launch point we had read a list of administrative rules for this newly acquired state holding. Along the river and the lake, we learned, were designated camping sites for small groups and for large parties. The large-party sites had to be reserved with the local forest ranger—a difficult task, at best, since the nearest phone was 20 miles away and the forest ranger, no doubt, was out guarding the forest. The catch-22 was this: one could camp *anywhere* as long as a few requirements were met—set back from water, and similar, less arbitrary rules of common sense. Since this was late October and no other canoes were in sight, we chose to be creative in our camping and to adhere to the spirit of the law, if not to the letter. Ashore, we found a group campsite and pitched our tent.

That night we ate a hot meal of javelina chili, fired a salvo to clean the oil out of our rifles, and told the deer they were in for trouble.

Loading a flintlock at five in the morning by the light of a Coleman lantern is a ticklish feat. It is hard to tell if the powder goes down the barrel or down your boots. The temptation is to stand smack next to the light and see what you are doing, until the thought of the lantern igniting the powderhorn in your hand soaks through your coffee-laced brain. Then you step back even farther and forget if you have tossed a charge down the barrel or not. "This," says Hatfield, "is why Indians attacked at dawn."

Our plan was to still-hunt, then rendezvous at camp in midmorning. I was the last to leave, and as I zipped up the tent, I heard a deer scuffle along a ridge 40 yards from where I stood. But there was no chance of a hasty shot. I took the deer as good sign and headed toward a mountain above camp.

I hit a road right off and met another hunter. That depressed me. Company is fine for rifle season, but a flintlock cradle in the arm makes a man lust for endless space and for neighbors a lot less than few. Back in camp we decided, although we had all seen or heard deer, to move on—away from the road and the trucks and the kids camped down the river.

We packed up and paddled for the rest of the day, into the lake, into a hard-quartering wind, past loons and beavers and a shoreline this century has ignored. We came to a pretty bay at dusk. A small sign on a tree identified another forbidden group campsite, so we circled the bay looking for an alternative. Finding none, we pulled into the designated camp. A clearing set back 30 yards from the water showed signs of considerable use—old boards, trash, a partially covered dump of rusted cans. We would move if a party with a reservation came in; anyway, we had seen no other canoes on the water. We pitched the tents and settled in for the evening.

The road was still with us, we discovered at first light, but we had run out of lake and were running out of time, so there was no escape. We ate breakfast and split up to hunt.

I do not brag about my deer-hunting skills. I am mediocre at best. My talent, if I have one, is this: I have been around long enough to have distilled out the essence of deer and the ways of hunting them. I believe that deer are found where sign of deer are found. So when I found deer sign not 50 yards from the camp—scrapes and rubs and fresh tracks—I took them under advisement and kept walking, to the top of the mountain, where the sign diminished, then disappeared, but where the view was great and the exercise invigorating. Mediocrity can have its own rewards.

I got back to camp before noon. Davey was there, heating the coffee. We had a cup and told our stories and speculated on BJ's and Ted's success. Then the ranger arrived. He drove up to our camp, radios squawking, along the road we had been trying to escape for two days. He wore a big handgun on his hip and tight lips on his face. "Damn," I thought, "this guy is going to stick it to us." He did.

He ticketed us, summonses that turned into two $25 fines, and delivered a spiel about how, by all rights, he should haul us in to the local JP, 50 miles away. But since we were cooperative (we admitted our guilt immediately and said we would gladly strike camp and move), he would let us plead guilty by mail. That we had paddled the better part of a day to that camp, that no one else was on the water, that we would have been legal had we camped 20 yards away, had no effect. The ranger drove off. Davey and I were left to stew.

Then it started to rain.

When Ted and BJ returned, we told them of our run-in with the ranger. BJ stretched out in the tent; Davey and I, irritated from our scrape with the law, paced about; and Ted, bless him, just cracked a grin and wisely sauntered off to where he had seen deer sign, not 100 yards from where I had seen sign.

In two hours the big boom of a flintlock rolled through the woods. In 20 minutes Ted strutted into camp, rooster proud. We pumped him for the details. He led us to a eutrophic beaver pond. A six-point buck had ambled down to the clearing, 110 yards—honest paces from Ted's stand. He had drawn a fine bead and drilled a ball through the deer's heart.

We dragged him out, each fighting for a chance to pull, to share the glory that comes from being close to the kill. At camp we sliced the liver and fried it up fast, serving it pink and tender with sliced onions and great gurgling, sputtering slugs of Hatfield's corn whiskey. That was all so fine that we paid little attention to the increasing rain.

I started to pay attention to it in the middle of the night when the tent began to leak and puddles spread across the floor like overweight amoebae. Everyone was paying attention by morning, when our makeshift kitchen had a mud floor two inches deep and each step said *squoosh*. Too much rain to hunt. We thought about it, long and hard, even tried plastic around the locks and wax on the pan. But blackpowder sucks up moisture all too well, sucks it through the barrel and the touchhole like Lana Turner once sucked sodas at Schwab's. *Pffft*, says a flintlock in the rain.

We broke camp, loaded the canoes, and paddled out the lake and down the river. We camped again near where we had camped that first night, but at a legal site.

We tried to hunt, on and off, for another day and a half. We would load our rifles when the rain let up and slink through the heavy mist in the woods until the rain began again. Back at camp we would have a shoot-off. *Pffft*, said our rifles, time after time.

And so that hunt ended. Wet. Cold. Fraught with frustration. One deer down.

But, in truth, a lot of hunting trips balance out less successfully. Blackpowder was a special catalyst on this hunt. It added dimensions that enhanced the memories, and that is good. Maybe, too, it heightened the irritation of our run-in with the bureaucracy; that was not so good. In the balance, however, the fun and romance of blackpowder left us eager to go again, knowing the next time could be better still. We might wear skins and woollies like mountain men; it is so easy to be swept up in the romance of flintlocks that dressing up hardly sounds foolish at all. Certainly, we would stick to the wilderness where a man can camp where he chooses, as long as he obeys the less capricious laws of conscience and good sense.

And like a lot of pioneers who listened to their flintlocks go *pffft* as arrows flew over their heads, we would pray for blue skies, dry air and no rain.

Mobley Pond

DAVID FOSTER

Sixty million years ago, give or take five or ten million, some theorists believe the Earth either struck a small comet or passed close enough to it to create a massive meteor storm that struck most of what is today the Southeastern coast, leaving strangely shaped craters from the coastal lands of Georgia all the way to Nebraska. Or, some 175 thousand years ago, give or take five or ten thousand, hydrologic, soil and geological conditions along the same path shifted and flowed in such a way as to cause the same effect. Either way, what we got was some 500,000 wetlands from the size of backyard bathing pools to 24,000-acre behemoth swamps called Carolina bays, named not for the water that may or may not stand or have stood within them but for the bay trees that often line them, especially in the South. What makes Carolina bays unique—and mysterious, not to mention controversial—is that they are shaped like teardrops, the fat end of the tear facing southeast.

From this tower stand I can peer out across one of the largest of these tears, though not one of the best known as it sits on private land. Locally, this Carolina Bay is called Mobley Pond, named for the man who first tried to tame it more than two centuries ago. Or maybe somebody else. Depends on which local lore you choose to believe, just as its origin depends on which scientific theory you care to believe. Being a fellow who loves a good fireworks display, I go with the comet.

Mobley Pond isn't a pond, not in the way you think of a pond: a depression full of green water, lined with cattails, shallow at the back where the basses and other sunfishes congregate to make their lives and provide you sport. In fact, nowhere in Mobley Pond will you find standing water, but it is home to monster alligators, not to mention panfish, coyotes, fox, rabbits (cottontails and their larger cousins, the swamp rabbits), weasels, opossums, bobcats, the late-coming armadillo, songbirds too numerous to enumerate in this space, wild turkey, ducks, geese, bobwhite quail, mourning doves, wild hogs and deer, not to mention for a fleeting time during late December and early January, woodcock.

But it is the deer that bring most folks to ask for an invite back. Big-racked bruisers, the kind that make a hunter's pulse race when seen from a distance; close enough to shoot, they can give even the veteran hunter a bad case of gun-quivering, mirage-making buck fever.

That kind of deer. And shooting one looks as though it would be so easy. Mobley Pond isn't home to a tree larger than a scrub. Not one, except for the alders and bays that line the old alligator-inhabited drainage canals and the odd pine sports growing short in wet loamy soil where the aquifer kisses the surface. It is just approximately five square miles of natural grasses and boggy black dirt, crisscrossed by deep-rutted deer and hog trails and 155-year-old canals dug by W. W. Starke, looking to turn a swamp into cropland. Except at the edges, none of these labors amounted to much. And nobody's tried to tame it since.

Interesting thing, that lack of trees. Early histories speak of some large cypress, but those are long gone. Instead, as you sit in this tower you see almost a mile of waist-high brown grasses and briar heads to the front, with a few agricultural fields creeping tentatively into the crater from the sides. Behind is a 40-foot "hill" that rings the entire crater/sink with tall hardwoods and, at the top, massive pines, where the wet black loamy soil ends and turns mostly to sand.

Hence, the plethora of wildlife. There is vastly more cover, feed and browse than a casual tourist could ever comprehend, from wild grasses and the shoots thereof to the weeds and seeds and berries that grow with them. Normally you hunt deer at Mobley Pond two ways: from stands in the fields above when the deer come out to feed in the green patches, and from stands in the pond itself when they pass into and out of the pond to the same green patches. More does are taken here every year than at any other location on the farm. Bucks, however, are, as they say in the nearby town of Girard, a whole 'nother story.

It's enough to drive you crazy. Hunting in Georgia, even in a bean field, isn't really all that much of a long-distance project; down in the forests and swamps, shooting is so close that, unless you just love your rifle so much you can't do without it, a shotgun is often a much better tool. But in Mobley Pond, the bucks know the routine much better than the humans, and they prove it almost every season.

It is true, I suppose, that deer seldom look up, hence our love for stands. But with only that waist-high grass to impede vision for up to half a mile, it's easy from a deer's field of view to see a stand and the fellow wriggling around in it from a long way off. Second, the agricultural ditches are three to five feet below the waist-high grass, which means the ten- to 14-pointer you're looking for can walk past fewer than 50 feet from the best setup and the hunter will never know he was ever closer than New York. Third, and the cruelest deer trick of all, is seeing through your binoculars a huge rack attached to a hidden body making its way nonchalantly through the grasses, always—always—600 or more yards distant. This brings on the commonly heard whine back at camp: "Oh, Lord, you should have seen . . ."

Four years ago, a hunter took a very nice ten-pointer in one of the green patches at the pond. Another shot one at dusk seven years ago along the very edge of the wild grasses. An eight-pointer fell at dawn three years ago in a fallow cornfield. And that was the end of big bucks after 15 years of hunting the pond for one week every year. You can almost hear that old big-racked Boone-and-Crockett champion laughing from the bottom of a canal. No, you can hear him.

On the other hand, you come to appreciate his victory over our high-tech tools. You can bet the Native Americans had only slightly better luck, unless they burned the grasses and forced the deer out, and the early settlers, once the canals went in during that fruitless battle against Mother Nature, probably didn't fare much better than us. Mobley Pond has fought the plow, pollution and well-armed men. It has protected its wildlife well without the help of a government or the first tree hugger.

So another season comes around and again it all looks so easy, though you know come Sunday the chances of having Old Mose in the cooler are much smaller than not. But you love the red sunrise over Mobley Pond. Maybe you ponder on that comet while glassing the seemingly empty, yet, you know, so full terrain. Here the animals win almost every time, even against you. But ask yourself: Does it really get any better than this?

As Near to Perfect

BOB BUTZ

Given the choice between a plane trip and a road trip, I'll always hit the road. There's something liberating about throwing all your belongings into the back of a pickup and driving day and night to some faraway spot on the horizon.

Still fresh in my mind are those echoings of Kerouac and those long, lazy summers when my half-baked college friends and I left responsibility behind for the uninhibited freedom and possibility we found on the road.

Even though I work for a living now and have what my boss calls *culpability*, I still have chronic, fevered bouts with restlessness; no doubt a consequence of all those summer road trips, all those unabated meanderings fostered in my college years.

But perhaps I've always been a vagabond and a heathen at heart, for truthfully that urge to roam has always been there. It's been a chronic infection that comes in waves that ebb and flow with the changing of seasons. This, of course, makes me think that my propensity for wandering is rooted in some primitive instinct held over from the days when human beings were joined together in nomadic tribes that hunted, gathered, and moved over the land with the animals.

At least, that's my excuse anyway.

For another one of my shortcomings is that I just happen to be a hunter—a bowhunter. And to hell with the social implications and political correctness of it all; my desire to sneak around the woods with a bow in my hand is like an itch I gotta—yes, *gotta*—scratch. My need to move is insatiable sometimes. It's a hunger that grumbles in my belly and makes my bones ache, a voice in my head like a siren's song that calls me out into the fields and forests in the fall.

A note came over the fax machine early last November (neighboring tribes don't use smoke signals anymore). It said: *Bob, the rut is on. Call me.* It wasn't signed or anything, but the Mahaska Custom Bow Company letterhead told me the note was from my friend Kent Ostrem.

The whitetail rut was just beginning to peak down in southeast Iowa. According to Kent, who sounded downright giddy over the phone, the bucks were madly running scrapelines. According to Kent, the river bottom where he hunted was "an absolute zoo," what with all the bucks around chasing does. And one particular buck—a four by four that Kent said was *gargantuan*—got particular mention for having twice been in bow range that week alone.

I suspected from the obvious omission of any further details that a miss or two had probably occurred. Kent was calling for reinforcements, a call I was all too eager to answer. By the end of the conversation I was already plotting my temporary escape from the nine-to-five.

It was not so much the story of the big buck that helped me make up my mind (although it certainly didn't hurt). It was Kent's breathless enthusiasm, his bewilderment at seeing so much chaos in the woods. "I've never seen so many deer," he kept saying. "They're running around like rabbits." Morning, afternoon, and evening. Every time he got on stand. In the past week, Kent had seen close to a dozen bucks. "All shooters," he said, "plus that big boy who's been givin' me fits."

Kent's never been one to exaggerate the details. But the whole thing sounded easy, as if getting a shot at a deer would be incidental to simply getting my butt down to Oskaloosa by daybreak Saturday morning.

Now I appreciate a *hard* hunt just as much as the next guy—perhaps even more so. In fact, most of my hunts where the longbow is involved tend to fall into that category (most would be dubbed *unsuccessful,* too, but that is another matter). By design or happenstance, I seem to walk more miles, miss more shots, and get myself into more wild predicaments than other hunters prowling the woods with more high-tech weaponry. Call it a lack of efficiency or downright foolishness. Because of it, I seem to eat up more vacation days than anyone else back home in the office (doing things like missing your boat and getting marooned on a small island in Alaska for an extended period of time has a way of really cutting into your personal days—but again, that's another story.)

My motives then for sneaking out of the office for a couple days without telling anyone were made even more lecherous by my want of an easy hunt. Though I relished the idea of watching many thick-necked, rut-crazed whitetail bucks tearing through the woods with reckless abandoned, the fact remains: It had been a very lean year. The Gods had not been good to me, you might say, which simply meant my freezer was near empty and I longed to pack it full of prime, Iowayan venison.

I being a sneak, yes: my boss was away on business and my girlfriend was down in Grand Rapids for a few days doing something with computers I don't understand. The plan was to get down to Kent's by Friday evening, hunt all day Saturday and Sunday morning, if need be. If I played it right I'd be home by Sunday afternoon with nobody the wiser. And if I got caught . . . well, there's an old saying: "It's always easier to beg for forgiveness than ask for permission."

Back in college, the provisions that went into any roadtrip consisted of simple amenities such as an ample supply of beef jerky, pork rinds, and beer. Even now I have a hard time leaving one of those all night convenience stores without a bag of chips, a pack of cheap cigars, or one of those big bottles of Crazy Horse in hand.

However, it was fourteen hours to Oskaloosa from my tiny rat-shit cabin in northern Michigan, so granola bars and a big cup of coffee were on order that morning.

I left a note on the kitchen table should my girlfriend come home early (she, as always, would understand) and a cryptic message on the answering machine at work. The phone at the office has a crackling-bad connection somewhere, made even worse if you finger the cord when you talk. Its come in handy when talking with salesman or irate customers and it proved its worth again; if you took up a handful of the cord and twirled it around, the cracks and whines that came out of the receiver were quite enough to make all of my erroneous babble completely undecipherable.

After packing my longbow, tube full of arrows, and a change of clothes, I was off. The drive itself passed like a dream. I rode most of the way with the radio turned off and the window rolled partway down.

Because of suicidal deer and the reputation of small town Iowa police, Kent warned me to keep the pedal off the floorboard after turning off 180. And it was a good thing, too, as I avoided one speed trap in Montezuma and a small spike buck that jumped up onto the road and froze up in my headlight five miles outside Oskaloosa. Still, I was standing at Kent's door at one hour under time.

Kent Ostrem founded Mahaska Custom Bows in his basement almost a decade ago, back when competent traditional bow makers were scarce. He started by making longbows and recurves for himself and friends. But the operation grew. The orders started coming in. So many, in fact, that he up and quit his regular job and build a little shop out behind his garage.

It's where I found him that night, working late as always. Kent came to the door covered with sawdust and wearing a thing that looked like a gas mask and goggles. He shook my hand and said something inaudible before pulling the mask down and smiling. "Hey Bob. C'mon in," he said. Then, looking outside, "What the hell time is it?"

I told him it was eight and he said, "Cripes. Where'd the day go, huh?"

He had taken my hand upon opening the door, and hadn't let go until I was standing inside. "Be done in a minute here. Just hold on." He fixed the mask on his face then and kicked on the belt sander. In his other hand was a bow—always a bow. He bent over the machine, and while he labored away over the drone of the thing I stood there looking around.

The shop was small, like a hermit's den, dusty and smelling of sawdust. Wood and machines for making bows occupied every inch of the place. Bows hung from clasps on the ceiling, all in various stages of production. Longbows, recurves, and flatbows. Everyone with a tag made out in black marker with names of bowhunters as faraway as Australia and Spain.

Kent shut off the sander and fingered the tips of the bow he'd been working. He was transfixed for a moment, turning the bow this way and that in the light. Then he said something aloud, but to no one in particular; something that was garbled what with the respirator on his face. I imagined for a moment him spending his days like that—alone. Airing his every thought in that tiny room. He walked over to me still holding the bow—scrutinizing it—and finally, handing it over for a look.

"Perfect, huh?" he said, to which I soon agreed.

Like all of Kent's work this bow was exquisite. Its gently curving limbs, smooth and elegant. There is a beauty in a finely crafted bow, just as there is beauty in the painting and the sculpture and the written word. But the bow is a living art, one that can never be fully be realized unless used as the maker intended. It's the difference between reading a Shakespearean play and watching one acted out on stage.

Kent had gone from the room, walked across the yard to the house, and returned a moment later with a six-pack of beer. "Long day," he said. He scrutinized the bow I was holding one last time before fixing the corresponding tag back on the riser and placing it gently on the workbench.

His is akin to an artist life, one totally enveloped by his devotion. In fact, whenever Kent and I get together we rarely talk of anything other than bows and arrows and hunting. We like retelling the same old stories, tales of animals we've killed and shots we've missed. We laugh a lot. But admittedly, it's mostly caveman talk—banter that's best shared in the firelight or off in some ramshackle hunting cabin where men can still talk like men.

That late night spent in dull light of Kent's little shop, we talked as we always did—as I hope we always will. Kent, damn near old enough to be my father, turned giddy as a teenage retelling the events of the previous week. "That big buck," he said. "God! What a whopper." He stretched out his hands to show me the size of the rack. Then he pitched back in his chair and stared at something on the wall. Remembering.

"Man, I feel good about tomorrow," he said. "Real good."

Though my friend is a little unorthodox when it comes to bowhunting, it's hard to debate his proficiency at taking deer. Throughout the years I've known him, he's never gone a year without bringing home a whitetail. Almost all of them have been bucks, and everyone was taking at close range on the ground. Kent was never that fond of heights; therefore, he makes it a point to stay out of the trees. He also doesn't believe in using scents or lures, he doesn't wear camo, and if the impulse strikes he's not at all worried about smoking a cigarette or two while sitting on stand—that is, of course, as long as the wind is right.

He's one of those guys who make deer hunting look remarkably simple. Therefore, hunting with Kent has always been something of an education, not so much in whitetail habits and habitat (Kent keeps all this knowledge to himself), but rather in what a bowhunter can get away with while hunting for whitetail deer.

We didn't leave the house the next morning until the civilized hour of 7:00 a.m. Though a bit concerned by this, I said nothing. Just as I said nothing when Kent climbed into my truck and started smoking one cigarette after another. Clad in rubber boots, blue jeans, sock hat, and a brown Filson cape coat, Kent looked more like an old trapper than a bowhunter.

We drove out of town, crossed a bridge over a river named Skunk, then took a hard turn onto a dirt road that we followed until Kent pointed a cigarette out over the big fields toward a long line of trees on the horizon. "That's where we'll be hunting," he said.

The sun had only just begun rising over the trees. And in the gray light I could see for the first time how vast the land was here. The field, which a month ago had been covered with corn, was now barren and unbroken save for that single line of trees in the distance.

Kent pointed his cigarette again at an old rusty gate at the side of the road. "Here she is," he said.

We came to a stop and he climbed out of the cab and fumbled with the lock, checking with a breath of cigarette smoke the direction of the wind, which he watched ride away on the breeze. The gate finally opened, he gave me a smile and a thumbs up when I passed.

For somebody used to hunting the rolling hills and cedar swamps of Michigan, this wide-open country seemed like grossly inadequate deer cover to me. With the cropland now harvested, there was nothing left but the cover along the river bottom. The whole place was like one big natural funnel, exactly what all those deer hunting experts always tell you to look for. It explained our leisurely start; bumble around in the dark in a place like this and you'd easily spook every deer in the woods.

With light upon us, however, we fast parked the truck and ducked into the woods. A deer trail along the muddy bank of the Skunk made for easy walking. Around every bend, we scared up mallards and buffleheads lounging in the muddy backwater sloughs. Each time we hunkered down to watch. Geese sounded somewhere above us. And I looked for them, but the canopy was too dense overhead to see.

Everywhere were these scraggly locust trees and waist-high grass the color of ripe wheat. The grass was covered with in a hoarfrost that soaked my wool pants clean through before we finally stopped and knelt down on the edge of that big opening in the trees. Kent whispered something about seeing the big buck here just the other day. He spread his hand, the one without the bow in it, and put it up to his head to imitate an antler. Then he whispered something else about this being a good spot and that I might want to consider sitting here.

Two big scrapes marked the far side of the clearing and the ground was crisscrossed and trampled with tracks. Though I wish I could say that a little more scouting than this initial observation went into my deciding to wait out the morning here, but there wasn't.

I made a nest down in the grass on the high bank of the river. But ten minutes into sitting there I got to thinking that the grass would never been enough to break my silhouette if any deer did happen to amble by. Farther back in the woods I spotted a tangle of vines, tree limbs, and stumps that looked more inviting. I collected my things and repositioned here, again clearing a space to hunker down. Yet when I finally got situated I found that, although this new place offered enough cover to break my outline, there was barely enough room to draw my bow.

Things had quieted down and I got to thinking how silly and stupid I had been for moving. As it was, unless I held the bow practically horizontal, I could not even pull it partway back without the limbs hitting or scraping up against something. If any deer did come into the clearing to check those scrapes, the only shot I'd have now looked better than twenty paces, which was a long one for me.

But I sat there for a little while more, afraid to move for everything had fallen so still. There came the calling of more geese overhead and a cock pheasant sounding off somewhere out in the stubble fields across the river. I watched for sometime a fox squirrel, an enormous red and brown one, up in the crooked limbs of a pin oak tree. And then I saw the buck working his way through the tall grass and brush.

Head down, he plodded out into the clearing toward me. It was not the big-racked buck Kent had been seeing all week. But I guess it very well could have been, as I only looked at his antlers long enough to see that he had them. There in the sunlight he was beautiful, a soft color of chestnut in the sun. And I knew right away that I was going to kill him.

As awkward a shot as it was, I felt somehow disconnected from it when it all finally came to pass. The buck took off across the opening, my arrow deep in his chest and a big splash of blood trailing down over his shoulder and leg. But he never made it to the trees.

There was no need to sit and wait, no time to replay what had just happened, or second-guess the shot. That buck was dead, and lying there in sunlight in the open like that I remember thinking he looked as dead as anything I had ever seen. I stood and walked over to where he lay. And though I'm almost always in somewhat of a haze at this moment—the moment when the hunt has ended and the magic of the moment is realized—this time I remember feeling as detached as an executioner.

I don't think it's possible to have too clean a kill when bowhunting, but too clean a hunt, yes. The shot I'd made was as near to perfect as any I have ever made, and I'm sure some would probably say that the events of the hunt seemed pretty much perfect, too. After all, I had not even been on stand fifteen minutes—in fact, I had not been in Iowa more than fifteen hours—and already I was standing over a deer.

But frankly, I felt as if I had cheated somehow.

Yet the feeling abated when I set about the field dressing chores. Whereas the killing of the buck seemed so quick and easy as to not be believed, there was no mistaking the reality of its blood, the warmth and stickiness of it on my fingers, and the smell of bowel and gut so heavy in the air that I could almost taste it going down.

I dragged the deer back to our meeting place, liking the feel of the rope digging into my shoulder and the subtle burn in my legs coming up. Noticing myself breathing heavy again, for the first time in months, I thought how frantic I had become—not simply to kill a deer—but to have again the very feeling that came over then. The weight of the tiny buck was real. And I suppose I come all this way to be reminded of that—to feel the weight—and in the knowing realized once again that there is still another life outside my ordinary one, and that I, along with most men, do indeed live what Thoreau called lives of quiet desperation.

The Third Deer

BOB BUTZ

I believed in deer long before I'd ever actually seen one. Looking back, it is not a stretch to say that I grew up revering them as something sacred. To me, a deer was the incarnation of God albeit one that left its tracks and sign upon the earth and occasionally came out from behind the curtain of brush to reveal something in its teaching.

My memory is sharp as glass recalling the first deer. It passed my hiding place by way of happenstance. After school I would often hide inside the massive trunk of a tree killed by lightning. I'd squeeze into that damp and darkened chamber through a gaping hole between the roots. I recall the footfalls in the leaves, held my breath thinking surely I'd been followed. Looking back on it now, my hiding place was little more than a rotted old stump, cut it in half so that a couple feet over my head was splintered and open to the sun. Through a knothole I spied the deer browsing down the trail, closer. I reached my arm through a woodpecker hole hoping to sweep my fingers over her back, hoping to touch as she craned he neck picking crabapple blossoms. But then she snorted and was gone.

Growing up, I spent a lot of time wondering about deer. The gnarly black locust swamp, my childhood haunt, had its share of raccoons, opossums, skunks, and squirrels. Cottontail rabbits and a few whitetail deer. I loved all those creatures, but the deer I found most fascinating. Perhaps it was their size and the fact that the swamp was so small. Deer seemed as big as cows, yet they lived in the shadows like rabbits. Until that first deer, all I ever saw were tracks and piles of their dropping like shiny black pearls.

The sign, those black heart-shaped tracks, deepened for me the mystery of deer. The tracks lent a silent record of their passages, their trails left for me to decipher like some forgotten language more mystifying than Egyptian hieroglyphics or the cave paintings at Lascaux.

I killed a deer when I was fourteen; a doe that took my arrow and came up kicking like a bronco. I remember the air, so cold, the zip of the arrow piercing her ribs, and the white vapor puffed from the gory hole. She took a little hop and the smoke, a twirling, wispy trail like from a candle blow out streamed upward. Her breath had quickened a little, too, so that all around was a fog and the pattering of blood spilling onto the leaves.

She bolted away, taking wonderful, high, bounding leaps. I remember she appeared flying until in midair she died and fell a skidding crash, legs tangled in a mass of thorny bushes and old logs.

I used to believe that if I lived good and honest and true that I could make deer appear simply by closing my eyes and filling my head with images of them. I still think there's something to this, even though on the surface it sounds absurd.

To me, deer were a making of wind and light, a vestige of the shadows in the morning and the sound of cawing crows. In the woods, every stick that snapped, every rustle of leaves, carried the promise of deer. Deer were everywhere and all around me. And if I concentrated hard enough on trying to draw the elements together, if I opened my heart and became the vessel, deer would appear seemingly out of nowhere, conjured as if by magic.

It happened this way often enough that I believed the power some kind of gift. But then I killed a deer, thinking the killing would lend proof to my power, my understanding. I killed to make their wildness my own. Following her blood, finding her dead. In her ebony eye my reflection. I ran my hand over her walnut colored hide, the rounded belly, the putrid smell and searing heat of her twisted insides. Her blood on my hands. I peeled the hide away, marveling at the corded muscles under the fur intertwined, and in doing so parted some of the mystery. But not all. Something remained, something wild and untouchable. The third deer, a buck, I conjured out of the morning mist, a buck whose antlers appeared a mass of tangled, jagged, ivory-tipped tines. His shoulder and flank creased with muscle. He stopped on the edge of my range and pawed at the ground, then raised his head to sniff the air and those antlers fell across his back like those of a bugling bull elk.

I remember the buck turning and the arrow streaking along its path. The white feathers flashed on his side. The arrow thumped and cracked as if striking bone, then disappeared, and the buck wheeled around and was gone, and nothing moved for a long time after that.

When the fog finally burned away, I fully expected to see the deer—my deer—lying there dead somewhere in the valley below, revealed to me with the morning mist like a gift. But he was not there, nor was there any sign of him in the place where he had been standing. The woods had changed so much since the half-light that I thought maybe I was standing in the wrong place. But then I saw the black Earth, the overturned leaves and the fresh dirt kicked up along the path the buck had fled. Then I saw my arrow, stuck in a tiny sapling with not a speck of blood on the shaft.

There was nothing in that moment but silence, a swift and passing silence. And it's that silence I remember most and how it seemed the only thing that belonged to me.

The Ghost Buck of Chitlin Creek

J. WAYNE FEARS

The narrow valley Chitlin Creek flowed through was not known for producing trophy bucks. In fact, the area didn't have a large deer population, and few hunters ever ventured into the jungle-like tangle of small trees, vines, and brush covering the valley and surrounding slopes.

A homestead had once occupied the little out-of-the-way valley, but the Great Depression had doomed the small farm. Following that era, the valley had grown up in pine trees, but a few years ago the lumber company that owned the land had cut all the pines, leaving nothing but scrub hardwoods and brush. It simply wasn't the kind of place that keeps whitetail deer hunters awake at night.

I discovered Chitlin Creek quite by accident. I had spent two hot days in August scouting some nearby land owned by the lumber company, trying to find a good area to hunt whitetails the coming season. Deer sign was scarce, and it was obvious why few hunters bothered to hunt there.

Early the third morning of my scouting trip, I sat in front of my tent and studied a topographical map of the area. Chitlin Creek caught my attention, but not for deer hunting; I had an ultralight spinning outfit in my truck, and I thought a few fish would be good for dinner.

After a third fruitless day of scouting, I decided to forget this area for deer hunting and got my rod and reel to catch some fish. Chitlin Creek, with its banks of low-growing brush, wasn't a scenic place, but the water was swift, clean, and refreshingly cool on a hot afternoon. It was ideal for wade fishing.

I hadn't been fishing long when I waded around a bend and saw another fisherman working a pool with a cane pole. He grinned when he saw me and motioned me to come up to the pool.

He was a slim, slightly bent fellow of at least 75 years. His wading attire was faded blue denim overalls and an old pair of tennis shoes. A tomato can of worms protruded from one of his pockets.

With an elfin twinkle in his eyes, he watched me without speaking until I reached his side. "I never seed anyone in hare a'fore," he finally spoke. I explained this was my first time and that I had given up on deer scouting and decided to fish to help ease my disappointment.

"Thar's a big buck down the creek a little ways, hangs out round the ol' Hixon place. Must be eight points or bet'r," he confided.

"Do you see him often?" I queried.

"Sorta," my new friend grinned. "Sometimes I think I see 'im, and the next second he's gone. Leaves me scratch'n my head, he does. But I got one good look at him last August, I believe it was. I turned a bend in the creek and thar he was, standing in the creek. Just stood and looked at me, not mor'n ten yards, for nigh on to a minute, then high-tailed it."

Now I was really interested. "Where would you suggest I look for a sign?" I asked.

He pointed a bony finger down the creek. "The ol' Hixon homestead is about 200 yards down the creek. The cabin was on the left bank. The smokehouse was ten yards behind the cabin. Not much left of neither one, but ye can tell the cabin by the ol' chimney. Whar the smokehouse was thar's only a dug-out spot whar the Ghost Buck—that's what I call him—gets his'n salt."

He continued, "Ol' Ghost Buck is plenty smart. Ye won't find many tracks. He only crosses the creek at gravel bars so he won't leave tracks."

I thanked the old angler and fished my way back toward the truck.

Early the next morning I was standing next to the rock chimney that had once served the Hixon cabin. The site of the smokehouse in the honeysuckle vines behind the cabin was just as the old man had described, a well-used salt lick. The Hixons would be surprised to know the same salt that kept their hams and bacon from spoiling was now being used by deer.

The honeysuckle offered the buck plenty of food, the thick vegetation gave him cover, water was plentiful, and no one ever hunted the little valley. What a perfect hideaway for a buck. I would return in the fall.

The area around the Chitlin Creek homestead would be ideal for handgun hunting. The thick cover made long shots impossible, and it made traveling or stalking with a long-barreled gun a difficult chore.

After much consideration, I elected to hunt there with my Remington XP-100 bolt-action, single-shot handgun. It is a favorite brush gun of mine due to its short, 14½-inch barrel and light weight; with scope, it weights only a little over five pounds. Its nylon stock is virtually indestructible, so I knew it could take the abuse of crawling through thick brush.

Another reason I chose my XP-100 is that is chambered in .35 Remington. Firing Remington 200-grain soft point Core-Lokt ammunition, this caliber is a sledgehammer on big whitetail bucks at ranges out to 150 yards.

To be equipped for any range shot the Chitlin Creek hunt might present, I mounted a Simmons 2.5-7x28 handgun scope on the XP-100 using a Burris mounting system.

The handgun, scope, and load combination proved to be an accurate team on the range. From a sand-bag rest at 100 yards, the 200-grain load printed one and half to two-inch groups. Not only did I practice from the bench, but I spent several afternoon practicing with the handgun in field positions, such as bracing on the side of a small tree. I didn't want poor marksmanship to keep me from taking the buck.

Many evenings that fall were spent studying topographical maps and aerial photographs of the Chitlin Creek area. I got to know the terrain as best one can with a limited amount of time on the property. I wanted to be ready when opening morning rolled around.

Long before daylight on the first day of the whitetail season, I groped my way to a hillside that rose behind the homestead site. I found an opening on the slope and sat down to await dawn.

As the pink fingers of light in the east gave way to a rising sun, I realized I could see no more than 20 yards in any direction. I wasn't sure I could find a spot with more visibility in the thick tangle without making too much noise, so I stayed on the cold slope for most of the morning. All I saw were two gray squirrels playing in a distant red oak tree.

By midday I had concluded that I must get to know the area much better; just sitting in the woods was not the way to hunt this buck. I spent most of the afternoon scouting the area slowly and quietly. There was little sign to be found, but I did see old rubs on small trees near the old home site. Along the creek, true to the angler's word, I found deer tracks, but only on gravel bars. These were difficult tracks to locate. It was almost as though the buck knew that someone would be trying to track him.

Late that evening I took a stand on one of the creek crossings. On a slight rise overlooking the crossings grew a thick stand of wild plum and gum saplings. I backed into those bushes and sat where I could see the creek crossing and the approach from both sides.

As the sun slipped below the western horizon, the air in the damp valley grew colder. My hopes began to fade. Suddenly I spotted a movement to the left of the stream. I eased the XP-100 up on my knee and into a ready position. A doe eased out and slowly, cautiously waded the creek. I was enjoying watching her when I saw a second deer emerge along the same route. There stood the Ghost Buck. My heart raced as I watched the buck standing looking at the doe that was disappearing into the brush on the opposite side of the creek.

I took my eyes off the buck just long enough to spot a gum sapling nearby that I could ease the handgun up to for a shooting rest. When I moved my eyes back up to where the buck had stood, he was gone. Without a sound. No wonder the old man called him a Ghost Buck.

The next morning I returned to the same stand in the sapling thicket, but my only reward was to watch a red fox pass by with a cottontail rabbit in its mouth.

At lunch I walked back to the old homestead site to explore its remains and eat my lunch. As I was sitting next to the chimney thinking what a peaceful place this must have been to live, I was curious about where the barn might have been located. It had to be nearby. I began to walk around the house site in ever-widening circles, and down the little valley some 150 yards from the chimney, I found the remains of an old fence. There, on a fence post, hung the metal rim of a wagon wheel. I pushed my way through a thick growth of honeysuckle and poplar saplings to find a somewhat open area that was thinly forested in old apple and pear trees. I had stumbled upon the homestead orchard. Several small pine trees grew among the fruit trees, and some of the pines were freshly rubbed. I felt a rush of excitement!

Further scouting around the old orchard revealed five large scrapes along the edge of the opening. Each scrape was freshly pawed with a recently broken limb handing over it. I had found the Ghost Buck's honeymoon suite. Now to decide how to hunt it.

The orchard was at least two acres in size. When I tried several ground blind sites, my vision was blocked by low-growing vegetation. I needed to be in an elevated blind. Several large oaks grew around the edges, a couple in great locations to see all five of the scrapes, but none with low-growing limbs that could be climbed.

Back in camp in my truck was a new portable ladder stand. I could mount the ten-foot ladder stand and see the entire opening.

The remainder of the day was spent walking back to camp and packing the stand back into the old orchard at Chitlin Creek. By the time I had the stand in place, it was dark.

Two hours before daylight the next morning, I was on my way to the stand. It was the expectation of a successful hunt that carried me through the thick brush in the darkness of that cold, pre-dawn morning.

As the first light appeared, I checked out the padded guard rail on the stand. It made a perfect rest for the XP-100, and I could get a clear shot at many areas in the old orchard. Most importantly, I would be able to see all five scrapes.

With the growing light came a fog that gave the opening an unearthly appearance. I hoped the fog would burn off quickly. Within an hour it abruptly disappeared, and there, to my surprise, lay a doe near one of the scrapes. She seemed to be waiting for the Ghost Buck to appear. Occasionally she would look around as though expecting company at any time.

The morning advanced and no buck appeared. I became concerned that in my haste to put up a stand, I may have unknowingly scared the buck. As I sat in the stand thinking of what all could have gone wrong, I heard a faint grunt off at a distance. I couldn't tell which direction the sound came from. The doe heard it, too, and she looked into the thick woods behind her. Then came two loud grunts. At this, the doe jumped up and ran across the old orchard, passing almost directly under my stand. I sat the XP-100 on the padded guard rail and watched the woods line near where the doe had been lying.

Without a sound, the buck emerged, his nose in the air and his lips curled back. I pushed the safety off and found the buck's shoulder in the scope. As he turned back toward the thick cover, I squeezed the trigger. The handgun jumped in my hand, and I heard the bullet hit home. The Ghost Buck went down.

It took me three hours to get the buck to a point where I could get my truck to it. As I loaded the nice eight-pointer, the old fisherman walked up with his short cane pole on his shoulder.

"I see ye got him, Sonny," he grinned. "Thought ye might."

He paused, then continued. "Did I tell ye about the big ten-pointer I've been seeing a little further down the creek at the ol' Taylor place? He's sort of a Ghost Buck, too."

"Let's sit down and talk," I said to my friend. He had my full attention.

Reprinted with permission of the author. The author's many books are available on his website: www.jwaynefears.com

Chloe's First Buck

GREG RODRIGUEZ

My daughter Chloe and I gathered our gear for the long walk to the blind. As we walked, she whispered excitedly the whole time, seemingly oblivious, or perhaps not caring, that this would be her last chance to take her first buck before we had to leave the ranch. Her excitement was contagious, and my fear of going home empty-handed was quickly replaced by pride in her patience and understanding.

"Don't worry, Daddy. We'll get one. And even if we don't, I had a great time just being with you."

I grabbed her hand and smiled, trying to keep it together. We walked the last few yards in silence. The gravity of the moment subsided when we got to the blind and the preparation began. The placement of the rifle, ear muffs, juice boxes, and coloring books was paramount. Hunting with a five-year-old requires careful planning and patience. Heck, I couldn't believe she hunted with me for two whole days without a complaint, despite the fact that our hunt, while a great success on so many levels, had yielded no buck.

Opportunities were presented and lost due to fickle alarm clocks, coughing brothers, and a clumsy dad, but Chloe never lost her cool. Yes, Daddy, the Great White Hunter, was having a remarkable outing. Thank goodness Chloe was not one of my paying clients.

We had fun waiting for a buck to appear. We laughed at the squirrels' acrobatic antics, colored, and had a real conversation. I enjoyed talking with my daughter away from ringing phones and Sponge Bob

Squarepants, but I could not quit thinking about the effect that going home empty-handed might have on Chloe. Silently, I prayed for a buck to emerge from the cedars.

A plump doe emerged 30 minutes before dark. It calmly fed less than 60 yards away, just the chip shot I hoped for.

"Do you want to shoot her, Chloe?"

"No, Daddy. We still have time. Let's wait."

I smiled at her. She smiled back and squeezed my hand. *Wasn't I supposed to reassure her?*

"Daddy, look. Is that a good buck?"

I looked past the end of her tiny finger just in time to see an ancient axis buck amble out of the brush, harem in tow. Without a word, I helped her don her ear muffs and climb into my lap, then picked up her rifle and helped her ease it out the window.

"Chloe, do you remember where I told you to shoot him?"

"Yes, Daddy, right on the shoulder."

Just then the axis buck fed behind a cedar.

"Daddy, he went behind that big bush."

"I know, baby. Stay on him. He'll come out the other side in a minute."

The buck disappeared for what seemed like an eternity. I feared we would run out of daylight before he moved, but just as I was about to safe the rifle, the buck stepped clear.

"Daddy, I am going to shoot him."

She fired before I could respond. The buck disappeared so fast I would have thought she missed had I not heard the solid smack of the slug striking bone. Seconds later, after a big hug and a frantic piggy back run through the cacti, my Chloe wrapped her tiny hands around the horns of her first deer and smiled like I have never seen her smile before. It was a smile and a moment I will never forget.

I was elated and proud of my daughter. A lot of people told me that a five-year-old could not do it, and even if she could she would not understand the gravity of what she did. That may be true of their five-year-old, but not mine.

Chloe was happy and proud, but she was respectful of the deer and even expressed that she felt she deserved "her deer" because she had worked so hard and been so patient. She told her mother and brother that she couldn't wait to eat it. She told her friends that God put animals on this earth for us to eat, and our family likes to kill our own food. There was true reverence for the game and for the sport, not rhetoric learned by rote. Chloe is a hunter. All 33 pounds of her.

Reprinted with permission of the author. To book a hunt through Greg Rodriguez's hunting agency, go to www.mbogo.net.

The Rack

JAY CASSELL

"I found his antler, Dad," the throaty voice of my six-year-old son, James, crackled over the telephone. "I saw it in the woods when Mom was driving me home from school, right near where we went hunting! Are you coming home tonight?"

When I told him that my flight wouldn't get in until 11:00, and that I wouldn't be home until midnight, there was a disappointed silence over the phone. Then, "Well, okay, but don't look at it until morning, so I can show you. Promise?"

I promised. We had a deal. I told him I'd see him soon, then asked to talk with his mother.

"Love you, Dad."

"Love you too, James."

Unbelievable. My son had found the shed antler of the buck I had hunted, unsuccessfully, all season. The big ten-pointer I had seen the day before deer season, the one with the wide spread and thick beams. He had seen me that day, having winded me as I pussyfooted through some thickets for a closer look. I think he somehow knew that he was safe, that he was far enough away from me.

I had scouted the 140-acre farm and adjoining woods near my home in suburban New York, the farm that I had gotten permission to hunt after five years of asking. "You can hunt this year," Dan the caretaker had said to me during the summer, when I asked my annual question. "I kicked those other guys off the property. They were in here with ATVs and Jeeps, bringing two and three friends every day they hunted, without even asking. Lot of nerve, I thought. Got sick of 'em, so I kicked 'em off. Now I'll let you hunt, and your buddy John, three other guys, and that's all. I want some local people on here that I know and trust."

When Dan had told me that, I couldn't believe it. But there it was, so I took advantage of it. Starting in September, I began to scout the farm. I had seen bucks on the property in previous years while driving by, but now I got a firsthand look. There was sign virtually everywhere: rubs, scrapes, droppings in the hillside hayfields, in the mixed hardwoods, in the thick hemlock stands towering over the rest of the woods. I found what were obviously rubs left by a big deer. In a copse of hemlocks near the edge of the property, bordering an Audubon nature preserve, were scrapes and, nearby, about five or six beech saplings absolutely ripped apart by antlers.

With James's help, I set up my tree stand overlooking a heavily used trail that seemed to be a perfect escape route out of the hemlocks. James and I also found an old permanent tree stand, which he and I repaired with a few two-by-fours and nails. This would officially be "his" tree stand—or tree house, as he called it.

Opening day couldn't come fast enough. James and I talked about it constantly. Even though he's only six, and can't really hunt yet, he couldn't wait for deer season. He knows what deer tracks and droppings look like; can tell how scrapes and rubs are made; can even identify where deer have passed in the leaf-covered forest floor. My plan was to hunt the first few days of the season by myself while James was in school, and then take him on a weekend. If luck was with me, maybe I'd take the big buck and could then concentrate on filing my doe tag with my son's help.

Opening day came and went, with no trophy ten-pointer in sight, or any other bucks, for that matter. A lot of other days came and went too, most of them cold, windy and rainy. Three weeks into the two-month-long season, on a balmy Sunday in the 50s, James and I packed our camo backpacks with candy bars and juice boxes, binoculars and grunt calls, and at 2:00 p.m. off we went, on our first day of hunting together. When we reached the spot where I always park my car, on a hillside field, I dabbed some camo paint onto James's face, which he thought was cool. Then we started hiking up the field and into the woods, toward the hemlocks.

We saw one white tail disappear over a knob as we hiked into James's stand. I didn't really care, though. This was the first time I was taking my son hunting! It would be the first of many, I hoped. I wouldn't force it on him, just introduce him to the sport, and keep my fingers crossed.

At James's stand, we sat down and had a couple of candy bars. "Can I blow on the deer call now, Dad?" I said yes, and he proceeded to honk away on the thing like a trumpet player.

"Do it quietly," I advised. "And remember, always whisper, don't talk loudly. And don't move around so much!"

What with James honking on the call and fidgeting—checking out my bow, looking around, pointing to the hawk soaring overhead, crumpling up his candy bar wrapper and stuffing it into his pocket—I was sure no self-respecting deer would come within a mile of us. None did, not to my son's stand, or to mine, or to the rocks where we later sat, overlooking a trail and those ripped-up beech saplings, until darkness finally settled over the woods. But that was okay.

Hiking out of the woods, we met my friend John coming from his tree stand.

"I saw that ten-pointer today," he began, giving James a poke in the ribs with his finger.

"Where?"

"Up near those hemlocks, the same area you and I have been hunting. We were probably 100 yards away from each other."

"Well, what happened?" Part of me was saying, *Great, he got the buck!* The other part of me was saying, *Pleeeease tell me you didn't shoot him.* John looked at me sheepishly.

"I was watching that trail, and I saw a doe headed my way, right where I always put my climbing tree stand. Then, right behind her, I saw a buck—you know that six-pointer we've seen over by the lake? Well, I started to draw back on him—he was only 30 yards away—but then I saw some movement to my left. It was HIM! Cutting through the hemlocks. That six-pointer and doe got out of there fast, and the ten-pointer got to within ten yards of my stand, stopped broadside to me, and then looked up straight at me!"

"Did you shoot? Did you shoot?"

"I couldn't. I was shaking too much. I mean, I could even hear the arrow rattling against the rest. Eventually, he just took off down the trial. Man, he was something. Must weigh 200 pounds!"

Later, driving the short ride home, James said, "Hey, Dad, how come. John didn't shoot that deer?"

"Shooting a deer is a lot harder than many people think. Even if everything else is right, sometimes you can get so nervous that you just can't shoot, no matter how much you want to. John's time will come, though. He works at it."

I didn't see the buck until two days after Christmas. Hunting by myself, I left my normal tree stand and circled around to the backside of the hemlocks. At 4:00 p.m., I was wedged between some boulders that overlook a well-used trail. It was 20°F, getting dark, and I was cold and shivering uncontrollably. But I kept hearing a rustling behind me. *Another squirrel.* But it wasn't. Suddenly, 60 yards through the trees, I could see a big deer headed my way. It was moving with a purpose. It stopped at what appeared to be a scrape, and I could see a huge symmetrical rack dip down as the buck stuck his nose to the ground. Then he stood up, urinated into the scrape, turned, and headed back into the hemlocks. If he had kept coming down the trail, I would have had a clean 15-yard shot. It wasn't meant to be.

That was my season. I didn't see that ten-pointer again, and I missed my only shot of the year, a 35-yarder at a forkhorn that sailed high. Such is deer hunting.

So now I was returning home from my trip. I walked in the door at midnight, quickly read through some mail on the counter, soon slipped into bed. My wife rolled over and whispered, "Don't forget to wake up James before you go to work. He really wants to show you that rack."

The alarm went off at 6:30, and I got up to take a shower.

"Psst, Dad, is that you?" came a sleepy voice from my son's room.

"Yes, buddy, how are you?"

"Wait here, Dad!"

Before I could say another word, he jumped out of bed, put on his oversized bear-paw slippers, and went padding down the stairs to the basement. When he returned, he had the biggest grin on his face that I've ever seen.

"Look, Dad!"

And there it was, half of the ten-pointer's rack. A long, thick main beam, four long, heavy points, the back one eight inches. Amazing. And that buck will be there next year.

"Dad, can I put it on my wall?"

"Of course."

"And can we go look for the other half of his antlers tomorrow, because tomorrow's Saturday, and I don't have school, and you once told me that their antlers usually fall off pretty close together. Please?"

"Sure, James. If you're good in school today."

The deal was made. We never found the other half of the shed, though. It snowed, and we couldn't really look. Mice probably ate the other half.

But you know what? I think maybe my future hunting companion was born this past season.

On Stand

JAY CASSELL

The air is still and cold. The breath rolls out of my mouth like a wisp of fog, hanging there as if frozen before finally dissipating. My gloved hands, tucked deep inside my pockets, have had no sensation in the fingertips for almost an hour. My toes are numb little clubs, stored in boots that seem detached from my body; if I wiggle them, needlelike sensations stab through them. I shiver uncontrollably for a minute, then force myself to stop. Something is coming.

Swish, swish. Swish, swish, swish. Ever so slowly, I roll my eyes to the left, toward the direction of the sound. Now I swivel my head, an eighth of an inch at a time. After what seems an eternity, I'm looking toward the old rock wall just uphill from me. The deer trail comes through a broken-down part of that wall, straight in front of me, 15 yards away. This is where the buck will come, when it's time. *Swish, swish, crunch.*

A doe appears, cautiously headed down the trail. She's followed by two smaller does. No buck. Their gray, ghost-like forms move at a deliberate pace in the fading light. They stop ten yards from me and look around nervously. The last doe stares directly at me. I avoid eye contact and don't move and, eventually, she pays me no more attention. I'm not a threat. They continue down the trail. The sounds of their hooves *swishing* through the frozen leaves grow farther and farther away, then are gone. I'm alone again.

I've been sitting in this stand from 2:00 until dark for the past four days. I've seen eight does, more squirrels than I care to count, one red fox and a red-tailed hawk overhead, screeching. I did see one large deer body moving through the woods some 70 yards away, but my grunt call made it run from me, tail up.

I think about my family, my job, friends, places. Christmas is coming soon and, once again, I've put off shopping until the last minute. I've got to put up the Christmas tree, put the lights up outside; I haven't even taken the screens out of the windows yet. Yet here I sit, a frozen man in a frozen tree.

I've logged a lot of days in a lot of tree stands over the years. There was the stand up on the Neversink, the one that I built after patterning a buck for more than two years. I shot that ten-pointer the third year I was after him; he was five and half years old.

Then there's the stand I use in the Catskills during rifle season. It's an old one, one that I found and fixed up. I've hunted there for two years now and still haven't taken anything from it. But it overlooks a well-used trail, and I've got a good feeling about it. It just looks too good not to produce. If I'm persistent, sooner or later I'm going to take a deer out of it. I know.

I remember the V stand, made out of cut saplings wedged between two trees and a boulder, the one with the red Dellwood milk crate as a seat. I shot a seven-pointer out of that stand five years ago. A new hunter in our group, Ken, came over at the shot and helped me drag that buck back to camp, and we've been friends ever since. But the days I really remember in that stand are the cold ones, the 10°F days when the wind was howling. That stand was out in the open, and it seemed as if every wind in the mountains funneled through that spot, whistling between the cut saplings, before continuing up the mountain. One day it snowed hard for four hours, yet I didn't budge because deer were moving all around me. When Ken came by to pick me up for the hike back to camp and lunch, he laughed at my appearance. Said he thought I was dead, totally covered with snow, ice-rimmed beard and mustache, and not moving.

It's 4:20 now. The last faint glow of the sun has disappeared from the leaden winter sky. I survey my surroundings. This is a mixed hardwood forest, grown up on land that was farmed 60 years ago. It's hard to imagine how anyone could have scratched a living out of the rocky soil in this area. In the fading light, all the trees appear the same—vertical black lines stretching upward, lines that blend together as one if you stare at them long enough.

I refocus my eyes, moving them from right to left across the drab forest floor, searching for movement. Darkness is setting in. When you're in these stark December woods, and you're watching daylight slowly turn to gray and then black, the feeling is almost as if you're going to sleep, except your eyes are open. There are maybe 15 more minutes of shooting light, and then I'll have to lower my bow and pack to the ground, climb down, and hike out to my car in the dark. I can hear the noise from the interstate a mile away. Traffic's picking up, people are heading home from work. A train whistle knifes through the stillness. I wonder if my wife is on that train.

I wiggle my toes, move my fingers, suppress another shiver. The cold is freezing on my beard, and I suspect that I again must look as if I'm frozen dead . . . .

To me, the one thing that all stands seem to have in common is that they're cold. Maybe in the beginning of the season the weather will be warm, and there will be pleasant days spent watching the woods, seeing the sun rise, the wildlife start to move. But as the season moves on, the cold creeps in, inevitably, uncaring. And those are the days you remember, the days you suffered, pinning your hopes on the chance that this might be the day he will come down the trail. You can envision him coming now, a big buck that walks right in front of your stand, his rack magnificent, his coat thick, his visage majestic. You can see the cold air billowing from his flared nostrils. You picture yourself slowly settling the sight pin on his heart. Then you let go and . . .

I fish a Milky Way out of my pocket, pulling the paper off with one hand to minimize my movements. Inching my hand to my mouth, I pop the candy in and slowly force my hand back down into my pocket. The bar is frozen, but I work it with my teeth and soon finish it.

Swish, swish. Another sound, one I didn't hear over my teeth crunching the candy bar. It's almost dark, but something is definitely coming . . . not down the trail, though, but through the thickets behind me. I deliberately remove my hands from my pockets and wrap them around my bow. My arrow is nocked. *Swish, crack, swish* . . . stop. He's right behind me now, maybe 15 yards away, probably with his nose in the air, warily checking the wind, maybe catching my scent. He's probably looking right at me. Should I try to move? Try to swivel around slowly? Should I stay still, on the chance he'll keep coming and walk right under my stand?

I decide to pivot around, slowly, very slowly. Maybe I'll get a chance at a shot. First my eyes, then my head. My heart is in my throat. *Swish, swish, swish, swish.* The tension is unbearable, but this is a feeling that only hunters know, a feeling that hunters live for. My fingers tighten on the bowstring. . . .

The gray squirrel suddenly decides to run down a log next to my tree. He hops on the crunchy, leafy ground and bounds away. I relax and let out a deep breath. The shivering returns. It's almost too dark to see now anyway. I put the arrow into my quiver and stand up, letting the blood flow down my legs, making them tingle unbearably. I tie my bow to the rope with stiff fingers, then lower it to the ground. I undo my safety belt and begin to climb down.

Tomorrow he'll come. I'll be here.

PART IX

Africa and Asia

Karamojo

W. D. M. BELL

I.—Into the Unknown

MY earliest recollection of myself is that of a child whose sole ambition in life was to hunt. At a very early age I conceived the idea of hunting the American bison. With this end in view I gathered together a few oddments, such as the barrels of a double-barrelled pistol, a clasp knife, a few bits of string and all the money—chiefly pennies—that I could lay hands on. This bison-hunting expedition was prematurely cut short at the Port of Glasgow by the critical state of its finances, for after buying a pork pie for two-pence its treasury was found to be almost empty. This was a sad blow, and it was while thinking it over on a doorstep that a kindly policeman instituted proceedings which resulted in the lost and crestfallen child being restored to his family. But the growth of years and the acquirement of the art of reading—by which I discovered that bison no longer existed in America—my ambition became fixed on becoming an elephant hunter. The reading of Gordon Cumming's books on Africa finished the business. An elephant hunter I determined to become; this idea never left me. Finally, after all kinds of vicissitudes I arrived in Africa and heard of a wonderful new and unexplored country called Karamojo. Elephants were reported by the black traders to be very numerous with enormous tusks, and there was no sort of administration to hamper the hunter with restrictions and game laws. Above all there appeared to be no other person hunting elephants in this Eldorado except the natives, and they had no firearms. My informants told me that the starting point for all safaris (caravans) was Mumias, a native town and Government Post at the foot of Mount Elgon, which formed the last outpost of civilisation for a traveller proceeding North.

At the time of which I write Mumias was a town of some importance. It was the base for all trading expeditions to the Lake Rudolph basin, Turkana, Dabossa and the Southern Abyssinia country. In the first few years of the trade in ivory this commodity was obtained for the most trifling sums; for instance, a tusk worth £50 or £60 could be bought for two or three shillings' worth of beads or iron wire. As time went on and more traders flocked to Karamojo to share in the huge profits of the ivory trade, competition became keener. Prices rose higher and higher. Where once beads and iron wire sufficed to buy a tusk, now a cow must be paid. Traders were obliged to go further and further afield to find new territory until they came in violent contact with raiding parties of Abyssinians away in the far North.

When most of the dead ivory in the country had been traded off the only remaining source was the yearly crop of tusks from the elephants snared and killed by the native Karamojans. For these comparatively few tusks competition became so keen and prices so high that there was no longer any profit when as much as eight or ten cows had to be paid for a large tusk, and the cows bought down at the base for spot cash and at prices of from £2 to £5 each. Hence arose the idea in the brains of two or three of the bolder spirits among the traders to take by force that which they could no longer afford to buy. Instead of traders they became raiders. In order to ensure success to a raid an alliance would be made with some tribe which was already about equal in strength to its neighbours through centuries of intertribal warfare. The addition of three or four hundred guns to the tribe's five or six thousand spearmen rendered the result of this raid by the combined forces almost beyond doubt, and moreover, conferred upon the raiders such complete domination of the situation that they were able to search out and capture the young girls, the acquisition of which is the great aim and object of all activity in the Mohammedan mind.

Complete and magnificent success attending the first raiding venture the whole country changed magically. The hitherto more or less peaceful looking trading camps gave place to huge armed Bomas surrounded by high thorn fences. Everyone—trader or native—went about armed to the teeth. Footsore or sick travellers from caravans disappeared entirely, or their remains were found by the roadside. Native women and cattle were heavily guarded, for no man trusted a stranger.

Into this country of suspicion and brooding violence I was about to venture. As soon as my intention became known among the traders at Mumias I encountered on every side a firm barrage of lies and dissuasion of every sort. The buying of pack donkeys was made impossible. Guides were unobtainable. Information about the country north of Turkwell was either distorted and false or entirely withheld. I found that no Mohammedan boy would engage with me. The reason for all this apparently malicious obstruction on the part of the trading community was not at the time known to me, but it soon became clear when I had crossed the Turkwell and found that the peaceful, polite and prosperous looking trader of Mumias became the merciless and bloody Dacoit as soon as he had crossed that river and was no longer under European control. Numbering among them, as they did, some pretty notorious ex-slavers, they knew how unexpectedly far the arm of the law could sometimes reach and they no doubt foresaw that nothing but trouble would arise from my visit to the territory they had come to look upon as theirs by right of discovery. It surprises me now, when I think of how much they had at stake, that they resorted to no more stringent methods than those related above to prevent my entry into Karamojo. As it was I soon got together some bullocks and some pagan boys. The bullocks I half trained to carry packs and the Government Agent very kindly arranged that I should have eight Snider rifles with which to defend myself, and to instill confidence among my Baganda and Wanyamwere and Kavirondo boys. The Sniders looked well and no one knew except myself that the ammunition for them was all bad. And then I had my personal rifles, at that time a .303 Lee-Enfield, a .275 Rigby-Mauser and a double .450-.400, besides a Mauser pistol which could be used as a carbine and which soon acquired the name of "Bom-Bom" and a reputation for itself equal to a hundred ordinary rifles.

While searching through some boxes of loose ammunition in the store at Mumias in the hope of finding at least a few good rounds for my Snider carbines I picked up a Martini-Henry cartridge, and while looking at its base it suddenly struck me that possibly it could be fired from a Snider. And so it proved to be. The base being .577 calibre fitted perfectly, but the bullet, being only .450 bore, was scarcely what you might call a good fit for a .577 barrel, and there was, of course, no accuracy to the thing at all. But it went off with a bang and the propensity of its bullet to fly off at the most disconcerting angles after rattling through the barrel from side to side seemed just to suit the style of aiming adopted by my eight askaris (soldiers), for on several occasions jackal and hyena were laid low while prowling round the camp at night.

Bright and early next morning my little safari began to get itself ready for the voyage into the Unknown. The loads were got out and lined up. First of all an askari, with a Snider rifle very proud in a hide belt with five Martini cartridges gleaming yellow in it. He had carefully polished them with sand for the occasion. Likewise the barrel of the old Snider showed signs of much rubbing, and a piece of fat from the tail of a sheep dangled by a short string from the hammer. Then my chop-boxes, and camp gear borne by porters, followed by my boy Suede and Sulieman, the cook, of cannibal parentage be it whispered. As usual, all the small loads seemed to be jauntily and lightly perched on the massive heads and necks of the biggest porters, while the big loads looked doubly big in comparison to the spindly shanks which appeared below them. One enormous porter in particular drew my attention. He was capering about in the most fantastic manner with a large box on his head. From the rattle which proceeded from the box I perceived that this was the cook's mate, and as I possessed only a few aluminium cooking pots, his was perhaps the lightest load of any, and I vowed that he should have a good heavy tusk to carry as soon as possible. This I was enabled to do soon after passing the Turkwell, and this splendid head-carrier took entire charge of a tusk weighing 123 lbs., carrying it with pride for several hundred weary miles on a daily ration of 1 lb. of mtama grain and unlimited buck meat.

Usually when a safari started from Mumias for the "Barra"—as the bush or wilderness is called—the townsfolk would turn out with drums and horns to give them a send off, but in our case we departed without any demonstration of that sort. We passed through almost deserted and silent streets, and we struck out for the Turkwell, the trail skirting the base of Elgon for six days, as we travelled slowly, being heavily laden. I was able to find and shoot enough haartebeeste and oribi to keep the safari in meat, and after two or three days' march the boys became better and better and the bullocks more and more docile. I purposely made the marches more easy at first in order to avoid sore backs, and it was easy to do so, as there were good streams of water crossing our path every few miles.

On the seventh day we reached the Turkwell River. After descending several hundred feet from the high plateau we crossed by the ford and pitched camp on the opposite or north bank. The Turkwell has its sources in the crater of Elgon and its slopes. Its waters reach the dry, hot plains of Karamojo after a drop of about 9,000 ft. in perhaps twenty or thirty miles. In the dry season—when it is fordable almost anywhere—it totally disappears into its sandy river bed while still some days' march from its goal, Lake Rudolph. It is a queer and romantic river, for it starts in lava 14,000 ft. above sea-level, traverses bitterly cold and often snow-covered heath land, plunges down through the dense bamboo belt, then through dark and dripping evergreen forest to emerge on the sandy plains of Karamojo. From this point to Rudolph its banks are clothed with a more or less dense belt of immense flat-topped thorn trees interspersed with thickets of every kind of thorny bush, the haunt of rhino, buffalo and elephant. Throughout its entire course its waters were drunk, at the time of which I write, by immense herds of elephant during the dry season. Even after disappearing underground, elephant and natives easily procured water by simply making holes in the soft clean sands of its river bed.

At that time the Turkwell formed the northern boundary of European rule. North of it was no rule but disrule. The nearest cultivated settlement of Karamojo natives was at Mani-Mani, some 150 miles to the north, but scattered about in the bush were many temporary settlements of poor Karamojans who got their living by hunting and snaring everything from elephant downwards.

Dreadful tales of murders of peaceful travellers had been related by Swahilis, and we were careful not to let anyone straggle far from the main body. At night my eight askaris mounted guard and kept a huge fire going. Their vigilance was extraordinary, and their keenness and cheerfulness, fidelity and courage of a very high order, showing them to be born soldiers. Their shooting was simply atrocious, in spite of practice with a .22 I had, but notwithstanding their inability to align and aim a rifle properly, they used sometimes to bring off the most brilliant shots under the most impossible conditions of shooting light, thereby showing a great natural aptitude to point a gun and time the shot.

While we were drying out the gear that had got wet while crossing the Turkwell two natives strolled into the camp. These were the first Karamojans we had seen, and I was very much interested in them. They showed great independence of bearing as they stood about leaning on their long thrusting spears. I had some difficulty in getting into conversation with them, although I had an excellent interpreter. They seemed very taciturn and suspicious. However, I got it explained to them that I had come for one purpose only, *i.e.*, to hunt elephant. They admitted that there were plenty of elephant, but when I asked them to show me where to look for them they merely asked me how I proposed to kill them when I did see them. On showing them my rifle they laughed, and said they had seen Swahili traders using those things for elephants and, although they killed men well enough, they were useless against elephant. My answer to this was that I had procured some wonderful medicine which enabled me to kill the largest-sized elephant with one shot, and that if they would like to see this medicine working all they had to do was to show me where the elephant were and that I would do the rest and they should have as much meat as they wanted. They retorted that if my medicine was truly sufficiently powerful to kill an elephant instantaneously, then they could not believe that it would fail to show me their whereabouts also. This grave fault in my medicine had to be explained, and I could only say that I grieved heartily over the deficiency, which I attributed to the jealousy of a medicine man who was a rival of him who had given me the killing medicine. This left them not altogether satisfied, but a better impression was produced when I presented them with a quarter of buck meat, while telling them that I killed that kind of meat every day. They went off without holding out any hope of showing me elephant, and I thought that I had seen the last of them. I sat until late in my long chair by the camp fire under a brilliant sky and wonderful moon listening to the talk of my Nzamwezi boys and wondering how we were going to fare in the real wild land ahead of us.

An early start was made next morning and we had covered perhaps six or seven miles when the two natives, visitors to our camp of yesterday, came stalking along appearing to cover the ground at a great rate without showing any hurry or fuss. I stopped and called the interpreter and soon learned that four large elephants had that morning passed close to their camp in the bush and that when they left to call me the elephants could still be heard in the vicinity. At once I was for going, but the interpreter and the headman both cautioned me against treachery, declaring that it was only a blind to separate us preparatory to a general massacre. This view I thought a bit far fetched, but I ordered the safari to get under weigh and to travel well together until they reached the first water, where they were immediately to cut sufficient thorn trees to completely encircle themselves in camp, to keep a good look-out and to await my coming.

Taking my small boy and the gigantic cook's mate—whose feather-weight load I had transferred to the cook's head—I hastily put together a few necessities and hurried off with the two Karamojans at a great pace. We soon struck off from the main trail and headed for the Turkwell Valley. Straight through the open thorn bush we went, the elephant hide sandals of my native guides crunching innumerable darning-needle-sized thorns underfoot, the following porters with their light loads at a jog trot, myself at a fast but laboured walk, while the guides simply soaked along with consummate ease.

Supremely undemonstrative as natives usually are, there was yet observable a kind of suppressed excitement about their bearing, and I noticed that whenever a certain bird called on the right hand the leader would make a low remark to his companions with an indescribably satisfied kind of gesture, whereas the same calling on the left hand drew no notice from them beyond a certain increased forward resolution and a stiff ignoring of it.

The significance of these signs were lost on me at that time, but I was to come to learn them well in my later dealings with these tribes. They were omens and indicated success or failure to our hunting.

On the whole they were apparently favourable. At any rate, the pace never slackened, and I was beginning to wish for a slowing down. As we drew nearer the Turkwell Valley signs of elephant became more and more numerous. Huge paths worn perfectly smooth and with their edges cut as clear as those of garden walks by the huge pads of the ponderous animals began to run together, forming more deeply worn ones converging towards the drinking places on the river. Occasionally the beautiful lesser koodoo stood watching us or loped away, flirting its white fluffed tail. Once we passed a rhino standing motionless with snout ever directed towards us. A small detour round him as we did not wish to get mixed up with his sort and on again. Halt! The little line bunches up against the motionless natives. A distant rumble resembling somewhat a cart crossing a wooden bridge, and after a few seconds of silence the crash of a broken tree.

Elephant! *Atome!* (in Karamojo). Word the first to be learned and the last to be forgotten of any native language. A kind of excitement seizes us all; me most of all, the Karamojans least. Now the boys are told to stay behind and to make no noise. They are at liberty to climb trees if they like. I look to my .303, but, of course, it had been ready for hours. Noting that the wind—what there was of it—was favourable, the natives and I go forward, and soon we come upon the broken trees, mimosa and white thorn, the chewed fibrous balls of sansivera, the moist patches with froth still on them, the still steaming and unoxidised spoor, and the huge tracks with the heavily imprinted clear-cut corrugations of a very recently passing bunch of bull elephants. In numbers they were five as nearly as I could estimate. Tracking them was child's play, and I expected to see them at any moment. It was, however, much longer than I anticipated before we sighted their dull grey hides. For they were travelling as well as feeding. It is remarkable how much territory elephant cover when thus feeding along. At first sight they seem to be so leisurely, and it is not until one begins to keep in touch with them that their speed is realised. Although they appear to take so few steps, each step of their lowest gait is about six ft. Then, again, in this feeding along there is *always* at least one of the party moving forward at about three-and-a-half miles per hour, although the other members may be stopping and feeding, then catching up again by extending the stride to seven ft. or more.

As soon as they were in sight I got in front of the Karamojans and ran in to about 20 yds. from the stern of the rearmost animal. Intense excitement now had me with its usual signs, hard breathing through the mouth, dry palate and an intense longing to shoot.

As I arrived at this close proximity I vividly remember glancing along the grey bulging sides of the three rearmost animals, who all happened to be in motion at the same time in single file, and remarking a tusk of an incredible length and size sweeping out from the grey wall. I instantly determined to try for this one first. With extraordinary precautions against making a noise, and stoopings and contortions of the body, all of which after-experience taught me were totally unnecessary, I got away off at right-angles to the file of elephants and could now grasp the fact that they were all very large and carried superb ivory.

I was now almost light-headed with excitement, and several times on the very verge of firing a stupid and hasty shot from my jumping and flickering rifle. So shaky was it when I once or twice put it to my shoulder that even in my then state of mind I saw that no good could come of it. After a minute or two, during which I was returning to a more normal state, the animal with the largest tusks left the line slightly, and slowly settled into a halt beside a mimosa bush. I got a clear glimpse at his broadside at what looked about 20 yds., but was really 40 yds., and I fired for his heart. With a flinch, a squirm and a roar he was soon in rapid motion straight away, with his companions in full flight ahead of him. I was rather surprised at this headlong flight after one shot as I had expected the elephant here to be more unsophisticated, but hastily concluding that the Swahili traders must have been pumping lead into them more often than one imagined, I legged it for the cloud of dust where the fleeting animals had disappeared. Being clad in running shorts and light shoes, it was not long before I almost ran slap up against a huge and motionless grey stern. Recoiling very rapidly indeed from this awe-inspiring sight, I saw on one side of it an enormous head and tusk which appeared to stick out at right-angles. So drooping were the trunk and ears and so motionless the whole appearance of what had been a few seconds ago the very essence of power and activity that it was borne straight to even my inexperienced mind that here was death. And so it was, for as I stared goggle-eyed the mighty body began to sway from side to side more and more, until with a crash it fell sideways, bearing earthwards with it a fair sized tree. Straight past it I saw another elephant, turned almost broadside, at about 100 yds. distance, evidently listening and obviously on the point of flight. Running a little forward so as to get a clear sight of the second beast, I sat quickly down and fired carefully at the shoulder, when much the same performance took place as in the first case, except that No. 2 came down to a slow walk after a burst of speed instead of to a standstill as with No. 1.

Ranging rapidly alongside I quickly put him out of misery and tore after the others which were, of course, by this time, thoroughly alarmed and in full flight. After a mile or two of fast going I found myself pretty well done, so I sat down and rolled myself a cigarette of the strong black shag so commonly smoked by the Swahilis. Presently my native guides came with every appearance of satisfaction on their now beaming faces.

After a few minutes' rest we retracked the elephant back to where our two lay dead. The tusks of the first one we examined were not long but very thick, and the other had on one side a tusk broken some 2 ft. outside the lip, while on the other was the magnificent tusk which had filled me with wonder earlier on. It was almost faultless and beautifully curved. What a shame that its companion was broken!

As we were cutting the tail off, which is always done to show anyone finding the carcase that it has been killed and claimed, my good fellows came up with the gear and the interpreter. Everyone, including myself, was in high good humour, and when the Karamojans said that their village was not far off we were more pleased than ever, especially as the sun was sinking rapidly. After what appeared to the natives no doubt as a short distance, but what seemed to my sore feet and tired legs a very long one, we saw the welcome fires of a camp and were soon sitting by one while a group of naked savages stood looking silently at the white man and his preparations for eating and sleeping. These were simple enough. A kettle was soon on the fire for tea, while some strips of sun-cured haartebeeste biltong writhed and sizzled on the embers. Meanwhile my boys got the bed ready by first of all cutting the grass and smoothing down the knobs of the ground while another spread grass on it to form a mattress. Over this the canvas sheet and blankets and with a bag of cartridges wrapped in a coat for a pillow the bed was complete. Then two forked sticks stuck in the ground close alongside the bed to hold the rifle and all was ready for the night.

II.—Ivory and the Raiders

After a hearty supper of toasted biltong and native flour porridge, washed down with tea, I cleaned my rifle, loaded it and lay down utterly tired out and soon dropped off to the music of hyenas' howling. As soon as ever it was light enough to see, we left for the dead elephant, and the way did not seem half so long in the fresh morning air as it had appeared the evening before. We quickly arrived, followed by all the villagers, men, women and children, every one in high spirits at the sight of the mountains of meat. In this country the meat of elephants is esteemed more highly than that of any other animal, as it contains much more fat. The Karamojan elephants are distinguished for their bodily size, the quality and size of their ivory and for the quantity of fat on them.

I was anxious to get the tusks out as rapidly as possible in order to rejoin my caravan, so I divided the Karamojans into two gangs and explained to them that no one was to touch the carcasses until the tusks were out, but that then they could have all the meat. They set to with a will to get all the skin and flesh off the head. It is necessary to do this so as to expose the huge bone sockets containing the ends of the tusks. About a third of their length is so embedded, and a very long, tedious and hard job it is to get all the skin and gristle cut away. Nothing blunts a knife more quickly than elephant hide, because of the sand and grit in its loose texture.

When the skull is clean on one side the neck should be cut. This alone is a herculean task. The vertebra severed, the head is turned over by eight or ten men, and the other side similarly cleaned. When both sockets are ready an axe is used to chop them away chip by chip until the tusk is free. This chopping should always be done by an expert, as otherwise large chips off the tusk itself are liable to be taken by the axe.

This chopping out of ivory is seldom resorted to by natives, requiring as it does so much hard work. They prefer to leave the sun and putrefaction to do the work for them. On the third day after the death the upper tusk can usually be drawn without difficulty from the socket and the underneath one on the following day.

On this particular occasion no one was at all adept at chopping out, and it was hours before the tusks were freed. Later on my Wanzamwezi boys became very expert indeed at this job, and twelve of them, whose particular job it became, could handle as many as ten bull elephants in a day provided they were not too distant one from the other and that they had plenty of native assistance.

While the chopping out was going on I had leisure to watch the natives, and what struck me first was the remarkable difference between the men and the women. The former were tall, some of them quite 6'4" slim and well made, while the latter were distinctly short, broad, beefy and squat. The married ones wore aprons of dressed buckskin tied round the waist by the legs of the skin and ornamented with coloured beads sewn on with sinew thread. The unmarried girls wore no skins at all and had merely a short fringe of black thread attached to a string round the waist and falling down in front. As regards hair, all the women wore it plaited and falling down all round the head and giving somewhat the appearance of "bobbed" hair. Some of the men wore the most extraordinary-looking periwigs made up of their own and also their ancestors' hair mixed with clay so as to form a kind of covering for the top of the head and falling down the back of the neck. In this pad of human felt were set neat little woven sockets in such a way as to hold upright an ostrich feather in each.

The people with whom we are dealing at the moment were poor and therefore hunters. Africans differ from us entirely on the question of hunting; whereas among us it is the well-off who hunt, among them it is the poor. Having nothing but a few goats and sheep, these hunters inhabit the bush, shifting their village from site to site according to the movements of the game.

Their system of taking game is the snare; their only weapon a spear. The art of snaring has been brought to a unique development by these people, for they have snares varying in size for all animals from elephant down to dik-dik.

The snare for elephant is a great hawser, 4½ ins. in diameter, of twisted antelope or giraffe hides. One may find in the same rope haartebeeste hide, eland, zebra, rhinoceros, buffalo and giraffe hide. If made of haartebeeste alone no less than eleven or twelve skins are required. The skins are scraped and pounded with huge wooden mallets for weeks by the women before being twisted or "laid" into the rope which is to form the snare. The running nooses at both ends are beautifully made. Besides the snare there is a thing like a cart wheel without any hub and with scores of thin spokes meeting in the centre where their points are sharp. The snare is laid in the following manner:

A well frequented elephant path is chosen and somewhere near the spot decided upon for the snare a large tree is cut. Judgment in the choosing of this must be exercised as if it is too heavy the snare will break, and if too light the snared elephant will travel too far. A tree trunk which ten or twelve men can just stagger along with seems to be the thing. This log is then brought to the scene of action and at its smaller end a deep groove is cut all round to take the noose at one end of the rope. After this noose has been fitted and pulled and hammered tight—no easy matter—the log is laid at right angles to the path with the smaller end pointing towards it. A hole a good bit larger than an elephant's foot is then dug in the path itself to a depth of two feet or so. Over this hole is fitted the cart wheel. Round the rim the large noose of the snare is laid and the whole covered carefully over with earth to resemble the path again. The snare is now laid, and if all goes well some solitary old bull comes wandering along at night, places his foot on the earth borne by the sharp spokes of the hubless wheel, goes through as the spokes open downwards, lifts his foot and with it the wheel bearing the noose well up the ankle, strides forward and tightens the noose. The more he pulls the tighter draws the noose until the log at the other end of the snare begins to move. Now alarmed and presently angry, he soon gets rid of the cart wheel, but as its work is already done, that does not matter. The dragging log is now securely attached to the elephant's leg, and it is seldom that he gets rid of it unless it should jamb in rocks or trees. Soon he becomes thoroughly alarmed and sets off at a great pace, the log ploughing along behind him. Should a strong, vigorous young bull become attached to a rather light log, he may go twenty or thirty miles.

As soon as it becomes known to the natives that an elephant has been caught, everyone within miles immediately seizes all his spears and rushes to the spot where the snare had been set and from there eagerly takes up the trail of the log. When they come up with the somewhat exhausted animal they spear it to death. Then every scrap of meat is shared among the village which owns the snare, the tusks becoming the property of the man who made and laid the snare. The spearing of an elephant, with its enormously thick hide, is no easy matter, as the animal can still make short active rushes. Casualties are not infrequent, and should anyone be caught he is, as a rule, almost certain to be killed.

While the tusk-getting operations were going on I took the opportunity to examine the respective positions of the heart, lungs and brain in relation to the conspicuous points of the animal's exterior, such as the eye, the ear, the line of the fore leg and the point of the shoulder. In order to fix the position of the heart and lungs I made some boys get the stomach and intestines out. This was a terrific job, but we were ably assisted by the powerful native women. The "innards" of elephant are very greatly prized by all natives who eat elephant. The contents of the stomach must have weighed a ton, I should think, and I saw the intestine or sack which contains the clear pure water so readily drunk by the hunter during the dry season when he finds himself far from water. It is from this internal tank that the elephant can produce water for the purpose of treating himself to a shower bath when there is no water. He brings it up into his throat, whence it is sucked into the trunk and then delivered where required. The first time I saw an elephant doing this I thought he must be standing by a pool of water from which he was drawing it. I was many weary miles from water and the sun was scorching, and I and the boy with me were very thirsty, so we hastened towards the elephant, which moved on slowly through the bush. Very soon we arrived at the spot where we had seen him at his shower bath, but no spring or pool could I find. I asked the Karamojan about it and he then told me, with a smile at my ignorance, that the nearest water was at our camp and that all elephant carried water inside them and need not replenish their stock for three days. Coming up with the elephant I killed him and got Pyjalé (my Karamojan tracker) to pierce its water tank, and sure enough water, perfectly clear barring a little blood, gushed out, which we both drank greedily. It was warm certainly, but quite tasteless and odourless and very wholesome and grateful.

When everything had been got out, except the lungs and heart, I had spears thrust through from the direction from which a bullet would come. I meanwhile peered into the huge cavity formed by the massive ribs and when a spear pierced a lung or the heart, I immediately examined its situation and tried to commit it to my memory. One thing I noticed was that with the animal lying on its side the heart did not occupy the cavity which was obviously intended for it when upright, therefore an allowance had to be made. Another thing I was impressed with was the size of the arteries about the heart. It extended the killing area a considerable distance above the heart, and I have often since killed elephant with a shot above the heart. About the situation of the brain I also learned a lot. I thought I had its position fixed to a nicety in my mind, but I subsequently found that all I had learned was one of the many positions the brain does not occupy. And it was by a series of these misplacings that I finally came to know where the brain really does lie. It is a small object contained in a very large head. It lies so far from the exterior that a very slight and almost unnoticeable change of angle causes the bullet to miss it completely.

From this my first dealing with Karamojans it began to be borne in on me that they were not so bad as the Swahili traders had tried to make out. And my subsequent dealings with them confirmed this impression. As far as I was concerned I had hardly any trouble with them. But at the same time some terrible massacres took place while I was in their country. These affairs were the most completely successful operations I have ever heard of from the native point of view. On three occasions massacres of well-armed trading caravans were attempted, and on two there were no survivors among the traders and no casualties among the natives, while on the third there was one trader survivor who escaped. I will describe later on the methods employed by the natives so successfully, for it was not until my Karamojan friend Pyjalé came to me that I heard the inside of the thing. For the next few days nothing of note happened except that we passed the remains of two black men by the roadside—stragglers from some trading caravan probably, judging by the bits of cloth lying about. Now here was a state of things requiring explanation. We were now close to Mani-Mani, the up-country base for all trading caravans. Mani-Mani was also a populous centre for Karamojans, with whom the traders were perforce at peace. And yet here on the roads were two murdered men obviously belonging to the traders. On my arrival at Mani-Mani I found the explanation. It was thus: among Karamojans, as among Masai, Somals and other tribes, a young man is of no consideration, has no standing with the girls, until he has killed someone. It does not matter how he kills him, he may be asleep or unarmed. When he has "done someone in," either man or woman, other than Karamojan of course, he has the right to tattoo the right side of his body for a man victim and the left side for a woman. Moreover, at the dances he mounts a very tall ostrich feather dipped blood red, and then he is looked upon as a man. He may and does now demand anything from the unmarried girls. He may flog them should they resist. And this atrocious incitement to murder is the cause of death to any leg-weary straggler from caravans. That the Swahili leaders never made these wayside murders a *casus belli* shows them to be what they are, callous snivellers. That they could have put down this custom was shown when some of my boys lost their way among the villages. As soon as it was reported to me I at once got together five of my askaris and raced off among the herds of Karamojan cattle. We rounded up a huge mob and held them more or less in one place. Spearmen rushed about, women holloaed, and shields were produced from every hut. I was so hot and angry—thinking that the missing boys had been murdered—that I was eager to begin by attacking straightaway. It looked as if about 400 spearmen were assembled and I meant to give them a genuine shaking up with my 10-shot .303, followed by my ten-shot Mauser pistol. I felt confident that as soon as I let loose on them and killed one or two the others would run like rabbits. It never came to a fight, for some old unarmed men and women came tottering up, picking grass at every step, biting it in two and casting the bits to the winds. This meant peace; peace at any price. Where were my porters? They did not know, really they did not. But they would be all right. Nobody would harm them. I told them to go and produce every one of them unharmed or I would take and kill all their cattle and a lot of them besides. Moreover, if any armed man approached anywhere near to the cattle I would shoot him dead. The cattle would remain there—between ourselves we could not have handled them—until the porters were produced.

And produced they were, very quickly. They had merely lost their way among the villages and had been guided back.

I did not regret having had this opportunity of showing the natives that as far as my people were concerned we were prepared to fight savagely for any member of the safari and not—as did the traders—let stragglers be murdered without even a protest. The noise of this affair travelled far and probably saved us a lot of trouble in our after dealings.

Another reason for this apathy on the part of the Swahili leaders was, I think, that the certainty of murder awaiting anyone on the road prevented desertion. They were enabled by this means to keep their boys for years without payment of wages. So long as they could prevent the boys from reaching Mumias alive there was no redress. Hence it was difficult for the Government representative at Mumias to get reliable information of the internal state of Karamojo.

On our arrival at Mani-Mani we were met by one Shundi—a remarkable man. Kavirondo by birth, he had been captured early in life, taken to the coast and sold as a slave. Being a man of great force of character he had soon freed himself by turning Mohammedan. Thence onward fortune had smiled upon him until at last here he was, the recognised chief *Tajir* (rich man) of all the traders. Having naturally the intelligence to recognise the value of bluff and from his primitive ancestors the nerve to carry it off, he was at this time the greatest of all the traders. Just as he had been a leader while slave-raiding was the order of the day, so now he led when ivory had given place to slaves as a commodity. One other thing makes him conspicuous, at any rate, in my mind, and that was the fact that he had owned the slave who had laid low the elephant which bore the enormous tusks, one of which now reposes in the South Kensington Museum. These tusks are still, as far as I know, the record. The one which we have in London scales 234 lbs. or thereabouts. According to Shundi his slave killed it with a muzzle-loader on the slopes of Kilimandjaro.

Shundi was accompanied by a large body of traders of all sorts. There were Arabs, Swahilis, one or two Persians and a few African born Baluchis, and a pretty tough lot they looked. Beside their mean and cunning air Shundi—the great coal-black Bantu—appeared like a lion among hyenas. What an extraordinary calm and dignity some of these outstanding black men have. Here was a kin spirit to Buba Gida.

They hated my appearing in their country, but did not show it. Shundi took it in the spirit that what had to be had to be, but some of the lesser villains were obviously nervous. They pretended to wish me to camp inside the town, but I preferred to remain outside. The town was of very considerable size, although the buildings were of a temporary construction. I remarked an extraordinary number of women about and thought that I recognised Masai types among them. This was so, as I afterwards learnt that Shundi alone had over eighty women, many of whom were Masai from Kilimandjaro.

With native politeness gifts of food, etc., were offered and presently all withdrew, intimating that they would return when I had rested.

They must have been feeling rather uncomfortable about the appearance in their midst of a white man, possibly an agent of that detestable Government so troublesome about raiding. I did not actually know at the time, but learnt afterwards that at the very moment of my arrival in their midst they had an enormous raid on the Turkana underway.

In the afternoon they came again and we had the usual ceremonial palaver. Every one was strictly guarded, but they made a distinct effort to embroil me with the natives in the hope, I suppose, of getting me so mixed up in some shooting affair that I would become more or less one of themselves. I refused to have anything to do with their intrigues. I got little information regarding elephant from these people. In fact, neither side could quite overcome a severely suppressed but quite strong hostility to the other.

I stayed a few days at Mani-Mani as there were repairs to be attended to and man and beast required a rest. The first sign of trouble soon appeared, caused, I feel certain, by Swahili intrigue. It was the dry season and all animals were watered once a day at the wells dug in the otherwise dry river-bed. My animals were being watered as usual. That is, water was drawn from the well in buckets and emptied into a watertight ground sheet laid over a suitable depression in the sand. Word was suddenly brought to me that the natives refused to allow my animals to be watered. I went at once to the scene and asked the natives what all the trouble was about. There were about forty young bloods leaning against their spears and they laughed in the most insolent manner without giving me any answer. I turned to my herds and beckoned them to bring up the animals. As they began to do so three of the bloods strode over and began flogging the thirsty bullocks in the face and driving them off. It was now or never, first impression and so on. I seized from the nearest Karamojan his cutting-edged club, sprang over to one of the bullock obstructors and dealt him the hardest blow on the head I possibly could. I was fairly hefty, in good training, and meant all I knew. To my astonishment the native turned on me a smile instead of dropping dead or at least stunned, while the club flew to atoms. I had hit his shock-absorbing periwig, previously described. I might as well have hit a Dunlop Magnum.

I must confess it was rather a set-back. However, one good effect it had was that everyone, except myself, roared with laughter, and then when even I began to see the humour of it I spotted a mischievous devil calmly jabbing his spear through our priceless waterproof ground sheet. This would not do, so I drew my Mauser pistol. Now these natives were then at a most dangerous stage of ignorance with regard to firearms. Their experience of them had been gathered on raids with the Swahilis, and they all firmly held the conviction that all you had to do to avoid being struck by the bullet was to *duck when you saw the smoke.* While I was fitting the wooden holster to the Mauser they watched me carefully. They had probably never seen such a gun before if they even recognised it as such. When therefore I had it fitted up and was covering them no one moved. They were waiting, I suspect, for the smoke. And when they heard the particularly vicious bang of the little Mauser and saw no smoke, the laugh this time was rather on them, and especially on the gentleman who had been so busy with his spear and my ground sheet; for he now stood looking at a half severed and completely spoilt spear in his hand with a ridiculous air of surprised injury. In a few seconds the humour of this phase struck all concerned, although the natives began to edge nervously away. All their swagger was gone now. I had been approaching the fellow with the damaged spear, and now suddenly set upon him, relying upon my herds to help me. Never have I felt anything like the sinewy strength of that greasy native; he was all but off when the boys secured him just in time. Seeing some flourishing of spears going on among the others, I began pasting dust about them with the little Mauser. Seeing no smoke again, yet getting whing whang right and left of them, they turned and bolted. I got in another clip of ten and kept them dodging dust-bursts for 400 or 500 yds.

On returning I put it out among the natives that our prisoner would be released when ten goats and sheep had been paid by his family as a fine. They were soon forthcoming.

Up till now I had been looked upon by the natives as a sort of poor Arab. In this idea they were no doubt helped by the traders. They had never seen white men, and they saw my mean little safari and drew their own conclusions from appearances. But after the affair at the water hole I was treated with much greater respect, and with a kind of good-humoured indulgence, much as a very persistent headstrong child might be looked upon. And eventually, after a few more "incidents," we became fast friends and they would do almost anything for me or for my people. One instance of this I may as well here record, although it happened long afterwards.

Away down in civilised parts I had left two aged Wanyamwezi boys in charge of my cattle ranch. This was situated a few miles from Nandi Boma (Government Post). At the Boma post office I had left directions for my letters to be forwarded to another Boma on the slopes of Elgon, where I used to send every six months or so to get them. All my letters went as directed until there occurred a change of District Commissioner. Now one of my old pensioners looking after the ranch had orders to report every fortnight to the D.C. that all was well or otherwise. In pursuit of these instructions the old boy appeared one day before the new D.C., who asked him who he was. He said he belonged to me, naming me. The D.C. said he had some letters for me, and told the boy to *take them to me*, thinking that I was at the ranch a few miles off, instead of which I was actually over 600 miles away. That dear old man took the letters without a word, went straight back to the ranch and prepared to follow me into what was much of it quite unknown country. He told the other boy, who was also about sixty-five years of age, that he would have to look after everything himself as he was going after the Bwana (master). Being a thrifty old soul, he had by him much stock of dry smoked beef from cows which had died. His preparations were, therefore, almost complete. An inveterate snuff-taker, he had only to grind up a good quantity for the journey and he was ready. Shouldering his Snider and with the packet of letters cunningly guarded against wet, off he set through the wilderness, steering due north. Sleeping by night alone by his camp fire and travelling the whole of the day, he came wandering through what would have been to anyone else hostile tribe after hostile tribe. Countries where if I sent at all I sent at least five guns as escort he came through without trouble. How often he must have been looked upon by the lecherous eyes of would-be bloods as fair game for their spears and as means of gaining the coveted tattoo marks and the blood-red ostrich feather. But so sublimely unconscious was he of any feeling of nervousness and so bold and confident his bearing that nothing happened. Being old and wise, he courted the routes which led through the most populous centres instead of dodging along the neutral zones between tribes as a nervous man would have done. Had he done this he would to a certainty have been killed. Wherever he went he slept in the largest village, demanded *and got* the best of everything, and eventually reached me intact. It was a splendid effort. He walked into camp as if he had left it five minutes before, and he still had smoked beef and snuff when he arrived. The dear old hoarder had lived to some purpose on the natives as he passed through. He arrived, if you please, escorted by a number of Karamojan big-men, this dingy and, I have to say it, very dirty old man. The letters, alas! proved to be most uninteresting in themselves, but, nevertheless, they formed a link with civilisation. They were chiefly bills from unscrupulous Coast merchants being rendered for the third and fourth time although already paid at least once.

The newspapers were, of course, very old, but produced an extraordinary feeling of uneasiness or disquietude. Leading the life I then was, with its freedom from financial care—money was valueless and never handled—from responsibility—there was no law in the land except that of force—it had rather the effect of a sudden chill to read of strikes, famines, railway accidents, unemployment, lawsuits, and the other thousand and one unhappinesses usually contained in newspapers. Although I read them, every word, including the advertisements—here again remedies for ills—I felt distinctly perturbed for two or three days after. The happiest literature I ever had in the bush was "Pickwick Papers," and the happiest newspaper the dear old *Field*.

III.—The Coming of Pyjalé

From Mani-Mani we moved on to Bukora, another section of Karamojans. I was warned by the Swahilis that Bukora was a very bad country. The people were very rich in cattle and correspondingly insolent. Everyone who passed through Bukora had trouble. Either stock was stolen or porters murdered.

I cannot say that I believed all this, or perhaps I would not have been so ready to go there. But that there was some truth in their statements I soon found. In fact, there were moments when it was touch and go. Looking back on it calmly I can see that nothing but chance luck saved us. It was thus: we pushed our way smartly right into the middle of Bukora, intending to camp near some large village. But to our disappointment the catchments of water were nearly dry. What remained in them was merely mud. We were obliged therefore to move on to some wells on the outskirts of the villages. This is always a bad place to be attacked in. Natives are much more willing to attack people outside than when they are right in their midst. When you are close alongside a village and there is any question of hostilities, the people of that particular village feel that they will probably come in for more than their share of the trouble when it begins. They have their goods and chattels there, their corn, cows, babies, fowls, etc. For these reasons they are against hostilities. Another advantage to the travellers when close to stockaded villages—as these were—is that such a village can be rushed and then held against the rest of the tribe.

However, I was young and without much thought of anything in those days, and camp by the wells I would. We accordingly did so. And presently the camp began to fill with apparently friendly natives. They dropped in by twos and threes and stood around, each man with two spears. I thought they seemed a nice friendly, sociable crowd, and took little further heed of them. Then comes my headman, a Swahili, to me. "Bwana, there is no good brewing. These people mean trouble. Look around, do you see a single woman anywhere?" I laughed and asked him what he thought they would do. He said that at a given prearranged signal they would start spearing everyone. And then it dawned on me how absurdly easy it would be for them to do so. When you came to look around with this thought in your mind it became apparent that every man was being marked by several spearmen. If he moved they also lounged about until they were again close to him. I must say they appeared to me to act the indifference part very well. When I had convinced myself that something of this nature really was afoot, I naturally got close to my shooting irons, ready to take a hand when the fun started. In those days I always wore fifty rounds in my belt.

Now I thought that if I could only supply something sufficiently distracting the affair might never begin. There over the plains were plenty of game. I took my rifle and got the interpreter to tell the Karamojans to come as I was going killing meat. They came at once in fair numbers. They had already heard of my wonderful rifles, and wherever I went I always had an audience eager to see them or the Bom-bom (Mauser pistol) at work.

Hardly had we gone a few hundred yards, and while we were still in full view of the camp, when a herd of zebra came galloping across our front. They had been alarmed by some abnormal movement of natives and had somehow got mixed up and lost.

They came well spaced apart and just right for my purpose. I shot one after the other as hard as I could fire. I was using a 10-shot .303, and when I had fired the ten shots the survivors of the herd were too far off. I was careful not to reload in the ordinary way, for I carried another charged magazine. Consequently the natives thought I might have any number of shots left in this quite new and terrifying weapon. No smoke and such a rapid fire of death—they had never seen the like. Bing! bing! bing! bing!

bing! they kept saying to themselves, only much more rapidly than the actual rate of fire. And the zebras, strong brutes, knocked right down one after the other. No! this was something new. They had better be careful about fooling around with this *red* man. He was different from those red men among the Swahilis, who used to fire great clouds of smoke and hit nothing.

After an episode of this kind one *feels* somehow that a complete mental transformation has taken place. One is established right above these, in some ways, finer but less scientific people. But this knowledge comes to both at the same time. I now ordered these previously truculent, now almost servile, savages to flay, cut up and carry to camp every bit of meat and skin. When I saw anyone sneaking a bit of fat or what-not I blackguarded him soundly. I rushed the whole regiment back to camp loaded with several tons of meat, many of them forgetting their spears in their hurry. But had I ventured to bullyrag them like this before the zebra incident I would have had a spear thrust for answer and right quickly too.

I now began to push enquiries about elephant, but with no great success at first. One day a Bukora boy came to camp and while in conversation with some of my people casually told them that he had recently returned from no man's land, where he and some friends of his had been looking for Kumamma. The Kumamma were their neighbours to the west. They had been looking for them in order to spear them, should things be right—that meaning should the enemy be in sufficiently small force for them to easily overcome. When the numbers are at all equal, both sides retire smartly to the rear. This is the normal kind of state in which these tribes live. It leads to a few deaths certainly, but it keeps the young men fit and out of other mischief. Every young man goes looking for blood frequently, and as they carry no food except a few handfuls of unground millet simply soaked in water, and as they never dare to sleep while in the neutral zone, it acts as a kind of field training.

This youth, then, had seen no Kumamma but had seen elephant. My boys told me this and I tried to get the lad to go with us to hunt. He said he would come back and let me know. He did so and brought a friend. This friend of his was a most remarkable-looking man. Strange as it may seem, he had a most intellectual head. He was a man of perhaps thirty-five years of age, most beautifully made and tattooed for men victims only, I was relieved to see. Pyjalé was his name, and now began a firm and long friendship between this distinguished savage and myself. I cannot say that I have ever had the same feelings for any man as I came to have for Pyjalé. He was, I found, a thorough man, courageous, quiet, modest, with a horror of humbug and untiring in our common pact, the pursuit of elephant. He was with me during the greater part of my time in Karamojo, and although surrounded by people who clothed themselves, never would he wear a rag even. Nor would he sleep comfortably as we did on grass and blankets. The bare hard ground out by the camp fire with a hole dug for his hip bone and his little wooden pillow had been good enough for him before and was good enough now. No one poked fun at Pyjalé for his nakedness; he was the kind who do not get fun poked at them.

Pyjalé was game to show us elephants, but said we would have to travel far. His intelligence was at once apparent by his saying that we ought to take tents as the rains might come any day. He was right, for come they did while we were hunting.

I took to Pyjalé right at the start and asked him what I should do about the main safari. He said I could leave it where it was; no one would interfere with it. If I liked I could leave the ivory in one of the villages. This I gathered was equivalent to putting one's silver in the bank at home. And so it is, bizarre as it may seem. You may leave anything with natives—ivory, beads, which are money, trade goods, stock, anything—and not one thing will they take provided you place it in their care. But if you leave your own people to look after it they will steal it, given the chance.

Thinking that it might save trouble I put all my trade goods and ivory in a village, and leaving the safari with plenty of rations, I left for a few days' hunting, taking a sufficient number of porters to bring home any ivory we were likely to get. This was necessary at this time as the natives did not yet follow me in hundreds wherever I went, as they did later on.

We trekked hard for three days and came once more in sight of the Debasien range, but on its other side. On the night of the third day the rains burst upon us. The light calico bush tents were hastily erected in a perfect gale and downpour. Even Pyjalé had to shelter.

In the morning Pyjalé said we were certain to see elephant if we could only cross a river which lay ahead of us. When we reached its banks it was a raging torrent, red with mud and covered with patches of white froth. There was nothing for it but to camp and wait until the spate subsided.

While this was being done I saw a snake being carried down by the swollen river. Then I saw another and another. Evidently banks were being washed away somewhere.

A boy pointed to my shorts and said that a *doodoo* (insect) had crawled up the inside of one of my legs. Thinking, perhaps, it was a fly, or not thinking at all, perhaps, I slapped my leg hard with open hand and got a most frightful sting, while a huge scorpion dropped half crushed to the ground. But not before he had injected quite sufficient poison into me. "Insect," indeed! how I cursed that boy. And then, by way of helping me, he said that when people were stung by these big black scorpions—like mine—they always died. He was in a frightful state. And then another fool boy said: "Yes, no one ever recovered from that kind." I shouted for whisky, for you certainly could feel the poison going through the circulation. I knew that what the boys said was bunkum, but still I drank a lot of whisky. My leg swelled and I could not sleep that night, but I was quite all right next day.

The river had gone down somewhat, so I proposed to cross. No one was very eager to go across with a rope. A rope was necessary, as some of the boys could not swim and the current was running too strong for them to walk across the bottom under water, carrying stones to keep them down, as they usually did.

I carried at that time a Mexican rawhide lariat and thought that this stretched across would do nicely for the boys to haul themselves over by. So I took one end to the other side and made it fast, when the safari began to come over. Once the plunge had been taken I found that more of them could swim than they had led me to believe. Then the inevitable—when rawhide gets wet—happened and the rope parted. As luck would have it there was a boy about mid-stream at the instant. The slippery end slid through his fingers and he went rapidly down-stream. His head kept going under and reappearing I noticed, but thought that, as he had a smile on his face each time he came up, he was another humbug pretending to be unable to swim. His friends, who knew perfectly well that he could not swim a yard, said, of course, not a word. And it was not until he gushed water at the mouth instead of air that I realised he was drowning. I ran down the bank while another boy plunged in at the crossing place. I reached the boy first by a second and we soon had him towing to bank. Black men are good to save, they never seem to realise their close call and do not clutch and try to climb out on you. While towing to the bank I felt something on my head and put up a hand to brush it off. Horrors, a snake! It was merely trying to save itself on anything above water level, but I did not realise this. Whenever I knocked it off it seemed to come again. Luckily we just then reached the bank or in another instant I would have abandoned my drowning porter to save myself from that beastly serpent. It was all very silly, and the snake was nearly at its last gasp, but I did not see the humour at the moment. Needless to say, the boy was perfectly all right in ten minutes after vomiting up a bucket or two of water.

While we were getting ready again for the march we heard elephant. To my inexperienced ear the sound seemed to come from some bush 400 yds. or 500 yds. away. But Pyjalé said, to my astonishment, that they were a long way off and that unless we hurried we should not see them before sundown. As the sun then indicated about one o'clock, I thought he was wrong. But he was not; for it was half an hour from sunset when we saw them, still far away. I remember looking industriously about all those miles expecting momentarily to see elephant, while Pyjalé soaked along ahead of me without a glance aside. The only explanation of this extraordinary sound-carrying that has ever occurred to me is humidity of atmosphere. During the dry season the earth becomes so hot that when the first rains fall much is evaporated in steam and the humidity is remarkable.

Here we were face to face with such a gathering of elephant as I had never dared to dream of even. The whole country was black with them, and what lay beyond them one could not see as the country was dead flat. Some of them were up to their knees in water, and when we reached their tracks the going became very bad. The water was so opaque with mud as to quite hide the huge pot-holes made by the heavy animals. You were in and out the whole time. As we drew nearer I thought that we ought to go decently and quietly, at any rate make some pretence of stalking them, if only out of respect to them. But no, that awful Pyjalé rushed me, splashing and squelching right up to them. He was awfully good, and I began to learn a lot from him. He treated elephant with complete indifference. If he were moved at all, and that was seldom, he would smile.

I was for treating them as dangerous animals, especially when we trod on the heels of small bogged-down calves and their mothers came rushing back at us in the most alarming fashion, but Pyjalé would have none of it. Up to the big bulls would he have me go, even if we had to go under infuriated cows. He made me kill seven before sundown stopped the bloodshed.

With great difficulty we found a spot a little higher than the surrounding country and fairly dry. As usual at these flood times the little island was crawling with ants of every description. How comes it that ants do not drown, although they cannot swim? They appear to be covered with something which repels water.

Scorpions and all kinds of other horrors were there also. One of the boys was bitten and made a fearful fuss all night about it.

I expected to do well on the morrow, but when it came, behold, not an elephant in sight. Such are the surprises of elephant hunting. Yesterday when light failed hundreds upon hundreds in sight and now an empty wilderness.

We had not alarmed them, as I noticed that when a shot was fired only the animals in the vicinity ran and that for a short distance only. There were too many to stampede even had they been familiar with firearms. And the noise was such as to drown the crack of a .303 almost immediately.

I asked Pyjalé what he thought about it. He said that at the beginning of the rains elephant wandered all over the country. You could never tell where they might be. With water and mud and green food springing up everywhere they were under no necessity to frequent any one district more than another. Pyjalé's advice was to get the ivory out and take it home, and then he would show me a country where we were certain to get big bulls. Accordingly the boys set about chopping out while I went for a cruise around to make certain there was nothing about.

I saw nothing but ostrich, giraffe and great herds of common and Topi haartebeeste. On crossing some black-cotton soil I noticed that it clung to the boots in a very tiresome way. Each time you lifted a foot, ten or fifteen lbs. of sticky mud came with it. At this stage the ground was still dry underneath, only the top few inches being wet. From the big lumps lying about where antelope had passed it was obvious that they had, too, the same trouble as I was having, *i.e.*, mud clinging to the feet.

But on watching Pyjalé it appeared that it did not stick to naked human feet to anything like the same extent. Pyjalé told me, and I afterwards saw it actually done, that it was possible to run down ostrich and the heavy antelope, such as eland, when the ground was in this state.

Returning we found the boys well on with their chopping out. Towards evening we started for home, being much troubled with swollen rivers. Most of the boys walked through the rivers when we could find a place where the current was not too strong. The heavy tusks, of course, kept them on the bottom. But it was a curious sight to see them calmly marching in deeper and deeper until their heads went right under, reappearing again close to the other bank. Of course, the distance they thus traversed was only a few yards, but for fellows who cannot swim it was not bad.

One camp from home (the safari) we slept near some flooded wells. The boys took their tusks to scrub them with sand and water, the better to make an appearance on the morrow when we should rejoin the safari. This is always a source of joy to Wanyamwezi, to carry ivory to the base. When allowed to do so they will spend hours dancing and singing their way into the camp. The women turn out, everybody makes a noise of some kind, from blowing a reed pipe, to trumpeting on a water buck horn or beating a drum or a tin, in fact anything so that it produces noise.

While they were scrubbing the tusks one of these slipped from the boy's hands into a well. I heard of it and went to see what could be done. To test the depth I tried one of Pyjalé's nine-ft. spears. No good. Then I tied another to it, but even then I could not touch bottom. Pyjalé said the bottom was very far. Then I looked at one of my boys squatting on the edge of the well. He had been a coast canoe-man shark-fisher—than whom no finer watermen exist—and knew what I meant without a word passing. He tied his cloth between his legs and stripped his upper body. Then jumping into the air he twisted half round and went down head first into the very middle of the well. It seemed ages before his head reappeared. At last it did so, but only for an instant. Down again; apparently he had not found it the first time. After another long wait he came up with the tusk and swimming or treading water. Eager hands clutched the tusk and drew it out; the boy crawled out himself. This particular tusk weighed 65 lbs., the length being almost the diameter of the well, so it had to be brought up end on. How he did it I cannot imagine. The water was the colour of pea-soup, and a scrubbed tusk is like a greasy pole to hold. Of course, it would not weigh 65 lbs. when submerged, but it was a pretty good effort I thought. I know I would not have gone 20 ft. or 30 ft. down that well for any number of tusks.

These boys have the most extraordinary lungs. I once sent one of them down to disentangle the anchor of a motor launch, which had got foul of something. There were about four fathoms of chain and the boy went down this hand over hand. I only wanted him to clear the anchor, when we would heave it up in the ordinary way. But presently up the chain came the boy and the anchor.

On the morrow we entered Bukora again, with fourteen fine white tusks. We had a great reception at our camp. The natives, too, were rather astonished at our rapid success. Pyjalé stalked along without any show of feeling.

The boys who had stayed behind had nothing to report except the loss of three of our sheep by theft. Now it was essential to nip this kind of thing in the bud. I did nothing that day, merely sending Pyjalé to his home with a handsome present. I knew he would put it round as to the kind of people we were. Natives always exaggerate enormously when back from a scurry in the bush, and his account of our doings would probably have made me blush had I heard it.

Next day when Pyjalé came with a pot of fresh cow's milk as a present, I asked him if he had heard anything about our sheep. He said no. I asked him to point me out the village which had stolen them. He said they would kill him if he did so. Therefore he knew. I then said that he need not go with me, if only he would indicate it. He said the village with the three tamarind trees was where the thieves lived.

I went over quietly, as if looking for guinea-fowl, in the evening. The village was quite close to our camp. When their stock began to come in I signalled up some boys. We walked up deliberately to the herds, no one taking any great notice of us. I separated out a mob of sheep and goats and we started driving them towards camp, but very quietly and calmly. It is wonderful how imitative Africans are. If you are excited they at once become so. If you are calm and deliberate, so are they.

A more dramatic thing would have been to take the cattle. But these native cattle are not used to boys wearing clothes, as mine did, and we found at Mani-Mani that they became excited and difficult to handle unless they see their black naked owners about. Pyjalé I had carefully left out of this business.

As soon as our object dawned upon the Karamojans there was the usual commotion. Women *wha! wha! wha*-ed while rushing from the huts with shields; warriors seized these and rushed with prodigious speed directly away from us; while we pushed our two or three hundred hostages slowly along.

Arrived at camp we just managed to squeeze them all into the bullock boma. There were noises all round us now. The boys were uneasy; there is always something in the alarm note when issued by hundreds of human throats. Dark was soon on us and we sat up by the camp fires till fairly late. Nothing happened, as I anticipated. Discretion had won. They hated that little bom-bom so.

What I wanted now was that they should come. I wanted to tell them why I had taken their sheep. No one appeared, but I consoled myself with the thought that they jolly well knew why I had taken them.

Presently there appeared to be great signs of activity in one of the nearer villages. Native men kept coming from all directions. My boys were all eyes for this, to them, impending attack. I thought they must be born fools to try anything of that sort in broad daylight. Night was their best chance.

Pyjalé had been absent, so I hoped that he was at the meeting. Presently he appeared. He said they had had a discussion and had concluded not to attack us. I told him to go straight back and invite them all to come; I wanted to be attacked. And moreover, if my sheep were not instantly brought I would proceed to kill the hostage sheep we held, and that then I would proceed to hunt the thieves.

This acted like magic; I suppose they thought that as I had known the village of the thieves, I also probably knew the actual men themselves. Our sheep were very soon brought and the hostages released.

I took the opportunity when the natives were there to impress upon them that we did not want anything from them. All we wanted was to hunt elephant in peace, but at the same time I hinted that we could be very terrible indeed. I got some of the older men to dry up and sit down, in a friendly way, and we had a good talk together. I now brought out the card to which I owed all my success in killing elephant in Karamojo. I offered a cow as reward for information leading to my killing five or more bull elephant. This was an unheard-of reward. There a cow of breeding age is simply priceless. Normally natives never kill or sell she-stock of any kind and cows could only be obtained by successful raiding. Now among Africans there are numbers of young men who just lack the quality which brings success to its lucky owner, just as there are in every community, and to these young men my offer appealed tremendously. That they believed in my promise from the very start was, I thought, a great compliment, not only to me, but to their astuteness in perceiving that there was a difference between white men and Swahilis.

When my offer had gone the rounds the whole country for many miles round was scoured for elephant, with the result that I never could have a day's rest. Everyone was looking for elephant. But had the reward been trade goods scarcely a soul would have bothered about it.

The first man to come was remarkable-looking enough to satisfy anybody. A terrible-looking man. A grotesquely hideous face above a very broad and deep chest, all mounted on the spindliest of knock-kneed legs. Chest, arms, shoulders, stomach and back heavily tattooed, denoting much killing. By reputation a terrific fighter, and very wealthy.

At first I thought that he was come to show me elephant. That was his intention, he said, but first he wanted to become my blood-brother. He said he could see that I was a kindred spirit and that we two should be friends. He said he had no friends. How was that? I asked. Pyjalé answered in a whisper that the lion never made friends of jackals and hyenas. And so we became friends. I was not going through the blood-brotherhood business, with its eating of bits of toasted meat smeared with each other's blood, sawing in two of living dogs or nonsense of that kind. I took his hand and wrung it hard, and had it explained to him that among us that was an extraordinarily potent way of doing it. That seemed to satisfy the old boy, for the act of shaking hands was as strange to him as the act of eating each other's blood is to us.

He started off then and I said: "What about those elephant?" "Wait," was the answer, and off he went, to return shortly with a fat bullock. And then I found that my friend was the wealthiest cattle owner anywhere about—a kind of multi-millionaire. I thought to myself, well, he will not look for elephant. Nor did he; but he had sons without number, being much married, whom he scattered far and wide to look for them. He had arranged the thing most perfectly. We went with food for a few days and returned laden with ivory. Besides which we had some of the jolliest nights in the bush.

This great man being now my friend, our troubles were at an end. Wherever we went we were followed by scores of the young unmarried girls and one old maid—the only one I have come across in Karamojo. She was so outstandingly above the average in good looks, so beautifully made and so obviously still quite young, that I often asked why she should remain a spinster. They told me that no man would marry her because she was so beautiful. But why should that be a bar? We white men like our wives to be beautiful. They thought this strange, even for white men. They said they never married very beautiful women as all men wanted them. They also gave as another reason that these very attractive women wanted all men. And I must say that our camp beauty gave decided colour to this latter statement.

No sooner were we arrived back with our imposing line of beautiful tusks than other natives clamoured to take us to elephant. They wanted me to go there and then, but I needed a rest.

In the evening I presented my friend with a heifer, when to my astonishment he refused it. He said he wanted nothing from his friend. I was rather suspicious about this at first, but I need not have been, as I subsequently found this man to be thoroughly genuine. I am convinced that he would have given me anything. It is a big affair in their lives, this blood-brotherhood. Apparently we now owned everything in common. He offered me any of his daughters in marriage, and, thank goodness, never asked me for my rifle. From now on he followed me about like a faithful dog, some of his young wives attending to his commissariat arrangements wherever he was. He even took my name, which was Longelly-nyung or Red Man. And he began now to call his young male children, of whom he was very fond, by the same name. He was a delightfully simple fellow at heart and as courageous as a lion, as I had proof later.

After a few more journeys to the bush lasting from four to ten days, I found suddenly that I had as much ivory as I could possibly move. And this, while still on the fringe of Karamojo. I decided to return to Mumias, sell my ivory, fit out a real good expedition capable of moving several tons of ivory, and return to Karamojo fitted out for several years in the bush.

The Thak Man-Eater

JIM CORBETT

Peace had reigned in the Ladhya valley for many months when in September '38 a report was received in Naini Tal that a girl, twelve years of age, had been killed by a tiger at Kot Kindri village. The report, which reached me through Donald Stewart, of the Forest Department, gave no details, and it was not until I visited the village some weeks later that I was able to get particulars of the tragedy. It appeared that, about noon one day, this girl was picking up windfalls from a mango tree close to and in full view of the village, when a tiger suddenly appeared. Before the men working near by were able to render any assistance, it carried her off. No attempt was made to follow up the tiger, and as all signs of drag and blood trail had been obliterated and washed away long before I arrived on the scene, I was unable to find the place where the tiger had taken the body to.

Kot Kindri is about four miles southwest of Chuka, and three miles due west of Thak. It was in the valley between Kot Kindri and Thak that the Chuka man-eater had been shot the previous April.

My most direct route to Kot Kindri was to go by rail to Tanakpur, and from there by foot via Kaldhunga and Chuka. This route, however, though it would save me a hundred miles of walking, would necessitate my passing through the most deadly malaria belt in northern India, and to avoid it I decided to go through the hills to Mornaula, and from there along the abandoned Sherring road to its termination on the ridge above Kot Kindri.

While my preparations for this long trek were still under way a second report reached Naini Tal of a kill at Sem, a small village on the left bank of the Ladhya and distant about half a mile from Chuka.

The victim on this occasion was an elderly woman, the mother of the Headman of Sem. This unfortunate woman had been killed while cutting brushwood on a steep bank between two terraced fields. She had started work at the further end of the fifty-yard-long bank, and had cut the brushwood to within a yard of her hut when the tiger sprang on her from the field above. So sudden and unexpected was the attack that the woman only had time to scream once before the tiger killed her, and taking her up the twelve-foot-high bank crossed the upper field and disappeared with her into the dense jungle beyond. Her son, a lad some twenty years of age, was at the time working in a paddy field a few yards away and witnessed the whole occurrence, but was too frightened to try to render any assistance. In response to the lad's urgent summons the Patwari arrived at Sem two days later, accompanied by eighty men he had collected. Following up in the direction the tiger had gone, he found the woman's clothes and a few small bits of bone. This kill had taken place at 2 p.m. on a bright sunny day, and the tiger had eaten its victim only sixty yards from the hut where it had killed her.

On receipt of this second report, Ibbotson, Deputy Commissioner of the three Districts of Almora. Naini Tal, and Gathwal, and I held a council of war, the upshot of which was that Ibbotson, who was on the point of setting out to settle a land dispute at Askot on the border of Tibet, changed his tour program and, instead of going via Bagashwar, decided to accompany me to Sem, and from there go on to Askot.

The route I had selected entailed a considerable amount of hill-climbing so we eventually decided to go up the Nandhour valley, cross the watershed between the Nandhour and Ladhya, and follow the latter river down to Sem. The Ibbotsons accordingly left Naini Tal on 12 October, and the following day I joined them at Chaurgallia.

Going up the Nandhour and fishing as we went—our best day's catch on light trout rods was a hundred and twenty fish—we arrived on the fifth day at Durga Pepal. Here we left the river, and after a very stiff climb camped for the night on the watershed. Making an early start next morning we pitched our tents that night on the left bank of the Ladhya, twelve miles from Chalti.

The monsoon had given over early, which was very fortunate for us, for owing to the rock cliffs that run sheer down into the valley, the river has to be crossed every quarter of a mile or so. At one of these fords my cook, who stands five feet in his boots, was washed away and only saved from a watery grave by the prompt assistance of the man who was carrying our lunch basket.

On the tenth day after leaving Chaurgallia we made camp on a deserted field at Sem, two hundred yards from the hut where the woman had been killed, and a hundred yards from the junction of the Ladhya and Sarda Rivers.

Gill Waddell, of the Police, whom we met on our way down the Ladhya, had camped for several days at Sem and had tied out a buffalo that MacDonald of the Forest Department had very kindly placed at our disposal; and though the tiger had visited Sem several times during Waddell's stay, it had not killed the buffalo.

The day following our arrival at Sem, while Ibbotson was interviewing Patwaris, Forest Guards, and Headmen of the surrounding villages, I went out to look for pug marks. Between our camp and the junction, and also on both banks of the Ladhya, there were long stretches of sand. On this sand I found the tracks of a tigress, and of a young male tiger—possibly one of the cubs I had seen in April. The tigress had crossed and recrossed the Ladhya a number of times during the last few days, and the previous night had walked along the strip of sand in front of our tents. It was this tigress the villagers suspected of being the man-eater, and as she had visited Sem repeatedly since the day the Headman's mother had been killed they were probably correct.

An examination of the pug marks of the tigress showed her as being an average-sized animal, in the prime of life. Why she had become a man-eater would have to be determined later, but one of the reasons might have been that she had assisted to eat the victims of the Chuka tiger when they were together the previous mating season, and having acquired a taste for human flesh and no longer having a mate to provide her with it, had now turned a man-eater herself. This was only a surmise, and proved later to be incorrect.

Before leaving Naini Tal I had written to the Tahsildar of Tanakpur and asked him to purchase four young male buffaloes for me, and to send them to Sem. One of these buffaloes died on the road, the other three arrived on the 24th, and we tied them out the same evening together with the one MacDonald had given us. On going out to visit these animals next morning I found the people of Chuka in a great state of excitement. The fields round the village had been recently plowed, and the tigress the previous night had passed close to three families who were sleeping out on the fields with their cattle; fortunately in each case the cattle had seen the tigress and warned the sleepers of her approach. After leaving the cultivated land the tigress had gone up the track in the direction of Kot Kindri, and had passed close to two of our buffaloes without touching either of them.

The Patwari, Forest Guards, and villagers had told us on our arrival at Sem that it would be a waste of time tying out our young buffaloes, as they were convinced the man-eater would not kill them. The reason they gave was that this method of trying to shoot the man-eater had been tried by others without success, and that in any case if the tigress wanted to eat buffaloes there were many grazing in the jungles for her to choose from. In spite of this advice, however, we continued to tie out our buffaloes, and for the next two nights the tigress passed close to one or more of them, without touching them.

On the morning of the 27th, just as we were finishing breakfast, a party of men led by Tewari, the brother of the Headman of Thak, arrived in camp and reported that a man of their village was missing. They stated that this man had left the village at about noon the previous day, telling his wife before leaving that he was going to see that his cattle did not stray beyond the village boundary, and as he had not returned they feared he had been killed by the man-eater.

Our preparations were soon made, and at ten o'clock the Ibbotsons and I set off for Thak, accompanied by Tewari and the men he had brought with him. The distance was only about two miles but the climb was considerable, and as we did not want to lose more time than we could possibly help we arrived at the outskirts of the village out of breath and in a lather of sweat.

As we approached the village over the scrub-covered flat bit of ground which I have reason to refer to later, we heard a woman crying. The wailing of an Indian woman mourning her dead is unmistakable, and on emerging from the jungle we came on the mourner—the wife of the missing man—and some ten or fifteen men, who were waiting for us on the edge of the cultivated land. These people informed us that from their houses above they had seen some white object, which looked like part of the missing man's clothing, in a field overgrown with scrub thirty yards from where we were now standing. Ibbotson, Tewari, and I set off to investigate the white object, while Mrs. Ibbotson took the woman and the rest of the men up to the village.

The field, which had been out of cultivation for some years, was covered with a dense growth of scrub not unlike chrysanthemum, and it was not until we were standing right over the white object that Tewari recognized it as the loincloth of the missing man. Near it was the man's cap. A struggle had taken place at this spot, but there was no blood. The absence of blood where the attack had taken place and for some considerable distance along the drag could be accounted for by the tigress's having retained her first hold, for no blood would flow in such a case until the hold had been changed.

Thirty yards on the hill above us there was a clump of bushes roofed over with creepers. This spot would have to be looked at before following up the drag, for it was not advisable to have the tigress behind us. In the soft earth under the bushes we found the pug marks of the tigress, and where she had lain before going forward to attack the man.

Returning to our starting point we agreed on the following plan of action. Our primary object was to try to stalk the tigress and shoot her on her kill: to achieve this end I was to follow the trail and at the same time keep a lookout in front, with Tewari—who was unarmed—a yard behind me keeping a sharp lookout to right and left, and Ibbotson a yard behind Tewari to safeguard us against an attack from the rear. In the event of either Ibbotson or I seeing so much as a hair of the tigress, we were to risk a shot.

Cattle had grazed over this area the previous day, disturbing the ground, and as there was no blood and the only indication of the tigress's passage was an occasional turned-up leaf or crushed blade of grass, progress was slow. After carrying the man for two hundred yards the tigress had killed and left him, and had returned and carried him off several hours later, when the people of Thak had heard several sambur calling in this direction. The reason for the tigress's not having carried the man away after she had killed him was possibly because his cattle may have witnessed the attack on him, and driven her away.

A big pool of blood had formed where the man had been lying, and as the blood from the wound in his throat had stopped flowing by the time the tigress had picked him up again, and further, as she was now holding him by the small of the back, whereas she had previously held him by the neck, tracking became even more difficult. The tigress kept to the contour of the hill, and as the undergrowth here was very dense and visibility only extended to a few yards, our advance was slowed down. In two hours we covered half a mile, and reached a ridge beyond which lay the valley in which, six months previously, we had tracked down and killed the Chuka man-eater. On this ridge was a great slab of rock, which sloped upwards and away from the direction in which we had come. The tigress's tracks went down to the right of the rock and I felt sure she was lying up under the overhanging portion of it, or in the close vicinity.

Both Ibbotson and I had on light rubber-soled shoes—Tewari was bare-footed—and we had reached the rock without making a sound. Signing to my two companions to stand still and keep a careful watch all round, I got a foothold on the rock, and inch by inch went forward. Beyond the rock was a short stretch of flat ground, and as more of this ground came into view, I felt certain my suspicion that the tigress was lying under the projection was correct. I had still a foot or two to go before I could look over, when I saw a movement to my left front. A goldenrod that had been pressed down had sprung erect, and a second later there was a slight movement in the bushes beyond, and a monkey in a tree on the far side off the bushes started calling.

The tigress had chosen the spot for her after-dinner sleep with great care, but unfortunately for us she was not asleep; and when she saw the top of my head—I had removed my hat—appearing over the rock, she had risen and taking a step sideways, had disappeared under a tangle of blackberry bushes. Had she been lying anywhere but where she was she could not have got away, no matter how quickly she had moved, without my getting a shot at her. Our so-carefully-carried-out stalk had failed at the very last moment, and there was nothing to be done now but find the kill, and see if there was sufficient of it left for us to sit up over. To have followed her into the blackberry thicket would have been useless, and would also have reduced our chance of getting a shot at her later.

The tigress had eaten her meal close to where she had been lying, and as this spot was open to the sky and to the keen eyes of vultures she had removed the kill to a place of safety where it would not be visible from the air. Tracking now was easy, for there was a blood trail to follow. The trail led over a ridge of great rocks and fifty yards beyond these rocks we found the kill.

I am not going to harrow your feelings by attempting to describe that poor torn and mangled thing; stripped of every stitch of clothing and atom of dignity, which only a few hours previously had been a Man, the father of two children and the breadwinner of that wailing woman who was facing—without any illusions—the fate of a widow of India. I have seen many similar sights, each more terrible than the one preceding it, in the thirty-two years I have been hunting man-eaters, and on each occasion I have felt that it would have been better to have left the victim to the slayer than recover a mangled mass of flesh to be a nightmare ever after to those who saw it. And yet the cry of blood for blood, and the burning desire to rid a countryside of a menace than which there is none more terrible, is irresistible; and then there is always the hope, no matter how absurd one knows it to be, that the victim by some miracle may still be alive and in need of succour.

The chance of shooting—over a kill—an animal that has in all probability become a man-eater through a wound received over a kill, is very remote, and each succeeding failure, no matter what its cause, tends to make the animal more cautious, until it reaches a state when it either abandons its kill after one meal or approaches it as silently and as slowly as a shadow, scanning every leaf and twig with the certainty of discovering its would-be slayer, no matter how carefully he may be concealed or how silent and motionless he may be; a one in a million chance of getting a shot, and yet, who is there among us who would not take it?

The thicket into which the tigress had retired was roughly forty yards square, and she could not leave it without the monkey's seeing her and warning us, so we sat down back to back, to have a smoke and listen if the jungle had anything further to tell us while we considered our next move.

To make a machan it was necessary to return to the village, and during our absence the tigress was almost certain to carry away the kill. It had been difficult to track her when she was carrying a whole human being, but now, when her burden was considerably lighter and she had been disturbed, she would probably go for miles and we might never find her kill again, so it was necessary for one of us to remain on the spot, while the other two went back to the village for ropes.

Ibbotson, with his usual disregard for danger, elected to go back, and while he and Tewari went down the hill to avoid the difficult ground we had recently come over, I stepped up onto a small tree close to the kill. Four feet above ground the tree divided in two, and by leaning on one half and putting my feet against the other, I was able to maintain a precarious seat which was high enough off the ground to enable me to see the tigress if she approached the kill, and also high enough, if she had any designs on me, to see her before she got to within striking distance.

Ibbotson had been gone fifteen or twenty minutes when I heard a rock tilt forward, and then back. The rock was evidently very delicately poised, and when the tigress had put her weight on it and felt it tilt forward she had removed her foot and let the rock fall back into place. The sound had come from about twenty yards to my left front, the only direction in which it would have been possible for me to have fired without being knocked out of the tree.

Minutes passed, each pulling my hopes down a little lower from the heights to which they had soared, and then, when tension on my nerves and the weight of the heavy rifle were becoming unbearable, I heard a stick snap at the upper end of the thicket. Here was an example of how a tiger can move through the jungle. From the sound she had made I knew her exact position, had kept my eyes fixed on the spot, and yet she had come, seen me, stayed some time watching me, and then gone away without my having seen a leaf or a blade of grass move.

When tension on nerves is suddenly relaxed, cramped and aching muscles call loudly for ease, and though in this case it only meant the lowering of the rifle onto my knees to take the strain off my shoulders and arms, the movement, small though it was, sent a comforting feeling through the whole of my body. No further sound came from the tigress, and an hour or two later I heard Ibbotson returning.

Of all the men I have been on shikar with, Ibbotson is by far and away the best, for not only has he the heart of a lion, but he thinks of everything, and with it all is the most unselfish man that carries a gun. He had gone to fetch a rope and he returned with rugs, cushions, more hot tea than even I could drink, and an ample lunch; and while I sat—on the windward side of the kill—to refresh myself, Ibbotson put a man in a tree forty yards away to distract the tigress's attention, and climbed into a tree overlooking the kill to make a rope machan.

When the machan was ready Ibbotson moved the kill a few feet—a very unpleasant job—and tied it securely to the foot of a sapling to prevent the tigress's carrying it away, for the moon was on the wane and the first two hours of the night at this heavily wooded spot would be pitch dark. After a final smoke I climbed onto the machan, and when I had made myself comfortable Ibbotson recovered the man who was making a diversion and set off in the direction of Thak to pick up Mrs. Ibbotson and return to camp at Sem.

The retreating party were out of sight but were not yet out of sound when I heard a heavy body brushing against leaves, and at the same moment the monkey, which had been silent all this time and which I could now see sitting in a tree on the far side of the blackberry thicket, started calling. Here was more luck than I had hoped for, and our ruse of putting a man up a tree to cause a diversion appeared to be working as successfully as it had done on a previous occasion. A tense minute passed, a second, and a third, and then from the ridge where I had climbed onto the big slab of rock a kakar came dashing down towards me, barking hysterically. The tigress was not coming to the kill but had gone off after Ibbotson. I was now in a fever of anxiety, for it was quite evident that she had abandoned her kill and gone to try to secure another victim.

Before leaving, Ibbotson had promised to take every precaution, but on hearing the kakar barking on my side of the ridge he would naturally assume the tigress was moving in the vicinity of the kill, and if he relaxed his precautions the tigress would get her chance. Ten very uneasy minutes for me passed, and then I heard a second kakar barking in the direction of Thak; the tigress was still following, but the ground there was more open, and there was less fear of her attacking the party. The danger to the Ibbotsons was, however, not over by any means for they had to go through two miles of very heavy jungle to reach camp; and if they stayed at Thak until sundown listening for my shot, which I feared they would do and which as a matter of fact they did do, they would run a very grave risk on the way down. Ibbotson fortunately realized the danger and kept his party close together, and though the tigress followed them the whole way—as her pug marks the following morning showed—they got back to camp safely.

The calling of kakar and sambur enabled me to follow the movements of the tigress. An hour after sunset she was down at the bottom of the valley two miles away. She had the whole night before her, and though there was only one chance in a million of her returning to the kill I determined not to lose that chance. Wrapping a rug around me, for it was a bitterly cold night, I made myself comfortable in a position in which I could remain for hours without movement.

I had taken my seat on the machan at 4 p.m., and at 10 p.m. I heard two animals coming down the hill towards me. It was too dark under the trees to see them, but when they got to the lee of the kill I knew they were porcupines. Rattling their quills, and making the peculiar booming noise that only a porcupine can make, they approached the kill and, after walking round it several times, continued on their way. An hour later, and when the moon had been up some time, I heard an animal in the valley below. It was moving from east to west, and when it came into the wind blowing downhill from the kill it made a long pause, and then came cautiously up the hill. While it was still some distance away I heard it snuffing the air, and knew it to be a bear. The smell of blood was attracting him, but mingled with it was the less welcome smell of a human being, and taking no chances he was very carefully stalking the kill. His nose, the keenest of any animal's in the jungle, had apprised him while he was still in the valley that the kill was the property of a tiger. This to a Himalayan bear who fears nothing, and who will, as I have on several occasions seen, drive a tiger away from its kill, was no deterrent, but what was, and what was causing him uneasiness, was the smell of a human being mingled with the smell of blood and tiger.

On reaching the flat ground the bear sat down on his haunches a few yards from the kill, and when he had satisfied himself that the hated human smell held no danger for him he stood erect and turning his head sent a long-drawn-out cry, which I interpreted as a call to a mate, echoing down into the valley. Then without any further hesitation he walked boldly up to the kill, and as he noted it I aligned the sights of my rifle on him. I know of only one instance of a Himalayan bear eating a human being; on that occasion a woman cutting grass had fallen down a cliff and been killed, and a bear finding the mangled body had carried it away and had eaten it. This bear, however, on whose shoulder my sights were aligned, appeared to draw the line at human flesh, and after looking at and smelling the kill continued his interrupted course to the west. When the sounds of his retreat died away in the distance the jungle settled down to silence until interrupted, a little after sunrise, by Ibbotson's very welcome arrival.

With Ibbotson came the brother and other relatives of the dead man, who very reverently wrapped the remains in a clean white cloth and, laying it on a cradle made of two saplings and rope which Ibbotson provided, set off for the burning that on the banks of the Sarda, repeating under their breath as they went the Hindu hymn of praise *'Ram nam sat hai'* with its refrain, *'Satya bol gat hai.'*

Fourteen hours in the cold had not been without its effect on me, but after partaking of the hot drink and food Ibbotson had brought, I felt none the worse for my long vigil.

II.

After following the Ibbotsons down to Chuka on the evening of the 27th, the tigress, sometime during the night, crossed the Ladhya into the scrub jungle at the back of our camp. Through this scrub ran a path that had been regularly used by the villagers of the Ladhya valley until the advent of the man-eater had rendered its passage unsafe. On the 28th the two mail-runners who carried Ibbotson's dak on its first stage to Tanakpur got delayed in camp, and to save time took, or more correctly started to take, a short cut through this scrub. Very fortunately the leading man was on the alert and saw the tigress as she crept through the scrub and lay down near the path ahead of them.

Ibbotson and I had just got back from Thak when these two men dashed into camp, and taking our rifles we hurried off to investigate. We found the pug marks of the tigress where she had come out on the path and followed the men for a short distance, but we did not see her, though in one place where the scrub was very dense we saw a movement and heard an animal moving off.

On the morning of the 29th, a party of men came down from Thak to report that one of their bullocks had not returned to the cattle-shed the previous night, and on a search being made where it had last been seen a little blood had been found. At 2 p.m. the Ibbotsons and I were at this spot, and a glance at the ground satisfied us that the bullock had been killed and carried away by a tiger. After a hasty lunch Ibbotson and I, with two men following carrying ropes for a machan, set out along the drag. It went diagonally across the face of the hill for a hundred yards and then straight down into the ravine in which I had fired at and missed the big tiger in April. A few hundred yards down this ravine the bullock, which was an enormous animal, had got fixed between two rocks and, not being able to move it, the tiger had eaten a meal off its hind quarters and left it.

The pug marks of the tiger, owing to the great weight she was carrying, were splayed out and it was not possible to say whether she was the man-eater or not; but as every tiger in this area was suspect I decided to sit up over the kill. There was only one tree within reasonable distance of the kill, and as the men climbed into it to make a machan the tiger started calling in the valley below. Very hurriedly a few strands of rope were tied between two branches, and while Ibbotson stood on guard with his rifle

I climbed the tree and took my seat on what, during the next fourteen hours, proved to be the most uncomfortable as well as the most dangerous machan I have ever sat on. The tree was leaning away from the hill, and from the three uneven strands of rope I was sitting on there was a drop of over a hundred feet into the rocky ravine below.

The tiger called several times as I was getting into the tree and continued to call at longer intervals late into the evening, the last call coming from a ridge half a mile away. It was now quite evident that the tiger had been lying up close to the kill and had seen the men climbing into the tree. Knowing from past experience what this meant, she had duly expressed resentment at being disturbed and then gone away, for though I sat on the three strands of rope until Ibbotson returned next morning, I did not see or hear anything throughout the night.

Vultures were not likely to find the kill, for the ravine was deep and overshadowed by trees, and as the bullock was large enough to provide the tiger with several meals we decided not to sit up over it again where it was now lying, hoping the tiger would remove it to some more convenient place where we should have a better chance of getting a shot. In this, however, we were disappointed, for the tiger did not again return to the kill.

Two nights later the buffalo we had tied out behind our camp at Sem was killed, and through a little want of observation on my part a great opportunity of bagging the man-eater was lost.

The men who brought in the news of this kill reported that the rope securing the animal had been broken, and that the kill had been carried away up the ravine at the lower end of which it had been tied. This was the same ravine in which MacDonald and I had chased a tigress in April, and as on that occasion she had taken her kill some distance up the ravine I now very foolishly concluded she had done the same with this kill.

After breakfast Ibbotson and I went out to find the kill and see what prospect there was for an evening sit-up.

The ravine in which the buffalo had been killed was about fifty yards wide and ran deep into the foothills. For two hundred yards the ravine was straight, and then bent round to the left. Just beyond the bend, and on the left-hand side of it, there was a dense patch of young saplings backed by a hundred-foot ridge on which thick grass was growing. In the ravine, and close to the saplings, there was a small pool of water. I had been up the ravine several times in April and had failed to mark the patch of saplings as being a likely place for a tiger to lie up in, and did not take the precautions I should have taken when rounding the bend, with the result that the tigress, who was drinking at the pool, saw us first. There was only one safe line of retreat for her and she took it. This was straight up the steep hill, over the ridge, and into sal forest beyond.

The hill was too steep for us to climb, so we continued on up the ravine to where a sambur track crossed it, and following this track we gained the ridge. The tigress was now in a triangular patch of jungle bounded by the ridge, the Ladhya, and a cliff down which no animal could go. The area was not large, and there were several deer in it which from time to time advised us of the position of the tigress, but unfortunately the ground was cut up by a number of deep and narrow rain-water channels in which we eventually lost touch with her.

We had not yet seen the kill, so we re-entered the ravine by the sambur track and found the kill hidden among the saplings. These saplings were from six inches to a foot in girth, and were not strong enough to support a machan, so we had to abandon the idea of a machan. With the help of a crowbar, a rock could possibly have been pried from the face of the hill and a place made in which to sit, but this was not advisable when dealing with a man-eater.

Reluctant to give up the chance of a shot, we considered the possibility of concealing ourselves in the grass near the kill, in the hope that the tigress would return before dark and that we should see her before she saw us. There were two objections to this plan: (*a*) if we did not get a shot and the tigress saw us near her kill she might abandon it, as she had done her other two kills; and (*b*) between the kill and camp there was very heavy scrub jungle, and if we tried to go through this jungle in the dark the tigress would have us at her mercy. So very reluctantly we decided to leave the kill to the tigress for that night, and hope for the best on the morrow.

On our return next morning we found that the tigress had carried away the kill. For three hundred yards she had gone up the bed of the ravine stepping from rock to rock, and leaving no drag marks. At this spot—three hundred yards from where she had picked up the kill—we were at fault, for though there were a number of tracks on a wet patch of ground, none of them had been made while she was carrying the kill. Eventually, after casting round in circles, we found where she had left the ravine and gone up the hill on the left.

This hill up which the tigress had taken her kill was overgrown with ferns and goldenrod and tracking was not difficult, but the going was, for the hill was very steep and in places a detour had to be made and the track picked up further on. After a stiff climb of a thousand feet we came to a small plateau, bordered on the left by a cliff a mile wide. On the side of the plateau nearest the cliff the ground was seamed and cracked, and in these cracks a dense growth of sal, two to six feet in height, had sprung up. The tigress had taken her kill into this dense cover and it was not until we actually trod on it that we were aware of its position.

As we stopped to look at all that remained of the buffalo there was a low growl to our right. With rifles raised we waited for a minute and then, hearing a movement in the undergrowth a little beyond where the growl had come from, we pushed our way through the young sal for ten yards and came on a small clearing, where the tigress had made herself a bed on some soft grass. On the far side of this grass the hill sloped upwards for twenty yards to another plateau, and it was from this slope that the sound we had heard had come. Proceeding up the slope as silently as possible, we had just reached the flat ground, which was about fifty yards wide, when the tigress left the far side and went down into the ravine, disturbing some kaleege pheasants and a kakar as she did so. To have followed her would have been useless, so we went back to the kill and, as there was still a good meal on it, we selected two trees to sit in, and returned to camp.

After an early lunch we went back to the kill and, hampered with our rifles, climbed with some difficulty into the trees we had selected. We sat up for five hours without seeing or hearing anything. At dusk we climbed down from our trees, and stumbling over the cracked and uneven ground eventually reached the ravine when it was quite dark. Both of us had an uneasy feeling that we were being followed, but by keeping close together we reached camp without incident at 9 p.m.

The Ibbotsons had now stayed at Sem as long as it was possible for them to do so, and early next morning they set out on their twelve days' walk to keep their appointment at Askot. Before leaving, Ibbotson extracted a promise from me that I would not follow up any kills alone, or further endanger my life by prolonging my stay at Sem for more than a day or two.

After the departure of the Ibbotsons and their fifty men, the camp, which was surrounded by dense scrub, was reduced to my two servants and myself—my coolies were living in a room in the Headman's house—so throughout the day I set all hands to collecting driftwood, of which there was an inexhaustible supply at the junction, to keep a fire going all night. The fire would not scare away the tigress but it would enable us to see her if she prowled round our tents at night, and anyway the nights were setting in cold and there was ample excuse, if one were needed, for keeping a big fire going all night.

Towards evening, when my men were safely back in camp, I took a rifle and went up the Ladhya to see if he tigress had crossed the river. I found several tracks in the sand, but no fresh ones, and at dusk I returned, convinced that the tigress was still on our side of the river. An hour later, when it was quite dark, a kakar started barking close to our tents and barked persistently for half an hour.

My men had taken over the job of tying out the buffaloes, a task which Ibbotson's men had hitherto performed, and next morning I accompanied them when they went out to bring in the buffaloes. Though we covered several miles I did not find any trace of the tigress. After breakfast I took a rod and went down the junction, and had one of the best day's fishing I have ever had. The junction was full of big fish, and though my light tackle was broken frequently I killed sufficient mahseer to feed the camp.

Again, as on the previous evening, I crossed the Ladhya, with the intention of taking up a position on a rock overlooking the open ground on the right bank of the river and watching for the tigress to cross. As I got away from the roar of the water at the junction I heard a sambur and a monkey calling on the hill to my left, and as I neared the rock I came on the fresh tracks of the tigress. Following them back I found the stones still wet where she had forded the river. A few minutes' delay in camp to dry my fishing line and have a cup of tea cost a man his life, several thousand men weeks of anxiety, and myself many days of strain, for though I stayed at Sem for another three days I did not get another chance of shooting the tigress.

On the morning of the 7th, as I was breaking camp and preparing to start on my twenty-mile walk to Tanakpur, a big contingent of men from all the surrounding villages arrived, and begged me not to leave them to the tender mercies of the man-eater. Giving them what advice it was possible to give people situated as they were. I promised to return as soon as it was possible for me to do so.

I caught the train at Tanakpur next morning and arrived back in Naini Tal on 9 November, having been away nearly a month.

III.

I left Sem on the 7th of November and on the 12th the tigress killed a man at Thak. I received news of this kill through the Divisional Forest Officer, Haldwani, shortly after we had moved down to our winter home at the foot of the hills, and by doing forced marches I arrived at Chuka a little after sunrise on the 14th.

It had been my intention to breakfast at Chuka and then go on to Thak and make that village my headquarters, but the Headman of Thak, whom I found installed at Chuka, informed me that every man, woman, and child had left Thak immediately after the man had been killed on the 12th, and added that if I carried out my intention of camping at Thak I might be able to safeguard my own life, but it would not be possible to safeguard the lives of my men. This was quite reasonable, and while waiting for my men to arrive, the Headman helped me to select a site for my camp at Chuka, where my men would be reasonably safe and I should have some privacy from the thousands of men who were now arriving to fell the forest.

On receipt of the Divisional Forest Officer's telegram acquainting me of the kill, I had telegraphed to the Tahsildar at Tanakpur to send three young male buffaloes to Chuka. My request had been promptly complied with and the three animals had arrived the previous evening.

After breakfast I took one of the buffaloes and set out for Thak, intending to tie it up on the spot where the man had been killed on the 12th. The Headman had given me a very graphic account of the events of that date, for he himself had nearly fallen a victim to the tigress. It appeared that towards the afternoon, accompanied by his granddaughter, a girl ten years of age, he had gone to dig up ginger tubers in a field some sixty yards from his house. This field is about half an acre in extent and is surrounded on three sides by jungle, and being on the slope of a fairly step hill it is visible from the Headman's house. After the old man and his granddaughter had been at work for some time, his wife, who was husking rice in the courtyard of the house, called out in a very agitated voice and asked him if he was deaf that he could not hear the pheasants and other birds that were chattering in the jungle above him. Fortunately for him, he acted promptly. Dropping his hoe, he grabbed the child's hand and together they ran back to the house, urged on by the woman who said she could now see a red animal in the bushes at the upper end of the field. Half an hour later the tigress killed a man who was lopping branches off a tree in a field three hundred yards from the Headman's house.

From the description I had received from the Headman I had no difficulty in locating the tree. It was a small gnarled tree growing out of a three-foot-high bank between two terraced fields, and had been lopped year after year for cattle fodder. The man who had been killed was standing on the trunk holding one branch and cutting another, when the tigress came up from behind, tore his hold from the branch and, after killing him, carried him away into the dense brushwood bordering the fields.

Thak village was a gift from the Chand Rajas, who ruled Kumaon for many hundreds of years before the Gurkha occupation, to the forefathers of the present owners in return for their services at the Punagiri temples. (The promise made by the Chand Rajas that the lands of Thak and two other villages would remain rent-free for all time has been honored by the British Government for a hundred years.) From a collection of grass huts the village has in the course of time grown into a very prosperous settlement with masonry houses roofed with slate tiles, for not only is the land very fertile, but the revenue from the temples is considerable.

Like all other villages in Kumaon, Thak during its hundreds of years of existence has passed through many vicissitudes, but never before in its long history had it been deserted as it now was. On my previous visits I had found it a hive of industry, but when I went up to it on this afternoon, taking the young buffalo with me, silence reigned over it. Every one of the hundred or more inhabitants had fled, taking their livestock with them—the only animal I saw in the village was a cat, which gave me a warm welcome; so hurried had the evacuation been that many of the doors of the houses had been left wide open. On every path in the village, in the courtyard of the houses, and in the dust before all the doors I found the tigress's pug marks. The open doorways were a menace, for the path as it wound through the village passed close to them, and in any of the houses the tigress may have been lurking.

On the hill thirty yards above the village were several cattle shelters, and in the vicinity of these shelters I saw more kaleege pheasants, red jungle fowl, and white-capped babblers than I have ever before seen, and from the confiding way in which they permitted me to walk among them it is quite evident that the people of Thak have a religious prejudice against the taking of life.

From the terraced fields above the cattle shelters a bird's-eye view of the village is obtained, and it was not difficult, from the description the Headman had given me, to locate the tree where the tigress had secured her last victim. In the soft earth under the tree there were signs of a struggle and a few clots of dried blood. From here the tigress had carried her kill a hundred yards over a plowed field, through a stout hedge, and into the dense brushwood beyond. The foot-prints from the village and back the way they had come showed that the entire population of the village had visited the scene of the kill, but from the tree to the hedge there was only one track, the track the tigress had made when carrying away her victim. No attempt had been made to follow her up and recover the body.

Scraping away a little earth from under the tree I exposed a root and to this root I tied my buffalo, bedding it down with a liberal supply of straw taken from a near-by haystack.

The village, which is on the north face of the hill, was now in shadow, and if I was to get back to camp before dark it was time for me to make a start. Skirting round the village to avoid the menace of the open doorways, I joined the path below the houses.

This path after it leaves the village passes under a giant mango tree from the roots of which issues a cold spring of clear water. After running along a groove cut in a massive slab of rock, this water falls into a rough masonry trough, from where it spreads onto the surrounding ground, rendering it soft and slushy. I had drunk at the spring on my way up, leaving my foot-prints in this slushy ground, and on approaching the spring now for a second drink, I found the tigress's pug marks superimposed on my foot-prints. After quenching her thirst the tigress had avoided the path and had gained the village by climbing a steep bank overgrown with strobilanthes and nettles, and taking up a position in the shelter of one of the houses had possibly watched me while I was tying up the buffalo, expecting me to return the way I had gone; it was fortunate for me that I had noted the danger of passing those open doorways a second time, and had taken the longer way round.

When coming up from Chuka I had taken every precaution to guard against a sudden attack, and it was well that I had done so, for I now found from her pug marks that the tigress had followed me all the way up from my camp, and next morning when I went back to Thak I found she had followed me from where I had joined the path below the houses, right down to the cultivated land at Chuka.

Reading with the illumination I had brought with me was not possible, so after dinner that night, while sitting near a fire which was as welcome for its warmth as it was for the feeling of security it gave me. I reviewed the whole situation and tried to think out some plan by which it would be possible to circumvent the tigress.

When leaving home on the 22nd I had promised that I would return in ten days, and that this would be my last expedition after man-eaters. Years of exposure and strain and long absences from home—extending as in the case of the Chowgarh tigress and the Rudraprayag leopard to several months on end were beginning to tell as much on my constitution as on the nerves of those at home, and if by the 30th of November I had not succeeded in killing this man-eater, others would have to be found who were willing to take on the task.

It was now the night of the 24th, so I had six clear days before me. Judging from the behavior of the tigress that evening she appeared to be anxious to secure another human victim, and it should not therefore be difficult for me, in the time at my disposal, to get in touch with her. There were several methods by which this could be accomplished, and each would be tried in turn. The method that offers the greatest chance of success of shooting a tiger in the hills is to sit up in a tree over a kill, and if during that night the tigress did not kill the buffalo I had tied up at Thak. I would the following night, and every night thereafter, tie up the other two buffaloes in places I had already selected, and failing to secure a human kill it was just possible that the tigress might kill one of my buffaloes, as she had done on a previous occasion when the Ibbotsons and I were camped at Sem in April. After making up the fire with logs that would burn all night I turned in, and went to sleep listening to a kakar barking in the scrub jungle behind my tent.

While breakfast was being prepared the following morning I picked up a rifle and went out to look for tracks on the stretch of sand on the right bank of the river, between Chuka and Sem. The path, after leaving the cultivated land, runs for a short distance through scrub jungle, and here I found the tracks of a big male leopard, possibly the same animal that had alarmed the kakar the previous night. A small male tiger had crossed and recrossed the Ladhya many times during the past week, and in the same period the man-eater had crossed only once, coming from the direction of Sem. A big bear had traversed the sand a little before my arrival, and when I got back to camp the timber contractors complained that while distributing work that morning they had run into a bear which had taken up a very threatening attitude, in consequence of which their labor had refused to work in the area in which the bear had been seen.

Several thousand men—the conductors put the figure at five thousand—had now concentrated at Chuka and Kumaya Chak to fell and saw up the timber and carry it down to the motor road that was being constructed, and all the time this considerable labor force was working they shouted at the tops of their voices to keep up then courage. The noise in the valley resulting from axe and saw, the crashing of giant trees down the steep hillside, the breaking of rocks with sledge hammers, and combined with it all the shouting of thousands of men, can better be imagined than described. That there were many and frequent alarms in this nervous community was only natural, and during the next few days I covered much ground and lost much valuable time in investigating false rumors of attacks and kills by the man-eater, for the dread of the tigress was not confined to the Ladhya valley but extended right down the Sarda through Kaldhunga to the gorge, an area of roughly fifty square miles in which an additional ten thousand men were working.

That a single animal should terrorize a labor force of these dimensions in addition to the residents of the surrounding villages and the hundreds of men who were bringing foodstuffs for the laborers or passing through the valley with hill produce in the way of oranges (purchasable at twelve annas a hundred), walnuts, and chilies to the market at Tanakpur is incredible, and would be unbelievable were it not for the historical, and nearly parallel, case of the man-eaters of Tsavo, where a pair of lions, operating only at night, held up work for long periods on the Uganda Railway.

To return to my story. Breakfast disposed of on the morning of the 25th, I took a second buffalo and set out for Thak. The path, after leaving the cultivated land at Chuka, skirts along the foot of the hill for about half a mile before it divides. One arm goes straight up a ridge to Thak and the other, after continuing along the foot of the hill for another half-mile, zigzags up through Kumaya Chak to Kot Kindri.

At the divide I found the pug marks of the tigress and followed them all the way back to Thak. The fact that she had come down the hill after me the previous evening was proof that she had not killed the buffalo. This, though very disappointing, was not at all unusual; for tigers will on occasions visit an animal that is tied up for several nights in succession before they finally kill it, for tigers do not kill unless they are hungry.

Leaving the second buffalo at the mango tree, where there was an abundance of green grass, I skirted round the houses and found No. 1 buffalo sleeping peacefully after a big feed and a disturbed night. The tigress, coming from the direction of the village as her pug marks showed, had approached to within a few feet of the buffalo, and had then gone back the way she had come. Taking the buffalo down to the spring I let it graze for an hour or two, and then took it back and tied it up at the same spot where it had been the previous night.

The second buffalo I tied up fifty yards from the mango tree and at the spot where the wailing woman and villagers had met us the day the Ibbotsons and I had gone up to investigate the human kill. Here a ravine a few feet deep crossed the path, on one side of which there was a dry stump, and on the other an almond tree in which a machan could be made. I tied No. 2 buffalo to the stump, and bedded it down with sufficient hay to keep it going for several days. There was nothing more to be done at Thak, so I returned to camp and, taking the third buffalo, crossed the Ladhya and tied it up behind Sem, in the ravine where the tigress had killed one of our buffaloes in April.

At my request the Tahsildar of Tanakpur had selected three of the fastest young male buffaloes he could find. All three were now tied up in places frequented by the tigress, and as I set out to visit them on the morning of the 26th I had great hopes that one of them had been killed and that I should get an opportunity of shooting the tigress over it. Starting with the one across the Ladhya, I visited all in turn and found that the tigress had not touched any of them. Again, as on the previous morning, I found her tracks on the path leading to Thak, but on this occasion there was a double set of pug marks, one coming down and the other going back. On both her journeys the tigress had kept to the path and had passed within a few feet of the buffalo that was tied to the stump, fifty yards from the mango tree.

On my return to Chuka a deputation of Thak villagers led by the Headman came to my tent and requested me to accompany them to the village to enable them to replenish their supply of foodstuffs, so at midday, followed by the Headman and his tenants, and by four of my own men carrying ropes for a machan and food for me, I returned to Thak and mounted guard while the men hurriedly collected the provisions they needed.

After watering and feeding the two buffaloes I retied No. 2 to the stump and took No. 1 half a mile down the hill and tied it to a sapling on the side of the path. I then took the villagers back to Chuka and returned a few hundred yards up the hill for a scratch meal while my men were making the machan.

It was now quite evident that the tigress had no fancy for my fat buffaloes, and as in three days I had seen her tracks five times on the path leading to Thak, I decided to sit up over the path and try to get a shot at her that way. To give me warning of the tigress's approach I tied a goat with a bell round its neck on the path, and at 4 p.m. I climbed into the tree. I told my men to return at 8 a.m. the following morning, and began my watch.

At sunset a cold wind started blowing and while I was attempting to pull a coat over my shoulders the ropes on one side of the machan slipped, rendering my scat very uncomfortable. An hour later a storm came on, and though it did not rain for long it wet the to the skin, greatly adding to my discomfort. During the sixteen hours I sat in the tree I did not see or hear anything. The men turned up at 8 a.m. I returned to camp for a hot bath and a good meal, and then, accompanied by six of my men, set out for Thak.

The overnight rain had washed all the old tracks off the path, and two hundred yards above the tree I had sat in I found the fresh pug marks of the tigress, where she had come out of the jungle and gone up the path in the direction of Thak. Very cautiously I stalked the first buffalo, only to find it lying asleep on the path; the tigress had skirted round it, rejoined the path a few yards further on and continued up the hill. Following on her tracks I approached the second buffalo, and as I got near the place where it had been tied two blue Himalayan magpies rose off the ground and went screaming down the hill.

The presence of these birds indicated (a) that the buffalo was dead, (b) that it had been partly eaten and not carried away, and (c) that the tigress was not in the close vicinity.

On arrival at the stump to which it had been tied I saw that the buffalo had been dragged off the path and partly eaten, and on examining the animal I found it had not been killed by the tigress but that it had in all probability died of snake-bite (there were many hamadryads in the surrounding jungles), and that, finding it lying dead on the path, the tigress had eaten a meal off it and had then tried to drag it away. When she found she could not break the rope, she had partly covered it over with dry leaves and brushwood and continued on her way up to Thak.

Tigers as a rule are not carrion eaters but they do on occasions eat animals they themselves have not killed. For instance, on one occasion I left the carcass of a leopard on a fire track and, when I returned next morning to recover a knife I had forgotten, I found that a tiger had removed the carcass to a distance of a hundred yards and eaten two thirds of it.

On my way up from Chuka I had dismantled the machan I had sat on the previous night, and while two of my men climbed into the almond tree to make a seat for me—the tree was not big enough for a machan—the other four went to the spring to fill a kettle and boil some water for tea. By 4 p.m. I had partaken of a light meal of biscuits and tea, which would have to keep me going until next day, and refusing the men's request to be permitted to stay the night in one of the houses in Thak, I sent them back to camp. There was a certain amount of risk in doing this, but it was nothing compared to the risk they would run if they spent the night in Thak.

My seat on the tree consisted of several strands of rope tied between two upright branches, with a couple of strands lower down for my feet to rest on. When I had settled down comfortably I pulled the branches round me and secured them in position with a thin cord, leaving a small opening to see and fire through. My 'hide' was soon tested, for shortly after the men had gone the two magpies returned, and attracted others, and nine of them fed on the kill until dusk. The presence of the birds enabled me to get some sleep, for they would have given me warning of the tigress's approach, and with their departure my all-night vigil started.

There was still sufficient daylight to shoot by when the moon, a day off the full, rose over the Nepal hills behind me and flooded the hillside with brilliant light. The rain of the previous night had cleared the atmosphere of dust and smoke and, after the moon had been up a few minutes, the light was so good that I was able to see a sambur and her young one feeding in a field of wheat a hundred and fifty yards away.

The dead buffalo was directly in front and about twenty yards away, and the path along which I expected the tigress to come was two or three yards nearer, so I should have an easy shot at a range at which it would be impossible to miss the tigress—provided she came; and there was no reason why she should not do so.

The moon had been up two hours, and the sambur had approached to within fifty yards of my tree, when a kakar started barking on the hill just above the village. The kakar had been barking for some minutes when suddenly a scream which I can only, very inadequately, describe as 'Ar-Ar-Arr' dying away on a long-drawn-out note, came from the direction of the village. So sudden and so unexpected had the scream been that I involuntarily stood up with the intention of slipping down from the tree and dashing up to the village, for the thought flashed through my mind that the man-eater was killing one of my men. Then in a second flash of thought I remembered I had counted them one by one as they had passed my tree, and that I had watched them out of sight on their way back to camp to see if they were obeying my instructions to keep close together.

The scream had been the despairing cry of a human being in mortal agony, and reason questioned how such a sound could have come from a deserted village. It was not a thing of my imagination for the kakar had heard it and had abruptly stopped barking, and the sambur had dashed away across the fields closely followed by her young one. Two days previously, when I had escorted the men to the village, I had remarked that they appeared to he very confiding to leave their property behind doors that were not even shut or latched, and the Headman had answered that even if their village remained un tenanted for years their property would be quite safe, for they were priests of Punagiri and no one would dream of robbing them; he added that as long as the tigress lived she was a better guard of their property—if guard were needed—than any hundred men could be, for no one in all that countryside would dare to approach the village, for any purpose, through the dense forests that surrounded it, unless escorted by me as they had been.

The screams were not repeated, and as there appeared to be nothing that I could do I settled down again on my rope seat. At 10 p.m. a kakar that was feeding on the young wheat crop at the lower end of the fields dashed away barking, and a minute later the tigress called twice. She had now left the village and was on the move, and even if she did not fancy having another meal off the buffalo there was every hope of her coming along the path which she had used twice every day for the past few days. With finger on trigger and eyes straining on the path I sat hour after hour until daylight succeeded moonlight, and when the sun had been up an hour, my men returned. Very thoughtfully they had brought a bundle of dry wood with them, and in a surprisingly short time I was sitting down to a hot cup of tea. The tigress may have been lurking in the bushes close to us, or she may have been miles away, for after she had called at 10 p.m. the jungles had been silent.

When I got back to camp I found a number of men sitting near my tent. Some of these men had come to inquire what luck I had had the previous night, and others had come to tell me that the tigress had called from midnight to a little before sunrise at the foot of the hill, and that all the laborers engaged in the forests and on the new export road were too frightened to go to work. I had already heard about the tigress from my men, who had informed me that, together with the thousands of men who were camped round Chuka, they had sat up all night to keep big fires going.

Among the men collected near my tent was the Headman of Thak, and when the others had gone I questioned him about the kill at Thak on the 12th of the month, when he so narrowly escaped falling a victim to the man-eater.

Once again the Headman told me in great detail how he had gone to his fields to dig ginger, taking his grandchild with him, and how on hearing his wife calling he had caught the child's hand and run back to the house—where his wife had said a word or two to him about not keeping his ears open and thereby endangering his own and the child's life—and how a few minutes later the tigress had killed a man while he was cutting leaves off a tree in a field above his house.

All this part of the story I had heard before, and I now asked him if he had actually seen the tigress killing the man. His answer was no; and he added that the tree was not visible from where he had been standing. I then asked him how he knew that the man had been killed, and he said, because he had heard him. In reply to further questions he said the man had not called for help but had cried out; and when asked if he had cried out once he said, 'No, three times,' and then at my request he gave an imitation of the man's cry. It was the same—but a very modified rendering—as the screams I had heard the previous night.

I then told him what I had heard and asked him if it was possible for anyone to have arrived at the village accidentally, and his answer was an emphatic negative. There were only two paths leading to Thak, and every man, woman, and child in the villages through which these two paths passed knew that Thak was deserted and the reason for its being so. It was known throughout the district that it was dangerous to go near Thak in daylight, and it was therefore quite impossible for anyone to have been in the village at eight o'clock the previous night.

When asked if he could give any explanation for screams having come from a village in which there could not—according to him—have been any human beings, his answer was that he could not.

And as I can do no better than the Headman, it were best to assume that neither the kakar, the sambur, nor I heard those very real screams—the screams of a human being in mortal agony.

IV.

When all my visitors, including the Headman, had gone, and I was having breakfast, my servant informed me that the Headman of Sem had come to the camp the previous evening and had left word for me that his wife, while cutting grass near the hut where his mother had been killed, had come on a blood trail, and that he would wait for me near the ford over the Ladhya in the morning. So after breakfast I set out to investigate this trail.

While I was fording the river I saw four men hurrying towards me, and as soon as I was on dry land they told me that when they were coming down the hill above Sem they had heard a tiger falling across the valley on the hill between Chuka and Thak. The noise of the water had prevented my hearing the call. I told the men that I was on my way to Sem and would return to Chuka shortly and left them.

The Headman was waiting for me near his house, and his wife took me to where she had seen the blood trail the previous day. The trail, after continuing along a field for a short distance, crossed some big rocks, on one of which I found the hairs of a kakar. A little further on I found the pug marks of a big male leopard, and while I was looking at them I heard a tiger call. Telling my companions to sit down and remain quiet, I listened, in order to locate the tiger. Presently I heard the call again, and thereafter it was repeated at intervals of about two minutes.

It was the tigress calling and I located her as being five hundred yards below Thak and in the deep ravine which, starting from the spring under the mango tree, runs parallel to the path and crosses it at its junction with the Kumaya Chak path.

Telling the Headman that the leopard would have to wait to be shot at a more convenient time, I set off as hard as I could go for camp, picking up at the ford the four men who were waiting for my company to Chuka.

On reaching camp I found a crowd of men round my tent, most of them sawyers from Delhi, but including the petty contractors, agents, clerks, timekeepers, and gangmen of the financier who had taken up the timber and road construction contracts in the Ladhya valley. These men had come to see me in connection with my stay at Chuka. They informed me that many of the hillmen carrying timber and working on the road had left for their homes that morning and that if I left Chuka on 1 December, as they had heard I intended doing, the entire labor force, including themselves, would leave on the same day; for already they were too frightened to eat or sleep, and no one would dare to remain in the valley after I had gone. It was then the morning of 29 November and I told the men that I still had two days and two nights and that much could happen in that time, but that in any case it would not be possible for me to prolong my stay beyond the morning of the first.

The tigress had by now stopped calling, and when my servant had put up something for me to eat I set out for Thak, intending, if the tigress called again and I could locate her position, to try to stalk her; and if she did not call again, to sit up over the buffalo. I found her tracks on the path and saw where she had entered the ravine, and though I stopped repeatedly on my way up to Thak and listened I did not hear her again. So a little before sunset I ate the biscuits and drank the bottle of tea I had brought with me, and then climbed into the almond tree and took my seat on the few strands of rope that had to serve me as a machan. On this occasion the magpies were absent, so I was unable to get the hour or two's sleep the birds had enabled me to get the previous evening.

If a tiger fails to return to its kill the first night it does not necessarily mean that the kill has been abandoned. I have on occasions seen a tiger return on the tenth night and eat what could no longer be described as flesh. On the present occasion, however, I was not sitting over a kill, but over an animal that the tigress had found dead and off which she had made a small meal, and had she not been a man-eater I would not have considered the chance of her returning the second night good enough to justify spending a whole night in a tree when she had not taken sufficient interest in the dead buffalo to return to it the first night. It was therefore with very little hope of getting a shot that I sat on the tree from sunset to sunrise, and though the time I spent was not as long as it had been the previous night, my discomfort was very much greater, for the ropes I was sitting on cut into me, and a cold wind that started blowing shortly after moonrise and continued throughout the night chilled me to the bone. On this second night I heard no jungle or other sounds, nor did the sambur and her young one come out to feed on the fields. As daylight was succeeding moonlight I thought I heard a tiger call in the distance, but could not be sure of the sound or of its direction.

When I got back to camp my servant had a cup of tea and a hot bath ready for me, but before I could indulge in the latter—my forty-pound tent was not big enough for me to bathe in—I had to get rid of the excited throng of people who were clamoring to tell me their experiences of the night before. It appeared that shortly after moonrise the tigress had started calling close to Chuka, and after calling at intervals for a couple of hours had gone off in the direction of the labor camps at Kumaya Chak. The men in these camps hearing her coming started shouting to try to drive her away, but so far from having this effect the shouting only infuriated her the more and she demonstrated in front of the camps until she had cowed the men into silence. Having accomplished this she spent the rest of the night between the labor camps and Chuka, daring all and sundry to shout at her. Towards morning she had gone away in the direction of Thak, and my informants were surprised and very disappointed that I had not met her.

This was my last day of man-eater hunting, and though I was badly in need of rest and sleep, I decided to spend what was left of it in one last attempt to get in touch with the tigress.

The people not only of Chuka and Sem but of all the surrounding villages, and especially the men from Talla Des where some years previously I had shot three man-eaters, were very anxious that I should try sitting up over a live goat, for, said they, 'All hill tigers eat goats, and as you have had no luck with buffaloes, why not try a goat?' More to humor them than with any hope of getting a shot, I consented to spend this last day in sitting up over the two goats I had already purchased for this purpose.

I was convinced that no matter where the tigress wandered to at night her headquarters were at Thak, so at midday, taking the two goats, and accompanied by four of my men. I set out for Thak.

The path from Chuka to Thak, as I have already mentioned, runs up a very steep ridge. A quarter of a mile on this side of Thak the path leaves the ridge, and crosses a more or less flat bit of ground which extends right up to the mango tree. For its whole length across this flat ground the path passes through dense brushwood, and is crossed by two narrow ravines which run east and join the main ravine. Midway between these two ravines, and a hundred yards from the tree I had sat in the previous two nights, there is a giant almond tree; this tree had been my objective when I left camp. The path passes right under the tree and I thought that if I climbed half-way up not only should I be able to see the two goats, one of which I intended tying at the edge of the main ravine and the other at the foot of the hill to the right, but I should also be able to see the dead buffalo. As all three of these points were at some distance from the tree, I armed myself with an accurate .275 rifle, in addition to the 450/400 rifle which I took for an emergency.

I found the climb up from Chuka on this last day very trying, and I had just reached the spot where the path leaves the ridge for the flat ground, when the tigress called about a hundred and fifty yards to my left. The ground here was covered with dense undergrowth and trees interlaced with creepers, and was cut up by narrow and deep ravines, and strewn over with enormous boulders—a very unsuitable place in which to stalk a man-eater. However, before deciding on what action I should take, it was necessary to know whether the tigress was lying down, as she very well might be, for it was then 1 p.m., or whether she was on the move and if so in what direction. So making the men sit down behind me I listened, and presently the call was repeated; she had moved some fifty yards, and appeared to be going up the main ravine in the direction of Thak.

This was very encouraging, for the tree I had selected to sit in was only fifty yards from the ravine. After enjoining silence on the men and telling them to keep close behind me, we hurried along the path. We had about two hundred yards to go to reach the tree and had covered half the distance when, as we approached a spot where the path was bordered on both sides by dense brushwood, a covey of kaleege pheasants rose out of the brushwood and went screaming away. I knelt down and covered the path for a few minutes, but as nothing happened we went cautiously forward and reached the tree without further incident. As quickly and as silently as possible one goat was tied at the edge of the ravine, while the other was tied at the foot of the hill to the right; then I took the men to the edge of the cultivated land and told them to stay in the upper verandah of the Headman's house until I fetched them, and ran back to the tree. I climbed to a height of forty feet, and pulled the rifle up after me with a cord I had brought for the purpose. Not only were the two goats visible from my seat, one at a range of seventy and the other at a range of sixty yards, but I could also see part of the buffalo, and as the .275 rifle was very accurate I felt sure I could kill the tigress if she showed up anywhere on the ground I was overlooking.

The two goats had lived together ever since I had purchased them on my previous visit, and being separate now, were calling lustily to each other. Under normal conditions a goat can be heard at a distance of four hundred yards, but here the conditions were not normal, for the goats were tied on the side of a hill down which a strong wind was blowing, and even if the tigress had moved after I had heard her, it was impossible for her not to hear them. If she was hungry, as I had every reason to believe she was, there was a very good chance of my getting a shot.

After I had been on the tree for ten minutes a kakar barked near the spot the pheasants had risen from. For a minute or two my hopes rose sky-high and then dropped back to earth, for the kakar barked only three times and ended on a note of inquiry; evidently there was a snake in the scrub which neither he nor the pheasants liked the look of.

My seat was not uncomfortable and the sun was pleasingly warm, so for the next three hours I remained in the tree without any discomfort. At 4 p.m. the sun went down behind the high hill above Thak and thereafter the wind became unbearably cold. For an hour I stood the discomfort, and then decided to give up, for the cold had brought on an attack of ague, and if the tigress came now it would not be possible for me to hit her. I retied the cord to the rifle and let it down, climbed down myself, and walked to the edge of the cultivated land to call up my men.

V.

There are few people. I imagine, who have not experienced that feeling of depression that follows failure to accomplish anything they have set out to do. The road back to camp after a strenuous day when the *chukor** bag is full is only a step compared with the same road which one plods over, mile after weary mile, when the bag is empty, and if this feeling of depression has ever assailed you at the end of a single day, and when the quarry has only been *chuker*, you will have some idea of the depth of my depression that evening when, after calling up my men and untying the goats. I set off on my two-mile walk to camp, for my effort had been not of a single day or my quarry a few birds, not did my failure concern only myself.

Excluding the time spent on the journeys from and to home, I had been on the heels of the man-eater from 23 October to 7 November, and again from 14 to 30 November, and it is only those of you who have walked in fear of having the teeth of a tiger meet in your throat who will have any idea of the effect on one's nerves of days and weeks of such anticipation.

Then again my quarry was a man-eater, and my failure to shoot it would very gravely affect everyone who was working in, or whose homes were in, that area. Already work in the forests had been stopped, and the entire population of the largest village in the district had abandoned their homes. Bad as the conditions were they would undoubtedly get worse if the man-eater was not killed, for the entire labor force could not afford to stop work indefinitely, nor could the population of the surrounding villages afford to abandon their homes and their cultivation as the more prosperous people of Thak had been able to do.

The tigress had long since lost her natural fear of human beings, as was abundantly evident from her having carried away a girl picking up mangoes in a field close to where several men were working, killing a woman near the door of her house, dragging a man off a tree in the heart of a village, and, the previous night, cowing a few thousand men into silence. And here was I, who knew full well what the presence of a man-eater meant to the permanent and to the temporary inhabitants and to all the people who passed through the district on their way to the markets at the foothills or the temples at Punagiri, plodding down to camp on what I had promised others would be my last day of man-eater hunting; reason enough for a depression of soul which I felt would remain with me for the rest of my days. Gladly at that moment would I have bartered the success that had attended thirty-two years of man-eater hunting for one unhurried shot at the tigress.

* Hill partridge

I have told you of some of the attempts I made during this period of seven days and seven nights to get a shot at the tigress, but these were by no means the only attempts I made. I knew that I was being watched and followed, and every time I went through the two miles of jungle between my camp and Thak I tried every trick I have learnt in a lifetime spent in the jungles to outwit the tigress. Bitter though my disappointment was, I felt that my failure was not in any way due to anything I had done or left undone.

VI.

My men when they rejoined me said that, an hour after the kakar had barked, they had heard the tigress calling a long way off but were not sure of the direction. Quite evidently the tigress had as little interest in goats as she had in buffaloes, but even so it was unusual for her to have moved at that time of day from a locality in which she was thoroughly at home, unless she had been attracted away by some sound which neither I nor my men had heard; however that may have been, it was quite evident that she had gone, and as there was nothing further that I could do I set off on my weary tramp to camp.

The path, as I have already mentioned, joins the ridge that runs down to Chuka a quarter of a mile from Thak, and when I now got to this spot where the ridge is only a few feet wide and from where a view is obtained of the two great ravines that run down to the Ladhya River, I heard the tigress call once and again across the valley on my left. She was a little above and to the left of Kumaya Chak, and a few hundred yards below the Kot Kindri ridge on which the men working in that area had built themselves grass shelters.

Here was an opportunity, admittedly forlorn and unquestionably desperate, of getting a shot; still it was an opportunity and the last I should ever have, and the question was, whether or not I was justified in taking it.

When I got down from the tree I had one hour in which to get back to camp before dark. Calling up the men, hearing what they had to say, collecting the goats, and walking to the ridge had taken about thirty minutes, and judging from the position of the sun which was now casting a red glow on the peaks of the Nepal hills, I calculated I had roughly half an hour's daylight in hand. This time factor, or perhaps it would be more correct to say light factor, was all-important, for if I took the opportunity that offered, on it would depend the lives of five men.

The tigress was a mile way and the intervening ground was densely wooded, strewn over with great rocks and cut up by a number of deep nullahs, but she could cover the distance well within the half-hour—if she wanted to. The question I had to decide was, whether or not I should try to call her up. If I called and she heard me, and came while it was still daylight and gave me a shot, all would be well; on the other hand, if she came and did not give me a shot some of us would not reach camp, for we had nearly two miles to go and the path the whole way ran through heavy jungle, and was bordered in some places by big rocks, and in others by dense brushwood. It was useless to consult the men, for none of them had ever been in a jungle before coming on this trip, so the decision would have to be mine. I decided to try to call up the tigress.

Handing my rifle over to one of the men I waited until the tigress called again and, cupping my hands round my mouth and filling my lungs to their utmost limit, sent an answering call over the valley. Back came her call and thereafter, for several minutes, call answered call. She would come, had in fact already started, and if she arrived while there was light to shoot by, all the advantages would be on my side, for I had the selecting of the ground on which it would best suit me to meet her. November is the mating season for tigers and it was evident that for the past forty-eight hours she had been rampaging through the jungles in search of a mate, and that now, on hearing what she thought was a tiger answering her mating call, she would lose no time in joining him.

Four hundred yards down the ridge the path runs for fifty yards across a flat bit of ground. At the far right-hand side of this flat ground the path skirts a big rock and then drops steeply, and continues in a series of hairpin bends, down to the next bench. It was at this rock I decided to meet the tigress, and on my way down to it I called several times to let her know I was changing my position, and also to keep in touch with her.

I want you now to have a clear picture of the ground in your mind, to enable you to follow the subsequent events. Imagine then a rectangular piece of ground forty yards wide and eighty yards long, ending in a more or less perpendicular rock face. The path coming down from Thak runs on to this ground at its short or south end, and after continuing down the center for twenty-five yards bends to the right and leaves the rectangle on its long or east side. At the point where the path leaves the flat ground there is a rock about four feet high. From a little beyond where the path bends to the right, a ridge of rock, three or four feet high, rises and extends to the north side of the rectangle, where the ground falls away in a perpendicular rock face. On the near or path side of this low ridge there is a dense line of bushes approaching to within ten feet of the four-foot-high rock I have mentioned. The rest of the rectangle is grown over with trees, scattered bushes, and short grass.

It was my intention to lie on the path by the side of the rock and shoot the tigress as she approached me, but when I tried this position I found it would not be possible for me to see her until she was within two or three yards, and further, that she could get at me either round the rock or through the scattered bushes on my left without my seeing her at all. Projecting out of the rock, from the side opposite to that from which I expected the tigress to approach, there was a narrow ledge. By sitting sideways I found I could get a little of my bottom on the ledge, and by putting my left hand flat on the top of the rounded rock and stretching out my right leg to its full extent and touching the ground with my toes, retain my position on it. The men and goats I placed immediately behind, and ten to twelve feet below me.

The stage was now set for the reception of the tigress, who while these preparations were being made had approached to within three hundred yards. Sending out one final call to give her direction, I looked round to see if my men were all right.

The spectacle these men presented would under other circumstances have been ludicrous, but was here tragic. Sitting in a tight little circle with their knees drawn up and their heads together, with the goats burrowing in under them, they had that look of intense expectancy on their screwed-up features that one sees on the faces of spectators waiting to hear a big gun go off. From the time we had first heard the tigress from the ridge, neither the men nor the goats had made a sound, beyond one suppressed cough. They were probably by now frozen with fear—as well they might be—and even if they were, I take my hat off to those four men who had the courage to do what I, had I been in their shoes, would not have dreamt of doing. For seven days they had been hearing the most exaggerated and blood-curdling tales of this fearsome beast that had kept them awake the past two nights, and now, while darkness was coming on, and sitting unarmed in a position where they could see nothing, they were listening to the man-eater drawing nearer and nearer; greater courage, and greater faith, it is not possible to conceive.

The fact that I could not hold my rifle, a D.B. 450/400, with my left hand (which I was using to retain my precarious seat on the ledge) was causing me some uneasiness, for apart from the fear of the rifle's slipping on the rounded top of the rock—I had folded my handkerchief and placed the rifle on it to try to prevent this—I did not know what would be the effect of the recoil of a high velocity rifle fired in this position. The rifle was pointing along the path, in which there was a hump, and it was my intention to fire into the tigress's face immediately it appeared over this hump, which was twenty feet from the rock.

The tigress, however, did not keep to the contour of the hill, which would have brought her out on the path a little beyond the hump, but crossed a deep ravine and came straight towards where she had heard my last call, at an angle which I can best describe as one o'clock. This manoeuver put the low ridge of rock, over which I could not see, between us. She had located the direction of my last call with great accuracy, but had misjudged the distance, and not finding her prospective mate at the spot she had expected him to be, she was now working herself up into a perfect fury and you will have some idea of what the fury of a tigress in her condition can be when I tell you that not many miles from my home a tigress on one occasion closed a public road for a whole week, attacking everything that attempted to go along it, including a string of camels, until she was finally joined by a mate.

I know of no sound more liable to fret one's nerves than the calling of an unseen tiger at close range. What effect this appalling sound was having on my men I was frightened to think, and if they had gone screaming down the hill I should not have been at all surprised, for even though I had the heel of a good rifle to my shoulder and the stock against my cheek I felt like screaming myself.

But even more frightening than this continuous calling was the fading out of the light. Another few seconds, ten or fifteen at the most, and it would be too dark to see my sights, and we should then be at the mercy of a man-eater, plus a tigress wanting a mate. Something would have to be done, and done in a hurry, if we were not to be massacred, and the only thing I could think of was to call.

The tigress was now so close that I could hear the intake of her breath each time before she called, and as she again filled her lungs, I did the same with mine, and we called simultaneously. The effect was startlingly instantaneous. Without a second's hesitation she came tramping with quick steps through the dead leaves, over the low ridge and into the bushes a little to my right front, and just as I was expecting her to walk right on top of me she stopped, and the next moment the full blast of her deep-throated call struck me in the face and would have carried the hat off my head had I been wearing one. A second's pause, then again quick steps; a glimpse of her as she passed between two bushes, and then she stepped right out into the open, and, looking into my face, stopped dead.

By great and unexpected good luck the half-dozen steps the tigress took to her right front carried her almost to the exact spot at which my rifle was pointing. Had she continued in the direction in which she was coming before her last call, my story—if written—would have had a different ending, for it would have been as impossible to slew the rifle on the rounded top of the rock as it would have been to lift and fire it with one hand.

Owing to the nearness of the tigress, and the fading light, all that I could see of her was her head. My first bullet caught her under the right eye and the second, fired more by accident than with intent, took her in the throat and she came to rest with her nose against the rock and knocked me off the ledge, and the recoil from the left barrel, fired while I was in the air, brought the rifle up in violent contact with my jaw and sent me heels over head right on top of the men and goats. Once again I take my hat off to those four men for, not knowing but what the tigress was going to land on them next, they caught me as I fell and saved me from injury and my rifle from being broken.

When I had freed myself from the tangle of human and goat legs I took the .275 rifle from the man who was holding it, rammed a clip of cartridges into the magazine and sent a stream of five bullets singing over the valley and across the Sarda into Nepal. Two shots, to the thousands of men in the valley and in the surrounding villages who were anxiously listening for the sound of my rifle, might mean anything, but two shots followed by five more, spaced at regular intervals of five seconds, could only be interpreted as conveying one message, and that was, that the man-eater was dead.

I had not spoken to my men from the time we had first heard the tigress from the ridge. On my telling them now that she was dead and that there was no longer any reason for us to be afraid, they did not appear to be able to take in what I was saying, so I told them to go up and have a look while I found and lit a cigarette. Very cautiously they climbed up to the rock, but went no further for, as I have told you, the tigress was touching the other side of it. Late in camp that night, while sitting round a camp-fire and relating their experiences to relays of eager listeners, their narrative invariably ended up with, 'and then the tiger whose roaring had turned our livers into water hit the sahib on the head and knocked him down on top of us and if you don't believe us, go and look at his face.' A mirror is superfluous in camp and even if I had had one it could not have made the swelling on my jaw, which put me on milk diet for several days, look as large and as painful as it felt.

By the time a sapling had been felled and the tigress lashed to it, lights were beginning to show in the Ladhya valley and in all the surrounding camps and villages. The four men were very anxious to have the honor of carrying the tigress to camp, but the task was beyond them; so I left them and set off for help.

In my three visits to Chuka during the past eight months I had been along this path many times by day and always with a loaded rifle in my hands, and now I was stumbling down in the dark, unarmed, my only anxiety being to avoid a fall. If the greatest happiness one can experience is the sudden cessation of great pain, then the second greatest happiness is undoubtedly the sudden cessation of great fear. One short hour previously it would have taken wild elephants to have dragged from their homes and camps the men who now, singing and shouting, were converging from every direction, singly and in groups, on the path leading to Thak. Some of the men of this rapidly growing crowd went up the path to help carry in the tigress, while others accompanied me on my way to camp, and would have carried me had I permitted them. Progress was slow, for frequent halts had to be made to allow each group of new arrivals to express their gratitude in their own particular way. This gave the party carrying the tigress time to catch us up, and we entered the village together. I will not attempt to describe the welcome my men and I received, or the scenes I witnessed at Chuka that night, for having lived the greater part of my life in the jungles I have not the ability to paint word-pictures.

A hayrick was dismantled and the tigress laid on it, and an enormous bonfire made from driftwood close at hand to light up the scene and for warmth, for the night was dark and cold with a north wind blowing. Round about midnight my servant, assisted by the Headman of Thak and Kunwar Singh, near whose house I was camped, persuaded the crowd to return to their respective villages and labor camps, telling them they would have ample opportunity of feasting their eyes on the tigress the following day. Before leaving himself, the Headman of Thak told me he would send word in the morning to the people of Thak to return to their village. This he did, and two days later the entire population returned to their homes, and have lived in peace ever since.

After my midnight dinner I sent for Kunwar Singh and told him that in order to reach home on the promised date I should have to start in a few hours, and that he would have to explain to the people in the morning why I had gone. This he promised to do, and I then started to skin the tigress. Skinning a tiger with a pocket-knife is a long job, but it gives one an opportunity of examining the animal that one would otherwise not get, and in the case of man-eaters enables one to ascertain, more or less accurately, the reason for the animal's having become a man-eater.

The tigress was a comparatively young animal and in the perfect condition one would expect her to be at the beginning of the mating season. Her dark winter coat was without a blemish, and in spite of her having so persistently refused the meals I had provided for her she was encased in fat. She had two old gunshot wounds, neither of which showed on her skin. The one in her left shoulder, caused by several pellets of homemade buckshot, had become septic, and when healing the skin, over quite a large surface, had adhered permanently to the flesh. To what extent this wound had incapacitated her it would have been difficult to say, but it had evidently taken a very long time to heal, and could quite reasonably have been the cause of her having become a man-eater. The second wound, which was in her right shoulder, had also been caused by a charge of buckshot, but had healed without becoming septic. These two wounds received over kills in the days before she had become a man-eater were quite sufficient reason for her not having returned to the human and other kills I had sat over.

After having skinned the tigress I bathed and dressed, and though my face was swollen and painful and I had twenty miles of rough going before me, I left Chuka walking on air, while the thousands of men in and around the valley were peacefully sleeping.

I have come to the end of the jungle stories I set out to tell you and I have also come near the end of my man-eater hunting career.

I have had a long spell and count myself fortunate in having walked out on my own feet and not been carried out on a cradle in the manner and condition of the man of Thak.

There have been occasions when life has hung by a thread and others when a light purse and disease resulting from exposure and strain have made the going difficult, but for all these occasions I am amply rewarded if my hunting has resulted in saving one human life.

Leopard: A Most Dangerous Game

JIM CARMICHEL

You do not hunt a leopard, you plot a confrontation. It is a chess game of will and patience; you make a move and the leopard makes a move, over and over until a wrong move is made. Then you win or the leopard wins.

We had been making our moves for more than a week, somewhere in western Tanzania where a parched scrub plain is split by the Rungwa River. It is not an unexplored region, perhaps avoided is a better word. Livingstone passed near there, and Stanley and Speke and possibly Baker. But they all went on, leaving the land veiled behind its curtain of bloodsucking tsetse flies.

Few men travel there now, except nomadic bee hunters seeking wild honey and treasure hunters who wander the forests in search of teak and other rare woods. And when they have chopped their tree or robbed the killer bees of their honey, these men do not remain. That's why this savage and beautiful place is one of the richest hunting lands on earth.

Tanzania is a new name. When great books were written about the place, it was known as Tanganyika. It is the land of Kilimanjaro, Ngorongoro Crater, and the Serengeti. It is also one of the last hunting areas in Africa where the traditions of great safari still live. If you turn off the electric generator, the adventure of safari life is the same as when Britain was an empire. Lions roar at night, hippos grunt, and barefoot black men in white coats say, "Morning B'wana" when they bring you tea.

That's why we were there; I wanted the first safari for my wife and friends to be like those I had experienced nearly a generation before when I had first gone out to Africa. There is still plenty of good hunting in Africa, but the days of the classic safari are numbered. The reason is simply because there are so few professional hunters of the old school remaining. These were the professional hunters of legend—educated and cultured gentlemen who organized and guided safaris for sportsmen and sportswomen of, presumably, similar tastes and backgrounds. Their exploits were the stuff of storybooks: On a normal hunting day, a Finch Hatton or a Von Blixen would track elephants from dawn to dusk, oversee a camp and staff, discipline rebellious porters, save a client from a charging buffalo, then appear starched and polished for sundowners, ready to knock off a decanter of gin and determined to take all necessary precautions to protect his honor and reputation from a spoiled and determined heiress.

No one in the safari business today better fills this description than Michael Rowbotham. Born and educated in England, and a Scots Guard officer in World War II, he was a natural for the professional hunting business. Landing in Kenya after the war, young Rowbotham signed on as an assistant hunter with some of the great professionals of the era, including Tony Henley and Harry Selby. Those he didn't work with he at least knew and learned from. In time, he earned his professional hunter's license and a reputation as a tough, resourceful hunter who not only brought his clients home alive, but got them great trophies as well. When *King Solomon's Mines* was filmed in the early 1950s, Rowbotham was hired as hunter-in-residence to look after the well-being of the movie's stars. Who better than the dashing Rowbotham to guard Deborah Kerr's tent and bedstead from marauding lions and other African rascals?

Today, after more safaris than one can imagine, Mike Rowbotham is owner of Hunter's Tracks safari company, and he is one of the few members of the original East African Professional Hunter's Association still practicing his craft. If your idea of a professional hunter is some galoot with elephant hair bracelets on his arms, a gold chain with a lion's claw dangling from his neck, and Banana Republic labels on his kit, Rowbotham is not your man. The only time you would recognize Rowbotham for what he is is in the African bush; then there is no mistaking. Swahili is the language of his trade, and his tool is a double rifle.

I'd hunted with Mike before (see "The Croc That Wouldn't Croak," *Outdoor Life*, May 1985), and I insisted that he take personal charge of this safari. Because there were three hunters in our party plus two non-shooters, Mike arranged for another professional hunter, Lou Hallimore, a savvy Rhodesian, to share the guiding chores. Mike's son, Ian, came along as assistant hunter.

Our KLM flight from Amsterdam touched down before dawn at the Arusha airport, and while customs officers busied themselves counting our rifles and ammunition, we witnessed the spectacle of an African sunrise. The first light glinted from a golden crown floating above the plain. Then the light gathered around the crown, causing it to take shape and grow higher. As the sun continued to rise, the crown of gold became a mantle of shimmering white. Kilimanjaro. Driving into Arusha, we passed herds of cattle tended by Masai tribesmen, their robes pulled tight against the morning cold. It was July, the time of cool days and dry air—the hunting season.

I'd hunted Africa before, plenty of times, from the Nile to the Cape of Good Hope, and each time with a manic determination to explore the land, study the game, and earn the trophies. I was a student of the hunting rifle, and Africa was my classroom. But now I wanted to relax with good friends, sharing with them the discoveries and exultations of a first safari. There was my wife, Linda, Don Crowe, Allen Harris, and his daughter, Stanley. Don, a pal since college days, is into more business ventures than I can list, and Allen is one of the world's largest manufacturers of hardwood flooring. Stanley is a pixie to whom the world is a beach ball and life a garden party. Her first safari would not be her last.

Life in a safari camp soon settles into a relaxed daily routine. Because we were not hunting any particular species, we spent the days scouting the plains, watching the game, and occasionally putting a stalk on especially good trophies. The area had not been hunted for several years, so it was not difficult to find record-class animals. Some days we lunched in the field, but more often we would meet back at camp at midday to unload whatever game we might have taken. After lunch and an afternoon nap, we would hunt until the sun touched the horizon. Then it was time for sundowners by the fire and happy talk about the day's events while waiting turns for the shower. Dinner was followed by bed, and soon a new hunting day would begin. It was an easy hunt, and likely would have remained so had not Saleem, one of our trackers, found a track in the sandy bottom of a dry river bed. "Chui," he said in Swahili. "Leopard."

Leopards change things. When the presence of a leopard is discovered, you can try to ignore it, which is impossible, or you try to hunt the animal. When you hunt a leopard, it changes everything about your day. It changes the way you think and the way you act. Your schedule revolves around the leopard. The deadly chess game begins, and the first move is yours.

The leopard is impossible to explain. Not because of what it is but because of what it does to men's minds. It is difficult to look at a leopard and then, looking away, quite remember what you saw. Instead, your memory flashes images from your subconscious. The leopard's eyes are mirrors that reflect things you do not want to see. When we understand fear, we will understand the leopard. In African culture, the leopard is the symbol of savagery. Whereas lions are the symbol of bravery, leopards signify invincibility. Warriors wear leopard skins as displays of their strength, and witch doctors invoke the spirit of the leopard to cast magic spells. Even in death, the leopard is a force to be reckoned with.

I once knew a professional hunter who could have been one of the best. But he became afraid of leopards. It was not ordinary sensible fear, but the kind of fear that rots a man's mind. I haven't seen this individual for more than a decade, but I hear that he hangs out in the lobby of a cheap hotel in Hirarie, swilling gin and selling elephant hair bracelets to gullible tourists. Strangely, he was never attacked by a leopard.

The leopard is one of Africa's so-called "Big Five" trophies. If size were the only measure the leopard wouldn't qualify because a big tom will seldom weigh more than 180 pounds; females are smaller. But what the leopard lacks in size is more than made up for in savage efficiency. Pound for pound and inch for inch, it is one of the most cunning and efficient killers ever to stalk the earth. Its power is difficult to describe because the measures of strength we ordinarily use simply don't apply. But to give you an idea, let's say that you weigh 200 pounds and stand six feet tall and possess such superhuman strength that you can make a standing jump onto a ledge a foot or two over your head, landing gracefully on your feet. If you were a leopard, you could perform the same feat carrying 200 pounds of dead weight.

You kill a leopard by using its rules: The only honor is deceit, and quickness is the only measure of sportsmanship. Glory is survival. The only reasonable chance of killing a leopard is from a blind, and that is the most difficult hunting of all.

Building a proper leopard blind is probably a professional hunter's greatest challenge. It is a skill based on several skills—and luck. All too often, leopard hunting is described as being a simple matter of hanging a bait in a tree and waiting for the stupid beast to come looking for any easy meal. But leopards aren't stupid, and they aren't easily tempted by free food. That is why a leopard hunt is carried out in stages—not at all unlike a battle plan, or a game of chess.

It is exceedingly unusual to see a leopard during daylight. The pretty pictures and television "documentaries" we see of leopards are made in game parks and reserves, where leopards' normal habits have been radically altered. Filming truly wild leopards in their natural environment would be virtually impossible because they remain hidden during the day. That's why leopards are almost always shot at first light or just before dark. The only evidence a hunter usually has of a leopard's presence is the track. Everything else about the leopard is an abstraction—pieces of a spotted puzzle scattered in the thorny bush.

The first stage of the hunt is hanging bait—not just one but several. And not in just any tree. Each hanging site must be just right in a number of ways. It must be a fairly large tree with limbs thick enough to support the leopard without swaying. It must offer a clear line of fire from the blind, and the area around the tree must be open so that the leopard, dead or alive, can be seen. Too, the tree has to be situated so that both the bait and the leopard are outlined against the sky. Naturally, it's usually impossible to find the perfect tree, so compromises have to be made. One compromise that no smart hunter will ever make, however, is safety. A wounded leopard is a professional hunter's worst nightmare, so the selection of bait trees is made with this worst case scenario uppermost in mind.

The next stage is actually hanging the bait. Just about any meat will do—preferably waterbuck or something else that is less than desirable fare for the camp table—but it must be hung with exacting care. If it is hung too low, it will be ripped away by hyenas; too high, and the leopard might not take notice. Also, it has to be tightly bound to the tree so that the leopard or some scavenger can't make off with it. Mike's technique is to secure the bait with a chain passed through tendons and bone. Sometimes we would use the truck to hoist the bait into place, but more often we simply muscled it into the tree. All the while, we worked as quickly and quietly as we could and left as little human scent and sign as possible.

It all takes time. Hours that might have been pleasantly filled hunting other game are now spent killing and hanging bait and watching for additional bait trees. Our safari was scheduled to last three weeks—plenty of time for a relaxed general-bag hunt—but a leopard demands extra time. Precious hours and then days are invested while other trophies go unhunted. Many is the hunter who has used up his safari hunting leopards. It is always a gamble, you gamble your money, your time and your effort. Then, at the moment of payoff, you may gamble your life. The leopard becomes an obsession; nothing else really matters.

In the beginning, we hung bait in two trees. When nothing came, we baited more trees, hanging small antelope among the branches and slitting their bellies open so that their gut stench would drift to where the leopard hid, tempting it out. Leopards are eaters of foul, rotted meat. It is an unspeakable irony of evolution that a creature of such charismatic beauty should bury its face among the maggots and feed on carrion.

Every morning we would check each bait, approaching the trees silently and with caution, looking for sign that a leopard had come—searching for a track, a ripped bait or a claw mark. Each day the baits rotted more, stinking so that it was hard to go near. Flies swarmed, and rotted strips of flesh fell among pools of maggots. And then one night the leopard came.

We did not see the leopard, and unskilled eyes would never have known that it had been there. There was no track on the hard ground, and the bait was not eaten. The only sign was a slit in the tree's bark and three honey-colored hairs snagged in a broken twig. It wasn't much to go on, but it was all we had. The leopard had made a move, so now it was time for the hunt's second stage. It was time to build a blind.

When a leopard is feeding on a bait, it is vulnerable, but that is only because it has convinced itself, utterly, that it is in no danger. Until then, the leopard moves like a nervous shadow. Each step is an exercise in caution—the eyes consider everything, searching for a reason to flee. The bait is not natural to the leopard, and the cat is bewildered. It is free food, but whose? Did another leopard put it there? If so, the leopard is trespassing and risking a savage fight. Perhaps it has seen bait before and even felt the hot breath of a bullet. Every instinct tells it that the bait is danger.

A hunter almost never knows that he has spooked a leopard. That is because the leopard remains hidden as it approaches the bait, often freezing into total stillness as it considers everything in the area. If it sees or senses something it doesn't like, the leopard retreats as carefully as it came. That's why a blind has to be built so that no trace of the hunter is visible.

But hiding the hunter isn't the only consideration when building a blind. The blind also has to permit the hunter a clear view of the bait and surrounding area; it has to be situated so that any wind will not alert the leopard; and—because the hunter must remain virtually motionless for hours at a time—it must be relatively comfortable.

Reason tells us that a blind should be a good distance from the bait—100 yards or even more. That way the blind is in less risk of being detected by the leopard, and the hunter himself is in less risk of being attacked should he only wound the quarry. Distance, however, is a luxury that the professional hunter cannot afford. His single overwhelming concern is that his client's bullet be dead on target. To this end, he risks all else and puts his skill on the line by putting the blind as close to the bait as possible. I've heard of blinds being closer than ten yards, especially when the professional hunter didn't have much faith in his client's marksmanship. The longest shooting distance I know of was some 80 yards—the distance at which I nailed a leopard a few years ago in Zimbabwe—but then there was no other choice.

A similar situation now existed because the area around the shootable side of this tree was open and packed hard. That meant that the blind had to be about 60 yards from the bait and situated on a slight knoll covered with scrub brush. The distance was acceptable to both Mike and me, and the scrub cover would help conceal the blind. What was not good, however, was a rather deep dry wash just behind the tree. Beyond that was a flat plain of thorny bush that stretched out of sight. If I wounded the leopard, it could instantly disappear into the wash or the dense thorn. Either way, there would be hell to pay.

We've all read those wonderful stories about how brave hunters armed with shotguns and buckshot waded into the brush after wounded leopards. Shooting a leopard on the wing with a load of buckshot is a chancy business at best, but it is the only sane way (if it can be called that) to deal with the cats when they are wounded and lying in ambush.

We didn't have a shotgun, thanks to a bureaucratic snag, and Mike's double rifle was being held by customs officials wanting more paperwork. If the leopard didn't die in its tracks, we would have to go into that thorny hell armed only with scope-sighted, bolt-action rifles. In other words, I would have only one chance to do it right, and my bullet had better, by gawd, be dead on the mark. Leopards are tough; they die hard. They have been known to absorb two slugs from an elephant gun and still have enough fight to kill the hunter. It has happened again and again, and it will surely happen yet again.

Mike didn't say much about the danger, but I could tell that he was bothered. While the blind was being built, I would see him studying the dry wash and the endless thicket of thorn beyond. It was like looking at a pair of dice and trying to decide whose number would come up. Nothing he saw gave him consolation. Professional hunters like to have faith in their clients, but those who have survived as long as Mike have learned that it is best to put their faith in themselves. This time, he had to put all his faith in someone else because some bureaucrat hundreds of miles away had decided that paperwork was more important than a hunter's safety.

The blind was some consolation. Designed by Lou Hallimore, it was made of woven bamboo slats fitted around a box frame. Its advantages, other than being quick to set up, were that it offered some-what more comfort than a typical blind made of brush while at the same time almost totally hiding the occupants. The risk of any blind is that the leopard will decide that it is not part of the landscape, so we piled green brush around the front and sides so it looked more natural. When everything was in place, I went inside and propped my rifle on a forked shooting stick that had been cut for that purpose. Leaving nothing to chance, I wanted to make sure that I had a steady rest and a clear line of fire to the bait. While Linda and Ian piled more brush around the windows so that no light could reflect off my rifle and scope, I studied the shooting situation and tried to anticipate problems that might arise.

One difficulty I spotted immediately was a large leafy branch that formed a curtain behind the bait. In bright daylight I could see well enough, but in dim twilight a leopard could very well blend into the foliage, making it difficult, if not impossible, to see the cat's outline and aim at its vital area. I wanted to see the leopard clearly outlined against the sky, so I ordered that the limb be cut. Saleem climbed the tree and hacked at the limb with his hook-bladed panga until I could see the sky beyond. The way I figured, the leopard would leap from the ground to a low limb, and from there to a thick, horizontal limb just under the bait. When it began feeding, it would be in a broadside position, giving me a clear shot at its heart. Even in dim light, its sky-outlined silhouette would offer me a reasonable target. A reasonable chance is all a leopard hunter can ever ask for.

"Come look here." It was Mike. "We need a fail-safe plan. When the leopard falls, it may very well drop into that depression beyond the tree. We won't be able to see it from the blind, so we must get out quickly and run to where we can see better. When you fire, I'll dash to that little bluff to our right. You be right behind me, ready to fire again." Twice we practiced the maneuver; if the leopard was still alive, speed would be vital. With luck, I'd be able to put another bullet into the cat before it disappeared.

The last thing that I did that morning was to go back into the blind and try, once again, to imagine what could go wrong—how I could fail. Linda came in and sat beside me, looking through the hole to see what I would see. She had been with us all along, helping select the trees and hang the baits. She is a professor of literature and has read the hunting stories of Hemingway, Ruark and Faulkner. Now the stories would have a new focus, a special meaning all her own. She took my hand, and we went out of the blind together, counting our steps to the tree. It was 57 paces. An easy shot?

That day at lunch there was news of another leopard. At least we hoped it was another. Mike and Lou decided that the second track was so far from the first that we were dealing with two different animals. Yet, if the whim strikes them, or if they are forced out of their territory, leopards will relocate miles away. Was this what had happened to my leopard? We'd soon know. Anyway, the immediate plan was for Lou to proceed with selecting trees and hanging baits as if they were onto a different leopard. If it was the cat I'd been working for, there was nothing I could do except hope that Don or Allen would get a crack at it.

Soon after lunch, the rest of the party left to begin killing and hanging baits. It would keep them occupied for the next couple of days. Would it be possible to bag two leopards on one safari? It was too much to hope for, I decided. It takes a lot of luck to get even one.

That afternoon, we stayed at camp later than usual. There were things to do and thoughts to be thought. Sleep would have been a blessing, but there was no chance of that. Mike and Ian spent time alone and talked about the things a father and son talk about when they are about to do a dangerous thing. They talked for a long time. Linda tried to read, but mostly the book lay closed in her lap while she thought about what women think about when their husbands go to kill leopards. I suppose they are the same thoughts born of women whose husbands go to do battle, to race fast cars or to fight bulls.

Near our camp, I set up a target and paced off 57 steps. The purpose was to learn where my rifle would hit in respect to point of aim at that exact distance. When rifles are sighted-in for long-range hunting, as mine was, the short-distance point of impact can be somewhat off point of aim. The first bullet was off the mark a bit—less than an inch—so I adjusted the 4X Leupold scope slightly and fired again. This time, the 250-grain Nosler bullet split the aiming mark. Sebbi, a camp worker, and Saleem watched with rapt attention, their ebony faces twin studies in solemn concentration. It takes powerful magic to kill a leopard, and they wanted to know if any bad spirits were lurking in my bullets. The target was carried back to camp, where a small crowd gathered to discuss the magical power of my rifle. It was a .338 Winchester Magnum built on a Mauser action by the David Miller Company. A veteran of many hunts, the blue was wearing thin in places and the stock wore a few dents and scars, but it still had all its magic.

"Sebbi," Mike bellowed, "bring tea," and instantly there was the rapid slapping sound of bare feet on packed earth, quickly followed by a rattling of pots and china in the cook tent.

Within moments, fresh tea came to the thatch-shaded dining table, and Mike, as only an Englishman can, presided over the service. For a while, we sipped the hot brew silently, our thoughts very much on what we were about to do. In the background, I could hear the truck being loaded, the tank being filled with gas, everything being done with cautious quietness as if the leopard, miles away, could hear us.

"Linda," Mike broke the silence, "what are your plans? Will you stay in camp, or are you going with us?"

"I'm going."

"Very well then; you will stay in the truck with Ian. The flies will be bad before dark, so take your bug jacket. The way I have this figured," he went on, speaking to me, "this fellow should cause us no trouble. But if we should get in a mess and he gets at you, try to get on your belly and cover your head with your arms. And for gawd's sake, if he is on me, don't shoot unless you're absolutely sure."

One of a professional hunter's greatest fears is being shot by a companion trying to save him from an attacking lion or leopard. It has happened often enough that some hunters warn their clients to never use a gun no matter how bad the situation looks.

"And another thing," Mike continued, "the leopard may be close by, guarding the bait, so let's not show our hand by strolling into the blind like a couple of poffs on parade. Ian, you will drive, and Jim and I will be in the back. Drive close to the rear of the blind, but *don't stop*. Just slow down enough for us to step out, and you keep on going. If the leopard is watching, his attention will be on the truck, and he'll think it is just passing by. Then circle back and park. When you hear a shot, come like bloody hell. Otherwise, don't come until full dark." After that, we finished tea and tried to talk about other things, but the image of a clawing leopard raged in my mind.

In the back of the truck was a large chest that I had not seen before, but I knew what it contained. It was a hospital kit with bottles of powerful antiseptics. Leopards are horribly infectious; their bites and claw rips almost always lead to infections, fever and even blood poisoning. That's why first-aid for a leopard attack means drenching the wounds with antiseptic. The chest would also contain surgical equipment, sutures and hypodermic syringes. For pain, there would be morphine.

Ian slowed the truck a few feet from the blind, and Mike and I were quickly inside—he carrying two canvas camp chairs and a hemp bag of water, and me toting the rifle, a small leather case of extra cartridges and the one other thing a leopard hunter always needs: a book. Quickly we went to the small windows and searched the landscape, first with unaided eyes, then again, more slowly, with binoculars. Finally satisfied that the leopard was not there, we unfolded the chairs and made ourselves comfortable for the long watch. It would be more than two hours until dark, and I knew from past experience that time would creep by with excruciating slowness.

My book was *The White Nile*, Allen Moorehead's great story of hunter-explorers who came to Africa searching for the source of the river Nile. I'd read it before, twice, and now was the time to read it again because some of the adventures in its pages happened just where we were. Probably some of the explorers had passed by the very place where we were sitting. I looked out the window and wondered whether what I saw was different from what Living-stone might have seen when he came that way. Probably not.

My routine was simple: I'd read a page, then carefully survey the bait tree and the surrounding landscape, tracing every branch, every bush, every feature, straining to detect anything different from the last look. Then I would read a page and begin another search.

It was a warm day with no wind to drive away the tsetse flies, and within an hour, they had found us. The tsetse flies have silent wings and feet like padded snowshoes. They can land on your face so softly that you won't feel a thing until they bore under your skin. Then there is pain like a bee sting, and the voracious bloodsucker is gone. They bite through clothing; no repellent yet made will deter them; and no insect is more wary. That's why killing one is a victory. A slap won't do it; you have to roll them under your fingers until they pop open and the blood spurts out. It's your blood, and you're amazed at how much they can hold in their accordion-pleated bellies. So you sit there, squashing flies and praying for the leopard to come and end the waiting. Why in hell doesn't it come? Where is it? Will it come?

Gradually the shadows shifted, giving a new perspective to every outline. The sky faded from blue to pink, then erupted in a blaze of such brilliant color that the sun seemed to be pouring itself across the earth. Then the sky cooled and became burnished copper, against which the leopard tree was a solitary black outline. Now was the time for the leopard to come.

Moving with breathless caution, I eased the rifle through the window and settled it on the shooting stick. The crosshairs of the Leupold first found the bait, then moved cautiously through the tree, inspecting every branch.

"Can you still see?" Mike whispered.

I nodded the affirmative. If the leopard came soon, I would have a good shot. Though I could no longer see into the shadows, the big limb was clearly outlined. The cat would be easy to see if it came in the next ten minutes, 15 at the most. The minutes ticked by, covering us with darkness, and the leopard did not come.

The next day there was plenty of excitement in camp. The other hunters had made an early morning check of their freshly hung baits and found where a leopard had been feeding. We had checked our baits, too, and found nothing; layers of maggots were sucking at the rotting meat, but no leopard had been there. It had been two days since the leopard had come, and even then it had not eaten any of the bait. I did not believe that the cat would come again. We had already lost too much time, and I felt that we should resume our normal hunting and salvage what we could of the few remaining days. It was a disappointment, but what would hunting be if there were no failures? I'd hunted leopards before and lost, but this was a first time for Linda. She had been involved from the beginning, had shared in the work, had suffered the tsetse flies, had hoped the hardest, and would most keenly feel the sting of failure. She doesn't give up without a fight.

"Here's what we'll do," I announced at lunch. "We'll try my leopard one more time. Win or lose, we'll dismantle the blind and bring it back tonight. You guys can set it up in the morning and be in business by tomorrow evening."

It was agreed. That afternoon, we were in the blind again. The tsetses were particularly vicious, but in a way, I suppose I welcomed them. We hunters have a way of rationalizing discomfort that suggests that we are somehow convinced that if we work harder, climb higher, suffer more cold, more heat, and endure more physical torture, we will be rewarded. So the tsetses bored into my hide, the bug repellent stung my eyes, and I waited for my reward. Like the day before, the afternoon crawled by with only the occasional cackle of a francolin to punctuate the monotony. Then time gathered speed, and the sky turned cold and dark. There was no leopard, no reward. But there was the satisfaction of having made a final effort. I was glad for that. We had played the game the best way we knew how, and had been beaten by an opponent who played the game better. There was no disgrace in that. So we took the blind apart in darkness and arrived in camp ready for a tall drink. I toasted the leopard, and wished it a long life.

The next day was a good one; it was a relief to have the leopard episode behind us. After a long and difficult stalk, I shot a hartebeest that will rank high in the world's records, and I looked forward to three more days of good hunting. Don and Lou had even better luck. As easy as you please, they had set up the blind near their working bait and had waited only an hour or so for a leopard to appear. Don had killed the cat with his .300 Winchester Magnum, and they had been back in camp, sipping gin and tonic, before sundown. The whole affair had been so quick and easy that Don hadn't been especially impressed. He had been incredibly lucky, and he didn't even know it. Anyway, it was good to have a leopard in camp. Including the two lions taken by Allen and Don plus our exceptional plains trophies, the safari had been a fantastic success.

We would never have gone back to the bait tree had not Mike needed to retrieve his bait chain. "Hurry," he ordered Saleem as we drove near, "climb up there and take the bolts out." We were on our way to a distant vlei where we'd seen roan antelope two weeks earlier. It would be a long drive, and we didn't have time to waste. Saleem, running ahead of the truck, never made it to the tree because suddenly he reversed direction and came racing back, pointing over his shoulder as he ran.

"Chui, chui." I recognized the Swahili word again and again in the rapid exchange that then took place between the hunter and tracker. Leopard! They were talking about the leopard! "Here's the story," began Mike, using his best British phrasing to hide his excitement, "Saleem says a leopard has been eating the bait. We may have spooked it just now, which is good because it will still be hungry and want to come back. What is your pleasure?"

"Let's go back to camp and get the blind. We'll hunt roan another day."

There wasn't time to camouflage the blind as carefully as before. A few withered branches were propped here and there, possibly blurring the outline, but if a leopard looked twice, it would see us. Looking out of the window with my binocular, I could see ripped strips of flesh hanging from the bait. Very little had been eaten. I was confident that the leopard would come back. I was more than confident; I was *sure*. Everything around me whispered the leopard's presence.

Could a creature be possessed of such powerful presence that it radiates around the animal like a charged current? I could feel it. Linda, in the truck a half-mile away, felt it, too. It was like standing in the wind that comes before a thunderstorm—all of nature bends to its force. Yet, not a leaf moved. From somewhere in the brush came a sound that I'd never heard before, similar to the sound of a small dog crying in pain. It did not stop for a long while. Mike raised his eyebrows and shrugged his shoulders in silent questioning. The noise was strange to him also.

A hyena came, whimpering the external frustration of its species—ugly, its back hunched and its crooked little hind legs scurrying after the larger, more powerful front legs. The hyena stopped under the tree and studied the bait for a long minute. It could see the bait; it could smell it, and the hyena desperately wanted to eat it. But the scavenger could not reach it. Such is the lot of a hyena's existence. Suddenly, the hyena seemed to realize that it had no business there, and like a frightened thief, it spun around and disappeared.

The leopard was close. So very close; I knew it. It was just over there, or over there. The certainty of the leopard's presence was so overpowering that I could resist no longer. My hand went to the rifle and guided its muzzle through the window, the butt touching my shoulder at the exact instant that the leopard appeared.

It was there! Walking slowly, utterly confident of the force it radiated, the biggest wild leopard I'd ever seen. It moved toward the tree with unmistakable arrogance, each stride a study in measured power. I could have killed the cat at any one of several moments—my finger was tight on the trigger—but I wanted *that* moment to be the best moment. We'd waited too long and worked too hard for me to botch it now.

Suddenly, I was aware of Mike close beside me. *My gawd,* I realized, *he doesn't see the damn thing!* Mike's concentration was so intently focused on another spot that he hadn't seen the leopard. *He should be watching the leopard when I shoot. What should I do? The hell with Mike!*

The leopard stopped, looked up at the bait, and then, to my total disbelief, sat down! Sat down just like a dog begging a tidbit. Until that instant, I had been convinced that I would shoot the leopard after he was in the tree. That's how leopards are killed; it's the time-honored way, the way hunting books are written. It's the *safe* way. A cat on the ground is not a clear target—one leap and it could be out of sight.

The cat moved; I could see its muscles tense. Was it going to leap into the tree or was something wrong? Was it about to run? It was my turn. Now!

The blaze of muzzle fire reached out like a long arm, torching the landscape like lightning. Momentarily blinded by the fireball, I could not see the leopard. Where was it? Was it dead? Then I remembered our practiced routine and charged out of the blind and ran to the knoll. Mike was already there, his eyes, like mine, struggling to see again.

"Shoot again," he commanded, "it's under the tree. Shoot."

The leopard was very still, it was dead, I knew it. Its heart was gone, and so was its magic. There was no need to make another hole in its magnificent hide. "Shoot." I raised the rifle, aimed casually at a spot on the tree and pulled the trigger. Harmless shreds of bark showered the lifeless form.

"Good, now he's dead," Mike said.

Moments later, headlights were darting through the brush. Linda was coming, laughing, crying, Ian shouting. Mike and I stood in the glare of the lights so that they could see we were safe. Linda was laughing and crying, Ian shouting. We would go to the leopard together.

Saleem turned the leopard over and poked a finger into the hole where a heart had been. He tried to act casual, unimpressed, as if killing a leopard was just part of a day's work. Later when he thought we would not see, he knelt beside the leopard and looked at it for a long while. Then he took my rifle and held it close, letting its power—its magic—flow into his body.

On the way to camp, a foraging hippo charged the truck; we got lost and arrived late. Linda held the leopard all the way. And Mike never asked why there was only one hole.

Dreaming the Lion

THOMAS MCINTYRE

Part One

Along the River

> *Such are the hardships to be endured when discovering new lands in the manner we set about it!*
> —Bernal Díaz

History of the Conquest of New Spain

As waterholes went, it wasn't much. Bright-green reeds grew jaggedly around it, and the standing water was a less bright, oily green. Still, we could dip our canteens into it and purify its water with iodine pills or draw out a bucketful of it to wash with; and if you dropped a bottle of beer into it, it would eventually turn the beer coolish and soak off the bottle's label that showed an elephant's head printed on a red oval. Though it was only eight miles from our starting point in Ouanda Djallé, we had made a tardy beginning on this our first day's walking (what caravaners call "the little start"), so we decided to pitch our camp beneath a large banyan tree near this waterhole called Mie Mai.

The ground was black with ashes in late January, the height of the dry burning season. As we all drifted across the bare earth under the midday sun to where we would make camp in the shade, it was impossible to calculate with any degree of certainty, counting professional or "white" hunters (one white, one very much black), trackers, gun bearers, water bearers, a cook, the cook's helpers, porters carrying crates and bundles on their heads with long-accustomed ease, camel drivers leading four camels and four horses, and bewildered hunters on safari, what our exact number might be.

That morning back in Djallé—the phrase "back in *Jolly*" began to acquire the cachet of a punch line among us as we marched on, describing all manner of equipage, from extra shoes to spare eyeglasses to additional ammunition to laxatives, that to save weight we had jettisoned, only to discover a crying need for farther on in the country—back in Jolly, at any rate, it had been entirely too confounding to take anything like an accurate tally. It had been hard enough, among the whitewashed headquarters buildings of the French safari company we were hunting with, just to organize the gear, animals, and hired men into the semblance of a unit a tad more cohesive than, say, a Chinese fire drill. Thirty souls, give or take, would not have been far off the mark.

Here in the northeast of the Central African Republic, the safari had initially called for a dozen camels, half a dozen horses, and two donkeys to transport our burdens. We were to strike off east into an unexplored portion of the safari company's vast concession toward the border with Sudan, going afoot because motor vehicles had never been there and roads were nonexistent. No one knew if there was even any game to be found there, but it would nonetheless be the rarest of opportunities to be the first hunting party into an area where only Africans had been before and to conduct a safari along the antique principle of putting one foot deliberately in front of the other. It seemed, simply and anachronistically, the right thing to be doing even, or maybe especially, at the close of this shocking twentieth century.

What we had not bargained for was a band of highly placed Saudi sportsmen sweeping in ahead of us and making off, to a well-appointed hunting camp on the small Koubo River sixty kilometers to the north, with most of the safari company's stock of camels (for no better reason, I assume, than severe *maladie du pays*, since they did all their traveling exclusively in vehicles). Claims of miscommunication were made, but obviously the fix had been put in somewhere. So because "money talks and all the rest walks," we had to recruit porters, many of them at first refusing the offer of employment when the harebrained nature of our excursion became clear to them, then accepting with the utmost reluctance when it became equally clear that the manager of the safari company meant to take names and to remember them when future job opportunities arose. As we straggled in a quarter-mile file out of the village, past the adobe houses and fields of maize, porters running off to bid goodbye to their families, the first of numerous loads spilling from the humped backs of the green-mouthed, braying, balking, sad camels the Arabs had seen fit to bequeath us, and wound our way around the base of the tall naked rock, the djebel called Kaga Moumo that marked Ouanda Djallé's position in the tropical geography, "plans" were jettisoned as well and we began to learn the invaluable art of living extemporaneously.

The Central African Republic in the language of the travel guides is a lightly populated, landlocked, Texas-sized nation lying just above the equator. It is encased, beginning clockwise from the north, by the countries of Chad, Sudan, Zaire, the Republic of the Congo, and Cameroon. When it was part of French Equatorial Africa it was called Oubangi-Chari. It is bled by those two great river systems: the Oubangui in the south, draining on into the Congo of Stanley and Mr. Kurtz; and the Chari which is nourished by the many smaller rivers of the north before flowing on into Lake Chad.

Transitional in climate between the sub-Saharan and the equatorial, the C.A.R. is for the most part a two-thousand-foot-high rolling plateau, a "Guinea" savannah of tall grass and trees. It is the country, particularly in the northeast area known as Ouandjia-Vakaga, of the giant eland, equinoxial buffalo, the Western roan antelope, and the lion.

The riparian folk of the country's south, the Ubangi, were once noted for their platter-lipped women who would purposely disfigure themselves by slitting their lips and inserting large wooden disks into them as an expedient against being selected for the harems of the Arab slaving sultans who raged unchecked across the territory for generations. In Ouandjia-Vakaga the slavers exterminated many tribes, from the Bingas to the Challas to the Bongos to the Melas, in the conduct of their enterprise. Various sultans based in Ouanda Djallé carried on their grim commerce until by main force the French Military was able to place it in foreclosure—though not until 1912. Independence was declared on December 1, 1958, and with it came immediate native military rule. In the late 1970s the republic briefly attained imperial status when the infamous Colonel Jean-Bédel Bokassa had himself crowned emperor in what eyewitnesses categorized as a profoundly bizarre and fantastic ceremony. The emperor's excesses rapidly escalated to legendary and deranged proportions, including a reported taste for human flesh, and he was relieved of his duties and permitted to scuttle off into comfortable exile in lieu of the firing squad. (Unaccountably, Bokassa chose to return some years later and now resides in prison, serving a sentence of life at hard labor.)

The inhabitants of the C.A.R. who were working around us now, laying out our beds on the ground under the banyan tree and putting the white mosquito nets over them, cutting sticks to tie together into a crafty dining table with benches, rolling out their own sleeping mats, and building cooking fires, were for the most part of the Goula and Youlou tribes, while the camel drivers were Sudanese. Except for the Sudanese, they all shared the Sango trading language, the C.A.R.'s *lingua franca*. As I sat in the shade, one of the trackers, a suspected reprobate and retired poacher, approached the professional hunters and presented his credentials—letters of recommendation from hunters in whose employ he had previously been. He was bare-headed and had removed his shirt, and the stump of his left arm hung limply. He had lost the arm, it seemed, when his black-powder musket exploded on him a decade earlier, when he may or may not have been up to something. The truth, as is so often the case, varied with the teller.

Flopped in exhaustion in the dirt, one of the paying hunters, a largish American gentleman from parts unknown—let's leave it at that—was already complaining bitterly and loudly about the pace we had set and the sorry state the new boots he hadn't had the sense to break in before the safari had left his feet in. The professional hunters, the white one and the black one, tried to ignore him as they nodded cautiously over the tracker's yellowed letters.

Contrary to rumor, the letters said the tracker was perfectly reliable, and for some reason I took to him at once. Impulsively I located a spare camouflaged cap I still had in my duffel and gave it to him. Putting it on at once, he smiled dazzlingly. Taking back his letters with a nod and tucking them under his stump, he shook hands all around. Bidding us "Hello" in English, he retired to his place among the other trackers. He was called "Djouma," and his was the first tracker's name I learned. The annoyed white hunter informed me then that one never gave a gift to the trackers until *after* the safari, for fear of its leading to insubordination.

The black white hunter, François, was of the Banda tribe and had hunted in Ouandjia-Vakaga for several years. Yet even he had never been in this neck of the bush before. A track star while in high school, known as *"la soucoupe volante"* ("the flying saucer"), he had lit out one day, during one of the C.A.R.'s not infrequent periods of political upheaval, for the territories from the capital city of Bangui, where his father was then *chef de police* and he was a college philosophy major, to become a P.H. He spoke English with effort (far better, of course, than I spoke either French or Sango), was a giggler, and showed no fear of any kind in the face of dangerous animals. He was also found to have an insatiable appetite for reggae music.

The white white hunter, the W.W.H., was a short, round, bearded, blustery, British colonial whom, though I never came truly to dislike, I cannot say that I ever came to understand. My first guess was that he was in it only for the money, but there may have been a less cynical explanation for it, and him. I just never knew for sure. He had arranged for the foot safari with the French company, even though he had never before hunted the C.A.R. after living and hunting most of his life in many other parts of Africa. At times he grew downright martial and would speak fondly of his war years in Rhodesia, now Zimbabwe, spent killing "gooks."

The paying hunters included the Gentleman-from-Parts-Unknown and an Old Boy accompanied by his wife. The Old Boy and his wife were in their late fifties but still unmistakably preppy and Ivy League and Old Money. In their Willis & Geiger safari-wear and with their copy of *Rowland Ward's Records of Big Game*, Eighteenth Edition (Africa), tucked under the Old Boy's arm, they cut the perfect figure of the Sporting Rich, though of the most unspoiled variety. The Old Boy's wife, although an indefatigable walker, had lost her interest in hunting, but the Old Boy hadn't and had seen more of it at the best of times than I knew I ever would, from Kodiak bear in the fifties to polar bear off Kotzebue and shikars in the Madhya Pradesh in the sixties to the big game of Tanzania, Namibia, and South Africa. One night he mentioned to us in passing that his grandfather had died of blood poisoning after reaching out to shake his jockey's hand in the winner's circle and receiving a severe nip on the wrist from his own thoroughbred.

Unlike the Old Boy's, the Gentleman-from-Parts-Unknown's grandfather, the Gent told us, had not died from the bite of his racehorse. And he, himself, had made his money in the hardest of ways, and meant for no one ever to forget it. He had been to Zimbabwe to shoot once, for a week or two, but had no sense of Africa or of hunting either, at least as I comprehended them. I didn't know what his reasons for being here were, and I don't think he actually did either, except that to him the word "unexplored" held the promise of being able to kill bigger and less wary wild animals with which to populate his living room.

That left three others: my nonhunting friend—a Beverly Hills attorney—a Missionary-Photographer, and me.

My attorney friend had come with no romantic preconceptions about Africa. His only wish was to see someplace wild, someplace that was not a city, and the C.A.R. sounded as likely a choice as any. Thinking he needed to justify his presence, he concocted an outlandish story about being a cinematographer and went so far as to haul along an elaborate 16mm movie camera and hundreds of feet of film. But after exactly thirty-seconds of trying to film the loading of the camels back in Jolly, he took one hard look at the device and packed it sensibly away in its padded aluminum carrying case, never to remove it again. He owned the only L.A. Dodgers cap in Ouandjia-Vakaga (until he presented it to our young camp helper Idriss), dragged continually on a Marlboro, never complained, and was the all-around class clown. The Africans titled him *Patron Sans-souci* (the "carefree boss").

The Missionary-Photographer came from missionary stock. He was a bilingual hunting parson, had been involved with the W.W.H. in organizing the foot safari, and had been invited by the French safari company to come along to act as the W.W.H.'s interpreter, take photos, and try for a giant eland. The blunt and brazen W.W.H. soon proved an arduous trial to him: after the hunt, both would behave extraordinarily unpleasantly toward each other, and for months afterward I would receive tedious letters from one attacking the character and behavior of the other, and vice versa. So the Missionary-Photographer attached himself at once to François, engaging him in interminable conversations in the French language to the exclusion of the rest of us. He was far from unfriendly, though, during the safari and would never hunt on Sunday.

I, I'm afraid, *would* hunt on Sunday or Christmas or the Fourth of July, and when I had heard that someone was going to walk across African savannahs in a place where there was a chance of seeing giant eland, I made shameless inquiries and wrangled myself an invitation from the French safari company to come along. I outfitted myself with a .375 with a 1.5-6X scope, Dorst & Dandelot's *A Field Guide to the Larger Mammals of Africa* that I'd picked up in Nairobi years before, Serle & Morel's *Les Oiseaux de L'Ouest Africain* that I'd bought in Paris on the way over, Bernal Díaz del Castillo's 400-year-old first-hand account of Hernan Cortés's adventure in Mexico, *History of the Conquest of New Spain,* a Webster's pocket dictionary, notebooks, pens, cameras, film, tins of Copenhagen snuff, binoculars, and a sturdy pair of well-broken-in boots. Nevertheless, by the second day my feet went south, I let the gun bearer bear my gun, I drank enough water for three people each day, ate salt tablets by the fistful, and still sweat so much that I would never need to urinate on the trail and would often break out shivering in the sun from heat exhaustion. Yet after too many years of being out of Africa I was happier to be back than I could possibly explain.

Our first night in Africa, following an afternoon of sighting in the rifles when the Gentleman-from-Parts-Unknown demonstrated an uncanny inability to make his shots find the target, ended with the W.W.H. sitting at the stick table in the blue light of the battery lanterns, drinking whiskey, and defaming (I now think primarily for our benefit) the French, both individually and as a race, for having only four sorry camels to grant us. The rest of us had already crawled into our beds when he at last got up and arranged himself in his with his .460 Magnum at his side. The air was startlingly cold and the full moon immense and round as a dollar. The W.W.H. lay with his head toward the lighted clearing of our camp. Never lie with your head toward the brush, he advised aloud, because that was where, in the "lion hour" between midnight and dawn, the lion came. Let him take you by the feet and you had at least the ghost of a chance of blowing his brains out before he dragged you off. I changed position instantly.

No lions came that night. Leaving the other Africans behind to strike camp and pack the animals, we (with our weekly antimalarial chloroquine phosphate pills for Saturday breakfast) set off with our trackers, gun bearers, and water bearers at dawn. We made twelve-and-a-half miles that day to the Ouandjia River, seeing on the way only the fresh dung of small elephants (the size of the dung corresponding to body size) and a troop of baboons lumbering away from us, displaying red rumps. The Ouandjia is one of the rivers which, flowing north into the Bahr Aouk, goes on to feed the Chari in Chad. When I hobbled down to it, I tugged off my boots and socks and stood in the cool water and decided never to move. It was clear and running, and after seeing the W.W.H. dip up a tin cup and drink it, with the water spilling silvery over his beard and onto his chest, I took the cup from him and, disregarding the dire predictions of Boy Scout manuals the world over, drank the sweetest drink of my life ("For thirst," said Bernal Díaz, "knows no laws"). And nothing befell me, mystifyingly enough.

As we lay on the sandy riverbank, the Africans went downstream to burn the tall grass to clear our campsite, and we could see swallows looping in the smoke of the wide fire, plucking insects rising out of the grass. Our food stocks were already so low that we were reduced to sardines for lunch. That afternoon, though, the Old Boy and François went out to look for game.

While they were gone, the W.W.H., the Gent, the Patron Sans-souci, and I found two square rock pools the size of small swimming pools in the river just above camp and went there to bathe. As we were all undressing beside one of them, the Gent started in on one of his reactionary political commentaries, which I had not yet learned to ignore, and I thought I might enjoy soaking in the other pool alone. As I was about to slip into the neck-deep water a hundred feet from them, the W.W.H. made sure he called out to me, "Mind the crocs!" I remembered with some disquiet a photo I had once seen of the legs of a white man who had gone swimming in an African river he was *convinced* could not contain any crocodiles, a photo of just his legs in a cardboard box. I peered into the pool intently, then climbed in, staying in the water a long, somewhat uneasy time while a hadada ibis harangued me from the branches of a nearby ironwood tree.

As we limped back into camp in the evening, our feet still stinging from the New-Skin we had painted over our blisters, François and the Old Boy returned, packing an excellent Lelwel hartebeest on one of the gaunt horses. At dinner we were fiends for meat, eating long into the dark as the fire, which had jumped the river, continued to flare up. The camels lay placidly below us in the sand in full view of the flames. A few of the Africans crossed the river, and we could see one of them, backlit, climbing into a tree wish a bundle of burning grass, directing the smoke at something. In a while they all crossed back, carrying combs heavy with wild honey.

I went hunting the next day with an assistant guide, while the W.W.H. and the Gent, mounted now on a rickety but remarkably resilient stallion led by a water bearer in a ragged shirt, went one way, and the Old Boy, his wife, and François another. On my walk I saw oribi, hartebeest, western bush duiker, a sounder of warthogs, an unforgettably blue *rollier d'Abyssinie* (as it said in Serle & Morel), ground hornbills resembling grazing antelope in the distance among the trees, and killed my first game in the C.A.R., shooting a dove and a rock hen with a .22 rifle, the Africans wanting them for the pot.

Back in camp the Old Boy came in with a nice duiker, a very small antelope whose Afrikaans name means "diver" for the way it plunges into the underbrush, which we would eat in its entirety for lunch. Then the W.W.H. returned to tell us that he and the Gent had heard poachers' gunfire and even their voices, and seen no game. It would be wise for us to move on tomorrow. That night I heard hyenas crying for the first time in ten years.

As we were about to leave camp the next morning, the Missionary-Photographer asked me how old I was. Thirty-two, I told him. Thirty-two today.

We made almost twenty gameless hallucinatory miles to the south that day, getting aridly lost for several hours until we back trailed and relocated the upper Ouandjia in an utterly exquisite grove of cool green trees. I spent the rest of my birthday sitting fully clothed in the river, that fell across large smooth rocks, drinking red wine from a foil pouch.

"How's the water?" the shirtless Patron Sans-souci inquired, a wet bandanna tied around his head.

" 'The marvelous thing is that it's painless,' " I said, taking one more sip of wine. For dinner we ate some small fish François trapped out of the river.

On the trail the next day we found Arabic runes carved into the bark of a tree. It was the poachers' newsletter and apparently warned of our presence in the country. The poachers, on camelback, had at first come over from Sudan for ivory; then after shooting out the elephants, they turned to poaching just for meat to sell back in Sudan. Because professional hunters, who are the de facto game wardens in most of Africa, never ventured into this area, the poachers considered it their private preserve. I did not know what it would take to dislodge them, but it would be a force superior to ours.

Farther along, the Gent dismounted from his weary horse long enough to gut-shoot a big dog baboon in hopes of expanding his collection. He was well pleased with the full-body-mount one he already had on display at home, dressed in one of his young son's old suits, seated at an old-fashioned school desk in the kitchen. The Missionary acted as Samaritan and finished the baboon off for him.

We left the carcass beside the trail for the porters to pick up. They were supposed to skin it out, but instead burned all the hair off it, then butchered it up and cooked it in the camp we made that day at noon after thirteen miles of walking. We made that camp in a dense thicket of trees at the Ouandjia's source, a deep hole in volcanic rock where the chtonian water sprang up cold and clear and reasonably pure. The Old Boy's bowels, we now learned, had been malfunctioning for some days by, oddly for the place and circumstances, refusing to function. He could see no alternative now but to walk all the way back to Jolly for the laxatives he had seen absolutely no need for and so had left behind. A bicycle trail used by diamond prospectors, that we had circled away from on our exploration, ran thirty miles from here back to the headquarters. Tomorrow morning he, his wife, and François, with the Missionary tagging along, would set out on it.

The Patron Sans-souci and I were faced with the glum prospect of at least *days* alone with the W.W.H. and the Gent and their considered opinions of Africans, the Red menace, and the very end of the world as we knew it, or, rather, as they perceived it to be. Worse was the very real possibility that the Old Boy and his wife, who to the Patron and me had become nothing less than Ward and June to our Wallace and the Beav', were fed up with the whole affair and would not come back at all. In them we had found two people we could talk with out here in Africa, while with the W.W.H., and even more so with the Gent, the most that could be hoped for was ugly arguments. We were not happy.

That afternoon I listened to the Africans making their camp in the open outside our thicket, singing lilting falsetto songs that I wished I understood, and felt this prefatory lonesomeness. That night at dinner, deciding there was no dishonor in eating it even if the Gent had shot it, I requested some of the baboon, and tasting it for the first time I found it delicious. I was put in mind of a story a famous Mexican big-game hunter told of the time he tried baboon on safari. He enjoyed it immensely too, so much so that he asked for seconds. To his dismay, he was brought on a platter a curled, charred child-sized hand—considered the finest cut—and instantly lost his appetite.

"Listen," the grinning Gent, still infuriated over the loss of his trophy but with a belly full of its rich meat, was boasting now to the W.W.H., "I hate them as much as you." François happened to be conveniently away from our newest table of sticks at the time.

"You don't understand," the W.W.H. explained with chilling mildness. "Hate has nothing whatsoever to do with it. The simple fact is, they're twenty thousand years behind us." I stared away from the lantern into the night, turning my back to the table.

The next dawn, when the Patron Sans-souci and I walked with the Old Boy and his wife from our cove of leaves to say farewell, we found the Africans clustered sheepishly around one of the sad camels. Branded with three scars on its flank, lying bent-necked on the ground, it had expired in its sleep. We looked at it, then at one another. Come back, Shane, I wanted to tell the Old Boy and his wife. Don't leave us.

Part Two

Over the Divide

> *Without knowing our way, we found some good meadows—which they call savannahs—on which deer were grazing.*
>
> —Bernal Díaz

The nameless waterhole was all that remained of the river our map had no name for. It stood shaded in a hollow of leafy trees, looking brown and zoetic and smelling like an old bar towel.

One of the trackers sank into it a round terra-cotta pot we had found that morning on the trail at the site of a poacher's deserted camp and drew out some water. After letting the water settle awhile in the pot, he presented it to the white white hunter who after drinking deeply pronounced it "ice cold." Then the Gentleman-from-Parts-Unknown partook, followed by the Patron Sans-souci. When my turn came, I asked the Patron how it had been. If you strained it a little through your teeth, he allowed, it was not completely foul. Though I had long ago abandoned all pretense of drinking only pure water on this safari, the thought of schistosomes performing vigorous wee scissor kicks and synchronized backstrokes in my intestines was too much for me. I tapped the plastic container of warm filtered water (our last) set beside me, and finding it still half full, drank sparingly from it instead.

We were now some ten miles west of the camp at the source of the Ouandjia River. After our dawn parting yesterday with the Old Boy and his wife beside the deceased camel, I had lain down and slept through to dinner, arising only long enough to go off into some tall grass and, setting fire to my toilet paper afterward to help keep Africa beautiful, accidentally burned over not more than an acre or two of tall grass, the fire swift and cool, doing no visible harm to any of the trees. The Gent had occupied his day with an unprofitable horseback hunt around the country, failing to slay a thing (though a duiker he wounded with his .375 did, heaven only knows how, manage to escape). Today, at least, his feet felt sufficiently healed for him to walk and spare the pony further abuse. We would lie here under the trees by this waterhole now until the sun passed its zenith and then, with our trackers, gun bearers, porters, horses, and the remaining camels, move on to the next water that the Africans indicated, by snapping their fingers in the air to count off increments of distance, was another ten miles or more farther on. It would take several hours, they showed us by pointing to where the sun would be in the western sky when we reached our destination.

As I rested on a bed of fallen leaves and roaming ants, I recalled the lurid misfortunes, from arrow wounds to fevers to witnessing his comrades sacrificed by the Aztecs, that Bernal Díaz had described in his history. What we were enduring here, I realized, was in comparison a very rich slice of cake, with frosting. Then, almost before I knew it, it was time to go on again.

The heat of the afternoon was baking and windless. The country, though, was beginning to be not so scorched and blasted looking as it had been before, showing green trees now and shady park lands. And when I became lost in the unbroken rhythm of my walking, there would also be *animals* to wheel me out of my daze: bounding triplets of oribi; herds of hartebeest; dark elk-looking sing-sing waterbuck; and equinoxial, or Nile, buffalo. These are an intermediary between the Southern, or Cape, buffalo and the dwarf buffalo of West Africa's jungles. Though smaller horned than the Cape, the Nile buffalo is of about equal body size. We saw a large herd of them late in the day, and I got to watch the W.W.H. and the Gent put a sneak on the big-muscled animals who were every color from sleek black to bright red. As I watched from a crouching position, dreaming of oxtail soup and sincerely wishing the Gent all the luck in the world, it was as bracing as iced bourbon to see the wild cattle of Africa once more. None of these creatures seemed to measure up to the Gent's trophy requirements, though, while I could only keep thinking over and over, my God they're *meat*. When he and the W.W.H. stood to break off the stalk, a lioness, who from the opposite side of the herd had been hunting the now stampeding buffalo as well, could be seen running away.

The long day went on until at sunset, my sore-footed hobbling come to resemble the pirouetting of a trained bear, we crossed the Galénguélé Ridge, the divide between the Oubangui and the Chari watersheds, and made a camp on the flowing Poto Poto River at the foot of a grassy hillside. This time, with the Old Boy's wife gone, I stripped off not only my boots and socks, but all my clothes and lay down in the shallow stream.

A delegation of the Africans, who had been subsisting for some days solely on cooked manioc, confronted the W.W.H. after setting up camp, and holding their stomachs for dramatic effect, implored him to make the Gent shoot *something* fleshy first thing "Yesterday" (meaning "Tomorrow"—or maybe they actually did mean yesterday), never mind about bloody horns! It appeared that I had not been alone in my carnivorous lusts.

At dinner, while the Gent treated us to a tirade of embarrassing political and racial inanities as we sat in beerless paralysis, we four were served a single, very small can of cooked chicken, the absolute last of our iron rations. We sat before that chicken like Bugs and Elmer isolated in a cabin in the snow, contemplating the single boiled bean that will comprise their last supper. Above us on the hill one or two campfires flickered. A strong wind and a huge light awakened me at midnight from my hunger-filled sleep, and I saw the entire hillside no longer flickering but entirely engulfed, the tall flames whipping down onto us. The Sudanese poachers, to emphasize what was the Central African equivalent of "my beach, my wave," had sent us a grassfire as an invitation for us to move on. As I stood in my slippers and underwear outside my mosquito net, feeling the heat on my face and unsure in which direction to bolt, the Africans lying near us at the foot of the hill arose and, yawning, adroitly ignited backfires. They then went back to sleep, leaving the three surviving camels tied down five yards from me to growl their outrage at this disturbance and the fire to consume itself. *Les chiens aboient, la caravane passe*, in more than a manner of speaking.

The next morning was sheer bathos when after only an hour's walk we discovered a maintained road, then a quarter-mile along it a hunting camp of round thatched-grass huts, called *bougarous* in Sango, with real beds inside. This camp was Pipi, and here I truly hoped the Old Boy and his entourage would rejoin us, driving down on the Ouadda Road from Jolly in a safari-company vehicle. If they did it would once again be time on this safari to adapt.

The small staff at Pipi greeted us and offered us startlingly cold filtered water from a kerosene refrigerator and rank buffalo jerky that shimmered like verdigris. For luncheon they would prepare some tasty fillets of male lion the previous hunter had left behind. ("We were pleased enough in camp with the very little food they brought us, for evils and hardships vanish when there is enough to eat," wrote Bernal Díaz, only too rightly.)

Still the Patron and I waited in glum silence. Then around noon, just as the Gent was launching into a paean to gold and other "hard currencies" which he had gleaned from his reading of some deranged survivalist manifesto, we heard the unbelievable sound of a vehicle engine. The Patron Sans-souci and I fled from the Gent's lecture in mid-screed to greet loudly the Old Boy, now purged and looking fabulously jaunty in a pair of motorcycle goggles, his wife, François, and the Missionary-Photographer as they arrived in a total wreck of a windscreen-less Land Rover piled with trackers and food and fuel and beer and multicolored bottles of flavored syrups for soft drinks. It seemed as if everything might be all right for a time.

Fixed as my mind is on the archaic, when walking across Africa made far more sense than it appears to today, I could not leave the camel-and-foot aspect of our safari so quickly behind. Now that there was a vehicle, a couple of hartebeest got taken in short order. The next day the camp staff cut the meat, as they do throughout Africa with meat not eaten fresh by the hunters and staff, into thin ten-foot strips and hung it out like laundry on a line to dry. In the afternoon I found myself wandering up behind camp, past the lines of meat, to where the three Sudanese camel drivers sat around the ashes of their fire. The youngest was patiently dissolving some yellow lumps in a bucket of water, to medicate the camels with the minerals. The middle-aged one had a callous on his forehead from his five-daily bowed prayers in the direction of Mecca. And the eldest one was splitting a hartebeest shank with his steel dirk to free the raw marrow—for "power" as he would explain through explicit pantomime.

"*Salaamu al laikoum!*" he greeted me, raising both hands into the air in a gesture of peace, still holding the greasy knife. He was tall and desiccated, and the sparse hair around his taut black scalp was white. His eyes were lidless slits that had stared at desert suns much too long. He wore leather sandals, a long white cotton *djellaba*, a white-and-red sheath for his dirk tied to his upper left arm, and a string of leather phylacteries containing bits of paper inscribed with Koranic passages bound around his upper right. I salaamed him in return and made a note to ask with him later, somehow, about caravans, bandits, and the crossing of burning sands, armed primarily with a faith in the Prophet's words. In short, Real Life.

That evening, still on foot after roughly 120 miles of walking in eight days, I shoot my first antelope. It is a western bush duiker the Missionary and trackers and I spot in a woody place five miles from camp. The Missionary whispers that the antelope looks exceptional. Remembering our duiker lunch on the Ouandjia, I creep up to a dead tree 50 yards from where he is feeding on fallen leaves, get a rest, and put a 300-grain solid through him. And watch him run. We take off after him, and the trackers soon find blood, then I find another dull dusty splash of it ahead, and another, until there the thirty-pound animal lies 150 yards from where he was hit, dead. His orange-brown coat is graying and the ridges of his straight black horns have been smoothed with age. The Missionary enthuses that these horns are really big—enormous, in fact—and will rival the top-listed in the Old Boy's *Rowland Ward*, now our camp bible. Later, various professional hunters from the safari company will declare that after literally *years* in the Central African Republic they have never encountered bigger. With all that, though, what we are talking about is an awesome 4⅝ inches of horned fury, and the praise is strikingly like being congratulated on having just bagged the world-record cocker spaniel. My main concern is, how'll he eat?

What I had walked all this way for was a chance to hunt giant eland, *Taurotragus derbianus gigas*, the grander Central African version of the already grand-enough Lord Derby's eland found in far-western Africa. The "largest and handsomest, and one of the least known, of African antelope," according to Theodore Roosevelt who hunted them in 1910, it is in a league with the bongo, the greater kudu, and the mountain nyala as one of the continent's most beautiful large wild animals. Called *bosobo* in Sango, the giant eland would have to be placed not only among Africa's, but the earth's grandest wild animals, alongside the royal elk, the Marco Polo sheep, even the elephant. Its sandy coat is slashed by a dozen white stripes, a curly black ruff of hair surrounds its thick, dewlapped neck. Standing six feet at the shoulder and weighing nearly a ton with its heavy horns spiraling out well beyond three feet, it is acutely wary and virtually incapable of remaining still—so that it will move all night and right through the heat of the day, browsing at a brisk walk on the large green leaves of young *Isoberlinia doka* (a short, faintly purplish-red vuba hardwood tree). I had yet to see a photo of a live giant eland when it was not on its feet, usually in midstride, nor heard of anyone who knew precisely when it was that the animal slept. The giant eland would have to be put not only among Africa's, but the earth's grandest wild animals, alongside the royal elk, the Marco Polo sheep, even the elephant.

Nonetheless, when I strode back into camp at dusk I was fully prepared to brag on the duiker one of the trackers now carried on a stick laid over his shoulder like a bindle. The Old Boy and his wife, François, the W.W.H., the Gent, and their trackers had all succeeded in wedging into the clunking Land Rover that morning and had seen, against all known odds, a truly fine giant-eland bull *lying* in the shade beneath a tree. The Gent was, by a previous cutting of cards, the one with the right of first shot; but as he fumbled with his radically customized .375 (a "bells-and-whistles" gun the Patron, who didn't know a Mauser from a muzzle-loader, had accurately characterized it), the Old Boy had sighted in on the animal with his own rifle. Matters became confused, then heated, and the eland managed to get up and lope off without a shot being fired at it. The Gent had then gone off on foot in a rage with François for many hours, never laying eyes on the eland again. The day ended with them running all the oil out of the Rover, stealing the quarters of a young eland freshly killed and abandoned by a lion, and the Gent firmly convinced that everyone was out to screw him. They were all sitting around the oil-cloth-covered dining table now, powdered with red dust like cookie people sprinkled with cinnamon, drinking gin, and not speaking. No one seemed overly interested in hearing about my Colossus of Duiker just then.

A long safari, removed from any outlet to the rest of the world, can be like a mail-order marriage for the strangers thrust together on it, and for at least the duration of the hunt there is no possibility of divorce. Our marriage had now obviously become a rocky one. I picked up a bottle of flavored syrup and attempted some cleverness to lighten the mood.

"Will you have lime juice or lemon squash?" I inquired of the Patron Sans-souci, who had wisely spent his day alone in camp reading Le Carré. He went on reading in silence.

Later, in the dark, the Gent demanded belligerently of the W.W.H., "Can't you get one of these *chimpanzees* to go back to Jolly and get us some oil?"

"You son of a bitch," the Old Boy snarled at the Gent, throwing down his napkin and leaving the table.

I was here to write about the hunt, and as much as possible to stay out of the way of the paying hunters. I knew my place. But I exceeded my authority now, went even beyond cleverness, as I folded my hands and leaned across the table to get close to the Gent's face. I wanted to ask him the question that had been on my mind from the very moment I met him, though I was almost certain he could not answer it: Why, I wondered out loud, my eyes unblinking, did someone like him ever come to Africa?

Leaning far back away from me, hugging his arms tightly around his chest, and blinking his eyes rapidly, he sneered, "Don't waste any of your sympathy on me." I wasn't aware that I had.

The next morning at the Missionary's urging, "for the sake of the safari," the Old Boy apologized to the Gent. But the Gent, after a quite audible private argument in the middle of camp with the W.W.H., resolved, it seemed, to punish us all by refusing to hunt. So the W.W.H. and I went off with Djouma and some other trackers, a long hot walk through a grassy valley that produced only more sore feet. We sighted only a small roan antelope, who snorted at us before galloping away, and a lone giraffe who ran off the way one imagines a startled television-transmission tower might. (Nobody, of course, has yet explained the existence of the giraffe to my personal satisfaction. Like those aircraft engineers who contend that by all the known laws of aerodynamics the bumble bee cannot fly, I can imagine no known law of Nature which adequately accounts for an animal who has much greater difficulty bowing to drink than it has in stripping from a tree with its blue tongue a leaf fluttering twenty feet above the ground.)

Back in camp that afternoon, we found that the safari company had sent us an extra vehicle, a working four-wheel-drive diesel Toyota, and the Gent, relieved to have some *decent* equipment under him at last, agreed once more to go shoot at animals. And returned at sunset with a buffalo, probably from the same herd he had turned down on the trail when we had all wanted meat so desperately.

The very next noon, mirabile dictu, he and the W.W.H. pulled in with a superb giant eland. How it had happened no one who knew, I think, ever really said, but everyone else was flatly shocked. Suddenly the Gent was downright expansive. He even invited me to go out with him that afternoon in the Toyota so I could look for a buff, or whatever else he had already killed. I knew that to see more game I was going to have to travel farther from the area around camp than I could reasonably walk to and back before dark, so I sighed and thought, What the hell. I made sure I rode in the open back, while the Gent sat inside the cab.

It was passing strange to be bouncing across the country in a vehicle after so long on foot. I let the wind flow over me and kept my eyes moving all around as we traveled. We drove back past the camp where we had very nearly become midnight barbecue and found an old bull buff with nubby horns all by himself. I passed, deciding that we had enough meat for now and that I might find something bigger later. And I did.

As we drove in I was standing up, holding onto the roll bar, when I saw a flash of tawny-golden color a quarter-mile ahead of us through a stand of tall teak trees. I leaned down and whispered sharply through the driver's window for the W.W.H. to stop and back up. I sighted the tawny thing once more. Putting my 7X binoculars on it, I saw in the late afternoon sun the folded, heavy skin of a huge walking animal's rump, something so big my first reaction was, rhino. My immediate second reaction was that there were probably no rhinos in the C.A.R. anymore outside a *parc national.* I knew then what it must be: a giant-eland bull, solitary as Bugs and Elmer's bean.

I jumped down from the Toyota and grabbed my .375.

"What is it?" the W.W.H. whispered.

"Eland."

From the ground I had lost sight of the bull, and I slipped forward to try to find him again, the W.W.H. and Djouma following closely behind. Then I saw him, walking easily, undisturbed. Djouma could not yet see him, so I took him by the shoulders and pointed him at the big mature eland bull.

"Yes," he said excitedly, "yes. Thank you, Tom," pronouncing it *Tome.* Now the W.W.H. saw him too and commanded me to shoot him from this very spot. The eland was well over three hundred yards away.

"Out of the question," I said.

Djouma understood our argument, if not our words, and hissed, "Yes," going off at once in a swift duck-walk, flitting from tree to tree. I went after him, leaving the W.W.H. frozen and speechless where he was. We moved to where the trees ended at a wide bare field of black volcanic rock. The eland was on the other side where another stand of the big trees began, turned sideways to us. The distance had been cut to under two hundred yards, and Djouma gestured for me to shoot. I rested the rifle against a tree and let off the safety, putting the crosshairs into the middle of the eland's shoulder hump, trying not to let his wonderfully long horns distract me. As my finger lay on the trigger, the eland turned and wandered into the tall timber and a thicket of *Isoberlinia doka* within it.

"No," Djouma whispered. I lowered the gun and slipped the safety back on. Djouma caught hold of my sleeve and, bent double, we crossed the open ground like some single, rare specimen of trotting mammal.

Inside the timber, Djouma circled downwind in wide arcs around the dense patch of short green-leafed trees the eland must have been feeding his way through. The African moved in a deft half-run, his plastic-sandaled feet never touching a twig. Jogging heavily behind him, I crunched down on a dry leaf, and Djouma wheeled on me, *tsk*-ing in reproach. We proceeded this way for many minutes, Djouma biting his lip as he searched through the trees for a glimpse of the eland.

Djouma suddenly halted, taking my arm and whispering rapidly to me in the French language. He pointed to the solid wall of trees, then held his thumb and forefinger a small distance apart. Too small? Wait a moment? What *is* it, Djouma?

Impatient, I started to raise my rifle, but he pushed it down. "*No. No. No,*" he insisted.

The bull eland glides out of the cover eighty yards away. He is quartering toward us with his ears up and the light through the trees behind him. He stands looking, unable to define us, and Djouma whispers, "*Yes. Yes. Yes.*"

I bring the .375 up slowly, putting the duplex reticle of the scope on the point of the bull's left shoulder and let the safety off.

Dust lifts off the eland's shoulder where the 300-grain soft-nosed bullet strikes him. The eland bucks and spins, disappearing into the cover. We run full out through the trees after the wounded bull, then Djouma snatches my arm, and there is the enormous animal staggering ahead of us, his shoulder broken and the bullet deep in his chest.

I am going to shoot him again, but I see that he is about to fall. He drops his heavy-horned head as if its weight has suddenly become too much for him and begins to sway, then lies down. He has his legs folded under him, and now he lifts his head and looks straight ahead, silent. I walk up to twenty yards from him, trying to control my panting from the run. Working the rifle's bolt, I angle in another round in back of his ribs and into his chest. He rolls over dead.

He is sandy golden and half-again as big as a horse. The clean white vertical stripes, black neck ruff, and heavy hump are just as I have always heard them described. He has a powerful warm sweet smell that I will be unable to put out of my mind as long as I live, and his black spiraled horns are nearly forty inches long on a straight line from the bases to the tips, and over forty-eight inches around the spiral. One-armed Djouma throws off his cap *and* his shirt and bounces into the air ecstatically, proclaiming himself a "grand tracker" again and again. He daubs his finger in the eland's shoulder wound and bloods himself. Then he comes over to where I sit on an old termite hill, staring stunned at this perfect creature, my unloaded rifle laid across my knees. As he reaches, grinning wildly, to mark my forehead too, a distant lion begins to roar.

It had been a better, more "successful" stalk than any I had ever known. The sole bad part was that in the middle of the lion hour two nights earlier, the night of the lost eland, amid the brays and protestations of the camels, the old Sudanese had arisen and with the two younger ones packed the animals in the darkness and gone back to Jolly. Now I could not show the old man this fine, astonishing eland or salaam him or discuss the finer points of caravan life and the art of putting one foot in front of another.

Part Three

After the Game

> *As for the horrible noise when the lions . . . roared . . . it was so appalling that one seemed to be in hell.*
> —Bernal Díaz

I floated in the waterhole whose water was chill and sparkling. Tini Falls fell in a two-hundred-foot veil into it, and I did my level best not to consider the five-foot crocodile that had slid into its den at the water's edge when we had arrived. It was a sanctuary of sorts here, and nothing, no matter how possibly red in tooth and claw, was about to make me let go of it until I was perfectly ready to.

Djounia, to whom I had given all my Copenhagen after the eland hunt, lay sleeping sweetly on a large flat rock above the pool, while the Old Boy's wife paddled in the water in her Willis & Geiger clothes. The Patron Sans-souci and François had come swimming too. The W.W.H., though, refused to enter the water on grounds of the croc, and the Old Boy just wanted to sit, smoking his pipe, The Gentleman-from-parts-unknown stood apart from us again, diligently fishing for perch with bloody hunks of wormy reedbuck liver, unwilling to waste one minute of his vacation on leisure.

Our safari was now nearly done. Begun on foot, it was ending in Toyotas. Four weeks, through the cycle of the moon, and it was almost time to leave.

We were now based in the Chari watershed one hundred kilometers north of Pipi in the large Koubo camp previously occupied by the infamous Saudis. It was mid-February and this was country of wild palms and grassy plains—by the map the flats of the Koumbal, Yata, Mbongo, and even the Ouandjia (that had wound its way through our journey) rivers, all gathering strength for Chad. In places there were pockets of volcanic-red and green-forested hills where the Old Boy had hunted for giant eland, as hard as I had ever seen a human hunt. And across it all were good numbers and varying types of wildlife.

Two weeks earlier at Pipi, when I had come in at dark with my giant eland, I found that the Missionary-Photographer had stumbled across and killed an excellent full-ginger-maned lion that he really didn't want, giving us two record-book eland and a lion on the same day. That is the way Africa can work, sometimes: windfall on the heels of famine. And now meat no longer presented a problem for us, eland proving to be the best I had ever tasted.

So a day later we decided all to hunt one more morning then break camp and drive back to Jolly. The Patron and the Old Boy's wife, who were not here to hunt anyway, announced that they would set out ahead of us and walk the twenty-five miles back to Jolly on the one-lane dirt road the rest of us would be driving up late in the day.

At dawn of that day, the Old Boy handed his wife the over-and-under 12-gauge he had brought, loaded with double-aught buckshot, and kissed her goodbye as she, the Patron, and young Idriss set off on foot. We hunted till noon, then returned to Pipi and gathered our gear and headed for Jolly. As we drove in during the late afternoon and evening, we kept expecting to see the marchers at any time, waiting exhausted for us along the road. But when we reached Jolly, they were already there—beaming, sunburned, and freshly bathed, the Patron in a tweed sportscoat and wrinkled shorts sitting at the open thatched-roof bar, drinking an ice-cold beer from a bottle with an elephant head on a red oval label. Later the Patron would tell me that as soon as they were out of sight of Pipi, the Old Boy's wife had broken open the 12-gauge and removed the shells. Whenever they reached the infrequent villages along the old colonial road, the villagers would all come out to welcome them and bring them tea to drink and straw mats to lie on while they rested in the shade.

From Ouanda Djallé, trading the rattletrap Land Rover in on another Toyota, we headed farther north to Koubo, held to be among the finest areas in the French safari company's concession. At Koubo the Patron and I selected a bougarou at the farthest reach of camp on the margin of the narrow Koubo River, and the very first night there I was awakened by hyenas trotting around outside the flimsy grass walls.

I found a penlight and flashed it into the night, catching a pair of yellow hyena eyes. These most peculiar, distant relations of the cat—not dog, as one might suspect—are noted, according to Dorst & Dandelot, for occasionally attacking human sleepers and "causing serious mutilation by *biting off the face* [italics definitely mine]." Their jaws are some of the strongest in Africa and are ideal for crushing bone—their droppings are ashy white piles, pure skeletal residue. They are very far from the cowardly slinkers of legend. Yet they are fastidiously clean creatures, essential scavengers, and to love Africa in all its stark relief is to love, or at least appreciate, the hyena. Killing one could not for me be hunting, merely shooting. (The Gent, to be sure, later shot one—badly.)

All the same, as this one *ooooooUP*-ed merrily in the darkness and ran away from my feeble light in his sloping uphill lope, I resolved then and there never to be without my rifle in my hut at night.

The next day I hunted a handsome Buffon's kob, a reddish-orange antelope the size of a black-tailed deer and related to the waterbuck, lechwe, and reedbuck. The buck was running in a herd of twenty or thirty other kob out on one of the big grassy flats, trying to cover a doe. Then he stopped, winded by the pursuit, and I crept up to about 150 yards from him and rested the fore-end of my .375 in the crook of the German shooting stick the Old Boy had given me. The kob looked farther than he was, and I made the amateur's mistake of holding high and shot over his back with the first bullet. He sprinted off in a wide circle and stopped again.

There were three tall trees growing together on the flat and I kept them between us until I got just a little over one hundred yards from the kob. His ringed horns had a deep S-curve to them, and in the late-afternoon light the look of his muscles under his hide had a sculpted, austere, somehow ancient quality. There was a timeless feel in this whole affair of stalking an animal across the clean, well-lighted heart of Africa. It seemed so familiar—not so much a matter of my having been here before, but that in our own fashions the kob and I were in this together, and always had been. My bullet took him behind his shoulder and off he went once more, dying in midstride.

For the most part, the Gent and the Old Boy were doing the bulk of the hunting, it being their safari after all. The Gent got to shoot things on a fairly regular basis and this, presumably, was what pleased him most. Djouma, spotting vultures circling one day, even led him into the tall grass after a beautifully maned, large lion, who proceeded to sit up ten yards in front of them, then flee before the Gent could manage to fire.

There were lions most everywhere (we counted thirty-two—young and old, male and female, one for every year of my life—before the safari was done), and on another day I watched the Gent, Djouma, and the W.W.H. cross a small creek and stalk a pair of them feeding on a buffalo the lions had battered to the ground. I was thirty yards away and could see that the lions had just started to feed, having gotten to the favored first parts by chewing out a large hole around the buffalo's anus and then pulling his intestines out through a tear in his lower abdomen (often a buffalo is not yet dead while all this is taking place). Now one of the powerfully built lions was worrying the big red buff's head the way a dog worries a rag. I could also see the three men advancing slowly on them, the Gent raising his rifle two or three times, always when he was beside a tree, but never thinking to use it as a rest to steady his aim. During all this I had a round in the chamber, my scope turned down to 1.5X, and my thumb on the safety, fully expecting that any second now I would be dealing with a wounded lion coming at me in a full-roaring charge. Luckily there were no manes on these lions and the Gent held his fire, letting the big cats crash off into the brush once they sighted the creeping humans.

On our way back to the Toyota I made what I thought to be a rather modest and reasonable proposal, that in the future the Gent might consider taking advantage of a rest when one was available.

"Let me tell you, *scribe*," he began, as he now always began, going on to explain how he did not much care for my offering him advice. The W.W.H. sniffed, "He'll probably be writing about some bloody theory of *rests* when he gets back."

So when we spotted the decent Nigerian bohor reedbuck, with his forward-hooking Panic horns, a quarter-mile farther on, and I slipped down with Djouma from the Toyota and we snuck behind cover to where there was 150 yards of open grass flat between us and the animal standing quartered away, and knowing that the two back at the vehicle were studying me closely with their binoculars, I very pointedly rested the fore-end of my rifle in the fork of the shooting stick. I broke the reedbuck's neck—even though I was aiming for his left shoulder—and Djouma, who had been subjected for weeks now to the Gent's haphazard shooting, erupted in delight, pounding my back, giving me a thumbs-up salute and pumping my hand as we walked to the buck. I heard the Toyota grinding up behind us (and the W.W.H. saying drily, "Nice shot; not quite as big a reedbuck as I had thought, though"), and knew I had shot for every wrong reason imaginable, for the worst of all reasons for killing any animal: to prove something. And hoped I would never do it for that reason again.

All this while, the Old Boy was dogging eland. He was pursuing herds of them around the rocky hills, sometimes for ten or fifteen miles a day on foot, never able to overtake them. When he would return in the afternoon, he'd be so tired he would let me go hunting for roan antelope and buffalo with François while he rested in camp.

One long, exciting stalk François and I had after a very good bull buffalo was botched by one of his trackers, Alamine. We had dubbed him "The Torch" for the wooden match he carried at all times between his white teeth, ready to ignite every last blade of dry grass he encountered to clear the soil for new growth. Part way through our buffalo stalk, we told Alamine to wait behind, since fewer people had a better chance of closing with the buffs. But as we crept up on the small group of bulls, here came Alamine looking for us, strolling right into them, scattering them like a busted covey of three-quarter-ton quail. *C'est la vie* was about the best light I could put on the incident, remembering the sight of a meter or so of sweeping buffalo horn.

The winter trade wind, the *harmattan*, had begun to blow down out of the Sahara, yellowing the sky with the fine dust it bore and tatting up the sunsets like carnival gold fish. Some call this dry breeze "the doctor" for the way it remedies the summer's dampness, but *harmattan* has roots similar to *harem* in Arabic and describes something forbidden, the wind known to bear with it such diseases as meningitis. On one of these hazy harmattan afternoons, François spotted a long file of grazing buffalo, and we went after them on foot to see if the herd held any good bulls.

We arced around them for a mile or two, trying to position ourselves where we could best see the buffalo without spooking them. With François' chief tracker Tchekel in the lead, and François, me, my gun bearer Alamine, and the water bearer Amath behind, we climbed up onto a bare spine of rocks. We were beneath a large dead snag, craning for a view of the buffs, when Alamine pushed past me, spit out his match, and began hissing Sango words at François. Which sent them all flying of for dear life, leaving me standing by myself, gaping, watching Alamine running away with my .375. For one second, as I snapped my head around, I could not discover what it was that was surely about to kill me—buffalo stampede? lion attack? tribal uprising? Then the furious swarm of African bees pouring out of the hollow honey tree engulfed my face.

I overtook and passed François and the team at about the 100-yard marker. At 200 yards a small band of hartebeests looked up with a start as one white man and four black ones were bearing down, howling and flailing their arms around their heads: a sight they hadn't seen for at least several millennia, sending them racing off in half a dozen different trajectories. At 300 yards the bees gave up the chase and I could halt, miraculously unstung, while the others tallied their wounds.

I assumed that would pretty much be that for the buff hunting today. *Au contraire*, said François, rubbing a sting on his neck, they have paid no heed to our capering. So we sneaked back toward them—this time I bore my own rifle—and finally closed to within ten yards of the whole grunting, feeding herd. Hunkered down, we watched them for several minutes at this exceptionally unsettling range, seeing tickbirds pecking on them and the huge red and black animals tossing their heads and flicking their ears at the annoyance. They paid us no mind, but the herd held only one young bull. "Too small," François dismissed him with a flick of his wrist. In the end François merely stood and shooed all fifty of the wild oxen away, their running hooves making the earth vibrate like a drumhead.

As we made our way back to the Toyota in the dusk, François, the trackers, and I all began to giggle at the same time as we remembered the bees. I could not resist teasing François, noting that for a fellow with so little apparent fear of big, potentially obstreperous mammals, he certainly did let a few *insects* get the better of him.

"Well, Tome," a teary-eyed François explained, "you can shoot ze buffalo; you cannot shoot ze bee!"

The Missionary, who through his command of the French language had monopolized François in conversation every night at dinner, each day on the trail, and in the Toyota—until the Old Boy's wife coolly but firmly asked him please to speak with François in English when we were all together so the whole class could share in the conversation—had to leave a week early to return to his ecclesiastic duties at his office in Europe. And after his departure, François' English underwent a marked improvement. One night at dinner, while we were discussing wildlife conservation in his country, he mentioned a European "game expert" who was continually criticizing the Central Africans' own honest efforts in this area. The expert was noted for his very vocal opinions that Africans were in general many years "behind" certain other, unnamed races.

Smiling in a private way as he carefully turned down Bob Marley on the Patron's cassette player, François asked, in a precise, rhetorical voice that everyone could hear clearly, "Why does he come to Africa if he believes this?" The W.W.H. and the Gentleman-from-Parts-Unknown spooned oxtail soup to their lips in silence, not lifting their eyes from their bowls, while François went on smiling.

The next morning I was out with the Old Boy when one of François's trackers spotted a trotting herd of giant eland in the trees ahead. The Old Boy had been chasing eland for weeks now, and when he took off with the Africans, his wife and I waited behind, hoping that this would be one herd he overtook. We waited half an hour before we heard the distant shot. Then a minute or two later there was a second. It was an hour before the Old Boy returned. I had walked off a few hundred yards into the cool trees, unable to bear the tension of sitting. Then I looked back and saw the Old Boy standing there with his wife. There was no reaction from either for a moment as he spoke beyond my hearing. Then the Old Boy's wife put her arms around him, rising on her toes as he bent forward, and they kissed and I knew he had his eland, the trackers now back in the trees skinning and quartering it. I jogged up to him and employed my last line from American Lit. on the safari.

"You god damned bull fighter," I said, shaking his hand.

Now all the hunters wanted roan. These horsy antelope (*Hippotragus equinus*) are the largest in Africa next to the eland, weighing over six hundred pounds on the hoof. Their bodies are gray and with their long (more mulish than horsy, actually) tufted ears and their faces painted in black and white, they resemble circus clowns nearly as much as they do their jet-black relative the sable. Their scimitar-curved horns give them a sturdy handsomeness, though, and they are among the most challenging antelope to hunt. They inhabit the same country as the eland, and if you start trailing them they can lead you on for hours. If wounded they have also been known, like the buffalo, to charge or to lie in ambush for the hunter.

There was an excellent bull in a large herd of roan very near camp, so near, in fact, that the roan had grown used to vehicles and hunters driving past them and would move off in the easiest of fashions when approached. At Koubo there was an unwritten rule (the most important kind for a hunter to adhere to) that these antelope were to be left alone. Even the Saudis, who had received a special dispensation to shoot an eland cow and who had all craved roan as much as we (and who all did not kill one) had not tried to shoot this bull. Then one afternoon the Old Boy went out with the W.W.H. and the Gent in their Toyota, and minutes later the sound of a shot came from just around the bend in the dirt road. Several minutes later the Old Boy came marching back down the road alone, his rifle laid across his shoulder and his face flushed with anger.

"What?" I asked, knowing.

"They shot the camp roan," he said matter-of-factly, placing his rifle with exaggerated care in the rack in the thatched-roof dining area and looking around for the Scotch bottle.

(Strangely, in spite of everything else, it was at this moment that the Gentleman-from-Parts-Unknown and I ceased to be on speaking terms. I for my part was no doubt just being childish.)

The Old Boy finally found his roan far out on the bright river flats a few days later. He had missed a very good herd bull earlier in the day in the timbered hills, missed twice with his .375 at close range, and was disgusted with his shooting. As we came down out of the hills, he wanted to head directly in to lunch and forget about roan altogether.

François and I were standing together in the back of the Toyota when we saw a large brown marsh mongoose rippling across the ground by the edge of a waterhole.

"*Rikki-tikki-tavi*, eh?" I said, acting insufferable.

"Ah yes," François replied, savoring the thought. "Keepling."

Then François sighted a good bull standing alone in the shade of a tree out in the open. The Old Boy slid out, with his 7mm this time, and slipped low across the open to a tree to get a rest. He killed the roan at well over 200 yards with a single 160-grain bullet, distant baboons barking in the heat of the day as the antelope collapsed.

"Shook one in," the Old Boy said as he stood beside the roan.

Several toasts were proposed for the Old Boy that night, and I recall the Patron Sans-souci making mention as he toddled off to our bougarou about how red wine always made him *so* sleepy.

Those who have heard one will assure you that a tornado roaring toward you sounds like an approaching express train, and that is the way the lion sounded when his roar crashed through my sleep at one-thirty the next morning. Actually, trains and tornadoes probably sound much more like a lion roaring than the other way around. I sat up and found my .375 beside me, leaning against the aluminum carrying-case housing the Patron's redundant movie camera. The lion was across the shallow stream of the Koubo, maybe fifty yards off, just seconds away if he were to charge all out. His chest-deep roar would come full, then trail off in a series of grunting coughs, but as long as he roared I knew where he was. Often there would be intermissions of ten or fifteen minutes when he was silent except for the sound of his walking in the now-moonless dark of the lion hour.

Everyone else in camp, with the infuriating exception of the Patron, had been awakened, too, and in the bougarous spread out around the clearing I could hear rifle bolts being run home. The camp staff, sleeping around the campfire, piled more wood on it to send the flames high into the sky and illuminate the area around them. No one spoke.

Sitting in the blackness of a wispy grass hut, meditating on the possibly parallel fates of myself and Three Little Pigs, I was something more than apprehensive.

"*For Christ's sake, wake up,*" I whispered loudly to the Patron. I figured he would rather I woke him than have the lion do it by leaping onto his bed. Also, I'd be damned if I was going to sit here being scared witless all by myself. But the Patron, true to his name, just went on snoring, as free of worry as a newborn.

For an hour and a half the lion roared, walking up and down beside the stream, meaning no harm, I suppose, merely being a lion. Then he unceremoniously wandered off, and I put down my rifle and fell asleep again. I woke past dawn, just as the Patron Sans-souci was opening his little eyes, rubbing his knuckles in them. He announced with a wide yawn that his uninterrupted night's sleep had left him thoroughly refreshed. Right as rain. He was somewhat confounded, however, when I, bags big as dopp kits under my eyes and my hair standing out in spikes, began shrieking at him wholeheartedly.

The Old Boy and his wife and I drove off with François that late morning, planning to meet up with the others at Tini Falls at noon for a picnic and our swim in the waterhole. The falls was a famous, if remote, sight in Ouandjia-Vakaga, and we all wanted to visit it. Hunting our way there, we spotted an excellent roan bull by himself in the timber, and François and his trackers and I set off after him.

We chased him through the green *Isoberlinia doka* trees for two hours on foot, getting up on him once and having him stare us down, then snort, like a steam locomotive getting under way, and gallop off before I could get a shot. The trackers and François were able to follow the trail in the volcanic dirt, over rocky lava ground, across every terrain until we saw him again and once more he snorted, running away through a stand of timber with his neck-mane erect, like the knight's on a chess board. I followed him in my scope but would not risk a shot through the trees. We went on tracking him, the Africans always locating his track until he entered a large grove of trees whose fallen leaves blanketed the ground deeply for an acre all around so he could no longer be trailed. He was gone now, and we went out and found the road again.

Alamine, perhaps just nostalgic for flame, immediately built a small fire and sat in its smoke. The rest of us simply sat covered in tiny flies called "sweat bees" while Amath ran back to bring up the Toyota. As I waited for the vehicle, I believed I could be content if this long safari were to end on this spot, after that last fine chase.

It went on, though, up the road to where we crossed the Oumyawa River, the route posted with an old eland skull-and-horns hung in the fork of a tree, to the Tini River branch and its falls and waterhole where I floated. For our picnic we had cold roan meat, bread, and beer. Then I floated some more until I was ready to leave, seeing at last that you have to let go of it all sometime.

The final days slipped by impossibly fast. The others were ready for home; I was mostly ready to be away from the Gent's unique brand of "sport." Back at Koubo after the picnic, the Old Boy, his wife, François, his trackers, and I decided to go out on foot, to make a long circle around the country and once again put one foot, astonishingly, in front of the other. I took a spiral-horned harnessed bushbuck on the walk, giving the camp workers more meat for them to dry and take home. A day or two later the Gent, of course, killed the *de rigueur*, almost maneless, young male lion while standing in the back of a Toyota. Then on the next to last day, I got to chase with the Old Boy and François after a buffalo the Old Boy had wounded, and to put in the last round when the old bull, who had been waiting for us in the shade of a bush, refused to go down from an assortment of .375s and .458s from the other two's rifles, and was gathering himself for a charge. ("Uh," I asked, "may *I* shoot?" absurdly standing on etiquette as they struggled with the bolts on their rifles and the standing fierce buffalo rocked from side to side thirty yards from us; *Please do*, they replied, *please do*. I did and the buffalo lurched forward with a bellow, lying still and black on the ground.)

The very last day, after circling the country with François all afternoon without seeing any game, we were on our way in when at one minute to six in the African evening we spotted a very decent roan bull in a herd. I stalked toward him in the twilight, then raised my rifle and squeezed the trigger, harder and harder—the way you do when you're hunting the animals who migrate through your dreams—until I realized I hadn't taken off the safety. The roan bull started to drift off with the herd, and I followed in a slink until I came to a big tree with the roan standing out at seventy yards in the dimming light. This time I remembered the safety but crept up on my scope. When I shot the rear of the eyepiece ringed my forehead and the herd ran. I saw through the blood running into my eyes the bull walking very slowly, then lying down. And at the very last minute, as I stood marked with my own blood, the hunting was done.

The next morning, the lion roaring off a ways from camp, we began to make our way back to jolly. Along the way I watched all the running herds of ancient game and could feel the sun on their hides and the air in their lungs as if their hides and lungs were my own, just as I could feel within me the motion of their strides. It felt like a promise, and I hoped not a false one. I was going on, but the running animals would remain, with luck and care, for a long time. There were even to be seen round shallow tracks and broken trees along the road, fresh signs of elephants. Then we saw the naked stone of Kaga Moumo rising above the village of Ouanda Djallé.

I had followed the moon and rivers in a cycle through Africa, and now I was back among adobe and daub-and-wattle houses, with cities and the world just beyond the horizon. And the only thing I really wanted to do, I knew, was turn right around and take the long way back again.

Bernal Díaz, writing (as a cranky yet obviously still noble old man in pinched circumstances, having ended up an insignificant magistrate and the owner of worthless estates, in Guatemala) of his days half a century earlier, tells us that he and a number of his comrades after gaining the wild lands of Mexico, mostly because they had seen no better prospects in their lives, callowly abandoned them for someplace they thought would be much better. But, he says, "we were thoroughly deceived." It might very well be that these wild lands of Africa, which I felt shamelessly were somehow more than ever "mine" alone, were for all the hard and hungry and thirsty parts—and the apparently failed attempt to relive the past of foot safaris; the certainly failed brotherhood of all hunters—as good as it got for me. Yet now I was leaving it all.

Then as we drove into the dusty yard among the whitewashed buildings of the safari company's headquarters, I saw the Sudanese camel drivers sitting around the cold ashes of their last night's fire, and everything seemed all right. I remembered something that I had known for ten years, since I last laid eyes on Africa, that it was a land that was always with you no matter how far from it you thought you had gotten. You never let it all go, not even in your wildest dreams.

"*Salaamu al laikoum!*" the old Sudanese shouted to me above the accumulated clatterings of the motor vehicles, raising his bony arms toward me.

I raised my arms back to him.

"*Wa al laikoum salaam!*"

Reprinted with permission of the author and Countrysport Press.

Second-Best Buffalo

CRAIG BODDINGTON

One of the wonderful things about hunting Cape buffalo is it is all about the experience. Any buffalo taken in fair chase, on foot, offers the stuff memories are made of, and any mature bull taken under such circumstances is a great trophy by any definition. That said, most hunters would prefer a *big* buffalo. That's easier said than done. Any area that has a lot of buffalo will have a few exceptional bulls, but finding them isn't ever a certainty. It's a matter of time, patience, and the hunter's greatest imponderable, plain old luck.

Over the course of thirty years of African hunting I have been very lucky with big buffalo. Let's put it another way: Lady Luck has been a major factor with almost all of my really good bulls! On the other hand, she has been most fickle. There have been a number of hunts where I have tried extremely hard to find the kind of bull buffalo hunters dream of: wide spread; deep hooks; and the wide, heavy, and completely hard boss of a mature bull. I have never taken such a bull in such an attempt. The great bulls I've taken—enough that I do consider myself charmed on buffalo—have almost always come on days when I'd have been perfectly happy with *any* mature bull.

The biggest one came on fine October day in Tanzania's Masailand, in the famous old Mto wa Mbu block that straddles the Great Rift Valley north of Lake Manyara. That particular hunt didn't exactly fall into either of the above categories, and I'm not even sure luck was on my side. You can be the judge of that.

It started on the first day of a three-week safari with Geoff Broom. Our primary goal was to strike far to the west on the Upper Ugalla and prospect some new country that should hold sitatunga, roan, sable, and some cats. But we started with a few days in Masailand, and on that first afternoon, still jet-lagged, we drove across dusty plains and started up into the cooler hills above the valley floor. We hadn't gone far before we spied a nice herd of buffalo feeding along two ridges to our south. As I recall we weren't specifically hunting buffalo at all, just enjoying a quick first-day outing. But I had buffalo on license, three to be precise, and Geoff Broom loves to hunt buffalo as much as I do. Even if you don't love them, when you see a herd you will stop and look—and if you have a buffalo on license, you will probably stop whatever you're doing and approach for a closer look.

We scrambled up and over the first ridge, and the herd was spread out on the next ridge, feeding slowly upward. It was a nice herd, perhaps sixty buffalo. They were too far for a shot, but just right for a really good look. There were several younger bulls, but on the left side of the herd there was one bull that stood out. He was a herd bull, with his horn tips still sharp, but he was hard-bossed and fully mature. His horns were coal black and extremely wide, almost certainly forty-four inches, with a nice curve. Most distinctive were those sharp tips, not curving in or back but jutting straight up like long spikes.

We were pinned down, unable to move until the buffalo crossed that next ridge. They took their time, and it was almost sundown before we could move. We dashed down the ridge and up the next and we caught the van of the herd at close range. Had that bull been there we would have shot him with no hesitation, but he was not. We maneuvered a bit, but the quartering wind was dicey and the light was starting to go. We backed off without spooking them, certain we could find them again in the morning.

The sun was just hitting the hills when we pulled up to an old Masai well on the valley floor and began glassing the ridges above us. Geoff found buffalo almost immediately, feeding along far above us. They weren't all that far from where we'd left them, and the number looked correct; it almost had to be the same herd. The wind was coming down the hills, so we climbed straight up from the well, hoping to come onto them from the valley side.

The ridge was taller, steeper, and rockier than it had looked like from the well, so the buffalo were long gone by the time we got to the top. No problem. The spoor was fresh and we took it, keeping to the left side for the best advantage with the wind. As we dropped down into a little *korongo* a very good lesser kudu bull jumped, ran a few yards, and stood and stared at us, iron gray with bright white side stripes and wonderful spiraling horns. A primary reason for being in this area was because my hunting partner desperately wanted a lesser kudu—but he was off hunting elsewhere. I didn't want a lesser kudu, and he never saw one. We continued on after the buffalo.

We caught them quickly enough, but they must have fed on the open ridges through the night, because although it was still early they were already in heavy thornbush on the benches beyond. So began the game of cat and mouse that is one of the best parts of hunting buffalo. They were moving slowly, already seeking a place to bed, and we worked along with them, circling and cutting as we tried to locate that big bull with the high, sharp tips. We got very close, smelling their cattle smell and hearing them break branches, but it was very thick and we were seeing only bits and pieces of a few animals at a time, blacker animals in black shadows.

With a half-century of experience in Rhodesia's even thicker thornbush, Geoff Broom is a master at this game. We stayed with them for a couple of hours, and although a couple of cows spotted us now and again we had the wind and they never spooked. On the other hand, we couldn't find that bull. The day heated quickly, and in the late morning they found what they were looking for and lay down in a really nasty patch of thick, green bush.

We crawled this way and that, glassing clumps of buffalo through thorny screens from thirty or forty yards, but we just couldn't find that bull. A couple more hours passed and we had done what we could. We weren't sure we had seen them all, but we couldn't press any farther without spooking them. So we backed off to our own patch of shade and lay down, clumps of buffalo still plainly visible.

Now it was early afternoon, and we had a problem. Expecting to stroll up the ridge and shoot a buffalo, we had committed the cardinal sin of leaving the truck without water. We rested in the shade for a bit, quietly weighing our options. The buffalo would get up and start feeding and might give us a better look . . . but that might not happen for another three hours. It was very hot now, and by late afternoon we'd be in trouble. It would have been worth the misery if we knew that big bull was there, but Geoff and I were of the same mind: though in bits and pieces, we'd seen the herd pretty well. It seemed all too likely that he had split off during the night, and we were wasting our time.

The Rhodesian, now Zimbabwean, hunters grow up tracking buffalo in dense cover, where the biggest problem is always seeing the bulls in a herd. They have a last-ditch tactic for this. We rested for a while, decided it was time, and then we crept a bit closer, stood up, and charged the herd. Buffalo erupted from their beds, milled for a few seconds, then stampeded off in panic. We ran with them, not quite keeping pace, and in a little clearing on the far side they did exactly what we had hoped they would do. Uncertain of the danger, and having not caught our scent, they turned and faced us, a solid wall of shifting black bodies.

We pulled up short and got our best look. The bull we wanted wasn't visible. The standoff lasted for a few seconds, and then the herd turned and thundered off, down a little cut, up the far side, and lost in the thorn. Geoff scratched his head. "Craig, I don't think he's there, but they were so packed we couldn't see the last of the herd. They shouldn't go far, so let's give them one last go."

The tracks led us over that low ridge and another, and then to the edge of a deep, steep-sided brushy ravine that cut all the way down to the valley floor. We stopped, glassing the ascending ridges beyond, hoping to see black bodies moving. Nothing. Then, almost simultaneously, we glanced down the *korongo* to our left, and we saw something black. It wasn't the herd, but it was three buffalo feeding on the far side, almost at the bottom of the cut. Even at five hundred yards two of them looked very big.

This was the simplest stalk I have ever made on a buffalo—or most anything else. All we had to do was stroll down our side of the ravine, then follow a little finger straight to the buffalo. In ten minutes we were sitting on a little open patch of gravel overlooking the bottom of the ravine. Little more than a hundred yards below us, on the far side, three black forms were partially visible in a little patch of green bush.

This would be a very long shot on a buffalo, but if we dropped down any farther we would be in the brush on our side, noisy, and we would almost certainly spook them. I was carrying a scoped .416 Rigby and I knew it was accurate. I got into a good sitting position and wrapped the sling around my arm, and we waited.

In a few minutes the first buffalo took a few steps downhill and came into the clear. He was the widest buffalo I have ever seen, horn tips far beyond his ears. His boss was massive, and he had plenty of curve. In fact, he had it all. He was facing directly to me with his head down, and since he was on the opposite slope I had his entire neck and the thick muscle at the top of his shoulder. The crosshairs were steady just where the neck joins shoulder, and I knew I put the bullet down through his spine and into his chest. Geoff and I have often talked about this moment in the years since. I have no idea why I didn't complete the squeeze, and he has no idea why he didn't tell me to. Neither of us had ever seen a buffalo like this, nor have we since, nor are we likely to.

Perhaps I was greedy, wanting it perfect. Surely he would turn broadside and give me just a bit of shoulder. So I waited, and he took a couple more steps straight to me. We hadn't realized that the roll of our slope hid the bottom of the ravine. He took a couple more steps, still straight to me, and then he dropped into that dead ground and was gone.

Long moments passed while we hoped he would reappear, but I think we both knew what we had just done. Then another bull stepped out into exactly the same place. This one had deeper curls, a prettier shape, and bosses almost as heavy. He was the second-widest buffalo I had ever seen.

"Craig, that's also a lovely buffalo. I don't know where the other one has gone, but I think you should shoot this one."

As he said it the bull turned just a bit, and I shot him high in the shoulder, angling down. He ran up the far side, and I jumped up and ran along our edge to get a better view, hitting him twice more before he gained heavy cover. We waited a bit, then crossed the bottom and picked up the spoor. I traded the .416 for the .470 double our tracker had carried, and Geoff had his little .375 double. We were only fifty yards into the bush when the bull heaved to his feet in front of us. I shot him again with the big .470, and this time he went down, stayed down, and in a few moments gave his death bellow.

The next couple of hours were extremely thirsty while we fetched the truck. Then we got the buffalo organized, took some pictures, and spent some time admiring him. He was indeed a lovely buffalo, all the buffalo anyone ever needs. His horns spread to forty-seven inches, heavy throughout with the beautiful, deep curls the best East African buffalo are known for.

He was, and is, the best buffalo I have ever taken, so I was not, and am not, lamenting for the one that got away. We checked the tracks where he had stood, and there was much more dead ground than we had imagined. We had simply let him walk away from us, down the *korongo*. But not quite, as they say, "out of our lives forever."

We tried to find him the next day, to no avail, and then we went on to the west. Another PH thought he saw him in the same area a few days later, but when we came back at the end of the safari we failed to find him yet again. Two seasons later, in the same place, Geoff Broom found the scattered bones of an old buffalo bull long since killed by a lion. The horns were cracked and weathered, but still intact. Geoff maintains he would know that buffalo anywhere. Even dried in the African sun they spread to fifty-four inches.

Reprinted with permission of the author. For information on his books and DVDs, visit his website at www.craigboddington.com

Among the San

E. DONNALL THOMAS, JR.

The Bushmen were the first. They're still the best.

As a culture, we have lost the honorable art of sitting still. Bowhunting and wildlife photography have given me lots of practice and I do it better than most, but I still have my limitations. As I watched Ghao settle into the dirt at the base of the shepherd's tree, I realized I was watching a master in action. He didn't fidget. His eyes didn't drift shut. He simply sat, elegant and motionless, and waited for the next phase of the stalk to begin as if he had all the time in the world, which I suppose he did.

We had kept pace with the wildebeest for over two hours while the sun burned the last of the overnight winter chill from the sands beneath our feet. The herd was grazing slowly into the wind, and the big bull we were after refused to detach himself from his company long enough to let us try to slip in for a shot. Left to his own devices, I'm sure Ghao would have headed off into the bush to look for a more promising track, but I wanted a wildebeest. So there we sat.

As the dark, strange-looking animals frisked about the dry pan, the sounds of the Kalahari filled my ears: the buzz of insects, the three-note dirge of the doves roosted in the acacias, a springbok ram's distant snort. Yielding to the spell of the place, I soon found myself watching and listening with an infinite supply of patience. As we waited for the animals to make their next move, I found myself reflecting idly upon our remarkable circumstances: a visiting American bowhunter and a representative of the world's oldest surviving hunting culture, improbably joined together against the long odds and difficult geometry of capricious winds and wary eyes.

And I realized that during all my bowhunting adventures around the world, I'd never run into anyone quite as intriguing as Ghao and his fellow Bushmen.

The San

An ethnically and linguistically unique people, the Bushmen—or San—were southern Africa's original inhabitants, ranging in nomadic fashion from modern Zimbabwe and Zambia all the way to the Cape. No one knows just how long the San have been around, but their abundant rock paintings date back at least 5000 years. Early in the last millennium, the area experienced an influx of pastoral, Bantu-speaking tribes from the north. Agriculturalists and cattle-tenders, the new arrivals' social structure conflicted sharply with the Bushmen's hunter-gatherer lifestyle. Furthermore, the northern tribesmen introduced a new concept to the region, one that the San had fortuitously managed to avoid: organized warfare.

The results were inevitable. Relentlessly displaced from their original homelands, the San slowly retreated to the inhospitable Kalahari, where their finely honed survival skills and an incredibly harsh environment provided them with a natural means of insulation from their enemies. While the arrival of European colonialists four centuries ago certainly increased their isolation, the San had given up much of their original territory long before our own ancestors arrived on the scene to add to their woes. And the San endured only by the most demanding means imaginable: by learning to thrive in terrain that others could barely survive for days.

Short, finely featured, and almond colored in complexion, the San appear physically distinct from all other indigenous African peoples. Punctuated by baffling clicks, their unique speech has intrigued linguists for years. Their democratic social customs also distinguish them from other inhabitants of the region. In San culture, for example, women have always enjoyed full participation in the decision-making process, a rarity in Africa. But as a bowhunter, I have to admit that all these unique physical and cultural traits pale before my appreciation of their hunting and tracking abilities. Simply stated, they are the best, and every time I've hunted with them I've come away from the experience in awe.

Reserved without being diffident, the Bushmen are quick to laugh and provide unfailingly good company in the field. The only flash of animosity I ever saw from them came one morning when we stumbled across a horned adder while trailing a gemsbok. The Bushmen quickly armed themselves with sticks and beat the nasty looking little snake to a pulp. Allan translated the flurry of discussion that followed for our benefit: *We might walk this way again tomorrow.*

Please note that one does not simply arrive in Africa and go hunting with the Bushmen. Today, most Bushmen live in Botswana and Namibia. Many have lost contact with their traditions through inevitable cultural assimilation. Those who have not often live in geographic isolation compounded by formidable language barriers. My own opportunities to hunt with the San have come through Allan Cilliers, an accomplished and widely renowned Namibian PH who enjoys a unique relationship with the

Bushmen based on years of experience with their culture. Despite his own accomplishments and abilities, Allan clearly holds the Bushmen in the highest esteem, and it's equally obvious that the sense of respect extends both ways. In Allan's camp, the Bushmen are more hunting partners than employees, and even the simplest walk through the bush with Allan quickly turns into a fascinating lecture on the local flora and fauna and how the Bushmen utilize them in their daily life. Furthermore, Allan's huge, game-rich hunting concession borders immediately on Bushmanland, a huge trackless area where the San still enjoy their traditional way of life in as unspoiled a manner as possible.

Bushman Archery Equipment

While architects and engineers have debated the relationship between form and function for years, the design of Bushman archery tackle begins on an even more basic level: they had to make do with the raw materials at hand.

Bushman bows are simple affairs. Whittled down from a variety of woods, especially the brandybush *(Grewia flava)*, they are usually only 30–35 inches long and draw no more than 20 pounds. Oil derived from the sour plum *(Ximenia caffra)* keeps the wood from cracking in the dry desert heat. Strings come from a variety of material including hide and sinew, but most are made from plant fiber harvested from a tough succulent known as mother-in-law's tongue *(Sanseviera aethiopia)* which the Bushmen roll into cord upon their thighs. The Kalahari San fashion lovely cylindrical quivers from the root bark of the umbrella thorn *(Acacia luerdertzii).* Farther to the south, bark from the aptly named *kokerboom* (quiver tree) serves the same purpose.

As often seems to be the case in indigenous hunting societies, bow design ultimately reflects the availability of suitable arrow materials, and the traditional Bushman hunting arrow clearly represents the most sophisticated and imaginative element of their hunting tackle. Shafts are made from sections of a variety of stiff grasses similar to our own river cane. These grasses are not widely distributed, and on our last trip into hunting camp Allan thoughtfully stopped by the side of the road as we passed a known thicket of the stuff and harvested a supply for his hunters.

Between joints, the cane is quite straight and true, but single segments are too short to make an effective arrow. The Bushmen solve this problem by whittling a male-male ferrule from giraffe bone with which they can link two segments together, resulting in an arrow approximately 20 inches long. Shafts are unfletched and completed with a simple self-nock. Tips traditionally came from carved bone, but nowadays most are made from scavenged steel laboriously filed into delicate triangular heads. As nearly as I can tell, steel points represent one of only three ready concessions to modern society, the other two being the surplus Namibian military jackets the Bushmen wear against the cool Kalahari winters and—inevitably, I suppose—tobacco.

By itself, this simple, lightweight equipment obviously lacks the punch needed to bring down gemsbok and other large antelope. Bushmen hunters overcome these limitations by poisoning the tips of their arrows. Under certain conditions, they use a variety of plant-derived toxins for this purpose, but most arrows are embellished with potent poison derived from several species of flea beetle grubs, especially

Diamphidia simplex. Bushmen carefully harvest the larvae from known locations at certain times of year and store them to treat arrows as needed. Eight or ten grubs are needed to treat one arrow. Based on descriptions of the poison's effects, I surmise that it affects the autonomic nervous system, leading to incoordination, stupor and eventual collapse as it absorbs into the blood stream. The poison takes hours to days to work depending on the nature of the hit and the size of the animal. The poison does not affect the edibility of the meat.

All this makes the bushman arrow design appear especially ingenious. The toxin is applied only to the distal segment of the shaft, not the tip itself, so the arrows remain relatively safe to handle. Furthermore, arrows tend to break off at the ferrule, leaving the toxic segment embedded in the quarry. Arrowmaking remains a highly esteemed art in Bushman culture. Hunters frequently pass arrows back and forth as tokens of gratitude and respect, and in the elaborate formula Bushmen use to divide meat among the band after a kill, the maker of the lethal arrow receives first share no matter who actually fired the killing shot. (Attention, American arrow-makers: does that sound like a good deal or what?)

Hunting Techniques

San hunting practices ultimately depend upon their legendary tracking skills, which we'll discuss below. But first, a few observations made about the methods they employ in the field, especially as they contrast to our own.

Hunting with Ghao, I was surprised to note that when we came to open areas I often spotted game at a distance before he did even without my binoculars. At first I thought there might be something wrong with his eyes as he is quite old, but I quickly realized that when he needed to he could spot game in the brush far better than me. I finally realized that he just didn't care about spotting animals hundreds of yards away. Seeing game told him nothing that he didn't already know based on the sign underfoot.

The Bushmen seemed fairly indifferent to terrain features when planning stalks and were often quite willing to advance upon sharp-eyed animals in plain sight. They get away with this because of their spooky ability to anticipate the quarry's head movements. Ghao always seemed to know just when to freeze and when to start moving again. They only stalk game early in the morning and late in the afternoon when there are long shadows on the ground and they stick to the shadows meticulously. They regard stalking at midday and during low light as a complete waste of time.

In traditional Bushman culture, hunting is very much a group effort, largely because of the need to have lots of help at hand upon the successful conclusion of a hunt to avoid meat loss to spoilage or scavengers. When I hunted with two or more of Allan's trackers, I noticed that they conversed in animated fashion on the trail, especially when the track demonstrated some unique or confusing feature. In this regard, their unique language seemed especially adaptive as their flurry of clicks usually disappeared on the desert breeze with little trace of the human voice. Allan confirms that he has often observed the Bushmen holding one of these discussions within earshot of wary game without spooking the animal.

The Bushmen use two gaits to close within bow range. The first is a stooped-over duck walk that they can sustain at brisk speed indefinitely. The second they call the "leopard crawl": down on all fours, with long feline strides that result in almost no change in profile from the quarry's perspective. Watch the family cat stalk a robin on the lawn and you will have a good idea of what this method entails. Of course, the short, light Bushman bows prove ideally suited to this kind of stealthy maneuvering.

Once within bow range, the Bushmen shoot with a quick, plucking style: a short draw, free floating anchor and thumb release. Shot placement as we know it matters very little to them. The idea is simply to get the tip of an arrow (or two) into the animal anywhere and let the poison go to work. Several times when we stalked together, Ghao obviously expected me to take a shot at what I considered an unacceptable angle and rolled his eyes in frustration when I declined. I tried my best to explain my reservations in pantomime, but I'm not sure I ever made much of an impression.

Tracking

As finally adapted as their equipment and hunting methods may be, the Bushmen truly distinguish themselves from the competition when it comes time to track game, wounded or otherwise. Over the course of multiple trips to Africa, I've hunted with a number of African trackers whose skill level ranged from not much better than my own to very good indeed. But none could begin to approach the remarkable level of skill I observed when hunting with Ghao, Tsisaba, and the rest of Allan's incredible crew.

The soil in Allan's new hunting area consists mostly of soft, sugary sand. Granted, that kind of footing can hold lots of tracks, but individual hoof prints rapidly loose their distinction. Furthermore, game densities are so high that every square foot of ground contains tracks left by multiple animals. Nonetheless, the Bushmen could easily follow the trail of an individual animal through this riot of sign at a dead run. They could also tell exactly how far away the animal was, its condition, the precise nature of any wounds, and what it was likely to do next . . . even when tracking at night by moonlight supplemented occasionally by matches.

One day, during our last visit with Allan, Lori shot a kudu bull while hunting alone. The shot placement sounded perfect, but she was shooting from a pit blind and Lori doesn't stand that far off the ground to begin. The steep upward track of the arrow resulted in a one-lung hit . . . and an opportunity for the Bushmen to do what they do best.

As we listened to Lori's description of the shot, one of the younger trackers started immediately for the edge of the brush where Lori had last sight-tracked the bull. Ghao called him back sharply and delivered what sounded like a stern lecture. As Allan explained, Ghao was chiding him for ignoring the first part of the track even though we all knew where it led. Ghao explained that it was always important to take the track from the very beginning, to learn as much about the animal as possible. In fact, by the time we reached the acacias, Ghao knew the age and size of the kudu, exactly what Lori's arrow had done, and what the likely outcome of the pursuit would be: estimates that all proved remarkably accurate by the time we were through.

I'll spare readers most of the long, hot miles through the thorns. The only tracking hitch came in a flurry of sand some two miles into the chase. As the trackers sat down to smoke and consider the situation, Allan explained Ghao's interpretation of events. Lori's bull had run into the middle of a large herd of kudu and the sight of the bright arrow protruding from its chest had scattered the herd in all directions. Half an hour later, Ghao had sorted out the mess and we were back on track again.

After five hours and an estimated eight miles, Ghao stopped trotting and began to creep forward like a cat, fully aware that we were about to make contact with the wounded bull. Several hundred yards farther ahead, he suddenly pointed to a dense patch of thorns from which two spiral kudu horns protruded, and it was time for a strategy discussion. Allan's rifle offered an effective if unattractive option. Ghao explained that based on the spoor he felt the kudu was distracted and that Lori should be able to slip in for a killing shot, and after some last minute discussion between the two of us I watched her leopard crawl into the brush.

After one of the longest hours in my life, Ghao suddenly leapt to his feet in excitement. Moments later, the bull charged past trailing another one of Lori's brightly fletched arrows from its previously healthy side. When the kudu piled up a hundred yards away, Lori enjoyed the distinction of becoming the first modern woman archer to kill a big-game animal in Namibia . . . with a little help from her friends.

Back in the dry riverbed, the wildebeest have finally started to stir. Rising slowly from his lair at the base of the shade tree, Ghao tests the wind. Using hand signals and crude diagrams scrawled in the dirt, we offer one another thoughts on our next approach, each shaking off a suggestion or two from the other, like pitchers who want to throw curves when their catchers are calling for fastballs. Finally we reach a tentative agreement of sorts and begin to ooze forward through the brush.

And suddenly I realize just what a remarkable life experience bowhunting can be. Here we are, two men separated by apparently impossible gulfs in culture, language, and background, setting off together on one of the most seminal—and difficult—tasks our species can face. But a simple realization tempers my high spirits: as a fifty-two-year-old American, I will never be able to emulate Ghao's remarkable talents here on the veld. While he was learning how to stalk and track, I was studying calculus, Spanish, and biochemistry, noble efforts in their own right that suddenly feel strangely devoid of meaning.

A century ago, our culture tried to destroy Ghao's with rifles, roads and fences. Today, we threaten the same end through the process of assimilation: radios, money, Coca-Cola and all the empty promises of easy living. How will the story of the San conclude? Perhaps it's foolish to be optimistic. But in the meanwhile, I'll do my best to keep to the shadows and start every track at the beginning, just as I'll remain grateful for the opportunity to appreciate the potential skills that lurk inside us all.

Reprinted with permission of the author. To order his books, go to www.donthomasbooks.com.

Vengeance

TERRY WIELAND

The border post at Namanga comes up suddenly as you climb through the heat haze from the Tsavo plain of Kenya toward the sweeping highlands around Mount Kilimanjaro. Namanga itself isn't much. A collection of ramshackle buildings, a scattering of trucks, a lopsided bus, and everywhere, like shifting flocks of tropical birds, the bright-beaded Masai in their crimson robes. There are a few trees, and under every tree in the dust is a seller of something: Beads. Pens. Pots. A few have board *duccas* thrown together—a two-foot counter fronting a one-shelf store. Those who aren't selling are begging. When they crowd around, it's hard to tell one from the other.

Years ago, every safari passed through Namanga, hot and dusty and two days out from Nairobi, heading for Arusha to draw licenses and have a cold beer at the Greek's. Nobody does that anymore. Today the safari trade is airborne; sleek six-seaters whisk you from Nairobi's Wilson Airport to Kilimanjaro in an hour; pay the bribes, pick up licenses, and continue on west by air. By sundown you're in camp with a cold one in your hand and Tommies prancing on the plain. You don't even hate the safari car. Not yet.

The border post at Namanga, deprived of the high-rent safari trade, has been reduced to shaking down busloads of package-deal tourists, who stand there looking helpless as they are deftly disencumbered of their loose belongings by the bony fingers of the crimson-dad crones who trade on their Masai appearance to ply city-bred skills. The old Africa hands avoid making eye contact, stride purposefully, and snarl *hapana* as they wade through the crowds to get their passports stamped. Sometimes it works. By the time you finally roll out of Namanga with Mount Meru looming in the distance, you truly feel you are in Tanzania—land of great beasts and grubby beggars, and more than enough of each.

When Tanzania gained its independence in 1963, the new government embraced a philosophy of crackpot socialism that over the next 30 years managed to undo what little economic progress the country had made in the last 100. On the social front, the newly minted politicians with their pseudo-Oxonian accents and Savile Row suits found their less-enlightened brethren rather an embarrassment, and none more so than the Masai. The Masai, with their spears and their buffalo-hide shields, their crimson cloaks and elaborate beads, their herds of cattle and lion-mane headdresses, were great for the tourists but bad for the image of a socialized society. In quick order, the Masai had their spears confiscated, their red robes banned, and their children locked up in school. In far-off Dar es Salaam, the politicians and United Nations do-gooders congratulated each other over cool ones on the veranda and discussed whose lives they could screw up next.

For 30 years the Masai in Tanzania lived under proscription. Their entire way of life—all the things that made them Masai, and hence made life worth living—had been legislated out of existence. The old men crouched in the dust and drank beer, and the lions went unhunted.

Then came the end of the old government. Julius Nyerere, darling of the aid agencies, retired to reflect on his accomplishments, and a new crowd took over a country that had become an economic basket case. Disenchanted with socialism, they unleashed free enterprise (or tried to) and backed it up with a more-or-less blanket endorsement of the old ways. Not many Masai would return to their traditional way of life anyway, they reasoned. Not after 30 years. What harm can it do? And so the proscription was lifted. Announcements went out.

Within days the spears had come out of mothballs and every scrap of red cloth had been swept from the ducca shelves. The elaborate blue, white, and red beads and headdresses sprouted from every Masai head, and the school desks sat empty. The smiths on the plain stoked their forges to begin once again making the long-bladed spears and *simis*, the short swords that, together with shield and spear, announce to the world that this red-clad dandy is a blooded Masai *moran*.

It's a funny thing about Tanzania: you can pull the Land Cruiser over to the side in the middle of nowhere, with nothing in sight for miles across the plain except dust devils, and within five minutes there will be a couple of urchins crowding around the truck with their hands out. Give it a couple more minutes and there will be a half-dozen locals begging for handouts. Even if you don't pull over, when they see you coming in the distance they lock their eyes on yours and stand by the road with their arms straight out, palms upward, gaze unwavering as you roar on by, muttering. In Tanzania, begging at the personal, regional, and international level has been elevated to the status of national pastime.

But just when you think you've got that figured, you round a bend and see a Masai by the road. His hand is not out. It's holding a spear, or fingering a *simi*, and if he stares at you at all it is down his long, straight nose. The Masai—the *real* Masai, not the sheep in wolf's clothing that infest Namanga—asks nothing from anyone except to be left alone with his herds and his flocks and his lion scars.

About 20 miles south of Namanga you are in the heart of Masai country. Mount Meru looms in the distance, and on the other side lies Arusha, the metropolis of the north; but here the plain stretches away with only the occasional spiral of smoke to indicate a dwelling. Off to the southeast, Kilimanjaro drifts in and out of its constant clouds and haze. As you drive, a line of hills appears on your left, rising starkly from the plain. It is not really a line of hills, though; it is the rim of a long-extinct and worn-down volcano called Mount Longido, which rises 3,000 feet from the Masai plain.

Eroded to a stump, Longido is dwarfed by its sisters, Mount Meru and Mount Kilimanjaro, and is now little more than a high crater encircled by steep, rocky hills. The crater is several miles across and grown over with trees. The name comes from the Masai *Ol Donyo Ngito. Ngi* is a type of black rock found on the mountain, and for centuries the Masai have climbed Longido to sharpen their spears and simis on the black rocks. The highest remaining point of Mount Longido is a sheer rock pinnacle like the prow of a ship. It is usually obscured by clouds, and on the higher slopes the thick brush turns to rain forest. From the upper reaches you can see all the way to the border post at Namanga, 20 miles north, and into Kenya as far as Amboseli National Park.

There is a Masai village, also called Longido, at the base of the mountain. It consists of a few buildings, a ducca, a police post. Under the spreading acacias, two saloons grace the main drag, which is nothing more than a wide spot in the dust. One establishment is called the Lion, the other the Vatican. The Lion is the more upscale of the two, which is to say it has a door. Right now the door to the Lion stands open and beckoning, and inside a stack of beer crates reaches to the low ceiling. The bar is a plank, and the seats are planks that run around the edge of the one small room. Two Masai moran in blinding red robes sit with a glass of ale, their spears leaning against the wall, discussing stock prices. They nod as we enter and do not stare overlong.

Ever since the army I have not been a lover of warm beer, but sometimes it isn't bad. This was one of those times. Then we continued on out of town and around the base of the volcano and into our camp, on the southern slope facing Kilimanjaro far out across the Ngasarami Plain.

The plan was fairly simple. Mostly what people hunt around Longido are lesser kudu and some plains game. Sometimes they venture up the outer slope in hopes of a klipspringer, but mountain climbing in the heat is not a lot of fun, and as you get higher the going gets rougher. Like most mountains, it looks a lot easier from a distance.

Longido is shaped like a huge bowl. There are one or two passes where you can climb up over the hills and down into the crater, and in some spots these hills rise higher and higher, eventually simulating real mountain peaks, shrouded in cloud with rain forest and heavy mists. The crater is several miles across; a few Masai live up there and raise crops in the crater, carrying on a running battle with the baboons who raid from the forested hillsides. The Masai run their cattle on the hillsides as well, sharing the sparse grazing with a few dozen Cape buffalo. Rumor had it that high on Mount Longido there lurked a few buffalo bulls, too old to breed, too cantankerous to associate with, living out their lives alone. A few people had been up there and seen tracks. That was all. But they were big tracks. I had hunted Cape buffalo waist-deep in swamp water and dry as dust in sand and thornbush. Why not on a mountain top?

Cape buffalo-hunting today consists all too much of roaming around in a safari car. No one we knew of had ever climbed Mount Longido looking for a big old bull off by himself on a distant mountainside, but preliminary investigation suggested there might well be a good one up there if we were willing to sweat. Jerry Henderson thought that hunting such a bull would make good publicity for his new-found safari company and reminded me in his soft Texas tones that I like mountain hunting.

Sure enough, I do. And sure enough, I will. The company had a small group of very good professionals from Zimbabwe—Gordon Cormack, Duff Gifford, and a third I will just call Frank. Frank was a youngster of Afrikaner stock, and he was to be my PH when Jerry and I went off up the mountain. Jerry had dispatched him earlier to go up and look around, and Frank had returned determined that once was enough, although he did not say it in so many words. Instead, he decided the best way out was to discourage me from going up there. One conversation with Frank was enough to persuade me that I wanted no part of hunting Cape buffalo with someone I didn't trust, and it was obvious, as he lectured me on the perils of mountain hunting, that he himself did not want to go up that mountain.

"I'll go," I told Jerry. "I *want* to go. It can't be any steeper than the Chugach, or any thicker than coastal Alaska. But I ain't going with *him*."

Frank, to his relief, was out. Duff Gifford, to my relief, was in. The next morning we rolled out of camp and edged along the base of the mountain toward the winding trail up and over the hills to the Masai settlement in the crater.

Our party looked, as we made our laborious way up the mountainside, much like those porter safaris from Teddy Roosevelt's day. In addition to Duff, Jerry, and me, we had our cook and camp boy, both laden down with equipment. A couple of Masai retainers trailed along as well. Then there was the government game scout, Swai, a grinning citizen of legendary corruption who was based in Longido. By law we had to have him along; by custom he surrounded himself with his own retinue of flunkeys, including a gunbearer, a gunbearer's assistant, and who knows what all. Altogether, we had a dozen people strung out along the dry watercourse that cut through the thick brush on the mountainside and afforded the easiest route over the hills and down into the crater.

We reached the Masai huts around noon with the sun directly overhead and overbearing as only the equatorial sun can be. We flopped down under an acacia while Swai went off to negotiate with the locals. While we waited they brought us tea and maize, scorched by the fire and not half bad. When Swai returned, he brought with him three Masai to guide us. They wore their working clothes—gym shorts and spears. Ceremonial garb is fine for standing around wowing the tourists, but climbing a mountain in search of buffalo calls for something a little more practical. We divided up the baggage, formed a line, and swung on up the mountain.

To anyone accustomed to the Chugach, or any of the mountains of the American West, the going was not that hard. It was steep in places, and stony, but there were trails through the thorn brush where generations of goats and cattle and buffalo had browsed. The worst part was the heat. The sun was a physical weight on our shoulders as we struggled upwards, panting and sweating. The Masai suffered not at all, moving ever upwards in a loose, swinging gait, bare feet oblivious to rocks and thorns, bare shoulders shrugging off the sun.

Below us the Masai settlement was soon reduced to a few dots and postage-stamp fields, and we were high enough to look out across the crater. The peaks still loomed above, but the ancient volcano had lost its shape and unity, and we felt as though we were climbing among jumbled hills. There were ravines and gullies overgrown with a jungle of tangled brush. There were boulders that blocked our path as we wended our way back and forth, ever upward toward a high meadow that bordered a patch of rain forest just below the peak. There we would camp and, with luck, glass the hillsides below for a glimpse of buffalo.

We reached the meadow in late afternoon and made camp—a couple of small tents and a fire pit. Dinner was a laudable effort under the circumstances, eaten around the fire in the chill brought on by the sudden darkness of the equatorial night. Then our cook produced a precious few ounces of Scotch—barely enough for a sniff apiece, but it lent the illusion of a safari camp—and Duff and Jerry and I sat around our cheerful little blaze talking guns and buffalo and mountains.

That night was one of the coldest and most miserable I can remember. With darkness the temperature plunged and the rain came. We had no bedding—a slight mixup—and I spent the hours huddled on the damp plastic of the tent floor with the stock of my Model 70 for a pillow. I didn't know it at the time, but the sheer misery of that cold, wet night on the mountain was to prove a great benefit to us.

As soon as the sky turned grey I crawled out into a soupy mist that swirled and drifted and soaked the air as the rain had soaked the grass. Everyone was gathered around the fire, which smoked and hissed as it tried to produce enough heat to boil water. A more forlorn looking group I have never seen in a hunting camp. Swai, the game scout, huddled close to the tiny flame wrapped in an army blanket with his teeth chattering and his retainers bunched close around. Duff handed me a coffee and smiled his wolfish smile. The wet misery of the mountainside had robbed him of none of his assurance.

"Shall we go take a look?"

"In this stuff?"

"It'll clear. We want to be out there when it does."

Duff said a few words to Swai, who mumbled in response but made no move to leave the warmth of the fire.

"Is he coming?"

"Not right now. I told him we're just going to glass. No need to disturb himself." The wolfish smile again.

Duff and Jerry and I gathered our rifles and binoculars and picked our way through the grass along a ridge to a rocky promontory. The fog was shifting now, swirling gently at first, then a little stronger. Somewhere up there the sun was rising and bringing with it a breeze, and soon that breeze would become a wind and clear the fog away for good. Meanwhile, we could see little and do nothing but wait. But at least we were waiting alone.

For those who have not had the pleasure, hunting in Tanzania is, by law, a group activity. By law, you must have a game scout with you at all times. By the letter of the law, that means *all* times. No self-respecting game scout, however, goes out alone. He needs at least as many retainers as the professional hunter has, to show his equality. So if the PH has two trackers and a boy to carry the water jug, the game scout needs at least three flunkeys and preferably four. That adds up to a hunting party of ten, traipsing through the bush and scaring the wildlife.

In hunting, one is company and two is pushing it. Hunting with a cast of thousands, all arguing about what the tracks mean and debating whether we should go left or right, critiquing *bwana's* shooting and generally having a hell of a time, is not my idea of a perfect hunting scenario. If the game scout insists on coming, though, you don't have much choice.

Now we found ourselves, thanks to that blessed, wonderful, beautiful mist and rain and cold, allowed to leave camp unencumbered while Swai the Ungodly attempted to thaw himself out. And if Swai did not need to venture forth, neither did anyone else. For us, it was like being let out of school early.

The slopes of Mount Longido are cut by dozens of ravines carved by centuries of torrential rains. Some are so deep they could be called canyons, others are just dongas, but all are overgrown with vegetation and jumbled with boulders. We found a lookout and settled in, each watching a different valley. It was like being high up in an enormous stadium—or would have been but for the thick, shifting fog. We shivered and waited. A sporadic wind began to blow. The clouds came and went, clearing one minute, enveloping us the next. It was during one of these brief clear moments that I happened to catch sight of a grey-black object disappearing into some brush on a far hillside. Just a quick glimpse, and then the fog rolled back in.

"Duff, I saw one," I said, not quite sure I really had. Maybe all I had seen was a rock. But when the fog drifted away again, there was no grey rock right there. It must have been a buffalo. He had shown himself in a clearing for a split second at the precise moment a window had opened in the fog, and I just happened to have my binocular trained on the spot.

We sat and willed the fog to clear. By now it was 9:30; the sun was well up and the rising wind made short work of what was left of the clouds. The slopes and the crater were all in plain sight, and for half an hour we studied the hillside across the valley. For Duff and Jerry, I pinpointed as best I could where I thought I had seen the buffalo disappear. There was the bare face of a large boulder just to the right of the spot. That was the only real landmark in the hodgepodge of brush. As the minutes passed, I became less and less sure. Had I really seen a buffalo? Had I really seen *anything*?

"What'd you see, exactly?"

"Just the back end, and just for a second."

"Which way was he moving?" Duff is from Zimbabwe, and his Rhodesian voice was clipped and military as he gathered information. But he seemed to have no doubts.

"Along the hillside, from left to right. About halfway up."

Half an hour went by. By that time I was almost convinced I had been hallucinating. When the buffalo did not reappear, Jerry wandered back to watch the other valley.

"I've got an idea," I said to Duff. "Let's have Jerry stay here to spot for us, and you and I go down and look for him." Duff grinned. "Sounds good to me," he said, and padded off to get Jerry.

"We'll cross straight over to the hillside and use that tree as a start line," Duff told him, pointing to a bare-trunked acacia that rose taller than the others. "When we get there, we'll work straight along toward the big boulder on the right. If you see us get off course in that thick stuff, signal. Or if you see the buffalo . . ."

Jerry nodded a quick assent, gave me a clap on the shoulder, and a soft, Texan "Good luck." Then we dropped down the steep hillside with Duff leading. Almost immediately we came upon a scraped-out hollow. The musky urine smell of buffalo hung in the air, and we found hoof prints the size of dinner plates. "Well, we know there's one here," Duff whispered. "Big old boy, too."

We continued down along one of the bull's established trails. There was a wart hog skull under a bush and, a few feet away, one of its ivory tusks, slightly rodent-chewed. I put it in my pocket for luck.

We were across a creek bed and climbing again. Now we could look back and see Jerry perched high on the rock opposite, watching us. Through the binocular, he gave a thumbs up. We were on course and almost immediately found the bare-trunked tree. A clearing stretched along the slope in front of us, and at the far end I could just make out the big rock face.

It was approaching 10:30. The sun was high, and the air had warmed. I was sweating in my goose-down shirt. Worse, it was noisy, catching on every thorn and twig. I tore it off and stuffed it into my belt. Duff, in shorts and khaki vest, moved through the brush like a leopard, and his cropped hair and compactly muscled shoulders reinforced the image. We were edging along the clearing now, a few feet apart, communicating by signs and instinct as if we had hunted together for years.

He was watching for tracks and I was looking past his shoulder when the bull stuck his head out of the bushes about 150 yards in front of us, right beside the boulder. I hissed and pointed. We froze. The buffalo had not seen us. He swung his head from side to side, and the boss of his horns was so big it made his horns look stubby, but they were not. His boss was heavy and black and met on the top of his skull without a gap. He was, indeed, a big old boy.

The bull looked around, then slowly withdrew into his sanctuary. We breathed again and melted into the thick brush out of sight.

"He's big, he's wide," Duff whispered. "You want him?"

"I sure do."

We crawled along inside the screen of brush until we came up against a large rock, then crept back up to the clearing. We found ourselves on the edge of a deep donga jammed with a jungle of scrub. On the other side, 60 yards away, was the rock face where we had seen the bull. This was as close as we were going to get.

"Can you shoot from here?"

I nodded, found a clear spot to sit down, jacked the scope up to four power and wrapped the sling around my arm. Just as I leaned forward the big buffalo came out again, right on cue. He seemed to be going somewhere. I put the crosshair on his shoulder and squeezed. As the .458 bucked up into my face, the bull hunched and roared and dashed down into the donga, deep into the thickest of the thick brush.

"Shoot again," Duff yelled, but there was no time, and then the bull was out of sight. We could hear him, moving around down in the donga a few yards away. Then the rustling stopped and all we heard was his breathing, heavy and rasping. We stood together on the lip of the donga, looking down into the undergrowth. I replaced the spent cartridge in the magazine of the Model 70 and turned the scope down to one. Then we waited.

"He's hard hit," Duff said. "He blew blood out his mouth as soon as you shot. Hear him?"

From the brush, the sound of heavy panting came to us. He was no more than 15 yards away, maybe less.

"Hear him? Can you hear him? He's *kuisha*," Duff said. "Finished. That was a good shot, *bwana*. You got him in the lungs. We'll give him ten minutes, see what happens."

We stood side by side, trying to pierce the brush with our eyes, listening to the harsh breathing, waiting for the long, drawn-out bellow that would signal the end. But the only sound from the donga was the rough grating of each painful breath, in and out, in and out, in and out.

The old bull had lived alone on the mountainside for many years. There was a small herd of younger Cape buffalo up there, too, cows and calves and bulls, maybe a dozen in all, but they wanted nothing to do with him and they avoided his valley. He bedded on a slope overlooking the crater and each day visited the creek that bubbled down the mountain, then browsed up and along his favorite hillside as he made his way toward his own special place.

There was a boulder there, and some thick acacias, and in the shadow of the boulder it was cool for him to doze through the heat of the day. On one side was a donga and a narrow trail that led down into it and back up out of it. He crossed through that donga each day. Although the brush looked as solid as a wall, with his four-foot horns he could force his way through.

On this day, as the clouds cleared (cleared as they did almost every day up here, away from the plain, away from the big buffalo herds) the old bull sensed there was something wrong. He caught a whiff of something—smoke, perhaps—but there was no smoke on the mountain; the Masai stayed down in the crater, and the smoke from their fires rarely drifted this far up.

But there was something, something; once or twice he emerged to look along his backtrail before withdrawing back into his hideaway. Finally, he decided he would climb the hill to a better vantage point. As he came out he caught it again, that scent—not leopard, not Masai—a scent he had known only once or twice before in his long life, and just as he quickened his pace he was slammed in the ribs and a tremendous roar slapped his head and a cough was forced out of his lungs by the impact of the bullet and blood sprayed from his mouth.

Involuntarily he bucked and sprang. His trail was at his feet, the familiar trail down into the donga, and he let it carry him into the friendly gloom. Once there, he paused. His head was reverberating from the crash of the rifle and he could feel his breathing becoming heavy as a huge vise tightened on his chest. From the embankment above came the murmur of voices, and his rage began to build as his lungs filled up with blood.

The bottom of the donga was a tunnel through the vegetation, scoured clean of debris when the heavy rains came. The old bull slowly walked a few yards up the creek bed, then turned and lay down facing the trail. On each side of him were high earthen banks, and over his head was a roof of solid vegetation. They would have to come down that trail. He fixed his eyes on it, six feet away. Now let them come.

And there he waited as blood spurted out the bullet hole, his heart pumping out a bit of his life with each beat. Each breath came a little shorter, and the pool of bright red blood under his muzzle spread wider, and his rage grew inside him like a spreading fire. He heard them whisper "Kuisha . . ." Well, not just yet. And he heard them say "Give him ten minutes . . ." Yes. Ten minutes. He was old and he was mortally wounded. But he was not dead yet. The old bull fixed his gaze on the trail and concentrated on drawing each breath, one by one, in and out, in and out.

The minutes ticked by: three, four, seven, eight.

Duff and I waited on the bank. Only the wounded buffalo's rasping breath broke the silence on the mountainside.

"I know you want to see . . ." Duff whispered.

"Not me, *bwana*," I answered. "I can wait here forever."

"When you hear him bellow . . ." he began.

The old bull watched as the pool of blood grew and he felt himself growing weaker. Ten minutes. They weren't coming. Not much time left now. He heaved himself to his feet and a gout of blood poured from his mouth.

The bull could have eased silently down the donga and died, off by himself. But he did not want to go quietly. He wanted to take those voices with him. And since they would not come to him . . .

He bunched his muscles and sprang, charging up the trail. His horns plowed through the brush and shook the trees. He could not see them yet, but he was coming hard. There was not much time, and he had to reach the bated voices.

"He's moving, get ready!" Duff yelled.

We saw the brush trembling and his hoofs rocked the hillside, but we could not see the bull. Not yet. He was only yards away and moving fast, but where would he come crashing out? We couldn't see a damned thing. And then a black shape burst from the bushes five yards down and to my right.

"Shoot!"

I tried to get the scope on him, but all I could see was black. I fired, hoping to catch a shoulder, then worked the bolt and Duff and I fired together.

As we did, the bull turned his head toward us. His murderous expression said, "Oh, there you are!" and his body followed his head around. I was between Duff and the buffalo, and the buffalo was on top of me, and all I could see was the expanse of horn and the massive muscles of his shoulders working as he pounded in.

No time to shoulder the gun now—just point and shoot and hope for the best. I shoved the .458 in his face and fired as I jumped back, and the bull dropped like a stone with a bullet in his brain, four feet from the muzzle of the rifle.

"Shoot him again!" Duff shouted. "In the neck!"

"With pleasure," said I, weakly, and planted my last round just behind his skull.

Duff and I looked at each other.

"We're alive!"

We gave the meat to our Masai guides, and they brought the skull and cape down the mountain for us the next day. It took three hours to skin him out. They built a fire, and we roasted chunks of Cape buffalo over the flames as the skinner worked, carving off bites with our belt knives and tossing the remains to the Masai dogs. The meat was tough, but juicy and rich tasting. Duff and I ate sparingly and chewed long. If you are what you eat, we were one mean bunch of bastards when we came down off that mountain.

Then the reaction set in. For two days I did little except stay in camp, sometimes talking, but mostly just off by myself. I set up a camp chair in the shade where I could catch the breeze through the day and look out across the plain to the smoke rising off the slopes of Kilimanjaro. I had a well-worn copy of Hemingway that has travelled with me around the world, and it was then I discovered that there are times when you cannot read. Mostly I just sat and stared at Kilimanjaro in the distance, or rose and walked to the edge of our camp and looked back up the slopes of Mount Longido.

In the first split second when my buffalo burst from the bushes, I thought he was the most wonderful creature that ever lived, and when he dropped at my feet with a bullet in his brain and his eyes still open and fixed upon me, at that moment I knew a thousand times more about Cape buffalo than I had even minutes before.

We were driving back into camp late one afternoon when a brightly clad Masai elder flagged us down. A roving trio of lions, two young males and female, had killed a cow that afternoon. The dead animal was in the brush, guarded by four morani who had driven them off the kill with spears. Could we help them get the cow back to their village?

By the time we got there, nosing gingerly through the brush with Duff at the wheel and me riding shotgun with my now thoroughly beloved .458, it was pitch black. Our headlights picked up a Masai, waiting for us in the bush beside the dirt track to guide us in. The Land Cruiser forced its way through and over the thorny acacias to a tiny campfire beside the dead cow and four heavily armed Masai, standing in the darkness with three hungry lions somewhere nearby.

They hauled and heaved the carcass up into the back, and Duff put the Land Cruiser in gear. As the headlights swung in an arc, they picked up three pairs of eyes in the bush not 20 yards away. The lions had not gone far. As we pulled out onto the track, we met two Masai youngsters swinging along the road, armed like their elders with tiny spears and scaled down swords, driving two donkeys ahead of them, coming to start ferrying the beef back to camp if we had not shown up. Two little boys with two little spears, driving two tiny donkeys through the darkness, with three hungry lions lying up somewhere in the bush nearby. Three hungry and bitterly disappointed lions who, to the best of our knowledge, never did get a meal that night. Standing up in the back with the .458, I suddenly felt a little foolish.

The door of the Lion was still open and beckoning when we pulled into Longido the next day. Beer crates still reached to the ceiling, and the propane refrigerator was still not working. We had a beer anyway.

Three Masai in full regalia sat in the bar with their spears against the wall, drinking Tusker and discussing stock prices. We bought them a beer, and they gravely returned the favor. A few days later, bribing my way back out of the country at Namanga, a scarlet-robed native pawed at me and begged for alms, all the while proclaiming, "I am Masai!" To which I replied, "Like hell you are, bucko."

Epilogue
About a year later, an envelope arrived in the mail with a Houston postmark. Inside was a newspaper clipping from The Daily Telegraph *with the headline, "Peer's Son Killed By Charging Buffalo," and the story of how Andrew Fraser, the youngest son of Lord Lovat (of World War Two commando fame) had been charged and killed while on safari near Mount Kilimanjaro.*

"Mr. Fraser shot and wounded the buffalo, but it took cover in thick bushes from where it made its charge, tossing him and causing severe injuries," it read. The clipping was dated March 17, 1994—one year to the day after our encounter on Mount Longido.

In the margin was a note: "Terry, does this sound familiar? Jerry."

Long Stalk for Marco Polo

CRAIG BODDINGTON

It was freezing cold and still gray when we climbed to the top of the divide and set up to glass. Pale sun wouldn't touch the far valley for at least two hours, and there would surely be sheep. There is no grass up in the rocky ridges of the Pamirs, and not much in the valleys, just lonely blades here and there where the snow has blown away. It is enough, and the Marco Polo argali will come down to graze. Undisturbed, they will come down in the late afternoon and alternately feed and ruminate through the night. In the morning you will find them in the open alluvial valleys, and you can watch them from afar and put them in their beds. The grass is so sparse that they do not feed like other wild sheep, grazing contentedly. Instead they feed like caribou, constantly on the move.

In good country they are surprisingly plentiful, and from such divides I have seen hundreds of them in one vista, moving up from the valley floor in long lines to find their resting places on the ridges. There was no such spectacle in this valley, but there were sheep. Not far away was a band of young rams, and beyond them scatterings of ewes and lambs. We set up the spotting scope on a flat patch of snow and discounted all of these quickly. Glassing beyond these visible sheep, Attobek found two more at the base of a distant finger ridge, dark boulders showing through the snow. In the spotting scope I could only see that these were rams, and one was larger than the other. But Attobek was excited, and he was sure. Through a bit of English and much more Russian he explained that one was a younger ram, but the other was the kind of ram we sought. His nephew Shoudi, former Russian paratrooper, veteran of their excursion into Afghanistan, took a quick look and confirmed.

We watched while the two rams made their way up the hogback, then they disappeared over the far side. The cold was getting to me and I would have moved then. Attobek knew better. We waited and watched, and in a little while the two rams reappeared, working their way up the big mountain above the ridge. They climbed up into the pale sun, and the two distant specks gained contrast and resolution. Now I could see what my Tajik friends had seen instantly in the shadowed valley. One ram was just a ram; the other was the kind of Marco Polo argali that sheep hunters dream of. At this distance no man could see the tips with any optics, but the curl came well below the jaw, and the horns were heavy throughout, much heavier than those of his companion. The pair climbed up onto a shallow knob, circled and lay down, facing downhill.

The lay of the land was simple. If we could reach the base of that first hogback we would be covered. It would be an easy matter to climb up, and from this distance it appeared we would have a shot from the top. But that lower ridge was miles away. The valley and the lower slopes were broad, snow-covered, and completely devoid of any cover. We had all day, and we were wearing snow camouflage. It was about eight o'clock when we started to crawl.

After an hour my mittens and my knees were frozen solid, and that rock-studded ridge didn't look much closer. I truly can't recall whether I thought this insane stalk was going to work; if Attobek and Shoudi were willing to try it, then I had to try as well. We had been at this for more than a week now, and we'd made other stalks. Early on we had stalked a monstrous ram and spooked him at the last minute, catching only a glimpse of him as he made his exit. A couple of days earlier we'd stalked another band in some horrible high country, 17,000 feet by altimeter. They were bedded peacefully and we had just a hundred yards to go—and then the wind kissed the back of my neck, and they were gone into Afghanistan.

Exhausted and frustrated, we'd sat for a long time before starting the long hike down. This was my second hunt for these Marco Polo argali. I'd gotten a nice ram, good enough, but I'd had a serious bout with altitude sickness. They'd wanted to take me down, and they'd been right. I'd refused, pretty much at gunpoint, and I'd fought my way through it. But I'd never felt good on that hunt, had never been right. I wanted to do it again, partly because it is one of the world's greatest hunts, and partly because I needed to know I could do it. Tajikistan's Marco Polo country, with China to the east and the Afghan border to the south, is the end of the Earth. They don't get much return business, and the warmth of the welcome had surprised me.

Much had passed in the four years since I'd been in the Hot Springs Camp of the Attobek Clan. I'd done my own time in Afghanistan, with my own military, and we had some interesting notes to compare. Attobek assigned himself as my guide, assisted by Shoudi, and they were determined to find me one of the big ones. They had willingly passed innumerable rams, and after our failed stalks they had shrugged and kept looking. Now we had yet another chance. It wasn't my job to weigh the odds; all I could do was keep crawling, Attobek in the lead, Shoudi to my rear.

We stopped occasionally and lay prone in the snow, easing our aching backs and frozen knees. The rams were still there, bedded peacefully, surveying the valley where wolves and other dangers might lurk. Slowly, slowly, that rocky ridge drew nearer. At three o'clock, in the shade of the ridge, Attobek stood up and stretched, a broad grin on his face. I slithered the last few inches to his feet, and he helped me stand up. Shoudi pulled in beside me, and we laughed and shook our heads as we looked back across the clean expanse we had covered.

Despite the jumbled boulders the ridge was the easy part. Less than an hour and we were near the top, working our way up through a battlement of frozen rocks. Shoudi went ahead and found a good spot, and I followed him into my designated position and raised my binoculars. The rams were there, straight up a ridge that was much too clean. One ram was medium-sized, with nicely flaring horns. The other was a monster, with wonderful mass and deep curls and flaring tips. He seemed almost close enough to touch across that expanse of snow and ice, but my crazy Tajiks already knew what I must now accept. Perhaps they knew it all along: The two rams were still seven hundred yards away, far up a slope that was much too clean and open. I was so horrified that long moments passed before I realized that Attobek and Shoudi were still smiling.

Keeping his movements below the stone ramparts, Attobek motioned to the sun, now on top of the ridge behind the rams, and spoke a few words in various languages. Slowly, through my despair, I understood. When the sun dropped over the ridge the rams would get up, and they would come down that open ridge to us. Moving slowly, we prepared a rest for the rifle and I tried the position. Then I dropped back down and settled in to wait.

The cold didn't creep in at all. It rushed in, a palpable thing. I had good wool under the snow camo, more layers under that, and still I was cold. My feet and hands burned, and the cold spread through my legs from my frozen knees. There was nothing to do except lean against the frozen rocks and take it—and hope that Attobek was right. At least it was dead calm.

Few people in the world have done more sheep hunting than the Tajik tribesmen, and no one knows wild sheep better. When the sun left them the rams began to stir, rising slowly from their beds and stretching like bird dogs after their nap. Then, moving slowly and deliberately, they came straight down the ridge to us. When they dropped into the low spot between our false crest and the main ridge I got into position, and then we waited some more.

For long minutes it appeared they would come right to us, but there was unseen broken ground to our front, and at a bit beyond three hundred yards they veered, moving across our front. This was the time, and the big ram was in the lead. He stopped for a moment, quartering to me. No wind, serious uphill angle, a fast 140-grain bullet in the .270 WSM. I held just at the midpoint and squeezed the trigger.

The ram took the bullet hard and I thought he would go down. He did not. He recovered, turned and headed up around the toe of the big ridge, hidden in seconds. Later I would understand that I had hit him exactly where I had aimed—but I had aimed at an optical illusion. I couldn't possibly have seen his shoulder at the angle he presented, because it would have been covered by his right horn. So instead of his shoulder I had shot past the horn and hit him too far back. At the moment this didn't matter at all. What did matter was the ram wasn't down, and darkness was coming fast. We got up and ran, cold and altitude forgotten.

Shoudi, youngest and strongest, got to the top first. I don't know how I got there at all, because I don't remember the run. I remember being surprised at how the ridge suddenly dropped off into a narrow ravine, with scrub brush on the far side. Shoudi had our ram in view when Attobek and I puffed up beside him. He had made the far side and was struggling up through the brush, badly hurt but still on his feet. The range was now five hundred yards, but it was dead calm, and we had to end this now.

Swallowing my heaving lungs, I slid in behind a boulder. The stricken ram was going up the far side. I waited until his broad back was straight to me, then raised the crosshairs above those beautiful horns. Though I didn't yet know how, I knew I had blown a much easier shot. Oddly, then, there was now no uncertainty. I fired, and I think I was already standing and shouting when we heard the bullet hit and saw the great ram dashed to the ground, then slide backwards in the snow.

Reprinted with permission of the author. For information on Craig Boddington's books and DVDs, visit his website at www.craigboddington.com.

The Classic Fall-on-Your-Arse Double

ROBERT F. JONES

As I write this, it's dead, dreary winter in Vermont—a foot of squeaking, crusted snow on the ground, with the barn thermometer registering well below zero at sunup and rarely topping 20 degrees on even the sunniest days. Gloom prevails. The bird season is quits until next fall and my major outdoor activity is lugging in cartloads of frost-crusted logs to feed the insatiable woodstove. As always during these bleak times of year, my memories turn to warmer climes and skies full of fast-moving gamebirds. Some of the best shooting I ever enjoyed occurred in Kenya, back in the 1960s and '70s, the last years of East Africa's golden era as a hunting venue. Here's a taste of it:

The big Bedford lorries had arrived the day before, so by the time we wheeled into the campsite along the Ewaso Nyiro River the tents were up—taut, green, smelling of hot canvas and spicy East African dust. It was a sandy country, red and tan, and the river rolled silently but strong, dark almost as blood, under a fringe of scrawny-trunked doum palms and tall, time-worn boulders. Sand rivers cut the main watercourse at right angles, and the country rolled away to the north and west in a shimmer of pale tan haze. The fire was pale and the kettle whistled a merry welcome.

This was the last camp of the month-long shooting safari through Kenya's arid Northern Frontier Province, a hunt that had begun three weeks earlier at Naibor Keju, in the Samburu country near Maralal, then had swung northward through the lands of the Rendile and Turkana tribes to Lake Rudolf and back down across the Chalbi and Kaisut deserts past Marsabit Mountain to the Ewaso Nyiro.

"I call it EDB," Bill Winter said as we climbed down out of the green Toyota safari wagon. "Elephant Dung Beach. The first time I camped here the lads had to shovel the piles aside before we could pitch our tents, it was that thick. *Ndovus* everywhere."

Not anymore. On the way in from Archer's Post, Bill had pointed out the picked skeleton of an elephant killed by poachers—and not long before, judging by the lingering smell. We'd stopped to look it over—vertebrae big as chopping blocks, ribs fit for a whaleboat, the broad skull still crawling with ants, and two splintered, gaping holes where the ivory had been hacked out.

"*Shifta*," Bill had said, and when we got into camp the safari crew confirmed his diagnosis. *Shifta* were even then the plague of northeastern Kenya, raiders from neighboring Somalia who felt, perhaps with some justification, that the whole upper right hand quadrant of Kenya belonged to them. When the colonial powers divided Africa among themselves, they all too often drew arbitrary boundaries regardless of tribal traditions. The Somalis—a handsome, fiercely Islamic people related to the Berbers of northwest Africa and the ancient Egyptians (theirs was the Pharaonic "Land of Punt")—were nomads for the most part, and boundaries meant as little to them as they do to migrating wildebeest. But these migrants armed with Russian AKs and plastic explosives had blood in their eyes. They poached ivory and rhino horn, shot up *manyattas* (villages) and police posts, mined the roads and blew up trucks or buses with no compunction. Sergeant Nganya, a lean old Meru in starch-stiff Empire Builders and a faded beret, led us over to a lugga near the riverbank. In the bottom were the charred, cracked leg bones of a giraffe, scraps of rotting hide, the remains of a cook fire and an empty 7.62mm shell case stamped "Cartridge M1943"—the preferred diet of the Soviet AK-47 assault rifle. Nganya, who had been with Winter since their days together in the Kenya game department, handed the shell over without a word.

"I'm sure they'll leave us alone," Bill said as we drank our chai under the cool fly of the mess tent. "They know we're armed, and the lads will keep a sharp lookout around the camp. Just to ensure sweet dreams for one and all, though, I'll post guards at night. Not to worry."

We would finish out the safari with some serious bird shooting. It was a welcome relief, a slow, leisurely cooling-out from the high tension and dark tragedy of big game, and for me doubly so because bird hunting has always been my first love among the shooting sports. But this was a different kind of bird hunting: I'd grown up on ruffed grouse, woodcock, sharptails and pheasants in the upper Middle West, and that kind of gunning had meant cold mornings, iron skies, crisp wild apples, the crunch of bright leaves under muddy boots. It had been all tamaracks and muskegs, old pine slashings, glacial moraines and ink-black ponds. In the one-horse logging towns we'd whiled away the evenings on draft beer, bratwurst and snooker. The great unspoken fear in that land of Green Bay Packer worship hadn't been *shifta* but something far more fearsome, in those days at least: the Chicago Bears.

The contrast between American and African bird shooting became quickly clear. We were up before dawn, but even this coolest part of the day was T-shirt weather. Hyenas giggled downriver and a great fish eagle winnowed the air overhead as we sipped strong Kenya coffee at first light. There were lion tracks outside the tents, fresh ones—great bold pug marks that circled the camp twice, evidently made during the night. But our guards, the wry Turkana named Otiego and the big, slab-faced Samburu we called Red Blanket, reported no signs of *shifta* during their watches. Yet they hadn't seen the lion either. . . .

Not far from the river was a hot spring, a *maji moto* in Swahili, and we walked in quietly through a low ground fog, armed only with 20-gauge shotguns. Soon the sand grouse would be flying. Lambat lead the way, peering intently into the mist. He raised a hand: Halt. We heard a huffing sound in the fog, then dimly made out two dark bulky shapes. "*Kifaro,*" Lambat hissed. "*Mama na mtoto.*"

Either the fog thinned or adrenaline sharpened my vision, for suddenly they came into focus: a big female rhino and her calf. The mother whuffed again, aware that something was wrong but unable with her weak eyes and the absence of wind to zero in on the threat. She shook a head homed like a Mexican saddle and shuffled off into the haze followed by her hornless offspring, which looked at this distance like an outsized hog. I'd often jumped deer while bird hunting in the US, and once a moose had gotten up and moved out of an alder swale I was pushing for woodcock near Greenville, Maine. But rhinos are somehow different. If only for the heightened pucker factor.

The sun bulged over the horizon, a giant blood-orange, and instantly the fog was gone, sucked up by the dry heat of the day. But then it seemed to return, in the whistling, whizzing form of a million sand grouse, chunky birds as quick and elusive as their distant relatives, the white-winged doves and mourning doves I'd shot back home.

These were chestnut-bellied sand grouse, *Pterocles exustus*, the most common of some six species that inhabit the dry thorn scrublands of Africa. They fly to water each morning, hitting the available water-holes for about an hour soon after dawn, fluttering over the surface to land, drink and soak up water in their throat feathers for their nestlings to drink during the dry season.

I promptly began to miss them, overwhelmed and wild-eyed at their sky-blackening abundance. Then I settled down as the awe receded and began knocking down singles and doubles at a smart clip. It was fast, neck-wrenching shooting, with the birds angling in from every direction. I stood under the cover of an umbrella acacia, surrounded by shell husks, the barrel of my shotgun soon hot enough to raise blisters, shooting until my shoulder grew numb. Bill stood nearby, calling the shots and laughing at my misses.

"Quick, behind you, *bwana!*"

I spun around to see a pair of sand grouse slashing in overhead, mounted the gun with my feet still crossed, folded the lead bird and then leaned farther back to take the trailer directly above me. *Pow!* The recoil, in my unbalanced, leg-crossed stance, dropped me on my tailbone. But the bird fell too.

"Splendid," Bill said with a smirk. "Just the way they teach it at the Holland & Holland Shooting School. The Classic Twisting, Turning, High-Overhead, Passing, Fall-on-Your-Arse Double. Never seen it done better, I do declare!"

Then it was over. The sand grouse vanished as quickly as they had appeared. The trackers began to pick up the dead birds and locate any "runners." There were few wounded birds. I'd been shooting No. 6s, the high-brass loads we'd used earlier in the safari for vulturine and helmeted guinea fowl. The heavy shot had killed cleanly when I'd connected. We could have used No. 7½ shot, perhaps even 8s on these lightly feathered, thin-skinned birds and increased the bag a bit, but there really had been no need to. By using heavier shot, we'd ensured swifter kills, and there never had been a dearth of birds.

Or so I was thinking. Just then one of the birds—a cripple, far out near the white-scaled salt of the hot spring's rim—scuttled away, trailing a shattered wing. Lambat stooped like a shortstop fielding a line drive, grabbed a stone and slung it sidearm. It knocked the bird dead at 20 yards. He picked up the grouse and brought it to me, walking long and limber, dead casual, a look of near-pity on his face as he placed it in my hand. Ah, the sorry, weak *Mzungu* with his costly firestick, blasting holes in the firmament with those expensive shells, when there were rocks right there for the picking. "His lordship," indeed.

Reprinted with permission of Louise H. Jones.

Everything Your Heart Desires

ROBERT F. JONES

The camp was in an uproar when we returned. *Shifta*—four of them, scruffy little men with dirty shirts and heads wrapped in hand towels, accompanied by even scruffier dogs—had approached the camp. Ganya had driven the poachers away with warning rifle fire. No, they hadn't shot back, merely eased themselves into cover and out of range. They had faded southward, into the tangled vegetation of the riverbank. Everyone was excited. Even the old *mpishi*—the safari cook—was muttering and shaking his head as he poked at his perpetual fire. Normally the *mpishi* was Mister Cool.

After a lunch of grilled sand grouse breasts, we drove up the river to Merti, the last town before the Ewaso Nyiro makes its great bend and loses itself in the wastes of the Lorian Swamp, hard by the Hothori and Sabena deserts. There is a police post at Merti, and Bill wanted to check in, letting them know we were in the area. Along the way I kept seeing wrecked vehicles beside the twisting, twin-rutted road—fully a half-dozen of them in the course of a 30-mile drive. Some were badly rusted and nearly buried with windblown sand, but others seemed newer. We stopped to examine one. The frame was bent like a steel pretzel, the hood ripped as if by a giant can opener. Even the wheel rims were twisted. The vehicle was barely recognizable as a Land Rover. But what could have torn up the truck so badly? On this barely traveled road, it could hardly have been a multi-truck collision.

"Plastique," Bill said. "C-4 or Semtex, the Communist equivalent. A land mine did this work—the *shifta* use them all over the province."

Merti, when we got there, had the look and feel of a besieged "strategic hamlet" in Vietnam. The police post was encircled ten feet high with barbed wire, its corners guarded by machine-gun towers. The town itself resembled the old, grainy sepia-tone photographs of laagers during the Boer War, and you almost expected to see wide-hatted, leathery *voortrekkers* hung with bandoliers lounging outside the *duka* drinking beer, waiting for the order from Smuts or Botha that would send their commando back into the field. The Kenya police were definitely on the defensive in this undeclared war.

Yellow-necked spurfowl were part of a healthy mixed-bag rough shoot.

"Oh, yes indeed, sir," the sergeant in charge said, smiling widely. "There are *shifta* about. Perhaps a hundred of them. Bad men, yes. *Mbaya sana.*" But he wasn't doing anything about them. And rightly so, Bill pointed out later. If he sortied from the town, the *shifta* might lure him and his men deeper into the waterless thorn-scrub while others swung back to loot the *dukas* in town and make off with whatever supplies and weapons they could lay their hands on.

"Well," Bill told him, "we're upriver in Block Seven near Kittermaster's Camp, hunting, and I'm sure they won't bother us."

"Oh no, sir." The sergeant smiled. "Of course not. Not with the police so close at hand." They both laughed heartily.

We stopped at the *duka* and drank a warm Tusker beer. The dusty, cool shop was pleasant but poorly stocked.

"I came off safari once, years ago, into a little *duka* like this," Bill recalled. "Back in my anti-stock-theft days with the Kenya constabulary. I'd been chasing Turkana cattle thieves all over hell and gone. God, it was hot. What I wanted more than anything was a good, clean shave, and I'd run out of razor blades days earlier. I came into the *duka* and asked the owner what he had in stock. A big, happy, smiling chap he was, like that police sergeant we were talking to just now. 'Oh, *bwana*,' he said, 'we have everything your heart desires!' He gestured around at his shelves.

" 'By chance, would you have a razor blade?' I asked him.

" '*Hakuna*,' quoth he rather sadly. 'I have none.' "

Bill laughed.

" 'Everything your heart desires.' Don't you love it, *bwana?*"

I think I'll go out this afternoon with the shotgun," I told Bill at lunch on our last day at Elephant Dung Beach. "A rough shoot—see what I can walk up. There must be plenty of birds right around camp."

"Sounds like a fine idea," Bill said. "I've got to stay here and organize the packing, though. You can take Lambat and Otiego along with you to push the birds up. There's no end of *ndeges* around here. I hear them calling in the morning—guinea fowl, francolin, yellow-necked spur fowl, maybe even some button quail. You'll have a good time, I'm sure. *Ndeges mingi sana* hereabouts, birds galore."

And *shifta* as well, but we left that unspoken. It was too beautiful a day to worry about them, at least out loud. This was my last day afield, and the bird shooting so far had been an alien form—there'd been the sand grouse, of course, and I'd shot driven guinea fowl in an old coffee shamba that had previously belonged to Karen Blixen, aka Isak Dinesen, of *Out of Africa* fame. It had been good shooting, but too formal—too much like an English driven pheasant shoot for my rough-and-ready American taste. The boys had formed a line at the top of a long, brushy slope and pushed the birds down to us where we stood above the jungly banks of the Tana River near where it rises beyond Thika, the guineas lurching into the air well above us, big dark birds heavier than pheasants but just as fast as they poured past, cackling, and we shot fast and furious, folding some nicely but seeing others slant down, heavy-hit, legs trailing, to land in the riverside tangle. When we went in to finish them we found fresh buffalo sign—steaming mounds of shiny dung, trampled shrubbery.

"What do we do if they come?" I asked Bill, hefting the 20-gauge pitifully in my hands.

"Climb," Bill laughed. "*Panda juu.* There are plenty of trees at hand."

"I don't know if I'm still that arboreal," I said doubtfully.

"You will be, *bwana*," he said. "Don't worry about it. Nature will take its course. I was in a situation like this with a fat old English nobleman once. He scampered up a thorn tree like a bloody *nugu*—just as agile as a monkey. Never even let out a yelp from the thorn stabs. Didn't feel them."

We'd gone in then and collected our birds, and the buff left us alone. Just as the *shifta* would leave me alone today, I hoped.

Yet deep down it was *because* of the *shifta*—the chance of them being there—that I wanted to do this. Every bird hunter knows the neck-itching feeling that crawls up from your kidneys when you walk into a good covert. As if something deadly were waiting there, silent in the mottled green dark. What's waiting, though, is no deadlier than humiliation if you blow the shot. Yet when the bird gets up with a rattle and a roar, it's as if some bogey man suddenly sprang out at you, heart-stopping, remorseless: Abdul the Objectionable in his final, fatal pounce. The adrenaline rush is beyond comparison. This would be even better.

The country upstream from camp was thick with wait-a-bit thorn and elephant grass, tough going as we pushed into it. Behind us the sounds of camp life—clanking pots, happy conversation in English and Swahili—quickly faded; ahead the doum palms and borassus swayed, their shadows shifting black on the bright grass. A heavy silence, broken only by the buzz of flies and bees and the rusty creak of nooning birds.

Otiego swung wide to the right and slapped his spear at a low thorn thicket. A bird got up with the forever-startling feathery whirr—a long brown bird, big as a pheasant—and I centered it, *pow!* Then another, and three more. I didn't hear my second barrel fire, but there were two birds down. Feathers still falling through the hot, hard light. Otiego brought them back—yellow-necked spur fowl, their throats pale orange, conspicuously bare, their wet dead eyes rimmed with bare skin, pebbly red.

We could hear others ahead calling back and forth—*graark, grak, grak.* They ran as we approached, and we could see them scuttling gray-brown through the scrub. Then from the left a different bird got up—darker, chunkier—and Lambat dropped flat as he saw me swing past him, then shoot. The bird fell down. Its white throat and legs and mottled belly proclaimed it a Shelley's francolin, counterpart of the sharp-tailed grouse of my boyhood.

In the denser forest back of the riverbank another variety abounded—Heuglin's francolin, dark-feathered and plump as European partridge. They got up like ruffed grouse, with a great spooking thunder of wings, in there under the confining forest canopy, and had the same maddening habit of waiting until you were past, then lining out with a tree trunk between them and your gun barrel.

In the open, with the pheasant-like spur fowl and the tight-holding, sharp-tail-like Shelley's francolin, I couldn't seem to miss; now it was hard to score a hit. Otiego grinned wickedly and clucked his mocking disapproval.

Back out in the open we jumped a small covey of buff-colored, round-winged birds that buzzed off like outsized bumblebees. Button quail. I dropped two before they pitched in less than a hundred yards ahead. Lambat scooped the pair up on the run, but when we got to where the singles had landed we couldn't trigger a single reflush. Yet there had been at least eight in the covey, perhaps ten—slow fliers at best—that had landed in the tall grass. We could hear them scuttling, hear their frog-like *whoo-whoo-whoos* as they ran. We didn't see them again. The dead birds in hand looked vaguely like quail, but there was something odd about their feet. Then I noticed that they lacked the hind toes of the quail back home. It certainly didn't seem to hinder their speed on the ground.

For three hours we zigzagged through that wild, thorn-fanged riverside bush, a gamebird heaven, the trackers working like clever gundogs, spotting each possible hiding place, circling beyond it, then pushing through to put the birds out toward the gun. On some I shot nicely; on others I might as well have thrown the gun at them. But it was a time machine—no, a time-and-place machine. At one moment I was back in a southern-Wisconsin pheasant field, swinging on a fast-moving rooster with the corn tassels crunching underfoot; in the next I was kicking the soybean stubble for Georgia quail. Then I was up in Minnesota working the shortgrass prairie for sharptails, and in the next step jumping a woodcock out of alder edges in Vermont.

Yet at the same time I was aware that this was Africa: there could be a surly old bull buffalo just under the bank to my left, very angry at having his midday snooze disrupted; or a lion behind the next bush, sleeping off his midnight gluttony but not too lazy to get up and chomp a clumsy *Mzungu*. And above all there was the chance of encountering Abdul & Co., with automatic rifles, plastique land mines and a total lack of compunction when it came to killing unwary travelers.

By the time we swung back into camp, Lambat and Otiego each had ten birds dangling from their hands and I had a few more slapping my hip, their heads forced through my belt loops. The three of us were laughing as we came out of the *nyika*.

Bill was sitting outside the mess tent at his afternoon tea. He looked up with a quizzical smile.

"Did you have a decent shoot, *bwana?*"

"Everything my heart desired."

Shadows in the Bush

PHILIP CAPUTO

Part I

"Cape buffalo do not bluff a charge. When one of them comes at you, he's not voicing an opinion—he wants to meet you personally."

My mental tape recorder played back those words when, on the third morning of a ten-day walking safari in Tanzania's Selous Game Reserve, the trackers found the fresh spoor of a lone Cape buffalo bull. The commentary on the animal's personality had been delivered earlier by my guide, Wayne Stanton, a professional hunter, or PH as they're called in Africa. Several species of plains game were on my license—wildebeest, impala, hartebeest, zebra, warthog—but they were to be afterthoughts in a quest for the black-hided beast that is called *Syncerus caffer caffer* in scientific argot, *mbogo* in Swahili, and *nyati* in Ndebele, and is by an name one of the most dangerous big-game animals on the planet.

Awesome in size—a big bull will weigh 1,600 pounds—armed with sharp, curving horns that average a yard from tip to tip and form a boss resembling poured concrete, the Cape buffalo can be highly aggressive when surprised and vindictive when it's wounded or merely in a bad mood. It is also cunning, despite its dull, bovine appearance. Pursued by man or lion, its only predators, it will retreat into dense scrub, wait in ambush, then conduct the "personal meeting" of which Stanton had spoken, doing all in its considerable power to gore and stomp its pursuer to death.

I don't know how many people have been killed or badly injured by Cape buffalo in the annals of African hunting. I do know that the casualty list numbered four in the weeks prior to my arrival in Tanzania: one dead, three seriously hurt—ample evidence that the animal is not a cow on steroids.

Fair Chase Means 'Walk'

Safari is a Swahili word derived from the Arabic for "traveling on foot." Since the 1930s, however, both hunting and photographic safaris have become motorized. In the hunting variety, the client rides about until game is spotted. He or she then gets out, toddles off a short distance, and pots it. In Tanzania, the rules of fair chase require the hunter to be only 200 meters from a vehicle when the quarry is shot. That didn't strike me as hunting; it was shooting. If I was going to kill an animal like a Cape buffalo, my personal rules of fair chase stipulated that I should pay for it in the currency of sweat, effort, and risk.

I wanted to make the most of the experience, believing that in hunting, as in most things, you get out of it only what you put into it. Miombo Safaris Ltd., an outfitter started ten years ago by an American, Scott Coles, and a Tanzanian of Greek ancestry, Michel Mantheakis, went out of its way to accommodate me. Our hunting party, consisting of eight men, would be supported by a ten-man logistics staff, responsible for transporting food, tents, and heavy equipment by vehicle to a series of fly camps.

On the first two days, the hunting group trekked some eight miles from Miombo Safaris' base camp to a fly camp near a water hole, overnighted, then walked another 11 miles to a second fly camp on the Ruaha River. Stanton and I soon realized we could not imitate the African hunts of yore, when safaris lasted weeks or months and the hunter had the leisure to march from one campsite to the next. With only ten days, I could well use up my limited time merely traveling from point A to point B. So we decided to modify our plans by scouting for tracks and sign in the Land Rover and doing everything afterward on foot.

We had driven about three miles from camp on the third day when the trackers, Pius Raphael and Fabian Mora, spotted a solitary bull's hoof-prints, leading down the road before they turned into a patch of low trees bordered by tall, yellow grass. Pius opined that the buffalo had passed through the previous night.

Looking at the prints, each roughly the size of a coffee saucer, I felt fear and excitement, apprehension and anticipation—an emotion that mimicked one I had experienced on patrol in Vietnam. I was reminded of a remark my friend and sometime marksmanship coach, Ted Fedun, had made a few weeks before I left the United States. Fedun had urged me to so familiarize myself with my rifle that it became an extension of myself. "Because you're not going hunting," he had explained. "You're going into combat."

Pius, Fabian, and Stanton pushed off into the grass, followed by me, then gun bearer Hassani Msologoni, photographer Hendrick "Stoney" Steyn, Andrew Walden, the assistant PH, and finally a Tanzanian government game scout who was there to record what was shot and where, and to make sure we complied with the country's game laws. He carried a .375 Holland & Holland. Stanton and I were each armed with a .458 Lott, his a Brno with express sights, mine a Ruger Model 77 with a Leupold 1.5X–5X scope—a concession to my 63-year-old eyes and to the bushveldt. (That's a general term for scattered grasslands and mixed forests, in the shadows of which a whole herd of buffalo can be difficult to see.)

Several friends experienced in hunting dangerous African game had advised me to bring the .458 Lott, a formidable gun firing a 510-grain bullet from a cartridge resembling an anti-aircraft round. The first time I shot it at the range, I felt as if I'd been punched in the shoulder by the young Mike Tyson.

Smaller calibers down to the .375 H&H are adequate for Cape buffalo so long as nothing goes wrong. However, when they do go wrong, they go dreadfully wrong, and the hunter will be thankful for a rifle that will stop the charge of a quadruped pickup truck pumped full of adrenaline.

The Story in the Dirt

We followed the buffalo's trail for well over two hours, through swales of grass six or seven feet high, through patches of light woods, into thick riverine forests bordering the dry sandy-bottomed streams called *korongos.* I should say that Pius, Fabian, and Stanton followed the trail, while I followed them. For me, interpreting the confusing language written in the dirt by half a dozen different species was like trying to make sense of *Finnegans Wake.* I would look right where the trackers and Stanton looked and could not for the life of me see whatever it was they saw.

Stanton attempted to educate me. "Those are new," he said, pointing at a couple of scrape marks on the pavement-hard earth. "They were made by his front hooves. You can tell he's an old bull because the edges are rounded off." Although he was only 34, Stanton, raised on a cattle ranch in Zimbabwe, had been hunting in Africa for almost 20 years, so I would have to take his word for it. Still, a suspicion lurked in the back of my mind that he and the trackers were faking things, putting on a show for their ignorant client.

The suspicion faded when we crossed another road. There, clear in the reddish dust, were the bull's prints. He was traveling southeast, conveniently into the wind. I was grateful for that spasmodic wind, and not only because it carried our scent away from our quarry. Between the hours of 7:30 and 11 in the morning, the dry-season climate in the Selous (pronounced Sell-*oo*) goes from pleasant to warm to hot to very hot to beastly hot. The numerical equivalent of *beastly* is 104 degrees Fahrenheit, making every puff of breeze feel as welcome and unmerited as grace.

We continued on, the trackers reading the text in the ground, and came across a mound of soft buffalo dung with flies on it. This was sign that didn't require expert analysis—the bull could not be far ahead. But the role luck plays in any form of hunting should not be underestimated. Half an hour later, we found his trail obliterated by the prints of a herd of cows, calves, and young bulls and gave up the pursuit.

"He had a pretty big track on him," Stanton remarked. "It's a pity there weren't three or four with him. It would have been so much easier to follow them."

Any Old Bull Will Do

Cape buffalo are gregarious animals, but when a male grows old, he leaves the herd to wander alone or with a small band of other geezers. Tanzanian game laws allow the shooting of females, except when they are pregnant or with calves. As buffalo cows are almost always pregnant or with calves, this effectively limits legal animals to males. Those approaching the end of their life spans—about 20 years—are preferred, and if none presents himself, any mature male will suffice. There are two reasons for this custom: (1) Older bulls generally sport the most impressive horns; (2) Cape buffalo have fairly short breeding lives, so in killing an older one, the hunter does little or no harm to a herd's ability to propagate itself.

I wasn't after a trophy for the wall or the record books. I was collecting horns and skulls for the American Museum of Natural History in New York, as well as liver samples for DNA analysis by researchers in the museum's Department of Mammalogy. I had volunteered my services to this institution because of my early education as a blue-collar hunter in the woods and fields of Illinois, Wisconsin, and Michigan.

According to the ethic I had been taught, one doesn't hunt purely for the sport of it but to serve some practical and beneficial end. In my youth, that meant putting food on your table or someone else's. We were going to eat whatever I shot and distribute the rest of the meat, but I thought the safari also presented an opportunity to make a contribution to science, however minor.

It was also a way of paying homage to Frederick Courteney Selous, for whom the vast reserve (at 21,000 square miles, it is considerably larger than Switzerland) is named. Selous came to southern Africa as a young man in the 1870s and is generally acknowledged to have been the greatest African hunter of all time. He was also a keen amateur naturalist as well as a gifted author, explorer, and soldier.

The Vision Thing

The day after our fruitless pursuit of the lone bull, we came upon the fresh spoor of a large herd about ten miles from camp near a dry water hole. We tracked the buffalo for the next four hours. They led us into the tangled forests that border the Ruaha to a depth of 2 or 3 miles. I was becoming slightly more literate in the language written in the earth and could distinguish the scrape marks of recent passage from older prints.

But I was in kindergarten while Stanton and the trackers held doctoral degrees. All three seemed to have superhuman vision that was doubtless the product of lives spent in the bush, away from artificial light, from TV and computer and movie screens. Maybe they saw the way our early ancestors did, when quickness of the eye spelled the difference between eating and going hungry.

Did I notice that large, dark circle in the grass? Yes, now that it was pointed out to me. That was where a buffalo had urinated, perhaps only minutes ago. Soon we could hear ruminant rumbles, an occasional bellow, branches cracking as the herd browsed in the scrub. Finally, Pius and Fabian spotted several animals, which remained invisible to me until I saw their tails switching back and forth.

Crouched low, communicating with hand signals, we began a stalk, trying to move quietly over a woodland floor carpeted in dead, dry-season leaves. It was like trying to sneak across a bed of broken glass. Cape buffalo have good eyesight and hearing, but their sense of smell is keenest. We tossed dirt and crumbled leaves into the air to test the wind, which swirled and eddied in unpredictable ways. Sure enough, an errant current spun around behind us, and the herd crashed off with a sound like a waterfall or a brushfire. Stanton climbed a termite mound as big as a haystack to see where they had gone, but the woods had swallowed them completely.

We started all over again and after another hour caught fleeting glimpses of the herd, each animal a massive, three-dimensional shadow in the shadows of the forest. Stealing up to within 30 or 40 yards,

Stanton raised his binoculars to look for mature bulls, which can be distinguished from cows and younger males by the development of the boss. He found one and, in a whisper, told me where it was.

In the twilight, I could not tell the animals apart. I could only see huge shapes the color of cast iron and the occasional flick of a tail. We moved closer, but the wind again betrayed us. Now I saw the bull, pounding away. Tossing all caution aside, Stanton ran in pursuit and I ran after Stanton. To our amazement, the bull, indeed the entire herd of 80 to 100 animals, stopped its flight. The bull stood a mere 20-odd yards off, behind a cow that masked all of him except his haunches.

With the scope turned down to its lowest power, I got down on one knee, raised the .458, and put his rear quarters in the crosshairs, waiting for the cow to move and give me a clear shoulder shot. A tsetse fly drilled through my shirt, another through my thick sock. It felt as if I were being stuck with hot hatpins, but I could do nothing but endure it. Stanton and I were utterly still, almost breathless. Behind us, the others were equally quiet. I assume it was the capricious wind that spooked the herd once more, and this time they ran a long way. In a display of the Cape buffalo's power, when the bull took flight his shoulder bumped a tree 30 feet tall and six inches in diameter, and it shook like a stick.

The Worst Bug in the World

The following day was a copy of the previous two. We began by attempting to relocate the herd but were seduced by the spoor of three or four old bulls that lured us into another long search, which accomplished nothing more than to put several more miles on our bodies' odometers and to add to our collection of tsetse bites.

This savage, bloodsucking insect, larger than a common housefly but slightly smaller than a horsefly, caused me to wonder whether a benevolent God truly reigns over the universe. It can be considered the hunter's friend because it transmits a fatal disease called *nagana* to domestic animals, so herdsmen keep their cattle out of areas where the tsetse is prevalent, thus preserving those areas for wildlife. On the other hand, it transmits *encephalitis lethargica*, a.k.a. sleeping sickness, to people. Tsetse flies do have one virtue, however; they have slow reactions, making them easy to kill.

Slogging toward a water hole, where we hoped to ambush the buffalo as they came in to drink, we heard a loud, alarming roar. Seventy-five yards away, a lioness lay, guarding a kill and a cub. It was awfully civil of her to warn us that we were getting too close, and we returned her politeness by backing off. Pausing to look through my binoculars, I saw her blood-smeared muzzle and her gaze fixed on me with an intense, unsettling concentration. She seemed to be looking at me and through me at the same time. "Your knees really start shaking when one of them charges you and you can see the yellow in its eyes," said Stanton.

We reached the water hole, sat under trees 60 yards downwind, and waited. Sometimes, scenery can compensate for the frustrations of a difficult hunt, but the landscape in our part of the Selous wasn't charming. In the dry season, its miombo forests—*miombo* being a term that covers many species of acacia and tropical hardwoods—had a strangely autumnal look, the lifeless orange leaves reminding me of a North American woods in mid-November. To this, the brushfires burning everywhere lent the aspect of a battleground. We saw a female sable—surely one of Africa's most beautiful animals—and two magnificent eland, but the band of aged bulls did not cooperate with our ambush plan. At dusk, the vehicle was summoned by radio to return us to camp.

Our camp was situated at a bend of the Ruaha, commanding a fine view downstream, where low hills rose above the tree-shrouded banks. A pod of hippopotami wallowed in the middle of the broad river, making their laughter-like call. The shores were attended by egrets and yellow-billed storks, and wedges of Egyptian geese flew overhead. Compared with the base camp, which had large wall tents, flush toilets, and showers, the fly camp was primitive—bell tents, a pit toilet, and bucket baths.

But in contrast to the spartan conditions I was accustomed to on hunts in Alaska, it was embarrassingly luxurious. The staff attended to and anticipated my every wish and need. If I left so much as a pair of socks in my tent, they would be washed that very day. If I went to fetch a cold beer from the cooler, someone would leap ahead and fetch it for me. If I wanted to wash up, someone else would escort me to the river, fill a five-gallon bucket—at some risk to himself, for crocodiles lurked in the Ruaha—and hand me a towel and a bar of soap.

And the meals prepared by the head cook, Rashidi Hussein, were splendid. It amazes me how African camp cooks, with one or two assistants and a couple of cast-iron pots, can accomplish more over an open fire than a New York chef can with a squad of sous-chefs and batteries of Viking ranges.

All of this—the view, the bath, the cold beer, and the fine dinner of spicy soup followed by chicken with roast potatoes and dessert—gave me a much needed lift. The hunt was nearing the halfway point, with nothing to show for it, and I was anxiously facing the possibility of reporting to the editors of this magazine that all I'd done was walk across miles of Africa, and to the director of the museum's Mammalogy Department that he would have to find another source for the horns, skulls, and DNA samples.

Stanton worked up a plan. All the buffalo sign we'd seen had been in a triangle formed by three water holes. The next morning, we would scout each one and, if necessary, cover the territory between them until we found something.

"We need to," he added. "We're running out of meat."

Shadows in the Bush

PHILIP CAPUTO

Part II

We left at first light and by 7:30 had picked up the spoor of a large herd, probably the same one we had chased two days before. The prints appeared to have been made earlier in the morning; the dung was soft. Fabian and Pius followed the track into some woods, then out into a meadow of golden grass dotted with trees. The easterly wind favored us, though I had learned not to trust it. After an hour we sighted the animals, resembling huge, gray-black boulders, some 200 yards away. It was the back end of the herd. Bulls are almost always in the lead, so we cut off to the left, cautiously working our way around to come nearer the front. The buffalo plodded into thicker scrub, lowing, bellowing, and breaking branches.

The stalk went on for an hour more and led in a U back to the road. With Wayne Stanton, the trackers, and I kicking dust to gauge the wind, we crept forward. In minutes, we'd caught up to the herd—it was off to our left. Each of us falling into a crouch, we came as close as ten yards to some animals. I saw a cow grazing so close by that I couldn't figure out how she hadn't seen me.

This was still the rear of the herd. The rest had crossed the road and gone down into a wide, deep *korongo,* more a valley than a riverbed. We turned off to stalk above it, concealed by tall grass as dense as the bristles on a paintbrush.

Stanton paused to point at a group of cows and calves 75 yards downhill, their backs to us. Dropping to all fours, like a pride of lions, we moved parallel to the *korongo,* came to a narrow gully, and crawled through it until we emerged onto a hillside stripped bare of grass by a brushfire. Blackened trees were still standing.

Looking down, Stanton scrutinized the herd, which had moved farther into the riverbed, grazing slowly, preparing to bed down for the day, showing no signs of alarm. The stalk was now well into its third hour, the sun was burning through broken clouds, and I was getting impatient. I had to caution myself not to rush things. One false move would make all this careful effort futile.

Trigger Time

The herd was about 150 yards away, a bit too far for shooting buffalo. Leaving the others behind, Stanton and I, cradling our rifles in our laps, went downhill on our backsides. Fabian followed with the shooting sticks. Using trees to hide our movements, it took a full quarter of an hour to cover 75 yards. Fabian set up the sticks, spreading the three legs wide so that I could fire sitting or kneeling.

"There's a mature bull with his head hidden by a tree and a cow alongside him, in front of him," Stanton whispered, pointing. "But his shoulder is exposed. Do you see him?" It took me several tries to spot him through my scope because the color of the animals blended so well into the charred hillside on the opposite side of the *korongo*. "There's a lump on his shoulder, with the sun on it, do you see that?" I answered that I did. "Aim for that," said Stanton.

Up to this point, with everyone doing the spotting and tracking, I had felt somewhat superfluous to the entire enterprise. Now I was at center stage and I had better do my job as well as the others had done theirs. What a difference between this and the photographic safari I'd taken in Kenya. Nothing was at stake there—miss a shot with a camera and I would get another.

Here everything was at stake. Miss with the rifle and I might kill the cow, which would be a disgrace, and might get me in trouble with the authorities. Wound the bull and I would be in more serious trouble with him, possibly getting myself or someone else killed or maimed. Stanton and I had agreed at the beginning of the hunt that he would not shoot backup for me, except in the most dire emergency. It was, in short, the moment of truth, at once scary and almost unbearably thrilling.

Resting the .458 in the crotch of the sticks, I cleared myself of all thought and emotion, centered the crosshairs on the lump on the bull's shoulder, drew in a breath, and exhaled slowly, squeezing the trigger at the same time. At the shot, the entire herd thundered off as one, a torrent of muscle and horn racing up over the opposite hill.

"You smoked him, Phil, good job!"

What was Stanton talking about? When I looked at where the bull had been, I saw nothing but burnt grass. In fact, there was something wrong with my vision. Things were clear out of my left eye but blurred out of my right.

"Where the hell is he?" I asked. "I don't see him."

Stanton reached down and picked up the right lens of my prescription shooting glasses. The Ruger's powerful recoil—which I hadn't felt in the excitement of the moment—had thrown my trigger hand against my glasses, popping the lens out of the frame.

With it replaced, I saw the bull atop the hill, some 40 yards from where I'd shot him. He was facing us, down on his knees, and as we approached for a finishing shot, he struggled to rise. I was close enough to see his eyes, baleful beneath his glinting horns. His intent was obvious—he meant to charge and kill the thing that had hurt him, but the bullet in him wouldn't allow his body to respond to his will. Moving to one side, I put a round in his spine. He fell, let out a bellow, and died.

I took everyone's congratulations with what I hoped was humility and grace, and thanked them all, then silently did the old Indian thing by thanking the buffalo's spirit. I didn't realize how much adrenaline was pouring through me until I held my hand out with the fingers spread. They were shaking.

All Heart

The skinning and butchering took over an hour, and I was pleased to see that very little, not even the intestines, would be left to the vultures and hyenas. I cut a piece of the liver and placed it in one of the tissue tubes from the American Museum of Natural History, for which I was collecting samples. This I tagged with the name of the species, my name, and the date and GPS coordinates of where it was taken.

Pius showed me the bull's heart, pierced by my first shot. It was another demonstration of how strong and tenacious of life a Cape buffalo is. This one was only an average bull, but he had run 40 yards and was prepared to do battle with a .458 soft-nose through his heart. I felt then, in roughly equal measure, pride in my shooting skills and sadness for what those skills had done. It seemed peculiar that something as puny as I could take the life of something this big and strong. Killing such a creature, whether for food, science, sport, or all three, was no cause for public or private chest thumping.

There was rejoicing at camp. Buffalo meat is quite tasty, and the staff were looking forward to their portion. Chef Hussein's dinner—buffalo tenderloin prepared in a relish of sweet caramelized onion—was preceded by the African version of Rocky Mountain oysters. Hussein had cut the bull's testicles into medallions and sautéed them in butter and oil. Stoney Steyn, who is very particular about what he eats, didn't realize the nature of the appetizer until he remarked, "These mushrooms are excellent," causing Stanton, assistant PH Andrew Walden, and me to double over in laughter. The whole camp chuckled at Steyn's expense as, with a grimace, he set the delight aside. Walden urged him to finish it. "You have a young wife waiting for you in Durban," he said to the 54-year-old photographer. "Don't you feel the power?"

Buffalo No. 2

It was back to business the next day. I had license to shoot two Cape buffalo, and there was a general feeling among the staff that this foot safari would not be successful until I bagged the second. That was my feeling as well. Before leaving the States, in a moment of overconfidence, I had promised the museum two sets of buffalo horns and skulls. We saw a trio of bull elephants shambling along in the early-morning light. Later there were sable, impala, hartebeest, and zebra, all of which I could shoot, except for sable; but we passed them up, intent on another buffalo bull.

Late in the morning we found a herd, then it was track and stalk once again. We came close to several males, which Stanton deemed too young to shoot. He added that if we were patient, we would find a mature one. Patient we were, but the ever shifting wind tricked us for the umpteenth time and the herd spooked off into woods so thick that it was almost impossible to see them.

We then lunched on buffalo burgers in a sand river, napped, and waited for the animals to settle down before resuming the hunt. Two hours later, we had to quit.

I took my usual bucket bath at the river, washing off a thick veneer of dirt and dried sweat, and delighted in the evening wind blowing on my naked skin. At dinner—buffalo tongue for an appetizer, a buffalo kebab for the main course—Stanton reminded me, as if I needed reminding, that seven days had been allotted for buffalo hunting. Tomorrow was the seventh day, after which I would have to content myself with lesser game.

It was all of a piece with the day before: a seven- to eight-mile tramp in punishing heat, bedeviled by tsetse flies, my hands and arms scratched by thorns. Getting close to a herd, only to have the cursed wind turn on us and panic the animals into a cross-country race. Once more, we wound up in a jungle-like forest, where the only thing we saw of note was a gorgeous trogon with a luminous green body and a red throat, a bird so rare that it was the first one Stanton had ever seen, though he'd lived all his life in Africa.

About an hour before dusk, we resigned ourselves—the buffalo hunt was finished. Madebe, the driver, was radioed to pick us up. As the Land Rover approached, Fabian and Pius said in whispers that sounded like shouts, "*Nyati!*" and sprinted down the road. "An old bull!" Stanton said, jogging behind them. I took off and caught up with Fabian as he was setting up the shooting sticks.

He pointed down a hill. I didn't see a thing that looked like a buffalo or any animal for that matter. "Look more to your left," Stanton told me. Sixty to 70 yards away, the bull stood in the woods, staring at us. A moment later, he turned and moved off. Stanton and the trackers ran along the road, parallel to the buffalo's line of travel. Fabian set up the sticks a second time. Resting the rifle, I followed Stanton's directions, swinging the scope till I saw the bull, which had again stopped. He was facing me at about a 45-degree angle.

"Aim for the left side of his chest and you should break his shoulder or hit his lungs."

I was a bit shaky from the run and had trouble keeping the rifle steady, despite the rest afforded by the sticks. When the scope settled on the bull's chest, the left side, I fired. I knew I'd hit him solidly, but he was running nevertheless. My blood was up, or maybe I was just feeling mean from all the heat and frustration and fly bites. At any rate, I dashed downhill after him, and this time it was Stanton and the trackers following me. The old bull was stumbling. I ran till I was broadside of him, then, from 20 yards, slipped a hasty sling around my arm and shot him through the lungs. It took a third round to bring him down for good.

Fabian and Pius began to clap their hands with a syncopated beat, singing some chant that contained the word *babu*. Walden, gun bearer Hassani, and driver Madebe took up the song, dancing in a circle.

"What are they doing?" I asked Stanton.

"They're singing about you," he replied. "*Babu* means 'grandfather' in Swahili. They're singing about how the old grandfather killed the old bull."

I looked at the buffalo. It was an old one indeed, with short but well-developed horns, a prominent boss, and a hide scarred from many battles with other males. I rested my hand on his massive neck.

"You needn't feel any regrets about this one," Stanton said. "He had about a year to go. Old age or the lions would have gotten him."

It was full night by the time we returned to camp with the quartered carcass. Madebe had radioed ahead, and the whole camp was waiting for me, calling out *"Babu, ahyay! Babu, ahyay!"* as I climbed out of the vehicle. Four men lifted me up in a camp chair and carried me to the fire, around which they and the others danced and sang. It was an elemental scene: the African rhythms of chant and handclap, the fire reflecting off the faces of the men, while the hippos chortled in the river and a hyena whooped, far off in the darkness.

Reprinted with permission of the author and *Field & Stream Magazine*.

The Wire

DAVID E. PETZAL

We found the carcasses at 11 in the morning. The Zimbabwean sun had mummified them in the positions of agony in which they died. There were six, a young sable cow and five impala, spaced in a line 200 yards long. Their killer was the principal author of death and suffering among Africa's wildlife, the poacher's snare. They had been grabbed by the neck or the leg or the body and had perished from thirst and hunger and exhaustion. Whoever set the snares had never come back to collect the bodies while they were still usable as meat.

Clive Perkins, my PH, watched as our trackers collected the wire and said in a voice as filled with bitterness as any voice I have ever heard:

"Welcome to Africa, David Petzal."

We were, however, to see worse.

Two days later I killed a dry Cape buffalo cow whose hoof had been ensnared at the hock. She had managed to break free, but the wire had dug so deeply that we could not dig it out with a knife, and the whole lower leg was grotesquely swollen. We heaved her into the truck and drove her back to camp, and on the way we saw another buffalo cow that had stepped in the wrong place. This one, however, had amputated her left foreleg halfway up.

Africa deals with the halt and the maimed in the form of lions and hyenas, which do not always bother with the formality of killing what they dine on, and while it would have been merciful to shoot the second cow then and there, we couldn't. She was only 75 yards away, but she was on another hunting concession, and woe betide the professional hunter who lets his clients trespass for whatever reason. The only thing we could do, said PH Wayne Van Den Bergh, was go back to camp, call the manager of the neighboring concession, and get permission. Then it would be a simple job to backtrack and shoot her.

"Of course," said the concession manager, so back we went, and she wasn't there. We didn't think she would move far because animals, particularly crippled ones, do not like to travel in the heat of an African high noon. We dismounted the truck and began to track her.

There were six of us: Clive Perkins; Wayne Van Den Bergh; PH Theo Bronkhorst, who ran our concession; Willard Ncube, who tracked for Wayne; Elias (he pronounced it *EEL*ias) Mathe, who tracked for Clive; and me. When you trail game, the trackers normally go a few yards ahead of the people with rifles, but when you follow a wounded Cape buffalo, the people with rifles stay up front. The trackers look for sign, and you keep your eyes forward, watching for a gray shape that will come hurtling at you with jackrabbit speed.

Her track led us out of the *mopane* woods where we began and into the open. She had gotten into a dry riverbed that was overgrown with waist-high grass. Elias shouted, and we got a glimpse of her head. She was cantering on three legs, moving much faster than we could, and there was no time to even snap a shot at her before she vanished into the grass.

We followed, and the grass changed to progressively taller reeds, which soon were head-high. We were now trailing blind, and it was apparent that if we were tracking her, she was leading us. The reeds were so dense that if you thrust your arm into them you could not see your hand. Theo and Clive left the riverbed for the bank; if she came out of the reeds they would be able to see her and shoot her.

Within another few hundred yards the reeds were ten and 12 feet high and we were reduced to crawling through tunnels left by buffalo that used this place as a refuge during the heat of the day. Sometimes our quarry left the tunnels and pushed her way through standing reeds, and we were forced to claw our way after her.

That she was going to charge eventually was a given, and there would be no warning, no time to aim. If we got a chance to shoot at all it would be point, pray, and pull the trigger. Wayne made his way back to me.

"Listen," he whispered, "if you have to shoot her off one of us, for Christ's sake shoot upward so you don't hit us."

Our own rifles were as much danger to us as they were to the buffalo. A trigger can snag, or a muzzle can cross a human back, and that is as good as a horn through the chest. A PH with whom I hunted years ago, as careful an individual as you would want, shot a colleague while trying to stop a leopard charge. The man he shot lived, but will never really recover.

Theo and Clive yelled at us to come up on the bank. One of the other PHs had arrived, and we lurched out of the reeds and into the shade. A water bottle was passed around and I took a couple of swallows, but it made no difference. It was like pouring water on a hot stovetop.

There seemed to be nothing else to do, so the four of us prepared to wade back in.

"If she gets her head into you, grab her horns and twist," Theo said. "She can't stay on her feet with that missing leg."

I waited for him to smile and show he was kidding, but he was not.

Back we went. By now we had crowded her into the end of the reedbed. She had perhaps two acres in which to maneuver, but all she had to do was keep a few steps ahead of us and pick her time to charge.

She did. There was no warning at all. There was simply a crash of reeds and a massive gray shape blotted out the sun. Wayne fired at it from a crouch; I shot across my chest while falling backward. Then the shape vanished. I could almost have touched it with my rifle barrel. There was a patch of blood on the ground and Elias was smiling.

"Did we kill her?" I asked.

"No," he said, and I realized he was smiling because she had not killed him. I think the combination of nearly impassable reeds and the missing leg saved us. She could not keep her footing in that tangle, fell, scrambled up with possibly one or two bullets in her, and fled. If she had charged with four legs, she would have killed one of us.

We kept going, and after only a few yards Willard froze.

"Shoot," he said, pointing into the reeds.

I couldn't see beyond my rifle barrel, but I fired where he pointed.

"Shoot," he said, pointing in a different direction, and I did.

"Reload," said Willard, but I was already doing that.

We stumbled onward, and Wayne suddenly lurched back in agony. A reed stalk had speared him in his eye, and he was now down to one usable eye and one round of ammunition. Wayne, Willis, and Elias had a short talk in Ndebele, the sum of which was: "We're not going to get lucky twice and it's time to get the hell out of here."

So we left the reeds, and Theo summed up our efforts perfectly: "Man, that was stupid."

There was only one thing left to try. Willard and Elias climbed an acacia tree while Theo and I stood on the roof of the truck. We would try to look down into the reeds and shoot from above. Clive blocked off the end of the reedbed, and Wayne, who has a wife and two children, borrowed ammunition from Clive and headed back into the riverbed.

We could see the reeds waving as the buffalo maneuvered, and Clive got a glimpse of her. He shot, and was sure he connected, but it was a standoff. She would not leave the reedbed in daylight, and we could not go in after her. Theo called an end to it, and Wayne came out of the reedbed. We drove along the riverbank for a while, checking for tracks, but there was really no chance of finding any. It ended.

A few days later I asked Theo if he would ever know what happened to her, and he said no, something would drag her down and she would vanish. In fact, she was almost certainly dead as we spoke.

So be it. We failed. I would like to think that we got a few bullets into her and at least shortened her suffering if we could not end it outright.

There is one thing more. I would like to think that somewhere in one of the nastier neighborhoods in hell there is a wire loop waiting for the foot of the poacher who snared her.

PART X

Reflections on Our Sport

To Hunt: The Question of Killing

THOMAS MCINTYRE

At sixteen I hunted and killed a barren-ground caribou. He bedded on Alaska tundra under a lead sky, and I bellied to the rim of the basin and shot him through the lungs with a rifle I borrowed from my father. The bull shuddered and rolled to his side, big-hoofed legs stiffening, heavy-antlered head sinking. I rose and bolted another round, setting the safety. Pink blood frothed from his nostrils; and as I walked to him, he gasped, drowning. The big hooves kicked, and a round staring eye clouded from ice-water clear to bottle green. The caribou stopped shuddering. I trembled still . . .

To arrive at an at best imperfect understanding of the hunt in these latter days, it is almost impossible not to rely on the Spaniard José Ortega y Gasset, again. A cranky, rather-more-than-elitist existentialist critic of "mass man," Ortega y Gasset remained a meritocratic republican. Although quoted to the brink of emesis by hunters desperate to demonstrate their literacy, his book-length essay, *Meditations on Hunting*, was the 20th century's most luminous explication of the hunt. And at the heart of *Meditations* lay the truth that after his spotting, pursuit, and stalking of an animal, "The hunter is a death dealer."

Hunting deals, inescapably, in death. Or, more precisely, killing. Killing is what places the hunter (animal and human) apart from every other walker in the woods. Not that this always explains the kill to the satisfaction of our friends, especially those of the more doctrinaire environmentalist or animal-zealot stripe, or often to our own families. Sometimes not even entirely satisfactorily to ourselves.

This killing is, of course, not homicide or the martial hunting of "armed men," but the legal killing in the hunt of wild animals (traditional game animals, ones neither endangered as a species nor representing members of an imperiled population), with the recovery and consumption of the animal's body moral and ethical obligations of that killing. The killing in hunting is not murder incognito—assuming a relative absence of psychopathological impulse. It is killing not for the sake (or thrill) of killing, and therefore causes hunters, oddly, to be excruciatingly tongue-tied about what draws them to the hunt, of which the kill is such an indissoluble component. Partly that's a matter of trying to tell a stranger about rock 'n' roll, but also because, as Ortega y Gasset says, hunting means "accepting reason's insufficiencies." The desire to hunt, which must inevitably lead to killing (at least by intent), comes from a place well before consciousness and words, so that when it arises today it does so almost beyond articulation. Most hunters cannot even say when it began for them, yet some try.

At four I entered a small dark Lascaux of a den in my father's best friend's house. Both men were employed in aerospace, the industry just then becoming the ample bosom of the Southern California economy; but on the paneled walls of the inner space of that den were not heroic photos of rocket launches but the mounted heads of a deer, an elk, and a wild boar, with a black-bear skin on the hardwood floor. There were also the head of a red African forest buffalo and a pair of perfect rose-ivory tusks, my father's friend having taken all his savings, cashed out his wife's life-insurance policy, and gone to (then) French Equatorial Africa to kill an elephant at less than thirty paces in dense jungle. No such icons would ever be found on the avocado-hued walls or aqua pile carpet of our home; and it was inconceivable to me that they could be found anywhere else inside suburban Los Angeles county tract housing.

In later years there would be my walking behind on desultory hunts for farm-raised pheasants set out by the State of California and fetching birds during the once-a-year San Joaquin Valley mourning-dove shoots that my father approached as social requirements rather than outings, "outing" in its earlier connotation representing a letting loose for which my mad parent in his life was never entirely prepared. Through it all my mind grew into its own Lascaux of feathers and horns and tusks, until I was old enough to shoulder my own gun. Then the painted walls expanded only more.

The summer I convinced my father to let me go to the Talkeetna Mountains, taking the rifle he owned but never used, was the summer of '68, of Chicago police in Lincoln Park and Soviet tanks in Wenceslaus Square, which were matters of minor note to me compared to my desire to hunt something "bigger than me." Then, looking at the caribou, the summit of Denali beyond, and the sky above, I realized that everything around me in the hunt was bigger than me, bigger than the caribou, too. It was bigger than both of us.

So, I had killed. What was it, though, I had really done? Killing is the most incomprehensible aspect of the hunt to a large extent because we have almost no widespread experience of the reverential or even prosaic forms of killing animals, no longer sacrificing, or even slaughtering, our own livestock. The writer Reynolds Price said, in one of those plummy commentaries National Public Radio so dotes on broadcasting, that "death has become almost the last obscenity, the single thing we're loath to discuss in public." This could, with all due respect, only be the opinion of an intellectual who must prattle on almost ceaselessly with his peers about death. It is based on an assumption that no one outside the cloister of the academy discusses so fraught a subject, when in fact we as a population have become further steeped than Aztec priests in a cult of death. It is impossible not to hear a constant drone about the "end-of-life experience" or oxymoronically termed "living wills," "doctor-assisted suicide," "death with dignity," and the "right to die" (more an obligation, isn't it?). The highest compliment to be paid fashion and food is that they are "to die for." Death be not just proud, these days, but darn-near haughty.

With this peculiar exaltation of death, though, killing, as identified above, remains a conundrum. People can pruriently covet the sight of death at a remove (the fiery crashes on stockcar tracks, exploding space shuttles, fatal accidents memorialized on the Web, network-televised euthanasia, and as Susan Sontag wrote, "What pornography [both rampant and tolerated, I would add] is really about, ultimately, isn't sex but death") while believing it iniquitous, even inhuman, to participate in the killing of the hunt. And yet that killing can never be genuinely understood or experienced without direct participation (which is what makes most writing about it, and almost all visual depictions of it—such as some hideously obscene televised hunting shows dwelling in the depths of the cable morass—abysmal). The best that can be done is to try to answer the questions such killing raises.

Is it fun? Is it wicked? Most important, is there anything erotic about it?

Bull, bedded, belly, shuddering, stiffening, rolled, gasped, trembled—what other conclusion could there be than that killing must be leather-and-latex erotic? This is possible to conclude because (aside from the Freudianization of all human behavior, and the view of some that the hunt is a form of "rapism") hunting and sex can appear to be the last natural acts humans enjoy on earth. Not for nothing is intercourse vulgarly characterized as the "wild thing"; for a great many of us sex is the final bivouac in the wild, our only first-hand experience of it anymore. So sex becomes the template we, knowing no better, place over all wild experience, unable to recall that there was once for humans, and yet for animals, a little more to it than that. Sex in the wild, as it were, is an intense (often perilous) but seasonal activity, and only one of many wild conditions, far more time taken up by gestation, birth, nurturing, feeding, gathering, divination, migrating, concealment, flight—and killing. It is a subsequence of modernism that everything be classified as erotic (and practically a shibboleth of postmodernism that "all sex is rape"); but killing is not a division of a corporation established by Eros: in the wild it is its own going concern.

What about fun?

The correct response given by the more enlightened hunter of the day is that he takes no pleasure in killing. He does it solely in pious acknowledgement of the cost of his food, or as a desperate, unavoidable, altruistic, anguished conservation measure ("thinning the herd"). Which is all, if you will forgive me, more than passing strange. Very few people in the industrialized world are hunters for any reason other than personal choice; far from bumming out its participants, hunting is, in the words of another Spaniard, Felipe Fernández-Armesto, in his history of food, "an attractive way of life, which still exercises a romantic appeal for some people in sedentary and even urban societies: thousands of years of civilization seem insufficient to scratch out the savage under the skin . . ."

Aldo Leopold, the "father of wildlife management," wrote, "We seek contacts with nature because we derive pleasure from them," and hunting is contact with nature at the most elemental level. It is a mistake, though, to equate *pleasure* with *fun*, with its implication of frivolousness. Pleasure is a primary constituent of life, and not necessarily just human life. You can see this in real "savages," those indigenous hunters for whom killing is hardly a style-of-life option. What experience I have had of such hunters, for whom killing can be both arduous and precarious, is that they tend to display something akin to sacred delight when an animal is brought down: why not, when a kill can provide food, clothing, craft material, even objects of veneration, all in a tidy bundle? Outside the human realm, watch the predators on the

Discovery Channel or Animal Planet, if you cannot witness them elsewhere. Even in close-up it's hard to detect much solemnity or remorse as the cheetah tumbles the Thomson's gazelle in a billow of ochre dust, or the croc rolls in the black river mud, the wildebeest calf in its toothsome grin. There aren't even crocodile tears.

The question should be whether one hunts for some sort of "joy of killing." I can say only that I hunt to hunt. I could find far less taxing means of satisfying an obsessive love of killing, had I one, than by hiking for miles through chaparral to shoot a plateful of quail. And in fact, the too-easy, "lucky" kill can rob the hunt of much of its savor. Killing, though, I must admit, does give me pleasure when I do it well. I believe this is the raw response to good killing by all those who truly love to hunt. I know of nothing we do that is not, without coercion, finally rooted in pleasure, however postponed or sublimated or lofty. Denials of the pleasure inherent in the good kill are less heartfelt than they are hunters' p.c. means of throwing an increasingly denunciatory public off the scent.

Then does this make it wicked?

In his NPR soliloquy, Price, quoting A. E. Housman's translation of lines from the Roman poet Horace—*Feast then they heart, for what the heart has had / The fingers of no heir will ever hold*—counseled that unless "a heart craves blood and cruelty, its owner should feed it lavishly." What Price did not explain was how blood and cruelty are intrinsically linked, making it wrong to feed with blood—certain kinds, anyway. Blood can be holy, sacrificial, celebratory, and yet not cruel. Some of the most profound cruelties involve the shedding of not a single drop.

In our ever-more denatured world, though, we can recognize nothing in spilled blood but heartlessness. This due not to any special characteristic of blood so much as of our stunted perception that makes us want to place our faith in a chimera like the one evoked by such phrases as "cruelty-free" or "no animals were harmed in the . . . etc." Never mind that it is most often utilized as a marketing ploy by cosmetics companies or a goad animal-rightists brandish for extorting contributions from media conglomerates; it represents a real desire (perhaps to deny the "savage under the skin"), although one that fails to account for each second of sentient existence that rides upon (or at the very least owes an irredeemable debt to) an innate bow wave of cruelty from which we are powerless to exempt any living creature, ourselves included. Which is not to say that blood/killing cannot be cruel.

In true hunting, though, cruelty is never the goal and is either inadvertent or the result of inexperience. Good hunting means good killing. Good killing means possessing the skill, knowledge, and empathy to be able to inflict a wound that will end an animal's life in a matter of heartbeats, honorably, and with a minimum of sensation, let alone pain. When an animal is killed well, to appropriate (who else?) Hemingway's words, all of him will race all the rest of him to the ground, leaving the hunter with almost no opportunity for regret. Bad killing—fumbled, prolonged, visibly painful—can fill a hunter with physical unease, even disgust, both for the unintended cruelty and the dishonor to the animal. Bad killing, though, to paraphrase Ortega y Gasset a final time, exists only at the expense of good killing.

There was a time when good killing mattered, when men were expected to be good killers. There is D. H. Lawrence's oft-repeated chestnut, referring to James Fenimore Cooper's *Deerslayer*, about how the "essential American soul is hard, isolate, stoic, and a killer." What never gets quoted is Lawrence's next sentence: "It has never yet melted." Maybe not in Lawrence's day; but since then the essential American soul, at least that of sensitized man (I hesitate to use the now rather passé neologism "metrosexual"), has turned into nothing less than a sump of goo.

Killing has never been the exclusive route to manhood (or personhood), but neither has being abstractly repulsed by or irrationally ignorant of it. A soul that has neurotically diagnosed itself as unfit to kill, and wishes to advertise itself as such, can, curiously, all too often be a soul unfit for trustworthiness, commitment, self-sacrifice, and courage, as well.

I kill, and try to kill well, because it is a difficult and complex physical act, involves moral and ethical reflection, compels me to look at death—and life—without an arbiter, and is an authentic thing in a grotesquely inauthentic world.

An end to good killing will lead not to a sounder environment, but will merely be evidence of one too deteriorated to sustain any longer the most primeval of nature's processes. Seeing a better world in the cessation of killing is like the conscious refusal of the "environmental movement's leading intellects" to bear children for the sake of a better planet, because they consider it, puzzlingly, the "most humane thing" to do. Hardly humane; more like unearthly, and an endeavor to prove a negative: That it *enriches* the world to withhold a child from it. Similarly, how it will be a poorer world that can no longer afford human hunting. (In the end, neither the child nor the hunt is what impoverishes the earth.)

Within his environment all of a caribou's life—all of the life of the caribou I killed—is an anticipation of the hunter, the killer, in whatever shape he assumes (the caribou's existence, in fact, owes itself to being hunted and killed, because that is how the caribou was shaped by evolution: *What but the wolf's tooth whittled so fine/The fleet limbs of the antelope?* as Robinson Jeffers wrote). If the killer were not me, then it would be the wolf's tooth or Old Ephraim the grizzly or winter, no animal going gentle into any good night (of them all, death by hunter may actually be gentlest). And yet the caribou never fears dying, is never enthralled by it, never once goes on the FM radio to meditate upon its meaning. If it were possible for death's lovers to tell the caribou how vital (*sic*) it is to embrace, even cherish death, it probably would shrug, if caribou shrug, and graze on.

Standing beside the body of a dead caribou, the trembling ebbing, I wondered at the thing of killing, which now seemed quite small, too. Against the sweep of the tundra, against the snows of Denali, against the curtain of light that would flourish late in the night sky, it was small and frail. All that I saw was greater than killing—this kind of killing. It made death itself, even my own someday, not some supreme Moloch, but something perceptibly withered and feeble, hardly worth mentioning. Hunting and killing gave me that. It let me shrug, too.

Would I have learned this without first having hunted and killed? There is no way now in which it will ever be possible for me to know.

Hunting According to Ortega

NELSON BRYANT

The day is gray and damp. The wet snow that fell during the night is nearly gone from the ground and the last messes of it have long since slipped from the dark green spruce branches.

I am alone in a hunting cabin, my companions having gone forth into the forest; the cylindrical sheet-iron wood stove sends forth a circle of warmth and the pungent smell of wood smoke pervades the room, an aroma that never fails to fill me with leisure that is nostalgia and anticipation.

Last night we talked of hunting and the reason for it, and today that talk is still with me, not only because of our conversation, but also because I have in my duffle bag a dozen letters from readers who expressed shock, bewilderment, sarcasm and sadness at a recent column which, after describing a day of shooting woodcock, I closed with the observation that there is no sweeter sight or sound in the natural world than the singing, spiraling courtship flight of the male woodcock in spring.

One man wrote that the experience of observing the courtship flight was apparently so sweet that I couldn't bear it and had to, therefore, endeavor to eliminate its source.

One wonders if non-hunters can ever be persuaded to understand, let alone endorse the hunter's raison d'être.

Probably the best explanation of why man hunts is in Jose Ortega y Gasset's *Meditations on Hunting*, recently republished by Charles Scribner & Sons. Ortega, Spain's foremost twentieth-century philosopher, has, according to Dr. Paul Shepard of Dartmouth College, "grasped that essential human nature is inseparable from the hunting and killing of animals and that from this comes the most advanced aspects of human behavior."

In *Meditations*, Ortega writes: "Thus the principle which inspires hunting for sport is that of artificially perpetuating, as a possibility for man, a situation which is archaic in the highest degree: that early state in which, already human, he lived within the orbit of animal existence."

And again: ". . . hunting has perpetually occupied the highest rank in the repertory of man's happiness . . . it is not essential to the hunt that it be successful. On the contrary, if the hunter's efforts were always inevitably successful it would not be the effort we call hunting, it would be something else."

Of great importance is Ortega's awareness that success is not an essential ingredient of the hunt. There are men who have, for example, gained a great deal of pleasure for more than a decade of unsuccessful hunting for deer. They would, one should hasten to say, have got the same pleasure from pursuing the animals with an empty rifle. It is important that there is a potential for bringing the confrontation between deer and man to a conclusion. Yet there are men, and there is one hunting out of this cabin today, who, when given an opportunity to kill a deer, have passed it up on several occasions. The animals may have been too small, it may have been a doe rather than a buck, the shot offered may not have been ideal—that is to say that there was a good chance the animal could not be killed cleanly—or it may have been that the beauty of the deer, perhaps standing half in sunlight, half in shade, stayed the hunter's trigger finger.

All this is to suggest that most hunters are not brutish men with a lust to kill. Their relationship with wild creatures is much more complicated and sensitive than the average opponent of the pursuit would suppose.

Twilight is descending early outside the cabin. Under the spruces the gloom is deep; the bare lean trunks of the leafless hardwoods on the near hillside are half obscured by mist, and coming through them, empty-handed, is one of my companions.

The Wealth of Age

LEE WULFF

From the front cover of the magazine, a big caribou bull stared at me. In my youth, that would have set me dreaming of going on a caribou hunt. Instead, my mind flashed back to Jim John and what he called the "harvest fields" of the upper Gander River in Newfoundland. The year was 1940, and I was 35.

Jim was a full-blooded Micmac Indian. His home was on the south coast of Newfoundland some seventy miles away. He was one of the best guides in the province, and he had brought me to this, his favorite hunting area. We had a few days of fruitless hunting behind us when we spotted a stag (the Newfoundlanders use the English "stag" for males instead of the American "bull"). The animal was about a mile away, and he looked good through the binoculars. If we hurried, Jim said, we could intercept him, and we took off.

We were making a film, so there were three of us on the lookout point—Jim, my cameraman, and I. Halfway along, the came man gave Jim has magazine camera and promised to come with the big camera and tripod as soon as he heard a shot. Jim was over 50 then, but he was still a traveling fool, and we ran more than we walked across the rough, going till we came to a jutting finger of the forest that penetrated the muskeg. We were still breathing hard when the caribou came into the open just where Jim, knowing the caribou trails, knew he'd show. The bull stood there, a little more than 100 yards away. He looked just like the caribou on the magazine's front cover. He was facing us and staring right at us.

By prearrangement, I would tell Jim when to start the little camera for its 20-second run. I had to be sure he'd start filming before I shot and that I would be able to shoot before the camera ran out of time. I knelt to take the shot.

It was a tableau. None of us moved, including the caribou. I looked along the iron sights and thought, "If I shoot now, I may hit the head or antlers and spoil them and the pictures. Should I wait? If I do, will he bolt and leave me with a running shot and a poor chance for a clean kill?" The seconds ticked by.

Slowly, the antlered head started to swing, a sign that he was ready to run. Without a word from me, Jim started the camera. I heard it running, and as the head lifted and the antlers cleared the white of his neck, I squeezed off the shot.

The bullet hit the spine in the neck, and he dropped in his tracks. It was a lucky shot under great pressure. Anything other than an instantaneous kill cannot be shown in a film.

That's just one of the animals I remember when my thoughts turn to caribou country. In memory, I recapture the look and smell of the yellow muskeg and the red blueberry barrens lying between the patches of dark timber. I close my eyes, and I am there.

The wealth of age comes in having past reality to reflect upon instead of future uncertainty to dream about. It lies in knowing firsthand instead of relying on the word of someone else to make decisions. It comes from having done most of the things you really wanted to do at least once and knowing those you enjoy most and want to do again and again. It lies in wisdom, which can only come from experience. Knowledge is something youth may have as well as old-timers. Wisdom comes from testing mere knowledge and being able to use it effectively.

Physical things, too, can be the gift of age. I remember 1938 and a fishing trip in the northern bush. The black flies were as thick and as fierce as I ever remember. The fly dopes of that day were not very effective, and in a few days we ran out of them. My guide said, "Wait long enough, and you'll get used to the bugs like I am."

He was right. I was bitten so much that I grew nauseated and felt physically ill for two days. He called it "fly fever."

Then the miracle happened. After that, I could watch a black fly bite me and feel no pain. The fly would go off, leaving a tiny, round, red mark on my flesh. Within a day the red spot would turn black. There was no swelling, and by the third day, even that small black reminder of the fly's visit was gone. That immunity is still with me, though perhaps not to the same degree, and I'm seldom bitten. When others around me are complaining of bites, I'm comfortable and disdain fly dope. It's truly a gift of having lived and experienced.

I was about 45 when I admitted to myself that my muscles would never again be what they once were and that I'd have to start using my head to make up for their failings. I couldn't race full tilt across a bog to intercept a caribou. I couldn't lift and carry as much or more than anyone else in the party and race to be the leader on the trail. Thinking comes harder when good muscles have previously given you a great advantage, but thinking helps you to do your share of the physical things when you grow older.

I had the first light seaplane in Newfoundland and Labrador. Flying a hydroplane let me fish the then-uncharted rivers, and I fished them before the other planes came and today's crowds moved in. As a result, I have a special sense about playing Atlantic salmon that came only with time and long experience. I have caught at least 3,000 salmon, and the total may be 4,000. I can watch one of the old movies of me playing a salmon in the late 1930s and see how much my tactics have changed. I've learned how well angle and pressure changes can be used to control a fish's runs and his position in a pool. I have learned that in playing stream fish, the best position for the angler is downstream of the fish so that it fights not only your pressure, but the flow of the stream as well. I used to race downstream to keep ahead of the fish, relying on my fleetness of foot and balance to get to the right places. With time, I learned to use only light pressures so the fish stayed in the pool, instead of pressuring them into wild, downstream runs, and I brought them in more swiftly than before.

With the big fish of the sea, there was a greater need to use my strength efficiently. I learned to work with static pressure so that the boat traveled on the same course and at the same speed as the fish as often as possible. The line neither comes off the reel nor is reeled in, so that maximum strain can be put on the fish with the minimum effort. I learned to break down the fish's will to resist.

At 40, when my muscles were beginning their downward slide, it would have been hard to imagine that at 72 I'd be able to set a new 80-pound-test line-class record for giant bluefin tuna. I had to play that fish for two hours and 15 minutes, and I did it more with my mind or just as much as I did it with my muscles. That 895-pound record fish has been bettered, but as I write this, I'm in my 70s and I'm still trying for a tuna record. I came close to a new record in 1982, when I was 77, with a 960-pound bluefin tuna I caught in Nova Scotia. After 50, it is an interesting game to see how much you can accomplish with a minimum of physical effort.

Flycasting, like many other things, is a matter of skill and timing—of easy rhythm rather than power. Such things can be enjoyed all through life and perhaps most of all in the more-relaxed years of age. Paddle easily. Climb slowly. Choose the right places from the experience of other days, and enjoy the view to the fullest.

I have been flycasting since I was nine, but it was not until I was over 40 and started flying a light seaplane that I really learned to cast a fly into the wind. Newfoundland, the old pilots told me, was too windy for a light plane like my J-3 Cub, but the Cub and I survived and I learned to live with wind.

The gales would pour viciously over the mountains and beat down hard on the lakes and bays I had to land on. Watching, I saw that winds are rarely constant. They flowed over the earth like water over a rapid run, gusting along at varying speeds. I used to look down fearfully at the pattern of hard, black squalls in which I was about to risk my airplane and my life. Then it dawned on me that the way to beat the wind was to land into the wind at the tail of one of the black squalls. The wind was strong, and my ground speed was slow when I approached. Then, just as I lit on the water, I'd enter one of the slack wind periods and my plane could settle quickly onto the water.

And that's the best way to cast a fly into the wind. Let the tail of a gust take your line out on a hard back cast, and then, in the lull that follows, drive hard into and through the relatively calm spots behind the gust. Casts should be timed to the wind. Though you can't make as many casts as you can on a calm day, it's possible, without too much effort, to fish quite effectively when most anglers have retreated to the taverns.

When it comes to deer hunting, it's obvious that the older hunter has to slow down. He can't cover the terrain he did in his youth. However, his growing experience should give him a better understanding of the animal so that he will be at the right places at the right time more and more. Most of the time, he can plan to signal a friend to help drag out the deer. Failing that, he can often shoot where the dragging is all downhill. Old bird hunters, too, manage to get their share of the game, using slower-working dogs that cover the ground more thoroughly, and they know just when, in a bird's flight, is the best time to shoot.

An old man can build up out of his years a fund of knowledge that stands him in good stead when there are decisions to make. Watching trout in the small brooks as a boy, I learned that the hardest strikes always come when two fish are racing each other to get to the bait. Whenever I encounter an extra-hard strike, I still remember those racing trout of boyhood. As quickly as I play one fish, I cast back to the same spot, because another hungry fish should be there.

When I went up to Newfoundland in 1938 to pioneer that island's tuna fishing for the government, I knew the fish were big, and I hoped to set a record. I used stout hooks and stainless-steel wire-cable leaders headed up with a large bright-brass swivel. I hooked only one bluefin that looked like a record-breaker. I tossed a mackerel bait to that monstrous fish and watched him take it and race away just under the surface in smooth water. Then I saw his companion, equally large, rush in alongside. My line went slack. My tuna's friend had snapped at the flash of the big brass swivel and the bright bubble of air it made as it raced through the water. The second fish cut the doubled line. Since then, I've used no swivel at all or the smallest, dullest one I thought would not break before the leader did.

All of us are seeing things now that will vanish with the changing world, leaving those who hold such memories with a deeper realization of the inevitability of change. I had heard that the old north-woods trappers could build their cabins without a single nail and with an ax as the only tool. One of the great north-country guides built a cabin for me. I helped him cut and peel the poles of spruce and fir and then notch and place them. Using pressure and pegs and undercuts to hold things together or to hinge them, he made a beautiful cabin. Its roof was of birch bark overlaid with soil on which he planted sod to hold the whole thing steady. It was a beautiful cabin that I think is still standing. Its creation gave me a sense of similar skills our civilization has already lost.

Another wonderful thing that makes the late years great is that your kids grow up and go off on their own. They were so big a part of your life that the change when they go is a dramatic one. You would have thrown yourself in front of an oncoming car to push them out of the way. You had them in your mind in all your waking hours. They gave you a lot of pleasure, and you'll always remember the tow-headed three-year-old, now 40 with hair as black as yours once was, catching his first sunfish with squeals of pure delight. You remember flying back to a salmon camp and looking down to see his ten-year-old brother standing in the river. You watched the salmon he was playing, his first, leap in a splash of spray and sunlight.

When they were small, you worried that they'd fall into the Battenkill and drown. One of their playmates in the village had done that. As they grew up, you wondered at night if their delayed return meant that they'd been in an accident and you had a twinge of fear if the phone rang in the wee hours and they were still out.

When they finally went off on their own, there was a great sense of loss at first. Then you realized that bringing them to maturity as good, healthy citizens was your real goal and that you had achieved it. They are no longer the kids you cuddled. Now they are grownups you love in a different way. And you've passed on to them an understanding of the wild world that endures.

Mature, experienced people do their best creative work. It is a time to enjoy with the richness of friends, doing the things you most want to do.

There is a wealth in having sat around many campfires in a multitude of camps. It lies in the friends you make. When you have lived with them on the waters and in the woods and time has seasoned the friendship, it is far more secure and satisfying than those that develop casually, each person showing the other only a part of what he is. It may be that the greatest wealth of all lies in our friends.

Old friends can wade a trout stream together or walk a woodland cover and not encounter just the fish or the game of that day but also the memories of other days and other places. They've taken the bitter with the better and found it all rewarding.

The years beyond 50 have been by far the best of my life. I've had the physical capacity to do a great many things and the judgment to do them better than ever before. I haven't had to do anything I really haven't wanted to do during those years. I know I put my heart fully into each effort. Because of maturity and depth of interest in what I do, whether writing, making films, or playing a fish, each thing I do should be more complete and better than the things I did in my energetic youth.

It is good for the young to realize how rewarding the over-50 years can be—years when the mind has sorted out the things of greatest value. When I look back, it seems I spent my youth and middle age preparing to enjoy my final years.

Reprinted with permission of Joan Wulff.

My Colter

RICK BASS

The next week, back home, I cut my knees badly with the chainsaw while thinning brush. The blade had torn through almost to the kneecap, slicing open the bursa over the patella, so that it would not stop bleeding. I finally had to go in that night for stitches. The next day, a Friday, I worked in the cabin all day. The leg was stiff and I could barely walk. It rained all day but broke to clearing sun shortly before dusk.

I was supposed to keep my foot, my hurt leg, elevated, and so like some old person I lay upstairs on my bed reading and watching that autumn light on the aspen. At about six o'clock, I put the book down and dozed. Elizabeth and the girls were downstairs. I heard a tremendous baying—the sound the dogs make whenever a car comes down the long gravel driveway—but then I heard nothing else, and so I got up and went to the window. The pups were on their chains, looking up the driveway. Old Homer came walking stiff-legged down the drive, the way he does after a car or truck has left—after he has vanquished it.

I didn't see Colter. I figured he was down by my writing cabin. I went back and lay down. The doctor had said no hunting for ten to fourteen days, but I was hoping it would only have to be two or three.

An hour later, I knew somehow that he was gone. I could feel a huge absence, a strange emptiness. Alone, Colter never left the space between the house and the writing cabin. The pups would run rabbits whenever they got loose together, but never Colter.

I waited up all night that first night, and for many night afterward. My knee healed quickly, and I scoured the woods with the other dogs for sign of a lion or wolf attack, but found nothing.

Earlier that afternoon, when Elizabeth and the girls had gotten back from town, I had lifted the baby out of the truck, despite my knee, and carried her a short distance before setting her down to walk. Colter had come running up and had darted all around us, licking the heck out of her, like a puppy, and making her laugh. It was funny for a while but then he kept licking her and wouldn't stop, and surely my last words to him, as I helped bring Lowry and the groceries inside, were something like, "Go on, now."

I remembered every hunt—every moment, every tree, every bush, the plucking of every bird. I remembered examining every crop, and what each bird had been eating. A dog creates, transcribes, a new landscape for you. A dog like Colter sharpens your joy of all the seasons, and for a while, sometimes a long while, such a dog seems capable, by himself alone, of holding time in place—of pinning it, and holding it taut. And then when he is gone, it is as if the world is taken away.

Dogs like that are young for what seems like a very long time.

On the second day, I took Superman up the road. Hobbling on a cane, but carrying the gun, I was grieving already, as I watched Superman try to work the same woods Colter had raced through, and knowing he could never, ever be the dog Colter was.

Just as I was thinking that—at that precise moment—I saw that Superman had gone on point, and that in front of him a young ruffed grouse was fanning. The late-day sun was shining on the bird and I knew then that someone, somewhere—perhaps Colter himself—was telling me Colter's hunt was over.

The bird flushed and I hit it and Superman ran over to examine it, though again with a kind of professionalism—not the gonzo wild-eyed glee of Colter. I suspect Superman will be a perfect little grouse dog, but I realize now that that is not what I wanted—though all along, it is what I believed I wanted.

Once you have lost a dog—especially the fist you trained from a pup, the one you first set sail into the world with—you can never fully give all of yourself to another dog. You can never again look at a dog you love without hedging a tiny bit, if only subconsciously, against the day when that dog, too, must leave. You can never again hunt or enter the future so recklessly, so joyously, without that weight or knowledge of forethought.

Jarrett, who helped train Colter—who worked with him two summers, and helped light the fire within him—wanted to use Colter as a professional guide dog. Jarrett often compared Colter to Michael Jordon. Unlike Superman, Colter didn't hunt so much to please me, in those first years, as to please the universe; and even as he began to mature, there was still always that feeling, that knowledge, that it was between the bird and him, and that I was merely fortunate enough to get to watch it.

He did not have to be "built up," in his training, nor whittled down. Jarrett and I tried simply to bring in his borders and focus, bit by bit, year by year, and bird by bird. His joy, his fury to be in the field, was pure and irreducible. His two little brothers possess his talent but not his genius. Point is more like Mike Tyson then Michael Jordon, and Superman is like The Professor on Gilligan's Island. They are only three years his ghosts, but it might as well be ten thousand years.

You never know when the last hunt is going to be. If you think about it at all, it is with the vague pleasure of distant daydreams, after thousands of hunts, not mere hundreds. You picture it at season's end, amidst snow and ice, and with the hunter, the dog, barely able to creep, but still pushing resolutely forward, nearly blind and shivering but with his blood still as hot as when he was young.

Colter had his name and number on his collar. All I can guess is that someone drove down the driveway, stopped, turned around when they saw our house—a lost tourist, perhaps, mistaking our driveway for a back road—and that for some reason, Colter followed that vehicle. Believing, somehow, that that vehicle was going hunting. He'd never done such a thing before, but there must have been something different about this one. Perhaps it had another dog, or dogs, in it. Maybe he was just desperate to go hunting.

I liked to imagine that he was still out there somewhere—perhaps a long way from Montana, hunting for someone else, or simply being a yard dog, sweet with children. I could not shake the hope that someday he would show up on the porch, ready to hunt again, or that I might get a phone call from someone saying, "I have a dog that sounds like he might be yours."

He liked to lie in the dry autumn-yellow grass at the edge of the marsh outside my writing cabin, and snooze in the sun. He followed me down to that cabin each morning, waited hours, then followed me back up to the house when I was done: he attended, guarded the door, of my every word.

He could tell, by scent alone, whether the pheasants he chased were roosters or hens. When I called his name, he would grin and show all his teeth. He would sneak in the open window of trucks and eat the lunches he found: sandwiches, cupcakes, baklava, everything. Once when he was a pup my friend Tim and I gave him a rest and took Tim's retriever, Maddie, out for a run, and left Colter in the back of Tim's truck. We heard Colter screaming, wailing his disapproval, and then there was a brief silence, after which he came bounding up to join us, having torn his way through the screen window of Tim's camper-shell to get out.

There is no closure. One way or the other, he is still out there running. He will never rest. There will always be this small gulf between us. I will always want him to know a moment's rest, and peace, and he will always know in his hot heart that the only peace to be gotten is by never resting, by always pushing on.

As I sleep restlessly, night after night, or more often, as I lie there awake, he runs, and I feel guilty that I am not there to honor the birds he is finding; that I am not there to shoot them for him, as he keeps finding them.

He is my Colter. Someone else may have fallen into possession of him—perhaps not knowing of his past—but when he runs, I am still his, and he is still mine.

1

After the Fire

TERRY WIELAND

In 1917, a great fire swept through the woods west of the village of Apsley in southern Ontario. It destroyed everything, leaving nothing but miles of burnt-over country and charred stumps.

I know this because I have seen pictures—faded, black-and-white photographs carefully pinned to a homemade board that hangs on the wall of a hunting camp that was rebuilt after the fire.

The camp is at the eastern end of a long, narrow lake, one of hundreds of small, undeveloped lakes that dot the southern edges of the Canadian Shield. I came upon it late one fall day while I was grouse hunting, miles from home and somewhat turned around in the heavy overcast. It was close to dark. The door was unlocked and there were candles and matches on a shelf. By the light of the candle, I studied the photographs as I sat by the fire, sipping coffee made with coppery lake water and coffee from a can I found on the same shelf. The firewood came from a stack under the eave by the cabin's only door.

On the wall beside the pictures was a penciled note, almost illegible it was so old, that said simply, "You are welcome to use whatever is here. Please bring in more kindling and close the door when you leave. Thank you."

The photographs showed the camp as it had been before the fire, a tiny cabin in a grove of giant pines. That photo was faded to almost nothing, on paper with scalloped edges. Then came the others, larger and blacker, from a different camera.

There was one of a harsh, barren landscape devoid of trees and only the stumps to show where they had been. Others showed a horse-drawn farm sled from the era before the wars, hauling in lumber through fresh, white snow; the new, larger cabin standing naked on the point with no trees around; a group shot of the men who built her and then pictures from the next year and the year after that, showing the same men with the deer they killed.

It was amazing to me, having hunted that country every year virtually for the past quarter century, that the devastation of a fire could be replaced within a year or two by so much wildlife that a dozen men could take 25 or 30 or 40 deer in the first few days of a month-long season, when limits were generous and provided their winter meat supply.

In those photographs, the deer are packed tightly and evenly on the meat pole. There is no room left on it and a second pole was put up above the first and then that one was filled. No laws were being broken, neither God's nor man's. This was life being lived the way it was meant to be, a group of men gathering each year to partake of what nature provided.

In the old days, camps like this were common in Ontario, in Quebec, in upstate New York, in Michigan. They are not so common today. In fact, they are disappearing like frost in the sun.

When I was ten years old, my parents decided we needed a place in the country, somewhere to go on weekends, where my father could fish. We ended up buying property on a lake that was just opening up. A new road had been bulldozed in from the highway and there was a landing for boats where the road met the lake. Our place was two miles up the lake by boat on the northwest shore with nothing behind it but hundreds of square miles of swamp and bush.

It had been a hunt camp. There were two buildings. One was a large one-room cabin with a complete propane system—lights, stove, heater. The inside was paneled and had glass windows that fit snug and even all around. It had been built by men who knew what they were doing. The other was an abandoned two-room shack that had been the hunt camp before the newer one was built to replace it.

That summer, in a fit of ambition, we set about cleaning up the old shack. In the course of doing so, we found it was quite sound and, once the garbage and cobwebs were swept out and the windows opened, it was quite a livable place. There were dates and names penciled on the bare wooden walls showing that one room dated from before World War I; the other had been added on after. There was a tongue-and-groove table built into the wall made from rough two-by-fours; there was a gun rack built into another wall and up in the eaves I found a treasure: a Hoppe's gun cleaning kit of indeterminate age with a partly filled tube of gun grease and a bottle of solvent. When I removed the top, I smelled Hoppe's No. 9 for the first time.

Eventually, we made the old place usable as a sleeping cabin that we called, logically, "the cabin." The newer building became "the cottage." I mention all this because it has a bearing on what happened later.

In the fall of our first year at our new camp—it would have been 1959—my father went up during deer season to make sure everything was all right. He was naturally protective of his new property and wanted to ensure everything was shipshape for the winter. In those days, there were no snowmobiles and almost no one went to their cottage after the first snow.

When my dad returned home, he had with him a gaunt and shivering deerhound bitch he had found curled up beneath the cottage, half-starved and weak from running. She had recently whelped and was leaking milk from her unused teats. Not knowing the ways of deer hunters, Dad brought her home and put an ad in the local paper. About three nights later, we got a call. It was a farmer up in Apsley who had been running deer, lost his dog and would be grateful to have her back.

We had christened her "Duchess" and made her a place beside the furnace in the basement. The whole family was pretty incensed that this could happen to a dog and we were going to make sure that farmer knew how we felt. When the weekend came, we all went along to drive her home and go to the cottage one last time.

When we got there, we found someone camped out in the cabin. There was a box of canned goods and a couple of duffle bags and sleeping bags. There was a low fire burning in the woodstove, which was damped right down. I forgot to mention that the previous owners always left the key under a cement block and we had seen no reason to change. So when one of the members of the camp who did not know it had been sold showed up for a couple of days hunting late in the season, the key was there and he moved right in.

By this time, Dad was getting a little weary of all this. First the dog, then unwanted guests. It meant he was going to have to come up yet again the next weekend to check up, and since it was nearing the end of November, the weather was getting more than a little unpredictable for crossing two miles of lake in an open boat. Up there, we get bad storms in November and when the wind sweeps in out of the west, it can roll up waves in the channels that make it impossible to cross.

Dad left a stiff note on the table saying the men were welcome to finish out this hunt, but would they please note the property had changed hands and was no longer their hunt camp?

Next weekend, back we went. The hunters were gone. The cabin was carefully swept, the firewood in the box replenished and on the table was a long, handwritten letter on four or five pages of foolscap. It began by apologizing for the intrusion and then went on to give the whole history of the camp, from the time three men trekked in overland in the winter on snowshoes to pick out the site back before the 1914–18 war.

It told of hauling lumber in by horse and sleigh, up the portages from three lakes down below. It told of adding on the second room when the group outgrew the first one. It told of abandoning the original camp in 1946 and building the spiffy new one (the cottage, as we knew it) with materials hauled in the same way—lumber, cement blocks, four-by-eight sheets of paneling as heavy as lead, glass windows, the propane system, everything. When they were finished, they had a state-of-the-art hunting cabin. Then the rug was pulled out from under them when somebody decided it was time for a little civilization and put the road in from the highway and opened up the lake.

By that time, of course, ownership had changed anyway.

Most deer camps in Ontario, the newer ones anyway, are built on land that belongs to the Crown and is loaned out for seven-year stretches. If you have a cabin on Crown land, you display your hunt camp permit in one window where it can be checked by a warden if he ever comes around. Every seven years you have to get your permit renewed.

Our place, however, was older than that system. Somebody in the original group had gained title to the land and then promptly lost the whole place in a poker game to another member of the group. When the lake opened up, the new owner had a windfall. Since he figured its days as a decent hunting area were over anyway, he might as well sell it—which he did, without bothering to tell anyone else in the group.

For my part, I'm glad he didn't. If he had, I would have never met Clare Irwin—uninvited guest and writer of that long letter to my father.

Clare's father was one of the originals who built the place in the 1920s. When Clare was old enough to hunt, he became a member of the group himself and by the time I met him he was in his 50s. His father was over 80 and nearing the end of his hunting days. In that year, Clare and his father had gone up on their own, assuming they could use the place the way they always had.

The letter impressed my father considerably and Clare became a friend of the family. He was a small-town bank manager, medium height and painfully thin. Even in his 50s, his face was heavily lined from so much time spent outdoors. The crow's feet at the corners of his pale blue eyes crinkled when he smiled, which was frequently, and he always found time to talk with me.

It used to be that deer hunting in Ontario was built around the camp system, and because of some peculiar regulations and practices the traditions of those camps seem strange to outsiders. One thing that has long been common practice is allowing "group" hunting. This means that if you have six men in camp with licenses, you can shoot up to six deer (it used to be 12), but not everyone has to shoot his own. One hunter can shoot all six, just so long as the total limit is not exceeded. And, you must have a license to take part.

This gives deer hunting here a different flavor. The "every man for himself" approach I have found in camps in Pennsylvania, for instance, is not much fun. Also, because you can continue to hunt even after you have filled your own tag, everyone goes out together before dawn each day. The camp does not slowly divide into the "haves" and the "have-nots" as tags are filled. Even better, older members who cannot get around as well can still go hunting, but stay in camp occasionally while the younger ones hunt on their behalf.

Having grown up with this system, it seems quite natural and logical to me. And having lived with it and experienced the other approach, which is more common, I like our practice better for fostering tradition among a group of hunters who go out together every year.

From the turn of the century until well into the 1960s, camps and hunting clubs were the most common way of hunting. You became part of one of these groups by invitation and some of the hunters were third- and even fourth-generation members. Sometimes they did not see each other from one year to the next; deer hunting was the only bond that held them together. Inevitably, whoever lived closest to the camp (and most were accessible only on foot or by boat and portage) drew the assignment of trekking in during the winter to clear snow off the roof or cut firewood.

Members who lived farther away would compensate by contributing material or, less often, money for expenses. It seemed that every group contained one good rough carpenter, another who could do roofing and a third who was good with ax and chain saw. At least one would be a farmer who had horses and heavy sleighs and could haul in lumber and full propane tanks when the lakes and swamps froze over.

In our area, there were at least a dozen other camps strung out through the woods, each a couple of miles apart. Over the years, I've visited all of them, sometimes intentionally. The groups knew each other, of course, and knew each other's dogs. In the old days, every camp had its own dogs, and every camp I know of up here has a few kennels scattered around where the dogs hole up when they are in camp.

People today do not understand hunting deer with dogs, at least not the way I know it. They think you unleash the pack, they go racing away on a scent, nipping at the heels of some terrified buck, and deliberately herd him right past where you are sitting. You, of course, promptly gun him down and go home. Easy as pie.

Naturally, it is not at all like that in practice. People up here started using dogs because of the terrain. The country is very broken and rough, with many swamps and marshes, and every year the beavers create more. The deer come out at night to feed on acorns in the scrub oaks or the thin grass that grows among the pines and hemlocks. By and large, though, there is no open country where they come out at sunset to feed, as there is in the south. The bush up here is thick; you'd be hard pressed to find a spot where you could get a shot over 75 yards and 40 is more likely.

I've stood and watched a buck cross behind a screen of trees, maybe 60 yards away from me. I could see him plainly, yet I never got a view clear enough to take a shot.

During the day, the deer go deep into the swamps and lie up and the only way to have any chance of success is to get them moving again. Driving is sometimes effective, but the best method is to put men on stands where they have at least a couple of sighting lanes and then put a half dozen dogs out. The dogs roam around until they pick up a scent, then follow it wherever it leads, going into the swamps and moving the deer out. With luck, once the deer are moving, one or two will come within shooting range of someone on a stand.

Needless to say, when a good hound gets on a scent, he can be gone for days. Lost dogs are common and throughout the season strays wash into every camp like flotsam, gaunt and panting, hoarse from baying and willing to eat anything softer than a birchbark canoe. Periodically, the camps gather up the strays and head into town. There's always a coffee shop where they meet to exchange stray dogs and news and have a hot piece of pie before heading back to camp.

Duchess, the dog my father found under our cottage, was one of those strays that ended up miles from home. Probably she should not have been hunting, having had puppies so recently, but how can you keep a dog in once the season starts? It's what they live for all year.

The nice thing about the system is that you do not need dogs yourself to benefit. Each camp has its own unofficial territory, with runs and stands and everyone respects everyone else's domain. We had a camp to the north of us with dogs and one to the south. Once either started to run deer, they could go anywhere—even to us.

Clare washed up on a distant camp one night, like a dog that had paid too much attention to the trail and lost track of where he was. He was up with his dad, had put him on a stand and then headed off to do the dog's work of stirring things up. There was a sprinkling of snow and he got on a track that led him in a great arc to the north. When darkness came, he was in a labyrinth of connected swamps with miles of timber between himself and the camp.

He told me he just started walking generally south, feeling his way in the darkness until he picked up a scent of woodsmoke. He began walking upwind, at one point wading through swamp water up to his armpits, as he concentrated on keeping the friendly smell in his nostrils. He stumbled into a strange camp shortly after midnight, bedded down there, and got home at mid-morning the next day, having covered something like 20 miles through thick brush. His main worry was his father, in camp by himself and undoubtedly worrying about Clare out in the woods overnight in the wet snow.

When he finally made it back, his dad was sitting by the fire with a pot of fresh coffee and some stew on the stove. He figured Clare would be hungry when he got in.

Clare told me that story years later, after I had my own first brush with a night in the woods.

"There's nothing to worry about if you're careful," he said, "but there sure seems enough to worry about at the time."

There came the year, my 16th, when I was ready to go deer hunting myself—or so I thought. I'd gone out and bought a .35 Remington Marlin 336, seeing no need to bother my parents by asking permission. This was a calculated risk. My father was not a hunter, but he loved to handle Clare's Model 94 whenever he got the chance. I was hoping that one look at my gleaming beauty and he would be more interested in trying it out than in punishing me for buying it without permission. He was.

The year I got my first license Dad called Clare, who came down for dinner the next Sunday. We sat in the living room a long time. Clare looked at my rifle and asked me all sorts of questions about it. He asked why I had chosen to replace the open sight with a Williams receiver sight. He looked at my choice of ammunition. We discussed when and how I would load it if I was hunting, and a bit about woodsmanship. Finally, Clare looked me in the eye and asked:

"How would you like to come hunting with me on Saturday?"

Friday night I barely slept. I had read that deer hunters were up at four and there I was, making coffee and bacon and eggs. My dad got up and ate breakfast with me and I had been fully dressed for an hour when Clare drove up. He had a spot in mind where it would not matter that we had missed the dawn.

It was midway through the season; the cold weather had brought the first snow and the deer were starting to yard up, migrating down from north of our lake to the preserve a few miles south. Clare knew the main gathering points and he figured to put us on one where we would wait through the day and let them come to us.

In the car driving north, the Statler Brothers sang "Flowers on the Wall," while Clare talked to me about the past, which I was about to become a part of.

"I remember one year, hunting down in the Flatiron where we're going, back in the '30s," he told me. "The limit in those days was two deer and there were animals everywhere. I got down in there and shot four deer in one morning. Most I ever got.

"Everybody was getting deer that year. We'd shoot one, clean it, haul it up in a tree and keep on hunting. We figured we'd come back and get them all later. Then the weather turned real warm for a couple of days and all those deer started to go. You could smell them as you walked through the woods. We couldn't get them out fast enough and the hot weather ruined a lot of the meat."

By 1965, though, those days were only a memory for people like Clare. For such a vast territory, Ontario does not have a huge deer herd and in the 1960s it was on a down swing. In those years, if we found a reasonably fresh track or some droppings, it was an event. One day, eating lunch by the stove in the cabin while the rain drummed down, Clare said to me, "You know, I don't really mind not getting deer myself. I just like to be up here hunting them. I'd like to see you get your first one, though."

Looking back to those lean years when the woods were so empty and silent, I think Clare's comment was the thing that kept me going back year after year. I wanted him to see me get my first one, too.

Along about that time, his wife died and Clare took it very hard. We didn't see much of him. After a while, he retired from the bank and took up flying; he would fly back and forth across the continent. Twice he crashed his plane in the mountains and walked out, once on a cracked ankle. He spent winters in Mexico, beachcombing. In the fall, most of his hunting time was spent farther north, after moose.

In 1967, I went deer hunting on my own for the first time, rowing across two miles of rough lake in the darkness with a box of canned goods in the stern, a duffle bag of clothes and my rifle in its vinyl case across the seat behind me. I slept in the old, original cabin and kept my rifle in the ancient gun rack.

It was the second week of the season and the weather was turning cold. During the day, I walked the woods looking for sign. At night I sat by the stove and read books on deer hunting. One day, I came on a fresh track in the snow and followed it through the afternoon as the sky clouded over and snow began to fall. It was almost dusk and the tracks were filling in when I glanced to my left and realized I was just brushing the northernmost tip of the last in a line of long swamps that drained into the bay beside our cabin. It was late and I was a long way out.

I made my way back as the snow thickened, skirting the edges of the swamps, trying to hunt as I went, although there was a certain lurking panic in my stomach. At one point, I climbed a tall pine to see where I was and discovered that I was in the top of a pine in the middle of a swamp in the midst of a snowstorm—nothing more. A ruffed grouse landed on a log 20 feet from me and I shot its head off with the .35 Remington, reflecting that I would at least have something to eat. But by remembering Clare's advice and listening for the sound of water on rocks, I was able to make it home just after dark. The grouse did not get eaten until a few days later.

This went on for several years. I would take a week of my vacation and go hunting, alone. I had no friends who hunted and I was very conscious, in a subconscious sort of way, that by being there every year, just by being there, I was somehow linking with the past, Clare's past, with whatever the future might be. And Lord knows, I did not see how the future could hold fewer deer than the present.

And then one day I returned to find a red seaplane tied up to our dock and Clare inside by the fire. He looked older, and thinner if that was possible, and his face was brown and stubbly and heavily lined. He seemed a little hunched, or maybe I had grown a bit. Anyway, he was back. Moose hunting was over and Mexico beckoned, but he had stayed on for a day or two of deer hunting.

"I had a hunch you might be here," he said, and his smile followed the lines of his face and crinkled his eyes.

We hunted together that year and the year after. From then on, whenever I was up, I watched for the red seaplane and always left coffee on the stove. Sometimes he came, sometimes he didn't, but whether he came or not, he was always there.

By the mid-1980s, the deer population had bounced back considerably. Ontario went to an antlerless permit draw system, which seemed to help. At any rate, the population doubled, from 100,000 to 200,000, which is minuscule when compared to Pennsylvania or Michigan but substantial by our standards. In fact, everything was on a high cycle. Since 1985, ruffed grouse have been abundant around our camp and moose, which have come and gone over the centuries, are once more pushing south and overlapping the whitetail range.

The last decade has been very good to wildlife, but it has not been good for the deer camps. Too many of them are on trails that are used by snowmobiles and many have been vandalized or burnt. The old system is breaking down as people move away, lose touch, and die.

A few miles west of us, the government decided to establish a park smack in the middle of some of the best deer and grouse cover I know of. They told the hunt camps their permits would not be renewed and gave them 12 months to remove all trace of them. Then the park was delayed indefinitely, but the camps were already gone and the hunters with them.

The advent of all-terrain vehicles has not helped, either. Where once remote little lakes were barely accessible and you could backpack in and hunt in peace, now you get there to find a half dozen city men with ATVs and walkie-talkies. But I guess it is the same everywhere. And all along the road into the lake, which I used to walk with a backpack to get to the rowboat to cross to our cabin, you now find row on row of cars and trucks on opening morning and hunters elbow to elbow in bushes 20 feet in from the road. Some of them, I am told, know how to use the guns they carry, but I have no proof of it.

A dozen years ago, a friend of mine down the lake began trying to put together an old-time hunting club, which would hunt out of his cottage. With hot showers and a microwave oven, Brian's place is not exactly a camp like the old days. Whether that was a factor, I don't know, but the club never really worked out. Three of us have stuck it out to hunt together every year and we have stopped trying to enlarge the group. We've staked a claim to a nice little plateau where the deer like to pass through, other hunters know we are there and go around and we are accepted by the other hunt camps in the area.

Still, our annual deer-hunting ritual always ended with us coming back empty-handed and it was wearing very thin. I was hunting other game in other places—caribou in Quebec, pronghorns in Montana, Dall sheep in Alaska; Brian made an annual trip to British Columbia for elk and one year he shot a mountain goat. Between us we managed to show up for deer hunting in November with enough game meat to give the camp a certain legitimacy, but I could see in Brian's eyes, every so often, a kind of wildness, a desperation maybe, that said that until we started getting deer here in the cradle of our hunting careers, we could not call ourselves hunters.

And strangely enough, things started to happen. In 1986 (20 years after I first hunted there with Clare), we not only saw two real, live animals, but Brian actually shot a yearling doe. Two years later, we got two more and in 1989 added a large doe. Our expectations began to change and we not only expected to see deer, we became determined that we would be satisfied only when we brought home a whitetail buck.

I have told these things to friends who live in places like Texas, with its population of four million deer and Pennsylvania, where the annual road kill is almost as large as our total deer herd, and they simply do not understand. They hunt whitetails with the same expectations I bring to woodchuck hunting and I am not sure they comprehend such a sparsity of deer or such a lack of skill on our part. Or maybe they just cannot see why I keep on doing it. Frankly, I am not sure myself, until I try to envision a year in which I miss deer season up there.

At least once every season, I leave Brian's place on my own and cut across country and come into our old camp from the back. It is not exactly a pilgrimage, at least I don't think of it as such. I could take a boat and be there in five minutes, but it would not be the same. The only way I want to see it is with a rifle in my hand, coming in the trail, saying hello to a few blackened stumps that still lurk in the undergrowth, three-quarters of a century after the big fire that swept the land clean.

That was how I saw Clare the last time.

As I walked past the cabin down to the shore, there was his plane tied up to the old dock. I waited there for him as the afternoon wore on and eventually he stalked in, in his rubber boots and old wool jacket. When he saw me, his eyes lit up and we sat and talked for half an hour. Then he climbed into the plane and took off. It was an hour's flight home and he had to make it before dark. I stood and watched as the plane disappeared behind the pines on the long point and then walked slowly home through the woods. It was dark and snow was blowing when I got to Brian's; inside, there was a cheerful blaze in the fireplace and the warmth reached all the way to the door. Brian was mixing Manhattans.

The following year, I heard that Clare had some sort of brain tumor. I wanted to go and see him or write to him, but I was advised that he no longer recognized people and in a lucid moment had asked that his friends not come to see him because he felt bad when he did not know who they were.

And then the year after that, our old hunt camp—the building we called the cabin that had stood on that spot for more than 70 years—mysteriously caught fire and burned to the ground. It was dry as tinder, of course, and in 15 minutes it was all over.

And about that same time, Clare Irwin died.

There is probably no connection between any of these occurrences. Even in my most superstitious moments, late at night, I can see nothing to connect them except my imagination—or maybe my wish. Clare Irwin, my old, old friend, and that building, the old, old friend of ours, were inextricably entwined in my mind and when they both were gone, within months of each other, all I had left was a large nothingness. I was so accustomed to them being there, I had never acknowledged that a day could come when they might not be.

And then a third event occurred.

It was something I would never have dared to predict or even to consider, but it now seems logical to the point of inevitability: On the second morning of the season, nature completed the triangle by placing an eight-point buck on a distant point of land and giving me one clear unforgettable shot.

A fire, a friend's death, a rifle shot, a whitetail buck, a few photographs, some antlers to go on the wall. They are all pieces of a puzzle that I have thought about, off and on, for more than a year. The puzzle is now complete, and even though I look at it and think about it and can never understand exactly what the picture means, it is amazing how the pieces all fit together so very, very well.

A Hunting Memory

RICK BASS

Having already been blessed with an elk and an antelope, I had spent the rest of the month walking around trying to work up a desire for deer, but the electricity I had felt as a young man, as well as the need, just wasn't there. I was mostly just out walking, now, carrying my rifle the way I might carry a rolled-up map. Sometimes, particularly at first light, I would feel a mild hunger and a curiosity, but there was none of the old fire, the old necessity. For most of the rest of the month, I was just out walking around with my rifle, to see what I might see, rather than hunting.

It was almost as if I was looking for something lost.

Some days I felt myself moving closer to that thing, however—that lost fire, or desire—and when it finally did return, on the last day of the season, I was overjoyed, for I had it figured out now that there would probably be a day when it might not return at all: or might simply drift past in moments, and in occasional memories.

And that would be all right. It would be whatever it ended up being. But when I went to bed the night before the last day of the season, I finally wanted a deer, and when I woke up early the next morning—the first of December—I really wanted one.

I had three different places that I wanted to try. I hadn't been seeing many deer, but that morning, hiking in to the first place, a young whitetail buck stood in the middle of the trail, illuminated in my flashlight beam, and he would not leave, nor would he move out of the path.

I took it as a good omen.

I hunted that area hard, farther in, at first light and for an hour beyond, sitting silently in the deep cold and watching the frozen silvery world become light. I didn't see anything else, but it didn't matter, because finally I was hunting instead of just watching. It's not something you can fake or force, and I had not realized how much I had missed it.

By midmorning I had gone over to another mountain, where I watched a small herd of whitetail does for a while and then, much higher on the mountain, a young spike a long way off. I hiked all the way to the top of the mountain and then down the back side, touched the Canadian line, then turned around and hiked out, following a different watershed and hunting carefully, intensely, all the way. And mid-afternoon, I was rewarded with the heartpounding sight of the back half of a big, beautiful whitetail standing behind a giant larch tree on a steep slope. Gold larch needles were falling slowly through the stillness for no reason other than the frosted weight of their own existence: the very last ones to fall.

I eased back up the slope until I could see the front half of the deer—how I wanted it to be a buck!—and felt the delicious joy of disappointment that it was not. The cold sun was directly in her eyes, igniting them the way it sometimes can, making the eyes look like liquid, or burning glass—and I lay there for about twenty minutes, hoping there might be a late-season buck nearby—particularly for her to be so motionless, for so long—but if there was, I never saw it, and finally, too cold to lie still any longer, I got up and eased on down off the slope.

On the way out, I was thinking about old hunts: about amazing things that had happened to me in the woods, and about some of the stories my father and uncle and grandfather had told me about various hunts they'd made. Certainly, it wasn't as if something phenomenal happened every time you went out into the woods, but it added up over the years—a handful of astounding, luminous happenings—and I was thinking about how it had been a while since I'd had one of those amazing incidents. I wasn't really asking for one, but was just kind of wondering when there might be another. Always, if you put in enough miles, and enough hours, there would be one more. It might be years in the coming, but always, there would be one more.

On my walk out—headed over toward my third mountain of the day—I started to daydream about some of the old hunts, the old amazing stories, and remembered some of my own. I thought about some of the old stories in which I, or someone I'd been hunting with, had been fortunate enough to get an animal on the last day, sometimes in the waning dusk-moments of that last day. The animal surely presenting itself to the hunter, at the end of the long season.

I don't think I was quite asking for such a thing, but I definitely was thinking of a place where I wanted to be sitting, high on a ridge of that third mountain, when dusk came; and if I hurried, I could just barely get there.

What a glutton! At first all I had wanted was to get my desire, my intensity, back—to want a deer—and next, I wanted not just the intensity, but the deer itself. And now here I was thinking about a miracle. Maybe not being audacious enough to ask for one, but definitely thinking about working hard to position myself in a place where, if one occurred, it would be spectacular. A beautiful ridge, one of my favorite views in the valley. A wonderful place to watch the sun go down on the last day, whether a deer wandered by at dusk or not.

The place where I was going was at the top of a cleft, a long vertical crevice that creased the mountain like a chimney. Four times previously in sixteen years I've seen a magnificent animal in that chute, sometimes at the top of it, as if the animals are born from that one rock, venting from it as if in miraculous, igneous expulsion. It has been much the same way with the elk I'd been fortunate enough to take this year, the animal falling far in the backcountry, but not thirty yards from where I'd previously killed other elk.

I know that one explanation for such happenings might be that a hunter can become so familiar with a stretch of landscape—so wedded and connected to it—that his or her chances of success are sharply enhanced. And to some extent I believe that's true—that there are certain specific areas, like individual fields or wild gardens, that speak deeply to a hunter—areas where that hunter's comfortable, landforms which he or she understands more deeply and intuitively than others, though for no known or apparent reason.

But I think that within those wild gardens, there are smaller areas or pockets that are more akin to what I consider not so much the body of the earth, but its wild DNA: or individual cells, at least, within the larger body, which—as long as all else remains healthy—will continue to regenerate, producing their various mysteries like magma upwelling through a vent or fissure in ceaseless birthings. I want to believe that.

A hunter who knows his or her half-million acres, or million acres, may hold a dozen or two such places in his or her mind, like talismans in a small leather pouch. There is a joy to be had in finding new places—particularly in following the winter tracks of animals into a new wellspring-place—but there is a deep pleasure also to be had in returning to those specific sites with which the hunter is already so intimately familiar—some unique flex or crevice or compilation of landscape that draws, and nurtures, a certain species of animal, and a certain kind, year after year (and in that manner, nurturing the hunter, too).

All the way up, this last afternoon, I was pushing hard—hunting attentively, on the way up, but focusing also on the singular image of picturing myself up in that quiet place at the top, sitting there in the last moments before dusk, and watching. If I pushed hard, I could still make it: I was right on schedule.

A herd of does crossed the steep slope in front of me, passing from north to south, and I paused to watch them in the early gloom. The first of December, with good snow and ice underfoot. It felt more like winter already than autumn. The does passed on by, and I hurried upslope, on through the place where they had crossed. I was hunting hard, but strangely, I had stopped wanting a deer again, and was wanting only to get to the top of that ridge, to sit quietly for a few minutes before dark and watch the light fade from the sky, and from the season. That was the only image I had, and it was an idea that brought me peace.

As I got closer to the top, the slope grew even steeper, and the snow became more wind-scoured, until it was like a shield, a frozen skin sculpted to fit perfectly the curve of the mountain. There was no purchase for either my hands or my feet, so that I had to kick little footholds, step by step, into the frozen shell: but I knew that once I reached the top—very soon now—I would be able to rest in my hiding spot and watch and wait.

And now that I was closer—maybe twenty yards from the top, but moving slowly, punching out each step one heel-divot at a time—I was, almost as if bidden to do so, beginning to imagine a buck passing through that spot.

It wasn't about desire, any more—or rather, not desire for a deer—but instead, the desire to be in that spot, that place—that cell—at that one certain end-of-season dusk—and that in so doing, the drift of a deer might be intercepted.

So intent was I upon gaining the ridge that I had stopped hunting, and was instead only mountain climbing: ascending into the icy, windy fog, with the mist hurtling past. I was taking caution not to slip and fall, I was concentrating on the last few steps, and then, finally, the last handhold of exposed wind-scrubbed rock, with which I could pull myself over the top.

I'm not sure why I paused and looked to the north, over to the other side of that stone chute, the stone chimney. But something turned my head, as I paused to rest for half-a-moment before pulling myself up over the ridge; and when I looked north, I saw a wonderful mule deer buck walking through a little opening about a hundred and fifty yards away. He had just come out of the trees and was crossing the ridge on the other side of that chimney: circling around, perhaps, to the very place I was hoping to get to, and where I'd been imagining a deer. It seemed that we were both angling in on the same place, and that I just happened to have glanced over and seen him converging—as if previously, he might almost have been traveling in parallel with me.

He stopped and lifted his head to test the wind. I crouched quickly and kicked in another foothold, and an elbow-hold, and tried to find the quickest and best fit of my body against the curve of that slab of ice. My heart was still pounding from the exertion of the climb and I was not yet ready to fire—I watched the big deer through my scope, but the image danced and wavered—and although I was anxious and eager, I was not overly so; it was enough of a wonder just to be seeing such a deer, and particularly under such dream-like circumstances.

There was another, smaller buck with him, hanging back, half in and half out of the trees, but my focus was on the one out in front. I don't know why he remained there, looking around—he had glanced in my direction, but I do not think he had seen me, tucked in tight against that snowy cliff-face, and with the wind gusting and the blue-black hues of nightfall rushing in—and it's even possible to believe that that big buck understood somehow that it was the end of the season, and that with the challenge of the hunting season draining away in the last of the day's light, he was pausing, preparing already to step ahead into the next challenge, the greater depth of winter.

My breathing had stabilized, the deep raggedness was gone. I braced against the cold rock, held steady, and squeezed.

A complete miss: the deer did not even flinch. He turned and looked in my direction, and took one step forward. I bolted another bullet in, braced, squeezed—and missed. Again the deer stood still. The brass of my bullets rained onto the rock and made a tinkling sound. I fired again, elevating a notch—believing that the deer might be farther out than I'd estimated—but again he merely stood there for a moment, though seconds later he whirled and ran back into the forest from which he had come. For a long time afterward, I could hear the thunderous compression of his stot as he galloped, flying for thirty feet in a bound, straight back down that chimney.

After he was gone, I sat there for a long while in the new silence. I had not even finished absorbing all of the onrush of good luck, so that while I was disappointed at missing, I was still feeling great about having seen the animal, and having had a chance. Always, in this kind of situation, you wish you could do it over again, you wish for one more chance—but certainly, I couldn't complain.

I traversed back down the ice-shield, kicking new steps, and crossed the chimney and waded through the deeper snow to go check out the tracks—to be absolutely certain the animal had not been nicked, and to follow his tracks on down the mountain. I knew I wouldn't get another shot at him—the light was sliding away as if following him all the way down the mountain—but I could at least follow his tracks out.

I had completely forgotten about the smaller buck. I suppose subconsciously I had assumed he had galloped on off down the hill with the big deer, but I wasn't thinking of him at all when I reached the tracks, and was instead examining the snow carefully for blood sign.

I heard some little noise back in the trees, or glimpsed some movement, I'm not sure—and looked up and saw the face and antlers of a mule deer looking at me, from not fifteen yards away.

I didn't know if it was the big one or the small one—I just saw antlers—and though I'd found no sign, my first thought, for the deer to still be there after all my shooting, and so close, was that it was wounded.

The deer saw me, and whirled and bounded. Without thinking, I raised the rifle and swept the scope over it and fired just as it jagged around some trees.

I had no idea whether I'd hit it. I'd only been trying to get another bullet into it, believing it was wounded, in the snow, at dusk. I went to the spot where it had been standing, watching me, expecting to find blood or hair, which I could then track, regardless of whether the snap-shot had connected, but there was nothing. Oh, I thought, a mistake, a bad one, a dumb one. I shouldn't have made the snap shot.

I took a few more steps, looking for possible new blood from my hasty shot—fearing the worst—and found some.

It was nearly true dark, now. Maybe thirty seconds of legal shooting light remained, or maybe a full minute, by the clock: but it was dark, cloudy, wintry, waning.

Ten more steps—true dark, now—and I came upon the incredible gift of a mule deer buck lying stone dead in the snow, as if he had been there forever. It was the smaller deer, and the bullet had gone in at an angle, striking almost every vital organ in him.

I think that there is a difference between fortune and luck. I was almost too rattled to even know how to begin to address my gratitude to the deer, the mountain, the season, and the chimney. It had been great fortune to get to see the big buck at dusk—to have been so indisputably summoned by it. But this—this embarrassing, in-your-face presentation of fool's luck—almost shamed me, and I barely even knew how to feel about it. Grateful, sure; but shocked, too, by the rampant, excessive generosity of it.

I tried to calm myself down by telling myself that clearly, it was meant to happen this way—but that didn't so much calm me down as agitate me further, as I realized again that so much of it seemed to have already existed as if in some fluid, dynamic design. Why was I uncomfortable with such forcefulness, such generosity of both spirit and matter? Would I have really preferred to believe that I, and not the great world, was in control?

I cleaned the buck in the new darkness, still disbelieving at my luck. I'd be home late that night, and my family would be thrilled. The weather was perfect for aging—I'd be able to drag the deer all the way down the steep mountain, atop the winter-deep snow, loose fur and redstain scribing a wandering sentence of success—of phenomenal luck—all the way down—and then I'd be able to hang the deer for ten or even fourteen days, no problem. It was still a couple of miles to the car, but downhill all the way— I wouldn't even have to quarter the animal; wouldn't have to return later in the night for a second trip.

This, I thought, is my lucky year.

After I'd cleaned the animal, I cached the entrails under a spruce tree for a marten, wolverine, coyote or wolf, and started down the mountain, rifle gripped in one hand and the deer's mahogany antlers in the other.

The sky was clear, it was gloriously cold, I was honored and ecstatic to have had such a hunt—to have hunted hard the whole season, which in itself was reward enough, without this incredible bonus— and because the mountain was so steep, and the snow so deep, I grew tired, though the deer slid along behind me almost as if flying.

Sometimes the deer would accelerate and would slide into me from behind, trying to travel down the mountain faster than I could go; other times it would skate around in front of me, so that I was running along behind it. Once, I tripped and fell, but held on to the deer, as well as to my unloaded rifle, and rode the deer quite some distance down the snowy mountain, holding onto it as I might grip the neck of a horse swimming in the surf.

I had to stop and rest often, panting. It was gloriously exhausting work, I was drenched with sweat and my old man's muscles were aflame. The season was over, and someone, or something, had given me a deer, and I understood now to let go of the guilt and simply enjoy, and revel in, the generosity of that gift. At each rest-break, I would lie on my back, panting and staring up at the stars, ass-whipped, but knowing I'd be even older and more tired next year, and that these were the good old days.

Go ahead and enjoy it, I thought, lying back in the snow and looking north, down into the snowclad bowl of the valley in which I lived. It won't last forever, nothing lives forever: enjoy it. And while I was lying there, leaning against the body of the deer, my old body steaming despite the great cold, and with plumes of breath rising from my lungs, I noticed some electricity overhead: and as I watched, the first faint strobes of northern lights began to pierce the starry sky.

And while I understood this was coincidence or perfection—that it was not about me, that I was but a gnat on one mountain in one valley on one cold winter night in one world—I was once again amazed by the extravagant density and perfection of this last day—the richness.

Why is the world showing off, part of me wondered, and how wonderful it must be feeling, to be revealing so many secrets, and, What does it mean?

I couldn't answer any of those questions, of course. I could only keep saying thank you to everything I saw, and everything I remembered. And to write it down, when I got home, so that one day my children, if they ever wonder about such things, will know what it was sometimes like, late in the autumn, to go up into the mountains looking for meat.

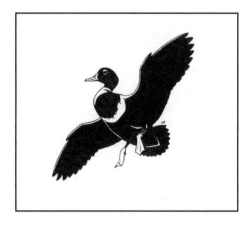

River Notes: Three Days of the Savage Life

BOB BUTZ

Friday, November 21

I'm all by myself in this canoe, maybe on this whole river, given the time of year and the fact that for days they've been calling for one hell of a storm.

Snow. There's over a foot on the ground already, which makes it great for spotting deer. Shortly after the put-in this morning, I drifted by a pair of them—two does—bedded down under a cedar tree a stone's throw from the water's edge. For a moment, I considered my bow lying there unstrung in the bow. But then I thought better of it: the deer were too close, too soon. I paddled past without looking at them, without looking directly into their eyes, and they let me by without bolting, without so much as twitching an ear.

I'm remembering now the color of their fur—a soft color of gray, like soot, almost as gray as the sky that weighs down so heavy now.

Anchored now in a quiet backwater slough where the Boardman River flows into Brown Bridge Pond . . .

A moment ago, there were mallards here—five drakes and a hen that shot up over the trees and circled twice before flying out high over the lake.

Ducks are fair game on this float, and had these given me the opportunity I would not have been as disinterested in arrowing one as I had been with the deer. The only food in my canoe is a three-pound bag of potatoes and three cans of tuna fish. A Spartan diet. One I hope to supplement with some freshly killed meat before long.

Trout fishing here earlier this summer, it seemed as if I was constantly walking up on deer bedded down on the riverbank. Of course, this got me thinking about swapping my fly rod for a bow come autumn. But the plan got pushed back to now what looks like winter.

Certainly, there are wilder rivers in northern Michigan—more secluded waters to hunt and lose one's self for a while. I fished much of the Boardman this summer, so I know the meandering course the river makes. Scattered along the upper reaches are cottages and summer homes, while the lower part is usually choked with canoers and beer swilling inner-tubers in summertime. But all of them are gone now thanks to the cold, gray promise of snow.

As for the river—truth is, even an inexperienced paddler could float the length of the Boardman in a day. But I'm hunting, so I plan on stretching that a little. In *A Witchery of Archery*, Maurice Thompson wrote of "Three Weeks of the Savage Life." I have less than three days.

The Boardman is a river the young Ernest Hemingway fished on random sojourns from his parent's northern Michigan home. And what fly-fisherman hasn't heard the story of Leonard Halladay and the now famous dry fly he invented for fishing these waters, named after his friend Judge Charlie Adams. The river will take me back to the city—Traverse City—the place I moved to for a job one year ago, almost to the day.

And as for my job, well, let's just say I knew before I took it that I wasn't cut out for the nine-to-five. But those paychecks that started coming in like clockwork sure beat the hell out of what I was making packing worms a bait shop. They had a way of making me overlook the fact that my back was starting to hurt all the time and my legs were atrophying to such an appalling degree that I would be embarrassed to bear my spindly shanks come summertime. Unlike others who seem to bulk up with inactivity, I've always gone the other way.

In a moment, I'll pull the anchor and ferry myself over to shore. My plan is to set up camp and spend what's left of the afternoon hunting. Waiting for the storm. After dragging the canoe ashore, I pulled it under the boughs of a cedar tree. There I cleared away a place to sleep. A shallow bed in the snow dug down into the leaves, down into the bear, black earth. I laid out a ground cover (a blue tarp folded in half), my sleeping pad, cold-weather bag, and the rest of my gear. The canoe placed over top formed a perfect makeshift bivouac.

I hunted the hill up behind camp for nearly two hours and then made my way back toward the river. My bow is a 64-inch hickory selfbow. It's one of the first bows I ever made, so it's kind of clumsy and heavy looking. Although selfbows can be particular in inclement weather—specifically the rain—this one has never given me a lick of trouble. I've killed with it before, and so I have that much-needed air of confidence.

The snow was soft and made for quiet walking. But instead of deer, all I crept up on were squirrels. Three grays and a black. I took a shot at the black squirrel where he sat on fallen log. It was a hurried shot and I missed, then spent the better part of a half hour digging for my arrow lost in the snow.

It started snowing soon after that, a fine, heavy snow. There was no wind or anything, just the snow-flakes wafting down like a million tiny moths, so beautiful that I decided to sit and watch it pile up for awhile before heading back to camp.

I cut down the hill toward the sound of the river, peeling a little bark from every birch tree I passed. Bark from the white birch makes good fire starter. It lights even when wet. It wasn't long before my pockets were bulging with the stuff, and it pleased me beyond measure to be thinking of such necessary things.

From deer to rabbits, I found tracks of both down in the alders and Juneberry bushes along the river. Having already reserved myself to a dinner of tuna fish and boiled potatoes, I didn't hold much hope of spotting either. And then I heard the ducks chattering out on the water, right back in the slough where I chased them from a couple hours before. The snow was still coming down, falling now as fine as dust. Everything was so crisp, clear, and cold. It sounded as if the ducks were right there, just around the next bend.

But creeping closer, I found them some distance away; surely the same ducks that had been here earlier in the afternoon. The drakes were tipping over one another to get their fill of whatever was down below. I sat hunkered down behind a drift of snow watching until it was clear they didn't have any intention of coming closer.

It was a long shot, but a makable one. And in less time than it takes to write it, I picked out a drake in the middle of the paddling and let go an arrow. But by the time it got there another duck had climbed over the back of the one I wanted. At first it appeared as if I had missed all of them. Up and away I watched them, not quite believing that I'd missed. And as it turned out I hadn't.

One of them faltered and went limp and fell just before they cleared the trees. It splashed down on the edge of the slough and I set off running along the bank to intercept him. A drake: a beautiful greenhead. The killing shot, a small gash on his neck where the broadhead passed an inch or so under the bill.

After that, I felt damn near invincible walking back to camp. I tried to take in everything: the soul-quieting snow; the heft of the mallard in my hand; the wood rattle of my arrows in the quiver as I walked. Everything. All while knowing it might be quite sometime until I felt this way again.

After plucking the duck clean (the breast skin the color of autumn corn), I found my little hide under the boughs of a cedar tree and there built a fire with the birch bark I'd collected. The flames I fed with snow-covered limbs that hissed and popped. The duck cooked at a miserably slow paced, only to come out a little dry—and a little burnt, too—when it was done. But in spite of that it tasted as good as any duck I've ever eaten.

It's dark outside as I remember all this to paper. I put a candle lantern up on the underside of the canoe seat, and I'm lying here now packed in by down sleeping bag barely able to see the page under its dull glow. My quarters are tight, though wonderfully comfortable. For warmth, I wrapped in a towel a stone from the fire ring and stuffed it down into the foot of my bag. Before going to sleep I will take a look outside just to make sure it hasn't stopped snowing.

I hope it snows all night. I hope to be covered over with the stuff by morning.

Saturday, November 22

Cold this morning and wakened every couple of minutes or so because of it. But in spite of that, I felt strangely refreshed—alive—when I rose from my snow-covered tomb this morning.

The sun was just coming over the trees, but it was miserable cold out in the air. A cup of coffee would have tasted fine, but I hadn't had the foresight to bring any. So I settled for a cup of river water, which was so chilly going down it made my throat ache.

The snow stopped sometime during the night. But so much of it had fallen that a passerby would never have noticed my camp. Even the fire pit was covered over, and my tracks all but obliterated.

While getting my gear together, I ate a couple handfuls of granola from the bag I had ferreted away in my pack. Then I set off across the slough to retrieve my arrow that had killed the duck for me last evening.

The sky this morning was powder blue and streaked with clouds the color of fire. All the trees along the banks were bent over, their branches hanging down, laden with snow that everywhere glowed with a soft pink light. The arrow stuck in the riverbank, only its fletching showing, I pulled it free and then paddled in close to shore, paddling slowly, languidly, watching for deer, for squirrels—anything that I might arrow for lunch later that afternoon.

The river below the Brown Bridge impoundment runs faster than above. Almost too fast for hunting. Past the first bend, I surprised another paddling of mallards . . . 25, 50 . . . too many to even begin to count. They all lifted up from the water, a literal wall of mallards, and were gone so fast I didn't even try to reach for my bow.

I drifted tight to the shoreline, veering away only when a log or fallen tree—a "sweeper"—got in the way, spooking tiny trout that darted under the boat and disappeared in the black water midstream.

Not long after the ducks, I came upon the mouth of Swainson Creek and what remains of the old bridge. "October 1907" is etched upon one of the crumbling cement trusses.

The bridge seemed a good place to stop and hunt for a while. I fished here this summer and had twice walked up on deer bedded down in the red diamond willow and switch alders.

The wind this morning was perfect, blowing right out of the North. So after stringing my bow, I slipped on my waders and started still-hunting my way along the riverbank.

The gurgle of the river made for quite walking, and the snow was piled so high on the banks it was like peering over a wall to see if anything was hidden on the other side.

I hadn't gone far before spotting a deer, a doe, deep in the alders. I saw her ears first, then the soft curl of her back. She was close and looking away but in too tricky a spot to manage a shot.

One step on the bank and the snow packed down underfoot sounding exactly like it does when you sit down in a leather chair. She sprung to her feet and bolted. Then more deer appeared, flashes of them, making off ahead of me through the alders like rabbits. They left a half dozen empty beds, one much bigger than the others and standing over it I could smell that sweet, mucky scent of rut. A buck, no doubt. And a big one, judging by the size of the tracks, the old October rubs on trees I found as soon as I started following their trail.

The tracks led into a stand of white pines. I followed, not because I thought I could ever catch up with them but because I would have liked to have just gotten a glimpse of that buck standing there in the snow. But the tracks never did stop running, and finally I gave up on the trail and headed back toward the river.

I will eat a can of tuna fish before shoving off again. And maybe a potato, which I'll wash in the river and eat raw.

A grouse! A big gray one. Rounding a bend I saw it just glide across the river—so close I could see its black beady eye—then set down right inside the trees on the riverbank close to shore. I dropped anchor, taking one arrow from my quiver—one shot—knowing I probably wouldn't get even that.

It landed on the other side of a sweeper—a big fallen maple that looked as if lightning had blasted it into toothpicks in the middle. The entire crown of the tree was hanging in the water and made for a perfect bit of cover to sneak up behind.

But this grouse was a wary one. He went up and out of there like a clap of thunder without me ever getting so much as a glimpse of him.

I crawled up on the bank and found in the snow where he had been sitting. And where I knelt down to get a closer look at the track, another grouse flushed from a deadfall to my left. I got a good long look at this one; perhaps too much of one, as another grouse flushed then from the same spot. Expecting another, I looked for another grouse in that tangle—trying to separate brush from bird . . . staring as hard as I have ever looked at anything. And when I was positive they'd all gone, I took a step and another shot out.

I paddled hard through a long stretch where it seemed as if around every bend was one vacated summer home after another. But the river would again find its way back into the woods, and once there under the cool of the cedars, the snow-covered hills rose up from the water from either shore.

The rest of the afternoon I still-hunted the top of a ridge, finding only the old tracks of deer, trails leading down toward the river into a bowl-shaped hollow, dark with cedar and white pine.

Tuna fish and boiled potatoes for dinner. And a restless night in cold, wakened regularly by thumps on the canoe from a snow pack falling from the branches above.

Sunday, November 23

The deer you see while float-hunting are almost always bedded down. And sometimes they are sleeping, which to me is one of the most unnatural things to behold in the world. I mean, human hunters just aren't supposed to *see* things like that. Only rare that we ever get a glimpse inside.

Stalking along the river, I once crept upon a deer kicking and twitching in its dreams like a dog. This morning, the one I find is cloaked in hoarfrost. Still as stone. Even as I sit here writing it, looking at what's left of her sprawled in the canoe at my feet, it seems impossible, as if the past couple days have culminated in a dream.

When I woke this morning, I had been in fact dreaming of the past couple days. Dreaming of what's real. Seeing myself and reliving the hours and postcard visions of a world covered in snow. I never understood that feeling of being outside oneself until this morning.

Three days within earshot of a river and all of a sudden to hear the gurgling rush of the current I have to really listen, as if it were the pulse of my own heart or the sound of blood coursing through my veins. All of a sudden, what has come to me is a feeling of belonging to this world, a idea most every hunter entertains: a sense that we could make it out here if we wanted to . . . if everything else went bad and we *needed* to.

The doe had dug out a place for herself in the fork of a fallen, snow-covered tree. I first thought her a stump. But then the image took shape. A deer! Drifting past, I anchored the canoe downriver and stalked back against the current.

I watched her dozing for a moment, waiting for the wind to carry my scent toward her. She didn't leap to her feet, but instead rose like a tired old cow. The arrow skimmed over the snow bank between us, and when it passed through her chest a tiny cloud of white air puffed from the hole.

And with that the spell was broken. I found her fallen in the cattails along an oxbow frozen over. She dragged easily back over the snow. And now, as I remember it to paper, I feel an urgency to be gone from here, a sudden revelation coming as quickly as the felling of belonging, that I am not the savage this story suggests or that I often pretend.

I'm thinking of my wife waiting at the railroad bridge downriver and how good it will be to see her. How good it will be to shed these boots and layers of wool, to just sit with her in the warm cabin with the air smelling of orange peels and cinnamon sticks simmering in a pot on the woodstove. Three days, though it suddenly feels as if I've been away forever.

Pushing away from the bank, I dig the paddle deep, letting the river take hold of the living and the dead, pulling away on a strong current running the shortest way home.

Forty Crook Branch

TOM KELLY

If you happen to hunt a great deal, or if you spend a lot of time in the woods for any other reason, there always seems to be a half section of land, somewhere, that fits you better than it fits anybody else.

Any number of things can attract you to a certain place. It may be that you killed a particularly difficult turkey there, or you may find some specific bend in a creek to be unusually attractive. It could be an outcropping of rock, maybe a special view, or perhaps a stand of trees; but it seems that you never go to that place without the distinct feeling that you are coming home, that every tree and rock and fold in the ground is an old friend, and that nothing but good things are ever going to happen to you while you are in there.

Almost invariably, you keep quiet about it.

If, by design, you have hunted with the same man for a number of years, he will be aware of this flaw in your character—though he will never discuss it—and will respect your idiosyncrasy. If you are not a wholly insensitive and barbaric clod, you will very likely detect a similar flaw in him and return the favor.

I know, for example, a man who gets distinctly uneasy whenever the area just north of Whetstone Creek creeps into the discussion. He does not fidget, particularly, or shift his eyes rapidly from side to side, or anything quite so obvious. But his face takes on that carefully expressionless look you use when you are being introduced fulsomely as an after-dinner speaker, or when you fill an inside straight.

Anytime we hunt near there, I am as careful to go in the direction he suggests—and stay there—as I am to listen to the location of the guest bathroom in a strange house and to refrain from opening any other doors on my way down the hall.

I open no strange doors whatever along Whetstone Creek. I do it to be polite. But even if I were impolite and opened them, whatever I saw might not strike my fancy particularly. I only know that somewhere in there something strikes his. Somewhere in there is something he considers private and wants to keep for himself. Obviously, he has found a combination of associations that soothe his soul, and it would be as inappropriate for me to pry into it as it would be to ask to see the love letters he wrote his wife when they were courting.

Besides, I am not all that interested, anyway, so long as he leaves Forty Crook Branch alone.

I am not really the sole owner of Forty Crook Branch. To be perfectly honest about it, I hold no color of title whatsoever. I pay no taxes on it, run no lines, and have no fences. I know that other people go there. I even know that somebody else hunts it. Some bastard killed a hen turkey in there last fall and picked her at the head of the hollow before he smuggled her out. I found her feathers.

But I have never seen anyone there, and if I am lucky, I never will. On those sleepless nights when I prowl around the house, I take a power of comfort in the hope that perhaps the hen murderer has died of leprosy, or maybe some infinitely more loathsome and disgusting disease I never even heard of.

The fact that unknown people may go there doesn't really matter. My lack of proprietorship does not really get into the quick. The core of the matter is that while I am there, I own it; and that is enough.

Now that I have committed the impropriety of discussing the place at all, I cannot tell you exactly what it is that makes it so appealing. God knows I have looked at enough land and timber during my life to be selective, and I have the added advantage of knowing precisely and exactly what my limits are in this respect.

I found this out a good many years ago, when I was assigned to make a critical assessment of the value of a tract of nearly a quarter million acres that had been purchased and was to be divided into five equal parts.

We had a timber cruise, naturally, and had spent some little time poring over stand types and acres and volumes and all the other things that constitute value. But it was decided that a careful appraisal of the property, section by section, made by a single head that had been relieved of all other duties, could best put together an objective opinion of the relative values of the individual fifths.

I began the job on Thanksgiving Day and finished March 1st. Every morning I was waiting in the woods for daylight, and when it got too dark to see, I quit and drove home. With the exception of Christmas Day, when I rested, I spent the entire time, with no distractions whatsoever, in a careful and conscientious examination of a block of land with an excellent road net. At just about the 200,000-acre mark, I made a discovery.

Until then, I could take the map and put my finger on a section at random, shut my eyes, and picture the area in my head with a high degree of accuracy. After that point, old sections passed out of my mind as fast as new ones were added.

Obviously, then, I have a 200,000-acre head.

I have not offered these senile meanderings in an attempt to be impressive, but rather to establish the fact that there is a basis for judgment, that I do have a head full of timber, and that this is not the opinion of a necktie salesman with Grandmother's eighty acres for comparison.

Forty Crook Branch and its environs are something special. If you draw the line from the upper end of Mobile Bay to the northeast corner of the state, go partway up the line and a little to the right, you will be able to locate it—and that is as complete a description as you are ever going to get.

The name of the branch itself no longer appears on the map, and I have no idea who named it originally. Most of our place names in this part of the world, except along the very coast itself, are either Indian or Scotch-Irish in origin. Whatever other abilities the Celts may have, they have a marvelous flair for pungent and distinctive place names and have left the mark of this descriptive poetry on natural landmarks all over the southeast. Names like Burnt Corn Creek and Oven Bluff and Gin House Branch and Goat Hobble Bald, the list is almost endless. The Indian names may be even more pungent but I cannot tell since I speak neither Creek nor Choctaw.

I suspect that Forty Crook Branch was named for the number of curves in it, rather than in any illusion to the companions of Ali Baba, but you never know. At any rate, it is remarkably crooked, and the terrain on both sides of the branch and its tiny feeder streams are as steep as any we have. The most pronounced feature of the area is a single central ridge that runs northeast and has a hollow on either side of it that is distinctly different from its matching hollow on the other side.

The hollow on your left—west—is a mixed stand of pine and hardwood and is almost an even mixture of each. I killed a turkey there one fall, early in the morning, that has the unique distinction of being the only flying bird I ever shot from above. I had missed them on the roost and they were down in the hollow fighting and squalling at one another to work off the ill humors of early morning when I heard the racket. I was able to stay under the crest of the ridge on the east side, until I got abreast of all the noise, and then run across the top and shoot down into the hole. They were all the way down in the bottom of the hollow, 120 yards away, and as they came up, one of them flew up the hill to my right, turned, and crossed along the slope of the ridge right to left and thirty yards below me.

The lead is identical and the swing is exactly the same, but the feeling is decidedly peculiar. I suppose shooting downhill is appropriate for hunters of mountain goats and bighorn sheep, but it is not all that common to bird hunters. Bird hunters get awfully used to looking up when they shoot. Every time I go along that ridge now, I stop and go over to the west side, and in my mind's eye, watch him cross below me. I usually take a practice swing or two there in the highly unlikely event that the situation will ever come up again. I hope it never does. I am batting a thousand in such instances, and lightning never strikes twice.

This remarkable event notwithstanding, the west hollow is not my favorite side. My choice is the one on the east, and its choicest point is at the head of the hollow, just as you walk onto the central ridge.

The central ridge begins as a nonentity. It breaks off from a perfectly ordinary looking hill with some scrubby-looking old-field loblolly pine mixed thinly among a stand of ratty-looking post oak, and falls gently away to a pile of limestone in a thicket of mountain laurel. There is an abrupt right-hand turn in the gap between two rocks the size of elephants, and an equally abrupt left-hand turn behind them. Then you step beyond the screen of laurel and down into an open area the size of a small room.

The room is ringed with limestone rocks that have been broken by weather and frost. Fossilized clamshells are visible along all of the breaks. The ring is nearly waist-high, and the area commands a view of both hollows and looks along the path that follows the crest of the ridge.

Just below the ring, the ridge saddles, and the path beyond, the saddle gently rises and passes from sight among the trees. The central ridge then curves gently to the right, beginning at a point just beyond the disappearance of the path, and you have a fine view along the eastern slope.

The first ten chains of the east hollow is an almost pure stand of beech.

I have never understood why the druids fooled away their time deifying an oak tree when beech was available. Sargent's manual lists nineteen commercial species of oak indigenous to south Alabama and four species of scrub. After you get past cherrybark oak, there is not fourteen cents worth of class in the lot of them.

Live oak has limbs that twist away from a central trunk for as much as twenty yards and is prone to festoons of Spanish moss, which you always associate with funerals and pallbearers.

Overcup has a regrettable tendency to have sucker sprouts all along the trunk, which ruin the symmetry of the bole. All of the red oaks produce a staple food for game, and we have to have them, but corn bread and collard greens with side meat are the same kind of staple. You may eat them all the time, but you don't put on your necktie and specifically take your wife out to dinner just to buy them. They may be good, but they do not go with candlelight and damask napkins and brandy and a good cigar afterward.

Beech does.

Not only is a beech tree handsome, but it has a nut that is perfectly delicious. If I were rich and powerful, I would have beechnuts collected by faithful family retainers and put them in my fruitcake rather than pecans. I might even eat them on my cereal for breakfast. A stand of beech, with its smooth blue-gray bark all the way to the stump, is cool and dim and hushed early in the year, when the leaves are on, and light and open and airy in the fall and winter, when the white bark on the thin, naked branches shines in the afternoon sun.

Forty Crook Branch itself starts in this hollow and makes up from a spring that first appears from under a monstrous limestone rock. The branch runs in a series of abrupt turns almost from its beginning and on the inside of most of the bends is what can only be called a sandbar, even though most of them are less than ten feet long and eighteen inches wide. The sand in these bars is clean and gray and has tiny flecks of mica in it.

Once, years ago, when she was very small, I took the Colonel's daughter there—the last half mile on my back—and cut her name and the date in small, dainty block letters low down on a beech tree. In my pocket I had brought a little block of wood with a hole through it, and we set up a flutter mill there in the creek made out of forked and split sticks with halves of magnolia leaves for blades. The whole thing was tied together with strips of bearpaw.

She watched the wheel run, with delight, and got both feet wet in the branch. Then she ran her fingers over her name cut in the bark and asked me if the shiny flecks of mica were tiny diamonds. I assured her that they were, with the utmost solemnity, and congratulated her upon her perspicacity in finding them.

We swore never to disclose the location of our mine to anybody, but agreed that if, later on, either of us ever needed money, he or she could come back and gather some.

I have never killed a turkey in this hollow, though there is a perfect place to do it. There is a beech there that overlooks an arena exactly one gunshot across. The tree has two buttressed roots which come away from the bole on both sides of your butt exactly the right distance apart and curve down at just the proper height to support each elbow. The ground in front of the tree drops away just gently enough to allow you to dig your heels in properly and not leave your knees propped up too high. It is as comfortable as a rocking chair, and I have done some of my very best sleeping there, in the fall, after I have scattered turkeys in the morning and had come back after lunch, and it made no real difference where I sat.

I have run a couple of turkeys off the roost there in the spring—turkeys that were gobbling fit to choke themselves—by crowding them in the last few yards of my approach in a futile attempt to get to that tree. In both instances, it was one of those pieces of stupidity that you carefully commit while your native good judgment is shrieking at you continuously to stop.

I am going to do exactly the same the next time it happens, too, because just one time, before I die, I am going to kill a turkey out of that rocking chair. It is important. It gets more important every year I don't get to do it.

Below the rocking chair, the hollow begins to widen and you move out of pure beech and begin to run through the mixed stands of upland oak and hickory common to the upper coastal plain. It is at this point that I usually climb the central ridge and walk along it, rather than staying down in my favorite hollow. If you are hunting, you have an opportunity to listen in both hollows simultaneously; and if you are just visiting, you get a marvelous overview of either side. The ridge is so narrow and the sides so steep, that as you walk along, you are level with the tops of eighty-foot trees down in either hollow and it is the next best thing to flying.

Right out on the point of the ridge, nearly a mile from its beginning and just before it drops off, there is a clump of shortleaf pine, not all that big, but old as hell. You can sit there and listen to the wind in the needles and look out over three-quarters of a county. In cold weather, you don't want to stay too long because the wind gets such a clear shot at you out there. But cold or hot, it is always worth the trip. Even if the sun is not shining and the rain has wet you straight through, it is still worth it, because the woods are always gloomy as hell on rainy days and there is a perverse pleasure, in one sense, at looking out over a quarter million acres of gloom.

When I leave Forty Crook Branch, I always try to go out so as to pass by the tree in the curve where we built the mill. I never go in to the site itself. I go close enough to see that the tree is still there, that lightning has not struck it, or a summer windstorm blown it flat since the last visit. But I never go far enough to see over the little hill and look in the bottom of the branch.

Because I have never gone back for my share of the diamonds.

In point of fact, I have not put my eyes on her name since the day I cut it in the tree. The mill cannot still be there. It was hardly built for the ages and could not have survived the first rainstorm. I would rather not go back and look at the scene of the ruin. The tree and the mill belong to the day itself, not to any other.

I never will go back.

So long as I never do, my shares are still there, still held in escrow. So long as I never do, she is still there, always four years old, always under the tree with her name on it, stooped in the sand by her mill with the utter absorption of a little child, enchanted with her diamonds.

I hope she never needs them.

Excerpted from *Better On a Rising Tide* with the author's permission. To order his books, go to www.tomkellyinc.net.

Acolytes

TOM KELLY

Of all the social customs that are in use along the Gulf Coast, one of the more civilized is that of calling older people by their first names, and preceding the name by the honorific. A stranger to the region will hear these references to Miss Laura or Mr. George and come to the logical conclusion that all these people are either spinsters or aged bachelors. The conclusion may be logical, but it is in error. The custom is not grounded on the marital status of the individual. It is, rather, a combination of affection and respect and is a method whereby the younger person can simultaneously avoid the callow presumption of the Christian name and the stiff formality of the family name. It is used properly only in friendship and only after long familiarity with the older person. It helps to bridge those gaps formed by either rank or years.

If the custom had not been firmly entrenched at the time Robert Cobb's years made him eligible for its benefits, it would have been necessary to invent it—specifically for him. I have never met a man it fitted better.

Kindly, courteous, considerate, white haired, member of a distinguished family, Robert Cobb has all the attributes and qualifications. He is the very epitome of the fatherly old regimental commander beloved by all his troops. Except for one thing. Any regiment unfortunate enough to go into action with Robert Cobb as its commander would need a five-ton truck to bring back the dog tags.

Ever since the American Revolution, it has been customary for former members to poke fun at the United States Army. Not only do they poke fun at it, some of them write rather bitter exposes of its criminal stupidity. The army, God love it, manages to muddle through somehow despite these waspish attacks, and it is not nearly as stupid as it is made out to be. It was astute enough, in 1917, to immediately recognize the quality of one of its newest recruits and see to it that Robert Cobb remained a private throughout his service. Mr. Robert made no objection and accepted his station cheerfully and without resentment. The Cobb family, as a matter of practice, invariably offers its services in emergencies of all kinds and accepts whatever assignment is given. Mr. Robert's rank was no real handicap to him at the time he served. It was only of minor importance later, because of where he lives. It was important because it effectively denied him a courtesy title.

It is customary in this region for a man to carry his title to the grave. The country abounds with people who are called "Judge" or "Senator" or "Colonel" because at one time or another they have been one. But nobody ever seems to use the courtesy title of private. We have a lot more ex-privates than we have of anything else, but none of the former privates clings to the title. It just doesn't seem to have the proper ring to it.

Mr. Robert has never alluded to this handicap in my hearing because I do not think he feels hurt over it. He served the nation to the best of his ability in the position the nation selected for him, and he considers that to be sufficient. What did hurt his feelings was that the army declined his services in 1942. A forty-five-year-old rifleman is hardly a pearl of great price to begin with, and it is possible that the army remembered his performance as a twenty-year-old. But the fact remains that he was not invited to the war, and he has never forgiven the army for its omission.

Unfortunately, there are a great many things that Mr. Robert does not understand. I do not mean for a minute to say that he is simpleminded, for he is not. He just thinks differently. He has a genius for bad luck and disaster and, were it not for the fact that the Cobb family is both wealthy and influential, he would have had a pretty hard time of it over the years. His family, and everybody else, makes excuses for him, finds things for him to do, and no one ever overrides his opinions pointedly or insinuates that he is anything other than a full member of the lodge, with all rights and privileges. It is easy to do all this because he is so thoroughly nice.

He has one premier and transcendental quality.

He is the worst turkey hunter in southwest Alabama.

The statement is accurate, is made carefully and with due deliberation, and you should consider the source. With no intention of being offensive to a sister state, calling a man the worst turkey hunter in Rhode Island, for instance, is no real star in his crown. It is sort of like your mother's thinking you are handsome. She has no real basis for comparison, and her judgment must be considered suspect.

Southwest Alabama abounds with turkey hunters, and they come in all shapes, sizes, and levels of expertise. To be considered the worst of all this multitude is to be a rare bird indeed. I do not mean simply to imply that Mr. Robert is ignorant. There are whole swamps full of turkey hunters who are simply ignorant. They have stumbled upon a particularly stupid turkey while deer hunting and killed it.

Somebody walking through the woods has flushed one over their head, and they killed it. Somebody has taken them along one spring morning and called a turkey up on their side, and they killed it. And they pass then, in their own minds, from one side of the salt to the other and become full voting members of the board.

They enter avidly into all the telephonic transmission of intelligence that goes on at night during the spring season. They become the life and soul of those early morning discussions on tactics and techniques in small-town cafés. They give freely of their advice on shot sizes, attend with critical ears all the turkey calling contests held south of the Tennessee line, pontificate at cocktail parties about the difficulties of their sport and, along about here, invest in a three-inch Magnum with a 30-inch barrel. They remind you of a 14-year-old girl struggling with her first pair of high heels—willing but awkward, and a little bit pitiful.

Mr. Robert is different. Mr. Robert suffers from that most tragic defect of all: experienced incompetence.

He was born in the middle of turkeys in the last year of the nineteenth century, and was presented with his first shotgun in 1908. If you believe half the stories you have heard about the era, it was perfectly possible, in 1908, to feed a family with a backyard garden and a 12-gauge. The hunting seasons opened when the summer ducks got big enough to fly, turned into serious business at the first cool snap, and ended only when the turkeys quit gobbling on the first of May. Here was a boy from a family of considerable financial resources, who could begin hunting at his back gate and who, except for school, had nothing else to do with his time. He turned himself into a superb shot—he is still one. Slow now, as you would expect, but given time to get ready, as good as anybody. He should be able to get inside a turkey's head and think like one. But he cannot, and I have never been able to figure out exactly why. And he is not alone. Their ranks are much diminished now, but thirty years ago, a great many of his contemporaries were still active, and a disproportionate number of them suffered from the same defect.

I suspect it is because the first decade of this century concerned itself largely with numbers. The browning, faded old photographs all bear that out. Pictures of boatloads of ducks or 30 feet of deer, hanging side by side on the same pole. A Model-T Ford with two men holding the ends of a string of fish far longer than the car. An angle in a rail fence with the hunters standing behind a pile of doves ten feet in diameter and knee-high. They seem to have taken a lot of pride in things like this. There was plenty to shoot, the supply was obviously inexhaustible, and you demonstrated your expertise by coming home with a back load of game.

Nobody, even then, was going to kill a boxcar full of turkeys, and I think they got so wrapped up in their numbers that turkeys were considered too slow to fool around with.

When the doldrums came—that period between World War I and 1950, when turkeys nearly went away—almost nobody fooled around with them. And after 1950, when turkeys, like Lazarus, rose from the sepulcher, it was, for most of that generation, then too late.

Those, like Mr. Robert, who could still make it past the front-porch swing, came out of retirement, accepted what they considered was a bounden duty to pass their skills on to the next generation, and showered their ignorance upon us. In certain instances, this ignorance fell as the gentle rain from heaven. Now and then there was a deluge.

I am being a trifle unfair, and I know it, because some of these creaky old folks knew exactly what they were doing. These knowledgeable individuals got the job done. Unfortunately, there were many, many more whose only qualification was the simple fact that they had lived through the era. Because I am a member of our peculiar society, a civilization that believes in its soul that expertise in one field automatically creates expertise in another, at first I was delighted to have Mr. Robert take me under instruction. There are not all that many turkey hunters willing to waste a morning on a rookie under the best of circumstances—and in those days there was a dreadful shortage of experts. Slowly I began to find out there was even one fewer than I had thought there was to begin with.

Here was a man whom I had seen call ducks across a quarter mile of marsh, a man whose delicate touch with a fly rod had to be seen to be believed, and a man whose careful, courteous, generous instruction was a perfect pile of horseshit. Naturally, I didn't know it at the time and spent several seasons under his careful tutelage, patiently committing all this useless excrement to memory. I would have been infinitely better off if he had refused to help me at all.

Mr. Robert is of that school that feels you should never get closer than a quarter of a mile to a gobbling turkey and is, in addition, a charter member of the Soft and Seldom Yelping Society. We would tiptoe to a point just inside the 500-yard mark, sit under a tree while he fiddled around and got out his wing bone, and then he would emit three tentative, plaintive, hesitant peeps at about the same volume you would expect from a baby hummingbird.

Then he would carefully put his wing bone back in his pocket, deliver a whispered homily about how many turkeys had been run off by too much yelping, and we would sit at the base of the tree and commune with nature for thirty minutes. During this time, the turkey would continue to gobble on the roost, hens would answer, hens would run or fly through the woods on their way to the gobbling, and the turkey would finally fly down, gather the ladies under his wing, and go off. I don't know whether or not these turkeys would have come to our calling, but we gave them no chance. They never heard us.

One morning, in the middle of one of these affairs, we made a mistake. We tiptoed in and sat down in the same township with a gobbling turkey, and just as Mr. Robert did his imitation of an orphaned hummingbird, a turkey we had not even suspected was in the country gobbled in a tree a scant 200 yards to our left. The turkey flew down in a matter of minutes, came steadily and directly to us in a full strut, and Mr. Robert shot him neatly in the head at a distance of thirty steps.

On the way out of the woods, in the same delicate, carefully chosen terms you use to suggest a possible lack of virtue in another man's wife, I ventured to suggest that maybe we ought to try getting a little closer and yelping a little louder. Mr. Robert put the turkey down in the middle of the logging road, turned around so that I could get the full effect of his snow white hair and senatorial diction, and made me feel as if I had suggested we sell the First Presbyterian Church to the Hindus so they could have a place to stable their water buffalo.

I was not a child at the time of this incident. I was a grown man in my middle twenties. But when he got through with me I could have crawled under a leaf and hidden.

In some detail, the lecture covered ingratitude, callow ignorance, disrespect of elders, a blatant disregard of tradition, and the possibility of prior cases of misidentification of certain babies in certain hospitals. He even managed to work in the gallantry of the Confederate Army and the purity of Southern womanhood. It was a masterful performance, and it is a pity that it could not have been recorded. It could serve as a shining example to public-speaking classes all the way from Virginia to Texas.

Impressive as it may have been, it had one of the characteristics of four volleys from a battalion of eight-inch artillery. It was far more enjoyable on the sending end than it was on the receiving.

Mr. Robert did not turn me out into the world alone from that moment, although I suspect he wanted to. He is far too generous and far too conscientious. Even though ignorant and ungrateful, the young must be instructed. But the incident always lay between us.

It lies there yet.

No matter what I do, no matter what I may become, no matter what rank or fame or wealth I may acquire, I will always remain the unlicked cub who asked, in effect, wouldn't we all be just as well off with only Nine Commandments. I suspect he is secretly relieved that I am safely married. There is little chance that I might, some bleak day, ask to form an alliance with the daughter of some member of his immediate family.

I did begin to hunt a great deal more with other people. He began, more and more, to spread around his instruction. There were, after all, far more deserving swine before whom he could cast his pearls. And then one day we both looked up and realized that we had not hunted together for a long time.

In the more than thirty years that have passed since I blotted my copybook, Mr. Robert has not learned a thing. He is still moderately active now, though much enfeebled. He goes through life serene and confident in the sure knowledge that he is absolutely right, giving roosted buzzards to people in the firm conviction that they are turkeys. He calls at night to present unscattered droves of nonexistent turkeys to innocent bystanders. He is the life and soul of every turkey-calling contest held in a five-county area, sits firmly in the middle of the front row, and makes no comment whatsoever if I appear upon the platform as a judge.

The Cobb household goes through no single Thanksgiving or Christmas dinner with the shame of a tame turkey upon the table. One or another of his ex-students always manages to get one into Miss Sally's kitchen with some flimsy excuse about not having time to get it plucked, or the pressures of a forthcoming business trip or some other such transparent fiction. The ones that come from me—the bad seed—get there through an intermediary, sworn to secrecy.

Any day now, and considering how fast he appears to be fading, someday soon, Miss Sally is not going to be able to wake him up one morning, and we are going to have the biggest funeral the county ever saw. The cars are going to stretch from the First Presbyterian Church all the way down to the courthouse on both sides of the street—after the parking lot gets full. There will be three preachers at the church, and another at the cemetery, and the honorary pallbearers will fill the entire first four rows of the left-hand side of the congregation. There is going to be a firing party from his old company of his old regiment; and the first volley is going to be presentable, the second ragged, and the third a disgrace. The boy from the high school band who plays taps is going to do some ugly things to the notes that make up the sixth bar, and when the flag is put in Miss Sally's lap, it is going to be folded a little crooked and have the wrong corner showing.

If you happen to be a stranger driving through town that day on your way to someplace important, you might wonder about the reason for the size of the turnout.

If you ask, you are going to express surprise when you are told it is for a man who never rose above the rank of private, never held a public office, was never a power behind anybody's political throne, and who never, in all his life, amassed a sizable estate or made any substantial fortune.

If you are still curious, do not ask the family. They won't be able to help you.

Go down to the barbershop, or visit the boat dock. Go by the depot or, better yet, go talk to that pack of loafers who play dominoes under the oak tree on the courthouse square. Ask any of these.

These are his acolytes.

Any one of them will be happy to explain.

Excerpted from *Better On a Rising Tide* with the author's permission. To order his books, go to www.tomkellyinc.net.

A Sudden Silence

TERRY WIELAND

Sometimes it is Not What Happens so Much as What Happens Afterwards

The buffalo came in a rush of heaving shoulders, out of the thicket, head up, hunting. The bullets struck and his body followed his head around and down on top of me.

The bolt worked on its own, firing, ejecting, firing again as the buffalo came on with our eyes locked, and part of me loved him as the other part worked the rifle in a concentration of conscious effort and subconscious analysis, counting down the shots remaining . . . *three, two, one . . .*

We cut strips from his loins and blackened them over a fire as the skinners worked. The meat was rubbery-fresh and juicy, and we chewed and chewed and chewed in the silence that persisted in spite of the chattering voices and the breeze ruffling the trees.

Then a part of me withdrew. I would sit in camp and look out across the plain to the smoke rising from the lower slopes of Kilimanjaro. They were burning off the grass and the smoke mingled with the clouds that shrouded the peak. I stared at it for hours at a time. Sometimes I would walk to the edge of camp and look back up the mountain where the Cape buffalo had died with his eyes still fixed on me, muzzle to muzzle with my rifle. Then my other self returned, haggard but intact. It was very quiet in that camp, I remember. That part of it lasted two or three days.

Magic

TERRY WIELAND

It was a day like you find late in the fall, when the leaves are off the trees and the snow comes gently in wet flakes—when the sky is gray and motionless and you learn how good canned soup can be, steaming on a woodstove, and the snow you stamp off your boots lies unmelting on the cabin floor.

Claire was an old man even then, a man who had hunted deer up there for longer than I had been alive. He started with his father just after the first war, saw his father's last hunts, taught his son what it was all about, and then sort of adopted me when his sons went off and married. I was not an orphan, except in the sense of being a kid in thrall to hunting but trapped in a family of indoorsmen, and I took to Claire and his old '94 like a tack to a tire.

It was the last day of the season, a Saturday when everyone was out for one last time. The deer were starting to yard up, and even seeing one was a long shot at best. With a new rifle and a pair of new dub-bined boots and my first deer license, out in the woods with real ammunition, it did not matter to me how long the odds were; I still expected a big buck to appear the way bucks did in *Outdoor Life*, heavy-horned and silhouetted against the snowy timber. Wet and cold but supremely unmiserable, even the long trip back across the lake to the cabin, with the waves slapping and ice building up on my precious Marlin, felt good to me. And the smell of that soup on the stove as I lugged more firewood into the cabin—I can still feel it all today.

We were on the last of the coffee when Claire took his pipe out of his mouth and started to talk, looking into the fire. It felt awfully good, that fire, and if Claire wanted to talk for a while rather than get right back out there, it was okay with me. It was a long way across the lake with only a chilly stand to look forward to. Afternoon optimism is tough.

"We might see a deer later, and we might not," he said. "There aren't as many as there used to be. Haven't been for quite a few years. I'd like to see you get your first one, but other than that, I don't much care if I shoot another one. I just like to be up here hunting them."

Many fall days have slipped away since that one. Many big wet flakes have drifted down, and now a few of them sift gently onto the place where Claire is buried. There have been mountaintops in Alaska and plains in Tanzania and swamps in Botswana; I've made a few good shots and missed more than a few easy ones, and I've stared into a lot of campfires, and every one is as good as the last. Sitting by the fire in Alaska one time, a fire that was built with wet alders and camp scrap and was more wishful thinking than anything else, a sheep guide said to me that he'd climb over an entire mountain range and down a dozen hanging glaciers if there was the chance of a big ram at the end of it, but he couldn't understand people who would do that just to get a photograph.

"It ain't the meat and it ain't the horns," he said. "I don't know what it is, but that's what makes it all worthwhile."

I don't know exactly what it is either, truth to tell, any more than Dale did, although actually I suspect we both knew, we just could not explain it.

One of the great things about big game hunting, more than any other activity known to man, is that one minute you can be poor as a church mouse, soaked through, shivering, with a thousand dollar rifle rusting into scrap before your very eyes, and the next minute you can be richer than Solomon—all because an animal walked out of the woods and threw his head back, and you made one of those wonderful miraculous shots that was as much luck as anything, but at least it was luck you made yourself. This is a fact that has been true since man first killed something to eat and hung the antlers in a tree over the campfire; it has been true since there has been a god of hunting (or a goddess, depending on who and what you are); and it will still be true long after all the other artificial pastimes we have invented to take the place of hunting are gone and forgotten. That is why there has always been a god of hunting, and why there will never be a god of racquetball.

It is why what you get will never be as important as what you gave to get it, and why sometimes you find, when the search has failed, that the search itself was what you were really looking for. That is when you look at a big Dall ram on the wall and remember what it took to get him back down the mountain, long since out of water with darkness coming on, and having to dig deeper into yourself than you ever did before. And why, forever after, you could say, "No matter what happens, no one can take away from me that on that night, in that place, I did those things." That is why, looking at your cat curled up asleep on the bear skin, you can remember what that bear looked like when he came down off the hill at a dead and silent run. That is why the Cape buffalo will always be a memory of heaving shoulders and blowing blood and shooting from the hip, and to hell with how wide he was. He was plenty wide enough.

Then there are the times when a plan works to the letter, and the buck is exactly where he is supposed to be, when he's supposed to be there, and your pal drops him with one perfect shot as you come out of the woods, grinning. He's only a forkhorn, with one tine broken at that, but the plan simply worked too well to waste. The meat will be damned good, anyway, and those little antlers are just the right size to make a rattle. There's a buck just like that one hanging up outside my window right now, beside the woodpile. That hunt was 27 minutes from start to finish, like clockwork, but I'll remember it the rest of my life, just like the five-point bull in Colorado that Jim flushed out of the bush that time. Half the bunch went one way, the other half the other, but the one big bull came straight and nearly ran me down. I shot him at ten yards, in self-defense as much as anything. He was good meat, too.

It is fall again now, and last night for the first time we had those big heavy flakes. They covered the little buck where he hangs from the high branch, coated him like frosting, and I look at him every time I go out for more wood. He's high enough the wolves won't get him, but the shotgun is by the door anyway.

All of those are real things. The buck is real. The shotgun is real. God knows the wolves are real. None of it is magic, unless it all is. Claire was right all along. The magic lies just in being there.

Struggle and Chance: Why We Do It

DATUS PROPER

You never know when you will catch what you are chasing, but in good country you have faith. You stop and swing your gun three times where bright, unmown hay pushes against a thicket of twisted limbs. You dare the pheasant to flush. He is in the geometry of leaf and trunk, hill and field; you see how his colors will shine in the sun. Enough of this will conjure him up. You keep going. You do not intend to do violence to yourself, but the harder you try, the better your odds. This knowledge draws you out.

At the edge of fatigue comes relief: your head floats free of your legs. It feels a little like the sensation you get from a portable radio playing music in both ears as you ride a bus to work—but better. (I tried the recorded music once and did not like it because it got between mind and world. Bad as the commuter's environment was, an impermeable membrane between it and me was worse.) The hunter's high brings a heightened perception of wind in the aspens, mud squishing around boots, places where a pheasant ought to be. At this point it becomes easy to understand how visions came to Indians seeking them. A person who does mostly mental work needs this feeling; craves fresh air in the confines of brain and body. Perhaps everyone needs it.

You can get a runner's high, too, so it may have something to do with the blood pumped from legs that are weakening to a brain growing more active—a passing of the baton from the tired part of you to the fresh. I don't know, but the effect has a name: euphoria.

Euphoria feels as good as it sounds. According to the *American Heritage Dictionary*, it means: "1. A feeling of great happiness or well-being; bliss. 2. *Psychiatry.* An exaggerated sense of well-being in pathological cases involving sympathetic delusions." I leave the pathology to the pathologists and the physiology to the physiologists. What I think I understand is the music that the brain plays without benefit of radio. It is quite real, and here is how it works.

Your brain is constantly thinking, out there in the fields. You can confirm that easily next time you take a walk. You may not realize, however, that you are thinking in a language—presumably English, for most readers of this book. You are in a language mode even when you do not think aloud. This is by no means my discovery. I did not even grasp it till I came to know my own language by learning others. In time I found myself thinking in a couple of them, recognizing the words because they did not come so naturally as those in English. Language, it seems, is a way of forming thoughts, not just expressing them.

Your language is timed by your breathing. (This is easy to feel if you talk aloud to yourself as you walk.) Your breaths, in turn, are timed by the needs of your legs and heart and emotions. Musicians play the rhythms of the chase as if they were pounded out by a horse's four hooves—but you march to the same drummer, biped, after you get going. Your chair-bound muscles stretch. Your tempo becomes upbeat, as regular as the farmland where pheasants live: andante for the most part, allegro when dog strikes scent, presto when he trails the bird. And by now you are thinking in meter. You cannot help it.

Hunting is the oldest song, I guess. It would be nice to know the mother language that our ancestors evolved on the African plains. This much I can report: English is right because it has feet—literally. Feet (sequences of stressed and unstressed syllables) are the units of meter. Modern English-language poets sometimes soar above their language's feet, just to be different, and when they do, readers walk away. Conventional Spanish and French poets do not use meter, and their poems do not move my boots. I dream in Portuguese, sometimes, but I hike in English.

By the time you hear the beat, the thing that caused it has become important. It *must* be important to have done this to you. Therefore you try very hard to shoot the bird when your chance comes. You try even if you were not eager when you started walking. If you have not had the experience, you may find this baffling, but I imagine the long-distance hunters nodding yes, yes.

Whether you miss your chance or make it, you fix the pheasant's place by its coordinates. You will need to call it back later at the edge of sleep. The spot will be precise, then: the intersection of struggle and chance. Your energy carries you far enough to cross the pheasant's path at some random place. Your dog's search meets the bird's collusion with cover. Your gun swings to intercept the path of flight. Your brain sends your trigger-finger a signal at the millisecond when the curves cross. The trajectories in time and space all intersect. True sports have such junctions and so does life, if played as a participant sport. Watching does not count.

One day you get no chances for all your struggle. Or, worse yet, you fail chances that you should have seized. Another time you make them all. If you consistently get limits, however, consider making the rules more difficult for yourself. Field sports are not about targets and scores. Score-keeping is necessary in competitions between humans, unattractive in competitions with weaker adversaries. Consistent scores of many to zero do not smell of struggle and chance. They smell of greed.

We oscillate between excess and fastidiousness, these days. We do not kill chickens in the kitchen and save their blood, as old recipes instruct, or make a holiday of butchering our pigs, as the Portuguese still do. We insulate ourselves from natural human death, too. I do not know whether it is a coincidence that our television sets are Roman circuses, displays of gladiators killing each other for the pleasure of an audience. Then there is the violence on streets, drug-pushers slaughtering for the privilege of selling effort-free thrills to the self-indulgent. Either this is not civilization or Freud was wrong when he saw civilization as holding unconscious impulses in check.

My family escapes most of the nastiness. We have no television set, see few films, live far from big cities. It is a boycott and more. The fact is that I am squeamish. So is my son, who never had a chance to get used to television. My wife is made of sterner stuff; I can bribe her to trap mice, which would take over the place if I were in charge.

Shooting our food is not like that. Sometimes I do feel sorry for woodcocks, ducks, bobwhites, and deer, in that order, but I hunt them, with restrictions to placate myself. We all draw the line somewhere. In Virginia, a neighbor installed an electric bug-zapper behind his opulently landscaped house. All night the infernal machine drew pretty moths to its light and fried them with sparks and sizzles. On the other hand, he would not teach his son to shoot an air rifle. Few of us today would kill a panda; many (but not me) are happy to squash spiders. I have no problem shooting rattlesnakes that threaten my pup. I do not want to kill any primate, any relative of the dog, anything young with big eyes. Do not bother to tell me that this makes no sense. I know that. It is anthropomorphism: the Panda or Cuddle Factor. It explains, I suppose, why the debate between anti-hunters and hunters is a dialogue of the deaf, between those who see hunting as an atrocity and those who suspect that the rest of life is the atrocity.

I feel few pangs for the cock pheasant. He is a dragon. If this be sympathetic delusion, make the most of it.

When I slay the pheasant, I kill, first, the dragon in me, which is the ugly one appearing in most Western art. Western painters have known about that greedy creature for as long as it has been threatening to consume us. They have, however, been ignorant of nature's dragon, the one that lures rather than repels. You are not to think that all dragons are ugly. Watch those that appear in Chinatown parades. These are the lovely dragons of the swamps, the ones that a Chinese artist could see running around in a rice paddy: serpent's tail, eagle's wings, hawk's beak and eyes, cruel spurs. I have watched the cock pheasant chase off a fox.

At night I slay my dragon by the edge of the twisted forest. My son tells me that he does it too, and from the way Huckleberry runs and yips in his sleep, I conclude that pointer pups are in on the game. My wife, on the other hand, reports that the dragons in her country have been rendered extinct by a knight in shining armor. Perhaps the meaning of dragons is sex-linked. I do not know about this, but you may have confidence that *my* dragons are the real thing.

I clutch this reality as an antidote to indifference. We think of hunting and fishing as escape, and they are. They are escape from a society of escapism: from pervasive complacency, from media pitched to the lowest common denominator, from trivialization of thought, from the politics of blandness, from gladiators, celebrities, entertainment, scandals, the life synthetic. A hunter chasing pheasants feels everything except anomie.

Pheasants make the fields and roadsides glow with feathers; women make the town swirl with skirts and fresh-washed hair. It is (I guess) no coincidence that the goddess of the chase is female, or that wives wear T-shirts reading, "This marriage has been interrupted for the hunting season." Diana's pheasants and Eros's women populate adjacent sections of the male landscape.

Once, clothed in old jeans before old jeans were fashionable, I rode a decrepit motorcycle from my home in Montana to college in New York. North Dakota was the best part because the sun was shining and girls were on the sidewalks. My form of transportation seemed as romantic to me as it must have looked forbidding to anyone in her right mind. The streets shone with possibilities. As dungeon holds fair maiden, so might Fargo hold The Girl. I would scarcely have known what to do with her even if, by some miracle, her mother had not whisked her away from the hoodlum with bugs squashed between his black leather helmet and Lindbergh goggles. Thinking that she might appear was enough to make North Dakota beautiful.

"A trip to Florence or to Athens is one thing for a young man who hopes to meet his Beatrice on the Ponte Santa Trinita or his Socrates in the Agora," says Allan Bloom, "and quite another for one who goes without such aching need. The latter is only a tourist, the former looking for completion."

Diana the huntress is another kind of completion: perhaps the only kind besides Beatrice the woman and Socrates the thinker. Hunting aches as much as the other two needs. Diana is distinctly older than thinking and older even than Eros, properly speaking. (Do not confuse Eros with mere reproduction.)

You can hunt with a bow and arrow or fishing rod instead of a gun. Perhaps you can hunt with binoculars and camera. I like them, but I use them mostly at comfortable times. The people I see hunting with lenses are near roads, in wildlife refuges, after breakfast, and sometimes in groups. They are more tourist than hunter. It seems to take a gun to get one into the lonely, thorny places before winter dawns.

In Diana's company you are not a tourist. You are not trying to peer into a distant secret magnified eight times by a lens. You are a hunter/forager like all wild animals. You have accepted the risks and discomfort that go along with climbing through the looking glass, into the secret.

When you descend from Diana's world and get back into your car, you leave the secret but take some of its emotions with you. You are now as far from real things as a tourist, but you see them differently. Bent cornstalks and collapsing barns are no longer objects, pretty or ugly. They are possibilities, sparks of excitement, stars that shine in the fields as you drive by. You must check them out next time. Hunting has populated the countryside with needs and meanings. The farm has become the faerie. It hides a pheasant.

There is a future in this. We will increasingly value bird hunting, especially with pointing dogs. The conviction settled on me, oddly, when a friend and editor asked me to investigate trends in trout flies over the last thirty years. What I discovered was that there had been a boom in dry flies, and in imitative dry flies at that—those representing specific natural insects. Fishing with such flies is effective. It takes science, art, magic. It is visual, rational, demanding. It is fun. It is like hunting with a pointer, though more cerebral, not so relentlessly honest.

Call the dog's point a miracle or spell; either is close enough. Or consider it a gamble for high stakes between predator and prey. At core, the point is a prolongation of the pause before pouncing. All canids and felids (or at least all I have seen) do it. Why? Why not just jump on the prey without wasting time?

The answer became clear when Jeff Koski loaned me a "recall pen" so big that I could walk inside. We stocked the pen with a dozen bobwhites. For each training session, I catch a couple and put them out in the grass for the pup to point. At the end of the session, the birds remaining in the pen call the loose ones back in through a one-way door.

The catching is not as easy as it sounds, even in a pen. I cannot just walk in and start grabbing. If I do, all of the birds run or fly around. They confuse me. I reach for everything and catch nothing. Instead, I must stop and study, isolate one bird in my mind, ready my hand, then grab accurately. The pause gives me the advantage of surprise: I know exactly what I am going to do and choose when to do it. The bird must react to my initiative.

In the wild, however, the bird can conceal itself, which means that it too may gain something by waiting rather than flushing. The predator may pass by without knowing what it is missing. Gallinaceous (chickenlike) birds around the world often choose to hide rather than fly, when the ground-cover is thick enough. They know that they are most vulnerable at the moment when they jump from the ground: fully exposed, but still moving slowly. Predators are skilled at exploiting this moment.

The point, then, is tension. The pointer's art is tension crystalized, frozen in time like an insect in amber. Dog must persuade bird that any other course of action carries more risks than sitting still. It is a game of nerves. The pheasant is superbly adapted to it.

- On the one hand, its reluctance to fly means that it is exposed to the dog for protracted periods. (A bird that flies takes itself out of the game either because it escapes or is killed.)
- On the other hand, the pheasant lays a longer trail than any other bird hunted by dogs, and at the end of the trail must still be persuaded to sit until the human gets in a position to shoot.

The game, then, is easy to join, long of play, and difficult to win: sporting, in a word. And the key to winning is tension.

The emotion of the point makes the game worth playing even off-season: Huck and I do it for half an hour on most winter afternoons. As opportunities for shooting constrict, more people will try no-kill hunting with a pointer, just as they now do catch-and-release fishing with a fly rod. They will get everything except the shot. The point will provide enough emotion (and complication) to compensate, for awhile. I would like to tell you that hunting under no-kill rules can keep dog and man keen forever, but canine and human pups both need the consummation. Old dogs and men do not need the shot as often as they did when they were young, but they need it sometimes. And all human families need the pheasant dinner.

Whatever the rules, we will need more of them to keep struggle and chance in balance as the natural world shrinks. Will our hunting mean less when it is more constricted? No: not if it is real hunting. Rules are part of that. Rules assure us that we are doing the thing right. The hunters who painted in the cave of Lascaux had art, so I would guess that they also had rules. If you have thought of those people as savages halfway down from the tree, have a close look at their paintings. They were as good as art gets. They had Picasso's economy and at least as much emotion. Artists then were like us, except that they stayed with two natural subjects: game, mostly, and then women. (A liberated 21ˢᵗ century person like you would be bored with that old stuff, of course.)

Those ancient hunters would have wanted to stalk the wild bull according to traditions and codes, even when he needed no protection. They would have had myths.

Perhaps all of this seems primitive and forbidding. Perhaps you got this book to give to someone who deserves a present. You do not hunt yourself but you have read a little bit, trying to understand inexplicable tastes. How can a hunter shoot and love? Given a bit of time and sensitivity, it is natural—as natural as Achilles killing Hector, John D. Rockefeller turning philanthropist, or any teenage boy becoming a husband. Love and death are no harder to believe now than ten thousand years ago.

From *Pheasants of the Mind*. Reprinted with permission of Anna Proper.

Choices

T. EDWARD NICKENS

There is a particular expression that fixes my daughter Markie's face when she is watching for a white-tailed deer to step gingerly out of the thick tangle of greenbrier along Black Creek. It is a look unlike any other I have witnessed, at any other time, under any other circumstances. Markie leans slightly forward from the waist, eyes boring into the brambles a hundred yards distant. She does not move. Her lips are pressed thin. She holds her eyes open so long that the corneas glisten with tears, then she forcibly blinks, as if she might miss that exact, exquisite moment when a deer emerges from the shadows and into the open cypress flats. She simply watches, with an intensity that suggests a belief, or wish, that sheer force of will can draw a deer from the thicket and into view from where our two-person tree stand perches 18 feet up a giant chestnut oak.

Her expression is hopeful and expectant, and it is predatory. Not, perhaps, in the sense that mine is predatory, for I am holding the rifle. But it is predatory in that it carries her fervent desire to comprehend the wildness that manifests itself in a large mammal living unfettered in the woods, and her wish to make that deer, in some meaningful way, her own.

I have lived 30 years as a hunter, but in the last two years my perspective of what hunting is, and can be, and should be, has changed in ways that have changed my relationship to my most passionate avocation. My two children, Markie, nearly ten, and Jack, seven, are now old enough to spend time with me in the field. In the past, their connection to hunting had been a step removed. They'd run out the door when I pulled in front of the house and squabble over who would get the duck feathers or who might score the deer hooves. Then, three years ago, I began taking Markie to the woods. Our trips were nothing as intense as hours on a deer stand, but purposeful walkabouts through the squirrel woods, with a shotgun in hand. Last year was Jack's year to try to stay still long enough for an animal—a squirrel, a bird, any animal at all—to wander into view of a bundle of camouflage-clad fidget. They are hooked. For now.

I want my children to grow up to be hunters for selfish reasons, and for reasons far beyond self—mine or theirs. Keep my kids hooked on hunting, and in years to come I'll have hunting companions for life. Each morning chasing squirrels in the next county over is the seed for a greater adventure in years to come—ducks in the Dakotas, grouse in Vermont, deer in the big bottoms of Georgia.

But an embrace of hunting can also be the starting point for a concept of nature unsullied by the overly animated version of the natural world kids are subjected to from birth. To truly understand hunting is to understand that nature's beauty is found not only in the spirited, liquid eyes of a fawn, but in its spotted flanks, in that sun-dappled pattern whose sole purpose is to confound the wolf. What we take for nature's exquisite and primeval elegance—the rabbit's laughably long ears, the butterfly's patterned wings—is often an expression of nature's irrepressible calculus of eat-or-be-eaten.

And that calculus is not limited to life beyond the sidewalk. I want my children to know that even the most modern life, the life lived closest to the cubicle and the subway, involves tremendous consequences for wildlife. We make a thousand choices every day—to wear cotton clothing dyed with ink, to eat fish, to operate an internal combustion engine on the way to a soccer field that once was a meadow filled with nesting meadowlarks—with little to no regard to their impacts on what Henry Beston called those "other nations." Hunter or vegan, city boy or farmer's daughter, life requires life. I want them to understand this fundament of existence in an elemental and clear form: a gun in hand, a finger on a trigger, a choice to make. And one not to make lightly.

Markie is tender-hearted, empathetic to every bug that splats on the windshield. She has a love of nature that manifests itself in a collection of bones displayed near a family of stuffed tigers. She is beginning to process this push-pull of hunting—the love of the woods and its wild lives with those awkward still moments after the blast of the gun. She walks on my right, away from the muzzle, down the path at Edie Pie's farm. She likes to look for the squirrels herself, wants me to shoot them as they dash through the treetops, swift as quail. "It's only fair, Dad," she shrugs. "You miss a lot, you know."

This is good, I think. Already she is fashioning an ethic of fair chase in which the jaws sometimes snap on thin air or tail feathers. "Are you going to take a gun?" she asked, the last time I proposed a deer hunt.

"We are hunting, you know. That's part of it."

She wrinkled her nose. "No mamas, then, promise?"

"No does," I agreed. "We'll hold out for a big buck. And maybe we'll just watch him hang out for a while."

Jack, however, is a bottom-line guy. The sight of a squirrel in the woods where we hunt, as we hunt, sends him into white-knuckled fits of excitement that threaten to burst through every pore of his body.

"Daddy! Daddy! See him? Do you see him? Are you gonna shoot? Shoot! Daddy, Shoot!"

He sits beside me, at the base of the tree, rocking back and forth in an attempt to stay still. He holds his little Buck BB gun in his lap, forgetting to pout because I won't let him load it yet. Another year, perhaps.

There is, after all, a process to this. It began, and continues, with uncountable forays into the wilds of backyard and backcountry. Long before Markie and Jack held a BB gun, they held a bug net. We live deep inside a city of a half-million people surrounded by a metro area of a million more, but we spent hours ferreting out creekbanks and strips of greenspace where frogs and salamanders could still be found. Our playroom stills sports air hockey and art easels and three glass aquaria regulated by a seven-day rule: live animals are returned to natural habitat within a week of capture. Frogs, snakes, fish, snails, lizards, insects, slugs—bring 'em home. Watch. Feed. Water. Learn to care. Every box of PetSmart crickets carried a lesson: big or small, man or beast, scale or fin or exoskeleton—we rely on each other.

Another part of that process involves the gun in hand. Vice President Dick Cheney's recent relationship with a Perazzi 28 gauge shotgun—a dainty firearm compared to the workhorse 12 gauge—caused a national spotlight on hunting safety, and it's one I welcome. I want gun safety front and center. I want my kids to know what I knew at age ten, forwards and backwards—the Ten Commandments of Gun Safety. (Yes, there is such a thing.) I want them to pick up a firearm and without thinking check the safety, point the muzzle up, and peer into the chamber to make sure it's unloaded, even if they saw me do this five seconds before. In my house, there is nothing mysterious about a gun. Unless it is on its way to the truck, it is locked in a safe. But guns are used, and regularly. My kids think of a gun as they think of an axe or a roll of duct tape. It is a tool. (And truth be told, nowhere near as cool as duct tape.)

But I don't take my kids hunting just to teach them firearm safety, and I don't take them hunting solely so I will have playmates for my dreamy forays to distant woods. I take them because I want them to experience the natural world in a way that puts them in the picture. The more my kids know about nature—real nature, beyond the pixel-perfect world of Pixar Studios—the better they will understand why their particular species bears so much responsibility for the future of all the others.

There will come a time when my children will choose whether they wish to hunt or not. It may be a precise moment of great weight and consequence—I imagine a particular animal, a particular smear of blood on fur, an instant in which fire is kindled or extinguished, forever. Or it may be a gradual dawning of self apart from nurture and experience: *This is not for me.*

I'd be lying if I said that their choice does not matter. But I'm working on that.

Hard Times

NORMAN STRUNG

The hard times. We don't care to remember them; we concentrate instead upon the golden days when birds were as thick as autumn leaves and fish jumped in the boat. Yet when you dig deeply enough, it is the hard times that mold us as outdoorsmen and friends.

Having had my share of mean experiences, I find they fall into two categories: disasters of our own making, and those that are the consequences of bad luck I could cite many illustrations of the first state of graceless ignorance, but the one that comes most quickly to mind happened over two decades ago.

It was the first deer season of my life: the first year I could legally hunt big game. Without a mentor or personal transportation, but charged with enthusiasm at the chance of taking a deer, I made sketchy plans with two equally green friends to hitch to upstate New York for opening weekend.

We had no idea where we were going, and our equipment was so scant as to be skeletal: guns, knives, shells, cheap kapok sleeping bags, a Sterno stove, a pot, a pan, paper plates and cups, instant coffee, and lots of canned spaghetti.

Miraculously, we were picked up by two deer hunters who called themselves Jay and Tee and who dropped us off at a campground they knew of, in the middle of public hunting lands. But after that, everything went wrong. It started to rain around three in the morning, and by six our bags were soaked and soggy. We arose wet, shivering, and lusting for a hot drink, but it was so cold and damp that the Sterno didn't generate enough heat to dissolve the coffee crystals. After an hour of this had assured us that, indeed, watched pots never boil, it was breaking light and there was no time to heat the spaghetti. We ate it cold.

It rained all that morning. By blind chance and the custom of the day, we wore checkered-wool jackets. So long as we kept moving, we at least kept warm. As might be expected, we saw no deer.

The rain changed to snow that afternoon. We ate tepid spaghetti under the boughs of a dripping fir. Somehow deer hunting had lost most of its glamour. We started a fire by borrowing coals from a neighboring camper and tried to dry out our bags against the coming night.

To their credit and our gratitude, Jay and Tee stopped by to check on us just as night was falling. They had killed their deer and were headed home.

It took us all of five seconds to weigh the glory of another day afield against their offer of a round trip. We cased our guns, crammed our meager belongings into a duffel bag, and thanked them profusely when they dropped us off near our homes.

There's more to this story, however, than testimony to our bright-eyed stupidity. In the shared misery of those sodden mountains, each of us received an education that would have been denied us under more benign circumstances: the worth of wool, the wisdom of careful planning, to name a few. We also learned to expect the unexpected and, in my case at least, to develop a distaste for canned spaghetti.

Although classes taught in the school of hard knocks seldom need repeating, disasters of your own making aren't limited to the untutored and tender-footed. I now consider myself an accomplished outdoorsman, yet errors in judgment still visit me with their ruler-on-the-knuckles lessons.

I count whitewater rafting among my outdoor passions, as much for the superb fishing that usually comes attached to inaccessible canyons as for the thrills. Knowing that your life depends upon the quality and condition of your equipment, I always keep mine in perfect shape. But on one trip that very perfection cost me and my companions dearly.

Sam Curtis, Brett Freidah, and I were floating the Middle Fork of Montana's Flathead River during the bull trout run. The raft I was using was old, but it had been cared for immaculately—blown dry and powdered after each use, stored in a cool cellar, and preserved without so much as a patch to blemish its smooth skin.

But the invisible deterioration of age had taken its toll, and that factor, compounded by unusually abrasive rocks, shallow water, and a two-foot misjudgment on a narrow passage, found us slamming into a sharp rock shelf that ripped the bottom of a tube wide open. The raft became a bathtub in an instant, and we were scoured into the water at the head of a particularly vile rapid. We lost the raft, but not our lives. Thanks to a previous education, we all knew to stay upstream of the raft; to point our legs downstream and use them as shock absorbers should we collide with a rock; and to angle toward shore with the current rather than against it. Since that trip I reserve older rafts for more leisurely floats and use only new equipment when there's danger to life or limb.

That Flathead trip also revealed another of the disguised gifts that accompany hard times. It was a five-star foulup in ways other than the dunking. What was forecast to be sunny July weather turned into four downhill days that went from cool and showery to a persistent downpour, ending with snow on the mountains. The only time we were dry and warm was in our bags at night. We could not even take comfort in good fishing. The bull trout had lock jaw.

It was a ripe environment for gripes, fault-finding, and games of pin-the-blame-on-the-next-guy, but there was none of that. Rather, there was a willingness to shoulder the burden and share our mutual disappointment. This smoothed out what could have been a human conflict even stormier than the weather. We pulled together, made the best of a bad situation, and made it together. To this day, I'd be willing to pitch a camp on the rimrocks of Hell if I knew Sam and Brett would be my partners.

Hard times teach you to pick a partner carefully!

Mettle of that caliber doesn't require great drama to be revealed, however. Bad luck will bring it out in smaller ways. For example, there was the week I once spent in a backpack tent, on the shores of one of the best trout lakes in the Rockies, during unexpected mountain monsoons. There were four of us, and the fishing was fair between the raindrops, but the gloomy weather, the close confines, and the incessant accommodations to the weather could easily have driven our spirits down. Instead, each of us seized every opportunity to lighten a heavy situation. We hatched an elaborate plot to lynch the weatherman. We read to each other from the labels of soup cans. We made a deck of cards from a notepad, and played poker, using the seeds of pine cones for chips. Looking back upon that week I remember a lot of laughs; despite everything, it had actually been enjoyable. That's another thing about hard times—they teach you to pick your hunting and fishing partners carefully.

I once went broadbill hunting with a fellow I'd known for several years. We'd fished together a few times, and walked the uplands for grouse, and he seemed a likable sort. We'd rigged thirty blocks on a deepwater point with a small pram and paddles. Around midday, a front came through, and the wind freshened from the northwest. The shooting improved as the wind grew in intensity. By three it was blowing a gale, and the decoys started dragging their anchors.

We agreed that we'd had enough for the day, and paddled out to pick up the stool, but as we reached the farthest block and turned around, it was apparent that the wind and waves were a force to be reckoned with. We paddled till our arms ached, and seemed to make no progress. Five miles of icy, open water licked at our backs.

"We're not gonna make it . . . I can't fight it any more," he wailed, shipping his paddle.

Half in shock, I yelled that if he didn't keep paddling, I'd throw him overboard to lighten the load. (I never would have. One person with one paddle in that high-profile pram was a certified dead man.) But it worked. Fear of certain drowning overcame his acceptance of probable drowning. He found a new reserve of strength and we made it inside the lee of the point, and finally to shore. But I never fished nor hunted with the man again.

Hard times can also forge partnerships as strong as the links in a log chain. My closest companion afield was only an acquaintance at the time, and a tough situation brought us a little closer together. We were hunting black ducks on the marshes of Long Island on a Christmas morning, and had driven a Jeep down the beach to a place recommended to us by a friend. It was bitter cold that day, and the soft sand and marsh mud were frozen so hard that we didn't even have to engage the front hubs. With such firm footing, we drove our decoys right to the blind over salt meadows that would never support the vehicle in warmer weather. Although we had enough sense to return the Jeep to solid ground in case of a thaw, the hard freeze belied its location. Later that morning the weather clouded and warmed, and when I tried to move the vehicle, the wheels dug in up to the frame.

It was noon, and we were due at a family Christmas dinner at two. We shored and we jacked and we levered in that accursed jelly for an hour. The Jeep fell off the jack, and slid off the slick boards we'd placed under the wheels. It started sleeting, then it poured rain. We built a corduroy road of sticks and cattails and driftwood, and we worked so hard that my partner vomited from overexertion.

We made it to the dinner 15 minutes late, and we were on the same marsh the next day, for the gunning had been good, and we agreed it was worth the price.

We were almost constant companions on trout streams the next spring, and bass ponds that summer. We endured a few other hard times during that period, but for the most part, good times prevailed. And then early that fall, before the obligations of establishing a more formal partnership could intrude upon the impending hunting season, we were married.

Reprinted with permission of Silvia Strung.

The Measure of a Hunter

NORMAN STRUNG

We mature as hunters as we mature as human beings and the process is no less complex than the journey that leads us from childhood to adulthood. I can still recall my first year with a gun. I was 14 then, with a 16-gauge bolt-action shotgun and an unbridled blood lust. Throughout that fall, I would venture from the family's summer home every Saturday and Sunday at dawn, and walk the woods all day long, a boy possessed.

My intent was to bag limits of grouse, quail, pheasants, rabbits, squirrels, raccoons, oppossums, ducks, geese, and even crows and fox. This fantasy of mayhem was not blind of reason, however. I couldn't articulate it then, but I equated being a hunter and sportsman with all the elusive qualities of manhood: courtliness, confidence, knowledge, and above all, freedom. It seemed obvious that the shortest, most direct route to that state of grace was to bring home limit after limit of game. After all, what better proof existed that one was a good and able hunter?

There is, fortunately, a law of inverse proportions at work in the woods when you are young, inexperienced, and bloodthirsty. Although I would have decimated Long Island's game populations had I been given the opportunity, my aimless wanderings, flock shooting, and sky blasting resulted in a season's bag of one rabbit and one quail. I came to the painful conclusion that I was not a very good hunter.

The next year proved better. I had begun to learn from experience where and when game was likely to be found. I discovered that the twilight hours of dawn and dusk might be good for trout fishing, but that quail generally stayed under cover until the sun burned off the frost and went back to their roosts around sundown. I noted that rabbits preferred clearing edges rather than deep woods, and that grouse tended to hole up where laurels grew. Occasionally, I shouldered my gun fast enough, and shot straight enough, to bag a few.

Sadly, I had no mentors during those green years. None of my family, nor friends of my family, hunted. But I did have a role model, a man of casual acquaintance who lived next door. He had a pair of sleek bird dogs kenneled behind his home. He carried a fine, engraved shotgun from his house to his car when I left on Saturday mornings. And soon after he returned, a brace of mallards or pheasants, or two quail and a rabbit, were usually hanging below the eaves of his garage, catching the low, fall sunlight like a still life by the Old Masters.

One Friday in late November, it snowed heavily. Then the snow changed briefly to rain, and it got bitterly cold. I went hunting the following day and surprised a small covey of quail in a flattened, white field, scratching through the crust for ragweed seeds.

I can still recall my elation at that stroke of good fortune. There was literally no place for the quail to hide, and the shooting was wide open. I took my first double ever from the covey rise, then hunted each single down until I reached my limit; that, too, a first. In the afternoon, six quail turned slowly on a string that was secured under the eaves of our garage.

I waited idly until my neighbor returned, and then pretended to fiddle with the quail and the string. I waved to him as he kenneled his dogs. He saw the birds and smiled, returning my wave. He stepped into our yard.

"Did pretty well today, son," he said through pipe-clenching teeth.

"Sure did," I replied, and recounted the circumstances of the hunt.

Like the ticking of a clock, each detail removed one weathered wrinkle around his eyes and mouth. When I was done, his smiling face had become as flat, featureless, and somber as the crusted snow. He tapped his pipe thoughtfully on the palm of his hand, gazed at the quail, and smiled a different smile.

"You're young," he began, "and I was too, once. You got your birds, and you're proud, and I don't want to take that away from you. But someday, when you get a little older, you'll come to find there's a difference between killing and hunting. It's a distinction that people who aren't hunters seldom understand."

I was devastated. A rite of passage that spanned two years and had at last been successfully run was disqualified in half a minute. If numbers were not the name of the game, by what yardstick was I to measure?

I would like to report that an epiphany occurred that night, or soon after, but such was not the case. I continued to hunt with a laser focus that stretched from the barrel of my gun to the game that rose in front of it. A good day equaled a heavy game pocket.

But I had been sensitized. Long hours in the woods gradually taught me how to spot hiding rabbits and squirrels by the telltale pinprick of light in their shiny, black eyes. I concluded that gift was advantage enough, and chose to walk them up and flush them, rather than shoot them where they hid. I once did the same thing with a pheasant on the ground. I rushed the bird to make it fly before I shot. I missed.

Aside from those small gestures, though, I was not tested again until my early twenties. By then I had entertained and discarded a dozen friendships with people I had met afield, and had found a handful of special friends called hunting buddies, with whom strong bonds had been formed through times good and bad.

I was hunting black ducks on Moriches Bay with one of them when a norwester arrived with the suddenness and power of a hammer blow.

We were on a long point, and a raft of at least 1,000 birds lay to the east. The fierce winds tore loose a sheet of ice that stretched for three miles along the western shore of the bay, and as it bore down on the raft, the birds were forced to move. The wind was so strong that the only way they could make headway was to fly into the teeth of the gale, flat on the deck, where backcurrents and eddies broke some of the blow. Their route took them right over the point where we hid.

At first we were astonished as singles, doubles, and small flocks arrived as if on an assembly line, flying so low that we could touch some of them with our barrel ends. There was also a short time of humbling shooting until we figured out that a bird pumping along at five miles an hour into a 55-mile-an-hour headwind had to be led the same distance as one sizzling along at 55 miles an hour on a calm day. But once we got the lead down, there was no contest, and no sport. We found each other reluctant to shoot, saying, "You take this one," and "Poor devils," as the confused ducks poured into our decoys.

At some point, one of us spoke for both of us and said, "Enough." We broke our guns, lay back, and enjoyed the spectacle, leading birds with our fingers, and yelling "boom." To this day, when I tell the story, someone will allow as how we must have been nuts not to take advantage of such a once-in-a-lifetime opportunity, but I recall both of us feeling uncommonly good later that evening about what we had done.

The years went by and I grew in knowledge, experience, and I think, as a hunter. I acquired fine bird dogs of my own, expensive guns I knew how to shoot, and I learned the habits of game so well that I rarely returned from the field empty-handed. But along the way, a curious transformation took place. Armed with such sure knowledge in my callow youth, I would have killed all the limits I dreamed of. Yet now, I began to exercise restraint.

Sure, there were times when filling a table with a feast for friends led me to shoot a limit of ducks or pheasants, and big-game season represented sustenance as well as sport. But more often than not, I would swing on the most difficult bird in a covey rise, rather than taking the sucker shot. When a flock of fidgety mallards swung wide of the decoys and circled overhead, I would resist the long shot for the possibility that they might settle down, and treat me to the singular beauty of a classic toll, approaching the decoys on confident, cupped wings.

I also found that I preferred the company of others with a like mind. It wasn't snobbishness or elitism; just a matter of priorities. It gradually made more sense to enjoy the company of people who could savor the best of a morning on a marsh, then cap that memory when the bottle was full, rather than let it overflow with the excess of another two or three birds that could be bagged in an instant as a foregone conclusion. I also discovered another common denominator among those I called both hunter and friend: a mutual reverence for the things we hunted.

That one can have reverence and respect for something you are trying to hunt down is easy to imagine as a contradiction, but I have seen antelope hunters choose a tough, tricky stalk over an easy one in exchange for the certainty of a swift, clean kill, and bird hunters who spent half their afternoon finding a cripple. But no example speaks so eloquently of this abiding sense of reverence as the time a friend downed a six-point bull elk that we had hunted hard and well. It was a perfect shot and a magnificent trophy, yet in that ebullient moment of deserved triumph, he was moved to briefly touch the carcass and mutter, "I'm sorry. . . . It was not a statement of regret, but of humble apology and thanksgiving to a spirit that we both understood perfectly.

Upon that cold and windblown hillside, perhaps I arrived at the estate I first sought as an adolescent in thought and years, but I don't really know. It's like asking me now, at two score and three, if I've finally grown up, and to be honest, I hope I haven't, because when you stop growing, you stop living. At that moment of salute to the fallen elk, a quote ran through my mind. It has been a creed of mine ever since, and I recall these same words every time I sight down a barrel:

"We are measured more as hunters by the things we choose not to shoot, than by those that we do."

Reprinted with permission of Silvia Strung.

Integrity

ED GRAY

You'll know it when the time comes. There won't be any need for official regulations or the posting of seasons—those things take care of themselves, and they always manage to make things legal for you. The time comes late in the season, every year. It will come again this year.

The week before, it will snow. Hard. For three days. And the northeast wind will push drifts deep into the troughs of the sand dunes along the barrier beach. At the height of the storm the crests of the dunes will shed spumes of sand into the wind, hard stinging grit that rides in the snow across the channel and onto the marsh.

Then the snow will taper, clouds thin, and the tides will rework their sculpture on the hardened edges of the little creeks. Salt ice cover, a foot thick, will crack and fall in the draining marsh to lie like collapsed tunnels before the rising neap floats them again. Hardened spartina will bend up under the crusting snow, trapped by the weight until group pressure pops a jagged hole and the grasses rise in a mat above the lumpy white.

That night the clouds will blow to sea, and by midnight a hard starry sky will blink down on the subdued marsh. Cold northern night, quiet radiational chiller from the land of tapered meridians, this will be the dark that comes before the time.

False dawn, light without heat, faint hint of the eastern horizon, will find you, shadows moving on the marsh. Three of you, moving slowly, bent and bundled, stepping cautiously on the grass and snow mat, picking your way along the edge and moving toward the silver twinkle of open water.

At the point of the marsh, where two of the little creeks come together to form a small bay, you will stop, thump wet burlap heavily on the snow crust. The dog, still dry and carwarm, tail-high and excited, will prance and sniff at the decoy bags, then slide down the muck to the sludge ice edge of the creek.

Your partner will drag a line of decoys—cork bodies and pine heads, black, gray and tan, big Canadas—out into the water while you scrape at the snow on the grass, looking for beaten plywood that covers the pit.

The pit. You had found the spot earlier, in the high summer when you were pramming the creek with the little guys, scouting for periwinkles and cherrystones, and you had come back in bright September with your partner to dig the pit. Four feet down, three feet back, seven wide, lined with plywood; bench and shelf, drainage hose, hinged cover and woven grassing. Hours. Hammered thumb. Fishing time given up. The pit.

Now it's here. Ice cracks when you open the lid; inside the mud is frozen hard, like dark brown plaster spilled badly, and the bench is slick and crinkly when you step down on it. Your partner comes back for another string of blocks as you set out the gear in the blind.

Guns out of the canvas, thermos on the shelf, ammunition in utility boxes—a faint Army memory, bad, gone quickly—and then out of the pit to check the grassing. Snow has covered the storm-blown bare spots. No problem today.

It's coming on real dawn now, and with it the wind, cold beyond gradation, a solid pressure on your chest and pure pain in your face. You can't look into it. Look away.

Your partner is back and the decoys are all out, 19 pitching geese grouped according to his view of the order of things. Other days you'd need more silhouettes on sticks out in the flats, but not today, not this late and cold. Today is the time.

In the pit and waiting, you watch the sky. The rising wind brings clouds, gathering gray smothering the early yellow and red of the dawn and cutting off the sun before it can show itself. The cold flows deep, a dark sensation heightened by the shivering dog sitting between you. He'll be okay; underneath he's a furnace burning with focussed and retained energy.

So you focus yourself. You know where they will come from, and you have to look into the wind to stay with it. Up in the wind, over the little bay and the breadth of marsh, are the sand dunes, shields against the winter sea, low cover for the homing birds. They may be there right now, just outside the barrier, three feet off the water, fanned out and winging steady, coming fast and smooth downwind.

Look for them. Look for them on this last day. Hold fast into the bite of the wind, don't miss any of it. Any of it.

For now it has come down to the simple—the clean, hard end of it. No more ducks, no more shore birds, gulls; no more easy autumn, late sails up in the harbor; no other hunters, blue herons, distant horns or light planes overhead. No more days. One more chance, two tracks on a sure vector. The time. Take all of it. Look hard, don't turn.

There they come.

Over the dunes, half a dozen, rising. Ten, fifteen now, wings steadily beating. Twenty. Thirty, fanned out, coming in off the ocean, winging easily. More coming, fifty now.

There they come . . . there they come . . .

Here they come. Half a mile, straight at you. It had to be. You knew it, you knew it. Get your head down.

Hold now in the pit of winter, in the ending cold of it; hold now and watch them as they slide down the wind and spread out, twenty feet off the ground, coming at you. Three hundred yards. Look at them . . .

The wings set. A hundred and fifty yards and coasting. Now you must look down and count the seconds. Count them. One . . . two . . . three . . . four . . . five . . .

Now. This is the time. This is the time.

Look up.

Mercy on Beeson's Partridge

SYDNEY LEA

It was my scream, not the knock on the head, that put white spots before my eyes. Nothing lay handy to attack but a metal barrel. I crashed it like a cymbal, spilling rubbish. The racket sent our cat flat-belly across the kitchen floor and downcellar; he'd been watching three chickadees at the window feeder: I half noticed them blow off their perches like seedpods. The dogs hid inside their kennel-houses.

I was, thank God, the only human on hand. But there was more than one of me.

And had always been. Just now I think for instance of a hot afternoon's baseball in my tenth summer, our playing field the back meadow at Sumneytown. I've misremembered my slot in the order, so that when it comes around my teammates all shout, "Syd! Syd!" I linger on the whale-shaped boulder near third, looking for the fellow they're calling. Then someone, not I, walks to home plate. From what seems the sudden height of my seat, I watch him pop lazily to first, then amble over to the rock and climb it to where I perch.

I am on the rock. I.

I—whose age, looks, character, and very gender seem as hazy as the August air.

My motives for connecting that boyish self to the self who decades later would beat up a trashcan may seem equally hazy and ill defined. I appear to inherit from my mother's mother a tendency to oblique association, without her tendency to lay positive emphasis upon it. In any case, pulling that barrel from under our sink, I rammed my skull against a countertop, and even though the blow was pretty light—no gash, no blood—my rage so lifted me that once again I looked down on someone else: a lame man teetering in my kitchen, waving a cane, searching for something further to smash. Could he have been the child who so languidly waved that old bat?

Like anyone, I'd been lamed before, though never seriously nor for long. The usual run of a young male's sports injuries, little more. Still I knew certain things, or thought I did: how in health we forget the body's primacy; how, when bodily health fails, the spiritual may soon follow; how even then, if we recover in due course, we simply take up our affairs again, none the wiser. Yet this time would be different, I was sure. It seemed impossible that memories of the preceding five weeks would ever dull, that I'd need to feel an identical wound to resharpen them—or else some jog as unpredictable, say, as that turn a moment ago to an ancient inning of ball.

I convinced myself that this time I'd seen into the suffering and despair the chronically ill must experience. Indeed, my hip scarcely better after a month than when I first crippled it, I imagined myself among their ranks. And so there'd be no more of anything that till now had made me what I was. I might sit in a blind or on a deer stand, but no more busting the puckerbrush; I might fish from bank or boat, but no more scrabbling among slippery rocks in a streambed.

In fancy I'd vainly squeeze two triggers on the thunderous getaway of a grouse. He lit too far to be chased up again, and thus in fancy I hobbled from thicket's edge to where I'd parked nearby. Or I pictured the head-and-tail rise of a trophy brown trout—there, against the opposite bank, too distant to reach without the deep wading I couldn't risk anymore. I envied the yellowlegs on that shore, trotting smartly into the riffle, smartly out, then strutting like arrogant pimps, bobbing their sound little asses.

At last the great outdoors would have turned dangerous. From now on, in an April like this I'd pick my way across our paltry meadow, staff in hand, a sharp eye out for swells and soft spots. Looking high over the ridge I might see the broadwing hen, spring's annual genie, and covet her view more than ever. I'd breathe the mud, the sap, the mist. Then I'd turn for the house in tears.

Come fall, I'd weep too, remembering the scents of a bird cover: frost-slackened apple, cinnamon whiff of dead fern, pungency of the slain grouse itself, pointer's breath in my face as I congratulated her or him on the find. In June I might drive to some old roadside trout haunt: dusk; bats; spinners in their egg-laying dance; slurping fish; the odors of water and weed and gravel. I'd take it all in through my rolled-down window, then start up the new truck, the one without a clutch.

Summer'd annoy and winter scare me. I wouldn't be one of those admirable souls who, squarely acknowledging the goneness of a prior life, start over in a new track. My deepest track was worn through those gamewoods and riverbottoms, and I followed it, even when inobviously, in the craft I had long since chosen. The very notion of another context for my writing spun the brain.

In short, he had vanished, that I I'd known for so many years.

I'm supposed to stand six feet, two inches tall, although—bones settling after half a century—I may have shrunk some. At all events, I felt shorter during this period of soreness than I had since eighth grade, when every last girl in town seemed a tower enfleshed. My wife is supposed to stand six feet one, and does, but just then she became one more woman looking down on me, for every good reason, physical and metaphorical: I made a miserable, nasty invalid, whom I myself despised.

I mention my wife in part because of this whole business started with her, whose statuesque height is all in her legs. I, on the other hand, am apelike, nothing but upper torso. While her inseam is a full six inches longer than mine, on taking over the wheel of a car from me, she must tilt the rearview mirror significantly down.

On Robin's thirty-fifth birthday, we contrived to put our preschoolers in the care of a babysitter. For the first time in years, she and I were free to ramble the hills, just the two of us, as we'd done on first marrying. While a good deal of our conversation was of course *about* those children, our outing felt—well, romantic and then some.

Robin herself is March's child, which might in an ordinary late New England winter seem inauspicious. But on this particular day we could halfway imagine all nature smiling in congratulation. The temperature climbed to the middle forties, the sun strong. A snow had fallen overnight, just enough to turn the woods crisp and clean, even as the freshets loosened and sang of springtime. We saw a mink track, a doe who'd made it through the cold months in fine shape, even a precocious warbler, its gilt plumage a shock against the sober hemlocks.

There was a certain steep tote road, about seven years old, near home. Though it meant a detour, we hiked it for the view of Moosilauke. On the way down my wife suddenly stopped and laughed out loud.

"What's so funny?" I asked.

She pointed at our footprints in the snow. I saw, not for the first time, that I needed two strides to cover the distance she made in one. But I laughed back anyhow, because it seemed such a long way from eighth grade, from those idiotic leg-stretching drills I'd invented in the hope of growing tall as my pretty second cousin Anne Longstreth—because here stood my wife, even taller, prettier.

Then Robin broke into a downhill run, catch-me-if-you-can, a willowy woman in a thermal undershirt, a pair of Johnson's green wool pants, a set of felt-lined Sorels, a weathered down jacket cinched around her waist, but—she was that beautiful, she was that desirable—I conjured a fleeing nymph. I took off, for all the world like a bassett on a hare's trail, but I caught and kissed her. She smelled like fresh air.

When she broke again, I tried to match strides with her, laying my feet down in her tracks. Though each pace felt like a broad-jump, I kept at it until I heard an odd little crackling just behind me. Three more strides and I went down like a shot boar.

That strange sound had been the wrenching of hyperextended hip ligaments, but it had taken my brain a moment or two to register the pain, the weakness.

Sound again, I'd recall that pain and that weakness and accompanying moods—mopery of March, fury of April, related miseries of May and June. They'd seem exotic enough by then that I likened my contemplation of them to the sort of research an archaeologist must do. So often and long has he studied, say, the mystic artifacts of the ancient Niger delta that he "knows" them backward and forward; yet they are not his by virtue of that knowledge. Nor will they ever become his unless he can somehow and improbably be drawn into a context where all their originative energies and *felt* meanings operate. He may consciously or unconsciously long for such transport; but he must also sense how awesome, even crushing, it could prove.

I have dug around sufficiently in my period of lameness to have the archaeological knowledge of it, but I can no longer truly feel it from within, even if in certain instants of magical thinking I may want to. Perhaps such a desire passes in my case for intellectual curiosity; a saner self, however, prays that if it should ever revisit the spiritual domain of those months, if it should ever again inhabit the I that I was then, it will do so not in a sickroom—to say nothing of ward or cellblock or nursing home, or any other place that literally shuts a soul in.

The physical end of this story arrived, none too soon, by July, and by August I was back on the track entirely. The mornings and evenings turned brisk, the less hardy trees began to blush, the grouse chicks pushed their adult feathers. I had two veteran gun dogs, but also a green one to work, and at last the time was right for him to meet wild birds.

A mile from my house lay a great beaver flowage, its eastern bank a strip of ground just under a cliff. Narrow as that strip was, its hedges of alder, sumac and berrystalk always held game. The water on one side and the sheer ledge on the other, moreover, were natural checks on a headstrong pup.

That summer the grouse were in cyclical decline, and the Beeson cover—as I called it for its absentee Connecticut owner—harbored only one brood. But this consisted of a half dozen birds, who liked to congregate in a certain northerly corner of the puckerbrush. I could park my truck in Beeson's field, leave the pointer yapping in his crate, walk to the spot, and flush the partridge. Then I could bring my novice back to hunt up the singles, which were mature enough by August that when we arrived the mother hen would simply fly out of the cover, abandoning them temporarily to their own devices. I had other wild thickets in which to train, but this one combined handy terrain with a decent number of grouse, well past being squealers but still adequately naive to stay put while I firmed up a point.

In one case, a spring chick sat *too* well. Before I could get there, my dog broke and grabbed the bird. He killed it, even if he can't have given much of a bite: I dressed and cooked the contraband partridge that evening, but I never found a toothmark. I ate a perfect meal for a single person, my wife and children off visiting her mother at the time.

Perhaps because everything about that meal was illegal—and I couldn't help thinking a bit immoral, despite my innocence—I remember offering a Paganish prayer to the hen, penance and gratitude mixed together in it. I'd been walking and even running steadily for several weeks, but the taste of her chick seemed a culminative rite in my healing.

There is a passage in Emerson that I've adored for so long I can all but recite it, and as I lingered at my table, sipping black coffee, missing my family, noting how short the evening shadows were becoming, it crowded my thoughts:

The writer wonders what the coachman or the hunter values in riding, in horses and dogs. It is not superficial qualities. When you talk with him he holds these at as light a rate as you. His worship is sympathetic; he has no definitions, but he is commanded in nature by the living power which he feels to be there present. No imitation or playing of these things would content him; he loves the earnest of the north wind, or rain, of stone and wood and iron. A beauty not explicable is dearer than a beauty we can see to the end of. It is nature the symbol, nature certifying the supernatural, body overflowed by life which he worships with coarse but sincere rites.

I couldn't speak for the coachman, but I could for the hunter, our values being identical, and likewise for the writer. Indeed, by the merest bending of Emerson's observations I could claim that to write and hunt in the same spirit was to be, as his title implied, "The Poet" . . . or at least a *sort* of poet.

My sort.

To be that way (the hell with fame and riches) seemed all I could wish for; and it still does. I recall looking at the backs of my hands, on which the Beeson brambles had prematurely inscribed a birdshooter's autumn tatoos. Strange that there'd been no pain in their making, and certainly none now. In fact, whether because it was a matter of "body overflowed by life" or not, those red scratches seemed to feel *good*. Healed, I'd already forgotten the despondencies of the prior months, forgotten what it was not to worship—nor be able to worship—nature in sympathy. I was again the I with whom I'd for so long been most familiar, steeped in a beauty whose end he could not see.

That I. He was among other things more than ready for his family to come home. He wanted to touch the good flesh of his children. He wanted even more to touch the flesh of his marvelous wife, and thus he simply leapt over his interlude of mental and physical pain to a snowy trail, in fancy watching her glide downhill ahead of him, virtually defining his notions of the erotic. This time, of course, he scripted a more appropriate close, in a wrangled bed.

It was as if he'd never fallen, would never fall again. He could barely remember the bitter human being who frothed at the mouth; who stood in his kitchen, dazed, chopping the air with his cane, ready to raze the whole world.

By further vague association, however, I'll now remember another person who brandished a cane, her grim lips likewise flecked with foam. I knew this woman only as Mrs. Greene. She was a friend of my grandmother's, though everyone in my family made a great joke of the friendship. For as unfailingly cheerful as that grandmother remained to the end of her astonishingly active life (she played tennis through her late eighties), so gloomy and angry was Mrs. Greene, although she hung on to her spectacular good looks till the end of *her* long but sedentary life. While my mother's mother was all good-natured non sequitur, Mrs. Greene was all fierce concentration. Indeed, everything about the two women seemed so different that they could scarcely resist—and usually didn't—falling into quarrel whenever they met. My father assumed that they called on one another in order, as he put it, to keep their batteries charged.

There is a certain very large cornsnake that figures prominently in my recall of this Mrs. Greene. One of my younger brothers had found it on a ramble over my uncle's farm and brought it home. By happy coincidence, a younger sister had recently been presented by some thoughtless adult with a pair of white mice. Since these were apparently of opposed sex, their numbers soon multiplied by tens. Before long, of course, my mother was stuck with tending both reptile and rodent, and she conceived the obvious plan: the snake would be fed, and the population of mice controlled.

Now anyone who has ever kept a constrictor knows that its appetite is unpredictable: it may hop right on its prey, or it may lie there for hours and even days, as if unconscious of the prey's existence. Corny, as the snake had been witlessly named, proved more energetic than some, and could generally be counted on to swallow his mouse within a half hour.

Practical-minded as my mother was and is, aware as she was and is of the natural world's stern-ness, still she felt a tinge of compassion for the mice, who tripped with such moronic fearlessness around Corny's glass cage. Having deposited a rodent, therefore, she would immediately set an egg timer for forty-five minutes. If the creature survived that span, he or she would be lifted out and another put in. My brothers and I called this arrangement Mouse Roulette.

Corny was provisioned well—and perhaps too effortlessly. Indeed, I sometimes surmise it was because he missed the challenge of a stalk that he finally broke from confinement. He did not, however, leave the house: now and then he'd make brief appearances, poking out of a heat register but always duck-ing back in before someone could nab him.

Enter, from stage left in the living room, Mrs. Greene, for her weekly cup of tea and her fight.

Enter, from stage right, Corny, who stretches more of himself than usual out of the wall-grate, shoots his tongue, weaves like a cobra.

Exit Mrs. Greene, rapidly, for all that she needs a cane. In her rush she scatters the tea service to the floor.

It's still easy, you see, to recall all this as farce, even without the snake. On that bright September afternoon just before Labor Day, I'd made an audience because at 21 I was young enough to be amused by an old woman's wrath, and by the hoarse and haphazard chastisement it always earned from another old woman. I never dreamed, though, of anything so comically appropriate as Corny's appearance, a touch that convinced Mrs. Greene that my grandmother—or at least someone from our evil clan—had contrived this whole show.

None of us would see Mrs. Greene again for more or less exactly a year, across which I'll hop here. Though by now the evenings had turned clear and cool, the women's reconciliation was to tran-spire not over tea but over dinner on the back porch—in the open air, where no serpent might be cached.

My parents were up in Maine, fishing. In their absence, I'd been sucking down beer all afternoon with my oldest chum Tommy White. Like most people, I could be much changed by drunkenness. Like most arrested adolescents, I liked to show off. The circumstance, in short, was volatile.

Tommy and I fixed ourselves sandwiches. On a whim I carried mine to the table where the old ladies sat, and he followed me. I gave my grandmother an exaggerated kiss on the cheek, and I greeted Mrs. Greene with a similar, but even more exaggerated one, together with compliments on her appear-ance, overdone even for so physically beautiful a person as she—who was no fool. She shrugged me off and muttered grimly.

A general silence fell till my grandmother offered a few cheery and diffuse platitudes. The last of the sweetcorn always tasted wonderful. The Phillies had the pennant sewed up at the end of a wonder-ful season. Lyndon Johnson was a wonderful man after all. It was wonderful too how the Pennsylvania mugginess was fading, and the September breezes starting, and you could just smell the garden's wonderful marigolds— "Naughty Mariettas," she called them, inhaling demonstratively.

"Yes, Bessie," growled Mrs. Greene, "everything is just so damned *wonderful*."

"Well," my grandmother answered, "better that way than some others."

I winked at my friend—the show was warming up, the batteries charging—but Tommy looked nervous.

"How old are you?" Mrs. Greene suddenly asked, her brilliant, ice-blue eyes seeming to recede into her skull as she studied her friend.

My grandmother, in spite of that fixed stare, justifiably supposed the question addressed to one of us boys. It took her a moment to catch on. "You know exactly how old I am," she finally answered. "Five years older than you are. Why ask such a stupid thing?"

"Stupid?"

"Stupid."

"Well, I was wondering exactly how *you* could live so long and be so stupid."

My grandmother deliberately folded her napkin and set it on the table, a prelude, I was sure, to the dressing down she meant to give her veteran adversary. I beat her to it: "Mrs. Greene," I asked, speaking softly, feigning respectful curiosity, "I was wondering something too."

She turned her gaze my way now, eye sockets become black holes, that glimmer barely discernible within—the frigid light, it suddenly occurred to me, of a snake's stare.

"I wonder why you're such a bitch."

I think back on this crudeness with horror, as if someone else—maybe Tommy—were responsible for it. I'd been irked by this broody woman's assaultive comments to my beloved grandmother, of course, but it was more than a mere rallying to flesh and blood that prompted my own assault. It was liquor, to be sure, but it was somehow hormones as well: for all Mrs. Greene's years, a bizarre, aggressive sexual edge had some part in my treatment of her just then.

All of which, perhaps, is only to say that I ached to be other than my same old well-raised self.

"Yes?" I prodded.

"Yes, what?" Mrs. Greene grunted. But for the eyes her face looked bored, as if she'd encountered—and now I'm sure she had—challenges that put my own dull insult to shame.

"How come—" I began.

"I don't have to answer *you*," she said, her voice drenched in condescension.

"Maybe you can't."

"Oh, I can. Or I could."

"Then you accept the fact that you're a bitch?"

"I accept the fact that you say so, and I accept the fact that you don't know the first thing about anything."

"You can't answer," I said, sensing how foolish and resourceless my taunts appeared, how desperate I was growing—I, who dreamed of becoming an author, a wordsmith.

"I said I don't have to explain."

"You can't."

"The *world* will explain it to you in time, young man. *All* of it."

I turned to my grandmother. She was a woman, God bless her, of whom I simply could not be afraid; but I was curious to see how my oafishness sat with her.

I would not see, for just then I glanced indoors, where my father—stationed so that I alone could detect his presence—beckoned me. I rose without making excuses and went in to him, and to my mother, who lurked even further back in the room.

Both were sun-browned and unkempt.

My father showed the full week's growth of beard.

I noticed that my mother, in a five-and-dime cotton dress, had long hairs on her legs.

They'd sneaked home to deposit their Maine salmon in the freezer and to pick up some clean clothes. They meant to extend their holiday by spending a couple more nights away, in my dead grandparents' cabin out in Montgomery County. I felt mildly hurt to witness their earthy energy, their mischief, their clear lust to be gone again, for in spite of the pleasant anarchy that I and my brothers and sisters always enjoyed under my grandmother's care, I had missed them both. Yet I was relieved as well: in their distraction and hurry, my parents overlooked the fact that I'd been drinking. Moreover, some part of me relished the prospect of further and better outrages toward Mrs. Greene.

By the time I returned to the porch, however, the two old women were onto some other topic of dissension, fairly mild. And I could tell that my friend Tommy, if he'd savored my boorishness in the first place, now wanted to leave as much as my parents had.

"Good night," I said to my grandmother. And then, the devil come back despite me, I made a deep actor's bow to Mrs. Greene. "And good night to you too, Madame Bitter."

"Bitter," she flatly repeated.

"*Madame* Bitter."

My barb seemed no less labored and puny than the others, but Mrs. Greene—wincing with the effort—laid her hands on the glass tabletop and pushed herself to her feet. Next she unhooked her cane from the chairback and raised it overhead. At last I'd made an impression.

"You wouldn't hit me?" I sneered.

"You stand where you are and find out!" she shouted, a runnel of spit flowing down the channel of her frown, that aged face's only groove.

"You'd smash up the whole world if you could," I said.

"I'd love to," she answered. "And you will too one day."

I took a few steps toward her and, her timing faulty, she came up empty as she swung the stick. I stood in my tracks till Tommy dragged me backwards off the porch. Even as I left Mrs. Greene made hatchery gestures in my direction.

The autumn after my lameness, the grouse remained as scarce as they'd promised to be during those summer training sessions by Beeson's beaver swamp. The male dog who'd caught and killed the young bird in August came along nicely, though given more plentiful upland game he'd have come along even better. All through the gun season I needed to return to Beeson's just to make sure he'd get his nose into *something*. Time and restiveness had dispersed the grown chicks to other places, but that faithful hen remained. She was smarter, flightier, harder to pin than the brood she had raised; but she was always there, and she saw my pup into college, as her chicks had seen him through high school.

On the final day of the season, I tramped through miles of woods behind that young dog. All the grouse in New England seemed gone. Dusk descending, I crated my pointer and headed for home. It had been a meager fall, but I remembered enough of the spring preceding to know how much worse it might have been. There'd be other seasons now; those angry and melancholic dreams of myself as an old man with a staff rather than a gun or rod in his hand would not come true for a considerable while.

And yet it was disappointing to think how soon we'd eat our way through the year's harvest of grouse in our freezer: I could feel saliva pool under my tongue at the thought of those few meals. And it was even more disappointing not to have shot a bird over the pup on his last hunt of the autumn, not to have lodged such a kill in his memory for the long coming winter. As I passed Beeson's bog, therefore, I slowed, my mind in conflict. There were some twenty minutes of shootable light remaining in the afternoon, all I needed to locate my hen partridge.

At length I backed up and parked. Breaking the shotgun, I slid one round only into a chamber; I meant to give that grouse all but every advantage. Then I opened the door of the dogbox, slipped the bellcollar over the pointer's head, and followed him toward the brush.

Halfway across the field beside the cover, I kicked a hidden wedge of granite. I must have done so, as they say, just right, for the hip I'd wounded eight months before cried out in pain, and so, falling to the ground, did I—I, who was again in that brief second the self of wan April and not bluff November.

When I got up, my legs were sound beneath me; yet I went on standing for minutes on end, till down in the thicket my dog's bell quieted: he'd found his bird. Still I stood, waiting for the inevitable fusillade of wings, and afterwards the clank of the moving bell. As soon as I heard these, I blasted my whistle.

It was time to go home; it was time for mercy on Beeson's partridge, the constant one, who'd even surrendered a chick to me and mine.

My eager young pointer was reluctant to come to heel, and I waited a long spell before he finally did. It was during that spell that I remembered not merely the bodily pain of a few short weeks ago, not merely the rage with which I clubbed a wastebasket but also that last evening with poor, dauntless Mrs. Greene, who wielded *her* cane like a weapon too.

I recalled the rough beard on my father, who would drop dead within eighteen months of that night.

I remembered my mother's silky leghairs.

I may even have remembered those pink-eyed mice, and how blithely they trotted the invisible confines of their glass world until—at the egg-timer's gong—they were lifted back to a more familiar realm, or, the gong too late, they were rapt by sudden coils.

Those coils would unravel, Corny's diamond head be smeared on the driveway by an unwitting neighbor kid's bike wheels.

My grandmother would fall and break her hipbone and never be the same woman again, her mind, so often delightfully scattered before, become a permanent and grisly chaos. She would not recognize her grandchild, me, for her last four years.

Standing in Beeson's field as the light went down, I scarcely knew that grandchild either. There was once a boy who could not quite understand his middle-aged parents' romantic silliness; nor the blackmindedness of his grandmother's quarrelsome companion; nor—as that wondrously handsome old companion claimed—much of anything at all.

Reprinted with permission of the author. Originally appeared in *Hunting the Whole Way Home.*

Three Days to Thanksgiving

T. EDWARD NICKENS

Rivers are funny like this: One minute you're paddling along absorbed in the moment, all senses fixed, then the river bends and you have the stern seat, so you quietly take a hard draw stroke because there could be a wood duck around the corner and Lee is hunched over in the bow, hand on his gun, leaning as far forward as he dares. Every detail is in fine relief, like hand-cut checkering, where you feel it in your palm. Heartbeats thud in your chest like the steady *thump-thump* of the dog's tail when you come into the dark kitchen before daybreak and she knows where she's going. The canoe inches forward, forward; any second now the ducks will see it and launch skyward, startled. If they're there at all.

But they're not, and five minutes later you're drifting through a languid pool and your head is a million miles away. One minute you're in the moment and the next you're off on a stream of consciousness down memory lane. At least that's how it is for me.

We launched our canoe in a trickle of black water through fall-spangled woods and wound up where the river broadened to 400 feet and turned brackish enough speckled trout. Three days and 15 dawdling miles untwined between the two spots. Looking back, nothing much happened. In that respect it was one of those unforgettable trips, a tile mosaic of small, glittering moments that coalesce into a grander work with just a few short days of distance.

Like the turkeys. Fifteen minutes after pushing off we eased around a kink in the creek and there were two gobblers standing on a sandbar not 50 feet away. We froze, drifting closer. The birds stood statue-still for long moments, silhouetted against the glare of the creek behind them as if cut and punched straight out of Audubon's *Birds of America*. Blue-white heads on slender necks, bronze shoulders, barred tails nearly dragging the ground. We cut the distance to 30 feet before one bird took a quick hop and crossed the creek with a flush of beating wings, followed by the other. In the woods unseen birds galloped through dry leaves like startled ponies.

Lee turned slowly and grinned as if any sudden movement would send the memory itself into startled flight.

"That was too cool," he whispered.

"Big toms," I said. "How many birds you figure?"

"I don't know. I was too impressed by those gobblers to even think about it. Can you believe how close we got?"

I could, because that's the nature of these coastal-plain streams. The river was a river in name only—not much more than a creek, really—uncoiling vinelike through dark woods where a few cypress trees towered over the floodplain, a handful old enough and tall enough to elicit whistles. Every coastal-plain county has one, or ten, of these floatable creeks—thin blue lines snaking across topographic maps in the blank spots between rural roads. Many offer get-gone-quick pockets of quasi-wilderness, two or three days' worth of quiet water and muddy banks pocked with mammal tracks. Some turn into, or spill into, full-size rivers. The best stretches have no more than one bridge crossing. Looking on the map, you'll think, *I could paddle that in a day easy.* Which you could. But then you must factor in the sneak time for 'round-the-bend woodies, the time you'll spend exploring beaver ponds, the fact that you'll need your tent up and firewood stacked by three p.m. because there are squirrels in the woods and supper beckons.

If you don't know the locals, you'll need public land for a campsite, or count on sandbars below the high-water mark. Don't expect primeval conditions. You'll hear the distant hum of traffic and the occasional barking dog and maybe a tractor, but they will be less bothersome than you might imagine. Expect that you'll pull your loaded boat over downed trees and logjams, sometimes so often that you'll swear it's the last time you'll try this. But it won't be, because you'll have a little piece of river to yourself and how often does that happen?

That first night we camped on a knoll of high ground overlooking the largest beaver pond I've ever seen. Two separate, parallel beaver dams, each hundreds of feet long, impounded a pond of swamp and dead timber that stretched to the horizon. It was easily a mile long, perhaps much larger than that, but even from the highest bank I couldn't see the far side. Amber water drained through the dams in gurgling cascades, like surf. We cooked a late supper as a nearly full moon rose over the beaver swamp, laying down a lane of shimmering white light through the trees. The Coleman lantern hissed, peppers and onions sizzled on a backpacking stove, wood crackled and popped in the fire. I lit a cheap cigar bought at the last minute from a country store just a few miles from the put-in. We'd paid $2.09 for a five-pack of Tampa Nuggets, and I thought of the pretentious days when I'd turned up my nose at any smoke that didn't cost twice as much as that entire pack.

"You remember those Garcia y Vegas you used to bring on our college backpacking trips?" Lee asked. I did. Each one came in its own plastic tube, which was the only thing differentiating them from every other cheap cigar. "Man, we thought we'd hit the top with those," he said. We counted off a few places and times we'd smoked them: Mount Mitchell's backcountry in 14 inches of new snow. Merchants Millpond in March, the time we hauled a bushel of oysters into the swamp woods by canoe. Who knew how many duck blinds?

And I began to understand, sitting there with cheap smoke trailing up to the stars. Like the turkeys on the sandbar and the swamp moon, each one of these memories was a gift. Each one a tiny tile in the mosaic of memory.

The next morning we woke to deerhounds that had struck scent north of the river. I made a quick cup of coffee and downed a handful of raisins. Ten minutes after waking, we were in the boat. Already the river had broadened; now it was twice as wide as our canoe was long—but it was just as crooked as ever. The trick to jump-shooting ducks by boat is to move slowly, steering the canoe into the shadows and along the inside of each bend. The hardest part is doing all this while positioning the gunner for a quick shot—and all with feather and sculling strokes, rarely removing the paddle from the water.

We hugged the bank and sliced through plumes of mist rising from the creek. Lee saw the ducks first, on the far side of the sixth or seventh bend. He dipped his hat brim and tightened his grip on the Ithaca over/under that his father had given him when he'd turned 12. It was a right-hand bend, and as I pried the boat away from the bank, there were the ducks—woodie drakes and hens, heads erect, nervous. The closest bird, a resplendent drake awash in sunlight, swam back and forth like a panicked squirrel in the road. Any second. And then the ducks flushed and the gun popped twice and a single bird came down.

"Whoa, nice one!" I said.

Lee picked up the hen. "She's banded," he said. "Don't see that every day." Pale-yellow feathers checked with black drifted on the water, and my thoughts went downstream with them.

Lemon feathers, we called them, and in college I worked at a drugstore lunch counter where I traded the delicate flank feathers of wood ducks to an older fellow who came in for coffee most days. He tied trout flies with them and treasured all I could garner, but I always was convinced I was getting the better end of the deal. For a brown lunch bag of wood duck feathers, I got to listen to his stories of trout fishing up in remote stretches of the Pisgah Forest. He brought me samples of flies—tawny tufts as small as peas—and told me about brown trout that sucked them down into dark pools and rainbows that slashed at them from riffles. At the time I'd never caught a trout, but leaning over the lunch counter, pouring his refills, I knew it was only a matter of time. I was 20 years old. Back then it was *all* just a matter of time.

On the second day we had a go of it finding high ground to camp. All day long tributary streams and swamp seeps flowed into the creek, which soon wound through low ground cloaked in cane and shrub. Hardwoods and cypress trees retreated from the banks. We could see where the river rose and fell with the ocean tides—not a lot, just a foot or so, but enough to make every piece of dry ground a question mark. Two good spots were clearly posted against trespassing, so we paddled on to a knuckle of public land that was our last hope before having to spend a long night in the bottom of the canoe. We cut briers and cane and wedged the tent into a tangle of brush. If we curled up just so, we fit between the cypress knees that poked under the tent floor.

Dinner was standard fare for my canoe camping trips; I long before had eaten my last can of Dinty Moore beef stew. To the wood duck breasts I added bacon and the boned squirrel I'd been able to pot, and I sautéed the lot in garlic and olive oil. I toasted pine nuts in the fire and boiled linguine, sun-dried tomatoes and dehydrated mushrooms. Parmesan cheese was the finishing touch—that and the cries of barred owls upriver. Then the Coleman lantern ran out of gas and we watched orange sparks rise from the fire and wink out amid the stars, and I wondered why we'd lit the lantern in the first place.

By most standards we ended up with little to show for our time. We shot two wood ducks and a squirrel. We never saw a deer, although we paddled through another flock of turkeys and drifted so close to a beaver that its tail-slap splashed the canoe with water. Simple pleasures. Gifts, if you look at them in just the right light. One morning after breakfast I sat on the riverbank watching leaves drift around an upstream bend and tried to guess which color would come next: a golden-yellow beech leaf, a nut-brown oak, perhaps an orange-tinted maple. We paddled under a huge aerie; whether it was the nest of an osprey or an eagle I can't say. I remember lying back by the fire and talking about old friends and our young kids and listening to the swamp water run over the beaver dam.

But most of all I remember the old man. He was the only human we saw on the entire trip until we cruised far into the tidal zone, where a few houses huddled over the marsh on sparse high ground and fishermen cast for speckled trout along marsh humps. He waited for us to break camp on our second day on the river, floating in the quiet water just downstream of a big logjam. He was quiet and patient as Lee and I struggled with our boat and load, each of us out of the canoe and gingerly balancing atop a slick sunken log while we pulled the boat—*one, two, three, heave!*—laterally between us.

The old man was alone and happy to chat. He'd snuck upstream for five miles that morning and never fired a shot. I asked him about his canoe, a battered fiberglass boat painted tan, with simple board seats. "Made it myself," he said proudly. "More than 25 years ago." All he carried in it was a weathered trapper's basket and a pair of shotguns at the ready. He chuckled at our mountain of gear.

He was 78 years old, lean, like musclewood, with a deeply lined face and a quick smile. His routine was to paddle upstream and then motor back to his truck with a 2-hp outboard. "I've hunted this river for 40 years," he said, then looked down into the water for a brief moment, the silence widening like ripples in a pond. "But you get to be my age and you wonder how much longer you can do these sorts of crazy things."

"I wonder the same thing myself," I said, and he grinned. He knew a gift when he heard one.

"Why, you boys are just getting started." I remember how good that made me feel.

After we'd paddled out of earshot, Lee turned from the bow seat and said, "I hope that's what I'm like when I'm his age." And I nodded in agreement. Then we paddled silently for a long, lovely stretch while we thought about the miles that had crossed under the khaki-colored hull of the old man's canoe, and the missed shots he'd cursed and laughed at, and the wonders he'd seen, and the wonders that remained for us around life's twists and turns if we would keep a firm hand on the paddle and an eye open for the random gifts that drift our way.

It was three days to Thanksgiving.

Why

GENE HILL

Once in a great while, when my wife shames me into it, we have a little party at the house. Invariably some meddling woman will notice the all-too-few woodcock shooting prints I have hanging on the wall or the all-too-few decoys in my sketchy collection. "You shoot *birds*? How *can* you?" And then I try to explain to her the difference between the swing-through method, the pointing-out method and maintained lead. If that doesn't confuse her out of any further remarks, she can be counted on to say "Oh I don't mean that. I mean how *could* you? The defenseless little things . . ." Mentioning the fact that she is wearing a leopard-skin coat that was probably poached by some African with a poisoned arrow, has absolutely no relation to the conversation. Save your breath. *Birds* are different.

It's of no help either to try to explain the ecology of so much land—so many birds. It does no good to explain about nature's law of the survival of the fittest; or that she's just knocked back second helpings on Pheasant Fricassee; or to point out that without the restraining laws of nature and predation etc., etc., she'd be up to her sweet derriere in bobwhite quail or wild turkey.

What she wants to know—or have you admit, is that you are one hell of a killer, teeming with blood lust, who comes home from a few hours in a meadow or marsh with enough stiff game slung over your bloody shoulder to pull the rivets on your truss.

This, for some reason *I* don't understand, *she* understands and will accept as a perfectly valid reason. A friend of mine who makes his living, more or less, by working, more or less, for a gun company, is by nature a big game hunter. His answer as to why his house is decorated from cellar to attic with heads of antelope, impala and the outer garments of lion and leopard and zebra, is guaranteed to stop the nonsense. He merely smiles a very mysterious smile that I'm sure he's practiced over African campfires, and says "Oh, I guess I just like to hear the thud of bullets smack against some solid flesh."

But what happens when you ask yourself the very same question? Some excellent recent anthropology, notably Robert Ardrey's fine book *African Genesis*, claims that man owes his evolution to the fact that he learned how to kill. Ardrey has satisfactory evidence that man's first tools were killing instruments.

Maybe we kill just to keep our hand in, in case the job folds and we lose the mortgage and end up back in the father-in-law's cave.

The non-hunter doesn't understand why you and I can go out and swamp it all day long, not popping a cap or cutting a feather and be delighted, if not satisfied, with a nothing-to-nothing tie.

I guess I don't really believe that hunting is a *sport*. I tend to agree with Hemingway who said something to the effect that only mountain climbing, bull fighting and automobile racing were sports and that everything else was a game.

To me sport entails some grave element of risk. And hunting so rarely involves danger—not counting stupidity—that it doesn't qualify.

So let's say that hunting is neither a game nor sport. Trap and skeet are games and delightful, but hunting is a thing apart. It requires some involvement.

A lot of deep thinkers claim that hunting is largely a sexual thing. I won't or can't argue that. I tend pretty much to agree, but hunting has more than sexual undertones.

I think each of us understands it in his own way. You hunt for your reasons and I hunt for mine. And each of us is satisfied in his own way.

I think I hunt because I'm afraid of death and shooting is to me a very deep and complex way of understanding it and making me less afraid or more reconciled to my inevitable end.

I think I hunt because I envy wildlife and by having this control over their life is to share in it.

And I think I hunt because I have been hunted.

I know I hunt without regret, without apology and without the ability to really know why. Let's say I get a sense of satisfaction out of it that stretches back to the beginning of man's mind. I hunt because I am a man.

We are still young animals ourselves. Chronologically speaking we are only hours old compared to the birds, the fishes, and the bug that lays us out with flu.

We hunters share some ancestor wrapped in stinking robes of skin who would greatly envy us our three dram load of 8s as he stares at the polished shin bone of an antelope he holds cocked and balanced in his hand.

As the dog has the ancestral wolf, we have an ancestral killer too, tucked away, and not too deep, inside.

Hunter's Moon

GENE HILL

An English astronomer once commented to the effect that the slight changing of the redness of a distant star could alter a hundred years of our mathematical calculations. This was his way of saying that the works of man are insignificant when faced with the whims of nature. Civilizations have been born or lost in earthquakes and the coming and going of volcanos and tidal waves. A degree or two of temperature change over a few thousand years melted away the ice cap that covered much of North America and a slight shifting in the rain patterns of the world has created bare and torrid deserts where years ago lay tropic jungle. Hairy mammoths that were born and raised in long-lost humid swamps are now chipped out of the light blue ice of our polar lands.

And you and I stand now in the coming of the fall speculating on the possibilities of an early frost that hopefully will skim the leaves from tenacious oaks . . . and yet not be severe enough to chill the ground so as to send the woodcock flying on to warmer soils and softer breezes. The slim balance of our sport so hangs on the vagaries of the unseen winds, the unknown seas—mysteries in their causes no less to us than to our apelike ancestors.

Yet, we will grow restive in the weeks ahead. The Hunter's Moon will see the shadow of a sleepless man who paces up and down his plot of grass, a morsel of dog as curious and as expectant as he is, tagging at his heels. He will stare at scudding clouds . . . wet his fingers to predict the vagrant wind . . . and hope that tomorrow will be kind enough to offer him a touch of frost or a heavy rain or a tracking snow. (And don't forget the days you have all three between the dawn and dark!)

But we'll go on out, if I know you, regardless. And come home wet or cold or both ten times to the single day we come home smiling at the red god's toss of dice. But that's all part of sport . . . small creatures are the birds and sheep and deer to us . . . and we, small creatures too, our wishes merely hopes sent up at night, cast out on the winds, in the light of the Hunter's Moon.

Log Fires

GENE HILL

There are few things most outdoor-minded men pride themselves on more than the ability to build a good fire.

I know I can start with a match, a nice dry chestnut log and a hatchet and bring a quart bucket of cold water to a rolling boil in less than five minutes. This particular accomplishment will not be whispered about in awed tones by my pals, but I take great pleasure in the fact. I think you can tell a lot about a man in the way he behaves around a fire—at home by the fireplace, in a gunning lodge, or the best of all fires—by the edge of a lake with only the wild voiced loons for company. They used to say that if you wanted to draw a crowd, start mixing a martini and suddenly six people would show up and tell you how to do it. But log fires are worse. People are forever poking and messing around with my fires; and never doing much good. I belong to the "start it right and leave it pretty much alone" school. I've just about gotten to the point where I hide my fireplace tools to keep meddlers from fussing around with a perfectly fine fire. To me a good fire doesn't roar and flame. It's obedient and thoughtful. It just burns quietly to provide a little background color to the stories and fill up the lulls in the conversation.

Ever notice how much the hunting dogs love a fire with their menfolk sitting around? Old Tip, my lovely lady Labrador, will snuggle up to a scorcher until I'll swear I can smell her singe. She'll toast one side, then the other. More often than not, when bedtime comes around she looks the other way or pretends she's deep in sleep because she wants to spend the night alone staring at the coals. Good fires make good friends.

And here's an old verse about wood that I've always wanted to memorize and never will:

> Beechwood fires are bright and clear
> If the logs are kept a year.
> Chestnut's only good, they say,
> If for long it's laid away.
> Birch and fir logs burn too fast,
> Blaze up bright and do not last.
> Elm wood burns like a churchyard mold;
> Even the very flames are cold.
> Poplar gives a bitter smoke,
> Fills your eyes and makes you choke.
> Apple wood will scent your room
> With an incense like perfume.
> Oak and maple, if dry and old,
> Keep away the winter cold.
> But ash wood wet and ash wood dry,
> A king shall warm his slippers by.

A Christmas Wish

GENE HILL

There are a lot of legends and stories about Christmas wishes . . . and how I wish this year that wishes were real and I had one now and then. My old dog Tip, I know, wishes she could run the fields again instead of having to shuffle slowly at my heels. And I'd like to wipe away the touch of winter that has come to stay forever with some of my old shooting friends. Some folks say to be careful of what I wish for because it might come true. But I don't think you and I would abuse the privilege. I don't know what I'd do if I were rich, so I wouldn't wish for that this Christmas. I'd like to take the friendships that I deeply treasure and really stretch them out for times to come. Old dogs, old friends, old brooks and quail meadows that I have learned to love especially should never change or go away. I think I know the wish that we'd all like to have. A handful of friends . . . a handful of dogs . . . would have their sweetest yesterdays become tomorrows.

We are all of

—*Oscar Wilde*

The phone call can   ped in a slow, undulating Southern drawl came blasting   ver of the phone and smiled broadly. He pulled me onto h   ld Fort Falls," he whispered. "I haven't heard from him in a   off the mouthpiece and said, "Fort, you don't have to yell! I ca

The voice on the   r me now, Kippy?"

"They can hear yo   n't have to talk so loud."

" 'S that better, Kip   perceptible decrease in his decibel level.

"That's just fine, Fo   igned to listening to what the earsplitting voice had to say. He knew it would be a sh   phone call. Fort came from a generation that counted the seconds on the telephone because a long-distance call could cost a morning's wages. "He's deaf, too," Kip whispered to me as I got off his lap to move a saucepan that was boiling over on the wood cookstove.

A minute later, my husband came into the kitchen. "Good old Fort," Kip said. "He practically raised me. Taught me to hunt and fish when I was a kid. I learned everything I know about the woods from Fort."

"He lived here in Hardscrabble?"

"Yep. He and his wife lived next door in the stone house and took care of Corey Ford for years. Before that, Corey had a plantation, and Fort was his estate manager. Then Corey moved here, and Fort and his wife, Louise, followed. When he left Hardscrabble in '53 for Dartmouth, Fort and Louise drew the line. They said Hanover was too fancy a place for country folk like them, so they opted to stay in Hardscrabble. They bought the farm down the road—the one beyond Ken's place—and lived there about fifteen years before moving back to Carolina when Louise's health started to fail."

"That's a funny name, Fort," I pondered.

"His full name is Fort Sumter Falls. There's a great story behind it. You'll have to have Fort tell you when he gets here."

"Oh, is he coming to Hardscrabble to visit?"

"Oh, didn't I say? Yes . . . he's coming for a visit."

"That's nice. Where's he staying?" I asked.

"Here. With us."

"With *us*?"

"Sure. He's only coming for a month."

"A *month*?" I couldn't believe Kip didn't ask me first. Here I was, with a large house, a small child, and more work than I could handle, and now I had to take care of a house guest for a month! I reined in my temper about as unsuccessfully as an unbroken stallion getting his first taste at a bit.

"Are you kidding?" I screamed.

"Sure . . . I mean, no," he continued, oblivious to my outburst or what it meant to have another person under our roof to feed and pick up after. "He's flying in on Saturday."

"*This* Saturday?"

"Laurie, that's three whole days away . . . plenty of time for us to get ready. (*"Us?"* I thought.) Besides, he's no trouble at all. You'll love Fort."

"How old is he?"

"Fort? Why, I guess he's pushing eighty by now."

This was one of those special moments in married life when I happily would have hung my husband by, uh . . . the thumbs.

Fort Arrives

Saturday arrived. Kip, Tommy, and I got ready to leave for the airport. The guest bedroom was all set, the refrigerator was stocked with food, sherried beef was simmering in the Crock-Pot for dinner, a batch of my homemade bread was rising in an enormous earthenware bowl on the kitchen counter, and some Joe Froggers were cooling on a wire rack out of Bess's reach.

I was prepared, and in the comfort that comes anytime you feel the contentment of having your own universe in order, I began to actually look forward to meeting the man that meant so much to my husband. Shortly after Fort had called a few days before, we got another phone call—this time, from Fort's granddaughter, who Kip had known since childhood.

"I'm sorry about Granddad," she said. "I don't know what got into him. Suddenly he announced that he wanted to go back to Hardscrabble one last time, and the next thing I knew, he was on the phone with you. I'm sure it has a lot to do with Grandma dying."

"Louise is dead?"

"Yes, Kip. She died about six months ago. But she'd been awfully sick for a real long time."

"Send Fort on up," Kip told her. "God knows he took care of me plenty when I was growing up. Laurie and I can surely take care of him for a mere month. Besides, it would be good for him to come home to Hardscrabble and be among his old friends."

"There can't be many left."

"Oh, you'd be surprised," Kip answered. "Hardscrabble doesn't surrender its own to the Grim Reaper graciously."

"Let me speak to her," I whispered to Kip, and after saying, "Of course it's all right, we'd be delighted"; and, "It means so much to Kip to have Fort visit"; I asked a battery of questions. The answers were consoling: "No," his granddaughter said, "he has no special dietary needs. He eats whatever you put in front of him." "Yes, he's entirely self-sufficient. Just give him a good book or a fishing rod and . . ."

So here it was, Saturday, and we were ready to leave for the Airport. As I said, everything was ready for Fort's arrival. I wasn't, however, prepared for the robust, elderly man who walked off the airplane.

He must have been very handsome as a young man. The square, cleft jaw was firm, his smile wide, and his blue eyes twinkled from under white brows that were arched in perpetual amusement. He had a full head of snow-white hair, stood as straight as an oak tree, and had a handshake as firm as a logger's. The only thing that betrayed his age (which I soon found out was actually eighty-three) was a hearing aid in one ear and a gimpy leg. ("Leg quit working right when I was a kid," he later explained. "I got in the way of the intentions of a hotheaded bull that got lusty over the cow I was milking. I took a horn right through the kneecap.")

"Fort!" Kip threw his arms around his old friend's broad shoulders.

"Why, Kippy," he purred in his Carolina drawl. "Good God, boy, it's good to see ya."

"How long has it been, Fort?"

"Lemme see. . . . Been about ten years, I reckon. You was just getting out of that fancy college your pa sent you to in Massachusetts."

"Williams. Yeah, I know. Well, that's behind me, thank God. Fort, I want you to meet my wife, Laurie, and my son, Tommy."

Fort held a box tied with a fancy ribbon in his hands and gave it to me. "Jest a little something for you, Laurie—pralines, a specialty down South. My wife, God rest her soul, she used to make the best pralines in all of Carolina. These are store-bought. Not too bad, but I can't say I've had a really good praline since Louise died."

"I'm sorry about Louise, Fort," Kip said.

"She had all kinds of problems at the end, then her heart just stopped beating one day." Fort's eyes got teary. "I'd just come in from sowing the corn—"

"Tell me," I interjected, anxious to reroute the course of the conversation. "How did you get your name, Fort?"

He brightened up. "Well, now, that's quite a story, Laurie," he smiled. "You see, my daddy was born and bred in Carolina. He and his kin never quite got over losing the War. . . ."

Tom whispered to me, "He's talking about the Civil War."

". . . so when I was born—I was the last of twelve children—it so happened that I came into the world on the day that Fort Sumter fell. So my daddy—his last name were Falls, you see—he named me Fort Sumter Falls —"

". . . because," I interjected, "you were born on the day that Fort Sumter fell."

"She's not only pretty, but she's smart, too." Fort winked at Kip. "You picked a good'un, Boy."

Maybe, I thought, having Fort for a month wouldn't be so bad.

We Meet Rebel

"How many bags do you have, Fort?" Kip asked as we made our way the short distance to baggage claim.

"Just one . . . and Rebel."

"No. . . ." Tom said, stopping in his tracks. "You didn't bring Rebel, did you?"

"Rebel?" I asked.

"Yes," Kip replied. "Why, he must be fifteen by now!"

"Sixteen, Kippy!" Fort beamed, and at that moment, an airport representative carried a small kennel into the baggage claim area.

"Rebel!" Tom cried. "How are you, old boy?" He opened up the wire cage, reached in, and took out a handsome beagle that, like his master, did not at all show his age.

"You didn't say anything about bringing Rebel," Tom said.

"Don't suppose I did, Kippy," Fort smiled, fondling his dog's ears, "but then I reckon I guess I didn't have to. You know I never go anywhere without my Rebel." Rebel pulled away from Kip to plant a series of wet kisses on his master's hand.

Tommy squealed with delight at the little dog.

"I don't know when there wasn't Rebel—that is, a Rebel," Kip explained to me. "Fort's been raising beagles . . . since when, Fort?"

"Since I was a tadpole myself, Kippy. One time, I had twelve beagles. Got Corey started on beagles for years and years before he took up with them high-hat setters of his. Though I gotta say, I did love 'em—Cider and Tober and, a' course, Trout. I always named one a my beagles, though, Rebel, and I've never been caught without one."

"This dog must be the great-great-grandson of the first Rebel I ever knew, right, Fort?"

"Yep, I reckon that's so. That was Rebel of the Wilderness. His son was Rebel of Gettysburg. This old boy is Rebel of Appomatox."

"He always named his Rebels after Civil War battles," Kip explained.

"Do you think he'll get along with Bess?" I whispered to Kip as we headed to the car with Fort, his bag, and Rebel in tow.

"Sure, if she ever wakes up long enough to get to know him. Besides," Kip added, "it's not like anything is going to happen."

"I see what you mean," I grinned. "I guess the most they could ever be is really good friends."

Fort Settles In

Fort and Rebel fit right in. Kip was delighted to have his old friend with us, who proved to be like a favorite uncle, not a guest. Rebel and Bess hit it off immediately and spent most of the day curled up, sleeping contentedly together like a couple of old folk, which in point of fact they were. It was hard to believe, but Bess was now getting on nine.

"Your dogs have always lived to a great old age," Tom asked Fort when we were sitting to dinner that evening. "What's your secret?"

"Can't say I do anything particular," Fort replied. Take care of 'em just like I take care of myself. We take a long walk every day, he gets a lot of loving and gives a lot of loving, and he eats what I eat." Fort took the side of his fork and shoveled some of the sherried beef and rice I had made over to the side of his plate. He could see I was concerned that perhaps he didn't like his dinner. "*Mmmmm*, that was a *reeeeal* good dinner, Laurie," he said. "That cow died good. I'm just saving a bit for Rebel. Like I said, he eats what I eat."

"There's plenty more, Fort," I said, lifting the casserole cover to offer seconds.

"I'm full, gal. Besides," he smiled, looking over to the counter. "I see them Joe Froggers sitting over there, and I'm particular partial-like to Joe Froggers."

Fort Reminisces

Fort told us stories, wonderful stories. About the plantation down South, and years before when Corey first bought it, and how back then some black folk wished the Civil War had never happened because the road to freedom was a hard road for them. "Corey was a great quail hunter," Ford reminisced, "and he bought the plantation so he could hunt birds. Of course, the business of the place was growing cotton, and there were black folk who tended to the crop just like their daddies and mammies had.

"They were poor folk. Corey was away most of the time in Hollywood, writing those movies for all those famous people like Hedy Lamarr and Robert Taylor and Greer Garson. He got mighty upset when he saw how poor people was. So he called me from Hollywood one day and he says, 'Fort,' he says to me, 'every week you butcher one of those big hogs we got on the farm, and you let the folk come down and give them some meat.' I remember how workers would gather round the slaughter yard, standing up along the ridge, waiting for the signal to come down for their pork parcels that me and my wife made up after some of the hands did the slaughtering. Corey made sure the families with children got the best cuts, then the sick and old people. Soon we was raising hogs like nobody's business and slaughtering three or four a week, just so the black folk that worked for Corey could have fresh meat.

"Well, then Corey gets another idea. You see, the nearest store was nine miles away, and folk had to walk to get their supplies. No one had a car back then, and only a few black folk could afford to keep a mule. One day, Corey calls me up from Hollywood and says, 'Fort, you go build us a store. That way the folk don't have to walk so far to get their supplies. And while you're at it,' he says, 'you go and build a school, for the youngsters. They need some education, too, you know.' He had a heart of gold, Corey did, and no one never gave him near enough credit, but he didn't want gratitude. He was rich and famous. 'I had a lucky break,' he'd say to me. 'If I can give other people a break, well then, that's payback enough for me.'"

Fort's Visit Sails By

And so the days melted into weeks, and Kip and I reveled in Fort's company. The two men went off just about every day to their old, secret trout streams and dark holes on the lake, fishing with Bess and Rebel in tow. They never came home without at least a couple of handsome rainbow, or a salmon, or a string of smallmouth bass.

All the while, Fort told us stories. There was the hilarious one about how the septic system got stopped up when Corey's mistress came from Hollywood to visit him at Stonybroke, his home in Hard-scrabble; or the time when Corey's best friend, W. C. Fields, came to stay with Corey at Christmas and how people here in Town took no notice. After all, Hollywood types didn't impress people in Hard-scrabble. Now, a ten-point buck . . . *that* was a different matter entirely.

Years later, when I started working on Corey Ford's literary archives, I discovered how deep the friendship was that he shared with Fields. Ford, a lifelong bachelor, always had difficulty coming to grips with Christmas and, until the day he died, gathered friends and friends' families about him and positioned himself as the benevolent Ebenezer Scrooge. Fields, likewise, had a great difficulty at Christmastime, but for a different reason. He was quoted as saying, "I believed in Christmas until I was eight years old. I had saved up some money carrying ice in Philadelphia, and I was going to buy my mother a copper-bottomed clothes boiler for Christmas. I kept the money hidden in a brown crock in the coal bin. My father found the crock. He did exactly what I would have done in his place. He stole the money. And ever since then I've remembered nobody on Christmas, and I want nobody to remember me either."

There was Fort's story about how Judge Parker and Corey founded the "Love the Little Kitty Society," a club complete with printed membership cards and a charter dedicated to "tiger hunting for the man with modest means." The two friends would sit on Corey's stone porch every night after supper and pot feral cats because, as Fort pointed out, "feral cats kill most of the wild birds, including pa'tridge—and the Judge wanted to pronounce and execute the sentence against those feline offenders."

But there was one story that Fort told us. It would take a number of years before I gathered up all the pieces and I could put the whole puzzle together. It is one of the most poignant stories I've ever known—and I daresay, I'm not alone.

Just a Dog

Farmer Boyden was tending to his chickens and pigs when he heard a shot ring out from below his barn. It was deer season. Fearful that one of his cows had been hit, he dropped what he was doing, grabbed his shotgun, and ran as fast as he could to the pasture. Gratified, after a quick glance, that his small herd appeared unscathed, his relief turned to outrage when a second shot was discharged not fifty yards away. It came from an adjacent field, which belonged to his neighbor, a country gentleman and a writer. There, beyond the stone fence, by the apple tree, stood a hunter. The farmer did not recognize the man. A cloud of dissipating smoke encircled the muzzle of a 30-30, freshly fired at point-blank range at what the farmer assumed was a small deer or coyote. But when he came upon the scene, he saw to his horror that the fallen animal was his neighbor's English setter.

"Whatinell do ya think yer doin'?" the farmer hollered at the hunter.

"Thought it was a deer," the hunter said offhandedly, as he unloaded the unspent bullets from the chamber of his gun. "I heard a rustle in the brush and saw a flash of white. Thought it was a whitetail deer. Honest mistake. It was an accident. . . . Anyone could have seen that white through this heavy cover and thought the same thing."

Indeed, the brush was heavy; and the dog was mostly white—a snow white English setter with orange ticks. But now she was a pitiful, lifeless heap. The farmer knelt down, hopeful of finding a sign of life, but finding none, he gingerly hoisted the poor animal onto his shoulder. As he was doing this, he caught a glimpse of the hunter turning heel and making his way to the road, where a car with Massachusetts license plates was parked.

"Mister," the farmer called. "Come back." The hunter turned around with a smirk on his face that was wiped clean when he realized he was looking into the shooting end of the farmer's double-barrel gun. "You come with me," Farmer Boyden ordered quietly, as he motioned toward his neighbor's house with the persuasive point of the gun muzzle.

"Look, I said it was an accident," the hunter mewled, turning pale. He groped for his wallet. "Here. . . . " he offered with hands shaking. "Here's five bucks. That should settle the matter."

The farmer replied with the determined cock of the right hammer of his gun.

"This dog was my neighbor's," the farmer said. "You owe him some explaining, not a darn fiver."

"Hell . . . it was just a dog," the hunter pleaded.

"You tell that to my neighbor," the farmer replied bitterly.

The farmer marched the hunter across the road and up the long, winding drive that led to an imposing stone lodge.

"Knock on the door," the farmer ordered, as he gently lowered the body of his neighbor's dog onto the front lawn.

A moment later, the country gentleman answered the door, beheld the scene—and fell to his knees.

Mabel, the housekeeper, related what happened. She had been in the kitchen baking pies when she heard a hollow cry. Running to the front door, she came upon her employer on his knees, cradling the body of his beloved setter, Trout. Sitting stiffly on the ledge of the stone porch, looking blankly over the valley vista, was a stranger. Standing nearby with a loaded shotgun trembling in his hand was Farmer Boyden.

"The stranger got up," Mabel recollected, "and said, 'It was just a dog.' Then Charlie Boyden said to the stranger, 'Get the hell outta here.' The man ran down the driveway like a frightened hare. Charlie carried Trout behind the house and buried her. Corey was too broken up. He went to his room and didn't come down for dinner."

The Day was November 23, 1940.

Farmer Boyden's neighbor was the legendary outdoor writer Corey Ford, who wrote a monthly column for *Field & Stream*. From 1952 until 1969, the antics and misadventures of an eccentric Down East group of hunters and fisherman known as the Lower Forty Shooting, Angling and Inside Straight delighted and captured the hearts of readers the world over. Not only were dogs an integral part of the fictitious Lower Forty, but they were fundamental to Corey's real-life existence. A lifelong bachelor, Corey's beloved setters were his family—and Trout especially was like a favorite child.

The night his little setter died, Corey made an entry in his diary that I happened upon but can't divulge. After all, a man, when confronted with the handiwork of the Grim Reaper, is due the privacy and respect of his sorrowing, and I found his diary unwittingly. Suffice it to say, the man mourned deeply, as you who have loved and lost a dog well know; and afterwards, he wrote a letter to his hunting buddy, chief editor of *Field & Stream* Ray Holland. Corey asked him to publish the following letter, and Holland stopped the presses to get it into the December issue of the magazine. It read:

Dear Ray:

I know this is a kind of unusual request; but I'd like to borrow some space in your columns to write an open letter to a man I do not know. He may read it if it is in your columns; or some of his friends may notice his name and ask him to read it. You see, it has to do with sport—a certain kind of sport.

The man's name is Sherwood G. Coggins. That was the name on his hunting license. He lives at 1096 Lawrence Street, in Lowell. He says he is in the real estate and insurance business in Lowell.

This weekend, Mr. Coggins, you drove up into New Hampshire with some friends to go deer hunting. You went hunting on my property here in Hardscrabble. You didn't ask my permission; but that was all right. I let people hunt on my land. Only, while you were hunting, you shot and killed my bird dog.

Oh, it was an accident, of course. You said so yourself. You said that you saw a flick of something moving, and you brought up your rifle and fired. It might have been another hunter. It might have been a child running through the woods. As it turned out, it was just a dog.

Just a dog, Mr. Coggins. Just a little English setter I have hunted with for quite a few years. Just a little female setter who was very proud and staunch on point, and who always held her head high, and whose eyes had the brown of October in them. We had hunted a lot of alder thickets and apple orchards together, the little setter and I. She knew me, and I knew her, and we liked to hunt together. We had hunted woodcock together this fall, and grouse, and in another week we were planning to go down to Carolina together and look for quail. But yesterday morning she ran down to the fields in front of my house, and you saw a flick in the bushes, and you shot her. You shot her through the back, you said, and broke her spine. She crawled out of the bushes and across the field toward you, dragging her hind legs. She was coming to you to help her. She was a gentle pup, and nobody had ever hurt her, and she could not understand. She began hauling herself toward you, and looking at you with her brown eyes, and you put a second bullet through her head. You were sportsman enough for that.

I know you didn't mean it, Mr. Coggins. You felt very sorry afterward. You told me that it really spoiled your deer hunting the rest of the day. It spoiled my bird hunting the rest of a lifetime. At least, I hope one thing, Mr. Coggins. That is why I am writing you. I hope that you will remember how she looked. I hope that the next time you raise a rifle to your shoulder you will see her over the sights, dragging herself toward you across the field, with blood running from her mouth and down her white chest. I hope you will see her eyes.

I hope you will always see her eyes, Mr. Coggins, whenever there is a flick in the bushes and you bring your rifle to your shoulder before you know what is there.

—Corey Ford

A furor followed. Mail poured into the New York offices of *Field & Stream* the likes of which the magazine had never seen before or possibly since. Hundreds of newspapers, magazines, dog and sportsmen's clubs, businesses, and community groups across the country seized upon Corey's poignant open letter and reprinted it to the same effect. Anyone who ever loved a dog understood. Most wept. Today the message garnered from Corey's letter is no less potent or poignant than when the ink and tears were still wet on his paper, and "Just a Dog" stands alone in the laurels of American sporting dog literature.

I wanted to tell you what happened because you understand. You understand what it is to love and be loved by a dog.

You know what it is come autumn to ramble in the woods with your canine companion by your side, under a shower of golden-tinged russet leaves; and catch a whiff of ripened apples warmed by streaks of sunlight filtering through a cathedral of lofty pines. If you hunt, you take more pride in your dog's retrieves and frolicsome flushes or stylish points than you do in the weight of your game bag come dusk.

You fall asleep at night to the rhythm of dog-snores and slumber-barks that come from the foot of your bed—or more likely, on it.

You know that a wet dog-kiss can lick your troubles clean.

And the warmth from his soft brown eyes can melt your worries.

We have them for such a short time, in the great scheme of life. Our four score and ten are a mere twelve or thirteen years to a dog. Dogs pack a lot of love into the time they share with us.

But then, you know.

Because you, too, know the love of a dog.

The Road to Tinkhamtown

COREY FORD

The road was long, but he knew where he was going. He would follow the old road through the swamp and up over the ridge and down to a deep ravine, and cross the sagging timbers of the bridge, and on the other side would be the place called Tinkhamtown. He was going back to Tinkhamtown.

He walked slowly, for his legs were dragging, and he had not been walking for a long time. He had not walked for almost a year, and his flanks had shriveled and wasted away from lying in bed so long; he could fit his fingers around his thigh. Doc Towle had said he would never walk again, but that was Doc for you, always on the pessimistic side. Why, here he was walking quite easily, once he had started. The strength was coming back into his legs, and he did not have to stop for breath so often. He tried jogging a few steps, just to show he could, but he slowed again because he had a long way to go.

It was hard to make out the old road, choked with young alders and drifted over with matted leaves, and he shut his eyes so he could see it better. He could always see it whenever he shut his eyes. Yes, here was the beaver dam on the right, just as he remembered it, and the flooded stretch where he had to wade, picking his way from hummock to hummock while the dog splashed unconcernedly in front of him. The water had been over his boottops in one place, and sure enough as he waded it now, his left boot filled with water again, the same warm, squidgy feeling. Everything was the way it had been that afternoon. Nothing had changed. Here was the blowdown across the road that he had clambered over and here on a knoll was the clump of thorn apples where Cider had put up a grouse—he remembered the sudden roar as the grouse thundered out, and the easy shot that he missed—they had not taken time to go after it. Cider had wanted to look for it, but he had whistled him back. They were looking for Tinkhamtown.

Everything was the way he remembered. There was a fork in the road, and he halted and felt in the pocket of his hunting coat and took out the map he had drawn twenty years ago. He had copied it from a chart he found in the Town Hall, rolled up in a cardboard cylinder covered with dust. He used to study the old survey charts; sometimes they showed where a farming community had flourished once, and around the abandoned pastures and under the apple trees, grown up to pine, the grouse would be feeding undisturbed. Some of his best grouse-covers had been located that way. The chart had crackled with age as he unrolled it; the date was 1847. It was the sector between Kearsarge and Cardigan Mountains, a wasteland of slash and second-growth timber without habitation today, but evidently it had supported a number of families before the Civil War. A road was marked on the map, dotted with Xs for homesteads and the names of the owners were lettered beside them: Nason, J. Tinkham, Libbey, Allard, R. Tinkham. Half the names were Tinkham. In the center of the map—the paper was so yellow he could barely make it out—was the word Tinkhamtown.

He copied the chart carefully, noting where the road turned off at the base of Kearsage and ran north and then northeast and crossed a brook that was not even named on the chart; and early the next morning he and Cider had set out together to find the place. They could not drive very far in the Jeep, because washouts had gutted the roadbed and laid bare the ledges and boulders, like a streambed. He had stuffed the sketch in his hunting-coat pocket, and hung his shotgun over his forearm and started walking, the old setter trotting ahead of him, with the bell on his collar tinkling. It was an old-fashioned sleighbell, and it had a thin silvery note that echoed through the woods like peepers in the spring; he could follow the sound in the thickest cover, and when it stopped, he would go to where he heard it last and Cider would be on point. After Cider's death, he had put the bell away. He'd never had another dog.

It was silent in the woods without the bell, and the way was longer than he remembered. He should have come to the big hill by now. Maybe he'd taken the wrong turn back at the fork. He thrust a hand into his hunting-coat; the sketch he had drawn was still in the pocket. He sat down on a flat rock to get his bearings, and then he realized, with a surge of excitement, that he had stopped for lunch on this very rock ten years ago. Here was the wax paper from his sandwich, tucked in a crevice, and here was the hollow in the leaves where Cider had stretched out beside him. He looked up, and through the trees he could see the hill.

He rose and started walking again, carrying his shotgun. He had left the gun standing in its rack in the kitchen, when he had been taken to the state hospital, but now it was hooked over his arm by the trigger guard; he could feel the solid heft of it. The woods were more dense as he climbed, but here and there a shaft of sunlight slanted through the trees. "And the forests ancient as the hills," he thought, "enfolding sunny spots of greenery." Funny that should come back to him now; he hadn't read it since he was a boy. Other things were coming back to him, the smell of the dank leaves and the sweetfern and frosted apples, the sharp contrast of sun and the cold November shade, the stillness before snow. He walked faster, feeling the excitement swell within him.

He had walked all that morning, stopping now and then to study the map and take his bearings from the sun, and the road had led them down a long hill and at the bottom was the brook he had seen on the chart, a deep ravine spanned by a wooden bridge. Cider had trotted across the bridge, and he had followed more cautiously, avoiding the loose planks and walking the solid struts with his shotgun held out to balance himself; and that was how he found Tinkhamtown.

On the other side of the brook was a clearing, he remembered, and the remains of a stone wall, and a cellar hole where a farmhouse had stood. Cider had moved in a long cast around the edge of the clearing, his bell tinkling faintly, and he had paused a moment beside the foundations, wondering about the people who had lived here a century ago. Had they ever come back to Tinkhamtown? And then suddenly, the bell had stopped, and he had hurried across the clearing. An apple tree was growing in a corner of the stone wall, and under the tree Cider had halted at point. He could see it all now: the warm October sunlight, the ground strewn with freshly pecked apples, the dog standing immobile with one foreleg drawn up, his back level and his tail a white plume. Only his flanks quivered a little, and a string of slobber dangled from his jowls. "Steady, boy," he murmured as he moved up behind him, "I'm coming."

He paused on the crest of the hill, straining his ears for the faint mutter of the stream below him, but he could not hear it because of the voices. He wished they would stop talking, so he could hear the stream. Someone was saying his name over and over. Someone said, "What is it, Frank?" and he opened his eyes. Doc Towle was standing at the foot of the bed, whispering to the new nurse, Mrs. Simmons or something; she'd only been here a few days, but Doc thought it would take some of the burden off his wife. He turned his head on the pillow, and looked up at his wife's face, bent over him. "What did you say, Frank?" she asked, and her face was worried. Why, there was nothing to be worried about. He wanted to tell her where he was going, but when he moved his lips no sound came. "What?" she asked, bending her head lower. "I don't hear you." He couldn't make the words any clearer, and she straightened and said to Doc Towle: "It sounded something like Tinkhamtown."

"Tinkhamtown?" Doc shook his head. "Never heard him mention any place by that name."

He smiled to himself. Of course he'd never mentioned it to Doc. There are some things you don't mention even to an old hunting companion like Doc. Things like a secret grouse cover you didn't mention to anyone, not even to as close a friend as Doc was. No, he and Cider were the only ones who knew. They had found it together, that long ago afternoon, and it was their secret. "This is our secret cover," he had told Cider that afternoon, as he lay sprawled under the tree with the setter beside him and the dog's muzzle flattened on his thigh. "Just you and me." He had never told anybody else about Tinkhamtown, and he had never gone back after Cider died.

"Better let him rest," he heard Doc tell his wife. It was funny to hear them talking, and not be able to make them hear him. "Call me if there's any change."

The old road lay ahead of him, dappled with sunshine. He could smell the dank leaves, and feel the chill of the shadows under the hemlocks; it was more real than the pain in his legs. Sometimes it was hard to tell what was real and what was something he remembered. Sometimes at night he would hear Cider panting on the floor beside his bed, his toenails scratching as he chased a bird in a dream, but when the nurse turned on the light the room would be empty. And then when it was dark he would hear the panting and scratching again.

Once he asked Doc point-blank about his legs. "Will they ever get better?" He and Doc had grown up in town together; they knew each other too well to lie. Doc had shifted his big frame in the chair beside the bed, and got out his pipe and fumbled with it, and looked at him. "No, I'm afraid not," he replied slowly, "I'm afraid there's nothing to do." Nothing to do but lie here and wait till it's over. Nothing to do but lie here like this, and be waited on, and be a burden to everybody. He had a little insurance, and his son in California sent what he could to help, but now with the added expense of a nurse and all . . . "Tell me, Doc," he whispered, for his voice wasn't as strong these days, "what happens when it's over?" And Doc put away the needle and fumbled with the catch of his black bag and said he supposed that you went on to someplace else called the Hereafter. But he shook his head; he always argued with Doc. "No," he told him, "it isn't someplace else. It's someplace you've been where you want to be again, someplace you were happiest." Doc didn't understand, and he couldn't explain it any better. He knew what he meant, but the shot was taking effect and he was tired. The pain had been worse lately, and Doc had started giving him shots with a needle so he could sleep. But he didn't really sleep, because the memories kept coming back to him, or maybe he kept going back to the memories.

He was tired now, and his legs ached a little as he started down the hill toward the stream. He could not see the road; it was too dark under the trees to see the sketch he had drawn. The trunks of all the trees were swollen with moss, and blowdowns blocked his way and he had to circle around their upended roots, black and misshapen. He had no idea which way Tinkhamtown was, and he was frightened. He floundered into a pile of slash, feeling the branches tear at his legs as his boots sank in, and he did not have the strength to get through it and he had to back out again, up the hill. He did not know where he was going anymore.

He listened for the stream, but all he could hear was his wife, her breath catching now and then in a dry sob. She wanted him to come back, and Doc wanted him to, and there was the big house. If he left the house alone, it would fall in with the snow and cottonwoods would grow in the cellar hole. There were all the other doubts, but most of all there was the fear. He was afraid of the darkness and being alone, and not knowing the way. He had lost the way. Maybe he should turn back. It was late, but maybe, maybe he could find the way back.

He paused on the crest of the hill, straining his ears for the faint mutter of the stream below him, but he could not hear it because of the voices. He wished they would stop talking, so he could hear the stream. Someone was saying his name over and over. They had come to the stream—he shut his eyes so he could see it again—and Cider had trotted across the bridge. He had followed more cautiously, avoiding the loose planks and walking on a beam, with his shotgun held out to balance himself. On the other side the road rose sharply to a level clearing and he paused beside the split-stone foundation of a house. The fallen timbers were rotting under a tangle of briars and burdock, and in the empty cellar hole the cottonwoods grew higher than the house had been. His toe encountered a broken china cup and the rusted rims of a wagon wheel buried in the grass. Beside the granite doorsill was a lilac bush planted by the woman of the family to bring a touch of beauty to their home. Perhaps her husband had chided her for wasting time on such useless things, with as much work to be done. But all the work had come to nothing. The fruits of their work had disappeared, and still the lilac bloomed each spring, defying the encroaching forest, as though to prove that beauty is the only things that lasts.

On the other side of the clearing were the sills of the barn, and behind it a crumbling stone wall around the orchard. He thought of the men sweating to clear the fields and pile the rocks into walls to hold their cattle. Why had they gone away from Tinkhamtown, leaving their walls to crumble and their buildings to collapse under the January snows. Had they ever come back to Tinkhamtown? Or were they still here, watching him unseen, living in a past that was more real than the present. He stumbled over a block of granite, hidden by briars, part of the sill of the old barn. Once it had been a tight barn, warm with cattle steaming in their stalls and sweet with the barn odor of manure and hay and leather harness. It seemed as though it was more real to him than the bare foundation, the empty space about them. Doc used to argue that what's over is over, but he would insist Doc was wrong. Everything is the way it was, he'd tell Doc. The present always changes, but the past is always the way it was. You leave it, and go to the present, but it is still there, waiting for you to come back to it.

He had been so wrapped up in his thoughts that he had not realized Cider's bell had stopped. He hurried across the clearing, holding his gun ready. In a corner of the stone wall an ancient apple tree had covered the ground with red fruit, and beneath it Cider was standing motionless. The white fan of his tail was lifted a little, his neck stretched forward, and one foreleg was cocked. His flanks were trembling, and a thin skein of drool hung from his jowls. The dog did not move as he approached, but he could see the brown eyes roll back until their whites showed, waiting for him. His throat grew tight, the way it always did when Cider was on point, and he swallowed hard. "Steady, boy," he whispered, "I'm coming."

He opened his eyes. His wife was standing beside his bed and his son was standing near her. He looked at his son. Why had he come all the way from California? he worried. He tried to speak, but there was no sound. "I think his lips moved just now. He's trying to whisper something," his wife's voice said. "I don't think he knows you," his wife said to his son. Maybe he didn't know him. Never had, really. He had never been close to his wife or his son. He did not open his eyes, because he was watching for the grouse to fly as he walked past Cider, but he knew Doc Towle was looking at him. "He's sleeping," Doc said after a moment. "Maybe you better get some sleep yourself." A chair creaked, and he heard Doc's heavy footsteps cross the room. "Call me if there's any change," Doc said, and closed the door, and in the silence he could hear his wife sobbing beside him, her dress rustling regularly as she breathed. How could he tell her he wouldn't be alone? But he wasn't alone, not with Cider. He had the old dog curled on the floor by the stove, his claws scratching the linoleum as he chased a bird in a dream. He wasn't alone when he heard that. They were always together. There was a closeness between them that he did not feel for anyone else, his wife, his son, or even Doc. They could talk without words, and they could always find each other in the woods. He was lost without him. Cider was the kindest person he had ever known.

They never hunted together after Tinkhamtown. Cider had acted tired, walking back to the car that afternoon, and several times he sat down on the trail, panting hard. He had to carry him in his arms the last hundred yards to the Jeep. It was hard to think he was gone.

And then he heard it, echoing through the air, a sound like peepers in the spring, the high silvery note of a bell. He started running toward it, following it down the hill. The pain was gone from his legs, it had never been there. He hurdled blowdowns, he leapt over fallen trunks, he put one fingertip on a pile of slash and floated over it like a bird. The sound filled his ears, louder than a thousand churchbells ringing, louder than all the heavenly choirs in the sky, as loud as the pounding of his heart. His eyes were blurred with tears, but he did not need to see. The fear was gone; he was not alone. He knew the way now. He knew where he was going.

He paused at the stream just for a moment. He heard men's voices. They were his hunting partners, Jim, Mac, Dan, Woodie. And oh, what a day it was for sure, closeness and understanding and happiness, the little intimate things, the private jokes. He wanted to tell them he was happy; if they only knew how happy he was. He opened his eyes, but he could not see the room anymore. Everything else was bright with sunshine, but the room was dark.

The bell stopped, and he closed his eyes and looked across the stream. The other side was basked in gold bright sunshine, and he could see the road rising steeply through the clearing in the woods, and the apple tree in a corner of the stone wall. Cider was standing motionless, the white fan of his tail lifted a little, his neck craned forward, one foreleg cocked. The whites of his eyes showed as he looked back, waiting for him.

"Steady," he called, "steady, boy." He started across the bridge. "I'm coming."

He had been sick when he wrote "Tinkhamtown," sick in body and soul, for a long time. Corey was sixty-seven that summer when, while traveling in Ireland, he developed an aneurysm that required immediate attention.

They flew him back home, to Mary Hitchcock, a stone's throw from his house, where he had an operation, and it was deemed a success. He was recuperating in Dick's House, a brick mansion dedicated to ailing members of the Dartmouth family; Corey was surely family, considering all he'd done for the college—founding a boxing squad, the rugby team, helping boys financially through college.

He called home.

"Bring me Tober," he said, meaning his English setter, the son of Cider. But in the few minutes it took for one of the boys to get Tober to Dick's House, Corey had suffered a crushing stroke.

He was half paralyzed. The doctors determined there was nothing they could do, not anymore, so he went home where his housekeeper and a nurse could care for him, and the boys could come in and out and keep him company.

One morning he made it known that he wanted to go to the bathroom to shave, alone. A couple of the boys carried him in and closed the door. Shortly after came the crash. Corey had suffered a second stroke, this one devastating: He was in a coma.

The ambulance came. It was a short distance to the hospital, and they put him in a private room. Meanwhile, one of the boys had followed in Corey's car with Tober. He would want Tober. A couple of boys were outside Corey's room. They gave their mate the signal, and he led Tober up the fire escape. When the coast was clear, they took Tober into Corey's room.

He lay there in a coma. Tober saw Corey and jumped on his bed and set down beside him. The setter put his head on his master's shoulder.

And in the coma, Corey Ford raised his arms, put them around his beloved dog's neck, and died.

A year to the day, despite a loving home, Tober followed his master to Tinkhamtown.

Is Tinkhamtown a real place? Yes, of course. Everything is the way Corey said it was, down to the lilac trees. Majestic elms surround the cellar holes, vestiges of homes that were once alive with people; but the elms died, too, from disease. The summer of the twenty-fifth anniversary of Corey's death, I went to Tinkhamtown. The dead elms were alive again with new, green growth and new life sprouting from saplings and branches thirty feet up.

I once brought someone to Tinkhamtown, the only time I ever did. When we came to the bridge, he stopped. He refused to cross.

He said it was not his time.

But then, how will we know when it is our time to cross the bridge?

And So, Farewell and Adieu

"This is the [Hardscrabble] of the past and present, and of the future, who shall speak? But whatever may betide—and if it be ill may we not be here to see it—the mountains will still keep a stately watch in their changing garb of green or russet gold or white, with the lakes spreading below in sparkling blue or armored ice. What man has created here can pass away, but the beauty with which God dowered this beloved corner of our great land will remain forever, even as it dawned upon the vision of that first white explorer three hundred years ago."

—Dorothy Peck Chapman

We have come to the end of our journey, and it is time to part. Do not say good-bye. Just say so long. We will meet again, and then, as Joe Gargery said to Pip in *Great Expectations*, what larks we shall have! In the between time, remember Hardscrabble; remember all the things you've been told and seen and heard. . . .

Whenever you hear the breast-bursting song of the first robin of spring, or whiff the sweet autumn perfume of rotting apples settling on a mossy bed of fallen leaves . . . When the deep blue of a bottomless summer's lake has the cast of a sapphire, and a trout breaks the surface and flashes his tail in the sun-glinted water . . .

Think of us. . . .

For Hardscrabble will always be just down the road apiece and as far away as a thought; as eternal as a memory, and evermore sheltered in the safekeeping of your dreams.

And now, dear friend, Godspeed.

Reprinted with permission of Dartmouth College.

A Spring Sermon . . . or Siberia

JIM HARRISON

Long before I understood what it meant, the vernal equinox was my most important annual holiday. I think I was 14 when I realized that I tended to go haywire—the current word is "depression"—during the dark winter months in northern Michigan. But around the middle of March and onward, the sap began to rise again. What is now called "seasonal affective disorder" is so widespread in northern climes that only the severest cases are recognizable. Sigurd begins to sob and rams his head through the glass of the jukebox to get closer to the music. That sort of thing.

Survival arrives in the new quality of light, even beneath close cloud cover. I have been reminded countless times that my home area receives less sunlight than any other place in the United States except a specific area in the Pacific Northwest. All of us think our weather is unique; some actually is.

By early April, spring fever is palpable as a barn fire, a kind of interior mange, whose itch is forever out of reach of any salve except physical exhaustion. I have long since stopped sorting my fishing tackle a month before the trout opener, as my father did. It only makes things worse. The ears perk up instinctively for new bird arrivals, and the somewhat pathetic crocuses and skunk cabbage are a welcome sight.

It doesn't matter that it snows on trout opener in late April or that the streams are turbid from the runoff. Even the whine of the first mosquito makes the heart glad.

By May it is time to address certain criminal activities, in which I too have been a guilty party. Put aside this magazine. Go to your freezer. How much and what kind of fish and game do you have left in there from the previous summer and fall getting freezer burn? Write it down and subtract it as penance from your bag limit this summer and fall.

If you're not going to prepare the game properly and eat it, don't shoot it. The bird carcasses and fish fillets you take to the dump during spring cleaning represent an unnatural act against the natural world. Pluck your birds, don't skin them. Don't breast ducks, use the whole bird. Otherwise, let it fly on. Our imagined dominion over the natural world, an offshoot of our illusions about manifest destiny, is exhausting our wild lands to the degree that our grandchildren will be stuck with only Nintendo and spectator sports. If you insist on going for numbers, stick to the skeet range or commercial trout ponds, or play the state lottery.

See how much you can do on foot. The sharp reductions of fish and game populations through hunting and fishing are invariably related to mechanization. Unfortunately, our government, when it offers up timber leases, does not demand that log roads be destroyed after cutting. Easy access means diminished quality, even in love.

Don't leave a trace of yourself in the wilds, whether on water or in the forest. The shores of the Great Lakes are lined with detritus on which perch cormorants, whose beaks have been distorted grotesquely by chemical pollution. Strangely, even the fitness-buff sportsmen I know who have cross-trained themselves to a frazzle like to drive the last foot to their destination. I have noticed on my own property that if there's a branch on the road, no one hesitates to expand the road. Traces you shouldn't leave behind also include the piles of bait and garbage that lure mammals into shooting range.

Outdoors writers are fond of prating that "a few bad apples spoil it for the rest of us." Perhaps—if ten percent comprises "a few"; that is roughly the same percentage of malevolently incompetent doctors and lawyers. We have discovered a principle here. Sadly, we could all do much better. If the writer of the outdoors column in your local newspaper betrays real ignorance of botany, forestry, ornithology, game biology and riverine morphology, holler until the paper hires a better one. It no longer suits our survival as sportsmen to indulge those bumbling sentimentalists and their tales of the old man and the boy and the dog and the 10-point swamp buck that gores the ten-pound brown trout while the American eagle hovers over the $10,000 worth of Japanese equipment the writer got as freebies for touting the stuff.

Another part of your spring coda might be to get involved—no matter your political leanings—in local environmental groups. It is in your interest as an outdoorsman to defend the integrity of your own backyard, your own bioregion, your prized watersheds. And remember that the land rapers of a dozen varieties are always waving their American flags to get themselves off the hook. This sort of patriotism is always the last refuge of scoundrels, as Samuel Johnson pointed out. A couple of thousand wolves roam freely in Minnesota, but to date not a single one has been reintroduced into Yellowstone Park for fear it might nail a cow or two on the surrounding, largely public, grazing lands. You can pay a couple hundred grand in federal taxes, but if you offer a modest suggestion, these entitled freeloaders will call you a tree hugger. The whole notion of "multiuse" public lands will continue to be a scandal as long as the policy is directed by cows and chain saws. I have no objection to grazing on public lands as long as the notorious abuses the government freely permits are corrected. In the end, if sportsmen don't firmly align themselves with centrist environmentalists, we'd better raise a big kitty and buy Siberia.

The Heart of the Game

THOMAS MCGUANE

Hunting in your own back yard becomes with time, if you love hunting, less and less expeditionary. This year, when Montana's eager frosts knocked my garden on its butt, the hoe seemed more like the rifle than it ever had before, the vegetables more like game.

My son and I went scouting before the season and saw some antelope in the high plains foothills of the Absaroka Range, wary, hanging on the skyline; a few bands and no great heads. We crept around, looking into basins, and at dusk met a tired cowboy on a tired horse followed by a tired blue-heeler dog. The plains seemed bigger than anything, bigger than the mountains that seemed to sit in the middle of them, bigger than the ocean. The clouds made huge shadows that travelled on the grass slowly through the day.

Hunting season trickles on forever; if you don't go in on a cow with anybody, there is the dark argument of the empty deep-freeze against headhunting ("You can't eat horns!"). But nevertheless, in my mind, I've laid out the months like playing cards, knowing some decent whitetails could be down in the river bottom and, fairly reliably, the long windy shots at antelope. The big buck mule deer—the ridge-runners—stay up in the scree and rock walls until the snow drives them out; but they stay high long after the elk have quit and broken down the hay corrals on the ranches and farmsteads, which, when you're hunting the rocks from a saddle horse, look pathetic and housebroken with their yellow lights against the coming of winter.

Where I live, the Yellowstone River runs straight north, then takes an eastward turn at Livingston, Montana. This flowing north is supposed to be remarkable; and the river doesn't do it long. It runs mostly over sand and stones once it comes out of the rock slots near the Wyoming line. But all along, there are deviations of one sort or another: canals, backwaters, sloughs; the red willows grow in the sometime-flooded bottom, and at the first elevation, the cottonwoods. I hunt here for the white-tailed deer which, in recent years, have moved up these rivers in numbers never seen before.

The first morning, the sun came up hitting around me in arbitrary panels as the light moved through the jagged openings in the Absaroka Range. I was walking very slowly in the edge of the trees, the river invisible a few hundred yards to my right but sending a huge sigh through the willows. It was cold and the sloughs had crowns of ice thick enough to support me. As I crossed one great clear pane, trout raced around under my feet and a ten-foot bubble advanced slowly before my cautious steps. Then passing back into the trees, I found an active game trail, cut cross-lots to pick a better stand, sat in a good vantage place under a cottonwood with the aught-six across my knees. I thought, running my hands up into my sleeves, *This is lovely but I'd rather be up in the hills*; and I fell asleep.

I woke up a couple of hours later, the coffee and early-morning drill having done not one thing for my alertness. I had drooled on my rifle and it was time for my chores back at the ranch. My chores of late had consisted primarily of working on screenplays so that the bank didn't take the ranch. These days the primary ranch skill is making the payment; it comes before irrigation, feeding out, and calving. Some rancher friends find this so discouraging they get up and roll a number or have a slash of tanglefoot before they even think of the glories of the West. This is the New Rugged.

The next day, I reflected upon my lackadaisical hunting and left really too early in the morning. I drove around to Mission Creek in the dark and ended up sitting in the truck up some wash listening to a New Mexico radio station until my patience gave out and I started out cross-country in the dark, just able to make out the nose of the Absaroka Range as it faced across the river to the Crazy Mountains. It seemed maddeningly up and down slick banks, and a couple of times I had game clatter out in front of me in the dark. Then I turned up a long coulee that climbed endlessly south, and started in that direction, knowing the plateau on top should hold some antelope. After half an hour or so, I heard the mad laughing of coyotes, throwing their voices all around the inside of the coulee, trying to panic rabbits and making my hair stand on end despite my affection for them. The stars tracked overhead into the first pale light, and it was nearly dawn before I came up on the bench. I could hear cattle below me and I moved along an edge of thorn trees to break my outline, then sat down at the point to wait for shooting light.

I could see antelope on the skyline before I had that light; and by the time I did, there was a good big buck angling across from me, looking at everything. I thought I could see well enough, and I got up into a sitting position and into the sling. I had made my moves quietly, but when I looked through the scope the antelope was two hundred yards out, using up the country in bounds. I tracked with him, let him bounce up into the reticle, and touched off a shot. He was down and still, but I sat watching until I was sure.

Nobody who loves to hunt feels absolutely hunky-dory when the quarry goes down. The remorse spins out almost before anything and the balancing act ends on one declination or another. I decided that unless I become a vegetarian, I'll get my meat by hunting for it. I feel absolutely unabashed by the arguments of other carnivores who get their meat in plastic with blue numbers on it. I've seen slaughterhouses, and anyway, as Sitting Bull said, when the buffalo are gone, we will hunt mice, for we are hunters and we want our freedom.

The antelope had piled up in the sage, dead before he hit the ground. He was an old enough buck that the tips of his pronged horns were angled in toward each other. I turned him downhill to bleed him out. The bullet had mushroomed in the front of the lungs, so the job was already halfway done. With antelope, proper field dressing is critical because they can end up sour if they've been run or haphazardly hog-dressed. And they sour from their own body heat more than from external heat.

The sun was up and the big buteo hawks were lifting on the thermals. There was enough breeze that the grass began to have directional grain like the prairie, and the rim of the coulee wound up away from me toward the Absaroka. I felt peculiarly solitary, sitting on my heels next to the carcass in the sagebrush and greasewood, my rifle racked open on the ground. I made an incision around the metatarsal glands inside the back legs and carefully removed them and set them well aside; then I cleaned the blade of my hunting knife with handfuls of grass to keep from tainting the meat with those powerful glands. Next I detached the anus and testes from the outer walls and made a shallow puncture below the sternum, spread it with the thumb and forefinger of my left hand, and ran the knife upside down to the bone bridge between the hind legs. Inside, the diaphragm was like the taut lid of a drum and cut away cleanly, so that I could reach clear up to the back of the mouth and detach the windpipe. Once that was done I could draw the whole visceral package out onto the grass and separate out the heart, liver, and tongue before propping the carcass open with two whittled-up sage scantlings.

You could tell how cold the morning was, despite the exertion, just by watching the steam roar from the abdominal cavity. I stuck the knife in the ground and sat back against the slope, looking clear across to Convict Grade and the Crazy Mountains. I was blood from the elbows down and the antelope's eyes had skinned over. I thought. This is goddamned serious and you had better always remember that.

There was a big red enamel pot on the stove; and I ladled the antelope chili into two bowls for my son and me. He said, "It better not be too hot."

"It isn't."

"What's your news?" he asked.

"Grandpa's dead."

"Which grandpa?" he asked. I told him it was Big Grandpa, my father. He kept on eating. "He died last night."

He said, "I know what I want for Christmas."

"What's that?"

"I want Big Grandpa back."

It was 1950-something and I was small, under twelve, say, and there were four of us: my father, two of his friends, and me. There was a good belton setter belonging to the one friend, a hearty bird hunter who taught dancing and fist-fought at any provocation. The other man was old and sick and had a green fatal look in his face. My father took me aside and said, "Jack and I are going to the head of this field"—and he pointed up a mile and a half of stalks to where it ended in the flat woods—"and we're going to take the dog and get what he can point. These are running birds. So you and Bill just block the field and you'll have some shooting."

"I'd like to hunt with the dog," I had a 20-gauge Winchester my grandfather had given me, which got hocked and lost years later when another of my family got into the bottle; and I could hit with it and wanted to hunt over the setter. With respect to blocking the field, I could smell a rat.

"You stay with Bill," said my father, "and try to cheer him up."

"What's the matter with Bill?"

"He's had one heart attack after another and he's going to die."

"When?"

"Pretty damn soon."

I blocked the field with Bill. My first thought was, I hope he doesn't die before they drive those birds onto us; but if he does, I'll have all the shooting.

There was a crazy old autumn light on everything, magnified by the yellow silage all over the field. The dog found birds right away and they were shooting. Bill said he was sorry but he didn't feel so good. He had his hunting license safety-pinned to the back of his coat and fiddled with a handful of 12-gauge shells. "I've shot a shitpile of game," said Bill, "but I don't feel so good anymore." He took a knife out of his coat pocket. "I got this in the Marines," he said, "and I carried it for four years in the Pacific. The handle's drilled out and weighted so you can throw it. I want you to have it." I took it and thanked him, looking into his green face, and wondered why he had given it to me. "That's for blocking this field with me," he said. "Your dad and that dance teacher are going to shoot them all. When you're not feeling so good, they put you at the end of the field to block when there isn't shit-all going to fly by you. They'll get them all. They and the dog will."

We had an indestructible tree in the yard we had chopped on, nailed steps to, and initialed; and when I pitched that throwing knife at it, the knife broke in two. I picked it up and thought, *This thing is jinxed.* So I took it out into the crab-apple woods and put it in the can I had buried, along with a Roosevelt dime and an atomic-bomb ring I had sent away for. This was a small collection of things I buried over a period of years. I was sending them to God. All He had to do was open the can, but they were never collected. In any case, I have long known that if I could understand why I wanted to send a broken knife I believed to be jinxed to God, then I would be a long way toward what they call a personal philosophy as opposed to these hand-to-mouth metaphysics of who said what to whom in some cornfield twenty-five years ago.

We were in the bar at Chico Hot Springs near my home in Montana: me, a lout poet who had spent the day floating under the diving board while adolescent girls leapt overhead; and my brother John, who had glued himself to the pipe which poured warm water into the pool and announced over and over in a loud voice that every drop of water had been filtered through his bathing suit.

Now, covered with wrinkles, we were in the bar, talking to Alvin Close, an old government hunter. After half a century of predator control he called it "useless and half-assed."

Alvin Close killed the last major stock-killing wolf in Montana. He hunted the wolf so long he raised a litter of dogs to do it with. He hunted the wolf futilely with a pack that had fought the wolf a dozen times, until one day he gave up and let the dogs run the wolf out the back of a shallow canyon. He heard them yip their way into silence while he leaned up against a tree; and presently the wolf came tiptoeing down the front of the canyon into Alvin's lap. The wolf simply stopped because the game was up. Alvin raised the Winchester and shot it.

"How did you feel about that?" I asked.

"How do you think I felt?"

"I don't know."

"I felt like hell."

Alvin's evening was ruined and he went home. He was seventy-six years old and carried himself like an old-time army officer, setting his glass on the bar behind him without looking.

You stare through the plastic at the red smear of meat in the supermarket. What's this it says here? *Mighty Good? Tastee? Quality, Premium,* and *Government Inspected?* Soon enough, the blood is on your hands. It's inescapable.

Aldo Leopold was a hunter who I am sure abjured freeze-dried vegetables and extrusion burgers. His conscience was clean because his hunting was part of a larger husbandry in which the life of the country was enhanced by his own work. He knew that game populations are not bothered by hunting until they are already precarious and that precarious game populations should not be hunted. Grizzlies should not be hunted, for instance. The enemy of game is clean farming and sinful chemicals: as well as the useless alteration of watersheds by promoter cretins and the insidious dizzards of land development, whose lobbyists teach us the venality of all governments.

A world in which a sacramental portion of food can be taken in an old way—hunting, fishing, farming, and gathering—has as much to do with societal sanity as a day's work for a day's pay.

For a long time, there was no tracking snow. I hunted on horseback for a couple of days in a complicated earthquake fault in the Gallatins. The fault made a maze of narrow canyons with flat floors. The sagebrush grew on woody trunks higher than my head and left sandy paths and game trails where the horse and I could travel.

There were Hungarian partridge that roared out in front of my horse, putting his head suddenly in my lap. And hawks tobogganed on the low air currents, astonished to find me there. One finger canyon ended in a vertical rock wall from which issued a spring of the kind elsewhere associated with the Virgin Mary, hung with ex-votos and the orthopedic supplications of satisfied miracle customers. Here, instead, were nine identical piles of bear shit, neatly adorned with undigested berries.

One canyon planed up and topped out on an endless grassy rise. There were deer there, does and a young buck. A thousand yards away and staring at me with semaphore ears.

They assembled at a stiff trot from the haphazard array of feeding and strung out in a precise line against the far hill in a dogtrot. When I removed my hat, they went into their pogostick gait and that was that.

"What did a deer ever do to you?"

"Nothing."

"I'm serious. What do you have to go and kill them for?"

"I can't explain it talking like this."

"Why should they die for you? Would you die for deer?"

"If it came to that."

My boy and I went up the North Fork to look for grouse. We had my old pointer Molly, and Thomas's .22 pump. We flushed a number of birds climbing through the wild roses; but they roared away at knee level, leaving me little opportunity for my over-and-under, much less an opening for Thomas to ground-sluice one with his .22. We started out at the meteor hole above the last ranch and went all the way to the national forest. Thomas had his cap on the bridge of his nose and wobbled through the trees until we hit cross fences. We went out into the last open pasture before he got winded. So we sat down and looked across the valley at the Gallatin Range, furiously white and serrated, a bleak edge of the world. We sat in the sun and watched the chickadees make their way through the russet brush.

"Are you having a good time?"

"Sure," he said, and curled a small hand around the octagonal barrel of the Winchester. I was not sure what I had meant by my question.

The rear quarters of the antelope came from the smoker so dense and finely grained it should have been sliced as prosciutto. We had edgy, crumbling cheddar from British Columbia and everybody kept an eye on the food and tried to pace themselves. The snow whirled in the window light and puffed the smoke down the chimney around the cedar flames. I had a stretch of enumerating things: my family, hayfields, saddle horses, friends, thirty-aught-six, French and Russian novels. I had a baby girl, colts coming, and a new roof on the barn. I finished a big corral made of railroad ties and two-by-sixes. I was within eighteen months of my father's death, my sister's death, and the collapse of my marriage. Still, the washouts were repairing; and when a few things had been set aside, not excluding paranoia, some features were left standing, not excluding lovers, children, friends, and saddle horses. In time, it would be clear as a bell. I did want venison again that winter and couldn't help but feel some old ridge-runner had my number on him.

I didn't want to read and I didn't want to write or acknowledge the phone with its tendrils into the zombie enclaves. I didn't want the New Rugged; I wanted the Old Rugged and a pot to piss in. Otherwise, it's deteriorata, with mice undermining the wiring in my frame house, sparks jumping in the insulation, the dog turning queer, and a horned owl staring at the baby through the nursery window.

It was pitch black in the bedroom and the windows radiated cold across the blankets. The top of my head felt this side of frost and the stars hung like ice crystals over the chimney. I scrambled out of bed and slipped into my long johns, put on a heavy shirt and my wool logger pants with the police suspenders. I carried the boots down to the kitchen so as not to wake the house and turned the percolator on. I put some cheese and chocolate in my coat, and when the coffee was done I filled a chili bowl and quaffed it against the winter.

When I hit the front steps I heard the hard squeaking of new snow under my boots and the wind moved against my face like a machine for refinishing hardwood floors. I backed the truck up to the horse trailer, the lights wheeling against the ghostly trunks of the bare cottonwoods. I connected the trailer and pulled it forward to a flat spot for loading the horse.

I had figured that when I got to the corral I could tell one horse from another by starlight; but the horses were in the shadow of the barn and I went in feeling my way among their shapes trying to find my hunting horse Rocky and trying to get the front end of the big sorrel who kicks when surprised. Suddenly Rocky was looking in my face and I reached around his neck with the halter. A twelve-hundred-pound bay quarter horse, his withers angled up like a fighting bull, he wondered where we were going but ambled after me on a slack lead rope as we headed out of the darkened corral.

I have an old trailer made by a Texas horse vet years ago. It has none of the amenities of newer trailers. I wish it had a dome light for loading in the dark; but it doesn't. You ought to check and see if the cat's sleeping in it before you load; and I didn't do that either. Instead, I climbed inside the trailer and the horse followed me. I tied the horse down to a D-ring and started back out, when he blew up. The two of us were confined in the small space and he was ripping and bucking between the walls with such noise and violence that I had a brief disassociated moment of suspension from fear. I jumped up on the manger with my arms around my head while the horse shattered the inside of the trailer and rocked it furiously on its axles. Then he blew the steel rings out of the halter and fell over backward in the snow. The cat darted out and was gone. I slipped down off the manger and looked for the horse; he had gotten up and was sidling down past the granary in the star shadows.

I put two blankets on him, saddled him, played with his feet, and calmed him. I loaded him without incident and headed out.

I went through the aspen line at daybreak, still climbing. The horse ascended steadily toward a high basin, creaking the saddle metronomically. It was getting colder as the sun came up, and the rifle scabbard held my left leg far enough from the horse that I was chilling on that side.

We touched the bottom of the basin and I could see the rock wall defined by a black stripe of evergreens on one side and the remains of an avalanche on the other. I thought how utterly desolate this country can look in winter and how one could hardly think of human travel in it at all, not white horsemen nor Indians dragging travois, just aerial raptors with their rending talons and heads like cameras slicing across the geometry of winter.

Then we stepped into a deep hole and the horse went to his chest in the powder, splashing the snow out before him as he floundered toward the other side. I got my feet out of the stirrups in case we went over. Then we were on wind-scoured rock and I hunted some lee for the two of us. I thought of my son's words after our last cold ride: "Dad, you know in 4-H? Well, I want to switch from Horsemanship to Aviation."

The spot was like this: a crest of snow crowned in a sculpted edge high enough to protect us. There was a tough little juniper to picket the horse to, and a good place to sit out of the cold and noise. Over my head, a long, curling plume of snow poured out unchanging in shape against the pale blue sky. I ate some of the cheese and rewrapped it. I got the rifle down from the scabbard, loosened the cinch, and undid the flank cinch. I put the stirrup over the horn to remind me my saddle was loose, loaded two cartridges into the blind magazine, and slipped one in the chamber. Then I started toward the rock wall, staring at the patterned discolorations: old seeps, lichen, cracks, and the madhouse calligraphy of immemorial weather.

There were a lot of tracks where the snow had crusted out of the wind: all deer except for one well-used bobcat trail winding along the edges of a long rocky slot. I moved as carefully as I could, stretching my eyes as far out in front of my detectable movement as I could. I tried to work into the wind, but it turned erratically in the basin as the temperature of the new day changed.

The buck was studying me as soon as I came out on the open slope: he was a long way away and I stopped motionless to wait for him to feed again. He stared straight at me from five hundred yards. I waited until I could no longer feel my feet nor finally my legs. It was nearly an hour before he suddenly ducked his head and began to feed. Every time he fed I moved a few feet, but he was working away from me and I wasn't getting anywhere. Over the next half-hour he made his way to a little rim and, in the half hour after that, moved the twenty feet that dropped him over the rim.

I went as fast as I could move quietly. I now had the rim to cover me and the buck should be less than a hundred yards from me when I looked over. It was all browse for a half-mile, wild roses, buck brush, and young quakies where there was any runoff.

When I reached the rim. I took off my bat and set it in the snow with my gloves inside. I wanted to be looking in the right direction when I cleared the rim rise a half step and be looking straight at the buck, not scanning for the buck with him running sixty, a degree or two out of my periphery. And I didn't want to gum it up with thinking or trajectory guessing. People are always trajectory guessing their way into got shots and clean misses. So, before I took the last step, all there was to do was lower the rim with my feet, lower the buck into my vision, and isolate the path of the bullet.

As I took that step. I knew he was running. He wasn't in the browse at all, but angling into invisibility at the rock wall, racing straight into the elevation, bounding toward zero gravity taking his longest are into the bullet and the finality and terror of all you have made of the world, the finality you know that you share even with your babies with their inherited and ambiguous dentition, the finality that any minute now you will meet as well.

He slid a hundred yards in a rush of snow. I dressed him and skidded him by one antler to the horse. I made a slit behind the last ribs, pulled him over the saddle and put the horn through the slit, lashed the feet to the cinch dees, and led the horse downhill. The horse had bells of clear ice around his hoofs, and when he slipped, I chipped them out from under his feet with the point of a bullet.

I hung the buck in the open woodshed with a lariat over a rafter. He turned slowly against the cooling air. I could see the intermittent blue light of the television against the bedroom ceiling from where I stood. I stopped the twirling of the buck, my hands deep in the sage-scented fur, and thought: This is either the beginning or the end of everything.

Lost

LAURIE BOGART MORROW

You gain strength, courage and confidence by every experience in which you really stop to look fear in the face. You are able to say to yourself, "I lived through this horror. I can take the next thing that comes along. . . . You must do the thing you think you cannot do.

—Eleanor Roosevelt

She knew the tears would come. They didn't come often, and she hated it when they did. But she was lost, really lost in the woods, and she was beginning to get frightened. She had never been frightened before, at least not like this—but it came from the same place, the fear. It came from within, that helpless place in her soul, the dark compartment she kept securely locked. She knew too well what it was to feel helpless. Helpless, like the day she lost her only daughter. She didn't want to think about that right now; she couldn't. She had to find her way out of the woods and get home. Home to her family. It was going to be dark in a couple of hours, and she was completely turned around.

They would be getting worried. Even her little springer spaniel seemed concerned as she stood alongside her, looking up expectantly. Her husband knew where she had gone, or at least where she was going.

Her sons knew this place well, too. They learned to hunt here. That was . . . what? Ten years ago . . . "Don't worry," her husband had assured her. "I'll take care of them. No, they're not too young. I was eight when my father took me bird hunting for the first time. . . ." Now their sons were at the cusp of adulthood, and yet it seemed like only yesterday. She wouldn't have been lost if they were with her; she shouldn't have gotten lost in the first place. After all, she learned to hunt here, too, all those years ago. But then she gave it up, had the children, kept the home fires burning. Then the baby died. Afterwards, when she learned to live with the terrible emptiness in her heart and tried to get on with it, she took up hunting again. Bird hunting, and now this fall she was going after deer with her husband and their boys. She loved the woods; it was so peaceful. And the hunting, well, that was a good way to fill the place her daughter was meant to fill, to dull the loss, to understand that expectation always falls short when you want something so very, very much.

No, she shouldn't have gotten lost, but she did. These woods went on and on for miles, through swamps and hills and valleys and on to nowhere, for all anyone knew.

Once it had been a thriving New Hampshire village with homesteads and even a meetinghouse. You could still make out the road that led to it, but now it was only forested trail. Here and there lay foundations of old houses and barns. A stone corral for sheep had tumbled with time, barely, an outline, bordered by ancient lilac bushes. Apple trees marked the foundation of an outlying farmhouse, out here, another there; they were overgrown and gnarled and shouldn't, but did, bear fruit, still, in the fall. She picked a ruby-red apple and pierced it lightly with her teeth, expecting bitter juice. But the apple was sweet, and she was hungry, and she ate it and picked another. Her pup jumped up, begging for a bite, and she gave her the core to devour. She stopped crying because the apple was comforting and she felt revived.

The leaves were brilliant, more brilliant against the blanket of darkening gray sky than they ever are on a cloudless, peacock-blue day. Good artists never attempted to paint autumn, she thought, because only nature knew how to mix the right palette. She used to paint, but she had given it up. When the baby died, she lost her inspiration. She couldn't deal with joy unrealized after she had been robbed of her only chance to raise a daughter. She wanted her so much. As time passed, it hurt more, and she didn't understand why. Tears again pinched her eyes, and she tried to fight them back.

Would she have raised her little girl to hunt? Probably not. When her sons and husband went hunting, she and her daughter would have gone shopping and done girlish things together. It would have become a joke. She would have threatened her husband with a big credit card bill as he and the boys took off for yet another weekend hunting deer. And he would have put her over his knee and pretended to spank her, and the children would have laughed. Yes, he and the boys would have gone hunting, and she and their daughter would have gone shopping, and everyone would have had a good time and lots to tell over Sunday night supper.

But her husband couldn't hold her over his knee anymore, not since he got sick. That was just after the baby died, when his legs got weak and he couldn't go hunting anymore, at least not like he used to. Now that the boys were older, they would drive their dad to a promising place, and he'd sit and wait for a deer while his sons went stalking in the forest. Last year, he took a fine buck that way, just under two hundred pounds dressed. Lately he felt better, and he could walk a mile sometimes. Last Sunday grouse season opened, and they took their hot little springer pup out for her first opening day. She put up four grouse. It was such a delight to finally have a good dog to flush their favorite coverts that they missed every single shot; and laughed, like they used to.

How did she get so turned around? She hefted her shotgun, breech open, over her shoulder and headed out of the old orchard, away from the once-was town. Stupidly, she left her compass in her other jacket, but the sun was setting, and she made that her marker. Her dog became lively again, as if to say, "Good, let's go home." But that wasn't it, she thought, that wasn't it at all. She brought her gun down, loaded a shell in each chamber, and no sooner had she closed the breech than her dog pounced on a fat grouse hen. The bird exploded from the forest floor with a whirrrr, hell-bent for safe haven. She swung her gun to her shoulder, pointed the barrels, and felled the bird with the second shot.

A sudden gust like a tailwind lifted the spaniel high over a crumbling stone wall as she bounded to retrieve the grouse. So majestic, the grouse, and she remembered the legend her husband told her of how Indians would say a prayer over their game, thanking their brother of the forest for sacrificing his life to sustain theirs. She whispered a tender prayer. She needed to speak to the silence; and the mighty pines arched overhead like a forest cathedral. The brisk evening wind blew her damp cheeks dry. It was at dusk eight Octobers ago today that her baby died in her arms.

Now she found herself in a fern-covered glen. The forest floor was awash with that golden cast peculiar to autumn sunsets. It reminded her of a happy time—how many years ago?—it must be going on twenty-five, when she and her husband first hunted together here. Here? Yes! She knew this place: She was at the beaver pond. They had brought a picnic and had drunk wine and then made love in the soft grass there, at the shoulder of the pond. The leaves shivered and shook loose the memory of a long-ago soft summer breeze that caressed their bare bodies, warmed by the sun, warmed from the loving. She wanted those days back, she wanted her daughter, she wanted to go home.

She saw the hill beyond the beaver pond and knew that uphill was the forgotten cemetery and beyond that, the road. It was a hard climb, but she was sure about it now, and it gave her renewed strength and hope. Her pup took the hill with trouble, for the ground was thick with brambles. She kept up with the little springer, her eye marking a birch tree that had splintered and fallen into the fork of a giant maple. Out of nowhere, a limb suddenly slingshot and cut her above her chin. She felt it sting, and a drop of blood trickled onto her red turtleneck, against her black hair, and she grabbed at the branch that dared injure her and broke it off with a snap. High above she could see the horizon through the pines, and she lunged forward, her arm bent to shield her face as tree limbs tore at her clothes as if trying to hold her back. There it was, the little cemetery. Seven headstones, that's all. Only seven, but they told the whole story. *"Their name was Eldridge,"* her husband's voice spoke to her across the years, *"and they owned that farm over there. Look. You can see the foundation."* She again turned her eyes in the direction he had pointed. It was still there, just a vestige of a place and a time that was no more.

"A father, a mother, and their five children. See this little marker with the lamb? She was the first, she died at birth." Just like my daughter, she thought; *just like my own baby. "And next to that,"* the memory voice of her husband continued through the past, *"three, all in a row. Two boys and a girl, ages two, three, and five. All within a week. It was smallpox. The epidemic took the whole village."* She thought, *Oh my God. I lost just one child. How did that mother survive?* Then she saw the fifth stone and remembered the mother

hadn't. *"Within a year,"* her husband's voice trailed, *"the mother . . . they say she died from grief."* And the sixth? The sixth tombstone was the last child, a son, killed in the First World War. Just turned eighteen. The last stone, the seventh. It was less tarnished by years than the others, dated six years after the soldier boy's. The father's. He was helpless. There was nothing he could do but watch each of his loved ones die. They say he finally went mad from grief. . . .

Helpless . . .

She didn't know how much time had passed, how long she sat pondering over the fate of the poor farmer and his family, how long she mourned for them, for herself. Her pup was asleep at her feet, and the autumn air was now cold with damp, the sky dark. This was a good place to leave her grief, she thought. Let it go, get on with it, find the road. But she felt the weight of her soul heavy upon her as she stood up to go.

She left the cemetery through the stone posts, squeezing past a sapling that had grown smack between them. How tremendous, she thought, as she realized it was a Gilead tree. She picked a leaf and rubbed it on her hand, aching for some balm to heal the wound within.

And ahead was the road. After that she knew her way. Her pace quickened as each step brought her closer to familiar ground. *It's time to get on with it*, she thought. Not to sorrow. She had blessings to enjoy, far more blessings than sorrows.

And then, with utter disbelief, she saw them. Ahead of her on the road were three grouse, dancing up and down and beating their wings all for joy, dusting the dry dirt road with their tails. Even the pup paused to look at the pageant. The birds continued to whirl and flutter, and the shiver of gold and red and orange leaves accompanied them like delicate music. All she could do was watch in wonderment.

The cover of night was gently descending upon the forest when, from a distance, there shone a light. Headlights. "Mom? Mom!" voices cried. "Are you all right?" Her sons raced toward her, scattering the grouse, which then pirouetted high into the air like fireworks and disappeared into the woods. Not far behind was her husband.

"Yes . . . I'm here. . . . I'm all right!" she cried as she ran to her family. Each step felt lighter. Each step carried her closer to the shelter of her loved ones. Each step took her farther and farther from the burden she left behind. For she had finally unlocked the compartment in her soul and gently, lovingly, laid her sorrow to rest in the holiness of the woods.

This episode is out of timing with the rest of this book. From cover to cover, *The Hardscrabble Chronicles* accounts for a mere two of the thirty years I've lived here. "Lost" happened to me about fifteen years ago.

Losing a child is hope dashed. The loss of hope, no matter how great or for what reason—whether for a brief time or for a period that lingers, festers, and disintegrates into blackness—is a cruel and heavy burden. I carried mine to Tinkhamtown where unexpectedly, a light filtered through the forest, and through my grief, and illuminated the dark place in my heart.

Loss is part of living. The Whys are seldom understood, often never known, but we can profit from loss. I was lost. I had lost faith. But in a single unplanned moment, I found it once again—or perhaps it found me. The rediscovery of faith is an act of grace.

Remember, in your own journey you don't have to look for a tranquil place like Tinkhamtown. Just search for the tranquil place in your heart. It's there, if you look hard enough.

You'll know when you find it.

Finding Your Way in the Woods

NELSON BRYANT

Although being lost in the woods is, at best, an unpleasant experience, thousands of deer hunters contrive to do it every year.

Death by exposure sometimes results, but the usual outcome is spending a cold, miserable night in the forest. There is also the embarrassment of possibly being the object of an organized search, a thing that would bother some men more than the physical discomfort.

All this could be avoided by carrying a map of the area and a compass, or, if the topography of the region to be hunted is committed to memory, the compass alone.

Anyone who spends a lot of time in a big forest sooner or later will become confused as to his whereabouts.

The first thing to do when you suddenly are aware that you don't know which direction to take to return to your car or camp is: sit down, think and compose yourself. You should realize that if you've been hunting properly—not moving too fast—you cannot be more than a few miles from your starting places; you haven't entered some strange never-never land.

If you have a map, or if you study the map of the region you are hunting, you should have a good idea, within a mile or so, of where you are. All other clues lacking, you can simply use your compass to backtrack to your start. Implicit in this is that you know, on the map, the point from which you began and the general direction of your travels.

If the sun is out, or if there are mountains or hills you can see and use as reference points, there is really no need for a compass. The same is true when the night is clear and the stars are visible. Every woodsman should, at the very least, be able to locate the North Star.

Sometimes, however, a bright, clear day becomes dark, snow begins to fall, or mist fills the woods, and you have nothing, except your compass, to go by.

Each of us has a sense of direction, and with most people it is thoroughly unreliable.

When you first realize that you don't know where you are and sit down to think it over, you will, after a while, often have a strong feeling about which way you should go to get out of the woods.

Checking that feeling against your compass, you will usually find that you are way off the mark.

This has happened to me several times, and I always marvel at the distinct act of will that is required for me to believe the instrument, not myself. I have even, in extreme cases, felt that there were magnetic rocks nearby pulling the compass needle awry. Always, however, the compass was correct.

Your compass should be of good quality, waterproof and liquid-dampened.

The only maps worth using are the topographic variety, available from both private and government sources.

If you study such maps carefully, you will eventually reach a point where you can actually envision the contours of the land.

If you are completely turned around, following a brook downstream will often lead you to civilization. This doesn't work all the time. To put it another way, the stream on one side of a mountain may lead you to a community in short order while one on the other side may take you deeper into the wilderness. You should, from your topographic map, know the direction in which streams drain if you are using them as a guide.

Following a brook can be a tough job. I once lost my way in the mist on a New Hampshire mountain and elected to use a stream. I was encumbered by a heavy pack, and the brook's boulder-strewn, twisting and often precipitous course down the mountain was a considerable challenge.

There may come a time when you are still deep in the woods at dark. If the walking is good and you are sure of where you are going, you might as well keep moving. If, however, you are on some rugged mountainside or deep in a blowdown where night travel is dangerous, the best thing to do is gather plenty of wood and light a fire.

If you are with other men in a deer camp, they won't start worrying about you—if you fail to appear—until after sundown.

Three shots, closely spaced, are regarded as a universal signal of distress, but don't touch them off until well after dark or they'll be mistaken for those fired at a deer.

Usually, and this should be arranged beforehand with the others, it is expected—if one of the party is missing—that the men at camp will fire three shots when it is truly dark.

If you hear those shots, respond with three of your own.

Thereafter, as the searchers start moving toward you, they will occasionally fire a single shot. Respond with one of your own.

Failing to hear their original three shots—or if you don't have a hunting party—the only thing you can do is fire groups of three at one-hour intervals after dark and hope for a response. (All this shooting presupposes that you have a full box of twenty cartridges with you.)

Some deer hunters, and I am one of them, bring along a small pack which contains a few packets of dried soup and tea or coffee, chocolate bars, a little bag of nuts and dried fruit, rope, a small hatchet and a canteen cup in which to heat water. It usually isn't necessary to carry water because streams, lakes and ponds are common in deer country, and if there is snow it can be melted for this purpose.

This little kit, which weighs only a few pounds, will help making a night in the woods more comfortable, and there will also be times when a cup of hot soup at midday is most welcome.

The pack should be draped with fluorescent orange so that some other hunter won't mistake it for a portion of a deer. An extra hunting vest of this color is ideal for this purpose.

The average hunter really doesn't need to achieve pinpoint accuracy in his woods navigation, but there are orienteering groups one may join, if they appeal to you. (Orienteering involves traveling as rapidly as possible from checkpoint to checkpoint through the woods.)

To return directly—assuming no impassable terrain is in the way—to one's point of entry into the woods requires keeping track of the distance traveled and the various changes of direction that were made. It is nearly impossible to do this and simultaneously hunt deer successfully. The best one can do is make an accurate guess.

Rather than striving to arrive at one's precise starting point, it is sometimes better to make a planned error. If, for example, one leaves his car on a road that runs east and west for several miles and then hunts to the south, one might simply head north near the end of the day. The difficulty with this is that when the road is reached one usually doesn't know whether the car is to the left or right. It is much better, on the return trip, to consciously veer ten or 15 degrees east or west of north. Then, upon reaching the road, there is no doubt about which way to go.

Although precise navigation isn't needed by most woodsmen, it can offer both a challenge and a reward. A trout fisherman who wants to visit a little pond five miles deep in the woods will, unless there is a trail to it, have to become truly proficient with map and compass. If the pond is, for example, only a quarter of a mile long, he hasn't much room for error.

For this, a specially designed compass—the orienteering models by Silva are excellent—is needed. The ordinary wrist, or watch-pocket-size instrument won't do.

There are government topographic maps available for most of the United States, and they may be obtained in many sporting goods stores and bookstores.

The Ledge

LAWRENCE SARGENT HALL

On Christmas morning before sunup the fisherman embraced his warm wife and left his close bed. She did not want him to go. It was Christmas morning. He was a big, raw man, with too much strength, whose delight in winter was to hunt the sea ducks that flew in to feed by the outer ledges, bare at low tide.

As his bare feet touched the cold floor and the frosty air struck his nude flesh, he might have changed his mind in the dark of this special day. It was a home day, which made it seem natural to think of the outer ledges merely as some place he had shot ducks in the past. But he had promised his son, thirteen, and his nephew, fifteen, who came from inland. That was why he had given them his present of an automatic shotgun each the night before, on Christmas Eve. Rough man though he was known to be, and no spoiler of boys, he kept his promises when he understood what they meant. And to the boys, as to him, home meant where you came for rest after you had had your Christmas fill of action and excitement.

His legs astride, his arms raised, the fisherman stretched as high as he could in the dim privacy of his bedroom. Above the snug murmur of his wife's protest he heard the wind in the pines and knew it was easterly as the boys had hoped and he had surmised the night before. Conditions would be ideal, and when they were, anybody ought to take advantage of them. The birds would be flying. The boys would get a man's sport their first time outside on the ledges.

His son at thirteen, small but steady and experienced, was fierce to grow up in hunting, to graduate from sheltered waters and the blinds along the shores of the inner bay. His nephew at fifteen, an overgrown farm boy, had a farm boy's love of the sea, though he could not swim a stroke and was often sick in choppy weather. That was the reason his father, the fisherman's brother, was a farmer and chose to sleep in on the holiday morning at his brother's house. Many of the ones the farmer had grown up with were regularly seasick and could not swim, but they were unafraid of the water. They could not have dreamed of being anything but fishermen. The fisherman himself could swim like a seal and was never sick, and he would sooner die than be anything else.

He dressed in the cold and dark, and woke the boys gruffly. They tumbled out of bed, their instincts instantly awake while their thoughts still fumbled slumbrously. The fisherman's wife in the adjacent bedroom heard them apparently trying to find their clothes, mumbling sleepily and happily to each other, while her husband went down to the hot kitchen to fry eggs—sunny-side up, she knew, because that was how they all liked them.

Always in winter she hated to have them go outside, the weather was so treacherous and there were so few others out in case of trouble. To the fisherman these were no more than woman's fears, to be taken for granted and laughed off. When they were first married they fought miserably every fall because she was after him constantly to put his boat up until spring. The fishing was all outside in winter, and though prices were high the storms made the rate of attrition high on gear. Nevertheless he did well. So she could do nothing with him.

People thought him a hard man, and gave him the reputation of being all out for himself because he was inclined to brag and be disdainful. If it was true, and his own brother was one of those who strongly felt it was, they lived better than others, and his brother had small right to criticize. There had been times when in her loneliness she had yearned to leave him for another man. But it would have been dangerous. So over the years she had learned to shut her mind to his hard-driving, and take what comfort she might from his unsympathetic competence. Only once or twice, perhaps, had she gone so far as to dwell guiltily on what it would be like to be a widow.

The thought that her boy, possibly because he was small, would not be insensitive like his father, and the rattle of dishes and smell of frying bacon downstairs in the kitchen shut off from the rest of the chilly house, restored the cozy feeling she had had before she was alone in bed. She heard them after a while go out and shut the back door.

Under her window she heard the snow grind dryly beneath their boots, and her husband's sharp, exasperated commands to the boys. She shivered slightly in the envelope of her own warmth. She listened to the noise of her son and nephew talking elatedly. Twice she caught the glimmer of their lights on the white ceiling above the window as they went down the path to the shore. There would be frost on the skiff and freezing suds at the water's edge. She herself used to go gunning when she was younger; now, it seemed to her, anyone going out like that on Christmas morning had to be incurably male. They would none of them think about her until they returned and piled the birds they had shot on top of the sink for her to dress.

Ripping into the quiet predawn cold she heard the hot snarl of the outboard taking them out to the boat. It died as abruptly as it had burst into life. Two or three or four or five minutes later the big engine broke into a warm reassuring roar. He had the best of equipment, and he kept it in the best of condition. She closed her eyes. It would not be too long before the others would be up for Christmas. The summer drone of the exhaust deepened. Then gradually it faded in the wind until it was lost at sea, or she slept.

The engine had started immediately in spite of the temperature. This put the fisherman in a good mood. He was proud of his boat. Together he and the two boys heaved the skiff and outboard onto the stern and secured it athwartships. His son went forward along the deck, iridescent in the ray of the light the nephew shone through the windshield, and cast the mooring pennant loose into darkness. The fisherman swung to starboard, glanced at his compass, and headed seaward down the obscure bay.

There would be just enough visibility by the time they reached the headland to navigate the crooked channel between the islands. It was the only nasty stretch of water. The fisherman had done it often in fog or at night—he always swore he could go anywhere in the bay blindfolded—but there was no sense in taking chances if you didn't have to. From the mouth of the channel he could lay a straight course for Brown Cow Island, anchor the boat out of sight behind it, and from the skiff set their tollers off Devil's Hump three hundred yards to seaward. By then the tide would be clearing the ledge and they could land and be ready to shoot around half-tide.

It was early, it was Christmas, and it was farther out than most hunters cared to go in this season of the closing year, so that he felt sure no one would be taking possession ahead of them. He had shot thousands of ducks there in his day. The Hump was by far the best hunting. Only thing was you had to plan for the right conditions because you didn't have too much time. About four hours was all, and you had to get it before three in the afternoon when the birds left and went out to sea ahead of nightfall.

They had it figured exactly right for today. The ledge would not be going under until after the gunning was over, and they would be home for supper in good season. With a little luck the boys would have a skiff-load of birds to show for their first time outside. Well beyond the legal limit, which was no matter. You took what you could get in this life, or the next man made out and you didn't.

The fisherman had never failed to make out gunning from Devil's Hump. And this trip, he had a hunch, would be above ordinary. The easterly wind would come up just stiff enough, the tide was right, and it was going to storm by tomorrow morning so the birds would be moving. Things were perfect.

The old fierceness was in his bones. Keeping a weather eye to the murk out front and a hand on the wheel, he reached over and cuffed both boys playfully as they stood together close to the heat of the exhaust pipe running up through the center of the house. They poked back at him and shouted above the drumming engine, making bets as they always did on who would shoot the most birds. This trip they had the thrill of new guns, the best money could buy, and a man's hunting ground. The black retriever wagged at them and barked. He was too old and arthritic to be allowed in December water, but he was jaunty anyway at being brought along.

Groping in his pocket for his pipe the fisherman suddenly had his high spirits rocked by the discovery that he had left his tobacco at home. He swore. Anticipation of a day out with nothing to smoke made him incredulous. He searched his clothes, and then he searched them again, unable to believe the tobacco was not somewhere. When the boys inquired what was wrong he spoke angrily to them, blaming them for being in some devious way at fault. They were instantly crestfallen and willing to put back after the tobacco, though they could appreciate what it meant only through his irritation. But he bitterly refused. That would throw everything out of phase. He was a man who did things the way he set out to do.

He clamped his pipe between his teeth, and twice more during the next few minutes he ransacked his clothes in disbelief. He was no stoic. For one relaxed moment he considered putting about, and gunning somewhere nearer home. Instead he held his course and sucked the empty pipe, consoling himself with the reflection that at least he had whiskey enough if it got too uncomfortable on the ledge. Peremptorily he made the boys check to make certain the bottle was really in the knapsack with the lunches where he thought he had taken care to put it. When they reassured him he despised his fate a little less.

The fisherman's judgment was, as usual, accurate. By the time they were abreast of the headland there was sufficient light so that he could wind his way among the reefs without slackening speed. At last he turned his bows toward open ocean, and as the winter dawn filtered upward through long layers of smoky cloud on the eastern rim his spirits rose again with it.

He opened the throttle, steadied on his course, and settled down to the two-hour run. The wind was stronger but seemed less cold coming from the sea. The boys had withdrawn from the fisherman and were talking together while they watched the sky through the windows. The boat churned solidly through a light chop, flinging spray off her flaring bows. Astern the headland thinned rapidly till it lay like a blackened sill on the gray water. No other boats were abroad.

The boys fondled their new guns, sighted along the barrels, worked the mechanisms, compared notes, boasted, and gave each other contradictory advice. The fisherman got their attention once and pointed at the horizon. They peered through the windows and saw what looked like a black scum floating on top of gently agitated water. It wheeled and tilted, rippled, curled, then rose, strung itself out and became a huge raft of ducks escaping over the sea. A good sign.

The boys rushed out and leaned over the washboards in the wind and spray to see the flock curl below the horizon. Then they went and hovered around the hot engine, bewailing their lot. If only they had been already set out and waiting. Maybe these ducks would be crazy enough to return later and be slaughtered. Ducks were known to be foolish.

In due course and right on schedule they anchored at midmorning in the lee of Brown Cow Island. They put the skiff overboard and loaded it with guns, knapsacks, and tollers. The boys showed their eagerness by being clumsy. The fisherman showed his in bad temper and abuse which they silently accepted in the absorbed tolerance of being boys. No doubt they laid it to lack of tobacco.

By outboard they rounded the island and pointed due east in the direction of a ridge of foam which could be seen whitening the surface three hundred yards away. They set the decoys in a broad, straddling vee opening wide into the ocean. The fisherman warned them not to get their hands wet and when they did he made them carry on with red and painful fingers, in order to teach them. Once the last toller was bobbing among his fellows, brisk and alluring, they got their numbed fingers inside their oilskins and hugged their warm crotches. In the meantime the fisherman had turned the skiff toward the patch of foam where as if by magic, like a black glossy rib of earth, the ledge had broken through the belly of the sea.

Carefully they inhabited their slipper nub of the North American continent, while the unresting Atlantic swelled and swirled as it had for eons round the indomitable edges. They hauled the skiff after them, established themselves as comfortably as they could in a shallow sump on top, lay on their sides a foot or so above the water, and waited, guns in hand.

In time the fisherman took a thermos bottle from the knapsack and they drank steaming coffee, and waited for the nodding decoys to lure in the first flight to the rock. Eventually the boys got hungry and restless. The fisherman let them open the picnic lunch and eat one sandwich apiece, which they both shared with the dog. Having no tobacco the fisherman himself would not eat.

Actually the day was relatively mild, and they were warm enough at present in their woolen clothes and socks underneath oilskins and hip boots. After a while, however, the boys began to feel cramped. Their nerves were agonized by inactivity. The nephew complained and was severely told by the fisherman—who pointed to the dog, crouched unmoving except for his white-rimmed eyes—that part of doing a man's hunting was learning how to wait. But he was beginning to have misgivings of his own. This could be one of those days where all the right conditions masked an incalculable flaw.

If the fisherman had been alone, as he often was, stopping off when the necessary coincidence of tide and time occurred on his way home from hauling trawls, and had plenty of tobacco, he would not have fidgeted. The boys' being nervous made him nervous. He growled at them again. When it came it was likely to come all at once, and then in a few moments be over. He warned them not to slack off, never to slack off, to be always ready. Under his rebuke they kept their tortured peace, though they could not help shifting and twisting until he lost what patience he had left and bullied them into lying still. A duck could see an eyelid twitch. If the dog could go without moving so could they.

"Here it comes!" the fisherman said tersely at last.

The boys quivered with quick relief. The flock came in downwind, quartering slightly, myriad, black, and swift.

"Beautiful—" breathed the fisherman's son.

"All right," said the fisherman, intense and precise. "Aim at singles in the thickest part of the flock. Wait for me to fire and then don't stop shooting till your gun's empty." He rolled up onto his left elbow and spread his legs to brace himself. The flock bore down, arrowy and vibrant, then a hundred yards beyond the decoys it veered off.

"They're going away!" the boys cried, sighting in.

"Not yet!" snapped the fisherman. "They're coming round."

The flock changed shape, folded over itself, and drove into the wind in a tight arc. "Thousands—" the boys hissed through their teeth. All at once a whistling storm of black and white broke over the decoys.

"Now!" the fisherman shouted. "Perfect!" And he opened fire at the flock just as it hung suspended in momentary chaos above the tollers. The three pulled at their triggers and the birds splashed into the water, until the last report went off unheard, the last smoking shell flew unheeded over their shoulders, and the last of the routed flock scattered diminishing, diminishing, diminishing in every direction.

Exultantly the boys dropped their guns, jumped up and scrambled for the skiff.

"I'll handle that skiff!" the fisherman shouted at them. They stopped. Gripping the painter and balancing himself he eased the skiff into the water stern first and held the bow hard against the side of the rock shelf the skiff had rested on. "You stay here," he said to his nephew. "No sense in all three of us going in the boat."

The boy on the reef gazed at the gray water rising and falling hypnotically along the glistening edge. It had dropped about a foot since their arrival. "I want to go with you," he said in a sullen tone, his eyes on the streaming eddies.

"You want to do what I tell you if you want to gun with me," answered the fisherman harshly. The boy couldn't swim, and he wasn't going to have him climbing in and out of the skiff anymore than necessary. Besides he was too big.

The fisherman took his son in the skiff and cruised round and round among the decoys picking up dead birds. Meanwhile the other boy stared unmoving after them from the highest part of the ledge. Before they had quite finished gathering the dead birds, the fisherman cut the outboard and dropped to his knees in the skiff. "Down!" he yelled. "Get down!" About a dozen birds came tolling in. "Shoot— shoot!" his son hollered from the bottom of the boat to the boy on the ledge.

The dog, who had been running back and forth whining, sank to his belly, his muzzle on his fore-paws. But the boy on the ledge never stirred. The ducks took late alarm at the skiff, swerved aside and into the air, passing with a whirr no more than fifty feet over the head of the boy, who remained on the ledge like a statue, without his gun, watching the two crouching in the boat.

The fisherman's son climbed onto the ledge and held the painter. The bottom of the skiff was covered with feathery black and white bodies with feet upturned and necks lolling. He was jubilant. "We got twenty-seven!" he told his cousin. "How's that? Nine apiece. Boy—" he added, "what a cool Christmas!"

The fisherman pulled the skiff onto its shelf and all three went and lay down again in anticipation of the next flight. The son, reloading, patted his shotgun affectionately. "I'm going to get me ten next time," he said. Then he asked his cousin, "Whatsamatter—didn't you see the strays?"

"Yeah," the boy said.

"How come you didn't shoot at 'em?"

"Didn't feel like it," replied the boy, still with a trace of sullenness.

"You stupid or something?" The fisherman's son was astounded. "What a highlander!" But the fisher-man, though he said nothing, knew that the older boy had had an attack of ledge fever.

"Cripes!" his son kept at it. "I'd at least of tried."

"Shut up," the fisherman finally told him, "and leave him be."

At slack water three more flocks came in, one right after the other, and when it was over, the skiff was half full of clean, dead birds. During the subsequent lull they broke out the lunch and ate it all and finished the hot coffee. For a while the fisherman sucked away on his cold pipe. Then he had himself a swig of whiskey.

The boys passed the time contentedly jabbering about who shot the most—there were ninety-two all told—which of their friends they would show the biggest ones to, how many each could eat at a meal provided they didn't have to eat any vegetables. Now and then they heard sporadic distant gunfire on the mainland, at its nearest point about two miles to the north. Once far off they saw a fishing boat making in the direction of home.

At length the fisherman got a hand inside his oilskins and produced his watch.

"Do we have to go now?" asked his son.

"Not just yet," he replied. "Pretty soon." Everything had been perfect. As good as he had ever had it. Because he was getting tired of the boys' chatter he got up, heavily in his hip boots, and stretched. The tide had turned and was coming in, the sky was more ashen, and the wind had freshened enough so that whitecaps were beginning to blossom. It would be a good hour before they had to leave the ledge and pick up the tollers. However, he guessed they would leave a little early. On account of the rising wind he doubted there would be much more shooting. He stepped carefully along the back of the ledge, to work his kinks out. It was also getting a little colder.

The whiskey had begun to warm him, but he was unprepared for the sudden blaze that flashed upward inside him from belly to head. He was standing looking at the shelf where the skiff was. Only the foolish skiff was not there!

For the second time that day the fisherman felt the deep vacuity of disbelief. He gaped, seeing nothing but the flat shelf of rock. He whirled, started toward the boys, slipped, recovered himself, fetched a complete circle, and stared at the unimaginably empty shelf. Its emptiness made him feel as if everything he had done that day so far, his life so far, he had dreamed. What could have happened? The tide was still nearly a foot below. There had been no sea to speak of. The skiff could hardly have slid off by itself. For the life of him, consciously careful as he inveterately was, he could not now remember hauling it up the last time. Perhaps in the heat of hunting he had left it to the boy. Perhaps he could not remember which was the last time.

"Christ—" he exclaimed loudly, without realizing it because he was so entranced by the invisible event.

"What's wrong, Dad?" asked his son, getting to his feet.

The fisherman went blind with uncontainable rage. "Get back down there where you belong!" he screamed. He scarcely noticed the boy sink back in amazement. In a frenzy he ran along the ledge thinking the skiff might have been drawn up at another place, though he knew better. There was no other place.

He stumbled, half falling, back to the boys who were gawking at him in consternation, as though he had gone insane. "God damn it!" he yelled savagely, grabbing both of them and yanking them to their knees. "Get on your feet!"

"What's wrong?" his son repeated in a stifled voice.

"Never mind what's wrong," he snarled. "Look for the skiff—it's adrift!" When they peered around he gripped their shoulders, brutally facing them about. "Down-wind—" He slammed his fist against his thigh. "Jesus!" he cried, struck to madness at their stupidity.

At last he sighted the skiff himself, magically bobbing along the grim sea like a toller, a quarter of a mile to leeward on a direct course for home. The impulse to strip himself naked was succeeded instantly by a queer calm. He simply sat down on the ledge and forgot everything except the marvelous mystery.

As his awareness partially returned he glanced toward the boys. They were still observing the skiff speechlessly. Then he was gazing into the clear young eyes of his son.

"Dad," asked the boy steadily, "what do we do now?"

That brought the fisherman upright. "The first thing we have to do," he heard himself saying with infinite tenderness as if he were making love, "is think."

"Could you swim it?" asked his son.

He shook his head and smiled at them. They smiled quickly back, too quickly. "A hundred yards, maybe, in this water. I wish I could," he added. It was the most intimate and pitiful thing he had ever said. He walked in circles round them, trying to break the stall his mind was left in.

He gauged the level of the water. To the eye it was quite stationary, six inches from the shelf at this second. The fisherman did not have to mark it on the side of the rock against the passing of time to prove to his reason that it was rising, always rising. Already it was over the brink of reason, beyond the margins of thought—a senseless measurement. No sense to it.

All his life the fisherman had tried to lick the element of time, by getting up earlier and going to bed later, owning a faster boat, planning more than the day would hold, and tackling just one other job before the deadline fell. If, as on rare occasions he had the grand illusion, he ever really had beaten the game, he would need to call on all his reserves of practice and cunning now.

He sized up the scant but unforgivable three hundred yards to Brown Cow Island. Another hundred yards behind it his boat rode at anchor, where, had he been aboard, he could have cut in a fathometer to plumb the profound and occult seas, or a ship-to-shore radio on which in an interminably short time he would have heard his wife's voice talking to him over the air about homecoming.

"Couldn't we wave something so somebody would see us?" his nephew suggested.

The fisherman spun round. "Load your guns!" he ordered. They loaded as if the air had suddenly gone frantic with birds. "I'll fire once and count to five. Then you fire. Count to five. That way they won't just think it's only somebody gunning ducks. We'll keep doing that."

"We've only got just two and a half boxes left," said his son.

The fisherman nodded, understanding that from beginning to end their situation was purely mathematical, like the ticking of the alarm clock in his silent bedroom. Then he fired. The dog, who had been keeping watch over the decoys, leaped forward and yelped in confusion. They all counted off, fired the first five rounds by threes, and reloaded. The fisherman scanned first the horizon, then the contracting borders of the ledge, which was the sole place the water appeared to be climbing. Soon it would be over the shelf.

They counted off and fired the second five rounds. "We'll hold off a while on the last one," the fisherman told the boys. He sat down and pondered what a trivial thing was a skiff. This one he and the boy had knocked together in a day. Was a gun, manufactured for killing.

His son tallied up the remaining shells, grouping them symmetrically in threes on the rock when the wet box fell apart. "Two short," he announced. They reloaded and laid the guns on their knees.

Behind thickening clouds they could not see the sun going down. The water, coming up, was growing blacker. The fisherman thought he might have told his wife they would be home before dark since it was Christmas day. He realized he had forgotten about its being any particular day. The tide would not be high until two hours after sunset. When they did not get in by nightfall, and could not be raised by radio, she might send somebody to hunt for them right away. He rejected this arithmetic immediately, with a sickening shock, recollecting it was a two-and-a-half-hour run at best. Then it occurred to him that she might send somebody on the mainland who was nearer. She would think he had engine trouble.

He rose and searched the shoreline, barely visible. Then his glance dropped to the toy shoreline at the edges of the reef. The shrinking ledge, so sinister from a boat, grew dearer minute by minute as though the whole wide world he gazed on from horizon to horizon balanced on its contracting rim. He checked the water level and found the shelf awash.

Some of what went through his mind the fisherman told to the boys. They accepted it without comment. If he caught their eyes they looked away to spare him or because they were not yet old enough to face what they saw. Mostly they watched the rising water. The fisherman was unable to initiate a word of encouragement. He wanted one of them to ask him whether somebody would reach them ahead of the tide. He would have found it impossible to say yes. But they did not inquire.

The fisherman was not sure how much, at their age, they were able to imagine. Both of them had seen from the docks drowned bodies put ashore out of boats. Sometimes they grasped things, and sometimes not. He supposed they might be longing for the comfort of their mothers, and was astonished, as much as he was capable of any astonishment except the supreme one, to discover himself wishing he had not left his wife's dark, close, naked bed that morning.

"Is it time to shoot now?" asked his nephew.

"Pretty soon," he said, as if he were putting off making good on a promise. "Not yet."

His own boy cried softly for a brief moment, like a man, his face averted in an effort neither to give or show pain.

"Before school starts," the fisherman said, wonderfully detached, "we'll go to town and I'll buy you boys anything you want."

With great difficulty, in a dull tone as though he did not in the least desire it, his son said after a pause, "I'd like one of those new thirty-horse outboards."

"All right," said the fisherman. And to his nephew, "How about you?"

The nephew shook his head desolately. "I don't want anything," he said.

After another pause the fisherman's son said, "Yes he does, Dad. He wants one too."

"All right—" the fisherman said again, and said no more.

The dog whined in uncertainty and licked the boys' faces where they sat together. Each threw an arm over his back and hugged him. Three strays flew in and sat companionably down among the stiff-necked decoys. The dog crouched, obedient to his training. The boys observed them listlessly. Presently, sensing something untoward, the ducks took off, splashing the wave tops with feet and wingtips, into the dusky waste.

The sea began to make up in the mounting wind, and the wind bore a new and deathly chill. The fisherman, scouring the somber, dwindling shadow of the mainland for a sign, hoped it would not snow. But it did. First a few flakes, then a flurry, then storming past horizontally. The fisherman took one long, bewildered look at Brown Cow Island three hundred yards dead to leeward, and got to his feet.

Then it shut in, as if what was happening on the ledge was too private even for the last wan light of the expiring day.

"Last round," the fisherman said austerely.

The boys rose and shouldered their tacit guns. The fisherman fired into the flying snow. He counted methodically to five. His son fired and counted. His nephew. All three fired and counted. Four rounds.

"You've got one left, Dad," his son said.

The fisherman hesitated another second, then he fired the final shell. Its pathetic report, like the spat of a popgun, whipped away on the wind and was instantly blanketed in falling snow.

Night fell all in a moment to meet the ascending sea. They were now barely able to make one another out through driving snowflakes, dim as ghosts in their yellow oilskins. The fisherman heard a sea break and glanced down where his feet were. They seemed to be wound in a snowy sheet. Gently he took the boys by the shoulders and pushed them in front of him, feeling with his feet along the shallow sump to the place where it triangulated into a sharp crevice at the highest point of the ledge. "Face ahead," he told them. "Put the guns down."

"I'd like to hold mine, Dad," begged his son.

"Put it down," said the fisherman. "The tide won't hurt it. Now brace your feet against both sides and stay there."

They felt the dog, who was pitch black, running up and down in perplexity between their straddled legs. "Dad," said his son, "what about the pooch?"

If he had called the dog by name it would have been too personal. The fisherman would have wept. As it was he had done all he could do to keep from laughing. He bent his knees, and when he touched, the dog hoisted him under one arm. The dog's belly was soaking wet.

So they waited, marooned in their consciousness, surrounded by a monstrous tidal space which was slowly, slowly closing them out. In this space the periwinkle beneath the fisherman's boots was king. While hovering airborne in his mind he had an inward glimpse of his house as curiously separate, like a June mirage.

Snow, rocks, seas, wind the fisherman had lived by all his life. Now he thought he had never comprehended what they were, and he hated them. Though they had not changed. He was deadly chilled. He set out to ask the boys if they were cold. There was no sense. He thought of the whiskey, and sidled backward, still holding the awkward dog, till he located the bottle under water with his toe. He picked it up squeamishly as though afraid of getting his sleeve wet, worked his way forward and bent over his son. "Drink it," he said, holding the bottle against the boy's ribs. The boy tipped his head back, drank, coughed hotly, then vomited.

"I can't," he told his father wretchedly.

"Try—try—" the fisherman pleaded, as if it meant the difference between life and death.

The boy obediently drank, and again he vomited hotly. He shook his head against his father's chest and passed the bottle forward to his cousin, who drank and vomited also. Passing the bottle back, the boys dropped it in the frigid water between them.

When the waves reached his knees the fisherman set the warm dog loose and said the his son, "Turn around and get up on my shoulders." The boy obeyed. The fisherman opened his oilskin jacket and twisted his hands behind him through his suspenders, clamping the boy's booted ankles with his elbows.

"What about the dog?" the boy asked.

"He'll make his own way all right," the fisherman said. "He can take the cold water." His knees were trembling. Every instinct shrieked for gymnastics. He ground his teeth and braced like a colossus against the sides of the submerged crevice.

The dog, having lived faithfully as though one of them for eleven years, swam a few minutes in and out around the fisherman's legs, not knowing what was happening, and left them without a whimper. He would swim and swim at random by himself, round and round in the blinding night, and when he had swum routinely through the paralyzing water all he could, he would simply, in one incomprehensible moment, drown. Almost the fisherman, waiting out infinity, envied him his pattern.

Freezing seas swept by, flooding inexorably up and up as the earth sank away imperceptibly beneath them. The boy called out once to his cousin. There was no answer. The fisherman, marvelling on a terror without voice, was dumbly glad when the boy did not call again. His own boots were long full of water. With no sensation left in his straddling legs he dared not move them. So long as the seas came sidewise against his hips, and then sidewise against his shoulders, he might balance—no telling how long. The upper half of him was what felt frozen. His legs, disengaged from his nerves and his will, he came to regard quite scientifically. They were the absurd, precarious axis around which reeled and surged universal tumult. The waves would come on and on; he could not visualize how many tossing reinforcements lurked in the night beyond—inexhaustible numbers, and he wept in supernatural fury at each because it was higher, till he transcended hate and took them, swaying like a convert, one by one as they lunged against him and away aimlessly into their own undisputed, wild realm.

From his hips upward the fisherman stretched to his utmost as a man does whose spirit reaches out of dead sleep. The boy's head, none too high, must be at least seven feet above the ledge. Though growing larger every minute, it was a small light life. The fisherman meant to hold it there, if need be, through a thousand tides.

By and by the boy, slumped on the head of his father, asked, "Is it over your boots, Dad?"

"Not yet," the fisherman said. Then through his teeth he added, "If I fall—kick your boots off—swim for it—down-wind—to the island. . . ."

"You . . . ?" the boy finally asked.

The fisherman nodded against the boy's belly. "—Won't see each other," he said.

The boy did for the fisherman the greatest thing that can be done. He may have been too young for perfect terror, but he was old enough to know there were things beyond the power of any man. All he could do he did, by trusting his father to do all he could, and asking nothing more.

The fisherman, rocked to his soul by a sea, held his eyes shut upon the interminable night.

"Is it time now?" the boy said.

The fisherman could hardly speak. "Not yet," he said. "Not just yet. . . ."

As the land mass pivoted toward sunlight the day after Christmas, a tiny fleet of small craft converged off shore like iron filings to a magnet. At daybreak they found the skiff floating unscathed off the headland, half full of ducks and snow. The shooting *had* been good, as someone hearing on the nearby mainland the previous afternoon had supposed. Two hours afterward they found the unharmed boat adrift five miles at sea. At high noon they found the fisherman at ebb tide, his right foot jammed cruelly into a glacial crevice of the ledge beside three shotguns, his hands tangled behind him in his suspenders, and under his right elbow a rubber boot with a sock and a live starfish in it. After dragging unlit depths all day for the boys, they towed the fisherman home in his own boat at sundown, and in the frost of evening, mute with discovering purgatory, laid him on his wharf for his wife to see.

She, somehow, standing on the dock as in her frequent dream, gazing at the fisherman pure as crystal on the icy boards, a small rubber boot still frozen under one clenched arm, saw him exaggerated beyond remorse or grief, absolved of his mortality.

Reprinted with permission of Bowdoin College, L.S. Hall papers, special collection.

Acknowledgments

This book could not have been put together without the help of many, many people. Listing them all is probably impossible, but I'll give it a try.

I would first like to thank Jim Range, George Cooper, Tim Zink and Cary Ridder of the Theodore Roosevelt Conservation Partnership for working so closely with me on this project. Having the Partnership's name on this book is an honor.

I'd also like to thank some of the many people who helped me assemble the stories within. My dear friend Tom McIntyre not only made suggestions of books to excerpt, but donated a significant section of one of his own books, "Dreaming the Lion." He also gave me a very insightful piece on what killing really means.

Lamar Underwood, the most voracious reader of outdoor literature that I know, made many valuable suggestions on what I might consider excerpting. While I was unable to obtain some of them, I was able to assemble many of Lamar's recommended chapters.

Nick Lyons, with whom I had the great pleasure of working at the old Lyons Press, lent me many hard-to-find books from his library, with his thoughts on what might be appropriate for this truly gigantic book.

Laurie Morrow was helpful in getting permission for me to use the Corey Ford pieces, plus she helped track down and get some other, difficult-to-obtain excerpts.

Phil Caputo, Dave Petzal, Rick Bass, Tom McGuane, Jim Harrison, Bob Butz, Ted Nugent. . . . I thank all the authors whose names appear on the table of contents.

Amy Berkley, *Field & Stream*'s photography editor, helped me find some crucial illustrations and photos for the book, some of them literally minutes before press time. Thank you Amy!

I also want to thank Steve Corcoran and Abigail Gehring of Skyhorse Publishing for all their hard work on this project. Without them, this book would never have come into existence.

Finally, I want to thank John Rice, who provided so many fine illustrations for this book.